Contents

KU-571-401

UNDERSTAND

SURVIVAL GUIDE

SPECIAL FEATURES

Welcome to the South Pacific

*Adrift in the daydreamy South Pacific –
deliciously remote and surprisingly
diverse – you can de-stress or ramp up
the action, with some superfresh seafood
awaiting at day's end.*

South Seas Dreaming

The South Pacific's paradisiacal reputation can be traced back to European explorers, returning home with tales of fertile soils, beautiful islanders and simple ways. These island nations have modernised since the late 1700s, but their allure remains undiminished: you'll still find gin-clear waters, smiling locals and gardenia-scented airs. But what's most amazing is how untainted by tourism most islands are. Blame it on remoteness, blame it on airfares...but few people who fantasise about the South Seas ever actually make the journey. Getting off the tourism grid and playing Robinson Crusoe is the true gift of the South Pacific.

Cultural Diversity

Even geography geeks crinkle their brows when contemplating this many islands, this far from anywhere else. On the map, all those dots look the same, their many-vowelled names tripping over the tongue. But on the ground there's a diversity befitting any such earthly expanse. Yes, there are Polynesian nations, Melanesian nations, Micronesian nations...but beneath these blanket names are myriad languages, customs, histories and landscapes that make each island group unique. It's not just homogenous beaches and reefs – bust out of your resort to find societies and experiences as rich as coconut cream.

Active Islands

Life moves slowly under the southern sun – it's no wonder sit-on-a-beach-and-read-a-book holidays are why most visitors are here. But what if you want a bit of action? Look around and you'll find world-class surf breaks, plus amazing snorkelling and diving sites. More surprisingly, you might try hiking to find crumbling *tiki* (sacred) statues in the jungle, trekking to the top of a volcano, swimming into a sea cave, rappelling down a waterfall or kayaking to a forgotten beach. The adventure-travel vein has scarcely been tapped here and, other than a few mechanised experiences like jet-skiing and 4WD tours, what's on offer is authentic, uncrowded and something you'll never likely forget.

Dinner Time

The South Pacific doesn't have a terrific rep' for fine food and wine. But sidestep the Westernised resort restaurants and be adventurous: you'll find hearty local stews cooked with coconut milk, fabulous fresh seafood (how's that lobster?), peppy Chinese noodle soups and even the odd Indian curry. And who needs shiraz when the weather is this humid? Sip a cold local lager instead – the perfect thirst quencher as the sun sets on another day in paradise.

South Pacific

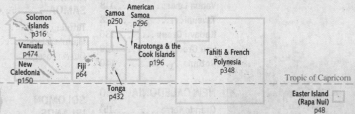

Equator

Solomon
Islands
p316

Samoa
p250

American
Samoa
p296

Vanuatu
p474

Rarotonga & the
Cook Islands
p196

Tahiti & French
Polynesia
p348

New
Caledonia
p150

Fiji
p64

Tonga
p432

Tropic of Capricorn

Easter Island
(Rapa Nui)
p48

SOUTH PACIFIC OCEAN

Cha   Carillet,
                                                                         d

Contents

HIKING IN RAROTONGA,
COOK ISLANDS P197

WILFRIED KRECICHWOST/GETTY IMAGES ©

BEACH FALES, SAMOA P250

ZSTOCKPHOTOS/GETTY IMAGES ©

Why I Love the South Pacific

By Charles Rawlings-Way, Writer

Sure, you've got the palm trees, the seafood, the hypercoloured reefs, the sweet scent of hibiscus on the evening breeze... But the best thing about the South Pacific is the pace of life. Or rather, the lack of pace. I spend most of my time careening around Australia's big cities, drinking too much coffee and talking a lot. Every slowed-down trip I make to the South Seas is an antidote to the mayhem, extending my allocated time on this lonely planet by unknown years.

For more about our writers, see page 612.

Above: Islands in Tonga's Vava'u Group (p453)

1. Traditional dance in Samoa

An important part of Polynesian cultures and an exciting way to enrich any South Pacific experience.

2. Bunglaows in Tikehau (p405), Tahiti

A uniquely South Pacific style of accommodation. .

3. *Moai* statue at Rano Raraku (p60)

Enigmatic symbols of Easter Island, the *moai* are thought to represent clan ancestors.

4. Ukeleles at Muri Night Market (p219)

This market is perhaps the biggest game in Muri, Cook Islands.

South Pacific

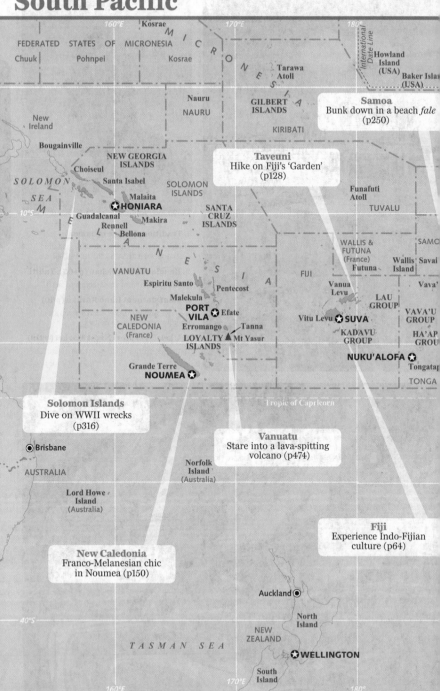

Samoa
Bunk down in a beach *fale*
(p250)

Taveuni
Hike on Fiji's 'Garden'
(p128)

Solomon Islands
Dive on WWII wrecks
(p316)

Vanuatu
Stare into a lava-spitting
volcano (p474)

New Caledonia
Franco-Melanesian chic
in Noumea (p150)

Fiji
Experience Indo-Fijian
culture (p64)

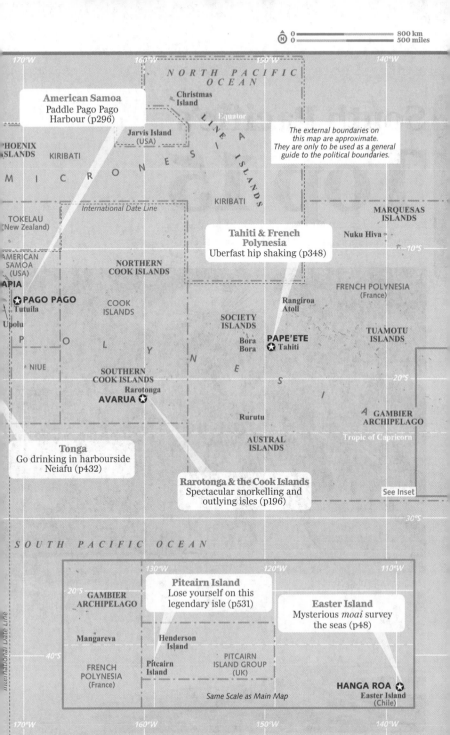

American Samoa
Paddle Pago Pago
Harbour (p296)

NORTH PACIFIC OCEAN

Christmas Island

Equator

Jarvis Island (USA)

PHOENIX ISLANDS

KIRIBATI

The external boundaries on this map are approximate. They are only to be used as a general guide to the political boundaries.

M I C R O N E S I A

International Date Line

TOKELAU (New Zealand)

KIRIBATI

MARQUESAS ISLANDS

Nuku Hiva

AMERICAN SAMOA (USA)

APIA

☆ **PAGO PAGO**
Tutuila

NORTHERN COOK ISLANDS

Tahiti & French Polynesia
Uberfast hip shaking (p348)

FRENCH POLYNESIA (France)

Upolu

COOK ISLANDS

Rangiroa Atoll

SOCIETY ISLANDS

TUAMOTU ISLANDS

P O L Y N E S I A

NIUE

Bora Bora

PAPE'ETE
☆ Tahiti

SOUTHERN COOK ISLANDS
Rarotonga
AVARUA ☆

Rurutu

Tonga
Go drinking in harbourside Neiafu (p432)

AUSTRAL ISLANDS

GAMBIER ARCHIPELAGO

Tropic of Capricorn

Rarotonga & the Cook Islands
Spectacular snorkelling and outlying isles (p196)

See Inset

SOUTH PACIFIC OCEAN

Pitcairn Island
Lose yourself on this legendary isle (p531)

GAMBIER ARCHIPELAGO

Henderson Island

Mangareva

PITCAIRN ISLAND GROUP (UK)

Easter Island
Mysterious *moai* survey the seas (p48)

FRENCH POLYNESIA (France)

Pitcairn Island

Same Scale as Main Map

HANGA ROA ☆
Easter Island (Chile)

International Date Line

South Pacific's
Top 15

Choose Your Own Paradise

1 Any of these countries could feature on that 'Travel to Paradise' poster that makes you want to quit your job and sit on a beach forever. But the South Pacific is far from a homogenised string of palms and blue sea. The cultures and landscapes spread across this vast ocean are incredibly diverse, from the low-lying atolls of the Cook Islands to the mangrove-encircled peaks of New Caledonia; from Euro-chic capitals to traditional jungle villages. Each island group is its own kind of wonderful, which makes travelling here all the more rewarding. Below left: Muri Lagoon (p211), Rarotonga

New Caledonian Scenes

2 With its seductive World Heritage–listed lagoons, New Caledonia offers aquamarine hues and white sandy beaches. This is the South Pacific with a French twist, especially around Noumea (p151). While the capital boasts sunny bays, waterside restaurants and a vibrant nightlife, head out to the Loyalty Islands to experience tribal accommodation and soak up the Kanak culture. Legendary Île des Pins is well worth exploring, and a road trip to the northern coasts of Grande Terre is highly recommended. Below right: Kanak totem pole

SORINOLAC/GETTY IMAGES ©

DELPIXEL/SHUTTERSTOCK ©

Tahitian Dance & Tattoos

3 Tahitians love to swing a hip! The hottest dance tickets in the country are for the annual Heiva festival (p359), held in Pape'ete every July. Through the rest of the year, professional groups offer performances at the big resorts. The men stamp, gesture and knock their knees together; the women shake and gyrate their hips – it's all very gendered and seductive. And while you're in the 'hood, check out Tahitian tattooing, another strong cultural trait that has surged back into popularity since the 1980s.

Hiking in Taveuni

4 Swap your beach blues for the jade jungles of Fiji's 'Garden Island'. Lush and humid, Taveuni (p128) is heaven for hikers, where even the shortest trails offer up rare birdlife, gargantuan trees and bizarre rock formations. In Bouma National Heritage Park, the Lavena Coastal Walk takes trekkers on a 5km journey past beautiful beaches, rainforest villages and over a suspension bridge to waterfalls. Serious sloggers can head up the steep Des Voeux Peak or to the muddy mountain crater of Lake Tagimaucia. Bottom: Lavena Coastal Walk (p135)

Easter Island's Moai

5 The enigmatic *moai* (p62) are the most pervasive image of Easter Island (Rapa Nui), and have intrigued archaeologists for generations. Dotted around the island, these massive figures on stone platforms supercharge the scene with mystical vibes. Like colossal puppets on a supernatural stage, it's thought that they represent clan ancestors. The biggest question is, how were these giants moved from where they were carved to their present positions? Never mind the answer – they have plenty to set your camera clicking without it.

South Pacific Diving

6 The South Pacific offers world-class diving (p35), with an irresistible menu of underwater treasures: reefs festooned with coral, waters teeming with rainbow-coloured fish, drop-offs that tumble into the abyss, and lots of pelagics, including sharks and manta rays – not to mention the odd passing whale. Another clincher is the eye-boggling array of diveable wrecks here – especially WWII ships, aircraft and even submarines – to keep you historically engaged but utterly in the moment. Bottom: Coral growing on wreck, Viti Levu (p65)

ROTHENBORG KYLE/GETTY IMAGES ©

Beach Fale in Samoa

7 These elongated, open-air huts on stilts (p291) hover over Samoa's trademark white sands, taking in panoramic vistas of turquoise seas while the cool breeze blows through. Few other South Pacific countries have retained their traditional architecture to the point that it's what they offer tourists, without design or modern fanfare: in Samoa, guests sleep on the *fale* floor and privacy is found by pulling down thatched louvres. *Fale* are basic and budget, but the views are worth a million bucks.

Solomon Islands' WWII Relics

8 The Solomon Islands serve up history by the bucketful. Above the surface, decaying WWII relics in the jungle will captivate history buffs. Outside Honiara, you can visit poignant WWII battlefields and memorials, as well as abandoned amtracks (small amphibious landing vehicles), Sherman tanks, Japanese field guns and the remains of several US aircraft. Strap on some scuba gear and dive sunken aircraft wrecks, warships and even tanks, tipped off the back of stricken carrier vessels.

Vanuatu's Volcanoes

9 Staring down into the real-life, lava-spouting mouth of a volcano is exactly the nerve-wracking experience you might expect it to be. And Mt Yasur (p494) in Vanuatu is one of the most accessible places in the world to do it. Set yourself up in a bungalow or tree house at the volcano's base, then climb the crater in the evening to watch the volcano light up the night. For more adventure, head to Ambrym island where you can scale the twin volcanoes of Mt Marum and Mt Benbow. Above far right: Formidable Mt Yasur (p494) in action

9

South Seas Surfing

10 Polynesians invented surfing, yet, apart from Tahiti, Samoa and Fiji, the South Pacific remains largely unexplored by surfers. Wave hounds are gradually discovering other breaks, such as Ha'atafu Beach (p436) on Tongatapu (Tonga), and finding uncrowded waves in warm, clear waters. Cyclone season (November to April) brings gnarly waves from the north, while during winter (May to August) low-pressure systems in the Southern Ocean and Tasman Sea bring big swells to islands with exposed southern coastlines. Right: Shredding Teahupoo (p363) in the Billabong Pro Tahiti

GREGORY BOISSY/STRINGER/GETTY IMAGES ©

10

TOM COCKREM/GETTY IMAGES ©

Indo-Fijian Culture

11 In Fiji, fab festivals and food give visitors a peek into Indo-Fijian culture. Diwali, the Festival of Lights, is celebrated in October or November. It's ushered in with nightly displays, from spotlit extravaganzas to candlelit driveways and households. Fireworks are obligatory. Fire of another sort takes centre stage during the fire-walking festival at Suva's Mariamma Temple in July or August. On the food front, curries and sweets can be found in cafes and shops across Fiji year-round, accompanied by blasting Bollywood music.

Top left: Indo-Fijian sweets

Bounteous Pitcairn Island

12 You probably know the infamous tale: in 1789 the irksome Captain William Bligh so thoroughly annoyed the crew of the HMS *Bounty* that master's mate Fletcher Christian launched a mutiny, setting Bligh and his few faithful sailors adrift in a dinghy. Pitcairn (p531) is where Christian ended up – an astoundingly remote island with a history that's almost tangible. There are few places in the world where you can feel so thoroughly lost, and yet so free (exactly the vibe Fletcher Christian was looking for).

Drinking in Neiafu

13 In Vava'u in Tonga's northern reaches, raffish Neiafu (p454) fronts onto one of the world's most photogenic natural harbours – a safe haven for yachts in a storm. Prop up the bar at one of the old town's harbourside booze rooms and sink a few cold beers. The conversation drifts between moorings, weather charts, trade winds and destinations – there might even be a South Seas duo strumming and harmonising in the corner, a kava session on the go...or at least some classic rock on the stereo.

Bottom right: Harbourside relaxation, Neiafu

Pago Pago Harbour

14 In American Samoa, 'Pago' (p304), as it's affectionately known, is a gritty working town full of fishers and canneries. But that's what makes its backdrop so surprising: vertical green peaks with jagged silhouettes, plunging dramatically into an elongated bay of dark teal. Launch a kayak to experience the bay at its best, at sunrise or sunset when the light plays off the mountains. You have an equal chance of paddling past children playing on the beach as you do stacks of shipping containers.

Surprising Cook Islands

15 Welcome to the Cook Islands (p196), one of the South Pacific's most accessible and surprising destinations. Ease into island time with Rarotonga's laid-back, family-friendly combination of snorkelling and hiking, day trips, markets and restaurants, and uptempo nightlife. Invest a few days to discover the Cooks' traditional outer islands: check out the birdlife and cave systems on 'Atiu; paddle your kayak to deserted islets around Aitutaki's lagoon; or go local in a village homestay on remote Ma'uke or Mitiaro. Bottom: Trader Jacks (p205), Avarua

Need to Know

For more information, see Survival Guide (p577)

Currency
Each country has its own currency; US dollars are readily exchanged.

Language
English in most tourist hubs; local languages in remote regions. French in French territories. Spanish on Easter Island.

Visas
Most South Pacific countries issue short-stay visas on arrival. New Zealanders don't need a Cook Islands visa.

Money
ATMs and money changers available in most large towns; cash only on most outer islands.

Mobile Phones
Use global roaming or buy a local SIM card. Reception varies but is available even on remote islands.

Time
Either side of the International Date Line, countries range from GMT +11 hours (New Caledonia, Vanuatu, Solomon Islands) to GMT -5 hours (Easter Island).

When to Go

Tropical climate, wet & dry seasons

Samoa
GO May–Oct

French Polynesia
GO Jun–Oct

Fiji
GO May–Aug

New Caledonia
GO Apr–Jul

Easter Island
GO Dec–Mar

High Season
(Jun–Aug & Dec–Jan)

➡ Many islanders living abroad come home to visit family.

➡ Book flights well in advance.

➡ June to August is dry, December and January are humid and wet. Cyclone season is October to April.

Shoulder Season
(May, Sep)

➡ Trade winds lower the humidity and keep temperatures pleasant.

➡ Flights are cheaper and less likely to be booked.

➡ Travel with company but very few crowds.

Low Season
(Feb–Apr & Oct–Nov)

➡ Expect hot temperatures and high humidity.

➡ Scour the web for deals on resorts looking to fill empty rooms.

➡ Diving visibility can be reduced due to heavy rains.

19

Useful Websites

➡ **Discover the South Pacific** (www.spto.org) Multicountry site run by the South Pacific Tourism Organisation: activities, accommodation and destination info.

➡ **Pacific Islands Report** (www.pireport.org) News from across the South Pacific.

➡ **Lonely Planet** (lonelyplanet.com/pacific) Destination info, hotel bookings, traveller forum and more.

Important Numbers

International country codes for South Pacific countries include the following:

Cook Islands	☏682
Fiji	☏679
New Caledonia	☏687
Samoa	☏685
Tahiti & French Polynesia	☏689

Exchange Rates

Cook Islands	NZ$1	US$0.68
Easter Island	CH$100	US$0.15
Fiji	F$1	US$0.47
New Caledonia	100 CFP	US$0.95
Samoa	ST1	US$0.39
Solomon Islands	S$1	US$0.13
Tahiti & French Polynesia	100 CFP	US$0.95
Tonga	T$1	US$0.45
Vanuatu	100 VT	US$0.90

For current exchange rates see www.xe.com

Daily Costs

Budget: Less than US$100

➡ Guesthouse bed: US$15–US$50

➡ Basket of fruit at a local market: US$3–US$10

➡ Bicycle rental per day: US$15–US$25

Midrange: US$100–US$400

➡ Double room in a boutique hotel or small resort: US$100–US$250

➡ Main course in a local cafe: US$10–US$20

➡ Snorkelling or glass-bottom boat trip: US$30–US$60

Top End: More than US$400

➡ Night in an over-the-water bungalow: US$500–US$3500

➡ Dinner at a restaurant with international chef: US$75–US$200

➡ Two-tank scuba dive: US$150

Opening Hours

Following are some generalised opening hours – time is flexible in the South Pacific! In many countries, everything closes on Sunday.

Banks 9.30am–3pm or 4pm Monday to Friday

Bars & Pubs 11am–midnight or later

Cafes 7.30am–8pm

Post Offices & Government Offices 9am–4pm Monday to Friday, from 7.30am in countries with French ties

Shops 9am–5pm Monday to Friday, to 1pm Saturday

Arriving in the South Pacific

Nadi International Airport (Fiji; p65) Frequent buses and plentiful taxis run into downtown Nadi, just 4km away. Many resorts offer free transfers.

Faa'a International Airport (Pape'ete, Tajiti; p430) Organise a direct hotel transfer or hire a car into town, 9km away. Local bus schedules often don't align with flights; taxis are expensive.

Tontouta International Airport (Noumea, New Caledonia; p194) Regular public and private buses run transfers into town, 45km away.

Fua'amotu International Airport (Tongatapu, Tonga; p434) Local taxis meet all flights, or organise a direct accommodation transfer into Nuku'alofa, 21km away.

Getting Around

Air The most efficient (and sometimes the only) way to island-hop; flights can be expensive.

Car & Motorcycle Car and motorcycle hire available on large islands; in remote areas it's usually not an option. Bring a current international driving permit and home driver's licence.

Ferry & Boat Ferries ply short distances between main islands; cargo ships make longer hauls. Or if you're lucky, hop on a yacht!

For much more on **getting around**, see p584.

If You Like...

Beaches

Ofu Beach (American Samoa) It's difficult to get here but this beach on the island of Ofu is divine defined. (p309)

Aitutaki Lagoon (Cook Islands) Necklace of compact island-trimmed beaches. (p224)

Yasawa Group (Fiji) Rugged volcanic interiors sloping down to delicate, idyllic stretches of sugar-white sand. (p109)

Ouvéa (New Caledonia) Twenty-five kilometres of perfect white beach line this Loyalty Islands lagoon. (p182)

Tikehau (French Polynesia) Incredible turquoise waters, pink sands and seclusion. (p405)

Diving & Snorkelling

Barefoot Manta Island (Fiji) Flip your fins with the eerily graceful manta rays that grace the northern passage of Drawaqa Island. (p111)

Solomon Islands Hundreds of sunken WWII ships and aircraft plus superb corals. (p316)

Rangiroa (French Polynesia) Shark week is every week on this massive coral atoll (dolphins too). (p397)

Espiritu Santo (Vanuatu) Dive on bright corals, wrecks and WWII artefacts. (p506)

Île des Pins (New Caledonia) Head to La Piscene Naturelle and meet the fish. (p185)

Hiking, Caves & Volcanoes

The Dog's Head (Vanuatu) Amble through a veritable cultural documentary: super scenery, caves and waterfalls. (p500)

Lake Tagimaucia (Fiji) This ancient volcanic crater rewards with a glimpse of the incredibly rare *tagimaucia* flower. (p130)

Mt Yasur (Vanuatu) Peer down into a gurgling volcanic abyss on Tanna. (p494)

Le Parc des Grandes Fougères (New Caledonia) Hike through the Park of the Great Ferns. (p170)

Cross-Island Track (Cook Islands) Waterfalls, peaks and fern-filled valleys on Rarotonga. (p213)

Swallows' Cave (Tonga) Boat-only access to this amazing cave: swim inside to see the birds. (p462)

Luxury Retreats

Ratua Private Island Resort (Vanuatu) Luxurious (but non-profit) private island donating to the Ratua Foundation to educate kids. (p512)

Vahine Island Private Island Resort (French Polynesia) Intimate boutique resort with an outrageous setting that makes up for its relative simplicity. (p384)

Jean-Michel Cousteau Fiji Islands Resort Adults get luxe dining and diving; kids get a nanny and a resort-like kids club. (p123)

Etu Moana (Cook Islands) Aitutaki's super-relaxed and understated yet downright plush hideaway. (p227)

Sandy Beach Resort (Tonga) Top of the hotel tree in Tonga, on a special stretch of white, crushed-coral beach. (p452)

Coconuts Beach Club Resort (Samoa) Stunning overwater *fale* putting a luxury spin on Samoa's traditionally humble beach huts. (p272)

Traditional Dance & Music

Heiva (French Polynesia) Fast hips, outrageous costumes, complex percussion and soothing harmonies at this July festival. (p359)

Island Nights (Cook Islands) Traditional song-and-dance evening show with fire juggling, acrobatics and a grand meal. (p221)

Fiafia (Samoa) Fire dancing, traditional 'slap' dancing, singing and a Samoan-sized buffet. (p289)

Rom Dance (Vanuatu) Watch feet pounding the dirt in this hypnotic, vibrant dance involving magic and custom. (p504)

Meke (Fiji) Sometimes gentle, sometimes frenzied trad dance performances: an authentic village *meke* is a show-stopper. (p143)

Tjibaou Cultural Centre (New Caledonia) Experience Kanak dance and music. (p153)

Traditional Dance Show (Easter Island) Authentic shows with brilliant costumes performed regularly at hotels. (p52)

Remote Escapes

Raivavae (French Polynesia) As beautiful as Bora Bora, but with some of the country's most authentic culture. (p421)

'Atiu (Cook Islands) Caves, bird-life and local drinking customs. (p229)

Uoleva (Tonga) A beach-bum island escape with whales breaching offshore. (p452)

Lau Group (Fiji) Blaze a trail through these little-visited, unspoilt gems. (p139)

The Maskelynes (Vanuatu) Engage with village life, hit the kava bars or try some mud crab. (p502)

Ta'u (American Samoa) Hump-back whales, birdlife, dramatic peaks, rugged coastline...and very little else on this island. (p311)

Maré (New Caledonia) Experi-ence Kanak culture in the Loyalty Islands. (p178)

Top: The serene, crystalline waters of Tikehau (p405), French Polynesia
Bottom: Traditional Fijian dance on Robinson Crusoe Island (p91)

Month By Month

January

January in the South Pacific is equal parts hot and wet. Cool off by the pool or step into the air-con and catch a flick.

☆ Fifo Pacific International Documentary Film Festival

Starting in late January and rolling into February, this fab festival in Tahiti (www.fifo-tahiti.com) screens the year's best Pacific documentary films, from Australia to Hawai'i. Year-round, 'Travelling Fifo' takes the films on the road, visiting even the remotest of islands.

February

It's still hot and humid, and it might be raining. Head for the resort pool (you'll possibly have it all to yourself), or get some Chinese food on your plate.

🎎 Tapati Rapa Nui

For two weeks at the beginning of February, Easter Island holds this eye-popping cultural celebration that includes music, dance and sport. The highlights are banana-tree sled races (Haka Pei) and bareback horse racing. (p53)

🎎 Chinese New Year

The date changes each year (it's based on the Chinese lunar calendar) but this two-week-long celebration on islands that have a Chinese community usually includes dancing, martial arts, fireworks and loads of food. The party is at its most effervescent in Tahiti.

April

Easing out of the South Pacific cyclone season, April can be a bit hit-and-miss as far as the weather goes, but it's a good time to sidestep the tourist crowds.

☆ Te Mire Kapa

The Cook Islands' annual 'Dancer of the Year' competition is held throughout April. There are events for all ages from juniors to 'Golden Oldies', enticing hip-swingers from right across the islands.

🏃 Naghol

From April to July, these unbelievable 'land-diving' rituals (www.fest300.com/festivals/naghol-land-diving) happen on Pentecost in Vanuatu, in a bid to ensure a plentiful yam harvest. Local men strap their ankles to vines and plummet from 30m towers – their heads must touch the ground! Wow! (p517)

May

The southeast trade winds (all-natural air-conditioning) start to pick up in May – the perfect time to windsurf, kitesurf or jump on a yacht for some island-hopping.

🍴 Stag & Prawn Festival

This food-focused fiesta (www.visitnewcaledonia.
com/stag-and-prawn-
festival) lures thousands of visitors to the country town of Broussard, New Caledonia. Expect sausage-eating, shrimp-peeling and stag-calling competitions, plus dog events, singing, dancing and the mandatory 'Miss' competition.

June

The stable weather of June marks the start of the busy tourist season, when Australian and Kiwi visitors flee the southern winter. Many islanders gear up for July's festivals with drum rehearsals and sports practise aplenty.

🏃 Pacific Nations Cup

Fiji, Tonga and Samoa join Canada, the USA and Japan in a condensed program of play-offs for this annual rugby prize (www.
worldrugby.org/pnc). The games are held from May to late June in all the participating countries.

July

Warm and dry July is festival time for many island groups, highlighted by sports competitions, beauty pageants, traditional song and dance, and plenty of partying. You can also expect booked-up hotels – reserve early.

Top: Pro surfer CJ Hobgood at the Billabong Pro Tahiti, Teahupoo (p363)
Bottom: Dancers at the Heiva i Tahiti festival (p359)

✪ Festival of Pacific Arts

Held every four years in a different country, this vibrant festival (www.pacificarts.org/art_festivals) showcases traditional and contemporary arts from around the Pacific.

✪ Heiva i Tahiti

Held in Pape'ete, French Polynesia's big-ticket festival (www.tahiti-tourisme.pf/heiva) lasts an entire month and is truly impressive (probably worth timing your trip around). Dancers and singers perform alongside parades and traditional sports comps. (p359)

✪ Bula Festival

Held in Nadi, this charitable event is one of Fiji's biggest and longest-running festivals, featuring rides, music, cultural shows and the crowning of 'Miss Bula' (beauty pageants are *big* in the South Pacific, and are much more modest than Western-style bikini-fests).

☆ Heilala Festival

Celebrating the flowering of the *heilala*, Tonga's national flower, this is Tonga's biggest excuse for a party, with music from hip-hop to church choirs on block-party stages. Dance performances, talent shows, parades and the Miss Heilala Pageant also make the grade.

✪ Independence Day

The good folks of the Solomon Islands celebrate their independence from Great Britain with traditional dance performances, a police-band parade, sports and lots of family gatherings. The biggest events take place in Honiara.

August

The July festivities spill over into sunny-and-dry August, with music festivals and cultural happenings. This is the height of the tourist season so you'll enjoy it all with plenty of company.

🏃 Tahiti Billabong Pro

This month-long comp (www.worldsurfleague.com/events) is one of the biggest events in world surfing: the gnarly waves at Teahupoo are as beautiful as they are scary. Take a boat ride to watch the surfers get tubed in the green room.

✪ South Indian Fire Walking

Indo-Fijian devotees pierce their tongues, cheeks and bodies with skewers, smear themselves with yellow turmeric and dance 3km to Mariamma Temple in Suva where they walk over hot embers. Wild times! It's a cleansing culmination of a 10-day ascetic period every August.

✪ Te Maeva Nui

Originally called the 'Constitution Celebrations', the new name of this festival (www.cookislands.travel/temaevanui) translates to 'The Most Important Celebration'. Marking the Cook Islands' shift from New Zealand governance to self-rule, festivities include traditional song and dance, a parade, and arts and sporting events.

☆ Live en Août

New Caledonia's biggest music festival (www.live-en-aout.nc) brings local and global acts to stages in and around Noumea. Expect everything from ska to jazz. The whole shebang lasts for two weeks.

✪ Bourail Country Fair

Held in Bourail on New Caledonia's Grande Terre, this is a true cowboy fest (www.gitesnouvellecaledonie.nc/decouvertes/foire-de-bourail), complete with rodeo, lumberjacks, the 'Miss Bourail Fair'... It's a side of New Caledonia that visitors might not even know exists. (p172)

September

September is lovely in the South Pacific. School holidays are over, the trade winds keep humidity down, the cyclone season hasn't ruffled any rooftops yet and tourists are few.

🏃 Pacific Games

Every four years, the Olympics-like Pacific Games feature 4000 athletes from 22 Pacific nations competing in around 34 sporting events. Epic! The 2019 games are slated for Nuku'alofa, Tonga's capital (watch this space though – financial factors may send them elsewhere).

✪ Teuila Festival

Samoa's capital Apia reels in the crowds with canoe races, food and craft stalls, traditional dancing and a beauty pageant (www.facebook.com/teuilafestivalsamoa).

🎎 Loyalty Islands Fair

Enjoy all things Loyalty during three days of activities at this New Caledonian fair (www.iles-loyaute.com), held in turn by Lifou, Maré and Ouvéa. There's dancing, art, fishing and a 'Miss Loyalty Islands' comp.

October

You never know what kind of weather you'll encounter in October in the South Pacific. The cyclone season officially kicks off, but they're rare at this time of year, and temperatures aren't too high.

🎎 Rise of the Palolo

Time to celebrate procreating *palolo* (coral worms) rising from the reef at midnight! The worms are netted and eaten – 'the caviar of the Pacific'! Observed in Samoa and Fiji in October or November, seven days after the full moon. (p273)

🏃 Oceania Sevens

Held at alternating venues across the South Pacific (from Fiji, Tahiti and Samoa to Australia and New Zealand), this annual rugby comp (www.oceaniarugby.com) features as much dance and celebration as collisions between massive men.

🎎 Diwali (Festival of Lights)

Hindus worship Lakshmi (the goddess of wealth and prosperity). In Fiji, this annual festival (www.diwalifestival.org/diwali-in-fiji.html) sees candles and lanterns decorating houses, set on doorsteps and along driveways to light the way for the goddess.

☆ Fest'Napuan

This annual five-day music festival (www.festnapuan.info) in Port Vila, Vanuatu, showcases contemporary Pacific music (you like reggae?). Around 40,000 people rock up each year – book your beds in advance! The parallel Fest'Nalenga offers more traditional sounds.

🎎 Samoana Jazz & Arts Festival

Local and international artists criss-cross between venues in Samoa and American Samoa over a weekend packed with music and other performing arts (www.samoanajazz.com).

🎎 Tisa's Tattoo Festival

Traditional Samoan *tatau* and modern-day needlework are on display – and on offer – at Tisa's (www.tisasbarefootbar.com), a chilled-out beach bar just outside of American Samoa's Pago Pago.

November

Pessimists call this the beginning of the rainy season, but Pacific islanders know it as the beginning of the season of abundance. The fishing is great, and most fruits start to come in season.

🏃 Vaka Eiva

Held in Rarotonga, Vaka Eiva (www.vakaeiva.com) is the Cooks Islands' big-ticket sporting event. Outrigger-canoe races take centre stage in a week-long paddle fest, featuring around 1200 breathless canoeists. (p203)

🏃 Hawaiki Nui Canoe Race

French Polynesia's major annual sporting event (www.hawaikinuivaa.pf), this three-day *pirogue* (outrigger canoe) race is an epic ocean-going affair, from Huahine to Ra'iatea, Taha'a and Bora Bora. Big crowds turn up to watch the paddlers and attend adjunct beachy events.

December

Celebrating Christmas is serious stuff for Melanesians and Polynesians and, as in many places in the world, December is defined by heavy shopping and lots of churchgoing.

🎎 Marquesas Arts Festival

This outrageously visceral French Polynesian arts festival celebrating Marquesan art and identity is held every four years, the next in 2019. Expect lots of trad tattooing, sculpture, woodcarving and *pahu* (drum) displays. There are also 'mini' festivals held between main festival years. (p418)

Itineraries

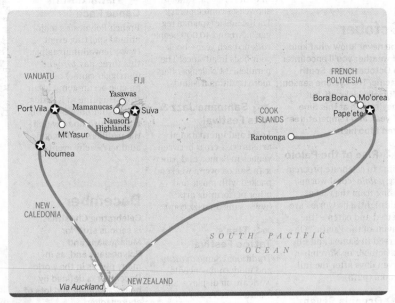

The Grand Tour

Fly to Fiji, the South Pacific's happening-est hub, and boat out to the **Yasawas** or **Mamanucas** where countless islets offer fabulous accommodation and brilliant beaches. Back on Viti Levu, take a bus to the **Nausori Highlands** to experience traditional Fiji. In bigsmoke **Suva**, shopping malls and markets coexist in distinctly South Seas style.

Fly to Vanuatu and join a kava session in a *nakamal* (men's clubhouse) around **Port Vila**, then check out **Mt Yasur** glowing after dark – one of the world's most accessible volcanoes.

Next stop, **Noumea** in New Caledonia, fronting the world's second-largest coral-reef lagoon. Don't miss the Pacific culture at the Tjibaou Cultural Centre and a *pirogue* (outrigger canoe) trip around Île des Pins.

Refine your *bonjour* on your flight to French Polynesia via Auckland. Start with a great Tahitian or French-influenced meal in **Pape'ete**, then take the ferry to **Mo'orea** for superb hiking and snorkelling. Alternatively, fly to **Bora Bora** and fool around with the jet set in an over-the-water bungalow.

Backtrack to Pape'ete, then wing it west for cold beers and hot restaurants on **Rarotonga** in the Cook Islands.

2 MONTHS South Seas Secrets

Lost in the empty ocean way out east, the remote **Marquesas Islands** in French Polynesia are your launch pad, accessed through the Galapagos Islands, Hawai'i or Pape'ete in Tahiti. Expect amazing art, photogenic peaks, fab tropical fruit and not many tourists.

The barren but beautiful **Tuamotus**, the largest group of atolls in the world, are next. It's a good thing you're flying: known as the Dangerous Archipelago, the reefs around here are strewn with shipwrecks.

Reacquaint yourself with civilisation in **Pape'ete** in Tahiti (bars, shops, restaurants – take your pick), followed by some Society Islands lagoon time in laid-back **Huahine** and mysterious **Ra'iatea**. From Pape'ete, jet into Rarotonga in the Cook Islands and beat a hasty retreat to the idyllic beachscapes of **Aitutaki**, an internal flight away.

From Rarotonga, wing through Auckland to **Apia** in Samoa – disorganised and soulful in equal measure. For a weird west-meets-south experience, detour to **Pago Pago Harbour** in nearby American Samoa – greenbacks and gorgeous scenery. Paddle a kayak around the waterfront to take it all in.

Flying out of Apia, raffish **Nuku'alofa** in Tonga is next: check out the Royal Palace and see if you can spy King Tupou VI from the gates. There are few tourists hereabouts: the vibe is low-key, unhurried and unharried. From Nuku'alofa, take an internal flight north to bend elbows with some ancient mariners in the **Neiafu** waterfront bars in Vava'u, fronting onto one of the word's most photogenic natural harbours.

Back in Nuku'alofa, jet out to **Vanuatu** (via Nadi in Fiji) – a nation still recovering from Tropical Cyclone Pam in 2015, and authentic to the core. There's some seriously wild terrain here (volcanoes!), plus this is the culture that invented bungee jumping (using vines, not giant rubber bands).

All this is only mild preparation for the numerous adventures ahead in the untrammelled wilds of the **Solomon Islands**. If you're interested in WWII history, don't miss diving on sunken wrecks or aircraft and warships, and peeling back the foliage from rusty tanks in the jungle.

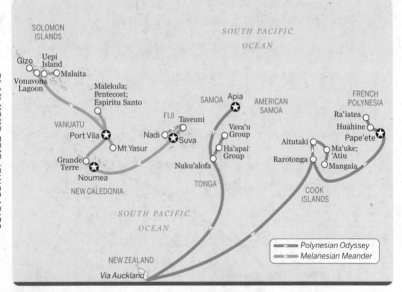

Melanesian Meander
1 MONTH

Get started in **Nadi** in Fiji and fly to **Taveu-ni** to hike along the Lavena coast, then dive over soft corals at the Rainbow Reef. Head back to Viti Levu via cosmopolitan **Suva** and chow down on Indo-Fijian curries.

Next up, fly into New Caledonia's capital **Noumea**, blending Melanesian culture and French chic. Dip into classy restaurants and boutiques, then explore the mangroves, silent forests and barren vistas of the vast main island, **Grande Terre**.

Jet into Vanuatu's colourful **Port Vila** with its rich English and French colonial history. Take a dip at the Mele Cascades and sip some kava before swaying into the Port Vila nightlife. Active **Mt Yasur** volcano on Tanna island is a show-stopper, as is the two-day trek across the Dog's Head on **Malekula**, past cannibal sites, caves and traditional villages. Continue to **Pentecost**, where farmers invented bungee jumping, then **Espiritu Santo** for world-class diving.

Another flight delivers you to the Solomon Islands: boat around gorgeous **Von-avona Lagoon**, snorkel or dive off **Uepi island** and chill out in **Gizo**. Finish up in **Malaita**, where locals summon sharks and live on artificial islands.

Polynesian Odyssey
1 MONTH

Kick things off in **Apia**, Samoa's capital: check out the Robert Louis Stevenson Museum, explore Upolu and spend at least one night on the beach in a traditional *fale* (house). Take the ferry to Savai'i for cave tunnels, lava fields and white beaches, then visit the forest-engulfed Pulemelei Mound, Polynesia's largest ancient monument.

Fly to **Nuku'alofa** in the ancient Kingdom of Tonga: eyeball the Royal Palace en route to lively Talamahu Market. To the north, the **Ha'apai Group** offers beachy living in thatched *fale*, while the **Vava'u Group** delivers active adventures like sea kayaking, diving and sailing.

Jag through the duty-free shops at Auckland Airport en route to the Cook Islands' capital **Rarotonga**. Hike the cross-island track, snorkel at sublime Muri Beach, or catch a plane to exquisite **Aitutaki**. Explore the caves of the *makatea* (raised coral islands) of **'Atiu**, **Mangaia** and **Ma'uke**.

From Rarotonga, fly to **Pape'ete**, the chic capital of the French Pacific, and squeeze in a visit to sleepy **Huahine** and the Polynesian spiritual capital of **Ra'iatea**.

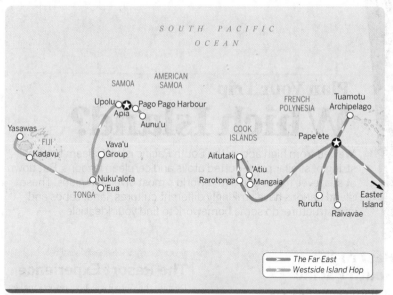

SOUTH PACIFIC OCEAN

SAMOA AMERICAN SAMOA

Upolu Pago Pago Harbour FRENCH POLYNESIA Tuamotu Archipelago
Apia
Aunu'u COOK ISLANDS Pape'ete
Yasawas Vava'u Group
FIJI Aitutaki
Kadavu 'Atiu
Rarotonga Mangaia
Nuku'alofa
'Eua Rururu Easter Island
TONGA Raivavae

The Far East
Westside Island Hop

3 WEEKS Westside Island-Hop

Island-hopping the western central region of the South Pacific from Australia or New Zealand is an easy South Seas jaunt.

Start with a week in Fiji exploring the blissful small islands and beaches of the **Yasawas** before heading off-grid for a few days to dive, hike and relax in an eco-attuned resort on **Kadavu**.

Fly into untouristy Tonga for a week, with a short stop in **Nuku'alofa** before taking the world's shortest commercial flight to little **'Eua** for some hiking. Further north, the **Vava'u Group** offers brilliant sailing and snorkelling, some harbourside daiquiris or more resort time.

Spend your final week in the Samoas, driving around **Upolu** for a few days discovering empty white-sand beaches and enjoying the friendly chaos of **Apia**.

Spend your last few days around glorious **Pago Pago Harbour** in American Samoa, where sheer mountains plunge down to colonial architecture and fishing industry humbleness. Be sure to visit the trad villages spectacularly sited around the island's remote north bays, and also walk around the car-free, carefree isle of **Aunu'u**.

3 WEEKS The Far East

This island galaxy is far, far away, even from the rest of the South Pacific. So while you're here, make the most of it!

First fly into **Rarotonga** in the Cook Islands to swim in the dreamy lagoon and hike the island's many inland trails. Take a side trip either to kayak around the turquoise lagoon nooks in **Aitutaki**, go bird-watching on **'Atiu**, or visit the mysterious limestone burial caves on **Mangaia**.

Back on Rarotonga, take the short flight to **Pape'ete** in Tahiti then fly out to either the **Tuamotu archipelago** for diving, snorkelling and castaway coral atolls, or to the Austral Islands: **Rururu** for some more cave exploration or **Raivavae** for traditional island culture, hiking and scenery to rival Bora Bora's.

If you're not ready for the adventure to end yet, continue your journey eastward with a long flight to **Easter Island**. There's nothing quite like the first time you see the island's iconic *moai* (statues), standing sentinel on grassy slopes, gazing out across the chilly spans of the South Pacific Ocean.

Plan Your Trip
Which Island?

Viewed from high above, the South Pacific islands seem to be a string of similar palm-dotted atolls and cerulean lagoons. But down at sea level, this is one of the world's most diverse regions. These island nations have strikingly different cultures, landscapes and infrastructure: do some homework to find your ideal isle.

Best of the South Pacific

Best Romantic Resorts

Vahine Island (French Polynesia), Matangi Island Resort (Fiji), Etu Moana (Cook Islands), Havannah (Vanuatu), L'Escapade (New Caledonia), Sandy Beach Resort (Tonga), Sunrise Beach Cabanas Eco Resort (Vanuatu)

Best for Backpackers

Beachcomber Island Resort (Fiji), Namu'a Island Beach Fale (Samoa), Chez Guynette (French Polynesia), Traveller's Budget Motel (Vanuatu), Aremango Guesthouse (Rarotonga), Hideaway (Tonga), Tisa's Barefoot Bar (American Samoa)

Best Eco-Resorts

Treasure Island Eco-Resort (Tonga), Tetepare Descendants' Association (Solomon Islands), Papageno Eco-Resort (Fiji), Bokissa Eco Island Resort (Vanuatu), Jean-Michel Cousteau Fiji Islands Resort (Fiji)

Best Dreamy Locales

Erakor Island Resort (Vanuatu), Aitutaki Lagoon Resort (Cook Islands), Le Meridien Île des Pins (New Caledonia), Coconuts Beach Club Resort (Samoa), Namena Island Resort (Fiji), Matafonua Lodge (Tonga)

The Resort Experience

Despite the stereotype, luxe resorts make up only a fraction of South Pacific accommodation. Big international chains have moved into tourist hot spots like Fiji, Tahiti and Vanuatu, but you'll also find endearing boutique resorts that blend local style and warmth with comfort and opulence.

Resorts: Which Island?

American Samoa As per Samoa, there's not a lot of swoon-worthy accommodation here, but there are a few simple, international-style hotels and upmarket B&Bs to choose from.

Easter Island This island has a handful of surprisingly posh choices – although few have pools or beaches and all are geared towards getting out to see the sights more than lounging around.

Fiji Got kids? Fiji is the best family resort destination in the region. It also caters well to active honeymooners and value seekers. Friendly service has been perfected.

New Caledonia On par with Tahiti for price but with modern Melanesian twists, resorts here cater less to the masses and usually offer sublime lagoon-front locations.

Rarotonga & the Cook Islands A good mix of international standards and boutique charm. Families are well catered for and there are plenty of activities and fun nightlife.

Samoa There's nothing too luxurious here but the beaches are dazzling, the atmosphere authentic and stress nonexistent (with or without the swanky spa).

Solomon Islands Honiara and Western Province are the only places with real resorts. The best (found at the latter) are diving and ecology oriented. Think: total disconnection from the world.

Tahiti & French Polynesia If you're ever going to pamper yourself silly, this is the place to do it. Many top hotels are on isolated *motu* (islets).

Tonga Head out to the Ha'apai or Vava'u groups for a scant number of eclectic, though not necessarily fancy, resorts in remote settings. Many have an eco bent; none have swimming pools.

Vanuatu Port Vila is swarming with sumptuous resorts. Espiritu Santo has some decadent choices well placed for diving; Tanna has a fun resort scene geared towards climbing Mt Yasur.

Resorts: What to Expect

Most resorts have restaurants, bars and a swimming pool (at bigger places), plus a shop and an activities desk. There are several accommodation-block-style resorts, but many feature individual bungalows (*fale, fare, bure* etc, depending on the local lingo). Superswanky places may have overwater bungalows (particularly in French Polynesia).

You'll usually be met at the airport and transferred to your resort by speedboat, plane or minivan. From the front desk onward you'll be invited to partake in organised activities, or you can just chill and explore the island on your own.

Food & Drink Resort-Style

All resorts have at least one restaurant, serving a mix of Western, Polynesian or

---

Melanesian, Asian and fusion specialities, usually with an imported chef. The bar will be well stocked and, in the French territories at least, the wine list will be decent. Some bigger outfits also stage a traditional dance performance and buffet weekly. Breakfast is often a buffet and other meals à la carte, with simple options like burgers and sandwiches for lunch.

The Local Experience

Away from the resorts, the South Pacific offers up a wide range of sleeping options, from sandy campsites to small, locally run hotels. If you want to travel independently and experience the culture at ground level, go local and adjust your standards accordingly (the hot water and wi-fi may be patchy, but the cheery vibes are worth it). Note that smaller, family-owned places, especially on remote islands, may not take credit cards.

Local: Which Island?

Each country has its own local accommodation style, from humble family pensions in Tahiti and New Caledonia to open traditional *fale* in Tonga and Samoa. Yet it's not all budget: small boutique hotels and guesthouses are increasingly popular.

American Samoa Local B&Bs and guesthouses are the way to go in American Samoa, with loads of Polynesian charm.

Easter Island Easter Island has about 120 places to stay, with mostly *hostales* and *residenciales* (homestays) on offer. Small and sociable, these range from a few bare rooms in someone's house to simple, comfortable bungalows.

Fiji Fiji offers everything from bare-bones backpackers to cultural-connection homestays and gorgeously designed, upscale beach bungalows. There's a party scene in tourist hot spots; things are quieter on less-visited islands like Kadavu and Taveuni.

New Caledonia Even basic, dirt-cheap accommodation in New Caledonia comes with power points, lights, pristine cotton sheets and, often, gardens, restaurants and pools. Campsites occupy some of the best beachy spots here.

Rarotonga & the Cook Islands On Rarotonga and Aitutaki stay at laid-back backpackers with activities aplenty, or in good-value, self-contained

---

HOLIDAY RENTALS

Holiday rentals (private homes or rooms rented by an individual) are becoming more popular in the South Pacific, particularly in Fiji. These often self-catering options can be fun and economical for families or groups that plan on staying in one place for more than a night or two. Handy websites to peruse include www.homeaway.com, www.vrbo.com, www.flipkey.com and www.airbnb.com.

holiday rentals. On the Cooks' smaller outer islands, go local at family-run homestays.

Samoa Samoa's signature accommodation is the beach *fale,* an elongated octagonal hut on stilts with no walls but coconut-thatch louvres to drop or raise, depending on your privacy and ventilation requirements.

Solomon Islands Resthouses and hostels here are inexpensive, with shared bathrooms and local guests. 'Lodges', mostly in Marovo, are simple but authentic with loads of character. Some villages have a leafhouse (bungalow with a thatched roof) set aside for visitors.

Tahiti & French Polynesia Family pensions or hotel-like *fare d'hôte* are everywhere here – and are often the only choice on remote islands. These range from a hard bed in someone's back room with a shared cold-water bathroom, to stylish but homey boutique hotels.

Tonga The Kingdom of Tonga has a wide variety of sleeping options from *fale* to bog-basic back-packers, though not much camping. For a cultural experience, stay at a Tongan-run place, such as Port Wine Guest House (p458) in Vava'u, Hideaway (p447) on 'Eua or Nerima Lodge (p439) in Nuku'alofa.

Vanuatu Around 90% of accommodation here is simple, with thin foam mattresses adding some comfort. Choose between guesthouses or bungalows: the former are usually comprised of rooms in a concrete building; the latter are more atmospheric thatched houses. Bathrooms are usually separate. Food is served in another hut.

Local: What to Expect

Some small lodgings on main islands do have air-con, but most will be fan-cooled and offer mosquito nets and coils. Swimming pools are almost nonexistent. All but the most rudimentary should have towels

CAMPING & HOSTELS

Camping options come and go, but generally it's a matter of small hotels and guesthouses having areas where you can pitch a tent outside and use the facilities inside. Western-style hostels are extremely rare. Locally owned budget guesthouses that offer simple rooms with shared bath-rooms do a good job of filling this gap, although few have dorm beds.

and linen; most can provide airport trans-fers if arranged in advance.

On the main islands you'll find every-thing from simple guesthouses to boutique hotels. On remote islands, however, you may encounter faulty plumbing, cold showers, unreliable electricity and 'rustic' vibes. If you need wi-fi, check in advance.

Food & Drink Local-Style

Many options on outer islands may offer (and sometimes insist on) half board, which usually means breakfast and dinner with other guests. Full board includes all meals. In many cases, the food is delicious and special needs are catered for where possible.

Activities

Resorts, upscale boutique accommodation and even hard-core budget lodges usually have activities available for guests, or work with independent operators they know and trust.

Millions of square kilometres of balmy tropical water, pristine lagoons and empty beaches are the obvious attraction here. But there's more to the South Pacific than watery pursuits. Opportunities abound for hiking, cycling, horse riding, birdwatching and caving, plus the chance to visit archae-ological sites and WWII relics.

Church on Sundays The South Pacific is devoutly Christian and Sunday is solemnly observed as a day of rest: some activities in some areas might be regarded as disrespectful. Rolling into church on a Sunday to hear the beautiful singing is, for many, a highlight of their South Pacific travels.

Diving Many resorts have dive centres, and local accommodation operators can usually hook you up with diving if it's available on the island.

Fishing The South Pacific is nirvana for anglers, with great sportfishing and excellent big-game fishing. Common catches include yellowfin and skipjack tuna, wahoo, barracuda, sailfish, and blue, black and striped marlin.

Hiking The loftier Pacific islands offer ter-rific opportunities to hike through magnificent forested interiors, with waterfalls, lava-formed coastal trails, archaeological sites and even live volcanoes to ogle. Some walks require local guides – resorts and guesthouses can assist.

PLANNING & BOOKING

Outside of high season (June through August and mid-December through mid-January) you can arrive just about anywhere in the South Pacific without any idea of where you're staying or what you're doing tomorrow. But during the seasonal rush, the better places will be booked out – plan in advance.

Note that, as many tracks cross land under customary ownership, you may need permission or possibly have to pay a small fee. You'll find excellent hiking in Fiji, French Polynesia, New Caledonia, Samoa and the Cook Islands. Walking in the heat can be miserable and/or dangerous: sun protection, insect repellent and plenty of water are mandatory.

Island & Lagoon Tours Minivans, private cars or 4WDs may take you around to see the island sights. More often than not though, the real adventure is on the water: boats (posh catamarans, ferries or old outboard skiffs) tour the lagoons and can whisk you away to deserted beaches of unimaginable beauty – plus you'll often get a picnic.

Sailing BYO yacht to the South Pacific or get a berth on someone else's. All Pacific countries have yacht clubs: many people charter yachts in French Polynesia and Vava'u in Tonga, with or without a crew.

Snorkelling If you're into snorkelling, the South Pacific is made for you! Reef and lagoon trips on boats of all kinds abound, but it's a good idea to bring your own gear (rental equipment may be in shabby shape). Some of the best spots include Somosomo Strait and Great Astrolabe Reef in Fiji, Motu Nui on Easter Island, the Loyalty Islands and Île aux Canards in New Caledonia, Tikehau and Bora Bora in French Polynesia, and Rarotonga's lagoon in the Cook Islands. Perhaps the best of the lot is off Uepi Island in the Solomons' Marovo Lagoon, with reef sharks, giant clams, fish and corals in dizzying abundance.

Spas Day spas aren't as big in the South Pacific as you might expect. Internationally owned and larger resorts will often have dedicated spas offering massage and exotic treatments, but these are touted as perks more than a central aspect of what's on offer. Some smaller boutique resorts may also have spas, but these are the exception rather than the rule. Local business-targeted, service-oriented day spas in island capitals can be less expensive than those geared towards tourists.

Surfing Polynesians invented surfing! Surfers come in bushy-blonde droves to French Polynesia, which hosts the Billabong Pro Tahiti (www.worldsurfleague.com) at Teahupoo. Fiji is popular too, but for uncrowded waves head to the Solomon Islands, Samoa, the Cook Islands, Vanuatu and Tonga. The reef breaks in these places are heavy, man, often with a long paddle across a lagoon and a gnarly coral landing if you get that take-off wrong: surfers need to be intermediate at least, and should get some local advice before paddling out. Few islands have surfboards for sale or hire – BYO.

Water Sports Most resorts have a water-sports centre (check before booking). These vary enormously: some offer a basic array of canoes and windsurfers; others run the gauntlet from waterskiing to kitesurfing and wakeboarding. Sea kayaking is big here, and tours are offered in a handful of countries, including Fiji, Tonga and Samoa. Kitesurfers have discovered the wonders of Aitutaki's superb lagoon in the Cook Islands, Uoleva island in Tonga and Mo'orea in French Polynesia. New Caledonia is also good for kitesurfing and windsurfing.

Wildlife Watching Migrating humpback whales spend much of the second half of the year in the South Pacific, and several countries, including New Caledonia, Tonga, the Cook Islands and Rurutu in French Polynesia, offer the opportunity to view them. It's big business here, but not without controversy: have a read of the boxed text Whale-Watching Ethics (p461) to make an informed choice before you book. Twitchers and bug fans won't need to search far to spy seabirds and gloriously coloured butterflies.

Top: Overwater bungalows in Bora Bora (p385), Tahiti
Bottom: Hanging out in Tonga (p432)

South Pacific Diving

The South Pacific is as much a Garden of Eden below the waterline as on land. Expect awesome walls, close encounters with sharks and manta rays, iconic wrecks and gorgeous reefs replete with multihued tropical fish. As if that weren't enough, waters are warm year-round and each island has its own personality.

French Polynesia

Society Islands

The Society Islands have a profusion of walls, reefs and passes, many teeming with marine life ranging from small critters to large predators.

Tahiti is a great place to brush up your skills, with a variety of uncomplicated dives a mere 10- to 20-minute boat ride away from Pape'ete, the capital. For something different, head to Tahiti Iti, which boasts untouched sites that are only used by one dive centre. The underwater scenery is the main draw, with a profusion of steep drop-offs, canyons, arches and caves.

Nearby Mo'orea is a perfect introduction to more challenging dive sites in the Tuamotus. Most diving is focused at the entrances to Cook's Bay and Opunohu Bay, and off the northwestern corner of the island. The reefs here slope gently away in a series of canyons and valleys. In Ra'iatea, be sure to log the *Nordby*, the only real wreck dive in French Polynesia.

Bora Bora is a great place to learn to dive, and sightings of eagle rays, manta rays and lemon sharks are common. From Bora Bora, fly to Maupiti and enjoy the aptly named Manta Point, in the lagoon. This cleaning station is visited by manta

Best Underwater Adventures

When to Go

Diving is possible year-round, although conditions vary according to the season and location. Visibility is reduced in the wet season, as the water is muddied by sediments brought into the sea by rivers. In most South Pacific countries the water temperature peaks at a warm 29°C during the rainy season, but can drop to 20°C in some areas, including New Caledonia and Easter Island, at certain times of the year.

Best for Wreck Diving

Vanuatu, Solomon Islands, Tonga

Best for Underwater Photographers

French Polynesia, Fiji, Solomon Islands, Vanuatu, New Caledonia, Tonga

Best for Shark Encounters

Tuamotus (French Polynesia), Fiji, Solomon Islands, New Caledonia

Best for Beginners

Society Islands (French Polynesia), Viti Levu & Mamanucas (Fiji), Cook Islands, New Caledonia, Tonga

rays; small fish come out of the coral heads to scour the mantas of parasites, in less than 10m.

Tuamotus

Consistently billed as the South Pacific's best diving destination, the Tuamotus are brimming with adrenaline-pumping dive sites. What makes diving here exceptional are the pass currents and the density of predators just offshore. Base yourself in Rangiroa and dive Tiputa Pass amid a swirl of grey sharks and reef species. The atoll of Fakarava shares similar characteristics, with two sensational passes, Garuae Pass and Tumakohua Pass. Fans of manta rays should head to Tikehau, which claims a manta cleaning station in the lagoon. Although they're less charismatic than Rangiroa, Fakarava or Tikehau, the atolls of Mataiva, Makemo and Ahe deserve attention for offering pristine sites.

Solomon Islands

Guadalcanal

Wrecks galore! With such turbulent history, it's no surprise that Guadalcanal has number of world-class sunken WWII vessels lying close to the shore. Most sites can be reached by car from Honiara. A few favourites include Bonegi I and II, about 12km west of Honiara. Bonegi I, a giant-sized Japanese merchant transport ship, also known as the *Hirokawa Maru,* lies in 3m of water descending to 55m, just a few fin strokes offshore. About 500m further west, the upper works of Bonegi II,

or *Kinugawa Maru,* break the surface, a towel's throw from the beach. Experienced divers will make a beeline for the *Seminole* and the USS *John Penn*, east of Honiara.

Tulagi

Easily accessed from the Honiara, Tulagi is a must for wreck enthusiasts. By far, its main attraction is its sunken WWII US and Japanese ships and planes of varying shapes and sizes lying off Tulagi Harbour. This underwater graveyard, which includes a 106m-long US Navy destroyer, a 150m-long oil tanker and two seaplanes, makes for a fantastic collection of vibrant artificial reefs. The only drawback on Tulagi is the depth. Most wrecks are deep dives, in the 30m to 60m range. Visibility is not the strong point here; expect 5m to 15m on average.

There are also a couple of awesome reef dives, such as Twin Tunnels, which features two chimneys that start on the top of a reef at a depth of about 12m.

New Georgia

The Munda area is a diver's treat, with a good balance of scenic seascapes, elaborate reef structures, dense marine life and atmospheric wrecks, including a WWII US fighter that rests undamaged on a sandy bottom.

Marovo Lagoon is another stunner. The main diving area is around Uepi island to the north. It has a vibrant assemblage of dramatic walls (on the ocean side), exhilarating passages and uncomplicated reef dives, all within close reach of Uepi island.

DIVING IN THE SOUTH PACIFIC – AN OVERVIEW

Country	Wrecks	Fish	Special Features
Cook Islands	✓	✓	easy dives
Easter Island	N/A	✓	water clarity, underwater topography
Fiji	✓	✓✓	soft corals, shark dives
French Polynesia	✓	✓✓✓	shark dives, manta rays, drift dives
New Caledonia	✓	✓✓✓	shark dives, drift dives
Samoa	✓✓	✓	pristine dive sites
Solomon Islands	✓✓✓	✓✓	muck dives, corals
Tonga	✓	✓✓	caves
Vanuatu	✓✓✓	✓✓	corals

Another not-to-be-missed area is Ghizo Island, further west. Here again the diving is superlative, with a stunning mix of WWII wrecks, including a virtually intact Japanese freighter, superb offshore reefs and plummeting walls. Kennedy Island is a lovely spot to learn to dive, with a parade of reef fish on the sprawling reef.

Fiji

Viti Levu

Viti Levu is normally the visiting diver's first glimpse of Fiji. The best diving is found off Nananu-i-Ra to the north, which is renowned for its healthy reefs, dense marine life and atmospheric underwater terrain. However, it tends to be overshadowed by Beqa lagoon, to the south, which is famous for its impressive shark-feeding sessions – up to eight species of sharks, including bull sharks, tiger sharks and lemon sharks, can be seen in one single dive. While it's certainly thrilling, it's more a show than a dive. And although these tightly choreographed dives are conducted in a professional way by experienced guides, such interactions may disrupt natural behaviour patterns and carry an element of risk. Diving in Beqa lagoon is not limited to shark dives; it also features fantastic soft coral sites.

Taveuni

Taveuni has gained international recognition in the diving community. The Somosomo Strait, a narrow stretch of ocean funnelled between Taveuni and Vanua Levu, offers exhilarating drift dives in nutrient-filled waters and steep drop-offs mantled with healthy soft corals. Purple Wall, Great White Wall, Rainbow Passage, Vuna Reef and Annie's Bommies are the perennial faves in this area.

Kadavu

Kadavu's highlight is Great Astrolabe Reef, a 100km-long barrier reef that hugs the southern and eastern coasts of the island. This reef acts as a magnet for countless species. The seascape is a mind-boggling combination of canyons, crevices and arches.

PRETRIP PREPARATION

➡ Make sure you possess a current diving-certification card (C-card) from a recognised scuba-diving instructional agency and bring it with you. Dive operators will need to see it. It's a good idea to have your dive logbook with you as well.

➡ When you prepare your itinerary, remember to allow 24 hours after diving before you fly. Careful attention to flight times is necessary in the South Pacific because so much of the interisland transportation is by air.

Mamanucas

Diving in the Mamanucas is less spectacular, but still rewarding, especially for novice divers, with a wealth of easy, relaxing dives. Most dive sites are scattered along the Malolo Barrier Reef or off the nearby islets.

Bligh Water & the Lomaiviti Group

If you have the chance to embark on a live-aboard, you'll probably dive the Bligh Water area and the Lomaiviti Group. Two seamounts rising from the abyss to just below the surface include E6 and Mt Mutiny – both act as magnets for pelagics and reef species. Off Gau island, Nigali Passage is an adrenaline-packed drift dive.

Vanuatu

Vanuatu's diving spots are based around the main islands of Santo and Efate. Most divers come to Vanuatu for one thing and one thing only: the legendary USS *President Coolidge*, which lies a few strokes from Santo's shore. She's trumpeted as the best dive wreck in the world and, being 200m long and 25m large, one of the biggest. The USS *President Coolidge* was a luxury cruise liner converted to a troop carrier during WWII. In 1942 the ship struck two mines and sank very close to the shore. Amazingly, more than 70 years after her demise, she's still in good shape. The only downside is that the *Coolidge*

Diver exploring a Hellcat wreck, Solomon Islands (p336)

has overshadowed other wrecks worthy of exploration, including the nearby USS *Tucker*.

If you need a break from wrecks, sample some truly excellent reef dives off Santo. Cindy's Reef is a favourite, as is Tutuba Point. At Million Dollar Point, divers swim among thousands of tonnes of military paraphernalia that were discarded here by the US Navy when they left the country.

Although Efate can't compete with Santo, it offers a good mix of reef dives, wall dives and wrecks.

New Caledonia

Diving is a well-established activity in New Caledonia. The country's main claim to fame is its lagoon – one of the largest in the world. It's protected by a barrier reef that extends over 1600km.

You could start your diving adventures in Noumea, the capital, which offers some truly spectacular diving near the passes

of Boulari and Dumbea. Coral is not the strong point of these areas but for fish action they're unbeatable. About eight different dives can be done here. And for wreck buffs, there are the *Dieppoise*, New Caledonia's best shipwreck, which was scuttled in 1988 and lies 26m deep, and the *Humboldt*, a 45m-long trawler.

Some great diving is also found off Hienghène to the east of Grande Terre, which boasts outstanding topography and prolific marine life. Off Poindimié, the reef structures are blanketed in a bright mosaic of soft corals.

Don't miss diving off Île des Pins, which has superb dives near Gadji's reef and Récif de Kasmira. For something unusual, try Grotte de la Troisième (Cave of the Third), which features an inland cave filled with crystal-clear fresh water. You'll navigate inside the cave, at about 6m deep, wending your way among stalactites and stalagmites.

The sites around the Loyalty Islands are also well worth bookmarking. Lifou's signature dives are Gorgones Reef and Shoji Reef, with sea fans wafting in the current the main attraction. Keep your eyes peeled for pelagics, including tuna, sharks, rays and barracuda. Ouvéa is an emerging destination for divers. You'll be rewarded with pristine sites, including the sensational Pass du Styx, which is said to be one of the best drift dives in Melanesia.

Easter Island

Easter Island is still a secret, word-of-mouth diving destination. But don't look for throngs of big fish or psychedelic corals – they are rare here. What's the pull, then? In a word, visibility. The lack of pollution, run-off, particles and plankton guarantees maximum water clarity – 40m is the norm. Another highlight is the dramatic seascape, with breathtaking drop-offs, arches and overhangs. Most sites are scattered along the western and northern coasts, with Motu Nui as a prime diving and snorkelling spot. They are suitable for all levels.

Since the island is devoid of protective barrier reefs, be prepared to cope with sometimes-difficult conditions to get to the sites, especially from June to September.

Cook Islands

The Cook Islands offers relaxed diving for recreational divers in a safe environment – it's got a bit of everything, but on a small

PLAN YOUR TRIP SOUTH PACIFIC DIVING

RESPONSIBLE DIVING

The Pacific islands and atolls are ecologically vulnerable. By following these guidelines while diving, you can help preserve the ecology and beauty of the reefs:

➡ Encourage dive operators in their efforts to establish permanent moorings at appropriate dive sites.

➡ Practise and maintain proper buoyancy control.

➡ Avoid touching living marine organisms with your body or equipment.

➡ Take great care in underwater caves, as your air bubbles can damage fragile organisms.

➡ Minimise your disturbance of marine animals.

➡ Don't support interactions with animals, such as shark feeding.

➡ Take home all your rubbish and any litter you may find as well.

➡ Never stand on corals, even if they look solid and robust.

scale. On the south side of Rarotonga you'll enjoy some good dives in the passages and along the sloping reef. Expect canyons, caves and tunnels. Rarotonga also has three wrecks that are regularly dived. It's possible to dive off Aitutaki as well (there's one dive centre on the island).

THE FIRST TIME

The South Pacific provides ideal and safe conditions for beginners, with its warm, crystalline waters and prolific marine life. Arrange an introductory dive with a dive centre to give you a feel for what it's like to swim underwater. It will begin on dry land, where the instructor will run through basic safety procedures and show you the equipment.

The dive itself takes place in a safe location and lasts between 20 and 40 minutes under the guidance of the instructor, who will hold your hand if need be and guide your movements at a depth of between 3m and 10m. Some centres start the instruction in waist-high water in a hotel swimming pool or on the beach.

There is no formal procedure, but you shouldn't dive if you have a medical condition such as acute ear, nose and throat problems, epilepsy or heart disease (such as infarction), if you have a cold or sinusitis, or if you are pregnant.

LIVE-ABOARDS

For hard-core divers, there are also a few live-aboard dive boats operating out of various countries to access remote locations. Check operator websites for itineraries.

Here's a selection:

➡ **Aqua Polynésie** (www.aquatiki.com) Tuamotu Islands, French Polynesia

➡ **Bilikiki** (www.bilikiki.com) Solomon Islands

➡ **Solomon Islands Dive Expeditions** (www.solomonsdiving.com) Solomon Islands

➡ **Nai'a** (www.naia.com.fj) Fiji

➡ **Fiji Aggressor** (www.aggressor.com/fiji.php) Fiji

Tonga

Whale watching is so popular in Tonga that it has stolen the show. While Tongan waters will never be mistaken for those of, say, French Polynesia, there's some excellent diving off Ha'apai and Vava'u. The reefs are peppered with caves, swim-throughs and chimneys that make for atmospheric playgrounds and eerie ambience. You'll also find lots of varieties of hard and soft corals. A few wrecks add a touch of variety.

Samoa

Samoa isn't a hard-core diver's destination, but for those looking for uncrowded sites, it's hard to beat. Novice divers in particular will feel comfortable – the dive conditions are less challenging than anywhere else but still offer excellent fish action. Many of the popular dive sites are close to the villages of Maninoa and Si'umu on the south coast of Upolu; and off the north coast of Savai'i.

Dive Centres

In most cases, the standards of diving facilities are high in the South Pacific.

➡ All dive centres are affiliated to internationally recognised certifying agencies: Professional Association of Diving Instructors (PADI), CMAS, Scuba Schools International (SSI).

➡ Dive centres welcome divers provided they can produce a certificate from an internationally recognised agency.

➡ They offer a range of services, such as introductory dives, Nitrox dives, night dives, exploratory dives and certification programs.

➡ In general, you can expect well-maintained equipment, well-equipped facilities and friendly, knowledgeable, English-speaking staff.

➡ Be aware that each dive centre has its own personality and style. Visit the place first to get the feel of the operation.

➡ Dive centres are open year-round. Most are land-based and many are attached to a hotel. They typically offer two to four dives a day.

➡ Diving in the South Pacific is expensive compared with most destinations in Asia, the Caribbean or the Red Sea; expect to pay US$90 to US$120 for an introductory dive and US$80 for a single dive (without gear). Dive packages (eg five or 10 dives) are usually cheaper.

➡ Gear hire may or may not be included in the price of the dive, so bring your own equipment if you plan to dive a lot.

➡ Almost all dive centres accept credit cards.

Travel with Children

Few regions in the world are as family friendly as the South Pacific. With endless sunshine, boundless beaches and swimming and snorkelling on tap, there's plenty to keep kids engaged. Family is profoundly important and children are cherished in island cultures – your kids can expect plenty of cheek-tweaking attention!

South Pacific For Kids

Water Activities

Diving, Snorkelling & Swimming Toddlers will be happy on a soft beach with a hermit crab to hassle. Anywhere with a shallow, sandy bottom is great for learning to swim, while seasoned swimmers can cruise the lagoons. Many dive centres offer introductory Professional Association of Diving Instructors (PADI) courses for kids; see www.padi.com.

Wildlife Watching Whale and dolphin watching is big business hereabouts; see **Whale-Watching Ethics** (p461) to help you make an informed decision on participation. There are also sea turtles and myriad birds to spy, plus saltwater crocodiles in the Solomons and Vanuatu. Fruit bats (flying foxes) hang around everywhere east of the Cook Islands; and the further east you travel, the more interesting the reptile life becomes.

Surfing It can be hard to rent a board on many islands, but some hotels keep them for guest use. Boogie boards are often sold in local shops; if you can, buy one and make a local kid's year by leaving it with them when you leave! Hit the beach breaks with little kids; reef-breaking monsters are for experienced wave hounds only.

On Dry Land

Hiking & Adventure Over-eights will love tropical island interiors, studded with waterfalls with icy

Best Regions for Kids

Fiji

With family-oriented resorts on mellow beaches, interesting culture (Fijian and Indo-Fijian) and magical interior landscapes, Fiji is our top pick for families.

Tonga

There's lots of roomy accommodation in Tonga, and plenty of things to keep kids entertained (caves, snorkels, boats, lagoons...). The food isn't spicy, and Tongans love kids!

Vanuatu

Volcanoes and cannibal caves may lure you away from Vanuatu's idyllic coasts. European-tinged Port Vila is a very family-friendly capital.

Rarotonga & the Cook Islands

Beyond the beach there are fruit smoothies aplenty, and activities from lagoon tours and snorkelling to gentle backroad cycling and exploring Rarotonga's reefs on a semisubmersible boat.

New Caledonia

An aquarium, a cultural centre and cool critters (fruit bats!) – great fun when you need a break from the beach.

Snorkelling past coral and seashells in Tonga (p432)

pools, dark caves, lakes and – on Vanuatu, Tonga and American Samoa – active volcanoes!

Archaeology Many ancient sites in the South Pacific aren't cordoned off: you can climb on almost anything, but apply common sense and be respectful.The surrounding jungles often hold other discoveries, like wild passionfruit and huge banyan trees.

Horse Riding & Cycling All-ages trail rides through hills and plantations is an option in the larger South Pacific countries. Bicycles can be rented on most islands; kid-sized bicycles are harder to find (check gears and brakes are working, too).

Eating Out

Most visiting kids will happily munch on South Pacific fish, fruit, chicken and coconut. Many urban eateries offer kid-pleasers (hamburgers, fried rice), while unfamiliar local foods are generally soft, unspicy and inoffensive (taro, *kumara* – sweet potato – and breadfruit). Baby supplies are available in most places...and when all else fails, there's ice cream!

Teens After Dark

It's normal for whole families to party together here: teens are welcome at any sort of local dance or show. Nightclubs in places like Pape'ete and Suva also swarm with high-schoolers. Be warned, though – the booze flows (among other substances) and the vibe can sometimes be rather 'meat-market'.

Children's Highlights
Beach Yourself

➡ **Fiji** Swimming, baby turtles and minigolf at Treasure Island Resort. (p105)

➡ **Tonga** Snorkelling and watching the surfers at Ha'atafu Beach. (p445)

➡ **Cook Islands** Snorkelling in the shallow marine reserve waters off Rarotonga's south coast. (p210)

➡ **Samoa** Bigger kids will adore staying in traditional open-air *fale* (houses) right on the beach.

Get Cultured

➡ **Easter Island** Larger-than-life archaeology. (p49)

➡ **Vanuatu** Cultural shows at Ekasup Cultural Village. (p478)

➡ **French Polynesia** Visiting the Musée De Tahiti et des Îles. (p360)

Natural Encounters

➡ **Fiji** Sliding down rock chutes at Waitavala Water Slide (p130) or going nose-to-beak with rare birds at Kula Eco Park (p94).

➡ **Tonga** Birdwatching and butterfly-spotting on jungle walks at 'Ene'io Botanical Garden. (p461)

➡ **Samoa** Ogling the amazing saltwater sprays at the Alofaaga Blowholes (p284) and exploring the eerie lava fields of northern Savai'i (p275).

Planning

There are a few sweeping kiddie generalisations that can ease your South Pacific passage. One essential is sunscreen (expensive on many islands), plus insect repellent and rain gear. BYO kid-size snorkelling gear, too.

At flashy resorts there may be organised kids' activities as part of the deal. Some hotels and resorts have no-children policies; others let kids stay for free – check when you're booking.

Note that child-rearing is often a communal responsibility here – you might find your toddler on the hip of a motherly eight-year-old, or see your older kids absorbed into games with local children.

Babies & Toddlers

A folding pushchair is handy, despite scrappy (or nonexistent) footpaths. Strap-on baby carriers are a better idea for hiking or exploring archaeological sites.

Public baby-change facilities are rare: bring a portable change mat and disinfectant handwash gel. Disposable nappies (diapers) and powdered milk (formula) are available from pharmacies and supermarkets in many large towns, but they can be expensive. Don't expect high chairs anywhere beyond the fancy resorts.

A lightweight mosquito net to drape over your toddler's cot is also a good idea.

Six- to 12-Year-Olds

Help middle-sized kids get more out of their South Seas experience: pack binoculars to zoom in on wildlife, surfers etc; a camera to inject some fun into 'boring' grown-up sights and walks; and field guides to island flora and fauna ('Is that a red shining parrot or a kingfisher?').

Teenagers

Getting teenagers to attempt some local language is a sure-fire way to shake off sullenness: pick up Lonely Planet's *South Pacific Phrasebook*. A dog-eared copy of *Mutiny on the Bounty* or the funny *The Sex Lives of Cannibals* will keep them in the here and now.

Pack teen-sized masks, snorkels and flippers if your 16-year-old isn't as big as you are.

Countries at a Glance

It would take a lifetime to visit every island in the vast South Pacific. So unless you're immortal, you'll have to pick and choose your destinations. Within most South Pacific countries are regions that are well set up for families, for romantic escapes, for diving, for cultural experiences... The trick is to see what else sparks your fancy. Like digging into history? Try Easter Island, the Marquesas Islands in French Polynesia or the WWII remnants in the Solomon Islands. Vegetarian? Look forward to spicy curries in Fiji (...conversely, carnivores will enjoy some South American beef on Easter Island). Another surprise is that not every island here is laced with accessible, swimworthy beaches: sand fans should beeline for Samoa, New Caledonia, Tonga or Vanuatu.

Easter Island

History
Activities
Scenery

Open-Air Museum

Easter Island is a mind-boggling open-air museum, with a wealth of pre-European archaeological remains – including the iconic *moai* statues, gazing out over the sea, loaded with both mystery and portent.

Outdoor Adventures

Outdoorsy types will be in seventh heaven in Rapa Nui, with hiking, diving, cycling, snorkelling and horse-riding activities all widely available.

Dramatic Landscapes

Stand on the edge of Ranu Kau, a lake-filled crater, or walk across the ruggedly beautiful Península Poike: hold on to your hat, lift your jaw off the floor and grab your camera.

p48

Fiji

Diving
Beaches
Culture

Soft Corals & Sharks

Fiji's underwater landscapes wave and waft with soft corals. Offering a few more thrills are shark, manta ray and turtle encounters, plus shimmering schools of barracuda, jacks and much more.

Super Sands

Fiji's beaches – especially the superstar stretches of the Mamanuca and Yasawa Groups – beckon with white-powder sands, perfect palms and splendid cerulean seas.

Kava to Curry

If Fiji's kava-offering, fire-dancing cultural encounters aren't enough for you, get into Indo-Fijian culture with a visit to a Hindu temple, a delicious curry for dinner or by catching a firewalking ceremony.

p64

New Caledonia

Diving
Beaches
Food

World Heritage Reef

With dive operators ready and willing to take you below on most islands here, there are myriad opportunities to explore New Caledonia's World Heritage–listed reefs.

Just Offshore

It's not only bleach-white beaches that impress here – it's the natural aquariums, deep swimming holes and just-off-the-beach coral gardens that make a trip to the beach a joy.

Bon Appétit

French culinary influences have rubbed off on New Caledonia: bakeries bake amazing goodies in Noumea, while even the simplest meal has a flavour you're unlikely to forget. Fresh, local, French: the three keys to New Caledonian cuisine.

p150

Rarotonga & the Cook Islands

Scenery
Food
History

Mountains to the Sea

Explore Rarotonga's mountainous interior, before discovering your own slice of Pacific perfection sea kayaking to tiny *motu* (islands) around amazing Muri lagoon. On isolated 'Atiu, Ma'uke and Mangaia, rugged sea cliffs conceal impossibly compact beaches.

Culinary Adventures

Be surprised by Rarotonga's dining scene. There's a growing emphasis on things organic and traditionally grown here: a highlight is trawling the easygoing food stalls at Saturday morning's Punanga Nui market.

Ancient Polynesia

Discover the spiritual and historical significance of Avana harbour – departure point for the 14th-century Great Migration to New Zealand. The burial caves on Mangaia and 'Atiu are equally fascinating.

p196

Samoa

Beaches
Hiking
Culture

Choose Your Slice of Sand

Beaches here offer spectacular variety, from wide, white beauties tumbling into aqua lagoons to sandy pocket paradises wedged between black lava formations.

Journey to the Centre of the Earth

Hike to spectacular waterfalls and along lava-shaped coasts, and explore the lush grounds of Robert Louis Stevenson's villa. Or head underground via extensive lava tubes that gush with subterranean rivers.

The Heart of Polynesia

Independent and proud of their Polynesian culture, Samoans have Facebook and mobile phones but adhere to old values, living in villages with meeting houses, chiefs and strict customs. And they'll welcome you with genuine warmth.

p250

American Samoa

Hiking
Scenery
Culture

National Park of American Samoa

National parks are rare in the South Pacific, but the National Park of American Samoa covers a huge swath of the country. There are well-maintained trails here, from short jaunts to all-day adventures from mountain to sea.

Dreamy Silhouettes

The sky-piercing peaks here look more like a Disney paradise than reality. Surround this with lava-formed coves, blue water and ribbons of sparkling cream-coloured beach – hard to beat!

Village Life

Travel beyond Pago Pago and the airport to where small-town American Samoa is all about church bells, village customs and welcoming smiles... all in sublime natural surrounds.

p296

Solomon Islands

Diving
Adventure
History

Wrecks & Reefs

The Solomons offers an unbeatable repertoire of diving adventures, including world-class sunken WWII vessels lying close to the shore and incredibly healthy reef ecosystems.

Hiking in the Jungle

Live out your Indiana Jones fantasies and blaze a trail through the Solomons' wild jungles. Be prepared for a culture shock, too: these islands are home to tiny villages where people lead lives that have changed little over centuries.

WWII Relics

The WWII history of the Solomons is compelling and tangible. As well as the wrecks offshore, you'll find rusting tanks, jeeps and military installations slowly being absorbed by the jungle throughout the archipelago.

p316

Tahiti & French Polynesia

Diving
Outdoors
Culture

Underwater Wildlife

Scattered over a marine area the size of Europe, these 117 islands are nirvana for diving enthusiasts and snorkellers. Expect to see some serious fish – and sharks aplenty.

Action Stations

There's plenty to keep your pulse ticking over in French Polynesia, on land and at sea – think lagoon excursions, hiking, horse riding, kitesurfing, surfing and sea kayaking.

Past & Present

South Seas culture just like you've seen on TV: flower garlands, fast-shaking hips and earth-oven feasts. Explore further to find historic moss-covered *tiki* (sacred statues) and temples.

p348

Tonga

Islands
Activities
Drinking

Beachy Stays

Postcard-perfect tropical islands abound in Tonga. Book yourself into a luxurious beach resort (they're few but fabulous) or beach-bum it in a breezy waterside *fale* (house).

Boots & Snorkels

There's plenty to keep you busy in Tonga, from hiking on 'Eua to snorkelling in Vava'u or wetting a fishing line in the brine pretty much anywhere. Going to church to hear the Tongans sing is an activity in itself!

Beer O'Clock?

Nothing happens in a hurry in Tonga! Slow down to Tonga time with a few cold local lagers at the waterfront bars in Neiafu, or along Nuku'alofa's main drag.

p432

Vanuatu

Diving
Culture
Beaches

Wreck Diving Spectacular

Most of Luganville's accommodation is geared towards divers: just offshore are the wreck of a luxury liner and an undersea dumping ground for WWII military paraphernalia...not to mention some eye-popping coral.

Hanging with the Locals

Watch a traditional dance or buy a traditional carving by all means, but you'll learn most about Ni-Van culture by spending some time the locals.

Two-Tone Sands

Check out Champagne Bay, a sweet horseshoe of azure and white, or bask your bones on a black volcanic-sand beach. Some beaches you'll have to yourself; others you'll share with hordes of laughing, splashing kids.

p474

On the
Road

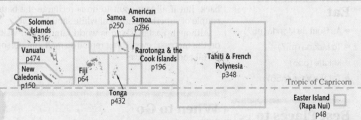

Equator

Tropic of Capricorn

SOUTH PACIFIC OCEAN

Easter Island (Rapa Nui)

↗ 032

Best Places to Eat

➡ Au Bout du Monde (p57)

➡ Te Moana (p57)

➡ Mikafé (p55)

➡ Tataku Vave (p56)

Best Places to Sleep

➡ Cabañas Ngahu (p52)

➡ Hare Noi (p54)

➡ Cabañas Christophe (p52)

➡ Camping Mihinoa (p52)

➡ Cabalgatas Pantu – Pikera Uri (p54)

Why Go?

Few areas in the world possess a more mystical pull than this tiny speck of land, one of the most isolated places on Earth. It's hard to feel connected to Chile, over 3700km to the east, let alone the wider world. Endowed with the most logic-defying statues in the world – the strikingly familiar *moai* – Easter Island (Rapa Nui to its native Polynesian inhabitants) emanates a magnetic, mysterious vibe.

But Easter Island is much more than an open-air museum. Diving, snorkelling and surfing are fabulous. On land, there's no better ecofriendly way to experience the island's savage beauty than on foot, from a bike saddle or on horseback. But if all you want to do is recharge the batteries, a couple of superb expanses of white sand beckon.

Although Easter Island is world famous and visitors are on the increase, everything remains small and personable – it's all about eco-travel.

When to Go
Easter Island

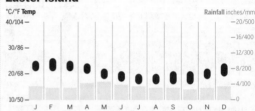

Jan–Mar Peak season. Highest prices and scarce hotels around February's Tapati Rapa Nui festival.

Jul–Aug Chilly weather, not ideal for beaches but a good time for hiking and horseback riding.

Apr–Jun & Oct–Dec The shoulder season is not a bad time to visit; the climate is fairly temperate.

HANGA ROA

POP 6700

Hanga Roa is the island's sole town. Upbeat it ain't, but with most sights almost on its doorstep and nearly all the island's hotels, restaurants, shops and services lying within its boundaries, it's the obvious place to anchor oneself. It features a picturesque fishing harbour, a couple of modest beaches and surf spots, and a few archaeological sites.

◎ Sights

Museo Antropológico Sebastián Englert   MUSEUM

(Map p55; ☑ 032-255-1020; www.museorapanui.cl; Tahai s/n; ☉9.30am-5.30pm Tue-Fri, to 12.30pm Sat & Sun) FREE This well-organised museum makes a perfect introduction to the island's history and culture. It displays basalt fishhooks, obsidian spearheads and other weapons, circular beehive-shaped huts, the ceremonial houses at Orongo and a *moai* head with reconstructed fragments of its eyes. It also features replica Rongo-Rongo tablets, covered in tiny rows of symbols resembling hieroglyphs.

According to oral tradition, these wooden tablets were brought here by Hotu Matua, along with learned men who knew the art of writing and reciting the inscriptions. Researchers have proposed various theories on the nature of the script, but it's still an enigma to decipher.

Caleta Hanga Roa & Ahu Tautira   ARCHAEOLOGICAL SITE

Your first encounter with the *moai* will probably take place at Ahu Tautira (Map p55; Av Te Pito o Te Henua), which overlooks Caleta Hanga Roa, the fishing port in Hanga Roa at the foot of Av Te Pito o Te Henua. Here you'll find a platform with two superb *moai*.

Ahu Tahai   ARCHAEOLOGICAL SITE

(Map p55) Ahu Tahai is a highly photogenic site that contains three restored *ahu*. Ahu Tahai proper is the *ahu* in the middle, supporting a large, solitary *moai* with no topknot. On the north side of Ahu Tahai is Ahu Ko Te Riku, with a topknotted and eyeballed *moai*. On the other side is Ahu Vai Uri, which supports five *moai* of varying sizes and shapes. Along the hills are foundations of *hare paenga* (traditional houses resembling an upturned canoe, with a narrow doorway).

Ahu Akapu   ARCHAEOLOGICAL SITE

(Map p55) You'll find this *ahu* with a solitary *moai* along the coastline, north of Hanga Roa.

Caleta Hanga Piko & Ahu Riata   HARBOUR

(Map p55) Easily overlooked by visitors, the little Caleta Hanga Piko is used by local fishers. Facing the *caleta,* the restored Ahu Riata supports a solitary *moai*.

Iglesia Hanga Roa   CHURCH

(Map p55; Av Tu'u Koihu s/n) The unmissable Iglesia Hanga Roa, the island's Catholic church, is well worth a visit for its spectacular wood carvings, which integrate Christian doctrine with Rapa Nui tradition. It also makes a colorful scene on Sunday morning.

Playa Pea   BEACH

(Map p55) For a little dip, the tiny beach at Playa Pea, on the south side of Caleta Hanga Roa, fits the bill.

🏃 Activities

Diving & Snorkelling

Scuba diving is increasingly popular on Easter Island. The strong points are the gin-clear visibility (up to 50m), the lack of crowds, the dramatic seascape and the abundance of pristine coral formations. The weak point is marine life, which is noticeable only in its scarcity.

Easter Island is diveable year-round. Water temperatures vary from as low as 20°C in winter to 26°C in summer.

Most sites are scattered along the west coast. You don't need to be a strong diver – there are sites for all levels. A few favourites include Motu Nui and the very scenic La Cathédrale and La Pyramide.

Mike Rapu Diving Center   DIVING, SNORKELLING

(Map p55; ☑ 032-255-1055; www.mikerapu.cl; Caleta Hanga Roa s/n; ☉8am-6.30pm Mon-Sat) This well-established operator offers introductory dives (CH$40,000), single-dive trips (CH$30,000) and courses. Prices drop by about 15% for more than three dives. Also runs snorkelling trips (CH$15,000) to Motu Nui three days a week.

Orca Diving Center   DIVING, SNORKELLING

(Map p55; ☑ 032-255-0877; www.orcadivingcenter.cl; Caleta Hanga Roa s/n; ☉8am-5pm Mon-Sat) This state-of-the-art outfit offers the full slate of diving adventures, including introductory dives (CH$55,000), single dives (CH$44,000), courses and packages, as well as snorkelling trips to Motu Nui (CH$28,000).

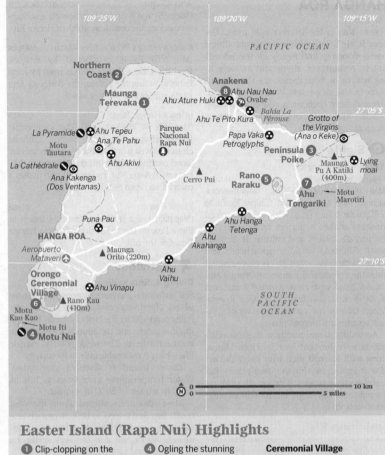

Easter Island (Rapa Nui) Highlights

❶ Clip-clopping on the flanks of the extinct volcano **Maunga Terevaka** (p59).

❷ Hiking along the ruggedly beautiful **northern coast** (p51).

❸ Seeking solace on the mysterious **Península Poike** (p60).

❹ Ogling the stunning limpid blue waters of **Motu Nui** (p49) on a snorkelling or diving trip.

❺ Taking a lesson in archaeology at **Rano Raraku** (p60), the 'nursery' of the *moai*.

❻ Pondering the island's mysterious past at **Orongo Ceremonial Village** (p59), perched on the edge of Rano Kau.

❼ Watching the sun rise at the row of enigmatic statues at **Ahu Tongariki** (p60).

❽ Taking a snooze under the swaying palms at **Anakena** (p59).

Anchors' Reef/The Moai DIVING

A relaxing dive in Hanga Roa Bay, with corals, anchors and even a recently submerged *moai* to round out the fun – all in less than 22m of water.

Cathedral DIVING

Features an underwater lavatube broken up by numerous faults in about 15m of water.

Lost Arch DIVING

The Lost Arch may well be Rapa Nui's most scenic dive, with a huge arch in 35m.

Motu Nui DIVING

Rapa Nui's signature site. Bottom depth is about 80m. A truly magical drop-off, wreathed with corals.

Motu Kao Kao
DIVING

It looks like a giant *moai* rising from the sea bed at 55m. The typical dive plan consists of swimming around the structure, starting at about 25m. Shoals of sea chubs are common.

Surfing

Easter Island is hit with powerful swells from all points of the compass throughout the year, offering irresistible lefts and rights – mostly lava-reef breaks, with waves up to 5m. The most popular spots are scattered along the west coast. For beginners, there are a couple of good waves off Caleta Hanga Roa.

A handful of seasonal (usually from December to March) outfits based on the seafront offer surfing courses and also rent surfboards.

Hare Orca
SURFING

(Map p55; ☑032-255-0877; Caleta Hanga Roa s/n; rental per half-day CH$10,000-15,000; ⊙8am-5pm Mon-Sat) This shop rents bodyboards, surfboards, stand-up paddle-boards and snorkelling gear. Surfing lessons are also available.

Horseback Riding

A network of trails leading to some of the most beautiful sites can be explored on horseback – a typical Rapa Nui experience.

Cabalgatas Pantu
HORSEBACK RIDING

(Map p55; ☑032-210-0577; www.pikerauri. com; Sector Tahai s/n; half-/full-day tour CH$35,000/75,000; ⊙daily by reservation) Offers guided trips that take in some of the sites near Hanga Roa or more remote places, such as Terevaka, Anakena and the north coast. Beginners are welcome. There's an extra fee if you pay by credit card.

Hiking

You can take some fantastic trails through the island. A memorable walk is the way marked 'Ruta Patrimonial', which runs from Museo Antropológico Sebastián Englert up to Orongo ceremonial village (about four hours, 7km). Other recommended walks are the climb to Maunga Terevaka from near Ahu Akivi (about three hours) and the walk around Península Poike (one day). For the walk between Ahu Tepeu and Anakena beach along the northern coastline, you'll need a guide because the path is not marked.

Cycling

Cycling is a superb way of seeing the island at your leisure, provided you're ready to come to grips with the winding roads around the southern parts. An easy loop is from Hanga Roa up to Ahu Tepeu, then east to Ahu Akivi and back to Hanga Roa (about 17km).

Makemake Rentabike
BICYCLE RENTAL

(Map p55; ☑032-255-2030; Av Atamu Tekena; per day CH$10,000; ⊙9am-1pm & 4-8pm Mon-Sat, 9am-1pm Sun) This venture rents mountain bikes in tip-top condition. A helmet and a map are provided.

Tours

We recommend joining an organised tour since you get the benefit of an English-speaking guide who can explain the cultural significance of the archaeological sites.

Plenty of operators do tours of the sites, typically charging CH$45,000 for a full day and CH$25,000 for a half-day. Entrance fees to Parque Nacional Rapa Nui (CH$30,000 or US$60) aren't included.

Aku Aku Turismo
CULTURAL TOUR

(Map p55; ☑032-210-0770; www.akuakuturismo.cl; Av Tu'u Koihu s/n; ⊙8.30am-5pm) A well-established company that employs competent guides.

EASTER ISLAND IN...

Four Days

Start the day by visiting the **Museo Antropológico Sebastián Englert** for some historical background. Next, take a half-day tour to **Rano Kau** and **Orongo Ceremonial Village** and soak up the lofty views. On day two take a full-day tour to marvel at **Rano Raraku** and **Ahu Tongariki**. On your return to Hanga Roa head straight to an atmosphere-laden bar on Av Atamu Tekena for the night vibe. Day three is all about Hanga Roa. Hit the *mercado* (market) to put a dent in the wallet and amble down Av Te Pito o Te Henua to enjoy the sunset at **Ahu Tahai**. Attend a traditional dance show later in the evening. Day four should see you lazing the day away at **Anakena** beach.

One Week

Follow the four-day agenda then make the most of the island's outdoor adventures. Book a horse-riding excursion along the north coast, spend a day diving off **Motu Nui**, scramble up and down **Maunga Terevaka**, and explore **Península Poike**.

Kava Kava Tours CULTURAL TOUR
(Map p55; ☏9352-4972; www.kavakavatours.
com; Ana Tehe Tama s/n; ☺by reservation) Run
by a young, knowledgeable Rapanui lad
who offers private, customised tours as well
as hiking tours.

Kia Koe Tour CULTURAL TOUR
(Map p55; ☏032-210-0852; www.kiakoetour.cl;
Av Atamu Tekena s/n; ☺9am-1pm & 3-6pm) Has
good credentials and uses knowledgeable
guides.

Rapa Nui Travel CULTURAL TOUR
(Map p55; ☏032-210-0548; www.rapanuitravel.
com; Av Tu'u Koihu; ☺by reservation) Run by a
Rapa Nui–German couple.

🛏 Sleeping

Unless otherwise stated, most places come
equipped with private bathroom, and breakfast is included. Air-con is scarce but fans
are provided in the hottest months. Airport
transfers are included.

Camping Mihinoa CAMPGROUND $
(Map p55; ☏032-255-1593; www.camping-
mihinoa.com; Av Pont s/n; campsites per person
CH$5000, dm CH$10,000, d CH$20,000-30,000;
☏) You have options here: a clutch of well-
scrubbed rooms (the dearer ones offer more
privacy), several two- to six-bed dorms, some
with their own bathroom, or a campsite
on a grassy plot (no shade). The ablution
block has hot showers (mornings and evenings). Perks include tent hire, wi-fi access
(CH$5000 flat fee), a well-equipped commu-
nal kitchen and laundry service.

DON'T MISS

TRADITIONAL DANCE SHOWS

If there's one thing you absolutely *have* to
check out while you're on Easter Island,
it's a traditional dance show. The most
reputable groups include the following:

Kari Kari (Map p55; ☏032-210-0767;
Av Atamu Tekena s/n; tickets CH$15,000;
☺show 9pm Tue, Thu & Sat) This elaborately costumed and talented group
performs island legends through song
and dance at a venue on the main street.

Vai Te Mihi – Maori Tupuna (Map
p55; ☏032-255-0556; Av Policarpo Toro
s/n; ☺show 9pm Mon, Thu & Sat) Features
excellent traditional dance shows. Front
row seats cost CH$17,000.

Location is ace; you're just a pebble's
throw from the seashore.

⭐**Cabañas Christophe** BUNGALOW $$
(Map p55; ☏032-210-0826; www.cabanaschris
tophe.com; Av Policarpo Toro s/n; d CH$60,000-
90,000; ☏) Hands-down the best-value
option in Hanga Roa, this charming venue
seduces those seeking character and comfort,
with three handsomely designed bungalows
that blend hardwoods and volcanic stones.
They're spacious, well appointed – think king-
size beds, kitchen facilities and a private ter-
race – and inundated with natural light. It's
at the start of the Orongo trail, about 1.5km
from the centre. Reserve well in advance.

Cabañas Ngahu CABIN $$
(Map p55; ☏8299-1041, 9090-2774; www.nga
hu.cl; Av Policarpo Toro s/n; d CH$40,000-80,000;
☏) A great choice where we encountered
helpful service, friendly owners and happy
guests. It consists of five well-equipped cabins of varying sizes and shapes, most with
sea views. The casual atmosphere and prime
sunset-watching make this the kind of place
where you quickly lose track of the days.
Good value (by Rapa Nui standards) considering the price and location. No breakfast.

Hare Swiss BUNGALOW $$
(Map p55; ☏032-255-2221; www.hareswiss.com;
Sector Tahai; s/d CH$62,000/85,000; ☏) Run
by a Rapanui-Swiss couple, this venture is a
solid option, with three immaculate cottages
perched on a slope overlooking the ocean.
They come equipped with sparkling bath-
rooms, king-size beds, tiled floors, kitchen fa-
cilities and a terrace with sea views. It's a bit of
a schlep from the center (you'll need a bike).

Tau Ra'a HOTEL $$
(Map p55; ☏032-210-0463; www.tauraahotel.cl;
Av Atamu Tekena s/n; s/d CH$75,000/90,000; ☏)
Here's one of the most commendable bets
in the midrange category. The 16 rooms are
spotless and flooded with natural light, and
they come equipped with back-friendly beds
and prim bathrooms. Alas, no sea views. The
substantial breakfast is a plus, and there are
plans to set up air-con. Bill, the Aussie owner,
is a treasure trove of local information.

Its peerless location, just off the main
drag, makes this an excellent base for roaming about town.

Aukara Lodge CABIN $$
(Map p55; ☏7709-5711, 032-210-0539; www.
aukara.cl; Av Pont s/n; s/d CH$40,000/70,000; ☏)

A good pick, though the 'Lodge' bit is a gross misnomer. Where else could you find an establishment with an art gallery featuring various paintings and woodcarvings by Bene Tuki, the proprietor? The rooms themselves are nothing outstanding but spruce enough, and the shady garden is a great place to chill out. It's easy walking distance from the action.

Bene's wife, Ana Maria, speaks excellent English and is very knowledgeable about the history of the island. Clearly a solid choice for the culturally and artistically inclined.

Cabañas Mana Nui CABIN $$
(Map p55; ☑ 032-210-0811; www.mananui.cl; Sector Tahai; s/d CH$40,000/60,000; ☞) This well-run venture is a reliable bet. The seven adjoining rooms are nothing to crow about but the general feel of cleanliness, the location, in a quiet area, and the million-dollar views over the ocean make it a steal. There are also two stand-alone cottages for self-caterers as well as a kitchen for guests' use.

Inaki Uhi CABIN $$
(Map p55; ☑ 032-210-0231; www.inakiuhi.com; Av Atamu Tekena s/n; s/d CH$50,000/80,000; ☞) Can't speak a single word of Spanish? Here you'll be glad to be welcomed in flawless English by Alvaro Jr, who spent 15 years in Australia. The 15 smallish rooms, which have been thoroughly modernised, occupy two rows of low-slung buildings facing each other. No breakfast, but there are four shared kitchens. It's right on the main drag, close to everything.

Alvaro Jr has plenty of experience in helping visitors with logistics and trip planning.

Aloha Nui GUESTHOUSE $$
(Map p55; ☑ 032-210-0274; haumakatours@gmail.com; Av Atamu Tekena s/n; s/d CH$37,000/70,000) This agreeable place features six well-organised rooms and a vast, shared living room that opens onto a flowery garden. But the real reason you're staying here is to discuss Rapa Nui archaeology in flawless English with Josefina Nahoe Mulloy and her husband Ramon, who lead reputable tours. No wi-fi.

Hostal Raioha CABIN $$
(Map p55; ☑ 7654-1245, 032-210-0851; off Av Te Pito o Te Henua; s or d CH$55,000) Run by a friendly couple, this discreet number is a valid, safe and comfortable option that's great value for the town's centre. The seven rooms are no-frills but are well maintained and open onto a verdant garden. No breakfast is served

TAPATI RAPA NUI

Easter Island's premier festival, the Tapati Rapa Nui, lasts about two weeks in the first half of February and is so impressive that it's almost worth timing your trip around it (contact the tourist office for exact dates). Expect a series of music, dance, cultural and sport contests between two clans that put up two candidates who stand for the title of Queen of the Festival. The most spectacular event is the Haka Pei: on the flanks of the Cerro Pui, a dozen male contestants run downhill on a makeshift sled at speeds that can reach 70km/h. No less awesome is the Taua Rapa Nui. This triathlon unfolds in the magical setting of the Rano Raraku crater. The first stage consists of paddling across the lake on a reed boat. Then the contestants race around the lake carrying banana bunches on their shoulders. The last leg consists of swimming across the lake using a reed raft as a board. On the last day the parade throughout Hanga Roa is the culmination of the festival, with floats and costumed figures.

but there's a communal kitchen. No wi-fi, but there's an internet cafe up the street.

Vaianny GUESTHOUSE $$
(Map p55; ☑ 032-210-0650; www.residencial vaianny.com; Av Tuki Haka He Vari; s/d CH$40,000/55,000; ☞) This well-established and central guesthouse is a good choice if you're counting the pennies, with basic but well-scrubbed rooms that are cluttered in a tiny garden area. There's a kitchen for self-caterers. The prime selling point here is the location, within hollering distance of some of the town's best bars and restaurants.

Hostal Petero Atamu GUESTHOUSE $$
(Map p55; ☑ 032-255-1823; www.hostalpeteroat amu.com; Petero Atamu s/n; with/without bathroom s CH$40,000/25,000, d CH$60,000/40,000; ☞) Popular with Japanese backpackers, this guesthouse is a simple affair not too far from the centre. Shoestringers will opt for the bare but acceptable rooms with shared bathroom, while wealthier travellers will choose the rooms with a private bathroom and a terrace; rooms 1, 2 and 3 are the best. There's a TV lounge and a kitchen.

Hostal Tojika
GUESTHOUSE **$$**

(Map p55; ☑7125-2210; www.rapanuiweb. com/hostaltojika/hostal.htm; Av Apina s/n; d/tr/q CH$45,000/55,000/65,000; ☎) A good bet for budgeteers, Hostal Tojika has several rooms that are all different and a communal kitchen in a single building overlooking the sea. Some rooms lack natural light but they get the job done. No breakfast is served but there's a small eatery at the entrance of the property.

★Cabalgatas
Pantu – Pikera Uri
BUNGALOW **$$$**

(Map p55; ☑032-210-0577; www.rapanuipan tu.com; Tahai s/n; d CH$190,000-210,000; ☎) A spiffing location plus decorative touches make this venture one of Hanga Roa's best retreats. Digs are in cute-as-can-be bungalows perched on a gentle slope overlooking the ocean; the Rito Mata and Uri offer the best sea views. They're all commodious, luminous and beautifully attired, and open onto a small corral where the owner, Pantu, gathers his horses every morning.

★Hare Noi
BOUTIQUE HOTEL **$$$**

(☑032-255-0134; www.noihotels.com; Av Hotu Matua s/n; s/d CH$600,000/800,000; ☎☒) A top-drawer hotel, without the stiff upper lips. Digs are in wood and stone bungalows dotted on an alluring property not far from the airport. They are roomy, light-filled and judiciously laid out, with elegant furnishings, solid amenities and a private terrace. It's quite spread out so you can get a decent dose of privacy, and it features an excellent on-site restaurant.

It's a bit far from the centre, but bikes are available for free.

Altiplanico
HOTEL **$$$**

(Map p55; ☑032-255-2190; www.altiplanico.cl; Sector Tahai; s/d CH$350,000/390,000; @☎☒) The best thing about this well-run venture with a boutique feel is its excellent location on a gentle slope in Tahai. Try for bungalows 1, 2, 3, 10, 11 or 17, which have panoramic sea

---

SLEEPING PRICE RANGES

The following price ranges refer to the price of a double room with private bathroom and breakfast.

$ less than CH$40,000

$$ CH$40,000–CH$80,000

$$$ more than CH$80,000

---

views. The 17 units are all sparkling clean and quirkily decorated, but they're fairly packed together and we found the rack rates somewhat inflated.

The on-site restaurant is elegant but pricey (pizzas cost US$30).

Hanga Roa
Eco Village & Spa
LUXURY HOTEL **$$$**

(Map p55; ☑032-255-3700; www.hangaroa.cl; Av Pont s/n; s/d from CH$125,000/150,000; ✳☎☒) ✎ Entirely renovated in 2012, this sprawling establishment is one of the best hotels on the island, with an array of creatively designed rooms and suites facing the sea. All units are built of natural materials and their layout is inspired by caves, with curving lines and shapes. The on-site restaurant serves refined food and the spa is a stunner. It's ecofriendly: there's a water and electricity saving system.

Cabañas Morerava
BUNGALOW **$$$**

(Map p55; ☑9319-6547, 9499-1898; www.more rava.com; Sector Tahai; d/q CH$110,000/170,000; ☎) There's not much in the way of a view here as this establishment is located inland, but there's nothing to disturb your dreams on this bucolic property. The four cottages are stylishly built with natural materials – it helps that the owners are architects – and can sleep up to four people. It's on the outskirts of town, but bikes are provided.

Cabañas Tokerau
BUNGALOW **$$$**

(Map p55; ☑8478-1444, 7887-5803; www.caba nastokerau.cl; Sector Tahai; d CH$80,000; ☎) A good choice if you're looking for a relaxed place in a chilled-out setting. It comprises two all-wood bungalows that come equipped with a handy kitchenette and a terrace with (partial) sea views. The larger unit can accommodate five people while the much smaller one is suitable for a couple. No breakfast.

Explora en Rapa Nui
BOUTIQUE HOTEL **$$$**

(☑in Santiago 02-395-2800; www.explora. com; 3-night all-inclusive packages from s/d CH$2,040,000/3,120,000; ✳☎☒) ✎ Rapa Nui's most luxurious establishment, this property blends into a forested patch of volcano-singed countryside. Rooms, all overlooking the Pacific and fiery sunsets, are abundant with indigenous materials (local Rauli wood, volcanic stone) that instil a sense of place. Prices include excursions. One proviso: it feels cut off from the rest of the island (it's about 6km east of Hanga Roa).

Hanga Roa

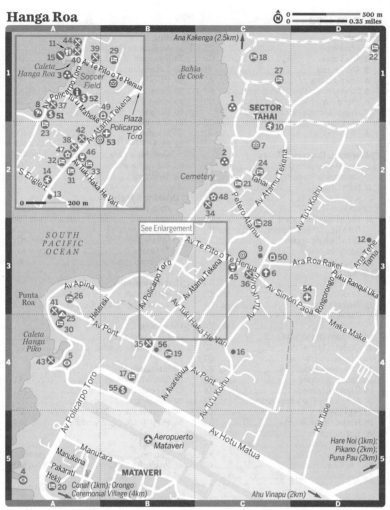

🍴 Eating

For self-caterers, there are a couple of well-stocked supermarkets on Av Atamu Tekena.

★ Mikafé   CAFETERIA, SANDWICHES $
(Map p55; Caleta Hanga Roa s/n; ice cream CH$1800-3200, sandwiches & cakes CH$3500-6000; ⊙9am-8.30pm Mon-Sat) Mmm, the *helados artesanales* (homemade ice creams)! Oh, the damn addictive banana cake! Other treats include panini, sandwiches, muffins and brownies. Also serves breakfast (from CH$3500).

Motu Hava Kafe   FAST FOOD $
(Map p55; Caleta Hanga Roa s/n; mains CH$2500-7000; ⊙9am-7pm Mon-Sat) Blink and you'll miss the entrance of this funky little den overlooking the Caleta Hanga Roa. It whips up freshly prepared empanadas, sandwiches and delicious daily specials at wallet-friendly prices. Good breakfast too (from CH$2800). Takeaway is available.

Casa Esquina   FAST FOOD $
(Map p55; ☎032-255-0205; Av Te Pito o Te Henua; mains CH$5000-9000; ⊙noon-11.30pm) A great-value option with a breezy terrace overlooking the church. Choose from pastas,

Hanga Roa

pizzas, sandwiches, salads and (yes!) seriously authentic sushi. Wash it all down with a *jugo natural* (fruit juice).

Mara Pika   FAST FOOD **$**
(Map p55; Av Apina s/n; mains CH$2500-6000; ⊙8am-8pm) You'll find no cheaper place for a sit-down meal in Hanga Roa. It's very much a canteen, but a good one, with friendly service and family-style Chilean cuisine, including empanadas and daily specials.

Caramelo   CAFETERIA **$**
(Map p55; ☑032-255-0132; Av Atamu Tekena s/n; mains CH$6500-8500; ⊙10am-9pm Mon-Sat) Caramelo is your spot for voluminous salads

and gourmet sandwiches. It also features a tantalising array of pastries and cakes as well as tea, coffee, smoothies and hot chocolate.

Moiko Ra'a   CAFETERIA **$**
(Map p55; ☑032-255-0149; Av Atamu Tekena s/n; snacks CH$2500-7000; ⊙9am-10pm; ☑) This delectable little cafeteria has a wide variety of cavity-inducing pastries, as well as excellent sandwiches, tarts and empanadas. Be sure to try the unctuous hot chocolate.

Tataku Vave   SEAFOOD **$$**
(Map p55; ☑032-255-1544; Caleta Hanga Piko s/n; mains CH$11,000-19,000; ⊙noon-10.30pm Mon-Sat) Tucked behind the Caleta Hanga

Piko, Tataku Vave is that easy-to-miss 'secret spot' that locals like to recommend, with a delightfully breezy terrace that's just metres from the seashore. Munch on superb fish dishes while the ocean crashes nearby. Call ahead for free transportat from your hotel.

Au Bout du Monde   INTERNATIONAL **$$**
(Map p55; ☑ 032-255-2060; Av Policarpo Toro s/n; mains CH$11,000-18,000; ◷ 12.30-2.30pm & 6-10pm Thu-Tue, closed Jun & Jul) In this agreeable venue run by a Belgian lady, every visitor ought to try the tuna in Tahitian vanilla sauce, the homemade tagliatelle or the organic beef fillet. Leave room for dessert – the Belgian chocolate mousse is divine.

Haka Honu   CHILEAN **$$**
(Map p55; Av Policarpo Toro s/n; mains CH$11,000-16,000; ◷ 12.30-10pm Tue-Sun) Fish dishes, steaks, homemade pasta, burgers and salads round out the menu at this well-regarded eatery blessed with unsurpassable ocean views. The grilled fish with papaya chutney is particularly flavoursome.

Kanahau   SEAFOOD, CHILEAN **$$**
(Map p55; ☑ 032-255-1923; Av Atamu Tekena s/n; mains CH$10,000-16,000; ◷ 11am-11.30pm) Whether you satisfy yourself with ultrafresh tuna or sample the *lomo kanahau* (beef with a homemade sauce), among a variety of hearty dishes, you'll be pleased with the careful preparation, attentive service and atmospheric decor.

Kuki Varua   SEAFOOD, CHILEAN **$$**
(Map p55; ☑ 8192-1940; Av Te Pito o Te Henua s/n; mains CH$9000-13,000; ◷ noon-11pm Wed-Mon) The Kuki Varua has a great selection of fish delivered daily from the harbour, including tuna and *mero* (grouper). The upstairs terrace is perfect for enjoying the cool, ocean breezes. Room should be kept for desserts – hmm, the crème brûlée flavoured with passion fruit...

★ Te Moana   CHILEAN **$$$**
(Map p55; ☑ 032-255-1578; Av Policarpo Toro s/n; mains CH$10,000-21,000; ◷ 12.30-11pm Tue-Sun) One of the most reliable options in Hanga Roa, this buzzy restaurant boasts a spiffing location, with an atmospheric veranda opening onto the ocean. It's renowned for its tasty meat and fishes dishes. The Polynesian decor is another clincher, with woodcarvings and traditional artifacts adorning the walls.

La Taverne du Pêcheur   FRENCH **$$$**
(Map p55; ☑ 032-210-0619; Caleta Hanga Roa s/n; mains CH$12,000-25,000; ◷ noon-3pm & 6-11pm

---

Mon-Sat) This French institution right by the harbour provides an enchanting, albeit expensive, dining experience with classic French fare with a Chilean twist – try the *thon Rossini* (tuna served with foie gras and flambéed with Cognac). The spiffing upstairs terrace is a great place to soak up the atmosphere of the seafront. Some readers have complained about the grumpy service, though.

🍷 Drinking & Nightlife

Most restaurants feature a bar section.

Te Moana   BAR
(Map p55; Av Policarpo Toro s/n; ◷ 12.30-11.30pm Mon-Sat) Come for the good fun, good mix of people and good cocktails.

Kopakavana Club   BAR
(Map p55; Av Te Pito o Te Henua s/n; ◷ 6pm-2am) You come here as much for a cocktail as for the trendy atmosphere.

Toromiro   BAR
(Map p55; Av Atamu Tekena s/n; ◷ 10am-midnight Mon-Fri, 10am-2pm & 6pm-midnight Sat & Sun) A funky drinking spot right in the centre. Food is only so-so.

Haka Honu   BAR
(Map p55; Av Policarpo Toro s/n; ◷ 12.30-10pm Tue-Sun) The outside terrace catches every wisp of breeze and is perfect for watching the world surf by.

Kanahau   BAR
(Map p55; Av Atamu Tekena s/n; ◷ noon-midnight) Kick off the night with a strong pisco sour at this cheerful hangout decked in wood. Serves excellent *picoteos* (tapas), too.

Mikafé   CAFE
(Map p55; Caleta Hanga Roa s/n; ◷ 9am-8.30pm Mon-Sat) In search of a real espresso or a cappuccino? Mikafé is your answer.

Pikano   BAR
(cover CH$3000; ◷ 11pm-4am Wed & Fri) Not your average watering hole, Pikano is

AHU TEPEU TO ANAKENA BEACH

If you want to experience Easter Island from a different perspective, consider exploring the coastline between Ahu Tepeu and Anakena beach. This wild area is extremely alluring: vast expanses of chaotic boulders, towering sea cliffs, barren landscapes and ocean views. There are also plenty of archaeological sites dotted along the way as well as caves adorned with impressive petroglyphs. From Ahu Tepeu it takes six to seven hours to reach Anakena beach on foot. Then hitch back or arrange a taxi back to Hanga Roa. It's not marked and the archaeological sites are not signed; you'll definitely need a guide. Contact the tourist office or your lodging to secure one.

isolated on the road to Anakena about 3km from the airport. This multifaceted venue is very popular on Wednesdays and Fridays with an eclectic crowd gulping down glasses of beer or noshing on grilled meat while listening to live bands. Later in the night it morphs into a club.

🛍 Shopping

Hanga Roa has numerous souvenir shops, mostly on Av Atamu Tekena and Av Te Pito o Te Henua.

Feria Artesanal ARTS, CRAFTS
(Map p55; cnr Avs Atamu Tekena & Tu'u Maheke; ⊙10am-8pm Mon-Sat) Good prices. Look for small stone or carved wooden replicas of *moai* and fragments of obsidian.

Mercado Artesanal ARTS, CRAFTS
(Map p55; cnr Avs Tu'u Koihu & Ara Roa Rakei; ⊙10am-8pm Mon-Sat) Across from the church, this place has a bit of everything.

ℹ Information

BancoEstado (Map p55; Av Tu'u Maheke s/n; ⊙8am-1pm Mon-Fri) Changes US dollars and euros. There's also an ATM but it only accepts MasterCard.

Banco Santander (Map p55; Av Policarpo Toro; ⊙8am-1pm Mon-Fri) Currency exchange (until 11am), and has two ATMs that accept Visa and MasterCard. Credit-card holders can also get cash advances at the counter during opening hours (bring your passport).

Farmacia Cruz Verde (Map p55; Av Atamu Tekena; ⊙8:30am-10pm Mon-Sat, 9.30am-9pm Sun) Large and well-stocked pharmacy.

Hare Pc (Map p55; Av Atamu Tekena s/n; per hr CH$1200; ⊙8.30am-2pm & 4-7pm Mon-Sat, 8:30am-2pm Sun; 🛜) Internet and wi-fi access.

Hospital Hanga Roa (Map p55; ☑032-210-0215; Av Simon Paoa s/n) Recently modernised.

Omotohi Cybercafé (Map p55; Av Te Pito o Te Henua s/n; per hr CH$1000-1500; ⊙9am-9pm; 🛜) Internet and wi-fi access, and call centre.

Police (☑133)

Puna Vai (Map p55; Av Hotu Matua; ⊙8.30am-1.30pm & 3-8pm Mon-Sat, 9am-2pm Sun) This petrol station also doubles as an exchange office. Much more convenient than the bank (no queues, better rates, longer opening hours).

Sernatur (Map p55; ☑032-210-0255; www.chile.travel/en.html; Av Policarpo Toro s/n; ⊙9am-6pm Mon-Fri, 10am-1pm Sat) Has various brochures, maps and lists of accommodations. Some staff speak good English.

PARQUE NACIONAL RAPA NUI

Since 1935, much of Rapa Nui's land and all of the archaeological sites have been a **national park** (www.conaf.cl; adult/child CH$30,000/15,000; ⊙9am-4pm) administered by Conaf, which charges admission at Orongo and Rano Raraku that is valid for the whole park for five days as of the first day of entrance. You're allowed one visit to Orongo and one visit to Rano Raraku. There are ranger information stations at Orongo, Anakena and Rano Raraku.

◉ Sights

◌ Northern Circuit

North of Ahu Tahai, the road is rough. Your best bet is to explore the area on foot, on horseback or by mountain bike.

Ana Kakenga CAVE
About 2km north of Tahai is Ana Kakenga, or Dos Ventanas. This site comprises two caves opening onto the ocean (bring a torch).

Ahu Tepeu ARCHAEOLOGICAL SITE
This large *ahu* has several fallen *moai* and a village site with foundations of *hare paenga* (elliptical houses) and the walls of several round houses, consisting of loosely piled stones.

Ana Te Pahu   CAVE

Off the dirt road to Akivi, Ana Te Pahu is former cave dwellings with an overgrown garden of sweet potatoes, taro and bananas. The caves here are lava tubes, created when rock solidified around a flowing stream of molten lava.

Ahu Akivi   ARCHAEOLOGICAL SITE

Unusual for its inland location, Ahu Akivi, restored in 1960, sports seven restored *moai*. They are the only ones that face towards the sea, but, like all *moai*, they overlook the site of a village, traces of which can still be seen. The site has proved to have astronomical significance: at the equinoxes, the seven statues look directly at the setting sun.

★ Maunga Terevaka   MOUNTAIN

Maunga Terevaka is the island's highest point (507m). This barren hill is only accessible on foot or on horseback and is definitely worth the effort as it offers sensational panoramic views.

Puna Pau   ARCHAEOLOGICAL SITE

The volcanic Puna Pau quarry was used to make the reddish, cylindrical *pukao* (topknots) that were placed on many *moai*. Some 60 of these were transported to sites around the island, and another 25 remain in or near the quarry.

◉ Southwestern Circuit

Ana Kai Tangata   CAVE

(Map p55) This vast cave carved into cliffs sports beautiful rock paintings. However, entrance is forbidden due to falling rocks.

★ Rano Kau &
Orongo Ceremonial Village   CRATER LAKE

Nearly covered in a bog of floating totora reeds, this crater lake resembles a giant witch's cauldron – awesome! Perched 400m above, on the edge of the crater wall on one side and abutting a vertical drop plunging down to the cobalt-blue ocean on the other side, **Orongo ceremonial village** (adult/child CH$30,000/15,000; ◷9am-4pm) boasts one of the South Pacific's most dramatic landscapes. It overlooks several small *motu* (offshore islands), including Motu Nui, Motu Iti and Motu Kau Kau.

Built into the side of the slope, the houses have walls of horizontally overlapping stone slabs, with an earth-covered arched roof of similar materials, making them appear partly subterranean. Orongo was the focus

---

🛈 BEST PLACES FOR...

Sunrise

Wake up very early and arrive before dawn at Ahu Tongariki just in time to watch the sun rise behind the superb row of *moai* (giant statues). Afterwards enjoy breakfast near the *ahu* – this is the life!

Sunset

Be sure to come to Ahu Tahai at dusk and watch the big yellow ball sink behind the silhouetted statues – a truly inspiring sight.

---

of an islandwide bird cult linked to the god Makemake in the 18th and 19th centuries. Birdman petroglyphs are visible on a cluster of boulders between the cliff top and the edge of the crater.

Orongo is either a steepish climb or a short scenic drive 4km from the centre of town.

Ahu Vinapu   ARCHAEOLOGICAL SITE

Beyond the eastern end of the airport runway, a road heads south past some large oil tanks to this ceremonial platform, with two major *ahu*. One of them features neatly hewn, mortarless blocks akin to those found in Inca ruins. Both once supported *moai* that are now broken and lying facedown.

◉ Northeastern Circuit

★ Anakena   BEACH

Beach bums in search of a place to wallow will love this picture-postcard-perfect, white-sand beach. It also forms a perfect backdrop for **Ahu Nau Nau**, which comprises seven *moai*, some with topknots. On a rise south of the beach stands **Ahu Ature Huki** and its lone *moai*, which was re-erected by Norwegian explorer Thor Heyerdahl with the help of dozen islanders in 1956.

Facilities include public toilets as well as food and souvenir stalls.

Ovahe   BEACH

This beach offers more seclusion than Anakena for wannabe Robinson Crusoes but is considered dangerous because of falling rocks.

Ahu Te Pito Kura   ARCHAEOLOGICAL SITE

Beside Bahía de La Pérouse, a nearly 10m long *moai* lies face down with its neck broken; it's the largest *moai* moved from Rano Raraku and erected on an *ahu*. A topknot – oval rather than round as at Vinapu – lies nearby.

ⓘ TICKETS FOR PARQUE NACIONAL RAPA NUI

Tickets for Parque Nacional Rapa Nui can be bought on arrival at the airport – look for the small booth. It's usually cheaper to pay in US dollars (US$60) than in Chilean pesos (CH$30,000). Children pay half price. Tickets are valid for five days from the first day of entrance. It's also possible to buy them at **Conaf** (☏032-2100-827; www.conaf.cl; Sector Mataveri; tickets adult/child CH$30,000/15,000; ⊙9am-4pm). Note that tickets are not sold at Orongo or Rano Raraku.

Papa Vaka Petroglyphs   ARCHAEOLOGICAL SITE

About 100m off the coastal road (look for the sign), you'll find a couple of massive basaltic slabs decorated with carvings featuring a tuna, a shark, an octopus and a large canoe.

Península Poike   PENINSULA

At the eastern end of the island, this high plateau is crowned by the extinct volcano **Maunga Pu A Katiki** (400m) and bound in by steep cliffs. There are also three small volcanic domes, one of which sports a huge mask carved into the rock that looks like a giant gargoyle. Also worth looking for is a series of small *moai* that lie face down, hidden amid the grass, as well as the **Grotto of the Virgins** (Ana O Keke).

Legend has it that this cave was used to confine virgins so that their skin would remain as pale as possible. It's worth crawling inside if you don't feel dizzy (there's a little path that leads to it, on a ledge, with the unbroken sweep of the Pacific below) to admire a series of petroglyphs.

The best way to soak up the primordial rawness of Península Poike is to take a day hike with a guide, as the sights are hard to find.

★**Ahu Tongariki**   ARCHAEOLOGICAL SITE

The monumental Ahu Tongariki has plenty to set your camera's flash popping. With 15 imposing statues, it is the largest *ahu* ever built. The statues gaze over a large, level village site, with ruined remnants scattered about and some petroglyphs nearby; some figures include a turtle with a human face, a tuna fish and a birdman motif.

The site was restored by a Japanese team between 1992 and 1995. A 1960 tsunami had flattened the statues and scattered several topknots far inland. Only one topknot has been returned to its place atop a *moai*.

★**Rano Raraku**   ARCHAEOLOGICAL SITE

(adult/child   CH$30,000/15,000;   ⊙9am-4pm) Known as 'the nursery,' the volcano of Rano Raraku, about 18km from Hanga Roa, is the quarry for the hard tuff from which the *moai* were cut. You'll feel as though you're stepping back into early Polynesian times, wandering among dozens of *moai* in all stages of progress studded on the southern slopes of the volcano. At the top the 360-degree view is truly awesome. Within the crater are a small, glistening lake and about 20 standing *moai*.

On the southeastern slope of the mountain, look for the unique, kneeling Moai Tukuturi; it has a full body squatting on its heels, with its forearms and hands resting on its thighs.

UNDERSTAND EASTER ISLAND

Easter Island Today

In 2008 Easter Island was granted a special status. It is now a *territoria especial* (special territory) within Chile, which means greater autonomy for the islanders. But independence is not the order of the day – ongoing economic reliance on mainland Chile renders this option unlikely in the foreseeable future.

The main claim is for the return of native lands. Indigenous Rapa Nui control almost no land outside Hanga Roa. A national park (designated in 1935) comprises more than a third of the island, and nearly all the remainder belongs to Chile. Native groups have asked the Chilean government and the UN to return the park to aboriginal hands. Since 2010 a land dispute has opposed one Rapa Nui clan to the owners of the Hanga Roa hotel.

The Rapa Nui are also concerned about the development and control of the tourism industry. Mass tourism it ain't, but the rising number of visitors – from about 30,000 10 years ago to approximately 95,000 tourists in 2014 – has an impact on the environment.

In October 2015 the Chilean government unveiled an ambitious environmental plan for Easter Island, namely the creation of a vast marine park to protect the island's fish stocks that are under threat from illegal fishing by industrial vessels. This marine sanctuary would be the world's largest.

Subsistence fishing would only be allowed in a small designated area.

The recent influx of mainland Chileans (mostly made up of construction workers) has fostered tensions with some locals, who see mainland Chileans as 'troublemakers'. There are plans to establish tighter immigration controls for the island, similar to those in place in Ecuador's Galapagos Islands.

History

The first islanders arrived either from the Marquesas, the Mangarevas, the Cooks or Pitcairn Island between the 4th and 8th centuries.

The Rapa Nui developed a unique civilisation, characterised by the construction of the ceremonial stone platforms called *ahu* and the famous Easter Island statues called *moai*. The population probably peaked at around 15,000 in the 17th century. Conflict over land and resources erupted in intertribal warfare by the late 17th century, only shortly before the arrival of Europeans, and the population started to decline. More recent dissension between different clans led to bloody wars and cannibalism, and many *moai* were toppled from their *ahu*. Natural disasters, such as earthquakes and tsunamis, may have also contributed to the destruction. The only *moai* that are left standing today were restored during the last century.

Contact with outsiders almost annihilated the Rapa Nui people. A raid by Peruvian blackbirders (slavers) in 1862 took 1000 islanders away to work the guano (manure) deposits of Peru's Chincha islands. After pressure from the Catholic Church, some survivors were returned to Easter Island, but disease and hard labour had already killed about 90% of them. A brief period of French-led missionary activity saw most of the surviving islanders converted to Catholicism in the 1860s.

Chile officially annexed the island in 1888 during a period of expansion that included the acquisition of territory from Peru and Bolivia after the War of the Pacific (1879–84).

By 1897 Rapa Nui had fallen under the control of a single wool company, which became the island's de facto government, continuing the wool trade until the middle of the 20th century.

In 1953 the Chilean government took charge of the island, continuing the imperial rule to which islanders had been subject for nearly a century. With restricted rights, including travel restrictions and ineligibility to vote, the islanders felt they were treated like second-class citizens. In 1967 the establishment of a regular commercial air link between Santiago and Tahiti, with Rapa Nui as a refuelling stop, opened up the island to the world and brought many benefits to Rapa Nui people.

The People of Rapa Nui

Rapa Nui is a fairly conservative society, and family life, marriage and children still play a central role in everyday life, as does religion.

More than a third of the population is from mainland Chile or Europe. The most striking feature is the intriguing blend of Polynesian and Chilean customs. Although they will never admit it overtly, the people of Rapa Nui have one foot in South America and one foot in Polynesia.

Despite its unique language and history, contemporary Rapa Nui does not appear to be a 'traditional' society – its continuity was shattered by the near extinction of the population in the last century. However, although they have largely adapted to a Westernised lifestyle, Rapa Nui people are fiercely proud of their history and culture, and they strive to keep their traditions alive.

Arts

As in Tahiti, traditional dancing is not a mere tourist attraction but one of the most vibrant forms of expression of traditional Polynesian

EASTER ISLAND (RAPA NUI) HISTORY

SUSTAINABLE TRAVEL

Easter Island is a superb open-air museum, but it's under threat due to the growing number of visitors. A few rules:

➡ Don't walk on the *ahu* (ceremonial stone platforms), as they are revered by locals as burial sites.

➡ It's illegal to remove or relocate rocks from any of the archaeological structures.

➡ Don't touch petroglyphs, as they're very fragile.

➡ Stay on designated paths to limit erosion.

➡ Motor vehicles are not allowed on Península Poike or Terevaka.

➡ Don't pitch your tent in the park.

culture. A couple of talented dance groups perform regularly at various hotels. Tattooing is another aspect of Polynesian culture, and it has enjoyed a revival among the young generation since the late 1980s.

There are also strong carving traditions on Easter Island.

The Landscape

Easter Island is roughly triangular in shape, with an extinct volcanic cone in each corner – Maunga (Mt) Terevaka, in the northwest corner, is the highest point at 507m. The island's maximum length is just 24km, and it is only 12km across at its widest point. Much of the interior of Easter Island is grassland, with cultivable soil interspersed with rugged lava fields. Erosion has created steep cliffs around much of the coast, and Anakena, on the north shore, is the only broad sandy beach.

Although some coral occurs in shallow waters, Rapa Nui does not have coral reefs. In the absence of reefs, the ocean has battered the huge cliffs, some of which rise to 300m.

Erosion, exacerbated by overgrazing and deforestation, is the island's most serious problem. In the most dramatic cases, the ground has slumped, leaving eroded landslides of brownish soil (it's particularly striking on Península Poike). To counteract the effects of erosion, a small-scale replanting program is under way on Península Poike.

SURVIVAL GUIDE

ℹ️ Directory A–Z

ACCOMMODATIONS

If you come here from mainland Chile, be prepared for a shock. Despite a high number of establishments – about 150 when we visited – accommodation on Easter Island is pricey for what you get. All accommodation options are located in Hanga Roa, except for one luxury hotel. *Residenciales* (homestays) form the bedrock of

---

LEARN HOW TO TELL YOUR AHU FROM YOUR MOAI

You don't need a university degree to appreciate the archaeological remains on Easter Island. The following explanations should suffice.

Ahu

Ahu were village burial sites and ceremonial centres and are thought to derive from altars in French Polynesia. Some 350 of these stone platforms are dotted around the coast. *Ahu* are paved on the upper surface with more or less flat stones, and they have a vertical wall on the seaward side and at each end.

Of several varieties of *ahu*, built at different times for different reasons, the most impressive are the *ahu moai* that support the massive statues.

Moai

Easter Island's most pervasive image, the enigmatic *moai* are massive carved figures that probably represent clan ancestors. From 2m to 10m tall, these stony-faced statues stood with their backs to the Pacific Ocean. Some *moai* have been completely restored, while others have been re-erected but are eroded. Many more lie on the ground, toppled over.

For several centuries, controversy has raged over the techniques employed to move and raise the *moai*. For many decades most experts believed they were dragged on a kind of wooden sledge, or pushed on top of rollers, but in the early 2000s archaeologists came to the conclusion that the *moai* were not dragged horizontally but moved in a vertical position using ropes. This theory would tally with oral history, which says that the *moai* 'walked' to their *ahu*. As you'll soon realise, it's a never-ending debate, which adds to the sense of mystery that makes this island so fascinating.

Topknots

Archaeologists believe that the reddish cylindrical *pukao* (topknots) that crown many *moai* reflect a male hairstyle once common on Rapa Nui.

Quarried from the small crater at Puna Pau, the volcanic scoria from which the topknots are made is relatively soft and easily worked. Carved like the *moai*, the topknots may have been simple embellishments, which were rolled to their final destination and then, despite weighing about as much as two elephants, somehow placed on top of the *moai*.

accommodation on the island but there's a growing number of luxury options. At the other end of the scale, there are also a couple of camping grounds in Hanga Roa. Note that wild camping is forbidden in the national park.

INTERNET ACCESS

You'll find internet cafes in Hanga Roa. Wi-fi is also available at most hotels and guesthouses but connections can be very slow at times.

MONEY

The local currency is the Chilean peso (CH$). A number of businesses on Rapa Nui, especially *residenciales*, hotels and rental agencies, accept US cash (and euros, albeit at a pinch). Travellers from Tahiti must bring US cash (or euros) as Tahitian currency is not accepted.

ATMs Easter Island has only three ATMs, one of which accepts only MasterCard. Don't rely solely on your credit card and make sure you keep some cash in reserve.

Credit cards Many *residenciales*, hotels, restaurants and tour agencies accept credit cards.

Moneychangers There are two banks and an exchange office in Hanga Roa. US dollars are the best foreign currency to carry, followed by euros. Note that exchange rates on Easter Island are slightly lower than those offered in mainland Chile.

Taxes All prices are inclusive of tax.

Tipping and bargaining Tipping and bargaining are not traditionally part of Polynesian culture.

OPENING HOURS

The following are normal opening hours for Easter Island.

Offices 9am to 5pm Monday to Friday

Restaurants 11am to 10pm Monday to Saturday

TELEPHONE

Easter Island's international telephone code is the same as Chile's (☑ 56), and the area code (☑ 032) covers the whole island. You'll find several private call centres in town. Entel offers GSM cell-phone service, and prepaid SIM cards are available for purchase. Ask your service provider about international roaming agreements and the charges involved.

TOURIST INFORMATION

Easter Island Foundation (www.islandheritage.org) Background information on the island.

Lonely Planet (www.lonelyplanet.com/chile/rapa-nui-easter-island) Has travel news and tips.

❶ Getting There & Away

AIR

The only airline serving Easter Island is **LAN** (Map p55; ☑ 032-210-0279; www.lan.com; Av Atamu Tekena s/n; ☺ 9am-4.30pm Mon-Fri, to

12.30pm Sat). It has daily flights to/from Santiago and one weekly flight to/from Pape'ete (Tahiti). A standard economy round-trip fare from Santiago can range from US$550 to US$900.

SEA

Few passenger services go to Easter Island. A few yachts stop here, mostly in January, February and March. Anchorages are not well sheltered.

❶ Getting Around

Outside Hanga Roa, the entire east coast road and the road to Anakena are paved.

TO/FROM THE AIRPORT

The airport is on the outskirts of Hanga Roa. Accommodation proprietors wait at the airport and will shuttle you for free to your hotel or *residencial*.

BICYCLE

Mountain bikes can be rented in Hanga Roa for about CH$10,000 per day.

CAR & MOTORCYCLE

Some hotels and agencies rent 4WDs for CH$40,000 to CH$60,000 for 24 hours depending on the vehicle. A word of warning: insurance is *not* available, so you're not covered should the vehicle get any damage. Don't leave valuables in your car.

Scooters and motorcycles are rented for about CH$20,000 to CH$25,000 a day.

You can contact the following outfits.

Haunani (Map p55; ☑ 032-210-0353; Av Atamu Tekena s/n; ☺ 9am-8pm) On the main drag.

Oceanic Rapa Nui Rent a Car (Map p55; ☑ 032-210-0985; www.rentacaroceanic.com; Av Atamu Tekena s/n; ☺ 8am-8pm) On the main drag.

Insular Rent a Car (Map p55; ☑ 032-210-0480; www.rentainsular.cl; Av Atamu Tekena s/n; ☺ 9am-8pm) Also rents mountain bikes (from CH$10,000 a day).

TAXI

Taxis cost a flat CH$2000 for most trips around town and CH$3000 to the airport.

Fiji

📞 679 / POP 881,065

Best Places to Stay

➡ Bibi's Hideaway (p133)

➡ Matava Resort (p137)

➡ Beachcomber Island Resort (p105)

➡ Maqai Resort (p136)

➡ Blue Lagoon Beach Resort (p114)

Best Places to Eat

➡ Eco Café (p96)

➡ Governors (p76)

➡ Taste Fiji (p83)

➡ Surf and Turf (p124)

➡ Navutu Stars (p112)

Why Go?

While Fiji's ludicrously blue skies, perfectly swaying palms and eye-smarting white sands provide the backdrop to many a tropical-paradise daydream, there's much more to the country than languid sun-lounge lying and coconut dodging. With eminently diveable undersea marvels, lush interiors begging to be hiked and a fascinating culture to explore, Fiji's 330-plus islands offer something special for every type of traveller. Billed as 'The Happiest Place on Earth', Fiji is extraordinarily welcoming, with a population as warm as its famous sunshine. It's also arguably the easiest place in the South Pacific to get around, and there's accommodation – from bare-bones *bures* to upmarket resorts – to suit every budget. Whether you're looking for relaxation, romance or rollicking adventure, chances are you'll discover the island holiday of your dreams in Fiji.

When to Go
Suva

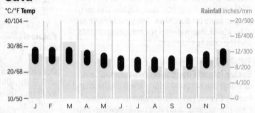

Jun–Sep
High season, with costs peaking in June and July.

May & Oct
Shoulder season and the beginning and end of the dry season.

Nov–Apr
Expect wet and humid weather.

VITI LEVU

POP 600,000 / AREA 10,400 SQ KM

Everyone who visits Fiji passes through Viti Levu, the country's largest island, but it's often looked at as no more than an unavoidable stop for those en route elsewhere. Yet there are plenty of attractions to make you linger longer.

Away from the gateway hub of Nadi, the southern Coral Coast offers a lively mix of resorts aimed at families and backpackers, plus a host of adventure sports including scuba diving with massive tiger sharks.

While sultry Suva, the South Pacific's largest city, has a rich cultural heritage to explore, northern Viti Levu's best attractions are on the water, from the dolphin-spotting and kite-surfer paradise of Nananu-i-Ra, to the coral reefs of the Bligh Passage. Tie this in with visits to traditional villages and breathtaking waterfalls, and you'll find that Viti Levu has what it takes to be the centrepiece of any Fijian trip.

ⓘ Information

Suva, the country's capital, largest city and main port, is in the southeast. Most travellers arrive in the west at Nadi International Airport, 9km north of central Nadi and 24km south of Lautoka.

Nadi and Suva are linked by the sealed Queens Rd that runs along the southern perimeter of Viti Levu (221km) and contains the scattering of villages and resorts known as the Coral Coast.

Heading north from Suva, the Kings Rd is mostly sealed and travels for 265km through Nausori (where Suva's airport is located), the eastern highlands, Rakiraki, Ba (on the north coast), and Lautoka. South of Rakiraki is Fiji's highest point – Tomanivi (Mt Victoria) at 1323m.

Three roads head up from the coast to the Nausori Highlands villages of Navala and Bukuya (via Ba, Nadi and Sigatoka).

DANGERS & ANNOYANCES

Travelling around Viti Levu is easy and safe, and most visitors will encounter a warm reception, particularly in rural areas. Walking around towns during daylight hours is perfectly safe; as soon as night descends, however, this is a no-no. This is particularly pertinent in Suva – from dusk onwards, locals will catch a taxi, even for a distance of 300m, and you should as well. Muggings and sexual assaults are a common risk, especially for solo travellers.

ⓘ Getting There & Away

Most travellers arrive in Fiji at Nadi International Airport. Nadi and Suva are both domestic transport hubs, offering flights to many of the other islands, as well as boat services and cruises to offshore islands.

ⓘ Getting Around

AIR

For those in a hurry or after a scenic flight, there are cheap, regular flights between Nadi and Suva for around $89.

BUS

Viti Levu has a regular and cheap bus network. Express buses link the main centres of Lautoka,

---

FIJI IN...

One Week

From **Nadi** follow the Coral Coast Hwy south to the **Momi Guns**, and **Natadola Beach** for horse riding. Chug into the verdant interior on the **Coral Coast Scenic Railway** or trek to the top of the **Sigatoka Sand Dunes**. Make your way to **Pacific Harbour** for diving with sharks in **Beqa Lagoon**. Don't miss the chance to raft the canyons of the **Navua River** before heading to **Suva**. Complete your loop via the Kings Rd, windsurfing at **Nananu-i-Ra** or scuba diving at **Rakiraki**. Head back to sugar country and visit **Lautoka**, the second-largest city and a great base for exploring the **Nausori Highlands**. If you have an extra night, spend it at the traditional village of **Navala** before heading back to Nadi.

Two Weeks

Thanks to a high-speed catamaran that weaves daily from **Port Denarau** through the **Yasawas** and back, this chain is readily explored. The boat passes a few of the **Mamanucas** on the way, so these islands are a good place to start. Spend the next few days on the sliver of sand that connects **Wayasewa** to **Waya** before drifting north to **Naviti** to snorkel with manta rays. Dash up to **Nacula**, or **Nanuya Lailai**, where you can paddle in the **Blue Lagoon**. From here, leapfrog back down the chain, stopping at **Matacawalevu** and Naviti once more.

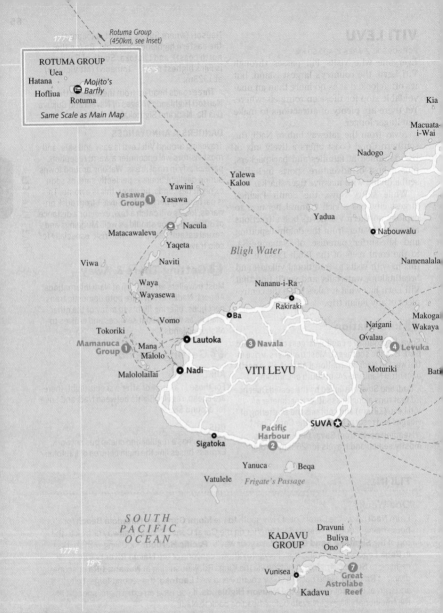

ROTUMA GROUP

Uea
Hatana
Hofliua

*Mojito's
Bartly*
Rotuma

Same Scale as Main Map

Rotuma Group
(450km, see Inset)

Kia

Macuata-
i-Wai

Nadogo

Nabouwalu

Namenalala

Yalewa
Kalou

Yadua

Bligh Water

Yawini
Yasawa

**Yasawa
Group**

Nacula

Matacawalevu

Yaqeta

Naviti

Viwa

Waya
Wayasewa

Nananu-i-Ra

Rakiraki

Vomo

Tokoriki

**Mamanuca
Group**

Mana
Malolo

Malololailai

Ba

Lautoka

Navala

Naigani

Ovalau

Makoga
Wakaya

Levuka

Moturiki

Bati

Nadi

VITI LEVU

SUVA

*Pacific
Harbour*

Sigatoka

Yanuca
Beqa

Vatulele
Frigate's Passage

*SOUTH
PACIFIC
OCEAN*

Dravuni
Buliya
Ono

**KADAVU
GROUP**

Vunisea

**Great
Astrolabe
Reef**

Kadavu

Fiji Highlights

1 Relaxing in the cobalt waters and somniferous sun of the **Mamanuca** (p103) and **Yasawa** (p109) islands.

2 Remembering to breathe when the first bull shark swims into view in the waters off **Pacific Harbour** (p97).

3 Having a drink at the *tanoa* bowl in the traditional village of **Navala** (p88).

4 Strolling around the colonial architecture of Fiji's first capital, **Levuka** (p115).

| 0 | | 100 km |
| 0 | | 60 miles |

Cikobia

Vetauua

Drua Drua

Quelevu

Mali
Labasa

Nukusemanu

Nukubasage
Nukubalati

VANUA LEVU

Rabi
Cobia

Buca Bay
Kioa
Yanuca

Nanuku
Lailai

Savusavu
Matei
Somosomo Somosomo Strait
Nanuku
Levu

Wailagi Lala

Savusavu Bay

Lavena Coastal Walk

Nanuku Passage

Naitaba

Koro

Taveuni

Malima

Vanua Balavu

Avea

Yacata
Kaidu
Kanacea
Moana's Guesthouse
Cikobia-i-Lau

LOMAIVITI GROUP

Nukutolu

Namalata

Susui
Munia

Vatu Vara

Mago

Karafaga
Vekai

Nairai

Cicia

LAU GROUP

Tuvuca

Yarous

Gau

KORO SEA

Nayau

Lakeba

Aiwa

Vanua Vatu

Oneata

Moala

Olorau

Komo

Moce

Same Scale as Main Map

Ono-i-Lau

Tavua Na Sici

Namuka-i-Lau

Ono-i-Lau (290km, see Inset)

MOALA GROUP

Totoya

Vuaqava

Kabara

Navutu-i-Ra
Yagasa

Same Scale as Main Map

Vatoa

Marabo

Navutu-i-Loma

Matuku

Vatoa (140km, see Inset)

Fulaga

Ogea Levu

⑤ Dropping anchor with the yachties at **Savusavu Bay** (p119).

⑥ Diving Taveuni's stunning **Somosomo Strait** (p129).

⑦ Swimming with manta rays at Kadavu's **Great Astrolabe Reef** (p137).

⑧ Hiking or kayaking Taveuni's **Lavena Coastal Walk** (p135) then staying the night in Lavena village.

Nadi and Suva, along both the Queens and Kings Rds. Most will pick up or drop off at hotels and resorts along these highways. Slower local buses also operate throughout the island and even remote inland villages have regular (though less frequent) services. Before heading to an isolated area, check that there is a return bus, as sometimes the last bus of the day stays overnight at the final village.

Coral Sun Express (☑ 672 3311; www.touristtransportfiji.com) Runs comfortable, air-conditioned coaches between Nadi and Suva ($20, twice daily), plus resorts on the way, including those at Coral Coast ($15) and Pacific Harbour ($18).

Pacific Transport (☑ 330 4366; www.pacifictransport.com.fj) Nine buses run daily to Suva ($15, five hours express or six hours regular) via the Coral Coast ($7.20) and Pacific Harbour ($11). It's $3.50 to Lautoka.

Sunbeam Transport (☑ 927 2121; www.sunbeamfiji.com) Eight daily buses run along the Queen's Rd from Nadi to the Coral Coast ($7.75) and Pacific Harbour ($11.60) resorts en route to Suva ($15.70). Frequent services to Lautoka ($3). Services along the King's Rd include Rakiraki ($11.50, 90 minutes) and Suva ($21, six hours).

Feejee Experience (☑ 672 5950; www.feejeeexperience.com) Offers hop-on-hop-off coach transfers (from $458) from Nadi to destinations all over Viti Levu.

MINIBUS, CAR & TAXI

Minibuses and carriers (small trucks) also shuttle locals along the Queens Rd. Taxis are plentiful: insist your driver turns on the meter. Viti Levu is also easy to explore by car or motorbike, although for the unsealed highland roads you'll generally need a 4WD.

Suva

POP 167,975

Suva (*soo-va*) is the heart of Fiji, home to half of the country's urban population and the largest city in the South Pacific. It's a lush green city on a hilly peninsula, that gets more than its fair share of rain, and has a vibrant cultural scene.

Downtown is as diverse architecturally as the populace is culturally. A jigsaw of colonial buildings, modern shopping plazas, abundant eateries and a breezy esplanade all form the compact central business district. Small passages are lined with curry houses, sari shops and bric-a-brac traders. Bollywood and Hollywood square off at the local cinema and within the same hour you're likely to see businessmen in traditional *sulu* (skirt) and student hipsters from across the Pacific region rocking the latest styles.

◉ Sights

★**Fiji Museum** MUSEUM

(Map p74; ☑ 331 5944; www.fijimuseum.org.fj; Ratu Cakobau Rd; adult/child $7/5; ⊙ 9am-4.30pm Mon-Sat) This museum offers a great journey into Fiji's historical and cultural evolution. To enjoy the exhibits in chronological order, start with the displays behind the ticket counter and work your way around clockwise. The centrepiece is the massive **Ratu Finau** (1913), Fiji's last *waqa tabus* (double-hulled canoe), over 13m long and with an enclosed deck for rough weather. Other attractions in the main hall include war clubs, a gruesome display about cannibalism and the rudder from *The Bounty* (of Mutiny fame).

★**Colo-i-Suva Forest Park** FOREST

(Map p70; ☑ 332 0211; adult/child $5/1; ⊙ 8am-4pm) Colo-i-Suva (pronounced tho-lo-ee-*soo*-va) is a 2.5-sq-km oasis of lush rainforest, teeming with tropical plants and vivid and melodic bird life. The 6.5km of walking trails navigate clear natural pools and gorgeous vistas. Sitting at an altitude of 120m to 180m, it's a cool and peaceful respite from Suva's urban hubbub.

Slipping and sliding through the forest over water-worn rocks is the Waisila Creek, which makes its way down to Waimanu River and forms the water swimming holes along the way.

University of the South Pacific UNIVERSITY

(USP; Map p69; ☑ 331 3900; www.usp.ac.fj; Laucala Bay Rd) While not necessarily a must-see from a tourist's perspective, this is the foremost provider of tertiary education to the island nations of the Pacific region. The USP's main Laucala Campus offers some fascinating people-watching and picturesque strolling through a small **botanical garden**. At the **Oceania Centre for Arts & Culture** (Map p69) you can also see temporary exhibits of paintings and carvings. The **USP Bookshop** nearby is particularly well-stocked.

Suva Municipal Market MARKET

(Map p69; Usher St; ⊙ 6am-6pm Mon-Fri, to 4.30pm Sat) It's the beating heart of Suva and a great place to spend an hour or so poking around with a camera. The boys

Suva

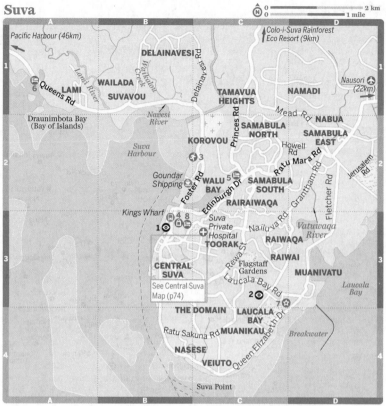

Suva

with barrows own the lanes and they aren't afraid to mow down a few tourists to deliver their cassava on time. Besides the recognisable tomatoes, cabbages and chillies, look out for bitter gourds, jackfruit, *dalo*, cassava and yams. Produce is cheaper than in supermarkets and there's no need to haggle – prices are clearly marked.

🏃 Activities

The **Suva Olympic Swimming Pool** (Map p74; 224 Victoria Pde; adult/child $3/1.50; ⊙10am-6pm Mon-Fri, 8am-6pm Sat) is slap bang in the middle of town. Other sports open to the public include golf and lawn bowls, and a brisk walk along the waterfront promenade (in daylight hours only) is a must.

Viti Levu

FIJI SUVA

Naviti

YASAWA
GROUP

SOUTH
PACIFIC
OCEAN

Waya

Wayasewa
(Waya Lailai)

Vatia
Point

Bligh Water

Tavua Rabula

Nailaga

Ba Back Rd

Ba

Vatukoula
Nadele

Nadarivatu

See Nadi & the West Map (p84)

Bekana

Vitogo

Tivua

Lauwaki

Viseisei

Lomolomo

Vakabuli

Lautoka

TAVAKUBU

Abaca

Toge

Navala

Balevuto

Nagatagata

9

Koro

Nadrau

Ba River

MAMANUCA
GROUP

Mana

Wadigi

Malolo

Malolo
Lailai

Malolo
Barrier
Reef

Uciwai
Landing

Yako

Denarau

Nadi

Nawaka

Naboutini

Nadi
Bay

Nadi
International
Airport

Natawa

Bukuya

Nausori
Highlands

Tubenasolo

Mt Mangondro
(889m)

Vaturu
Dam

Nanoko

Nabutautau

Nadrau
Plateau

Korolevu

Monavatu
(913m)

Keiyasi

Navula
Reef

Momi
Bay

Nawau

Nawagadamu

Vunimoli

Sigatoka River

Viti Levu

Mbavu

Tubairata

Mavua

Tuvutau
(Mt Gordon)
(933m)

Lomawai

Likuri
Landing

15

14

Vusama

Tilivalevu

Cuvu
Beach

Butoni

Naduri

Nadrala

Nabukelevu

Natadola
Beach

13

Nakabuta

Savu Na
Mate Laya
Waterfall

Upper Navua
River

Sanasana

16

Cuvu

Sigatoka

18

3

Korotogo

Coral Coast
Scenic Railway

See Sunset
Strip Map
(p95)

Coral Coast

Vatukarasa
Korolevu

Biausevu

Naboutini

Namatakula

Namaquaqua

Korovisilou

Naivabale
Reef

Blade
Rock
Reef

SOUTH
PACIFIC
OCEAN

Frigate
Passage

Frigate
Walls

Vatulele

2

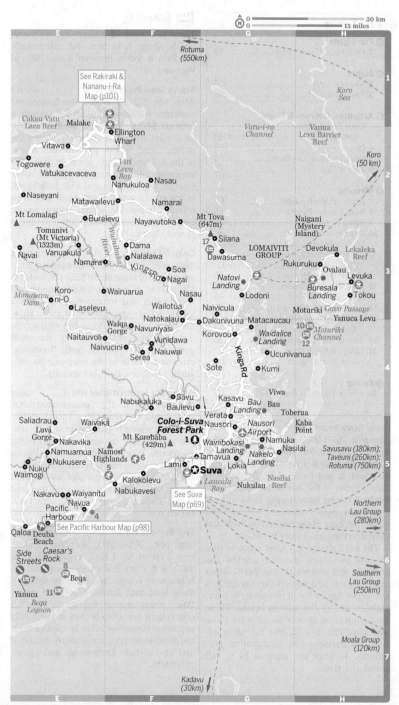

0 —————————— **30 km**
0 —————————— **15 miles**

Rotuma
(550km)

Koro
Sea

See Rakiraki &
Nananu-i-Ra
Map (p101)

Cakau Vatu
Laca Reef
Malake

Vitawa

Ellington
Wharf

Vatu-i-ra
Channel

Vanua
Levu Barrier
Reef

Koro
(50 km)

Togowere

Vatukacevaceva

Viti
Levu
Bay

Naseyani

Nanukuloa   Nasau

Matawailevu   Namarai

Mt Lomalagi

Burelevu   Nayavutoka   Mt Tova
(647m)

Naigani
(Mystery
Island)

Tomanivi
(Mt Victoria)
(1323m)

Vanuakula

Dama

Silana   17

Devokula

Lekaleka
Reef

LOMAIVITI
GROUP

Navai

Namara

Nalalawa

Dawasuma

Rukuruku

Ovalau

Levuka

Waimbuka
River

Soa

Nagai

Natovi
Landing

Buresala
Landing

Tokou

Monasavu
Dam

Koro-
ni-O

Wairuarua

Nasau

Lodoni

Moturiki   Gavo Passage

Laselevu

Wailotua

Naivicula

Matacaucau

Yanuca Levu

Waiqa
Gorge

Navuniyasi

Natokalau

Dakunivuna

Korovou

Waidalice
Landing

10   Moturiki
Channel

Naitauvoli

Vunidawa

12

Naivucini

Naiuwi

Ucunivanua

Serea

Sote

Kumi

Kings Rd

Viwa

Nabukaluka

Savu

Baulevu

Kasavu   Bau
Bau   Landing

Toberua

Saliadrau

Waivaka

Verata

Nausori

Nausori
Airport

Kaba
Point

Luva
Gorge

Nakavika

Mt Korobaba
(429m)

1   Wainibokasi
Landing

Namuka

Nasilai

Savusavu (180km);
Taveuni (260km);
Rotuma (750km)

Namuamua

Namosi
Highlands

6

Tamavua

Nakelo
Landing

Nukusere

5

Lami

Lokia

Nuku
Waimogi

Kalokolevu

Suva

Laucala
Bay

Nukulau

Nasilai
Reef

Northern
Lau Group
(280km)

Nakavu   Waiyanitu

Nabukavesi

Pacific
Harbour

Navua

4

See Suva
Map (p69)

Qaloa   Deuba
Beach

See Pacific Harbour Map (p98)

Side
Streets

Caesar's
Rock

7

8

Beqa

Southern
Lau Group
(250km)

Yanuca

11

Beqa
Lagoon

Moala Group
(120km)

Colo-i-Suva
Forest Park

Kadavu
(30km)

Viti Levu

Royal Suva Yacht Club SAILING
(Map p69; ☎331 2921; www.rsyc.org.fj; ☺office 8am-5pm Mon-Sat, 9am-4pm Sun) The Royal Suva Yacht Club is a popular watering hole for yachties and locals alike. It has great sunset views of the Bay of Islands, though the food can be hit and miss. Even without a yacht, overseas visitors are welcome and the atmosphere at the bar can be lively and salty; everyone has a story to tell.

The noticeboard is a good place to find crewing positions and the marina has dockside fuel and water. The **Yacht Shop** handles parts and repairs. Anchorage fees are $5 per day, or $50 if you prefer to overnight in one of the marina berths. There are laundry and shower facilities for those who have just arrived, and the office advises on customs and immigration procedures. Yachties use channel 16 to call ahead of arrival.

🛏 Sleeping

There is a swag of budget and midrange hotels along Robertson Rd, particularly the loop it forms between Anand St and Waimanu Rd.

South Seas Private Hotel HOSTEL $
(Map p74; ☎331 2296; www.fiji4less.com/south.html; 6 Williamson Rd; dm $25, s/d without bathroom $47/60, r with bathroom $77; ☺) Set on a quiet street just a step away from the museum and botanic gardens, this is one of the few truly budget places in Suva. The sweeping interior verandah, classic white exterior, high ceilings and wide halls speak of the romance of a bygone era. This large colonial house has simple, clean rooms, comfortably ageing lounge furniture and a shared kitchen.

Colonial Lodge GUESTHOUSE $
(Map p69; ☎330 0655; www.facebook.com/colonialloge; 19 Anand St; dm $35, r $75, treehouse $140) This home-cum-hostel caterers to backpackers and volunteers. It operates a lot like a homestay (and you'll get to know the owner's cats and dogs), but with simple dorm accommodation through the main house. There's a cute if rustic 'treehouse' extension annexe at the rear, with its own kitchen facilities. Basic but friendly.

Peninsula International Hotel HOTEL $
(Map p74; ☎331 3711; www.peninsula.com.fj; cnr McGregor Rd & Pender St; s/d from $125/140; ☺❄☎) Pleasantly situated in a leafy residential area, the Peninsula provides pretty good value. From the outside, it looks like an apartment block and is recognisable by the overhanging window canopies (which get in the way of what would have been excellent views). There is a small pool, restaurant and bar on site.

Five Princes Hotel BOUTIQUE HOTEL $$
(Map p69; ☎338 1575; www.fiveprinceshotel.com; 5 Princes Rd; d $240, bungalow $280, villa $400; ❄@☎☎) This one-time colonial villa is a great retreat away from the centre of Suva. Solid teak furniture, polished timber floors, power showers, satellite TV and wi-fi connections are all to be had in beautifully appointed rooms. Set in landscaped gardens, the stand-alone villas are similarly decorated and also include kitchenettes and private verandahs.

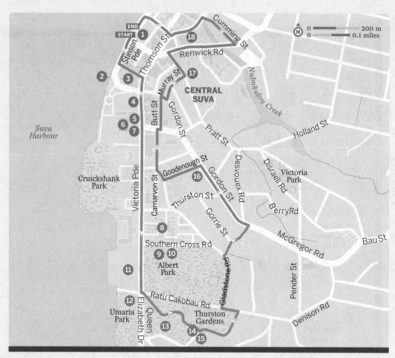

🏃 City Walk
A Taste of Suva

START STINSON PDE
END STINSON PDE
LENGTH 3.5KM; TWO TO FOUR HOURS

Downtown Suva has a scattering of colonial buildings and places of interest, making it a pleasant place to wander around.

Start on Stinson Pde at the **1 Suva Curio & Handicraft Market** (p78). Cross the street and follow the esplanade south, enjoying the views of Suva Harbour. Once you reach **2 Tiko's Floating Restaurant** (p77), cross the road and amble through the tree-lined **3 Ratu Sukuna Park**. Continue south down Victoria Pde, past the 1926 **4 Fintel building** and the 1904 **5 old town hall**. The **6 Suva Olympic Swimming Pool** (p69) is set back between this building and the 1909 **7 Suva City Library**.

Continue down Victoria Pde. On your left are the stately **8 Government Buildings**. Just south is **9 Albert Park**, a large sporting field. The **10 Kingsford Smith Pavilion**, named after the famous aviator who landed here, is on Southern Cross Rd. Opposite the park is the glorious **11 Grand Pacific Hotel** (p76). Just past Ratu Cakobau Rd is **12 Umaria Park & Suva Bowls Club**, where you can take a breather with a cold drink.

Cross the road at Queen Elizabeth Dr and enter **13 Thurston Gardens**. Meander through this colourful park, stopping at the **14 Botanic Gardens Clock Tower** and the **15 Fiji Museum** (p68).

Turn left and walk along the edge of Albert Park along Gladstone Rd, before cutting up the pedestrian path to McGregor Rd. Head downhill and turn left at **16 St Andrew's Church**, follow Goodenough St and dog-leg onto Carnarvon St. Stroll north past the bars and clubs to the **17 Roman Catholic Cathedral**, one of Suva's most prominent landmarks.

Turn left, then right and window-shop your way to Cumming St, then turn left to immerse yourself in Suva's little India – streets lined with Indian-run shops.

Make your way past the stately old **18 Garrick Hotel**, then head back to the Curio & Handicraft Market (p78). If you've got any energy left, spend it on a bout of souvenir shopping.

Central Suva

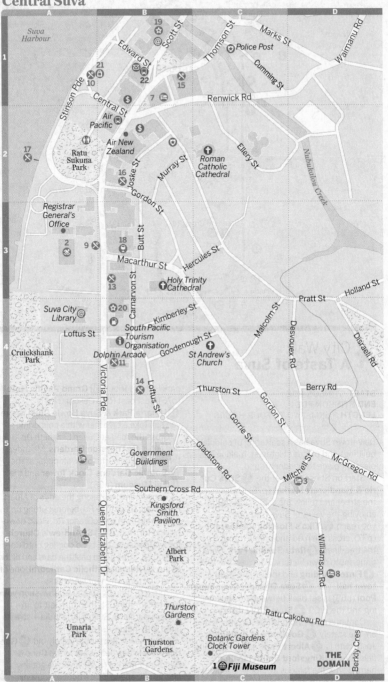

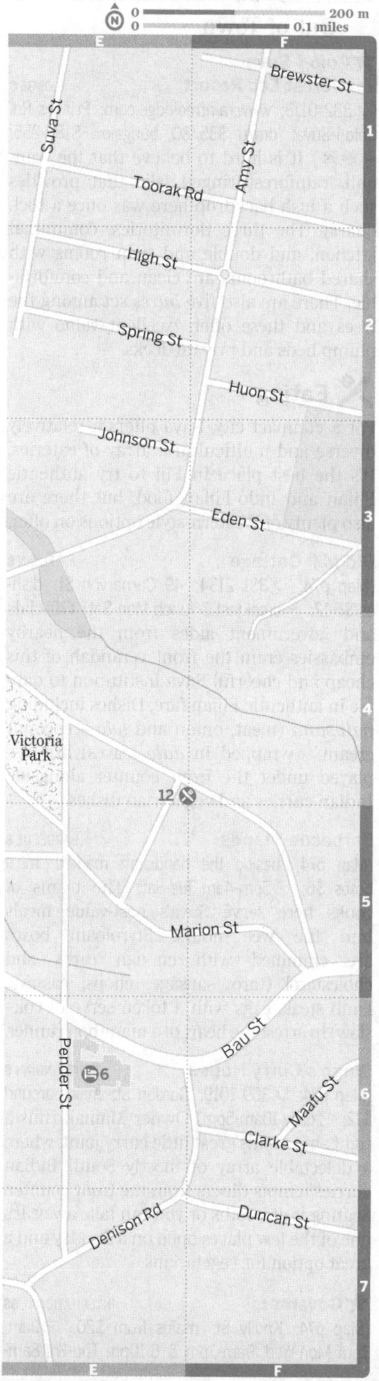

Central Suva

Top Sights
1 Fiji Museum C7

Activities, Courses & Tours
2 Suva Olympic Swimming Pool A3

Sleeping
3 Best Western Suva Motor Inn D5
4 Grand Pacific Hotel A6
5 Holiday Inn A5
6 Peninsula International Hotel E6
7 Quest Serviced Apartments B1
8 South Seas Private Hotel D6

Eating
9 Ashiyana A3
10 Barbecue Stands A1
11 Daikoku B4
12 Governors E4
13 Maya Dhaba B3
14 Old Mill Cottage B4
15 Shanghai Seafood House B1
16 Singh's Curry House B2
17 Tiko's Floating Restaurant A2

Drinking & Nightlife
18 O'Reilly's B3

Entertainment
19 Damodar Village Cinema B1
20 Traps Bar B4

Shopping
21 Suva Curio & Handicraft Market B1

Transport
22 Pacific Sun B1
Qantas .... (see 22)

De Vos Hotel HOTEL $$
(Central St; r $118-208; 📶) This hotel has a great location, opening straight onto Ratu Sukuna Park. It's all 1970s concrete and undeniably a little tatty around the edges, but the rooms are generously sized for the price (get one with park views), the service is friendly, and there's a reasonable restaurant on the ground floor.

Quest Serviced Apartments APARTMENT $$
(Map p74; ☎331 9117; www.questsuva.com; Thomson St; studio/one-bed apt $260/296) You'd never know these gems of apartments were here, tucked away on the 6th and 7th floor of the Suva Central building. Central, quiet, well-maintained and secure, they are popular with the long-stay embassy and development agency crowd, but there are always a few units available – there's a two-night

minimum stay. There's an air-conditioned gym on-site too.

Best Western Suva Motor Inn
HOTEL $$

(Map p74; ☑ 331 3973; www.hexagonfiji.com; cnr Mitchell & Gorrie Sts; studio/two bed apt $165/240; ❄ @ ☎ ☰) The four-storey Best Western (no lift) is shaped like a 'U' around a richly-planted courtyard with a small pool into which snakes a water slide. All rooms have balconies (the best with views to Albert Park) and the larger two-bedroom apartments sleep four and have kitchens. It's a good, solid midrange choice. Wi-fi costs $30/day.

Holiday Inn
HOTEL $$

(Map p74; ☑ 330 1600; reservations@holiday innsuva.com.fj; Victoria Pde; r $272-497; ❄ ❄ @ ☎ ☰) This inn occupies a great location on the harbour shore, across from the Government Buildings and near the museum. Rooms are generically spacious, cool and comfortable and will please picky travellers. The inn patently appeals to business travellers and those on coach tours, and it has the facilities, including wi-fi throughout, to match.

★ Grand Pacific Hotel
HERITAGE HOTEL $$$

(Map p74; ☑ 322 2000; www.grandpacifichotel. com.fj; Victoria Parade; r $490-550, ste $650-1200; ❄ ☎ ☰) The GPH, as it's locally known, is one of Suva's jewels. This iconic 1914 building facing Albert Park has undergone extensive renovation to return it to its former glory. The original white porticoed building holds sumptuous suites, while the majority of rooms are in a sensitively-designed new annexe at the rear. All rooms have pool or ocean views.

The restaurant is well-priced for the venue, and one of the few places in Suva where you can sit outside next to the sea. There's a Swiss coffee shop out front, as well as a gym and spa for less calorifically indulgent moments.

Novotel Suva Lami Bay
HOTEL $$$

(Map p69; ☑ 336 2450; www.novotel.com; Queens Rd, Lami; r from $190-300; P ❄ ☎ ☰) The low-slung Novotel offers no-nonsense business-style accommodation, but it has an unexpectedly great waterfront location and a pleasantly fresh and open restaurant with views across Draunimbota Bay. The only drawback is the location – Lami is a 10-minute drive from central Suva.

▦ Out of Town

★ Colo-i-Suva

Rainforest Eco Resort
LODGE $

(☑ 332 0113; www.raintreelodge.com; Princes Rd, Colo-i-Suva; dm/d $35/80, bungalow $185-255; ☻ @ ☰) It is hard to believe that the tranquil, rainforest-fringed lake that provides such a lush backdrop here was once a rock quarry. The three dormitories, communal kitchen, and double and twin rooms with shared bathrooms are clean and comfortable. There are also five *bures* set among the trees and these offer excellent value with plump beds and private decks.

✖ Eating

For a compact city, Suva offers a relatively diverse and multicultural array of eateries. It's the best place in Fiji to try authentic Fijian and Indo-Fijian food, but there are also plenty of Western-style options on offer.

Old Mill Cottage
FIJIAN $

(Map p74; ☑ 331 2134; 49 Carnarvon St; dishes $5-12; ⊙ breakfast & lunch Mon-Sat) Officials and government aides from the nearby embassies cram the front verandah of this cheap and cheerful Suva institution to dabble in authentic Fijian fare. Dishes including *palusami* (meat, onion and *lolo* – coconut cream – wrapped in *dalo* leaves) are displayed under the front counter alongside Indian curries and vegetarian dishes.

Barbecue Stands
BARBECUE $

(Map p74; beside the handicraft market; meal boxes $6; ⊙ 5pm-4am Tue-Sat) The teams of cooks here serve Suva's best-value meals into the wee hours. Styrofoam boxes are crammed with enough carbs and cholesterol (taro, sausage, chops, cassava, lamb steak, eggs with a token serve of coleslaw) to arrest the heart of a marathon runner.

Singh's Curry House
SOUTH INDIAN $

(Map p74; ☑ 359 1019; Gordon St; mains around $12; ⊙ daily 10am-5pm) Owner Mamaji runs a tight ship at this great little curry joint, where a delectable array of mostly South Indian curries tempts diners from the front counter. Seating is at booths or you can take away. It's one of the few places open on a Sunday and a great option for vegetarians.

★ Governors
INTERNATIONAL $$

(Map p74; Knolly St; mains from $20; ⊙ 9am-3pm Mon-Wed, 9am-3pm & 6-10pm Thu-Fri, 8am-

4pm Sat, to 2.30pm Sun) Housed in a converted colonial bungalow that was once home to Ratu Sir Lalu Sukuna, Governors is the newest fashionable eating place on the block. You can see why: great food (Italian and Thai notes on a Fijian base), plus great decor with vintage travel posters and luggage. Weekend brunch is incredibly popular, as is the live weekend evening music.

If you've got space for dessert, we counted six (!) different types of cheesecake, so plan for a return visit.

Ashiyana   INDIAN $$

(Map p74; ☑ 331 3000; Old Town Hall Bldg, Victoria Pde; mains $10-20; ⊙ 11.30am-2.30pm & 6-10pm Tue-Sat, 6-10pm Sun) This pint-sized restaurant is a long-standing Indian favourite with some of the best butter chicken in town and curries so spicy even the taxi drivers consider them hot. It has something of the feel of a downtown English curry house to it, but is always packed out (not that it takes much), so call ahead for a table.

Maya Dhaba   INDIAN $$

(Map p74; ☑ 331 0045; 281 Victoria Pde; mains $15-25; ⊙ 11am-2.30pm & 6pm-10.30pm; ✱) Maya Dhaba is one of Suva's most urbane restaurants, serving up Indian dishes in bright, modern surroundings. The meals are excellent: wrap your naan around any number of familiar and not so familiar North and South Indian classics. Takeaway options are also available.

Shanghai Seafood House   CHINESE $$

(Map p74; ☑ 331 4865; 6 Thomson St; mains $13-20; ⊙ lunch & dinner) In the heart of the shopping district, this 1st-floor restaurant is plush in a kitschy, fake-flower kind of way. The encyclopaedic menu and al fresco seating on the 1914 building's balcony induce long and lazy lunches.

Tiko's Floating Restaurant   INTERNATIONAL $$$

(Map p74; ☑ 331 3626; Stinson Pde; mains $19-55; ⊙ noon-2pm & 5.30-10.30pm Mon-Fri, 5.30-11pm Sat; ✱) The only way you could be any more harbourside would be if you were standing in the water. This permanently moored former Blue Lagoon cruise ship has excellent surf-and-turf fare including good steaks, fresh local fish (*walu* and *pakapaka*) and an extensive wine list. Everything is served on white linen and in fine china and glassware.

Daikoku   JAPANESE $$$

(Map p74; ☑ 330 8968; Victoria Pde; mains $25-40; ⊙ noon-2pm, 6-10pm Mon-Sat) Upstairs past the closet-sized bar, the acrobatic culinary skills of Daikoku's teppanyaki chefs are reason enough to spend an evening here. The seafood, chicken and beef seared on the sizzling teppanyaki plates would hold up in any Tokyo restaurant; the sushi is nearly is good. The lunch specials are popular with the international crowd, and tables fill up fast.

FIJI SUVA

MOVING TO THE BEAT OF A DIFFERENT DRUM

Dancers pay homage to the steady beat of the drums, seemingly oblivious to the spectators. The poorly lit room is crowded with both tourists and locals yelling '*bula*' to one another over the din. As a big, indigenous Fijian man – who better meets the image you may have of a traditional Fijian chief – approaches with a flower behind his ear and a pitcher of beer on his tray, you don't need any reminding that this is no *meke* (dance performance that enacts stories and legends). This is Saturday night in Suva, when the country's urban youth let down their hair and pole dance to pop music.

Fiji's urban youth face many of the same difficulties as young people around the globe: teenage parenting, crime, drugs and skyrocketing unemployment. However, these youths also find themselves straddling two opposing worlds: the traditional, conservative society of the villages many have left behind, where life was filled with cultural protocols, and the liberal, individualistic lifestyle of the modern and increasingly Westernised city. On the positive side, the rising club and cafe culture is bringing together youths from indigenous and Indo-Fijian backgrounds, in the midst of a city filled with ethnic tension. On the negative side, many have difficulty finding a job and returning 'home' to a village sporting dreadlocks and skin-tight jeans isn't much easier. Youth have little room to voice their own opinions and it's not entirely surprising that many look for routes out of the country.

This is not the Fiji of postcards, of grass skirts and beachside *lovo* (Fijian feast cooked in a pit oven). However, it's well worth grabbing a cappuccino or putting on your dancing shoes to check out Fiji's rising urban youth culture. It's an unexpected eye-opener.

Suva Municipal Market MARKET
(Map p69; Usher St) The best place for fish, fruit and vegetables.

Drinking & Nightlife

Suva has a good mix of drinking and dancing dens. The place to be on Thursday, Friday and Saturday nights is at the bars around Victoria Pde and Macarthur St. Dress standards are generally relaxed. Although some of the bars may seem rough, the ones we recommend are fairly safe. If a band is playing or the hour late, expect a small cover charge (usually no more than $10). If you arrive early, entry is free and drinks are discounted between the happy hours of 6pm and 8pm.

Be cautious around other nightclubs. They tend to become dodgier as the night progresses and most locals attend them only with a group of friends – you should do the same. Watch out for pickpockets on the dance floor and always take a taxi after dark, even if you're in a group. The *Fiji Times*' entertainment section lists upcoming events.

O'Reilly's PUB
(Map p74; ☑ 331 2322; cnr Macarthur St & Victoria Pde) O'Reilly's kicks the evening off in relatively subdued fashion: relaxed punters eating, playing pool or watching sport on the numerous TVs. But it brews quite a party as the hours tick by and come 11pm-ish, the place is generally throbbing with a diverse crowd shaking their bits to anything that keeps the crowd moving.

☆ Entertainment

Fijians are fanatical about their rugby, and even if you aren't that keen on the game it's worth going to a match. The season lasts from April to September, with teams toughing it out at the **National Stadium** (Map p69; Laucala Bay Rd) east of central Suva. The atmosphere is huge.

Damodar Village Cinema CINEMA
(Map p74; www.damodarvillage.com.fj; Scott St; adult/child $6/5) Recently released Hollywood and Bollywood films battle it out at Suva's six-screen cinema complex.

Traps Bar LIVE MUSIC
(Map p74; ☑ 331 2922; Victoria Pde) Something of a subterranean saloon bar with a series of cavelike, dimly lit rooms. Take a seat in the pool room with wide-screen TV (yes, with sports) or join the happy din at the main bar. The crowd is generally young, trendy, relatively affluent and dancing by 11pm. Live music is frequent (usually on Thursdays).

Shopping

Your best chance of finding something truly unique is to skip the mass-produced stuff found in the chain tourist stores (which are carbon copies of their Nadi parents) and head straight to the markets.

Suva Curio & Handicraft Market HANDICRAFTS
(Map p74; Stinson Pde) Strap on your barter boots: this market has endless craft stalls and, if you know your stuff, can offer some fantastic deals. Just be aware that not many of the artefacts are as genuine as the vendor would like you to believe. Only pay what the object is worth to you. A 2.1m by 1.2m *ibe* (mat) goes for between $45 and $75

HINDU SYMBOLISM

Tiny Hindu temples and shrines dot the Fijian countryside, each one symbolising the body or residence of the soul. For Hindus, union with God can be achieved through prayer and by ridding the body of impurities – hence no meat in the belly or shoes on the feet when entering a temple.

Inside the temples, Hindus give symbolic offerings and blessings to their many gods. Water and flowers symbolise the Great Mother who personifies nature, while burning camphor represents the light of knowledge and understanding. Smashing a coconut denotes cracking humans' three weaknesses: egotism (the hard shell), delusion (the fibre) and material attachments (the outermost covering). The white kernel and sweet water represent the pure soul within.

Hindus believe that a body enslaved to the spirit and denied all comforts will become one with the Great Mother. Life is compared to walking on fire: a disciplined approach, like that required in the fire-walking ceremony, leads to balance, self-acceptance and the ability to see good in all.

(depending on how fine the weaving is) and a completely plain white *tapa* cloth costs around $45 for a 3.6m by 0.6m length.

Suva Flea Market   HANDICRAFTS
(Map p69; Rodwell Rd) Less touristy than the curio and handicraft market, this is another great place to buy *masi* and traditional crafts, but you might have to sort through the Hawaiian shirts to find them. There's a great secondhand bookshop out the back.

USP Book Centre   BOOKS
(University of the South Pacific; Map p69; ☑323 2500; www.uspbookcentre.com) The bookshop at the University of the South Pacific campus is probably the best bookshop in the country. It has an excellent selection of local and international novels, travel guides and books about the region.

ℹ Information

Internet access is cheap and abundant in Suva. Convenient places include **Connect Internet Café** (Map p74; Scott St; per hr $3; ⊘8am-10pm Mon-Fri, 9am-10pm Sat, 9am-8pm Sun) and **Suva City Library** (Map p74; Victoria Pde; per hr $3; ⊘9.30am-5.30pm Mon-Fri, to noon Sat).

Police (Map p74; ☑911, 331 1222; Pratt St) There is also a police post on Cumming St (Map p74; ☑911; Cumming St).

Post Fiji (Map p74; Edward St) For parcels as well as regular post.

Suva Private Hospital (Map p69; ☑330 3404; www.sph.com.fj; Amy St)

ℹ Getting There & Away

Suva is well connected to the rest of the country by air and inter-island ferries. Keep in mind that most international flights arrive at Nadi International Airport.

TO/FROM THE AIRPORT

Nausori International Airport (Map p70) is 23km northeast of central Suva. A taxi between the airport and Suva costs around $30.

BUS

Frequent local buses operate along the Queens Rd and the Kings Rd from Suva's **main bus station** (Map p69; Rodwell Rd). They all stop at resorts along the way upon request. Try to catch a faster express service instead of those that stop at every homestead between Suva and Nadi.

Sample times and fares include: Pacific Harbour ($4.40, one hour), Sigatoka ($10.25, three hours), Nadi ($17.80, four hours) and Rakiraki

($14, 4½ hours). If you're going to Lautoka, it's faster via the Queens Rd ($17.80, 4½ hours).

ℹ Getting Around

It is easy to get around central Suva on foot. Metered taxis are cheap for short trips.

Nadi

POP 42,285

Most travellers go to Nadi (nan-di) twice, whether they like it or not: its indecently warm air slaps you in the face when you first step from the plane, and kicks you up the backside as you board for home.

For some, this is twice too often and many people ensure their Nadi exposure is as brief as possible: this ramshackle town doesn't offer much, though it's a good place to stock up on supplies, plan trips and make use of facilities that may be lacking elsewhere.

Just north of downtown, between the mosque and the Nadi River, Narewa Rd leads west to Denarau island, where you'll find Nadi's top-end resorts. There's also a busy tourist shopping and eating area at Denarau Marina, where boats depart for the Mamanuca and Yasawa Groups.

◉ Sights

Sri Siva
Subramaniya Swami Temple   HINDU TEMPLE
(Map p82; admission $3.50; ⊘5.30am-7pm) This riotously bright Hindu temple is one of the few places outside India where you can see traditional Dravidian architecture; the wooden carvings of deities travelled here from India, as did the artists who dressed the temple in its colourful coat and impressive ceiling frescos. Dress modestly and remove your shoes at the entrance; photos are okay in the grounds, but not the temple. The inner sanctum is reserved for devotees bringing offerings. The on-site temple custodian can help you make sense of it all.

Garden of the Sleeping Giant   GARDENS
(Map p84; ☑672 2701; www.gsgfiji.com; Wailoko Rd; adult/child $16/8; ⊘9am-5pm Mon-Sat, to noon Sun) More than a garden, this must-see spot is an absolute botanic bonanza. A'bloom with more than 2000 varieties of orchids, plus indigenous flora and other tropical beauties, the 20-hectare plantation makes for a gorgeous getaway. Peak flowering seasons are June-July and November-December, but expect a brilliant

FIJI NADI

Nadi

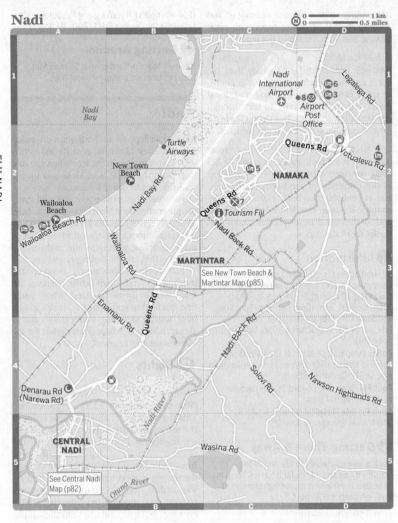

FIJI NADI

soothing massages for about \$30. A taxi here will cost around \$50 (return) from Nadi.

display year-round. Tours are included in the entrance fee, or go on a solo meander along the jungle boardwalk. A taxi here will cost around \$50 (return) from Nadi.

Sabeto Hot Springs HOT SPRINGS
(Map p84; admission \$20; ☉9am-5pm Mon-Sat) Never mind the pricey resort spas: slopping around this natural mud pit and geothermal hot pools will have you feeling like a million bucks, even if it's just from all the therapeutic giggling you'll be doing. If all the mud-glooping and pool-dipping proves too much of an exertion, local villagers offer

🏃 Activities & Tours

Nadi is a good base from which to explore the west side of Viti Levu and take day trips to the Mamanuca and Yasawa islands.

🛏 Sleeping

The black-sand New Town and Wailoaloa beaches will disappoint anyone with visions of white sands and aqua oceans, but they are quiet and peaceful and the best beaches

Nadi

Nadi has to offer. Hotels along the Queens Rd and near the airport have easy access to buses going to and from downtown. Most accommodations offer free transfers from the airport if they know to expect you.

New Town Beach

★**Bamboo** HOSTEL $
(Map p85; ☏672 2225; www.bambootravellers. com; 33 New Town Beach; dm $15-25, r with fan/AC $60-75/85-95, Bamboo Tropic r $80-120; ❄🛜⛱) Cheap and chilled, Bamboo is a wonderful old-school backpackers. A destination unto itself with a dedicated band of repeat visitors, Bamboo isn't fancy, but it is friendly and loads of fun. As well as breakfast, a variety of beach/sport/cultural activities and kava sessions come free. The more upmarket **Bamboo Tropic** – a beachfront mansion – is 100m from the hostel.

Smugglers Cove
Beach Resort & Hotel RESORT $
(Map p85; ☏672 6578; www.smugglersbeach fiji.com; Wasawasa Rd; dm $38-48, r $185-385; ❄🛜⛱) Fun, well-run and with major buzz, this is one of Nadi's most popular choices. Though it offers family rooms, it's geared towards young budget travellers looking for a social spot with facilities and activities galore: parties and programs (kava sessions, knife throwing, fire dancing) rock on through the night, while non-motorised water sports and golf gear come free for those functioning in daytime.

Aquarius on the Beach RESORT $
(Map p85; ☏672 6000; www.aquariusfiji.com; 17 Wasawasa Rd; dm $35-45, d $145-160; ❄🛜⛱) Set in a former luxury home, the Aquarius swims with warm party vibes. There's a lively **restaurant** (mains $8-28) and, for those who overdo it on the nightly cocktail specials, the refreshing pool and beach hammocks are but a stagger away. The 12-bed dorm gets cramped: cough up a bit extra for a two-, four- or six-bedder. All rooms have attached bathrooms.

Wailoaloa Beach

Oasis Palms Hotel BOUTIQUE HOTEL $$
(Map p80; ☏777 7337; www.oasispalmshotel. com; Wailoaloa Beach Rd; dm $42, bungalow $168, r $183-365; ❄🛜⛱) Spanking new and utterly sparkling, this is a welcome addition to Nadi's by-the-beach options. Dorms are airy and slick, while polished bungalows and upmarket rooms have balconies and mountain views. It's a short walk to the beach, but dragging yourself from the two pools, hot tub and superb Japanese restaurant **Mamasake** (mains $13-32) – try the ridiculously more-ish 'Mama's Balls' – takes supreme willpower.

Deals available for longer stays, or those going on to the hotel's sister resorts in the Yasawas, Octopus, Paradise Cove or Blue Lagoon.

Club Fiji Resort RESORT $$
(Map p80; ☏672 0150; www.clubfiji-resort.com; Wailoaloa Beach Rd; apt $174, bungalow $210-330; ❄🛜⛱) This smiley spot is less frenzied than some other budget beach options but has enough buzz to keep things interesting. Scattered among native gardens, the tidy *bures* all have private verandahs. There's a great selection of daily activities; it also runs tours, including game fishing and surfing. The great **restaurant** (mains $15-50) changes menus throughout the week, with Fijian, Teppanyaki, Mongolian barbecue and Mexican theme nights.

Queens Road

Dulcinea Hotel Oasis APARTMENT $
(Map p85; ☏672 2044; www.dulcineahotel oasis.com; Ragg St, Martintar; s/d/tr $85/95/110; 🅿❄🛜⛱) Formerly the Sandalwood Lodge, this is an oldie but a goodie. The complex has a retro-Fiji feel, and while the colourful apartments aren't for those after a 'resort' experience, they're wonderful for families and self-caterers: kids love the rambling grounds and cute pool. Kitchenettes are well-equipped; stock up at the huge supermarket a five-minute walk away.

Central Nadi

0 — 100 m
0 — 0.05 miles

Central Nadi

Nadi Bay Resort Hotel RESORT $

(Map p85; ☎672 3599; www.fijinadibayhotel.
com; Wailoaloa Rd, Martintar; dm $39-44, s/d with-
out bathroom from $80/95, s/d with bathroom &
air-con $130/180, apt from $220; ❋@☀) One
of Nadi's best-equipped budget resorts, this
sociable spot serves up a jovial mixed bag
of package-tour guests and backpackers.
The two **restaurants** (mains $8-35) and bars
are outstanding, the rooms are comfortable and clean, and there's even a free mini
movie theatre, games room and library. The
day spa offers traditional Fijian treatments
starting at $35.

Rabosea Bed & Breakfast B&B $

(Map p85; ☎946 7857; www.raboseafiji.com;
2 Jalil's Drive, Martintar; shared bathroom/private
bathroom $80/140; P❋☎) This splendid,
central B&B is a fantastic budget alternative
to Nadi's hostels. With only three bedrooms,
a communal kitchen and a comfy lounge,
a stop here feels like a homestay, thanks
in large part to the amiable Fijian/German
owners, who can whip your trip plans into
shape, rent you a bicycle, or take you for a
visit to their nearby 300-acre farm.

Nadi Downtown Hotel HOTEL $

(Map p82; ☎670 0600; www.fijidowntownhotel.
com; Main St, Nadi Town; dm/r $15/$105-135;
P❋☎) The name doesn't lie: this place is
as downtown as it gets in Nadi, with bars,
eateries, the handicraft market and the
Hindu temple all within skipping distance.
Though recently renovated, it's not flash, but
for cheap and central, it can't be beaten. Free
breakfast and airport transfers.

🛏 Near the Airport

Tanoa Skylodge LODGE $

(Map p80; ☎672 2200; www.tanoaskylodge.
com; Queens Rd, Namaka; dm $35, r $85-140;
❋☎☀) Nestled amid four acres of gardens
with loads of facilities, this is a fine choice
for families, budget travellers and business-
folk. For the little ones, there's an indoor soccer and basketball court, games room, kids'
pool and on-site hair braider; grown-ups
can recover at the CU cocktail bar. Rooms
are spotless and sunny; family rooms have
extra space and well-equipped kitchenettes.

Tokatoka Resort Hotel RESORT $$

(Map p80; ☎672 0222; www.warwickhotels.
com/tokatoka-resort; Queens Rd, Namaka; r $120-
300; P❋@☎☀) This sprawling, low-rise
resort is a 'village' of villas in varying sizes.

The designer pool and waterslide are loads of fun (though safety-conscious parents will give the rickety playground a wide berth). It's a popular stop for families flying in or out of Nadi, as it's right across from the airport (free transfers). Other facilities include a good **restaurant** (mains $18-55) and wheelchair-accessible rooms.

Raffles Gateway Hotel RESORT **$$**
(Map p80; ☑672 2444; www.rafflesgateway. com; Queens Rd, Namaka; r/ste $105-165/$320; P🅿❄🛜🏊) Directly opposite the airport, Raffles is a sound choice behind its ostentatious entrance. A Nadi favourite since 1969 and recently refurbished, the cheaper rooms are small but serviceable; superior rooms offer more space, facilities and private patios. Kids love Raffles for their two pools, a waterslide and a tennis court; those under 16 stay free. There's a pool bar and two restaurants; one casual (mains $10-35) and one more upmarket (mains $15-50).

Tanoa International RESORT **$$**
(Map p80; ☑672 0277; www.tanoainterna tional.com; Votualevu Rd, Namaka; r/ste from $165/280; ❄🛜🏊) Loaded with facilities and distractions (including five restaurants, tennis courts, a spa, gym and a pool), this place oozes Fijian tropicana with its lush gardens and bright rooms. Kids under 12 stay free.

🛏 Nadi Outskirts

⭐**Stoney Creek Resort** RESORT **$**
(Map p84; ☑746 669; www.stoneycreekfiji. net; Sabeto Rd; dm $55, s/d with shared bathroom $65/80, d $135, bungalow from $150; @🏊) Minutes from the airport but tucked away in a verdant valley, Stoney Creek is less 'resort' than retreat, with brilliant hosts Michelle and Gary on-hand to make your escape as easygoing or energetic as you like: loungers will love the pool, comfy chair-scattered common area and *bure* Jacuzzis, while active types can take advantage of mountain bike hire and organised treks to nearby attractions.

🍴 Eating

Most Nadi eateries serve a mixture of traditional Fijian, Indian, Chinese and Western dishes, and there are lots of cheap lunchtime places downtown. The restaurants at most resorts welcome nonguests.

Nadi has a large **produce market** (Map p82; Hospital Rd), selling fresh fruit and vegetables, as well as several bakeries and large supermarkets on Main St.

⭐**Tata's** INDIAN **$**
(Map p82; Nadi Back Rd; mains $5-10; ⏰8am-8pm Mon-Sat) This rough-looking joint just down from the temple dishes up some of the most authentic and flavoursome curries on Viti Levu: just ask the droves of locals crowding the open-air deck. There's a menu, but for the best experience, let the friendly staff pick for you (though the 'Uncivilised Chicken' curry is worth seeking out).

⭐**Taste Fiji** FUSION **$$**
(Map p85; ☑672 5034; www.tastefiji.com; Lot 1 Cawa Road, Martintar; mains $15-25, breakfast $12-22; ⏰6.30am-6pm Mon-Thu, to 10pm Fri, to 5pm Sat, 7am-2pm Sun; ❄🛜) Stylish, professionally-run and with a cosmopolitan menu featuring stand-out dishes created from local produce, this fabulous restaurant is not just 'good for Nadi': it's GOOD. Egg-centric breakfasts are hearty and delicious, and the mains – including the utterly divine caramelised Vuda pork belly – are simple yet sophisticated. The strong coffees and sweets are dangerously addictive. Gluten-free options galore.

Tu's Place FUSION **$$**
(Map p85; ☑672 2110; www.tusplace.webs.com; 37 Queens Rd, Martintar; mains $14-28; ⏰7am-10.30pm) Come hungry: the chefs at this popular spot aren't shy when it comes to portion control. Though they do Western-style breakfasts and some tasty Thai meals, the focus here is on Fijian cuisine, especially seafood: this is a great place to try *kokoda* (raw fish marinated in lemon juice and served in coconut milk). Try to squeeze in some *vakalavalava* (baked cassava pudding) for dessert.

Bounty Bar & Restaurant INTERNATIONAL **$$**
(Map p85; ☑672 0840; www.bountyfiji.com; 79 Queens Rd, Martintar; mains $18-45; ⏰9am-11pm; ❄) This convivial spot is named in honour of the local rum, and has an aptly nautical theme. Surf-and-turf-style meals are the go, but it also does decent curries. Its speciality – creamy chicken in a pineapple boat – is tropicana at its tasty best. There's a fun bar attached, with a large TV screening sports, and live music on weekends.

Nadi & the West

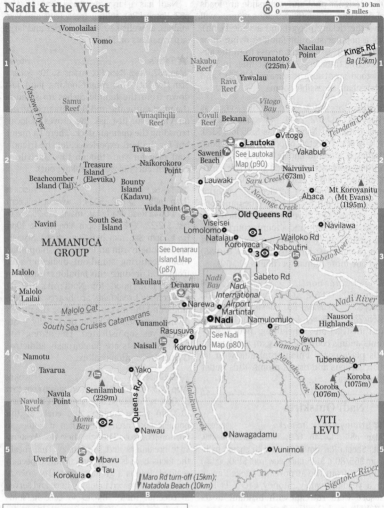

0 — 10 km
0 — 5 miles

FIJI NADI

Nadi & the West

⊙ Sights
1 Garden of the Sleeping Giant C3
2 Momi Guns..B5
3 Sabeto Hot Springs C3

🛏 Sleeping
4 Anchorage Beach Resort....................B3
5 DoubleTree Resort Resort..................B4
6 First Landing Resort...........................B3
7 Rendezvous Beach Resort A4
8 Seashell@Momi A5
9 Stoney Creek Resort D3

ⓘ Transport
Vuda Point Marina ....(see 6)

Bulaccino and Hemisphere Wine Bar

CAFE $$

(Map p80; ☎672 8638; www.bulaccino.com; Queens Rd, Namaka; mains $8-30; ⊙7am-8pm Tue-Sun, to 3pm Mon; 🅿🅰) Rightfully famous for its coffee, this Western-style hangout is also gaining renown for its gigantic sandwiches, tasty mains and scrummy cakes: its Lazy Gourmet selection of heat-at-home meals is a superb option for self-caterers. The open-air bar out the back is cool, leafy and has a decent wine and tapas menu.

Mama's Pizza PIZZA **$$**

(Map p82; ☑ 670 0221; Main St; pizzas $10-28; ☺ lunch & dinner; ✸) In Fiji, the word 'pizza' often seems open for interpretation. Not so at Mama's: these prodigious pies could hold their own anywhere in the world. Absolutely loaded with toppings ranging from the traditional to the gourmet, these whoppers are good to the last chomp, with a thick, crunchy American-style crust. There's an equally awesome branch at Port Denarau.

Drinking & Nightlife

Most of Nadi's beach hostels have sociable watering holes, and are open to nonguests.

Ed's Bar PUB

(Map p85; ☑ 672 4650; Lot 51, Queens Rd, Martintar; ☺ 5pm-late) It doesn't look like much, but this is one of Nadi's best drinking spots. Cheap beer, friendly crew, pool tables and the occasional live band draw locals and visiting social animals. Tables outside fill by early evening.

New Nadi Farmer's Club BAR

(Map p82; www.nadifarmersclub.com; Ashram Rd; ☺ 10am-late Mon-Sat) The cool, inviting beer garden at this riverside bar/restaurant is a top spot for a relaxing ale (or a decent feed). The staff are incredibly attentive, and the atmosphere is such that any ideas of 'just the one' go immediately out the window. And why leave? Fire dancing kicks off at 7pm (Thur-Sat), followed by live local bands (Wed-Sat).

Shopping

Nadi's Main St is a tribute to souvenir and duty-free shops, and their mass-produced products are aimed unashamedly at mass tourism.

Handicraft market MARKET

(Map p82; Cnr Main St & Koroivolu Ave; ☺ daily) Nadi's handicraft market is a far better bet than the souvenir shops along the main drag: goods are more authentic, there's less hassle, and stallholders make interesting chat.

❶ Information

You won't have any trouble finding banks and ATMs; there's also an ANZ bank (with ATM) at the airport, open for all international flights. Internet access and wi-fi is thick on the ground in Nadi.

New Town Beach & Martintar

⌂ Sleeping

1 Aquarius on the Beach........................A1
  Bamboo..(see 1)
2 Dulcinea Hotel Oasis B3
3 Nadi Bay Resort Hotel.........................A3
4 Rabosea Bed & Breakfast....................A3
  Smugglers Cove Beach
    Resort & Hotel.............................(see 1)

✖ Eating

5 Bounty Bar & Restaurant B3
6 Taste Fiji...B2
7 Tu's Place..B3

◉ Drinking & Nightlife

8 Ed's Bar...B2

DSM Centre (Map p82; ☑ 670 0240; www.dsmcentrefiji.com; 2 Lodhia St; ☺ 8.30am-4.30pm Mon-Fri, to 1pm Sat) Specialises in travel medicine; also has radiology and gynaecology departments.

Police (☑ 917, 670 0222; Koroivolu Ave)

Post Office There are post offices in Nadi's downtown (Map p82; www.postfiji.com.fj; Sahu Khan Rd), at the airport (Map p82; www.postfiji.com.fj; Nadi International Airport) and at Port Denarau (www.postfiji.com.fj; Port Denerau).

Tourism Fiji (Map p80; ☑ 672 2433; www. fiji.travel; Suite 107, Colonial Plaza, Namaka; ⊙ 8am-4.30pm Mon-Thu, to 4pm Fri) Crazily, there's no official visitor centre in Nadi (though most hotels have a tours and information desk). Tourism Fiji is more geared towards online info and marketing, but drop in if you're desperate.

TRAVEL AGENCIES

Arrivals at Nadi Airport will find scores of operators located on the ground floor upon arrival. Some well-regarded agencies:

Rosie Holidays (Map p80; ☑ 672 2755; www.rosiefiji.com; Nadi airport concourse) The largest and best-resourced agency in Fiji. Rosie Holidays manages the tour desks at many resorts and organises trips, treks and transport. It's the agent for Thrifty Car Rental.

Tourist Transport Fiji (Map p80; ☑ 672 2268; www.touristtransportfiji.com; Nadi airport concourse) This company operates the twice-daily **Coral Sun Express** Nadi–Suva bus services, and the **Feejee Experience** hop-on-hop-off transfers and package tours. It also runs the Great Sights Fiji (☑ 672 3311; www.touristtransportfiji.com/great-sights-fiji; Nadi airport concourse) small-group tours to Viti Levu's interior.

ℹ️ Getting Around

BUS

Nadi International Airport is 9km north of downtown Nadi; there are frequent local buses just outside the airport that travel along the Queens Rd to town ($0.90). Buses travel regularly between New Town Beach and downtown Nadi ($0.70, 15 minutes, Monday to Saturday).

TAXI

Taxis are plentiful in Nadi: insist your driver turns on the meter. It's about $15 between downtown and the airport.

Around Nadi

Denarau Island

Like a cruise ship docked at a port, Denarau Island (2.55 sq km) is an artificial enclave of top-end resorts, manicured gardens, heavenly pools and professionally run tourist facilities. Although it bears little resemblance to the rest of Fiji, it's a popular place to indulge in some pampering at one of the international resorts. Be warned – what the brochures and websites don't advertise is that Denarau is built on reclaimed mangrove mudflats, and the beach has dark-grey sand and murky water unsuitable for snorkelling.

🏃 Activities

Big Bula Inflatable Waterpark   WATER PARK
(Map p87; ☑ 776 5049; www.bigbulawaterpark.com.fj; Denarau Island; adults/kids/family of four $65/55/220; ⊙ 10am-5pm) This year-round waterpark is tons of fun for the kids (or the slightly-built adult: weight limit 85kg), with bright, cartoonish inflatable waterslides, jumping castles and obstacle courses. There's also a less full-on gated play area for the very young, and a small cafe for grown-ups needing to match the kids' energy via caffeine. Get there and back on the Bula Bus.

Adrenalin Fiji   WATER SPORTS
(Map p87; ☑ 675 0061; www.adrenalinfiji.com; Port Denarau Marina; ⊙ 8am-8pm) Adrenalin runs the watersports shops at all Denarau resorts and Port Denarau Retail Centre. It specialises in jet-ski safaris ($538/575 solo/tandem) to select Mamanuca islands and Cloud 9, plus parasailing, gamefishing, waterskiing and more. It can also tailor kids' activities based on age (from 2 years).

Denarau Golf & Racquet Club   GOLF, TENNIS
(Map p87; ☑ 675 9710; sg_gl2@tappoo.com.fj; Denarau Island; ⊙ 7am-sunset) This club has an immaculate 18-hole golf course with bunkers shaped like sea creatures. Green fees are $130/85 for 18/nine holes (club hire 18/nine holes $65/45) and the tennis court is $20 per hour. The breezy bar and cafe overlooks the course.

🛏️ Sleeping & Eating

The rates at Denarau's resorts vary drastically with season and occupancy. They're *very* popular with families during the Australian and New Zealand school holidays. Rooms are of a high standard, all pools are magnificent, and each resort has loads of dining options. If you want to stay in Denarau but a full-blown resort doesn't appeal, try the Terraces Apartments (Map p87; ☑ 675 0557; www.theterraces.com.fj; 1/2/3 bedroom apt $495/655/790; P ❄ 🛜 🏊).

The Denarau Marina is lined with restaurants and cafes.

Radisson Blu Resort Fiji   RESORT $$$
(Map p87; ☑ 675 6677; www.radissonblu.com/resort-fiji; r from $540; P ❄ 🛜 🏊) The Radisson gets top marks from little travellers for its sandy-edged lagoon pools, whitewater tunnel slide and squeal-inducing activities including fish feeding and the nightly torch-lighting run; grown-ups dig the hot

Denarau Island

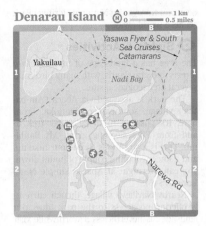

Denarau Island
N 0 ———— 1 km
  0 ———— 0.5 miles

Yasawa Flyer & South Sea Cruises Catamarans

Yakuilau

Nadi Bay

Narewa Rd

tub, day spa, adults-only pool and swim-up bar. And who doesn't love free kayaks, windsurfers and catamarans? There are four good restaurants; the new **Chantra Thai** (mains $32-42) gets rave reviews.

Sheraton Fiji Resort   RESORT $$$
(Map p87; ☑ 675 0777; www.sheratonfiji.com; r from $600; ⊕✴@🛜) While this sprawling resort is lovely on its own, the fact that guests can make use of all facilities at sister property **Sheraton Denarau Villas** (www.sheratondenarauvillas.com, from $865) and the Westin gives it a definite edge: choose from six pools – including its own 1200 sq m lagoon – and 14 restaurants. The kids club (ages four-12) is free, and children eat for $5.

**Westin Denarau Island
Resort & Spa**   RESORT $$$
(Map p87; ☑ 675 0000; www.westindenarauisland.com; r from $540; P⊕✴🛜🏊) This is a longtime family fave, though an adults-only lap pool and good gym and their posh Heavenly Spa attract couples by the drove. Free extras like farm tours and local rum and chocolate tastings are fun. Guests have use of the facilities at the Sheraton and Sheraton Denarau Villas, though unlike the Sheraton, there's a one-off $25 fee to join the kids club.

**★Nadina Authentic
Fijian Restaurant**   FIJIAN $$$
(Map p87; ☑ 672 7313; Denarau Marina; mains $30-55; ⊙10am-11pm) This fantastic restaurant specialises in local cuisine, using homegrown and foraged ingredients; it's a great

place to try *kokoda,* or opt for the divine fresh prawns with *ota* (a local bush fern) and chef-squeezed coconut cream.

ℹ Getting There & Away

West Bus Transport runs frequently (less so on Sunday) between Nadi bus station and Denarau ($1). A taxi from the airport/downtown costs $25/14. Be wary of the taxis going *from* Denarau: they often charge up to three times the actual fare. Call ☑ 6000 or ☑ 2000 and order a Nadi cab instead.

The inter-resort, thatched-roof Bula Bus ($8 per person, unlimited daily travel) trundles between resorts (and the port) on a continuous circuit.

Sonaisali Island

There's plenty of white sand at Sonaisali's **DoubleTree Resort** (Map p84; ☑ 670 6011; www.sonaisali.com; r incl breakfast $500-700; ⊕✴@🏊) but unfortunately none of it is on the beach. Like Denarau, Sonaisali is on the edge of mangroves, and the dark sand disappoints some. To compensate there is a large pool with a swim-up bar and an endless array of activities including a kids club, and it remains a popular destination for antipodean package tourists. The resort has had a recent makeover, and in 2016 is due to come under the Hilton hotel brand.

Sonaisali is a 25-minute drive south from Nadi airport. A taxi from the airport costs $30.

Uciwai Landing

Uciwai Landing, used by surfers to access the Mamanuca breaks and island resorts on Namotu and Tavarua, is 25km southwest of Nadi, the last 7km of which is on a slow and pot-holed road. Surfing is really the only reason to head here, and the only place to stay is **Rendezvous Beach Resort** (Map p84; ☑ 628 1216; www.surfdivefiji.com; dm $28, r with fan/air-con $52/74-98; ❄@❄). It's fairly basic and the staff are as languid as the seasoned surfers who visit, but they will organise trips to Mamanuca surfbreaks. Resort transfers from Nadi/airport are $40/60, or local buses to Uciwai from Nadi bus station ($2.50) depart a couple of times a day from Monday to Saturday.

Viseisei & Vuda Point

About 12km north of Nadi is Viseisei village, which, according to local lore, is the oldest settlement in Fiji. The story goes that *mataqali* (kinship groups) here are descendants of the first ocean-going Melanesians who landed 1km north of here circa 1500.

The quaint **Vuda Point Marina** (Map p84; ☑ 666 8214; www.vudamarina.com.fj; Vuda Point) is a well-organised boaties' lure. Facilities include a great cafe and restaurant-bar, free showers, a laundry, a general store, yacht-repair specialists, a chandlery and the largest travel hoist in Fiji.

If you're staying here, choose between two decent resorts – **First Landing Resort** (Map p84; ☑ 666 6171; www.firstlandingresort. com; Vuda Point; bungalow from $300, apts from $680; P❄❄❄) and **Anchorage Beach Resort** (Map p84; ☑ 666 2099; www.anchor agefiji.com; Vuda Point; mountain/ocean room from $198/275, villas from $390; P❄❄❄) – or try a Visesei homestay: local lady **Finau Bavadra** (☑ 925 5370; dawfinfijitravel@yahoo. com; Viseisei village) can organise this for you.

Koroyanitu National Heritage Park

Just an hour's drive from Nadi or Lautoka, and deep within Viti Levu's interior, the beautiful Koroyanitu National Heritage Park seems a world away.

◉ Sights & Activities

The area has a landscape of native *dakua* forests and grasslands, with many birds and several archaeological sites.

The park is accessed via Abaca ('Am-batha') village, southeast of Lautoka. From here, it's possible to make a day trek to and from Fiji's sleeping giant, Mt Batilamu. This is a strenuous three-hour hike up, and a knee-wobbling couple of hours down. You can overnight at Abaca's simple **Nase Lodge** ($45).

Nearby Navilawa village, though currently offering no access to the park (due to a landslide), is nevertheless a worthwhile visit for those seeking an authentic village atmosphere. The village is set in an old volcanic crater surrounded by forest and mountains. There's a short rainforest hike to a cave beside a clear-flowing creek. Visitors should take a *sevusevu* (gift for the chief) and make themselves known on arrival for a low-key and very authentic kava welcoming ceremony

Contact **Kalo Baravilala** (☑ 8077 147, 6253 792; www.exoticholidaysfiji.net) for information on transport, hikes and accommodation in the region.

❶ Getting There & Away

There is no local transport to Navilawa or Abaca, and getting to both villages requires 4WD; drivers would be wise to check directions with anyone on the road, as there are many small turnings.

To Navilawa from Nadi, take the Sabeto Rd and turn off left, 3.9km beyond Stoney Creek Resort; it's a further 9.3km to Navilawa. To Abaca from Lautoka, take Tavakubu Rd and turn off right, 4.7km from the main road. It's a further 10km of gravel road to Abaca.

Nausori Highlands & Navala

The grassy slopes of the Nausori Highlands snake their way into the mountainous interior, leaving the coastline and panoramic views in their wake. This region is one of the best places to experience traditional Fijian culture and hospitality, and although the region shares the same name as the airport town of Nausori near Suva, its small villages and scattered settlements are quite different.

On the banks of the Ba River, tiny Navala is by far Fiji's most picturesque village. The houses here are all traditional *bures,* built with local materials using time-honoured techniques. Navala is a photographer's delight, but you need to get permission and pay the $15 entrance fee before wandering around. If arriving independently, ask the first person you meet to take you to the *turaga-ni-koro* (the chief-appointed headman who collects the entrance fee). A traditional *sevusevu* is not required, although all other village etiquette applies.

🛏 Sleeping & Eating

Bulou's Eco Lodge   LODGE $
(Map p70; ☑ 628 1224; sipirianotui@gmail.com; dm/bungalow per person incl meals $75/180) To experience Fijian hospitality at its finest, a night (or two) spent with Bulou and her son (and hereditary chief) Tui is highly recommended. Their home and ecolodge is 1km past Navala village; phone ahead and they'll meet you at the bus stop. Tui is an excellent guide and accompanies all guests around the village introducing them to his relatives and friends (tours for nonguests $20 per group of four).

Tui can also arrange horse riding ($25) and trekking ($20) in the surrounding hills.

Guests can choose between two simple traditional *bures* in the garden and a 10-bed dorm attached to the house. There are cold-water showers, flush toilets and a limited electricity supply.

It is polite to bring a small *sevusevu* (a $5 pack of ground kava is enough) to present to the hosts during the welcoming ceremony (though they will neither ask for nor expect it).

❶ Getting There & Away

BUS
The local buses from Ba to Navala ($3, 90 minutes) leave Ba bus station at 12.30pm, 4.30pm and 5.15pm Monday to Saturday. Buses return to Ba at 6am, 7.30am and 1.45pm Monday to Friday. Ring Bulou's Eco Lodge in advance and they will pick you up from Navala.

CAR & 4WD
If driving from Ba, there are a couple of turns to watch out for: at the police post turn left, passing a shop on your right, and at the next fork in the road keep left. The road is rough and rocky, but usually passable.

TOURS
Several tour companies run day tours from Nadi to Navala.

Lautoka
POP 52,900

According to legend, Fiji's second-largest city derives its name from a battle cry that means 'spear-hit'. The story goes that when an argument erupted between two local chiefs, one cried out the words '*Lau toka!*' as he killed the other by spearing him through the chest, simultaneously stating the obvious and naming the location.

Lautoka's recent history is entwined with the fortunes of sugar: the mill here has been operating since 1903. During the cutting season, sugar trains putt along the main street; in September, the city crowns a Sugar Queen at the annual Sugar Festival.

From a traveller's perspective, there's not much to do. If you wander the wide streets amid swaying saris and aromatic curry houses, stroll along the picturesque esplanade towards the mill, or take a peek at the small botanical gardens and the Hare Krishna **Sri Krishna Kaliya Temple** (Map p90; ☑ 666 4112; 5 Tavewa Ave; ⊙ 8am-6pm), you have pretty much seen the best of the city.

🛏 Sleeping

Sea Breeze Hotel   HOTEL $
(Map p90; ☑ 666 0717; seabreezefiji@connect.com.fj; Bekana Lane; s $54-70, d $60-76; ☀ ❋ ⚜) From the outside, the Sea Breeze resembles a jaunty blue-and-white apartment building. Inside, the austere rooms are a clean and tranquil sanctuary for noise-weary travellers. The fan-cooled digs are the cheapest, but the sea-view rooms with air-con are the nicest. The well-maintained pool looks over the water, as does the TV lounge which serves breakfast ($10).

Cathay Hotel   HOTEL $
(Map p90; ☑ 666 0205; www.fiji4less.com; Tavewa Ave; dm $24-26, r $66-88; ❋ ⚜) This low-key, budget hotel is the choice of travelling government and NGO workers. Dorms here are good value: they have a maximum of four people to a room and each has its own bathroom. Otherwise, choose between spacious rooms with air-con and simpler, but still roomy, fan-cooled rooms with shared bathrooms.

Tanoa Waterfront Hotel   HOTEL $$
(Map p90; ☑ 666 4777; www.tanoawaterfront.com; Marine Dr; r $250; ☀ ❋ @ ⚜) Lautoka's top-end hotel has a great waterfront location. The cheapest rooms are spotless and have the

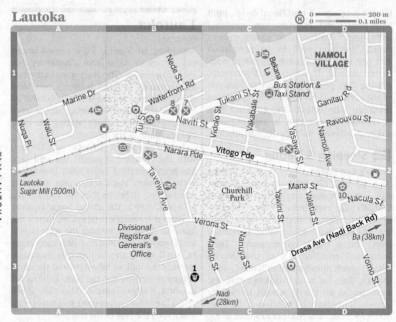

Lautoka

Lautoka

◎ Sights
1 Sri Krishna Kaliya Temple B3

🛏 Sleeping
2 Cathay Hotel...B2
3 Sea Breeze Hotel C1
4 Tanoa Waterfront Hotel.........................A1

✖ Eating
5 Blue Ginger Café & Deli B2
6 Chilli Bites...C2
7 Chilli Tree Café.. B1
8 Nang Ying B1

✪ Entertainment
9 Ashiqi Nightclub B1
10 Damodar Village Cinema.......................D2

ambience and trimmings of a midrange US hotel chain. The more expensive rooms have contemporary interiors, flat-screen TVs and small balconies overlooking two pools. There is a gym, a small children's playground, a bar and restaurant on site. Prices tumble if you book online.

✖ Eating

Lautoka has fewer restaurants than Nadi or Suva but lots of inexpensive lunchtime eateries.

★ **Blue Ginger Café & Deli**   CAFE $
(Map p90; Post Office Roundabout; meals from $6; ☺ 7.30am-5pm Mon-Sat; ▣) Delicious breakfasts (the menu includes homemade yoghurt, fruit and poached eggs) and lunches of wholemeal sandwiches, interesting wraps, fresh salads and lovely cakes and biscuits. Blue Ginger is run by a Swiss–Filipina couple and also serves truly good coffee (and/or a decent glass of wine) to go with the food.

Chilli Bites   INDIAN $
(Map p90; Yasawa St; meals from $10-15; ☺ breakfast, lunch & dinner Mon-Sat, lunch & dinner Sun; ▣) Ignore the scratched formica tables and enjoy the authentic north Indian food made by authentic north Indian Indians. The tandoor breads, rich and flavoursome curries, and sweet or salt yoghurt lassis are cheap and delicious.

Chilli Tree Café CAFE $

(Map p90; ☑665 1824; 3 Tukani St; meals $8-15; ☺7.30am-5pm Mon-Sat; ❉) This corner cafe is a good place to grab a paper and coffee, build a sandwich, wrap or slice of cake and settle into a chair for some serious people watching behind the plate-glass windows.

Nang Ying CHINESE $$

(Map p90; ☑665 2668; Nede St; mains $15-35; ☺lunch & dinner Mon-Sat, dinner Sun) Twinkly lights, backlit pictures and fake flowers give this place an air of Chinatown authenticity that would do San Francisco proud. Fragrant poultry and noodle dishes, sizzling seafood hotplates and fried-rice specials demonstrate that these cooks know their way around their chopsticks.

🍷 Drinking & Entertainment

Lautoka has a limited number of pubs and clubs, which generally veer towards the seedier side. The best place for a relaxing drink is the bar at Tanoa Waterfront hotel; for a loud Friday or Saturday night out, head to Ashiqi Nightclub (Map p90; Lautoka Hotel, Tui St; ☺8pm-1am Fri & Sat) in the Lautoka Hotel.

Hollywood and Bollywood are screened in harmony at Damodar Village Cinema (Map p90; Namoli Ave).

ⓘ Getting There & Around

BUS

Local buses depart for Nadi ($2.50, one hour, 33km) via the airport every 15 minutes. Sunbeam Transport and Pacific Transport also have frequent services to and from Suva ($17.80, five hours) via the Queens Rd. Sunbeam has seven daily departures to Suva via the Kings Rd ($18, six hours). Both companies have offices in Yasawa St, opposite the market.

TAXI

Taxis are plentiful: make sure drivers turn on their meters.

Southern Viti Levu & the Coral Coast

Skirting the southern half of the mainland, the Queens Rd winds through cane fields and snakes over dry hills along the stretch of shore known as the Coral Coast. This region is peppered with small towns, all manner of accommodation options, and some interesting local attractions. Despite the name, the Coral Coast doesn't offer particularly good snorkelling and the coral shelf is often exposed at low tide. Further east the weather turns more inclement, and the road near Pacific Harbour is flanked by waves of green hills on one side and a fringing reef that drops off dramatically into the deep blue of the ocean on the other.

Momi Bay

Coming from Nadi, the first of the Coral Coast attractions you'll pass are the Momi Guns (Map p84; $5; ☺9am-5pm), an evocative WWII battery built to defend Fiji against the Japanese Imperial Army; an army that had already swept through Papua New Guinea, the Solomon Islands and parts of what is now Vanuatu. A quick scan of the horizon will reveal why this spot was chosen for the installation. The guns (and now tourists) have unobstructed views to Malolo Barrier Reef, the Mamanuca islands and Navula Passage.

🛏 Sleeping & Eating

Seashell@Momi RESORT $

(Map p84; ☑670 6100; www.seashellresortfiji.com; dm/4 $32/96, bungalow $160-248, apt $240; ☺❉@☎) The Seashell is 13km from the main road and has an undiscovered air about it. It offers great value if you don't mind the dated decor. Accommodation comes in all shapes and configurations, from self-contained *bures* and apartments to roomy dorms. On-site facilities include a tennis court, a children's playground, two pools, a restaurant (mains $15-30) and enough palm trees for a whole island.

ⓘ Getting There & Away

The turn-off to Momi is about 20km from Nadi. Dominion Transport buses leave Nadi Bus Station for Momi Bay at 8am, 12.30pm, 2.30pm and 4pm and cost $3.50. Buses drop off at the door, but do not operate on Sundays.

Robinson Crusoe Island

Robinson Crusoe Island Resort (Map p70; ☑628 1999; www.robinsoncrusoeislandfiji.com; dm $49, bungalow $79-160, lodge $199-249; ☎) covers all of the tiny coral island of Likuri. Once a determined backpacker resort, it's spruced itself in recent years and offers good-quality accommodation, ranging from tidy dorms to some charming thatched, airy *bures* tucked away in the greenery. For all this, there's a heavy focus on group activities.

Central to the action is the **Pacific Island Dance Show** (Monday, Wednesday and Saturday, adult/child $199/99) (including fire-walking), part of a whole-day tour that involves snorkelling and a bush walk. Guests will also enjoy free activities from crab-racing and jewellery-making – though parents may end up biting their nails to the quick when the little ones beg to learn how to climb to the top of the coconut palms. There's snorkelling too, although it's poor compared to further along the coast. Transfers from Nadi cost $100.

Natadola Beach

Gorgeous Natadola Beach is one of Viti Levu's best. Its vast bank of white sand slides into a cobalt sea, which provides good swimming regardless of the tide; the absence of coral allows for enough surf to satisfy beginners and bodysurfers. Rather persistent locals offer **horse riding** ($30) along the beach to some nearby caves. It's a picturesque ride but be prepared to bargain hard.

🛏 Sleeping & Eating

Yatule Beach Resort APARTMENT **$$**
(Map p70; 🖉 672 8004; reservation@yatulere sort.com.fj; villas $420-675; P✿❄🛜🏊) The thatched roofs of the self-contained *bure* make this small resort look like a Fijian village. Originally built to house the big-wigs involved in the building of the Inter-Continental, it now offers some excellent chic beachside accommodation. All the villas have mini-kitchens, bedrooms and separate lounges. The family villa has four separate bedrooms and is ideal for teenage kids who need privacy.

Eat in the upscale Na Ua Restaurant, or during the day at the Pool Bar.

Natadola Beach Resort RESORT **$$**
(Map p70; 🖉 672 1001; www.natadola.com; ste $250; 🏊) This intimate adult-only resort has only 11 suites in two blocks. The resort was built in the faux-Spanish colonial style popular a few years back and has a certain *casa del Fiji* charm about it. Each suite has a spacious bathroom and private courtyard. The pool meanders through tropical gardens, with plenty of poolside shade for those wishing to snooze.

The restaurant-bar offers tasty food with small, no-frills servings, is open to nonguests and is a popular stop for day trippers.

Fiji Golf Resort & Spa RESORT **$$$**
(Map p70; www.intercontinental.com; r from $684, ste from $1150; ❄✿❄🛜🏊) This mammoth Intercontinental-run resort, is a conglomeration of slate-grey buildings somewhat at odds with the tropical land- and seascape, occupying a prime piece of real estate on the beach. The 266 rooms and 91 suites are beautifully appointed and equipped, with spa baths on each balcony. The three indoor/outdoor restaurants all offer sunset views along with an occasional howling trade wind.

ⓘ Getting There & Away

Paradise Transport buses head to and from Sigatoka ($3, one hour, four daily Monday to Friday), although most travellers arrive on organised day trips from Nadi or on the Coral Coast Scenic Railway. Keen walkers could follow this track from Yanuca (about 3½ hours) and catch the train or bus back.

Those with a rental car should turn off the Queens Rd onto Maro Rd, 36km from Nadi.

Yanuca & Around

Past the turn-off to Natadola, the Queens Rd continues southeast, winding through hills and down to the coast at Cuvu Bay and blink-and-you'll-miss-it Yanuca, about 50km from Nadi.

🏃 Activities

Coral Coast Scenic Railway SCENIC RAILWAY
(Map p70; 🖉 652 0434; Queens Rd; adult/child $69/35) The station for the railway is at the causeway entrance to Shangri-La's Fijian Resort. It offers scenic rides along the coast in an old diesel sugar train, past villages, forests and sugar plantations, to beautiful Natadola Beach. The railway was once used for transporting cane and passengers to the Lautoka Mill. The 14km trip takes about 1¼ hours, leaving at 10am on Monday, Wednesday and Friday and returning at 4pm (adult/child $92/46 including barbecue lunch). On Tuesday, Thursday and Saturday, a Sigatoka shopping trip runs east and costs $46/23.

🛏 Sleeping & Eating

Namuka Bay Resort RESORT **$$**
(Map p70; 🖉 670 0243; www.namukabaylagoon resort.com; dm incl meals $95, villa $200) These eight, roomy beachfront villas, each comprising two guest rooms with a shared verandah, are tucked 6km down a side road. It's *very* bumpy, but OK for all vehicles in

good weather. The resort fronts a lagoon and 2km of beach, with a historic (deserted) village site on the hill behind and a cave walk just along the coast.

It's very secluded and you'd want good weather – or a good supply of books – to fully enjoy it. There's power for a few hours each evening, though there are plans to bring mains electricity the extra mile required. The turn-off is about 5km from the Fijian on the Nadi side.

Gecko's Resort &
Kalevu Cultural Centre   RESORT $$
(Map p70; ☑ 652 0200; www.fijiculturalcentre. com; r/f $130/250; ☻ ✴ @ ☎) Directly opposite the scenic railway station, this resort has 35 new, simple-but-nice-and-roomy hotel rooms. Several have interconnecting doors and convert to family rooms. The restaurant (mains $25 to $50) is recommended and is often busy with dining escapees from the Shangri-La.

The complimentary South Pacific dance show on Friday and Sunday evenings is popular. In the landscaped grounds is a purpose-built cultural centre showcasing a collection of traditionally built huts and *bure*, pottery, *masi* and carvings (one-hour guided tour $20 per person between 9.30am and 4pm).

Shangri-La's Fijian Resort   RESORT $$$
(The Fijian; Map p70; ☑ 652 0155; www. shangri-la.com; r incl breakfast from $490; ☻ ✴ @ ☎) Anchored offshore on its own private island, this resort is one of the Coral Coast's premier (and biggest) hotels. Linked to the mainland by a causeway, the 442 rooms come in a variety of configurations and packages. If you like big resorts, and armies of squealing kids don't daunt you, you'll enjoy the three swimming pools, excellent restaurants, tennis courts and – possibly – even the lovely wedding chapel.

While mum and dad nip off for a round of golf (nine holes $35) or toddle down to one of the Fijian's swanky day spas or the adults-only pool, they can (lovingly) shunt junior into the child-care centre.

ⓘ Getting There & Away

The Fijian and Gecko's are about a 45-minute drive from Nadi and 11km west of Sigatoka. There is regular public transport and express buses along the Queens Rd.

Sigatoka & Around
POP 9500

Sigatoka ('sing-a-to-ka') is a neat, orderly town that serves as the commercial hub for the farming communities that live in the fertile Sigatoka Valley. It's also a popular day trip for tourists, and while all its major attractions are a short taxi ride out of town, its riverside location, bustling produce market, supermarket, souvenir shops and local mosque mean that it's a pleasant place to while away a few hours. There are no great places to stay in Sigatoka town but options are plentiful at nearby Korotogo on the coast.

◉ Sights

Sigatoka Sand Dunes   NATIONAL PARK
(adult/child/family $10/5/25, child under 6yr free; ⊘8am-5pm) One of Fiji's natural highlights, these impressive dunes are a ripple of peppery monoliths skirting the shoreline near the mouth of the Sigatoka River. Windblown and rugged, they stand around 5km long, up to a kilometre wide and on average about 20m high, rising to about 60m at the western end. They were made a national park in 1989.

Tavuni Hill Fort   HISTORIC SITE
(Map p70; adult/child $12/6; ⊘8am-5pm Mon-Sat) Although there are many forts like it scattered all over Fiji, Tavuni Hill Fort is the most accessible for visitors. Built in the 18th century by Tongan chief Maile Latumai, this fort was a defensive site used in times of war and is one of Fiji's most interesting historical sights.

The steep 90m-high limestone ridge at the edge of a bend in the Sigatoka River is an obvious strategic location for a fortification. The views over the valley are tremendous.

Naihehe Cave   CAVE
(Map p70) This cave is popular with package tour groups.

⚡ Activities

For surfers, Sigatoka has Fiji's only beach break, over a large, submerged rock platform covered in sand and at the point break at the mouth of the Sigatoka River.

☞ Tours

Adventures in Paradise   TOUR
(☑652 0833; www.adventuresinparadisefiji. com; tours per person incl Coral Coast/Nadi hotel transfers $99/119, child 5-12yr half-price) Offers day trips to the Naihehe Cave on

Tuesdays, Thursdays and Saturdays. Lunch and a *bilibili* (bamboo raft) ride downstream are included – children love it. The Savu Na Mate Laya Waterfall tour leaves Mondays, Wednesdays and Fridays and involves non-strenuous walking to a waterfall-fed swimming hole.

Sigatoka River Safari TOUR
(☑650 1721; www.sigatokariver.com; jet-boat tours per person incl Sigatoka/Coral Coast hotel transfers $249/289, child 4-15yr $125/145) These popular half-day jet-boating trips include a 45km whirl up the Sigatoka River, a village visit and lunch.

🛏 Sleeping & Eating

If you're stuck, you'll find a basic hotel room in Sigatoka, but you're better off heading to the superior accommodation in nearby Korotogo.

True Blue Restaurant INDO-FIJIAN $
(☑650 1530; mains $15-45; ⊗7am-11pm) The draw at this local hangout is its elevated position and lovely views from the cavernous, dancehall-like restaurant and balcony along the mangrove-lined Sigatoka River. It's all pretty informal. The food leans heavily to Indo-Fijian, with a dash of Chinese thrown in for good measure.

Vilisite's Seafood Restaurant SEAFOOD $$
(Map p70; ☑650 1030; Queens Rd; mains $18-35; ⊗lunch & dinner) First impressions can mislead: picture a tatty tropicana restaurant from the late '70s and you might give perennial favourite Vilisite's a miss. Don't. While there are Chinese and curry options on the menu, everyone goes for the seafood (three-course set menus from $30, or blow out on the $60 lobster), followed by an ice-cream cone from the shack outside.

❶ Getting There & Around

Pacific Transport and Sunbeam Transport run several express buses a day between Nadi and Sigatoka ($5.50, 1¼ hours) and between Sigatoka and Suva ($10.25, three hours).

Korotogo & Korolevu

The Coral Coast begins its dazzling thread in earnest at the small village of Korotogo. From here the road winds along the shore, skirting clear blue bays and scaling progressively greener hills as it heads east. Unexpected glimpses of coral reefs and deserted beaches make this the most photogenic stretch of the Queens Rd. Villages are plentiful and each is announced by a series of judder bars designed to slow traffic and reduce accidents. East of Korolevu, the road turns away from the shore and climbs over the southern end of Viti Levu's dividing mountain range towards Pacific Harbour.

⊙ Sights

Kula Eco Park WILDLIFE RESERVE
(Map p95; ☑650 0505; www.fijiwild.com; adult/child $25/12.50; ⊗10am-4pm)✎This wildlife sanctuary is supported by the National Trust for Fiji and several international parks and conservation bodies, and showcases some magnificent wildlife. This includes Fiji's only native land mammal, the Fijian flying fox; and an aviary full of quarrelsome kula parrots, Fiji's national bird and the park's namesake. The park runs invaluable breeding programs, with success stories for the Pacific black duck (Fiji's only remaining duck species) and the crested and banded iguana.

☂ Activities

The Korolevu stretch of coast offers spectacular diving, and most of the resorts in the area are serviced by **Dive Away Fiji** (☑926 3112; www.diveawayfiji.com) or **South Pacific Adventure Divers** (☑653 0555; www.spadfiji.com). Both operators will collect guests from nearby resorts; prices for a two-tank dive/PADI Open Water Course. average out around $150/950.

🛏 Sleeping

The resort stretch of coast at Korotogo is locally known as Sunset Strip.

Beachhouse HOSTEL $
(☑653 0500; www.fijibeachouse.com; Korolevu; dm/d incl breakfast $45/140-180; ➰🐾🔊) Aimed squarely at backpackers, this long-time favourite combines simple digs with heady social activities in a consistently winning formula. The dorms (including a women-only dorm) are in two-storey houses and the doubles are in colourful duplex bungalows. Buses will stop right outside and there's a pretty pool, a cheap cafe and on-site cooking facilities. A great place to meet travellers.

Crow's Nest Resort RESORT $
(Map p95; ☑650 0230; www.crowsnestresort fiji.com; Sunset Strip; villa $199-239; ➰❄@🔊) Nautical terms abound at these smart grey split-level timber bungalows. Each has a

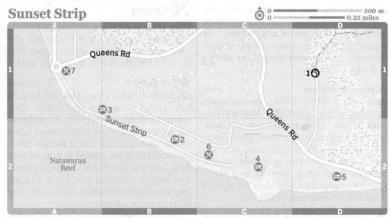

Sunset Strip

FIJI SOUTHERN VITI LEVU & THE CORAL COAST

lovely balcony and ocean views, and they're in good nick and are good value. The slightly more expensive rooms are self-contained, but all can accommodate a family of four. The **restaurant** (mains $17-25) faces the hillside pool and has a cosmopolitan menu (we enjoyed the pastas with various shellfish).

Tubakula Beach Bungalows RESORT $
(Map p95; ☑ 650 0097; www.fiji4less.com/tuba. html; Sunset Strip; dm $30, s/tw $70/77, chalet $140-198; ❄ ☎) If it weren't for the palm trees, pool and waterfront setting, this low-key resort would be right at home in the mountains. Simple dorms, singles and twins have shared facilities. The A-frame chalets have strapping timber frames, modern kitchens and verandahs with slouchy wooden seats. It's ideal for self-driving, self-catering, self-sufficient types wishing to escape the crowds.

Mango Bay Resort HOSTEL $
(☑ 653 0069; www.mangobayresortfiji.com; Korolevu; dm incl breakfast $40, d incl breakfast $200, bungalow incl breakfast $280; ❄ @ ☎ ☎) The dorm, cabins and *bures* are scattered through 16 acres of parklike grounds. Facilities are excellent for the budget – the dorms are modern, the *bures* have atrium showers and the beach is one of the best on the Coral Coast. Mango mainly targets a younger crowd with plenty of activities of the full-moon-party, crab racing and sunset-bonfire variety. Snorkelling is available.

★ **Waidroka Surf & Dive Resort** RESORT $$
(☑ 330 4605; www.waidroka.com; Korolevu; r $275, bungalow $375-425; @ ☎) Over a hilly 4.5km of dirt road, Waidroka caters to serious surfers

and divers looking for an upmarket alternative to the Yanuca island surf camps. Check out the variety of combined packages on their website. There's a small flotilla of boats on hand to take guests to local breaks and Frigate Passage.

Crusoe's Retreat RESORT $$
(☑ 650 0185; www.crusoesretreat.com; Korolevu; r incl breakfast from $235; ☎ ☎) Driving down the long dirt track to Crusoe's Retreat off the Queens Road, you'd be forgiven for thinking you were heading to the middle of nowhere, but there's a real gem at the end of the road. Many of the 28 spacious and fan-cooled *bure* are located on a hillside and the stairs are not ideal for older guests, but it's a truly tranquil retreat for others.

Wellesley Resort RESORT $$
(☑ 603 0664; www.wellesleyresort.com.fj; Man Fri Rd, Korolevu; d from $249, ste incl breakfast $349-559; ❄ ❄ ☎) This top-end adults-only resort oozes comfort, style and tranquility. The 15 suites saddle a small valley that leads

to a pretty cove and even the most ardent adrenalin junkies will soon rediscover their inner sloth. The restaurant (anyone for 'Fijian tapas' meets contemporary Pacific?) is excellent, and you can ease off the calories in the indulgent spa.

Bedarra Beach Inn INN $$
(Map p95; ☑650 0476; www.bedarrafiji. com; Sunset Strip; r $180-260; ❄☎📶🏊) This modern hotel is a gem. It offers spacious, spotlessly clean rooms with tiled floors and plenty of natural light, most of which have ocean views. There's a good balance between resort-style comfort and do-it-yourself practicality. The open bar area is designed for maximum sociability.

★Outrigger Fiji Beach Resort RESORT $$$
(Map p95; ☑650 0044; www.outrigger.com/fiji; Sunset Strip; r from $639, bungalow from $1069; ❄❄@📶🏊) The 7m outrigger canoe suspended from the ceiling in the main lobby and the stunning balcony views create a powerful first impression at this much-touted resort. From the main building, an artificial stream meanders through lush gardens to a huge, lagoon-style pool. It can get noisy with excited kids, but there's an adult-only pool for others to retreat to if needed.

Warwick Fiji Resort & Spa RESORT $$$
(☑653 0555; www.warwickfiji.com; Korolevu; r incl breakfast $554, ste incl breakfast $745; ❄❄@🏊) Owned by the same crowd that own Naviti (there's a free shuttle between the two and guests can use both resorts' facilities), the Warwick is another feature-laden, activity-rich resort. The public areas feature tile, wooden floors, cane furniture and soft brown furnishings. There are five restaurants, seven bars (one of which has Middle Eastern water pipes) and lagoons with all-tide swimming areas.

Naviti Resort RESORT $$$
(☑653 0444; www.navitiresort.com.fj; Korolevu; r incl breakfast $285-799; ❄❄@🏊) Heavy on the greenery and light on the concrete, the Naviti's 220 rooms have access to all the goodies – four restaurants, five bars, a nine-hole golf course, a swim-up bar, a health spa and a kids club. Unlike most resorts, all-inclusive packages include beer, wine, Sigatoka shopping excursions, a sunset cruise and a choice between à la carte or buffet dining. The two tiny islands offshore are used for weddings and there's an all-tide swimming lagoon to compensate for the poor beach.

✕ Eating

Many of the resorts have restaurants and bars – in some cases, multiple restaurants and bars – and they all welcome the opportunity to steal a few clients from their neighbours.

★Eco Café ITALIAN $$
(☑653 0064; Votua village; pizza $25-38, pasta $25; ⊙2-9pm Fri-Tue) This joint Italian-Fijian enterprise doesn't disappoint. It's a charming open-fronted wood and bamboo facing directly onto the sea with a mellow beach bar vibe. Pizzas are cooked in a wood-fired oven, and the focaccia is excellent. There's also some great Fijian food (with a strong emphasis on fresh veggies), but you'll need to call a day in advance to order.

Eco Café doesn't have an alcohol license, but welcomes BYO (a small corkage fee applies). Otherwise, enjoy the excellent Italian coffee or the refreshing home-made lemonade. The restaurant is on the Queens Rd between the Naviti and Warwick resorts.

★Beach Bar & Grill BISTRO $$
(Map p95; ☑652 0877; Sunset Strip; mains $15-38; ⊙5.30-9.30pm) Formerly Le Café, the Beach Bar & Grill is deservedly popular with those wanting to eat outside their resorts. It's a simple thatched outfit, but has an impressive menu, with lots of excellent local seafood and an interesting blend of Fijian, Thai and French flavours in the offerings (if that sounds odd, we can attest that it works).

Koko's Bar INTERNATIONAL $$
(Map p95; Sunset Strip; mains $14-29; ⊙noon-2pm & 5pm-late) This diner-style restaurant facing the sea is a good place to refuel. A smart open-fronted wooden building with a sports bar at the back, it has a decent line in Fijian dishes such as Ika Vakalolo (fish cooked in coconut), Indo-Fijian curries, plus some good pizzas and burgers and great service. The cocktails are great, and there's a kids' menu for $12.

Vilisite's Restaurant FISH & CHIPS $$
(☑650 1030; Queens Rd; mains $15-40; ⊙breakfast, lunch & dinner) If you're wearing your bula shirt you'll feel right at home, as this place drips tropical garb. It's a couple of kilometres beyond the Naviti, and has sweeping sea views. There's Chinese, seafood curries and lobster on offer, but everyone seems to order the fish and chips.

ⓘ Getting There & Away

The Korotogo area is about 8km east of Sigatoka, and Korolevu village is 31km east of Sigatoka. Regular buses ply the Queens Rd and will drop guests off outside most resorts. For the more isolated resorts it is best to phone ahead and arrange collection or a taxi once you have reached the Coral Coast vicinity.

Pacific Harbour

Billed as the 'Adventure Capital of Fiji', Pacific Harbour offers a range of adrenaline-fuelled activities including shark diving in nearby Beqa (*Ben-ga*) Lagoon, and rafting and trekking in the Namosi Highlands. You'd never guess this was Thrillseeker HQ from looking at it: originally a swamp, Pacific Harbour has been tamed, drained, subdivided and pedicured into a brochure-perfect housing development quite unlike the rest of Fiji. The next big development is the Pacific Palm Marina: a large marina is planned, plus restaurants, spa, a golf course and residential units.

🏃 Activities

The beach at nearby Deuba is reasonable for swimming.

Freedive Fiji   FISHING
(☏973 0687; www.freedivefiji.com; half-day per person $240) If spear- or game-fishing is your thing, this is the outfit for you. There are set departures each day, but you can organise whole boat charters too.

Rivers Fiji   ADVENTURE TOUR
(Map p98; ☏345 0147; www.riversfiji.com; Pearl South Pacific) Rivers offers excellent kayaking and white-water rafting trips into the Namosi Highlands north of Pacific Harbour. The day trip ($310 per person including lunch) to Wainikoroiluva (Luva Gorge) is highly recommended and the scenery alone is worth the bumpy two-hour carrier trip up to Nakavika village. After the obligatory kava session with the chief, you paddle downstream (four hours) by inflatable kayak over stretches of gentle rapids and past waterfalls to Namuamua village.

Zip Fiji   ADVENTURE SPORTS
(Map p70; ☏672 6045; www.zip-fiji.com; $225; ⊗8am-8pm) This outfit lets squealing thrill-seekers whoosh from one platform to another through dense forest canopy in a series of eight aerial zip lines that stretch 2km – the longest zip is a dizzying 210m.

The zipline is 25 minutes drive from Pacific Harbour, but the cost includes transfers.

Kila Eco Adventure Park   ADVENTURE SPORTS
(Map p70; ☏331 7454; www.kilaworld.com; half/full day adult $122/170, half/full day child $97/142, nature walk only $15; ⊗10am-4.30pm) This adventure park is aimed at the whole family. There are high and low rope walks, a zip line, abseiling and what bills itself as Fiji's biggest swing – at 12m high, it almost feels like a bungee jump. For those who prefer a little less adrenaline, there are also 10km of nature walks, with picnic *bures* along the way, and waterfalls where you can take a dip. Individual activities cost $60 if you don't want to buy a whole tour. The park is near Navua.

Diving

There are more than 20 excellent dive sites near Pacific Harbour, mostly within **Beqa Lagoon**, but these are overshadowed by the opportunity to dive with 4m-long tiger sharks and massive, barrel-chested bull sharks without being caged (or sedated). The dives are well organised (they would have to be), and not nearly as intimidating as many imagine. The tigers don't always show but the bulls are regularly seen between February and early September.

Aqua-Trek Beqa (Map p98; ☏345 0324; www.aquatrek.com; Club Oceanus) specialises in this activity; prices include $282 for a two-tank dive, $346 for a two-tank shark-feeding dive (Mondays, Wednesdays, Fridays and Saturdays) and $1018 for the PADI Open Water course.

☞ Tours

Arts Village   CULTURAL TOUR
(Map p98; ☏345 0065; www.artsvillage.com.fj; day pass per adult/child from $60/30; ⊗9am-4pm Wed-Sat) This faux village is unashamedly 'Fiji in a theme park', and within its Disney-like confines are a temple, chiefly *bure*, cooking area with utensils and weaving hut. Fijian actors dressed in traditional costumes carry out mock battles, preach pagan religion and demonstrate traditional arts. Tours include an canoe tour (for the kids), Island Temple Tour and Arts Village Show, and fire-walking (11am). It's fun for families, but not much to do with authentic village life.

Discover Fiji Tours   ADVENTURE TOUR
(Map p70; ☏345 0180; www.discoverfijitours. com) Discover runs several tours to the

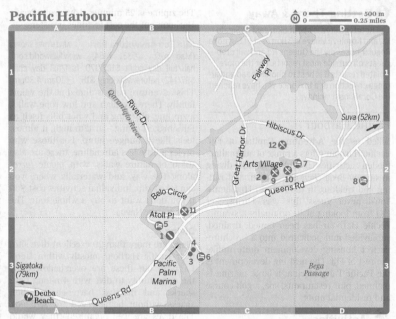

Pacific Harbour

Activities, Courses & Tours

Navua River area. Tours include waterfall visits, 4WD trips, trekking, kayaking and white-water rafting – there seem a dizzying number of permutations on offer – and cost between $225 and $469. Prices vary according to transfers: they'll pick you up anywhere between Nadi and Suva. All day tours last about six hours and include lunch.

Jetski Tours   ADVENTURE TOUR
(Map p98; ☑ 345 0933; www.jetski-safari.com; 158 Kaka Pl) Jetski Tours takes travellers on a four-hour, full-throttle, 65km jet-ski tour (solo rider $530, twin share $290 per person) around Beqa Lagoon. Lunch, snorkelling gear, wetsuits and life jackets are included. Book at least a day in advance.

Sleeping

Tsulu Backpackers   HOSTEL $
(Map p98; ☑ 345 0065; dm $35, d $70-90, apt $150; ✴@✽) Attached to the Arts Village, the Tsulu has picked up the artistic gauntlet and run with it. The walls of the dorms and double rooms are painted in vibrant murals. It's super cheap, but has something of a school dormitory feeling to it that even the cheery walls can't overcome. All bathroom facilities are shared.

Club Oceanus   MOTEL $
(Map p98; ☑ 345 0498; www.cluboceanus. com; 1 Atoll Pl; dm $30, r $150-190; ⊖✴🕾✽) This waterside resort (all rooms face the river) has a selection of clean and comfortable rooms in a long, compact block. The cosy 'loft' sleeps four, and there are kitchen

facilities in the 12-bed dorm. It's good value, located in a convenient spot on the canal close to the Arts Village complex and with Brizo's Grill bar-restaurant on site.

Uprising Beach Resort RESORT $$
(Map p98; ✆345 2200; www.uprisingbeach resort.com; dm incl breakfast $60, bungalow incl breakfast $255-300, villa from $355; ✱🗩🎿) The Uprising continues to give other resorts a run for their money, recently raising the bar with 12 very swish villas to add to the 12 spacious *bure*. There are nifty outdoor showers and bifolding doors to catch the ocean breeze. The 'treehouse' dorm is spotlessly clean and although it isn't in a tree, it does afford beautiful views from the verandah.

Pearl South Pacific RESORT $$$
(Map p98; ✆345 0022; www.thepearlsouth pacific.com; Queens Rd; r $485, ste from $550; ➌✱@🎿) This resort was undergoing a massive extension programme when we visited to almost double its size. It's high end stuff – Fijian-Asian fusion rooms that come themed in six flavours including Red Passion and Moody Blues. Style gurus will overdose on the marble bathrooms, low-slung beds and private decks with cushioned sun loungers – even if some of the final finish is a bit lacking.

🍴 Eating

⭐ Baka Blues Cafe FUSION $$
(Map p98; Arts Village Marketplace; mains $20-30; ⏰11am-10pm Tue-Sun) New Orleans blues accompanies the Cajun-influenced menu at this restaurant, which is the marketplace's standout offering. There's live music on Wednesday, Friday and Sunday evenings.

Tiki Bar & Melting Pot Restaurant INTERNATIONAL $$
(Map p98; Arts Village Marketplace; mains $8-30; ⏰lunch & dinner) In keeping with the faux-Fijian theme of the Arts Village, this open-air eatery is on the sand banks of a swimming pool. Overlooked by an 18m-tall, Aztec-like tiki head, this place is great for kids, who can swim in the pool or pickle themselves in the cannibals' 'hot pot' spa. Oh...and the food's not bad either. Day visitors can swim too (adult/child $5/2.50).

Oasis Restaurant INTERNATIONAL $$
(Map p98; Arts Village Marketplace; mains $16-36; ⏰breakfast, lunch & dinner; ✱) Burgers, sandwiches, tortillas, curries and a whole lotta seafood is served at this long-time local favourite. The secondhand books for sale may not be great literature but go really well on a sun lounger.

Mantarae Restaurant FUSION $$$
(Map p98; ✆345 0022; Pearl South Pacific; mains $28-40; ⏰dinner Tue-Sat) This place offers interesting contemporary, fusion-style cuisine that has diners licking their lips from entrée to dessert. The Thai night when we visited was delicious. Sprawled out on a day bed, or sequestered behind the bar with its mirror-backed water feature, it's fine dining all the way – with a wine list to match.

Sakura House JAPANESE $$$
(Map p98; ✆345 0256; River Dr; mains $25-40; ⏰dinner) Although it features other Asian dishes, the Japanese tempura, sashimi, shabu-shabu (thinly sliced meat and vegetables cooked tableside in a pot of boiling water) and teriyaki are Sakura's speciality.

ℹ️ Getting There & Away

Pacific Harbour is about an hour's express bus ride from Suva ($4.15) and around 3½ hours from Nadi ($15). A taxi to Suva costs about $40.

Namosi Highlands

The steamy Namosi Highlands, north of Pacific Harbour, have Fiji's most spectacular scenery, complete with rainforests, steep ranges, deep river canyons and tall waterfalls. The simplest way to see these highlands is to sign up with one of the Pacific Harbour tour companies that specialise in this remote area or, if you have your own wheels (preferably 4WD), take a detour inland from Nabukavesi.

Offshore Islands

Offshore from Pacific Harbour, a 64km-long barrier reef encloses the exquisite Beqa Lagoon, world-famous for its dizzying dive sites including Side Streets and Caesar's Rocks. Divers are joined by avid surfers, who test their mettle on the powerful left-hand breaks at Frigate Passage. Anchored amid the lagoon are Beqa and Yanuca islands, untouched except for a handful of inconspicuous resorts.

BEQA
AREA 36 SQ KM

The volcanic and rugged island of Beqa is best known for its villagers, who practise traditional fire-walking – but the best place

FIJI SOUTHERN VITI LEVU & THE CORAL COAST

to see them isn't on Beqa; they now perform chiefly for tourists at the Coral Coast resorts.

🛏 Sleeping

Lawaki Beach House LODGE $

(Map p70; ☑ 992 1621, 368 4088; www.lawaki beachhouse.com; sites per tent incl meals $93, dm/s/d $139/159/198) 🍃 This small resort sits in front of an isolated beach on the southwestern side of Beqa. The place comprises two double *bures* with en suites and verandahs, and a six-bed dorm. The unobtrusive and cosy set-up blends well with the surrounding environment, as do the solar, recycling and water-use practices. Guests mingle together in the communal lounge, soaking up the relaxed mood.

There is good snorkelling off the secluded, pristine white-sand beach, as well as visits to the nearby village, diving and surfing. Transfers from Pacific Harbour cost $220 one-way (one or two guests). Alternatively, you catch the small public ferry from the Navua Jetty. The ferry usually leaves between noon and 2.30pm Monday through Saturday, and costs $40 per person one way. It returns to Navua at 7am every day but Sunday.

Beqa Lagoon Resort RESORT $$$

(Map p70; ☑ 330 4042; www.beqalagoonresort. com; three night stay with meal plan from $845; ❇ @ ≋) The 25 stylish and well-maintained *bure* here come with opulent bathrooms and traditional interiors, and some with plunge pools. The surrounding landscape and calm bay in front lends itself to excellent snorkelling and kayaking. There's a **restaurant-lounge** serving fabulous food, and a spa and a pool beside a coconut tree-fringed beach. It's a dive resort fair and square, offering all-inclusive packages.

YANUCA

Tiny Yanuca island is a beautiful, hilly speck inside Beqa Lagoon, about 9km west of Beqa. The beaches here are lovely, but it's Yanuca's proximity to the surf breaks of Frigate Passage that lures travellers here.

Many a surfer hits **Batiluva Beach Resort** (Map p70; ☑ 992 0021, 345 0384; www. batiluva.com; all inclusive $175, transfer from Pacific Harbour $50) for a week, only to wake a month later in a hammock wondering where the time went. Spotless and airy dorms and semi-private double rooms are rented on a per-person basis, with couples getting dibs on the doubles. All meals are included in the tariff, as is the daily boat out

to Frigate Passage for the surf-til-you-drop clientele. Transfers from Pacific Harbour are $50 return, per person.

Tiny, locally run surf camp **Yanuca Island Resort** may also be open; ask around.

Viti Levu's Kings Road

The less-travelled Kings Rd is a scenic delight, with ribboning, highland ascents, gorgeous views over the Wainibuka River and, from Viti Levu Bay, a coast-skirting run to Lautoka past rugged cliffs and sugarcane fields. After years of neglect, the once-infamously bumpy road has finally been paved and upgraded; some locals say it's now the best highway in the country. A coastal road runs parallel to Natovi Landing (about a 20-minute drive from Korovou), from where there are combined bus and ferry services to Levuka on Ovalau. Beyond the landing, **Takalana Bay Retreat** (Map p70; ☑ 991 6338; http://takalana.blogspot. co.uk; s/d incl with shared bathroom $115/220, d with bathroom $250, bungalow $285) offers access to fabulous **Moon Reef** and its spinner dolphins (boat trips $55 per person). In the north, a turn-off from the highway will take you to Ellington's Wharf, gateway to the wonderful island of Nananu-i-Ra.

Vaileka, Rakiraki & Ellington Wharf

Northwest from Korovou, the Kings Rd slides alongside Wainibuka River, past small villages, towards Viti Levu Bay. West of Rakiraki junction, a turn-off leads past the sugar mill to the small service town of Vaileka. This is where buses arrive and depart from, and it's a good place to stock up on provisions before heading offshore. Town amenities include a supermarket, a taxi rank, internet, a produce market, banks with ATMs and several fast-food restaurants.

Heading out of Rakiraki towards Nadi, look out for **Udreudre's Tomb** (Map p101), the resting place of Fiji's most notorious cannibal, whose personal tally reached at least 872 corpses. It's about 100m west of the Vaileka turn-off, on the left, and resembles a rectangular slab of concrete.

The turn-off to Ellington Wharf is about 5km east of Rakiraki junction, and it is here that resorts collect their guests for the short boat ride across to Nananu-i-Ra.

Rakiraki & Nananu-i-Ra

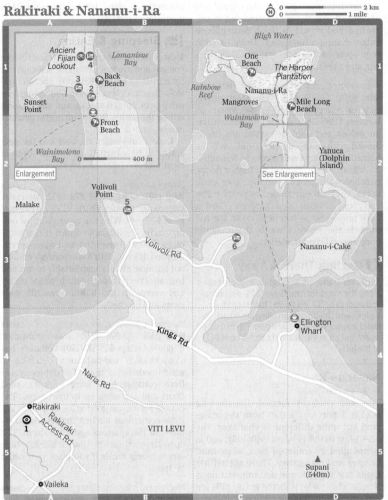

FIJI VITI LEVU'S KINGS ROAD

🏃 Activities

The reefs of Rakiraki offer some excellent **scuba diving**, with dense marine life and beautiful coral gardens. Volivoli Beach Resort and Wananavu Beach Resort have on-site dive shops and knowledgeable staff.

🛏 Sleeping & Eating

Volivoli Beach Resort   RESORT $$
(Map p101; ☎ 669 4511; www.volivoli.com; Volivoli Rd; bungalow $330-485 ; ❋ 🛜 ⛲) Located on the northernmost point of Viti Levu, Volivoli has a variety of modern, crisp *bure*

Rakiraki & Nananu-i-Ra

that wrap themselves around a curved spit of land, all with decks and views out to sea. are in a modern and spotlessly clean hillside lodge, sharing a huge deck. There's a great semi-open restaurant (mains $20-35) and bar, and a small beach with snorkelling.

Wananavu Beach Resort   RESORT $$$
(Map p101; ☎ 669 4433; www.wananavu.com; bungalow incl breakfast from $495-845, honeymoon bungalow $1185-1280; ❄ @ ☒) Wananavu has an indoor and outdoor restaurant (mains $16-40) with gorgeous views out over the beautiful pool area and across to Nananu-i-Ra island. All the *bures* have timber floors, panelled walls, air-con and their own small decks. They are surrounded by pretty palm- and bougainvillea-filled gardens. Garden *bure* prices rise as you head down the hill towards the water, towards the romantic honeymoon accommodation.

❶ Getting There & Away
Sunbeam Transport has regular express buses along the Kings Rd from Suva ($14, 4½ hours) and Nadi ($12.50, 2¼ hours) that stop at Vaileka and the turn-off to Ellington Wharf. To avoid lugging groceries and gear 1.3km to the wharf, get off at Vaileka and catch a taxi ($15) to the jetty.

Nananu-i-Ra
AREA 3.5 SQ KM

Tiny and perfectly formed, Nananu-i-Ra is only a hop and a skip from the mainland but quite different in character. The 3.5-sq-km island is beautifully hilly, and is surrounded by scalloped bays, white-sand beaches and mangroves. There are neither roads nor villages, and accommodation is simple. Those who walk the grassy hills are rewarded with fine views across the water to the volcanic Nakauvadra mountain range on the mainland.

☗ Activities
Nananu-i-Ra is renowned for its offshore reefs, and great windsurfing and kiteboarding. It can get very windy on the east side of the island from May through to July and again from late October to December during the cyclone season.

Safari Lodge (Map p101; ☎ 948 8888, 628 3332; www.safarilodge.com.fj; two-tank dive $250, PADI Open Water Course $890) hires gear for kitesurfing and windsurfing, as well as offering lessons. It's also the only PADI operator on the island.

🛏 Sleeping & Eating
Most places accept credit cards (check before you go) and are well set up for self-caterers. Safari Island Lodge, Betham's and McDonald's Beach Cottages have indoor-outdoor cafes with limited menus and small stores selling the basics. Fresh fruit and vegetables can be limited.

Expect cold-water showers and the generator to be switched off around 10pm at most places.

Safari Lodge   LODGE $
(Map p101; ☎ 948 8888, 628 3332; www.safarilodge.com.fj; dm/d/q $30/110/150, r $150, bungalow $295) 🖋 With the great range of outdoor activities available, Safari Lodge is the place to stay for the wind- and water-sports-inclined. It's run with a windsurfer's chilled-out attitude. Simple, comfortable rooms and balconies peep through foliage to the ocean, and creep up the hillside towards wide views and breezes.

Betham's Beach Cottages   CABIN $
(Map p101; ☎ 992 7132; www.bethams.com.fj; dm/tw/cottage $35/110/160) Betham's has some sound, old-fashioned beach-house accommodation options. The duplex beach-front cottages have large kitchens, tiled floors and can sleep up to five people. The double rooms are good value and there is a large communal kitchen that is shared by those in the spacious eight-bed dorm. The open-air restaurant (mains $25-35) here serves hearty meals if you place your order by 1pm.

McDonald's Beach Cottages   CABIN $
(Map p101; ☎ 628 3118; www.macsnananu.com; dm/tw $30/95, cottage $150) McDonald's offers a scattering of supertidy self-contained cabins on a nicely landscaped property right in front of the jetty. The cute blue and yellow cottages are self-contained and it's popular with do-it-yourself types. The restaurant specialises in pizzas.

❶ Getting There & Away
Nananu-i-Ra is a 15-minute boat ride from Ellington Wharf, and each resort runs its own transfers (around $50 per person return). Arrange your pick-up in advance.

MAMANUCAS DIVING & SURFING

Diving

Mamanuca diving sites teem with fantastically gaudy fish circling impossibly psychedelic corals. The visibility here astounds first-time divers and you can see for up to 40m through the water much of the year. The following are the big fish in the pond, with dive shops on multiple islands; other resorts have their own dive operators.

Tropical Watersports (☑ 995 9810; www.fijitropicalwatersports.com) This outfit services Treasure, Bounty, Beachcomber and Navini resorts. Two-tank dive $289, PADI openwater course $850.

Subsurface Fiji (☑ 999 6371; www.fijidiving.com) Runs dive shops at resorts including Plantation Island, Lomani, Musket Cove and Malolo Island Resort. A two-tank dive costs $295, and a three-day PADI open-water course is $975 ($860 if online course completed).

Surfing

The reefs off the southern Mamanuca islands have some of the world's most formidable breaks, including legendary left-handers **Cloudbreak**, **Restaurants** and **Namotu Left**.

Fiji's surfing guru Ian Muller is at **Fiji Surf Company** (Map p82; ☑ 992 8411; www.fijisurfco.com; cnr Main St & Hospital Rd, Crown Investment Bldg). Ian and his crew offer surf trips and surf school for all levels. Resorts on Malolo Lailai and Malolo will also get you out to the breaks (around $70 per person).

MAMANUCA GROUP

The Mamanuca islands tick every 'tropical paradise' box, with brochure-blue seas and beaches so brilliant they're Hollywood celebrities unto themselves. With romance, relaxation and a disproportional number of fantastic resorts on offer, the group is one of Fiji's most popular destinations. Kaleidoscopic coral reefs and masses of marine life await those who take the plunge into their crystal-clear waters. The islands themselves have enough facilities, activities and adventure opportunities to satisfy every visitor, whether they drop in for a day or stay a week.

❶ Getting There & Away

Thanks to their proximity to both Port Denarau and Nadi airport, the Mamanuca islands are easily reached by catamaran, speedboat (www.mamanucaexpress.com), seaplane (www.turtleairways.com) or helicopter (www.helicopters.com.fj).

Most people arrive on one of the high-speed catamarans departing Port Denarau; prices include pick-up from hotels in the Nadi region. Prices are for one-way adult fares. Children aged five to 15 are half-price.

South Sea Cruises (Map p87; ☑ 675 0500; www.ssc.com.fj) Five daily fast catamaran transfers to islands including South Sea ($80), Bounty ($90), Beachcomber and Treasure ($105), Malolo ($115), Castaway ($115), Mana ($120), Matamanoa ($145), Tokoriki ($145) and Vomo ($165).

Awesome Adventures Fiji (☑ 675 0499; www.awesomefiji.com) Runs the *Yasawa Flyer* (also known as the 'Yellow Boat'), which connects with South Sea Island ($80), Bounty Island ($90), Beachcomber and Treasure islands ($105) and Vomo ($165) on its way north to the Yasawas.

Malolo Cat (Map p87; ☑ 675 0205; www.malolocatfiji.com; $70) Runs daily transfers between Port Denarau and Plantation, Musket Bay and Lomani resorts on Malolo Lailai Island. A boat leaves Port Denarau at 7.30am, 10.30am, 2pm and 5.30pm; from the island, it leaves at 5.45am, 8.45am, 12.15pm and 4pm. The trip takes 50 minutes.

South Sea Island

South Sea is the smallest of the island resorts and little more than a bump of sand – albeit a beautiful bump – with some trees growing on top. You can walk around the whole island in three minutes. It's hugely popular with day trippers.

🛏 Sleeping

South Sea Island Hostel HOSTEL **$**
(Map p104; ☑ 675 0500; www.ssc.com.fj; dm $120; 🖥🌊) Many backpackers spend a night on South Sea on their way to or from the Yasawas. Accommodation is in a breezy

Mamanuca Group

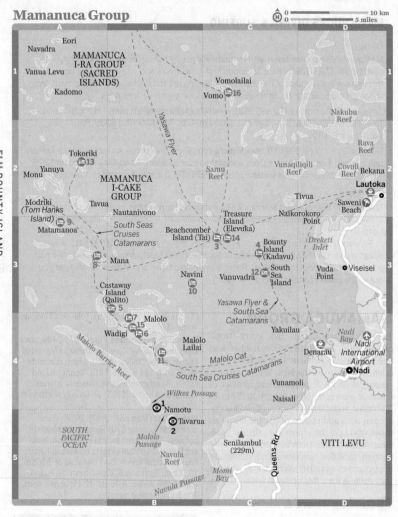

32-bed upstairs dorm. Night-time crowds are limited: dinner is a pleasant low-key event on the beach, and the cute bar never gets too crazy. The price includes all meals and the use of all nonmotorised water-sport equipment.

Bounty Island

AREA 0.2 SQ KM

Bounty (Kadavu) is bigger than its immediate neighbours but still takes only 30 minutes to walk around or, if you don't stop to tease the clownfish, 1½ hours to snorkel.

The white-sand beach attracts both endangered hawksbill turtles and day trippers.

🛏 Sleeping

Bounty Island Resort RESORT $$
(Map p104; ☑776 3391; www.fiji-bounty.com; dm/bungalow $45/145-175; ❋☎❋) This friendly, low-key resort is an excellent choice for backpackers and families on a budget. The air-conditioned 20- and 14-bed dorms have comfy, oversized bunks, though island *bures* are a good value step-up if you're after privacy. The beachfront *bures,* a short, sandy hike from the bar/restaurant, have

Mamanuca Group

FIJI BEACHCOMBER ISLAND

verandahs and hammocks. Bonus points for hot showers, 24-hour electricity and potable water.

Beachcomber Island

AREA 0.2 SQ KM

Pretty Beachcomber Island (Tai) is circled by a comely coconut palm-studded beach. Its quintessential cuteness belies a reputation of being *the* party island in the Mamanucas. True this may be, but Beachcomber's white sands, water-sports options and turtle sanctuary also attract flocks of families: somehow, the debauched and the (slightly more) decorous manage to co-exist quite nicely.

🛏 Sleeping

★ **Beachcomber Island Resort**　　RESORT $$
(Map p104; ☑666 1500; www.beachcomberfiji. com; dm/r/bungalow from $39/249/400; ❅🛜⛱) This resort is a wonderful oddity: beloved by backpackers for its anything-goes, sandbar and huge, somehow airy – even with 84 beds! – dorm, the sprawling Beachcomber also welcomes equal numbers of families, who keep to *bures* and (very) beachfront rooms far from the nighttime revelry. Surprisingly, there aren't any young vs younger battles over the water trampoline and putt-putt course.

Treasure Island

AREA 0.06 SQ KM

Like nearby Bounty and Beachcomber, Treasure Island (Elevuka) is a sweet little speck that takes mere minutes to walk around. It's supremely popular with holidaymakers and day trippers taking advantage of the many facilities and activities on offer.

🛏 Sleeping

Treasure Island Resort　　RESORT $$$
(Map p104; ☑666 0380; www.treasureisland-fiji. com; bungalow $845-1173; ❅🛜⛱) Opened in 1972, this is one of the Mamanucas' oldest resorts and a long-time family favourite (though the annual 120 weddings held in its sleek chapel point at another popular market). There's a fantastic kids club, plus a baby turtle sanctuary, mini-golf, toddler pool and the Kidzspa. Adults dig the spa, tennis court and infinity pool. The on-site medical centre is a major plus.

Vomo

AREA 0.09 SQ KM

This wedge-shaped island rises to a magnificent high ridge and has two lovely beaches (one or the other will be sheltered if it's windy) and some of the best snorkelling in the group.

🛏 Sleeping

Vomo Island Resort　　RESORT $$$
(Map p104; ☑666 7955; www.vomofiji.com; $2280-9550; ❅@⛱) This five-star escape has everything you might imagine – gorgeous beach, gourmet meals, golf course – and some things that you might not: unlike many resorts in this class, children are most welcome here. The *bures* are stunningly appointed in dark-brown Pacificana with separate living areas and Jacuzzis: those by the beach are walk-in-flippers-close to the water, and those on the hill have fantastic views.

TOUR THE MAMANUCAS

Day cruises to the Mamanucas from Nadi are exceedingly popular and generally include transfers from Nadi hotels, lunch, nonmotorised water activities and as much sunburn as you can handle.

South Sea Cruises (Map p87; ☑ 675 0500; www.ssc.com.fj; Port Denarau Marina) Runs three-hour catamaran sightseeing cruises (adult/child $66/33) that follow its resort-transfer routes, plus day trips to islands including South Sea (adult/child $113/56), Treasure ($132/66), Mana ($129/69), Castaway ($138/101) and Malolo ($132/69).

Captain Cook Cruises (Map p87; ☑ 670 1823; www.captaincookcruisesfiji.com) Offers a day cruise (adult/child $193/129) from Denarau to the tiny coral island of Tivua, and a sunset dinner cruise (adult/child $149/95, three hours).

PJ's Sailing, Snorkelling & Fishing (Sailing Adventures Fiji; Map p87; ☑ 672 5022; www.pjfishsailfiji.com) This lively outfit does popular day sails to Bounty Island (adult/child/family $185/95/510); the trips include lunch, guided snorkelling and use of Bounty's facilities.

Seaspray (Map p87; ☑ 675 0500; www.ssc.com.fj; cruise per adult/child $135/79) Travel by catamaran to Mana Island, then onwards on the *Seaspray* schooner to Modriki Island (where the Tom Hanks film *Cast Away* was shot). Cruises cost $135/79 per adult/child.

Navini

AREA 0.25 SQ KM

This itty bitty islet is ringed by a glowing white beach and vibrant reef just snorkelling distance offshore.

🛏 Sleeping

Navini Island Resort　　　　RESORT $$$
(Map p104; ☑ 666 2188; www.navinifiji.com.fj; bungalow $645-860, villa $960; 🛜) This boutique resort gets top marks, not only for its stunning surrounds and tasteful, airy accommodations, but for possibly having the most hospitable staff in the Mamanucas. With only 10 *bures* and no distracting daytrippers, staff actually outnumber holidaymakers: it's a rare guest that leaves without feeling like a family member. All rooms have their own slice of beachfront and private courtyards.

Malolo Lailai

AREA 2.4 SQ KM

Tranquil Malolo Lailai is the second-largest island of the Mamanuca Group and encompasses three resorts, a marina and an airstrip. The lagoon offers protected anchorage for yachties but the beach is extremely tidal and not ideal for swimmers.

⊙ Sights

Musket Cove Marina　　　　MARINA
(Map p104; ☑ VHF Marine channel 68 666 2215; www.musketcovefiji.com/marina) This excellent marina attracts yachties from all over the world. There are 27 moorings ($15 per day), 25 marina berths (from $2 per metre, per day), dockside fuel and water (0.10 cents per litre, though this can be limited in the dry season), drop-mail services, a laundry, rubbish disposal, hot showers, book swap, bike hire ($30/150 per day/week), a noticeboard and limited repair services.

🛏 Sleeping & Eating

The **Trader Market Store** (Map p104; Musket Cove Marina; ⊙ 8am-7pm) is probably the best-stocked shop in the Mamanucas (don't expect mainland prices); the attached **coffee shop** makes a mean cuppa.

Plantation Island Resort　　　　RESORT $$$
(Map p104; ☑ 666 9333; www.plantationisland. com; r from $620, bungalow $470-985; ❄🛜🏊) If children aren't your thing, be sure to check your calendar for school holidays as this huge place is a family favourite. While the littlies go berserk with the excellent Coconut Kids Club, waterslide, mini-golf course and dozens of squeal-inducing activities, parents relax with beachside massages, in the grown-ups pool or on the nine-hole golf course (from $32).

Musket Cove Island Resort RESORT $$$

(Map p104; ☑664 0805; www.musketcove fiji.com; bungalow $720-950, villa $1190-1220; ❄️🛜🏊) With oodles of accommodation, eating, drinking and activity options, this sprawling resort is truly a world unto itself. Children are welcome in the garden *bures* and self-contained garden villas, but age limits apply at the beachfront *bures*, island villas and lagoon *bures*, a cluster of six airy cottages with private overwater verandahs.

Lomani Island Resort RESORT $$$

(Map p104; ☑666 8212; www.lomaniisland. com; bungalow $990, ste $740-810, breakfast incl; ❄️🛜🏊) This glamorous, adult-only resort has a long, lazy pool, a classy colonial-style bar and a twinkling outdoor restaurant (optional meal plan $140 per person): romantic on-sand meals can be arranged. There are only 24 rooms in the resort, and none are further than 30m from the sand (the impossibly stylish beachfront *bures* are but a stumble from it).

❶ Getting There & Away

The **Malolo Cat** (p103) operates transfers from Port Denarau.

Malolo

The big daddy of the Mamanuca Group has two villages, several resorts, mangroves and coastal forest. The island's highest point, **Ul- uisolo** (218m), offers panoramic views of the Mamanucas and southern Yasawas.

🛏 Sleeping & Eating

Funky Fish Beach & Surf Resort RESORT $

(Map p104; ☑666 1500; www.funkyfishresort. com; dm $46, r $99-400, bungalow $279-500; ❄️🛜🏊) With some of Fiji's best breaks less than half an hour away, and top-notch kite-boarding spots a stroll from the door, Funky Fish is a thrillseekers' delight. Daily boats head out to spots including Cloudbreak, Restaurants and Swimming Pools, and stay until guests' wave-lusts are quenched. Ten-bed dorms and cheaper privates are clean but basic, while *bures* and Cloudbreak view rooms are a class above.

Malolo Island Resort RESORT $$$

(Map p104; ☑666 9192; www.maloloisland.com; bungalow $821-1942; 🚭❄️@🏊) This crisp, 100% Fijian-owned resort caters to both families (school holidays) and couples looking for a romantic escape (rest of the year). All 46 tropical-plantation-style *bures* have sea views; some are a footstep from the white sand. Young'uns like the kids club, their own pool and beach games; bigger folks love the adults-only pool (with swim-up bar and lounge), spa, and intimate Tadra beach *bures*.

Likuliku Lagoon LUXURY HOTEL $$$

(Map p104; ☑666 3344; www.likulikulagoon.com; overwater bungalow $2990, other bungalows $1790-2590, all meals included; ❄️🛜🏊) The first (and so far only) island resort with overwater *bu- res*, this exclusive, adults-only resort offers supreme luxury, intimacy and privacy. The 10 *bures*, accessible by a boardwalk, loom over a tidal lagoon; views are unsurprisingly in-credible. Interiors are equally gasp-inducing. Back on the sand, beachfront *bures* are no less stupendous; the deluxe upgrades have private plunge pools.

Tropica Island Resort RESORT $$$

(Map p104; ☑665 1777; www.tropicaisland.com; rm $699, bungalow $999, ste $1199; ❄️🛜🏊) The Tropica has left its former incarnation as Walu Beach Resort (purpose-built for an Australian reality TV show) far, far behind to become a slick adults-only destination. There are 30 totally refurbished *bures,* suites and rooms (all but the latter have out-door showers, patios and cosy deck swings), plus a 25m infinity pool, and spa. The res-taurant serves gourmet Fijian cuisine; meal plans $160.

Castaway Island

AREA 0.7 SQ KM

Stunning, reef-fringed, 70-hectare Castaway Island, also known as Qalito, is 27km (1.5 hours) from Denarau.

🛏 Sleeping

★ Castaway Island Resort RESORT $$$

(Map p104; ☑666 1233; www.castawayfiji.com; bungalow $1140-1450; ❄️🛜🏊) This is an oldie but a very-goodie. A huge hit with families (and couples, outside of school holidays), there's something for everyone here: great kids club, family-friendly pool with water-fall, adults-only pool with swim-up bar, free non-motorised water sports, bushwalks, vil-lage excursions, shadowboxing lessons and squillions more. All free-standing *bures* are spacious and stylish, with privacy screens between parents' and kids' bedrooms.

Mana

Beautiful Mana has a good selection of beaches and a peppering of hills with spectacular views. Check out the south-beach pier for a night snorkel; the fish go into a frenzy under the wharf lights.

Sleeping & Eating

A manned guard post and a high fence separate the backpacker places from the Mana Island Resort. Escapees from the resort's dining rooms are welcome at the budget spots, but it's harder to move in the other direction.

Mana Lagoon Backpackers   HOSTEL $
(Map p104; ☑924 6573; www.manalagoon backpackers.com; tent site/dm/r incl meals $60/85/210) Owned and run by locals, this endearingly ramshackle place feels more like a village homestay than a typical backpackers. Unlike the larger resorts, there's a charming family feel here, and the thatched-roof beach shelters and sandy-floored restaurant/bar define 'mellow island holiday'. Rooms are basic and electricity is sporadic; you'll be too busy snorkelling (free) and taking part in organised activities to notice.

Ratu Kini Backpackers
and Dive Resort   HOSTEL $$
(Map p104; ☑628 2375; www.ratukinidiveresort. com.fj; camping/dm/r/bungalow incl breakfast $35/39-65/180-230/200-250; ﹡ ☎) This fun and friendly stripside spot is a longtime Mamanucas drawcard: it even attracts guests from the fancier resorts to its social sunset bar and excellent seafood restaurant. No-fuss, no-frills, decent-sized dorms share cold-water showers; quieter rooms and bures have private facilities and loads of space.

Mana Island Resort   RESORT $$$
(Map p104; ☑665 0423; www.manafiji.com; bungalow $380-900, r $470, ste $840, honeymoon bungalow $1080; ﹡ ☎ ☒) One of the oldest and largest (at 300 acres) island resorts in Fiji, the 152 rooms, suites and bures span the spacious, beautifully landscaped low-lying grounds between the north and south beaches. Mana caters for everyone – couples, honeymooners and families – the latter dominating during Australian and New Zealand school holidays. Extensive renovation work in mid-2015 hadn't stopped a near-constant flow of guests.

ⓘ Getting There & Away

Mana is serviced by South Sea Cruises catamarans, and the Mana Flyer transfer boat ($75 one way, 55 minutes) makes a daily trip to and from Nadi's New Town Beach.

Matamanoa

Matamanoa is a small private island notable for its pointy volcanic cone and ludicrously white sand beach.

Sleeping

Matamanoa Island Resort   RESORT $$$
(Map p104; ☑672 3620; www.matamanoa.com; villa/bungalow/r incl breakfast $995/895/565; ﹡ ☎ ☒) As would be expected from an up-market, adults-only resort, Matamanoa is stylish, sophisticated and peaceful. Its 33 beachfront bures and villas overlook a blindingly white, soft-sand beach, while cheaper studio-sized resort rooms have carved-wood interiors and private garden verandahs. Its refined restaurant overlooks the ocean: meal plans are $170, or $110 for dinner only; there's also an à la carte option.

Modriki

Tiny, uninhabited Modriki (ironically, not Castaway Island) featured in the 2001 Tom Hanks movie Cast Away; almost every resort sells day trips to what is increasingly referred to as 'Tom Hanks Island' (somewhat confusingly, it's also known as Monuriki). Trips cost around $100 to $140 depending on where you start out, and what kind of lunch, if any, is included.

Tokoriki

The small, hilly northern island of Tokoriki has a beautiful, fine white-sand beach facing west to the sunset.

Sleeping

Tokoriki Island Resort   RESORT $$$
(Map p104; ☑672 5926; www.tokoriki.com; bungalow $1195-1495, villa $1695; ﹡ ☎ ☒) This orchid-strewn, adults-only playground makes for the ideal swoony getaway, with all manners of honeymoon packages, deserted-island picnics and photogenic proposal nooks on offer; there's even an on-site Romance Co-ordinator! All bures and villas have outdoor showers and divine interiors; many

have private pools. Naturally, dining options are romantic, including star-lit dinners, free-flow champagne breakfasts and the intimate eight-seat teppanyaki restaurant.

Namotu & Tavarua

Namotu and Tavarua are islands at the southern edge of the Malolo Barrier Reef, which encloses the southern Mamanucas. **Namotu Island** (Map p104; www.namotuislandfiji.com) is a tiny (1.5 hectares) and pretty island; bigger **Tavarua Island** (Map p104; www.tavarua.com) is 12 hectares, rimmed by beautiful white sand. Both islands are primarily package surf resorts, geared to the American market. There is no public access.

YASAWA GROUP

Rugged, remote and more dramatic than the sugardrop islands of the Mamanucas, the mighty Yasawas were once off-limits to all but those determined to play out their Robinson Crusoe fantasies. Today, ferries, cruise ships and seaplanes make daily deposits of sun-and-fun-seekers keen to explore both its looming landscapes and eminently diveable depths.

The chain is composed of 20 or so sparsely populated and surprisingly barren islands. There are no roads, cars, banks or shops, and most of the locals live in small remote villages. Electricity is intermittent at best in many resorts, and often off at night: bring a torch in case.

🛈 Getting There & Around

Half the fun of staying in the Yasawas is getting on and off the comfortable *Yasawa Flyer* as it works its way up the chain towards Nacula. The catamaran is operated by **Awesome Adventures Fiji** (☑ 675 0499; www.awesomefiji.com; Port Denarau) and with an accommodation booking desk on-board (credit cards accepted), island-hopping travellers are often able to book their beds as they go (although resorts appreciate direct bookings, and in peak season you must book ahead.) The boat departs Denarau at 8.30am daily, calling into South Sea, Bounty, Beachcomber, Treasure and Vomo Islands in the Mamanucas before reaching the Yasawa Group. From Denarau, it takes about two hours to Kuata or Wayasewa ($137), 2½ hours to Waya ($148), three hours to Naviti ($157) and 4½ hours to Yaqeta and Matacawalevu/Tavewa, Nanuya Lailai and Nacula ($167). In the afternoon it follows the same route back to the mainland, again calling in at all of the resorts, arriving in Denarau about 5.45pm. Island-hoppers should consider a 'Bula Pass' (seven/15/21 days $490/765/845) that enables unlimited travel but only one return to Denarau. Most islands don't have wharves, so the *Flyer* pulls up seemingly in the middle of the sea to meet a swarm of dinghies (called tenders) that bounce alongside to collect and deposit guests and bags.

Seaplane charters are another option for travel from Nadi: check out **Pacific Islands Air** (☑ 672 5644; www.pacificislandair.com; from $360) and **Turtle Airways** (☑ 672 1888; www.turtleairways.com; from $275). Be sure to inform your resort so they can send their boat out to collect you from the plane!

YASAWA ISLANDS TOURS

Blue Lagoon Cruises (☑ 670 5006; www.bluelagooncruises.com) Cruises on the 55m *Fiji Princess* take a maximum 68 guests. The three-night (twin per person $1922 to $2513, single $2513 to $3252), four-night (twin $2562 to $3350, single $3350 to $4336) and seven-night (twin $4138 to $5518, single $5518 to $7243) cruises meander through the Mamanucas and Yasawas; the company has exclusive use of the best part of Blue Lagoon beach.

Captain Cook Cruises (☑ 670 1823; captaincookcruisesfiji.com) Offers all-inclusive cruises ranging from three to seven nights (from $1950 per person) in various classes and sleeping arrangements on board *Reef Endeavour*. The 68m boat has a swimming pool, bars, lounges and air-conditioned accommodation for 135 people spread over three decks.

South Sea Cruises (p103) Runs daytrips to Barefoot Kuata, Octopus and Botaira resorts. Prices are about $210/120 per adult/child.

Southern Sea Ventures (www.southernseaventures.com) This Australian-operated group offers eight-day ($3600) and 11-day (from $4070) kayak safaris through the Yasawas between May and October.

Kuata

Petite Kuata is the first Yasawa stop for the *Flyer*: its unusual volcanic rock formations make a fine first impression. The best snorkelling is off the southern end of the island; the summit can be conquered in a hot and sticky 30 minutes.

🛏 Sleeping

★ **Barefoot Kuata Island**   RESORT $$
(Map p111; ☎896 2090; www.thebarefootcollection.com/kuata-island; Kuata Island; dm $90-130, bungalow $310; 🛜🗙) ✎ This former beachbum hostel has undergone a complete overhaul to become a spectacular, stylish hideaway (without the hefty price tag). New, spacious beachside six- and eight-bed dorms offer million-dollar views; *bures* are modern with cute interiors; privates have fabulous outdoor showers. Beautiful design elements are everywhere, from the seaside footprint-shaped pools to the carved handiwork lending major 'wow' to the sand-floored restaurant/bar.

Wayasewa

Also known as Waya Lailai (Little Waya), Wayasewa is dominated by Vatuvula (349m), a volcanic rock plug that dramatically towers over the beaches below. The hike to the top is an hour's hard scramble, and views take in the whole Yasawa Group. A 15-minute boat ride from the resorts is a spot renowned for shark snorkelling. Though the mostly white-tip reef sharks are harmless, this is a heart-stopping trip. Snorkelling with the sharks with/without gear costs about $50/25: arrange through your resort.

🛏 Sleeping

Naqalia Lodge   LODGE $
(Map p111; ☎932 2650; www.naqalialodge-fiji resort.com; Wayasewa Island; camping/dm/d bungalow incl meals $60/100/250; @) These wonderful, community-owned digs may not be fancy, but if you're looking to experience life as part of a Fijian family, drop your bags. Run by Wayasewa villagers, Naqalia (pronounced *nun-GA-lia*) has five traditionally built *bures* with handpainted interiors and wooden verandahs, and a simple 12-bed dorm; camping is also available.

Waya Lailai Resort   HOSTEL $
(Map p111; ☎603 0215; www.wayalailairesort.com; Wayasewa Island; camping $70, dm from $120, room from $200, bungalow from $270; @) Owned and operated by Wayasewa villagers, this rustic hostel enjoys a dramatic setting at the base of the Vatuvula volcanic plug. Accommodation is tiered over two levels above the beach, and includes dorms (five- or 26-beds), private singles and doubles in a former hilltop schoolhouse, and spacious traditional *bures* – two of which have cool lofts – with private balconies above the beach.

Waya

With rugged hills, beautiful lagoons and a periphery of long sandy beaches, Waya is easy on the eyes. Walkers can tackle the summit of Ului Nakauka (three hours return from Octopus Resort) and snorkellers can explore the thick rim of coral that traces the island.

🛏 Sleeping

★ **Octopus Resort**   RESORT $$
(Map p111; ☎777 0030; www.octopusresort.com; Waya Island; dm $38-68, bungalow $213-640, ste $915, family villa $1214-2080; two-night minimum stay; ❄🛜🗙) From good, no-bunk dorms to stand-alone *bures* in an array of configurations, all the way up to top-end suites and family villas, Octopus offers something for everyone. Despite the disparity, it all works out: this is a favourite Yasawas getaway for both family and free-wheeling types. With a beach perfect for slacking or snorkelling, super-friendly staff and amenities galore, what's not to love?

Naviti & Around

AREA 33 SQ KM

One of the largest (33 sq km) and highest (up to 380m) of the Yasawa islands, Naviti has a rugged volcanic profile and a dazzling snorkelling site where you can swim with manta rays. The best time to see the giant rays is between June and August, although they may be around as early as May and as late as October. Resorts in the area offer snorkelling trips for around $45 per person plus snorkel hire, with spotters heading out in the mornings ahead of the tours to check where the animals are.

Yasawa Group

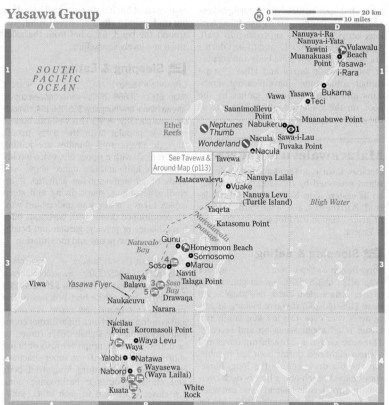

N 0 ————————— 20 km
   0 ————————— 10 miles

FIJI NAVITI & AROUND

🛏 Sleeping & Eating

★ **Mantaray Island Resort**   RESORT **$$**
(Map p111; ☎776 6351; www.mantarayisland.
com; Nanuya Balavu Island; dm $41, bungalow $150-
285, villa $485; ☀☎) This happening hideaway
can be whatever you want it to be: backpacker
party central or high-end escape. Lodgings
are spread across a small hill and two pretty
beaches: the 32-bed dorm and treehouse *bu-
res* are tucked away up a forested path, while
self-contained jungle *bures* and posh new
beachfront villas skirt the sand, far enough
from the lively bar to be peaceful.

Barefoot Manta Island   RESORT **$$**
(Map p111; ☎707 7328; www.thebarefootcollec
tion.com/manta-island; Drawaqa Island; dm $45-65,
bungalow $310, compulsory meal package $75; ☎)
This refurbished and rebranded resort hasn't
let its (continuing) upgrade go to its head:
though magnificent, Barefoot Manta is decidedly low-key. Most guests are here to take

---

Yasawa Group

◎ Sights
1 Sawa-i-Lau Cave D2

🛏 Sleeping
2 Barefoot Kuata Island B4
3 Barefoot Manta Island.......................B3
4 Korovou Eco-Tour Resort...................B3
5 Mantaray Island Resort......................B3
6 Naqalia Lodge B4
7 Octopus Resort B4
8 Waya Lailai Resort B4

---

part in underwater activities; as the name im-
plies, this is a top spot for goggling at manta
rays, with swim safaris running between May
to October. Custom dive packages, kayaking,
hikes and village visits are also available.

Korovou Eco-Tour Resort   HOSTEL **$$**
(Map p111; ☎925 5370; www.korovouecotour
resort.com; Naviti Island; dm/bungalow/villa incl
meals $140/350/450; ☎☀) This recently

renovated spot attracts chatty backpackers and sociable families for its fish-filled reef, long activities list and super-friendly staff. Surprisingly spacious 17- and 31-bed dorms are notable for their solid beds and surplus of toilets, while *bures* and villas – some timber, some stone – have pleasant verandahs and ensuites. Guests gather by the pool, on the giant restaurant deck and at the good-timey Bula Bar.

Matacawalevu & Yaqeta

Matacawalevu is a 4km-long hilly volcanic island protected by the large Nasomo Bay on its eastern side. Nanuya Levu (Turtle Island) is to the east, and to the south, across a protected lagoon used for seaweed farming, is Yaqeta.

🛏 Sleeping & Eating

Long Beach Backpackers HOSTEL **$**
(Map p113; 📞 925 5370; www.longbeachresort fiji.com; Matacawalevu Island; dm/bungalow incl meals $105/180-260) If you're looking to party, avert your eyes: this low-key, family-run hostel is all about seclusion and serenity. There are garden and beachfront *bures* and a clean eight-bed dorm: both are liveable, but the big draw here is the long, horseshoe-shaped beach and a breezy deck overlooking tiny Deviulau island – you can wade over at low tide and scramble to the top for great views.

Navutu Stars BOUTIQUE HOTEL **$$$**
(Map p113; 📞 664 0553; www.navutustars fiji.com; Yaqeta Island; bungalow incl breakfast $747-1264; ❄🛜🏊) This intimate resort specialises in Pacific-style decadence: think petal-sprinkled baths, romantic sunset dining and complimentary massages on arrival. The nine whitewashed *bures* have exquisitely detailed 8m-high roofs, space galore and fantastic views. If you can haul yourself out of your king-sized bed, there's free yoga every morning. Food is fabulous, a fusion of Italian specialities with local ingredients. Optional full/half meal plan is $185/120.

Tavewa

AREA 3 SQ KM

This small, low island houses some of the Yasawa Group's northernmost resorts. A pleasant beach unfurls itself on the south-eastern coast but it's often plagued by buffeting trade winds. Head to Savutu Point, just around the bend, for relief from the gales and some lovely snorkelling.

🛏 Sleeping & Eating

Coralview Resort HOSTEL **$**
(Map p113; 📞 666 2648; www.coralview.com.fj; Tavewa Island; dm/bungalow $55/156-194; compulsory meal plan $89; ❄🛜) This well-run budget resort is popular with the party people (though adventurous families are joining their ranks): with a ripper bar, twice-weekly *lovo*/disco/knife-and-fire dance show, and loads of adrenalin-spiking activities – including jet-skiing, shark diving and steep sunset hikes – it's easy to understand why. Air-conditioned dorms with partitions offer a semblance of privacy; garden and beachfront *bures* have patios and nice interiors.

★Coconut Beach Resort RESORT **$$**
(Map p113; 📞 945 7505; www.coconutbeach fiji.com; Tavewa Island; bungalow $250-350; 🛜) Occupying one of the best beaches in the Yasawas, this brand-new resort is an up-and-coming star. Set on a huge former copra plantation, its five stylish *bures* (more, to be dotted along the preposterously enticing shoreline, are planned) are super-spacious, comfortable and feature king-sized beds and stunning outdoor bathrooms; none are closer than 40m to each other, guaranteeing an immensely laid-back, private-paradise feel.

It's not a 'resorty' resort – there's no pool or kids club – but rather an ideal spot to unwind, snorkel (there's a vibrant marine sanctuary right off the sand) and eat yourself into a happy stupor: the chef is renown for his hearty meals and legendary afternoon teas (compulsory meal plan adult/child $89/49).

Nanuya Lailai

This is it, folks – home to the most famous of all the Yasawas' beaches, the **Blue Lagoon**. Crystalline and glossy, it doesn't disappoint the bevy of swimmers, snorkellers, divers, and people on cruise boats or yachts who dabble in its gorgeous, lucent depths.

The settlement of Enadala is on the exposed eastern side of Nanuya Lailai; a well-trodden track connects it with the Blue Lagoon.

Tavewa & Around

🛏 Sleeping & Eating

Gold Coast Inn
HOMESTAY $

(Map p113; 📞 925 5370; www.goldcoastinn-yasawas.com; dm/bungalow incl meals $105/250) This is a smallish affair – there are only five *bures* and a small 10-bed dorm – but it's run by a lovely family with a big heart. It's not the place for those expecting luxury: showers are cold and electricity can be sporadic. The beach, however, is gorgeous, and the Fiji-style meals are wholesome. A plus for parents: free babysitting!

Nanuya Island Resort
BOUTIQUE HOTEL $$$

(Map p113; 📞 666 7633; www.nanuyafiji.com; villas incl breakfast $389-1250; two-night minimum stay; ❄🛜) A short walk from the azure waters of the Blue Lagoon, this swish spot is the epitome of holiday indulgence and serenity (no kids under seven). The new Australian owners have given the romantic resort a makeover (work was still underway in 2015),

Tavewa & Around

with the addition of a luxurious honeymoon villa, four thatched-roof 'superior' villas (with spas and sundecks) and 24-hour solar power.

Nacula

Blanketed with rugged hills and soft peaks, the interior of the third-largest island in the Yasawas (22 sq km) is laced with well-trodden paths leading to villages and small coves. Nacula's **Long Beach** is one of the best in the Yasawas.

🛏 Sleeping & Eating

Nabua Lodge HOSTEL **$**
(Map p113; ☑ 925 5370; www.nabualodge-yasawa. com; dm $110, bungalow from $260; 🛜) Nabua's utterly relaxed vibe and welcome-to-the-family sociability make this budget spot stand out from the crowd almost as much as their pink *bures* do. Staring down at the sea from a well-maintained, hammock-strewn grassy plot, this is a good place for catching up on holiday reading, taking part in nightly Fiji-flavoured events or hopping out on a cave tour. All meals are included.

⭐ Blue Lagoon Beach Resort RESORT **$$**
(Map p113; ☑ 603 0223; www.bluelagoonbeach resort.com.fj; dm $30, r from $172, bungalow $316-870; 🌬🛜🏊) Blue Lagoon ticks all the right boxes: its beach is gorgeous, staff are friendly but unobtrusive, and while it's small enough to be low-key, it's big enough (about 100 guests when full) to have a bit of buzz. It caters for all budgets in a compatible way; *bures* are stylish (the beachfront digs are divine) and the two eight-bed air-conditioned dorms are sparkling.

Sawa-i-Lau

Must-see Sawa-i-Lau is a stand-out limestone island – housing two **caves** – amid a string of those formed by volcanoes. The underwater limestone is thought to have formed a few hundred metres below the surface and then uplifted over time. Shafts of daylight enter a great dome-shaped cave – its walls soar 15m above the water surface – where you can swim in a mind-bogglingly beautiful natural pool. With a guide, a torch and a bit of courage, you can also swim through an underwater passage into an adjoining chamber. The walls have carvings, paintings and inscriptions of unknown meaning.

Most Yasawa resorts offer trips to the caves for around $60 per person.

OVALAU & THE LOMAIVITI ISLANDS

POP 12,065 / AREA 409 SQ KM

Despite its proximity to Viti Levu, the Lomaiviti group is often overlooked as a tourist destination in Fiji. Its residents may moan this is unfair, and if you make it here you'll understand why. It was in Levuka, the capital of the main island Ovalau, that the first Europeans settled and eventually made this the country's first capital. Its wild and immoral colonial days are long over but you'll likely be seduced by its laid-back charms and welcoming atmosphere.

South of Ovalau, the tiny coral islands of Leleuvia and Caqalai have sandy beaches, good snorkelling and simple budget resorts.

Ovalau and the Lomaiviti group were badly affected by 2016's Cyclone Winston. On little Koro Island, 100% of homes were reportedly destroyed.

❶ Getting There & Around

From Suva **Northern Air** (☑ 347 5005; www. northernair.com.fj) flies to Ovalau ($86 one way, 12 minutes, Monday to Saturday) at 8am and returns to Suva at 8.40am. The airstrip is about 40 minutes' drive from Levuka. A taxi costs about $30.

Patterson Brothers Shipping (☑ 344 0125; Suite 2, Level 2, Epworth Arcade, Nina Street, Suva; ◷ 8.30am-4.30pm Mon-Fri, to noon Sat) has a daily combined bus-ferry service from Suva to Levuka via Natovi Landing ($35, four to six hours), leaving from Suva Bus Station at 1.30pm, and from Levuka at 5am. Arrive 30 minutes before departure.

The resorts on the islands near Ovalau (all except Koro) offer private transfers in their own boats to either Natovi, Bau or Waidalice landings on Viti Levu and to Levuka.

Ovalau

Ovalau is the largest island in the Lomaiviti Group. At the centre of the island is an extinct volcano and several mountains which offer nice hiking, as well as the captivating old colonial centre of Levuka, the only place in the Lomaiviti Group with decent banks, shops and services.

🏃 Activities

Diving & Snorkelling
The Lomaiviti waters offer some wonderful, little-visited dive sites where you can encounter manta rays, hammerheads, turtles, white-tip reef sharks and lionfish. Blue Ridge, off Wakaya island, is famous for its bright-blue ribbon eels. There is stunning soft coral at Snake Island, just off Caqalai, in the Moturiki Channel, and excellent hard coral at Waitovu Passage.

Wakaya Club, Leleuvia Island Resort and Naigani Island Resort offer diving.

Yachting
Levuka is a port of entry into Fiji for yachties and there are a few good spots to put down anchor in the Lomaiviti Group. You can anchor in Levuka harbour to explore Ovalau, and good desert-island spots to park include Leleuvia island and Dere Bay on Koro island. Try VHF marine channel 16 to reach the appropriate authorities if entering the country at Levuka, but if no one answers, anchor near Queen's Wharf and make your way ashore.

👉 Tours

The Ovalau Tourist Information Centre offers walking tours around Levuka.

Tours with Nox   WALKING TOUR
(☑344 0077) Offers historical walking tours of Levuka ($10) and hiking to waterfalls in the hills. Contact Nox through Levuka Homestay (p116).

Epi's Tours   TOUR
(☑977 9977, 746 0700; epistours@gmail.com; Levuka historical tour $10; Lovoni day trip $50-80; Nadelaiovalau Peak $20-30) Offers historical tours of Levuka town, day trips to the volcanic crater or Lovoni (with river swimming and traditional Fijian lunch), and a half-day hike to The Peak (487m), a summit overlooking Levuka, where you can learn about Ovalau's

wild foods and medicinal plants, as well as doing a trek up Nadelaiovalau Peak (626m), the highest point on the island.

Levuka

POP 3750

There's no denying Levuka's visual appeal. It's one of the few places in the South Pacific that has retained its colonial buildings: along the main street, timber shopfronts straight out of a Hollywood western are sandwiched between blue sea and fertile green mountains. The effect is quite beguiling – you can almost taste the wild frontier days of this former whaling outpost. In 2013 Levuka was listed by Unesco as Fiji's first World Heritage Site.

Buildings to keep an eye out for include the **Sacred Heart Church** (1858); Levuka's **original police station** (1874); the **Ovalau Club** (1904), Fiji's first private club; and the **former town hall** (1898). You'll also find the stone shell of the South Pacific's first **Masonic Lodge** (1875) and Levuka's only Romanesque building. It was burnt to a husk in the 2000 coup by villagers egged on by their church leaders.

Many of Levuka's historic buildings were badly damaged by Cyclone Winston in 2016.

👁 Sights

Former Morris Hedstrom   HISTORIC BUILDING
(Map p116; Beach St) The 1868 former Morris Hedstrom (MH) trading store is the original MH store in Fiji. Behind its restored facade are the Levuka Community Centre, a library and a branch of the Fiji Museum, which holds a small exhibition detailing the history of Levuka, including some wonderful old photos of the town from colonial days.

199 Steps of Mission Hill   HILL
(Map p116) There are many old colonial homes on Levuka's hillsides, and the romantically named 199 Steps of Mission Hill are worth climbing for the fantastic view – although if you count them, you might find there are closer to 185 steps.

🛏 Sleeping

Royal Hotel   HOTEL $
(Map p116; ☑344 0024; www.royallevuka.com; s/d/tr $32/53/73, cottages $90-150; ❋❄) The Royal is the oldest hotel in the South Pacific, dating back to the 1860s (though it was rebuilt in the early 1900s after a fire) and it's got the character to back it up. This proud

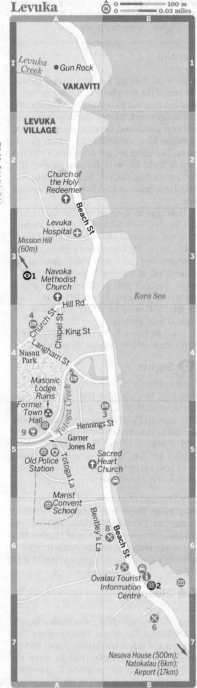

Levuka

⊙ Sights

🛏 Sleeping

⊗ Eating

⊕ Drinking & Nightlife

timber building is thick with colonial atmosphere, although the creaking wooden floorboards is sometimes matched by a similarly creaky approach to customer service.

Clara's Holiday Lodge   HOSTEL $
(Map p116; ☏ 344 0013; clarasholidaylodge@
rocketmail.com; Beach St; dm/s/d with shared
bathroom incl breakfast $25/40/50) The white-
washed wooden rooms at Clara's Holiday
Lodge are pretty basic, as are the shared
bathrooms. It's friendly enough though
and central, and meals can be prepared on
request ($15).

★ Levuka Homestay   B&B $$
(Map p116; ☏ 344 0777; www.levukahomestay.
com; Church St; s/d incl breakfast $60/180, extra
person $50; 🛜) Far and away the most chic
choice in Levuka – a multi-level house with
four large, comfortable, light-filled rooms
with terraces, each one on its own level. The
laid-back owners live on the highest level,
where guests come to eat a truly spectacular
breakfast or swap stories with them on their
enormous deck overlooking the sea.

🍴 Eating

★ Whale's Tale   WESTERN $
(Map p116; ☏ 344 0235; Beach St; mains around
$13.50; ⊙ 9.30am-2pm, 5-9pm Mon-Sat) This
perennial Levuka favourite is a charming
little place with big windows for watching
the world go by and a bamboo thatched
kitchen at the back. The fish and chips is a
classic, but look out for local river prawns,
deliciously light cassava cakes, and other
specials. It doesn't sell alcohol but allows

BYO (the mini-market next door sells booze).

Kim's Paak Kum Loong CHINESE $
(Map p116; ☑ 344 0059; Beach St; mains $9-15, breakfast $4-10.50; ☉ 7am-3pm, 5-9pm Mon-Sat, 11am-2pm, 6-9pm Sun) This is the best place to get Chinese food in Levuka, sat above the Westpac Bank. The menu has a bit of Thai and Fijian influence thrown in, while if you come in the morning it does a good line in cooked breakfasts. There's a good street-side balcony for voyeurs. Serves alcohol.

Horizon Restaurant PIZZA $
(Map p116; ☑ 344 0429; Beach St; mains $9-17, pizza from $13.50; ☉ 8am-2pm, 5-9pm Mon-Sat, 5-9pm Sun) You can get curries, fish and chips, and other European meals here, but locals recommend it because of the pizza, which is, apparently, very hit and miss – 'either one of the best pizzas you've ever tasted or a total disaster' was one comment. If you're willing to take the risk, go for one of the many fishy toppings – the tuna is the most fitting since the cannery's right on the doorstep.

🍷 Drinking & Entertainment

There are a number of pool halls where locals like to pot balls to pop music.

Ovalau Club BAR
(Map p116; Nasau Park) This extremely atmospheric and the white timber colonial-style building is a sight in its own right. Once Levuka's favourite drinking spot, it's currently closed due to a dispute over ownership, but we list it here in the hope that its door may re-open soon.

Vintage Bar BAR
(Map p116; Beach St; ☉ 10am-2pm & 4pm-1am Mon-Sat, 4pm-1am Sun) In the same building as the Horizon Restaurant, but tucked around the back, this is currently Levuka's main place to drink.

ℹ Information

There are Westpac and BSP Bank ATMs right next to each other on Beach St.
Levuka Hospital (Map p116; ☑ 344 0221; Beach St; ☉ outpatient treatment 8am-1pm & 2-4pm Mon-Fri, to noon Sat, emergencies only after hours) A good, new hospital at the northern end of town.
Ovalau Tourist Information Centre (Map p116; ☑ 330 0356; Levuka Community Centre, Morris Hedstrom Bldg; ☉ 8am-1pm

& 2-4.30pm Mon-Fri, to 1pm Sat) Has an information board detailing Ovalau's accommodation and food options and also organises Levuka town tours.
Police Station (Map p116; ☑ 344 0222; Totoga Lane)
Post Office (Map p116; Beach St) Near Queen's Wharf at the southern end of town; there's a cardphone outside.

Caqalai

Teeny little Caqalai island (pronounced 'Thangalai') lies just south of Moturiki. It only takes 15 minutes to walk around the island perimeter's beautiful golden-sand beaches, which are fringed with palms, electric-blue water and spectacular reef.

Walk out to **Snake Island** (named after the many black-and-white-banded sea snakes here) at low tide and swim around the reef: it's a veritable wonderland of soft and hard corals and home to a mind-boggling array of fish including massive Napoleon wrasses. Take reef shoes; the walkway can be hard on the feet.

🛏 Sleeping

Caqalai Island Resort RESORT $
(Map p70; ☑ 362 0388; www.fijiislandresort caqalai.com; camping (own tent)/dm/bungalow per person full board $55/65/75, boat transfers $40) Caqalai Island Resort is a gem of a backpackers and is run by Moturiki's Methodist Church, but don't let that scare you – you'll find more kava here than kumbaya (but bring your own alcohol if you prefer that to the muddy stuff). Accommodation is in big, basic *bures*, scattered between the palm trees and hibiscus. Cold-water showers are in a shared block.

Locals come over from Moturiki or Leleuvia in the evenings and there's often some singing and dancing and a kava session. The resort offers village trips to Moturiki ($10), boat trips to tiny Honeymoon Island ($15) and day trips to Leleuvia ($10). Boat transfers from the mainland are from Waidalice Landing, a 90-minute bus ride from Suva.

ℹ Getting There & Away

Boat transfers ($40) to the resort from the mainland are from Waidalice Landing, a 90-minute bus ride from Suva.

Leleuvia

Just south of Caqalai sits beautiful Leleuvia, another stunning palm-fringed coral island (slightly larger than Caqalai) wrapped in white, powdery beaches with outstanding views out to sea.

🛏 Sleeping

⭐ **Leleuvia Island Resort** RESORT **$$**
(Map p70; ☑ 999 2340; www.leleuvia.com; dm $40, bungalow $160, meal package $50, boat transfers adult/child return $84/42) Leleuvia Island Resort is a decent choice for couples looking for comfort and a fantastic choice for families thanks to the sandy bottom and shallow swimming at the island's point. Thatched *bures* here are basic but classy with views of the sea and trade winds pouring through for natural ventilation.

A large, open, sand-floored bar and restaurant area serves cold beer and tasty meals and at the resort's 'entrance' is a gorgeous wide stretch of beach with sun loungers and kayaks. There's even an art gallery. The staff put on all kinds of entertainment (such as kava drinking and beach bonfires). While the snorkelling is not on a par with Caqalai, it is still excellent and you can hire equipment. Village trips, diving and fishing excursions are also possible. Leleuvia is popular with the weekend crowd from Suva, so advance bookings are recommended. Boat transfers from the mainland are from Waidalice Landing, a 90-minute bus ride from Suva.

❶ Getting There & Away

Return boat transfers to/from Waidalice or Bau Landing are $84 (call in advance for a pick-up). Waidalice is about a 1½-hour bus ride from Suva; Leleuvia is one hour from Levuka.

VANUA LEVU

POP 135,961

Though it's Fiji's second-largest island, Vanua Levu ('Big Island') is one of the tropics' best-kept secrets. It's another world from the bustle of Viti Levu and the more touristed islands: many roads are little more than rutted dirt tracks, and Labasa, the island's largest 'city', is a one-street strip of shops. To the south, Savusavu entices yachties, divers and dreamers looking for a tropical idyll. The rest of 'Big Island' is given over to sugarcane and copra plantations, hideaway villages, mountain passes streaming with waterfalls, endless swaths of forest and an ever-changing coastline forgotten by the world. Take it slow, keep a smile on your face and savour rural Fiji on its grandest scale

❶ Getting There & Around

AIR

Flying is the easiest way to get to Vanua Levu. **Fiji Airways** (p147; billed as Fiji Link for domestic services) runs regular flights to/from Labasa, Nadi, Suva and Taveuni; for the brave (landings are notoriously bumpy), there are also flights in and out of Savusavu. The smaller **Northern Air** (p147) flies to Labasa and Savusavu from Suva.

The Labasa airport is about 11km southwest of Labasa. There's a bus that passes the airport about every hour, but it doesn't link up with flights and you'll have to go out to the main road to flag it down. A taxi from Labasa costs about $15.

Savusavu's airstrip is 3km south of town.

BOAT

To/From Taveuni

Two ferries ply the waters between Natuvu (Buca Bay) on Vanua Levu's east and the 'Korean Wharf' at Lovonivonu in Taveuni.

Grace Ferry (☑ 995 0775; ⊙ Sun-Fri; $15 each way) runs every day but Saturday. It leaves Taveuni at 8am and arrives at Natuvu on Vanua Levu at 9am; it returns to Taveuni at 9.30am. Express buses leave Labasa (bus-ferry ticket $35) at 4.30am and Savusavu (bus-ferry ticket $25) at 7am and arrive at Natuvu with plenty of time before the ferry departs.

The **Egi One** (☑ 708 0390; ⊙ Mon-Sat; $10 each way) runs Monday to Saturday. It leaves Taveuni at 7.30am, and departs Vanua Levu for the return trip around 9.30am or 10am. The company runs a bus from Savusavu to Natuvu ($7) at 7am; plans were afoot in 2016 to include a Labasa leg as well.

In addition to the ferries, the *Lomaiviti Princess* run by **Goundar Shipping** (☑ 330 1035; www. goundarshipping.com; Kong's Shop, Main St, Savusavu) leaves Savusavu for Taveuni (adult/ child $30/10) on Tuesday and Saturday mornings around 9am as part of its Suva route.

To/From Suva

Bligh Water Shipping (☑ 999 2536; www. blighwatershipping.com.fj) and Goundar Shipping both ply the waters between Suva and Savusavu; check their websites for timetables.

CAR

Vanua Levu's remote, tropical roads are crying out to be explored by 4WD. Hire cars are available in Labasa and Savusavu. Petrol stations are scarce and usually closed on Sundays, so plan to fill up in Labasa, Savusavu or Seaqaqa.

It's also possible to navigate the island by bus, but timetables can be erratic and journeys take far longer.

Just remember, you cannot wander on foot through the countryside without permission from the landowners.

Savusavu & Around

Before you book your tickets, a word of warning: once in Savusavu, there is a very good chance you won't ever want to leave. Preposterously picturesque and affable beyond all expectations, Savusavu is a swashbuckling throwback to the days of high-seas adventure and tall tales told in rollicking, rickety taverns. The storybook Savusavu Bay was once a gigantic volcano, and boiling springs still bubble up across town, perhaps accounting – at least in part – for the palpable energy that surrounds this enchanted outpost. As the sole point of entry for yachts on Vanua Levu – and home to two excellent marinas – Savusavu is constantly abuzz with dropped-anchor old salts mingling with lively locals and travellers looking to escape the well-trodden trail.

◉ Sights & Activities

Diving & Snorkelling

Far and away the best diving around Vanua Levu – and arguably in all of Fiji – is at Namena Marine Reserve (Map p120; www.namena.org; park fees $30, valid one year), a protected 70 sq km park housing corals so vibrant and marine life so plentiful that it's become the poster child for Fiji's underwater world. It's about a two-hour boat ride from Savusavu.

The best sites closer in are just outside Savusavu Bay (about a 20-minute boat ride) and include the suitable-for-all-levels Dreadlocks, with its multicoloured hard- and soft-coral garden; Dreamhouse, home to hammerheads, great schools of barracuda, jacks and tuna at a coral outcrop; Dungeons and Dragons, a towering maze of dive-throughs; and Nasonisoni Passage, an incredible drift dive that sucks thrillseekers along by a strong current.

Some resorts have in-house dive centres; others can arrange diving trips for guests.

KoroSun Dive   DIVING

(Map p120; ☑970 6605, 934 1033; www.korosundive.com; Savasi Island resort) Colin and Janine run an attentive and professional centre that caters just as well to beginners as it does to advanced divers. Two-tank dives/PADI Open Water Courses, including all gear, cost $230/850; snorkelling trips are $35. Multi-day dives are recommended, as discounts apply. In addition to spectacular dives just 15 minutes from shore, they also offer trips to the Somosomo Strait and Namena Marine Reserve.

Jean-Michel Cousteau Diving   DIVING

(Map p120; ☑885 0694; www.jeanmichelcousteaudiving.com) As befitting the name, this is a top-notch centre that gets rave reviews from seasoned divers from around the world; it's also the only outfit that regularly visits the drift-dive Nasonisoni Passage. It's based at Jean-Michel Cousteau Fiji Islands Resort. Two-tank dives/PADI Open Water Courses cost $335/1145.

Aboard A Dream   DIVING

(☑828 3030, 929 7041; www.aboardadream.com) This highly regarded outfit offers two- to five-day charters (two/four people from $2000/2800; includes diving for those certified) and half- and full-day snorkelling charters ($1100/1800) of Namena Marine Reserve and other fantastic nearby spots. These are intimate trips: there's a maximum of four guests on live-aboard trips, and 14 on day tours. Hosts Tommy and Nadine have a wealth of local diving experience.

Tui Tai Expeditions   DIVING

(Map p124; ☑999 6365; www.tuitai.com; five nights from s $4045-12,090, d $8956, seven nights from s $3191-9208, d $6821) A voyage with Tui Tai Expeditions is a fantastic way to see and do a lot in a short time. Sailing between Vanua Levu, Taveuni, and remote islands including Kioa, Rabi and the Ringgold Attols, you'll get to snorkel, kayak, bike, trek, swim, fish, dive or just lounge on deck to your heart's content. Prices include all meals and activities except diving.

Diving on the five-/seven-night trips costs $1160/1480; individual dives are $150.

Other liveaboard options that visit the region include Nai'a (www.naia.com.fj; from US$3626) and Siren Fleet (www.sirenfleet.com; liveaboards from €2995).

Vanua Levu

FIJI SAVUSAVU & AROUND

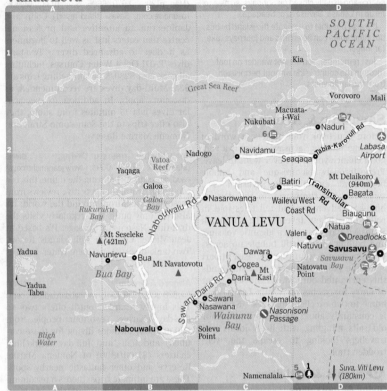

Vanua Levu

◎ Sights
1 Namena Marine Reserve D4

✦ Activities, Courses & Tours
Jean-Michel Cousteau Diving........(see 4)
KoroSun Dive................................(see 9)

🛏 Sleeping
Bayside Bure ....(see 4)
Daku Resort..................................(see 3)
2 Emaho Sekawa Luxury Resort............. D3

3 Gecko Lodge D3
4 Jean-Michel Cousteau Fiji Islands
Resort D3
5 Namena Island Resort.............................D4
Naveria Heights Lodge.................. (see 3)
6 Nukubati Island Resort..........................C2
7 Palmlea Farms Resort.............................D2
8 Salt Lake Lodge E3
9 Savasi Island E3
Vosa Ni Ua Lodge........................... (see 9)

Other Activities

There are **hot springs** behind the playing field and near the wharf. The shallow streams are literally boiling and locals come to cook food in them. You'll scald yourself if you touch them.

Rafa's Adventure Tours ADVENTURE TOUR
(☎838 0406; www.rafasadventuretours.weebly.com) These fun tours get top marks for their

friendly and knowledgeable guides. Set trips include an island adventure (including snorkelling, hiking and *lovo* lunch, $150), village and snorkelling tours ($125), waterfall visits ($95) and four-hour hikes up the Nakula Trail ($95); you can also customise your own tours.

J Hunter Pearls BOAT TOUR
(Map p124; ☎885 0821; www.fijipearls.com; $25; ☉tours 9.30am & 1.30pm Mon-Fri) Learn

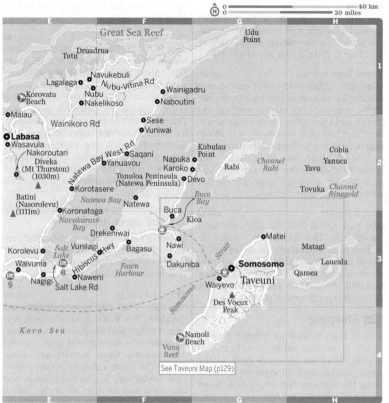

all about how black pearls are farmed before heading out on a glass-bottom boat to the floating farm. If you want to snorkel the oyster lines, bring your own gear and jump in; otherwise you can see everything from the boat. During seeding seasons (April to May and October to November), watch 'pearl technicians' implanting and harvesting pearls from the oysters.

Trip n Tour ISLAND TOURS
(Map p124; ☑ 992 8154, 885 3154; tripntour@connect.com.fj; Copra Shed Marina) These friendly folks offer a range of tours around Vanua Levu, including trips to a copra plantation and Waisali Rainforest ($69; minimum two people). They can also organise fishing trips and rent scooters.

Bagata Eco Tours CULTURAL TOUR
(☑ 961 5942; www.bagatavillage.com; $200) If you've had your fill of water-based activities, try a deep-end dive into village life. These tours explore Bagata, a small settlement 20km from Savusavu. Guests are welcomed into village homes and the church, and are treated to a *meke* and afternoon tea. Dress modestly and bring a *sevusevu* (customary gift for the chief) of dried kava: pick this up at the Savusavu markets.

Tours are $200 per group of six. Money from the tours funds village projects and provides scholarships for local kids.

You'll have to make your own way to Bagata: taxis ($40) or buses ($3) run regularly. The tours run from 2pm to 4pm daily.

Hot Springs HOT SPRING
(Map p124; ☑ 923 9043; savusavumedicalcentre@yahoo.com; $15; ⊙8am-4pm Mon-Fri) The Savusavu Medical Centre, beside the Hot Springs, has three therapeutic spa baths (40°C), and welcomes visitors. No appointment necessary.

Marinas

Use VHF marine channel 16 for assistance in locating moorings on arrival. The marinas can arrange for the relevant officials to visit your boat to process your arrival into Fiji.

Copra Shed Marina MARINA
(Map p124; ☑885 0457; www.coprashed.com) Starting life as a copra mill back in the late 1800s, this charming marina now attracts yachties and passerbys for its range of services and laid-back waterfront vibe. Moorings in the pretty harbour between Savusavu and Nawi Island cost $13.25/342.45 per day/month; berths per foot per day/week $0.50/3. Salty dogs will appreciate the hot showers and laundry facilities.

Waitui Marina MARINA
(Map p124; ☑835 3913, 885 3057; www.waitui marinafiji.com) This endearingly ramshackle marina is as atmospheric as all-get-out. It has 25 well-maintained helix moorings, plus showers, laundry and a wonderful club in a beautiful, restored boat shed. Moorings cost $12/80/300 per day/week/month.

🛏 Sleeping

Stay in town to soak up South Sea sailor charm, or venture out to some incredible resorts, either on Lesiaceva Point to the southwest, Savusavu Rd to the northwest or along the Hibiscus Hwy to the east. Buses service all locations regularly.

🛏 In Town

Savusavu Budget Lodge GUESTHOUSE $
(Map p124; ☑999 3127; www.savusavubudget lodge.com; Main St; s/d with fan $45/60, s/d with air-con $65/75, f $95; ❄🕸) The best low-budget option in Savusavu, this place is clean, welcoming and just a skip from the centre of town. Rooms are small but bright, with private hot water bathrooms, and there's an upstairs lounge and a balcony overlooking the street and the water. Breakfast is included.

Naveria Heights Lodge B&B $$
(Map p120; ☑885 0348; www.naveriaheights fiji.com; r incl breakfast $200-500; 🕸🛁) This boutique B&B can be as active or as chilled as you want it to be: choose between yoga classes, river tubing, mountain biking, snorkelling, hiking, or doing sweet nothing at all. It can also organise diving trips. Perched on a jungly hill, the lodge's three elegant, polished-wood rooms

have stunning bay views and open up to a fabulous sun deck.

Hot Springs Hotel HOTEL $$
(Map p124; ☑885 0195; www.hotspringsfiji.com; Nakama Rd; r with fan/air-con $105-165, studio $215, f from $310, apt $370; P❄🕸🛁) Every room in this huge hotel has a balcony with picture-postcard views over Savusavu Bay and an expanse of technicolour-green lawn. The rooms don't have a world of personality, but they are very clean and spacious; good-sized studios and apartments have well-equipped kitchenettes. It's a great option for families and self-caterers. The hotel also has a bar, restaurant and a pool overlooking the bay.

🛏 Lesiaceva Road

Lesiaceva Rd runs southwest along the peninsula from Savusavu for about 10km; it's home to some great places to stay and several white-sand beaches.

★ Gecko Lodge LODGE $
(Map p120; ☑921 3181; www.geckolodgefiji.com; r from $100; P❄🕸) Gecko's is a fantastic new budget option that combines Savusavu convenience (it's a three-minute drive to town) with away-from-it-all serenity and scenic vistas. The three colourful rooms-with-a-view are all very big, air-conditioned, and have their own en suite and fridge: there's a great communal kitchen too, though the hugely hospitable owners prepare fantastic meals upon request ($15). It also offers Indian cooking lessons.

Bayside Bure BUNGALOW $
(Map p120; ☑885 0556, 992 8154; Lesiaceva Point Rd; bungalow $120; 🕸) This sweet, bright-white little cottage sleeps two and has a decent kitchen with a gas stove, and TV and DVD player. There's a beach across the road that is excellent for snorkelling and kayaking. It's 6km out from Savusavu.

Daku Resort RESORT $$
(Map p120; ☑885 0046; www.dakuresort.com; Lesiaceva Point Rd; bungalow/villa from $235-555; ❄🕸🛁) A resort-cum-self-improvement centre, Daku offers a diverse array of courses from gospel singing and watercolour painting to meditation and yoga. If doing nothing makes your chakras sing, flop down by the inviting pool or book a massage. Accommodation is in neat *bures,* villas with plunge pools, or private three- or four-bedroom

houses (from $365) that are ideal for groups. All have wonderful views.

Jean-Michel Cousteau
Fiji Islands Resort RESORT $$$
(Map p120; ☑ 885 0188; www.fijiresort.com; bungalow $1850-5515; ☎✆) ⚑ This outstanding luxury eco-resort was started by the son of Jacques Cousteau. Unsurprisingly, it attracts divers, but families love it too: the kids club is exceptional, and practically a mini-resort unto itself, with a pool, flying fox, cooking classroom, play areas galore and a nanny-per-child for everyone under five. The beautiful *bures* are massive and feature handmade furnishings, large decks and private garden areas.

Emaho Sekawa Luxury Resort RESORT $$$
(Map p120; ☑ 995 3576; www.emahofiji.com; villas $2870-390, residence $9730; ☀☎✆) If you're looking for your own private slice of rainforest, tawny beach and decadence with your own staff, gourmet chef and dive master, this retreat hits the dream mark. Accommodation is Balinese Crusoe-chic with heart-stopping sunset views; you get a golf cart to tool around the two-hectare grounds. It's a five-minute walk to a 2km-long private beach where kayaks await.

No kids under 12. All meals are included, and there is a three-night minimum stay.

Hibiscus Highway

The Hibiscus Hwy runs along the south coast of Vanua Levu, starting about 5km from Savusavu.

Dolphin Bay Divers Retreat, the Remote Resort and Sau Bay Fiji Retreat are southeast of Buca Bay; accessible only by boat, they are most easily reached from Taveuni.

Vosa Ni Ua Lodge LODGE $$
(Map p120; ☑ 820 8648; www.flyseastay.com; bungalow from $200; ☎) The *bures* here are classy, comfortable and have insane sea views, but you'll likely be so busy you won't have time to appreciate them. The lodge is adrenaline HQ on this stretch of coast: from its wonderfully windy spot, staff offer professionally run kitesurfing courses, and arrange paragliding, diving, surf safaris and heaps more. Mountain bikes available to rent. The snorkelling out the front is superb.

★ Salt Lake Lodge LODGE $$$
(Map p120; ☑ 828 3005; www.saltlakelodgefiji. com; per night from $395 ; ☎) ⚑ For peace and

personalised service, this remote lodge is tough to beat. Sitting on a five-acre organic farm beside the Qaloqato River, the timber complex is yours alone, as are a personal chef, maid and all the fresh fruits and veggies you can pick. It's an absolutely idyllic location, and opportunities abound to explore it on fishing, snorkelling and kayak trips.

There's a strong eco ethos here: all toilets are compost, rainwater is used for bathing and cooking, and there's 24-hour solar power.

Savasi Island RESORT $$$
(Map p120; www.savasiisland.com; villas from $1255; ☀☎✆) This is the place to come for seclusion, scenery and getting spoiled senseless. The seven gorgeous villas all have incredible sea views, cloistered gardens and decks and impeccably designed interiors; most have their own pool. Gourmet meals are served in the tasteful restaurant, or in keeping with the privacy theme, on a deserted stretch of sand (or in a beach cave!).

The excellent KoroSun Dive (p119) is based here.

Savasi Island is connected to Vanua Levu by a causeway: it's about ten minutes' drive from Savusavu.

🍴 Eating

Savusavu Wok CHINESE $
(Map p124; ☑ 885 3688, 836 6898; mains $7-15; ⊙ 11am-9pm; ❋) Like so many eateries in Savusavu, this place looks a bit woebegone from the outside. But don't be fooled by the flaky paint and misspelled signs: the Wok dishes up `incredible, authentic Chinese food. It's locals' favourite for its low prices and huge portions. The menu is extensive: we tried to eat our way through it and found every dish divine.

Decked Out Café INTERNATIONAL $
(Map p124; ☑ 885 2929; meals from $6-15, pizzas from $20; ⊙ lunch & dinner; ☎) This no-frills, friendly pad is one of the more popular yachty hangouts: there's always a few old (or young) salts yakking over a beer and nosh in its street-facing covered beer garden. It dishes up all the standards: curries, fish and chips, pizzas and burgers. Daily happy hours run between 5pm to 7pm, and there's live music from Thursday to Sunday evenings.

Mum's Country Kitchen INDIAN $
(Map p124; ☑ 927 1372; meals $3.50-10; ⊙ 8am-6pm) One step up from a hole-in-the-wall, this place is popular with local Indo-Fijians

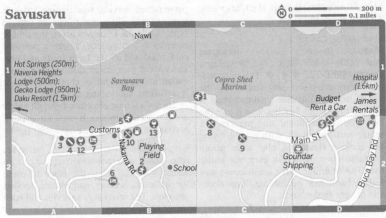

Savusavu

0 _____ 200 m
0 _____ 0.1 miles

Nawi

Hot Springs (250m);
Naveria Heights
Lodge (500m);
Gecko Lodge (950m);
Daku Resort (1.5km)

Savusavu
Bay

Copra Shed
Marina

Hospital
(1.6km)

Budget
Rent a Car

James
Rentals

Customs

Main St

Nakama Rd

Playing
Field

School

Goundar
Shipping

Buca Bay Rd

Savusavu

Activities, Courses & Tours
1 Copra Shed Marina C1
2 Hot Springs B2
3 J Hunter Pearls A2
  Trip n Tour .... (see 1)
4 Tui Tai Expeditions A2
5 Waitui Marina B2

Sleeping
6 Hot Springs Hotel B2
7 Savusavu Budget Lodge A2

Eating
8 Decked Out Café C2

9 Mum's Country Kitchen C2
10 Savusavu Wok B2
11 Surf and Turf D2

Drinking & Nightlife
12 Planters' Club A2
13 Savusavu Wines & Spirits B2
  Savusavu Yacht Club .... (see 1)
  Waitui Marina .... (see 5)

Entertainment
  Uros .... (see 11)

for its curries. It's not a creative menu, but a solid one. Takeaway meals come in plastic bags (and *dahl* is poured into old juice bottles), but don't be put off: this is the real, delicious deal. If you like it super-spicy, staff are happy to oblige.

★ Surf and Turf   INTERNATIONAL $$$
(Map p124; ☑ 885 3033; Waterfront Bldg; mains $25-65; ⊙ 10am-9.30pm Mon-Sat) This is the poshest restaurant in town, though you wouldn't know it from its dilapidated entrance. It has a beautiful deck overlooking the water, great wine list and lobster on the menu, yet it's as laid back as Savusavu itself. Tasty pastas, curries and exceptional fish and chips are to be had; it also has pricier steaks and upmarket seafood dishes.

🍷 Drinking & Nightlife

Savusavu Yacht Club   BAR
(Map p124; Copra Shed Marina; ⊙ 10am-10pm Sun-Thu, to midnight Fri & Sat) Tourists are considered temporary members of this friendly little drinking hole. There are tables out by the waterside, plenty of cold beer and lots of mingling between yachties and expats.

Waitui Marina   BAR
(Map p124; ☑ 835 3913; ⊙ 10am-10pm Mon-Sat) Sit on the balcony upstairs to enjoy classic South Pacific views of the yacht-speckled, palm-lined bay. The bar is well-stocked and all foreigners on holiday are considered temporary members. Expect locals playing guitars and heavy drinking as the night wears on.

Planters' Club   BAR
(Map p124; ⊙ 10am-10pm Mon-Sat, to 8pm Sun) This was traditionally a place for planters to drink when they brought in the copra, and some of their descendants can still be found clustered around the bar. It's got a whiff of colonialism and teems with expats. Happy hour is from 5.30pm to 6.30pm. It holds a monthly

Sunday *lovo*. Ignore the 'members only' placard; staff will happily sign in visitors.

Savavu Wines & Spirits LIQUOR STORE
(Map p124; ☑885 3888; Main St; ⊙9am-5pm Mon-Thu, to 9pm Fri & Sat) It's amazing what you can find in this little bottle shop: a great wine and international spirits selection as well as imported gourmet coffees, cheeses, cereals and more. There are a couple of tables outside if you wish to sit down and imbibe as many do.

☆ Entertainment

Uros CLUB
(Map p124; admission $5; ⊙8pm-midnight) Meaning 'sexy' in Fijian, this is where everyone comes to bump and grind to local and international music. It's a smallish room up a dark flight of stairs and great fun.

ℹ Information

Being an official point of entry for yachts, there are customs, immigration, health and quarantine services available. ANZ, BSP and Westpac banks all have branches in the main street.

Customs (Map p124; ☑885 0727; ⊙8am-1pm & 2-5pm Mon-Fri) Located west of the marinas on the main street.

Hospital (☑885 0444; Cross Island Rd) The hospital is 1.5km east of town on the road to Labasa. Call the hospital if an ambulance is required.

Police (☑885 0222) The police station is 600m past the Buca Bay Rd turn-off.

Post Office (Map p124) At the eastern end of town near Buca Bay Rd.

ℹ Getting There & Around

BUS

Savusavu's bus station is in the centre of town, beside the market. Buses travelling the scenic, sealed (yet bumpy) highway from Savusavu over the mountains to Labasa ($10, three hours, four times daily) depart from 7.30am to 3.30pm. Some buses take the longer route from Savusavu to Labasa along Natewa Bay, and these should depart at 9am ($18, six hours).

Buses from Savusavu to Napuca ($9, 4½ hours), at the tip of the Tunuloa Peninsula, depart three times daily. The last bus stays there overnight and returns at 7am. A 4pm bus only goes as far as Naweni ($3). There is no bus from Savusavu to Nabouwalu; catch a morning bus to Labasa and change buses there.

From Monday to Saturday there are five bus services from Savusavu to Lesiaceva Point ($1.20, 15 minutes) between 6am and 5pm. For

WORTH A TRIP

NUKUBOLU

Deep in the mountains north of Savusavu, reachable by 4WD, lies the ruins of Nukubolu, an ancient Fijian village whose old stone foundations, terraces and thermal pools are in surprisingly good condition. The setting is lovely: a volcanic crater with steaming hot springs in the background. Nukubolu has myriad uses for the local villagers, who dry kava roots on corrugated-iron sheets laid over the pools and use the hot springs as a healing aid. The ruins are on the property of the village of Biaugunu, so take a *sevusevu* (gift) for the chief and ask permission before wandering around. The turn-off is about 20km northwest of Savusavu; continue about 8km inland and over a couple of river crossings. You can also rent a carrier from town to take you there; combine it with a trip to Waisali Rainforest Reserve.

confirmation of bus timetables, ring **Vishnu Holdings** (☑885 0276; admin@vhlbuses.com).

CAR

Rental car agencies include **Budget** (Map p124; ☑881 1999; www.budget.com.fj), **Carpenters** (☑885 0274; www.carprentals.com.fj) and **James Rentals** (Map p124; ☑867 3375; www.jamesrentalsfiji.com). **Trip n Tour** (p121) rents scooters for $75.

TAXI

Taxis are easy to find in Savusavu; the main taxi stand is right next to the bus station.

Namenalala

The volcanic island of Namenalala rests on the Namena Barrier Reef, now one of the most spectacular protected marine reserves in the country, 25km off the southeastern coast of Vanua Levu and about 40km from Savusavu. Namenalala has the best diving and snorkelling in the region. The island also has lovely beaches and is a natural sailors' refuge. There's just one small, upmarket resort, which also runs daytrips to the island.

🛏 Sleeping & Eating

★**Namena Island Resort** RESORT $$
(Map p120; ☑828 0577, 885 3389; www.namenaislandresort.com; bungalow $360, roundtrip transfers $200; 🖘) This small dive and

snorkel retreat is outrageously located on Namenalala Island in the paradisaical Namena Marine Reserve. Namena was badly damaged in 2016's Cyclone Winston, and was closed at the time of research. Contact the resort for updates.

Labasa

POP 27,950

Labasa (pronounced 'Lam-basa'), Vanua Levu's administrative centre, is a dusty sugar and timber town that doesn't hold much allure for the average traveller. Sitting about 5km inland on the sweltering banks of the Labasa River and reclaimed mangrove swamps, the top sights in town are a large sugar mill and the seasonal trains that ka-chunk bushels of cane through Labasa's centre. The local population is predominantly Indo-Fijian, many of whom are descendants of *girmitiyas* (indentured labourers brought from India to work on the plantations).

Out of town are nearly undeveloped coastal areas that get great surf and have awesome diving.

Sights & Activities

Wasavula Ceremonial Site   HISTORIC SITE
This site has a cryptic – and cannibalistic – history. At the entrance, there's a sacred monolith that villagers believe grew from the ground; behind is a cemetery and the area that was used during cannibalistic ceremonies, with a *vatu ni bokola* (head-chopping stone), another rock for the severed head and a bowl-like stone where the brain was placed for the chief. The site is found in Wasavula village (Vunimoli Rd) south of town; a taxi should be about $7.

Sleeping

Hotel Northpole   HOTEL $
(Map p127; ☏881 8008; www.northpole.com.fj; Nasekula Rd; r $85-110; ⓟ❈🅥) Smack in the middle of town, the refurbished Northpole is an excellent option: it's friendly, clean and as modern as it gets in Labasa. 4WDs can be rented from here; they do worthwhile room and rental deals. The hotel is atop The Lunch Box fast food joint; don't be surprised if the wafting dinner smells induce a fried chicken craving.

Friendly North Inn   HOTEL $
(Map p127; ☏990 8611; www.cjsgroup.com.fj/ friendly.html; Butinikama-Siberia Rd; r $75-95; ❈)

A 15-minute walk to town, this well-maintained hotel offers a rare peace in Labasa. There are several surprisingly classy duplex villas set in a mellow, flower-studded garden; guests have free access to a large pool a couple of minutes' walk away. Breakfasts are included, and if you order in advance, staff can arrange other meals as well. A taxi to town is $5.

⭐**Grand Eastern Hotel**   HOTEL $$
(Map p127; ☏881 1022; www.cjsgroup.com. fj/grand_eastern.html; Rosawa St; r $90-200; ⓟ❈🅥🛏) This is the plushest hotel in Labasa. There's an airy, somewhat colonial atmosphere and the staff are helpful. Standard rooms have porches facing the river, but it's worth paying the extra for the deluxe rooms that open out onto the courtyard swimming pool. All rooms are clean but slightly careworn. There's also a decent restaurant and bar.

Palmlea Farms Resort   RESORT $$
(Map p120; ☏828 2220; www.palmleafarms. com; Tabia-Naduri Rd; bungalow incl breakfast from $295; ❈🅥🛏) 🌱 This remote-feeling resort makes for a gorgeous getaway. Overlooking the Great Sea Reef, simple *bures* with verandahs sit on a gentle green slope a short walk to the resort's jetty – from here you can kayak to a private white-sand beach or enjoy fantastic snorkelling. Organic fruit and veg is grown on-site and every effort is made to manage the resort in an ecofriendly fashion.

Other activities including hiking, diving ($250 two-tank dive), fishing and crabbing with a local guide.

It's a 20-minute drive from Labasa; there are also frequent buses passing daily, making it easy to get to Savusavu.

Eating

Labasa is full of basic cafes serving cheap plates of Indian and Chinese food. Note: most restaurants, although open for dinner, close by 7pm. There's also a cavernous **market** (Map p127) next to the bus station and a few well-stocked supermarkets.

Horse Shoe   FAST FOOD $
(Map p127; Reddy Place; $3-15; ⊙8am-7pm) This place is locally famous for its creative burgers, homemade chicken nuggets and vegetarian options. It gets especially packed at lunchtime: you can amuse yourself by chortling at the cheeky menu.

Labasa

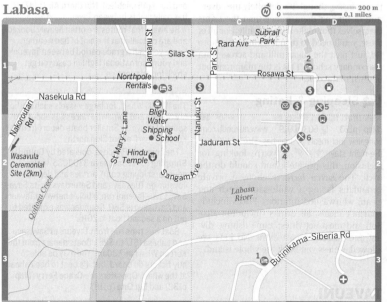

Subrail Park

Rara Ave

Silas St

Damanu St

Park St

Rosawa St

Northpole Rentals ●🏠3

Nasekula Rd

Nanuku St

Bligh Water Shipping ● School

Jaduram St

Nakoroutari Rd

St Mary's Lane

Hindu Temple 🛕

Sangam Ave

Wasavula Ceremonial Site (2km)

Qoitoga Creek

Labasa River

Butinikama-Siberia Rd

Oriental Seafood Restaurant CHINESE **$$**
(Map p127; ☎ 881 7321; Jaduram St; meals
$5-23; ⊗10am-3pm & 6-10pm Mon-Sat, 6-10pm
Sun) Look for the bright-orange door and
pink balcony overlooking the bus station.
Although you wouldn't guess it from the
outside, this is one of Labasa's most upmar-
ket and atmospheric restaurants, with a
well-stocked bar and a wide choice of tasty,
well-portioned Chinese dishes, including
plenty of veggies and a few Fijian options.

🛈 Information

ANZ, BSP and Westpac banks all have branches
in the main street and have 24-hour ATMs.

Hospital (Map p127; ☎ 881 1444; Butinikama-
Siberia Rd) The hospital is southeast of the
river.

Police (☎ 881 1222; Nadawa St)

Post Office (Map p127; Nasekula Rd) There
are several cardphones outside.

🛈 Getting There & Around

BUS

There are regular buses that chug along the
scenic mountain route between Labasa and
Savusavu ($10, three hours, five times Monday
to Saturday, four on Sunday) departing between
7am and 4.15pm. There is also a daily bus that
takes the long route ($18, six hours) to Savusavu

Labasa

🛏 Sleeping
1	Friendly North Inn	C3
2	Grand Eastern Hotel	D1
3	Hotel Northpole	B1

🍴 Eating
4	Horse Shoe	C2
5	Market	D1
6	Oriental Seafood Restaurant	D2

around the northeast, following the scenic Nate-
wa Bay. Buses to Nabouwalu depart three times
per day Monday to Saturday ($14, six hours).
Call **Vishnu Holdings** (p125) to confirm time-
tables.

TAXI & 4WD

There is no shortage of taxis. You'll find the
majority of them at the main stand near the bus
station. **Northpole Rentals** (Map p127; ☎ 777
7224; www.northpole.com.fj/rentals.html; Hotel
Northpole) has an office at the hotel of the same
name on the main drag. You can rent 4WD Suzuki
Jimmys from $120 per day. Free airport pick-up
and drop-off.

Around Labasa

The area around Labasa is a great place for
4WD exploration. There are some interesting

things to see, though it's definitely the adventure of finding them rather than the sights themselves that make it worthwhile. For all of these, you'll need to turn left onto Wainikoro Rd, just past the sugar mill and across from a secondary school. This is the main road out of town to the east.

🛏 Sleeping & Eating

Nukubati Island Resort   RESORT **$$$**
(Map p120; ☑603 0919; www.nukubati.com; bungalow incl meals & activities $1677-2420; min five-night stay; 🐾) 🌿 If you're looking for seclusion, this private island should do the trick. The seven *bures* each have private verandahs facing a white-sand beach and clean, whitwashed interiors. Prices include gourmet meals, all drinks (including alcohol) and most activities; game fishing, diving and massages cost extra. No kids are allowed, unless you book the whole island.

TAVEUNI

POP 12,000

Taveuni is renowned as Fiji's Garden Island, though its tangled, steamy interior is more reminiscent of a prehistoric jungle than anything that might yield to a hedgetrimmer and set of pruning shears. Hot and often wet, this impossibly green volcanic bump is covered by a riotous quilt of palms, monster ferns and tropical wildflowers, one of which, the *tagimaucia*, is found nowhere else on Earth. Its dense rainforest is a magnet for colourful bird life.

Much of Taveuni's coastline is rugged: Des Voeux Peak reaches up 1195m and the cloud-shrouded Mt Uluigalau, at 1241m, is Fiji's second-highest summit. A massive swath of the island's east is protected national park: here, you can get sweaty on hillside hikes, cool off under waterfalls, tramp along a coastal walk beside impossibly beautiful beaches or glide through impossibly clear waters on a traditional *bilibili* (bamboo raft).

Taveuni's beauty doesn't fade at the water's edge: the dazzling corals and diverse marine life of the Somosomo Strait, Waitabu Marine Park and Vuna Reef draw divers and snorkellers from around the world.

ℹ Getting There & Away

AIR

At Matei airport, **Fiji Airways** (p147) has at least one flight a day to/from Nadi (1½ hours)

and Suva (45 minutes). **Northern Air** (p147) has daily flights between Taveuni and Suva.

Be aware that routes are often heavily booked and are cancelled at the hint of bad weather. Leave yourself a grace period between Taveuni and your international flight in case you get stuck for a day or two.

BOAT

The Wairiki Wharf, for large vessels such as the MV *Suliven* and *Lomaviti Princess*, is about 1km south of Waiyevo. Smaller boats depart from the Korean Wharf, about 2km north

The *Lomaiviti Princess*, operated by **Goundar Shipping** (☑in Savusavu 330 1035; www.goundarshipping.com), arrvies and departs Taveuni on Tuesdays and Saturdays on its Suva–Savusavu–Taveuni run: a ticket between Taveuni and Savusavu is $30. Goundar was expected to put on a second boat in 2016.

Boat-bus trips run from Taveuni to Savusavu and Labasa ($17 to $25). Boats depart from the Korean Wharf at 7.30am. You may be able to buy tickets on board, but it's best to book ahead at the wharf. Operators are **Grace Ferry** (Map p132) and **Egi One** (p118).

ℹ Getting Around

The one main road in Taveuni follows the coast, stretching from Lavena in the east, up north and around to Navakawau in the south. It is sealed from Matei to Wairiki, and there's also a sealed (though slightly potholed) section through Taveuni Estates. There are also a couple of inland 4WD tracks. Getting around Taveuni involves a bit of planning – the main disadvantage being the sporadic bus service. To get around cheaply and quickly you need to combine buses with walking, or take taxis – the driver will probably act as a tour guide too.

TO/FROM THE AIRPORT

From Matei airport expect to pay about $30 to Waiyevo, and $90 to Vuna (about one hour) in a taxi. Most upmarket resorts provide transfers for guests.

BUS

Pacific Transport (Map p132; ☑888 0278) has a depot in Naqara, opposite the Taveuni Central Indian School. Buses start at the depot and travel north to Matei and beyond to Lavena in the southeast, as well as south to Navakawau, just past Vuna. They run three times per day Monday to Staurday, and once on Sunday.

You can find a schedule at www.taveuni.com.au/services/bus.htm. Be aware that times can and do change; buses may show up early or an hour late. Double-check the time of the return bus when you board, just to make sure there is one.

Taveuni

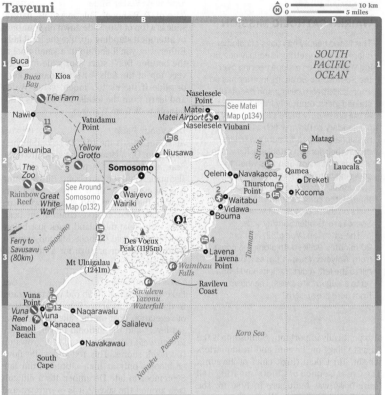

CAR

Give **Budget Rent a Car** (p125) a call, though keep in mind the roads here can be really rough. Locals are often willing to hire out their cars for around $130 per day. This of course means that there is no rental agreement and you will not be insured.

TAXI

It's easy to find taxis in the Matei, Waiyevo and Naqara areas, though on Sunday you might have to call one in advance. Hiring a taxi should cost from around $140 for the day, depending on how far you want to go. For destinations such as Lavena you can go one way by bus and have a taxi pick you up at the end at a designated time (but arrange this before you go).

Waiyevo, Somosomo & Around

This isn't the most beautiful part of Taveuni, but it holds most of the island's facilities. It's

Taveuni

WORTH A TRIP

WAIRIKI CATHOLIC MISSION

This faded beauty has bags of colonial charm, and the setting is equally beguiling – standing on a slope peering over the Somosomo Strait. Its interior has an impressive beam ceiling and beautiful stained glass, reputedly from France. In the presbytery there's a painting of a legendary battle in which a Catholic missionary helped Taveuni's warriors defeat their Tongan attackers. It's worth attending Mass on Sundays when the congregation lets rip with some impressive vocals. There are no pews here, though: the congregation sits on woven mats on the floor; take off your shoes. Some resorts offer Sunday trips.

The **mission** (Map p132) is about 20 minutes' walk south along the coast from Waiyevo. You can't miss it on the hill to the left. A dirt track behind leads up to a huge white cross. The views from here are superb.

also politically important – Somosomo is the largest village on Taveuni and headquarters for the Tui Cakau (high chief of Taveuni). The **Great Council of Chiefs' meeting hall** (*bure bose*) was built here in 1986 for the gathering of chiefs from all over Fiji.

Just south of Somosomo is Naqara, Taveuni's metropolis – if you take metropolis to mean a few supermarkets, a budget hotel and the island's only bank. Head another 2km down the coast and you'll hit Waiyevo, which is Taveuni's administrative centre and home to the hospital, police station, more ferry links and a resort. About 2km further south of Waiyevo is Wairiki village, which has a general store and a beautiful old hill-top Catholic mission.

◎ Sights

International Dateline   LANDMARK
(Map p132) Though Fiji adheres to the single time convention, the International Dateline cuts straight through Taveuni, offering visitors a great photo-op and the chance to jump from one day to the next. Take the road uphill from Waiyevo (towards the hospital) and cross the field on the right: you'll find a big Taveuni map split in two to mark both sides of the dateline.

Waitavala Water Slide   WATERFALL
(Map p132) Wahooo! This awesome natural slide is a ton of fun. Slide down on your bum or attempt it standing up, like the local kids. Either way, you'll end up in a small pool at the bottom. Don't start your slide from the very top of the falls – it's too dangerous – or slide if there's too much water. Watch and learn from the locals. The slide is a 20-minute walk from Waiyevo.

Des Voeux Peak   MOUNTAIN
At 1195m, this is the island's second-highest mountain. On a clear day the views from the peak are fantastic: it's possible to see Lake Tagimaucia and the Lau Group. Birdwatching is great every day. Allow three to four hours to walk the 6km up, and at least two to return. It's a steep, arduous climb in the heat; start early. Take the inland track just before you reach Wairiki Catholic Mission (coming from Waiyevo), or arrange for a lift up and walk back.

Lake Tagimaucia   LAKE
Lake Tagimaucia is in an old volcanic crater in the mountains above Somosomo. Masses of vegetation float on the lake (823m above sea level), and the national flower, the rare *tagimaucia* (an epiphytic plant), grows on the lake's shores. This red-and-white flower blooms only at high altitude from late September to late December. It's a difficult trek around the lake as it is overgrown and often very muddy. You'll need a guide; ask in Naqara or arrange for one through your accommodation.

🏃 Activities

Taveuni Ocean Sports   DIVING
(Map p129; ☏ 888 1111; www.taveunioceansports.com) 🌿 The centre is dedicated to protecting the environment; each dive starts with a short lesson on local marine biology. With group maximums at four people per dive you'll want to reserve in advance. It's based at Nakia Resort and Dive (p131).

Exotic Holidays Fiji   TOUR
(☏ 625 3792; www.exoticholidaysfiji.net) Though it's based in Viti Levu, this outfit knows Taveuni – particularly its natural attractions – inside out. If you're keen on making a short visit to the Garden Isle, staff can arrange accommodation and tours of all the must-sees on the island. A four-night stay (with tours included) starts at $499.

🛏 Sleeping & Eating

Garden Island Resort
HOTEL **$$**

(Map p132; ☑ 888 0286; www.gardenislandre
sort.com; r $245-490; ❋ 🛜 ⛱) The oldest re-
sort on Taveuni (built 1971), this place has
a plain block-like exterior, which opens to
a surprisingly chic, streamlined nests. All
rooms have balconies or patios; more ex-
pensive rooms have private spas. There's a
stylish pool, good snorkelling off the rocky
beach and a wonderful tree dripping with
sleeping bats at the water's edge. It has an
on-site dive shop.

Taveuni Dive Resort
RESORT **$$$**

(☑ 891 1063; www.taveunidiveresort.com; bungalow from $400; 🅿 🛜 ⛱) 🏊 If you're a diver,
this spanking new resort may well prove impossible to beat. Built by the well-respected
Taveuni Dive outfit, it's the closest digs on
Taveuni to Rainbow Reef: from *bure* to bubbling takes just 15 minutes. There are eight
luxury *bures* available, but don't be fooled
by the opulence: this is an eco-resort, running on solar power and constructed out of
sustainable materials.

Its super-sociable Salty Fox Bar & Grill
(mains $14-40; 7am-10pm) is proving popu-
lar with guests and visitors, who congregate
over burgers and beers to swap diving notes
and tall tales.

Nakia Resort and Dive
BURE **$$$**

(Map p129; ☑ 888 1111; www.nakiafiji.com;
bungalow from $470-850; 🛜) 🏊 Four simple,
dark yet comfortable *bure* sit on a grassy
hillside looking out to sea at this raved-
about eco-resort. It uses alternative energy
wherever possible, as well as composting
and recycling, and they have a large organic
garden growing fruit and veg for the restau-
rant (optional meal plans from $106). The
dive shop is excellent and takes the same
eco-bent.

Aroha Resort
BURE **$$$**

(Map p132; ☑ 888 1882; www.arohataveuni.com;
bungalow $300-420; 🛜⛱) This quiet spot
(max 12 guests) offers simple but elegant
varnished-wood rooms with louvred windows looking out over a black-sand beach.
Each *bure* has its own airy kitchen and outdoor shower. The new Kai Time restaurant
(mains $15-35) does fantastic meals. There's
a small infinity pool, a barbecue, bikes and
kayaks. Diving is through Taveuni Dive. It's
a short walk to Wairiki.

ℹ Information

Bank South Pacific
(BSP; Map p132; Naqara;
⊙ 9.30am-4pm Mon, from 9am Tue-Fri) The
only bank on the island will exchange currency
and travellers cheques and has an ATM, which
has been known to run out of money.

Hospital
(Map p132; ☑ 888 0444; Waiyevo)
For emergencies.

Police
(Map p132; ☑ 888 0222; Waiyevo) The
main police station is at the government compound behind the Garden Island Resort in Waiyevo. There is also a police station in Naqara.

Post Office
(Map p132; ☑ 888 0019; Wai-
yevo; ⊙ 8am-1pm & 2-4pm Mon-Fri) Among the
shops beneath the First Light Inn.

Southern Taveuni

The southern part of the island isn't well serviced by public transport but it's a beautiful
place to visit. Check out the blowhole on the
dramatic, windswept South Cape. Southern
Taveuni is also home to Vuna Reef, which
is perfect for snorkellers and novice divers.
The main villages in southern Taveuni are
Naqarawalu (in the hills) and, on the southern coast near Vuna Reef, Kanacea, Vuna
and Navakawau.

🏃 Activities

Taveuni Dive
DIVING

(Map p129; ☑ 828 1063; www.taveunidive.com)
This long-running centre offers diving and
snorkelling – and cultural, fishing and other
watersports – tours. It's based at Taveuni
Dive Resort but does pickups from across the
island.

Dolphin Bay Divers
DIVING

(Map p129; ☑ 992 4001, 828 3001; www.dolphin
baydivers.com) Located at Dolphin Bay Divers
Retreat (on Vanua Levu but best accessed
from Taveuni), this is a well-regarded outfit
with excellent gear.

🛏 Sleeping

★ Dolphin Bay Divers Retreat
RESORT **$**

(Map p129; ☑ 828 3001, 992 4001; www.dol
phinbaydivers.com; Vanaira Bay, Vanua Levu; safari
tent/bungalow $35-85/150-210; ◉) 🏊 Tucked
away in a jungly cove on Vanua Levu (but
best accessed from Taveuni), this is a fantastically remote place with simple *bure*
and permanent safari tents. Divers, aware
of the excellent location and great reputation of the diving outfit here, make up most
of the guests; there's also good snorkelling

Around Somosomo

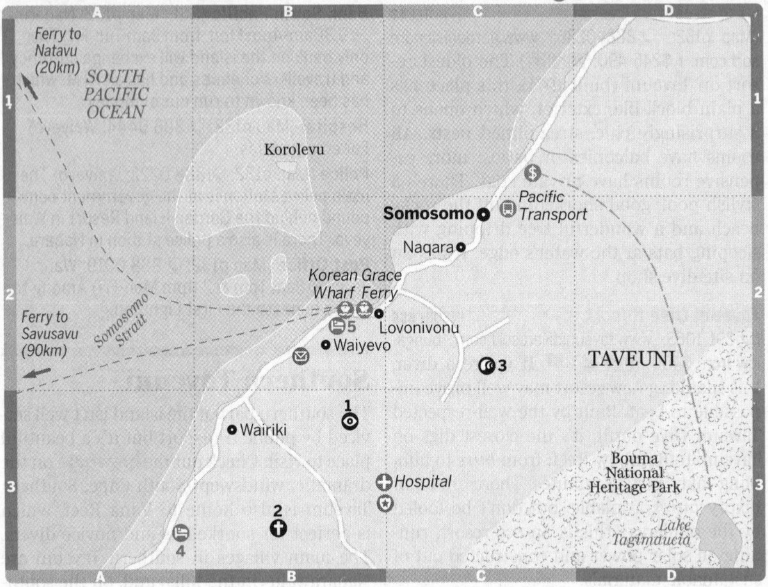

Around Somosomo

Sights

1 International Dateline B3
2 Wairiki Catholic Mission B3
3 Waitavala Water Slide C2

Sleeping

4 Aroha Resort A3
5 Garden Island Resort B2

from the stunning beach. The food is delicious (optional meal plan $105).

Vuna Lighthouse Lodge GUESTHOUSE $
(Map p129; ☎822 1963; dm/s/d $25/50/75) This simple blue wooden house is a few steps from a black volcanic rock beach. Run by a local family, there's a self-catering kitchen and laundry facilities. It's just a couple of minutes from Vuna Village; it's a great place to hang out and make friends with the locals. Good, home-cooked meals are available for between $7 and $12. Definitely call and book ahead.

Remote Resort RESORT $$$
(Map p129; ☎979 3116; www.fijiresort.com.fj; Vanua Levu; villas $1465-1740;) Private villas on the doorstep of the Rainbow Reef (it's only a 10-minute boat ride to the Great White Wall) make this luxury diving heaven. There's a spa, private plunge pools and as much or as little activity you could hope for on a beach like this. All meals are included and the views are beyond the imagination.

Paradise Taveuni RESORT $$$
(Map p129; ☎888 0125; www.paradiseinfiji.com; bungalow/r incl all meals & transfers from $550/600;) Set on a former plantation, this aptly named oceanfront place has stunning sunset views and plenty of hammocks and loungers from which to enjoy them. The *bures* and *vales* (rooms) are luxury all the way; all have outdoor Jacuzzis and rock showers, while *bures* and larger *vales* boast large private sundecks, some with locally handmade day beds.

Matei

A residential area on Taveuni's northern point, Matei is the main 'tourist hub', with a scarcely visible string of guesthouses, hotels and rental properties strewn along a long stretch of beachside road. Only a couple of beaches are suitable for swimming and sunbathing, but this is a good and friendly place to base yourself for diving and other activities.

🏃 Activities

Makaira Sports Fishing   FISHING
(Map p134; ☑ 888 0680; www.fijibeachfrontat
makaira.com; half/full day $950/1700) These
folks will take you fishing for big game
with Captain John Llanes Jr, who has over
30 years' experience on the water. Book
through Makaira Resort in Matei.

Peckham Pearl Farm Tours   PEARL FARM
(Map p134; ☑ 888 2789; Matei; $25) Snorkel this
saltwater black-pearl farm in Matei's Naselesele lagoon and buy pearls after the tour.

🛏 Sleeping

★ Bibi's Hideaway   BURE $
(Map p134; ☑ 888 0443; paulinabibi@yahoo.
com; bungalow $40-150; P) A rambling, quiet
five-acre hillside plot hides a selection of
adorable, colourful *bures* in varying sizes
among the fruit trees. Charming host Pauli-
na will welcome you with a heaving fruit
platter; once you've polished that off, you're
welcome to pick as much as you can gorge.
There are fantastic self-catering facilities
here and plenty of room for exploring. A
brilliant choice, especially for families.

Tovu Tovu Resort   BURE $
(Map p134; ☑ 888 0560; www.tovutovu.com;
bungalow from $95; 🛜) This friendly place has
a selection of ageing *bures* with wooden
verandahs, hot-water bathrooms and fans:
some have kitchenettes. It's built on a subdivided copra estate, and owned by the Pe-
tersen family, which once ran the plantation.
The resort is a 20-minute walk southeast of
Matei airport, past the Sun City Supermarket. The attached **Vunibokoi Restaurant**
(mains $15-20) does superb Fijian food.

Maravu Lodge   HOSTEL $
(Map p134; ☑ 888 0555; www.maravulodge.com;
dm $25-35, d $90, bungalow $120-150, villa $180;
🛜🏊) This is a little slice of backpacker heav-
en, with fun, frivolity and lots (and lots) of
kava. Accommodations are clean and comfy,
but what draws the crowds are the convivial
ambiance, huge home-cooked meals and the
majestic view over offshore islands. There's a
good bar here; if you can tear yourself away
from it, the awesome staff can organise
heaps of activities and tours.

Beverly's Campground   CAMPGROUND $
(Map p134; ☑ 907 4933, 888 0684; www.beverlys
campground.geewhiz.me; sites per person/perma-
nent tent/dm/r $15/17/20/50) This is one of
those magical spots where everybody makes
friends easily and camping isn't a chore.
The small site sits on a white-sand beach,
beneath huge rustling trees; basic facilities
include flush toilets, showers and a sheltered
area for cooking and dining.

Makaira by the Sea   BUNGALOW $$
(Map p134; ☑ 888 0680; fijibeachfrontatmakaira.
com; bungalow $415-530; 🛜) Makaira has three
bures, two of which have private plunge
pools. All have kitchenettes but there's also
a small cafe where breakfast and dinner can
be provided. The family that runs the resort
operates Makaira Sports Fishing; alternatively, try your luck on a fishing kayak trip
($110 per day). Guests are also invited to
take part in their coral gardening program
to help regenerate damaged reef.

Taveuni Palms   VILLA $$$
(Map p134; ☑ 888 0032; www.taveunipalms.
com; d villas all inclusive except alcohol $3190-
5320; ❄🛜🏊) Breathtakingly beautiful and
very private, Taveuni Palms boasts three
villas, each with its own beach, pool and
seven-strong staff, including a personal chef
and nanny. The cook will prepare a five-
course meal for you every night, but the
villas have kitchens anyway. All have huge
decks, ridiculous views and incredible entertainment centres with big TVs, DVD players
and loaded iPods.

Coconut Grove Beachfront
Cottages   BUNGALOW $$$
(Map p134; ☑ 888 0328; www.coconutgrovefiji.
com; bungalow $390-565; 🛜) These three taste-
ful, bright cottages enjoy beautiful beach
views and tranquility by the truckload. All
are breezy, tasteful and hard to leave, even
for the tempting golden-sand beach just
footsteps away. The attached **restaurant**
(mains $12.50-39) is possibly the best on the
island. The owners can arrange diving, snorkelling, sightseeing and birdwatching trips.
No children under 12.

🍴 Eating & Drinking

If you're here on a Wednesday, try the *lovo*
(feast cooked in a pit oven) or buffet (complete with entertainment) at Naselesele village; your accommodation can arrange this
for you. Profits go to the local school.

Really good rotis ($1.50) can had at Matei
airport.

Matei

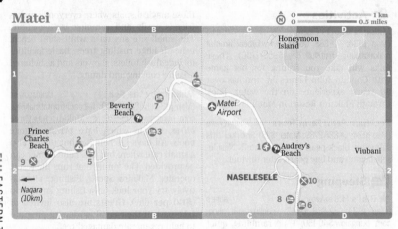

Matei

⊙ Activities, Courses & Tours
Makaira Sports Fishing .... (see 9)
1 Peckham Pearl Farm Tours C2

⊜ Sleeping
2 Beverly's Campground A2
3 Bibi's Hideaway B2
4 Coconut Grove Beachfront
　Cottages B1
5 Makaira by the Sea A2
6 Maravu Lodge D2
7 Taveuni Palms B1
8 Tovu Tovu Resort C2

⊗ Eating
　Coconut Grove Restaurant .... (see 4)
9 Restaurant Tramonto A2
10 Sun City Supermarket D2
　Vunibokoi Restaurant .... (see 8)

Sun City Supermarket　　GROCERY $
(Map p134; Matei; ☻7.30am-6pm Mon-Sat,
8-11am Sun) Sells a range of groceries (including disposable nappies), and accepts
credit cards. It has a public phone and
a petrol pump (no petrol on Sundays).
There's a bottle shop next door.

★Restaurant Tramonto　　WESTERN $$
(Map p134; ☑888 2224; pizza from $25, meals
$12-25; ☻lunch & dinner) If you're in the market
for a pizza the size of a small child, Tramonto
won't disappoint – they're huge, delicious and
mightily topped. The gasp-inducing sunset
views are equally scrumptious; get there early
to secure a table. It also does superb seafood.
Book in advance for the roasts on Sunday and
buffets on Wednesday.

Vunibokoi Restaurant　　FIJIAN $$
(Map p134; ☑888 0560; www.tovutovu.com;
dinner mains $15-20; ☻breakfast, lunch & dinner)
This downhome restaurant serves incredibly good, wholesome meals with a strong
emphasis on Fijian flavours: think crabs, coconut cream and chillis. It's attached to the
Tovu Tovu Resort, but everyone is welcome.
Come hungry for the Friday buffet (and live
tunes) or special Sunday roast.

Coconut Grove Restaurant　INTERNATIONAL $$$
(Map p134; ☑888 0328; www.coconutgrovefiji.
com; lunch $10-30, dinner $22-50; ☻breakfast,
lunch & dinner) Enjoy the sea views from the
deck of this popular restaurant. The menu
includes fresh vegetarian dishes, homemade
pasta, soups, salads and fish. You can just
turn up for breakfast or lunch, but you'll
have to let them know you're coming for
dinner. If you're lucky, you'll be serenaded
by local lads and their ukeleles.

Eastern Taveuni

The local landowners of beautiful eastern
Taveuni have rejected logging in favour of
ecotourism, under the banner of the Bouma
Environmental Tourism Project.

⊙ Sights

**Bouma National
Heritage Park**　　NATIONAL PARK
(Map p129; ☑867 7311; www.boumafiji.com)
This national park protects over 80% of
Taveuni's total area, covering about 150
sq km (57 sq mi) of rainforest and coastal
forest. The park includes the three Tavoro

DON'T MISS

LAVENA COASTAL WALK

The 5km Lavena Coastal Walk is well worth the effort. The trail follows the forest edge along the beach, past peaceful villages, and then climbs up through the tropical rainforest to a gushing waterfall. There's some good snorkelling and kayaking here and Lavena Point is fine for swimming.

The path is clearly marked and well maintained. To reach the falls at the end of the trail you have to clamber over rocks and swim a short distance through two deep pools. If you're visiting in the rainy season, the rocks near the falls can be slippery, if not flooded. It can be difficult and dangerous to reach the falls at this time.

The park is managed through Lavena Lodge. Park entrance is $20. You can also take a guided sea-kayak journey and coastal walk for $40 (including lunch). or arrange to take a boat one way and walk back ($220 for the whole boat).

Lavena village is about 15 minutes' drive past Bouma, 35 minutes from Matei. However, by local bus it takes about one hour from Matei or just under two from Waiyevo. Expect to pay about $75 for a taxi to/from Matei.

Waterfalls near the falls' visitor centre, each with natural swimming pools. The first waterfall is about 24m (78ft) high and only 10 minutes' walk along a flat cultivated path.

🏃 Activities

Birdwatching

Taveuni is one of Fiji's best areas for birdwatching. More than 100 species of bird can be found here. Try Des Voeux Peak at dawn for a chance to see the rare orange dove (the male is bright orange with a green head, while the female is mostly green) and the silktail. The forested Lavena coast is also a good spot to see orange or flame doves, Fiji goshawk, wattled honeyeater, and grey and white heron.

Hiking

Taveuni's wild interior makes it perfect for exploring on foot. Bouma National Heritage Park is the place to head for hiking action. Here you can amble beachside on the **Lavena Coastal Walk**, hike up and down hills to the **Tavoro Waterfalls** or take a guided trek on the **Vidawa Rainforest Trail** (🖉 820 4709; $60). If that's not hard-core enough you can slog it up Des Voeux Peak or around Lake Tagimaucia.

Waitabu Marine Park   MARINE PARK
(Map p129; 🖉 888 0451, 820 1999; www.waitabu. org; campground per person with own tent $12, incl hire tent $17) This area has decent snorkelling and a gorgeous white-sand beach. It is only possible to visit with a guide. Waitabu village has set up a half-day tour ($60 per person) that includes a guide, snorkelling, a *bilibili* (lashed bamboo raft) ride, and afternoon tea. There's also a Backpackers' Tour

($40 per person) with guided snorkelling. You must book in advance; trips depend on daily tides. You can arrange to sleep at the campground (own tent/hired $15/20); contact them for homestay options.

🛏 Sleeping & Eating

Lavena Lodge   GUESTHOUSE $
(Map p129; 🖉 877 9825; camping per person $25) Run by friendly, informative staff, the lodge was destroyed by Cyclone Winston in 2016. By the time you're reading this, it may have been rebuilt; contact them for updates. Otherwise, those with tents are welcome to camp on the beach.

Offshore Islands

Qamea, Matagi and Laucala are clustered just east of Thurston Point, across the Tasman Strait from northeastern Taveuni. All three islands have lovely, white-sand beaches.

Matagi

Tiny, horseshoe-shaped Matagi (1 sq km), formed by a submerged volcanic crater, is 10km off Taveuni's coast and just north of Qamea. Its steep rainforest sides rise to 130m. The bay faces north to open sea and there is a fringing reef on the southwest side of the island.

🛏 Sleeping & Eating

Matangi Island Resort   RESORT $$$
(Map p129; 🖉 888 0260; www.matangiisland. com; bungalow from $995-1610; 🛜🌊) The light-soaked *bures* here are huge, vaulted-ceilinged affairs with massive beds and

private verandahs; each one is surrounded by a neat tropical garden. It's romance run amok in the 'treehouse', perched 5m up in the tree canopy with wraparound decks, top views, outdoor Jacuzzis, lanterns aplenty and day beds. The pretty restaurant looks over Qamea and out to the ocean.

There are dozens of dive spots within 10 to 30 minutes of here. The resort is not suitable for children under 12.

Qamea

The closest of the three islands to Taveuni is Qamea (34 sq km), only 2.5km east of Thurston Point. Its coastline is riddled with deep bays and lined with white-sand beaches; the interior is fertile, green and rich in birdlife. The island is also notable for the *lairo* (annual migration of land crabs). For a few days from late November to early December, at the start of their breeding season, masses of crabs move from the mudflats towards the sea.

🛏 Sleeping & Eating

⭐ Maqai Resort   HOSTEL $
(Map p129; ☑ 990 7073; www.maqai.com; dm/bungalow from $80/185, compulsory meal plan $89;) A private white-sand beach, excellent snorkelling, epic waves and nightly entertainment: believe it or not, this is a backpackers. Accommodation is in sturdy, clean safari tents and shared *bures:* meals are taken in a common area with sand floors, couches and a pool table. There's a boat to take you out to the breaks and snorkelling, village visits and hiking.

Nadilo Bay Resort   RESORT $$
(Map p129; ☑ 820 8242; www.nadilobayresort.com; bungalow $175-195; 🛜) 🍃 This surf resort bills itself as sustainable, and it really does walk the walk. Power is via water turbine, all fruits and veggies are from its garden, and local fishermen provide their daily catches for the menu. *Bures* are super-traditional, and cut from the island's rainforest: they have not only thatched roofs, but walls as well.

The bay has top-notch right- and left-hand surf breaks; the resort rents long and short boards.

Kids are welcome, and are encouraged to play with local village children.

Qamea Resort & Spa   RESORT $$$
(Map p129; ☑ 888 0220; www.qamea.com; bungalow $1240-2070; ❄🛜🏊) These magnificently thatched *bures* lie on a long stretch of beautiful white-sand beach. Some have plunge pools, spa baths or rock showers. Rates include meals and transfers to and from Taveuni; children under 16 are not accepted unless you book the entire resort. There's excellent snorkelling just offshore, plus all manner of watersports, walks and village visits.

KADAVU GROUP

This is where you wish you were right now. Remote and authentic yet easily accessed from Viti Levu (it's 100km to the south) and home to comfortable, eco-friendly resorts, Kadavu blends Fiji's best assets. Your flight to the tiny airstrip will be followed by a long, and sometimes bumpy, boat ride to your resort past prehistoric-looking coves chirping with rare birds and fringed by the world's fourth-largest barrier reef, the incredible Great Astrolabe Reef. Handsome stretches of long, sandy beach and sheltered coves ring the islands' perimeters.

The group is made up of several islands including Kadavu (Fiji's fourth-largest island), Ono, Galoa and Yaukuve Levu.

Most visitors stay on Kadavu, where you'll find the bulk of the accommodation and the group's only town, petite Vunisea.

🏃 Activities

The Kadavu Group's rich landscape and underwater seascapes make it a perfect destination for nature lovers, divers, hikers and birdwatchers.

Hiking

Kadavu's hilly rainforest interior is sprinkled with waterfalls and hiking trails. There are good treks into the interior from several of the resorts.

Diving & Snorkelling

Buliya island, just north of Ono, is a great manta snorkelling site, where you're pretty much guaranteed an amazing encounter with the rays; Matava Resort takes people diving at a site off Kadavu accurately called Manta Reef. For novice divers, Yellow Wall and the Pacific Voyager wreck dive are on the more-protected western side of the island. All the resorts have either a dedicated dive centre or will find an outfit to take you out.

Fishing

The Great Astrolabe Reef is a fine location for blue water sport and big game fishing. Dogtail tuna, giant trevally and red bass are regulars on the line and many of Kadavu's resorts (Ono's Oneta Resort and Kadavu's Matava Resort in particular) will take you out beyond the reef for some serious fishing action. You may be able to take some of your catch home for dinner too.

Sea Kayaking

Organised kayaking trips take place from May to September and all of the resorts have two-person ocean kayaks free or for hire.

Tamarillo Sea Kayaking   KAYAKING
(☑761 6140; www.tamarillo.co.nz/fiji) These interesting and well-organised jaunts run five to seven days. All tours include meals and accommodation (at one of the Kadavu resorts) as well as a village stay. It also offers day and overnight trips. There's a two-person minimum.

Birdwatching

The lush rainforests, especially on Kadavu's eastern side, are home to a wide variety of birdlife, including the indigenous Kadavu honeyeater, Kadavu fantail, velvet fruit dove and the colourful Kadavu musk parrot. Most of the resorts will be able to arrange a guide but you'll see many of the birds fluttering around the resorts as well.

🛏 Sleeping

Take into account the time and cost of transfers when choosing your accommodation. In Kadavu, most of the places to stay are a fair way from the airport, and the only way to get there is by boat. Most places have a three-night minimum and offer package rates from their websites that are more economical than per-night rates. Prices listed include boat transfers.

🛏 Kadavu

Cooksley's Homestay   GUESTHOUSE $
(Map p138; ☑360 7970, 782 2505; osbornemck @yahoo.com; Vunisea; self-catering/full board $50/80, tent pitch $10) A minute's walk away from both Kadavu airstrip and the beach, this homely guesthouse is a basic but highly welcoming place from which to explore Kadavu if you're looking closer to regular island life instead of a dive resort. Rooms are partitioned by simple bamboo and woven palm

FIJI KADAVU GROUP

DON'T MISS

THE GREAT ASTROLABE REEF

The famous Great Astrolabe Reef is a major pull for most visitors to Kadavu and is the fourth-largest barrier reef in the world. Hugging the eastern side of the Group, it is bisected by the **Naiqoro Passage**, home to brilliantly coloured soft and hard corals, a fantastic assortment of tunnels, caverns and canyons, and a variety of marine life, including plenty of reef sharks and graceful manta rays. Recommended dive sites include **Eagle Rock** – a group of rock pinnacles with abundant hard corals and masses of fish life including pelagics – and **Broken Stone**, a beautiful underwater landscape with a maze of swim-throughs, caverns and tunnels. The weather often dictates which sites are suitable to dive, and visibility can range from 15m to 70m. Most of the resorts will also take snorkellers out to the reef.

---

walls. If you're self-catering, bring extra supplies from Suva.

★Matava Resort   RESORT $$
(Map p138; ☑333 6222; www.matava.com; d per person incl meals & transfers from $320; ☎) 🏊 Matava is a social, active and impeccably run place. Anything you want to do, from diving to sportfishing, birding or hiking, the team here can set you up. Meanwhile stay in spacious and clean hard-wood *bures* with heaps of windows to maximise the views (there are both garden and hillside options) and good solid beds.

Papageno Eco-Resort   RESORT $$
(Map p138; ☑603 0466; www.papageno resortfiji.com; Garden rooms s/d $232/292, bungalow incl meals s/d $339/515; ☎) 🏊 Low-key Papageno is the stuff of island fantasies. Large, dark-wood *bures,* with decks looking out to sea, are spread sparingly around manicured tropical gardens. Towards the back of the resort, the four connected 'garden rooms', which share a single verandah, are surrounded by greenery and overlook a small stream. All rooms are decked out with local artwork and have bigger-than-average bathrooms.

Kadavu Group

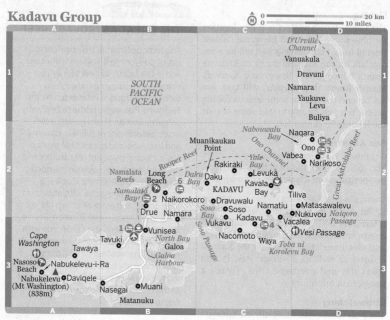

N 0 _____ 20 km
0 _____ 10 miles

SOUTH
PACIFIC
OCEAN

D'Urville
Channel
Vanuakula
Dravuni
Namara
Yaukuve
Levu
Buliya

Nabouwalu   Naqara
Muanikaukau   Ono
Point   Vabea   Narikoso
Rooper Reef   Rakiraki   Yale
Daku   Bay   Levuka
Namalata   Long   Daku   KADAVU   Kavala
Reefs   Beach   6   Bay   Bay   Tiliya
Namalata   2   Naikorokoro   Dravuwalu   Namatiu   Matasawalevu
Bay   Drue   Namara   Soso   Soso   Kadavu   Nukuvou   Naiqoro
Vukavu   Vacalea   Passage
1   Vunisea   Nacomoto   Vesi Passage
Cape   North Bay   Waya   Toba ni
Washington   Tavuki   Galoa   Korolevu Bay
Tawaya   Galoa
Nasoso   Nabukelevu-i-Ra   Harbour
Beach   Daviqele
Nabukelevu   Muani
(Mt Washington)   Nasegai
(838m)   Matanuku

Kadavu Group

Sleeping

Dive Kadavu   RESORT **$$**
(Map p138; ☎368 3502; www.divekadavu.
com; per person incl meals & transfers s/d/tr/q
$340/520/700/850; ☎) This resort has *bures*
with nearly all the walls covered in louvres
so you can open them up for plenty of ven-
tilation. They all have comfortable beds, ve-
randahs, hot water and tidy bathrooms, but
the brighter choices are the smaller units
at the southern end. It boasts an excellent
sheltered beach where the snorkelling and
swimming is wonderful.

Ono

★**Oneta Resort**   RESORT **$$**
(Map p138; ☎603 0778; www.onetafiji.com; d per
person incl meals from $300; ☎) The archi-
tecturally lovely thatched *bures* with hardwood floors, woven walls and louvred, netted
windows are among this region's classiest

accommodations. Mattresses have been imported from Italy and beds are draped with
gauzy white mosquito nets and topped with
Southeast Asian embroidered linens. All
units from the private honeymoon suite to
the stylish six-bed dorm complex have giant
open-to-sky bamboo showers.

★**Mai Dive
Astrolabe Reef Resort**   RESORT **$$**
(Map p138; ☎603 0842; www.maidive.com; r incl
meals from $390; ☎) Pretty tongue-and-
groove-built bungalows line the beach at this
very tidy, streamlined resort (just a few min-
utes' boat ride from the fantabulous Great
Astrolabe Reef) run by an Australian-Fijian
family. All *bures* have polished timber floors
and wooden verandahs and are right by the
water; they are simple but stylish and have
an incredibly happy feel to them.

ℹ️ Information

Many resorts offer wi-fi but service is very slow.
Some resorts, especially the more upmarket
ones, accept credit cards, but check before you
fly out. You can't change foreign currency in
Vunisea and there's no ATM, so bring however
much money you'll need.

Hospital (☎333 6008) Opened in 1996 with
the help of Australian aid, Vunisea's hospital
only has limited services. For more serious

ailments you're better off heading back to Viti Levu. Divers suffering from the bends can be transferred to the Fiji Recompression Chamber Facility in Suva by Medivac helicopter service.

Police (☑ 333 6007)

❶ Getting There & Away

AIR
Fiji Airways (p147) has daily flights to Kadavu from Nadi (from $195 one way, 45 minutes) except Sunday and Suva ($240 one way, 40 minutes). Prices can vary wildly, so book as far ahead as possible, but check timetables and confirm flights the day before departure as they are often late or cancelled.

BOAT
Goundar Shipping (☑ 330 1035; http://goundar shipping.com) runs the clean and reliable MV *Lomaiviti Princess*, which departs Suva every Wednesday at 10pm and arrives at Vunisea eight or nine hours later (economy seat/1st class seat/cabin $50/$70/$170); it departs Kadavu Thursday afternoon and arrives in Suva that night, connecting onwards to Vanua Levu and Taveuni. **Venu Shipping** (p148) operates the more basic MV *Sinu-i-Wasa* to Suva (from $55 one way) on Tuesday nights.

❶ Getting Around

Kadavu's few roads are restricted to the Vunisea area, except for one rough, unsealed road to Nabukelevu-i-Ra around the southern end of Kadavu. Small boats are the island group's principal mode of transport. Each resort has its own boat and will pick up guests from Vunisea airstrip. Make sure you make arrangements in advance. Boat trips are expensive due to fuel costs. In rough weather it can be a wet and bone-crunching trip to the more remote resorts.

LAU GROUP

The Lau islands are Fiji's final frontier. Though around 60 Lau islands dot the southwest corner of Fiji's vast archipelago, few visit here: those who do will find countless bays, deserted, reef-rimmed atolls and sparsely populated islands with hilly interiors.

Lau islanders are known for their woodcarving and *masi* crafts, and have been greatly influenced by neighbouring Polynesian cultures. Although the climate here is drier than most parts of Fiji, storms can be fierce and some of the bays are used as cyclone shelters by visiting yachts.

❶ Getting There & Away

AIR
Fiji Airways flies between Suva and Vanua Balavu on Wednesdays ($283 one way, one hour) and to Lakeba on Thursdays ($283 one way, 1½ hours). There's also a flight every Thursday from Suva to Cica ($272). There are no flights between islands.

BOAT
Goundar Shipping (☑ 330 1035; http://goundar shipping.com) operates a monthly trip to Vanua Balavu ($160) and Cicia ($150). Call well in advance to find out when the next sailing is. A new ship, the MV *Sea Rakino*, was coming into service in early 2016, offering a more regular service linking the Lau group to Suva, with the possibility of a stop at Savusavu and Taveuni.

Seaview Shipping (p148) has two ferries (the *Sandy* and the *Lady Sandy*), which sail from Suva to the southern Lau group. Schedules are a moveable feast.

Vanua Balavu
AREA 53 SQ KM

Vanua Balavu, 355km east of Nadi and about halfway to Tonga, is northern Lau's largest – and arguably most scenic – island. The celebrated Bay of Islands, also known as Qilaqila, sits in the northwest pocket and is a spectacular site for diving, kayaking and swimming.

Lomaloma, the island's largest village, was Fiji's first port, regularly visited by sailing ships trading in the Pacific. Today the people of Vanua Balavu rely largely on copra and *bêche-de-mer* (sea cucumber) for their income.

🛏 Sleeping & Eating

Moana's Guesthouse GUESTHOUSE **$**
(☑ 719 0929, 916 2684; r per person incl meals $95, children under 12yr $50; @) This hospitable place – the only accommodation on Vanua Balavu – covers all the basics with beach *bure* and guesthouse options. The simple *bures* are a 1km walk from Sawana village and mere metres from the lovely beach on Lomaloma Bay. The *bures* are simple, thatched affairs with mosquito nets, solar power, private bathrooms and mats laid over concrete floors.

Husband and wife owners Tevita Fotofili and Alumita can arrange boat, snorkelling and fishing trips, and collect travellers from the airstrip.

ROTUMA

POP 2000 / AREA 43 SQ KM

Far flung and isolated, the 43-sq-km volcanic island of Rotuma drifts in the Pacific 460km northwest of Viti Levu. The vast distance between the tiny island and the mainland may be an accident of geography, but this divide has allowed Rotumans to evolve ethnically and linguistically independent of the mainland. The best time to visit is during Fara, an annual six-week festival beginning on 1 December that sees Rotumans toss aside their strong work ethic for dancing, parties and general revelry. There are no banks or shops here.

The easiest way to stay on Rotuma is through a Rotuman contact (try www.rotuma.net or www.facebook.com/groups/rotumans). Alternatively, contact the Rotuman Island Council via the Fiji Visitors Bureau in Nadi.

Mojito's Barfly (✆889 1144; Motusa) has simple rooms with shared facilities, but they're generally reserved for government workers. Meals are also available, given plenty of notice.

✆ Getting There & Away

Fiji Airways flies from Nadi to Rotuma ($640) on Wednesdays; the trip takes 1½ hours.

Goundar Shipping (Map p69; ✆in Suva 330 1035; http://goundarshipping.com; 22-24 Tofua St, Walu Bay) sails to Rotuma once a month the first Saturday of every month. The journey takes 36 hours and the conditions on board are pretty basic.

Visiting yachts must obtain permission to anchor from the Ahau government station in Maka Bay, on the northern side of the island.

UNDERSTAND FIJI

Fiji Today

In recent years, Fiji's image as a tourist paradise has been tempered by a reputation as 'Coup-Coup Land' due to its army's predilection for sticking its nose (and its guns) into politics. But in 2014 the country finally returned to democracy. The road back hasn't always been without bumps, but Fiji is looking more stable than it has for years, even as it faces the challenges of globalisation, climate change and – of course – the continuing search for international rugby glory.

In 2016 the Category Five Cyclone Winston whaled into Fiji, causing widespread destruction. Visitors may notice residual damage to smaller villages – especially on the more remote islands – though nearly all resorts were spared major damage.

History

Crossroads of the Pacific

Fiji was settled by a wave or waves of Polynesians and Melanesians from Papua New Guinea who had descended from earlier Austronesian migrations from Southeast Asia.

The so-called Lapita people, possibly arriving from New Caledonia, left the earliest mark in the archaeological record through their distinctive pottery. It's theorised that a thousand years later, new arrivals from Melanesia assimilated, displaced or killed the descendants of the first Polynesian colonists and it was the blending of these two cultures that gave rise to the indigenous Fijian culture of today.

Around 500 BC a shift from a coastal, fishing lifestyle towards agriculture occurred, along with an expansion of population – probably due to further immigration from other parts of Melanesia – that led to an increase in intertribal feuding and cannibalism.

European Arrival & Settlement

In the early 19th century Fiji was known to European whalers, sandalwood and *bêche-de-mer* traders. By the 1830s a small whaling and beachcomber settlement had been established at Levuka on Ovalau. It became one of the main ports of call in the South Pacific, and was the centre of the notorious blackbirding trade.

The introduction of firearms by the Europeans resulted in an increase in violent tribal warfare, particularly from the late 1840s to the early 1850s. The eventual victor, Ratu Seru Cakobau of Bau, became known to foreigners as Tui Viti (King of Fiji), despite having no real claim over most of Fiji.

By the mid-19th century, London Missionary Society pastors and Wesleyan Methodist missionaries had found their way to Fiji, having entered the southern Lau Group from Tahiti and Tonga in the 1830s. They gradually displaced the priests of the old religion and assumed privileged positions in island society, instilling a legacy of influence.

In 1871 Cakobau formed a Fiji-wide government but, unable to maintain peace, it quickly crumbled. Two years later Britain agreed to annex Fiji, citing blackbirding as its principal justification. Fiji was pronounced a British crown colony on 10 October 1874.

Colonial Period & Independence

Fiji's economy became depressed following the slump in the cotton market at the end of the US Civil War. Unrest and epidemics ensued, with measles wiping out a third of the indigenous population. Fearing a racial war, the colonial government sought the support of the chiefs in order to control the masses. The existing Fijian hierarchy was incorporated into the colonial administration and, in order to curb quibbling, the sale of land to foreigners was forbidden.

Under increasing pressure to make the Fijian economy self-sufficient, the colonial government turned to plantation crops, which demanded large pools of cheap labour. Indentured labour seemed the perfect solution, and between 1879 and 1916 more than 60,000 Indians were transported to Fiji. Many came with hopes of escaping poverty, but were faced with heavy work allocations, low wages, unjust treatment and rationed food. Despite the hardship, the vast majority of *girmityas* (indentured labourers) decided to stay in Fiji once they had served their contract, and many brought their families across from India to join them. They were prohibited from buying land and discouraged from interacting with Fijians.

On 10 October 1970 Fiji regained its independence after 96 years of colonial administration. The new constitution followed the British model, although political seats and parties were racially divided.

Fiji's first postindependence election was won by the indigenous Fijian Alliance Party (FAP), and Fijians were at first optimistic about their future. However, underlying racial tensions grew as the economy worsened.

Era of the Coups

Greater unity among workers led to the formation of the Fiji Labour Party (FLP), and in April 1987 an FLP government was elected in coalition with the National Federation Party (NFP). Despite having a Fijian prime minister and majority indigenous-Fijian cabinet, the new government was labelled 'Indian dominated' and racial tensions rose. On 14 May 1987, only a month after the elections, Lieutenant Colonel Sitiveni Rabuka took over the elected government in a bloodless coup and formed a civil interim government supported by the Great Council of Chiefs.

In September 1987 Rabuka again intervened with military force. The 1970 constitution was invalidated, Fiji was declared a republic and dismissed from the Commonwealth, and Rabuka proclaimed himself head of state.

The coups, which were supposed to benefit all indigenous Fijians, in fact caused immense hardship. The economy's two main sources of income, sugar and tourism, were seriously affected, overseas aid was suspended and about 50,000 people – mostly Indo-Fijian skilled tradespeople and professionals – emigrated.

In the elections of May 1999 the FLP formed a coalition with the Fijian Association Party. Indo-Fijian Mahendra Chaudhry became prime minister, and indigenous Fijians were far from pleased. On 19 May 2000 armed men entered parliament in Suva and took 30 hostages, including Prime Minister Chaudhry. Failed businessman George Speight quickly became the face of the coup, claiming to represent indigenous Fijians. He demanded the resignation of both Chaudhry and President Ratu Sir Kamisese Mara and that a 1997 multiethnic constitution be abandoned.

Support for Speight's group was widespread, and Indo-Fijians suffered such harassment that many fled the country. Both Chaudhry and Mara eventually stepped down, the head of Fiji's military, Commander Frank Bainimarama, announced martial law and the 1997 constitution was revoked – but not for long.

In March 2001 the appeal court decided to uphold the 1997 constitution and ruled that Fiji be taken to the polls. Lasenia Qarase, heading the Fijian People's Party (SLD), won 32 of the 71 parliamentary seats in the August 2001 elections but defied the constitution by including no FLP members in his cabinet.

By 2004 the country was once again divided, this time by the Qarase government's draft *Promotion of Reconciliation, Tolerance and Unity (PRTU) Bill*, whose opponents saw the amnesty provisions for those involved in the coup was untenable. Backed by the military, Commodore Frank Bainimarama presented a list of demands to the Qarase government, which included dropping the PRTU and other controversial bills.

Although Qarase met several of the demands, it wasn't enough. On 5 December 2006 President Ratu Josefa Iloilo dissolved parliament on Bainimarama's order and Qarase was put under house arrest. Several key groups did not approve of Bainimarama's coup, including the Methodist Church and the Great Council of Chiefs, who refused to meet without Qarase, but it was to little avail when Bainimarama declared a state of emergency.

Bainimarama Secures His Position

In 2009 the constitution was annulled and the Court of Appeal was disbanded after it ruled the 2006 coup illegal. The same year Fiji was suspended from participation in the Pacific Islands Forum and dismissed (again) from the Commonwealth of Nations for failing to return to democracy. In 2012 Bainimarama consolidated power even further by abolishing the Great Council of Chiefs.

A new constitution was promulgated in 2013, promising a popular vote in 2014. When elections were finally held, Bainimarana was returned as prime minister with a large mandate, and Fiji was returned to the Commonwealth.

Bainimarama's plans for a new Fiji free of its old colonial ties came to a head in 2015, when his government unexpectedly announced the national flag – which has the British Union Jack in the corner – would be replaced. A public competition was held to design the new flag, and the national conversation drew sharp opinions both for and against the move. The new flag was due to be unveiled around the middle of 2016.

The Culture

The National Psyche

The Fijian people are the country's greatest asset. A smile goes a long way here, and Fijians of all backgrounds go to great lengths to make visitors feel welcome. Sometimes, however, these lengths can be too great. Not wishing to disappoint, a Fijian 'yes' might mean 'maybe' or 'no', which can be disconcerting if not confusing for visitors. Face-

KAVA

Few visitors will spend time in Fiji without being offered to join a kava ceremony at least once. This drink (more correctly called *yaqona*, and colloquially called 'grog') is made from an infusion of powdered roots from *Piper methysticum*, a type of pepper plant. Before the arrival of Christianity, *yaqona* was a ritual drink reserved for chiefs and priests, though nowadays gathering around a kava bowl for conversation with friends is an essential part of Fijian social life.

The ritual aspect of kava remains important. When visiting a village, you'll usually be welcomed with a *sevusevu* ceremony, centred on *yaqona* drinking. Visitors sit cross-legged facing their hosts and a large central wooden bowl (*tanoa*). Never walk around across the circle or turn your back to it, or step over the coir cord that ties the white cowrie shell to the *tanoa* (it represents a link to the ancestors).

The powdered *yaqona* is wrapped in cloth and mixed with water in the *tanoa*. The resulting infusion looks a little like muddy water. You'll be offered a *bilo* (coconut shell cup) with the drink. Clap, then accept the *bilo* and drink it down in one: bear this in mind if your hosts offer to fill your cup 'low tide' or 'high tide.' On drinking, everyone claps three times, and the *bilo* is passed back to the server. You needn't drink every *bilo* you're offered, but it's polite to at least drink the first. Bear in mind that once a kava session starts, it doesn't end until the *tanoa* is empty.

Kava is only very mildly narcotic. After a few drinks you might feel a slight numbness on the lips, but stronger mixes can induce drowsiness (kava from Kadavu is said to be the most potent). In 2014 a local drinks company started selling Tāki Mai, an 'anti-stress' shot drink with kava extract. Some Fijians we spoke to were skeptical, though: if you really want to de-stress, they told us, the best way is still to sit around all night chatting with your mates while drinking grog. Pass the *bilo*!

to-face confrontation is rare, but debate is a healthy component of daily life (just scan the readers' letters of any newspaper and you'll get the gist). The different challenges facing indigenous Fijians and Indo-Fijians remain key to a sense of national identity, and you're likely to hear both sides of the story in complete candour during any visit.

Multiculturalism

Fiji's population is the most multiracial in the South Pacific. Indigenous Fijians are predominantly of Melanesian origin, but there are Polynesian aspects in both their physical appearance and their culture. Most Indo-Fijians are descendants of indentured labourers. They constitute around 38% of the population, although large numbers continue to emigrate.

The government categorises people according to their racial origins, as you will notice on the immigration arrival card. 'Fijian' means indigenous Fijian, and while many Indo-Fijians have lived in Fiji for several generations they are still referred to as 'Indian', just as Chinese-Fijians are 'Chinese'. Fijians of other Pacific island descent are referred to by the nationality of their ancestors. Australians, Americans, New Zealanders – and Europeans – are referred to as 'Europeans'. Mixed Western and Fijian heritage makes a person officially 'part-European'.

INDIGENOUS FIJIANS

Most indigenous Fijians live in villages in *mataqali* (extended family, or kinship, groups) and acknowledge a hereditary chief, who is usually male. Each *mataqali* is allocated land for farming and also has communal obligations. Village life is supportive but also conservative; being different or too ambitious is seen to threaten the village's stability, and traditional gender roles are still very much in evidence.

Concepts such as *kerekere* (obligatory sharing) and *sevusevu* (a gift in exchange for an obligatory favour) are still strong, especially in remote areas. The consumption of *yaqona*, or kava, remains an important social ritual, and clans gather on special occasions for traditional *lovo* (feast cooked in a pit oven) and *meke* (dance and song performance that enacts stories and legends).

INDO-FIJIANS

Most of this group are fourth- or fifth-generation descendants of indentured

FIJIAN LITERATURE

Moving Through the Streets (Joseph C Veramu) An eye-opener about disaffected youth in Suva.

Fiji and **Stalker on the Beach** (Daryl Tarte) Historical saga that looks at the influence of outsiders on the country.

Kava in the Blood (Peter Thomson) Engaging memoir of Fiji's cultures and coups.

labourers. The changes these labourers were forced to undergo, such as adapting to living communally with Indians from diverse backgrounds, created a relatively unrestricted, enterprising society distinct from the Indian cultures they left behind. This is the basis for the Indo-Fijian culture of today.

Extended families often live in the same house, and in rural areas it's common for girls to have arranged marriages at an early age. Many women wear traditional dress, although dress codes are more cosmopolitan in Suva.

Religion

Religion is extremely important in all aspects of Fijian society. About 60% of Fijians are Christian (the majority of whom are Methodist), 30% are Hindu, 6% Muslim, and nearly 1% Sikh; The remaining 3% are a mix of Chinese religions and non-religious Fijians.

Arts

Indigenous Fijian villagers practise traditional arts and crafts, such as woodcarving and pottery, dance and music, and making *masi* (bark cloth). Some arts remain an integral part of the culture, while others are practised solely to satisfy tourist demand. Indo-Fijians, Chinese-Fijians and other cultural groups also retain many of their traditional arts.

Contemporary art includes fashion design, pottery, painting and photography. The most likely place to see contemporary work displayed is Suva.

Dance

Visitors are often welcomed with an indigenous *meke*, a dance and song performance

FIJI ARTS

FIJI ON FILM

Fiji's cobalt-blue waters have provided cinematic eye candy for films including the following:

The Blue Lagoon (1980) starring Brooke Shields

Cast Away (2000) starring Tom Hanks

Contact (1997) starring Jodie Foster.

enacting stories and legends. They vary from touristy performances accompanied by a disco-Fijian soundtrack (common in resorts) to traditional and low-key.

One of the best places to see contemporary dance in Fiji is the Oceania Centre for Arts and Culture at the USP Laucala Campus in Suva.

Music

Traditional Fijian music blends Melanesian and Polynesian rhythms. Along with native slit drums, guitar and ukelele are widespread accompaniments. Many visitors will experience this by hearing a rendition of *Isa Lei*, the lullaby-like national farewell song, with which many resorts serenade their guests on departure.

Modern Fijian music has been influenced by the currents of reggae, rock and even hip hop. Hindi pop and Bollywood soundtracks are also heard everywhere due to India's deep influence on Fijian culture. Church music, particularly gospel, is also popular.

Bark Cloth

You'll most likely become acquainted with tapa (also known as *masi* or *malo*), the Fijian art of making bark cloth, during your first shopping expedition. The cloth is made from the inner bark of the paper mulberry bush. Intricate rust and brown patterns are printed either by hand or stencil, often carrying symbolic meaning.

Environment

Geography

The Fiji archipelago has about 332 islands, varying from mere bumps a few metres in diameter to Viti Levu ('Great Land') at 10,400 sq km. Only about a third are inhabited. The smaller islands are generally of coral or limestone formation, while the larger ones are of volcanic origin; hot springs continue to boil on Vanua Levu. Fiji's highest peak is Viti Levu's majestic Tomanivi (Mt Victoria) at 1323m.

RESPECT & PROTECT

Many of Fiji's endangered animals and plants are protected by the Convention on International Trade in Endangered Species (CITES). Others are protected by national legislation. If you buy a souvenir made from a protected or endangered species and don't get a permit, you're breaking the law and chances are that customs will confiscate it at your overseas destination. In particular, remember the following:

➡ *Tabua* are *tabu* (sacred) – whale's teeth are protected.

➡ Turtle shell looks best on live turtles.

➡ Leave seashells on the seashore; protected species include giant clams, helmet shells, trochus and tritons.

➡ Tread lightly. Stepping on live coral is like stepping on a live budgie: you'll kill it.

➡ Many plants, including most orchids, are protected.

Trash & Carry

Your litter will become someone else's problem, especially on small islands; where possible, recycle or remove your own.

Don't Rush to Flush

Fresh water is precious everywhere, especially on small islands; take short showers and drink treated or rainwater rather than buy another plastic bottle.

Ecology

In February 2016 Fiji was mauled by Cyclone Winston. The Category Five system was the strongest cyclone ever recorded in the southern hemisphere, with savage winds reaching 325kmph. At least 44 people died, scores more were reported missing, and thousands of residents were displaced: on Koro Island in the Lomaiviti group, 100% of homes were destroyed.

Along with other Pacific island nations, Fiji is on the frontline of global warming. In 2014, following the innundation of their town and crops by rising seas, the residents of Vunidogoloa on Vanua Levu were moved to a new, specially constructed village under the government's 'climate change refugee' program. Rising sea levels also threaten marine life, and increased sea temperatures have led to the phenomenon of coral bleaching: two-thirds of Fiji's reefs have experienced large amounts of bleaching.

It's not all doom and gloom. On the islands, a reforestation program for the sandalwood tree, logged out by 19th-century merchants, is meeting with success. In many areas threatened by overfishing, Fijian environmental groups working in partnership with local communities are finding increasing success protecting fishing grounds by declaring them *tabu* (sacred) at particular times such as spawning season. On a larger scale, the Fijian government has declared its intent to protect 30% of its waters as marine parks by 2020 – potentially the largest marine park network in the world.

SURVIVAL GUIDE

❶ Directory A–Z

ACCOMMODATION

All room prices include bathrooms unless specified otherwise. Hotel websites commonly quote prices in various currencies (US$, A$, NZ$), although we usually quote prices in Fijian dollars for ease of comparison.

ACTIVITIES
Diving & Snorkelling

Fiji is a marvellous place to take the plunge. Among the best underwater spots are Taveuni, Nananu-i-Ra, Kadavu, Namena Marine Reserve and the Mamanuca and Yasawa groups. Fiji has scores of excellent dive operators. On average, an introductory dive costs about $200, a two-tank dive between $230 and $350 (including equipment rental), and an open-water certification course between $800 and $975.

Hiking

Viti Levu and Taveuni are the best islands for hiking. Suva's Colo-i-Suva Forest Park and Taveuni's Lavena Coastal Walk have marked trails that don't require guides or permission. Hiking hot spots in the Viti Levu highlands include Mt Batilamu and Koroyanitu National Heritage Park.

Kayaking

Sea-kayaking tours are available during the drier months (between May and November), and combine paddling with hiking, snorkelling, fishing and village visits. Two prime areas for kayaking safaris are the Yasawa and Kadavu Groups.

Surfing

Surfing usually requires boat trips as the majority of breaks are on offshore reefs. The best spots are in barrier-reef passages along southern Viti Levu (Frigate Passage) and in the southern Mamanucas (Cloudbreak, Namotu Left and Wilkes Passage). These should be tackled only by experienced surfers. The dry season (May to October) is the best time to surf due to low pressures bringing in big waves.

CHILDREN

Fiji is a major family destination and very child-friendly. Many resorts cater specifically for children, with babysitting, cots and high chairs, organised activities, children's pools and kids clubs. In many resorts children stay, and in some cases eat, for free.

EMBASSIES & CONSULATES

All embassies and consulates in Fiji are found in Suva. A full list of these – and Fijian missions abroad – can be found at www.fiji.gov.fj.

EMERGENCY

☑ 911

FESTIVALS & EVENTS

Fiji hosts loads of cultural festival throughout the year, including many Fijian-Indian Hindu

---

SLEEPING PRICE RANGES

The following price ranges are for twin or double rooms during peak season (July to September) and include Fiji's 15% value-added tax (VAT) and the 5% hotel turnover tax.

$ less than $150

$$ $150–300

$$$ more than $300

EATING PRICE RANGES

The following price ranges refer to the prices for standard main dishes:

$ less than $15

$$ $15–25

$$$ more than $25

events (these are lunar, and dates change annually). See www.fiji.travel for a full list.

Holi (February/March) Hindu festival of colours.

Bula Festival (July) Week-long party in Nadi.

Hibiscus Festival (August) Huge Suva festival.

Diwali (October/November) Hindu festival of lights.

INTERNET ACCESS

If you can get a phone signal in Fiji, you can normally find somewhere to get online. In remote areas, prepare for internet access to be limited, expensive (due to the need for connection by satellite) or completely nonexistent. Many resorts have wi-fi.

If you're carrying your own laptop or iPad you can sign up for a prepay account with a service provider such as Connect (www.connect.com.fj), Unwired Fiji (www.unwired.com.fj) or Vodafone (www.vodafone.com.fj). The latter sells modem sticks for $79 and 1GB of data costs $15.

MONEY

The local currency is the Fiji dollar ($); it's fairly stable relative to Australian and NZ dollars. The dollar is broken down into 100 cents. Bank notes come in denominations of $100, $50, $20, $10 and $5. There are coins to the value of $2, $1, $0.50, $0.20, $0.10 and $0.05.

ATMs ATMs are common in urban areas and most accept the main international debit cards, including Cirrus and Plus. Although they are increasingly commonplace, you won't find ATMs in remote areas, including the Yasawas, so plan ahead.

Tipping Not expected or encouraged; however, if you feel that the service is worth it, tips are always appreciated.

OPENING HOURS

Most businesses open weekdays from 8am to 5pm, and some from 8am to 1pm on Saturday. Many places close for lunch from 1pm to 2pm. Practically nothing happens on Sunday.

Banks 9.30am to 4pm Monday to Thursday and 9.30am to 3pm Friday

Government offices 8am to 4.30pm Monday to Friday (to 4pm on Friday).

Restaurants lunch 11am to 2pm, dinner 6pm to 9pm or 10pm

PUBLIC HOLIDAYS

Annual public holidays include the following:

New Year's Day 1 January

Easter (Good Friday & Easter Monday) March/April

Fiji Day (Independence Day) 10 October

Diwali Festival October/November

Christmas Day 25 December

Boxing Day 26 December

TELEPHONE

There are no area codes within Fiji. To dial a Fijian number from outside Fiji, dial the country code ☑ 679 followed by the local number. To use International Direct Dial (IDD), dial 00 plus the country code.

Collect (reverse-charge) calls are more expensive and a surcharge applies when using operator assistance ☑ 010 or international operator assistance ☑ 022. Outer islands are linked by cable and satellite to worldwide networks.

Mobile Phones Mobile phones in Fiji use the GSM system. There are two mobile phone companies: Digicel (www.digicelfiji.com) and Vodafone (www.vodafone.com.fj), both of which offer international roaming agreements. Alternatively, you can pick up a plan or prepaid SIM card (ID required) at any phone shop. Prices start from $10, but look out for offers.

TIME

Fiji is 12 hours ahead of GMT. When it's noon in Suva it's midnight the previous day in London, 4pm the previous day in Los Angeles, noon the same day in Auckland and 10am the same day in Sydney. Add one hour to these times if the other country has daylight saving in place.

TOURIST INFORMATION

The head office of the Fiji Visitors Bureau is in Nadi: though its website is excellent, it offers little to walk-in travellers.

The **South Pacific Tourism Organisation** (Map p74; ☑ 330 4177; www.spto.org; 3rd fl, Dolphin Plaza, cnr Loftus St & Victoria Pde, Suva) is a useful source for regional information.

VISAS

A free tourist visa for four months is granted on arrival to citizens of more than 100 countries. You can check www.immigration.gov.fj for a full list. You are required to have an onward ticket and a passport valid for at least three months longer than your intended stay.

Nationalities from countries excluded from this list will have to apply for visas through a Fijian embassy prior to arrival: see www.immigration.gov.fj

for full details. The website also has information on visa extensions.

Those entering Fiji by boat are subject to the same visa requirements as those arriving by plane. Yachts can enter only through the designated ports of Suva, Lautoka, Savusavu and Levuka. Yachts have to be cleared by immigration, customs and quarantine, and are prohibited from visiting any outer islands before doing so.

❶ Getting There & Away

AIR

Most international flights to Fiji arrive at Nadi International Airport, with very few flights landing at Nausori International Airport near Suva.

Air New Zealand (Map p74; www.air newzealand.co.nz) Flies to Nadi from Auckland once or twice daily.

Air Vanuatu (www.airvanuatu.com) Flights to Port Vila, Vanuatu

Fiji Airways (☑ 330 4388, 672 0888; www. fijiairways.com) For international and domestic flights.

Jetstar Airways (www.jetstar.com) A low-cost airline that flies between Australia and Nadi.

Qantas Airways (www.qantas.com.au) Operates direct flights from Australia (Brisbane, Gold Coast, Sydney and Melbourne), New Zealand (Auckland) and the United States (Honolulu) to Nadi.

Solomon Airlines (www.flysolomons.com) Direct flights to Honiara, Solomon Islands, or via Port Vila (Vanuatu)

Virgin Australia (www.virginaustralia.com) Operates flights from Sydney, Brisbane and Melbourne to Fiji.

SEA

Travelling to Fiji by sea is difficult unless you're on a cruise ship or yacht.

Yachts need to head for the designated ports of entry at Suva, Lautoka, Levuka or Savusavu, to clear customs, immigration and quarantine. Present a certificate of clearance from the previous port of call, a crew list and passports. Advance applications must be made to request Port Denarau as a port of entry.

You must email or fax a completed Advanced Notice of Arrival Form (C2C) to **FRCA** (Fiji Revenue & Customs Authority; ☑ 324 3000; www.frca.org.fj) a minimum of 48 hours prior to arriving. Forms can be downloaded from the website.

Fees payable on arrival are $150 (quarantine) and $172.50 (health). On arrival, contact port control on VHF channel 16 to be directed to quarantine and await the arrival of customs officials.

❶ Getting Around

By using local buses, carriers and ferries, you can get around Fiji's main islands relatively cheaply and easily. If you'd like more comfort, or are short on time, you can use air-conditioned express buses, rental vehicles, charter boats and small planes.

AIR

Domestic flights are in small, light planes. The two domestic carriers are **Fiji Airways** and **Northern Air** (☑ 347 5005; www.northernair. com.fj). Prices vary wildly, but sample one-way fares include Nadi–Suva $89, Nadi–Kadavu $230 and Nadi–Savusavu $320.

Charter Services

Charter services are most commonly used by those wishing to maximise their time at island resorts.

Turtle Airways (Map p80; ☑ 672 1888; www.turtleairways.com) Has a fleet of seaplanes departing from New Town Beach near Nadi. As well as joy flights, it provides transfer services to the Mamanucas and Yasawas.

Pacific Island Air (☑ 672 5644; www.pacific islandair.com) Offers helicopter, plane and seaplane transfers and scenic flights in the Mamanuca and Yasawa groups.

Island Hoppers (Map p87; ☑ 672 0410; www.helicopters.com.fj) Offers helicopter transfers to most of the Mamanuca islands resorts from Nadi Airport and Denarau; charter planes also fly to Taveuni, Savusavu and Kadavu.

BOAT

With the exception of the ferries, often the only means of transport between neighbouring islands is by small local boats or pricey water taxis. These rarely have radio-phones or life jackets. If the weather looks ominous or the boat is overcrowded, consider postponing the trip or opting for a flight.

High-speed, comfortable catamarans link Viti Levu to the Yasawas and Mamanucas. Less-reliable services link the mainland to Vanua Levu, Taveuni and Ovalau. Irregular boats also take passengers from Suva to the Lau Group, Rotuma and Kadavu. The fast catamarans aside, ferry timetables are notorious for changing frequently, and there is often a long

PRACTICALITIES

Languages Fijian, Fiji-Hindi, English

Maps Specialist marine charts are usually available at Fijian ports but are expensive.

wait at stopovers. Toilets can become filthy; take your own toilet paper.

Note that most car-rental agencies won't let you take their car on board.

Nadi–Mamanuca Group

Awesome Adventures Fiji (Map p87; ☑ 675 0499; www.awesomefiji.com) Calls into five Mamanuca islands on its daily run to the Yasawas.

Malolo Cat (Map p87; ☑ 675 0205) Runs four daily transfers between Port Denarau and Plantation, Musket Bay and Lomani resorts on Malolo Lailai Island.

South Sea Cruises (Map p87; ☑ 675 0500; www.ssc.com.fj) Operates two fast catamarans from Denarau Marina to most of the Mamanuca islands.

Nadi–Yasawa Group

Awesome Adventures Fiji (Map p82; ☑ 675 0499; www.awesomefiji.com) Owned by the same company as South Sea Cruises, it operates the lurid-yellow *Yasawa Flyer*, a large catamaran that services all of the resorts on the Yasawa islands. It's a large boat with a comfortable interior including a snack shop and toilets, but you'll still feel the swell on choppy days.

Suva–Vanua Levu/Taveuni

Two shipping companies connect Suva and Savusavu, often via Koro, Taveuni and/or Ovalau.

It takes around 12 hours to reach Savusavu. For those bound for Labasa, a bus often meets the boats at Savusavu and tickets can be bought in Suva that include the Labasa bus transfer. Sometimes the boats depart from Natovi Landing, a half-hour bus ride north of Suva.

Bligh Water Shipping (☑ in Suva 331 8247; www.blighwatershipping.com.fj; 1-2 Matua St, Walu Bay) Has regular Natovi–Savusavu departures aboard the MV *Westerland* in three classes, including super-comfy cabins, double bunks and economy seats. The ferry usually arrives in Savusavu in the wee hours of the morning.

Goundar Shipping (Map p124; ☑ in Savusavu 885 0108, in Suva 330 1035; www.goundarshipping.com; Kong's Shop, Main St, Savusavu) The comfortable *Lomaiviti Princess* departs Suva every Monday and Friday for a 12-hour voyage to Savusavu, and onwards for 2-3 hours to Taveuni. Accommodation ranges from economy seating to first-class cabins; facilities include a theatre room, kids' playground and cafe. A second ferry is due to be added to the route in 2016.

Suva–Kadavu

Viti Levu is connected to Kadavu by only two companies. Both sail out of Suva.

Goundar Shipping (☑ in Suva 330 1035; http://goundarshipping. com; 22-24 Tofua St, Walu Bay) Overnight voyage from Suva to Vunisea every Wednesday on the *Lomaiviti Princess*, departing 10pm and arriving around 6am. Accommodation ranges from economy seating to first-class cabins; facilities include a theatre room, kids' playground and cafe.

Venu Shipping (☑ 339 5000; Narain Jetty, Walu Bay, Suva) Weekly overnight service every Tuesday evening from Suva to Vunisea and Kavala Bay on the *Sinu-i-Wasa* cargo ship. The ferry is basic but there are a small number of cabins with bunkbeds.

Outer Islands

There are very few services to the Lau, Moala and Rotuma groups. Those that run are slow, uncomfortable and erratic. Many islands only receive one ferry a month, making this an unreliable option for anyone with a fixed timetable.

Goundar Shipping currently visits Vanuabalavu and Cicia in the Lau Group, and Rotuma once a month – call ahead for the schedule. A new ship, the MV *Sea Rakino*, was coming into service in 2016, offering a more regular service linking the Lau group to Suva, with the possibility of a stop at Savusavu and Taveuni.

Seaview Shipping (☑ in Suva 330 9515; www.seaviewshippingfiji.com; 37 Matua St, Walu Bay) MV *Sandy* regularly travels from Suva to Upper Southern Lau and Lower Southern Lau.

BUS

Catching a local bus on Fiji's larger islands is an inexpensive and fun way of getting around. While they can be fairly noisy, the buses are perfect for the tropics, with unglazed windows and pull-down tarpaulins for when it rains. There are bus stops but you can often just hail buses, especially in rural areas.

CAR & MOTORCYCLE

Ninety per cent of Fiji's 5100km of roads are on Viti Levu and Vanua Levu (about one-fifth are sealed). Both islands are fun to explore by car or 4WD.

Driving Licence If you hold a current driving licence from an English-speaking country, you are entitled to drive in Fiji. Otherwise, you will need an international driving permit, which should be obtained in your home country before travelling.

Hire Rental cars are relatively expensive, but are a good way to explore the larger islands, especially if you can split the cost with others. Rates for a week or more with an international company start at around $125 per day, excluding tax. It's usual to pay a deposit by credit card; if you don't have one, you'll need to leave a hefty cash bond. Generally, the larger, well-known companies have better cars and support, but are more expensive. The minimum age requirement is 21 or, in some cases, 25.

Insurance Third-party insurance is compulsory. Some car-rental companies include it in their daily rates while others add it at the end (count on $25 to $30 at least). Personal accident insurance is highly recommended if you are not already covered by travel insurance. Renters are liable for the first $500 damage. Common exclusions, or problems that won't be paid for by the insurance company, include tyre damage, underbody and overhead damage, windscreen damage and theft of the vehicle.

Road Rules Driving is on the left-hand side of the road. The speed limit is 80km/h, which drops to 50km/h in towns. Many villages have speed humps to force drivers to slow down. Seat belts are compulsory for front-seat passengers.

TOURS

Fiji has many companies providing tours within the country, including hiking, kayaking, diving, bus and 4WD tours. Cruises to the outer islands such as the Mamanucas and Yasawas are extremely popular. Check out www.fiji.travel or ask at your accommodation for suggestions.

New Caledonia

📞687 / POP 270,000

Best Places to Stay

➡ Le Lagon (p159)

➡ Hotel Hibiscus (p173)

➡ Relais de Poingam (p174)

➡ Nëkwéta Fish & Surf Camp (p172)

➡ Refuge de Farino (p170)

Best Beaches

➡ La Roche Percée (p172)

➡ Baie des Citrons (p153)

➡ Baie de Kanuméra (p186)

➡ Fayaoué Beach (p183)

➡ Yedjele Beach (p178)

Why Go?

New Caledonia's dazzling lagoon surrounds it with every hue of blue, green and turquoise. The light and the space simply delight your senses. By becoming a World Heritage site, the lagoon has helped bring the people together to celebrate and protect it, from village level through to government.

New Caledonia isn't just a tropical playground. There's a charming mix of French and Melanesian: warm hospitality sitting beside European elegance, gourmet food beneath palm trees, sand, resorts and bungalows. Long gorgeous beaches are backed by cafes and bars, with horizons that display tiny islets to attract day trippers. Be lured into kayaks or microlights, rock climb, sail, dive into a world of corals, canyons, caves and shipwrecks, go whale watching or snorkelling, or relax on the warm sand of a deserted isle. Natural wonders and manmade delights are at your fingertips.

When to Go
Noumea

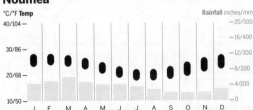

Apr–May Fresh from the heat and rains, the country is sparkling again.

Jul–Aug It may be cool for beachgoers, but that bodes well for hikers and whale-watchers.

Oct–Nov Catch life on the islands before folk head off on their summer vacation.

GRANDE TERRE

POP 245,000 / AREA 16,372 SQ KM

Orientated northwest to southeast, a chain of mountains sweeps down the middle of New Caledonia's main island, Grande Terre. Four hundred kilometres long, the island is 50km to 70km across for most of its length. To the west, in the lee of the mountains, are wide, dry plains dotted with country towns, while to the east, on the windward coast, lush vegetation descends to the sea.

The island is surrounded by its legendary World Heritage–listed lagoon, though this is not Grande Terre's only 'green gold'. The other is garnierite, a silicate rich in nickel that has fueled the country's economy since its discovery in 1864.

Administratively, Grande Terre is divided into two districts, Province Nord (the North) and Province Sud (the South). Île des Pins is officially part of Province Sud.

Noumea

POP 100,000

With its cheerful multi-ethnic community, New Caledonia's cosmopolitan capital is both sophisticated and uncomplicated, classy and casual. The relaxed city sits on a large peninsula, surrounded by picturesque bays, and offers visitors a variety of experiences. Diners can eat out at sassy French restaurants hidden in Quartier Latin, dine at bold waterfront bistros or grab a bargain meal from a nocturnal van in a car park. Meanwhile, shopaholics can blow their savings on the latest Parisian fashions or go bargain hunting for imported Asian textiles.

Central Noumea revolves around Place des Cocotiers, a large, shady square with landscaped gardens, a couple of blocks in from the waterfront. The main leisure area where locals and tourists hang out lies south of the city centre at Baie des Citrons and Anse Vata, with beaches, restaurants, bars and nightclubs.

While Noumea city has 100,000 residents, the greater Noumea area, including Le Mont-Dore, Dumbéa and Paita, is home to 164,000, or about 63% of New Caledonia's population.

◉ Sights

◉ City Centre

⭐ **Place des Cocotiers** SQUARE
(Map p156) This is the heart of the city. The square slopes gently from east to west and at the top is a band rotunda, a famous landmark dating back to the late 1800s. Place des Cocotiers is the perfect spot to watch the world go by. Near the band rotunda there's a popular *pétanque* pitch and a giant chessboard. Down the other end it's like a lush botanical garden, with palms and large spreading trees. There's free wi-fi throughout the square.

Regular concerts and street markets are held in Place des Cocotiers. Held twice a month, the popular Jeudis du Centre Ville street market has a different theme each time.

⭐ **Le Marché** MARKET
(Map p156; www.noumea.nc/en; ⊙5-11am Tue-Sun) This colourful multi-hexagonal-shaped market is beside the marina at Port Moselle. Fishermen unload their catch; trucks offload fruit, vegetables and flowers; and there's fresh-baked bread and cakes, plus delights like terrines and olives. The arts and crafts section includes a cafe. On Saturday and Sunday live music keeps shoppers entertained. The market is busiest early in the morning.

⭐ **Musée de la Ville de Noumea** MUSEUM
(Noumea Museum; Map p156; ☑26 28 05; Rue Jean Jaurès; admission 200 CFP; ⊙9am-5pm Mon-Fri, 9am-1pm & 2-5pm Sat) The beautiful colonial-style Musée de la Ville de Noumea, which overlooks Place des Cocotiers, is dwarfed by towering palm trees. It features fascinating temporary and permanent displays on the early history of Noumea.

Musée de Nouvelle-Calédonie MUSEUM
(Museum of New Caledonia; Map p156; ☑27 23 42; www.museenouvellecaledonie.nc; 42 Av du Maréchal Foch; adult 200 CFP; ⊙9-11.30am & 12.15-4.30pm Wed-Mon) The Musée de Nouvelle-Calédonie provides an excellent introduction to traditional Kanak and regional Pacific culture. Local exhibits are displayed on the ground floor and regional artefacts on the mezzanine level.

Mwâ Ka MONUMENT
(Map p156) Mwâ Ka is erected in a landscaped square opposite Musée de Nouvelle-Calédonie. The 12m totem pole is topped by a *grande case* (chief's hut), complete with *flèche faîtière* (carved rooftop spear), and its carvings represent the eight customary regions of New Caledonia. The Mwâ Ka is mounted as the mast on a concrete double-hulled *pirogue*, steered by a wooden helmsman, and celebrates Kanak identity as well as the multi-ethnic reality of New Caledonia.

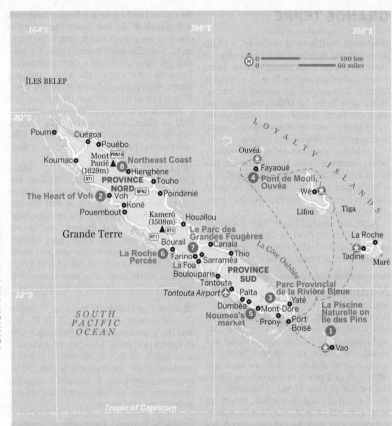

New Caledonia Highlights

1 Swimming with tropical fish at **La Piscine Naturelle** (p189) on Île des Pins.

2 Flying in a microlight over **The Heart of Voh** (p176) and the 'blue hole' in the lagoon from Koné.

3 Heading into the surprisingly isolated Far South for a hike in **Parc Provincial de la Rivière Bleue** (p165).

4 Admiring the stunning lagoon on Ouvéa and spotting turtles from **Pont de Mouli** (p183).

5 Drinking coffee with locals at Noumea's **market** (p151) while listening to a local Kanak band.

6 Checking out **La Roche Percée** (p172; Pierced Rock) and Le Bonhomme

(The Tubby Man) near Bourail.

7 Walking or biking among the great ferns at **Le Parc des Grandes Fougères** (p170) near Farino.

8 Riding the three-car ferry across the Ouaïème River when driving up the stunning **Northeast Coast** (p174).

Cathédrale St Joseph   CHURCH
(Map p156; 3 Rue Frédérick Surleau) The cathedral was built in 1888 by convict labour and is one of Noumea's landmarks. It has beautiful stained-glass windows and an elaborately carved pulpit, altar panels and confessional.

The main entrance is sometimes locked, but you should find the side doors open.

Musée de l'Histoire Maritime   MUSEUM
(Maritime Museum; Map p155; ☎26 34 43; http://museemaritime.nc; 11 Av James Cook; adult/child 500/250 CFP; ☼10am-5pm Tue-Sun) Looking sharp after recent refurbishments, the

Musée de l'Histoire Maritime, down past the Betico ferry terminal, has a mix of permanent collections and temporary exhibitions. The focus is on the maritime history of New Caledonia and, in particular, the voyages of the great French Pacific explorer, Jean-François de La Pérouse (1785–1788). There are interactive exhibits for children.

Baie des Citrons & Anse Vata

★ Baie des Citrons BEACH
(Map p158) Orientated north–south and less than 10 minutes from the city centre, trendy Baie des Citrons attracts locals and visitors alike. The beach is great for swimming, while the strip of restaurants, bars and nightclubs along the main road could well pull you in from breakfast until the wee hours.

★ Anse Vata BEACH
(Map p158) Orientated east–west, this popular beach is a hotspot for visitors to Noumea, with hotels, restaurants, shopping and other attractions. Only 10 minutes from the city centre, the locals relax here too, especially on the *petanque* courts next to the beach. On a breezy day at Anse Vata, you can watch the colourful kite- and windsurfers skimming up and down the bay. It's only five minutes by taxiboat from here out to Île aux Canards.

★ Aquarium des Lagons AQUARIUM
(Map p158; ☑ 26 27 31; www.aquarium.nc; 61 Promenade Roger Laroque; adult/child 1000/500 CFP; ☺10am-5pm Tue-Sun; 🚼) This aquarium is stunning. Species found in New Caledonian waters – including nautilus, sea snakes, stone fish, turtles, sharks and stingrays – have realistic surroundings in their huge tanks. Living coral displays are surprising but don't miss the emperor of coral reefs: Napoleon fish.

Ouen Toro VIEWPOINT
(Map p158) A sealed road winds up 132m Ouen Toro from just past Anse Vata beach. Two WWII guns still stand sentinel at the summit from where there are excellent views over Anse Vata and Baie des Citrons as well as the lagoon. Several trails weave through the wooded slopes of Ouen Toro.

Around the City

Tjibaou Cultural Centre ARTS CENTRE
(Map p166; ☑ 41 45 45; www.adck.nc; Rue des Accords de Matignon; adult/child 500 CFP/free,

---

ⓘ ONE PASS, SIX PLACES

On your first visit to a Noumea museum or site, ask about buying the 'Pass Nature & Culture'. It costs 1700 CFP but it gives you entry to three museums, the aquarium, the Tjibaou Cultural Centre and the zoo and botanical gardens.

---

guided tours 1000 CFP; ☺9am-5pm Tue-Sun) The cultural centre is a tribute to a pro-independence Kanak leader Jean-Marie Tjibaou, who was assassinated in 1989. It sits in a peaceful woodland and mangrove setting on Tina Peninsula. Displays include sculpture, paintings and photographs representing Kanak culture, as well as other cultures from around the Pacific. The main buildings are a series of tall, curved wooden structures which rise majestically above the trees.

The harmony between this contemporary architecture (designed by Italian architect Renzo Piano, who also designed Paris' Pompidou Centre) and the surrounding landscape is amazing. Behind the main building are traditional *grandes cases*; Kanak dance shows are held every Tuesday and Thursday at 2.30pm (2500 CFP). City bus 40 and the Noumea Explorer bus run regularly to the centre.

Parc Zoologique et Forestier ZOO
(Zoological & Botanical Gardens; Map p155; ☑ 27 89 51; Rte de Laubarède; adult/child 400 CFP/free; ☺10.15am-5.45pm Tue-Sun, to 5pm May-Aug; 🚼) Wander along a network of paths through gardens of native shrubs and trees, cactus and forest with a changing backdrop of sea views in the distance. You'll come across native species such as the flightless *cagou, roussette, notou* pigeon and various parakeets right in front of you. Speed around the Parc Zoologique et Forestier on a **Segway** (☑ 86 46 83; per person 7500 CFP) for something different.

Offshore Islands
The waters around Noumea are sprinkled with beautiful islets and the clear waters surrounding them are great for snorkelling.

Amédée Islet ISLAND
(www.amedeeisland.com) This islet, about 20km south of Noumea, is famous for its tall white lighthouse, **Phare Amédée** (admission 200 CFP), which was built in France, shipped out in pieces, and assembled on the postcard

NEW CALEDONIA IN...

One Week

Enjoy swimming at **Noumea's** beaches (Anse Vata and Baie des Citrons) and indulge in French pastries and bistro meals. Loll around the hotel pool, but emerge to visit the **market**, the gorgeous **aquarium** and, further out, the **Tjibaou Cultural Centre**. Ferry it to **Île des Pins**, pick up your awaiting rental car and explore the island, including visits to **Baie de Kuto**, **Vao** and **La Piscine Naturelle**. Walk in and along a river to a simple beachside restaurant where you can eat lobster. Return the car, catch the ferry back and dance like there's no tomorrow at an overwater nightclub.

Two Weeks

Follow the one week itinerary, then head north. Check out **Le Parc des Grandes Fougères** (Park of the Great Ferns), the beach and rock formations at **La Roche Percée**, and be sure to take a microlight flight over the **Heart of Voh** and the lagoon. Book ahead for a couple of magic days at **Relais de Poingam**, right at the tip, before heading down the east coast, discovering historical hotspots and buying up carvings and tropical fruits. Still time? Duck south and explore the **Parc Provincial de la Rivière Bleue** by canoe.

island in 1865. Climb up its spiral staircase to a narrow shelf with 360-degree views.

There's a snack bar and curio shop for visitors who come here on a day trip on the *Mary D*, which leaves from Port Moselle. Buy tickets at Palm Beach or Port Moselle.

Île aux Canards   ISLAND

(Duck Island; Map p158; www.ileauxcanards.nc; ⊙8.30am-5.30pm, restaurant 11am-3.30pm; 🚢) Île aux Canards is a cute postcard-perfect islet sitting five minutes by taxi boat off Anse Vata. It's all here, including an underwater snorkelling path, rental gear, a restaurant, and a stunning beach with loungers, hammocks, beach umbrellas and even VIP Lounges. Head to the water-taxi booth about halfway along Anse Vata beach (return trip 1200 CPF).

Îlot Maître   ISLAND

Only 15 minutes by boat from Port Moselle or Anse Vata, the gorgeous little island of Îlot Maître makes for a great day trip. Get out there with L'escapade (p160), which runs the island's resort, with Coconut Taxi (p165) or by taxi boat from Anse Vata. There's a beach and snack bar for day trippers, or ask the resort about using its facilities.

🏃 Activities

Diving

Abyss Plongée   DIVING

(Map p158; 📞79 15 09; www.abyssnc.com; Marina Port du Sud) Dives at many sites around Grande Terre and charges 7000 CFP for an intro dive and 11,000 CFP for a double dive, plus transport costs. It also offers PADI courses.

Alizé Diving   DIVING

(Map p158; 📞26 25 85; www.alizedive.com) Based at the Nouvata Park Hôtel in Anse Vata, Alizé Diving charges 13,000 CFP for an intro dive and 14,500 CFP for a two-dive package. Its boat leaves from Port du Sud Marina, but it includes transfers.

Amédée Diving Club   DIVING

(📞264 029; www.amedeediving.nc; 28 Rue du Général Mangin) Based on Amédée Island on the reef and in a marine reserve, these guys have some great options. Their Day Trip includes hotel transfers, boat transfers from Port Moselle, two dives and lunch. Departs 7am, returning 5pm, costing 15,000 CPF per person.

Water Activities

La Maison du Lagon   BOAT TOUR

(Map p156; 📞27 27 27; www.maisondulagon.nc; Port Moselle) This is a one-stop shop at Port Moselle for booking all your boat tours, whale-watching trips and anything else lagoon-and-water-related.

Centre Nautique Vata Plaisirs WATER SPORTS

(Map p158; 📞78 13 00, 29 44 69; www.mdplaisirs. com) On the beach at Anse Vata, this place offers up all kinds of water-sports activities including stand-up paddle-boarding, windsurfing, wakeboarding, kitesurfing, boating and kayaking. Ask about the MD Plaisirs Card, which gives you 40% discount and is usable here and at its other base in Poé Beach.

Locajet   WATER SPORTS

(Map p155; 📞77 79 79; www.locajet.info; 5hr 26,000 CFP + fuel) In Nouville on the western

Noumea

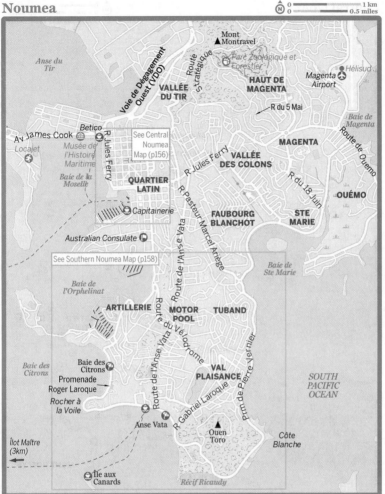

N 0 ——————— 1 km
0 ——————— 0.5 miles

NEW CALEDONIA NOUMEA

side of Baie de la Moselle, Locajet rents jet skis. Do a circular whiz from Baie de la Moselle to Île aux Canards, Îlot Maitre, a few more islets and back to the northern side of the Nouville peninsula.

Aquanature SNORKELLING
(Map p156; ☑26 40 08, 78 36 66; http://aqua nature.nc; Port Moselle; half-/full day 7000/8500 CFP) Specialising in snorkelling trips, Aquanature heads out from Port Moselle on half-day and full-day trips to snorkel on the reef with equipment included in the price.

Noumea Kite School ADVENTURE SPORTS
(Map p158; ☑79 07 66; www.noumeakiteschool. com; Port du Sud) Check out the website for all you need to know about kitesurfing and wakeboarding around Noumea.

Dream Yacht Charter BOATING
(Map p156; ☑28 66 66; www.dreamyachtcharter. com; Port Moselle) Dream Yacht Charter offers skippered or bare-boat catamarans and monohulls for 'the best lagoon in the world'. It also has a catamaran in Koumac on the Northwest Coast.

Central Noumea

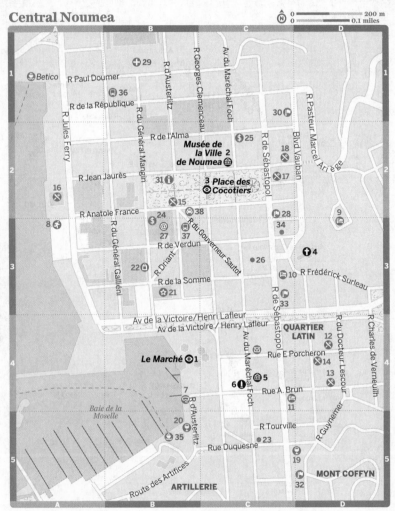

Land-Based Activities

You'll find all your favourite sporting activities are available in Noumea or around Grande Terre: golf, tennis, clay-pigeon shooting; just ask at the Office du Tourisme. It also has brochures for walks, cycling trips and climbs across islands, through forests and up creeks.

Noumea Fun Ride   BICYCLE RENTAL
(Map p156; ☑ 26 96 26, 78 40 25; www.facebook.com/noumea.funride.7; Gare Maritime; scootcars 1/2hr 5500/7500 CFP; 🚸) Based at the cruise ship quay, these guys rent wheels, including miniature cars, scooters, mountain and beach bikes. They also have helmets, child seats and roller blades. They're very busy when a cruise ship is in.

☞ Tours

Tchou Tchou Train   TOUR
(☑ 26 31 31; http://amedeeisland.com/tchou-tchou-train-excursion; adult/child 2000/1000 CFP; ⊙10am Mon, 3pm Wed & Sat; 🚸) Yes, that was a train you saw driving down the road. The bright yellow Tchou Tchou Train runs three times per week on entertaining and informative two-hour trips with an

Central Noumea

English-speaking guide. Book at the *Mary D* at Galerie du Palm Beach. If you see it out on the road at other times you'll know a cruise ship is in!

Mary D BOAT TOUR
(Map p158; ☑ 26 31 31; www.amedeeisland.com; Galerie du Palm Beach, departs from Port Moselle, Anse Vata; tour 14,250 CFP; ☺ 7.30am-6pm Mon-Sat) It's a grand day on one of Mary D's launches out to Amédée Islet. Visit the lighthouse, snorkel offshore or from the glass-bottom boat, feed sharks on the reef, indulge in a luscious three-course buffet lunch, and see fun dance and cultural shows. Includes hotel transfers.

Hélisud SCENIC FLIGHTS
(Map p155; ☑ 26 96 62; www.helisud.nc; 30min flight 43,500 CFP) Helicopters fly a maximum of three people over Noumea's bays, the islets sprinkled across the lagoon, shipwrecks and the barrier reef. You can even fly to Île des Pins or north to see the Heart of Voh. Based at Noumea's Magenta Airport.

✦ Festivals & Events

Noumea hosts a number of festivals through the year, including **Mardi Gras** in February, **Carnival** in August, **Régate des Touques** (Oil drum regatta) at Anse Vata in October, **Christmas Lights** in December and a major **New Year Fireworks** display.

In greater Noumea, there's a celebrated **Giant Omelette Festival** in Dumbea in April and a **Beef Festival** including rodeo in Paita in November.

🛏 Sleeping

Visitors need to make a conscious decision whether to stay in the middle of town or out at the beaches of Baies des Citrons and Anse Vata, a 10-minute drive away. The beaches offer up a lot more options.

🛏 City Centre

Auberge de Jeunesse HOSTEL $
(Map p156; ☑ 27 58 79; www.aubergesdejeunesse. nc; 51bis Rue Pasteur Marcel Ariège; dm/d 1800/4100 CFP; @ ⚮) This efficient and friendly hostel,

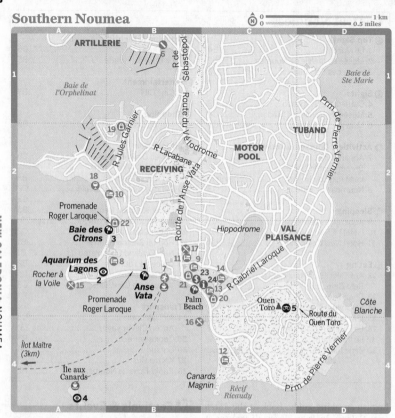

Southern Noumea

behind St Joseph's Cathedral, has a fantastic view of the city and Baie de la Moselle. The dorms and twin rooms share separate male/female bathroom facilities, while there is a kitchen, wi-fi, a television lounge and a ping-pong table. From the centre of town, head up the 103 steps at the top of Rue Jean Jaurès.

Hôtel New Caledonia HOTEL $$
(Map p156; ☑26 18 26; www.hotel-new-caledonia. com; 10 Rue Auguste Brun; d 9650 CFP; ✻☏) Simple and central says it all for this 28-room hotel in Quartier Latin in the city centre. It's just inland from Port Moselle, close to the action, and rooms have kitchenettes. There's wi-fi in the lobby and rates include breakfast.

Hôtel Le Paris HOTEL $$
(Map p156; ☑28 17 00; www.bestwesternleparis. com; 45 Rue de Sébastopol; s/d 11,450/12,350 CFP; ✻☏) With 24-hour reception in the centre of Noumea, Hôtel Le Paris is only a short stroll from Place des Cocotiers and right next

to Best Cafe. Rooms are spacious and simple and staff can arrange airport transfers.

⛪ Baie des Citrons

★**Hôtel Beaurivage** HOTEL $$
(Map p158; ☑24 24 77; www.grands-hotels. nc; 7 Promenade Roger Laroque; r from 9200 CFP; ⓟ✻☏) Nicely refurbished and in a brilliant location just across the road from the beach, the Beaurivage is a great option. Le Nahalie's Bar, the popular onsite bar and *snack* restaurant is open 6am to 10pm daily and Baie des Citrons' restaurant strip is only a short stroll away.

Casa del Sole HOTEL $$
(Map p158; ☑25 87 00; www.casadelsole.nc; 10 Rte de l'Aquarium; 1-bedroom apt from 12,150 CFP; ✻☏) This hard-to-miss skyscraper houses spacious and modern apartments with bright kitchenettes, comfy furnishings and private

Southern Noumea

terraces filled with views. It's a few minutes' walk from the beach, shops and restaurants.

Anse Vata

★ Le Lagon   HOTEL $$
(Map p158; ☑26 12 55; www.lelagon.nc; 149 Rte de l'Anse Vata; studio/ste 11,000/15,000 CFP; ✳@☎☀) Although back from the beach at Anse Vata, Le Lagon is the top boutique hotel in Noumea. An aquarium, lovely art and friendly staff welcome guests. The one-bedroom suites are double the size of the studios but all have modern kitchenettes, lovely king-sized beds and bathrooms with bath and shower. The pool's not huge, but the beach is nearby.

Nouvata Hôtel Complex   HOTEL $$
(Map p158; ☑26 22 00; 123 Promenade Roger Laroque; r from 9000 CFP; ⓟ✳☎☀) In the middle of the tourist atmosphere at Anse Vata, this complex has all the facilities you could need. There are three hotels: Le Pacifique, Le Nouvata Hotel and Nouvata Parc Hotel. Among them there are all levels of rooms and suites. The lounging areas, pool area and restaurants are welcoming. Look online for deals.

Ramada Plaza   HOTEL $$$
(Map p158; ☑23 90 00; www.ramadaplaza-noumea.nc; Rue Boulari; studio/ste from 18,000/22,000 CFP; ⓟ✳☎☀) With studios, suites and apartments at the twin-towered Ramada Plaza, the bases are covered. All are tastefully decorated in contemporary Pacific style and have racecourse or sea views. There's a gorgeous pool, a tropical garden, and the revolving restaurant features fine dining with fine views for all meals of the day.

Hilton Noumea La Promenade
Residences   APARTMENT $$$
(Map p158; ☑24 46 00; www.hilton.com/Noumea; 109 Promenade Roger Laroque; r from 20,000 CFP; ⓟ✳☎☀) A top spot on Anse Vata beach with gorgeous rooms ranging from studios to suites to apartments. The beach, restaurants and shopping are right outside. Exactly what you'd expect of a top-notch Hilton.

Le Méridien Noumea   RESORT $$$
(Map p158; ☑26 50 00; www.lemeridiennoumea.com; Pointe Magnin; r from 27,000 CFP; ⓟ✳☎☀) Out on the point beyond Anse Vata beach, this stunning hotel has landscaped grounds, a hypnotic pool area (the best in town) and several restaurants. You have transport to all sights and activities, should you ever wish to drag yourself off the premises. Check out the special deals on the website.

Outside of Town

Tour du Monde
B&B **$$**

(Map p166; ☎84 96 54; www.tour-du-monde.
nc; No 4 Les Fougeres, Col de Katiramona, Dumb-
ea; s/d 6000/7000 CFP; ❈ 🛜 ☀) It may seem
a suburban location, and it is out of town,
but you're in another world when you get
through the gates. Each cabin is themed
with pictures of the owner's travels, so take
your pic of the Orient, Broussard (think cow-
boy) or Melanesian cabin. There's a hot tub
and a small pool in a lovely communal area.

L'escapade
RESORT **$$$**

(☎26 05 12; www.glphotels.nc; Îlot Maître; garden/
beach/overwater bungalows from 18,000/
24,000/43,000 CFP; ❈ 🛜 ☀) This is overwater
bungalows at their best on Îlot Maître, a
couple of kilometres south of Anse Vata
beach, only 20 minutes from Noumea by
shuttle boat. There's a gorgeous restaurant,
a pool bar and myriad activities. Beach and
garden bungalows also await, and it's also
possible to head out there for a day trip.

Eating

Noumea has excellent restaurants specialising in French and international cuisine as
well as seafood. There are some great new
cafes in the city centre, plus plenty of options out at Baie des Citrons and Anse Vata.

City Centre

Aux Délices de Noumea
BAKERY **$**

(Map p156; ☎27 25 24; 21 Rue Eugène Pocheron;
⊙5am-7pm Mon-Sat, to 12.30pm Sun) There's nowhere to sit, but come here to Quartier Latin
for Noumea's best breads, cakes and pastries.
Beautiful displays and friendly service.

★ L'Annexe
CAFE **$$**

(Map p156; ☎25 33 15; www.facebook.com/lan-
nexe.noumea.7; Place des Cocotiers; ⊙6am-6pm
Mon-Fri, from 7am Sat) A great cafe right on Place
des Cocotiers that is perfect for a late break-

FOOD PRICE RANGES

The following price ranges refer to a
standard main course.

$ less than 1000 CFP

$$ 1000–2500 CFP

$$$ more than 2500 CFP

---

fast, lunch or coffee break. Sit back and watch
the world pass by with whatever tempts you.

Le Faré du Quai Ferry
CAFE **$$**

(Map p156; ☎20 67 60; www.cuenet.nc; ⊙6.30am-
5pm Mon-Fri; 🛜) This little oasis with free wi-fi
sits down at the cruise ship terminal on the
waterfront. Chic tables and chairs spill outside under bright sun umbrellas and a gorgeous shade tree. Beverages include freshly
squeezed juices, beer and wine, while the Bil'
Burgers and crêpes are superb.

Chez Toto
FRENCH **$$**

(Map p156; ☎28 80 42; 15 Rue August Brun, Quar-
tier Latin; mains from 2300 CFP; ⊙11.30am-1.30pm
& 7.30-9.30pm Tue-Sat) Head to this buzzing
little restaurant for terrific French meals; it is
truly so Frenchy, so classically chic, and, not
surprisingly, often full to the brim.

Zanzibar
RESTAURANT **$$**

(Map p156; ☎25 28 00; www.facebook.com/
restaurant.zanzibar.noumea; 51 Rue Jean Jaurès;
mains from 2300 CFP; ⊙11.30am-1.30pm Mon-Fri,
7.30-9.30pm Mon-Sat) It's all atmospheric timber and cloth, with a tiny upstairs verandah
and a range of dishes like duck with laven-
der. It's famous for its desserts.

Best Cafe
CAFE **$$**

(Map p156; ☎25 01 01; www.cuenet.nc; 47 Rue de
Sébastopol; mains 600-2950 CFP; ⊙6.30am-10pm
Mon-Thu, to 11pm Fri & Sat) Don't be fooled by
the look from the outside. Best Cafe is kind
of funky and hits all the right spots, no mat-
ter the time of day.

La Chaumière
FRENCH **$$**

(Map p156; ☎27 24 62; www.facebook.com/Res
taurantLaChaumiereNoumea; 13 Rue du Docteur Gué-
gan; mains from 1730 CFP; ⊙10am-10pm Mon-Sat,
to 2pm Sun) The atmosphere is warm and uncluttered in this old colonial building where
fabulous fine dining makes it very popular.
French favourites like fish soup or confit of
duck come with traditional accompaniments
that are hard to find elsewhere. Come for
lunch, share the menu, whatever – just don't
miss out.

Le Pandanus
CAFE **$$**

(Map p156; ☎29 75 75; 25 Rue de Sebastopol;
⊙6am-6pm Mon-Sat) With takeout bakery
products such as sandwiches, cakes and tarts
out front and a full sit-down restaurant out
the back, Le Pandanus is a haven for weary
feet just across the road from Place des
Cocotiers. A top spot to stop for a coffee,
brunch or lunch.

Baie des Citrons

The electric strip at Baie des Citrons has an oft-changing line-up of restaurants clamouring to be noticed: Italian, seafood, steak – you name it. Wander along, join all the other people soaking up the atmosphere, enjoy a drink or two, then pick your spot. The recommended Baie des Citrons drinking establishments usually serve good food too.

Sushi Hana JAPANESE **$$**
(Map p158; ✆23 88 87; Mirage Plaza; mains from 2000 CFP; ☺11am-2pm & 6-10pm Tue-Sun) Cool, quiet and frequently booked out, this restaurant has Japanese food brimming with fresh flavour. The best sushi in Noumea.

Anse Vata

Snack Ulysse FAST FOOD **$**
(Map p158; ✆28 69 28; 140 Rte de l'Anse Vata; sandwiches 5000-880 CFP; ☺11am-9pm) A popular *snack* that serves generously filled hot or cold sandwiches, burgers, chips and curry dishes. A good budget option. Eat in or take away.

★**Le Faré du Palm Beach** CAFE **$$**
(Map p158; ✆26 46 60; www.cuenet.nc; Galerie du Palm Beach; ☺6.30am-10pm; 🛜) In a garden setting streetside at the Palm Beach shopping centre, Anse Vata's version of Le Faré (the sister cafe is in town at the cruise ship quay) serves up tasty meals from early morning until late at night. The salads, burgers and crêpes really hit the spot, and the people-watching opportunities aren't bad either. Free wi-fi.

Fun Beach Restaurant & Grill INTERNATIONAL **$$**
(Map p158; ✆26 31 32; www.cuenet.nc; mains 2000-4900 CFP; ☺11am-2pm & 6.30-10pm; 🛜) Out on the peninsula between Baie des Citrons and Anse Vata, Fun Beach serves up salads, pasta, steak and seafood on a deck and surprisingly large indoor restaurant right by the bay. A very pleasant spot for a drink in the evening.

Le Roof SEAFOOD **$$$**
(Map p158; ✆25 07 00; www.cuenet.nc; 134 Promenade Roger Laroque; mains from 3500 CFP; ☺11.30am-2pm & 6.30-10pm; 🛜) It would be hard to miss Le Roof in Anse Vata. Out on the pier, spacious and open, Le Roof offers elegant fine dining with amazing sunsets, a cool terrace and, if you're really lucky, views down

on visiting sealife such as dolphins or sharks. Not surprisingly, the speciality is seafood.

Drinking & Nightlife

While there are places to drink in town, locals head out to the beaches, particularly the convivial bar and restaurant strip at Baie des Citrons, for a happy-hour beer after work.

City Centre

★**Art Cafe** BAR
(Map p156; ✆27 80 03; www.facebook.com/Artcafe-410011155804982; 30 Rue Duquesne, Quartier Latin; ☺6am-11pm Mon-Fri) Don't miss a drink at this terrific indoor/outdoor bar inland from the marina. You might chance upon live acoustic music while you eat pizza or drink cocktails on the terrace, and the crowd is friendly.

Le Bout du Monde BAR
(Map p156; ✆27 77 28; www.leboutdumondenoumea.com; 4 Rue de la Frégate Nivôse; ☺7am-11pm) Overlooking the Port Moselle marina, this is a pleasant place for a drink as well as a meal. It's open for breakfast, lunch and dinner, makes the most of the nautical atmosphere at the marina, and frequently has live music.

Baie des Citrons

★**Les 3 Brasseurs** BREWERY, BAR
(Map p158; ✆24 15 16; www.cuenet.nc; ☺11am-1am, to 2am Fri & Sat, to 10pm Sun) This brewery pub on the main drag in Baie des Citrons has it all; popular restaurant upstairs, brewery

---

NOUMEA FOR CHILDREN

Face it, the children just want to stay on the beach, swimming and building sand castles at Anse Vata or Baie des Citrons. But if anything will drag them away, it's a ride on the **Tchou Tchou Train** (p156). A visit to the **aquarium** (p153) is a must: endlessly entertaining and the perfect introduction to a trip out in a glass-bottom boat.

There's a **children's playground** at Baie de l'Orphelinat off Rue du Général de Gaulle, and another next to the public swimming pool at Ouen Toro, just past Anse Vata. Or head to **Le Marché** (p151): there's a buzz of activity, plenty to buy, and opposite, in the car park, children's fair rides.

Northern Grande Terre

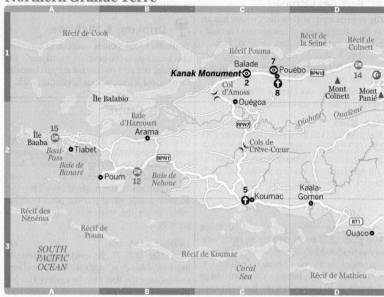

and bar downstairs with five of its own brews on offer, daily half-price happy hour running 4pm to 7pm and regular live music. It even does beer cocktails.

La Barca Cantina y Taqueria LOUNGE
(Map p158; ☑28 15 40; www.facebook.com/La-Barca-Noumea-506190522749625; ⏱9am-3am; 🕸) This fabulous spot transforms itself from quiet, relaxed lounge and cafe during the day to happy-hour pizza and beer 4pm to 7pm, to bar and nightclub later on with regular live music. Comfy couches, great decor and an extremely convivial atmosphere make La Barca a great place to hang out.

MV Lounge LOUNGE
(Map p158; ☑78 97 67; www.facebook.com/mv loungenoumea; ⏱10am-1am) At the city end of Baie des Citrons, MV Lounge sits so close to the water that waves are lapping the sand right in front of you. It's a relaxed and laid-back tapas-cocktail bar by evening; others turn up for breakfast, lunch and coffee by day.

🍷 Anse Vata

Code Bar COCKTAIL BAR
(Map p158; ☑26 05 51; ⏱10am-11.30pm) Streetfront at the Nouvata Parc Hotel complex, Code Bar offers up a lot more than a

regular hotel bar. Things get going in the evenings with regular live music, salsa nights and Latin dance evenings.

Le Bilboquet Plage WINE BAR
(Map p158; ☑26 46 60; www.cuenet.nc; Galerie du Palm Beach; ⏱11am-2pm & 6.30pm-midnight; 🕸) Upstairs at the back of the Palm Beach shopping centre, this brasserie serves tasty meals and snacks and has a spacious verandah that's a relaxing place for a drink amid plenty of greenery (as in potted plants).

Pop Light CLUB
(Map p158; ☑26 27 25; www.facebook.com/pop. light; Anse Vata; ⏱8.30pm-3am Tue, 10pm-3am Wed-Sat) This hugely popular venue in Anse Vata is fun, bright and as close to the water as you can get (without getting wet).

☆ Entertainment

For the latest, check out the *NC Pocket* (www.sortir.nc) entertainment guide, plus snap up a free copy of the English-language *Weekly* (www.newcaledoniaweekly.nc).

Ciné City CINEMA
(Map p156; ☑29 20 20; www.cinecity.nc; 18 Rue de la Somme; tickets 1200 CFP) Twelve theatres screen a large range of movies in French in central Nouméa. During La Foa Film Festival

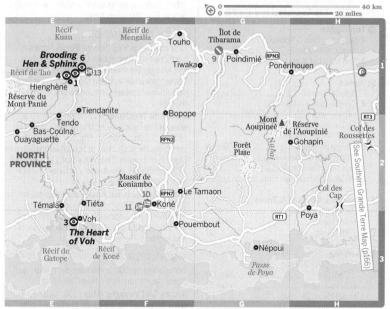

(June/July) movies are screened, both here and at La Foa's Cinéma Jean-Pierre Jeunet, in their original language.

Théâtre de l'Île   THEATRE
(Map p166; ☑25 50 50; www.theatredelile.nc; 161 Ave James Cook) This popular theatre is housed in a renovated old building at Nouville that has had former lives as a warehouse, a dance hall, a cinema and a boxing venue. Now a historic monument, the theatre offers a varied program.

 Shopping

In central Noumea you'll find shops selling French designer labels as well as prêt-à-porter outlets along Rue de Sébastopol, Rue de l'Alma and Rue Jean Jaurès.

Out of the centre, **Galerie Commerciale Port Plaisance** (Map p158; Baie de l'Orphelinat) is a pleasant mall on the way to the beaches, **Mirage Plaza** (Map p158) is at Baie des Citrons, and at Anse Vata **La Promenade** (Map p158), in front of the Hilton, and **Galerie du Palm Beach** (Map p158) have loads of boutiques and cafes.

Marine Corail   OUTDOOR, SPORTS
(Map p156; ☑27 58 48; www.marine-corail.nc; 26 Rue du Général Mangin; ☺8am-6pm Mon-Sat) For everything for water activities, from diving,

snorkelling and fishing gear to nautical maps, head to Marine Corail in central Noumea.

ℹ️ Information

INTERNET ACCESS

There is free public wi-fi around Place des Cocotiers and in a number of cafes and bars.

Cyber Nouméa Center (Map p156; ☑26 26 98; www.facebook.com/Cyber-Noum%C3%A9a-Center-872893476079877/; per 30min 250 CFP; ☺7.30am-5.30pm Mon-Fri, 8am-5pm Sat) Internet, printing, photocopying, DVDs, CDs.... you name it, they can do it here.

MAPS

The Office du Tourisme has excellent free maps of Noumea, New Caledonia and individual maps of the main islands.

MEDICAL SERVICES

Pharmacies, identified by a green cross, are dotted all over Noumea. Weekend on-call pharmacies and doctors are listed in the *Weekly*.

Decompression Chamber (Map p156; ☑26 45 26) A Comex 1800 decompression chamber, the only one in New Caledonia, is next to the hospital, open 24/7.

Hôpital Gaston Bourret (Map p156; ☑25 66 66, emergencies 25 67 67; www.cht.nc; 7 Rue Paul Doumer) Noumea's main hospital, this is the main medical facility in New Caledonia.

MONEY

ATMs that accept major credit cards are outside most banks.

Banque BNP Paribas (Map p158; ☑ 26 21 03; www.bnpparibas.nc; 111 Promenade Roger Laroque) Usefully located at the heart of Anse Vata.

Banque Calédonienne d'Investissement (BCI; Map p156; ☑ 24 20 60; www.bci.nc; 20 Rue Anatole France) Good location near Place des Cocotiers in central Noumea.

Banque Société Générale (Map p156; ☑ 25 63 00; www.sgcb.com; 44 Rue de l'Alma) Good location in the centre of Noumea; Western Union representative.

POST

Main Post Office (Map p156; www.opt.nc; 7 Rue Eugène Porcheron) The main office of the Office des Postes et Télécommunications (OPT) has a poste restante and fax service, and there's an ATM outside the building. There's also a post

office on Route de Anse Vata, on the way to the beach. Buy SIM cards here.

TOURIST INFORMATION

First chance, pick up the free *Weekly* from airports, tourist sites, hotels, Office du Tourisme etc. Also get the monthly entertainment guide *NC Pocket* (www.sortir.nc) for the month's festivals, exhibitions, concerts and Jeudis du Centre Ville themes.

Office de Tourisme (Map p156; ☑ 28 75 80; www.office-tourisme.nc; Place des Cocotiers; ⊙8am-5.30pm Mon-Fri, 9am-noon Sat) The very friendly staff offer practical information in English or French. The office walls are layered with pamphlets about every activity and service and the website is very good.

Office du Tourisme, Anse Vata (Map p158; ☑ 27 73 59; 113 Promenade Roger Laroque; ⊙9am-noon & 1-5pm) It's a little smaller than the office in the city centre, but the service is just as good.

TRAVEL AGENCIES

Companies that organise transport, tours and accommodation within New Caledonia:

Arc en Ciel Voyages (Map p156; ☑ 27 19 80; www.arcenciel.nc; 59 Av du Maréchal Foch) Arranges tickets for travelling or touring anywhere, including day trips to the islands.

Caledonia Spirit (Map p156; ☑ 27 27 01; www.caledoniaspirit.com; Le Village, 35 Av du Maréchal Foch) Expect friendly and efficient service at this small agency in Le Village. It specialises in the islands and has an excellent website.

❶ Getting There & Away

AIR

Noumea's domestic airport is at Magenta, 4km east of the city centre.

Air Calédonie (Map p156; ☑ 25 21 77; www.air-caledonie.nc; 39 Rue de Verdun; ⊙8am-4pm Mon-Fri, to 11.30am Sat) Air Calédonie is the domestic airline, with flights to northern Grande Terre, Île des Pins and the Loyalty Islands. It also has a ticket office (☑ 25 03 82) at the domestic airport in Magenta.

BOAT

The friendly and efficient **Capitainerie** (Harbour Master's Office; Map p156; ☑ 27 71 97; www.sodemo.nc; ⊙8am-4pm Mon-Fri, to 11am Sat) is at Port Moselle's southern end.

Betico (Map p156; ☑ 26 01 00; www.betico.nc) Noumea is connected to the Loyalty Islands and Île des Pins by the fast Betico ferry.

❶ Getting Around

TO/FROM THE AIRPORT

Tontouta International Airport is 45km northwest of Noumea. Public buses (Line C) operated by Carsud run between the city centre and the airport. A number of companies, including **Arc en Ciel Voyages** (Map p156; www.arcenciel-voyages.nc), run airport transfers (one way 3000 CFP). Taxis into Noumea cost 11,000 CFP (shared).

Magenta domestic airport is serviced by Karuia Bus. A taxi to the city or beaches costs around 1700 CFP (shared).

BUS

Carsud (Map p156; ☑ 25 16 15; www.carsud.nc; Gare de Montravel, Rue Edouard Unger) Operates buses on 12 lines between Noumea and the greater Noumea region. It goes as far north as Tontouta (400 CFP), passing through Dumbéa (320 CFP) and Païta (360 CFP), and south to Plum in Mont-Dore (400 CFP).

Karuia Bus (Map p156; ☑ 26 54 54; www.karuiabus.nc; Rue Austerlitz) This is the local bus service around Noumea city with 18 numbered lines. The red-and-white buses operate from 6am to 7pm. The ticket office is opposite the Compact Megastore; tickets are 190 CFP when bought there; 210 CFP when purchased on the bus.

Line 40 runs from the city centre to Magenta domestic airport and Tjibaou Cultural Centre. Lines 10 and 11 run out to Baies des Citrons and Anse Vata beaches.

On Saturday and Sunday only, Karuia Bus runs a hop-on, hop-off bus from the Ferry Quai. Line 12 Culturelle heads out to Parc Forestier and back, while Line 14 Panoramique runs out to Ouen Toro via Baies des Citrons and Anse Vata.

CAR & SCOOTER

The Office du Tourisme has a comprehensive list of car- and scooter-hire companies. Car rental costs from 3500 CFP per day, including free 150km per day – go for unlimited if you plan to tour the north or south.

TAXI

Radio Taxis de Noumea (Map p156; ☑ 28 35 12; www.noumea.nc/taxi) Noumea's taxis are operated by Radio Taxis de Noumea. Head to the main taxi rank on Rue Anatole France, across from Place des Cocotiers. There's also one near the aquarium at Anse Vata. City centre to Baie des Citrons costs 1400 CFP.

TAXIBOAT

Coconut Taxiboat (☑ 75 50 17; www.coconuttaxiboat.com) Hop on the Coconut Taxiboat to any of 14 spectacular islands. Your choice! Get dropped off and picked up later, or share your adventure with your skipper.

The Far South

The far south feels like a remote wilderness. The vast, empty region is characterised by

---

ⓘ ROAD WARNING

Before heading out to explore the far south by rental car, pick up a map from the Office du Tourisme. While the road from Noumea to Parc de la Riviére Bleue and on to Yaté is in good shape, things gradually deteriorate between Yaté, Touaourou and Goro, then become decidedly dicey from Goro to Port Boise, on to Prony and then to Plum. On this southern section we're talking total lack of signage, potholes that are more like bomb craters a small rental car could disappear into, and a massive nickel processing plant spewing smoke. Fill up with fuel and provisions in Noumea, and if you're planning on tackling the Goro to Plum section of road, mentally prepare for an adventure.

---

its hardy scrub vegetation and red soil, and offers a wide range of activities including hiking, kayaking and mountain biking. While Blue River Park sees the natural environment treated with care, the presence of a massive nickel-cobalt mine has seen sediments and toxic metals discharged into the lagoon offshore.

⊙ Sights

Monts Koghis   MOUNTAIN
Monts Koghis are clad in rainforest and rich native flora, and they have several walking trails; pick up a free route map. Or take a treetop trail on swinging bridges and rope walks with **Koghi Parc Aventure** (Map p166; ☑ 82 14 85; koghiparcaventure.e-monsite.com; trail 3000 CFP; ⊗ 10am-4pm Sat & Sun, by reservation Mon-Fri). The turn-off to these mountains is on RT1, 14km north of central Noumea.

★**Parc Provincial
de la Riviére Bleue**   WILDLIFE RESERVE
(Blue River Park; Map p166; ☑ 43 61 24; adult/student 400/200 CFP; ⊗ 7am-5pm Tue-Sun, entry closes 2pm) Protected Blue River Park is a reserve for many bird species, including the *cagou*. The landscape is a mixture of the far south's scrub vegetation and dense rainforest, and includes gigantic kauri trees. Take well-maintained RP3 from La Coulée to get to the western end of the hydroelectric dam, **Lac de Yaté**. It's a 2.4km drive from there to the park entrance.

There is a **visitor information centre** by the entrance gate which has good displays in English and French on the park's flora and fauna. At the entrance you will also find free

Southern Grande Terre

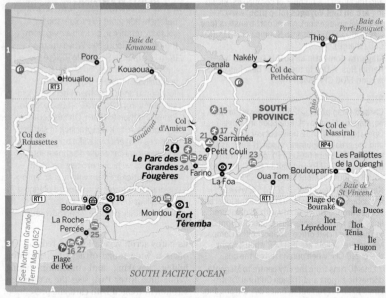

maps that outline the park's many walks, ranging from 30 minutes to six hours and from easy to difficult.

To the west and northwest of the park are Rivière Blanche and Rivière Bleue, Lac de Yaté's main tributaries. For the Rivière Bleue side, you can drive as far as Pont Perignon. A bus departs regularly (7.30am to 3.15pm, 400 CFP) from there to Vieux Refuge, taking 45 minutes each way. You can also walk, bike or kayak up the river. On the Rivière Blanche side, you can drive along the banks to the end of the road.

Le Site de Netcha   VIEWPOINT
(Map p166; day entry adult 400 CFP) Here, there are wooden platforms over the river and shelters and tables overlooking the water where you can picnic. You can camp here (500 CFP per tent) and rent canoes. From RP3, take the signposted road turning south at the eastern end of the Lac de Yaté. The 400 CFP entry fee also gets you into Chutes de la Madeleine.

Chutes de la Madeleine   WATERFALL
(Map p166; adult 400 CFP; ⏰8am-5pm) This ladylike waterfall, with its wide apron of tinkling water, sits in a botanic reserve in the middle of a vast plain. Swimming is forbidden at the waterfall, but allowed back towards the main road.

Touaourou Church   CHURCH
(Église de Touaourou; Map p166) If you do any driving around Grande Terre, you're bound to be stunned by the number of old churches. It seems that every village has at least one. At Touaourou, south of Yaté, the church demands a photo. Backed by a wall of mountains and tall pines, the bright white and blue *église* sits next to a makeshift soccer field.

Cascade de Wadiana   WATERFALL
(Map p166) At Goro on the east coast the road passes beside Wadiana falls, which cascade down a rocky slope into a natural pool where you can swim.

Port Boisé   BEACH
(Map p166) Port Boisé is an isolated bay surrounded by a forest of Cook pines, 6.5km from the turn-off on the main road. The ecolodge here makes a good base for the walking tracks along the coast and to a lookout point. It's also a top spot for lunch. You'll have to drive through heavy mining territory to get here.

Prony   VILLAGE
(Map p166) Once a convict centre, Prony sits in a lush hollow surrounded by forest beside Baie de Prony. A stream runs through the village of corrugated-iron cottages and overgrown stone ruins. The first European

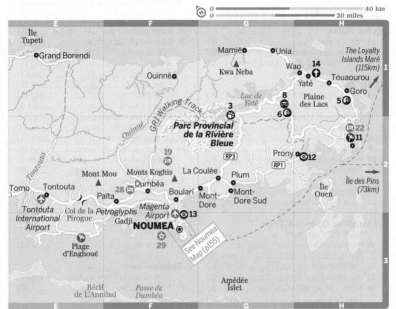

inhabitants were Captain Sebert and 29 convicts who landed here in 1867 to log timber for building materials for the growing colony.

The GR1 walking track starts about 500m south of the village at Baie de la Somme, which is part of the larger Baie de Prony.

🏃 Activities

There's a great range of activities waiting in the far south: canoeing, kayaking, mountain biking, walking, hunting or sitting by a stream.

Whale Watching   WILDLIFE WATCHING
(www.maisondulagon.nc) The whale-watching season runs from 11 July to 13 September, with great opportunities to head out and view humpback whales, especially in seas around the far south. La Maison du Lagon in Noumea can provide information on a dozen whale-watch operations that meet required industry standards. Expect to pay in the vicinity of 10,000 CFP per person.

GRNC1 Walking Track   HIKING
(Grande Randonnée 1; www.province-sud.nc/content/gr-nc1) The GR1 is a five-day (123.4km) hike from Prony through Parc Provincial de la Rivière Bleue and northwest to Dumbéa. This is a trek from the sea through plains, forests, hills, mountains and streams with huts

to bunk down in along the way. Download the seven stages of the hike from the website.

Aventure Pulsion   KAYAKING
(📞 26 27 48; www.aventure-pulsion.nc) There are lots of outdoor adventure options with these guys including canoeing, kayaking and 4WD trips. They'll also do drop-offs and pick-ups for GRNC1 hikers.

Sud Loisirs   BICYCLE RENTAL
(📞 77 81 43; www.sudloisirs.nc) Hire a mountain bike, a kickbike, a kayak, or take part in a bike/kayak combo tour in Parc Provincial de la Rivière Bleue. Ask the ranger at the park entrance for directions to the kiosk.

Pacific Free Ride   ADVENTURE SPORTS
(📞 79 22 02; www.pfr.nc) All sorts of activities including hiking, canyoning and kayaking at various spots around the far south.

🛏 Sleeping

Accommodation places serve meals to nonguests but you must book in advance.

Site de Netcha Camping Site   CAMPGROUND $
(Map p166; 📞 46 98 00; camping 1000 CFP; 🅿) Roofed campsites, set by the river, have camp fires, tables and benches, plus there

are bathroom facilities. There's no electricity and you'll need to take drinking water.

Gîte Iya　　　　　　　　　　BUNGALOW $
(Map p166; ☎ 46 90 80; www.office-tourisme.nc/en/gite-iya; camping 1500 CFP, bungalows 7000 CFP; ℗) The rustic but comfortable bungalows are in a coconut grove beside a small private beach. Meals are from 2100 CFP. You can snorkel along the fringing reef not far from the beach. There's a signpost to the gîte, just south of Wao.

Auberge du Mont Koghi　　　BUNGALOW $$
(Map p166; ☎ 41 29 29; koghiland@offratel.nc; Dumbéa; chalet/half-board 8500/17,500 CFP; ℗) Overlooking Noumea and its bays, 476m above sea level, the *auberge* has chalets and more remote huts about a 10-minute walk into the forest. The restaurant is open for lunch and dinner. It has a fireplace, warm timber interior, and specialises in melted-cheese *raclette*.

Loisirs Concept　　　　　CAMPGROUND $$
(Map p166; ☎ 83 90 13; http://loisirsconcept.nc; entrance 400 CFP, camping 70,000 CFP) A somewhat weird concept, but these guys have

tents suspended from trees a few metres off the ground in two locations at Parc Provincial de la Rivière Bleue. There are two tents at Pont Germain and three at Camp des Kaoris. You really need to check out photos on the website to get a handle on this!

Kanua Tera Ecolodge　　BUNGALOW $$$
(Map p166; ☎ 46 90 00; www.tera-hotels-resorts.com/hotel; bungalows with breakfast from 25,600 CFP; ℗ 🐾 🛜 ▨) This place is seriously isolated and hard to get to, on the seafront overlooking Port Boise Bay. There are 18 bungalows, plus a restaurant and bar. If you like seclusion, this could be the place for you.

ℹ Information

Visitor Information Centre (Map p166; ☺ 8am-12.30pm & 1.30-5pm Mon-Fri, 8am-12.30pm Sat) A small visitor information centre at Yaté (next to the market) has information on accommodation and activities, including walking-track brochures.

ℹ Getting There & Around

You'll need to hire a car to explore the far south. Head east out of Noumea towards Mont-Dore.

The road forks when it reaches the mountain at La Coulée: take RP3 to get to Parc Provincial de la Rivière Bleue and Yaté.

La Foa & Around

On Grande Terre's central west coast, the settlement of La Foa is a neat little town, 111km northwest of Noumea on RT1. La Foa is often seen as a staging point for exploring the nearby hotspots of Park of the Great Ferns, Farino, Sarraméa and Moindou.

ⓘ Getting There & Around

Several buses a day from Noumea stop in La Foa, but if you want to see what the region has to offer, it would be best to have your own wheels.

La Foa

The township and countryside around La Foa has an intriguing history. Atai, the initiator of the 1878 revolt, came from here, then later, groups of free settlers, convicts, Malabar Indians, Japanese, Indonesians and Polynesians from Wallis and Futuna established communities. You'll know you're hitting town when you look right from the highway bridge and see the Marguerite suspension bridge, designed by the disciples of Gustave Eiffel and opened in 1909.

La Foa township has everything you'll need stretched out along RT1, including supermarkets, restaurants, visitor information and a modern pharmacy. There is a weekly market next to the tourist information centre on Saturday mornings from 7.30am.

◉ Sights & Activities

La Foa Sculpture Garden GARDENS
(Map p166; ⊙6am-6pm) FREE The sculpture garden behind La Foa Tourisme features wonderful sculptures by artists from throughout New Caledonia. The garden is a pleasant place for a picnic, with a children's playground and public toilets.

🛏 Sleeping & Eating

Hôtel Banu BUNGALOW $$
(Map p166; ☑44 31 19; www.office-tourisme.nc/en/hôtel-banu; r 4350 CFP, bungalows 8350 CFP; [P][❄][🛜][🏊]) Right in the middle of La Foa on RT1, the Banu has both rooms and bungalows, though the latter, which are at the back near the refreshing swimming pool, are the best bet. The restaurant is open for all meals, or have a gourmet sandwich on the porch

(550 CFP) then try counting the 5000 caps on the bar's ceiling.

La Petite Ferme BUNGALOW $$
(Map p166; ☑44 34 05; www.office-tourisme.nc/en/la-petite-ferme; B&B per person 8100 CFP; ⊙Fri-Wed; [P]) For a farmstay experience about 12km east of La Foa township, head to La Petite Ferme, a 34-hectare ranch farming cattle and chickens. The bungalows with bunks are basic, but the reception is friendly and your English-speaking host, Jean Louis, runs 4WD night spins to see the deer. Meals are served in the garden, but book 48 hours ahead.

Dinner with wine is available for 4725 CPF.

Le Jasmin CREPERIE, ASIAN $$
(Map p166; ☑44 55 70; mains from 1300 CPF; ⊙11am-1.30pm & 7-9pm Tue-Sun; 🛜) This bright and friendly spot on RT1 in the middle of La Foa specialises in Asian cuisine and Brittany-style crepes. The food is good and there's free wi-fi if you're starving to hook up.

☆ Entertainment

Cinéma Jean-Pierre Jeunet CINEMA
(Map p166; ☑41 69 11; www.festivalcinemalafoa.com) A major event on New Caledonia's social calendar is the June/July film festival where international films, screened in their original language, are shown at La Foa's Cinéma Jean-Pierre Jeunet. Each year the festival is presided over by a famous person from the film industry.

ⓘ Information

La Foa Tourisme (Map p166; ☑41 69 11; www.lafoatourisme.nc; ⊙8.30am-4.30pm Mon-Sat, to 10.30am Sun) The friendly and efficient staff at La Foa Tourisme, the visitors information centre, can advise on accommodation and activities in La Foa, Farino, Sarraméa and Moindou.

Farino

Best described as a mountain village, Farino is only a 15-minute drive from La Foa, but it feels like a different world. New Caledonia's smallest district, Farino split from La Foa in 1911 and took its name from a synthesis of the name of a local Kanak clan and Farinole in Corsica, where many immigrants came from.

The road climbs steeply until you are presented with a majestic viewpoint over the plains and out to the lagoon from the Town Hall, at an altitude of 350m. Farino is known as the gateway to the Park of Great Ferns, but you'd better stock up in La Foa as there are no shops here. There is a market on the second Sunday of each month.

Activities

Sentier de la Petite Cascade   FISHING
(Little Waterfall Walk; Map p166) **FREE** This popular and easy short walk starts at the parking area below Refuge de Farino. It's about 1½ hours (3.6km) return to the small waterfall. Rainforest and an abundance of birds can be enjoyed along the way.

✸ Festivals & Events

Festival of the Bancoule Worm   FAIR
Held on the second Sunday in September: head to Farino to taste some fat, wriggling white worms. Becoming more popular by the year!

🛏 Sleeping

★**Refuge de Farino**   BUNGALOW $$
(Map p166; ☑44 37 61; www.office-tourisme.nc/en/le-refuge-de-farino; camping 800 CFP, bungalows 8900 CFP; P🐾) On a hillside in Farino's forest, Florence's superb timber bungalows have a kitchenette and forest views from their decks. There are barbecues, a hot tub (from 1890 CFP to use), a playground and 24-hour wi-fi around the bar. Breakfast is 950 CFP. BYO food is the way to go for other meals. Camping is also a great option.

Les Bancouliers de Farino   LODGE $$
(Map p166; ☑41 20 41; www.bancouliers.blogspot.com; Farino; camping per tent 1500 CFP, halfboard per person 8000 CFP; P) A lovely timber

---

PARK OF THE GREAT FERNS
....

Le Parc des Grandes Fougères (Park of the Great Ferns ; Map p166; ☑46 99 50; http://grandes-fougeres.nc; adult/child 400 CPF/free; ⏰ 7.30am-5.30pm Wed-Mon) This 4500-hectare park, in the mountains above Farino, features tropical rainforest with rich and varied flora and fauna. As the name suggests, tree ferns are in abundance, and most of Grande Terre's native birdlife can be spotted. A number of well-signposted hiking tracks range from 45 minutes to six hours, plus there are trails for mountain-bike enthusiasts. Head 6km up the unsealed road from Farino to the park entrance, where you can pick up a trail map.

The park sits between 400m and 700m in altitude.

---

bungalow with a mezzanine looks out over a river and sleeps six, or stay in one of the brightly decorated rooms that are attached to the house. It's friendly, rustic and you'll love the homemade (and often home-grown) food. Camping is another option.

ℹ Getting There & Around

From La Foa, head north on RT1 for five minutes, then turn right onto RP5, a major road which crosses the island. The road to Farino is signposted on the left after a couple of kilometres.

Sarraméa

Sarraméa, 15 minutes' drive north of La Foa, sits in a lush valley surrounded by mountains. There are good walking, biking and horse-riding opportunities. On the main road, just past the Sarraméa turn-off, is tribu de Petit Couli, where a beautiful old *grande case* stands at the end of a row of araucaria pines.

There is a market on the fourth Sunday of each month. Sarraméa hosts a coffee festival at the end of August.

✸ Activities

Sarraméa Randonnées   OUTDOORS
(Map p166; ☑76 60 45; www.sarramearandonnees.com; ⏰8am-5pm) Near the end of the road in Sarraméa, these guys offer a number of outdoor activities including horseback riding (from 4500 CPF) and quad bikes (from 7700 CPF). They also have a track available to hikers and mountain bikers for 500 CPF.

Trou Feillet   SWIMMING
(Map p166) At the end of the road in the Sarraméa valley, follow the signs for a five-minute walk to Trou Feuillet, a rock pool in a mountain stream that is popular for bathing.

Plateau de Dogny   HIKING
(Map p166) This popular hiking course covers 16km and rewards walkers with great views from a high plateau. With a vertical climb of nearly 1000m, it is a strenuous walk taking six to eight hours. Hikers should be well prepared before heading to the trailhead near the end of the road in the Sarraméa valley.

Stock up on provisions in La Foa and pick up a pamphlet on the hike at La Foa Tourisme.

🛏 Sleeping & Eating

Camping de Sarraméa Decouverte   CAMPGROUND $
(Map p166; ☑44 39 55; www.office-tourisme.nc/en/camping-de-sarramea-decouverte; tent 1500 CPF;

P) Right beside the road in the valley, this lovely shaded campground in tropical surroundings has shower and toilet facilities, plus tables and chairs. No shops, so bring your own food.

Hotel Evasion   HOTEL $$
(Map p166; ☑44 55 77; www.hotel-evasion.com; r/bungalows incl breakfast 9350/19,600 CFP; ✳@🛇🛇🛇) This upmarket eco-retreat has well-equipped rooms, plus smart bungalows with verandahs overlooking a stream at the end of the road in Sarraméa. There is a swimming pool, spa facilities, and an excellent restaurant that is open for breakfast, lunch and dinner. Meals (from 1860 CFP) are terrific.

🛈 Getting There & Around

From La Foa, head north on RT1 for five minutes, then turn right onto RP5. The road to Sarraméa is signposted on the right after 8km.

Moindou

A 15-minute drive straight up RT1 north of La Foa, Moindou is a small village with a long history. Visit reconstructed Fort Téremba, then stay in the village's beautifully restored inn. There is a market on the first Sunday of each month.

⦿ Sights

⭐**Fort Téremba**   HISTORIC SITE
(Map p166; ☑44 32 71; www.fort-teremba.com; RM9 Moindou; adult/child 800/300 CPF; ☺9am-4pm) Built in 1871, this historic fort originally held convicts brought to the area to build roads. Following a revolt by local Kanaks against French colonial rule in 1878, the fort was strengthened, then abandoned in 1898 when deportations came to an end. After years of neglect, it was restored from 1984 and is now classified as a historical monument.

The Fort Téremba Spectacle, held in October, features a play in period costume followed by fireworks. Explore the fort and view the interesting displays. It is 3km south of Moindou, signposted off RT1.

🛏 Sleeping & Eating

⭐**Auberge Historique
de Moindou**   HISTORIC HOTEL $$
(Map p166; ☑35 43 28; www.office-tourisme.nc/en/auberge-historique-de-moindou; RT1 Moindou; d 6650 CFP; P🛇) Right in the centre of the village and on RT1, this hotel, built in the 1890s, closed in 1976, has been beautifully restored and re-opened as the Moindou Inn, with

guestrooms and dining. Lovely furnishings and old photos make staying here a delight. Breakfast 580 CFP, Plate of the Day 1680 CFP.

Bourail & Around

With its strong Caldoche community, Bourail township is rural and inland, on RT1, 163km northwest of Noumea. The town itself is not the attraction for visitors. Most turn up for the nearby beaches of Plage de la Roche Percée and Poé Beach. The main road crosses the Néra River bridge at the southern end of town, and the turn-off to the beaches is immediately after the bridge when heading north.

Bourail

Bourail township has everything you need, from ATMs and petrol stations to *snack* restaurants and a supermarket. Get what you need before heading out to the beaches. There is a market on Friday and Saturday mornings from 6am.

⦿ Sights

Musée de Bourail   MUSEUM
(Map p166; adult/student 250/100 CFP; ☺9am-noon & 1-5pm Mon-Sat; P) An old stone building 500m south of the town centre houses the Musée de Bourail. Its displays include objects relating to the presence of US and NZ troops in Bourail during WWII and a guillotine complete with the basket where the decapitated head was placed. The guillotine was brought to New Caledonia in 1867.

New Zealand War Cemetery   CEMETERY
(Map p166) Nine kilometres east of Bourail on RT1 is the well-tended New Zealand War Cemetery, where over 200 NZ soldiers killed in the Pacific during WWII are buried. NZ troops set up a hospital in the area during the war, and many locals received free medical care there.

A ceremony is held at the cemetery on the Saturday closest to Anzac Day (25 April) and local children place a flower on each grave.

Arab Cemetery & Memorial   CEMETERY
(Map p166) Ten kilometres east of Bourail on RT1 is a mosque, an Arab cemetery and a memorial to Arabs, Kabyles, Algerians, Moroccans and Tunisians who were deported to New Caledonia between 1864 and 1896. Most took part in uprisings against French colonial rule in their homelands.

✦ Festivals & Events

Bourail Country Fair FAIR

(admission 500 CFP) Bourail holds a hugely popular country fair, first held in 1877, over the weekend closest to 15 August: there are farm animals on display; produce, arts and crafts for sale; children's rides; food stalls; and, the highlight, a rodeo. Campsites are available, and 25,000 people are expected.

⌷ Sleeping & Eating

Hôtel La Néra MOTEL $$

(Map p166; ☑44 16 44; s/d 8150/9150 CFP; ❋☎❋) This place has simple rooms with a river view, a pool and a children's playground, and is by the Néra River bridge. The cosy restaurant serves dishes such as deer curry, and you can head out on deer-hunting or cattle ranch tours.

ⓘ Information

Bourail Tourism (Map p166; ☑46 46 12; www. bourailtourisme.nc; ⊙9am-noon &1-5pm Mon-Sat; ☎) The town's helpful tourist information office is at the museum, on RT1 as you enter town from the south.

ⓘ Getting There & Around

Long distance buses heading up the west coast stop in Bourail, but if you want to head out to the beaches, you'll need your own wheels. There is talk of a shuttle service starting up from Bourail to the beaches, so ask around for the latest news.

La Roche Percée

Only a 10-minute drive from Bourail township, La Roche Percée has two famous rock formations: **La Roche Percée** (pierced rock), a headland with a hole in it that you can walk through, and **Le Bonhomme**, a stand-up rock off the end of the headland that's shaped like a tubby man.

The surf at Plage de la Roche Percée is caused by a break in the fringing reef, so you don't have to go out to the reef to catch a wave. The best spot is at the mouth of the Néra river. The beaches around here are also known as a nesting spot for sea turtles, and nests are monitored and protected by locals.

There are a couple of *snack* restaurants here, but no shops. The long beach is a popular swimming spot.

🏃 Activities

Three Bay Walk FISHING

(Sentier des Trois Baies) A walking track begins at the parking area at the base of the cliff near La Roche Percée headland, climbs the headland, then follows the coast past Baie des Tortues (Turtle Bay) to Baie des Amoureux (Lover's Bay). Allow 1½ hours for the 4km return walk.

There's a panoramic viewing point above Le Bonhomme where you can often spot turtles in the Baie des Tortues below.

Île Vert Eco-tour ADVENTURE TOUR

(☑78 40 26; www.nekweta.com/english; tour 6300 CPF) This fun half-day eco-tour, run by Manu at Nëkwéta Fish & Surf Camp, involves a visit to the offshore island, Île Vert (Green Island), snorkelling, observations of fish and fauna, plus explanations of local myths. Pre-booking required. Manu also operates a taxi boat to Île Vert (3150 CPF per person return).

Surf Charter SURFING

(☑78 40 26; www.nekweta.com/english; day trip 5250 CPF) Guided surfing tours out on the barrier reef run by Manu from Nëkwéta Fish & Surf Camp on a 7.4m banana boat. Opt for a four- to six-hour day trip or check out the website for full board and accommodation packages at Nëkwéta. Rental boards available.

⌷ Sleeping & Eating

★ **Nëkwéta Fish & Surf Camp** BUNGALOW $$

(Map p166; ☑43 23 26, 78 40 26; www.nekweta. com; d from 9150 CFP; ⓟ❋☎) One block back from the beach, Nëkwéta has a lovely tropical garden setting. Choose from an attractive *case* (bungalow) or one of the rooms in a two-storey building built from scratch by owner Manu. Meals are first class.

Plage de Poé

Plage de Poé is a beautiful, long white-sand beach 9km west of La Roche Percée. A 20-minute drive from Bourail township, Plage de Poé has *snack* restaurants, but no shops.

🏃 Activities

Poé Kite School WATER SPORTS

(Map p166; ☑77 60 59; www.poekiteschool. com) While the name says Poé Kite School, this place, at the western end of Poé, has all sorts of things on offer. Learn how to kite surf (3½ hours 13,000 CFP), ride the glass-bottomed boat (1½ hours, 2500 CFP), or rent a kayak (1100 CFP per hour) or stand-up paddle-board (1100 CFP per hour). *Snack* restaurant **L'alizé** is also here on site.

Poé Plaisirs WATER SPORTS

(Map p166; ☑75 00 01; www.mdplaisirs.com)
At the eastern end of Poé, these guys rent
out kayaks (1300 CFP per hour), windsurfers
(from 1500 CFP per hour) and stand-up
paddle-boards (1300 CFP per hour). Ask
about the MD Plaisirs discount card.

🛏 Sleeping & Eating

La Rêve de Némo CAMPGROUND $

(Map p166; ☑46 44 64; www.lerevedenemo.
com; per person/tent 300/1500 CPF; P) With a
great location along the Poé waterfront, this
campground has a *snack* restaurant on site
and good facilities.

★**Auberge de Poé** HOSTEL $$

(Map p166; ☑41 82 08; www.aubergesdejeunesse.
nc; dm/d 2500/7500 CPF; P❄🛜) This new
purpose-built hostel is as good as it gets, just
back from the beach. All rooms have ensuite
facilities, there's a laundry, a fully equipped
kitchen, a television room, free wi-fi and free
use of kayaks and snorkelling gear.

Hotel de Poé HOTEL $$

(Map p166; ☑44 22 00; www.facebook.com/hotel.
de.poe; d from 13,600 CPF; P❄🛜) This immaculate new hotel, a block back from Poé beach,
offers 14 fully equipped stylish bungalows
with bathrooms, refrigerators, TV and wi-fi.
The restaurant is open Thursday to Monday.
Highly recommended.

Sheraton Déva Resort & Spa RESORT $$$

(Map p166; ☑26 50 00; www.sheratonnewcale
doniadeva.com; r from 16,000 CPF; P❄🛜🏊) At
Domaine de Déva, a five-minute drive west
of Poé Beach, the Sheraton has everything
you'd expect to find at a new five-star re-
sort hotel, including two restaurants, a golf
course, a kids' club, a gym, a spa, bicycles
and water sports such as kayaking, stand-up
paddle-boards and jet skis.

Northwest Coast

Much of the northwest coast and its rolling
plains are taken up by cattle ranches. The
towns up here may have made their money
from nickel, but there is still plenty of interest.

Koné & Around

Koné, the Northern Province capital, is on
RT1, 274km northwest of Noumea. It has
all you'd expect of a growing rural town, in-
cluding a post office, *gendarmerie,* a clinic,
a pharmacy, supermarkets and banks with
ATMs.

One claim to fame is that the term 'Lapita'
was coined by archaeologists during a 1952
excavation near Koné on the Foué peninsu-
la. On mishearing a word in the local Haveke
language, which means 'to dig a hole', the
terms 'Lapita' and 'Lapita pottery' became
commonly used in research on the early peo-
pling of the Pacific islands. So-called 'Lapita
sites' have been uncovered in Melanesia and
as far away as Tonga and Samoa.

🛏 Sleeping & Eating

★**Hotel Hibiscus** HOTEL $$

(Map p162; ☑47 22 61; www.hotelhibiscus.nc; ⊙r
from 13,500 CPF; P❄🛜🏊) Be prepared for a
surprise. What doesn't look much from the
outside turns into an absolute oasis in the
middle of Koné township. Gorgeous swimming pool and gardens, immaculate bar, gallery and restaurant, plus tasteful rooms make
the Hibiscus one of New Caledonia's top boutique hotels. Co-owner Jean-Yves is a master
baker so you'll love the buffet breakfast.

Hôtel Koniambo HOTEL $$

(Map p162; ☑47 39 40; www.grands-hotels.nc; r
from 14,000 CFP; P❄🛜🏊) Named after the
nearby nickel-bearing mountain range, this
makes a very comfortable base to explore the
surrounding 'stockman's country'. There is a
heart-shaped pool, a restaurant and a *snack*
bar on hand. It's right next to the airport, just
north of town.

❶ Getting There & Around

Air Caledonie (www.air-caledonie.nc) flies three
days a week, taking 40 minutes from Noumea's
Magenta Airport to Koné airport, just north of
town. Buses head daily up RT1 from Noumea,
taking four hours.

Europcar (www.europcar.com) has rental cars
available from Koné airport.

Koumac

Koumac, 100km northwest of Koné, has
prospered from mining, both chromium and
nickel. The Tiébaghi mine (1902–64) was said
to be the most productive chromium mine in
the world.

The gateway to the far north and a sizea-
ble town, Koumac has an attractive marina
and an airport with direct flights to Nou-
mea. There are supermarkets, banks with
ATMs and plenty of *snack* restaurants. The

NEW CALEDONIA NORTHWEST COAST

town hosts one of New Caledonia's biggest Agriculture & Craft Fairs in September.

◉ Sights & Activities

Église Ste Jeanne d'Arc
CHURCH
(Map p162) Located near the roundabout, eye-catching Église Ste Jeanne d'Arc was constructed in 1950 out of a WWII aircraft hangar.

Reve Bleu
DIVING
(Map p162; ☑ 97 83 12; www.revebleucaledonie. com) Head to Koumac's impressive marina, La Marina de Pandop, where the dive club, Reve Bleu, is geared up to provide a grand professional experience. Intro dives are 6000 CFP, two-tank dives 12,000 CFP.

🛏 Sleeping & Eating

Gite du Lagon
CAMPGROUND, CABIN $$
(Map p162; ☑ 42 39 49; www.mairie-koumac. nc/Gite-du-Lagon_a420.html; camping/bungalows 1000/8400 CPF; P🛜) This attractive spot, right on the water a five-minute drive from town, has bungalows and camping and is a good budget option. The whole site is covered by wi-fi.

Monitel Koumac
HOTEL $$
(Map p162; ☑ 47 66 66; www.monitel.nc; d from 10,750 CFP; P❄🛜🏊) In the middle of town, Monitel Koumac has well-equipped clean rooms that look out on the pool with its inviting deck chairs. The restaurant meals (eat inside or out) are great and the service is friendly.

ℹ Information

Koumac Tourisme (Map p162; ☑ 42 78 42; www.mairie-koumac.nc; ☺ 9am-noon & 1-4pm Mon-Fri, 9am-noon Sat) Koumac Tourisme, the information centre, is at the northern end of town opposite the post office.

ℹ Getting There & Around

Air Caledonie (www.air-caledonie.nc) flies two days a week from Noumea's Magenta Airport to Koumac airport, just north of town. Buses head daily up RT1 from Noumea, taking 5½ hours.

The Far North

The remote region north of Koumac is known as the far north. Keep your eyes open for deer and wild horses, and if you're into bonefish fly-fishing, this is the place to set world records. Stock up on supplies before leaving Koumac, as there's next to nothing available in Poum.

🏃 Activities

New Caledonia Fishing Safaris
FISHING
(☑ 78 62 00; www.fishing-safaris.com) Richard Bertin's NCFS is for serious fishermen. Plan ahead for outstanding bonefish fly-fishing opportunities in the far north.

🛏 Sleeping & Eating

★ Relais de Poingam
BUNGALOW $$
(Map p162; ☑ 47 92 12; www.relais-poingam.nc; camping per person 900 CFP, bungalows 10,000 CFP; P🏊) On a long beach at the northern tip of Grande Terre, this place is a prime reason to fit the far north into your schedule. Comfortable bungalows have atmospheric 'outside' private bathrooms attached, there's a saltwater pool, and the restaurant serves wonderful dinners that include wine (3300 CFP). The camping area is right on the beach.

From the turn-off south of Poum, it's 23km to Poingam. The last 5km is on an unsealed road.

Hôtel Malabou Beach
HOTEL $$
(Map p162; ☑ 47 60 60; www.grands-hotels.nc; d bungalows from 12,500 CFP; P❄🛜🏊) This family-friendly place at Baie de Néhoué has newly renovated, well-equipped upmarket bungalows. The main restaurant's grand buffet (3900 CFP) specialises in seafood straight from the lagoon and there are plenty of activities – kayaking, trekking, tennis, minigolf. The hotel is signposted on the main road.

ℹ Getting There & Around

Air Calédonie has flights from Noumea to Koné and Koumac. There are daily buses from Noumea. Life will be a lot easier with your own wheels.

Northeast Coast

The stunning, relatively untouched coastline here features lush vegetation, gentle rivers, fascinating rock formations, waterfalls, deserted beaches and small villages.

Poindimié and Hienghène are the two main towns on the northeast coast. Both have grocery stores, a post office, clinic, pharmacy, bank and ATM, and *gendarmerie*.

ℹ Getting There & Around

Air Calédonie flies three times weekly from Noumea to Touho, halfway between Poindimié and Hienghène. **ALV** (☑ tel/fax 42 58 00; www.office-tourisme.nc/en/alv-poindimie; Poindimié; car hire per day from 5000 CFP) can meet you at the airport with a hire car.

Buses from Noumea run daily to Poindimié and Hienghène.

Poindimié

The largest town on the coast, Poindimié has a picturesque coastline and, stretching inland, the peaceful valleys of Ina, Napoémien and Amoa River, where you can admire the natural bush or pretty *tribu* gardens. These valleys are delightful places for a walk or a scenic drive. There are a number of *snack* restaurants in town.

🏃 Activities

Tiéti Diving   DIVING
(Map p162; ☑ 42 42 05; www.tieti-diving.com; dives from 7000 CFP) As well as dives, Tiéti Diving, which operates from a base next to Hotel Tiéti, offers transfers to Îlot de Tibarama (per person full day 2000 CFP), a great spot to relax, snorkel and swim just offshore from Poindimié.

🛏 Sleeping & Eating

Hotel Tiéti Poindimié   HOTEL $$$
(Map p162; ☑ 24 24 77; www.grands-hotels.nc; r from 15,000 CFP; P✳🛜🏊) At the northern end of Poindimié, this is the most upmarket place to stay on the northeast coast. There's a refreshing pool, renovated bungalows, a stylish bar and a topnotch restaurant, all right on the beach.

Hienghène

This serene village is tucked into the foothills on the shores of Baie de Hienghène, at the mouth of the Hienghène River. The area has fascinating rock formations, and it is known as the birthplace and home of Jean-Marie Tjibaou, New Caledonia's pro-independence leader who was assassinated in 1989. People speak of Tjibaou with great respect, and he is buried in Tiendanite, a *tribu* 20km up the Hienghène valley.

⊙ Sights & Activities

★ Brooding Hen & Sphinx   LANDMARK
(Map p162) Hienghène's renowned Poule Couveuse (Brooding Hen) rock formation sits on one side of the entrance to Baie de Hienghène, facing the Sphinx on the other. You can view these two rock formations

from the signposted lookout, 2km south of the village. There's a better profile of the Sphinx about 1.5km north of the village.

Lindéralique Rocks   LANDMARK
(Map p162) The Lindéralique rocks are towering black limestone rocks that stretch to 60m in height in places and are topped by jagged, sharp edges. They are best seen beside the road about 6km south of town.

**Centre Culturel
Goa Ma Bwarhat**   CULTURAL CENTRE
(Map p162; ☑ 42 80 74) This cultural centre on the eastern side of the river houses exhibitions, a museum and a sculptor's workshop. Undergoing renovation at the time of research, it was expected to reopen in 2016.

Babou Côté Océan   DIVING
(Map p162; ☑ 42 83 59; www.babou-plongee.com) Go diving around unique cliff faces and sheltered coral massifs (intro/double dives 8000/12,000 CFP), join an island trip to Îlot Hienga, which includes walking and snorkelling (4200 CFP), or rent a kayak (1500 CPF). There is also camping here for 500 CPF per person with free wi-fi. It's 10km southeast of Hienghène township.

🛏 Sleeping & Eating

In the Hienghène valley there are many *accueil en tribu* (per person around 3000 CFP), traditional homestays with Kanak families. Visitors usually take part in everyday activities and meals. Book through Hienghène's visitor information centre at least a day in advance.

Babou Côté Océan Camping   CAMPGROUND $
(Map p162; ☑ 42 83 59; www.babou-plongee.com; camping per person 500 CFP, tent hire 1000 CFP; P🛜) About 10km southeast of Hienghène, on the coast, this is the best place to camp. The Babou Côté Océan dive club is based here. Bring your own food. There's free wi-fi around the base building.

★ Ka Waboana Lodge   BUNGALOW $$
(Map p162; ☑ 42 47 03; www.kawaboana-lodge.nc; r/bungalows from 6500/10,500 CFP; P✳🛜) Opposite the marina in Hienghène, this is a top place to stay. The smallest rooms with shared bathrooms meet requirements and are good value for the price, while the bungalows with kitchenettes perch in the forest above the restaurant and terrace. It's spotlessly clean and very tastefully done, with views of the bay.

DON'T MISS

HEART OF VOH AND THE LAGOON FROM THE AIR

The Heart of Voh (La Cœur de Voh; Map p162) North of Koné, near the township of Voh, there's a mangrove swamp which has developed some unusual natural designs. The most intriguing is a perfect heart shape, La Cœur de Voh (The Heart of Voh), which is on the cover of *Earth from Above*, a book of aerial photography by renowned photographer Yann Arthus-Bertrand. There's a track up Mt Kathépaïk to a viewing point at an altitude of 400m (two hours' return), but the Heart is best seen from the air.

Hotel Hibiscus ULM Flights (☑ 47 22 61; www.ulmnc.com; from 17,000 CFP) These microlight flights that depart from Koné airport not only fly over The Heart of Voh, but also take in the magnificent lagoon and let you look right into a 'blue hole', a 200m-deep hole in the coral reef. The flight is spectacular, with the the pilot flying low enough to spot stingrays, turtles and sharks in the lagoon.

Koulnoué Village Hotel BUNGALOW $$
(Map p162; ☑ 24 24 77; www.grands-hotels.nc/koulnoue; bungalows from 15,000 CFP; P❄☎☀) Undergoing refurbishment at the time of research, this surprisingly large ex–Club Med complex was starting to regain some of its mojo. The bungalows are well equipped and have private porches out to the beach. Play tennis or *petanque*, canoe, or go horse riding. Meals are buffet style (breakfast 2100 CFP, dinner 4300 CFP). The turn-off is 8.5km south of Hienghène.

❶ Information

Visitor Information Centre (Map p162; ☑ 42 43 57; www.hienghene-tourisme.nc; Hienghène; ☺8am-noon & 1-5pm Mon-Fri, 8am-3pm Sat) This efficient visitor information centre looks over the Hienghène marina. Staff can book accommodation in *tribus*, help you contact guides for trekking in the area, and arrange traditional meals and dances. Contact them before you go for accommodation and trekking enquiries.

North of Hienghène

This is the wildest and most stunning stretch of the northeast coast. It's covered in tropical vegetation, and waterfalls and streams rush down the mountains to join the sea.

It's a captivating journey. A three-car ferry carries vehicles across the Ouaïème River, 17km northwest of Hienghène. It's free, runs 24 hours a day, and the crossing is a highlight. Expect to see roadside stalls selling fruit and carvings outside local thatched dwellings. Take care on one-lane bridges and watch out for dogs and chickens.

The area around Pouébo and Balade is a fascinating historical hotspot with places that mark the first contact between the Europeans and local Melanesians. While the Ouvanou Memorial is carefully tended by local Kanaks, other monuments celebrating European arrival and French annexation of New Caledonia have been left to virtually disappear in the undergrowth.

◉ Sights & Activities

The area north of Hienghène is an amazing drawcard for trekking enthusiasts and nature lovers. All activities, however, require a guide and authorisation for you to enter tribal territories. At the time of research, **Mont Panié**, New Caledonia's highest mountain, was closed to the public. Contact Hienghène Visitor Information Centre for the latest.

Pouébo Catholic Church CHURCH
(Map p162) Inside Pouébo's Catholic church there's a marble mausoleum where the remains of Bishop Douarre, who set up New Caledonia's first Catholic mission, are interred. The church complex, with school and grounds next door, is surprisingly large and impressive.

Ouvanou Memorial MEMORIAL
(Map p162) About 1km north of Pouébo, on the coast side of the main road, is a carefully tended, touching memorial to 10 local Kanak men who were guillotined by the French on 18 May 1868. They have very obviously not been forgotten, nearly 150 years on.

Balade Church CHURCH
(Map p162) The stained-glass windows in this cute little church tell the story from the first Catholic mass. In 1853 France officially laid claim to New Caledonia at Balade, the same year in which Bishop Douarre, who performed the first mass, died.

★ Kanak Monument MEMORIAL
(Map p162) Directly below Balade Church, this monument, a large Kanak flag, was

unveiled on 24 September 2011, 158 years to the day after France took possession of the colony at this exact spot, and a year after the Congress of New Caledonia voted to fly the Kanak flag alongside the French tricolor in the territory. Unlike the nearby Monument de Balade, which celebrates French possession, it is a call for Kanak and New Caledonian independence from France.

Next to the Kanak Monument is the original stone pillar erected by the French in 1853 when they took possession, though the commemoration plaque has since disappeared.

Mahamat Beach   BEACH, MEMORIAL

(Map p162) Captain James Cook became the first European to discover New Caledonia in 1774, on his second voyage. He landed at Mahamat Beach, and it was on climbing the mountains inland that he decided the new land reminded him of Scotland and called it New Caledonia. An altar at Mahamat beach commemorates the first Catholic Mass on Christmas Day 1843, though it may take some searching to find it. The turn-off to the beach is 1.5km north of Balade's church.

Monument de Balade   MONUMENT

(Map p162) This impressive monument was unveiled in 1913 to great fanfare to mark 60 years of French possession of New Caledonia. It has since been left to virtually disappear in the weeds. About 1km north of the Mahamat Beach turn-off, it sits atop a small hill that was the site for France's first fort in the colony, built in 1853. History buffs should look for a sign on the right, when heading north. Blink and you'll miss it.

Sleeping & Eating

There are a number of campsites along the coast where you can simply turn up. Allow for 1000 CPF per tent and stock up on groceries before you go.

Relais de Ouane Batch   BUNGALOW $

(Map p162; ☑42 47 92; www.gite-ouanebatch. com; camping 1100 CFP, bungalows with/without bathroom 5250/4200 CFP; 🅿 🛜) The bungalows and campsites that line the beach are simple at this friendly spot, but they do the trick. There's free wi-fi at the main building and meals are good (breakfast/dinner 950/2850 CPF). Activities include snorkelling and canoe hire (half-/full day 1500/3000 CFP). It's 20km north of the river ferry and 22km south of Pouébo.

LOYALTY ISLANDS

POP 22,000 / AREA 1980 SQ KM

Maré, Lifou and Ouvéa. Fairy-tale names for fairy-tale islands. In a line 100km off the east coast of Grande Terre, they're all sparsely populated with secluded beaches, hidden caves and deep holes. They all have large tracts of impenetrable bush, but their roads are so good that driving around is a dream.

Loyalty Islands? It is thought that British traders named them that at the end of the 18th century, perhaps because the people were so 'honest and friendly'.

The islands saw intense power struggles between Protestant pastors and Catholic missionaries in the 1840s, but the Protestants made greater headway, using indigenous languages while the Catholic missionaries preferred French. The Loyalty Islands still have a strong Protestant influence, English words in their languages and even a love of cricket!

The islands were only annexed by France in 1864, but, deemed unsuitable for intensive colonisation, they were left as a native reserve. The official language is French, but while it is generally spoken and understood, each island also has its own language.

The locals blend traditional and modern lifestyles with ease. You'll need to take cash (although each island has a bank with an ATM). You'll find a shop with limited groceries in each village. Dining is somewhat limited to your (or other) accommodation, or *snack*-type simple eateries.

★ Festivals & Events

Loyalty Islands Fair   FAIR

(www.iles-loyaute.com) Held each year in early September, the islands take turns hosting this three-day extravaganza. Musical performances, dancing, art, agricultural stalls, fishing and everything Loyalty is on display.

ⓘ Information

An excellent online source for information in English is www.iles-loyaute.com/en

ⓘ Getting There & Away

AIR

Air Calédonie (☑25 21 77; www.air-caledonie. nc) Flies at least twice a day between Noumea's Magenta Airport and each island. It also has flights between Lifou and Ouvéa on weekdays.

Air Loyauté (☑25 37 09; www.air-loyaute. nc) Flies between the Loyalty Islands in small aircraft daily.

BOAT

Betico (☑26 01 00; www.betico.nc) The Betico sails from Noumea to Lifou and Maré, once or twice a week.

❶ Getting Around

The islands have limited public transport so it's best to hire a car and have it waiting for you on arrival. Car-rental companies drop off vehicles at the airport, wharf or accommodation places for free.

Hitchhiking is common everywhere but it can take a while for a car to come along.

Maré

POP 7400 / AREA 641 SQ KM

With its scenic coastline, stunning beaches and coral cliffs, plus an interior that hides impressive sunken pools and a mysterious rock edifice, it is small wonder that Maré's geographical features have inspired legends.

The indigenous language is Nengoné, and while there are two small towns, Tadine and La Roche, most Maréans live in tribes associated with one of 29 chieftaincies. The coastal town of Tadine is Maré's main centre; if travelling by ferry you'll arrive or leave from the wharf there. Tadine has shops, a petrol station, a pharmacy, and a market on Tuesday and Friday mornings. The airport is near La Roche.

Maré proudly hosts three festivals: the **Avocado Festival** held in May; the **Ura Festival**, a celebration of agricultural and fishing abundance, in July; and the **Wajuyu (Snapper fish) Festival**, held in early November.

◉ Sights & Activities

Hotels and gîtes can organise tours of the island for around 3000 CFP per person.

Centre Culturel
Yeiwene Yeiwene   MUSEUM, RUIN
(Map p180; ☑45 44 79; ⊙7.30-11.30am & 1-4pm Mon-Fri) FREE Maréan Yeiwene Yeiwene was deputy to independence leader Jean-Marie Tjibaou and assassinated alongside him on Ouvéa in 1989. A statue of Yeiwene stands before the cultural centre, where there is a small exhibition of Kanak artefacts. Out the back are the stone ruins known as Hnaenedr wall, a mysterious rock wall that supposedly dates back to AD 250.

★ Yedjele Beach   BEACH
(Map p180) The southwest coast has several gorgeous beaches where you can swim or snorkel during the day and watch the glorious sunsets in the evening, but best of the lot is Yedjele Beach. There's an enclosed lagoon with turquoise water, coral outcrops and plenty of tropical fish.

★ Aquarium Naturelle   LANDMARK
(Map p180) About 3km south of Tadine is a large Aquarium Naturelle, a rockpool sunk in the cliffs and linked to the sea. Watch for Napoleon fish, perroquettes, picods and sometimes turtles swimming in the translucent water. It is signposted by a parking area beside the main road. No swimming.

Trou de Bone   CAVE
(Map p180) About 3km off the La Roche–Tadine Rd, on the road to Thogone, is Trou de Bone, a deep rock cavity that drops to a lush tropical garden and a pool. It's on the right-hand side of the road as you're heading to Thogone, about 1.5km from the turn-off. It isn't signposted, so look out for a metal guardrail beside the road.

La Roche   HILL
(Map p180) A huge limestone rock covered in vegetation near the coast gives the surrounding area of La Roche (the Rock) its name. The rock, known locally as Titi, rises above the impressive Catholic church. You can climb to the top of the rock with a local guide. Make enquiries in the *tribu*.

★ Le Saut du Guerrier   VIEWPOINT
(Warrior's Leap; Map p180) Seven kilometres east of La Roche by sealed road is this gap in the cliffs, 5m wide and 30m above the pounding surf. Legend tells of a warrior who escaped his enemies by leaping across the abyss. Try to imagine the jump as you look down at the rocks and pounding waves below.

Shabadran   HIKING
(Map p180) This isolated, exquisite sandy beach at the southeast corner of Maré is surrounded by cliffs and forest and makes a great day-hike. You must have a guide, so contact Damas Bearune (☑73 29 71) in Kurine, the *tribu* at the end of the road. Book in advance; allow for four hours walking, take plenty of water and wear sturdy footwear.

⨳ Sleeping & Eating

Chez Nath   BUNGALOW $
(Map p180; ☑45 10 93; Tribu de Kaewatine; camping/d 2000/3990 CFP; ℗) Head through the casual open-air restaurant (meals from 2000 CFP) and follow the coral paths to two smart traditional thatched-roof *cases* with an external shower and toilet block. There's

electricity, friendly faces and guides for local walks, though the beach is a good 40-minute walk away. Chez Nath is at Tribu de Kaewatine in the north of the island.

Seday   BUNGALOW, CAMPGROUND **$**
(Map p180; ☑84 86 42; camping 1200 CFP, case per person 2000 CFP; ℗) Up north, in the quiet *tribu* of Roh, is a little honeymoon bungalow (5600 CFP) set on a rock in the water, plus three thatched bungalows. Sit on the wooden platform over the water, or slither between the rocks where it's great to snorkel. The restaurant serves excellent meals (1800 CFP) based on fish and home-grown vegetables.

Waterloo   BUNGALOW, CAMPGROUND **$**
(Map p180; ☑87 05 93, 45 18 02; www.office-tourisme.nc/en/waterloo; Eni; bungalows/camping 4000/1260 CFP; ℗) There are two thatched *cases* here in pretty gardens beside the family home. Dinner is likely to be fish (2500 CFP), served with a delicious papaya salad. There are two bathrooms and shaded camping spots. Lovely Eni beach is a short walk away.

★Gite Yedjele Beach   BUNGALOW **$$**
(Map p180; ☑45 40 15; www.office-tourisme.nc/en/yedjele-beach; bungalows from 9000 CFP; ℗) A top spot to stay right on the island's most gorgeous beach. These sturdy bungalows, with kitchenette and mezzanine floor, can accommodate up to seven and are ideal for families. You'll need a rental vehicle and a smattering of French. Meals available with advance notice.

Hôtel Nengone Village   RESORT **$$$**
(Map p180; ☑45 45 00; www.hotelnengonevillage.nc; bungalows/ste 15,900/31,000 CFP; ℗✳🛜⛱) The island's only upmarket hotel, Nengone Village has spacious and comfortable bungalows that feature local timbers along a boardwalk. There's a refreshing pool by the excellent restaurant. Rental bicycles and kayaks are available. The meals are first class and the restaurant is open to nonguests with a reservation. The only place with wi-fi. Airport/wharf transfers cost 2800/1600 CFP.

ⓘ Information

BCI Bank (Map p180; ☑25 53 20; ⊙7.15am-noon & 1.15-4pm Mon-Fri) In Tadine; has an external ATM.
Post Office (Map p180; ☑45 41 00; ⊙7.45-11.15am & 12.15-3pm Mon-Fri) The main office is in Tadine, with a secondary office in La Roche.

Tourist Information Office (Map p180; ☑45 51 07; ⊙7.30-11.30am & 1.15-4pm) In Tadine; this place is helpful with advice and maps.

ⓘ Getting There & Away

Air Calédonie (Map p180; ☑45 55 10; www.air-caledonie.nc; ⊙8-11am & 2-5pm Mon-Fri) The domestic carrier has an office at the airport.

ⓘ Getting Around

You can try cycling around the island if you are fit but roads are long, straight and monotonous. Hôtel Nengone Village hires bicycles (half-/full day 650/1100 CFP).

The best way to get around Maré is by car, organised before you go.

ETTM (☑45 42 73; per day from 6300 CFP) Rental cars dropped off and picked up from the wharf and airport.
Golf Location (☑45 09 42; per day from 6300 CFP) Rental cars delivered to the wharf and airport.

Lifou

POP 10,320 / AREA 1207 SQ KM

Lifou is home to magnificent cliff-top views, sheltered bays with coral shelfs teeming with colourful tropical fish, secluded beaches, fascinating caves and a rich traditional culture. The indigenous language is Drehu.

The main centre in Lifou is Wé, where the Loyalty Island's provincial offices are based. Wé stretches for about 2km along the main road beside Baie de Châteaubriand. There's a market Wednesdays and Fridays, a good supermarket and a number of *snack* restaurants.

Lifou celebrates with a **Pahatr (Fern) Festival** in April, the **Sandalwood and Honey Festival** in August and the **Vanilla Festival** held in October.

⊙ Sights & Activities

★Chapelle Notre Dame de Lourdes   CHURCH
(Map p182) At the large white cross at Easo, stay on the coast road to a parking area below the small Chapelle Notre Dame de Lourdes. Steps lead up the hill to the chapel from where there are fantastic views of Baie de Jinek to the west and Baie du Santal to the east and south. The chapel was originally built in 1898 to commemorate the arrival of the first Catholic missionaries in 1858.

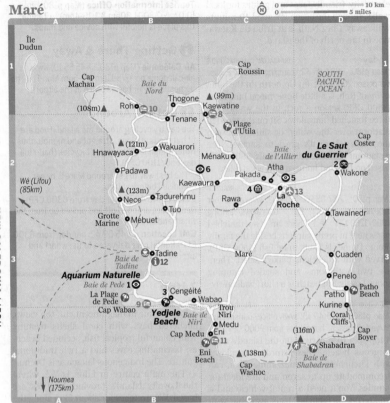

Maré

Peng BEACH
(Map p182) Don't miss the blissful, secluded beach at Peng on Baie du Santal, 3.5km off Wé–Drueulu Rd; turn off at the *tribu* Hapetra.

★**Luengoni Beach** BEACH
(Map p182) A stretch of fine white sand bordering a stunning lagoon. Locals boast that it is New Caledonia's most beautiful beach. The sheltered bay is a renowned turtle haunt.

Grotte les Joyaux de Luengoni GROTTO
(Map p182) Just west of Luengoni Beach are limestone caves both above and below ground; the underground caves have beautiful deep rock pools which shimmer emerald green when you shine a torch on the water.

Baie de Jinek SNORKELLING
(Map p182) At Easo, head down to Baie de Jinek, where steps from a wooden platform lead down to the water and an active snorkelling route in a fabulous coral-filled bay. The water teems with tropical fish in this popular snorkelling spot.

Jokin Cliffs SNORKELLING
(Map p182) Lifou's northernmost *tribu* sits on the cliff tops overlooking a vast bay with brilliant sunset views; the footpath to the left of the church lane leads to about 150 steps that take you down under the cliffs to a perfect snorkelling cove.

Lifou Diving DIVING
(Map p182; ☑78 94 72, 45 40 60; www.lifou-diving.com; 2-dive package 11,000 CFP) Based at Easo, Lifou Diving has qualified English- and French-speaking PADI instructors and divemasters, and runs dive trips to spectacular spots around the island. It offers night dives (7000 CFP), and can organise accommodation locally for clients.

Maré

🛏 Sleeping & Eating

À La Petit Baie   BUNGALOW $
(Map p182; ☑ 45 15 25; www.office-tourisme.nc/
en/la-petite-baie-0; Tribu de Joj; bungalows per person 2100 CFP; 🅿) À La Petit Baie's *case*, in lovely gardens, is one of the best you'll find, and
the dining room and bar is by the sea (organise your simple meals the day before). There's
a kayak club here, and ask Annette about her
outrigger trips.

★ L'Oasis de Kiamu   RESORT $$
(Map p182; ☑ 45 15 00; www.hoteloasisdekiamu.
nc; r from 12,000 CFP; 🅿❄🛜🏊) This oasis
right beside the main road and below limestone cliffs offers a variety of smart rooms,
a swimming pool, a superb restaurant, a
snack bar and its own beach just across
the road. There's friendly service, free wi-fi,
buffet breakfast (1850 CPF) and three course
dinners (3500 CPF).

Chez Jeannette   BUNGALOW $$
(Map p182; ☑ 45 45 05; www.office-tourisme.nc/
en/node/1243; bungalows d 5600 CFP, case 2100
CFP; 🅿) Jeannette's homestay buzzes with
energy as adventurers organise their day. It's
right on the beach at the northern end of Baie

de Châteaubriand. Follow the unsealed road
in front of *tribu* Luecilla along the waterfront.

Faré Falaise   BUNGALOW $$
(Map p182; ☑ 45 02 01; www.office-tourisme.nc/
en/fare-falaise; camping 2100 CFP, d bungalows
5775 CFP; 🅿🛜) Perched on the very edge
of the cliffs at Jokin at the northern tip of
Lifou, Faré Falaise offers rustic bungalows
and camping. The water is via 150 steps,
but it's great snorkelling. Campers have
a kitchen for cooking, while good meals
are available. You can also rent bicycles
and cars here.

Hôtel Drehu Village   BUNGALOW $$$
(Map p182; ☑ 45 02 70; www.hoteldrehuvillage.
nc; bungalows from 17,000 CFP; 🅿❄🛜🏊) Turn
down towards Châteaubriand beach and
you'll find Lifou's upmarket hotel where
comfortable bungalows spread through to
the grass and white-sand beach. The restaurant tables are romantically situated around
a pool and under a *faré* (breakfast 2400
CPF; dinner from 3250 CFP).

ℹ Information

BCI Bank (Map p182; ☑ 45 13 32; ⊙ 7.20am-
noon & 1-3.45pm Mon-Fri) On the main road
opposite the Air Calédonie office, it has an
external ATM.

Post Office (Map p182; ☑ 45 11 00;
⊙ 7.45am-3pm Mon-Fri) Located behind the
provincial offices in Wé.

Visitor Information Centre (Map p182; ☑ 45
00 32; ⊙ 7.30-11.30am & 12.30-4.30pm Mon-
Fri) The main office is next to the *mairie* in Wé.
There's also a booth at the airport with maps
and stacks of info.

ℹ Getting There & Away

Air Calédonie (Map p182; ⊙ 7.30-11.30am &
12.30-5.15pm Mon-Fri, 7.15-11am Sat) An office
in Wé (☑ 45 55 50) and a desk at the airport
(Map p182; ☑ 45 55 20; Airport).

ℹ Getting Around

The best way to get around Lifou is by car,
though you could take it on with a bike.

Alizée Locations (☑ 45 07 67) Rental cars
delivered to the airport.

Loca V (☑ 45 07 77; locav@lagoon.nc; per day
from 5700 CFP) Offers good rental cars delivered to the port or airport.

NEW CALEDONIA LIFOU

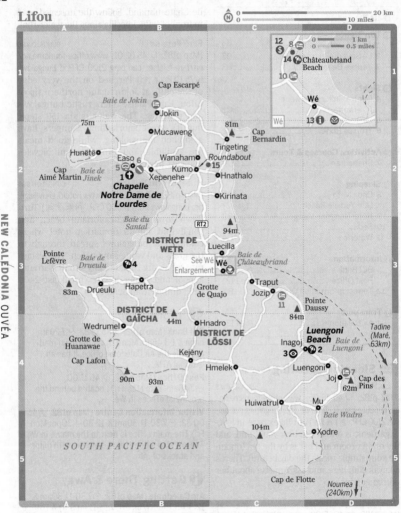

NEW CALEDONIA OUVÉA

Ouvéa

POP 4360 / AREA 132 SQ KM

Think 25km of perfect white beach backed with grass, tropical flowers, and thick forest inhabited by the endemic and protected Ouvéa green parrot. Look out over an exquisite turquoise lagoon stretching as far as you can see. Add a chain of tiny islets, the Pléiades. Sound unreal? Ouvéa may leave you shaking your head in wonder.

The Ouvéa lagoon was one of six marine areas in the New Caledonian archipelago to be listed as a Unesco World Heritage site in 2008. It's stunning.

Ouvéa has two indigenous languages. Iaaï is of Melanesian origin, while Faga-uvéa is spoken in the south and north of the island by descendants of Polynesian migrants who arrived in the 16th and 17th centuries.

A thin sliver of land, Ouvéa has administrative centres at Wadrilla and Fayaoué. The facilities in these villages, however, are so spread out that nowhere can really be described as a centre. There's a bank with outside ATM, a clinic and a pharmacy near the airport.

Lifou

◎ Top Sights
1 Chapelle Notre Dame de
    Lourdes B2
2 Luengoni Beach D4

◎ Sights
3 Grotte les Joyaux de Luengoni C4
4 Peng..B3

◎ Activities, Courses & Tours
5 Baie de Jinek B2
    Jokin Cliffs......................................(see 9)
6 Lifou Diving B2

◎ Sleeping
7 À La Petit Baie.....................................D4
8 Chez Jeannette C1
9 Faré Falaise B1
10 Hôtel Drehu Village C1
11 L'Oasis de Kiamu C3

◎ Information
12 BCI Bank... C1
13 Visitor Information Centre.................. D1

◎ Transport
14 Air Calédonie.. C1
15 Air Calédonie..C2

Ouvéa hosts its **Lagoon Festival** in June and the **Waleï (Sweet Yam) Festival** in August.

◎ Sights

★ Fayaoué Beach   BEACH
(Map p184) The highlight of Ouvéa is its magnificent beach and lagoon. While the east coast of the island is mainly rough cliffs pounded by the Pacific Ocean, the west coast faces the protected lagoon and this gorgeous beach stretches from Mouli in the south, fully 25km to St Joseph in the north. Make the most of the swimming, kayaking, sailing, windsurfing and other watersport opportunities.

★ Ouvéa Memorial   MEMORIAL
(Map p184) The large memorial in Wadrilla is a tribute to 19 Kanaks who died in 1988, when French military personnel stormed a cave to free French *gendarmes* being held hostage by the pro-independence movement. Tragically, pro-independence leaders Jean-Marie Tjibaou and Yeiwene Yeiwene were assassinated opposite the memorial at the first-year memorial ceremony. The perpetrator believed they had ceded too much to France. The names and faces of the 19 are inscribed on the impressive memorial.

DON'T MISS

HEAVENLY BRIDGE

Pont de Mouli (Map p184) It may seem unusual to recommend a road bridge as a top sightseeing spot, but at Pont de Mouli, Ouvéa's tip, Mouli island, is cut off by a wide channel that flows out of Baie de Lékiny into the lagoon. From the bridge, the display of dazzling white sand and shades of turquoise is occasionally broken by outlines of sharks, rays, turtles and fish swimming beneath you (unless it's the weekend, when all you'll see are kids jumping off).

Trou à Tortues   LANDMARK
(Turtles Hole; Map p184) Up in the north near St Joseph, the Turtles Hole is down an unmarked dirt road, then along a 50m path through the bush. An immense hole in the limestone is full of water and connected underground to the sea. Sit patiently and turtles are bound to appear. This is also a great place to spot the protected Ouvéa green parrot.

Trou Bleu d'Anawa   CAVE
(Map p184) The deep Trou Bleu d'Anawa is sunk in the coral rock and connected to the sea underground. If you're lucky, you may see fish and turtles in the blue water. Turn left along a track just past the Anawa shop, where the road curves sharply away from the coast. The pool is behind some abandoned bungalows.

Ouvéa Soap Factory   FACTORY
(Savonnerie D'Ouvéa; Map p184; ☑ 45 10 60; ⊙ 8-11.30am & 1.30-3.30pm Tue & Thu) **FREE** Take a free visit to the soap factory, next to the ferry quay in Wadrilla. Using coconut oil, it produces household soap, soap perfumed with *niaouli* (paper bark tea tree) and even soapflakes for laundry detergent. There's soap for sale.

◎ Activities

Plage de Tiberia   SNORKELLING
(Tiberia Beach; Map p184) At the north of Ouvéa, and almost at its easternmost point of Pointe Escarpée, this superb snorkelling spot is down a set of stairs beside the road. There's a sandy beach and an easily accessible reef teeming with coral and fish.

Ouvéa

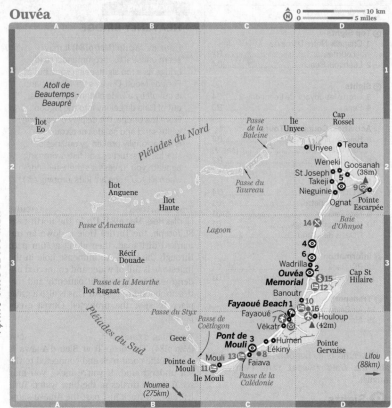

Charly Aema Tours BOAT TOUR
(📞 45 07 60; tour incl lunch 6500 CFP) Head out on a boat tour from Moague with Charly Aema. The trip heads out to Îlot Gee in the Pléiades du Sud where you can snorkel, fish and enjoy a picnic. Late each year sharks give birth in the warm shallow waters and with good timing you'll be able to see the 'shark nursery'. Book a day in advance.

Canio WATER SPORTS
(Map p184; 📞 75 45 45; ⊗ 8-11.30am & 1-4.30pm Tue-Sat) The interesting catamaran-shaped building on the beach in Fayaoué is the sailing club. Canio rents per one/two hours windsurfers (1500/2500 CFP), hobie cats (from 2000/3500 CFP) and kayaks (1000/1700 CFP).

Mio Palmo Plongée DIVING
(📞 84 47 38; www.facebook.com/miopalmo.plon gee.1; 2-dive package 12,000 CFP) You'll potentially be swimming with green turtles, Manta rays, humphead wrasse, parrotfish, surgeon-fish and sharks with this scuba-diving club. Take an intro dive for 8000 CFP, or a PADI Open Water course for 49,000 CFP.

Les Falaises de Lekiny ADVENTURE TOUR
(Map p184) These grey cliffs, pitted with caves, are 12km south from Fayaoue. Explore them with guide **Felix Alosio** (📞 92 55 12; per person 2100 CFP).

🛏 Sleeping & Eating

★ **Moague** BUNGALOW $$
(Map p184; 📞 75 08 89, 45 07 60; www.office-tourisme.nc/en/moague; Mouli; camping 2500 CFP, bungalows s/d 5500 CFP; 🅿) This friendly beachside accommodation in Mouli is run by Charly Aema, famous for his boat excursions. There's camping, five thatched-roof bungalows, separate bathroom facilities with hot water, plus an excellent restaurant. Join the island or boat tours with prior bookings. Airport transfers are 3000 CFP.

Chez Dydyce
BUNGALOW $$

(Map p184; ☑94 78 21, 45 72 87; www.office-tour isme.nc/en/chez-dydyce; camping 2300 CFP, bungalows 5500 CFP; P☏) This spot has a good camp kitchen, clean bathrooms and sunny camping spots. The restaurant Snack Champagne (complete with sand floor) is on-site, offering three-course dinners from 1575 CPF and free wi-fi. You can hire bikes (per day 1575 CFP) or join an excursion to the Southern Pleiades islets (7500 CPF).

Gîte Cocotier
BUNGALOW $$

(Map p184; ☑79 43 57, 45 70 40; www.office-tourisme.nc/en/cocotier; camping 2000 CFP, bungalows from 5500 CFP; P) Sammy has some good options at Cocotier, about 500m north of the church in Mouli. It's across the road from the beach, but you can pitch your tent on the beachfront. Hire bikes, go snorkelling or take an island tour for 3500 CFP. A set menu is 2200 CFP. Airport transfers cost 3000 CFP.

Hotel Beaupré
BUNGALOW $$

(Map p184; ☑45 71 32; www.hotelbeaupre. nc; bungalows from 14,900 CFP; P☏) Lovely bungalows, the restaurant specialises in seafood, plus you can join island and boat tours at this well-positioned place not far from the airport. No charge for transfers.

Hôtel Paradis d'Ouvéa
RESORT $$$

(Map p184; ☑45 54 00; www.paradisouvea.com; villas from 32,000 CFP; P☀☏☖) Step out of your luxurious spacious villa onto the stunning white-sand beach, or lie on your private deck and think about swimming in the azure sea. The tropical restaurant is top class and has soaring ceilings. Relax by the pool, hire bikes or head out on an island tour (4100 CFP). Airport return transfers are 2200 CFP

O'kafika
SEAFOOD $$

(Map p184; ☑45 90 27; ⊙vary) In the village of Hanawa and right next to the road and beach, O'kafika serves everything from sandwiches to tasty seafood meals on an outside terrace. Sandwiches from 500 CFP, meals from 1200 to 2600 CFP. This place is perfectly positioned if you are on a road trip to the north.

ⓘ Information

BCI Bank (Map p184; ☑45 71 31; ⊙7.20am-noon Mon-Fri, plus 1-3pm Wed) On the road to the airport; has an internal and external ATM.

Post Office (Map p184; ☑45 71 00; ⊙7.45-11.15am & 12.15-3pm Mon-Fri) There's an ATM inside the office in Fayaoué.

Tourist Information (☑94 97 14; Wadrilla; ⊙7.30am-4.30pm Mon-Fri) The office is on the beach road in Wadrilla and has info on tours and accommodation.

ⓘ Getting There & Away

Air Calédonie (Map p184; ⊙7.30-11am & 1.30-4pm Mon-Fri) Has an office in Wadrilla (☑45 70 22; Office) and a desk at the airport (☑45 55 30; Airport).

ⓘ Getting Around

There's no public transportation. The best option is to get a rental car delivered to the airport, or arrange transfers with your accommodation.

Julau Location (☑45 45 30; per day from 6300 CFP) Delivers to the airport.

Ouvéa Location (Map p184; ☑45 73 77, 79 55 58; per day from 6300 CFP) Delivers to the airport.

ÎLE DES PINS

POP 2000 / AREA 152 SQ KM

Known as Kunié to the Melanesians, Île des Pins (Isle of Pines) is a tranquil paradise of turquoise bays, white-sand beaches and tropical vegetation 110km southeast of Noumea.

According to legend, warriors of Tongan descent came from Lifou about three centuries ago and were invited to take over leadership of the island. Captain James Cook later named the island Isle of Pines when on his second voyage of Pacific exploration in 1774.

The 1840s saw the arrival of both Protestant and Catholic missionaries, and traders looking for sandalwood. The Kunies opted for the Catholic religion and thereby for French possession in 1853, though they may have regretted it 21 years later when their island became a settlement for 3000 political deportees from the Paris Commune. Nowadays the island is an indigenous reserve.

Administratively, Île des Pins is part of Province Sud. Vao is the administrative centre, while Kuto is the main tourist area. There's not much in the way of shops or restaurants and most people eat where they are staying. Restaurants attached to gîtes or hotels accept nonguests, but you'll need to book in advance. Seafood is popular, as are Île des Pins' *escargots* (snails), a local speciality.

The Île des Pins Fair is held in May or June over three days and features singing, dancing, crafts and gastronomic delights.

❶ Getting There & Away

Air Calédonie (☑ Vao 44 88 50, airport 44 88 40; ☺ 7.30-11am & 2-5pm Mon-Fri, 7.30-11.30am Sat) Air Calédonie flies to Île des Pins from Noumea at least twice daily.

Betico (☑ 44 22 42; www.betico.nc) The Betico sails from Noumea at 7am for a day trip on Wednesday. It also departs Noumea on Saturday at 7am and returns Sunday, arriving back in Noumea at 7.30pm. It docks at the wharf in Baie de Kuto.

❶ Getting Around

It is important to arrange a hire car, transfer or tour in advance, so you're not stranded at the airport or wharf, especially if you're on a day trip.

Edmond Location (☑ 76 69 96; per day 7500 CFP) Will deliver rental cars to the port or airport.

Nataiwatch Rentals (☑ 46 11 13; www.nataiwatch.com) Rental mountain bikes/cars per day 2000/7000 CFP;

Vao

Île des Pins' main village and administrative centre, Vao, is a serene place with not much going on. There's a market on Wednesday and Saturday mornings.

◉ Sights & Activities

Catholic Church   CHURCH
(Map p188) The attractive 19th-century Catholic church dominates Vao. It was established by the Marist priest Father Goujon, who managed to convert most of the island's population in just over 30 years following his arrival in 1848.

★ Statue of St Maurice   STATUE
(Map p188) At Baie de St Maurice, this statue commemorates the arrival of the first missionaries on the island and is also a war memorial. There's a solemn line of wooden totem poles just above the beach.

Baie de St Joseph   BAY
(Map p188) Two kilometres east of Vao and also referred to as Baie des Pirogues, this is where the Pirogue Excursion (p187) leaves from daily. Locals build their traditional canoes here.

✕ Eating

Snack Kohu   CAFE
(Map p188; ☑ 46 10 23; dishes 750-1450 CFP; ☺ 10am-3pm Mon-Fri) This is a pleasant place for lunch, just out of Vao on the road north towards the airport. There are tables under thatched shelters and everyone is very friendly. Meals include chicken or steak and chips, sandwiches from 450 CFP and a *plat du jour* (1650 CFP).

❶ Information

BCI Bank (Map p188; ☑ 46 10 45; ☺ 8am-noon & 1-3.30pm Mon & Fri, 8am-noon Tue & Wed, 1-3.30pm Thu) Has an outside ATM.

Post Office (Map p188; ☑ 46 11 00; ☺ 7.45-11.15am & 12.30-3.30pm Mon-Fri) Has a public telephone; there are other phones at the airport and wharf.

Visitor Information Centre (Map p188; ☑ 46 10 27; www.ile-des-pins.com; ☺ 8-11.30am Mon-Sat & 2-4pm Mon-Fri) Next to the bank. There's an information desk (☑ 46 14 00) at the airport which opens for flights.

Kuto & the West Coast

Kuto has two gorgeous aquamarine bays, separated by the narrow neck of Kuto peninsula. Baie de Kuto is the perfect place to lie on the beach or swim in the calm sea. For snorkelling go to Baie de Kanuméra, where coral grows not far from the shore. The ferry and cruise ship quay is on the north side of the Kuto peninsula.

◎ Sights & Activities

Convict Prison Ruins RUIN

(Map p188) Just north of Baie de Kuto, beside the main road, are the crumbling, overgrown ruins of an old convict prison built in the late 19th century. Île des Pins was initially used as a place of exile for convicts, including Paris Communards and Algerian deportees in the 1870s.

Grotte de la Troisième CAVE

(Map p188) About 8km north of Kuto, a signposted turn-off leads down a dirt road to the sunken Grotte de la Troisième. The cave is 100m down a path from the end of the road and if you climb into the wide opening, you can peer into its depth.

Nokanhui Atoll Boat Excursion BOAT TOUR

(☑45 90 66, 77 28 50; www.facebook.com/iledes pins.plaisance; per person with/without lunch 9500/7500 CPF) This day excursion by boat from Kuto Bay, departing at 9am, lets you take in the magnificent Nokanhui Atoll, to the south of Île des Pins. Lunch follows, then there's time to explore Île Môrô before returning to Kuto Bay around 3.30pm. Book at your accommodation.

Pic N'ga Track HIKING

(Map p188) Feeling energetic? Take a 45-minute climb up Pic N'ga (262m), the island's highest point. The path is mostly exposed, so it's best to go early morning or late afternoon. From the summit there are fantastic views over the entire island and its turquoise bays. The signposted path begins from the main road 200m south of Relais Le Kuberka.

Kunié Scuba Centre DIVING

(Map p188; ☑46 11 22; www.kunie-scuba.com; intro/2 dives from 9200/13,300 CPF) Based at Ouameo Bay, 10km north of Kuto, these guys have been organising dives, PADI training and snorkelling trips around Île des Pins since 1974.

🍽 Sleeping & Eating

★ Gîte Nataiwatch CAMPGROUND, BUNGALOW $$

(Map p188; ☑46 11 13; www.nataiwatch.com; camping 1800 CFP, bungalows 10,900 CFP, B&B s/d 9700/10,900 CFP; 🅿🛜) This is a popular gîte with a wide range of accommodation options in a wooded area towards the eastern end of Baie de Kanuméra. There's everything from camping to family bungalows, all with free wi-fi. Throw in a good restaurant, rental cars and mountain bikes, and a number of excursions on offer and you have a great spot to stay.

Relais Le Kuberka BUNGALOW $$

(Map p188; ☑46 11 18; www.office-tourisme.nc/en/relais-kuberka; s/d 7500/9400 CFP, bungalows 12,400 CFP; 🅿🛜🍽) A short walk from the beach, this home-away-from-home has tidy rooms and bungalows set around a small garden and pool. The restaurant serves an excellent range of meals (dishes 2100 CFP). Airport/wharf transfers 1500/500 CFP.

Hôtel Kou-Bugny HOTEL $$$

(Map p188; ☑46 18 00; www.kou-bugny.com; r/bungalows 22,600/26,600 CFP; 🅿❄🛜🍽) Kou-Bugny is right on Kuto beach, with rooms on the inland side of the quiet road and its restaurant almost on the sand. Sit on the terrace with a drink and catch the sunset. A great location with plenty of excursions on offer.

Ouré Tera Hotel RESORT $$$

(Map p188; ☑43 13 15; www.tera-hotels-resorts.com/hotel; r/bungalows from 36,900/45,900 CFP; 🅿❄@🛜🍽) This top place is right on the water at Baie de Kanuméra. The open bar and dining room (mains 2800 CFP to 3600 CFP) open on to a spectacular curving pool area. Rooms are superb. If you're not staying here, consider booking to eat at the restaurant.

Baie d'Oro & Around

North of Vao the road climbs gradually onto a central plateau. Follow the signs out to beautiful secluded Baie d'Oro. At the end of the road is a parking area, plus a lunch *snack* restaurant run by the local *tribu*.

Île des Pins

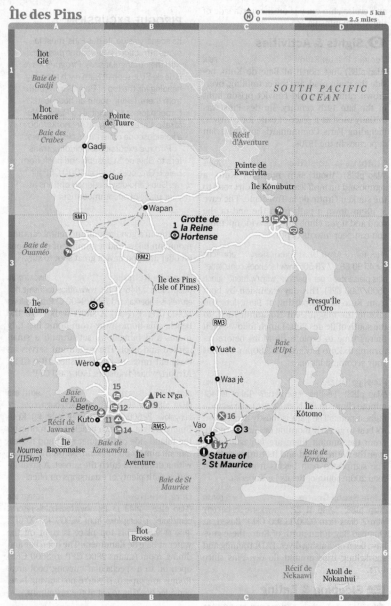

SOUTH PACIFIC OCEAN

Noumea (115km)

Sights & Activities

⭐ **Grotte de la Reine Hortense**   CAVE
(Map p188; admission 250 CFP) This impressive cave tunnels into a limestone cliff at the end of a path through wild tropical gardens. Queen

Hortense, wife of a local chief, is believed to have taken refuge here for several months during intertribal conflict in 1855; there's a smooth rock ledge where she slept. The sealed road down to the cave is signposted.

Île des Pins

★ **La Piscine Naturelle** SNORKELLING
(admission 200 CPF) A 20-minute signposted walk from the carpark at the end of the road, this pool of exquisite turquoise water is protected from the sea by a narrow waterway. The snorkelling is unbelievable and if you just sit in knee-deep water on the fine white sand, tropical fish will approach you! Highly recommended.

🛏 Sleeping & Eating

Camping/Restaurant
Le Kou-gny CAMPGROUND $
(Map p188; ☎70 25 35; camping 1000 CFP) This rustic campsite and restaurant is on the beach, five minutes east of Le Méridien. Tables are set under trees looking out over the water and it does a good trade serving lunch to Piscine Naturelle visitors. Try a dozen tasty Île des Pins snails here for 3100 CPF.

Le Méridien RESORT $$$
(Map p188; ☎26 50 00; www.lemeridienile despins.com; r/bungalows from 35,000/50,000 CFP; ⓟ❄☎☂) This is tropical luxury at its best. While the central lounge, bar and restaurant areas invite you to relax and enjoy, the rooms are as top-notch as you'll find in New Caledonia. The infinity pool is a stunner and there are plenty of excursion options on offer.

UNDERSTAND NEW CALEDONIA

New Caledonia Today

New Caledonia is approaching a crossroad. After often-violent independence struggles, in 1986 the UN put New Caledonia on its 'decolonisation list'. France was required to take 'immediate steps' to ensure independence for its colony. After much to-ing and fro-ing, it was agreed that a referendum on 'self-determination' must be held by the end of 2018, fully 32 years after the country was placed on the 'decolonisation list'.

With 2018 drawing ever closer, things are getting messy. In general, Kanaks are pro-independence and the French and big business (think nickel mining) are pro-France. In 2014 elections anti-independence pro-France parties won 29 of 54 seats, but a 2015 electoral law stating that only indigenous Kanaks and persons enrolled in 1998 will be automatically eligible to vote in the 2018 referendum is causing panic among anti-independence groups. This law was introduced to compensate for the huge time lag between the country being placed on the 'decolonisation list' in 1986 and actually holding the referendum in 2018 – and the fact that large numbers of French have immigrated to New Caledonia in the meantime.

With the population 40% Kanak and 29% European, it appears that the country is destined for independence.

There is a huge cultural and economic divide between New Caledonia's Kanak and Caldoche (locally born descendants of Europeans) populations. Kanaks suffered terribly after the arrival of the Europeans and the cuts still run deep. There is also an obvious financial gap, and it's not Kanaks who have benefitted from New Caledonia's nickel reserves.

History

New Caledonia was first populated by a hunter-gatherer people known as the Lapita, who arrived from the islands of Vanuatu around 1500 BC. From about the 11th century AD until the 18th century, groups of Polynesians also migrated to New Caledonia.

Europeans Arrive

English explorer James Cook spotted Grande Terre in 1774, naming it New Caledonia because the terrain reminded him of the highlands of Scotland (which was called Caledonia by the Romans).

During the 19th century British and US whalers, followed by sandalwood traders, were the first commercial Westerners to land on the islands.

The first missionaries from the London Missionary Society, arrived on Île des Pins in 1841. French Catholic missionaries established a mission at Balade on the northeast coast of Grande Terre in 1843.

French Colonisation

France officially claimed New Caledonia in 1853, initially establishing it as a penal colony. The first shiploads of convicts arrived at Port-de-France (present-day Noumea) in 1864.

Having served their sentences, many former convicts were given concessions to farm, and as more settlers arrived, an increasing amount of Melanesian land was taken over. This resulted in the revolt of 1878, led by chief Ataï, which lasted several months.

WWI & WWII

During WWI male Caldoches and Kanaks were recruited to fight on the French and Turkish fronts.

During WWII New Caledonian soldiers fought for the allied forces in North Africa, Italy and France. Meanwhile, 50,000 US and a smaller number of New Zealand soldiers set up a base in New Caledonia. The influence of the US soldiers in particular ushered New Caledonia into the modern era with their dollars, Coca-Cola and tobacco.

Postwar

Between 1946 and 1956 Kanaks were progressively given the right to vote, and in 1953 the first political party involving Kanaks was formed.

A nickel boom in the 1960s and '70s saw many New Caledonians abandoning their professions to work in the nickel industry. The boom also brought a large number of migrants.

Independence became an increasingly important issue for Kanaks, and the major-ity of Kanak parties joined to form the Front Indépendentiste (Independence Front) in 1979. In 1977 Jacques Lafleur established the loyalist Rassemblement pour la Calédonie dans la République (RPCR), the main adversary of the pro-independence movement.

The Independence Movement

In 1984, pro-independence parties joined the Front Indépendentiste to form the Front de Libération National Kanak et Socialiste (FLNKS), with Jean-Marie Tjibaou as leader.

In that same year, mounting political tensions resulted in Les Événements (the Troubles), a period of violent confrontation between pro-independence Kanaks and loyalist supporters.

In 1986 the UN General Assembly voted in favour of adding New Caledonia to its decolonisation list.

Conflict & Resolution

In January 1987 the French National Assembly approved a new plan for the territory and an election was called for 24 April 1988, the same day as the first round of voting for the French presidency. Pro-independence supporters ended up boycotting the election. The disagreement led to the Ouvéa hostage drama in which 21 people were killed.

The presidential elections saw the Socialists returned to power and a concerted effort was made to end the bloodshed in New Caledonia. Newly elected Prime Minister Michel Rocard brokered the Matignon Accords, a historic peace agreement signed by the two New Caledonian leaders, Jean-Marie Tjibaou and Jacques Lafleur.

In May 1989, when Tjibaou and his second-in-command, Yeiwene Yeiwene, were assassinated, their party split and lost power. President Mitterand brokered another deal which included education opportunities and economic benefits for Kanaks, and a clear path towards independence.

A Common Destiny

An agreement between the FLNKS, RPCR and French government was signed in Noumea in 1998. The Noumea Accord outlined a 15- to 20-year period of growth and development to culminate in a vote for self-determination by the end of 2018. It also called for the establishment of a common destiny for New Caledonians. Working together became a theme for both political and racial harmony, so while the

French tricolour was the country's flag until 2010, the independence movement's flag also obtained official status, making New Caledonia one of the few countries with two flags.

The Culture

The National Psyche

New Caledonia is a mix of Western efficiency and Pacific casualness with an unmistakable Frenchness. Noumea is where many French, Caldoches and people of Asian origin have made their fortunes in business, and there's plenty of conspicuous consumption. Noumeans are also very sporty: you'll see them cycling, jogging and walking along the city's picturesque southern bays.

Outside the capital, rural Caldoches are called Broussards (people from the bush). While rural Kanaks may be shy at first, the one thing all rural New Caledonians have in common is their generosity and hospitality.

Lifestyle

The lifestyles enjoyed by Kanaks and Caldoches are similar in many ways as both groups are family oriented and enjoy being outdoors in their leisure time. What sets them apart are cultural differences such as *la coutume,* the essential component of Kanak society.

La coutume is a code for living that encompasses rites, rituals and social interaction between clans. During important events such as birth, marriage and mourning, symbolic offerings are made and discussions are held.

Population

New Caledonia's population of around 270,000 includes 40% indigenous Kanaks, 29% Europeans, plus Polynesians, Asians and other minority groups. Two-thirds of the population live in the greater Noumea region.

Kanaks, the indigenous Melanesians, belong to clan communities known as *tribus,* and though many move to Noumea for education and employment, they maintain strong ties with their *tribus,* returning for holidays and cultural and family celebrations.

New Caledonia's European population has two distinct groups: the Caldoches and the Métros. Caldoches were born in New Caledonia and have ancestral ties to the penal colony or the early French settlers. The term Métro comes from Métropolitain, as in metropolitan France, and refers to those who were born in France and migrated.

There is a large Polynesian population in New Caledonia, mainly from the French territory of Wallis and Futuna. In fact, more Wallisians live in New Caledonia than in their homeland and they make up 9% of the population.

People of Asian origin, including Indonesians, Vietnamese, Japanese and Chinese, began arriving in New Caledonia in the early 20th century.

Arts

Wood sculpture is a popular form of artistic expression in New Caledonia, particularly in Kanak culture. For an overview of Kanak arts, visit the Tjibaou Cultural Centre.

Dance

Many dance styles are popular in New Caledonia, including *pilou* (traditional Kanak dance), Tahitian, Vietnamese and Indonesian. Performances are held regularly at festivals and public events.

Literature

New Caledonia has a dynamic literary scene.

➡ Déwé Gorodey is a Kanak politician and writer who evokes the struggle for independence in her writing and gives a feminist view of Kanak culture.

➡ Pierre Gope is another Kanak writer whose works include poetry and plays.

➡ Bernard Berger, also Caledonian, is a cartoonist whose *Brousse en Folie* comic-book series is immensely popular.

➡ Louis-José Barbançon, a Caledonian historian, has written books on the penal-colony history and the difficult political climate of the 1980s.

Music

In addition to popular Western music and hip hop, reggae has a huge following in New Caledonia, along with music from Tahiti, Vanuatu and Fiji. The immensely popular local music known as Kaneka is a mixture of reggae and traditional Kanak rhythms.

Environment

New Caledonia has a rich endemic biodiversity. The main threats to its natural environment are mining, deforestation, cattle farming and wildfires. Deer are also a significant threat and as a result deer hunting has become an intrinsic part of local life.

The barrier reef that surrounds New Caledonia is 1600km long and ranges from 200m to 1km in width. Inside the reef, the lagoon is seldom more than 25m deep.

Traditionally, Kanaks had a very sensible relationship with the environment, considering it their *garde-manger* (food safe), which meant the territory had to be managed properly in order to provide a sustainable food supply.

Open-cut nickel mining has caused deforestation, erosion, water pollution and reef damage. The last has occurred particularly along the midsection of the east coast of Grande Terre, as the run-off from the stripped mountains pours straight into the sea.

The emissions released from the nickel smelter in Noumea are another serious issue. International health and environmental agencies have classified nickel as an 'extremely hazardous substance' and have recognised that it can induce asthma.

Vale Nouvelle-Calédonie Goro nickel processing plant in the south is also causing controversy with its chemical extraction methods.

Bushfires, which lead to erosion and desertification, are a huge problem.

Geography

The territory is an archipelago that comprises the Grande Terre (16,500 sq km); Île des Pins (152 sq km); the Loyalty Islands (1980 sq km); and the tiny Îles Belep.

Grande Terre is 400km long with central ranges dividing the lush, mountainous east coast from the dry west coast and its plains. It is rich in minerals and has one of the biggest nickel reserves in the world.

The Loyalty Islands and Île des Pins are uplifted, flat coral islands. New Caledonia has 1600km of reef enclosing a magnificent 23,500 sq km turquoise lagoon.

Ecology

New Caledonia's flora and fauna originated in eastern Gondwanaland, evolving in isolation when Grande Terre became separated 80 million years ago. There are many unique plants and animals, and of the 3250 flowering plant species, 80% are native.

The most renowned indigenous land bird is the endangered *cagou (Rhynochetus*

jubatus), New Caledonia's national bird. Of the few land mammals, only *roussettes* (members of the fruit-bat family), a traditional Kanak food source, are indigenous. Introduced mammals include rusa deer, which are causing major damage to native plants and the environment.

New Caledonia's waters are home to around 2000 species of fish. Humpback whales visit between July and September. New Caledonia's sea snakes are often sighted on the water's surface or on land. The most commonly is the amphibious *tricot rayé* (banded sea krait). They are highly venomous but not aggressive and bites are extremely rare.

Parks & Reserves

There are many land and marine parks and reserves in New Caledonia. In the Far South, Parc Provincial de la Rivière Bleue is easily accessible, as is Le Parc des Grandes Fougères near La Foa.

SURVIVAL GUIDE

❶ Directory A–Z

ACCOMMODATION

Hotels have glorious garden and/or ocean views. Prices start around 7000/14,000/22,000 CFP per night for a room in a basic/midrange/top-end hotel for a single or double. Singles usually pay the same rate as a double.

Bungalow prices range from 4000 CFP to 21,000 CFP. Bungalows usually have private bathrooms, an on-site restaurant and sometimes a communal kitchen.

There are homestays *(accueil en tribu)*, gîtes and campsites everywhere, except in Noumea. Campsites have toilets and showers, usually with hot water, and cost between 1100 and 2100 CFP per tent (with two people). Homestays and farmstays are usually in a Melanesian family compound and have *cases* (with mattresses on the floor) or bungalows (with beds). They cost from 1000 CFP to 6000 CFP per person. Bring your own towels and soap; they're not usually provided. Meals are extra.

CHILDREN

Infants under three years stay free at most places. Children under 12 pay half the adult rate for accommodation and services.

DANGERS & ANNOYANCES

In general, New Caledonia is very safe for travellers. Always check that you're not walking or swimming in a taboo area, or on somebody's property.

EMERGENCY

In an emergency dial ☑17.

FESTIVALS & EVENTS

The Office du Tourisme website (www.office-tourisme.nc) and www.visitnewcaledonia.com have a calendar of events.

➜ **Festival of the Yam** (March) Kanak festival marking the beginning of the harvest.

➜ **Giant Omelette Festival** (April) At Dumbéa, a dozen chefs, 7000 eggs and many hands make a free-for-all 3.5m-diameter omelette.

➜ **Avocado Festival** (May) Held in Nece, Maré. It's the island's biggest fair, celebrating the end of the harvest.

➜ **Fete du Lagon** (early June) A day-long fishing festival in Ouvéa.

➜ **La Foa Film Festival** (late June) A week celebrating film in La Foa and Noumea.

➜ **Bastille Day** (14 July) France's national day. Fireworks on the 13th and a military parade in Noumea on the 14th.

➜ **Marathon Internationale de Noumea** (July/August) Held annually, attracts top athletes from all over the world.

➜ **Foire de Bourail** (August/September) Three-day fair featuring a rodeo, a cattle show, horse racing and a beauty pageant.

➜ **Fête du Bœuf** (October/November) Païta's popular fair and rodeo.

➜ **Sound & Light Show** (October/November) Impressive light shows staged at Fort Teremba, near La Foa.

GAY & LESBIAN TRAVELLERS

www.homosphere.asso.nc has events and information for gay and lesbian travellers to New Caledonia. Homosexuality is legal in New Caledonia.

INTERNET ACCESS

Most hotels offer free wi-fi access, sometimes in guests' rooms but usually in the lobby. Internet cafes are few and far between, but free wi-fi is sometimes available at cafes.

LANGUAGE

➜ French is spoken throughout New Caledonia.

➜ Twenty-eight Melanesian languages are spoken by Kanak peoples, including one on each of the Loyalty Islands.

➜ Ouvéa also has one Polynesian language.

➜ Outside of Noumea, English is not widely spoken.

MAPS

The Office du Tourisme in Noumea and Anse Vata has good free maps of New Caledonia and detailed maps of each island, with useful contact information on the reverse side.

> ### SLEEPING PRICE RANGES
>
> The following price ranges refer to a double room with bathroom.
>
> **$** less than 5000 CFP
>
> **$$** 5000–15,000 CFP
>
> **$$$** more than 15,000 CFP

MONEY

The currency is the Pacific Franc (CFP), also used in French Polynesia and Wallis and Futuna. Tipping is not expected.

OPENING HOURS

May vary, especially in rural areas or outer islands as compared to Noumea. Sundays are extremely quiet throughout the islands.

➜ **Government Offices** 7.30am to 11.30am and 1.30pm to 4.30pm Monday to Friday, some on Saturday mornings

➜ **Banks** 8am to 4pm Monday to Friday

➜ **Shops** 7.30am to 6pm Monday to Friday, Saturday mornings; some close for lunch

PUBLIC HOLIDAYS

➜ **New Year's Day** 1 January

➜ **Easter Monday** March/April

➜ **Labour Day** 1 May

➜ **Victory Day** 8 May

➜ **Ascension Day** 17 May

➜ **Whit Monday** 28 May

➜ **National Day** 14 July

➜ **Assumption Day** 15 August

➜ **New Caledonia Day** 24 September

➜ **All Saints' Day** 1 November

➜ **Armistice Day** 11 November

➜ **Christmas Day** 25 December

TELEPHONE

New Caledonia's international telephone code is ☑ 687. For directory assistance dial ☑1012.

➜ **Mobile (Cell) Phones** A local SIM card costs 6195 CFP and includes 3000 CFP credit – buy it from a post office (you need identification). Make sure you buy the correct recharge card (Liberté; 1000 CFP), which is available from post offices and tobacconists' stores.

➜ **Phonecards** Use IZI cards (1000 CFP or 3000 CFP) to make local and international calls from a public phone box, a landline or a mobile phone. Available at post offices and some tobacconists' shops in Noumea.

TIME

New Caledonia is 11 hours ahead of GMT. It's one hour ahead of Australian Eastern Standard Time

NEW CALEDONIA DIRECTORY A–Z

(Sydney, Brisbane and Melbourne) and one hour behind NZ and Fiji.

TOURIST INFORMATION

Good websites include Office de Tourisme (www.office-tourisme.nc), Tourism New Caledonia (http://www.nctps.com) and Loyalty Islands (www.iles-loyaute.com).

Getting There & Away

AIR

The following airlines fly into New Caledonia. Air France flies code-share with Aircalin (Air Calédonie International).

➡ **Air France** (www.airfrance.com)
➡ **Air New Zealand** (www.airnewzealand.co.nz)
➡ **Air Vanuatu** (www.airvanuatu.com)
➡ **Aircalin** (www.aircalin.com)
➡ **Qantas** (www.qantas.com)

Aircalin has direct flights to the following destinations:

➡ **Australia**: Sydney, Melbourne, Brisbane.
➡ **New Zealand**: Auckland
➡ **Japan**: Tokyo, Osaka
➡ **Fiji**: Nadi
➡ **French Polynesia**: Papeete
➡ **Vanuatu**: Port Vila
➡ **Pacific**: Wallis, Futuna

Airports

Tontouta International Airport (www.tontouta-aeroport.nc) is 45km northwest of Noumea – go by public bus or shuttle. Facilities include ATMs and a currency exchange office, tourist information office and all the big rental car outlets.

Magenta Domestic Airport is a further 20-minute bus ride from Noumea (Bus 40) – there is no direct connection by public transport between the airports. Take a taxi or pre-arrange a shuttle.

SEA

Cruise Ship

An endless stream of cruise ships visit New Caledonia.

➡ Cruise ships dock at Noumea's Gare Maritime.
➡ A tourist information booth opens at Gare Maritime on 'cruise ship days'.
➡ The ships also often have stops at Lifou and Île des Pins.
➡ P&O (www.pocruises.com.au) are regular visitors.

Yacht

➡ All yachts arriving in New Caledonia should proceed to Port Moselle, Noumea. All entry formalities are now only handled in Noumea.
➡ See www.noonsite.com for up-to-date details.
➡ www.cruising-newcaledonia.com is a good online cruising guide.

Getting Around

AIR

Air Caledonie

Air Calédonie (p164), New Caledonia's domestic airline, flies out of Magenta domestic airport in Noumea. The earlier you purchase, the better the chance of getting a cheap fare.

Destinations:
➡ **North Province** - Koné, Koumac, Touho
➡ **South Province** - Île des Pins
➡ **Loyalty Islands** - Lifou, Maré, Ouvéa

Air Caledonie is very strict on weights for check-in and cabin baggage. Unless you have a 'Flexible fare with 20kg baggage' ticket, you are restricted to 12kg for check-in baggage and 3kg for cabin baggage.

The website has flight schedules, Air Pass details and booking facilities. There are Air Calédonie agencies at all flight destinations, and a ticket office at Magenta domestic airport.

Air Pass

The Air Calédonie Pass offers a deal for four domestic flight segments. It's great in theory, but there are a limited number of pass seats for each flight. The pass is sold through the Air Calédonie office in Noumea; you'll need to send them a copy of your passport.

Other Airlines

Air Loyauté (p177) flies between Lifou, Maré, Ouvéa in the Loyalty Islands. It has smaller aircraft than Air Calédonie, but is very competitive on price.

BICYCLE

You'd have to be very keen to cycle round 400km-long Grande Terre. Drivers speed mercilessly and are not particularly courteous to cyclists.

Ouvéa and Île des Pins are ideal for cycling.

BOAT

Betico (p164) fast passenger ferry sails from Noumea to Île des Pins, and to Maré and Lifou in the Loyalty Islands. Tickets can be bought online.

To **Île des Pins** (adult/child 5450/2770 CFP one way; adult/child 10.700/5320 CFP day trip):
➡ Wednesdays: Noumea–Île des Pins–Noumea
➡ Saturdays: Noumea–Île des Pins
➡ Sundays: Île des Pins–Noumea

Noumea to Île des Pins takes 2½ hours.

To the **Loyalty Islands** (adult/child 7750/3600 CFP Noumea to Maré or Lifou; adult/child 4260/2030 between Maré and Lifou):
➡ Mondays: Noumea–Maré–Lifou–Noumea
➡ Thursday: Noumea–Maré–Lifou
➡ Fridays: Lifou–Maré–Noumea

Noumea to Maré takes four hours; between Maré and Lifou takes two hours; Lifou to Noumea takes five hours.

BUS

Rai (Réseau d'Autocars Interurbain; ☎ 05 81 61; www.rai.nc) Nearly every town on Grande Terre is connected to the capital by Rai's extremely efficient bus system. There are several departure points around Noumea, depending on your destination. Check when you buy your ticket.

Carsud (p165) Operates buses between Noumea and the greater Noumea region. They go as far north as Tontouta (400 CFP), passing through Dumbéa (320 CFP) and Païta (360 CFP), and south to Plum in Mont-Dore (400 CFP).

Karuia Bus (p165) Operates Noumea city buses. The ticket office is on Rue Austerlitz opposite the Compact Megastore (tickets are 190 CFP there, 210 CFP when purchased on the bus).

On the other islands there are practically no buses. It's essential to prearrange transport (or hitchhike).

Around Grande Terre by Bus

The following schedules are for services departing from Noumea. Fares range from 600 CFP to 2000 CFP.

Destination	Duration (hr)	Frequency
Bourail	2½	Mon-Sat
Canala	3½	daily
Hienghène	6½	Mon-Sat
Koné	4	daily
Koumac	5½	daily
La Foa	1¾	Mon-Sat
Poindimié	5	daily
Pouébo	6½	Wed & Fri
Thio	2	daily
Yaté	2	Mon-Sat

CAR, SCOOTER & CAMPERVAN

Touring New Caledonia by car allows you to explore places off the beaten track which aren't easy to reach by bus.

➡ Car-hire rates are reasonable.

➡ Petrol is the same price no matter how remote you are.

➡ Major roads and most minor ones are sealed and in good condition.

➡ Drink driving is common so be very careful, especially at night.

Driving Licence

A valid licence from your own country will suffice to drive in New Caledonia.

Hire

➡ Car-rental companies abound in Noumea and the larger ones have desks at Tontouta International Airport. The big players such as Avis, Hertz, Budget and Europcar are here, plus local operators.

➡ Most companies rent small sedans from 4500 CFP including 150km per day. Extra kilometres cost from 23 CFP per kilometre. Car hire with unlimited kilometres costs from 7000 CFP per day.

➡ Look for deals such as one-week's all-inclusive rental from 28,000 CFP.

➡ In the Loyalty Islands and Île des Pins, prices start at 6500 CFP per day with unlimited kilometres (it's not like you can go far). There's no extra cost to get your car delivered and picked up from your port of arrival and departure.

Insurance

No extra insurance is required when hiring a car. Some companies charge a security deposit of 100,000 CFP.

Road Rules

➡ Driving in New Caledonia is on the right-hand side of the road.

➡ The speed limit on a main road is 110km/h (though no one seems to pay attention to it) and in residential areas it is 50km/h.

➡ Seat belts are compulsory.

➡ The maximum permissible blood alcohol concentration is 0.05%, and random breath testing is carried out.

TAXI

➡ Taxis are confined to Noumea, the larger towns on Grande Terre and a couple of islands.

➡ In Noumea it's best to call and book (☎ 28 35 12), rather than stand on the side of the road and wait.

TOURS

Operators in Noumea organise tours and activities in and around the city, as well as throughout New Caledonia.

The Office du Tourisme has brochures for all kinds of optional tours, or try the following:

➡ **Arc en Ciel Voyages** (p164) Arranges tickets for travelling or touring anywhere, including day trips to the islands.

➡ **Caledonia Spirit** (p164) Arranges everything including accommodation and rental cars on the Loyalty Islands and Île des Pins.

Rarotonga & the Cook Islands

☎ 682 / POP 19,500

Best Places to Stay

➡ Sea Change (p217)
➡ Ikurangi Eco Retreat (p217)
➡ Beach Place (p217)
➡ Etu Moana (p227)
➡ Tiare Cottages (p235)

Best Places to Eat

➡ Vaima Restaurant & Bar (p219)
➡ Tamarind House (p206)
➡ Punanga Nui Market (p203)
➡ Mooring (p218)
➡ Trader Jacks (p205)

Why Go?

Fifteen droplets of land cast across 2 million sq km of wild Pacific blue, the Cook Islands are simultaneously remote and accessible, modern and traditional.

With a strong cafe culture, a burgeoning organic and artisan food scene, and a handful of bar and clubs, Rarotonga lives confidently in the 21st century. But beyond the island's tourist buzz and contemporary appearance is a robust culture, firmly anchored by traditional Polynesian values and steeped in oral history.

North of 'Raro', the lagoon of Aitutaki is ringed with deserted islands and is one of the Pacific's most scenic jewels. Venture further and Polynesian traditions emerge nearer the surface. Drink home brew at a traditional 'Atiuan *tumunu* (bush-beer drinking club), explore the *makatea* (raised coral cliffs) and taro fields of Mangaia, or swim in the underground cave pools of Mitiaro and Ma'uke. The remote Northern Group is a South Seas idyll experienced by a lucky few.

When to Go

Avarua

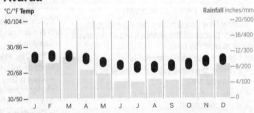

Mar–Apr The end of cyclone season usually brings clear, sunny days.

Aug Celebrate the nation's 1965 declaration of independence at the annual Te Maire Nui Festival.

Sep–Oct Look forward to warmer temperatures and reduced humidity.

RAROTONGA

POP 10,572 / AREA 67.2 SQ KM

The most populous of the Cook Islands is stunning in its natural beauty and physical drama. A halo of flame-orange coral reef encircles the island, and Rarotonga's sapphire-blue lagoon is trimmed by sparkling white beaches. Beyond the reef, breakers foam and crash like distant thunder.

Rarotonga's settlements are nestled on the coastal flatlands, with the island rising spectacularly through lush fields and rural farmland to the mountainous and thickly forested interior. These silent, brooding peaks dominate the landscape from every angle.

Rarotonga has plenty of history, too, with ancient *marae* (traditional meeting places) and monuments to explore, and some of the best-preserved coral churches in the South Pacific.

History

Legend tells that Rarotonga was discovered by Io Tangaroa, who arrived about 1400 years ago from Nuku Hiva in the Marquesas (French Polynesia). In the early 13th century two great warrior chiefs, Tangi'ia from Tahiti and Karika from Samoa, arrived in *vaka* (ocean-going canoes) to conquer the island and rule Rarotonga as joint kings. The land was divided among six tribes, each headed by an *ariki*. The first recorded European visitor was Philip Goodenough, captain of the *Cumberland*, who came in 1814 and spent three months looking for sandalwood. In 1823 missionaries John Williams and Papeiha set out to convert the Rarotongans, and in little more than a year Christianity had taken a firm hold.

ⓘ Getting There & Away

Air New Zealand links Rarotonga to Auckland, Sydney and Los Angeles, and Virgin Australia has flights between Auckland and Rarotonga. Air Rarotonga and Air Tahiti operate code-share flights linking Rarotonga with Tahiti.

ⓘ Getting Around

TO/FROM THE AIRPORT

Most hotels and hostels provide transfers from Rarotonga Airport. Raro Tours operates an airport-shuttle service (NZ$20 per person one way to anywhere on the island).

BUS

Circle-island buses run around the coast road in both directions, departing from the Circle Island Bus Stop at Cook's Corner in Avarua. Buses running clockwise depart hourly from 7am to 11pm Monday to Saturday, and from 8am to noon and 2pm to 4pm Sunday.

Buses running anticlockwise depart at 30 minutes past the hour, from 8.30am to 4.30pm Monday to Friday, and from 8.30am to 12.30pm on Saturday. There are no anti-clockwise buses on Sundays.

A night bus service runs clockwise on Friday at midnight and at 2am on Saturday. Note there is no 11pm bus on Friday.

Adult/child fares are NZ$4/3 for one ride, NZ$8/5 for a return trip (two rides) or NZ$30/19 for a 10-ride ticket. A family pass, valid for two adults and two children, costs NZ$26. There's also a day pass (NZ$16). The bus can be flagged down anywhere along its route. Tickets can be purchased on board.

Pick up bus timetables from the tourist office or the bus driver, or see the website for **Cook's Passenger Transport** (☑ 55215, 25512; www. busaboutraro.com). Several free publications, including the *Cook Islands Sun Rarotonga Map*, also contain timetables, and they are often posted in restaurants and shops.

CAR, MOTORCYCLE & BICYCLE

The speed limit is 50km/h outside town and 30km/h around Avarua. It's illegal for motorcyclists to ride two abreast (though many do), and if you exceed 40km/h on a motorcycle without a helmet you'll be fined. Driving is on the left-hand side of the road

To rent a car, your drivers licence from your home country is valid, but if you're planning on zipping around the island on a scooter, you'll need to get a Cook Islands drivers licence (NZ$20). If you're not licensed to drive a motorcycle at home, you'll also have to take a short practical test (NZ$5) including negotiating a simple slalom course of road cones. You can get your licence any day from 8am to 3pm, but turn up early as the police station issues many motorcycle licences daily and queues can be long.

The quintessential mode of transport in the Cook Islands is the scooter. Good rates for rental bikes are around NZ$50 for three days or NZ$100 per week. Cars and jeeps are available for around NZ$50 to NZ$70 per day. Mountain bikes are around NZ$7 per day or NZ$50 per week.

Avis Cook Islands Airport (☑ 21039; www. avis.co.ck); Avarua (Map p204; ☑ 22833; CITC Shopping Centre) Also has a branch at the Pacific Resort at Muri Beach (p218).

BT Rentals (Map p200; ✆23586; www.btrent
acar.co.ck; 'Arorangi) Scooter and motorcycle
hire.

Island Car & Bike Hire (Map p204; www.
islandcarhire.co.ck) Arorangi (Map p200;
✆22632; Ara Tapu); Avarua (Map p204;
✆24632); Muri (Map p200; ✆21632).

Polynesian Rental Cars (www.polynesianhire.
co.ck) Airport (✆21039; ☺open only for
international flights); Avarua (✆20895; 2 St
Joseph's Rd); Downtown Avarua (✆26895);
Edgewater Resort (✆21026; Edgewater Resort); Rarotongan Beach Resort (✆20838;
Rarotongan Beach Resort); Pacific Resort
(✆21838; Pacific Resort).

Rarotonga Rentals (Map p200; ✆22326;
www.rarotongarentals.co.ck) Opposite the
airport.

Tipani Rentals (Map p200; ✆22382; 'Arorangi) Near the Edgewater Resort in 'Arorangi.

TAXI

A number of operators around the island have
amalgamated into the Cook Islands Taxi Association. Look for the bright green cars and vans.
Rates are about NZ$3 per kilometre. From Muri
to the airport will cost around NZ$40, and there
is also the option of fixed-price airport transfers
of NZ$15 to NZ$20 per person to destinations
around the island.

Atupa Taxi (✆58252, 25517; Atupa) Contact
Panala & Ngaoa Katuke.

Executive Taxi (✆52355, 21400; ivorndot@
oyster.net.ck; Muri) Contact Ivor and Dorothy.

H-K Taxi (✆73549; teuiraka@oyster.net.ck;
Muri) Contact Teuira and Shirley.

JP Taxi (✆55107, 26572; 'Aorangi) Contact
Kim Pirangi.

Muri Height Taxi (✆58175, 25405; Muri)
Contact Junior Wichman.

Price Taxi (✆57303, 50908; larryprice38@
gmail.com; 'Aorangi) Contact Larry and Ina
Price.

Rainbow Taxi (✆72318; Takuvaine) Contact
Tere Poaru.

Seeplus Taxi (✆55297; Avatiu) Contact Rei
Enoka.

Avarua & Around

Fronting a pretty bay on Rarotonga's north
coast, Avarua is the Cook Islands' only proper town. Hardly an urban jungle, Avarua's
largest buildings are barely the height of a
coconut tree, and the atmosphere of shops
and cafes is extremely laid-back. Avarua
showcases the island's twin harbours, the
main market and some intriguing sights, including the National Museum and the Para
O Tane Palace.

There's one main road, the Ara Maire,
running through town, and past the shops
at the western end of Avarua is the Punanga Nui Market and Avatiu Harbour. This
is where interisland passenger freighter
ships depart from, and where the Port Authority is based. The airport is 1km further
west.

◉ Sights

★**Cook Islands Christian Church**   CHURCH
(CICC; Map p204; Makea Tinirau Rd) Avarua's
white-washed church was built in 1853. The
graveyard contains the graves of author Robert Dean Frisbie, and Albert Henry, the first
prime minister of the Cook Islands. The main
church service is at 10am on Sunday, and visitors are invited to stay for morning tea.

★**BCA Art Gallery**   HISTORIC BUILDING
(Map p204; ✆21939; Ara Tapu) This historical building was once an LMS missionary
school. These days it houses an excellent art
gallery, gift shop and courtyard cafe.

Para O Tane Palace   HISTORIC BUILDING
(Map p204) On the inland side of the main
road is this palace and its surrounding Taputapuatea *marae*. The palace is where
Makea Takau, the paramount *ariki* (chief)
of the area, signed the treaty accepting the
Cook Islands' status as a British protectorate

THE COOK ISLANDS IN...

One Week

Ease into **Rarotonga**'s holiday spirit with a relaxed combination of snorkelling, hiking and
casual dining, before hopping north to **Aitutaki** and exploring one of the South Pacific's
finest lagoons. Definitely find time to attend a wildly entertaining Island Night.

Two Weeks

From Aitutaki, fly to rocky and remote **'Atiu**. Sample the local coffee and *tumunu* (bush
beer), swim in shimmering underground pools, and discover 'Atiu's rare and idiosyncratic
birdlife. If your budget permits, return to Rarotonga and fly south to sleepy **Mangaia** for
reef fishing and to explore the island's fascinating burial caves.

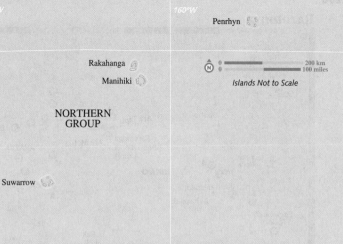

165°W

160°W

Penrhyn

10°S

Rakahanga

Manihiki

0 — 200 km
0 — 100 miles
Islands Not to Scale

Pukapuka

NORTHERN
GROUP

Nassau

Suwarrow

15°S

SOUTH PACIFIC OCEAN

Palmerston Atoll

Aitutaki **⑤**
Lagoon

Manuae

Takutea

Mitiaro

SOUTHERN
GROUP

20°S

'Atiu **⑥**

⑧ Ma'uke

①②③④
✪ AVARUA

Rarotonga

⑦ Mangaia

Rarotonga & Cook Islands Highlights

① Snorkelling, kayaking or paddle-boarding in the pristine azure waters of Rarotonga's **Muri Lagoon** (p211).

② Trekking Rarotonga's **cross-island track** (p213), inland trails and valley walks.

③ Feasting on the freshest of seafood and organic local produce in Rarotonga's excellent **restaurants** (p203).

④ Having fun and exploring Rarotonga's heritage and history on a two- or four-wheeled **tour** (p211).

⑤ Exploring **Aitutaki's stunning lagoon** (p224) by kayak, and finding your own deserted *motu* (island).

⑥ Exploring caves, coffee plantations and unique birdlife on **'Atiu** (p229).

⑦ Learning about **Mangaia's** (p238) ancient ways and exploring its mysterious limestone burial caves.

⑧ Discovering the story of the **Divided Church** (p236) on Ma'uke.

Rarotonga

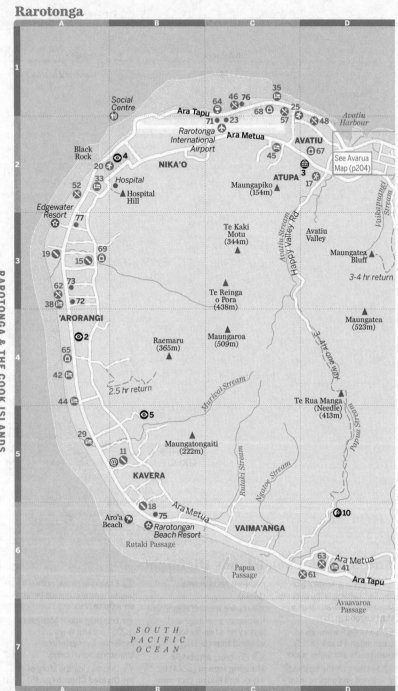

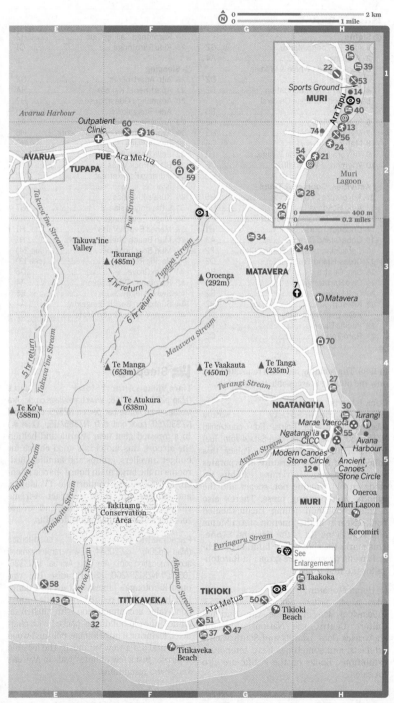

RAROTONGA & THE COOK ISLANDS

0 ———————————— 2 km
0 ———————————— 1 mile

Avarua Harbour

AVARUA

TUPAPA

PUE Ara Metua

Outpatient Clinic

Takuva'ine Stream

Pue Stream

Takuva'ine Valley

'Ikurangi (485m)

4 hr return

6 hr return

5 hr return

Takuva'ine Stream

Tupapa Stream

▲ Oroenga (292m)

MATAVERA

Matavera Stream

▲ Te Manga (653m)

▲ Te Vaakauta (450m)

▲ Te Tanga (235m)

▲ Te Atukura (638m)

Turangi Stream

▲ Te Ko'u (588m)

NGATANGI'IA

Turangi

Marae Vaerota

Ngatangi'ia CICC

Avana Harbour

Modern Canoes' Stone Circle

Ancient Canoes' Stone Circle

Avana Stream

Taipara Stream

Totokoitu Stream

Takitumu Conservation Area

MURI

Oneroa Muri Lagoon

Koromiri

Paringaru Stream

Turoa Stream

Akapuao Stream

See Enlargement

Taakoka

TITIKAVEKA

Tikioki

Ara Metua

Tikioki Beach

Titikaveka Beach

MURI

Sports Ground

Ara Tapu

Muri Lagoon

0 ———— 400 m
0 ———— 0.2 miles

Rarotonga

in 1888. The building has been renovated, but only the outside is accessible to the public.

Cook Islands
Library & Museum Society   MUSEUM
(Map p204; Makea Tinirau Rd; adult/child NZ$5/2.50; ⊙9am-1pm Mon-Sat, 4-7pm Tue) Inland behind the Para O Tane Palace, this collection of Pacific literature incorporates a small museum. Intriguing exhibits include an old whaling pot, spears and the island's first printing press. There's also a small bookshop selling Pacific-themed books. Nearby at the junction of Ara Metua and Takuva'ine Rd is the **Papeiha Stone**. This marks the spot where Tahitian preacher Papeiha preached the gospel in Rarotonga for the first time.

National Museum   MUSEUM
(Map p204; Victoria Rd; admission NZ$3; ⊙9am-4pm Mon-Fri) Inside the National Culture Centre, the National Museum showcases Cook Islands and South Pacific artefacts, and sometimes hosts temporary exhibitions. Books on the Pacific are also for sale.

🛏 Sleeping

Tiare Village Airport Motel   MOTEL $
(Map p200; ☑23466; www.tiarevillage.co.ck; Ara Metua; main house per person NZ$25, chalet s/d NZ$30/50, pool unit d/tr NZ$85/115; @🛜🏊) In a forested glen near Avarua and behind the airport, this motel is a good choice for budget travellers, groups and families. Bedrooms in the large main house share a kitchen, bathroom and comfortable TV lounge, and outside are three compact A-frame chalets with shared bathrooms, and several roomier self-contained poolside units.

Paradise Inn   GUESTHOUSE $
(Map p204; ☑20544; www.rarotongamotel accommodation.com; Are Tapu, Avarua; s NZ$85-105, d/f NZ$135/200; 🛜) Paradise Inn was once Rarotonga's largest and liveliest dance hall, but has been refitted to provide simple, good-value accommodation with kitchen facilities. The old building is packed with character, featuring a huge lounge, polished-wood floors and a sea-view verandah. The location is terrific, just a few minutes' walk to Avarua's shops and restaurants.

Islander   MOTEL $$
(Map p200; ☑ 21003; www.islanderhotel.co.ck; Ara Tapu; d NZ$265; ❋@☎❊) On the beachfront opposite the airport, the Islander offers ocean-view self-contained doubles that have been recently redecorated. There's a poolside barbecue restaurant, perfect for a cold beer and a final Cook Islands meal if you're leaving on an evening flight. Sun loungers and the attached Hula Bar – with an all-day happy hour – make for a social atmosphere.

Day use of the rooms is NZ$200.

Jetsave Travel   ACCOMMODATION SERVICES
(☑ 27707; www.jetsave.co.ck; Ara Maire, Avarua) Everything from rental houses through to luxury apartments.

Shekinah Homes   ACCOMMODATION SERVICES
(Map p204; ☑ 26004; www.shekinahhomes.com; Ara Tapu, Avarua) Holiday-house rental options from simple beachfront studios to larger family villas.

✖ Eating

★ Punanga Nui Market   MARKET $
(Map p204; www.punanganuiculturalmarket. co.ck; Ara Tapu, Avarua; ☺6am-noon Sat) Head here for fresh fruit and vegetables, fish and seafood, barbecued snacks, and stalls selling fresh bread and traditional Polynesian food. Foodie treats to discover include delicious fruit smoothies, local coffee, and the stand selling roast pork rolls with apple sauce, and delicious lemon meringue. Don't miss trying the homemade ginger lemonade either.

Hunt down local delicacies including *ika mata* (raw fish marinated in lime and coconut), *rukau* (steamed taro leaves), *poke* (banana with arrowroot and coconut) and *mitiore* (fermented coconut with onion and seafood). Also good are *firi firi,* Tahitian -style doughnuts with chocolate filling, and 100% organic artisan bread is available from 'Varaua mata, e te Miti, Vai'. There's also sourdough, croissants and wholegrain bread, and locally made dips, sauces and chutneys.

Body Fuel   CAFE $
(Map p204; ☑ 23575; Punanga Nui Market, Avarua; salads, juices & smoothies NZ$7-13; ☺7.30am-3pm Mon-Sat) Some of the healthiest food on the island is at this simple market food caravan that's open throughout the week. Smoothies and tropical juices go well with gourmet

Avarua

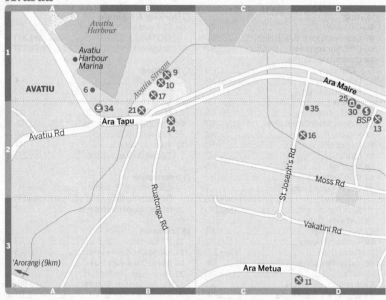

salads – try the smoked marlin one – and there's also sushi available from just NZ$1.

Bite Time
SEAFOOD $

(Map p204; ☑ 23577; Punanga Nui Market, Avarua; mains NZ$10-18; ⊙ 8am-4pm Mon-Thu & Sat, to 8pm Fri) Specialising in fresh fish, this Monday-to-Saturday market stall has great *ika mata*, brilliant tuna carpaccio, and a stonking seafood platter (NZ$18) combining all sorts of tasty marine goodies. There's also sashimi, and fish or chicken wraps for on-the-go dining. Phone orders are welcome.

LBV
CAFE $

(Map p204; Ara Tapu, Avarua; snacks NZ$7-10; ⊙ 7.30am-4pm Mon-Fri) Pop in for a fruit smoothie or coffee and croissant, and stock up on artisan breads, deli produce and other picnic-friendly goodies. Brunch and lunch is also available.

Waffle Shack
CAFE $

(Map p204; www.facebook.com/TheWaffleShack; Punanga Nui Market, Avarua; waffles NZ$6-9; ⊙ 7.30am-2.30pm Tue-Fri, 7am-noon Sat) Life's pretty simple really. Some days all you need is really good coffee and a freshly made waffle crammed with tropical fruit.

Rob's Charcoal Chicken
BARBECUE $

(Map p204; Cook's Corner Arcade, Avarua; mains NZ$10-15; ⊙ 9am-3pm Mon-Fri) Located in a quiet courtyard, Rob's offers expertly barbecued chickens, either served with a plate full of salad and taro chips, or doused with spicy *peri peri* flavours in a wrap. Whole chickens (NZ$20) are available for takeaway – a handy option if you're self-catering – and Rob's coconut curried fish is also very tasty.

BCA Café
CAFE $

(Map p204; Ara Tapu, Avarua; snacks NZ$5-12; ⊙ 9am-3pm Mon-Fri, to 1pm Sat) This courtyard cafe in the restored BCA Art Gallery building serves up excellent juices, bagels, toasted sandwiches, and coffee and cake. There's usually a selection of New Zealand magazines to browse.

Café Jireh
CAFE $

(Map p200; Ara Tapu, opposite the airport; snacks & mains NZ$7-18; ⊙ 8am-4pm Mon-Fri, from 1pm Sat) Near the airport, Café Jireh does excellent coffee and homestyle baking including creamy custard squares. It's also a popular spot for a lazy brunch.

Kai Pizza
PIZZA $

(Map p204; ☑ 53330; Ara Tapu, Avarua; pizza NZ$12-19; ⊙ 11am-2pm Tue-Fri, plus 4-9pm Mon-

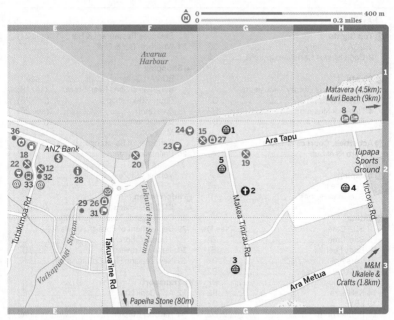

Sat) Wood-fired pizza is served from a colourful shipping container. Order the Hawaiian one with ham and pineapple, and celebrate all things Polynesian and Italian. There's outdoor seating, or oceanfront beach dining is a short drive away. Service can be slow so consider ordering by phone.

Ocean Fresh Seafood
SEAFOOD $

(Map p200; Ara Tapu, Panama; ⏰7am-4pm Mon-Sat) The best place to buy fresh fish if you're looking to barbecue up a storm or prepare your own sashimi. Fish could include wahoo, *mahimahi*, tuna, swordfish and broadbill, but it all depends on what's been caught that morning. Special export packs are also available if you're keen to take some fresh fish back on the plane.

Prime Foods
SUPERMARKET $

(Map p204; ☎22259; www.primefoods.co.ck; St Joseph's Rd, Avarua; ⏰8am-5.30pm Mon-Thu, to 6pm Fri, to 2pm Sat) Dining out on Raro can be expensive, so head to Prime Foods for barbecue-ready treats like gourmet sausages, and the island's best array of salami and ham for lazy afternoon snacking sessions.

CITC Supermarket
SUPERMARKET $

(Map p200; Ara Tapu, Avatiu; ⏰8am-6pm Mon-Fri, to 4pm Sat) Halfway to the airport from Avarua, the huge CITC Supermarket is great for tinned and packaged produce. There's also a liquor store attached.

Foodland
SUPERMARKET $

(Map p204; Ara Tapu , Avarua; ⏰8am-6pm Mon-Fri, to 4pm Sat) The best all-round supermarket is in the middle of Avarua's main shopping strip, with fresh bread, fruit and vegetables, packaged goods and a deli counter.

★ Trader Jacks
PUB FOOD, SEAFOOD $$

(Map p204; www.traderjackscookislands.com; Ara Tapu, Avarua; mains NZ$18-36; ⏰bar 11am-midnight, restaurant 11.30am-2.30pm & 6-9pm Mon-Sat) Trader Jacks is one of Rarotonga's iconic watering holes, and panoramic sea views and good food also make it a great place to eat. The front bar has top-notch pizzas, while the restaurant is more stylish and classy with meals including excellent sashimi and smoked marlin fish cakes. There's usually a live band on Friday and Saturday nights.

Tahiti Café
SEAFOOD $$

(Map p204; Ara Tapu, Avarua; mains from NZ$18, seafood platters NZ$40; ⏰11.30am-2.30pm Mon-Fri) Secure a table on the breezy deck and tuck into tasty Tahitian- and Asian-style spins on sashimi and *ika mata*. The concise

RAROTONGA & THE COOK ISLANDS AVARUA & AROUND

Avarua

seafood-only menu also extends to fried fish and fish platters, and it's all good, and all very fresh.

Café Salsa CAFE **$$**
(Map p204; ☑ 22215; www.salsa.co.ck; Ara Tapu, Avarua; mains NZ$14-27, pizza NZ$12-20; ⊙ 7.30am-3pm Mon-Sat) In downtown Avarua, Café Salsa is more Auckland-chic than Polynesian-rustic. The diverse menu combines Mediterranean and Asian flavours with local produce, and standout dishes include the Thai-style *eke* (octopus) curry, and the wood-roasted *mahi-mahi* fillet with slow-roasted tomatoes, feta and pine nuts. Gourmet pizzas are also good, and there's a decent NZ-centric winelist.

Cafe Ariki CAFE **$$**
(Map p204; ☑ 22772; Ara Metua, Avarua; mains NZ$18-26; ⊙ 10.30am-2pm Mon-Fri, plus 6-9pm Mon-Sat) Tucked away inland behind Avarua township, this good-value cafe and bar is a big favourite with locals. Sashimi, *ika mata* and huge burgers and salads for lunch give way to barbecues for dinner. Combine grilled tuna with a few beers, and definitely leave room for dessert of peach and yogurt cake.

Tamarind House INTERNATIONAL **$$$**
(Map p200; ☑ 26487; www.tamarind.co.ck; Ara Tapu, Tupapa; mains NZ$25-37; ⊙ 11.30am-2pm Mon-Fri, plus 5.30-10pm Mon-Sat, 9am-2pm Sun May-Oct only) The most elegant place to dine on Rarotonga is this colonial building on the island's north shore. Book a table on the grand verandah and enjoy the cool evening breeze with an inspired fusion of European, Asian and Pacific flavours. Try the island fish curry or the excellent blackened fish (usually tuna) with breadfruit chips and steamed *rukau* (local spinach).

From May to October Tamarind House is also open for Sunday brunch.

🍸 Drinking & Nightlife

The main after-dark action on Rarotonga is centred around Avarua. Raro's big night out is Friday, but Saturday is catching up in popularity. On Friday most places stay open to around 2am, but doors are bolted shut at midnight on Saturday out of respect for the Sabbath. Most restaurants double as bars, and resort bars are open to nonguests. Check out the *Cook Islands Sun* tourists' newspaper for what's on around the island.

For an organised Friday night out exploring Rarotonga's bars and clubs, join a Going Troppo tour (NZ$38 per person) with Raro Tours. After-dark tours on Friday nights are also arranged by Rarotonga's bigger resorts and hostels.

Trader Jacks (p205) in Avarua, and the Waterline Bar & Grill (p219) in 'Arorangi, are also good spots for a few quiet ones.

21.3 Vaiana Bistro & Bar   BAR

(Map p200; Ara Tapu, Avatiu; ⊘11am-10pm Tue-Fri, 4-10pm Sat) Fast track into an island state of mind with loping Pacific reggae, shimmering sunsets and cold beer at this relaxed beachside bar that's a favourite of locals and nearby accommodation owners. Weekend bands and DJs, and a pre-sunset happy hour from 4pm to 6pm, make it worth the short hop from downtown Avarua. Enjoying island life is really pretty simple.

Whatever Bar & Grill   BAR

(Map p204; ☑22299; Ara Tapu, Avarua; ⊘11am-midnight Mon-Thu & Sat, to 2am Fri) Who'd have thought – an open-air bar on a disused rooftop? Just out of Avarua, this place attracts trendy young things and gets very lively on Friday and Saturday nights. There are DJs and regular bands; check out the signboard out the front. Night-time views across town and the harbour are brilliant and there's well-priced bar food for lunch or dinner, including gargantuan burgers and fish sandwiches.

Staircase Restaurant & Bar   CLUB

(Map p204; ☑22254; www.facebook.com/stair caseraro; Ara Tapu, Avarua; ⊘6pm-midnight Thu-Sat) Upstairs behind the Topshape Health & Fitness Centre building, the Staircase is always popular. The bar is decked out with atmospheric island decor and has regular live bands, as well as good-value Island Nights on Thursday and Friday before DJs kick in from 10pm.

Hidie's Bar   BAR

(Map p204; Cook's Corner Arcade; ⊘9pm-midnight Wed, Thu & Sun, 4pm-2am Fri, 4pm-midnight Sat) On busy weekend nights everyone crams into Hidie's to check out the live bands, and there are usually DJs a couple of nights a week. The courtyard garden bar is a great place to be on a warm tropical night.

KEEP YOUR COOL, RARO STYLE

Exploring Rarotonga can be thirsty work, so here's our top-five picks to cool down, island-style.

➡ Dive into nature's very own electrolyte, a nu (young green coconut), chilled and ready to drink from the **Punanga Nui Market** (p203). Don't be surprised if it's also the drink of choice when you're served lunch on an island tour.

➡ Lots of tropical fruit equals lots of tropical smoothies. Recharge after snorkelling with huge servings of creamy, liquid goodness from **Saltwater Cafe** (p220) or **Charlie's Cafe & Beach Hire** (p218).

➡ Pull up a bar stool at **Trader Jacks** (p205), and toast Raro's dedicated crews of outrigger paddlers with a cocktail or a cold beer.

➡ Yes, the craft-beer movement has even washed up on Rarotongan shores. Take a tour and sample the beers at **Matutu Brewery** (p211), or cool down a west-coast sunset with a refreshing Mai Lager at the **Shipwreck Hut** (p221)

➡ Discover the unique flavours of banana wine at Muri's **Koteka Winery** (Map p200; Ara Tapu, Muri; ⊘9am-4pm Mon-Sat) or visit the winery's stall at Avarua's weekly market. The wine is mixed with whatever fruit is in season – anything from passionfruit to mango or orange. There's also vodka and fresh vanilla pods for sale. Look for the roadside signs just past Muri Beach as you're heading clockwise around the island.

Rehab CLUB

(Map p204; ☑ 25717; Ara Tapu, Avarua; ☺ 9pm-midnight Wed & Sat, 10pm-2am Fri) House and electro grooves thump 'n' bump under ultraviolet and stroboscopic lights. Rehab offers occasional drink specials if you arrive before 10pm.

🔒 Shopping

Shops around Avarua sell local basketwork, shell jewellery, necklaces, carvings and musical instruments. Many islands have their own speciality handicrafts, including *rito* (coconut-fibre) fans and hats from the Northern Group and *pupu ei* (shell necklaces) from Mangaia. Beware of cheap Asian imports. Most shops are closed on Sunday.

Printed *pareu* (sarongs) cost around NZ$20 to NZ$30, while handmade ones cost NZ$40 to NZ$50. There's always a good selection at Saturday morning's Punanga Nui Market. Great local T-shirts are also sold at the Punanga Nui market and at surfwear shops.

Only the Cooks and French Polynesia produce rarer black pearls. A single pearl costs from NZ$10 to over NZ$2000.

BCA Art Gallery ARTS & CRAFTS

(Map p204; www.gallerybca.com; Ara Tapu, Avarua; ☺ 10am-3pm Mon-Sat, to noon Sun) BCA houses a gallery specialising in contemporary Pacific art, an excellent gift shop selling pearls, clothing and designer homeware, and a relaxed courtyard cafe.

Island Craft SOUVENIRS

(Map p204; Ara Tapu, Avarua; ☺ 8am-5pm Mon-Fri, to 1pm Sat) The best-stocked souvenir shop is in Avarua.

Bergman & Sons Pearl Store JEWELLERY

(Map p204; www.bergmanandsons.com; Tutakimoa Rd, Avarua; ☺ 10am-4pm Mon-Fri, to noon Sat) Unique and modern settings including necklaces, rings and bracelets. Hillary Clinton was gifted some Bergman black pearls when she visited the Cook Islands in 2012 for the Pacific Islands Forum.

Dive Shop CLOTHING, SPORTS

(Map p204; ☑ 26675; www.palm.co.ck; Ara Tapu, Avarua; ☺ 9am-4pm Mon-Fri, to noon Sat) Sells good-quality fins, masks and snorkels and surfwear. See the website for an interactive map of Raro's best snorkelling sites.

Vonnia's Store CLOTHING

(Map p204; Ara Maire, Avarua; ☺ 8am-5pm Mon-Fri, to 1pm Sat) Centrally located.

Tuki's Pareu CLOTHING

(Map p204; Ara Tapu, Avarua; ☺ 8am-5pm Mon-Fri, to 1pm Sat) The locals' choice.

Mareko CLOTHING

(Map p204; Ara Tapu, Avarua; ☺ 8am-5pm Mon-Fri, to 1pm Sat) Good for T-shirts.

Bounty Bookshop BOOKS

(Map p204; Ara Tapu, Avarua; ☺ 8am-4pm Mon-Fri, to noon Sat) Historical and pictorial books

---

RAROTONGA IN...

Two Days

Take a **circle-island tour** or hire a scooter and buzz around the back roads to get acquainted with the island. Factor in kayaking or paddleboarding around **Muri Lagoon**, before settling in for sunset drinks at the **Shipwreck Hut** and dinner at **Vaima Restaurant & Bar**. Start your second day on an active note by conquering the **cross-island track** or bicycling with **Storytellers**. After the South Pacific's best fish sandwiches at the **Mooring**, relax with swimming and snorkelling near **Charlies Cafe & Beach Hire**, before heading out for an exciting **Island Night** combining local food, singing and dancing. Look forward to a high level of audience interaction.

Four Days

If you're on the island on a Saturday morning, a visit to the **Punanga Nui Market** is almost mandatory. Then head to **Highland Paradise Cultural Centre** for insights into traditional Cook Islands culture. Spend the evening exploring more contemporary local culture amid the nightlife of Avarua. Walk between the **Whatever Bar** and **Trader Jacks**, or head west through town to the beachside location of **21.3 Vaiana Bistro & Bar**. If you're in the mood for dancing, break out your best island moves at **Rehab**. After a well-earned lie in, have a lazy brunch at **Café Salsa** in Avarua, or at **LBV** in Muri, before a fun and exciting island tour with **Raro Safari Tours** or **Raro Buggy Tours**. If you're in town on a Monday or Thursday night, meet the locals on a **progressive dinner** around the island.

RAROTONGA FOR CHILDREN

Always check with the place you're staying about their policy on children, as some don't cater for kids under 12. For really little ones, you can hire strollers, car seats and port-acots from **Coco Tots** (☑56986; www.cocotots.com). Ask at your accommodation or the tourist information office about babysitting services.

The top draw for kids is the island's colourful lagoon and the spectacular beach that stretches around the island. Good spots for snorkelling are Muri, Tikioki and Aro'a Beach, and smoothies and ice creams are never far away at Fruits of Rarotonga or the Saltwater Cafe.

For an in-depth look at the island's underwater inhabitants, kids will adore a glass-bottom boat tour around Muri Lagoon with either Captain Tama's Lagoon Cruizes or Koka Lagoon Cruises. An option to explore the underwater world beyond the reef is on the Raro Reef Sub. From July to October you might be lucky enough to see humpback whales cruising past the island. If they're really keen on all things cetacean, visit the excellent Cook Islands Whale & Wildlife Centre.

Active kids will love exploring the island's jungle-covered interior on the Cross-Island Track, or Raro's quieter back roads on a bicycle ride with Storytellers. Alternatively, drop by Ride Rarotonga and rent a funky, go-anywhere beach cruiser with massive, knobbly wheels.

An entertaining jeep ride around the island with Raro Safari Tours will be sure to please, or you can take them for a quad-bike spin with Coconut Tours if they're eight years or older. Another exciting offroad option is with Raro Buggy Tours, but mum or dad will definitely need to be behind the wheel.

about the Cook Islands, and international and NZ magazines.

Philatelic Bureau STAMPS & COINS
(Map p204; Ara Tapu, Avarua; ☺8am-4pm Mon-Fri) Cook Islands coins and bank notes are sold here, plus Cook Islands stamps (highly prized by philatelists). The unique $3 Cook Islands note is available in two designs. Several new coins were minted for the country's 50th anniversary of independence in 2015.

ℹ Information

Internet access is widely available on Rarotonga. There are Bluesky wi-fi hot spots all around the island, including at most of the major resorts. Telepost shops and other stores sell pre-paid wi-fi access in denominations of NZ$10 (150MB), NZ$25 (500MB), and NZ$50 (1.25GB). Another option is to buy a local Kokanet 3G sim card (NZ$25) for your smartphone, and purchase additional data for 20 cents per MB up to 1GB for NZ$50. At the time of writing 3G service was limited to Rarotonga, but Bluesky hot spots were available on other islands including Aitutaki and 'Atiu.

ANZ (www.anz.com/cookislands; ☺9am-3pm Mon-Fri) ATMs at the main branch in Avarua, at Cook's Corner in Avarua, at Wigmore's Superstore at Vaimaanga, at Muri Beach, and at the Rarotongan Beach Resort at 'Arorangi.

Bluesky Teleshop (Map p204; www.tele com.co.ck; CITC Shopping Centre, Ara Maire; ☺8am-4pm Mon-Fri, 8.30am-1pm Sat) Wi-fi access, internet terminals and mobile phone services.

BSP (Bank South Pacific; www.bsp.co.ck; ☺9am-3pm Mon-Fri) The main branch is beside the Foodland supermarket in Avarua, and another airport branch opens for international flights – both have ATMs. ATMs are also at Oasis Service Centre (Nikao), JMC Store (Muri) and the Edgewater Resort ('Arorangi).

CITC Pharmacy (Map p204; ☑22000; CITC Shopping Centre, Ara Maire; ☺8.30am-4.30pm Mon-Fri, 9am-1pm Sat) Part of the CITC Shopping Centre.

Click Internet Lounge (Map p204; Cook's Corner Arcade; ☺8.30am-5pm Mon-Fri) Internet access via PCs.

Cook Islands Tourist Authority (Map p204; ☑29435; www.cookislands.travel; Avarua; ☺8am-4pm Mon-Fri, 10am-1pm Sat) The main tourist office can help with everything from accommodation and nightspots to interisland flights and shipping services. Ask here about Island Nights around Rarotonga, and attractions and accommodation on the outer islands.

Jetsave Travel (Map p204; ☑27707; www. jetsave.co.ck; Ara Maire, Avarua) Has good air-fare-and-accommodation packages and deals to the outer islands.

Post Office (Map p204; ☺8am-4pm Mon-Fri) Centrally located.

> ### ⓘ SADDLE SORE?
>
> We're not sure how many registered motorscooters there are in the Cooks, but this egalitarian form of transport is everywhere you look. To see a smartly dressed minister aboard his trusty Honda on the way to Sunday-morning church is a visionary sight indeed. People smoke and chat riding two-abreast, talk or text on the phone and maybe chew a sandwich at the same time. Robust Polynesian mamas perch on the side while tiny children cling on behind.
>
> Locals prefer the manual 110cc 'postie bike' but the scooters hired to tourists are usually the automatic type. They're easy to ride with push-button ignitions, brakes and throttle. Even if you've never ridden a motorcycle before, after 10 minutes you'll be riding like a pro, and after a few days you'll be walking like a cowhand. Be careful with the proximity of your suntanned legs to the hot exhaust pipe. Get too close and you'll be in danger of getting a 'Rarotongan Tattoo'. Watch out also for the occasional stray dog, and avoid riding at night as there's minimal street lighting on most parts of the island.
>
> Remember also if you don't have a motorcycle licence in your home country, you need to head along to the police station in Avarua and get local accreditation when you first arrive.

Around the Island

Though Rarotonga is the largest of the Cook Islands, it's still compact and accessible, and is circumnavigated by a 32km coastal road known as the Ara Tapu (Sacred Rd). Inland is a second road, the Ara Metua (Ancient Rd), built in the 11th century. The Ara Metua passes through farmland, taro plantations, and rambling homesteads in the foothills of Rarotonga's mountainous centre. The island's rugged interior can be crossed only on foot. There are no private beaches on Rarotonga, but take care not to cross private land in order to access the shoreline.

⊙ Sights

Cook Islands Whale & Wildlife Centre   MUSEUM
(Map p200; ☑21666; www.whaleresearch.org; Ara Metua, Atupa; adult/child NZ$12/6; ⊙10am-4pm Sun-Fri) Visit this centre to learn about whales and other wildlife frequenting the Cook Islands. It's an essential stop if you're planning on going whale watching, and the centre's cosy Whale Tail Café has good coffee, snacks and wi-fi. Live critters include a giant centipede and coconut crabs, and there are also exhibits on sharks, turtles and shipwrecks.

Black Rock   VIEWPOINT
On the northwest coast is Black Rock (Turou), traditionally believed to be where the spirits of the dead commenced their voyage to 'Avaiki (the afterworld). It's also one of the island's best snorkelling spots. Look out for the sign to the Rarotonga Hospital from where there are commanding views of the island's west coast.

'Arorangi   HISTORIC SITE
(Map p200) On Rarotonga's west coast, 'Arorangi was the first missionary-built village, conceived as a model for other villages on the island. The missionary Papeiha is buried at the 1849 CICC.

Highland Paradise Cultural Centre   CULTURAL CENTRE
(Map p200; ☑21924; www.highlandparadise.co.ck; self-guided admission adult/child NZ$30/15, guided tours adult/child NZ$75/37.50, island nights adult/child NZ$99/55; ⊙self-guided admission 9am-3pm Mon-Fri, village tours 9.30am-1pm Tue & Thu, island nights 5.30-9.30pm Mon, Wed, Fri) High above 'Arorangi, Highland Paradise stands on the site of the old Tinomana village with panoramic views over the west and south coasts. Members of the Pirangi family, descendants of Tinomana Ariki, take visitors on guided tours including weaving, dancing and drumming exhibits. It's also possible to explore the sacred site on a self-guided basis from Monday to Friday. On Monday, Wednesday and Friday, fabulous sunset Island Nights are held. Bookings are essential and transport is included.

Wigmore's Waterfall   WATERFALL
(Map p200) On the eastern edge of the abandoned Sheraton resort site, a road leads inland to Wigmore's Waterfall, a lovely cascade dropping into a fresh, cool swimming pool. Note that in the dry season, the cascade can be more of a trickle. The south coast also has the island's best beaches, with the best snorkelling to be found at Aro'a, Titikaveka and Tikioki.

★ Muri
BEACH

With its four *motu* (islets), Muri is the most beautiful section of Rarotonga's encircling lagoon. The blue water is packed with tropical fish, especially around the *motu* (Taakoka, Koromiri, Oneroa and Motutapu), and out towards the reef. Taakoka is volcanic while the others are sand cays. The swimming is wonderful over sparkling white sand. Water-sports equipment and lagoon cruises are available from Muri through Captain Tama's and Koka's Lagoon Cruises. Other attractions include kitesurfing, paddle-boarding and good restaurants.

Matutu Brewery
BREWERY

(Map p200; ☑26288; www.matutubeer.com; Ara Tapu, Takitimu; ☺10am-3pm Mon-Sat, tours noon & 1pm) Pop in to meet the guys behind Raro's very own craft brewery. Regular beers – also sold around the island – are Mai Lager and Kiva Pale Ale. Seasonal limited-run brews are also sometimes conjured up, and often available at the tiny brewery. Join a tour and tasting session, and don't leave the island without buying a Matutu T-shirt.

Te Vara Nui Cultural Village
BUILDING

(Map p200; ☑24006; www.tevaranui.co.ck; Muri; village tour adult/child NZ$39/19, dinner & show adult/child NZ$89/45; ☺village tour 5pm, dinner & show 7.30pm Tue, Thu & Sat) Te Vara Nui combines a purpose-built village showcasing local culture including traditional medicine, carving, tapa making and legends, with one of Rarotonga's most spectacular Island Nights. After-dark shows take place on pavilions and stages set above a manmade lagoon, and dinner is a sprawling *umu* (earth oven) buffet. A combination deal (adult/child NZ$109/59) for both the two-hour village tour and the dinner and show is also available.

Matavera CICC
CHURCH

(Map p200) The old CICC is lovely at night when the outside is lit up.

Arai-Te-Tonga Marae
HISTORIC SITE

(Map p200) A small sign points off the road to the island's most important *marae* site, Arai-Te-Tonga. Situated just off the Ara Metua, there's a stone-marked *koutu* (ancient open-air royal courtyard) site in front of you. This whole area was a gathering place, and the remains of the *marae*, the *koutu* and other meeting grounds are still visible.

🏃 Activities

Cycling

Ride Rarotonga
BICYCLE RENTAL

(Map p200; ☑27433; www.riderarotonga.com; Ara Tapu; ☺9am-5pm Mon-Fri, to 1pm Sat) Rarotonga's only bike shop has an excellent range of hire bikes, from cool beach cruisers (NZ$15/70 per day/week) to mountain bikes and road bikes (NZ$30/140 per day/week). Electric bikes are NZ$45/210 per day/week. At the time of writing, a project encompassing 28km of specialist bike paths was beginning on the island, including an exciting network of mountain-bike trails.

Drop in at the shop for the latest information on these initiatives, which will make Rarotonga one of the best mountain-biking destinations in the Pacific.

Storytellers Eco Cycle Tours
BICYCLE TOUR

(☑53450, 23450; www.storytellers.co.ck; per person NZ$69-109) These exceptionally well-run bicycle tours exploring the byways and backroads of the island come packed with information on the history, environment and culture of Rarotonga. Three different tours range from the easygoing Discover option – around 8km to 12km on easy roads – to the Excite tour which traverses streams and

---

HELPING RAROTONGA'S ANIMALS

You'll probably spy the cute animals from the **Esther Honey Foundation** (Map p200) at its stall at Saturday morning's Punanga Nui Market, but it's also worth visiting the main location to check out the excellent animal welfare work being undertaken.

Rarotonga has a much lower stray canine population compared to other Pacific islands, and significant credit is due to the Esther Honey Foundation. Dog numbers on the island have decreased from 6000 to around 2000, a reduction managed only by spaying and neutering animals, and the dog population of the Cook Islands is now noticeably healthier and more easygoing than in other Pacific destinations.

Drop by to have a chat with the international crew of vets and assistants, and there's also the chance to interact with a diverse menagerie of dogs, cats and other animals. Feeding times are in the morning.

switchbacks in a 20km adventure for more experienced and fitter riders.

All three tours end with a well-earned lagoonside lunch and the opportunity for a swim.

Deep-Sea Fishing

Deep-sea fishing is popular in the Cook Islands, with catches of *mahimahi* and tuna (from October to May), wahoo and barracuda (April to October), and sailfish and marlin (November to March). The following operators have safety gear; contact them by telephone or down at the Avatiu wharf where most boats tie up. A half-day tour – usually around five hours from 6am – costs around NZ$150 to NZ$170 per person.

Blue Water Rarotonga   BOATING
(☑53544, 23545; www.bluewaterrarotonga.com) Wide range of boat-based activities including fishing, whale watching, reef tours, and sunset cruises. Four- and seven-night outer-island tours are also available.

Cook Islands Game Fishing Club   FISHING
(Map p200) Just east of Avarua, anglers swap yarns at this friendly club. Non-fishing types are also welcome at the island's most affordable bar, and adjacent is the excellent Flying Boat Fish & Chips.

Akura Fishing Charters   FISHING
(☑54355; www.akurafishingcharters.com) Big-game fishing from NZ$170 per person.

Captain Moko's   FISHING
(☑73083, 20385; www.fishingrarotonga.com) Expect lots of Raro humour and the opportunity to eat your catch afterwards. Half-day trips from NZ$150 per person.

Marlin Queen   FISHING
(☑55202; www.marlinqueen.co.ck) Half- and full-day tours available.

Seafari Charters   FISHING
(☑55096; www.seafari.co.ck) On board the MV *Seafari*, a 1934 Canadian fishing trawler.

Wahoo Fishing Charters   FISHING
(☑73731, 25130; www.wahoofishingcharters.net) Morning and afternoon 4½-hour trips available.

Diving & Snorkelling

Diving is fantastic outside the reef, especially around the passages along the island's southern side. There are canyons, caves and tunnels to explore, and outside the lagoon the island drops off to around 4000m, although most diving is between 3m and 30m.

Rarotonga has several well-preserved shipwrecks, including SS *Maitai* off the northern shore. Other well-known diving

---

EXPLORING MURI

Start at the northern end of Muri Beach at Avana Harbour, one of the only deep-water passages into Rarotonga's lagoon. Maybe grab a fruit smoothie or fish sandwich from the **Mooring** (p218) to set you up for the walk ahead.

The great ocean-going *vaka* (canoes) set off from here in the 14th century to settle New Zealand – the so-called 'Great Migration'. There's often a replica – but still ocean-going – *vaka* anchored in the lagoon. Walk north onto the small promontory to see **Marae Vaerota**, the traditional *marae* of the Kainuku Ariki, where canoes were blessed and human sacrifices were made to the gods.

Head south to the picturesque **Ngatangi'ia CICC**, where you'll find some interesting headstones. Opposite in the park is the **ancient canoes' stone circle** and a plaque commemorating the seven canoes that completed the journey to New Zealand: *Takitumu, Tokomaru, Kurahaupo, Aotea, Tainui, Te Arawa* and *Mataatua*. There's a **modern stone circle** further south that commemorates the arrival of traditional Polynesian canoes during the sixth Festival of Pacific Arts in 1992.

To the south, glorious **Muri Beach** is one of the island's best snorkelling areas. It's a lovely walk along the shoreline with views over the four palm-covered *motu* (islets) in the lagoon. The remains of one of Rarotonga's oldest *marae* are on **Motutapu**, but you'll need to kayak out there. Pick up coffee and cake at **LBV** (p220) or a leisurely lunch at **Sails Restaurant** (p220).

If you're feeling active, sign up for kitesurfing, windsurfing or paddle-boardng with **Kitesup** (p214), or linger over a cocktail at **iSOBAR** (p221) before the **Muri Night Market** (p219) kicks off at 5pm four nights a week.

spots include **Black Rock** in the north; **Sandriver** and **Matavera Wall** on the island's east side; and the **Avaavaroa**, **Papua** and **Rutaki** passages in the south.

Rarotonga has five accredited diving operators, all offering twice-daily boat trips. Single-tank dives cost around NZ$95 and two-tank dives are about NZ$140 including gear. Introductory dives are available and three-day open-water courses cost around NZ$480.

Rarotonga's spectacular lagoon is fantastic for snorkelling and swimming. The water is crystal clear, warm and packed with technicolour fish and coral. The beaches along the island's southern and western sides are all good for swimming, but the northern and upper-eastern sides are not as good. The best snorkelling is around **Muri Lagoon**, **Aro'a Beach**, **Titikaveka** and **Tikioki** (Fruits of Rarotonga) in the south of the island, and Black Rock in the northwest. Many of these areas are protected by *ra'ui* (traditional conservation areas).

Snorkelling gear is available from the island's diving operators, and most accommodation also provides free gear for guests' use.

Cook Island Divers   DIVING
(Map p200; ☎ 22483; www.cookislandsdivers. com; 'Arorangi) Offers introductory dives in the Tikioki Marine Sanctuary.

Adventure Cook Islands   DIVING, SNORKELLING
(Map p200; ☎ 22212; www.adventurecookislands. com; Kavera Rd, 'Arorangi) Excellent company that offers everything from mountain treks and mountain biking through to diving, snorkelling and spearfishing. Gear rental includes sea kayaks, mountain bikes, snorkelling gear and bodyboards.

Dive Centre   DIVING
(Map p200; ☎ 20238; www.thedivecentre-rarotonga.com; Aro'a Beach) Also offers special 'Bubblemaker' scuba experiences for kids.

Dive Rarotonga   DIVING
(Map p200; ☎ 21873; www.diverarotonga.com; 'Arorangi) See the website for a map of Rarotonga's dive sites.

Pacific Divers   DIVING, SNORKELLING
(Map p200; ☎ 22450; www.pacificdivers.co.ck; Muri Beach) Also offers night snorkelling around Muri Lagoon.

Hiking

The island's mountainous centre is crisscrossed by walking tracks and trails. The top walk is the Cross-Island Track, but there are lots of others to discover. The best guide is *Rarotonga's Mountain Tracks and Plants* by Gerald McCormack and Judith Künzlé, also authors of *Rarotonga's Cross-Island Walk*. Guided hiking trips are offered by Pa's Mountain Walk (p214) and Adventure Cook Islands.

Wear light, breathable clothing and sturdy boots, and check the weather forecast before you go. Tell someone where you're headed and when you expect to return.

Cross-Island Track   HIKING
(Map p200) Passing through impressive natural scenery, the three- to four-hour hike from the north to south coasts via the 413m **Te Rua Manga** (Needle) is Rarotonga's most popular walk. Don't do the walk in a south–north direction, as the chances of taking a wrong turn are much greater. Wear adequate shoes, take plenty of drinking water, and use mosquito repellent.

Parts of the walk get extremely slippery in wet weather and the upper section is quite rugged and overgrown.

The tourist office recommends walkers join a guided tour, but it's possible to do the walk on your own. Follow the orange track markers carefully, and leave your name and details in the intentions book at the start of the hike. The road to the starting point is south of Avatiu Harbour. Continue on the road up the valley by Avatiu Stream until you reach a sign announcing the beginning of the walk. A private vehicle road continues for about 1km.

From the end of the vehicle road a footpath leads off and after 10 minutes drops down and crosses a small stream. Don't follow the white plastic power-cable track up the valley, but instead pick up the track beside the massive boulder on the ridge to your left, after the stream crossing.

From here, the track climbs steeply up to the Needle (about 45 minutes). At the first sight of the Needle there's a boulder in the middle of the path – a nice place for a rest. A little further on is a T-junction; the Needle is a 10-minute walk to the right. Don't try to climb up to the Needle itself, as there have been several rockfalls and landslides, and there's a long and probably fatal drop on either side of the trail. Follow the track round to the left instead and you'll begin the long, slippery descent towards the south coast.

After 30 minutes the track meets the Papua Stream and follows it downhill, zigzagging back and forth across the stream. After about 45 minutes the track emerges into fernland. Be sure to stick to the main track, as there are several places where minor tracks seem to take off towards the stream but these end at dangerous spots upstream from the waterfall. Another 15 minutes further on, the main track turns back towards the stream, bringing you to the bottom of Wigmore's Waterfall. A dirt road leads from the south coast up to the waterfall. It's about a 15-minute walk to the coast road, where you can flag down the circle-island bus or cool off in the nearby lagoon. You're likely to get muddy and sweaty, so don't make plans for a flash lunch immediately afterwards.

Pa's Mountain Walk HIKING
(☑21079; www.pastreks.com; per person NZ$70) A guided trek over the cross-island track is run by the dreadlocked Pa Teuraa. He's also a herbalist, botanist and traditional healer. Pa's cross-island walk runs on Monday to Friday (weather permitting), and he conducts nature walks on Tuesdays and Thursdays. A light lunch is included on both excursions and you'll need moderate fitness for the cross-island walk.

See the website for more information. Note that on some treks, Pa's nephew leads the activity in place of Pa.

Sailing & Water Sports
Muri Lagoon and the island's south coast are the best places for swimming, windsurfing, sailing and kayaking. Sailing races start at Muri Beach every Saturday and Sunday afternoon from around 1.30pm. Kayaks are readily available to explore the lagoon's deserted *motu* and many hotels provide them for guests' use. Kitesurfing and paddle-boarding are also very popular, and the lagoon's usually benign waters are a great place to learn these sports.

Surfing is in its infancy on Rarotonga. Bodyboarding is popular but local board riders are few and it's not the place to learn as the reef-breaks are steep and fast, and the water is shallow. Adventure Cook Islands (p213) offers bodyboard rentals.

Raro surfing is dangerous – for intermediates and experts only – and too fast for long-boarders. The island's north gets swells in the November-to-March cyclone season while the south works best during the May-to-August 'winter'. There are breaks at **Social Centre** in the northwest, off the **Rarotongan Beach Resort**, **Avaavaroa** and **Papua** on the south coast, and **Koromiri**, **Turangi** and **Matavera**

on the east side. Since the waves break outside the lagoon it's a long paddle to the action.

Ariki Holidays WATER SPORTS
(Map p200; ☑27955; www.arikiholidays.com; Ara Tapu, Muri; kiteboarding lessons NZ$90-350, night paddleboarding per person with/without barbecue dinner NZ$64/49) Kiteboarding and paddle-boarding is the focus at the family-run Ariki Holidays. Kiteboarding lessons take place on nearby Muri Lagoon, and Ariki also offers unique night paddle-boarding tours where waterproof lights suspended under the paddle-boards create a luminous halo in the lagoon's moonlit waters. Tours run Monday to Saturday by appointment for a minimum of two people.

Once you've had your fill of waterborne exercise, Ariki co-owner Julie offers sports, deep tissue and relaxation massage (NZ$80 per hour). She once helped New Zealand's All Blacks win the Rugby World Cup, so you're in safe hands.

Kitesup WATER SPORTS
(Map p200; ☑27877; www.kitesup.co; Ara Tapu, Muri Beach; ◷9am-4pm Mon-Sat) Lessons and gear rental to get you out kitesurfing, windsurfing or paddle-boarding on Muri lagoon. Kitesup also acts as a booking agent for many other activities around the island.

Learn to Sail SAILING
(☑73653, 26668; upwind@oyster.co.ck) Learn the ropes with Kiwi Ken Kingsbury on the super-sheltered waters of Muri Lagoon. Kick off with a two-hour lesson (NZ$120), a further one hour sail with Ken (NZ$60), and you can then hire his cute and compact sailboat for NZ$70 per hour. He can also hook you up with a treddlecat, a surprisingly speedy pedal-powered catamaran which he invented.

Captain Tama's
Lagoon Cruizes WATER SPORTS
(Map p200; ☑27350; www.captaintamas.com; Muri Beach) Beside the Rarotonga Sailing Club, Captain Tama's offers windsurfers for hire (NZ$30), and also offers windsurfing lessons (NZ$50) and paddle-boarding guidance and hire.

Rarotonga Sailing Club SAILING
(Map p200; ☑27349; www.sailsrestaurant.co.ck/sailingclub.htm; Muri Beach) Rents out kayaks and small sailing boats.

Other Sports

Volleyball is often played on Muri Beach. Tennis courts are available at Edgewater Resort and Rarotongan Beach Resort.

Golf Course   GOLF
(Map p200; ☑20621; www.rarotonga.nzgolf.net; ⏰8am-2pm Mon-Fri, members only Sat) Rarotonga's nine-hole course is near the airport.

👆 Tours

Underwater Viewing

Captain Tama's Lagoon Cruizes   BOAT TOUR
(☑55002, 27350; www.captaintamas.com; Muri Beach; adult/child NZ$79/40; ⏰11am-3.30pm) The entertaining crew from Captain Tama's runs glass-bottom boat tours, including snorkelling and a barbecue lunch on the tiny *motu* of Koromiri.

Koka Lagoon Cruises   BOAT TOUR
(Map p200; ☑55769, 27769; www.kokalagoon cruises.com; Muri Beach; adult/child NZ$79/40; ⏰10am Sun-Fri) Koka operates cruises around Muri including a barbecue fish lunch and snorkelling with friendly local guides. A percentage of all bookings is donated to support marine conservation.

Raro Reef Sub   BOAT TOUR
(Map p204; ☑55901; www.raroreefsub.com; Avatiu Harbour; adult/child NZ$65/35; ⏰9am, 11am & 2pm daily) Explore the outer reef on Raro's very own yellow submarine. Descend into the semi-submersible's underwater-viewing area to spy on shape-shifting shoals of giant trevally and the rusting hulk of the 1916 shipwreck of the SS *Maitai*. If you're lucky you might see turtles and eagle rays, and humpback whales are sometimes sighted from July to October.

Scenic Flights

Air Rarotonga   SCENIC FLIGHTS
(☑22888; www.airraro.com; min 2, max 3, per person NZ$129; ⏰9am-3pm Mon-Sat) Climb aboard for 20-minute scenic flights, complete with onboard commentary.

Walking Tours

Takitumu Conservation Area   BIRDWATCHING
(TCA; ☑55228, 29906; kakerori@tca.co.ck; Ara Tapu, Avarua; guided tour adult/child NZ$50/30) This private forest reserve in Rarotonga's southeast corner runs guided tours where you might see the endangered *kakerori* (Rarotongan flycatcher).

Whale Watching

Humpback whales visit the Cook Islands from July to October. Most diving, sailing and fishing charters offer whale-watching trips in season. Visit the Cook Islands Whale & Wildlife Centre (p210) to learn more about whales.

Vehicle Tours

A round-the-island tour is a great way to see Rarotonga, especially if you're only here for a few days.

Coconut Tours   ADVENTURE TOUR
(Map p200; ☑24004; www.coconuttours.co.ck; per person NZ$150; ⏰Mon-Sat) Lead a convoy of excited wannabe rally drivers on quad bikes through the backroads and streams of the island's rugged interior. Tours run rain or shine and kids from eight to 17 years can ride pillion on the quad bikes with an adult (NZ$190 for adult and child). Sorry, two adults on one bike isn't allowed.

Raro Buggy Tours   DRIVING TOUR
(☑75730, 74480; 1/2 persons NZ$125/150) Take a tour of Rarotonga – on and off road – in these cool self-drive vehicles that are a cross between a go-kart and a beach buggy. Three-hour tours are conducted as a convoy with the tour leader at the front, and the bright yellow machines are very easy to drive. Tours depart from the Muri Beach Club Hotel.

Drivers need to be at least 18 years of age and have a driver's licence from their home country, and passengers must be at least six years old.

Raro Safari Tours   TOUR
(☑23629; www.rarosafaritours.co.ck; morning tours adult/child NZ$80/40, afternoon tours adult/child NZ$70/35; ⏰9am & 1.15pm Sun-Fri) Raro's most entertaining excursions are these three-hour expeditions around the island's rugged mountains, inland valleys and historical points of interest in safari-style jeeps. A fresh-fish beach barbecue lunch is included on the morning departures, and costs include pick-up from your accommodation. Say hi to Mr Hopeless for us.

Raro Tours   TOUR
(Map p200; ☑25325; www.rarotours.co.ck; adult/child NZ$60/30; ⏰10am-1pm Mon-Fri) Join an Island Discovery Tour and explore ancient *marae* and the island's best snorkelling spots.

Tik-etours   TOUR
(☑53686, 28687; www.tik-etours.com; adult/child from NZ$55/35) Take a Lap of the Island Tour (90 minutes) in a colourful electric tuk-tuk

to get your bearings when you first arrive, or take the longer Highlights of Rarotonga tour (adult/child NZ$79/35) with lots of interesting stops. A fun sunset option is an island bar-hop (per person NZ$45, minimum four people) sampling the best cocktails on Rarotonga.

Airport, restaurant and market transfers are also available.

🛏 Sleeping

Rarotonga has accommodation options to suit all budgets, although postcard-perfect views can come at a premium. High-season prices are quoted.

Renting a house is often the best-value way to visit the island, especially for families. Fully furnished two-bedroom houses cost around NZ$1000 to NZ$1500 per week. Studio units – suitable for two people – begin at around NZ$500 per week. Check out **Bookabach** (www.bookabach.co.nz), **Holiday Houses** (www.holidayhouses.co.nz) and **Rent Raro** (☑ 55519; www.rentraro.com).

Muri Beach Shell Bungalows　　BUNGALOW $
(Map p200; ☑ 22275; www.shellbungalows.co.ck; Ara Tapu; d/q NZ$100/110) In a great location 100m from Muri Beach, these two large self-contained bungalows with full kitchens are great value. One has a mezzanine level that sleeps an extra two, and there's a flat that sleeps four.

Aremango Guesthouse　　GUESTHOUSE $
(Map p200; ☑ 24362; www.aremango.co.ck; Ara Tapu; s/d from NZ$55/69, cottages NZ$140; @ 🛜) Aremango has single and double fan-cooled rooms arrayed along a central hallway. The common lounge, bathroom and kitchens are clean and comfortable, and there's a pleasant garden area to relax in. Muri Beach and good restaurants are a short walk away. Check the website for details of Aremango's adjacent private self-contained studio. Bikes and kayaks are also available for use.

Rarotonga Backpackers　　HOSTEL $
(Map p200; ☑ 21590; www.rarotongabackpackers.com; Ara Tapu; dm NZ$25, s NZ$40, d NZ$50-130, bungalows NZ$85, beach house NZ$120-185; @ 🛜🏊) A west-coast beachfront site offers everything from dorms to fully self-contained suites. There's a pretty central pool, and self-contained units with private verandahs and fabulous views. Around 600m away there are new and good-value garden bungalows, and for families or groups there's the option

of another new beach house and absolute beachfront units along Raro's northern coast.

Aito Apartments　　APARTMENT $$
(Map p200; ☑ 20029; www.aitoapartments.com; Ara Tapu, Muri; d NZ$160) These two modern apartments represent excellent value just a short walk from the cafes, restaurants and water sports of Muri Lagoon. The Cook Island-Tahitian owners are a real delight, and the spotless apartments feature spacious verandahs, designer bedrooms punctuated with Pacific textiles, and lovely bathrooms trimmed with natural river stones.

Fire up the barbecue, prepare loads of tropical fruit in the self-contained kitchen, and you'll quickly ease into island time.

Avana Waterfront Apartments APARTMENT $$
(Map p200; ☑ 20836; www.avanawaterfront.co.ck; Ara Tapu, Avana; apt NZ$192-370; ❄🛜🏊) Tucked away down a quiet side road, this complex consists of 10 stylish self-contained apartments, some with front-row views of the spectacular sprawl of Avana Lagoon. There's a swimming pool if the ocean waters don't appeal – unlikely on most days – and a private jetty for island kayaking trips or fishing expeditions. There's a five-night minimum stay.

Ariki Bungalows　　BUNGALOW $$
(Map p200; ☑ 27955; www.arikiholidays.com; Ara Tapu, Muri; d NZ$130; 🛜🏊) These three modern units share a breezy location a short uphill walk from Muri Lagoon. Each of the three units is decorated in natural wood and bright colours, and are self-contained with a small kitchenette. There's an exceedingly laid-back bar and a plunge pool, and Ariki also offers a Polynesian dinner for guests most weekends (NZ$15).

The good-value accommodation is worthy of its own recommendation, but Ariki Bungalows is also a great option if you're planning to kiteboard or paddle-board (p214) while on Rarotonga.

Kura's Kabanas　　BUNGALOW $$
(Map p200; ☑ 27010; www.kkabanas.co.ck; Ara Tapu; units & cabanas NZ$150; ❄@🛜) Shady palms, Muri Lagoon views and a glorious china-white beach are just steps from the doors of Kura's airy timber-framed cabanas. Two larger 1st-floor family studios can sleep four (children under 12 free). Fully equipped kitchens, queen beds, TVs and a great location make this hard to beat for the price.

Check the website for details of Kura's two self-contained villas at the nearby Paku's Retreat (NZ$120 to NZ$200).

Palm Grove
BUNGALOW $$

(Map p200; ☑ 20002; www.palmgrove.net; Ara Tapu, Vaimaanga; d NZ$225-345; ※ ☀) Set among lawns and coconut palms on one of the south coast's best beaches, Palm Grove has a reputation for being somewhere that regular guests return to year after year. They're lured by the spacious bungalows – and equally expansive decks with lagoon views – and a welcoming vibe that's enhanced by features like shared barbecue facilities and a compact pool.

Across the road, Palm Grove's Yellow Hibiscus is a handy restaurant and bar with live music on a Friday night. Rates include a daily breakfast buffet.

Aro'a Beachside Inn
BUNGALOW $$

(Map p200; ☑ 22166; www.aroabeach.com; Ara Tapu, 'Arorangi; d NZ$205-290; ※ @ ☎) Choose from beachside units or ocean-view units at this super-friendly spot on Rarotonga's sunset-friendly west coast. Rates include a tropical breakfast and free use of everything you need to explore the nearby reef. After you've invested holiday energy in kayaking, paddleboarding or snorkelling, kick back in the Shipwreck Hut bar.

Manea Beach Villas
BUNGALOW $$

(Map p200; ☑ 25336; www.maneabeachrarotonga. com; Muri Beach; bungalows NZ$210-230, house NZ$400-590; ※ ☀) Down a quiet Muri road, Manea Beach combines spotless one-bedroom bungalows – some with lagoon views – and three larger three-bedroom houses that are perfect for families or groups of friends. The decor is a winning combination of modern and tropical, and there's a pleasant shared pool overlooking nearby Muri Lagoon.

Sunhaven Beach Bungalows
BUNGALOW $$

(Map p200; ☑ 28465; www.mysunhaven.com; Ara Tapu; studios & bungalows NZ$240-330; ※ ☎ ☀) Sunhaven offers good value in some of the largest self-contained rooms on the island, set around a beachfront swimming pool on a quiet stretch of west-coast beach. The bungalows are sparkling clean and simply finished, with white-tile floors, cane furniture and functional fixtures. There's also an on-site licensed cafe, and lagoon kayaking and snorkelling on tap.

Children must be 15 years and older.

Bella Beach Bungalows
BUNGALOW $$

(Map p200; ☑ 26004; www.shekinahhomes.com; Ara Tapu; bungalows NZ$180) With the waves all but licking the stilts of these four functional units at Titikaveka on the island's south side, they're about as close to the beach as you can get. Inside are tiled floors, kitchens, small bathrooms and comfortable king-sized beds, while outside are large sundecks overlooking the beach and lagoon.

★ Sea Change
BOUTIQUE HOTEL $$$

(Map p200; ☑ 22532; www.sea-change-raroton ga.com; Ara Tapu; villas NZ$450-950; ※ @ ☀) Many of Rarotonga's boutique hotels look to this place as a benchmark. The impeccably appointed free-standing thatched villas have fabulously appointed interiors with luxury king-size four-poster beds, entertainment systems, flat-screen TVs and private outdoor pools. The open-plan villas are finished in earthy tones and traditional materials, off-setting the contemporary design elements.

★ Ikurangi Eco Retreat
BUNGALOW $$$

(Map p200; ☑ 25288; www.ikurangi.com; Titama Rd, Matavera; villas NZ$249, luxury tents NZ$359-449; ☎ ☀) ✿ Glamping style comes to Rarotonga at Ikurangi Eco Retreat. Accommodation is either in luxury safari-style tents – each with their own spacious deck and private bathroom – or in well-equipped villas. Luxe highlights include top of the range bed linen, and there's a focus on sustainability – including solar electricity – with the design, construction and management of the property.

The inland location has excellent views of dramatic Mt Ikurangi, and is handily placed midway between Avarua and Muri. Free use of bicycles for guests, and breakfast is included.

★ Beach Place
RENTAL HOUSE $$$

(Map p200; www.airbnb.com/rooms/870875; Ara Tapu, Tikioki Beach; d NZ$280) With an absolute beachfront location, this spacious heritage villa has wooden floors, wraparound decks, and a winning combination of a well-equipped kitchen with lagoon views and a chic bathroom with a clawfoot bath. One double room and a pair of bunks make it good for families, but it's also a quietly romantic spot for holidaying couples.

It's just a 10-minute stroll to Muri Beach to the north, and there's good snorkelling at Tikioki to the south. Out front is good for swimming and for lazy days paddling in the property's colourful kayaks.

Black Rock Villas
VILLA $$$

(Map p200; ☑21233; www.blackrockvillas.com; d NZ$350; ❄@🔊☀) With an infinity pool and views towards Rarotonga's rugged north-west coast, the two self-contained apartments at Black Rock Villas are spacious, breezy and decked out with colourful local art. Tropical blooms frame the property's lovely gardens, and each villa has two bedrooms and two bathrooms, making them ideal for families or couples travelling together. Nearby is the excellent Tuoro Cafe.

Pacific Resort
RESORT $$$

(Map p200; ☑20427; www.pacificresort.com; units NZ$430-1180; ❄@🔊☀) Right on Muri Beach and shaded by palm trees, the Pacific Resort's 64 self-contained units are smart and elegant, harnessing local elements of design and decor – the best have sitting rooms and private verandahs. Amenities include the beachfront Barefoot Bar and the open-air Sandals Restaurant. Spa and beauty services are on tap so you can look your best in paradise.

Apartments Kakera
APARTMENT $$$

(Map p200; ☑20532; www.apartmentskakera. com; Ara Tapu; apt NZ$245-360; ❄@🔊☀) With three huge modern apartments blending sleek modern decor with lovely Polynesian touches, Kakera also boasts a long list of eco-credentials. The split-level apartments have high ceilings, private courtyard gardens with plunge pools, full kitchens and flat-screen TVs and entertainment systems. An excellent choice for travelling families.

WE DO

Many couples come to the Cook Islands to get married as it's a very romantic destination. Most hotels and resorts offer wedding packages and there are also several specialist wedding companies. Cook Islands marriages are legally binding worldwide. You'll need a copy of your birth certificate and passport. If you've been married before, you'll also need your divorce papers or a death certificate. The Marriage Registrar requires a minimum of three working days before the wedding day to issue a marriage licence, so you need to be resident in the country for that long before the nuptials. If you and your loved one simply can't wait, an additional NZ$50 fee can be paid to speed up the process.

Muri Beachcomber
RESORT $$$

(Map p200; ☑21022; www.beachcomber.co.ck; Ara Tapu; d units NZ$305-460; ❄@🔊☀) With a choice of garden and sea-view units and luxury villas overlooking lovely grounds and a tropical lily pond, the Muri Beachcomber has a relaxed family-friendly village feel. The accommodation is modern – clean lines and tasteful appointments – and on-site facilities include guest lounge, laundry, pétanque court, free kayak use and snorkelling gear.

Little Polynesian
BOUTIQUE HOTEL $$$

(Map p200; ☑24280; www.littlepolynesian.com; Ara Tapu; villas NZ$680-1140; ❄@🔊☀) The 10 beachfront and four garden villas at Little Polynesian are a superb blend of traditional Polynesian design (with traditional Mangaian coconut-fibre sennit binding) and modern architecture, and the uninterrupted lagoon view from the foyer, pool and villas is sublime. Check online for substantial discounts.

Magic Reef Bungalows
BUNGALOW $$$

(Map p200; ☑27404; www.magicreef.co.nz; Ara Tapu; d NZ$325-430; ❄@🔊☀) On a golden stretch of sand on the sunset side of the island, Magic Reef features tastefully decorated bungalows with four-poster beds, fans and air-con, galley kitchens, private outdoor showers and separate bathrooms with bathtubs.

🍴 Eating

★ Mooring
SANDWICHES $

(Map p200; Avana Lagoon; sandwiches NZ$13, salads $19; ⊘9.30am-3.30pm Mon-Fri, noon-3pm Sun) Tuck into tuna and *mahimahi* sandwiches on grilled Turkish bread at this funky blue shipping container on the edge of Avana Lagoon. Variations include Tijuana Tuna or Cajun Spiced, and other goodies include Rustys – marinated chicken pieces with pawpaw salsa. Refresh with a fruit smoothie or a *nu* (fresh coconut), and park yourself with views of Avana's sparkling waters.

Charlie's Cafe & Beach Hire
CAFE $

(Map p200; ☑28055; chosking@oyster.net.ck; Ara Tapu, Titikaveka; snacks NZ$10-12; ⊘10am-4pm Mon-Sat, from noon Sun) The biggest fish sandwiches on the island, fruit smoothies, and freshly baked muffins are all available at this family-run beachside shipping container that also doubles as a rental centre for gear to explore the nearby reef. Kayaks, paddleboards, and snorkelling gear are all available. Stay out there for long enough, and you might even be hungry enough to finish your sandwich.

Cook Islands Coffee Company   CAFE $

(Map p200; Ara Tapu, Matavera; coffee from NZ$3; ⊙ from 7.30am Sun-Fri) Kiwi expat Neil Dearlove blends and roasts gourmet coffee at his home in Matavera. Many locals stop in for their fix on the way into work or pick up a few fresh croissants. If the orange road cone is outside the shop, Neil is open and dispensing perfect espressos and flat whites. Ground coffee is also available for takeaway.

Deli-licious   CAFE $

(Map p200; www.delilicious.net; Ara Tapu, Muri Beach; lunch NZ$10-19; ⊙ 8am-3.30pm Mon-Sat; 🖀) Right in the heart of the Muri, Deli-licious serves up cooked breakfasts, and salads and sandwiches for lunch. Excellent coffee is served along with shakes and smoothies. This place is always buzzing and has an alfresco deck. Try the smoked marlin pie, with local fish caught from just beyond the lagoon.

Muri Night Market   MARKET $

(Map p200; Ara Tapu, Muri Beach; mains NZ$7-12; ⊙ 5-8pm Tue-Thu & Sun) Welcome to the biggest game in Muri for four nights a week. There's occasional live music to partner seafood curries, garlic prawns, and tuna with papaya salad, and dessert of a slab of coconut and chocolate pie is mandatory. It's OK to bring your own wine or beer, and the meals are so big you'll probably need a lie-down afterwards,.

Vili's   FAST FOOD $

(Map p200; Ara Tapu, Muri; burgers NZ$7-12; ⊙ 8am-8pm) Colourful outdoor tables, winning smiles from the kitchen team, and rocking Pacific ukulele beats combine at this humble spot on Muri's main drag. The fish burger is massive, so consider taking one of the beach cruiser bicycles for a spin (NZ$10 per day), and balancing the holiday ledger between virtue and vice. Of course the fish and chips (NZ$10) are briny-fresh.

Flying Boat Fish & Chips   FISH & CHIPS $

(Map p200; ☑ 22230; Ara Tapu, Game Fishing Club, Tupapa; snacks & mains NZ$7-20; ⊙ 11am-9pm Mon-Sat) Tuck into Raro's best fish and chips at this funky reconfigured fishing boat. The lagoon's waters are just metres away, and cheap-as-chips drinks are available from the bar at the adjacent Game Fishing Club. The club's a good place to drop by if you're looking to watch live rugby featuring New Zealand's mighty All Blacks. Phone orders are also welcome.

Fruits of Rarotonga   CAFE $

(Map p200; ☑ 21509; Ara Tapu, Tikioki; snacks & smoothies NZ$5-9; ⊙ 10am-4pm Mon-Sat) Homemade jams and tropical chutneys are divine at this shop opposite Tikioki beach, but it's good for cakes and fruit juices too. Kayaks are available for hire (NZ$5 per hour), and you can leave gear here when you go snorkelling in the lagoon. Don't leave Rarotonga without recharging on a creamy pawpaw-and-banana smoothie. Opening hours can be somewhat flexible.

Wigmore's Superstore   SUPERMARKET $

(Map p200; Ara Tapu, Vaima'anga; ⊙ 6am-10pm) The south coast's only proper grocery store is more expensive than Avarua's supermarkets. It's the only large supermarket that trades on Sunday though, and it has a small liquor store. Drop in on a Sunday afternoon for lots of still-warm freshly baked local produce.

Super Brown   SUPERMARKET $

(Map p200; Ara Tapu, Tupapa; ⊙ 24hr) Super Brown is Raro's only all-night convenience store and petrol station, with a fair selection of beer, wine, groceries and takeaway food.

★ Vaima Restaurant & Bar   POLYNESIAN $$

(Map p200; ☑ 26123; www.vaimarestaurant.com; Ara Tapu, Vaima'anga; mains NZ$28-34; ⊙ 4-9pm Mon-Sat, dining from 6pm) Perched near a sandy beach on the island's south coast, Vaima is one of Rarotonga's best eateries and bookings are essential. The stylish dining room features local artworks, and there's a beachfront patio and breezy outside terrace. Combine Pacific cuisine with the sand between your toes for a quintessential Raro experience. Partner seafood curry with a Matutu Mai lager.

Pizza is also available for takeaway from 4pm to 7pm, and there are happy-hour drinks deals from 4pm to 6pm.

Waterline Bar & Grill   INTERNATIONAL $$

(Map p200; ☑ 22161; www.waterline-restaurant.com; Ara Tapu, 'Arorangi; mains NZ$20-36; ⊙ 11.30am-2.30pm Tue-Fri, from 6pm Tue-Sat) Welcome to the South Pacific restaurant of your dreams with a rustic beachfront pavilion and absolute waterfront tables and chairs. Book in for around 30 minutes before sunset to enjoy a cocktail before graduating to a restaurant table for calamari, prawns and steak. Lunchtime is a more informal offering, with BLT sandwiches and kebabs.

LBV
CAFE $$

(Map p200; ✉28619; Ara Tapu, Muri Beach; lunch mains $21-27, dinner mains NZ$28-32; ⊗7.30am-late Tue-Fri, 7.30am-5pm Sat-Mon) Come for a morning combo of an espresso and a cinnamon doughnut or chocolate brioche – LBV is the best bakery for many miles – and then return for a more leisurely lunch of Caprese salad, or dinner of seafood paella. Cooked breakfasts are also available, and there's a good drinks list with local beers and wines from New Zealand.

The setting, in a restored colonial house nestled in gardens and lawns, is very peaceful, and local art is regularly displayed for sale. Get the kids burning off some holiday energy by running around on the grass or getting active in the small playground. Bookings are recommended for dinner.

Sails Restaurant
FUSION $$

(Map p200; ✉27349; www.sailsrestaurant.co.ck; Muri Beach; breakfast & lunch mains NZ$16-25, dinner mains NZ$25-34; ⊗8am-late) Overlooking the sands and sea of Muri Lagoon, breezy Sails is an open-air bistro-bar serving light breakfast and lunchtime fare, and heartier evening meals daily. Try the island-style fries with the yellowfin tuna *ika mata*. Bookings are recommended for dinner, and brunch is available from 9.30am on the weekend. The attached iSOBAR is a fun place for a few drinks.

Tuoro Cafe
CAFE $$

(Map p200; ✉21233; www.blackrockvillas. com; Black Rock Villas, Nika'o; tapas NZ$10-18, mains NZ$22; ⊗11am-3pm Tue-Fri & Sun) Asian-inspired tapas – try the steamed pork dumplings – combine with fish, chicken and steak lunch dishes at this welcoming elevated spot on Raro's northwestern coast. There's a good selection of beer, gin and tonics are served with a generous addition of the good stuff, and there are top views from the sunny deck to the landmark of Black Rock.

Kikau Hut
INTERNATIONAL $$

(Map p200; ✉26860; Ara Tapu, 'Arorangi; mains NZ$21-35; ⊗6-11pm) Candles and dim lighting make this circular restaurant in 'Arorangi a great place for an evening meal. The international cuisine is well prepared and the welcome is friendly and convivial. There's regular live music and a breezy relaxed atmosphere. Just come as you are and fast forward to an easygoing holiday state of mind.

Saltwater Cafe
CAFE $$

(Map p200; Ara Tapu, Titikaveka; mains NZ$19-28; ⊗10am-6pm Sun-Thu) This roadside eatery on the south coast at Titikaveka is a great place for lunch or a cold drink. The menu includes pad Thai and garlic prawns, and there's also cold beer and punchy tropical cocktails. The homemade cheesecake ($10) is excellent, and it's a handy spot on Sundays when not much else is open.

The kitchen normally closes around 2.30pm, but coffee, cocktails and cakes are served until 6pm. If you're traversing the island by scooter, you've just reached the halfway point from Avarua.

Hidden Spirit Café & Grill
CAFE $$

(Map p200; ✉22796; www.hiddenspirit.net; Ara Tapu, Titikaveka; mains NZ$18-26; ⊗10am-4pm Mon-Sat) Set in the verdant surroundings of the Maire Nui Gardens, this cafe offers delicious cakes and desserts – try the lemon meringue pie (NZ$16) – and healthy salads. Lunches are also available, and afterwards you can take a relaxing stroll around the gardens (NZ$5).

Rickshaw
ASIAN $$

(Map p200; www.facebook.com/TheRickshawRarotonga; Are Tapu, Muri; mains NZ$20-24; ⊗5.30-10pm Mon-Sat) Variations on dishes you enjoyed in Bangkok and Hanoi feature at this pan-Asian eatery. Reserve a spot on the breezy deck and feast on beef rendang, Vietnamese squid or Singapore chilli prawns. Covering lots of culinary bases, the flavours aren't always totally authentic, but considering you're dining on a far-flung Pacific island, the Rickshaw's still worth a visit. Bookings recommended.

La Casita
TEX-MEX $$

(Map p200; ✉20693; www.facebook.com/La CasitaRarotonga; Are Tapu, Muri; mains NZ$14-21; ⊗5.30pm-11pm Mon-Sat, 11.30am-2pm Sat) Combining Tex-Mex (burritos, quesadillas and enchiladas) with Italian (pizza and pasta), La Casita is a bustling and colourful spot that's a reliable standby after a busy day snorkelling, paddle-boarding, or just taking it easy on nearby Muri Lagoon. The pescado tacos come crammed with chunks of local fish. Bookings recommended.

Progressive Dining
POLYNESIAN $$$

(✉20639; per person NZ$90; ⊗dinner Mon & Thu) Eat your way around the island during this progressive dinner held in locals' homes. The relaxed, easygoing occasions run to three courses across four to five hours and include live music and visits to gardens and plantations. It's a great way to meet the locals and tuck into dishes including *ika mata* and pawpaw salad.

Booking ahead is essential, and note that dinners only take place when there are sufficient numbers.

🍸 Drinking & Entertainment

Shipwreck Hut   BAR
(Map p200; Ara Tapu, 'Arorangi; ⊙4-9pm) The Shipwreck Hut is a wonderfully rustic spot with an absolute waterfront location. There's regular live music, great pub meals and barbecue dinners, and it's a top west-coast location to watch Rarotonga's incredible sunsets. Come along on a Saturday night for the dulcet tones of Jake Numanga. He's the ukulele whiz who welcomed you when you flew in.

iSOBAR   BAR
(Map p200; Muri Beach; ⊙3-10pm Mon-Sat) Twelve-buck happy-hour cocktails and regular 3pm to 6pm DJ sets from Wednesday to Saturday make this a top lagoon-side spot to ease into another Raro evening. Live bands often raise the tropical tempo on Friday nights. There's also good dining in the associated Sails Restaurant.

🛍 Shopping

Mike Tavioni   ARTS, CRAFTS
(Map p200; ✆24003; Ara Metua, Atupa; ⊙Mon-Sat) Visit the workshop of Rarotonga's most renowned sculptor and carver on the back road near Avarua. See his stone carvings at the Punanga Nui Market and the National Culture Centre.

M&M Ukalele & Crafts   MUSIC
(Map p200; ✆20662; www.facebook.com/mmukalele682; Ara Metua; ⊙9.30am-4pm Mon-Fri) M&M sells handmade ukuleles and has a great selection of local music on CD. Phone ahead to make sure it's open.

Prison Craft Shop   ARTS, CRAFTS
(Map p200; 'Arorangi; ⊙8.30am-3pm Mon-Fri) A good spot for unique gifts including handmade ukuleles.

Tivaevae Collectables   ARTS, CRAFTS
(www.tivaevaecollectables.com; Nikao; ⊙9am-4pm) Visit for beautiful Cook Islands *tivaevae* (hand-sewn quilted fabrics) harnessing traditional designs such as bedspreads and bed linen, but also reworked as cushion covers, tablecloths and women's clothing. Shopping online and worldwide shipping are both possible if you're concerned about excess baggage.

Art Studio   ARTS, CRAFTS
(Map p200; www.theartstudiocookislands.com; 'Arorangi; ⊙10am-5pm Mon-Fri) Contemporary art from owners Ian and Kay George combines with works from other Pacific artists. Handpainted or printed textiles are available, as are spectacular wall-covering screen-printed photographs.

Tokerau Jim   JEWELLERY
(Map p200; ✆24305; www.tokeraujim.com; ⊙9am-3.30pm Mon-Fri) Located in Matavera, Tokerau Jim does beautiful and incredibly fine carvings on pearls and pearl shell. On

---

ISLAND NIGHTS

Rarotonga's traditional form of evening entertainment is the Island Night – a spectacular showcase combining traditional dance and music (*karioi*) with a lavish buffet of local food (*kai*). Dancing, drumming and singing are always on show, and fire juggling, acrobatics and storytelling are often thrown into the mix.

Island Nights are held regularly at the large resorts, and every night except Sunday you can catch a show somewhere on the island. Extravagant affairs are featured at the Pacific Resort (p218), Edgewater Resort (✆25435), Crown Beach Resort (✆23953) and the Rarotongan Beach Resort (✆25800). You'll pay between NZ$15 and NZ$35 for the show only, or NZ$55 to NZ$99 for the show and buffet.

On Monday, Wednesday and Friday nights, Highland Paradise (p210) offers a NZ$99 show that includes transport, a cocktail and an *umukai* (underground oven) feast. Another *umukai* is provided at Te Vara Nui Village (p211) on Tuesday, Thursday and Saturday nights. On Thursday and Friday nights the Staircase Restaurant & Bar (p207) features a show costing just NZ$35 including food (NZ$5 for show only).

Ask the tourist information office in Avarua for its handout listing the many Island Nights on offer around the island from Monday to Saturday.

Saturday mornings you'll find him at the Punanga Nui market.

Turtles & Ocean/Earth   CLOTHING

(Map p200; Avatiu; ⊗8am-4pm Mon-Fri) Interesting designs spoofing global brands and also that Cook Islands rugby shirt you've always wanted.

Perfumes of Rarotonga   GIFTS

(Map p200; www.perfumes.co.ck; ⊗9am-4.30pm Mon-Sat) Near the airport, this place makes its own perfumes, soaps, liqueurs and scented oils. There's another **outlet** (Map p204; Cooks Corner Arcade, Avarua; ⊗9am-4.30pm Mon-Sat) in Cook's Corner Arcade in central Avarua that also sells excellent fudge full of tropical fruit and coconut flavours.

Croc Tatau   TATTOOS

(Map p200; ☑76384; www.facebook.com/croc tatau; Muri) Englishman 'Croc' is the only man on Rarotonga crafting *tata'u* (tattoos) the traditional way, using pigment and hand tools. Check out his blog (www.croctatau. wordpress.com) for information and photos. He's sometimes off the island working in Europe, so email him before you travel. You'll find other local tattooists offering traditional designs but modern techniques at Avarua's weekly Punanga Nui Market.

ⓘ Information

Bluesky Teleshop (Map p200; www.bluesky. co.ck; Ara Tapu, Muri, opposite Pacific Resort; ⊗10am-6pm Mon-Fri, noon-4pm Sun; 🛜) Internet and wi-fi hotspot and data sales.

Cook Islands Pharmacy (Map p200; Ara Tapu, Muri Beach; ⊗10am-5pm Mon-Fri, 10am-2pm Sun) Convenient location in Muri.

Deli-licious (Map p200; Ara Tapu, Muri Beach; ⊗8am-3.30pm Mon-Fr; 🛜) Wi-fi internet access.

Dr Uka's Surgery (Map p200; ☑23680; Ara Tapu, Muri, opposite Pacific Resort; ⊗9.30am-1.30pm Mon-Thu, 9.30am-noon Fri) Handy for minor accidents and ailments if you're staying around Muri Beach.

Hospital (Map p200; ☑22664; ⊗emergency 24hr) On a steep hill behind the golf course.

Island Hopper Vacations (Map p200; ☑22576; www.islandhoppervacations. com; Turama House, Nika'o) Has good airfare-and-accommodation packages and deals to the outer islands.

Kavera Central (Map p200; Kavera; ⊗8am-4pm Mon-Sat) Internet access.

Outpatient Clinic (Map p200; ☑20065; ⊗8am-4pm Mon-Fri) About 1km east of Avarua. Also has emergency dental services.

AITUTAKI

POP 2035 / AREA 18.3 SQ KM

Aitutaki, the Cooks' second-most-visited island, curls gently around one of the South Pacific's most stunning lagoons. The aqua water, foaming breakers around the perimeter reef and broad sandy beaches of its many small deserted islets make for a glorious scene. From the air or on the water, Aitutaki will take your breath away.

It's just 45 minutes by air from Rarotonga but it feels like another world. Although there are some impressive, plush resorts, this island is slower and much less commercialised. Many visitors come on Air Rarotonga's day tour or opt to stay at upmarket resorts, but there are still good-value accommodation options, and it's worth spending a few days to slow down to island time.

Sunday is solemnly observed as the day of prayer and rest. Take the opportunity to see a local church service, as the singing is spine-tingling. Sunday flights from Rarotonga continue to inspire protest from elements of the island's religious community, and you may see a few banners and placards when you arrive.

Aitutaki is shaped like a curved fishhook, and you'll fly into the north of the island near O'otu Beach and the private Aitutaki Lagoon Resort. On the west side are most of the hotels and Arutanga, the island's main town. On the east coast are the small villages of Tautu, Vaipae and Vaipeka. The *motu* around the edge of Aitutaki's lagoon are uninhabited.

History

Legend tells that Ru from 'Avaiki (Ra'iatea in French Polynesia) arrived at Aitutaki by *vaka* (canoe). He came with four wives, four brothers and their wives, and 20 royal maidens at the Akitua *motu* (now the Aitutaki Lagoon Resort).

Aitutaki's first European visitor was Captain William Bligh, who arrived on the *Bounty* on 11 April 1789 (17 days before the famous mutiny). In 1821 John Williams left Tahitian preachers Papeiha and Vahapata here to convert the islanders to Christianity. Charles Darwin passed by on the 1835 *Beagle* voyage, and in the 1850s Aitutaki become a favourite port of call for

Aitutaki

whaling ships. During WWII American soldiers arrived to build two long runways, and in the 1950s the lagoon was used as a refuelling stopover for the Tasman Empire Air Line's (TEAL; Air New Zealand's predecessor) luxurious 'coral route' across the Pacific, flown by Solent flying boats. Hollywood acting legends John Wayne and Cary Grant were just two of the celebrities who spent time on Akaiami *motu* while their Solent was refuelled. Most lagoon cruises stop at Akaiami where the crumbling foundations of TEAL's absolute waterfront terminal are still visible.

⊙ Sights

The lagoon may be what draws the tourists here, but Aitutaki's ancient *marae* are also notable for their large stones and cultural significance. **Marae Orongo** (Map p223) is today in the main village of Arutanga. The main road runs through another large *marae*,

and on the inland road between Nikaupara and Tautu are the islands' most magnificent *marae* – including **Tokangarangi** (Map p223) and **Te Poaki O Rae** (Map p223) – mostly reclaimed by the jungle.

Arutanga   TOWN

Compared to Rarotonga, Arutanga, Aitutaki's only town, seems astonishingly quiet, with few signs of life even on weekdays when the shops are open. The island's main harbour is by the Orongo Centre. The lovely weather-beaten **CICC** church near the Administration Centre was built in 1828, making it the oldest in the Cooks. Beautifully restored in 2010, the church has lovely stained-glass windows, fine carved-wood panelling and an old anchor precariously suspended from the ceiling.

Try to attend a service on the first Sunday of every month, when Aitutaki's female parishioners wear pristine white dresses.

Aitutaki

RAROTONGA & THE COOK ISLANDS AITUTAKI

Maungapu VIEWPOINT

The 30-minute hike to the top of Maungapu (124m), Aitutaki's highest peak, provides splendid views over the entire atoll and the sapphire-blue lagoon. The track starts off pretty gently opposite the bungalows of Paradise Cove, but gets more challenging towards the summit.

★ **Aitutaki Lagoon** LAGOON

(Map p223) Aitutaki's stunning lagoon, brimming with marine life and ringed by 15 palm-covered *motu* (islets), is a South Pacific treasure. **Maina** (Little Girl) offers superb snorkelling and is home to the red-tailed tropicbird, once prized for its crimson feathers. Nearby is the wreck of cargo freighter *Alexander*, which ran aground in the 1930s. **Tapuaeta'i** (One Foot Island) is the best-known *motu*, fringed by white beaches and divided from its neighbour, **Te-kopua**, by a deepwater channel that's teeming with tropical fish.

Akaiami *motu* is where the old TEAL flying boats landed to refuel on the trans-Pacific

'Coral Route' between Fiji, Samoa and Tahiti – the remnants of the old jetty can still be seen.

🏃 Activities

The best swimming, snorkelling and beaches are around the *motu*, especially near Maina, accessible by boat. Just south of Black Rocks, on the main island's northwest coast, you can walk out to the outer reef on a coral causeway that starts 50m from the shore. The nicest swimming beaches on the main island are **O'otu Beach** (Map p223) and the wharves at **Vaipae** and **Tautu**. The island's east coast is mainly shallow mud and mangrove swamp.

Scuba diving is fantastic in Aitutaki. The visibility is great, and features include drop-offs, multilevels, wall dives and cave systems. Many divers ask to dive on the wreck of the *Alexander*, but it sits in a mere metre of water and is just as suitable for snorkellers.

In recent years the popularity of kite-surfing has really soared, and the skies and beaches around Honeymoon Island are often dotted with kitesurfers zipping along in robust tropical breezes.

Check out www.aitutaki.net, www.cookislands.travel/aitutaki/ and www.aitutaki.com for more activities listings.

Bubbles Below
DIVING

(Map p223; ☑31537; www.diveaitutaki.com; 1/2 dives NZ$105/170, PADI discover/open-water course NZ$170/550) Offers dive trips and courses. The entertaining manager Onu (Turtle) Hewett really knows the waters surrounding Aitutaki.

Wet & Wild
KITESURFING

(☑75980, 56558; www.wetnwild-aitutaki.com) This versatile outfit runs its own kitesurfing centre on Honeymoon Island – including gear hire and lessons for beginners – and also offers marine adventures as diverse as snorkelling, fishing, whale watching and spearfishing.

 Tours

Most tour operators on Aitutaki don't have offices. Arrange a cruise by calling the operator or ask the people you're staying with to arrange it. The operator will collect you from your hotel.

Fishing

Aitutaki Game Fishing Club
FISHING

(Map p223; ☑31379; 5pm-midnight Wed-Sat) Find out about the fishing scene at Aitutaki Game Fishing Club, by the wharf in Arutanga. It's also a good place for a cold beer from 5pm from Wednesday to Saturday. Bonefish are among the fastest and most exciting fighting fish in the world, and Aitutaki's lagoon has some of the biggest on the planet.

Black Pearl Charters
FISHING

(☑31125; www.blackpearlaitutaki.com) Hooking wahoo, giant trevally and *mahimahi* from NZ$180 per person. Spearfishing trips in the lagoon (half-/full day NZ$250/500) are also available.

Bonefish E2
FISHING

(☑52077, 31686; www.e2sway.com) Local guide Itu Davey has been hooking Aitutaki's bonefish since he was a boy. Half-/full-day charters per two people are NZ$350/450.

Slice of Heaven Charters
BOATING

(☑71847, 31747; www.sliceofheavencharters.com; half-day deep-sea fishing per person from NZ$180, lagoon tours for 2 people from NZ$350) Marine adventures ranging from deep-sea fishing excursions catching wahoo, *mahimahi*, barracuda and tuna, to lagoon trips incorporating island visits, snorkelling and lunch. Full-day combinations of deep-sea fishing and exploring the lagoon are also available.

Lagoon Cruises

For many travellers an Aitutaki lagoon cruise is a Cook Islands highlight. There are several operators that cruise around the *motu* and snorkelling spots. All provide snorkelling gear, a barbecue fish lunch and a stop at Tapuaeta'i (One Foot Island) – remember to take your passport to get it stamped at the One Foot Island 'post office' for NZ$2. You can also send Aitutaki postcards to the folks back home.

Aitutaki Adventures
CRUISE

(☑31171; captpuna@aitutaki.net.ck; adult/child NZ$99/45; ⊙10am-4pm Sun-Fri) Lagoon cruises with a family-owned company including snorkelling, fish-feeding and a terrific lunch on One Foot Island. Most trips also stop at Honeymoon Island to see the kiteboarders soar like frigatebirds.

Bishop's Cruises
BOAT TOUR

(☑31009; www.bishopscruises.com; per person NZ$95; ⊙ Mon-Sat) Lagoon tours visit Maina, Moturakau and Tapuaeta'i, and there are also honeymoon cruises and *motu* drop-offs.

Kia-Orana Cruises
CRUISE

(☑73750; www.kiaoranacruise.com; per person NZ$125; ⊙Sun-Fri) The main Seven Wonders of Paradise Cruise from 9.30am to 3.30pm visits Maina, Moturakau, Honeymoon Island and Tapuaeta'i. Sunset snorkelling excursions from noon to 6pm are also available.

Vaka Cruise
CRUISE

(☑31398; www.aitutaki.net; per person NZ$125; ⊙10am-4pm daily) Cruises are on a Polynesian-style catamaran, the *Titi Ai Tonga* (Wind from the South), which has a roof and onboard bar. Look forward to lots of on-board entertainment and the company of daytrippers from Rarotonga.

Teking
CRUISE

(☑31582; www.tekingtours.com) Offers a 'Snorkeling Safari' lagoon cruise (per person NZ$119) and a romantic sunset cruise for two with champagne (NZ$269). Expect tasty lunches and a healthy dose of Aitutaki humour.

Other Tours

Aitutaki Punarei Cultural Tours
CULTURAL TOUR

(Map p223; ☑50877, 31757; www.facebook.com/Punarei; adult/child NZ$80/40; ⊙9am-1pm Mon, Wed & Fri) Local guide Ngaa Pureariki is a keen archaeology buff, and this island experience visits the Punarei Cultural Village he has established to showcase traditional structures before the arrival of Christianity. Tours also incorporate a visit to an ancient *marae*, an *umukai* lunch, and Ngaa is a passionate advocate and learned source of information about earlier centuries on Aitutaki.

🛏 Sleeping

Matriki Beach Huts
BUNGALOW **$**

(Map p223; ☑ 31564; www.matrikibeachhuts. com; s/d NZ$79/99) These knocked-up beachfront fibro shacks with mural-painted walls and one self-contained garden unit comprise this most delightfully ramshackle place to stay. The split-level huts share toilet facilities but are otherwise self-contained with kitchenettes and showers and the most brilliant location. Matriki runs snorkelling trips outside the lagoon reef and can arrange fishing charters and activities.

Gina's Garden Lodges
LODGE **$**

(Map p223; ☑ 31058; www.ginasaitutakidesire. com; s/d NZ$75/120; 🏊) Set amid a peaceful garden of fruit trees and flowers in Tautu, these four large family-friendly lodges are the best value on Aitutaki. Queen Manarangi Tutai, one of Aitutaki's three *ariki* (high chiefs), is the proprietor and one of the island's most gracious and charming hosts. The self-contained lodges have high ceilings and large verandahs overlooking the gardens and swimming pool.

Each lodge has beds in a small loft that are perfect for kids. Gina's is a few kilometres from town, so you'll need transport.

Amuri Guesthouse
GUESTHOUSE **$**

(Map p223; ☑ 31231; s/d NZ$50/80) Amuri has six double bedrooms and two shared bathrooms with a large dining and kitchen area in the owner's house. Accommodation is very clean, friendly and excellent value, and fresh fruit is often supplied *gratis* for breakfast. You'll be around 100m from the beach, but handily placed for food shopping.

Aitutaki Seaside Lodges
BUNGALOW **$$**

(Map p223; ☑ 70458, 31056; www.seaside-aitutaki. com; Amuri Beach; d NZ$250; 🕾) These three comfortable self-contained bungalows enjoy an absolute beachfront location at the quieter northern end of Amuri Beach. Complimentary use of kayaks and sun-loungers makes it a tough decision how to spend most mornings.

Paradise Cove
BUNGALOW **$$**

(Map p223; ☑ 31218; www.paradisecove-aitutaki. com; garden/beachview bungalow NZ$150/180) Paradise Cove features beachfront bungalows on a glorious beach shaded by coconut palms. The thatched pole-house bungalows offer uninterrupted views across the lagoon from private verandahs. Inside are king-sized beds, kitchenettes with fridges, bathrooms and ceiling fans. They're not huge, but the larger garden suites can sleep up to four – a good option for families.

Its rustic beachside restaurant and bar is perfect for a sand-between-the-toes beer at the end of another Aitutaki day.

Amuri Sands
BUNGALOW **$$**

(Map p223; ☑ 50613, 31130; www.aitutaki-vacation.com; Amuri; s/d NZ$155/175) These beach bungalows offer all you need for an island sojourn: a lagoon-facing location, trade-wind-friendly decks and a grassy lawn studded with coconut palms and a few soaring pine trees. Decor is simple but trendy, and the bathrooms and self-contained kitchens are spotless and modern. Look forward to a central location near good restaurants and cafes.

Inano Beach Bungalows
BUNGALOW **$$**

(Map p223; ☑ 31758; www.inanobeach.com; lagoon-view/beachfront bungalows NZ$130/160, family bungalows NZ$170) Offering excellent value for money, Inano Beach Bungalows have been built using largely local materials and traditional methods. There are woven pandanus walls, ironwood balconies and mahogany tabletops. Near the end of the airport, fronting a nice stretch of beach, Inano's self-contained bungalows are large with good kitchen facilities.

Paparei Bungalows
BUNGALOW **$$**

(Map p223; ☑ 73275; www.papareibungalows.com; d NZ$225) Paparei offers two modern self-contained beachfront bungalows near the centre of town. They're large, clean, well equipped and nicely decorated in an unfussy way. Operators Trina and Steve are lovely hosts, and guests also receive a discount on food and beverages at the Koru Cafe near the airport.

Gina's Beach Lodge
BUNGALOW **$$**

(s/d incl transfers NZ$210/380) Queen Tutai from Gina's Garden Lodges also runs Gina's Beach Lodge on Akaiami island, and guests can choose to spend a while at each.

★**Etu Moana**　　　　BOUTIQUE HOTEL **$$$**
(Map p223; ☑31458; www.etumoana.com; villas NZ$505-750; ✱@☎☒) These boutique beach villas have thatched roofs and luxurious furnishings showcasing gleaming Tasmanian oak floors, loft ceilings, king-sized beds, private outdoor showers and teak sundecks. The design and decor are very classy, and there's a tear-drop pool complete with rock garden, sun-shaded tables and a deluxe honesty bar. If you prefer your luxe resorts understated, then this is the place. No kids under 12.

Pacific Resort　　　　RESORT **$$$**
(Map p223; ☑31720; www.pacificresort.com; beachfront bungalows/ste/villas NZ$600/1190/1890; ✱@☎☒) Pacific Resort Aitutaki is a benchmark in luxury Polynesian. From the Oriental lily ponds and enormous carved-timber reception desk of its sumptuous foyer to the rough-rendered walls and timber floors, decor and views of the split-level restaurant, the Pacific Resort is breathtaking. The rooms are superb, with commanding views, huge private beach decks and private garden bathrooms with outdoor showers.

Even if you can't afford to stay, come and enjoy the resort's restaurants. Our favourite is the more informal Black Rock Cafe.

Aretai Beach Villas　　　APARTMENT **$$$**
(Map p223; ☑31645; www.aretaibeachvillas.com; villas NZ$300; ✱@) The lovely two-bedroom villas at Aretai are among the largest on the island, and definitely the best presented and best value for money in this price range. Halfway between Arutanga and the airport, with wonderful sea views and outstanding facilities – including full kitchens, dining areas, gorgeous furniture and huge patios – these stylish villas are ideal for travelling families or groups.

Aitutaki Lagoon Resort　　　RESORT **$$$**
(Map p223; ☑31201; www.aitutakilagoonresort.com; beachfront/over-water bungalows NZ$750/1135; ✱@☎☒) Aitutaki Lagoon Resort, ensconced on its own Akitua island, has everything glam jet-set patrons would expect. It's truly beautiful, with great expanses of glistening white beach and a private ferryman to shunt you to and from the mainland. There are bars and restaurants, and a pool and day spa. The thatched garden and beachfront villas are large, light and comfortable

Over-water bungalows – the only ones in the Cook Islands – and premium beachfront bungalows are also special. Nonguests are welcome, so drop in for a visit and dine at its excellent restaurant with astounding lagoon views. The resort offers packages and discounts for extended stays – see the website.

Tamanu Beach　　　　RESORT **$$$**
(Map p223; ☑31810; www.aretamanu.com; bungalows NZ$340-550; ✱@☎☒) The elegant Tamanu Beach has chic bungalows ranging in size from studio to one-bedroom, all arrayed around a lush garden, or with excellent lagoon views. 'Casual luxury' is the resort's slogan and we reckon that's very accurate. There's also a breezy open-sided restaurant that does a good Island Night on Thursdays.

✖ **Eating**

Maina Traders Superstore　　SUPERMARKET **$**
(Map p223; ☑31055; ☺7am-8pm Mon-Sat) Centrally located in Arutanga.

Rerei's　　　　SUPERMARKET **$**
(Map p223; ☺7am-9pm Mon-Sat) Stock up on groceries at this Amuri store with a Heineken sign out the front. Unfortunately it's not a bar, but it does have a pretty good selection of beer and wine.

Neibaa　　　　SUPERMARKET **$**
(Map p223; ☺7am-8pm) On the island's east side in Vaipae, Neibaa is the only shop that opens Sundays.

Market　　　　MARKET **$**
(Map p223; Orongo Centre; ☺6am-2pm Mon-Fri, to noon Sat) Self-caterers can stock up on fruit, vegetables and fruit at Aitutaki's market.

Black Rock Cafe　　　　FUSION **$$**
(Map p223; Pacific Resort; mains NZ$20-35; ☺11am-5pm) The Pacific Resort's more casual daytime restaurant is a stunner. The lagoon is just a cocktail shake away, towering palms shade the swimming pool, and the easy-going staff serve up lighter lunch dishes and fruit-laden cocktails. Standouts are the tuna sashimi and the hearty grilled chicken wraps.

Flying Boat Beach Bar & Grill　　CAFE **$$**
(Map p223; Aitutaki Lagoon Resort; mains NZ$23-30, pizza NZ$25-25; ☺11am-6pm) Open to outside diners, the daytime restaurant at the Aitutaki Lagoon Resort has quite possibly the most stunning location in all of the Cooks. Lagoon views stretch for 180°, a few tiny *motu* feature on the near horizon, and the above-water deck is perfect for an afternoon

beer, cocktail or grilled seafood. Just maybe the Cooks' best pizzas too.

You'll need to make the short hop across the lagoon to the resort's private island. Just ask the boatman on the resort's nifty barge.

Blue Lagoon
CAFE $$

(Map p223; O'otu Beach, Aitutaki Village; lunch NZ$12-25, dinner NZ$25-37; ⊘11.30am-10pm) With a sandy floor and a thatched roof, this easygoing eatery at the Aitutaki Village resort is a cool and rustic place for a beer, lunch by the lagoon, or an evening meal at sunset. The food is simple – fish, burgers, steaks and salads – but the view is serene and the ambience relaxed. Try the excellent Thai-style red fish curry.

Blue Lagoon has regular Island Nights and a good Sunday afternoon barbecue from around noon. Live music often kicks off at 6pm on Sunday.

Koru Café
CAFE $$

(Map p223; ☑31110; www.korucafe.biz; O'otu Beach; breakfast NZ$10-19, lunch NZ$10-30; ⊘7am-3pm; 🛜) Koru is a spacious and breezy Aitutaki spin on a trendy New Zealand cafe. All-day cooked breakfasts and lunches – including Caesar salad, steak sandwiches, BLT, pasta and salt-and-pepper calamari – all complement the island's best coffee. Wi-fi is available, and you can call to arrange ready-to-eat meals, picnic lunches and barbecue packs.

Locally made arts and crafts, including weaving, jewellery and ukuleles, are also available.

Café Tupuna
POLYNESIAN $$

(Map p223; ☑31678; Tautu; mains NZ$20-27; ⊘11am-3pm) In a lovely rural setting in the hills behind Arutanga, Café Tupuna is Aitutaki's only independent restaurant offering fine dining. The menu features fresh local fish and seafood cooked with island flavours and exotic spices. On our last visit we enjoyed baked *mahimahi* stuffed with shrimps. The lush garden setting is very relaxed and there's a good wine list.

Bringing insect repellent is often a wise move.

Tamanu Beachfront
POLYNESIAN $$

(Map p223; Tamanu Beach; lunch NZ$15-25, dinner NZ$30-35; ⊘noon-3pm & 6.30-9.30pm) The breezy, thatched-roof, open-sided restaurant of the Tamanu Beach hotel is also open to outside guests. Here's your chance to dine at sunset on Pacific-style fresh fish, top-notch salads and other local dishes. Tama-

nu's Island Night on Thursday is renowned as one of Aitutaki's best, and bookings are recommended. Robust cocktails and a good winelist are other fine attractions.

Coconut Shack
CAFE, BAR $$

(Map p223; Paradise Cove; mains NZ$24-30; ⊘6-10pm Sun-Tue, Thu & Fri) With a circular bar built around a coconut tree, and plenty of absolute beachfront tables and chairs, the Coconut Shack at Paradise Cove fulfills every expectation of a rustic South Pacific watering hole. Cocktails come packed with booze and tropical fruit, hearty mains include fish curry and chicken stuffed with prawn salsa, and whole parrotfish for NZ$28 is good value.

Boatshed Bar & Grill
SEAFOOD, BAR $$

(Map p223; ☑31739; Popaara Beach; mains NZ$21-37; ⊘11am-11pm; 🛜) A sprawling array of maritime memorabilia and classic country music makes the Boatshed a very laid-back spot. Try to secure a space on the deck for reef views, and feast on seafood classics like fish and chips, *ika mata* and sashimi. The beer's cold, the wine's reasonably priced, and booking for dinner is recommended.

Don't be surprised to see the guys that were there at 2pm still downing cold ones a few hours later.

Tauono's Garden Cafe
CAFE $$

(Map p223; ☑31562; www.tauonos.com; cake & dessert NZ$10-22, lunch NZ$19-28; ⊘market 10am-5pm Mon, Wed & Fri, lunch noon-2pm, afternoon tea 3-5pm Mon, Wed, Fri only; 🛜) 🍃 Tauono's is a delight, a tiny garden cafe run by one-time Canadian-Austrian Sonja and her occasional team of travellers and WWOOFers (Willing Workers on Organic Farms). Renowned for its coconut cake, fruit smoothies, and afternoon teas, Tauono's also offers home-cooked cuisine served alfresco for lunch. The food is prepared according to what's been freshly picked from the on-site organic garden.

Stop by for homemade cake and fresh fruit and veg from Sonja's market shop, and ask about joining a plantation tour (per person NZ$35). Fresh and frozen meals are also available to take away. Sonja's tasty breadfruit lasagne is deservedly world famous in Aitutaki.

Rapae Bay Restaurant
FUSION $$$

(Map p223; ☑31720; Pacific Resort; mains NZ$27-55; ⊘5.30-10pm) The island's standout resort restaurant is in Pacific Resort. It offers superb Pacific fusion cuisine in a brilliant split-level patio setting. Look forward to interesting combinations of Pacific and Southeast Asian flavours including tuna sashimi and fresh Vietnamese-style spring rolls.

 Drinking & Nightlife

Puffy's Beach Bar & Grill   BAR
(Map p223; ⊙noon-2pm & 6-8.30pm Mon-Sat) Puffy's is a tiny bar popular with both locals and visitors from nearby Paradise Cove. Simple meals – mainly burgers and fish and chips – and cheap booze are served, and there's also a really good weekly Island Night, usually on a Friday at 7.30pm. Keep an eye on the noticeboard out the front for details of funky local bands too.

ⓘ **Information**

Ask at your hotel if you should boil the water before drinking it. Many places get their drinking water from separate rain tanks.

There are no dogs on Aitutaki (the island's canine population was blamed for a leprosy outbreak) but there are plenty of roosters – bring earplugs if you're planning on sleeping in.

The main police station is behind the Orongo Centre near the wharf in Arutanga.

Aitutaki Tourism (Map p223; ✆31767; www.cookislands.travel/aitutaki; ⊙8am-4pm Mon-Fri) Helpful office in Arutanga.

ANZ Bank Agent (Map p223; ⊙8am-3pm Mon-Fri) With an ATM outside.

BSP (Bank South Pacific; Map p223; ⊙9am-3pm Mon-Fri) Also has an ATM.

Hospital (Map p223; ✆31002; ⊙24hr) On the hill behind Arutanga.

Post Office & Bluesky (Map p223; ⊙8am-4pm Mon-Fri; 🛜) In the Administration Centre in Arutanga. Also offers phone, internet and has a wi-fi hotspot.

ⓘ **Getting There & Away**

AIR

Air Rarotonga (Map p223; ✆in Arutanga 31888, in Rarotonga 22888; www.airraro.com) Several flights to Aitutaki from Rarotonga Monday to Saturday, and one flight on Sunday. Regular one-way fares from NZ$181 to NZ$270. There's also a direct flight from Aitutaki to 'Atiu on Monday, Wednesday and Friday. One-way fares are priced from NZ$250. Also available is an Aitutaki/'Atiu combo fare combining travel from Rarotonga to Aitutaki to 'Atiu and back to Rarotonga.

Air Rarotonga also runs Aitutaki Day Tours from Monday to Saturday, leaving Rarotonga at 8am and returning at 5.30pm. The cost is NZ$493 per person, including hotel transfers, flights, and a lagoon cruise on Vaka Cruise (p225) with snorkelling gear and lunch.

BOAT

Cargo ships travelling to the Northern Group occasionally stop at Aitutaki.

ⓘ **Getting Around**

TO/FROM THE AIRPORT

Island Tours (✆31379) Island Tours offers a minibus transfer service that costs NZ$20 to and from the airport. The larger resorts provide transfers for their guests.

CAR, MOTORCYCLE & BICYCLE

Various places rent out bicycles (NZ$5 per day), scooters (NZ$25), cars and jeeps (NZ$70 to NZ$100). Try **Popoara Rentals** (Map p223; ✆31739; O'otu Beach), **Ranginui's Retreat** (Map p223; ✆31657; O'otu Beach) or, for the best range, **Rino's Beach Bungalows & Rentals** (Map p223; ✆31197; Arutanga).

PALMERSTON

POP 60 / AREA 2.1 SQ KM

Palmerston, 500km northwest of Rarotonga, is the Southern Group's only true atoll, halfway towards the Cooks' Northern Group. The lineage of all Palmerston Islanders can be traced to just one man – prolific Englishman William Masters, a ship's carpenter, who arrived from Manuae with two Polynesian wives in 1863. Having quickly added a third wife, over the next 36 years Masters created his own island dynasty. He came from Gloucester and his progeny spoke excellent English with a thick Gloucester accent. Today, there are three main families on Palmerston (who spell their name Marsters), and you'll find Marsterses scattered throughout the Cooks and the rest of Australasia – the total number of William's descendants is now well into the thousands.

There's no organised accommodation on Palmerston, but if you're planning to travel there, contact the island secretary **Tere Marsters** (✆37615, 37620; palmerstonisland@hotmail.com). The only way to reach the island is by interisland freighter or private yacht.

'ATIU

POP 470 / AREA 27 SQ KM

In pre-European times 'Atiu was an important seat of regional power and its warriors were renowned for ferocious fighting and ruthlessness. By contrast, the rocky, reef-fringed island is now known for gentler

'Atiu

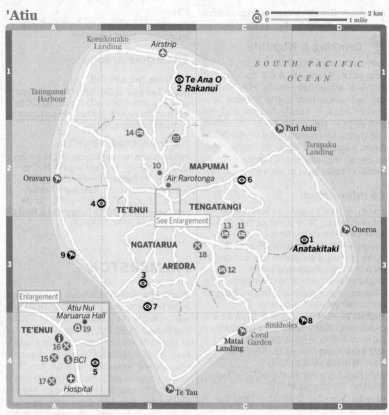

N
0 — 2 km
0 — 1 mile

pursuits. It's the Cooks' eco-capital and a haven for naturalists and bird lovers. It also attracts adventurous travellers in search of an island with a more traditional edge.

'Atiu's five main villages (Areora, Tengatangi, Mapumai, Te'enui and Ngatiarua) are clustered together on the island's central plateau, surrounded by a band of fertile swampland

and lush taro plantations. The *makatea* – the dramatic ring of upthrust rock that's rich in marine fossils and was once the island's exterior reef – is just one of 'Atiu's natural features. The island is also covered with forest and honeycombed with limestone caves. 'Atiu's most famous cave is Anatakitaki, the only known home of the *kopeka* ('Atiuan swiftlet).

History

'Land of Birds' or 'Land of Insects' is the translation of 'Atiu's traditional name 'Enua Manu. Along with its neighbours Ma'uke and Mitiaro, 'Atiu makes up the Nga Pu Toru (Three Roots). In the recent pre-European times, 'Atiuan *ariki* overlorded smaller Ma'uke and Mitiaro. 'Atiuan warriors also made incursions on Rarotonga and Aitutaki, but without success. James Cook was the first European to land on 'Atiu on 3 April 1777. Reverend John Williams landed on 19 July 1823. Rongomatane, the leading 'Atiuan chief, was converted to Christianity after Williams' missionaries boldly ate sugarcane from Rongomatane's sacred grove – he subsequently ordered all the idols on the island to be burnt. The arrival of missionaries Williams and Tahitian Papeiha is celebrated on Gospel Day (19 July).

◉ Sights & Activities

Deep limestone caves, hidden away deep in the bush-covered *makatea,* are the most famous feature of 'Atiu. A torch and sturdy walking shoes are essential, and the coral is razor sharp. The main caves are on private land and you'll need a guide to visit them. Many caves were used for burials – it's *tapu* (taboo) to disturb the bones, so unless you fancy taking home a curse...

★ Anatakitaki   CAVE
(Map p230) Eerie Anatakitaki is 'Atiu's most spectacular cave, a multichambered cavern surrounded by banyan roots and thick jungle. It's also home to the rare *kopeka*, or 'Atiuan swiftlet – listen for its distinctive echo-locating clicks.

★ Te Ana O Rakanui   CAVE
(Map p230) Te Ana O Rakanui is a burial cave packed with musty old skulls and skeletal remains. It's a tight squeeze inside – claustrophobics be warned.

Rima Rau   CAVE
(Map p230) Another of 'Atiu's burial caves, Rima Rau is reached by a vertical pothole and still contains skeletal remains. Many will find it claustrophobic.

Lake Te Roto   LAKE
(Map p230) Lake Te Roto is noted for its *itiki* (eels), a popular island delicacy. On the western side of the lake, a cave leads right through the *makatea* to the sea.

Taunganui Harbour &
Oravaru Beach   BEACH
'Atiu's barrier reef is close to shore. The surrounding lagoon is rarely more than 50m wide and its waters quite shallow. Taunganui Harbour, on the west coast where the water is clear and deep, is the best spot for swimming. About 1km south is Oravaru Beach, where Captain Cook's party made its landing.

Taungaroro & Tumai   BEACHES
(Map p230) South of Oravaru Beach, Taungaroro and Tumai are two of the most popular swimming beaches.

Takauroa Beach   BEACH
(Map p230) You can swim in the three lovely sinkholes west of Takauroa Beach only at low tide. Between Takauroa Beach and Matai Landing, the falling tide empties through the sinkholes and fish become trapped in a fascinating natural aquarium known as the Coral Garden.

Marae Orongo   HISTORIC SITE
(Map p230) Near Oravaru Beach, this was once 'Atiu's most sacred *marae,* and it's still a powerfully atmospheric place – many locals are reluctant to go near it. You'll need a guide as it's on private land.

Marae Vairakai   HISTORIC SITE
(Map p230) Along a walking track north of Kopeka Lodge, Marae Vairakai is surrounded by 47 large limestone slabs, six of which have curious projections cut into their top edges.

Marae Te Apiripiri   HISTORIC SITE
(Map p230) This *marae* is where the Tahitian preacher Papeiha first spoke the words

---

EATING PRICE RANGES

The following price ranges refer to the cost of a main meal.

$ less than NZ$15

$$ NZ$15–30

$$$ more than NZ$30

of the Gospel in 1823. There's not much left to see, but a stone commemorates the site.

Tours

Atiu Tours
TOUR

(☑ 33041; www.atiutoursaccommodation.com) Run by Englishman Marshall Humphreys, Atiu Tours offers an informative 3½-hour circle-island tour (NZ$50 per person) visiting *marae*, beaches and historical points of interest. Lunch includes probably the best banana muffins in the Pacific, and there's often the opportunity for bodysurfing. There's also an excellent 2½-hour tour to Anatakitaki (NZ$35 per person) and Rima Rau burial cave ($30 per person).

Don't miss having a candlelit swim in the beautiful underground pool in the Anatakitaki cave.

George Mateariki
BIRDWATCHING

(☑ 33047; per person NZ$50) Also known as Birdman George, George Mateariki is 'Atiu's resident ornithologist and a local celebrity thanks to his highly entertaining ecotour. George oversaw the release of the endangered *kakerori* (Rarotongan flycatcher) here from Rarotonga, and also the more recent introduction of the *kura* (lorikeet) from the French Polynesian island of Rimatara. George also offers a specialist tour for birdwatchers.

Ask about having a tropical feast at his 'Restaurant at the Beach' at 4pm on Sundays.

Paiere Mokoroa
TOUR

(Map p230; ☑ 33034; macmokoroa@gmail.com) Historical tours taking in *marae* and battle sites around the island cost NZ$30 per person. Paiere Mokoroa is based at Taparere Lodge.

Andrew Matapakia
FISHING

(☑ 33825) Offers reef and lagoon fishing tours (NZ$30), and also deep-sea excursions (around NZ$100 per person) trolling for tuna, wahoo and *mahimahi*, or catching flying fish at night. Give him a call or see him during his sideline as barman at Kura's Kabana at Atiu Villas.

Atiu Island Coffee
TOUR

(Map p230; ☑ 33088) Mata Arai, whose family had grown coffee in the 1950s, returned to 'Atiu in the 1990s and resumed production. Her coffee is hand picked, hand dried and hand roasted, using coconut cream to give the coffee its flavour. Tours are NZ$30 per person and include delicious pikelets and coconut cream.

🛏 Sleeping

Kopeka Lodge
LODGE $

(Map p230; ☑ 33283; kopeka1@kopekalodges.co.ck; s/d NZ$85/120) Three rustic plywood chalets sit in rural grounds southeast of Areora village, with one single and two double units complete with self-contained kitchen. The stained-wood and pale-green colour scheme is simple, but the units are quite comfortable. On Rarotonga contact **Eddie Drollet** (☑ 52884).

Taparere Lodge
LODGE $

(Map p230; ☑ 33034; macmokoroa@gmail.com; s/d NZ$50/100) With two large breeze-block units, Taparere is bright, airy and cheerfully decorated. Accommodation is self-contained with kitchen facilities and (sometimes) hot-water showers. Shady verandahs overlook a pleasant valley.

Atiu Villas
VILLA $$

(Map p230; ☑ 33777; www.atiuvillas.com; bungalows NZ$210-250, extra person NZ$20; @ 🛜 🏊) The extra money goes a long way at Atiu Villas, which was built from local materials around 35 years ago by Kiwi expat Roger Malcolm and his 'Atiuan wife Kura. Six delightful villas are arrayed around a shady garden and have decks from where you can take in the valley views. There's a pool, tennis courts and a large bar-restaurant.

Complimentary wi-fi is provided, as is internet access on resident computers. Prepaid bookings made 12 weeks in advance earn a 15% discount, and last-minute bookings (seven days in advance) attract a 40% discount.

Atiu Bed & Breakfast
B&B $$

(Map p230; ☑ 33041; www.atiutoursaccommodation.com; r per person NZ$60; @) Tour provider Marshall Humphreys rents out rooms in his very comfortable family home near Areora. A double and a twin comprise the accommodation (with shared bathrooms), and guests have the run of the house. A tropical breakfast is complimentary, and evening meals and packed lunches can be arranged.

Marshall's wife Jéanne is a celebrated local artist, and her colourful and tropical work is for sale (from NZ$30).

🍴 Eating & Drinking

Self-catering from the slim pickings at the grocery stores – largely tinned and frozen food – is the most reliable eating option. Ask George Mateariki about his regular Sunday afternoon 'Restaurant at the Beach'.

TUMUNU

Christian missionaries took to eradicating kava drinking among Cook Islanders, so 'Ati-uans developed home-brewed alcohol, and the *tumunu* (bush-beer drinking clubs) were born. Men would retreat into the bush and imbibe 'orange beer', made from fermented oranges and malt extract. *Tumunu* are still held regularly on 'Atiu; the *tumunu* is the hollowed-out stump of a coconut palm traditionally used for brewing beer. *Tumunu* retain some of the old kava-drinking ceremonies, but these days the vessel is likely to be plastic.

Most tours of 'Atiu can also include a visit to a *tumunu*, or ask at your accommodation. It's customary to donate $5 per person to help pay for ingredients for the next brew. Traditionally, it's for men only, but the rules are relaxed for tourists, and males and females are both welcome. Be warned – 'orange beer' can be pretty potent stuff, but it's actually pretty tasty with a subtle effervescence.

The 'Atiu Tumunu Tutaka, when there is a hard-fought competition and taste-off to find the best *tumunu* of 'Atiu, is held occasionally.

Akai Bakery BAKERY $
(Map p230; Mapumai; ⊙10.30am Sun-Fri, 11pm Sat) Fresh-baked bread is ready for the milling crowd by about 10.30am each day. Saturday is the Seventh-Day Adventist Sabbath and the baking doesn't begin until dusk – at 11pm there's that milling crowd again. Stocks usually last just a few minutes.

Super Brown FAST FOOD $
(Map p230; Areora; burgers NZ$7-10; ⊙6.30am-9pm Mon-Sat; 🖥) Drop in for burgers, toasted sandwiches and fish and chips at this friendly spot in Areora village. You can even have a cold beer while you wait. There's a handy BlueSky wi-fi hotspot and data vouchers are sold. Super Brown is also a good bet for takeaway groceries, beer and wine.

Jumbo Bakery BAKERY
(Map p230; Teenui; ⊙5.30-7am Mon-Sat) Early risers and fans of freshly baked doughnuts and buns should head to Jumbo when the doors open to eager locals at 5.30am.

Kura's Kitchen POLYNESIAN $$
(Map p230; ☑33777; Atiu Villas; dinner NZ$30; ⊙7pm Mon-Sat) Kura at Atiu Villas cooks up evening vittles whenever there's a quorum, and sometimes there's an informal Island Night that kicks off in the thatched restaurant-bar area (NZ$30 with food, or NZ$40 including the show). Kura's Kitchen is open to outside guests, but booking before 3pm is essential. Bring along your favourite flag to add to the Pavilion Bar's collection.

Terangi-Nui Café CAFE $$
(Map p230; ☑33101; Areora; dinner NZ$25; ⊙craft shop 9am-2pm, dinner from 6pm) The lovely Parua Tavioni offers a two-course dinner every night, but you'll need to book by noon, either by popping in to her small shop selling local crafts, gifts and *pareu*, or by phone.

🛍 Shopping

Around the villages, you'll occasionally hear the rhythmic percussion of local women beating tapa cloth, and most are happy to explain what they are doing.

Parua Tavioni HOMEWARES
(Map p230; ☑33101; Arerora; ⊙9am-2pm) Working from her village house – a corner residence that doubles as the Terangi-Nui Cafe for dinners – Parua Tavioni crafts intricate *tivaevae* (appliqué work) that makes beautiful bedspreads and other homewares. Some of the hand-sewn work can sell for around NZ$5000.

Vainetini Te Akapuanga CRAFTS
(Map p230; ☑33134, 33269; beside Atiu Town Hall) Local crafts are for sale at this centre next to the Atiu Town Hall. Opening hours are flexible.

ℹ Information

BCI (Bank of the Cook Islands; Map p230; Areora; ⊙9am-noon Mon-Fri) Can provide cash advances on credit cards, but note there is no ATM on the island.

Post & Telecom (Map p230; ⊙8am-4pm Mon-Fri) North of Mapumai village.

Tourist Information Office (Map p230; www.atiutourism.com; Areora; ⊙9am-1pm Mon-Fri) Very helpful local tourism office.

ℹ️ Getting There & Around

TO/FROM THE AIRPORT

Return airport transfers by accommodation owners are NZ$24 per person.

AIR

Air Rarotonga (Map p230; ☑ 33888; www.airraro.com) Air Rarotonga flies between Rarotonga and 'Atiu on Monday, Thursday and Saturday. One-way fares cost from NZ$213. On Monday, and from Wednesday to Saturday, you can fly direct from Aitutaki to 'Atiu from NZ$213. Also available is an Aitutaki/'Atiu combo fare for travel from Rarotonga to Aitutaki to 'Atiu and back to Rarotonga. Check the website for the latest fares.

CAR, MOTORCYCLE & BICYCLE

You'll need transport to get around 'Atiu. The circle-island road is fun for exploring by motorbike, and walking tracks lead down to the dramatic beach. Accommodation places and **Super Brown** (p233) can provide motorbikes (NZ$25 per day), and most also have mountain bikes(NZ$10 to NZ$12). Atiu Villas rents a soft-top Jeep for NZ$55 a day.

MA'UKE

POP 310 / AREA 18.4 SQ KM

Although much flatter than 'Atiu and only slightly larger than Mitiaro, Ma'uke is also characterised by its *makatea* and thick coastal forest. Ma'uke is a sleepy and quietly charming island, traditional in its ways, and circled by a rough coastal track. It's pock-marked with many underground caverns, including Motuanga, a network of limestone chambers said to stretch right out underneath the reef. Known as the Garden Island, Ma'uke is one of the Cooks' main exporters of tropical flowers, which means your goodbye *'ei* is likely to be particularly impressive.

◎ Sights

Like its sister islands, 'Atiu and Mitiaro, Ma'uke's raised-coral *makatea* is riddled with caves, many filled with cool freshwater pools. Interesting caves around the island include **Vai Ou** (Map p235), **Vai Tukume** (Map p235), **Vai Moraro** (Map p235), **Vai Ma'u** (Map p235) and **Vai Moti** (Map p235), reached by old coral pathways across the *makatea*.

★ Vai Tango   CAVE

(Map p235) Vai Tango is the best cave for swimming, a short walk from Ngatiarua village. Schoolkids often head there at week-

ends and after school, and they can show you where to find it.

★ Motuanga   CAVE

(Map p235) Motuanga (the Cave of 100 Rooms) is a complex of tunnels and caverns in the island's southeast that's said to extend all the way under the reef and out to sea. The cave was used as a hiding place from 'Atiuan war parties. Access is via a small crawlspace into a surprisingly compact subterranean atrium complete with an underground pool.

Circle-Island Road   BEACHES

An 18km-long circular road negotiates Ma'uke's secluded coves and beaches, which are among the island's main attractions. One of the nicest is **One'unga** (Map p235), on the east side, and **Teoneroa** (Map p235) and **Tukume** (Map p235) on the island's southwestern side are also delightful. **Anaraura** (Map p235) and Teoneroa have sheltered picnic areas that are popular with the island's pigs. **Kea's Grave** (Map p235) is on the cliffs above Anaiti, where the wife of Paikea (the Whale Rider) is said to have perished while waiting for her husband's return.

Just south of Tiare Cottages is **Kopupooki (Stomach Rock) Beach** (Map p235), with a beautiful fish-filled cave that becomes accessible at low tide. Around 3km south from Tiare Cottages, the fractured rusting hulk of the Te Kou Maru sits groaning on the edge of the reef. The cargo ship floundered in October 2010, but quick work from Ma'uke locals ensured most cargo was ferried by hand across the rugged *makatea* to safety. Walk towards the coast around 50m south of Ma'uke's rubbish tip to find the wreck.

Marae Rangimanuka   HISTORIC SITE

(Map p235) Marae Rangimanuka, the *marae* of Uke, is one of Ma'uke's many *marae* that are now overgrown, but you can still find it with a guide.

Marae Puarakura   HISTORIC SITE

(Map p235) Marae Puarakura is a modern *marae,* still used for ceremonial functions, complete with stone seats for the *ariki, mataiapo* and *rangatira* (subchief).

☞ Tours

Tangata Ateriano   TOUR

(Map p235; ☑ 73009, 35270) Based at Tiare Cottages, 'Ta' Ateriano takes visitors around the island (NZ$15 per person per hour), either in his 4WD or on a scooter tour. Highlights include the island's caves, beaches,

Ma'uke

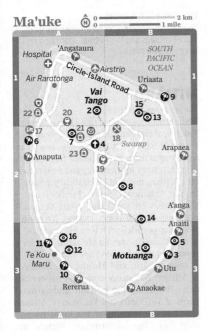

0 — 2 km
0 — 1 mile

Hospital 'Angataura
Circle-Island Road
Air Rarotonga Airstrip
Uriaata
SOUTH
PACIFIC
OCEAN

Vai Tango

Swamp
Arapaea

Anaputa

A'anga
Anaiti

Te Kou
Maru

Motuanga
Utu
Rererua
Anaokae

Ma'uke

◎ Top Sights

1 Motuanga	B3
2 Vai Tango	A1

◎ Sights

3 Anaraura	B3
4 Divided Church	A2
5 Kea's Grave	B3
6 Kopupooki (Stomach Rock) Beach	A2
7 Marae Puarakura	A2
8 Marae Rangimanuka	B2
9 One'unga	B1
10 Teoneroa	A3
11 Tukume	A3
12 Vai Ma'u	A3
13 Vai Morato	B1
14 Vai Moti	B2
15 Vai Ou	B1
16 Vai Tukume	A3

⊕ Activities, Courses & Tours

Tangata Ateriano	(see 17)

⌂ Sleeping

17 Tiare Cottages	A2

⊗ Eating

18 Takeaway Bar	B2

⊖ Drinking & Nightlife

19 Tua's Bar	A2
20 Tura's Bar	A1

⊙ Shopping

21 Ariki Store	A2
Kato's Store	(see 18)
22 Ma'uke Market	A1
23 Virginia's	A2

RAROTONGA & THE COOK ISLANDS MA'UKE

Kea's Grave, the Divided Church, and one of the world's largest banyan trees. Customised tours are also available.

🛏 Sleeping

Tiare Cottages GUESTHOUSE $$
(Map p235; ☎ 35270, 73009; www.maukeholiday.com; bungalows & lodges NZ$75-85, house NZ$150) The garden units are basic, with a main sleeping area and a simple kitchen, toilet and shower tacked on the end. The newer self-contained lodge is more comfortable, with a better-equipped kitchen and an airy and cheerily furnished bedroom. There's also a brilliant house – O'Kiva – with panoramic sea views from its cliff-top perch.

It's self-contained and excellent value, and one of the nicest places to stay on the Cooks' outer islands. Dinner costs NZ$20 per person, and you'll need to provide for your own breakfast and lunch.

Ri's Retreat BUNGALOW $$
(☎ 35181; keta-ttn@oyster.net.ck; bungalows NZ$125) Ri's Retreat has bungalows located near Anaraura Beach, and a few near the airport. The airport bungalows are all sparkling clean and brightly decorated, with large beds, modern bathrooms and verandahs. The seaside bungalows have the nicer location, built on stilts beside the gorgeous and remote Anaraura Beach, and are often enlivened by robust trade winds.

🍴 Eating & Drinking

The best of Ma'uke's grocery stores is **Virginia's** (Map p235) near the Divided Church, and a less-well-stocked back-up option is the **Ariki Store** (Map p235). **Kato's Store** (Map p235) is well stocked and is also the island's only bakery. Kato's also hosts a **takeaway bar** (Map p235; ⊙11am-1pm & 5-9pm Mon-Sat), turning out good burgers, fish and chips and milkshakes. Pull up a chair in the adjacent gazebo and get chatting to the locals.

From 8.30am on Friday morning you can buy fresh produce at **Ma'uke market** (Map p235; ⊙8.30-11am Fri), near the wharf.

Tura's Bar
BAR

(Map p235) Liquid refreshment is available at this humble spot opposite Ma'uke College. Opening nights vary, so ask Ma'uke locals for the latest. Tuesday night is usually darts night and Ma'uke players are renowned across the Cooks.

Tua's Bar
BAR

(Map p235) Another option for a relaxed beer with the locals, Tua's is near the island's rugby field and normally open on a Friday and Saturday night.

ⓘ Information

Hospital (Map p235; ☑ 35664; ⊙ 8am-noon & 1-4pm Mon-Fri) Ma'uke hospital.

Police Station (Map p235; ☑ 35086) Between the Administration Centre and the wharf.

Post Office & Telecom Office (Map p235; ⊙ 8am-noon & 1-4pm Mon-Fri; 🛜) There's a 24-hour Kiaorana cardphone outside and pricey internet access.

ⓘ Getting There & Around

TO/FROM THE AIRPORT
Transfers to/from the airport cost NZ$25.

AIR
Air Rarotonga (Map p235; ☑ Kimiangatau 35888, airport 35120; www.airraro.com) Air Rarotonga operates flights between Rarotonga and Ma'uke on Monday and Friday (one way NZ$318).

DON'T MISS

THE DIVIDED CHURCH

Ma'uke's **Cook Islands Christian Church (CICC)** (Map p235) was built by two villages, Areora and Ngatiarua, in 1882. When the outside was completed, there was disagreement between the villages about how the inside should be decorated so they built a wall down the middle. The wall has since been removed, though the interior is decorated in markedly different styles. Each village has its own entrance, sits at its own side and takes turns singing the hymns. The minister stands astride the dividing line down the middle of the pulpit. Look for the Chilean coins that are set into the wooden altar. Chilean currency was frequently traded throughout the South Pacific in the 19th century.

MOTORCYCLE & BICYCLE
You can hire scooters for NZ$30 per day from Tiare Cottages and Ri's Retreat. Tiare also rents out mountain bikes.

MITIARO

POP 180 / AREA 22.3 SQ KM

The tourism juggernaut that churns through Rarotonga and Aitutaki is a world away from sleepy Mitiaro. Here people live much the same way as their ancestors have for hundreds of years (except for electricity and motorscooters). Mitiaro may not be classically beautiful in the traditional South Pacific sense – the beaches are small and, where the land's not covered with boggy swamp, it's mainly black craggy rock – yet it is an interesting slice of traditional Polynesian life and makes for a rewarding place to spend a few days.

Like on 'Atiu and Ma'uke, the *maketea* of Mitiaro has many deep and mysterious caves, including the brilliant underground pools of Vai Nauri and Vai Marere. Mitiaro also has the remains of the Cook Islands' only fort. The islanders on Mitiaro are great craftspeople and you'll discover that the weaving, woodcarving and traditional outrigger canoes are all beautifully made. Another highlight is staying a few days in a homestay, either in a local's private home or in one of three *kikau* cottages dotted around the tiny island's only settlement.

◉ Sights & Activities

Vai Marere
LANDMARK

(Map p237) The Cook Islands' only sulphur pool is Vai Marere, a 10-minute walk from Mangarei village on the Takaue road. From the main road it's barely visible and easy to miss, but as you duck into the cave it broadens out into a gloomy cavern covered with stalactites. According to locals, the water here has healing properties.

★ Vai Nauri
LANDMARK

(Map p237) A real highlight in this region is the deep sparkling-blue Vai Nauri, Mitiaro's natural swimming pool. Local women used to hold gatherings known as *terevai* at Vai Nauri and at nearby Vai Tamaroa, where they met to swim and sing the bawdy songs of their ancestors. With Mitiaro's declining population, the *terevai* tradition is now largely limited to holiday periods like Christmas and New Year when islanders return to Mitiaro from their homes in Australia and New Zealand.

Mitiaro

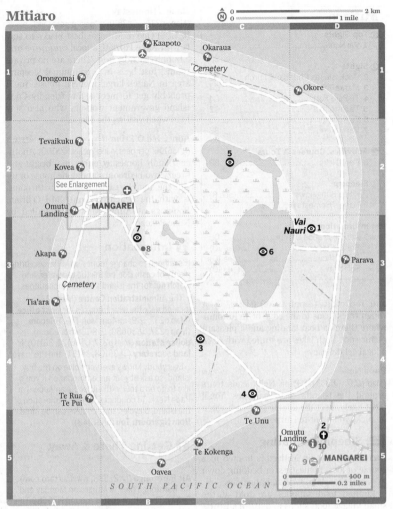

Marae Takero
HISTORIC SITE

(Map p237) The *marae* of Mitiaro are largely consumed by jungle, but you are still able to see the stone seat of the *ariki* and several graves at Marae Takero, located near the abandoned Takaue village.

Te Pare Fort
HISTORIC SITE

(Map p237) The remains of Te Pare Fort, set deep in the *makatea,* are Mitiaro's most impressive ancient ruins. The fort was built as a defence against 'Atiuan raiders. In times of danger, people would assemble in the underground shelter, while above stood a lookout tower from which approaching canoes

could be seen. The only tour guide to Te Pare Fort is Julian Aupuni (☑ 70131, 36180), who has permission to visit from the site's owner, Po Tetava Ariki.

Cook Islands Christian Church
CHURCH

(Map p237) The white-painted CICC is a fine sight, with its blue trim, stained-glass windows and parquet ceiling decorated with black-and-white stars. The Sunday church singing is inspirational.

Te Rotonui & Te Rotoiti
LAKES

Mitiaro is unique in the Cooks for its twin lakes, **Te Rotonui (Big Lake)** (Map p237)

Mitiaro

and **Te Rotoiti (Small Lake)** (Map p237). A rough track leads to the edge of Te Rotonui, where there's a boat landing and a pleasant picnic spot. Both lakes are stuffed with *itiki,* a local eel delicacy.

Papa Neke   TOUR
(Map p237; ☑ 36347) Papa Neke leads tours around the island's historical sites. You'll most likely meet the affable patriarch when he picks you up at the airport.

🛏 Sleeping & Eating

Accommodation on Mitiaro is limited to a couple of local homestays, or bedding down in one of the island's *kikau* bungalows.

Limited food supplies are sold at the small village food shops and at **Pa's Store**, but all accommodation includes meals.

Kikau Bungalows   BUNGALOW $
(Map p237; ☑ 20639; office@cookislandscon nect.co.ck; per person incl meals NZ$100) Made from woven panels of *kikau* leaves, this village accommodation is light and airy and features en suite bathrooms and spacious verandahs. The bungalows are arrayed around the main village of Mangarei, and meals are provided by host Vivian and local families. For reservations and more information, contact Cook Islands Tours (office@cookislandsconnect.co.ck).

Nane's Homestay   HOMESTAY $
(Map p237; ☑ 36106; per person incl meals NZ$100) One of Mitiaro's best places to stay is with Nane Pokoati, a local *mataiapo* and a bubbly, friendly host. There are no private rooms, just beds in a communal sleeping area in Nane's large, modern house. You'll probably get to meet a few friendly Cook Island government workers who also stay here when visiting the island.

Aunty Mii O'Brian   HOMESTAY $
(☑ 36106; per person incl meals NZ$100) Another friendly homestay, either in a bright and breezy two-bedroom standalone house or inside the main house with shared bathrooms, is with the delightful Aunty Mii O'Brian. Bookings at Aunty Mii's are handled by Nane Pokoati.

ℹ Information

It's difficult to change money on Mitiaro so bring plenty of cash. Don't drink the tap water, and watch out for the island's vicious mosquitoes.

The **Administration Centre** (Map p237), located near the wharf, houses the **post office** (Map p237; ☉ 9am-4pm Mon-Fri), **Telecom** (Map p237; ☑ 36680; ☉ 8-10am & 1-3pm), **police station** (Map p237; ☑ 36124, 36110), **island secretary** (☑ 36108, 36157) and the mayor.

Everybody knows everyone else on the tiny island, so ask at your accommodation if you'd like to go on a tour with either Julian Aupuni or Papa Neke. To conduct your own exploration of the island, bicycles and scooters can be hired from **Ngarouru Tou** (☑ 36148).

ℹ Getting There & Away

AIR

Air Rarotonga (☑ 22888; www.airraro.com) Air Rarotonga flies to Mitiaro on Monday and Friday. The return cost is around NZ$580. There are occasionally unscheduled flights linking Ma'uke and Mitiaro, and flights from 'Atiu to Rarotonga also occasionally stop on Mitiaro to pick up passengers.

MANGAIA

POP 573 / AREA 51.8 SQ KM

Next to Rarotonga, Mangaia (pronounced mung-EYE-ah) is the Cooks' most geographically dramatic island. It is the second largest of the islands – it's only slightly smaller than Rarotonga – with a towering circlet of black two-tiered raised-coral *makatea* (three-tiered in the island's north) concealing a huge sunken volcanic caldera that falls away on each side of the 169m Rangimotia ridge, the island's central spine. This sunken interior is swampland planted with taro fields and vegetables.

Mangaia is the Pacific's oldest island – at once craggy and lushly vegetated – and riddled with limestone caves that once served as sacred burial grounds and havens during tribal fighting. There are lakes in the island's centre, dramatic cliffs and many spectacular lookout points. Mangaians have a reputation for haughtiness and superiority, and they're perhaps a little less voluble on first meetings, but they are friendly, gracious and impeccably well mannered.

Mangaia's three main villages are on the coast: Oneroa in the west, Ivirua in the east and Tamarua in the south. Oneroa, the main village, has three parts: Tava'enga to the north and Kaumata to the south on the coast, and Temakatea high above the second *makatea* tier overlooking the ocean. The island's interior is cross-hatched by tracks and dirt roads, which are great for walking, but they can get very muddy after heavy rain. The airstrip is in the north of the island.

History

Mangaian legend tells that the island was not settled by voyagers on canoes, but that the three sons of the Polynesian god Rongo – Rangi, Mokoaro and Akatauira – lifted the island up from the deep, and became the first settlers and ancestors of the Nga Ariki tribe.

James Cook landed in 1777 but found the Mangaians were hostile and quickly moved on. Cannibalism had already been outlawed by Mangaian chief Mautara 100 years before the first missionaries arrived. John Williams was the first missionary to land in 1823 but, like James Cook, he was not welcome. Subsequent Polynesian missionaries had more success – the Mangaians were eventually converted to Christianity by the Rarotongan preacher Maretu.

◉ Sights

Mangaia has many spectacular caves, including Te Rua Rere (Map p240), a huge burial cave that has crystalline stalagmites and stalactites, and some ancient human skeletons. Other caverns worth exploring include the multilevel Tuatini Cave (Map p240) and the long, maze-like Toru a Puru Cave (Map p240).

Some of the finest old CICCs in the Cooks are on Mangaia. Tamarua CICC (Map p240) is especially beautiful, and still has its original roof beams, woodcarved interiors and sennit-rope binding. The interiors of the Oneroa (Map p240) and Ivirua (Map p240) CICCs were once even more impressive, but were sadly mostly removed in the 1980s.

The island also has 24 pre-missionary *marae*, but you'll need a guide to find them since they have been mostly overtaken by bush.

Avarua Landing   HARBOUR
(Map p240) Fishermen return from their morning's exploits around 8am or 9am in tiny outrigger canoes with several huge wahoo and tuna. Hang around for the cleaning and gutting because there are three giant green turtles that come to feed on the entrails and off-cuts that are cast into the water. Whales pass just beyond the reef in the July-to-October season.

★ Rangimotia   VIEWPOINT
At 169m, Rangimotia is the highest point on the island, with stunning coastal views. From the Oneroa side, a dirt road leads to the top.

Te-Toa-A-Morenga Lookout   VIEWPOINT
(Map p240) This stunning viewpoint is just inland from Ivirua.

Maumaukura Lookout   HISTORIC SITE
(Map p240) Has a glorious view inland from the top of the *makatea* cliff.

Te Pa'ata Lookout   VIEWPOINT
(Map p240) Above Oneroa.

☞ Tours

Doreen Tangatakino & Ura Herrmann TOUR
(☑ 34092; Babe's Place) Takes visitors on a full-day island tour for NZ$50, which includes the inland taro plantations and Lake Tiriara. Tours to Tuatini Cave cost NZ$30. Doreen's husband Moekapiti Tangatakino is the school history teacher and runs an informative three-hour tour that takes in the lookouts over the taro farms, lakes, the 1909 wreck site of the coal freighter *Saragossa* (only the anchor remains), the human *umu* (underground pit-oven used to cook human flesh), villages and *marae* for NZ$50.

Maui Peraua   FISHING
(☑ 34388) Maui Peraua leads tours to his family cave of Toru a Puru (NZ$35) and runs popular traditional pole-fishing tours on

RAROTONGA & THE COOK ISLANDS MANGAIA

Mangaia

Mangaia

◎ Sights

1 Avarua Landing	A2
2 Ivirua CICC	C2
3 Maumaukura Lookout	C4
4 Oneroa CICC	D1
5 Tamarua CICC	C4
6 Te Pa'ata Lookout	A3
7 Te Rua Rere Cave	B2
8 Te-Toa-A-Morenga Lookout	C2
9 Toru a Puru Cave	C2
10 Tuatini Cave	B4

⊟ Sleeping

11 Babe's Place	A3
12 Mangaia Lodge	D1
13 Mangaia Villas	A2

⊗ Eating

14 Akeke Trading	A3
Babe's Store	(see 16)
15 Kirikiri Store	C2

⊕ Drinking & Nightlife

Babe's Bar	(see 11)

ⓘ Information

16 Babe's Store	D1
17 Visitor Information Centre	D2

ⓘ Transport

18 Air Rarotonga	D1
19 Moana Rentals	D1

the reef (NZ$25) – you can have your catch cooked on the beach.

🛏 Sleeping

Babe's Place MOTEL $
(Map p240; ☏ 34092; mangaia@babesplace.
co.ck; Oneroa; s/d incl meals NZ$75/120) With all

meals included, a terrific location, and four large comfortable motel-style rooms, Babe's Place is good value for money. Babe is the island's entrepreneur, owning the island's main store, liveliest bar and this motel. The units have mosquito nets, colourful bedspreads and small patio areas.

Guests have 24-hour use of the main kitchen – with a fridge, tea and coffee – and the lounge area with a TV. Lively Babe's Bar, next door, parties on well into the night on Friday and Saturday.

Mangaia Lodge LODGE **$**
(Map p240; ☑34324; Oneroa; s/d NZ$40/70) This tumbledown colonial-style lodge has three plain bedrooms and a sunny, enclosed terrace overlooking the gardens. The accommodation is basic but the old building has a rustic charm and million-dollar views over the ocean. The separate shared toilet and shower block is pretty rustic. Meals are included.

★Mangaia Villas VILLA **$$$**
(Map p240; ☑29882; www.mangaiavillas.com; Oneroa; villas NZ$300) These six one-bedroom villas are hands-down the Cook Islands' finest accommodation beyond Rarotonga and Aitutaki. Spacious verandahs showcase ocean views, whale watching and tropical sunsets, and the villas are constructed of local Mangaia limestone with thatched roofs and shimmering hardwood floors. Modern touches include designer kitchens and bathrooms, and rates include a tropical breakfast. Dinner can be also be arranged.

🍴 Eating & Drinking

There's no eating out on Mangaia, but meals are usually provided with accommodation. A weekly Friday-morning **market** kicks off at 8am beside the Oneroa post office.

Babe's Store SUPERMARKET **$**
(Map p240; Tava'enga; ☺7am-9pm Mon-Sat) The best-stocked shop.

Kirikiri Store SUPERMARKET **$**
(Map p240; ☺7am-9pm Mon-Sat) North of Ivirua.

Akeke Trading SUPERMARKET **$**
(Map p240; ☺7am-9pm Mon-Sat) Inland from Oneroa.

Babe's Bar BAR
(Map p240; Oneroa; ☺5pm-midnight Fri-Sat) Opens Friday and Saturday nights.

🛍 Shopping

Basketwork, tie-dyed *pareu*, stone pounders and *pupu ei* are Mangaia's most famous handicrafts.

Mangaia Airport Shop ARTS, CRAFTS
(☺open when flights arrive and depart) This tiny shop opens for incoming flights. It also doubles as a booking office for tours and activities.

ℹ Information

Babe's Store (Map p240; Oneroa; ☺8am-7pm) The island's ANZ agent.

Post & Telecom (internet access per 30min NZ$5; ☺8am-4pm Mon-Fri) On the hill above Oneroa.

Visitor Information Centre (Map p240; ☑34289; ☺8am-4pm) In the Administration Centre at the bottom of the Temakatea road cutting.

ℹ Getting There & Around

AIR

Air Rarotonga (Map p240; ☑34888; www.airraro.com) Air Rarotonga flies between Rarotonga and Mangaia two to three times a week for around NZ$550 return.

MOTORCYCLE

Moana Rentals (Map p240; ☑34307) You'll need a motorbike to get around Mangaia. There are some very rough sections of road in the island's south, and the cross-island roads are muddy and perilous after rains. Moana Rentals hires out motorcycles for NZ$25 per day.

NORTHERN GROUP

These sparsely populated tropical idylls are breathtaking in their beauty and remoteness. This sublime isolation inspired writers Tom Neale and Robert Dean Frisbie, who both lived as castaways on these far-flung coral atolls. Only the hardiest and most intrepid travellers ever make it to the Northern Group. Flights are few and mind-bogglingly expensive but, if you can surmount the financial and logistical challenges, the rewards are sublime.

ℹ️ Getting There & Away

AIR

Air Rarotonga (☎ 22888; www.airraro.com) Flights from Rarotonga to Manihiki once every two weeks, and to Pukapuka occasionally. Flights take about 3½ hours, and the return fare is a staggering NZ$3100. Penrhyn is very occasionally serviced for a return fare of around NZ$4000. Bad weather, limited fuel supplies and too few bookings can cause the flights to be cancelled at short notice.

BOAT

The only other regular transport to the Northern Group islands is on the Taio Shipping cargo ship. To reach Rakahanga, you must fly to Manihiki and then take a boat.

YACHT

Suwarrow is accessible only by private yacht.

Manihiki

POP 243 / AREA 5.4 SQ KM

Manihiki, 1046km from Rarotonga, is where most of the Cooks' black pearls are farmed. It has a magnificent lagoon – one of the South Pacific's finest – and is a highlight of the Northern Group. Nearly 40 tiny *motu* encircle the enclosed lagoon, which is 4km wide at its broadest point. The island is the summit of a 4000m underwater mountain. The US ship *Good Hope* made the first European discovery in 1822, and Manihiki was a US territory until it was ceded in 1980.

Tauhunu is the main village, and the airstrip is at Tukao on this island's northern point. Black pearls are the island's economic mainstay and they're harvested from September to December. The lung-busting abilities of the island's pearl divers are legendary – they can dive to great depths and stay submerged for minutes at a time.

Beachside retreat **Manihiki Lagoon Villas** (☎ 43123; www.manihikilagoonvillas.co.ck; bungalow s/d incl meals NZ$110/200, guesthouse incl meals NZ$80) offers bungalows and a guesthouse built on the water's edge of the lagoon. The accommodation is simple but the location is deluxe.

Rakahanga

POP 77 / AREA 4.1 SQ KM

With two major islands and many smaller *motu* dotted in a turquoise lagoon, Rakahanga is another idyllic island. The lagoon here is unsuitable for pearl farming and the few families who live here are concentrated in Nivano village in the southwestern corner. The only export is copra, although the island is still renowned for its fine *rito* (coconut-fibre) hats, which are mostly sold on Rarotonga.

Penrhyn

POP 203 / AREA 9.8 SQ KM

Penrhyn is the northernmost of the Cook Islands and boasts one of the largest lagoons in the country – so huge that the twin islands on opposite sides of the lagoon are barely visible from each other. Penrhyn has three deepwater passages that make excellent harbours, a fact that attracted whalers and traders in the 19th century. Peruvian blackbirders (slave traders) also visited the island in the 1860s. Penrhyn is another centre for black-pearl production and some interesting shell jewellery is produced on the island. The remains of a crashed B17 bomber are reminders of the WWII US servicemen who were stationed here and built the airstrip.

Soa's Guesthouse (☎ 42181; Omoka village; r NZ$100) is run by Soa Tini, a local fisherman and pearl farmer, who has a three-bedroom family house in the centre of Omoka village.

Pukapuka

POP 453 / AREA 5.1 SQ KM

Well known for both its sensuous dancers and beautiful girls, remote Pukapuka is in many ways closer to Samoa than to the rest of the Cook Islands. Pukapuka's most famous resident was the American travel writer Robert Dean Frisbie, who lived here in the 1920s and wrote several evocative accounts of his life on the islands. Pukapuka sustained severe damage during the 2005 cyclones. In 2015 Pukapuka achieved 100% electricty sustainabilty through a solar energy network, and it is hoped this initiative will encourage emigre Pukapukans to resettle on their home island.

Contact the **island secretary** (☎ 41712) or the **island council** (☎ 41034) to arrange homestay accommodation.

Suwarrow

POP 0 / AREA 0.4 SQ KM

The Cook Islands' only national park is a nature-lover's paradise, home to colonies of seabirds and some of the country's richest marine life. Two atoll managers live here six months of the year to oversee the park. During cyclone season they head back to Rarotonga. Suwarrow is best known as the home of Tom Neale, who lived here for three long stints between 1952 and his death in 1977. You can relive his adventures in his classic book *An Island to Oneself*, and visit his old house on Anchorage Island – one room is still furnished just as it was when he lived here. The only way you're likely to be able to visit Suwarrow is by private yacht, or on the annual expedition on the SRV *Discovery*.

UNDERSTAND RAROTONGA & THE COOK ISLANDS

Rarotonga & the Cook Islands Today

Imbued with the cosmopolitan influence of Auckland, Rarotonga has developed as one of the Pacific's most versatile travel destinations. To the north, Aitutaki is morphing into a more upmarket option, while the nation's other outer islands are increasing the emphasis on authentic and eco-aware traveller experiences. Stay in a traditional *kikau* homestay on Mitiaro, discover 'Atiu's fascinating birdlife, or go underground in the storied burial caves on Mangaia. All around the Cook Islands, the welcome for visitors continues to be friendly and gregarious, so remember to pack a good sense of humour.

History

Cook Islanders are Maori people closely related to indigenous New Zealanders and French Polynesians. The Maori had no written history, but historians believe that Polynesian migrations from the Society Islands in French Polynesia to the Cooks began around the 5th century AD. Oral histories speak of around 1400 years of Polynesian activity on Rarotonga. A *marae* (religious meeting ground) on tiny Motutapu in Rarotonga's Muri Lagoon is estimated to be around 1500 years old. In the 14th century great ocean-going *vaka* (canoes) departed from Rarotonga for Aotearoa (New Zealand), and the settlers were ancestors of present-day New Zealand Maori.

During his disastrous second voyage from Spanish-occupied Peru, Don Alvaro de Mendaña y Neyra came upon Pukapuka on 20 August 1595 – he would die just months later in the Solomon Islands. Eleven years later, Mendaña's chief pilot Pedro Fernández de Quirós led another Pacific expedition, stopping at Rakahanga. James Cook explored the Cooks in 1773 and 1779. Only ever setting foot on Palmerston and never finding Rarotonga, Cook named the group the Hervey Islands in honour of a British Lord of the Admiralty. In his 1835 *Atlas de l'Océan Pacifique*, Russian explorer and cartographer Admiral Adam Johann von Krusenstern renamed them in honour of Captain Cook.

Reverend John Williams of the London Missionary Society (LMS) arrived on Aitutaki in 1821. In 1823 Papeiha, a convert from Ra'iatea in the Societies, moved to Rarotonga and set about converting the islands to Christianity. Though many *marae* were destroyed and sacred artefacts were carted off to British museums, much of the island's culture survived, including the traditional titles of *ariki* (chief) and *mataiapo* (subchief), the land-inheritance system and the indigenous language. The missionaries imposed a catalogue of strict rules and doctrines (known as the Blue Laws) and brought deadly diseases such as whooping cough, measles, smallpox and influenza, leading to a long-term decline in population numbers.

The Cook Islands became a British protectorate in 1888, in response to fears of French colonisation. In 1901 the islands were annexed to New Zealand, and the Southern and Northern Groups together became known as the Cook Islands.

During WWII the US built airstrips on Penrhyn and Aitutaki, but the Cooks escaped the war largely unscathed, unlike many of their South Pacific neighbours. In 1965 the Cook Islands became internally self-governing in free association with New Zealand.

Since self-governance was achieved, successive Cook Islands governments have struggled to maintain fiscal balance. In the early 1990s a series of bad investments – including the failed Sheraton resort on Rarotonga's south coast – left the country almost

NZ$250 million in debt, representing 113% of national GDP. An economic stabilisation plan in 1996 slashed public spending and the public sector workforce. Many Cook Islanders voted with their feet and left for greater opportunities in New Zealand and Australia.

Population decline and the country's national debt remain major issues. Growth in tourism is an ongoing opportunity, especially from New Zealand and Australia, and the country experienced strong visitor numbers in 2015 for the Cook Islands' celebrations for 50 years of independence.

The Culture

The National Psyche

Cook Islanders carry New Zealand passports, which allows them to live and work in New Zealand and, by extension (courtesy of the Special Category Visa), to live and work in Australia. This means many Cook Islanders are well travelled, worldly people. Rarotonga is a cosmopolitan place, yet beneath this Westernised veneer many Maori traditions remain, including traditional titles, family structure and the system of land inheritance. All native islanders are part of a family clan connected to the ancient system of *ariki*. Many still refer to themselves as from their 'home island' – Mangaian or Aitutakian.

But there is still a continuing exodus from the outer islands to Rarotonga, New Zealand and Australia, and some claim that Cook Islands' nationhood is undermined by that Kiwi passport – when the going gets tough the islanders move away to Auckland or Melbourne. Tourism is the Cooks' only major industry, but few tourists go beyond Rarotonga and Aitutaki. The outer islands have a fraction of the populations they had a few decades ago.

Politics, sport, dance, music, land and inheritance remain important, as do community, family and traditional values. Christianity is taken very seriously.

Lifestyle

Islanders from Rarotonga are thoroughly First World in their lifestyles, with modern houses, regular jobs and reasonable salaries. Elsewhere in the Cooks, people live a more traditional lifestyle by fishing, growing crops and practising traditional arts and crafts. Family and the church are the two most influential elements in most islanders'

lives, but people remain relaxed and informal about most aspects of day-to-day living. Like elsewhere in the Pacific, Cook Islanders are especially relaxed about timekeeping – things will happen when they do.

Population

The resident population of the Cook Islands is around 19,500, but around 80% of Cook Islanders live overseas. More than 50,000 Cook Islanders live in New Zealand, half that number in Australia, and several thousand more in French Polynesia, the Americas, Europe and Asia. Of those who do live in their country of origin, more than 90% live in the Southern Group, with 60% living on Rarotonga.

Like many Pacific islands, the Cooks are struggling with a long-term population drain, as islanders move overseas in search of higher wages. More than 90% of the population is Polynesian, though the people of some of the Northern Group islands are more closely related to Samoans than to other Cook Islanders.

Arts

Dance & Music

Cook Islanders love to dance and they're reputed to be the best dancers in Polynesia. Don't be surprised if you're invited to join them at an Island Night. Traditional dance forms include the *karakia* (prayer dance), *pe'e ura pa'u* (drum-beat dance), *ate* (choral song) and *kaparima* (action song). Men stamp, gesture and knock their knees together, while women shake and gyrate their hips in an unmistakeably suggestive manner.

The islanders are also great singers and musicians. The multi-part harmony singing at a Cook Islands' church service is truly beautiful, but pop music is popular too. Polynesian string bands, featuring guitars and ukuleles, often perform at local restaurants and hotels.

Arts & Crafts

Traditional woodcarving and woven handicrafts (pandanus mats, baskets, purses and fans) are still popular in the Cooks. You'll see women going to church wearing finely woven *rito* (coconut-fibre) hats, mainly made on the Northern Group islands.

Ceremonial adzes, stone taro pounders and *pupu ei* (snail-shell necklaces) are produced on Mangaia, and the best place to see traditional *tivaevae* (appliqué work, used for bedspreads, cushion covers and home decoration) is at the Atiu Fibre Arts Studio on 'Atiu. Black pearls are grown in the Northern Group and are an important export. *'Ei* (floral necklaces) and *'ei katu* (tiaras) are customarily given to friends and honoured guests. You're bound to receive a few, especially on the outer islands.

Traditional *tata'u* (tattooing) is also making a resurgence, with intricate designs often showcasing an individual's genealogy. Ask at Avarua's bookshops for *Patterns of the Past: Tattoo Revival in the Cook Islands* by Therese Mangos and John Utanga.

Literature

Purchase these in Avarua's bookshops.

An Island to Oneself by Tom Neale is the classic desert-island read, written by a New Zealander who lived as a virtual hermit on Suwarrow during the 1950s and 1960s.

Robert Dean Frisbie ran a trading outpost on Pukapuka in the 1920s and wrote two evocative memoirs, *The Book of Pukapuka* and *The Island of Desire*.

Sir Tom Davis (Pa Tuterangi Ariki) was – among many things, including medical doctor and NASA scientist – the Cook Islands' prime minister for most of the 1980s (he died in 2007). His autobiography is called *Island Boy*.

If you're after local legends, pick up *Cook Islands Legends* and *The Ghost at Tokatarava and Other Stories from the Cook Islands*, both by notable Cook Islands' author Jon Tikivanotau Jonassen. Pukapukan poet Kauraka Kauraka published several books of poems including *Ta 'Akatauira: My Morning Star*.

Akono'anga Maori: Cooks Islands Culture, edited by Ron and Marjorie Tua'inekore Crocombe, is an excellent book that looks at culture manifested in traditional Polynesian tattooing, poetry, art, sport and governance. *Patterns of the Past: Tattoo Revival in the Cook Islands* by Therese Mangos and John Utanga is a beautifully illustrated title on *tata'u* in the Cook Islands.

Guide to Cook Islands Birds by DT Holyoak is a useful guide to the islands' native birds, with colour photos and tips for identification.

Environment

The Cook Islands' small land mass (just 241 sq km) is scattered over 2 million sq km of ocean, midway between American Samoa and Tahiti.

The 15 islands are divided into Northern and Southern Groups. Most of the Southern Group are younger volcanic islands, although Mangaia is the Pacific's oldest island. The Northern Group are 'low islands', coral atolls with outer reefs encircling lagoons, that have formed on top of ancient sunken volcanoes. 'Atiu, Ma'uke, Mitiaro and Mangaia are 'raised islands' characterised by *makatea* – rocky coastal areas formed by uplifted coral reefs.

Waste management is a major issue in the Cook Islands. Glass, plastic and aluminium are collected for recycling, but there's still a huge surplus of rubbish. Water supply is also a major concern.

Rising sea levels associated with global warming are a huge threat to the Cooks. Many of the islands of the Northern Group are low lying and could be uninhabitable within the next 100 years. Climate scientists predict that severe cyclones are likely to become much more common.

In 2011, the Cook Islands' government announced plans to become the Pacific's 'greenest' destination, and was targeting 100% reliance on solar and wind-generated energy by 2020. In 2015 a new solar electricity farm funded by the New Zealand government was installed on Rarotonga for the Cooks' 50th anniversary of independence, and less-populated islands in the Northern Group achieved 100% energy sustainability.

Wildlife

Rarotonga's mountainous centre is covered with a dense jungle of ferns, creepers and towering trees, providing habitat for the island's rich birdlife. Coconut palms and spectacular tropical flowers grow almost everywhere in the Cook Islands, though the once-common pandanus trees are now rare on Rarotonga and 'Atiu.

The only native mammal is the Pacific fruit bat (flying fox), found on Mangaia and Rarotonga. Pigs, chickens and goats were introduced by the first Polynesian settlers, along with rats, which devastated the islands' endemic wildlife, especially native birds. The *kakerori* (Rarotongan flycatcher) was almost wiped out, but is now recovering thanks to the establishment of the Takitumu

Conservation Area on Rarotonga. Other native birds include the cave-dwelling *kopeka* ('Atiu swiftlet) on 'Atiu, the *tanga'eo* (Mangaian kingfisher) and the *kukupa* (Cook Islands fruit dove).

SURVIVAL GUIDE

ⓘ Directory A–Z

ACCOMMODATION

Officially, visitors are required to have booked accommodation before arriving in the Cook Islands, although you can usually arrange a hotel when you arrive at the airport. However, many places to stay on Rarotonga are booked up in advance, so it pays to plan ahead.

Rarotonga's accommodation includes hostels, motel-style units, self-contained bungalows and expensive top-end resorts. All the major Southern Group islands have organised accommodation. Even for couples, renting a house can be a good way to cut costs.

Manihiki and Penrhyn are the only Northern Group islands with simple accommodation.

For a dorm bed, budget travellers can expect to pay around NZ$30.

ACTIVITIES

The Cook Islands are perfect for relaxation, but there's plenty of activities to keep energetic travellers busy. Rarotonga is an excellent place for hiking, and Aitutaki's backcountry roads and deserted beaches are good for exploring. 'Atiu, Ma'uke, Mitiaro and Mangaia have many trails winding through the *makatea*. History enthusiasts will enjoy visiting the historic *marae* on most of the islands. Many of these traditional religious meeting grounds are still used today for formal ceremonies, such as the investiture of a new *ariki* or *mataiapo*.

Water Sports

The sheltered lagoons and beaches on Rarotonga and Aitutaki are great for swimming and snorkelling. Diving is also excellent, with good visibility and lots of marine life, from sea turtles and tropical fish to reef sharks and eagle rays. You can hire snorkelling gear on Aitutaki and Rarotonga, as well as kayaks, sailboards and other water-sports equipment.

Raro has just a handful of resident surfers, but there are serious waves outside Rarotonga's perimeter reef and a budding community of bodyboard riders.

Kite surfing, paddle-boarding and small-boat sailing are popular in Rarotonga's Muri Lagoon. Glass-bottomed boats also operate from Muri Beach, and there are several lagoon-cruise

operators in Aitutaki. Deep-sea fishing boats can be chartered on Rarotonga and Aitutaki, and bonefishing on Aitutaki lagoon is growing in popularity. From July to October, whale-watching trips are available on Rarotonga.

Caving

The Cook Islands has some extraordinary caves to explore including Anatakitaki and Rima Rau on 'Atiu, Motuanga on Ma'uke, Vai Nauri on Mitiaro, and Te Rua Rere on Mangaia.

CHILDREN

Travelling with kids presents no special problems in the Cook Islands, although many smaller hotels and bungalows don't accept children aged under 12 – ask about the policy before booking.

CUSTOMS

The following restrictions apply: 2L of spirits or wine or 4.5L of beer, plus 200 cigarettes or 50 cigars or 250g of tobacco. Quarantine laws are strictly enforced, and plants, animals or any related products are prohibited. Firearms, weapons and drugs are also prohibited.

DANGERS & ANNOYANCES

Swimming is very safe in the sheltered lagoons but be wary around reef passages, where currents are especially strong. Rarotonga's main passages are at Avana Harbour, Avaavaroa, Papua and Rutaki. They exist on other islands as well, often opposite streams.

Mosquitoes can be a real nuisance in the Cooks, particularly during the rainy season (around mid-December to mid-April). Use repellent; mosquito coils are available everywhere.

ELECTRICITY

240V AC, 50Hz, using Australian-style three-blade plugs. Power is available 24 hours throughout the Southern Group.

EMBASSIES & CONSULATES

Department of Foreign Affairs & Immigration (Map p204; ☑ 29347; www.mfai.gov.ck) Citizens from countries other than New Zealand seeking consular advice should talk to the Secretary of the Department of Foreign Affairs & Immigration on the 3rd floor of the Trustnet building in Avarua.

New Zealand High Commission (Map p204; ☑ 55201, 22201; nzhcraro@oyster.net.ck; PO Box 21, Avarua) New Zealand High Commission is located above the Philatelic Bureau in Avarua. New Zealand the only country with diplomatic representation in the Cook Islands.

EMERGENCY

Police ☑ 999
Ambulance ☑ 998

FESTIVALS & EVENTS

Dancer of the Year (April) Dance displays are held throughout April, culminating in the Dancer of the Year competition.

Gospel Day (July) The arrival of the gospel to the Cook Islands is celebrated with *nuku* (religious plays), held on 20 July on 'Atiu, 21 July on Mitiaro, 25 July on Rarotonga, and elsewhere on 26 October.

Constitution Celebration (Te Maire Nui; August) Celebrating the 1965 declaration of independence, this is the Cook Islands' major annual festival.

Tiare (Floral) Festival Week (August) Celebrated with floral-float parades and the Miss Tiare beauty pageant.

Vaka Eiva (November) This week-long canoe festival celebrates the great Maori migration from Rarotonga to New Zealand. There are many race events and celebrations of Cooks culture.

INTERNET ACCESS

BlueSky Teleshops in Avarua, Muri Beach and on Aitutaki offer internet access and sell prepaid wi-fi access which can be used at hotspots around the main islands and also on 'Atiu. Convenience stores also sell this pre-paid wi-fi access in denominations of NZ$10 (150MB), NZ$25 (500MB), and NZ$50 (1.25GB). Another option is to buy a local Kokanet 3G SIM card (NZ$25) for your smartphone or tablet, and purchase data for 20 cents per MB up to 1GB for NZ$50. Note that at the time of writing, 3G service was limited to Rarotonga. Most Telecom offices on the outer islands have small cyberbooths, though the connections are slow and expensive.

MONEY

New Zealand dollars are used in the Cook Islands. You'll probably get a few Cook Islands coins in change (in denominations of 5c, 10c, 20c, 50c, $1, $2 and $5). The Cook Islands prints a $3 note that's quite collectable and available at the Philatelic Bureau in Avarua. Note that Cook Islands currency cannot be exchanged anywhere in the world.

There are limited ATMs and banks on Rarotonga and Aitutaki, and credit cards are widely accepted on the nation's main two islands. Credit cards are accepted at the larger hotels on Aitutaki and at some places on 'Atiu, but for other islands cash is essential.

A 15% VAT (value-added tax) is included in the price of most goods and services. All prices quoted include VAT. A departure tax when leaving the Cook Islands is already incorporated into international air tickets.

Tipping is not customary in the Cook Islands, but it's not frowned upon for exceptional service. Haggling over prices is considered rude.

OPENING HOURS

Sunday is largely reserved for churchgoing and rest, although a few cafes and restaurants around Rarotonga and Aitutaki open in the afternoon.

Banks 9am to 3pm on weekdays. Only Avarua's Westpac is open on Saturday morning.

Businesses and shops 9am to 4pm Monday to Friday, most shops open until noon on Saturday.

Small grocery stores 6am or 7am until 8pm or 9pm.

PRACTICALITIES

Newspapers Rarotonga's *Cook Islands News* is published daily except Sunday, and the *Cook Islands Herald* comes out on Wednesday. Both feature local and international news.

Radio Radio Cook Islands (630 kHz AM; www.radio.co.ck) reaches most islands and broadcasts local programs, Radio New Zealand news and Radio Australia's world news. The smaller KC-FM (103.8 MHz FM) station can be received only on Rarotonga.

TV Cook Islands Television (CITV) screens across Rarotonga; international cable channels are available at some hotels. On outer islands, Sky Fiji is available and programming is usually controlled by each island's mayor. If you're engrossed in CNN or a wildlife documentary, there's every chance it will be switched mid-program to the rugby. Only in the Pacific! Aitutaki has a small station that broadcasts intermittently on local issues.

DVDs Can be hired all over Rarotonga and many accommodation places can provide DVD players.

Weights & Measures Metric system.

Language Cook Islands Maori – closely related to the Maori language of New Zealand – is the local language, but virtually everyone also speaks English.

POST

Poste-restante mail is held for 30 days at post offices on most islands. To collect mail at the post office in Avarua it should be addressed to you c/o Poste Restante, Avarua, Rarotonga, Cook Islands.

PUBLIC HOLIDAYS

New Year's Day 1 January
Good Friday & Easter Monday March/April
Anzac Day 25 April
Queen's Birthday First Monday in June
Gospel Day (Rarotonga only) 25 July
Constitution/Flag-Raising Day 4 August
Gospel Day (Cook Islands) 26 October
Christmas Day 25 December
Boxing Day 26 December

TELEPHONE

All the islands are connected to the country's modern telephone system. Each island has a BlueSky Telecom office, usually incorporating a payphone and an internet booth. Most of these offices also offer a pre-paid wi-fi service.

The country code for the Cook Islands is ✆ 682, and there are no local area codes. Dial ✆ 00 for direct international calls and ✆ 017 for international directory service. The local directory operator is ✆ 010. You can make collect calls from any phone by dialling ✆ 015.

For mobile phones, a GSM network is available through BlueSky, and international roaming and local SIM cards available. 3G data services are available on Rarotonga only.

TIME

The Cook Islands are east of the International Date Line, 10 hours behind Greenwich Mean Time (GMT). The country has no daylight-saving time. When it's noon in the Cooks it's 10pm in London, noon in Tahiti and Hawai'i, 2pm in LA, 10am the next day in Fiji and New Zealand, and 8am the next day in Sydney.

TOURIST INFORMATION

Aitutaki Tourism (www.cookislands.travel/aitutaki) Excellent for accommodation and activities on Aitutaki.

Bluesky Cook Islands (www.telecom.co.ck) Searchable telephone directories.

Cook Islands Government Online (www.cook-islands.gov.ck) Government news and press releases.

Cook Islands Herald (www.ciherald.co.ck) Online edition of the popular weekly newspaper.

Cook Islands News (www.cookislandsnews.com) Online edition of the daily Cook Islands newspaper.

Cook Islands Website (www.ck) Local business details including tourist operations.

Enjoy Cook Islands (www.enjoycookislands.com) Website for the *Cook Islands Sun* newspaper, including lots of traveller-friendly information.

Escape (www.escapemagazine.travel) Website for *Escape*, an excellent travel and lifestyle magazine covering the Cook Islands.

Lonely Planet (www.lonelyplanet.com/rarotonga-and-the-cook-islands) Author recommendations, traveller reviews and insider tips.

Tourism Cook Islands (www.cookislands.travel) Central information site for the main tourist office.

www.cookislands.org.uk Hosted out of the UK, this is the only noncommercial website covering the Cooks.

www.jasons.com New Zealand-based portal for Pacific travel including accommodation bookings.

❶ Getting There & Away

AIR

Rarotonga has international flights to Auckland, Sydney, Los Angeles and Tahiti. Low-season travel to the Cooks is from mid-April to late August, and the high season runs from December to February. There's heavy demand from New Zealand to the Cooks in December, and in the other direction in January. Demand for flights from New Zealand and Australia is also strong during those countries' respective school holiday periods.

Air New Zealand (www.airnewzealand.com) Regular flights between Auckland and Rarotonga (return fares around NZ$850). Weekly direct flights between Sydney and Rarotonga on a Saturday (return fares from around A$800). Weekly direct flights between Rarotonga and Los Angeles (return fares from around US$1300).

Virgin Australia (www.virginaustralia.com) Regular flights between Auckland and Rarotonga (return fares around NZ$850).

Air Tahiti (www.airtahiti.aero) Direct codeshare flights on Thursday with Air Rarotonga linking Tahiti with Rarotonga (return fares from around NZ$950).

SEA

Rarotonga is a favourite port of call for South Pacific cruise ships but they don't take on passengers, typically arriving in the morning and departing in the afternoon after quick island tours and souvenir shopping.

The Cooks are popular with yachties except during the cyclone season (November to March). Once you arrive at Rarotonga, fly your Q flag and visit the **Harbour Master** (Map p204; ✆ 28814; Avatiu Harbour, Rarotonga). There are other official ports of entry at Aitutaki, Penrhyn and Pukapuka, which have good anchorages.

Virtually uninhabited, Suwarrow Atoll is a trophy destination for cruising yachties, but isn't an official entry.

There's a slim chance of catching a crewing berth on a yacht from the Cook Islands to Tonga, Samoa, Fiji, French Polynesia or New Zealand. You can ask at Rarotonga's **Ports Authority** (Map p204; Avatiu Harbour), where yachties leave messages if they are looking for crew.

❶ Getting Around

Unless you're sailing your own yacht, travel between the Cook Islands is limited to slow cargo ships and Air Rarotonga flights. Flights to the Northern Group islands are expensive, and only Manihiki, Penrhyn and Pukapuka have airstrips.

AIR

Air Rarotonga (📞 22888; www.airraro.com), the only domestic airline in the Cook Islands, has several daily flights to Aitutaki, and several weekly flights between Rarotonga and the rest of the Southern Group. Other than the high-traffic Rarotonga–Aitutaki route, Air Rarotonga sometimes cancels or moves flights to consolidate passengers if there are too many empty seats.

Flights to the Northern Group are more erratic – there's a scheduled flight to Manihiki every second Tuesday, and flights to Penrhyn operate only when there's sufficient demand.

The baggage allowance for the Southern Group is 16kg, for the Northern Group it's 10kg. Passengers are allowed one piece of hand luggage not exceeding 3kg.

BOAT

Shipping schedules are notoriously unpredictable – weather, breakdowns and unexpected route changes can all put a kink in your travel plans. Ships stop off at each island for just a few hours, and only Rarotonga and Penrhyn have decent harbours. At all the other islands you go ashore by lighter or barge.

Taio Shipping (📞 24905; taio@oyster.net. ck; Avatiu Wharf) is the only interisland shipping company and its vessels are far from luxury cruise liners: there's limited cabin space and some ships have no cabins at all. Showers and toilets are available to all passengers. Return trips to the islands of the Southern Group cost NZ$250. To the Northern Group, return fares are NZ$1200 in a cabin and NZ$450 for deck space. Ships only run one or two times per month.

LOCAL TRANSPORT

All the islands are good for cycling. Rarotonga has a regular circle-island bus service, taxis, and bicycles, motorcycles and cars for hire. Aitutaki has a taxi service, and bicycles, motorcycles and cars for hire. 'Atiu has a taxi service, rental motorcycles and a couple of Jeeps. You can rent scooters and bicycles on Ma'uke, Mitiaro and Mangaia.

Hitchhiking is legal, though of course never entirely safe, and if you're walking along an empty stretch of road someone will stop and offer you a lift before too long.

TOURS

Circle-island tours on Rarotonga offer a good introduction to the island's history, geography and traditional culture. Guided tours are also offered on Aitutaki, 'Atiu, Ma'uke and Mangaia.

Rarotongan travel agencies can organise single-island or multi-island package tours. Day trips from Rarotonga to Aitutaki are available.

Samoa

☎ 685 / POP 190,372

Best Places to Stay

➡ Seabreeze Resort (p271)

➡ Namu'a Island Beach Fale (p270)

➡ Lupe Sina Treesort (p272)

➡ Dave Parker's Eco Lodge (p267)

➡ Joelan Beach Fales (p279)

Best Places to Eat

➡ Bistro Tatau (p264)

➡ Palusami (p263)

➡ Amoa Restaurant (p279)

➡ Sunday lunch (p281)

➡ Taefu T Matafeo Store (p279)

Why Go?

Serene but spirited, wild yet well-manicured, hushed but birthed by volcanic explosions; stunning Samoa is a paradisaical paradox. Despite its intense natural beauty – all iridescent seas, jade jungles and crystal waterfalls – this is a humble place, devoid of mega-resorts and flashy attractions, but with welcomes as warm as the island sun.

Geographically and culturally, this small nation is considered the heart of Polynesia. Though the missionaries of the 1800s were enormously influential, the country has nevertheless clung to *Fa'a Samoa* (the Samoan Way), making it one of the most authentic and traditional of all Pacific societies: in some parts of the islands you're more likely to see someone juggling fire than a house with walls.

Despite its isolation, Samoa offers accessible adventures. From the relative ruckus of Apia to the soul-stirring silence of Savai'i, you'll find a paradise that is safe, sweet and easy to get around.

When to Go

Apia

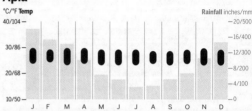

Dec–Jan
Peak holiday period when Samoans living abroad visit home.

May–Oct
Dry season and festival time.

Nov–Apr
Steamy weather and cyclone season.

UPOLU

POP 143,418 / AREA 1125 SQ KM

Enchanting Upolu may be small in size, but it's huge on options. Beach-bumming or bushwalking? Resort cocktails or billiard-hall beers? Diving or do-nothing? Whatever floats your holiday boat, odds are you'll find it here.

Home to the international airport, the capital city and the bulk of the country's population, Upolu is where nearly all travellers begin their Samoan sojourn. The majority get their first glimpse of local life on the 35km drive from the airport to Apia, where a procession of tidy villages, incongruously large churches and rickety fruit stalls line perhaps the slowest highway in the world (the speed limit is 40km/h).

Most visitors devote themselves to the dazzling strips of sand skirting Upolu's southern shoreline, with forays into pristine offshore lagoons that shelter colourful coral groves and schools of fish; the ethereal To Sua Ocean Trench attracts those keen on the surreal swim of a lifetime. But Upolu also has its fair share of terra firma treasures: the tangled rainforest of the interior, rough coastal cliffs formed by the cooling of lava rivers and fascinating craters and caves. The urban delights of Apia shouldn't be neglected either – not if you fancy the odd boogie, movie, or the country's best eating and drinking establishments.

ℹ Getting Around

TO/FROM THE AIRPORT

Faleolo Airport is on the coast, 35km west of Apia. Many resorts and hotels offer transfers; otherwise there's always an armada of taxis ready to ferry arrivals to the city or other Upolu destinations. The fare to Apia is around ST60.

If you're travelling alone, it's cheaper to catch an airport shuttle. It pays to prebook, but you'll usually spot them waiting across from the terminal for all of the major international flights. **Samoa Scenic Tours** (p255) has shuttles that stop at any of Apia's hotels (about ST47, 45 minutes); it also offers transfers to other Upolu resorts.

Many of the international flights arrive and depart at ungodly hours, but if you're lucky enough to have one at a reasonable time, buses are an option. Walk out to the main road and hail any bus approaching from your right to get to Apia. To get to Faleolo Airport from Apia (ST4), take any bus marked 'Pasi o le Va'a', 'Manono-uta', 'Falelatai' or 'Faleolo'.

BUS

Buses connecting Apia with almost every other part of Upolu leave from both Maketi Fou (the main market) and from behind the Flea Market. Drivers circle between the two until the bus is full (this can take up to an hour) and are liable to veer off route to deposit locals at their front doors. There are set bus stops on the coastal road, but if you hail the driver they'll stop almost anywhere. Pay as you leave the bus. Fares within Apia range from ST1 to ST1.80. The most you'll pay for a trip anywhere in Upolu is ST8.50. Buses begin running early in the morning and stop in the early afternoon, though services are limited on Sundays.

A bus schedule for Upolu that includes fare information is available by emailing the **Samoa Tourism Authority** (Map p258; ☑ 63500; www.samoa.travel; Beach Rd; ⊙ 9am-5pm Mon-Fri, 8am-noon Sat).

To reach the Aleipata district at the eastern end of the island, catch the Lalomso bus. To head east along the north coast, take the Falefa, Fagaloa or Lotofaga bus. For any point along the Cross Island Rd, take either the Si'umu or Salani bus. For Togitogiga and O Le Pupu-Pu'e National Park, take the Falealili or Salani bus.

CAR

The main roads in Upolu range from pristine to potholed. The national speed limit maxes out at 56km/h and drops to 40km/h through villages (omnipresent speed humps ensure you never forget to slow down); as there are very few stretches of road that don't pass through villages, expect to be driving at a snail's pace most of the time. The sealed Main Coast Rd winds its way around Upolu, while three roads cross over the island's east–west central ridge and divide it roughly into quarters.

Be aware: though there are very few main roads, there is an even greater dearth of street signs. Those that exist mostly point the way to obscure villages (rather than, say, the airport). Roads often veer off in the opposite direction of the one you might wish to take, with no notice at all. Don't be shy about asking for directions.

A high-clearance 2WD vehicle should be adequate for all but the roads to Uafato and to Aganoa Black Sand Beach (4WD only). Outside of Apia and the stretch between the city and the airport, petrol stations are in short supply.

Apia

POP 36,735

Few people come to a Pacific paradise to hang around in a small city with not much in the way of beaches. But it's worth taking some time to explore the (relative) sprawl

SAMOA APIA

Samoa Highlights

❶ Sleeping in a traditional Samoan *fale* such as those on **Namu'a island** (p270).

❷ Soaking up the village vibe while strolling around the white-sand-encircled island of **Manono** (p275).

❸ Stepping off the perfect flax-coloured sands into the turquoise waters of **Aleipata's beaches** (p267).

❹ Partying with the locals in the bars and nightclubs in **Apia** (p264).

❺ Admiring the sunset from the sacred sites of **Cape Mulinu'u** (p283).

❻ Bathing in the idyllic sunken waters of the **To Sua Ocean Trench** (p267).

❼ Exploring an old lava tunnel, swimming and getting covered in mud at Savai'i's **Dwarf's Cave** (p282).

❽ Having a lost-world moment battling overgrown weeds and lost trails before standing atop the mysterious **Pulemelei Mound** (p284).

of Apia: with an excellent cultural centre, three buzzy markets and an eclectic collection of local eateries and nightspots, the capital offers an immersive introduction to island life. Plentiful accommodation, facilities galore and proximity to some fascinating natural and historic attractions – and, given the island's small size, pretty much everything else on Upolu – makes Apia a handy base for visitors with their own wheels.

◎ Sights & Activities

Vaiala Beach BEACH
(Map p258; Vaiala) The closest beach to Apia town, immediately east of the harbour. The currents can be strong, so take care and avoid the area marked by buoys where there's a dangerous whirlpool.

⭐ **Samoa Cultural Village** CULTURAL CENTRE
(Map p258; www.samoa.travel; Beach Rd; ☺9am-5pm Mon-Fri, interactive sessions 10.30am-12.30pm Tue-Thu) **FREE** Though this 'village' is open every weekday, it's the interactive sessions that are an absolute must. Knowledgeable and extremely affable hosts take visitors through all aspects of Samoan cultural and traditional life, with workshops on weaving, woodworking, *siapo* cloth making, traditional *tatau*, dance and music. Guests are also treated to an *'ava* (kava) ceremony and lunch from the *umu* (hot-stone oven).

The village is tucked away behind the Samoa Tourism Authority's information *fale*.

Maketi Fou MARKET
(Food Market; Map p258; Fugalei St; ☺24hr) Abuzz with local merchants, shoppers, loiterers and men slamming it down over

games of *mu* (Samoan checkers), this 24-hour market is a must-see shopping and social experience. Though primarily a produce market, pretty much everything is sold here. Souvenir hunters will find *siapo* (decorated bark cloth), woodcarvings, coconut-shell jewellery, *lava-lava* (wraparound sarongs) and T-shirts. A cold *niu* (drinking coconut) will give you strength to shop on, despite the oppressive humidity of the place.

The ambience is somewhat enlivened by the fume-ridden chaos of the adjacent bus station.

Flea Market
MARKET

(Map p258; cnr Fugalei St & Beach Rd; ☺8am-4pm Mon-Fri, to noon Sat) Down on the waterfront, this steamy labyrinth is packed with small stalls selling craftwork, clothing and souvenirs. Don't bother to test your bargaining skills here, as haggling is not an element of Samoan commerce.

Fish Market
MARKET

(Map p258; off Beach Rd) A scramble takes place here at the crack of dawn every Sunday to snag the freshest catches for the post-church *to'ona'i* (Sunday lunch). Unsurprisingly, Apia's best fish and chips are also found here.

Falemata'aga
MUSEUM

(Museum of Samoa; Map p258; ☎26036; www.museumofsamoa.ws; cnr Ififi & Vaitele Sts; ☺9.30am-4pm Mon-Fri) FREE The German-era school building houses an enchanting collection of artefacts and displays focusing on four themes: history, culture, Pacific and environment. Donations are appreciated.

Government House
BUILDING

(Map p258; Beach Rd) While Government House isn't a thrilling landmark in itself (though the giant, modern rendition of a *fale* roof atop it is cause for a snapshot), it's worth a visit to see the Samoa Police Brass Band – in full regalia – toot out the national anthem as it raises the flag each weekday morning between 7.30am and 8am.

Immaculate Conception Cathedral
CHURCH

(Map p258; Beach Rd) Looming over the harbour, this lofty cathedral is breathtakingly beautiful. Originally constructed in 1884, the building was recently rebuilt at an estimated cost of ST13 million: it's a hefty price tag for a country that isn't exactly rolling in it, but the devout believe its ornate timber-crafted ceilings, dazzling stained-glass windows and gaspingly huge interior (2000-person capacity; it previously held 400) make it priceless.

Vanya Taule'alo Gallery
GALLERY

(Map p268; ☎20011; Mulivai Lane, Taumeasina; ☺8am-4pm Mon-Sat) This small but special gallery showcases the works of Samoan and other Pacific Island artists: prints, paintings, woodcarvings, jewellery, and other handicrafts are all top quality, and are all for sale. The gallery is attached to the equally worthy **Legends Cafe**. It's about a five-minute drive from the centre of Apia.

SAMOA IN...

Five Days

Spend a day or two exploring **Apia**, making sure to visit the Samoa Cultural Village, Palolo Deep Marine Reserve, the Robert Louis Stevenson Museum and catching a *fiafia* (dance performance) or fa'afafine show. The following day begin the loop around Upolu, heading east and soaking up the sights and village calm. Spend your first night at **Namu'a Island Beach Fale** then continue on around the island, stopping two more nights at the resort or *fale* of your choice. Don't miss splashing around the **To Sua Ocean Trench** and stopping at the stunning **beaches** of the south coast.

Ten Days

Follow the five-day itinerary, then continue north up the coast of Upolu, stopping for a night on the island of **Manono**. The following day take the ferry to **Savai'i** and spend the next four days leisurely driving around the island counter-clockwise: get covered in mud at **Dwarf's Cave**, take the eerie, scenic drive to **Fafa O Sauai'i**, and get blown away by the **Alofaaga Blowholes**. If you're keen on archaeology and adventure, search for the mysterious **Pulemelei Mound**.

Upolu

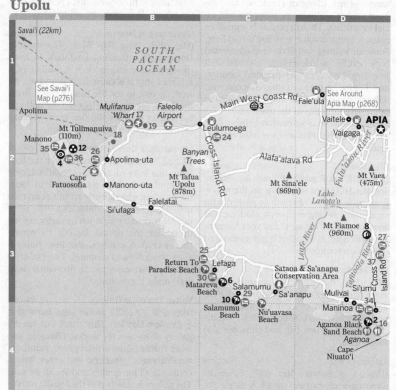

SOUTH PACIFIC OCEAN

Savai'i (22km)

See Savai'i Map (p276)

Apolima

Mulifanua Wharf 17
Faleolo Airport

Main West Coast Rd Fale'ula

See Around Apia Map (p268)

Vaitele APIA

Vaigaga

Mt Tulimanuiva (110m)
18
19

Leulumoega
24

Cross Island Rd

Alafa'alava Rd

Fuluasou River

Manono
35
12
26
4 36
Apolima-uta

Banyan Trees

Cape Fatuosofia Manono-uta

Mt Tafua 'Upolu (878m)

Mt Sina'ele (869m)

Lake Lanoto'o

Mt Vaea (475m)

Si'ufaga Falelatai

Mt Fiamoe (960m) 8 27

25

Return To Paradise Beach
Lefaga
30 6 Salamumu
Matareva Beach
10 29 Sa'anapu
Salamumu Beach
Nu'uavasa Beach

Sataoa & Sa'anapu Conservation Area

Leafe River

Tafitoala River

Cross Island Rd

37
Si'umu
Mulivai 34
Maninoa
22 2 16
Aganoa Black Sand Beach
Aganoa

Cape Niuato'i

Mormon Temple CHURCH

(Map p258; Vaitele St) One of the most impressive buildings in Samoa is this massive temple taking up 1736 sq metres on the western approach to town. Completed in 2005 after a fire destroyed the previous building, the white granite edifice has an elegant art-deco sensibility and is capped by a golden angel.

Palolo Deep Marine Reserve SNORKELLING

(Map p258; Vaiala Beach Rd; adult/child ST4/1, hire of mask & flippers/snorkel ST5/2; ⊗8am-6pm) Between Vaiala Beach and Apia's harbour, this reserve is a magnificent stretch of shallow reef (best visited at high tide) that features a deep, coral-encrusted hole thronging with marine life. To reach the drop-off, swim out from the beach to the dark patch of water to the left of the marker stick. It's around 100m from the shore, and you'll need flippers and a snorkel to get you out there without damaging the coral (or your feet).

A Touch of Samoa SPA

(Map p268; ☑843 0034; Falealili St (Cross Island Rd), Tanugamanono; 60min massage ST50; ⊗9am-7pm Mon-Sat, 11am-7pm Sun) Take a load off at this popular spa, where they use massage techniques based on both Samoan and European traditions. Waxing, pedicures, manicures, eyebrow and eyelash tinting and more also available.

Misiluki Day Spa SPA

(Map p258; ☑20759; www.misilukispa.com; Falealili St; massage per 30min from ST50; ⊗9am-7pm Mon-Fri, to 3pm Sat, 2pm-7pm Sun) For massage, as well as mani-pedis, waxing, facials and body treatment, this serene yet simple spa gets top marks from locals.

👉 Tours

Polynesian Xplorer TOUR

(Map p268; ☑26940; www.samoaaccommo dation.co; Falealili St) Full-service boutique

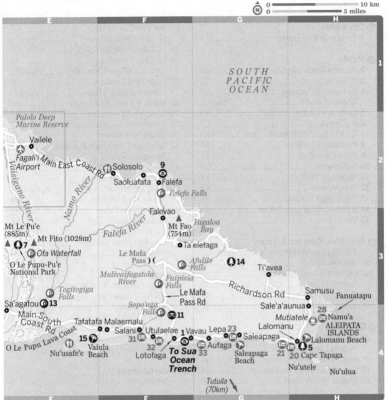

travel agency that runs recommended tours in Upolu (half-day ST120, full-day from ST220) and day tours to Manono (ST230) and Savai'i (ST397). Groups are small and you can design your own custom itinerary including lodging and transfers. Also has an airport office.

Samoa Scenic Tours   TOUR
(Map p258; ☑26981; www.samoascenictours.com) Runs a huge variety of tours around Upolu, Savai'i and to Manono: see the website for full listing and prices. It can also tailor tours for groups and special interests.

🛌 Sleeping

Most places in Apia include breakfast in their rates; many also offer airport transfers.

Just out of town, on Taumeasina Island, the upmarket **Taumeasina Resort** was nearing completion at research time: check www.taumeasinasamoa.com for details.

Aniva's Place   GUESTHOUSE **$**
(Map p268; ☑20501; www.anivasaccommo dationsamoa.com; off Falealili St (Cross Island Rd), Moto'otua; s/d ST120/140, without bathroom ST100/120; 🅿❄🛜🏊) Run by the exceptionally charming Aniva, this two-storey suburban dwelling offers a homey, welcoming atmosphere with clean, comfortable rooms, an honesty bar, a library and a small pool. Excellent home-cooked meals are available on request for a small fee.

Annabelle Inn   INN **$**
(Map p258; ☑20505; inbound@samoascenic.com; Beach Rd; r with/without bathroom from ST60/50; 🛜) Set in a quaint, early-20th-century home, this sweet place offers comfortable, homey rooms and a sunny, sociable verandah restaurant that looks over to the marina. It's a quick stroll to the Palolo Deep Marine Reserve; those interested in a different kind of wildlife will rejoice in Annabelle's

Upolu

proximity to Apia's best bars and clubs. Non-night owls, be warned: it can get noisy.

Taumesina Hideaway　　　　BUNGALOW $
(Map p268; ☏774 7905, 758 9255; taumesina.
hideaway@gmail.com; Taumesina Reserve, Moata'a;
bungalow from ST95; P☏) This quiet place,
crouched by a lovely lagoon, offers the only
beach *fales* in Apia. All are enclosed; three
have shared bathrooms, while the rest come
with ensuites and small fridges. Though
the ocean views were somewhat spoiled by
a nearby construction project at time of research, this is a good – if basic - getaway for
those seeking proximity to Apia without the
city buzz.

Su Accommodation　　　　APARTMENT $$
(Map p258; ☏27001; www.su-accommodation.
com; Fugalei St; r/ste ST190/290; P✳☏) This
friendly, family-run spot is an excellent
choice for self-caterers and families. While
there are clean motel-like rooms on-site,
the spacious, fully appointed suites are the

best option, with serviceable kitchens ide-
al for cooking up your finds from Maketi
Fou (directly across the road) or either of
the two large supermarkets bookending the
property.

The family also offers private units
(ST160) in the less urban surrounds of Vait-
ele, about 7km out of Apia.

Lynn's Getaway Hotel　　　　B&B $$
(Map p268; ☏20272; www.lynnsgetaway.com;
Salenesa Rd, Moto'otua; s/d ST150/170, without
bathroom ST130/150; P✳☏✵) This eccentric, social little spot attracts return visitors
and long-term guests by the boatload. The
two comfy common rooms, shared kitchen,
poolside barbecue area and library lend
Lynn's a true home-away-from-home feel,
as do the hearty, host-prepared dinners
(ST20, available on request). Discounted
rental car rates are available for guests; if
driving isn't your thing, island tours and
hiking expeditions can be booked here.

GET ACTIVE ON UPOLU

Diving

Diving is undeveloped in Samoa. On Upolu this means that experienced divers can partake in exploration trips with AquaSamoa Watersports and potentially get sites named after them! Top dives include the Manono Wall (just off of Manono island) and Magic Mushrooms, where you'll find the namesake unique mushroom-shaped coral formations that are frequented by schools of sharks.

AquaSamoa Watersports (Map p254; ☑ 45662; www.aquasamoa.com; Sheraton Aggie Grey's Lagoon Resort, Mulifanua) Upolu's only dive centre offers dives for beginner and skilled divers (two-tank dive ST340), plus PADI courses (open-water course ST1250), waterskiing, wakeboarding, and snorkelling tours (ST80); it's also got an on-site tattooist on hand!

Hiking

Shorter tracks that don't require a guide include the short but steep walk to Robert Louis Stevenson's grave near the summit of Mt Vaea and the Mt Matavanu crater walk. Even on short walks, the sun and hot, humid conditions can take their toll. Good walking shoes are essential. For longer hikes, a guide is imperative.

Based in Apia, Eti at **SamoaOnFoot** (p267) offers expert guided hikes to Lake Lanoto'o, Uafato Conservation Area and O Le Pupu-Pu'e National Park. On Savai'i, Mt Silisili offers a challenging multiday trek.

Surfing

Upolu has great surf but most of it is reef-breaking, far offshore and within limits of a village's water rights, so you'll need permission. It's best to go with an operator. **Salani Surf Resort** (p274), **Samoa Surf Secrets** (at Vaiula Fales; p274), **Offshore Adventures** (p274), **Sa'moana Resort** (p272) and **Manoa Tours** (Map p254; ☑ 777 0007; www.manoatours.com; Coconuts Beach Club resort) all offer surf packages; some offer shuttle services to the breaks for nonguests.

Other Activities

For information on fishing charters and tournaments, visit the Samoa International Game Fishing Association website (www.sigfa.ws).

Outdoor Samoa (Map p254; ☑ 45991; www.outdoorsamoa.com; Airport Lodge, Mulifanua) Based near Faleolo Airport and Mulifanua Wharf, this outfit offers a huge range of biking and kayaking adventures ranging from day trips to multi-day/week expeditions. It also hires kayaks (ST75 per day) and bikes (ST45/65 half-/full day) for solo jaunts.

Samoa Adventure (Map p254; ☑ 777 0272; www.samoa-adventure.com; Sheraton Aggie Grey's Lagoon Resort, Mulifanua) This lovely 35ft catamaran makes sunset tours (from ST110), and a slew of other excursions including cruises to Savai'i (10 hours, from ST320) and Manono (from ST250 per person including fishing, food and drinks) and personalised fishing trips.

Le Penina Golf Course (Map p254; ☑ 45611; www.sheratonsamoaaggiegreysresort.com/golf; Main West Coast Rd; 9/18 holes ST30/50, club hire ST15; ⊗ 8am-5pm Mon-Sat, noon-5pm Sun) This par-72 course winds around the Sheraton Aggie Grey's Lagoon Resort.

Oceanic Sportfishing Adventures (☑ 775 9606; www.grandermarlin.com) Go with Captain Chris to catch the big ones – from tuna to marlin – on the new, 37ft Merritt *Leilani*. Best from April to October.

Insel Fehmarn Hotel HOTEL **$$**
(Map p268; ☑ 23301; www.inselfehmarnsamoa.com; Falealili St (Cross Island Rd), Moto'otua; d from ST280; P❄🛜🏊) Blocky and nondescript from the outside, this large hotel is surprisingly welcoming and well equipped. All rooms have plenty of space (families should request a Garden Room on the ground floor) and excellent kitchens; ours had a full gas stove. Genuinely friendly staff are quick to

Apia

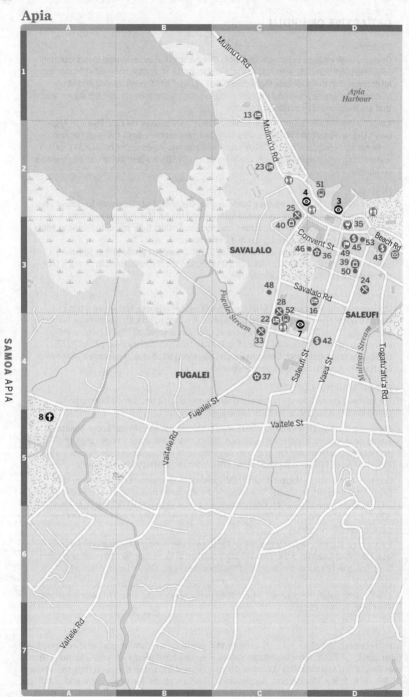

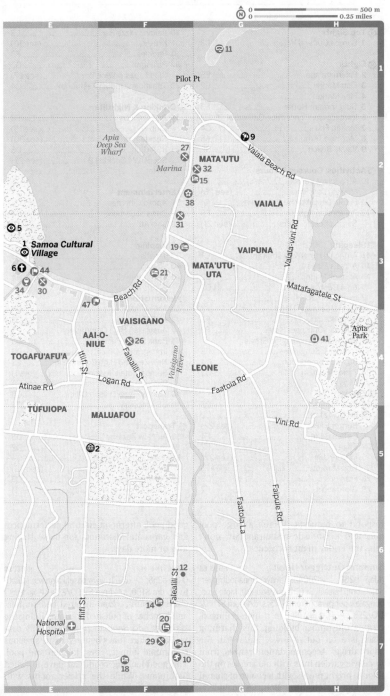

SAMOA APIA

Apia

respond to requests. There's a large pool area and a fantastic restaurant-bar; don't miss the Friday night barbecues.

Samoan Outrigger Hotel　　HOTEL **$$**
(Map p268; ☑20042; www.samoanoutrigger-hotel.com; Falealili St (Cross Island Rd), Moto'otua; bungalow per person from ST75, s/d/f from ST140/170/255; Ⓟ❄️🛜🏊) Set in a high-ceilinged, century-old timber building, this charming place is a bit out of town, but worth the short drive. Accommodation ranges from *fale*-style garden huts with mattresses on the floor to bright rooms with a choice of shared bathroom or ensuites. Bonuses include a

good pool, afternoon cultural performances and car-rental discounts for those staying four or more days.

Pasefika Inn　　HOTEL **$$**
(Map p258; ☑20971; www.pasefikainn.ws; Matautu St; dm ST50, s/d from ST190/220; Ⓟ❄️🛜🏊) Carved beams, *siapo*-inspired bed runners and bunches of polished coconuts lining the stairway add Samoan touches to this central, airy place that's bettered by its spacious communal lounge, guest kitchen and pool. The good-looking rooms all have attached bathrooms. While the pricier rooms with

terraces are bigger, they also pick up more noise from the busy road out front.

Apia Central Hotel HOTEL $$
(Map p258; ☏20782; www.apiacentralhotel.com; Savalalo Rd; s/d from ST140/170; P❋❈) As the name suggests, this is one for those who want to be in the thick of it; everything from Maketi Fou, supermarkets, restaurants and nightlife are but a short walk away. The hotel doesn't rest on its good-location laurels, however, with big, impeccably clean rooms, bend-over-backwards staff and a lovely outdoor courtyard for escaping the humid din of Apia.

★ Samoa Tradition Resort RESORT $$$
(Map p268; ☏25699; www.traditionresort.com; Papaseea Rd, Ululoloa Heights; r/apt/ste/villa ST320/410/450/490; P❋❈❈) Gorgeous grounds, divine digs and five-star service make this resort an absolute stand-out. Accommodation ranges from spanking new hotel rooms all the way up to massive luxury villas. The restaurant gets rave reviews; the Thursday night *fiafias* are superbly theatrical and shouldn't be missed. It's not cheap, but you'd be hard-pressed to find a more 'resorty' resort in Apia.

Sheraton Samoa Aggie Grey's Hotel & Bungalows HISTORIC HOTEL $$$
(Map p258; ☏22880; www.aggiegreys.com; Beach Rd; s/d/ste from US$138/160/350; ❋@❈) If you ever wanted to step into a 1940s-era

tale of the South Seas, this iconic hotel gives you the chance. Though completely refurbished in 2016, Aggie Grey's has retained its breezy, near-colonial atmosphere, while giving its spacious rooms a much-needed overhaul. In addition to the old-school ambience, the hotel boasts three on-site eateries, a bar, a spa, a gym and three pools, one with a swim-up bar.

Tanoa Tusitala HOTEL $$$
(Map p258; ☏21122; www.tanoatusitala.com; Mulinu'u Rd; r/ste from ST470/640; P❋❈❈) One of the swankiest and most professionally run places in town, this hotel – instantly recognisable by its huge, traditional-roofed lobby – is nestled in lush gardens across from the sea wall. Rooms are big and elegant. Facilities include a pool with plenty of lounge chairs (there's also a kids' pool and playground, a rarity in Samoa), tennis court and gym, plus an excellent bar-restaurant.

Amanaki Hotel & Restaurant HOTEL $$$
(Map p258; ☏27889; www.amanakihotel.com; Mulinu'u Rd; d ST285-360; ❋❈❈) This popular, two-storey hotel enjoys an excellent location – and equally excellent ocean breezes – across from the sea wall. The huge, comfortable rooms face a nicely landscaped pool. Guests and locals flock to the on-site restaurant for its breezy atmosphere and

SAMOA APIA

THERE'S SOMETHING ABOUT BLOODY MARY

Agnes Swann was the daughter of a Lincolnshire chemist who had migrated to Samoa in 1889, and a Samoan girl from Toamua village. In 1917 she married and had four children; after her first husband died, she married Charlie Grey, a compulsive gambler who lost everything they had. Aggie had to look for some means of supporting the family.

In 1942 said means arrived in the form of American soldiers in Apia carrying 'unimaginable wealth'. Aggie borrowed US$180, bought the site of a former hotel and began selling hamburgers and coffee to the servicemen. Response was overwhelming and, although supplies were difficult to come by during WWII, Aggie built up an institution that became famous Pacific-wide as a social gathering place for war-weary soldiers. She even succeeded in getting through the New Zealand–imposed prohibition of alcoholic beverages.

When James Michener published his enormously successful *Tales of the South Pacific*, Aggie was so well-known that it was widely assumed she was the prototype for the character of Michener's Tonkinese madam, Bloody Mary. Michener has said that he did visit Aggie's place whenever he could from Pago Pago, where he was frequently stationed, though he denied that anything but the good bits of Bloody Mary were inspired by Aggie Grey.

Over the next few decades, the snack bar expanded into a hotel where numerous celebrities stayed while filming or travelling in the area. If you'd like to read more about Aggie Grey, who died in June 1988 at the age of 91, track down *Aggie Grey of Samoa*, by Nelson Eustis.

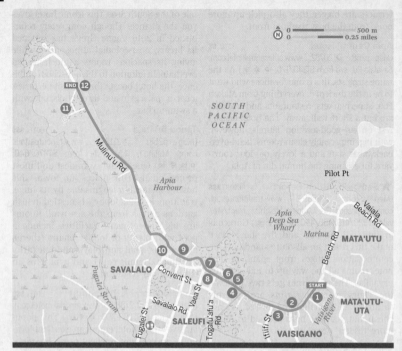

City Walk
Historical Apia

START SHERATON SAMOA AGGIE GREY'S HOTEL & BUNGALOWS
END INDEPENDENCE MEMORIAL
LENGTH 3.5KM; 1½ HOURS

Start from **1 Sheraton Samoa Aggie Grey's Hotel & Bungalows** (p261), Samoa's most famous address. Founded in 1933, it became a popular haunt of American servicemen during WWII. The late Aggie Grey is said to have been the inspiration for the Bloody Mary character in James Michener's *Tales of the South Pacific*.

Cross the road and walk west along the sea wall to the **2 John Williams monument**. It celebrates an early missionary who was killed and eaten in 1839 while evangelising in Vanuatu. His bones were recovered and buried under the church across the road. A little further along you'll pass the genteel wooden colonial-style building that once housed the **3 Supreme Court**.

As you continue along Beach Rd, gaze up at the grand and glorious **4 Immaculate Conception Cathedral** (p253) on your left and then the *fale*-style **5 Samoa Tourism**

Authority office (p266) on your right; if you time your visit right, stop at the **6 Samoa Cultural Village** (p252) behind the *fale* for an immersive and entertaining experience. Further along you'll see the **7 clock tower** (now in the middle of a busy roundabout), constructed in memory of those who fought and were killed in WWI. Across the road are the elegant arches of the Spanish Mission–style **8 Chan Mow's building**.

From the clock tower, take the smaller road heading behind the library to check out the **9 Fish Market** (p253) and then the **10 Flea Market** (p253).

Amble north through the park beside the sea wall that buttresses the eastern shore of the Mulinu'u Peninsula until you reach Samoa's parliament house, the **11 Fale Fono**. In case you had any doubts about Samoa's Christian leanings, cross the road to read the **12 Independence Memorial**. It was built to celebrate the independence of Western Samoa on 1 January 1962 and bears the inscription 'Samoa is founded on God', with thanks to each member of the Holy Trinity.

high-quality, reasonably priced seafood meals (supplied by the hotel's own fishing boats); the bar gets buzzy after dark too.

✕ Eating

Apia is the one of the few places in Samoa where you won't be held hostage to the culinary abilities (or lack thereof) of your accommodation provider. There's a decent selection of eateries scattered around town, with most of the upmarket ones lining the waterfront.

For self-caterers, Apia's best-stocked supermarkets are **Frankies** (Map p258; Fugalei St; ⏱6am-9pm) and **Farmer Joe** (Map p258; www.farmerjoe.ws; Fugalei St; ⏱6am-9pm); both are open seven days a week.

Krush   VEGAN $

(Map p268; ☑27874; Falealili St (Cross Island Rd), Tanugamanono; mains ST10-15; ⏱9am-5pm Mon-Fri, to 3pm Sat; ☑) Apia's only vegan restaurant has a small menu, but it's a tasty one that's sure to make visiting herbivores happy. Inventive salads and risottos are served by the scoop; other items include 'beefless burgers' and meat-free takes on Samoan cuisine. It also whizzes up a massive range of fresh juices and smoothies.

Burger Bill's   FAST FOOD $

(BB's; Map p258; ☑26388; Fugalei St; meals from ST9; ⏱9am-10pm Mon-Thu, to 1am Fri & Sat, 10am-10pm Sun) This much-beloved, locally owned fast-food chain serves up exceptional fish and chips that – despite hefty portion sizes – are ridiculously moreish. As per the name, it also creates great burgers; fried chicken is another speciality.

Fish Market   SEAFOOD $

(Map p258; off Beach Rd; fish & chips ST8; ⏱7am-3pm Mon-Fri, to noon Sat & Sun) Battle local crowds for the best and freshest fish and chips in town in an endearingly gritty, local-style setting.

Coffee Bean   CAFE $

(Map p258; www.thebeansamoa.com; Falealili St (Cross Island Rd); mains ST10-25; ⏱8am-4.30pm Mon-Fri, to 1pm Sat, to noon Sun; ☎) Along with excellent, strong coffees, the Bean serves big breakfasts like eggs Benedict (ST25) as well as lighter choices; at lunch choose from sandwiches, savoury pies and casseroles. It also operates **Bean Central** (Map p258; www.thebeansamoa.com; Vaea St; mains ST10-25; ⏱7am-3.30pm Mon-Fri, to noon Sat), about 1km west; it's just as good.

★Palusami   FUSION $$

(Map p258; ☑771 3177; www.palusami.biz; Beach Rd; mains ST13-50; ⏱5.30pm-midnight Tue-Sat) ☘ This wonderful place uses organic, locally sourced produce to create incredible meals that combine Samoan flavours with international favourites (coconut beef stroganoff, anyone?). Other inventive fare includes eggs Benedict with spicy taro cakes, grilled pork on a *palusami* gratin and a to-die-for *Koko Samoa* chocolate tart. *Niu* (coconut) cocktails – including a very, very good mojito – served in the shell are a must.

Edge   INTERNATIONAL $$

(Map p258; ☑775 5174; Apia Marina; mains ST10-30; ⏱8am-late Mon-Sat) An excellent addition to Apia's up-and-coming dining-entertainment precinct at the marina, this laid-back spot is a top choice for a lazy lunch or dinner. A diverse menu offers Samoan classics, international favourites and a long list of sinful all-day breakfast options; it also does excellent espressos. Stick around for cocktails (happy hour 4pm to 7pm) and DJ sets (7pm to midnight Thursday to Saturday).

Sips Tapas & Wine Bar   TAPAS $$

(Map p258; ☑770 1888; Apia Marina; tapas/mains from ST18/25; ⏱11am-10pm Tue-Thu, to midnight Fri & Sat, 5.30-10.30pm Sun) What this hip and happening spot lacks by way of an extensive menu (the pickin's are tasty, but slim), it more than makes up for with good vibes and top views. An extensive wine list makes this an excellent spot for sunset drinks; if you're in town on a Sunday afternoon, drop in for its lively pizza-and-barbecue parties.

Giordano's   ITALIAN $$

(Map p268; ☑25985; off Falealili St (Cross Island Rd), Moto'otua; small pizzas ST20-26; ⏱3-11pm Tue-Sat, 5-10pm Sun) Sit in the tropical back courtyard and tuck into exceptional pizzas featuring such exotic (for Samoa) toppings as olives, blue cheese, parmesan, pepperoni and anchovies. It was the first pizza place to open in Samoa and many think it's still the friendliest and the best. Gluttons take note: the XL pizzas are *really* XL!

Tifaimoana Indian Restaurant   INDIAN $$

(Map p258; ☑29604; Fugalei St; dishes from ST15; ⏱7am-9am, 11am-3pm & 5-10pm Mon-Sat; ☑) The chef here (from the Punjab region of India) orders ingredients from his homeland and you can taste it. The *thali* set meals (many vegetarian; prices from ST25) are Samoan-sized and include a lassi; if you're ordering à la carte, the chicken korma is memorable.

Italiano Pizza Bar
ITALIAN $$

(Map p258; ✆24330; Beach Rd; small pizzas ST16-25; ⏰9am-10pm Mon-Fri, to midnight Sat, 4-10pm Sun) Locals and travellers converge on this humble waterfront pizzeria to talk, drink jugs of lurid alcoholic mixtures and add their scrawl to the graffiti on the walls. On top of all that, the pizzas are great.

★Bistro Tatau
FUSION $$$

(Map p258; ✆22727; www.bistrotatau.ws; Beach Rd; mains ST40-70; ⏰noon-2pm Mon-Fri, from 6.30pm Mon-Sat; ⁂✎) This upmarket spot ranks as one of Samoa's best and most innovative restaurants, fusing local favourites such as *palusami* into soufflé and ravioli. Polished floorboards, white tablecloths, vibrant local art, tropical floral arrangements and efficient barefoot waiters in *lava-lava* complete the experience.

Paddles
ITALIAN $$$

(Map p258; ✆21819; Beach Rd; mains ST25-60; ⏰5-11pm Mon-Sat) A delightful Italian-Samoan family serves superb home cooking and ready conviviality at this attractive and rightfully popular terrace restaurant across from the seafront. It has that perfect balance of laid-back and chic. Try the smoked fish lasagne or the divine mushroom risotto.

Drinking & Nightlife

Apia's waterfront is well supplied with drinking options, though few places open their doors on a Sunday. Some of the dodgier pool halls aren't pleasant places to be at closing time.

Ace of Clubs
CLUB

(Map p258; ✆20430; off Beach Rd; ⏰club 5pm-midnight, bar from 10.30am Mon-Sat) Hitch your fancy threads on for Apia's newest and classiest nightclub. Laser-lit and loud, it attracts an enthusiastic crowd with pumping dance hits, good drinks menu and brilliant security staff that ensures everyone – especially women – have a great, safe night. There's a dress code, and cover charges apply most nights (ST5 to ST25). There's a more low-key bar and bistro on the ground floor.

Y-Not
BAR

(Map p258; Beach Rd; cover charge ST10; ⏰4-10pm Mon & Tue, to midnight Wed-Sat) Ask anyone of any age where to go for a drink in Apia and this is always the enthusiastic answer. It's no wonder. Looking over the Apia Harbour with deck seating, a pool table, live or DJ music on Friday and Saturday nights and a reliable mix of expats, locals and visitors, Y-Not is bucketloads of fun.

Club X
CLUB

(Map p258; Beach Rd; admission ST15-20; ⏰7pm-midnight Wed-Sat) This waterside club is a local institution for all the right reasons: blaring pop hits, cheap drinks, good bartenders and a sociable – if young – crowd. The small dancefloor gets packed and sweaty most nights.

Sheesha's Cocktail Bar
COCKTAIL BAR

(Map p258; ✆775 1500; Apia Marina; ⏰5-10.30pm Tue-Thu, to 12.30am Fri & Sat) One of the classiest bars in Apia – all chandeliers and fancy wallpaper – Sheesha's has a fantastic cocktail menu that attracts a slightly older (25 and up) clientele. It's a tiny place, but its size just adds to the intimate ambience (though there's more room outside overlooking the water).

Apia Yacht Club
BAR

(Map p258; ✆28584; Mulinu'u Rd; ⏰5-10pm Tue-Sun) Its private-club status makes it one of the few sure-fire places for a drink on a Sunday evening. Its location on the sea wall – and resultant breezes – merely reinforces the relaxing effects of a cold Vailima beer. Meals are also available.

Cocktails on the Rocks
BAR

(Map p258; Beach Rd; ⏰3-10pm Mon-Thu, to midnight Fri & Sat) Also known as 'Cocks on the Rocks' and 'The Hole in the Wall', this small bar is much loved by tourists, expats and locals for its mellow vibe, sea breezes, 5L 'towers' of Vailima beer and live music most nights (bar Mondays).

RSA Club
BAR

(Returned Services Association; Map p258; ✆20 171; Beach Rd; ⏰9am-10pm Mon-Thu, to midnight Fri & Sat) This down'n'dirty – but characterful – place is a top spot for meeting locals and checking out some live music (Thursday to Saturday). If you're after posh cocktails and a well-heeled crowd, best go elsewhere: you don't want to be here if a fight breaks out (avoid the pool tables at closing time).

☆ Entertainment

Many hotels and resorts in Apia host weekly *fiafia* nights, celebrations of Samoan culture through vibrant song, dance and storytelling performances. Ask at your accommodation, or pop into the Samoa Tourism Authority's information *fale* on Beach Rd for a full list of weekly shows.

Divas of Samoa   CABARET
(Map p258; Maliu Mar Bar & Restaurant, Fugalei St; adult/child ST10/5; ⊙from 9pm Wed) The only *fa'afafine* show in Samoa is outrageous fun, full of glitter, glamour and cheesy music. It's a drag show, but maybe not as you know it: children are enthusiastically welcomed at the performances.

Siva Afi   DANCE
(Map p258; ☑26029; Beach Rd; dinner & show ST75) Named after the Samoan fire dance that is its hallmark, this place has a commitment to training young performers and keeping the traditional arts alive. Check out its dramatic fire- and knife-dancing shows every Tuesday night (Samoan-style dinner 7.30pm, show starts at 8.30pm). Bookings are recommended.

Apollo Cinemas   CINEMA
(Map p258; ☑28127; Convent St; adult/child ST15/10; ⊙screenings from 9.30am Mon-Sat) Big Hollywood blockbusters often hit the screens here before they reach Australia or NZ and for a fraction of the price. Its two cinemas are blissfully air-conditioned, and there's a new cafe attached if popcorn isn't doing it for you.

🔒 Shopping

Memorable souvenirs can be bought at various shops around Apia, including *siapo, ie toga* (fine mats) and finely made, multi-legged *'ava* (kava) bowls. Such crafts, plus jewellery and clothes, are available from Maketi Fou (p252) and the Flea Market (p253).

Plantation House   HANDICRAFTS, GIFTS
(Map p268; ☑22839; Lotopa Rd, Alafua; ⊙9am-5pm Mon-Fri, to 1pm Sat) Stop in for high-quality, locally made art, craft and gifts, including hand-blocked fabric, *lava-lava,* prints, tailored shirts, bedding and jewellery.

Mailelani   BEAUTY
(Map p268; ☑22111; www.mailelani-samoa.com; Mailelani Rd (just off Cross Island Rd), Papauta; ⊙9am-5pm Mon-Fri, to noon Sat) The handmade soaps, creams and goodies here are made with organic coconut oil; everything smells and feels divine. Stop by and you'll

SAMOA APIA

PIMP MY RIDE

Samoa is a quiet and polite place, but a wallflower it ain't: from its blazingly blue waters to its ludicrously large and looming village churches, there's much about this country that screams 'Look at me!' And there's nothing that seizes the eye with more insistence than Samoa's wonderfully over-the-top buses (*pasi*).

More than just a means of transportation, *pasi* are a form of self-expression by their independent owners. While a few are content to merely splash their bus sides in solid blocks of lurid colours, the majority have gone down the airbrush route, creating rolling kitschmobiles as glorious as they are garish. There are buses plastered with knock-off odes to Bon Jovi and Guns-n-Roses, starburst-heavy declarations of support for Manu Samoa (the national rugby union team), a startling number of Jesus-and-Mary glamour portraits hovering above the muffler, and way too many featuring depictions of what appears to be a psychotic, perhaps vampiric, Mickey Mouse.

The fun continues inside, with carpeted ceilings, flags, family photos, plastic garlands, religious trinkets (often neon) and a few thousand dangling air fresheners prettily obscuring parts of the windscreen. Extremely loud music is a must on buses, and visitors will soon develop either a taste for Samoan pop or earplugs. Such distractions cleverly divert passengers' attentions from the fact that there is no air-conditioning and seats are made of bum-busting hardwood. If the bus is crowded, a Samoan will probably sit on your lap. Roll with it!

probably get a tour showing how the products are made.

Mena
CLOTHING

(Map p258; ☑ 31293; www.menashop.com; Mac-Donald Bldg, Fugalei St; ⊗ 8.30am-5pm Mon-Fri, to 2pm Sat) High Samoan fashion in the form of well-cut dresses in traditional fabrics or painted with floral patterns. It's a bit pricey but there's something for all shapes and sizes.

Pacific Jewell
HANDICRAFTS, GIFTS

(Map p258; ☑ 32888; Levili Blvd, Levili; ⊗ 8am-5pm Mon-Fri, to 2pm Sat) This little nook has an on-site gallery and beautiful outdoor cafe. Locally made jewellery, carvings, art and more are all of exceptional quality.

Janet's
HANDICRAFTS, GIFTS

(Map p258; ☑ 23371; www.janetssamoa.com; 2nd fl, Lotemau Mall, Vaea St; ⊗ 9am-5.30pm Mon-Fri, 8.30am-1.30pm Sat) Janet's stocks a large range of woodcarvings, *siapo* and gifts.

❶ Information

ANZ Bank (Map p258; Beach Rd; ⊗ 9am-4.30pm Mon-Fri, 8am-1pm Sat) The ANZ also has ATMs on Salenesa Rd (just off Cross Island Rd) and on Saleufi St opposite Maketi Fou.

Bank South Pacific (BSP; Map p258; ☑ 66100; Beach Rd; ⊗ 9am-4pm Mon-Wed, to 4.30 Thu & Fri, 8.30am-12.30pm Sat) Has an ATM out the front that accepts overseas cards.

Main Post Office (Map p258; ☑ 27640; www.samoapost.ws; Beach Rd; ⊗ 8.30am-4.30pm Mon-Fri, 8am-noon Sat) For poste restante, go to the separate office next to the main post office. Have mail addressed to you care of: Poste Restante, Chief Post Office, Apia, Samoa.

National Hospital (Map p268; ☑ 66600; Ilifi St, Moto'otua) Apia's main hospital.

Samoa Tourism Authority (Map p258; ☑ 63500; www.samoa.travel; Beach Rd; ⊗ 9am-5pm Mon-Fri, 8am-noon Sat) For information, assistance, bus schedules and maps. You'll find them in a prominently positioned *fale* across from the Catholic cathedral on the main drag.

❶ Getting Around

As visitors will soon discover (after hearing 'Taxi?' for the millionth time), Apia has an extraordinary number of cabs prowling its streets. Meters are optional, but fares are low; you shouldn't be charged more than ST5 for a ride within town. Be sure to agree upon a price before you hop in.

Buses are equally plentiful (though not so much on Sundays) and cheap; fares within town run at about ST1.

Around Apia

◎ Sights & Activities

★ Robert Louis Stevenson Museum & Mt Vaea National Reserve
MUSEUM

(Map p268; ☑ 20798; www.rlsmuseum.org; Cross Island Rd, Vailima; adult/child ST20/5; ⊗ 9am-4.30pm Mon-Fri, to noon Sat) The Scottish author's former residence is an enchanting estate, with a centrepiece lawn and perfectly manicured gardens. Stevenson's mansion, substantially destroyed in the cyclones in the early 1990s, was lovingly rebuilt and opened as a museum in 1994 on the centenary of Stevenson's death. Access is by a half-hour tour that leads through rooms filled with antiques and sepia family photographs.

Stevenson is buried in the adjacent Mt Vaea National Reserve (Map p268; Cross Island Rd, Vailima; ⊗ 6am-6pm Mon-Sat) FREE. Follow the signs for the path – known as the 'Road of Loving Hearts' – to the tomb. At the first unmarked fork, turn left. The path soon forks again: the right-hand trail (30 minutes) is steeper but shorter; the left-hand trail (50 minutes) is gentler but still involves a final slippery section. At the top you'll be greeted by wonderful views of Apia, Stevenson's stately Victorian tomb, and clouds of vicious mosquitoes. Cool off after after your hike with a dip in the natural swimming hole that was once the author's pool; it's right near the museum carpark.

A taxi from Apia to the museum costs ST10 one way, or take the Vaoala bus (ST2) from Maketi Fou.

★ Papase'ea Sliding Rocks
WATERFALL

(Map p268; off Maugafolau Rd; adult/child ST5/2; ⊗ 8.30am-5.30pm Mon-Sat, 11am-6pm Sun) Kids and adults have a brilliant time skimming down these natural slides – actually small waterfalls – into blessedly cool waterholes; you'll hear happy hoots even before you make your way down the long, precarious stairway to the pools. The longest slide is 5m long; there are a couple of smaller ones at the bottom of the stairs. During the dry season, check that the water is deep enough for sliding; if not, it's still a top spot for a dip.

The site is 6km from central Apia, well-signposted from the road past the Mormon Temple. Take the Se'ese'e bus (ST2.80) from Maketi Fou and ask to be dropped at the turn-off for Papase'ea. A return taxi trip is about ST25.

Papapapai-tai Falls WATERFALL
(Map p254; Cross Island Rd) About 14km south of Apia is the lookout for Papapapai-tai Falls, a 100m waterfall that plunges into a forested gorge; they're one of the longest falls in Samoa. Roughly 100m before the lookout, an unmarked track leads to the **Tiavi waterhole**, a delightful place to cool off on a hot day.

Lake Lanoto'o National Park LAKE
The pea-green crater of Lake Lanoto'o is about as removed from human habitation as you can get on Upolu. Its remote central-highlands location and alternating warm and cold currents lend it an eerie nature. Keep your eyes peeled for wild goldfish.

The steep trail leading to the lake from the car park (3km along a very rough side road) is overgrown and forks repeatedly. Many hikers (including locals) have gotten lost; a guide is a must. A dependable outfit is **SamoaOnFoot** (☑759 4199, 31252; www. bestsamoatours.com).

Bahá'í House of Worship RELIGIOUS SITE
(Map p268; ☑20385; www.bahaisamoa.ws; Cross Island Rd, Tiapapata; ⊙6am-6pm) **FREE** The architecturally interesting Bahá'í House of Worship is one of only eight such structures in the world; all are different except for being domed – this one is 28m high – and having nine sides and entrances, reflecting the faith's tenet of a basic unity of religions and peoples.

A taxi from Apia costs around ST30, or catch the Siumu bus (ST6) from Maketi Fou. Contact the temple if you wish to attend a Sunday session (10am); it may be able to offer you a free lift.

🛏 Sleeping

★ Dave Parker's Eco Lodge LODGE $
(Map p268; ☑842 8899; www.daveparker ecolodge.ws; Tapatapao Rd, Aleisa East; s/d bungalow ST45/65, lodge ST78/98, ste ST125/155; 🅿🛜❄) Surrounded by rainforest and boasting jaw-dropping views of the coast, this delightful hilltop spot is an excellent escape from the heat of the big smoke. The main lodge houses eight tidy rooms and a suite; those wishing to get even further away from it all should opt for one of four

bungalows set beside the very swimmable river.

Birdwatchers and hikers will find their bliss here; if the isolation gets too much, Dave offers free city transfers Monday to Saturday. There's also an excellent restaurant and bar on-site.

Eastern Upolu

The pointy end of Upolu is blessed with some of Samoa's best beaches, offering the winning combination of white sand, clear waters and excellent snorkelling. Heading east from Apia there's a succession of beautiful, sleepy villages along the surf-battered shoreline. The road turns sharply inland not far past Piula Cave Pool and skirts rainforest and plantations before hitting the glorious glowing sands of the Aleipata coast.

👁 Sights & Activities

Aleipata Beaches & Reefs BEACH
At the southeastern end of Upolu, Aleipata district has a reef system that's making a good comeback after being pummelled by the 2009 tsunami. It already has surprisingly good snorkelling, and the beaches here are among the most spellbindingly beautiful in the world. Check out the undersea magic by walking in off the spectacular white beach at **Lalomanu**. If you're lucky you might spot a turtle, but beware of strong currents.

The bus from Apia to Lalomanu (ST7.70) takes around two hours. If you're driving, don't be surprised if you get hit up for a fee for simply parking your car at a beach. Villages earn income from this, but some 'toll collectors' do push it a bit (one man tried to charge us ST50 for the pleasure); feel free to negotiate or move along elsewhere.

★ To Sua Ocean Trench LANDMARK
(Map p254; Main South Coast Rd; adult/child ST20/10; ⊙8.30am-6pm) This outrageously photogenic spot is a Samoan icon; skip it to your everlasting regret. Though the first thing you'll see upon entering the grounds is To Le Sua (a smaller, drier depression), it's To Sua that is the star of the show: more akin to a giant sinkhole than a trench, its sheer, green-draped rock walls plummet 20-odd metres to the almost hallucinatory-blue waters of the magnificent pool below. Swimming access is via a precipitous but sturdy

Around Apia

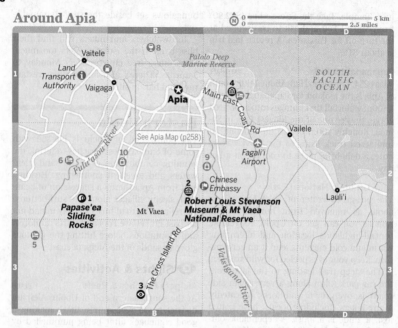

wooden ladder; believe us, it's worth the clamber.

When you've had your fill of this enchanted waterhole, take the short track to the wave-battered cliffs. The well-groomed garden is a great spot for a picnic.

Gorgeous though it is here, visitors still need to exercise caution: swimming through the underwater passage that feeds the waterhole from the sea is a big no-no, and if you're with kids, beware the child-sized gaps between the ground and the fence that circles the top of the trench.

Piula Cave Pool   LANDMARK

(Map p254; Main East Coast Rd; adult/child ST5/3; ⊙8am-4pm Mon-Sat) Secreted beneath the campus of Piula Methodist Theological College, Piula Cave Pool consists of two blue-green, fish-filled freshwater grottoes, only metres from the sea. The brave can swim between them via a creepy 3m underwater passage that's difficult to find in the darkness. The pools are concreted in so it's not a completely *au naturel* experience but it is refreshing and the college grounds are beautiful.

From Apia, take the Falefa or Lalomanu bus (ST4).

Lalomanu Crater   NATURE RESERVE

(Map p254; Lalomanu) A short but steep walk (10 to 15 minutes) leads to this extinct crater, blanketed in jungle overgrowth. Home to a huge colony of flying foxes, and with magnificent ocean and island views, it's worth the trek. If you go with a guide (about ST10; ask at your lodgings), they'll usually throw in a tour of the nearby taro plantation.

Uafato Conservation Area   FOREST

(Map p254) The 14 sq km of wild and rugged terrain that comprise the Uafato Conservation Area boast untouched rainforest that marches down from Upolu's northeastern hills to dip its toes in the ocean. Flora lovers can track down a rare stand of *ifilele* (the tree used for 'ava bowls), while fauna fans can observe numerous bird and bat species going about their aerial business. Uafato village is known for its traditional carvers, who are usually willing to demonstrate their art to visitors.

Uafato can be reached via a rough road that winds around Fagaloa Bay from the turn-off at Falefa Falls. This route offers beautiful views, but don't go past Saletele without a high-clearance vehicle. Another option is the road (4WD only; 10km) signposted off Le Mafa Pass Rd to the village of Ta'elefaga.

Around Apia

Contact SamoaOnFoot (p267) for tours and transport.

Sopo'aga Falls   VIEWPOINT
(Map p254; Le Mafa Pass Rd; adult/child ST5/free; ⏰8am-4pm) The 54m-high Sopo'aga Falls empty themselves into an enormous gorge close to where the Main South Coast Rd meets Le Mafa Pass Rd. The well-signposted lookout is quite a distance from the falls, but the owners make an effort to give value for the entrance fee by touring visitors around their well-labelled kitchen garden. Traditional artefacts are also displayed, including drums and an *umukuka* (cooking house).

🛏 Sleeping & Eating

🏨 Around Falefa

Le Uaina Beach Resort   RESORT **$$**
(Map p254; ☎40270; www.leuaina.com; Main East Coast Rd, Faleapuna; villas ST155-290; P❉🛜🏊) Located on a sweet stretch of coast just before the turn off leading to Aleipata (it's right next door to the Piula Cave Pool), friendly Le Uaina makes for an excellent base for exploring Upolu. Villas are clean with great beds; the best are on the beachfront. Steps lead from the white sand into calm, blue waters that are great for snorkelling or kayaking.

The restaurant dishes up big portions of Western standards (the burgers are excellent) and a few Samoan favourites; dining is indoors or outside on a big deck that surrounds a magnificent old tree.

HERE HE LIES WHERE HE LONGED TO BE

In December 1889 the already-famous Scottish author and poet Robert Louis Stevenson and his wife Fanny Osborne arrived in Apia. Stevenson had left Europe in search of relief from worsening tuberculosis and the general sickliness that had plagued him all his life. He was enchanted by Samoa, and in 1890 he paid £200 for 126 hectares of land in the hills above Apia; it was here he constructed Vailima, the grandest home ever seen on the island. They imported furniture from Scotland and dressed their Samoan employees in *lava-lava* patterned with the Stuart tartan.

In the 1890s, during the period of strife in Samoa between Britain, the USA and Germany, Stevenson became an activist for Samoan rights, maintaining that the people should be left to determine their own destiny in accordance with their customs. He came to be loved by the Samoans for his friendliness and his ability to entertain with stories; they affectionately referred to him as Tusitala (Teller of Tales).

On 3 December 1894 Stevenson died of a stroke at Vailima. When the Samoan chief Tu'imaleali'ifano spoke of Stevenson's death, he echoed the sentiments of many Samoans, saying 'Our beloved Tusitala. The stones and the earth weep.' Two months before his death, in gratitude for his kindness, a delegation of Samoan chiefs had arranged for a hand-dug road to be made between Apia and Vailima, which they called O Le Ala O Le Alofa, the Road of the Loving Heart.

Stevenson had stipulated that he wished to be buried at the top of Mt Vaea, part of the Vailima estate. After a Christian burial service, the coffin was laid on a base of coral and volcanic pebbles and the grave lined with black stones, a practice normally reserved for Samoan royalty.

Namu'a & Lalomanu

Lalomanu Beach stretches long and white in front of a lagoon so blue it looks radioactive. Beach *fale* on this strip are all right next to each other, making this the most 'built up' (take this term lightly) strip outside of Apia. The accommodation is all simple and local style; while it's not tops for privacy, it feels more social and fun than touristy or spoiled. There are a number of very basic places here, so you can easily shop around.

★ Namu'a Island Beach Fale BUNGALOW $
(Map p254; ☏ 751 0231; Namu'a Island; bungalow incl 2 meals & return boat transfers per person ST120) Namu'a is only a short boat ride from Mutiatele, but once you're on this tiny private island, Upolu seems light years away (though it's clearly visible across the strait). *Fale* are open, basic and right on the beach – there's no electricity so everything is lit by oil lamps at night. Meals are mostly local style: simple yet delicious.

It's a perfect place for lounging and languid swims; the more active can do a circumnavigation of the shoreline (low tide only), clamber up the steep central peak and snorkel the surrounding reef.

If you're driving, park (ST10 per day) at the shop with the Namu'a sign in Mutiatele; they'll call the resort to come pick you up.

Anita's Beach Bungalows BUNGALOW $$
(Map p254; ☏ 777 9673; anitasbeachbungalows@hotmail.com; Main South Coast Rd, Lalomanu; open/enclosed/ensuite bungalow, all incl breakfast & dinner ST155/215/360; P🖘) Unmissable in pink and green, Anita's is a longtime Lalomanu favourite: it's fun, friendly and its location can't be beaten. The open *fale* offer the usual mattress on the floor and pull-down plastic sheets, the enclosed ones have a modicum more privacy, while the ensuite *fale* have fans, lockable doors and their own bathroom. There's a sociable restaurant (mains ST13 to ST25) and bar.

Taufua Beach Fales BUNGALOW $$
(Map p254; ☏ 844 1051; www.taufuabeachfales.com; Main South Coast Rd, Lalomanu; s/d bungalow from ST120/180, unit from ST120/240, all incl buffet breakfast & dinner; P🖘) Yellow and mint-green *fale* are as bright as the smiles of the owner and staff, and the spectacular Lalomanu beach is steps away. Basic open *fale* have mattresses on the floor; closed

ones have walls, fans and proper beds. If *fale* aren't your thing, choose one of the simple units about 900m up the hill.

A *fiafia* (open to nonguests) is held on Wednesday and Saturday nights in the sociable dining *fale*; guests are treated to a full traditional lunch on Sunday afternoons.

Litia Sini's Beach Resort BUNGALOW $$
(Map p254; ☏ 41050; www.litiasinibeach.ws; Main South Coast Rd, Lalomanu; s/d bungalow garden ST265/300, beachfront ST295/365, all incl breakfast & dinner; 3-night minimum stay; P🖘) It's well worth shelling out for the enclosed beachfront *fale*, which have terraces right over the outrageous Lalomanu beach and are decorated in bright whites and blues; the garden *fale* are decent but drab. All have shared bathrooms and there's a big restaurant area overlooking the water. The prices are steep for *fale*, but you do get a ceiling fan, electric light and lockable door.

Aga Reef Resort RESORT $$$
(Map p254; ☏ 47800; www.agareefresort.com; Main South Coast Rd, Lalomanu; r ST550, villa ST790-1040; P✳🖘) This posh boutique resort, perched over a stunning stretch of water, is one for the luxury lovers: it's stylish, spotless and the staff is exceptional. There are beautiful rooms available in the large wooden main building, but for a real splurge, nab an Island Villa with an overwater deck (the VIP Villas take indulgence up yet another notch, with private plunge pools).

The picture-perfect lagoon is ideal for snorkelling and kayaking (both are free to guests), or lap up the views from the two wonderful pools.

Saleapaga to Aufaga

There are several beach *fale* places along Saleapaga Beach – a stretch almost as gorgeous as Lalomanu (nitpickers may notice a few pebbles blemishing otherwise perfect white sand).

Faofao Beach Fales BUNGALOW $
(Map p254; ☏ 844 1067; www.beachfalesamoa.com; Main South Coast Rd, Saleapaga; bungalow ST70, s/d r ST150/250, all incl breakfast & dinner ; P✳🖘) Faofao treats guests like family, and their charming, all-natural thatched *fale* make for a wonderful home away from home (the air-conditioned rooms are pretty pleasant too). The beach is a stunner, and great for swims or snorkelling (gear ST5 per

day). Mealtimes often feel like social events; nonguests are welcome to join the Saturday night *fiafia* and Sunday *umu* feasts.

Manusina Beach Fales BUNGALOW $$

(Map p254; ☑846 5398; www.manusinabeach fales.ws; Main South Coast Road, Saleapaga; s/d bungalow open ST80/150, enclosed ST100/180, all incl breakfast & dinner; P 🛜) This place may be simple, but if you're after a warm welcome, gorgeous views, fresh food and cleanliness (even the shared toilets are spotless, a *fale* rarity), it's a tough one to beat, especially at these prices. There are six beachfront *fale* (two of which are enclosed); all have glorious views and working power points. The family that runs it is exceptionally friendly and helpful.

★ Seabreeze Resort RESORT $$$

(Map p254; ☑41391; www.seabreezesamoa. com; off Main South Coast Rd, Aufaga; d/tr/q incl breakfast from ST587/806/1006; ❋ 🛜 ☲) Set in a black-lava-rock bay lined with palm trees and dotted with tiny islands, this exclusive resort has beautifully built bungalows decorated in minimal, tropical style. Kayaks are available or you can snorkel in front and swim to isolated patches of beach. There's an excellent restaurant and bar; optional full meal plan ST130 per day. No kids under 13.

Seabreeze Restaurant INTERNATIONAL $$$

(Map p254; ☑41391; www.seabreezesamoa. com; off Main South Coast Rd, Aufaga; mains ST35-75; ☺8am-9pm) Beautifully appointed and idyllically situated on the edge of the bay, this restaurant offers the best food by far at this end of the island. The slow-cooked smoky barbecue ribs melt in your mouth, as do the real Indian curries; for the ultimate experience, let the chef choose for you. Fridays are *fiafia* night; try the gourmet woodfired pizzas on weekends (noon to 4pm).

South Coast

The fact that Samoa's swankiest resorts are clumped on this stretch of coastline says much about its beauty. It's a delight to drive through the villages, with their brightly painted houses echoing the vibrant colours of the native flora. While the lowlands are impeccably manicured, those seeking untamed nature can explore the rugged the O Le Pupu-Pu'e National Park.

Many of the beaches are a bumpy drive from the main road, and give a welcome sense of seclusion after the road-hugging bays of Aleipata.

◉ Sights & Activities

The south coast of Upolu is dotted with secluded, surf-lapped beaches that you're likely to have all to yourself; if you've ever wanted to play castaway, this is the place to do it. You'll likely be asked to pay admission to most beaches; prices depend on the size of your vehicle (and who's doing the asking), but expect to shell out anywhere from ST15 to ST30.

Vaiula Beach BEACH

(Map p254; South Coast) There's decent surfing to be had at this pretty beach, accessed from Tafatafa village.

Aganoa Black Sand Beach BEACH

(Map p254; admission per car ST15, surf fee ST15) This gorgeous beach is a beautiful spot for a paddle or a picnic. The water is deep enough for swimming but there's no reef to protect you – the snorkelling, however, is some of the best on the island. There's a popular surf-break (for experienced boarders only) called **Boulders** (Map p254; Main South Coast Rd) here, just off Cape Niuato'i. The rough 3km track to Aganoa is 150m east of the stone bridge in Sa'agafou – don't attempt it without a 4WD. The beach is a 10-minute walk to the east.

Salamumu BEACH

(Map p254) This village is home to a beautiful set of beaches reached by a potholed 5.5km track.

Matareva BEACH

(Map p254) You'll find a series of delightful coves with shallow snorkelling areas and lots of rock pools.

O Le Pupu-Pu'e National Park NATIONAL PARK

(Map p254; Main South Coast Rd; ☺7am-6pm) **FREE** The name of this 29-sq-km national park means 'from the coast to the mountaintop'. There are some superb (if rough) hikes to be had here. A trail (six hours return) winds through thick jungle to **Pe'ape'a Cave**, a large lava tube inhabited by *pe'ape'a* (swiftlets); bring a torch. From here, the hardcore can continue along a heavily overgrown trail to **Ofa Waterfall** (three days return). For a less intense tramp, the 700m **Ma**

Tree Walk ends at a gigantic rainforest tree with huge buttress roots.

For the longer walks, a guide, such as Eti from SamoaOnFoot (p267), is essential.

At the park's western boundary, a bumpy 3km unsealed access road (open 7am to 4pm) leads to the magnificently rugged O Le Pupu Lava Coast, where a rocky coastal trail leads along lava cliffs, the bases of which are constantly harassed by enormous waves.

Togitogiga Waterfalls WATERFALL
(Map p254; Off Main South Coast Rd) `FREE` A glorious spot for a splash, this series of gentle waterfalls are separated by blessedly cool waterholes. It's best to visit in the wet season. To get here, take the access road for O Le Pupu-Pu'e National Park and stop at the parking area. There are changing rooms and toilets on-site.

🛏 Sleeping

Le Valasi's Beach Fales BUNGALOW $
(Map p254; ☑35221; www.valasisfales.com; Main South Coast Rd, Savaia-Lefaga; per person incl breakfast & dinner ST120; P) This sweet spot is a winner, with spotless, traditional *fale*, extremely welcoming owners, family-style fresh food and a wonderful location beside a giant clam reserve (snorkel it for ST5). It feels more like a homestay here than a hotel. Bikes, kayaks and snorkelling gear are available.

Tiavi Mountain Escape CABIN $
(Map p254; ☑774 7810; off Cross Island Rd, Tiavi; cabin ST95; P) This is a great little place: away from the swelter of the coast but with a million-dollar view of it. Cabins have small decks that catch the mountain breeze; there's also a guest kitchen, a friendly posse of dogs and a playground. Bring your own supplies, mossie coils and a deck of cards: there's a whole lot of wonderful nothing to do up here.

⭐ **Coconuts Beach Club Resort** RESORT $$$
(Map p254; ☑24849; www.cbcsamoa.com; Main South Coast Rd, Maninoa; ste/beach bungalow/villa/ overwater bungalow from ST1000/1200/ 1400/1800; P✳🛜🏊) This is the hippest resort in the country. Samoa's only overwater *fale* are found here, and what a find they are, with huge, luxuriously-appointed bedrooms, outdoor sunken tubs and two sun decks apiece. Back on land, beach *fale* have covered decks and stylish interiors; many of

the villas line a river and are accessed via bridges. 'Treehouse' suites are back from the beach but have good views.

No kids under three.

⭐ **Lupe Sina Treesort** BOUTIQUE HOTEL $$$
(Map p254; ☑773 5875; www.lupesinatreesort. net; off Cross Island Rd, Tiavi; treehouse ST520-730; P🛜) If you're looking for a (literal) lovenest, grab your bags – and your beloved – and head up the hill to Lupe Sina, home to two extraordinary treehouses. The bigger one is built 12m up a gigantic banyan tree; the other is 10m up an ava tree, with a suspended bedroom and a glass ceiling for unforgettable star-gazing.

The views, obviously, are magnificent; the professional staff, free pancake breakfasts and facilities are equally remarkable. There's an excellent on-site restaurant and tour desk. No kids under seven.

Return to Paradise Resort RESORT $$$
(Map p254; ☑35055; www.returntoparadise resort.com; Lefaga; r/ste/villa from ST600/ 1100/1700; P✳🛜🏊) Sitting smack on the beach that starred in the 1953 Gary Cooper film *Return to Paradise*, this sparkling, upmarket resort is a destination unto itself: with four pools, three restaurants and activities galore (including traditional spearfishing and kayaking lessons, turtle swimming and snorkelling over a giant clam reserve), there's no chance of tropical ennui setting in. Accommodation ranges from tidy hotel rooms to luxurious villas and suites.

Sa'moana Resort RESORT $$$
(Map p254; ☑842 8880; www.samoanaresort. com; Salamumu; fale ST520-890, beach house ST1200; ✳🛜🏊) Sa'moana has a divine location on a white-sand beach that tumbles past black lava formations into a stunning lagoon. Upscale bungalows sit directly on the beach; there's a two-storey house (with a private stretch of sand) for larger groups. As well as offering tons of tours and special surf packages, there are family-friendly activities galore, babysitters, fab pool and a free kids' menu for those under 11.

Saletoga Sands Resort & Spa RESORT $$$
(Map p254; ☑41212; www.saletogasands.com; Main South Coast Rd, Matatufu; villas ST610-1080; P✳🛜🏊) This new resort is more akin to one you'd find in Fiji than far-less-touristed Samoa: it's big, shiny, and draws everyone from honeymooners to families (it's one of the few resorts in Samoa that offer a kids'

club). Villas are modern and have outdoor showers. Flash facilities include a great pool (with swim-up bar), a gym, a spa and a splendid restaurant; its *fiafia* nights (Wednesdays) shouldn't be missed.

Sinalei Reef Resort RESORT $$$
(Map p254; ☑25191; www.sinalei.com; Main South Coast Rd, Maninoa; villas ST973-3000; P❋🛜🏊) If you like lazing around the pool and being handed cocktails by charming waiters, Sinalei is the place to do it. This beautifully landscaped plot by the ocean offers well-appointed stand-alone units, plus two restaurants, tennis courts, a golf course, a watersports centre and good snorkelling around an ocean spring. The staff are delightful; rooms are comfy but a bit plain for the price. No kids under 12.

Eating

Lupe's Cocktail Bar & Restaurant INTERNATIONAL $
(Map p254; ☑31223; www..lupesbeachfale.com; Main South Coast Rd, Maninoa; mains from ST12; ⏾8am-late) For a down-to-earth, filling and home-cooked meal by the sea, check this little place out. They whip up anything and everything here, from pasta to *palusami*, and their trademark burgers are outstanding. Sunday lunches aren't to be missed. You can sleep your meal off in one of the basic beach *fale* (from ST60).

Get there by taking the Coconuts Beach Club Resort entrance, then turn left.

Laumo'osi Fale Restaurant & Ava i Toga Pier Restaurant INTERNATIONAL $$$
(Map p254; ☑25191; www.sinalei.com; Sinalei Reef Resort, Main South Coast Rd, Maninoa; mains ST25-75; ⏾8am-9pm) Sinalei alternates evening meals between its two restaurants. The pier restaurant is the pick of the two, offering an eclectic menu of Samoan dishes, Japanese noodles, pastas, salad and grills in a romantic waterside setting. Themed buffet dinners are served in the *fale* restaurant. Wednesdays are *fiafia* nights (the knife-throwing show is famous); stuff yourself silly at the Saturday barbecue.

Mika's Restaurant INTERNATIONAL $$$
(Map p254; ☑24849; www.cbcsamoa.com; Coconuts Beach Club Resort, Main South Coast Rd, Maninoa; mains ST25-75; ⏾8am-9pm) Chef Mika travels the globe for inspiration, serving

THE RISE OF THE BLUE WORMS

Samoa's most anticipated party has an unlikely guest of honour: the humble worm. Called Palolo Rising, festivities begin on the seventh day after the full moon in October or November (or sometimes both) when the palolo reef-worm emerges from the coral reefs to mate. The blue-green vermicelli-shaped worms – rich in calcium, iron and protein – are a prized delicacy, and are said to be a powerful aphrodisiac. Parties take place on beaches at the worm-catching spots; when the creatures finally appear at around midnight, crowds carrying nets and lanterns hurriedly wade into the sea to scoop them up.

delicious Italian, French and Samoan dishes and a wonderful Hawaiian *ahi poke* salad (raw fish with sesame oil and chilli). Save room for a treat from the extensive tropical desserts menu.

Northwestern Upolu

The main reason for staying here is to be near the airport, the ferries to Savai'i and the boats to the Apolima Strait islands. The coastline is quite built-up (for Samoa, that is), particularly between Apia and the airport, and the brilliantly coloured lagoon is too shallow for a truly satisfying swim.

⊙ Sights

EFKS Museum MUSEUM
(Map p254; ☑42967; www.cccs.org.ws; Main West Coast Rd, Malua; adult/child ST10/5; ⏾8.30am-4.30pm Mon-Fri) About halfway between the international airport and Apia, this museum – run by the Congregational Christian Church – is Samoa's largest. While the displays aren't earth-shatteringly exciting, interesting local contemporary artworks and inspiring woodcarvings make this a worthwhile stop if you're in the area. As might be expected, there are also artefacts dating back to Samoa's early missionary days. An outdoor turtle pond will give the littlies respite from the collections within.

DO DROP IN

Upolu's south coast is blessed with top-notch breaks that draw experienced surfers (these waves are *not* for newbies) from around the world. Though one of the biggest attractions here is the lack of crowds, there is a cluster of surf camps and package tours catering to those who crave waves. Hang ten with any of these recommended operators:

Vaiula Fales (Map p254; ☑ 729 5595; www.samoasurfsecrets.com.au; Tafatafa; bungalow incl breakfast & dinner per person from ST60; P 🎓) Cheap *fale*, close to the breaks and with a sociable surf bar on the beach. **Samoa Surf Secrets** is based here.

Salani Surf Resort (Map p254; ☑ 41069; www.salanisurfresort.com; Salani; surfer package per d/share ST675/400, min 3-night stay; ❄ @ 🎓) On the mouth of the Fupisia River, with excellent left- and right-hand breaks in view.

Offshore Adventures (Map p254; ☑ 750 8825; www.offshoreadventures samoa.com; Salamumu; accommodation & surfing packages per person per day from ST320; P 🎓) Runs popular 'surfaris' for a maximum of five guests.

Sa'moana Resort (p272) A more upmarket resort that also offers surf packages.

🛏 Sleeping & Eating

Airport Lodge   HOTEL $$
(Map p254; ☑ 45584; www.airportlodgesamoa.com; Main West Coast Rd, Mulifanua; s/d bungalow from ST150/180, r ST280; P ❄ 🎓) As uninspiring as its name may be, Airport Lodge actually has a lot going for it. It's close to the airport and wharf, the hotel rooms are huge and clean (the cute enclosed garden *fale* are smaller but perfectly serviceable) and it's a lot cheaper than nearby resorts, though meals are expensive for what they are (the gigantic baked mac and cheese offers the best value).

There's no pool, but guests can swim off a private landing across the road. Outdoor Samoa (p257) is based here.

★ Ifiele'ele Plantation   B&B $$$
(Map p254; ☑ 42554; www.ifieleele.com; off Main West Coast Rd, Fasitoo-Uta; villa/studio ST560/460; P ❄ 🎓 🐾) 🍃 Set on a six-hectare working tropical fruit plantation, this self-catering retreat is the definition of intimate, with just one villa and a studio (both are modern and clean). Active guests can play tennis, tramp the private walking track or partake in cultural activities; those giving in to the languid surrounds can paddle in the lap pool or watch resident goats at play.

Full kitchens are provided, though catered meals can be arranged.

Sheraton Aggie Grey's
Lagoon Resort   RESORT $$$
(Map p254; ☑ 45663; www.sheratonsamoa aggiegreysresort.com; Main West Coast Rd, Mulifanua; r/ste from ST650/790; P ❄ 🎓 🏊) The best things about this sprawling resort are its large pool, spacious grounds, proximity to the airport and wharf, and long list of facilities, including a 160-acre golf course, free kids club (ages four to 12), two restaurants, Samoa's only **casino** (Map p254; ☑ 759 9909; www.whitesandscasino-samoa.com; Sheraton Aggie Grey's Resort, Mulifanua; ⏱ 2pm-4am) and AquaSamoa (p257), the lone dive centre on Upolu. Aggie's turns on a scintillating *fiafia* every Friday night (ST85). Rooms are comfy enough but lack pizazz.

The resort allows nonguests to use its facilities for ST25: kids will tell you that the resort pool is worth every cent.

Le Vasa Resort   RESORT $$$
(Map p254; ☑ 46028; www.levasaresort.com; Main West Coast Rd, Cape Fatuosofia; r ST200, bungalow ST300-375, villa ST600-675, all incl breakfast; P ❄ 🎓 🏊) A millennium ago the Tongans were booted out of Samoa at this grassy headland, but you can expect a warmer welcome at this personable little resort. It's set on a stunning lagoon (no beach, though there is one within strolling distance) and there's a good pool. All *fale* and villas have gorgeous sea views; cheaper rooms look over a landscaped garden.

Anyone is welcome at the open-air **restaurant** (mains from ST50) and the fun **Ugly Mermaid Bar**.

MANONO

POP 889 / AREA 3 SQ KM

If you thought Upolu was mellow, try the tiny, tranquil island of Manono on for size. Canines and cars have been banished here, and the only things that might snap you out of a tropical reverie are occasional blasts from stereos and the tour groups that periodically clog the island's main trail.

It's obligatory for visitors to do the 1½-hour circumnavigation of the island via the path that wends its way between the ocean and people's houses. They're friendly sorts here; expect to be greeted with a cheery '*malo*' a dozen or so times.

The trail winds through Lepuia'i, where you'll see the two-tiered **Grave of 99 Stones** (Map p254; Manono). Translated from the Samoan, the name actually means 'Grave of the Missing Stone' and is dedicated to high chief Vaovasa, who was killed after an unsuccessful attempt to abduct his 100th wife from Upolu. The missing stone at the grave's centre represents the missing wife. The trail's most beautiful section is Manono's less-populated northern edge, where little bays offer terrific views of Apolima. Apai village has the island's best beach.

If you follow the path behind the women's committee building in Salua, you'll eventually end up on top of Mt Tulimanuiva (110m), where there's a large **star mound** (Map p254; Manono). Nearby is the **grave of Afutiti** (Map p254; Manono), a chief who was buried standing up to keep watch over the island. Allow 90 minutes to two hours for this side trip.

Sleeping

Sunset View Fales BUNGALOW $
(Map p254; 759 6240; bookings@samoa-hotels.ws; Lepuia'i; bungalow per person with/without bathroom ST130/100) Rustic but bright beach shacks are offered here (now up on the hill since the 2009 tsunami wiped out the waterfront ones), along with a daily boat trip out to the edge of the reef for memorable snorkelling stints. Price includes all meals and boat transfers.

Sweet Escape BUNGALOW $
(Map p254; 728 0914; www.sweetescapesamoa.com; Faleu; bungalow per person incl breakfast & dinner ST120) Facing Upolu, these enclosed, bright-yellow *fale* are closely clustered together on a sandy spit looking over the lagoon. Tours and cooking classes are available.

Getting There & Away

Both **Samoa Scenic Tours** (p255) and **Polynesian Xplorer** (p254) offer day tours of Manono. **Outdoor Samoa** (p257) runs kayaking trips (from ST140) to the island.

If you'd rather go it alone, head for the jetty just south of Le Vasa Resort at Manono-uta village. Buses marked either 'Manono-uta' or 'Falelatai' (ST6.50) will get you here from Apia (allow 90 minutes). The boats leave when there are enough people (usually when the bus arrives) and the cost is ST5 each way. If you want to charter the whole boat expect to pay about ST40 each way. Although the boats are small, Manono is inside the reef so the 20-minute trip isn't usually rough.

APOLIMA

POP 80 / AREA 1 SQ KM

Few travellers make the trip out to the minuscule but marvellous Apolima. From a distance, its steep walls look completely inaccessible; when you get closer you can spy the narrow gap in the northern cliffs, through which small boats can enter the crater and land on a sandy beach. The small settlement consists of a handful of buildings interspersed with pigpens, jungly foliage and (naturally) a large church. To get an overview of the island, climb up to the small **lighthouse** perched high on the crater's northern rim.

Getting to Apolima isn't easy. You'll need an invitation to stay with a local family; Sunset View Fales (p275), on nearby Manono, may be able to arrange this – plus a boat to come and collect you – but you'll have to negotiate a fee.

SAVAI'I

POP 43,142 / AREA 1700 SQ KM

Samoa's 'Big Island' offers a spectacular scenic smorgasbord of riotous rainforest, sea-smashed cliffs, pristine waterfalls and ragged volcanic cones (around 450 of them). Though visitors will be taken by Savai'i's gentle, snoozy ambience, the island itself – the largest shield volcano in the South Pacific – has volatile tendencies, most dramatically displayed in the eerie lava fields,

Savai'i

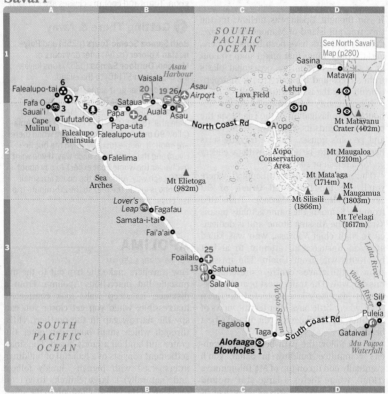

village ruins and craters of the north and the explosive blowholes of the south coast.

Though it's the largest island in Samoa (and the fourth largest in Polynesia), Savai'i is home to less than a quarter of the country's population, and has little in the way of facilities or infrastructure. *Fa'a Samoa* (the Samoan Way) remains strong in Savai'i's orderly villages, where the humid hush is broken only by the squeals of playing children, the buzz of weed-whackers and the soaring hymns of Sunday services.

ⓘ Getting There & Away

AIR

Samoa Air (p294) operates charter flights between **Maota Airport** (Map p276; Maota) and **Asau Airport** (Map p276) on Savai'i and Faleolo and Fagali'i airports on Upolu. Email for bookings and fares.

BOAT

Two car ferries tackle the 22km Apolima Strait between Upolu and Savai'i daily. The larger of the two boats, the *Lady Samoa III,* is the more comfortable. The trip across can take anywhere from 45 minutes to over an hour, depending on conditions.

Vehicles should be prebooked through the **Samoa Shipping Corporation** (p293); many hotels and car rental agencies can also do this for you. Before putting your car on the ferry at Mulifanua Wharf, you must have its underside cleaned (free) at the spraying station 100m before the boat terminal. This is done to prevent the spread of the giant African snail.

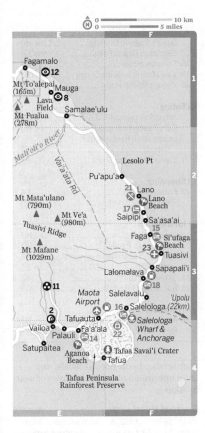

(map labels)

N 0 — 10 km
   0 — 5 miles

Fagamalo
⊙12
Mt To'alepai
(165m)   Mauga
▲ Lava ⊙8
  Field   Samalae'ulu
Mt Fualua
(278m)

Mali'oli'o River

Va'aiata Rd

Lesolo Pt
Pu'apu'a
Mt Mata'ulano
(790m)   21 Lano
▲   ⊗ Lano
  Mt Ve'a   17   Beach
  (980m)   Saipipi Sa'asa'ai
Tuasivi Ridge   Faga Si'ufaga
                   23   Beach
Mt Mafane   Tuasivi
(1029m)
         Lalomalava Sapapali'i
⊗11   18
      Maota   Salelavalu
      Airport   16 Salelologa   'Upolu
      2   Salelologa (22km)
     Tafuauta   Salelologa
Vailoa   Fa'a'ala   Wharf &
    Palauli 14   22 Anchorage
Satupaitea   Tafua Savai'i Crater
      Aganoa   Tafua
      Beach
   Tafua Peninsula
   Rainforest Preserve

❶ DON'T MISS THE BOAT

The ferries to and from Savai'i can get very full, especially on weekends, holidays and Friday afternoons. Arrive at least an hour early on these days and get in the queue (in your car if you're driving or in the departure lounge if you're on foot) or you'll risk not getting on – the captains are (fortunately) quite strict about not overloading the boats. If you're driving, buying your ticket in advance is a must.

Boats seldom run on 'Samoa time'. A 2pm departure means a 2pm departure.

Manase or Sasina bus. The Falealupo bus will take you around the Falealupo Peninsula, while the Salega or Fagafau buses trundle past the Alofaaga Blowholes and Satuiatua Beach. The most you'll pay for a ride is ST10 (to Asau). Buses to out-of-the-way destinations are timed with the ferries.

CAR

It's a joy to drive the sealed coast road that circles the island, but keep an eye out for stray children, pigs, dogs and chickens. Off the main road you'll encounter a few bumpy tracks where at the very least you'll need a high-clearance 2WD (if not a 4WD if there's been heavy rain). This includes the steep, rocky climb up Mt Matavanu.

There are several petrol stations around Salelologa but only a few scattered around the island.

Cars can be hired on Savai'i but, as there's more competition on Upolu, if you're staying several days it works out cheaper and easier to bring a car over on the ferry. A small 2WD Hyundai costs around ST170 per day.

The spanking new **MotoSamoa** (☏ 764 5435; www.motosamoa.com; per day ST59, discounts for longer hire) group rents out 110cc scooters from three locations on Savai'i (see website for details); they'll also deliver to your accommodation.

TAXI

A small army of taxis congregates around the Salelologa Market and the wharf.

Lady Samoa III 'Big Boat' Ferry Departures

Departs Salelologa	Departs Mulifanua
Sun 11am & 3pm	Sun 1pm & 5pm
Mon 6am, 10am & 2pm	Mon 8am, noon & 4pm
Tue 6am & 2pm	Tue 8am & 4pm
Wed 6am, 10am & 2pm	Wed 8am, noon & 4pm
Thu 6am & 2pm	Thu 8am & 4pm
Fri 6am, 10am & 2pm	Fri 8am, noon & 4pm
Sat 6am, 10am & 2pm	Sat 8am, noon & 4pm

❶ Getting Around

BUS

Salelologa's market is the main terminal for Savai'i's colourful, crowded buses. For the east-coast beaches take the Pu'apu'a bus, or to continue on to Fagamalo, take the Lava Field Express. To carry on to Manase, take the

Salelologa & the East Coast

Ragtag Salelologa stretches up from the ferry terminal, offering little of interest except for a fairly languid *market* (Map p276; Salelologa; ⊙early-late Mon-Sat); if your needs run more to groceries than geegaws, the

Savai'i

big **Frankies** (Map p276; Salelologa; ⊙ 6am-9pm) supermarket across the road has loads of fresh produce and groceries. There's nowhere better for supplies on the entire island.

Heading north you'll pass a tight series of villages fronting a shallow lagoon. It's only once you round the point at Tuasivi that things get exciting, as long white-sand beaches come into view, outlining the vivid aquamarine lagoon. The best of them, **Si'ufaga** and **Lano**, are among Savai'i's finest. The area also has numerous freshwater pools and springs for bathing.

🛏 Sleeping

Salelologa is handy to the wharf and makes a fine base, but it's only once you head out of town that you really start to experience the restful charms of Savai'i.

Salelologa & Around

Ieu & Winnie's Islands View Motel MOTEL $
(Map p276; ☎ 722 2557; islandsviewsavaii@gmail.com; Wharf Rd, Salelologa; 1-/2-bedroom units ST90/145; P❋🛜) This small, hospitable family-run motel is a short stumble from the wharf. There are six simple units, a restau-

rant serving home-cooked meals, and – as the name promises – splendid views of near-by islands.

Savaiian Hotel RESORT $
(Map p276; ☎ 51296; www.savaiianhotel.com; North Coast Rd, Lalomalava; s/d without bathroom ST55/80, bungalow ST85/115, unit ST175/205; P❋🛜🏊) The large enclosed *fale* here are many steps above your average beach hut, with balconies, fans and private bathrooms. The units have amenities including air-conditioning, while new budget rooms are basic but excellent value. They're all set in a sparse garden between the village and the sea; the water's too shallow for swimming, but there is a small pool.

It also rents snorkelling gear and kayaks, and can arrange tours of Savai'i.

Lusia's Lagoon Chalets BUNGALOW $$
(Map p276; ☎ 51487; www.lusiaslagoon.com; South Coast Rd, Salelologa; bungalow s ST70-270, d ST120-320, s/d 145/200; ❋🛜) Fall asleep to the lullaby of lapping waves at this charming, slightly ramshackle place. Accommodation varies dramatically: the cheapest *fale* teeter on stilts over the lagoon and are very basic (though their sea-gazing decks are adorably

atmospheric), while those with private facilities have air-conditioning, mod-cons and a sturdier feel. The on-site restaurant-bar is social, scenic and open to all.

Kayaks are free, and there's deep enough water for a proper swim off the pier.

Jet Over Hotel HOTEL **$$**
(Map p276; 51565; www.jetoverhotel.com; r/ste ST225/250;) Just off the main road behind a cluster of shops, this is a surprisingly stylish place: the pool and grounds are impeccable, the restaurant serves up sublime meals (pancake lovers may embarrass themselves at the free buffet breakfasts), and the sea views are glossy-mag gorgeous. While the cheapest rooms are decent enough (if plain), the two-storey, self-contained beach-facing suites get top marks.

It turns on a mean *fiafia* every Thursday night.

Tuasivi & Lano

★ **Joelan Beach Fales** BUNGALOW **$**
(Map p276; 722 9588; www.joelanbeachfales.ws; North Coast Rd, Lano Beach; open/enclosed bungalow incl breakfast & dinner ST120/140;) Long, languid Lano Beach easily rates as one of the best strips of sand on Savai'i, and Joelan's simple but well-kept thatched *fale* nab the best bit – some are so close to the water you could almost dangle your toes in the surf. The food here is bountiful and beautiful, as is the down-home hospitality. Ask about taking its *paopao* (traditional canoe) for a paddle.

Lauiula Beach Fales BUNGALOW **$**
(Map p276; 53897; www.lauiulabeachfales.com; North Coast Rd, Lano Beach; bungalow beach/garden per person incl breakfast & dinner from ST70/50;) Right next to Joelan's, the beach here has eroded away quite a bit but huddled-together *fale* are more 'posh' thanks to linoleum floors and a more sturdy thatch enclosure: for an extra ST10 you can have actual walls. There's a pro set-up with tours and transport on offer. Breakfast and dinner are served in a gorgeously carved seafront dining *fale*.

Amoa Resort RESORT **$$$**
(Map p276; 53518; www.amoaresort.com; North Coast Rd, Tuasivi; bungalow/villa ST520/640;) This recently revamped and rebranded boutique resort sits pretty across the road from an eye-smartingly turquoise lagoon. Large luxurious villas and beautiful bungalows hook around a lushly landscaped pool (with swim-up bar), and its magnificent restaurant – specialising in nouveau-Pacific cuisine – deserves many stars. It's easily the most upmarket choice on this stretch of coast.

Eating & Drinking

★ **Taefu T Matafeo Store** CAFE **$**
(Map p276; 764 5435; North Coast Rd, Asaga; snacks ST1-10; 7am-8pm Mon-Sat, 7am-9am & 5-8pm Sun;) If you're driving between Salelologa and the north coast, do yourself a favour and stop at this absolute gem of a place. It doesn't look like much, but there are sweet surprises in store: excellent espresso, indescribably wonderful homemade cakes (the chocolate is legendary), icy beers and light meals, including a mindblowing kimchi, all served in a delightful courtyard. There's even free wi-fi!

CC's Restaurant and Bar INTERNATIONAL **$$**
(Map p276; 51487; www.lusiaslagoon.com/dining; Lusia's Lagoon Chalets, Salelologa; mains ST19-45; 7am-10pm) Overlooking a lovely lagoon with views to Upolu, this casual place serves super-fresh seafood, traditional Samoan dishes, curries and hearty grilled meats. Pop by in the morning for strong espresso and homemade cake, or watch the sun set with a cold cocktail in hand.

LeSogaimiti Restaurant & Bar INTERNATIONAL **$$**
(Map p276; 51296; www.savaiianhotel.com; Savaiian Hotel, Main North Rd, Lalomalava; mains ST15-45) At the Savaiian Hotel, this decent, dependable restaurant offers water views and some truly filling meals. A varied menu lists everything from (very good) seafood, chicken, sausages and steak to Samoan classics and spicy curries. It also has a kids' menu and vegetarian options.

★ **Amoa Restaurant** INTERNATIONAL **$$$**
(Map p276; 53518; www.amoaresort.com; Amoa Resort, North Coast Rd, Tuasivi; mains ST25-75) This place is a true gem, and unlike anywhere else you'll find on Savai'i: it's a foodie destination unto itself. Fresh, locally sourced ingredients are used to create truly innovative takes on Samoan and Pacific classics, including *palusami* risotto balls, coconut-crusted chicken and homemade pasta infused with taro leaves.

North Savai'i

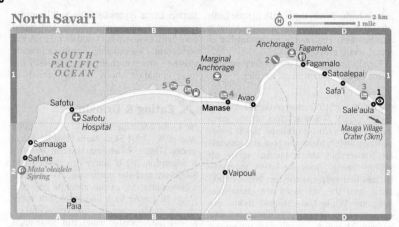

North Savai'i map showing South Pacific Ocean, Safotu, Safotu Hospital, Samauga, Safune, Mata'olealelo Spring, Paia, Manase, Avao, Marginal Anchorage, Anchorage, Fagamalo, Satoalepai, Safa'i, Safa'i, Sale'aula, Mauga Village Crater (3km), Vaipouli. Scale: 2 km / 1 mile.

ℹ Information

ANZ Bank (Map p276; Salelologa; ☺ 8.30am-3pm Mon-Fri, to noon Sat) Has an outdoor ATM.

Bank South Pacific (Map p276; Salelologa; ☺ 8.30am-3pm Mon-Wed, to 4pm Thu-Fri) The outdoor ATM accepts most cards.

Malietoa Tanumafili II Hospital (Map p276; ☑ 53511; North Coast Rd, Tuasivi) Has on-call doctors and a pharmacy. Other basic hospitals are at Safotu and Satua.

Post Office (Map p276; Blue Bird Mall, Salelologa; ☺ 8.30am-noon & 1-4pm Mon-Fri) Has telephones.

Central North Coast

Sporting surreal lava fields, captivating caves and arguably the best beaches on the Big Island, it's no surprise that this is the most popular stretch on Savai'i. The coast has an abundance of accommodation options ranging from traditional *fale* to sumptuous suites; lovely little Manase offers the most choice. The high chief here had the foresight to ban dogs, making this one of the most unstressful villages to explore outside of Manono.

The bus from Salelologa to Manase costs about ST7; there's an ATM and petrol station at Manase.

◉ Sights

The Mt Matavanu eruptions between 1905 and 1911 created a moonscape in Savai'i's northeastern corner as a flow of lava 10m to 150m thick rolled through plantations and villages. The North Coast Rd crosses this dark, fractured lava field.

Sale'aula Lava Fields HISTORIC SITE
(Map p276; North Coast Rd, Sale'aula; adult/child ST5/3; ☺ 8.30am-5pm) This striking spot offers a fascinating glimpse of the destruction wrought by the 1905 eruption of Mt Matavanu. Most photogenic is the ruined **LMS Church**: 2m of lava flowed through its door and was eerily imprinted by corrugated iron when the roof collapsed. Nearby, the **Virgin's Grave** purportedly marks the burial place of a girl so pure that lava flowed around her grave, leaving it untouched.

Amid all the lava, there are some nice grassy picnic spots here; littlies will enjoy chasing the squillion resident chickens.

Mauga Village Crater SCENIC AREA
(Map p276; North Coast Rd, Mauga) The modern, iron-roofed *fale* of Mauga village encircle a shallow, almost perfectly circular crater populated by banana palms. The access road is guarded by an enormous Catholic church. Approach a villager if you'd like to be shown around. It's 5km south of Sale'aula

Mt Matavanu Crater VOLCANO
(Map p276; ST20; ☺ 9am-4pm Mon-Sat) If you've got a 4WD and a sturdy pair of boots, a visit to the volcano responsible for the devastation visited upon northeastern Savai'i a century ago is worth a few hours of your time. In addition to the fun of the very bumpy ride and pleasant views, you'll also get to meet 'Da Craterman', who maintains the track and collects the fee for his village (charming as he is, don't let him charge you more than ST20 per person).

North Savai'i

From Safotu take the turn-off to Paia village, then follow the signposted track up the mountain. After a lengthy stint of bouncing over the old lava flow, you'll reach Craterman's *fale*: if he's not around, keep heading up and you'll doubtless find him. From here there's an even bumpier 2km to the car park, where a 10-minute trail leads to the crater's edge. Keep the kids tight at hand: there's a vertiginous drop into the lush greenness below. The whole route is lined with Craterman's cheesy signs representing the visitors from 110-and-counting countries who have made the trek.

Pe'ape'a Cave
CAVE
(Map p276; North Coast Rd; adult/child ST7/4; ☺8am-5pm) This cave sits beside the coast road just south of Letui. A round-trip guided exploration of this small lava tube takes only 10 minutes, but you'll see white-rumped Polynesian swiftlets and their nests up close. Bring your own torch.

✦ Activities

Dive Savai'i
DIVING
(Map p280; ☏54172; www.divesavaii.com; North Coast Rd, Fagamalo; ☺closed Sun) Besides diving interesting sites including a Missionary-era shipwreck (two-tank dives ST275), this family-friendly outfit offers PADI open-water courses (ST1260) and half-day snorkelling tours (ST65, snorkelling gear ST20); turtle and dolphin sightings aren't guaranteed, but they are common. It also hires snorkelling equipment on a casual basis (full set per 24 hours ST30).

⊨ Sleeping & Eating

There are many quality *fale* places lining the North Coast Rd. Most places include breakfast in the rates; those in Manase throw in lunch and dinner as well.

⊨ Sale'aula

★ Bayview Resort
RESORT $$
(Map p280; ☏54170; www.bayviewresort.ws; North Coast Rd, Sale'aula; bungalow ST220-300; 🅿❄🛜) First you'll be taken by its dramatic location on a solid river of black lava, then you'll be knocked for six by the dazzling turquoise bay it's named for, and by the time you're lounging on the massive deck attached to the best cottages, you'll be dead-set on extending your stay. Swimming and white-sand sunning is superb; check out the lava pool at high tide.

The restaurant means well, but is very hit-or-miss; if you're driving, there's an excellent pizza place five minutes up the road.

⊨ Fagamalo

Le Lagoto Resort & Spa
RESORT $$$
(Map p280; ☏58189; www.lelagoto.ws; North Coast Rd, Fagamalo; d ST775-900; 🅿❄🛜🏊) The wooden bungalows at this boutique beach-side resort are the plushest you'll find on the island; they're wonderfully atmospheric with intricate Samoan-style interiors and

---

SUNDAY LUNCH

On Sunday mornings you'll find the islands shrouded in smoke as villagers light fires to warm stones needed for the *umu* (ground ovens) used to bake *to'ona'i* (Sunday lunch). Visitors sometimes complain that nothing happens in Samoa on Sunday, but it's hardly true – after a small breakfast (on account of the looming lunch), Samoans go to church and sing their lungs out, at noon they eat an enormous roast dinner and in the afternoon they sleep.

You may be lucky enough to be invited to a family *to'ona'i*. A typical spread includes baked fish and other seafood (freshwater prawns, crabs, octopus cooked in coconut milk), suckling pig, baked breadfruit, bananas, *palusami* (coconut cream wrapped in taro leaves), salads and curry dishes.

SAMOA CENTRAL NORTH COAST

DWARF'S CAVE

Dwarf's Cave (Map p276; Near Paia Village; guide per group around ST20; ⊙8.30am-5pm Mon-Sat) This intriguing subterranean lava tube leads downwards as if to the centre of the earth. The cave is named after a legendary group of dwarves, who apparently still live in its depths, and leave the occasional footprint. It's said that no one – except maybe the dwarves – has reached the end of it, and your guides (the village *matai* or local boys) will keep leading you through its prodigious depths, crossed by underground rivers, until you tell them to turn around.

Bring your own torch and reliable footwear, and be prepared to swim and get seriously muddy.

The cave is signposted off the Main North Coast Rd, just west of the Mt Matavanu turn-off. In Paia, look for the faded signpost on the right and wait outside the blue *fale* at this intersection; someone should appear to guide you to the cave.

blue-sea views. The **restaurant** (⊙7.30am-9pm, mains ST20-70) is great some nights, uninspired the next, but it has an extensive kids' menu and good *fiafia* nights (Thursdays). It's open to nonguests.

Savai'i Lagoon Resort　　　RESORT $$$
(Map p280; ☑54168; www.savaiilagoon.co.nz; North Coast Rd, Fagamalo; studio ST350, bungalow ST315-450; P🖤) Taking the plum spot on one of Savai'i's best and most protected beaches, these large self-contained units are clean and inviting, but overpriced for their bland interiors and lack of air-conditioning. The resort owns Samoa's only glass-bottomed boat; tours run twice daily (except Sundays) and cost ST40/20 for adults/children. Free activities include bocce, volleyball, kayaking and zooming around in a dinghy.

Leilina's Pizza　　　PIZZA $$
(Map p280; ☑54454; North Coast Rd, Fagamalo; pizzas ST24-45; ⊙10am-8pm Mon-Sat, 11am-8pm Sun) If you're hankering for pizza – especially crunchy, super-thin-crust pizza – this place is a godsend. The smell emanating forth from the kitchen is enough to work up a good drool; you'll be positively slobbering after a few bites of the wickedly spicy 'diavolo' (with pepperoni, chilli and garlic). Take it with you for a beach picnic, or dine in the small courtyard restaurant.

🛏 Manase

Tailua Beach Fales　　　BUNGALOW $
(Map p280; ☑54102; tailuasbeachfales@gmail.com; North Coast Rd, Manase; bungalow per person incl breakfast & dinner ST70; P🖤) This is a small, family-run collection of recently upgraded *fale* that are a step above their competition for their sea-facing decks, raised beds and spotlessness. Snorkellers report an abundance of turtles in the reef channel here. Nothing is too much trouble for the wonderful hostess Lua; you'll dream of her cooking long after you leave.

Regina's Beach Fales　　　BUNGALOW $
(Map p280; ☑54054; reginabeachfales@gmail.com; North Coast Rd, Manase; bungalow per person incl breakfast & dinner ST60; P🖤) The *fale* here are of the traditional variety with woven blinds and mattresses on the floor, but they do have electric lights. Meals are low-key social events, with substantial local dishes such as roast breadfruit and taro served up at a communal dining table.

Tanu Beach Fales　　　BUNGALOW $
(Map p280; ☑54050; tanubeachfales@gmail.com; North Coast Rd, Manase; bungalow per person incl breakfast & dinner ST70, s/d ST95/170; P🖤) This long-standing establishment is huge, which is only fitting as it's owned by the village's *ali'i* (high chief; the man to be thanked for the dog ban). There are dozens of simple *fale* dotting the beach; the accommodation block across the road offers basic rooms with real beds and shared bathrooms. It runs occasional – and very lively – *fiafia* nights.

Stevenson's at Manase　　　RESORT $$$
(Map p280; ☑58219; www.stevensonsatmanase.com; North Coast Rd, Manase; bungalow/villa ST280/400, ste ST550-950; P🖤🖤) This is the most upmarket place in Manase, with accommodation ranging from enormous, super-modern suites and posh beach villas to boutique *fale*, complete with fridges and cool stone ensuites. Its popular outdoor bar overlooks a glorious beach, while across the road, its Tusitala Restaurant (mains ST28 to ST55) does the usual mix of international classics with a sprinkling of Samoan samples.

Northwestern Savai'i

Jutting out from the western end of Savai'i is the beautiful Falealupo Peninsula, rich with sites associated with significant Samoan legends. The peninsula's remoteness and protected tracts of rainforest lend it an almost unnerving calm.

In past years, burglars have targeted tourists in this area, so lock your car and don't leave anything of value in it or in your *fale*. Even if you don't have anything stolen, you'll likely feel robbed after having been asked for so many exaggerated 'custom fees' to tour the sites. It's definitely one of the more beautiful areas of the island, though, so weigh the pros and cons of feeling swindled.

◉ Sights & Activities

Cape Mulinu'u   VIEWPOINT
(Map p276; Falealupo Rd; ⊘8.30am-5pm Mon-Sat) The country's most western point is not only gorgeously scenic (until Samoa hopped the dateline, it was the last place in the world the sun set each day), but home to many fascinating cultural and archaeological sites. The **Fafa O Sauai'i** outlook was one of Samoa's most sacred spots in pre-Christian times; there's a great swimming hole here. Nearby is a **star mound**, **Vaatausili Cave** and the **Vai Sua Toto** (the 'Blood Well' – named after the warrior Tupa'ilevaililigi, who threw his enemies' severed heads in here).

You may be hit up for an exorbitant admission fee; you can probably get away with ST10 per person.

Falealupo Canopy Walk   NATURE RESERVE
(Map p276; Falealupo Rd; admission ST20; ⊘7am-6pm) This wobbly walk takes you across a 24m jerry-built bridge strung between two large trees almost 10m above the rainforest floor. After you cross the walkway to the second tree, climb via a slightly sturdier wooden ladder to a platform up a magical, nearly 230-year-old banyan tree. The walk is part of the **Falealupo Rainforest Preserve**, a customary-owned conservation area.

The ST20 admission also covers you for nearby attractions Moso's Footprint and the House of Rock.

Moso's Footprint   ARCHAEOLOGICAL SITE
(Map p276; Falealupo Rd; admission incl in Canopy Walkway ticket; ⊘7am-6pm) This ancient 1m-by-3m rock depression is decidedly un-remarkable apart from the legend that surrounds it: apprently, the giant Moso made the footprint when he stepped over from Fiji to Samoa. You'll find it well signposted in front of a tidy *fale*.

House of Rock   ARCHAEOLOGICAL SITE
(Map p276; Falealupo Rd; admission incl in Canopy Walkway ticket; ⊘7am-6pm) Legend says this site – a partially collapsed lava tube – is the result of a house-building competition between Falealupo's men and women, a contest the women won; it's a symbol of motivation for Samoan women to this day. It doesn't look like much (though it does make a handy cyclone shelter), but a good guide (ST5) with stories to tell will enliven the experience.

Falealupo Ruins   RUIN
(Map p276; Falealupo) Cyclones Ofa and Val struck the peninsula in 1990 and 1991, completely destroying the village of Falealupo. The decision was made to rebuild the village further inland and the ruined village was left in tatters, though some families have since moved back to rebuild. The ruins of the **Catholic church** (Falealupo Rd) are particularly enigmatic and eerily beautiful. You may be shaken down here, even if you just want to take a photograph.

A'opo Conservation Area & Mt Silisili   HIKING
The two- to three-day return trip to the summit of Mt Silisili (1858m), the highest point in Samoa, traverses some wonderful rainforested sections of the A'opo Conservation Area and Savai'i's mountainous backbone. To organise a guide, speak to the *pulenu'u* (a combination of mayor and police chief) of A'opo; ask in the town's small shop for directions.

You'll pay around ST50 per person per day and will need to supply food and water and all the requisite camping and hiking equipment.

⛖ Sleeping & Eating

Vaisala Beach Hotel   HOTEL $
(Map p276; ☏58016; South Coast Rd, Vaisala; s/d from ST100/120, bungalow ST75; ⓟ❉🛜) Quirky Vaisala has a distinct retro charm, with mismatched furnishings and a dated, barracks-like main building. Rooms are slightly oddball but comfortable, and all have terraces; the *fale* have traditional thatched roofs and louvres. The hotel's restaurant has an outdoor deck and serves

filling dinners, including a much-lauded lobster dish. It faces its own beautiful – and swimmable – beach.

Va-i-Moana Seaside Lodge BUNGALOW $$

(Map p276; ☑58140; www.vaimoanaseaside lodge.com; South Coast Rd, Asau; open bungalow per person ST95, closed bungalow s ST140-170, d ST250-300, ste ST320-400, all incl breakfast & dinner; P❋☎) This friendly place sits on a sparkling cove, with a hodgepodge of lodgings that range from traditional open *fale* and enclosed bungalows perched over the surf to blissfully air-conditioned luxe. There's a good restaurant and bar, free kayaks and fishing tours on offer (from ST800 for two anglers). Ask the lovely owners about the site's fascinating history.

South Coast

With less reef to protect it, Savai'i's south coast bears witness to dramatic confrontations between land and sea, resulting in blustering blowholes and some great surfing spots. Away from Mother Nature's theatrics, this delightfully drowsy, sparsely populated stretch is a wonderful place to do very little at all.

◉ Sights

★ **Alofaaga Blowholes** GEYSER
(Taga Blowholes; Map p276; via Taga Village; admission ST5; ⊙7am-6pm) These powerful blowholes are among the most spectacular on Earth, and well worth going out of your way for. Strong waves are pushed through a series of lava tubes, causing rip-roaring, geyser-like explosions that shoot dozens of metres into the air. If this wasn't dramatic enough, villagers throw coconuts

> ### GATEWAY TO THE UNDERWORLD
>
> The natural beauty of the Falealupo Peninsula befits its spiritual significance. In pre-Christian times it was believed to be the gateway for souls into the next world. According to tradition, there are two entrances to the underworld: one for chiefs and another for commoners. One entrance is through a cave near Cape Mulinu'u and the other is on the trail made by the setting sun over the sea.

(for a fee: don't pay more than ST10) into the blowholes, where they blast up like cannonballs: it's thrilling stuff, and photographs extremely well. DO NOT get too close to the blowholes, no matter what the locals do.

Pay admission at the first *fale* and park your car at the second *fale*, near the main blowhole. You shouldn't have to pay admission again, though you may be asked to; there are a few crafty sorts around here, so keep your doors locked, even when you're inside the car.

Pulemelei Mound ARCHAEOLOGICAL SITE

(Map p276; off South Coast Rd) Polynesia's largest ancient structure is the intriguing, pyramidal Pulemelei Mound (sometimes called Tia Seu Ancient Mound). Constructed sometime between AD 1100 and 1400, it measures 65m by 60m at its base and rises to a height of more than 12m. Its original purpose continues to baffle experts; for more information about its possible purpose see p303. It's a stirring place, with views from its stony summit to the ocean and into thick rainforest. The surrounding area is presumably covered in important archaeological finds but, for now, the jungle hides its secrets.

It's very difficult to visit the mound as it's located on disputed land. There's no signage or upkeep: the path to the site and the mound itself are very overgrown. Guides often refuse to take people here because they worry that someone who has an ambiguous claim to the land may hassle them into handing over an exorbitant fee, or worse, just kick them off. That said, it may be possible to pick up a guide; ask at the *fale* at nearby Afu-A-Au Falls.

If you want to try it sans-guide, head down the road flanked by iron poles that starts about 300m beyond the iron-girder bridge on the opposite side of the river from Afu-A-Au Falls (no sign). You'll soon reach a rocky ford over a stream (impassable without a good 4WD). Park here, cross the creek at the bend and enter an overgrown track between two poles. The track follows an old road bordered by stone walls, then continues up a fern-filled path to the mound. The walk takes about an hour each way: you'll need water and sturdy shoes.

This is a very secluded area – women especially should not walk alone, and don't leave any valuables in your car.

Afu-A-Au Falls WATERFALL

(Map p276; off South Coast Rd; adult/child ST5/2; ⊙8am-6pm Mon-Sat) Gorgeous Afu-A-Au Falls, also known as Olemoe Falls, are a dream come true on a steamy Samoan day (which is, truthfully, almost every day). Cascading down to a blessedly cool 3m-deep waterhole in a secluded jungle, the falls are spring-fed, meaning swimming is possible even during the dry season. It's only signposted if you're travelling from the east; if you're coming from the west, turn left immediately after crossing the steel bridge. Pay at the *fale* by the entrance.

Tafua Peninsula Rainforest Preserve NATURE RESERVE

(admission ST5) This preserve contains superb stands of rainforest and rugged stretches of lava coast studded with cliffs and sea arches. A highlight is the **Tafua Savai'i crater**: its sheer, deep walls are choked with vegetation, giving it a lost-world feel. This place is a birdwatcher's delight, and you will probably catch glimpses of flying foxes napping in the trees far below.

Take the side road signposted to Tafua opposite Ma'ota Airport and pay the 'custom fee' about 50m along. The hiking track to the crater is overgrown and can be hard to follow, so it's worth taking the services of a guide (be sure to agree on a price beforehand) or at least asking directions from the village kids.

🏃 Activities

At the western end of Fa'a'ala village, a track leads to lovely **Aganoa Beach**. There are strong currents here, so swim with care. Ask at at Aganoa Lodge before surfing.

Satuiatua SURFING

(Map p276; per person ST10) Surfers will find an excellent left-hand surf-break at Satuiatua; the fee is used to support the local school.

🛏 Sleeping & Eating

Satuiatua Beach Fales BUNGALOW $

(Map p276; ☏846 4119; South Coast Rd, Satuiatua; bungalow per person incl breakfast & dinner ST75; 🅿🛜) Run by a family of women, this spotless place is loaded with simple and effective touches. Open *fale* have proper beds and are well maintained, while enclosed *fale* are more like large cottages; there are also a couple of ensuite units. The marvellous treehouse (with swings!) perched in a huge banyan tree is reason alone to stay, though the idyllic snorkelling and fantastic surfing get high marks too.

The **restaurant** (lunch ST20) serves good, hearty meals. It's a good stop for lunch if you find yourself in these parts when the tummy rumbles.

Aganoa Lodge BUNGALOW $$$

(Map p276; ☏+1 310 990 6269; www.pegasus lodges.com; Aganoa Beach; 6-night surfer packages from ST5080; 🅿🛜) Recently rebranded and given a high-end makeover, this all-inclusive surf resort exploits the beauty of an exquisite little beach and its proximity to some of Savai'i's best breaks. Surfers (and their nonsurfing partners and families) shack up in luxurious *fale* with real beds, ensuites, open-air showers, electricity and surf-facing decks. Set meals are top-notch, locally sourced and served communally.

Surf package prices include all meals, accommodation, guided surf trips and return airport transfers.

UNDERSTAND SAMOA

Samoa Today

In 2012 Samoa celebrated 50 years of independence with huge pomp and partying. Though Samoa is very much its own country, it still relies heavily on foreign aid, particularly from Australia and New Zealand, with whom ties are very close. In 2014 Samoa hosted the third international Small Island Developing States (SIDS) conference, which culminated in the adoption of the Samoa Pathway, a document which – in part – saw global leaders pledge their support to sustainable development and the battles against climate change faced by small, vulnerable island nations.

History

Prehistory

The oldest evidence of human occupation in Samoa is Lapita village, partially submerged in the lagoon at Mulifanua on the island of Upolu. Carbon tests date the site to 1000 BC.

Archaeologists have discovered more than a hundred star-shaped stone platforms across the islands. It's believed that these platforms, dubbed 'star mounds', were used to snare wild pigeons, a favoured pastime of *matai* (chiefs). Savai'i's Pulemelei Mound is the largest ancient structure in the Pacific.

Around AD 950 warriors from Tonga established their rule on Savai'i, and then moved on to Upolu. They were eventually repelled by Malietoa Savea, a Samoan chief whose title, *Malie toa* (Brave warrior), was derived from the shouted tributes of the retreating Tongans. There was also contact with Fiji, from where legends say two girls brought the art of tattooing. The Samoans never really trusted their neighbours – *togafiti* (tonga fiji) means 'a trick'.

European Contact

Whalers, pirates and escaped convicts apparently introduced themselves to Samoa well before the first officially recorded European arrival in the region. This was the Dutchman Jacob Roggeveen, who approached the Manu'a Islands in American Samoa in 1722. Other visitors followed in his wake and over the next 100 years numerous Europeans settled in. The settlers established a society in Apia and a minimal code of law in order to govern their affairs, all with the consent of Upolu chiefs, who maintained sovereignty in their own villages. Along with technological expertise, the *palagi* (Europeans) also brought with them diseases to which the islanders had no immunity.

Missionaries

In August 1830 missionaries John Williams and Charles Barff of the London Missionary Society (LMS) arrived at Sapapali'i on Savai'i's eastern coast. They were followed by Methodist and Catholic missionaries, and in 1888 Mormons added to the competition for souls. Samoans were quite willing to accept Christianity due to the similarity of Christian creation beliefs to Samoan legend, and because of a prophecy by war goddess Nafanua that a new religion would take root in the islands. Although interdistrict warfare was not abolished until the start of the 20th century, schools and education were eagerly adopted.

Squabbling Powers

There were – and still are – four paramount titles relating to four '*aiga* (extended families equivalent to royal dynasties), in what is now Samoa: Malietoa, Tupua Tamasese, Mata'afa and Tu'imaleali'ifano. During the 1870s a civil dispute broke out between two of these families, dividing Samoa. Much land was sold to Europeans by Samoans seeking to acquire armaments to settle the matter.

The British, Americans and Germans then set about squabbling over Samoan territory, and by the late 1880s Apia Harbour was crowded with naval hardware from all three countries. Most of it subsequently sunk – not because of enemy firepower, but because of a cyclone that struck the harbour in March 1889. After several attempted compromises, the Tripartite Treaty was signed in 1899, giving control of Western Samoa to the Germans and eastern Samoa to the Americans.

Foreign Administration

In February 1900 Dr Wilhelm Solf was appointed governor, and the German trading company DHPG began to import thousands of Melanesians and Chinese to work on its huge plantations. But although the Germans had agreed to rule 'according to Samoan custom', they didn't keep their word. In 1908 there was widespread discontent, and the organisation of the *Mau a Pule* (Mau Movement) by Namulau'ulu Lauaki Mamoe; he and his chief supporters were sent into exile soon after.

In 1914, at the outbreak of WWI, Britain persuaded NZ to seize German Samoa. Preoccupation with affairs on the home front prevented Germany from resisting. Under NZ administration Samoa suffered a devastating (and preventable) outbreak of influenza in 1919; more than 7000 people (one-fifth of the population) died, further fuelling anger with the foreign rulers. Increasing calls for independence by the Mau Movement culminated in the authorities opening fire on a demonstration at the courthouse in Apia in 1929.

Following a change of government (and policy) in NZ, Western Samoa's independence was acknowledged as inevitable and even desirable, and in 1959 Prime Minister Fiame Mata'afa was appointed. The following year a formal constitution was adopted and, on 1 January 1962, independence was finally achieved.

Since Independence

The Human Rights Protection Party (HRPP) has been in power for most of the period since independence. Economic development has been excruciatingly slow or nonexistent, far below population growth, but at least the country has been politically stable.

Upolu and Savai'i have been battered by several huge tropical storms over the past two decades, including the severe Category Four cyclones Val (1991) and Evan (2012).

In 2009 the government switched driving from the right-hand side of the road to the left, apparently to allow access to cheap secondhand vehicle imports from NZ.

The Culture

Many visitors correctly sense that below the surface of the outwardly friendly and casual Samoan people lies a complex code of traditional etiquette. Beneath the light-heartedness, the strict and demanding *Fa'a Samoa* (Samoan Way) is rigorously upheld.

The National Psyche

'Aiga, or extended family groupings, are at the heart of the *Fa'a Samoa.* The larger an *'aiga,* the more powerful it is, and to be part of a powerful *'aiga* is the goal of all traditionally minded Samoans. Each *'aiga*

is headed by a *matai,* who represents the family on the *fono* (village council). *Matai* are elected by all adult members of the *'aiga* and can be male or female, but over 90% of current *matai* are male.

The *fono* consists of the *matai* of all of the *'aiga* associated with the village. The *ali'i* (high chief of the village) sits at the head of the *fono.* In addition, each village has one *pulenu'u* (a combination of mayor and police chief) and one or more *tulafale* (orators or talking chiefs). The *pulenu'u* acts as an intermediary between the village and the national government, while the *tulafale* liaises between the *ali'i* and outside entities, carries out ceremonial duties and engages in ritual debates.

'Ava (kava) is a drink derived from the ground root of the pepper plant. The *'ava* ceremony is a ritual in Samoa, and every government and *matai* meeting is preceded by one.

Beneath the *matai,* members of a village are divided into four categories. The society of untitled men, the *aumaga,* is responsible for growing food. The *aualuma,* the society of unmarried, widowed or separated women, provides hospitality and produces various goods such as *siapo* (decorated bark cloth) and the *ie toga* (fine mats) that are an important part of *fa'alavelave* (lavish gift-exchange ceremonies). Married women are called *faletua ma tausi.* Their role revolves around serving their husband and his family. The final group is the *tamaiti* (children). Close social interaction is generally restricted to members of one's own group.

Individuals are subordinate to the extended family. There is no 'I', only 'we'. The incapable are looked after by their family rather than by taxpayers, and with such onerous

SAMOA THE CULTURE

EARTHQUAKE & TSUNAMI DISASTER IN THE SAMOAS

On 29 September 2009 Upolu's southern and eastern coasts and the south coast of Tutuila in American Samoa were struck by a tsunami that killed approximately 190 people and left thousands homeless. It began with an 8.1 magnitude earthquake with its epicentre 190km south of Apia, which struck at 6.48am local time. Eight minutes later, a 10m-high wave demolished Upolu's south coast where people had little to no warning. On Tutuila, four tsunami waves between 4m and 6m were reported; these waves surged up to 1.6km inland, destroying homes and wiping out the electricity infrastructure.

In the years after the tsunami, resorts were rebuilt, new all-weather access roads were constructed, and visitors to many coastal regions will notice street signs pointing to tsunami evacuation routes leading to higher ground.

family (plus village and church) obligations, it's a struggle for any individual to become wealthy. Life is not about individual advancement or achievement, but about serving and improving the status of your 'aiga. The communal ownership of land and lack of reward for individual effort tend to stymie Western-style economic development, but have kept control of most of Samoa's resources in Samoan hands.

Lifestyle

Parents and other relatives treat babies with great affection, but at the age of three the children are made the responsibility of an older sibling or cousin. *Fa'aaloalo* is respect for elders, the most crucial aspect of the *Fa'a Samoa*, and children are expected to obey not just their immediate relatives, but all the *matai* and adults in the village as well as older siblings. Parents rarely hug or praise their children, so the youth often suffer from low self-esteem and lack confidence and ambition. Fun family activities are few and far between; a rare exception is White Sunday in October, when children eat first, star in church services, and are bought new clothes and toys. Some teenagers resort to *musu* (refusing to speak to anybody) as a form of protest.

Overriding all else in Samoa is Christianity. Every village has at least one large church, ideally a larger one than in neighbouring villages. These operate as the village social centre, the place where almost everyone makes an appearance on Sunday, dressed up in their formal best. Sunday-morning church services are inevitably followed by *to'ona'i* (Sunday lunch), when families put on banquets fit for royalty.

Sa, which means 'sacred', is the nightly vespers, though it's not applied strictly throughout all villages. Sometime between 6pm and 7pm a gong sounds, signifying that the village should prepare for *sa*. When the second gong is sounded, *sa* has begun. All activity should come to a halt. If you're caught in a village during *sa*, stop what you're doing, sit down and quietly wait for the third gong, about 10 or 15 minutes later, when it's over.

A rigid approach to Christianity has led to conservative attitudes on many social issues, including homosexuality, but this is tempered by a generally tolerant attitude to *fa'afafine* – men who dress and behave like women. The name *fa'afafine* means 'like

a woman' and has no obvious parallel in Western society. *Fa'afafine* fulfil an important role in the social fabric, often helping out with the children and looking after their parents in old age. A *fa'afafine* may have a relationship with a man, but this isn't seen as homosexual. Neither are they seen as women, per se.

Population

Three-quarters of Samoans live on the island of Upolu. The urban area of Apia houses around 21% of the nation's population, with the rest sprinkled around the small villages that mainly cling to the coastline. Minorities include both expat and Samoan-born Europeans (called *palagi* in Samoan) and a small number of Chinese; both minorities are centred on Apia.

Sport

Sport in Samoa is a community event, which might explain why this tiny nation turns out a disproportionate number of great sportspeople. Drive through any village in the late afternoon and you'll see people of all ages gathering on the *malae* (village green) to play rugby, volleyball and *kirikiti*. *Fautasi* (45-person canoe) races are held on special occasions. Samoa's main obsession is rugby union and the members of the national team, Manu Samoa, are local heroes – as are the many Samoan players who fill the ranks of rugby union, rugby league and netball teams in NZ, Australia, the UK and France.

Arts

Architecture

Traditional (not to mention highly practical) Samoan architecture is exemplified by the *fale*, an oval structure with wooden posts but no walls, thus allowing natural airflow. It's traditionally built on a stone or coral foundation and thatched with woven palm or sago leaves. Woven coconut-leaf blinds can be pulled down to protect against rain or prying eyes, but in truth, privacy in such a building is practically impossible.

Palagi-style square homes with walls, louvre windows and doors, though uncomfortably hot and requiring fans, have more status than traditional *fale* and are becoming more common in Samoa.

Fiafia

Originally, the *fiafia* was a village play or musical presentation in which participants would dress in costume and accept money or other donations. These days the term '*fiafia* night' usually refers to a lavish presentation of Samoan fire- and slap-dancing and singing, accompanied by a buffet dinner. But traditional *fiafia* are still performed during weddings, birthdays, title-conferring ceremonies and at the opening of churches and schools.

Drummers keep the beat while dancers sing traditional songs illustrated by coordinated hand gestures. A *fiafia* traditionally ends with the *siva*, a slow and fluid dance performed by the village *taupou* (usually the daughter of a high chief), dressed in *siapo* with her body oiled.

Literature

Towering over Samoan literature is Albert Wendt, a novelist, poet, academic and latterly visual artist, now resident in NZ. Many of his novels deal with the *Fa'a Samoa* bumping against *palagi* ideas and attitudes, and the loss of Samoa's pre-Christian spirituality; try *Leaves of the Banyan Tree* (1979), *Ola* (1995) or *The Mango's Kiss* (2003). Perhaps some of the prose is too risqué for the Methodists who run most of Samoa's bookshops, as copies are hard to track down in Samoa – you'll have better luck overseas or online.

The Beach at Falesa by Robert Louis Stevenson is a brilliant short story set in Samoa by a master stylist with inside knowledge of the South Pacific. Stevenson spent the last four years of his life in Samoa.

Music

Music is a big part of everyday life in Samoa, whether it be the exuberant drumming that accompanies *fiafia* nights, the soaring harmonies of church choirs or the tinny local pop blaring out of taxis.

Traditionally, action songs and chants were accompanied by drums and body slaps, but guitars, ukuleles and Western-style melodies are now a firm part of the *fiafia* repertoire. Songs were once written to tell stories or commemorate events and this practice continues today. Love songs are the most popular, followed by patriotic songs extolling local virtues. *We are Samoa* by Jerome Grey is Samoa's unofficial national anthem.

While clubs in Apia host local hip-hop and reggae-influenced acts, it's offshore that Samoan artists have hit the big time, especially NZ-based rappers such as King Kapisi, Scribe and Savage.

Siapo & Ie Toga

The bark cloth known as *siapo* is made from the inner bark of the *u'a* (paper mulberry tree) and provides a medium for some of the loveliest artwork in Samoa.

The fine mat called *ie toga* is woven from pandanus fibres split into widths of just a couple of millimetres and can involve years of painstaking work. *Ie toga*, along with *siapo*, make up 'the gifts of the women' that must be exchanged at formal ceremonies. Agricultural products comprise 'the gifts of the men'.

Tattooing

Samoa is the last of the Polynesian nations where traditional tattooing (*tatau*) is still widely practised (albeit against the wishes of some religious leaders). The traditional *pe'a* (male tattoo) covers the man's body from the waist to the knees. Women can elect to receive a *malu* (female tattoo), but their designs cover only the thighs.

The skills and tools of the *tufuga pe'a* (tattoo artist) were traditionally passed down from father to son, and sharpened shark teeth or boar tusks were used to carve the intricate designs into the skin. It was believed that the man being tattooed must not be left alone in case the *aitu* (spirits) took him. In most cases the procedure takes at least a fortnight. Noncompletion would cause shame to the subject and his '*aiga*.

Environment

Current environmental issues faced by Samoa include soil erosion, overfishing (including dynamite fishing), deforestation and invasive species. As a low-lying nation with the majority of its population living along the coast, Samoa is – like all islands in the region – vulnerable to effects

---

SLEEPING PRICE RANGES

The following price ranges refer to a double room or *fale*:

$ less than ST150

$$ ST150–300

$$$ more than ST300

---

of climate change including rising sea levels, increase in cyclones, drought and coral damage.

Geography

Samoa lies in the heart of the vast South Pacific, 3700km southwest of Hawai'i. Tonga lies to the south, Fiji to the southwest, Tuvalu to the northwest and Tokelau to the north, while the Cook Islands are to the southeast.

The country has a total land area of 2934 sq km and is composed primarily of high, eroded volcanic islands with narrow coastal plains. It has two large islands: Savai'i (1700 sq km) and Upolu (1115 sq km). The nation's highest peak, Mt Silisili on Savai'i, rises to 1866m. The small islands of Manono and Apolima lie in the 22km-wide Apolima Strait that separates Upolu and Savai'i. A few other tiny, uninhabited rocky islets and outcrops lie southeast of Upolu.

Ecology

The heights of Savai'i and Upolu are covered in temperate forest vegetation: tree ferns, grasses, wild coleus and epiphytic plants. The magnificent *aoa* (banyan tree) dominates the higher landscapes, while other areas are characterised by scrublands, marshes, pandanus forests and mangrove swamps. The rainforests of Samoa are a natural apothecary, home to some 75 known medicinal plant species.

Because Samoa is relatively remote, few animal species have managed to colonise it. The Lapita brought with them domestic pigs, dogs and chickens, as well as the ubiquitous Polynesian rat. But apart from two species of fruit bat (protected throughout the islands after being hunted close to extinction) and the small, sheath-tailed bat, mammals not introduced by humans are limited to the marine varieties. Whales, dolphins and porpoises migrate north and south through the islands, depending on the season.

Pili (skinks) and *mo'o* (geckos) can be seen everywhere, and various types of turtles visit the islands. The only land creature to beware of (besides the unloved and unlovely dogs) is the giant centipede, which packs a nasty bite.

SURVIVAL GUIDE

ⓘ Directory A–Z

ACCOMMODATION

It's fair to say that accommodation options in Samoa are limited. There's little budget accommodation outside the ubiquitous *fale;* and at the other end of the scale, only a handful of resorts qualify as truly luxurious. At both ends of the scale, many properties are overpriced given the quality offered. That said, much of the country's accommodation occupies idyllic settings on the beautiful sands that fringe the islands – this meets the minimum requirements for most visitors.

An excellent source of accommodation information is the **Samoa Hotels Association** (Map p258; ☑ 30160; www.samoahotels.ws; Samoa Tourism Authority information fale, Beach Rd, Apia). It also acts as a booking agent, taking its fee from the provider, not the guest.

Beach *fale* are the most interesting budget option. Hotel, motel and resort accommodation ranges from rooms in slightly dilapidated buildings with cold-water showers to well-maintained rooms with all the mod cons. There's sometimes access to a shared kitchen. Resorts tend to offer bungalow-style accommodation (sometimes called *fale* to sound exotic), with the bigger ones having swim-up cocktail bars and multiple restaurants.

Traditional village homestays can be organised through **Samoa Village Stays** (☑ 22777; www.samoavillagestays.com; ST100 per person per night).

ACTIVITIES

Visiting Samoa is less about seeing sights as doing things – particularly things that involve tropical beaches.

Diving

Samoa's dive industry is far less developed than those of some of its neighbours, meaning there are some fantastic sites to explore, with access to a multitude of tropical fish and larger marine creatures, such as turtles and dolphins. Two-tank dives start from ST275 and PADI open-water courses are around ST1250.

Fishing

Samoan reefs and their fishing rights are owned by villagers, so you can't just drop a line anywhere; seek permission first. If you'd like to go fishing with locals, inquire at your accommodation or speak to the *pulenu'u* of the village concerned.

Game fishing is becoming increasingly popular in the islands – in fact, Samoa has been rated one of the top 10 game-fishing destinations in the world. The Samoa International Game Fishing Tournament (www.sigfa.ws) heads out from Apia Harbour in late April.

Hiking

Samoa's rugged coastal areas, sandy beaches, thick rainforests and volcanoes all invite exploration on foot. However, trails can quickly become obscured due to tangled tropical growth and half-hearted track maintenance. Combine this with the effects of heavy rain and there's often a good chance of getting lost (or at the very least covering yourself in mud). For more remote treks, it pays to take a guide with you.

Costs vary enormously. Sometimes villagers will be happy to accompany you for nothing; at other times, they'll be seeking goods as a reward (like cigarettes), but mostly they'll be interested in cash.

Kayaking

Kayaks are perfect for pottering around lagoons; several accommodation providers have them available. Longer kayaking excursions can be organised through **Outdoor Samoa** (p257).

Snorkelling & Swimming

The novice snorkeller will find Samoa's waters fascinating and teeming with life. In places the reef has been damaged by cyclones, tsunamis and human contact, but will still reveal live corals and an abundance of colourful fish, often just a short paddle out from the beach. Some particularly good and accessible spots are Lalomanu, Namu'a and Palolo Deep Marine Reserve. Many places hire out snorkelling gear, but it's worth bringing your own mask and snorkel.

The majority of Samoan beaches are great for splashing about in, but too shallow for satisfying swimming. Always ask permission from local villagers before using their beach.

Surfing

Powerful conditions, sharp reefs and offshore breaks that are difficult to access mean that surfing in Samoa is challenging, to say the very least, and probably one of the worst places in the world to learn the sport. While the surf can be magnificent at times, offering waves of a lifetime in glorious surroundings, conditions are generally difficult to assess, with some very dangerous situations awaiting the inexperienced or reckless. That said, the islands are an increasingly popular destination for experienced surfers. The wet season (November to April) brings swells from the north; the dry season (May to October) brings big swells from the south.

It's best to hook up with a surfing outfit. They know all the best spots and provide boat transport to them and, perhaps more importantly, they have established relationships with local villagers and understand the culture – they know where it is and isn't OK to surf.

CHILDREN

The Samoan climate (discounting long periods of heavy rain or the odd cyclone), warm waters and dearth of poisonous creatures make the islands a paradise for children. You'll find that Samoans tend to lavish attention on very young children, and foreign toddlers will not be starved for attention or affection while visiting the islands.

Never leave your child unsupervised near beaches, reefs or on walking tracks, particularly those running along coastal cliffs (these

---

THE BEACH FALE: SAMOA'S SIGNATURE ACCOMMODATION

The simple structures called *fale* come in a variety of styles. At their most simple and traditional, they're just a wooden platform with poles supporting a thatched roof, surrounded by woven blinds for privacy. Woven sleeping mats are laid on the floor, topped by a mattress with sheets and a mosquito net. From this basic model, various degrees of luxury can be added: electric lights, ceiling fans, proper beds, wooden walls, lockable doors and decks. Avoid those with plastic-sheeting walls; they tend to flap around in the wind without letting much air through. Bathroom facilities are usually a communal block, with cold water being the norm. The price usually includes breakfast and often a set lunch and dinner as well.

Fale are usually priced per person, ranging from a reasonable ST70 (including meals) to well over ST200. As a result, couples or larger groups may find themselves paying much more than they would for a midrange hotel, for what is basically one step up from camping on the beach.

are never fenced). Typically only the upmarket resorts provide cots, and only some car-rental agencies have car seats (and these can be of questionable quality), so it may pay to bring your own.

EMBASSIES & CONSULATES

The following diplomatic missions are based in Apia.

Australian High Commission (Map p258; ✆23411; www.embassy.gov.au/ws.html; Beach Rd; ⊙9am-4.30pm Mon-Fri) Canadian consular services are also provided here.

Chinese Embassy (Map p268; ✆22474; www.ws.chineseembassy.org/eng; Cross Island Rd, Vailima; ⊙8.30am-noon & 2-4.30pm Mon-Fri)

New Zealand High Commission (Map p258; ✆21711; www.nzembassy.com/samoa; Beach Rd; ⊙8.30am-4.30pm Mon-Fri)

US Embassy (Map p258; ✆21631; www.samoa.usembassy.gov; 5th fl, ACC Bldg, Apia; ⊙9-11am Mon-Fri, phone enquiries to 5pm)

EMERGENCY

Ambulance ✆996
Police ✆994

FESTIVALS & EVENTS

Independence Day celebrations (1–3 June) Festivities commemorating Samoa's 1962 independence from New Zealand.

Teuila Festival (September) Apia reels in the tourists with canoe races, food and craft stalls, traditional dancing and a beauty pageant.

White Sunday (second Sunday in October) The day that Samoan children rule the roost.

Palolo Rise (October/November) Marking the annual emergence of the edible reefworm.

Samoana Jazz and Arts Festival (late October–early November) Hosts local and international artists, and jumps between Apia and American Samoa.

The first annual **Upolu-Savaii swim** (22km) event is due to take place in early April 2016.

EATING PRICE RANGES

The following price ranges refer to a meal. Unless otherwise stated tax is included in the price.

$ less than ST20

$$ ST20–35

$$$ more than ST35

INTERNET ACCESS

Wi-fi in Samoa is offered by LavaSpot (www.lavaspot.ws) or Bluezone (www.bluezone.ws) hotspots on a pay-by-the-minute basis. You can buy time directly from their websites, or at your accommodation's front desk.

Hotspots are found at restaurants and hotels all around Apia and at some resorts around Upolu and Savai'i.

Note that web connections can drop out with frustrating frequency on these remote islands.

MAPS

The free Jasons *Samoa Visitor Map* is updated annually and is widely available. It's reasonably basic but should suit most visitors' needs. They're also available to order online (free) at www.jasons.com/samoa.

MONEY

The tala (dollar), divided into 100 sene (cents), is the unit of currency in use in Samoa.

ATMs

Several branches of the ANZ and BSP banks are equipped with ATMs. Be aware that ATMs can be prone to running out of bills at the start of the weekend. Take plenty of cash with you (in small denominations) when you're heading outside the bigger settlements.

Tipping

Not expected or encouraged, though it is acceptable for exceptional service at finer restaurants.

OPENING HOURS

On Sunday almost everything is closed, although ripples of activity appear in the evening. Markets normally get underway by about 6am; Maketi Fou in Apia is active more or less 24 hours a day.

Standard opening hours:

Banks 9am to 3pm Monday to Friday, some open 8.30am to 12.30pm Saturday

Bars noon to 10pm or midnight

Government offices 8am to 4.30pm Monday to Friday

Restaurants 8am to 4pm and 6pm to 9pm

Shops 8am to 4.30pm Monday to Friday, 8am to noon Saturday (kiosks and convenience stores keep longer hours)

TELEPHONE

The country code for Samoa is ✆685. The nation does not use area codes.

The mobile phone providers in Samoa are Digicel (www.digicelsamoa.com) and Bluesky (www.blueskysamoa.ws). Prepay top-ups can be purchased from dozens of shops around both islands, including at the international airport. Reception is generally very good.

TOURIST INFORMATION

The excellent, comprehensive website of the Samoa Tourism Authority (www.samoa.travel) has easy-to-browse information on activities, attractions, accommodation and useful organisations, plus an up-to-date events calendar.

TIME

At midnight on 29 December 2011, Samoa officially switched to the west side of the International Date Line. This means its dates are the same as those of NZ, Australia and Asia. Local time is GMT/UTC plus 13 hours. Therefore, when it's noon in Samoa, it's 11am the same day in Auckland.

Samoa adopted daylight saving time in 2010. In early October the clocks go forward (to GMT/UTC plus 14 hours), returning to normal in late March.

VISAS

A free, 60-day visitor permit is granted to all visitors on arrival in Samoa (except for American Samoans).

Samoan visitor permits may be extended by several weeks at a time by the country's **Immigration Office** (Map p258; ☑ 20291; www.samoaimmigration.gov.ws; Convent St, Apia; ☺ 9am-4pm Mon-Fri). Take along your passport, wallet and two passport-sized photos and don't make any other plans for the rest of the day. You may also need to have proof of hotel accommodation, onward transport and sufficient funds for your requested period of stay.

➊ Getting There & Away

AIR

Aside from a few flights from American Samoa, all flights to Samoa arrive at **Faleolo Airport** (Map p254; ☑ 21675; www.apia.airport-authority.com; West Coast Rd, Upolu), 35km west of Apia. Many arrive and depart in the early hours of the morning, but airport transfer and accommodation providers are well used to this. **Fagali'i Airport** (Map p268; Fagali'i), on Apia's eastern outskirts, is mainly used for flights to/from American Samoa.

Direct flights head to Samoa from American Samoa, Fiji, Auckland, Brisbane and Sydney. If you're flying from the northern hemisphere, flights via Honolulu are likely to be the most straightforward.

Airlines that service Samoa include the following (phone numbers are local):

Air New Zealand (NZ; Map p258; ☑ 20825; www.airnz.com; cnr Convent & Vaea Sts, Apia; ☺ 8.30am-4.30pm Mon-Fri, 9am-noon Sat)

Fiji Airways (Map p258; ☑ 22983; www.fiji airways.com; Saleufi St, Apia; ☺ 8.30am-5pm Mon-Fri, 8am-noon Sat)

Inter Island Airways (☑ 42580; www.inter islandair.com; Faleolo Airport)

Polynesian Airlines (Map p258; ☑ 21261; www.polynesianairlines.com; Beach Rd, Apia)

Virgin Australia (www.virginaustralia.com)

SEA

Ship

Samoa Shipping Corporation (☑ 20935; www.samoashipping.com; one way adult/child ST12/6, vehicles from ST80) runs a car ferry/cargo ship (MV *Lady Naomi*) between Apia and Pago Pago (American Samoa) once a week. It departs from Apia every Thursday at 11pm; it departs Pago Pago the following day (also a Thursday, thanks to the bizarre dateline) at 4pm. The ferry takes foot passengers as well as vehicles. The journey takes about seven hours. Return deck fares are ST120/75 per adult/child. Note that American passport holders can only buy one-way tickets from Apia. All tickets must be purchased at least one day in advance: book online or ask your accommodation in Apia for assistance.

Cargo ships sail between Apia and remote Tokelau two to three times a month. Bookings for the 24- to 26-hour trip (return fares NZ$450) can be made in Apia at the **Tokelau Apia Liaison Office** (Map p258; ☑ 20822; www.tokelau.org.nz; Fugalei St, Apia; ☺ 9am-5pm Mon-Fri). You must obtain a Tokelau visa before booking.

Yacht

Between May and October (outside the cyclone season), South Pacific harbours swarm with yachts from around the world. Apia is the official entry point for private yachts visiting Samoa. In Savai'i, there are also anchorages at Fagamalo, Salelologa Wharf and Asau Harbour.

Before entering Apia's harbour, yachts must call Apia Port Control on VHF 16. Officially, yachties must contact each clearance department – customs, immigraton and quarantine –

SAMOA GETTING THERE & AWAY

separately (see www.samoagovt.ws for directories); however, Port Control will most likely do it for you once you've made contact.

ℹ Getting Around

AIR

Samoa Air (☑ 27905; www.samoaair.ws) operates charter flights between Upolu and Savai'i. Email them for bookings and fares.

BICYCLE

Touring Upolu and Savai'i by bicycle is a scenic, reasonably relaxed option – we say 'reasonably' because aggressive dogs are a prevalent problem. The roads are generally in good condition and traffic is minimal. The major roads encircling the islands are sealed and relatively flat, but you'd need a sturdy mountain bike to tackle most of the trails to beaches and other coastal attractions. You can transport a bike between Samoa's two main islands on the ferry.

A big challenge for cyclists is the heat. Even during the coolest months of the year (July, August and September), afternoon temperatures will still be high. Plan to avoid cycling long stretches in the heat of the day. Also bear in mind that buses are unlikely to be able to accommodate bicycles should you run out of leg power.

It shouldn't be hard to track down a bike repairer if you really need one, but it's best to bring your own repair kit, a decent lock and heavy-duty panniers. Some accommodation providers offer bike hire, but these are for day touring, not long-distance rides.

BOAT

The ferry from Mulifanua Wharf regularly plies the waters between Upolu and Savai'i. Small boats leave from Cape Fatuosofia for Manono.

The **Apia Yacht Club** (p264) is a good place to share information on sailing around the islands over a cold beer.

BUS

Travelling by public bus in Samoa is an experience in itself. The vibrantly painted, wooden-seated vehicles (more often than not blasting Samoan pop music at deafening volumes) each have their own character. Drivers are often as eccentric as the vehicles, and services operate completely at their whim: if a driver feels like knocking off at 1pm, he does, and passengers counting on the service are left stranded. Never rely on a bus after about 2pm. Buses are also scarce on Saturday afternoon and often only cater to church services on Sunday.

All buses prominently display the name of their destination in the front window. To stop a bus, wave your hand and arm, palm down. To get off, either knock on the ceiling or clap loudly. Fares are paid to the driver – try to have as near to the exact change as possible.

Although most visitors don't notice it at first, there is a seating hierarchy on Samoan buses. Unmarried women normally sit together, while foreigners and older people must have a seat and sit near the front of the bus. Don't worry about arranging this yourself – the locals will see to it that everything is sorted out. The way in which Samoans stack themselves on top of each other on crowded buses without losing any dignity is akin to a social miracle.

CAR

Getting around by car in Samoa is quite straightforward. The coastal roads on Upolu and Savai'i are sealed; most of the other main roads are pretty good. A 4WD will make trips down rough, unsealed side roads more comfortable, but nearly all of these can be tackled in a high-clearance 2WD (unless there's been heavy rain).

Petrol stations are few and far between on both islands.

Driving Licence

Visitors to Samoa need to obtain a temporary driving licence. Most car-hire companies issue these, or you can call into the **Land Transport Authority** (LTA; Map p268; ☑ 26740; www.lta. gov.ws; Off Vaitele St (opposite Vailima Brewery), Vaitele; licence per month ST21; ⊗ 9am-5pm Mon-Fri) in Apia. You'll need to present a valid overseas driving licence.

Hire

There are dozens of car-hire agencies in Samoa and, on top of this, some of the larger accommodation providers also hire vehicles. Most of the agencies are in or around Apia and the airport, and prices can be quite competitive. Note that you can usually take hire cars from Upolu over to Savai'i and back, but cars hired on Savai'i cannot be taken to Upolu. It's sometimes cheaper to hire in Upolu even given the ferry fee, especially if you obtain a discount for a longer booking.

When hiring a vehicle, check for any damage or scratches and note everything on the rental agreement, lest you be held liable for damage when the car is returned. Furthermore, fend off requests to leave your passport or a cash deposit against possible damages. Many places will require a credit card pre-authorisation by way of a deposit and it's usual to pay in advance.

Prices start at around ST110 per day, with discounts offered for longer-term rentals.

Insurance

It's essential to have your hire car covered by insurance as repair costs are extremely high in Samoa. Insurance costs aren't always included in the price of a quote, so always double-check this.

Road Rules

In 2009 the Samoan government decided to change the law from driving on the right-hand side of the road to the left-hand side. Still, don't be surprised to see a mixture of left-hand-drive and right-hand-drive vehicles on the road. When renting a car, insist on a right-hand drive vehicle. The speed limit within central Apia and through adjacent villages is 40km/h; outside populated areas it's 56km/h.

On Upolu, taxis can be a useful transport option for day tripping; however, the same can't be said for taxis on Savai'i, which are only convenient for short trips. It always pays to have the correct change as drivers can be (perhaps too conveniently) relied upon not to have any.

If you find a driver you hit it off well with early on, it can be worth getting their telephone number and using their service during your stay. You may be able to negotiate a decent day rate that compares favourably with a hire car.

Local buses are cheap and run all over the islands frequently (apart from on Sundays).

American Samoa

☏1-684 / POP 55, 519

Best Places to Stay

➡ Moana O Sina (p304)

➡ Vaoto Lodge (p310)

➡ Tisa's Barefoot Bar (p305)

➡ Le Falepule (p304)

➡ Homestays organised by the National Park Visitor Information Center (p308)

Best Beaches

➡ Ofu Beach (p309)

➡ Fagatele Bay National Marine Sanctuary (p302)

➡ Alega Beach (p303)

➡ Two Dollar Beach (p303)

Why Go?

There but for a more exotic name goes American Samoa. Mention of this distant archipelago more often than not elicits a blank stare, but despite its mundane moniker and confusing status (it belongs to, but isn't a part of, the US), American Samoa is one of the most breathtakingly beautiful pockets of Polynesia.

A photogenic feast of green jagged peaks, electric blue depths and idyllic beaches, American Samoa's islands are the stuff South Pacific daydreams are made of. Tutuila is home to Pago Pago, a blue-collar fishing town nestled beside one of the world's most stunning natural harbours; outside city limits, flower-scented villages cling to deep-rooted traditions. For more extreme escapism, head to the remote Manu'a Islands, believed to be the birthplace of Polynesia, or hike the trails of the National Park of American Samoa. Whichever adventure you choose, this is one Pacific paradise you're likely to have all to yourself.

When to Go

Pago Pago

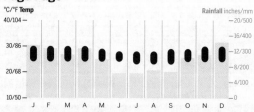

Dec–Jan
Peak holiday period when Samoans living abroad visit home.

May–Oct
Dry, cool season with minimal to no risk of cyclones.

Oct
Festival month and whale season.

TUTUILA

POP 54,145 / AREA 140 SQ KM

Tutuila is a dramatic mass of sharp edges and pointy peaks, softened by a heavy padding of rainforest. Its craggy green silhouettes loom over the island's blindingly white sands, turquoise shallows, inviting islets and the stunning Pago Pago Harbor, one of the best-protected natural harbours in the world.

While the airport road offers a disappointing first impression, rest assured that there's more to Tutuila than fast-food joints and shabby shacks: between the urban delights of Pago Pago, ancient sacred sites, secret swimming spots and scenic hiking trails, this is one of Polynesia's most eclectic – if little-known – destinations. The island's claims to fame don't stop there: the tiny village of Poloa, on Tutuila's west coast, is the last place on earth to see the sun set each day.

◉ Sights

◉ Pago Pago

While the urban environs of Pago Pago are as gritty as they come (two tuna canneries, a huge working seaport and potholed streets lined with ramshackle buildings), its evocative natural harbour, white-sand beaches and backdrop of magnificent geometric peaks give the city a dreamy, paradisaical feel. It's an incongruous combination, but somehow it works, lending Pago Pago a unique and explore-worthy charm.

Though pretty well stuck together, Pago Pago is technically a string of villages. Confusingly, 'Pago Pago' (pronounced pung-o pung-o) is used to describe the small village at the far end of the harbour, the harbour itself, the 'town', the whole island of Tutuila or even the whole of American Samoa.

AMERICAN SAMOA TUTUILA

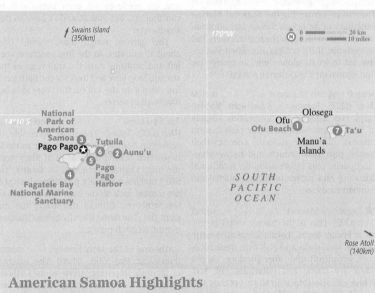

American Samoa Highlights

❶ Ogling rainforest-clad mountains and white sands while floating in the crystalline waters off **Ofu Beach** (p309).

❷ Strolling the plantations and crater lakes on the diminutive island of **Aunu'u** (p309).

❸ Hiking the jungle trails of the **National Park of American Samoa** (p301).

❹ Snorkelling and whale watching in **Fagatele Bay National Marine Sanctuary** (p302).

❺ Paddling about calm **Pago Pago Harbor** (p297), fringed by magnificently jagged peaks.

❻ Enjoying a traditional Samoan meal with a modern twist, beachside at Tutuila's **Tisa's Barefoot Bar** (p307).

❼ Exploring the mysteries of ancient Polynesia on the isolated island of **Ta'u** (p311).

Utulei is edged by a beach dotted with day *fale* (houses), offering shelter from the sun between swims. Fagatogo is the administrative centre and contains the Fono (Map p302; Fagatogo), a large, *fale*-shaped building that houses American Samoa's Senate and House of Representatives.

★ Fatu ma Futi   ISLAND
(Flowerpot Rock; Map p300; Fatumafuti) Get your camera ready: you'll spot these iconic offshore rock formations on your drive into Pago Pago from the airport. Legend has it that a couple named Fatu and Futi had sailed from Savai'i (Samoa), looking for Tutuila; their canoe sank, and the pair were transformed into these beautiful tree-topped mini-islands. You can swim here and cross between the two at low tide.

Tauese PF Sunia Ocean Center   MUSEUM
(Map p302; ☑ 633 6500; www.americansamoa. noaa.gov; Pago Pago Harbor; ⊙ 9am-4pm Mon-Fri) The visitor centre for the National Marine Sanctuary of American Samoa has informative exhibits relating to the region's reefs and ecosystems; if it's not playing when you arrive, ask to see this 'globe show', an interactive film shown on a 360-degree screen.

Jean P Hayden Museum   MUSEUM
(Map p302; Fagatogo; ⊙ 8am-4pm Mon-Fri) FREE Has a small but interesting display of Samoan artefacts, including *va'a* (bonito canoes), *alia* (war canoes), coconut-shell combs, pigs' tusk armlets and native pharmacopoeia, plus information on traditional tattooing and native medicinal plants and Samoan medicine.

★ Fagatogo Market   MARKET
(Map p302) This is the town's social centre on a Friday night. Locals come to gossip, ransack food stalls and pick over fresh coconuts, breadfruit and other produce; there's often live music and entertainment, too. When a cruise ship is in town (as they frequently are), stalls selling souvenirs, locally made crafts and clothes pop up in their dozens. There are a few 'fast-food'-style places at the back selling Samoan-sized meals (US$2 to US$5) for lunch.

The main bus station is behind the market.

⦾ Western Tutuila

Most of the western end of Tutuila is taken up by the rainforest-wreathed mountains that line the northern coast. The bulk of the population inhabits the flat plains to the south, particularly the strip-mall suburbs of Tafuna and Nu'uuli. Once you pass Leone, there's a succession of cute villages lining pretty beaches.

Nu'uuli Falls   WATERFALL
(Map p300; Nu'uuli) Standing in stark relief to Nu'uuli's scruffy strip of restaurants and convenience stores, this secluded waterfall with a deliciously cool swimming hole at its base is a magical place. The surrounding rainforest muffles the sound of the water cascading down 20m of jagged black lava rocks.

It's a little hard to find. Coming along the main road from the west, turn left at the Nu'uuli Family Mart and follow this side road, veering left at the pig farm. At the end, park on the grass to the left (you'll see a house downhill on your right); the start of the track is in front of you. If you see anyone, it's polite to ask their permission to continue on, but you shouldn't have to pay any money.

The narrow, rough track should take about 15 minutes. At the first juncture, veer left and continue until the trail reaches the stream. Stop here and look for the path leading steeply up the hill on the other side before wading across.

Tia Seu Lupe   ARCHAEOLOGICAL SITE
(Map p300; Tafuna) The most accessible of American Samoa's fascinating star mounds is secreted behind a statue of St Mary near the huge Catholic cathedral in Tafuna. Tia Seu Lupe has a viewing platform where you get a good look at the two distinct tiers of the structure, without disturbing the ancient site. The name literally means 'earthen mound to catch pigeons'.

Cathedral of the Holy Family   CHURCH
(Fatu-o-Aiga; Map p300; Tafuna) The exterior of Tafuna's imposing, snow white Catholic cathedral is striking, with a space-age bell tower and dissected dome, though a homier beauty lies in its Polynesian-meets-Western artworks, including an '*ava*-bearing, larger-than-life Samoan Christ, and a nativity featuring a *fale* as a stable and an '*ava* bowl as a manger.

Turtle & Shark Site   HISTORIC SITE
(Map p300; Vaitogi; access fee US$2; ⊙ Mon-Sat) The most famous of Tutuila's legends is set at this dramatic clifftop site. According to one version, an

old lady and her granddaughter were turfed out of their village during a famine, and jumped into the sea. The guilt-ridden villagers went to the shore and called their names; they appeared in the form of a turtle and a shark. The grandmother gave the villagers a song and promised they would come whenever it was sung; locals insist the song lures the pair to this day.

Whether the fabled creatures appear or not, you'll enjoy the rugged character of the place, with its black lava cliffs, heavy surf and blowholes. Don't swim here: this is a sacred site and the currents are treacherous.

Leone   VILLAGE

The village of Leone welcomed the first missionary to Tutuila in 1832. John Williams subsequently erected the island's first church, garnishing it with three towers, a stunning carved ceiling and stained glass. Try to attend a service here on Sunday morning, when villagers congregate in their best whites to sing hymns before heading home for a lunchtime banquet.

Leone was hit exceptionally hard by the 2009 tsunami; there's a memorial monument and healing garden dedicated to the victims overlooking the sea.

Cape Taputapu   AREA

For a memorable, perhaps romantic evening, this is a tough spot to beat: Tutuila's westernmost point is the last place on earth the sun sets each day.

Just past Amanave Village is the lovely, white-sand Palagi Beach. From there, a winding northern road brings you to a cluster of small villages, revealing spectacular coastline along the way.

Eastern Tutuila

Fale have given way to clunky concrete-block houses; otherwise, the small villages cling to the shoreline as they've done for centuries.

Rainmaker Mountain   MOUNTAIN

Also known as Mt Pioa, 523m-high Rainmaker Mountain traps rain clouds and gives Pago Pago the highest annual rainfall of any harbour in the world. From afar it looks like a single large peak, but a drive up Rainmaker Pass reveals a three-pronged summit. The mountain and its base area are national landmark sites due to the pristine tropical vegetation on the slopes.

Masefau & Sa'ilele   AREA

A cross-island road leads from the village of Faga'itua up over a pass before winding slowly down to Masefau, a village that looks too idyllic to be true.

Back at the pass, a turn-off takes you down a narrow, potholed road to Sa'ilele, which has one of the island's loveliest swimming beaches. The sandy area below the large rock outcrop at the beach's western end is an excellent place for a picnic.

Activities

Though its depths are home to hundreds of fish and coral species, diving is as yet a largely untapped market in American Samoa. On Tutuila, Pago Pago Marine Charters (p303) can organise dive trips.

Hiking & Walking

Hiking is one of American Samoa's biggest drawcards, with decently maintained trails winding through thick, pristine rainforest and dazzling coastlines.

AMERICAN SAMOA IN...

Two Days

Begin with breakfast at **DDW** in **Pago Pago** and then spend the day exploring the eastern end of Tutuila. Stop for a swim at **Alega Beach** and lunch at **Tisa's Barefoot Bar** before catching the ferry to **Aunu'u** for the afternoon. Head back to Pago Pago Harbor for dinner. Next morning, hit the **Mt Alava Trail** for a taste of Tutuila's dramatic landscapes, from forest to reef. That night catch the *fiafia* (traditional dance performance) at the **Equator** restaurant at the Tradewinds Hotel in Tafuna.

Five Days

Fly to **Ofu** and spend the first two days snorkelling, lying around the beach and exploring **Olosega** by foot. Catch a boat to **Ta'u** and explore the birthplace of Polynesia. Head back to Tutuila then follow the two days itinerary.

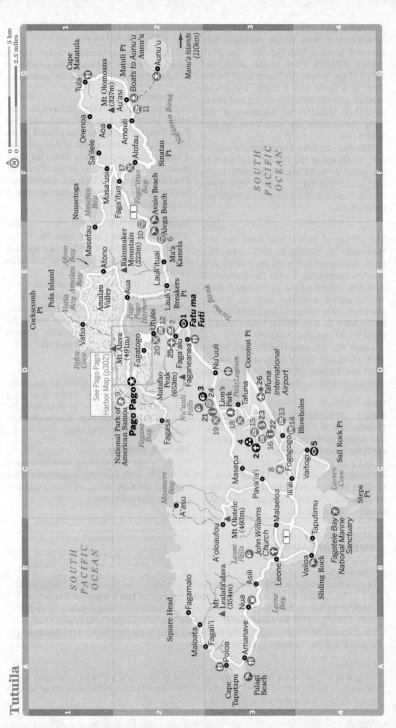

Tutuila

SOUTH PACIFIC OCEAN

SOUTH PACIFIC OCEAN

5 km
2.5 miles

Manu'a Islands (110km)

Cape Matatula

Tula

Mt Olomoana (327m)

Au'asi

Boats to Aunu'u

Aunu'u

Matuli Pt

Onenoa

Salele

Aoa

Amouli

Alofau

Sinatau Pt

Nusetoga

Masausi

Masefau

Faga'itua

Faga'itua Bay

Avaio Beach

Alega Beach

Masefau Bay

Afono

Amalau Valley

Mafia Bay

Amalau Bay

Afono Bay

Rainmaker Mountain (523m)

Lauli'ituai

Ma'a

Kamela

Breakers Pt

Lauli'i

Pola Island

Cockscomb Pt

Vatia

Tafeu Cove

Aua

Utulei

Fatu ma Futi

National Park of American Samoa

Pago Pago

Mt Alava (491m)

Fagatogo

Faga'alu

Faganeanea

Nu'uuli

Coconut Pt

PalaLagoon

Tafuna International Airport

Blowholes

See Pago Pago Harbor Map (p302)

Matafao Peak (653m)

Nu'uuli Falls

Lion's Park

Tafuna

Fagasa

Fagasa Bay

Pago Pago Harbor

Nafanua Bank

Fatumafuti Bank

Sail Rock Pt

Fogagogo

Vaitogi

Steps Pt

Larsen Cove

Massacre Bay

A'asu

Masepa

Pava'i'ai

'Ili'ili

Malaeloa

Taputimu

Mt Olotele (493m)

John Williams Church

Leone

Vailoa

Fagatele Bay National Marine Sanctuary

Leone Falls

Leone Bay

Asili

Nua

A'oloaufou

Mt Lealatalava (354m)

Sliding Rock

Square Head

Maloata

Fagali'i

Poloa

Amanave

Cape Taputapu

Palagi Beach

Fagamalo

Tutuila

AMERICAN SAMOA TUTUILA

★ **National Park of American Samoa** NATIONAL PARK, HIKING
(Map p300; www.nps.gov/npsa) **FREE** Created in 1988, the territory's sole national park protects huge swathes of pristine landscapes and marine environments on Tutuila and the Manu'a Islands. The 1000-hectare Tutuila section follows the north coast between the villages of Fagasa and Afono. Trails within park boundaries are often very well maintained. Be sure to bring strong mosquito repellant.

The National Park Visitor Information Center (p308) in Pago Pago is an invaluable source of information and maps.

There are scores of hikes within the park to choose from; brochures available at the information centre (and online) list them all. In order of difficulty (easy to challenging), here are three popular hikes:

➡ **Pola Island Trail**

Vatia is a peaceful village situated on a lovely, coral-fringed bay. Guarding the mouth of the bay, tiny Pola Island has magnificent, sheer, 120m-high cliffs populated by seabirds. For a close-up of soaring rocks and birds, head through the village and park at the school, then walk 300m to reach the wonderfully isolated beach at the base of the cliffs.

➡ **Amalau Valley**

From Aua, a surfaced road switchbacks steeply up over Rainmaker Pass and down to Afono and Vatia. Between these two villages is the beautiful, secluded Amalau Valley, home to many forest-bird species and to two rare species of flying fox. Stop at the lookout point just past the western side of Amalau Bay for some wonderful views.

➡ **Mt Alava**

Hiking the trail that leads up Mt Alava (491m) and then down to the coast is a wonderful way to experience the park's lowland and mountain rainforests, its thriving birdlife, and the peacefulness that permeates it. On Mt Alava, a metal stairway leads up to a TV transmission tower and the rusted remains of a cable-car terminal that once ran 1.8km across Pago Pago Harbor to Solo Hill. The 5.5km ridge trail (1½ to two hours one way) starts from Fagasa Pass. Behind the rest *fale* at the end of this section, a very steep trail (including ladders in places) leads 2km down to Vatia; allow an additional two hours for the descent.

Pago Pago Harbor

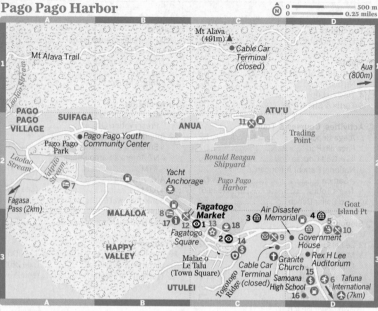

Pago Pago Harbor

Fagatele Bay
National Marine Sanctuary   HIKING
(Map p300; ☎633 6500; www.fagatelebay.noaa.
gov) A submerged volcanic crater, Fagatele
Bay is fringed by Tutuila's last remaining
stretch of coastal rainforest. Its depths
house more than 140 species of coral, and
are visited by numerous turtle species and
migrating southern humpback whales (June

to September). There are four marked trails
here, two of which are less than 1km from
the parking area at the bay's entrance.

The Tauese PF Sunia Ocean Center
(p298) in Pago Pago has free maps detailing longer hiking routes.

Massacre Bay   HIKING
A marvellous 4km hiking trail (allow four
hours return) leads from the scenic village

of A'oloaufou down to A'asu on Massacre Bay. Its foreboding name was given after a deadly skirmish (1787) between French sailors and Samoan villagers.

The track begins near the community garden in A'oloaufou. It's often overgrown, extremely muddy and difficult to navigate, particularly on the climb back up. Hikers should consider hiring a guide in A'oloaufou (between US$5 and US$10).

Swimming & Snorkelling

Many coastal areas are too rough or shallow for swimming but there are a number of easily accessible spots; you can get to the following beaches by bus. There's also a swimming beach in Utulei, just across from Samoana High School. In most cases swimsuits are a no-no – wear a T-shirt and long shorts or a *lava-lava* (wraparound sarong).

Alega Beach SNORKELLING, SWIMMING

(Map p300; admission US$5) A short drive east of Pago Pago, this is a lovely spot that gets crowded on the weekend. It's not only a great place to swim and snorkel (check currents and conditions with locals first), but it is also overlooked by Tisa's Barefoot Bar, the perfect spot for a cold drink. You can waive the access fee for the beach by buying a drink at Tisa's.

Two Dollar Beach SNORKELLING, SWIMMING

(Avaio Beach; Map p300; admission US$5; ⊙7am-6pm) This well-maintained strip of white sand sits beside calm, shallow water that's great for snorkelling. There's a small rocky island just offshore for exploring. It's an excellent spot for a day trip, and has good facilities including barbecues, showers and clean toilets. Despite the name, it's now US$5 to use the beach.

Faga'alu Park SWIMMING

(Map p300) At the outer southern part of Pago Pago Harbor, this grassy park with picnic tables and a small white-sand beach is a good, central place for a dip. The water here is much cleaner than the interior of the bay and the corals are in surprisingly good shape.

Kayaking & Canoeing

Some of the local outrigger canoe clubs welcome guests to paddle with them on Pago Pago Harbor; they often leave from the beach at Sadie's by the Sea. Ask around about times and availability.

South Pacific Watersports WATER SPORTS

(Map p302; ☑633 3050; www.southpacificwatersports.com; Utulei; ⊙5am-7pm Mon-Fri, 6am-4pm Sat) The friendly folk here rent out stand-up paddle boards (per hour/half-day/day US$15/45/80), kayaks (US$10 per hour), snorkel gear (US$5 per hour) and outrigger canoes. They can also organise hiking and paddling tours; a modicum of fitness is required.

Sadie's by the Sea KAYAKING

(Map p302; ☑633 5981; www.sadieshotels.com; Utulei) Kayaks and paddle boats are free for hotel guests (US$10 per hour for nonguests), and are a highly recommended way to explore Pago Pago's scenic harbour. The beach fee for nonguests (where you'll have to launch from) is US$5 per day.

Other Activites

Pago Pago Marine Charters FISHING

(☑733 0964; www.pagopagomarinecharters.com; Pago Pago Harbor) This professional outfit offers gamefishing and diving charters. A PADI dive centre, it rents and sells diving equipment; it also has the only re-compression chamber this side of Fiji. Email or phone for pricing.

Sidebar: AMERICAN SAMOA TUTUILA

STAR MOUNDS

More than 140 distinctive stone or earthen mounds dating back to late prehistoric times have been found scattered across the Samoan archipelago. Dubbed 'star mounds', the structures range from 6m to 30m in length, are up to 3m high and have from one to 11 raylike projections radiating from their base. Forty star mounds have been discovered (though not yet excavated) in Tutuila's east on the road between Amouli and Aoa.

The prominent theory regarding the star mounds is that they were used for pigeon-snaring, an important sport of chiefs. However, some archaeologists believe they served a much more complex function in Samoan society, including as sites for rituals related to marriage, healing and warfare. Archaeologists also believe the star mounds came to reflect the position of the *matai* (family group leader) and the notion of *mana* (supernatural power).

'Ili'ili Golf Course Golf   GOLF
(Map p300; ☑699 2995; 'Ili'ili; ☉dawn-dusk)
This is a 'very forgiving' 72-par course with
great views. Green fees for nine/18 holes are
US$4/7 on weekdays and US$5/10 on weekends. Club hire is US$20; carts are US$8/16
for nine/18 holes on weekdays and US$10/20
for weekends. Recap your game over a coldie
at its Nighthawk clubhouse.

☞ Tours

History buffs should check out the American
Samoa Historic Preservation Office's online
walking tour (www.ashpo.org) of Pago Pago.
Its detailed map links to fascinating titbits
about the city's lesser-known landmarks.

North Shore Tours   HIKING
(☑731 9294; rorywest@yahoo.com) Rory West
has an impressive knowledge of and passion
for the island's plants, legends and best secret spots. He caters to all levels but his ten-
dency veers towards hard-core; be prepared
for a real adventure.

Tisa's Tours   TOUR
(Map p300; ☑622 7447; www.tisasbarefootbar.
com) Island tours include lunch and swimming at Tisa's Barefoot Bar. Tisa can organise
tailored tours for guests.

🛏 Sleeping

Despite a surprising scarcity of waterside
options, Tutuila has a handful of excellent –
and occasionally quirky – places to stay.

🛏 Pago Pago

★Le Falepule   B&B $$
(Map p300; ☑633 5264; isabel@blueskynet.
as; Faga'alu; s/d US$140/150; P✳🛜) Sitting
on the terrace of this luxury boutique B&B
and gazing over the sublime ocean views,
you may never want to leave. It's a won-
derful place, with delightful staff, tropical
breakfasts, elegant rooms and a private yet
accessible location. Free laundry service is
a bonus. It's at the end of a steep driveway
200m north of the hospital turn-off.

Sadie Thompson Inn   HOTEL $$
(Map p300; ☑633 5981; www.sadieshotels.
com; Fagatogo; r US$137; P✳🛜) This wooden
inn was – apparently – where the original
Sadie Thompson (immortalised in Somerset
Maugham's novel *Rain*) set up her red light.
It's a bit less rollicking these days, but makes

for a clean, central place to stay. The identikit
rooms are – alas – not done in period style, but
the verandah-edged building itself is quaint
and charming. The restaurant is hit-or-miss.

Evalani's Motel   HOTEL $$
(Map p302; ☑633 7777; www.evalanis.com;
Pago Pago; r/ste/apt US$63/131/142; P✳🛜)
Also known as Motu-O-Fiafiaga Motel, this
friendly place is owned by a former show-
girl. Evalani may have left Vegas but Vegas
never left Evalani: the fabulously retro decor
here could best be described as brothel-chic.
Head down the creaky, scarlet-carpeted cor-
ridors and you'll find that the bright rooms
are very comfortable for the price. There's a
lively bar–Mexican restaurant attached.

Sadie's by the Sea   HOTEL $$$
(Map p302; ☑633 5900; www.sadieshotels.
com; Utulei; r US$167; P✳🛜🏊) 'By the sea'
is the big drawcard here; this is one of the
few places with a swimmable beach at its
doorstep. Rooms are characterless in that
midrange-hotel way, but are large and loaded with facilities. Shops, the harbour and
other attractions are steps away. Other perks
include the great on-site restaurant, Goat
Island Cafe, and a well-stocked shop selling
everything from souvenirs to booze.

🛏 Western Tutuila

Pago Airport Inn   HOTEL $
(Map p300; ☑699 6333; Tafuna; s/d US$78/99;
P✳🛜🏊) This friendly little hotel is a top
option for those who need to be close to the
airport (it's a three-minute drive away); that
it's extraordinarily cheap – for Tutuila – is
another bonus. There's a big pool, the rooms
are clean and large, and its free shuttles go
to the airport and nearby restaurants.

★Moana O Sina   B&B $$
(Map p300; ☑699 8517; isabel@blueskynet.
as; Fogagogo; s/d incl breakfast US$140/150;
✳🛜🏊) This elegant seaside B&B makes
for a stylish getaway, with gorgeous
grounds and well-appointed, Polynesian-
inspired rooms. The owners have made the
most out of their stunning surrounds, with
a delightful outdoor breakfast pavilion and
two small swimming pools overlooking
crashing waves and dramatic blowholes.
Other than the three friendly dogs on-site,
you may end up with this fantastic place all
to yourself.

AND GOD CREATED SAMOA

Samoans claim their land is the 'cradle of Polynesia', a place created by the sky god Tagaloa (Tangaroa). Before the sea, earth, sky, plants or people existed, Tagaloa lived in the expanse of empty space. He created a rock, commanding it to split into clay, coral, cliffs and stones. As the rock broke apart, the earth, sea and sky came into being. From a bit of the rock emerged a spring of fresh water.

At Saua in the Manu'a Islands, Tagaloa created man and woman, whom he named Fatu and 'Ele'ele ('Heart' and 'Earth'). He sent them to the region of fresh water and commanded them to people the area. He ordered the sky, called Tu'ite'elagi, to prop itself up above the earth.

Tagaloa then created Po and Ao ('Night' and 'Day'), which bore the 'eyes of the sky' – the sun and the moon. He sent their son, Manu'a, to be the people's chief. The Manu'a Islands were named after this chief, and from that time on, Samoan kings were called Tu'i Manu'a tele ma Samoa 'atoa (King of Manu'a and all of Samoa).

The world now consisted of Manu'a, Viti (Fiji), Tonga and Savai'i. Tagaloa then went to Manu'a and noticed that a void existed between it and Savai'i. Up popped Upolu and then Tutuila.

Tagaloa's final command was: 'Always respect Manu'a; anyone who fails to do so will be overtaken by catastrophe.' Thus, Manu'a became the spiritual centre of the Samoan islands and, to some extent, of all Polynesia.

Maliu Mai Beach Resort RESORT $$

(Map p300; ☑699 7232; maliumai@blueskynet. as; Fogagogo; r US$85-150; P❋🐾≋) Though a bit of a work in progress, this seaside resort is nevertheless a decent option, with helpful owners, a swimmable sea pool and a happening restaurant-bar attached. The new rooms are clean and serviceable; the pricier ones have lovely sea views.

Tradewinds Hotel HOTEL $$$

(Map p300; ☑699 1000; www.tradewinds.as; Main Ottoville Rd, Tafuna; r/ste from US$156/252; P❋@🐾≋) Tradewinds has everything you'd expect from a large business hotel – including an enticing resort pool, day spa, car-rental/tour desk and an ATM – and like many such hotels, it's opted for a generic look for its spacious rooms and broad corridors. Its **Equator Restaurant** (⊙6am to 9.30pm) is fine, but fits the same homogeneous-hotel bill, though *fiafia* (traditional dance performance) nights on Fridays are worth attending.

🏖 Eastern Tutuila

You may be able to arrange an overnight stay in Vatia through the homestay program of the National Park of American Samoa (p301).

★Tisa's Barefoot Bar BUNGALOW $

(Map p300; ☑622 7447; www.tisasbarefootbar. com; Alega Beach; fale per person incl breakfast & dinner US$50) Tisa's is possibly the most pop-ular place on Tutuila, and rightfully so. It's one of the rare spots to offer traditional *fale* (though these have proper beds instead of mattresses) and its superb setting on Alega Beach, brilliant bar-restaurant and the wonderful company of Tisa and her boyfriend Candyman combine to make this a very difficult place to leave.

Amouli Beach Fales BUNGALOW $

(Map p300; ☑254 2050; www.amoulibeachfales. com; Amouli; fale $25-75, electricity extra; P🐾) The open beachfront *fale* here are simple (electricity may be available, for an additional cost), and there's no restaurant (shops and eateries are but a stroll away), but who needs bells and whistles when you're parked on a glorious beach like this one? If you have kids, they'll love playing with the locals who come to take advantage of Amouli's top swimming.

Two Dollar Beach Apartments APARTMENT $$

(Map p300; ☑733 7011, 622 7656; www. twodollarbeach.com; Avaio Beach; apt US$150; P❋🐾) These two good-sized, two-bedroom self-contained apartments sit beside one of Tutuila's most popular beaches. If you don't feel like cooking indoors, pop down to the shore and crank up the barbecue; otherwise, there's a small bar-restaurant on-site.

🍴 Eating & Drinking

American Samoa's reputation for fatty fried foods is not generally contradicted by the eateries on Tutuila. The main road leading from the airport is a tribute to America's fast-food giants and a testimony to the high esteem they hold in the Polynesian palate. A scattering of Asian restaurants provides a lighter alternative.

Many hotels have bars that are open to nonguests.

✗ Pago Pago

Young's Mart SUPERMARKET $
(Map p300; ☑633 2655; Utulei; ⊙7am-8pm) This well-stocked supermarket is in a convenient location, and is open on Sundays.

★ DDW Beach Cafe AMERICAN $$
(Don't Drink the Water; Map p302; ☑633 5297; Utulei; mains US$6-30; ⊙7am-3pm Mon-Fri, 8am-2pm Sat) This bright waterfront cafe is a local favourite. Its huge breakfasts are legendary; lunches are equally gargantuan and span everything from well-cooked burgers to salads to seafood curries. It's also a top spot for a coffee.

Goat Island Cafe INTERNATIONAL $$
(Map p302; ☑633 5900; www.sadieshotels. com; Sadie's by the Sea, Utulei; mains US$10-35; ⊙6.30am-late) This popular restaurant has an incredibly extensive menu, offering everything from pizza and American-style sandwiches (its Philly 'steak bomb' is to die for) to the local version of haute cuisine. The outside dining *fale* overlook the beach. It's got the relaxed feel of an established hangout: you'll find plenty of locals and expats mixing it up, especially during happy hour (4pm to 6pm weekdays).

Evalani's Cantina MEXICAN $$
(Map p302; ☑633 7777; www.evalanis.com; Evalani's Motel, Pago Pago; mains US$5-22; ⊙7am-3pm & 5pm-late Mon-Sat) Attached to the flamboyant Evalani's Motel, this Mexican restaurant is no less gaudy, with over-the-top furnishings and flashing neon lights. The food is wonderfully cheesy too: the big burritos, enchiladas and nachos are fantastically fattening and so delicious that you won't care. It morphs into a fabulously kitsch nightclub as the evening wears on, and there's often live music. Don't miss it.

Paradise Pizza PIZZA $$
(Map p302; ☑731 6020; Satala, opposite Starkist Cannery; pizzas US$11-25; ⊙9am-10pm Mon-Sat) If you're craving big slices of American-style pizza, this is the place to indulge. It's got all the favourites, as well as those with interesting local toppings, including taro, Samoan pork sausage and one covered in tuna from the cannery across the road.

Sook's Sushi Restaurant ASIAN $$
(Map p302; ☑633 5525; GHC Reid Building, Fagatogo; mains US$7-20; ⊙9am-10pm Mon-Sat) Little has changed at this tiny seaside nook in the almost-20 years it's been running: that's a good thing. Fresh Japanese and Korean dishes – its beef *kalbi* (ribs) and tuna sashimi are locally famous – are prepared in an open kitchen beside the little dining room; there are small private rooms up the back if crowds aren't your thing.

Fia Fia Seafood Restaurant CHINESE $$
(Map p302; ☑633 0101; Fagatogo, Samoan News Building; mains US$6-25; ⊙10am-10pm) This clean, central place does Samoan-sized portions of Chinese food; thankfully, its quantity is matched by quality. While it's billed as a seafood restaurant, you'll find all the classics on the extensive menu.

ILLUSTRATING SAMOA

The full-bodied *pe'a* (male tattoo), which extends from the waist to just below the knees, is a prized status symbol in Samoa. It can take weeks to complete and is a very painful process: anyone who undergoes the ritual is considered extremely brave. Any adult member can, in effect, receive a *pe'a* if the *'aiga* (extended family), *tufuga* (tattoo artist) and village leaders agree that it is suitable. The *tufuga* is usually paid with traditional gifts of *ie toga* (fine mats) and food.

Tattooing was discouraged when the missionaries came, but as young Pacific islanders take more pride in their heritage, there has been a revival of interest in the traditional designs. Contemporary tattoos – made with the modern machine or by the traditional comb – come without social and cultural restrictions, but designs often signify a person's *'aiga*, ancestors, or reference to nature.

Western Tutuila

Mom's Place
SAMOAN $

(Map p300; 699 9494; Tafuna; mains US$5-15; 7am-2pm Mon-Sat) Mom's rich, diner-style cooking won't help keep your waistline under control, but to hell with it. Try your luck at getting through a plate of *panikeke* (the round doughnuts that Samoans call pancakes), or go island-style with corned-beef hash or spam and eggs.

Toa Bar & Grill
INTERNATIONAL $$

(Map p300; 699 5099; cnr Nu'uuli St & Lion's Park Rd, Nu'uuli; US$8-25; 4pm-midnight Mon-Thu, 2pm-2am Fri & Sat) Hungry locals congregate here for huge portions of seafood, steak and Samoan classics, as well as for the popular bar and regular screening of live sports. Toa rocks on into the night, with regular happy hours and live music throughout the week. It's friendly, but not fancy.

Eastern Tutuila

Da Tamalelei Seaside Grill
INTERNATIONAL $

(Map p300; 252 1488; Alofau; mains US$3-10; 10am-7pm Mon-Sat) This humble seaside place dishes up gigantic serves of belt-busting grub for pocket change. Its burgers are legendary (even ravenous carnivores will battle to finish the two-patty, toppings-loaded 'Da Monster'), and it also cooks a variety of Asian and Samoan dishes; all meals come with rice, macaroni and vegetables. It does deliveries as far west as Pago Pago and Faga'alu.

Tisa's Barefoot Bar
SAMOAN $$

(Map p300; 622 7447; www.tisasbarefootbar. com; Alega Beach; meals US$10-30) This social beachside restaurant specialises in super-fresh seafood with a Samoan twist. Opening hours can be sporadic, so it pays to call ahead. On Wednesday nights it fires up the *umu* (stone oven) for its legendary Samoan feast (US$40, bookings recommended), where traditional fare is given an international twist. Tisa's is also an exceptional spot for a cold beer or fruity cocktail.

⭐ Entertainment

For an all-singing, all-dancing, thigh-slapping Samoan *fiafia,* head to the Equator restaurant at Tradewinds Hotel (p305) on a Friday night. A buffet dinner is included in the price (US$35).

A handful of bars and cafes host local musicians (Sadie's by the Sea and Tisa's among them), while karaoke bars tend to cater to the seedier side of the fishing industry via Chinese prostitutes.

Regal Nu'uuli Place Twin
CINEMA

(Map p302; 699 3456; Fagatogo; adult/child US$7.50/5) Head here for some smash-'em-up Hollywood action.

🛍 Shopping

Tutuila's not quite Rodeo Drive, but you'll find what you need in the shopping centres and strip malls of Tafuna, Nu'uuli and Pago Pago. For souvenirs, head to Fagatogo Market (p298).

Off Da Rock Tattoos
TATTOOS

(252 4858; www.offdarocktattoos.com; Nu'uuli; 9am-4pm by appointment) The award-winning artists here specialise in clean, beautiful Polynesian designs; they take it easy on tourists with a modern electric needle.

ℹ Information

Many of American Samoa's hotels offer free wi-fi. ATMs are found throughout commercial areas of the island.

American Samoa Historic Preservation Office (Ashpo; Map p300; 699 2316; www.ashpo.org; Nu'uuli) Excellent contact for history, sociology, anthropology and archaeology buffs. Its walking tours (info available online and in a pamphlet) offer insight into the region's colourful past.

American Samoa Visitors Bureau (Map p300; 699 9805; www.americansamoa. travel; Level 1, Fagaima Center One, Tafuna; 8am-4pm Mon-Fri) Drop in if you're in the area, but you're better off with the National Park or National Marine Sanctuary info centres in town.

ANZ Amerika Samoa Bank (Map p302; Fagatogo) There are many branches around Tutuila, including in Fagatogo, Nu'uuli and Tafuna.

Bank of Hawai'i (Map p302; www.boh.com; Utulei; 9am-3pm Mon-Fri, ATM 24hr) Has a branch in Utulei, plus one in Tafuna, on the main road from the airport.

Blue Sky (Map p300; www.bluesky.as; Laufou Shopping Centre; ◷8am-4pm Mon-Fri) Blue Sky hot spots can be found all over Tutuila (see the website for a full list). Unlimited use for 24 hours/one week is US$10/20.

LBJ Tropical Medical Center (Map p300; ✆633 1222; Faga'alu; ◷emergency 24hr) American Samoa's only hospital.

National Park Visitor Information Center (Map p302; ✆633 7082; www.nps.gov/npsa; 2nd fl, MHJ Building; ◷8am-4.30pm Mon-Fri) This is the best place in American Samoa for tourist advice and information. It has excellent free maps, day-hikes pamphlets, information on WWII sites and a homestay program with choices on Tutuila, Olosega and Ta'u islands (US$35 to US$50 per night). Staff are helpful and professional.

Post office (Map p302; ◷8.30am-3.30pm Mon-Fri, 9am-1pm Sat) American Samoa's main post office.

ⓘ Getting There & Away

All international flights and boats to American Samoa head to Tutuila.

A Pago Pago–bound ferry departs Apia (Samoa) every Thursday at 11pm; it departs Pago Pago the following day (also a Thursday, thanks to the bizarre dateline) at 4pm. The journey takes about seven hours. Prices (and currencies) vary, depending on which country you're leaving from; see the Samoa Shipping Corporation (p315) website for details.

ⓘ Getting Around

TO/FROM THE AIRPORT

Frequent buses from Pago Pago Harbor to Tafuna International Airport are marked 'Tafuna' and stop right outside the terminal (US$2). If arriving at night you'll need to get a cab into Pago Pago (between US$15 and US$25). There's a taxi stand just outside the airport entrance.

BUS

Riding Tutuila's colourful 'aiga (extended family) buses is a must-do. These buses do unscheduled runs around Pago Pago Harbor and the more remote areas of the island from the main terminal at the market in Fagatogo. Fares range from US$1 to US$2.50.

Buses regularly head east to Aua and Tula, south to Tafuna and west to Leone. Less-frequent buses go to Fagasa, A'oloaufou on the central ridge, Amanave and Fagamalo in the far west; a trip to the northwest villages often means disembarking at Leone and catching

another bus from there. Buses also head over Rainmaker Pass to Vatia.

CAR

A 2WD is fine for motoring around Tutuila. Car hire is around US$80 per day.

Avis Car Rental (Map p300; ✆699 2746; www.avis.com; Tafuna International Airport)

Sir Amos Car Rental (Map p300; ✆256 4394; siramoscarrental@gmail.com; Tafuna International Airport)

Tropical Car Rental (Map p300; ✆699 1176; www.prtropicalcarrental.com; Tafuna International Airport)

TAXI

Taxis are plentiful and convenient in Pago Pago, Nu'uuli and Tafuna. Fares vary wildly and meters aren't often used; be sure to agree on a price before getting in.

MANU'A ISLANDS

POP 1160 / AREA 57 SQ KM

Ofu, Olosega and Ta'u, anchored about 100km to the east of Tutuila, are among the most ravishing – and remote – of all the Pacific isles.

The three share the same marvellous natural characteristics: enormous cliffs sheltering seabird colonies, expired volcanic cones, pristine lagoons stocked with a brilliant array of coral, and a soul-soothing sense of quiet. Ofu Beach ranks as one of the most splendid stretches of sand in the world.

The Manu'a Islands make the laid-back environs of Tutuila seem chaotic by comparison; be sure to pack plenty of extra reading material and a willingness to fall asleep in the middle of the day. While visitors are content to wallow in island inertia, the mosquitoes here are very active; bring repellent.

Plan to visit Manu'a near the beginning of your trip; any disruption in the weather could keep you here longer than you intended.

ⓘ Information

There are basic medical clinics in Ofu village and on Ta'u. There are post offices on each of the islands.

There are no banks in the Manu'a Islands (though one is apparently in the works for Ta'u), and most accommodation options don't take credit cards. Pack cash.

> **DON'T MISS**
>
> ## AUNU'U
>
> The 3-sq-km, tangled confines of Aunu'u are perfect for a half-day of exploring on foot. The walking tracks are manageable on your own, or you can arrange a guide when you get off the ferry (US$8 to US$10 is reasonable).
>
> At the north end of the island is Pala Lake, a deadly looking expanse of quicksand whose fiery red hue is best appreciated at low tide. Within Aunu'u's central volcanic crater lies Red Lake, filled with eels and suffused by a preternatural glow at dusk. On the island's eastern shore is Ma'ama'a Cove, a rocky bowl pounded by large waves. Legend says that this is the site where two lovers, Sina and Tigila'u, were shipwrecked. You can make out bits of crossed 'rope' and broken 'planks' embedded in the rocks.
>
> Below the western slope of Aunu'u's crater are the Taufusitele Taro Marshes. The safest place to swim on the island is in the little harbour, where the water's so clear that you can see the coral from the breakwater.
>
> Small launches head to Aunu'u from the dock at Au'asi (at the eastern end of Tutuila). If you catch a boat with the locals, it's US$2 each way. If you charter a boat, a return trip is around US$10 to US$15. Boats don't run on Sundays.

ⓘ Getting There & Away

AIR
Polynesian Airlines flies four times a week between Pago Pago and Ta'u Island (Fitiuta Airport) and once a week between Pago Pago and Ofu Airport.

Manu'a Airways (www.manuaair.com) – a new branch of **Inter Island Airways** (☑ in Pago Pago 699 7100, in Ta'u 677 7100; www.interislandair. com) – should be up and running by the time you read this, with direct flights between Pago Pago and Ofu and Ta'u islands, as well as flights between Ofu and Ta'u.

BOAT
The **MV Sili** (☑ 633 4160; www.american samoaport.as.gov/services/water-transport ation-division.html; 1 way/return US$30/50) cargo ship departs Tutuila for Ofu and Ta'u every second Thursday morning, and returns the following morning. Book in advance: you'll need to call to do so, or ask your accommodation to help out. The journey takes between eight to 12 hours, and seas can get rough.

Take all of this with a grain of salt. The ageing ship often breaks down, and the Manu'a Islands have previously gone for weeks without it calling in. This is no fun for travellers, and even worse for locals: they depend on it for food and supplies.

ⓘ Getting Around

Ofu and Olosega are joined by a bridge; to get to Ta'u, you'll need to hop a boat or fly.

Flights between Ofu and Ta'u islands on new airline Manu'a Airways should have commenced by the time you read this.

The *Segaula* – an aluminum catamaran – regularly plies the waters between Ofu and Ta'u; the MV *Sili* creaks between the two fortnightly. Otherwise, charter boats can be arranged (about US$200 for four people).

Getting around on the islands themselves involves walking or sticking your thumb out; though there are only a handful of vehicles on the islands, few drivers will pass a walker without offering a lift.

Ofu & Olosega

POP OFU 176, OLOSEGA 177 / AREA OFU 5.2 SQ KM, OLOSEGA 3 SQ KM

These twin islands, separated by a deep channel but linked by a bridge, are as close to paradise as it gets. Ofu's lone village crouches at its western end, leaving the rest of the island largely – and delightfully – uninhabited. Taking up its southern shoreline, exquisite Ofu Beach is 4km of shining, palm-fringed white sand, flanked by outrageously picturesque peaks that rise behind it like giant shark's teeth.

This, along with 140 hectares of offshore waters, comprises the Ofu section of the National Park of American Samoa. The reef here is considered to be one of the healthiest in all the Samoas. Huge schools of coloured fish dart through jaw-droppingly clear waters, occasionally pursued by reef sharks: they're harmless, to humans at least, but can induce heart palpitations for the novice snorkeller. Equally squeal-inducing (but just as benign) are the giant coconut crabs you'll likely see clattering around; they're the biggest land bugs in the world (not to mention very tasty).

Ofu & Olosega

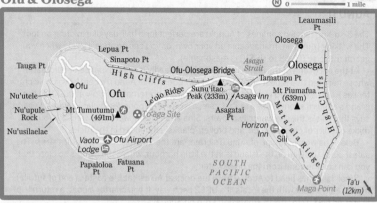

⊙ Sights & Activities

Olosega shares the same marvellous encircling reef system as Ofu. The two islands look conjoined, but are separated from each other by the 137m-wide Asaga Strait. From the cyclone-proof **bridge**, the water is impossibly clear. Local kids regularly jump off, letting the current carry them to shore. This isn't advised for visitors – if you get the wrong tides you could easily be carried straight out to sea.

To'aga Site
ARCHAEOLOGICAL SITE
(Ofu) While there's nothing to see here now, it was at this site (just behind Ofu Beach) where archaeologists found an unprecedented array of artefacts dating from early prehistory to the modern day. Samoans believe the bush between the road and the beach is infested with devilish *aitu* (spirits or ghosts), meaning you're likely to have one of the world's best beaches to yourself.

Mt Tumutumu
HIKING
(Ofu) The 5.5km-long, often indistinct track (five hours return) to the summit of Mt Tumutumu (491m) begins just north of Ofu village wharf and twists up to the mountaintop TV relay tower. You'll need sensible shoes, long trousers (to protect from cutting plants), heavy-duty mosquito repellent and a knife to hack through the foliage.

Maga Point
FISHING
(Olosega) The 1.5km walk to Maga Point on Olosega's southern tip offers unforgettable views of the point's steep cliffs, colourful reefs and distant Ta'u. To avoid local dogs, veer around Olosega village on the beach. After passing the rubbish tip, pick your way along the coral-strewn beach and look for the narrow hillside trail.

🛌 Sleeping & Eating

Ofu and Olosega villages have basic stores where you can stock up on provisions.

★ Vaoto Lodge
LODGE $
(☎ 655 1120; www.vaotolodge.com; Ofu; s/d US$80/90, cabins from US$120; 🛜) This friendly, family-run place sits pretty at the base of Mt Tumutumu. Its beach – and those nearby – offers sensational snorkelling; it's also within strolling distance of some terrific hikes. Units are simple but comfortable; all have en suites. Delicious home-cooked meals (US$10 to US$20) are served communal-style.

Asaga Inn
MOTEL $
(☎ 655 7791; www.asagainn.com; Ofu; r US$90; ❄🛜) In a plum location right beside the Ofu–Olosega Bridge, this small motel offers good-sized rooms and air-conditioning (a rarity in the islands); the lovely family that owns it also runs the local mini-market. Full meal plans (US$36 per day) are available.

Horizon Inn
INN $
(☎ 655 1302; www.horizoninn.yolasite.com; Olosega; s/d US$80/95; 🛜) This new inn is small, simple and right on the sand. Rooms are basic but clean. The bridge connecting Ofa and Olosega, as well the Maga Point hike, are within walking distance. The meals at

its restaurant (5am to 9pm) are gigantic and fantastically fattening.

Ta'u

POP 790 / AREA 39 SQ KM

On the dramatic south coast of this remote, sparsely populated volcanic island, some of the highest sea cliffs in the world rise 963m to Mt Lata, the territory's highest point.

The main settlement on Ta'u consists of the villages of Ta'u, Luma and Si'ufaga in the island's northwest. From Ta'u village there's a good walk south to secluded Fagamalo Cove. It was in Luma that Margaret Mead researched her classic anthropological work, *Coming of Age in Samoa*, in 1925. Despite the book's impression of a permissive society, Ta'u is the most conservative part of American Samoa.

The island's dense rainforests are home to flying foxes and numerous native birds. Ta'u is also the only habitat of the Pacific boa.

Sights & Activities

Saua Site   ARCHAEOLOGICAL SITE

This sacred site is where Tagaloa is said to have created the first humans before sending them out to Polynesia. Its volcanic boulders, wild surf and windswept beach lend it an ancient, supernatural atmosphere. Short trails lead to the main archaeological area, and *fale* have been erected for shelter. It's about 2.5km from Fiti'uta.

Keen hikers can continue from Saua via a rough track to Tufu Point. If you've arranged a guide, you could plug on for another 2km to a waterfall on the Laufuti Stream.

Judds Crater   HIKING

(Luatele Crater) Treks to this gigantic volcanic crater should only be undertaken by very experienced hikers, and guides are a must; contact the National Park of American Samoa (p301) to arrange one well in advance of your trip. The hike should take about three hours (one way) from the road near Fiti'uta.

Sleeping & Eating

At least three families on Ta'u offer village homestays (about US$80). These are facilitated by the National Park of American Samoa (p301): click on the 'homestay program' button on its website for more information.

SUBSEA SPECTACLE: THE VALLEY OF GIANTS

Ta'u, with its soaring sea cliffs, creation legends and preternatural sense of remoteness, is an extraordinarily exotic island. But its otherworldly feel isn't limited to land: Ta'u's surrounding waters are home to one of the largest, oldest and most mysterious coral colonies on the planet. Known as the Valley of Giants, this remarkable reef is populated by massive live boulder corals known as porites. The biggest is the gargantuan Big Momma, which looms 6.4m high, has a circumference of 41m and is believed to be at least 530 years old. How Big Momma and her colossal counterparts have managed to thrive despite centuries of climate change has baffled the few scientists that have been able to study this underwater wonder.

UNDERSTAND AMERICAN SAMOA

American Samoa Today

The two tuna canneries in Pago Pago account for 80% of American Samoa's employment, though the high costs of operating here makes their staying power shaky at best.

American Samoa's relationship with America is an unusual one. Though the people here are unquestionably Samoan, many speak with American accents and refer to the continental US as 'the mainland'. And whether due to patriotism or for economic reasons, American Samoa has the highest rate of military enlistment of any American state or territory. The 'American or not?' question was answered with some finality in 2015, when a court case (*Tuaua vs the United States*) pushing for full citizen rights for American Samoans was rejected.

History

Prehistory

Archaeological finds near the villages of Tula and Aoa at the eastern tip of Tutuila, and at To'aga on Ofu, reveal that the islands have been inhabited for more than 3000

Ta'u

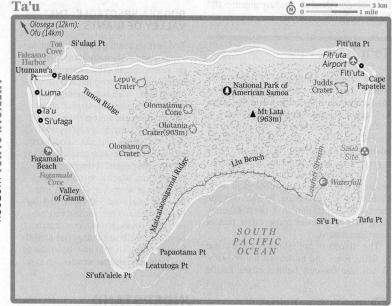

Olosega (12km);
Ofu (14km)

years. Traditionally Samoans believed that the Manu'a Islands were the first land to emerge at the hands of the god Tagaloa (see p305). The Tu'i Manu'a (paramount chief of the islands) was held in high esteem by Samoans. Although various conflicts ultimately split the islands, the paramount chief was still a powerful figure at the time of cession to the US at the beginning of the 20th century.

European Contact

In 1722 Dutchman Jacob Roggeveen sighted the Manu'a Islands, but sailed on without landing. In May 1768 French explorer Captain Louis-Antoine de Bougainville bartered with the inhabitants of Manu'a, but merely sighted Tutuila. The first expedition to set foot on Tutuila was headed by Frenchman Jean-François de Galaup, comte de la Pérouse, who landed at Fagasa in 1787. The encounter had a tragic finish, with the French and the Samoans fighting each other at A'asu: 12 sailors and 39 villagers were killed, and A'asu was christened Massacre Bay.

US Military Rule

A Samoan civil war in the 1870s and 1880s was co-opted by the US, Britain and Germany into an argument over which foreign power should rule the islands. By the time the dust had settled, control of western Samoa had been granted to Germany, and by 1900 the islands of eastern Samoa had been formally annexed to the US by a deed of cession signed by all local chiefs. Eastern Samoa became a naval station under the jurisdiction of the US Department of the Navy. In exchange, the US agreed to protect the traditional rights of indigenous Samoans. The inhabitants acquired the status of US nationals but were denied a vote or representation in Washington.

In 1905 the military commander of Tutuila was given the title of governor and the territory officially became known as American Samoa.

Increasing Democracy

Until the 1960s American Samoa retained its traditional social structure and subsistence economy. But under President Kennedy, American Samoa was swiftly modernised, with European-style homes replacing traditional *fale*, electrification and the construction of an international airport and tuna canneries.

Through the 1960s and 1970s a series of referendums resulted in the adoption of a constitution, a democratically elected governorship and a two-chamber legislature. In 1980 American Samoans were allowed, for the first time, to elect a (nonvoting) delegate to serve in the US House of Representatives.

Recent Decades

In January 1987 the territory was hit by Cyclone Tusi, one of the worst storms in recorded history. Several more cyclones ploughed through the area between 1990 and 2009. In 2009 much of Tutuila was pummelled by a massive tsunami.

While American Samoa relies heavily on funding from the US government, the relationship isn't as one-sided as it seems: many American Samoans play for US sporting teams (particularly gridiron), and plenty more serve in the US military.

The Culture

Samoans have maintained their traditional way of life and still closely follow the social hierarchies, customs and courtesies established long before the arrival of Europeans.

Population

Most of the population lives on the main island of Tutuila. The birth rate is high but is offset by emigration to Hawai'i and the US mainland. Some 1500 foreigners reside in American Samoa, most of whom are Koreans or Chinese involved in the tuna or garment industries. About one-third are *palagi* (Westerners), many of whom hold government jobs, usually in the teaching or health fields.

Arts

American Samoa shares its artistic traditions with Samoa, from the energetic song-and-dance routines called *fiafia* and the satirisation of their elders by village youth in the skit-based *Faleaitu* (meaning 'House of Spirits'), to the breezy architecture of the *fale*, intricate tattoos, and the lovely *siapo* (bark cloth) and *ie toga* (fine mats) used in customary gift exchanges.

Environment

Geography

American Samoa has a total land area of 197 sq km. The main island, Tutuila, is 30km long and up to 6km wide. The Manu'a group, 100km east of Tutuila, consists of the islands of Ta'u, Ofu and Olosega, all wildly steep volcanic remnants.

The easternmost part of the territory is tiny Rose Atoll, two minuscule specks of land (plus a surrounding reef) that were declared a Marine National Monument in 2009. This status helps protect the green turtle, as well as the extremely rare hawksbill turtle. Only scientific research expeditions are allowed to visit the atoll, though a charter there – at the discretion of the US Fish and Wildlife Service (www.fws.gov) – is theoretically possible

Equally tiny Swains Island (350km north-northwest of Tutuila) consists of a 3.25-sq-km ring of land surrounding a brackish lagoon. Both culturally and geographically, it belongs to Tokelau, but in 1925 the island's owners, the Jennings family, persuaded the US to annex it.

Ecology

The wild inhabitants of American Samoa include two species of flying fox, *pili* (skinks), *mo'o* (geckos) and the harmless *gata* (Pacific boa), which is found only on Ta'u. The surrounding waters are home to pilot whales, dolphins and porpoises, while hawksbill turtles occasionally breed on remote beaches. Bird species include the nearly flightless banded rail, the barn owl and the superb *sega* (blue-crowned lory). While walking in rainforests, listen for the haunting calls of the rare multicoloured fruit doves (*manuma*) and the beautiful green-and-white Pacific pigeons.

Tutuila is characterised by its broadleaf evergreen rainforest. Ofu, Olosega and Ta'u host temperate forest vegetation such as tree ferns, grasses, wild coleus and epiphytic plants.

SURVIVAL GUIDE

❶ Directory A–Z

ACCOMMODATION

Fale accommodation for tourists has never quite caught on in American Samoa. With a few

SLEEPING PRICE RANGES

The following price ranges refer to a double room with bathroom:

$ less than US$100

$$ US$100–US$150

$$$ more than US$150

exceptions, lodgings here come in the form of generic motels, hotels and a handful of B&Bs.

The National Park of American Samoa (p301) operates a village homestay program.

EMBASSIES & CONSULATES

All American Samoan diplomatic affairs are handled by the US. There are no consulates or embassies in American Samoa and no places that are able to issue visas for the US.

EMERGENCY

📞 911

FESTIVALS & EVENTS

Flag Day (17 April) American Samoa's main public holiday commemorates the raising of the US flag over the islands in 1900 with an arts festival and traditional fanfare.

Tisa's Tattoo Festival (October) Showcase of traditional and modern *tatau* at Tisa's Barefoot Bar on Tutuila.

White Sunday (second Sunday of October) Celebration of Samoan childhood, with a heavy religious slant.

Moso'oi Festival (last week of October) A week of sporting and cultural events.

Samoana Jazz and Arts Festival (late October/ early November) This new festival hosts local and international artists, and jumps between Tutuila and Apia.

INTERNET ACCESS

Most hotels and guesthouses offer wi-fi.

LANGUAGE

Samoan, English.

MAPS

The tourism and national-park offices produce free brochures with maps.

MONEY

The US dollar, divided into 100 cents, is the unit of currency in use in American Samoa.

ATMs are provided by the ANZ Amerika Samoa Bank and the Bank of Hawai'i on Tutuila.

Tipping is not expected or encouraged in American Samoa, though it's acceptable for exceptional service at finer restaurants.

OPENING HOURS

The following are standard opening hours in American Samoa:

Banks 9am to 4pm Monday to Friday, some open 8.30am to 12.30pm Saturday

Bars noon to midnight

Government offices 9am to 5pm Monday to Friday

Restaurants 8am to 4pm and 6pm to 10pm

Shops 8am to 4.30pm Monday to Friday, 8am to noon Saturday (village stores keep longer hours)

TELEPHONE

Blue Sky (p308) sells SIM cards and pre-paid mobile credit.

TIME

The local time in American Samoa is GMT/ UTC minus 11 hours. Therefore, when it's noon in American Samoa, it's 11pm the same day in London, 3pm the same day in Los Angeles, 9am the following day in Sydney and – just to be skull-crunchingly confusing for those booking flights to/from Samoa – 1pm the following day in Apia.

USEFUL WEBSITES

American Samoa Historic Preservation Office (www.ashpo.org) This site includes information on Samoa's history and a good walking tour.

American Samoa Visitors Bureau (www. americansamoa.travel) Loads of information on attractions and accommodation in American Samoa.

Busy Corner (www.amsamoa-busycorner. blogspot.com.au) Online magazine focusing on the culture and highlights of American Samoa.

Lonely Planet (www.lonelyplanet.com/ american-samoa) For planning advice, author recommendations, traveller reviews and insider tips.

National Park of American Samoa (www. nps.gov/npsa) This excellent site has a wealth of information on all aspects of the park, plus details of a territory-wide homestay program.

Samoa News (www.samoanews.com) For the latest American Samoan news.

VISAS

US citizens equipped with a valid passport and an onward ticket can visit American Samoa visa-free. Nationals of Australia, New Zealand, Canada, the UK and some EU countries equipped with a passport (valid for at least 60 days) and an onward ticket will receive a free one-month visa on arrival. Other nationals must apply in advance for their one-month visa (US$40). It's a good idea to check your status before you go.

Visas can be issued by the **Attorney General's office** (📞 633 4163; okboard.asag@gmail.com), but given that it has no official website, email queries often go unanswered and the phone connection can be dodgy, it's a better idea to ask your hotel if they can arrange a visa for you (fee about US$40).

Visa extensions are handled by the AG or the **Immigration Office** (Map p302; ☑ 633 4203; ground fl, Executive Office Bldg, Utulei; ⊙ 8am-4pm Mon-Fri), located within the government building in Pago Pago. Visas can only be extended by one month; the fee for this varies depending on what country you hail from. Again, larger hotels should be willing to play the middleman in what can be a confusing and convoluted procedure.

❶ Getting There & Away

AIR

There's no better illustration of the physical isolation of American Samoa than the fact that you can only fly directly to Tutuila from Samoa and Hawai'i.

All flights go via Tafuna International Airport, 15km southwest of Pago Pago Harbor. The following airlines service American Samoa (telephone numbers here are for dialling from within American Samoa).

Hawaiian Airlines (☑ 699 1875; www.hawaiian air.com) Flies on Mondays and Fridays to/from Honolulu; return fare from US$955.

Inter Island Airways (☑ 699 7100; www.inter-islandair.com) Two daily flights to/from Samoa; return fares from US$170. It also runs flights to the Manu'a Islands.

Polynesian Airlines (☑ 699 9126; www.polyne-sianairlines.com) Runs frequent daily flights between Samoa and Pago Pago, plus some to the Manu'a Islands.

SEA
Ferry

A car ferry/cargo ship called MV *Lady Naomi* runs between Pago Pago and Apia once a week. It departs Pago Pago each Thursday at 4pm for the trip (about seven hours). Return fares start at US$65. Tickets must be purchased at least one day in advance from **Samoa Shipping Corporation** (☑ 633 1211; www.samoashipping.com).

Yacht

Pago Pago's deep, spectacular harbour serves as the official entry point for private yacht owners.

All yachts and boats are required to contact the Harbour Master before entering American Samoan waters on VHF channel 16. Permission from Pago Pago is needed to sail to other islands in American Samoa. Yachts should be granted anchorage from US$7.50 per month in the harbour. Vessels arriving from Hawai'i need to present a US customs clearance document from Honolulu. See the **American**

Samoa Port Administration (☑ 633 4251; www.americansamoaport.as.gov) website for full details.

❶ Getting Around

AIR
Inter Island Airways (p315) and Polynesian Airlines (p315) fly between Tutuila and the Manu'a Islands. The new Manu'a Airways (p309) should be running flights between Ta'u and Ofu by the time you read this.

BICYCLE
Tutuila is not very conducive to cycling. The island is mountainous, traffic can be heavy, and a complete circuit is impossible as there are no roads across the rugged north coast. Dogs can also be a major hassle here.

BUS
Villages and towns on the island of Tutuila are serviced by '*aiga*-owned buses. Buses theoretically run until early evening, but don't test this theory after 2pm on Saturdays, or at all on Sundays. All buses display the name of their final destination in the front window. To stop a bus, wave your hand and arm, palm down, as the bus approaches. To signal that you'd like to get off the bus, either knock on the ceiling or clap loudly. Pay the driver; try to have the exact fare.

CAR
Hiring a car allows you to explore Tutuila quickly and comfortably via the island's good sealed roads. That said, going it alone will rob you of the unique cultural experiences that public transport offers.

When hiring a vehicle, check for any damage or scratches before you drive off, and note everything on the rental agreement, lest you be held liable for damage when the car is returned.

Vehicles drive on the right-hand side of the road. The speed limit is 40km/h (25mph) island-wide. A valid foreign driving licence should allow you to drive in American Samoa.

Insurance

It's essential to have your hire car covered by insurance as repair costs are extremely high. Some local car-hire firms offer contracts where there's no option of accepting a collision/damage waiver (CDW). The lack of a CDW technically means that the car hirer is liable for *all* costs resulting from an accident, regardless of whose fault it is, so sign such contracts at your peril. You should insist on a CDW, for which you pay an extra fee of around US$12 per day.

TAXI
Taxis on Tutuila are expensive and are only convenient for short trips.

Solomon Islands

677 / POP 538,000 / AREA 27,540 SQ KM

Best Historical Sites

➡ US War Memorial (p317)

➡ Tetere Beach & WWII Museum (p329)

➡ Vilu War Museum (p330)

➡ Skull Island (p334)

Best Places to Stay

➡ Rekona Flourish (p321)

➡ Tavanipupu Private Island Resort (p330)

➡ Urilolo Lodge (p338)

➡ Uepi Island Resort (p333)

➡ Sanbis Resort (p339)

Why Go?

Forget what travelling the Pacific *used* to be like – around the Solomon Islands it's still that way. These islands are laid-back, welcoming and often surprisingly untouched. From WWII relics scattered in the jungle to leaf-hut villages where traditional culture is alive, there's so much on offer. Then there's the visual appeal, with scenery reminiscent of a Discovery Channel documentary: volcanic islands, croc-infested mangroves, huge lagoons, tropical islets and emerald forests.

Don't expect white-sand beaches and ritzy resorts. With only a smattering of traditional guesthouses and comfortable hideaways, it's tailor-made for ecotourists. For outdoorsy types, lots of action-packed experiences await: climb an extinct volcano, surf uncrowded waves, snorkel pristine reefs or kayak across a lagoon. Beneath the ocean's surface, awesome WWII wrecks and dizzying drop-offs will enthral divers. The best part is that there'll be no crowds to mar the experience.

When to Go
Honiara

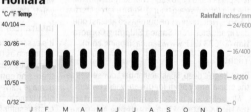

Dec–Mar Intervals of calm weather broken by storms, making for good reef breaks and diving.

Jun–Sep High season's mild weather (but rough seas) is good for hiking, but less ideal for diving.

Apr–May & Oct–Nov The shoulder seasons are relatively dry and aren't a bad time to visit.

GUADALCANAL

POP 109,000

The largest island in the Solomons, Guadalcanal hosts the national capital, Honiara. There's no iconic calling card but a smattering of cultural sights, including well-preserved WWII relics along the northern coast, as well as a few modest beaches. There's also fantastic diving at Iron Bottom Sound, the famous graveyard of WWII's Battle for Guadalcanal, just off the north coast. Outside the northern coast, the island has the genuine look of a lost world. The hills behind the capital eventually become a mighty mountain range rising to 2400m, which remains untamed and raw.

Honiara

POP 68,000

The first port of call for most visitors, due to its position at the hub of all activity within the archipelago, it's hard not to spend some time in Honiara, the closest thing you'll find to a city in the Solomons. Just over a decade ago it was little more than a sleepy South Seas port, but over the last few years it has undergone an urban boom, and traffic snarl-ups at peak hours are now increasingly common in the centre.

It's rarely love at first sight – the architecture wins no prizes and sights are sparse. But get under the city's skin and the place just might start to grow on you. Hang around the atmospheric wharf, wade through the shambolic market, grab a few gifts in the well-stocked souvenir shops and get your first taste of Melanesian culture by visiting the museum.

Honiara is also the optimal launching pad for exploring Guadalcanal's outdoor offerings and the various WWII battlefields around the city.

◉ Sights

★ Central Market   MARKET

(Map p324; Mendana Ave; ⊙6am-5pm Mon-Sat) While Honiara won't be mistaken for Lagos, the country's bubbling principal food market covers a whole block between Mendana Ave and the seafront. It has a huge selection of fresh produce, especially fruits and vegetables, that come from outlying villages along the northern coast and from Savo Island. Also on sale are traditional crafts. The fish market is at the back. There's no hassling to buy anything, but beware of pickpockets.

Holy Cross Catholic Cathedral   CATHEDRAL

(Map p324; Mendana Ave) Honiara's most prominent religious building is this cathedral perched on a hill to the east of the centre. Visitors are welcome to attend, but make sure you dress modestly.

National Parliament   BUILDING

(Map p326; Lower Vavaya Rd; ⊙8am-4pm Mon-Fri) The conical-shaped concrete building that's perched on the hill above Hibiscus Ave is the National Parliament. Inside, the dome boasts a rich tapestry of traditional art, including arching frescoes.

National Museum   MUSEUM

(Map p326; ☑24896; Mendana Ave; admission by donation; ⊙9am-4pm Mon-Fri, 10am-2pm Sat) This modest museum (it has only one room) features interesting displays and old photographs on traditional dance, body ornamentation, currency, weaponry and archaeology. It also covers the role of the coastwatchers during WWII and the influence of missionaries.

US War Memorial   HISTORIC SITE

(Map p324; Skyline Dr) This superb memorial is a five-minute taxi ride from the centre. The well-maintained compound has marble slabs bearing detailed descriptions of battles fought during the Guadalcanal campaign. It was unveiled on 7 August 1992, the 50th anniversary of the US beach landings. There are also great views of the northern coast.

★ Activities

Diving is Honiara's trump card; a fantastic collection of WWII wrecks lie offshore in an area known as Iron Bottom Sound, including Bonegi I and Bonegi II to the west, and USS *John Penn* to the east. For more, see p36.

Solomon Islands
Diving – Tulagi Dive   DIVING, SNORKELLING

(Map p326; ☑25700; www.tulagidive.com; Mendana Ave; single/double dive from S$900/1200; ⊙9am-5pm Mon-Fri, 8am-5.30pm Sat & Sun) This highly professional dive shop run by Australian Neil Yates adheres to strict safety procedures for deep dives. It specialises in dive sites along the northern coast but also organises day trips to the Florida Islands (S$1700 including two dives, equipment and lunch; minimum six divers) and snorkel trips (S$400) to Bonegi. It's beside Point Cruz Yacht Club.

Ko Kama Rafting   RAFTING

(☑7494788; aemmett04@gmail.com; trips S$700; ⊙Sat & Sun by reservation) East of Honiara, the

Solomon Islands Highlights

① Diving and snorkelling in fish soup in **Marovo Lagoon** (p330).

② Feeling free in an intimate lodge at **Langa Langa Lagoon** (p343).

③ Huffing to the top of the mount on **Kolombangara** (p340).

④ Spending the day spotting rusty **WWII relics** (p328) around Honiara.

⑤ Taking a dip in a natural pool at **Mataniko Falls** (p328).

⑥ Assisting rangers in tagging marine turtles on

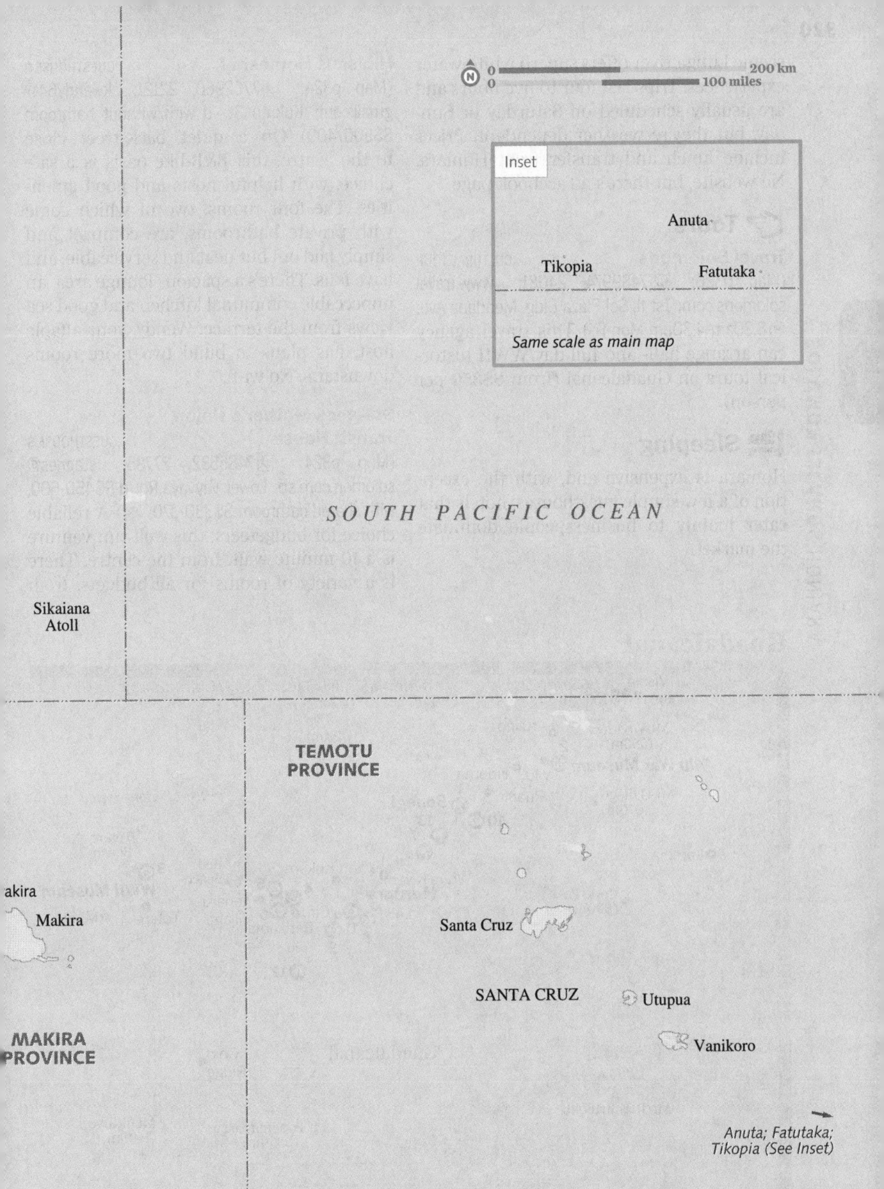

0	200 km
0	100 miles

Inset

Anuta

Tikopia   Fatutaka

Same scale as main map

SOUTH   PACIFIC   OCEAN

Sikaiana
Atoll

**TEMOTU
PROVINCE**

akira

Makira

Santa Cruz

SANTA CRUZ   Utupua

**MAKIRA
PROVINCE**

Vanikoro

*Anuta; Fatutaka;
Tikopia (See Inset)*

ecofriendly **Tetepare Island**
(p334).

❼ Chilling out at a laid-back
resort on **Mbabanga Island**
(p338).

❽ Flipper-kicking into
sunken WWII wrecks off **Tulagi**
(p329).

scenic Lunga river offers superb white-water experiences. Trips last four to five hours and are usually scheduled on Saturday or Sunday, but they're weather dependent. Prices include lunch and transfer from Honiara. No website, but there's a Facebook page.

🖝 Tours

Travel Solomons CULTURAL TOUR
(Map p326; ☑7489974, 24081; www.travel solomons.com; 1st fl, Sol Plaza Bldg, Mendana Ave; ☺8.30am-4.30pm Mon-Fri) This travel agency can arrange half- and full-day WWII historical tours on Guadalcanal (from S$350 per person).

🛏 Sleeping

Honiara is expensive and, with the exception of a few simple guesthouses, hotels that cater mainly to businesspeople dominate the market.

Hibiscus Homestay GUESTHOUSE $
(Map p324; ☑7762960, 22121; kwendy64@ gmail.com; Kukutu St; d with/without bathroom S$500/400) On a quiet backstreet close to the centre, this B&B-like oasis is a safe choice, with helpful hosts and good amenities. The four rooms, two of which come with private bathrooms, are compact and simply laid out but neat and serviceable, and have fans. There's a spacious lounge area, an impeccable communal kitchen and good sea views from the terrace. Wendy, your affable host, has plans to build two more rooms downstairs. No wi-fi.

St Agnes Mother's Union Transit House GUESTHOUSE $
(Map p324; ☑7485532, 27785; stagnes@ solomon.com.sb; Lower Vavaya Rd; d S$450-600, with shared bathroom S$330-370; ※) A reliable choice for budgeteers, this well-run venture is a 10-minute walk from the centre. There is a variety of rooms for all budgets, from

Guadalcanal

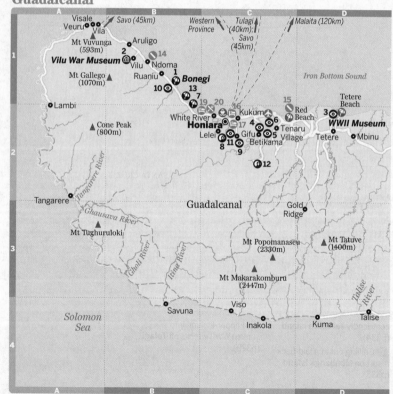

fan-cooled, two-bed rooms to self-contained units with private facilities (cold-water showers). Rooms are simply furnished but are in good nick, and the shared bathrooms are as clean as a whistle. It's also a safe choice for women travellers. No wi-fi.

Chester Resthouse GUESTHOUSE $
(Map p326; ☎26355; mbhches@solomon.com. sb; Lower Vayvaya Rd; r with shared/private bathroom S$330/750; ✷@) This budget set-up is popular with travellers and local families because it's spitting distance from the action. In the older wing, fan-cooled rooms are tiny, have thin mattresses and lack intimacy (windows open right onto the corridor and communal area). For more space and privacy, upgrade to a room with private facilities and air-con in the more recent wing.

No alcohol is allowed on the premises. No wi-fi but there's an internet terminal at the reception (S$10 per hour).

★**Rekona Flourish** GUESTHOUSE $$
(Map p324; ☎7832085, 21082; ptani.maike@ gmail.com; Lower Vayvaya Rd; d S$500-600; ☎) A pleasant surprise, this abode feels like a cosy bird's nest, with only six fan-cooled rooms and a kitchen for guests' use. Patricia, your helpful host, does a superb job in keeping her place shipshape. Angle for one of the upstairs rooms, which have balconies and wonderful harbour views. There's a watchman at night – very reassuring for women travellers. It's a 10-minute stroll to the centre.

Sanalae Apartments APARTMENT $$
(Map p320; ☎39218; sanalae.apart@solomon. com.sb; Panatina Ridge; r S$880-1100; ☎) A well-guarded secret among long-term visitors, this pert little number in a quiet neighbourhood is a reliable establishment despite being far from the action – it's 5km away from the centre – and up a steep road. The 15 rooms are self-contained, attractively furnished and squeaky clean. Upstairs rooms are more

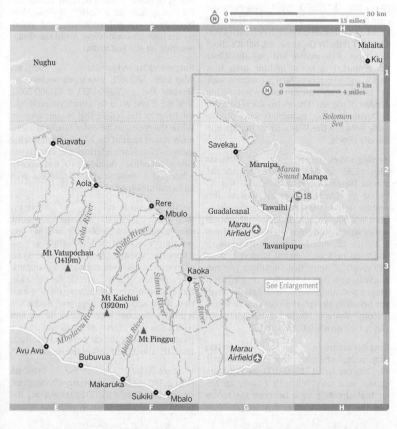

Guadalcanal

spacious and have balconies and great mountain views. Tip: angle for room 1, which affords sea views. You'll need to get a taxi here.

The Ofis B&B **$$**
(Map p320; ☑7355620, 20334; www.theofissolo mons.com; White River; d incl breakfast S$650; ⊛) This fair-value cafe-cum-B&B occupies a verdant plot right by the seashore, but it's about 3km west of the centre just past the White River market (a not-so-inviting area after dark), and two rooms face a concrete wall. Try for the aptly named Ocean View, within earshot of the sea. There's on-site security.

During the day, numerous vans ply the route between the White River market and the city centre.

Heritage Park Hotel HOTEL **$$$**
(Map p326; ☑24007; www.heritageparkhotel. com.sb; Mendana Ave; d S$2800-3100; ⊛⊛⊛) By far the fanciest hotel in Honiara, this venture right in the centre and on the waterfront is a hot favourite among international businessmen and consultants. It features a cluster of smartly finished, three-storey buildings in a well-tended garden and offers plenty of amenities, including two restaurants, two bars, a business centre, a gift shop, a pool and a disco. Nearly all the small but tastefully designed rooms have a sunny balcony; rooms in blocks 1, 2 and 3 have sea views. One proviso: there's no lift.

King Solomon HOTEL **$$$**
(Map p326; ☑21205; www.kingsolomonhotel. info; Hibiscus Ave; d S$900-1500; ⊛⊛⊛) Anchored on a steep hill with a kinky funicular that shunts people between the rooms and the reception area, this longstanding venture features a variety of spacious units scattered amid beautifully landscaped grounds and boasts a stress-melting swimming pool built into the hill. Like most hotels in Honiara, it starts to show its age but it's manageable for a couple of days. Most bungalows are self-contained, and many rooms have an ocean view. Avoid the disappointing on-site restaurant.

Solomon Kitano Mendana HOTEL **$$$**
(Map p326; ☑20071; www.kitanomendana.com; Mendana Ave; s S$1200-1700; d S$1200-2000; ⊛⊛⊛) If you want to launch yourself into the heart of the action, this is your answer. While the rooms in the older blocks are seriously frayed around the edges, the new wing showcases modern interiors and affords sea views. Amenities include two restaurants, a bar and a souvenir shop. Sadly, the pool lacks maintenance.

Pacific Casino Hotel HOTEL **$$$**
(Map p320; ☑25009; www.pacificcasinohotel. com; Kukum Hwy; d S$850-1350; ⊛⊛⊛) You certainly won't fall in love with this two-storey, barrack-style block at the eastern end of town – the neon-lit corridors feel oppressive and the rooms are bare. On the plus side, the extensive grounds encompass a restaurant, a bar and a swimming pool, and it has a great waterfront location. Ask for a room with a sea view otherwise you'll end up in a room overlooking the car park and the main road. It's about 2km east of the centre.

Honiara Hotel HOTEL **$$$**
(Map p324; ☑21737; reservation@honiarahotel. com.sb; Chinatown; d S$800-1900; ⊛⊛⊛) Reposed over sloping grounds with lots of tree

and flower coverage, this sprawling hotel has seen better days but the deluxe rooms in the more recent wings are light-filled and come with good sea views and a private terrace. The cheaper rooms feel gloomy and uninspiring in comparison. Amenities include a bar, three restaurants and, best of all, a large pool.

Caveat: there's no lift and the walk up to the highest units may leave you short of breath. It's a short taxi ride from the centre.

Coral Sea Resort RESORT $$$
(Map p324; ☎ 26288; www.coral-sea-resort.com; Mendana Ave; P❋☎) Honiara's most recent hotel, the Coral Sea Resort was built in 2016 and features a casino, a restaurant and a series of buildings that shelter rooms with sea views.

✗ Eating

Sky Horse FAST FOOD $
(Map p326; ☎ 25552; Mendana Ave; mains S$15-45; ☸ 6am-5pm) This sprightly little joint is the ideal pit stop for a midday nibble. It churns out delicious rotis ($15) as well as ready-made meals.

The Bakery CAFETERIA $
(Map p326; Sol Plaza Bldg, Mendana Ave; mains S$10-30; ☸ 7.30am-7.30pm Mon-Sat) Located inside the Sol Plaza building, this offbeat cafeteria is a handy spot for an affordable, uncomplicated, walk-in bite. Choose from

rotis, doughnuts, pizza slices and buns, all delicious and moderately priced. It also has excellent coffee drinks and first-rate smoothies (S$35).

Honiara Hot Bread Kitchen BAKERY $
(Map p326; Mendana Ave; buns S$3-6; ☸ 6am-7pm) For the most flavoursome buns and scones in town, take your sticky fingers to this unassuming outlet on the main drag. Come early: by 10am they're sold out. Bread also available.

Frangipani Ice ICE CREAM $
(Map p326; Mendana Ave; ice cream from S$4; ☸ 8am-6pm) This unassuming ice-cream parlour on the main drag is very popular with locals. It also has waffles, milkshakes and smoothies.

★Mambo Juice CAFETERIA $$
(Map p320; ☎ 28811; Mendana Ave; mains S$35-90; ☸ 7am-6pm Mon-Fri, 8am-5pm Sat & Sun) Just off Mendana Ave, this easy-to-miss cafeteria is a surprise, with its enticing outdoor seating area, super-fresh fare and explosively fruity juices and smoothies. It offers an appetising selection of gourmet sandwiches, salads, omelettes and homemade yoghurt. It's about 1km west of the centre.

Bamboo Bar & Cafe CAFETERIA $$
(Map p326; ☎ 21205; Hibiscus Ave; mains S$50-190; ☸ 7am-3.30pm Mon-Fri; ☎) This cheerful

---

ITINERARIES

One Week

In a week you'll be able to explore Guadalcanal and either Savo or Tulagi. Base yourself in **Honiara** (p317) and spend three days (four if you're a diver) visiting the capital and the historic sites dotted along the northern coast. Then catch a boat to **Savo** (p329) and settle in for a couple of days of relaxation. If you're keen on diving, opt for **Tulagi** (p329), which features superb wreck dives. Another option, if your budget permits, is to skip Savo and Tulagi in favour of **Tavanipupu Private Island Resort** (p330) – a luxurious yet laid-back hideaway tucked in a sweet eastern corner of Guadalcanal.

Two Weeks

With two weeks, you can easily include the Western Province in your itinerary. Start with your one-week itinerary, then hop west to **Munda** (p334), which offers great diving and snorkelling options and good day tours to some must-see WWII relics. Afterwards, grab a flight or catch a boat to **Gizo** (p336) where three to four days can easily be spent messing around in and on the water. You might also make time for a hike on **Kolombangara** (p340). Fly back to Honiara the day before your international flight out.

Three Weeks

With three weeks, fly to Seghe and devote a few days to **Marovo Lagoon** (p330), where all sorts of water activities and adventures await. Thanks to fairly reliable inter-island boat services, a trip to **Malaita** (p340) could even be on the cards – fly back to Honiara and catch a boat to **Auki** (p340) and chill out in **Langa Langa Lagoon** (p343) for a couple of days.

Greater Honiara

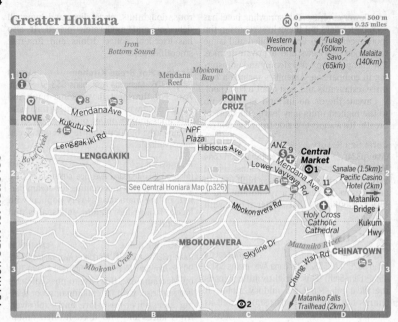

place is perfect for a comforting breakfast (fab banana pancakes!), lunch or a snack attack any time of the day. The menu is straightforward but scrummy and features tasty dishes such as chicken curry, vegetarian omelette and focaccia. Healthy smoothies, great coffee and sweet treats are also on offer, and there's outdoor seating. Free wi-fi.

Lime Lounge
CAFETERIA **$$**

(Map p326; ☑23064; www.limelounge.com.sb; off Mendana Ave; mains S$40-100; ⊙7am-4pm Mon-Fri, 8am-3pm Sat & Sun; 🛜) Funky little Lime Lounge is highly popular with expats. There's everything from satisfying breakfasts to palate-pleasing salads, well-made sandwiches, burgers and yummy pastries (hmmm, the banana cakes). No view and no terrace, but the walls are adorned with paintings by local artists, which gives the place a splash of style. Free wi-fi.

Breakwater Cafe
CAFE **$$**

(Map p326; ☑23442; Mendana Ave; breakfast S$80-110, pastries S$25-40; ⊙7am-4pm Mon-Fri, from 7.30am Sat & Sun) This slick venture that seems to have been imported direct from Oz is the meeting point for expats who are yearning for a satisfying breakfast. Desserts like carrot cake, cheesecake, doughnuts,

brownies, banana muffins and other pastries from the bakery window are not to be missed.

The Ofis
PIZZERIA, CAFE **$$**

(Map p320; ☑7355620, 20334; White River; mains S$60-180; ⊙5-9pm Wed-Fri, from 8am Sat & Sun) A very relaxing spot. Picture a lovely waterfront location, ample views of Savo, and good thin-crust pizza, wraps and salads. It also offers lovely coffee, juices and smoothies. For dessert, try the belt-bustingly good brownie with homemade chocolate sauce. Copious all-day breakfasts are available on weekends. It's in White River, about 3km west of the centre. Go by taxi as the area is a bit dodgy after dark.

Taj Mahal
INDIAN **$$**

(Map p326; ☑7478550; www.tajsolomon.com; Point Cruz Yacht Club, Mendana Ave; mains S$60-120; ⊙11am-3pm & 5-9pm Mon-Sat, 5-9pm Sun) The dining room is nothing fancy (think plastic chairs) but Taj Mahal serves authentic, richly flavoured Indian and Sri Lankan specialities at puny prices. Tandooris, tikkas, biryanis and masalas are all here plus a good selection of veggie options. Brilliant value. Also does takeaway.

Hong Kong Palace
CHINESE **$$**

(Map p326; ☑23338; Hibiscus Ave; mains S$50-200; ⊙11am-2pm & 5.30-9.30pm) This unmissa-

Greater Honiara

⊙ Top Sights
1 Central Market D2

◉ Sights
2 US War Memorial.................................C3

🛏 Sleeping
3 Coral Sea Resort...................................B1
4 Hibiscus Homestay A2
5 Honiara Hotel D3
6 Rekona Flourish C2
7 St Agnes Mother's Union
    Transit House...................................C2

✖ Eating
  Club Havanah...............................(see 5)
  Oasis Restaurant ....(see 5)

🍸 Drinking & Nightlife
8 Monarch Bar & Grill A1

ℹ Information
9 Honiara Private Medical Centre.........C2
10 Nature Conservancy A1

🚌 Transport
11 MV Fair Glory..D2

ble reddish pagoda on Hibiscus Ave brings an unexpected dash of orientalism in an otherwise dull area. Inside, it's much more sterile, with neons and tiles, but you'll be too busy choosing from the mile-long menu to bother.

Hakubai JAPANESE $$$
(Map p326; ☏ 20071; Solomon Kitano Mendana Hotel, Mendana Ave; mains S$100-250; ⏱ noon-2pm & 6.30-9pm Mon-Fri, 6.30-9pm Sat & Sun) If you have a sashimi or yakitori craving that must be met, head to Hakubai inside the Mendana Hotel for authentic Japanese food. On top of the classics, tuck into seductive offerings like *nikomi* noodles (udon noodles with half-cooked poached egg) or beef teppanyaki. Don't miss the sushi buffet on Saturday.

Club Havanah FRENCH $$$
(Map p324; ☏ 21737; Honiara Hotel, Chinatown; mains S$110-300; ⏱ 6.30-9pm) Inside Honiara Hotel, Club Havanah's adept French chef cooks up ambitious dishes with a strong French accent – think wild pigeon cooked in red-wine sauce or snails in garlic butter. Just one grumble: the big fake fish and siren at the back are ludicrous.

Capitana INTERNATIONAL $$$
(Map p326; ☏ 20071; Solomon Kitano Mendana Hotel, Mendana Ave; mains S$100-250; ⏱ noon-

2pm & 6-9pm) This popular restaurant inside the Mendana Hotel serves classic Western dishes and boasts a terrace overlooking the sea. Its Wednesday dinner buffet (S$260) draws the crowds.

Oasis Restaurant INTERNATIONAL $$$
(Map p324; ☏ 21737; Honiara Hotel, Chinatown; lunch mains S$100-120, dinner S$220-300; ⏱ 11.30am-2pm & 6.30-10pm) Part of the Honiara Hotel, the Oasis enjoys a great location next to the pool. The food is nothing spectacular, but there's a good choice ranging from burgers and salads to meat dishes and fish fillet. Catch the Melanesian dance show and dinner buffet Sunday nights at 7pm.

🍷 Drinking & Entertainment

If you've just arrived in the Solomon Islands, you'll find Honiara's bar scene pretty dull. But if you've just spent several weeks in the provinces you'll feel like you're in Ibiza! Hotel bars open to nonguests and are a good place to hook up with expats. Sometimes they offer live entertainment – bamboo bands, Micronesian hula dancers and karaoke. Many restaurants also double as bars.

Monarch Bar & Grill BAR
(Map p324; Mendana Ave; ⏱ 9am-10.30pm Mon-Thu, to 2am Fri & Sat) Skip the food; it's only so-so. The bar is definitely the main focus, and can get tremendously lively on a Friday or Saturday night when there's usually a live band. There's a pleasant deck that overlooks the water.

Disco Heritage Park CLUB
(Map p326; Heritage Park Hotel, Mendana Ave; cover S$30; ⏱ 6pm-2am Wed-Sat) Honiara's sole decent club is the elegant Disco Heritage Park, inside Heritage Park Hotel.

🛍 Shopping

Honiara is a good place to pick up souvenirs. On top of the souvenir shops, it's also worth considering the gift shops at top-end hotels and the stalls at the central market.

King Solomon Arts & Craft Centre HANDICRAFTS
(Map p326; Mendana Ave; ⏱ 8.30am-noon & 1-4.30pm Mon-Fri, 8.30-11.30am Sat) Has a wide selection of masks, basketwork and skilfully crafted wooden carvings.

Museum Handicraft Shop HANDICRAFTS
(Map p326; ☏ 20137; National Museum, Mendana Ave; ⏱ 9am-4.30pm Mon-Fri, 9am-3pm Sat) Next

Central Honiara

to the National Museum, this well-stocked store features a good selection of woodcarvings, basketwork, Malaitan shell money, souvenir shells and forehead ornaments made of fossilised clams.

ℹ Information

DANGERS & ANNOYANCES

It's safe to stroll around the centre by day, provided you use your common sense and avoid walking alone in deserted streets. After dark, take a taxi. Beware of pickpockets at the market and in crowded areas.

INTERNET ACCESS

You'll find a couple of internet cafes in the NPF Plaza building. There's a small internet outlet at the post office, too. Rates average S$20 per hour. Wi-fi is available at most hotels as well as at some cafes and restaurants, but a fee usually applies.

MEDICAL SERVICES

Honiara Private Medical Centre (Map p324; ☏ 7492434, 24027; Hyundai Mall, Mendana Ave; ⏰ 8am-5pm Mon-Fri, 9am-1pm Sat) A well-regarded clinic inside the Hyundai Mall. A consultation costs S$250.

Point Cruz Chemist (Map p326; ☏ 22911; Mendana Ave; ⏰ 8am-5pm Mon-Fri, 8.30am-1.30pm Sat) A well-stocked pharmacy. Also sells locally made cosmetics and soaps.

MONEY

You'll find a good dozen 24-hour ATMs in the centre. There's a small bureau de change at the airport.

ANZ (Map p324; Hyundai Mall, Mendana Ave; ⏰ 9am-4pm Mon-Fri) Changes major currencies and has one ATM inside.

Bank South Pacific (BSP; Map p326; Mendana Ave; ⏰ 9am-4pm Mon-Fri) Changes major currencies. Has ATMs (Visa only). Other ATMs are in the main BSP office near Heritage Park Hotel; there's also one ATM beside the reception at Heritage Park Hotel.

Bank South Pacific (BSP; Map p326; Mendana Ave; ⏰ 9am-4pm Mon-Fri) On the same side of the road as Sky Horse fast-food joint. Changes major currencies. Has two ATMs.

POST

Solomon Post (Map p326; Mendana Ave; ⏰ 8am-4.30pm Mon-Fri) Also houses a Western Union counter and a small internet cafe.

TELEPHONE

Bmobile/Vodafone (Map p326; ☏ 8444101; www.bmobile.com.sb; Mendana Ave; ⏰ 8am-5pm Mon-Fri, to noon Sat) Sells prepaid SIM cards.

Our Telekom (Map p326; ☏ 21164; www.ourtelekom.com.sb; Mendana Ave; ⏰ 8.30am-4.30pm Mon-Fri, 9am-noon Sat) Sells prepaid mobile phonecards and prepaid wi-fi access cards. Has a couple of other branches in town.

Central Honiara

SOLOMON ISLANDS HONIARA

TOURIST INFORMATION

Solomon Islands Visitors Bureau (SIVB; Map p326; ☏22442; www.visitsolomons.com.sb; Mendana Ave; ☺8am-4.30pm Mon-Fri) There's little printed material, but staff can provide advice and help with accommodation bookings. Also sells a map of the country (S$60).

ⓘ Getting There & Away

AIR

International flights land at Honiara's Henderson Airport, and all domestic routes begin and end in Honiara.

Guadalcanal Travel Services (GTS; Map p326; ☏22586; guadtrav@solomon.com.sb; Mendana Ave; ☺8am-4.30pm Mon-Fri, 9am-noon Sat) This well-established travel agency represents most international and regional airlines.

Solomon Airlines (Map p326; ☏20152, 20031; www.flysolomons.com; Hibiscus Ave; ☺8am-4pm Mon-Fri, 8.30-11.30am Sat) From Honiara, Solomon Airlines flies to most islands in the country.

BOAT

The cost and departure times are subject to change. All ferries and boats dock at Point Cruz.

To/From Tulagi and Malaita

MV 360 Flyer/Discovery (Map p326; ☏20555; Fera Pako Building, off Mendana Ave; ☺8am-4.30pm Mon-Fri, to noon Sat) This passenger boat travels between Honiara and Auki (S$250 to S$350 one way, three to four hours) three times a week; two days a week it makes a stop at Tulagi (S$200). Tickets can be bought at the ticketing office or on board.

MV Express Pelican II (Map p326; ☏28104; Fera Pako Building, off Mendana Ave; ☺8am-noon & 1-4pm Mon-Fri, 8-11am Sat) This passenger boat operates twice weekly between Honiara and Auki (S$200 to S$250 one way, three to four hours). The ticketing office is in a building close to Lime Lounge but tickets can also be bought on board.

To/From the Western Province

MV Anjeanette (Anolpha Shipping Services; Map p326; ☏22719; Point Cruz) This cargo

---

ⓘ GETTING AROUND THE NORTH COAST

Exploring the north coast by public transport is not really an option. Most sights are not signed and are not easy to find. Your best bet is to hire a taxi in Honiara; count on S$100 to S$120 per hour.

boat offers a weekly service between Honiara and Gizo via Marovo Lagoon (Mbunikalo, Nggasini, Chea and Seghe). The Honiara–Gizo trip costs S$460 (S$500 in 'first class') and takes about 27 hours (10 to 13 hours to Marovo Lagoon). To Mbunikalo it costs S$380. It leaves Honiara on Saturday evening (return on Tuesday). The ticketing office is at Point Cruz but tickets can be bought on board.

MV Fair Glory (Fairwest Shipping; Map p324; ☑ 22899; Mendana Ave) This cargo boat offers a weekly service between Honiara and Gizo via Marovo Lagoon (Mbunikalo, Batuna, Chea and Seghe). The Honiara–Gizo trip costs S$480 on the deck (S$1490 per cabin) and takes about 27 hours (10 to 13 hours to Marovo Lagoon). Deck passage to Mbunikalo is S$380. It generally leaves Honiara on Sunday morning (return on Tuesday); check while you're there.

The ticketing office is across the road from the cathedral but tickets are also sold on board.

To/From Other Provinces

Island hopping on the cargo boats that sail between Guadalcanal and other provinces is an inexpensive but adventurous and rough way to travel. Departure times and dates are unscheduled and the best way to find out what's available is to ask around at the docks.

❶ Getting Around

From the airport, the standard taxi fare into town is S$100.

Honiara's minibuses are cheap, frequent (in daylight hours) and relatively safe. The flat S$3 fare will take you anywhere on the route, which is written on a placard behind the windscreen of the bus.

There are taxis everywhere in Honiara. They don't have meters, so agree on a fare before hopping in – S$10 per kilometre is reasonable.

East of Honiara

You'll need a day to take in the sights.

◉ Sights & Activities

Solomon Peace Memorial Park   MEMORIAL
(Map p320; Mt Austen Rd; S$50) The road to Mt Austen begins in Kukum and climbs up to the historical sites where Japanese troops doggedly resisted the US advance. About 3.5km from the main coastal road, this large, white memorial was built by Japanese war veterans in 1981 to commemorate all who died in the WWII Guadalcanal campaign.

Mt Austen   MOUNTAIN
(Map p320) The clearing at the summit of Mt Austen (410m) offers a marvellous view northeast over Henderson. Americans in WWII dubbed this spot Grassy Knoll. There's a plaque that explains the strategic importance of the hilltop during WWII.

Betikama SDA Mission   HISTORIC SITE
(Map p320; Betikama; museum S$25; ⊙8am-noon & 1-5pm Sun-Thu, 8am-noon Fri) In Betikama village, this sprawling property comprises a small WWII museum with an outdoor collection of salvaged material (mostly US aircraft) as well as two small Japanese anti-tank guns. There's a handicraft shop, specialising in Western Province products and stylish modern copperware.

DON'T MISS

TAKE A DIP!

Short of dreamy expanses of white sand on Guadalcanal, you can take a dip in lovely natural pools.

Mataniko Falls (Map p320; guided walk S$200-250) One of the star attractions in Honiara's hinterlands is Mataniko Falls, which feature a spectacular thundering of water down a cliff straight into a canyon below. The hike to these waterfalls starts in Lelei village with a steep ascent to a ridge, followed by an easier stretch amid mildly undulating hills. Then you'll tackle a gruelling descent on a muddy path to reach the floor of the little canyon where the Mataniko flows. It's roughly two hours return.

A guide from Lelei is required – the tourist office in Honiara (p327) can make arrangements on your behalf.

Tenaru Waterfalls (Map p320; guided walk S$150) At 63m, these waterfalls are spectacular. They are a fairly easy four-hour walk (return) from a tiny settlement about 2km south of Tenaru Village. It's flat and shady all the way. The path follows the floor of the river valley and cuts across the river's many bends, crossing and recrossing a dozen times before reaching the falls.

Guides are available at Tenaru Village – contact the tourist office in Honiara.

WORTH A TRIP

TULAGI & SAVO

Another world awaits just a two-hour boat ride from Honiara, either on Tulagi or Savo.

In the middle of the Florida Islands, Tulagi was the Solomons' former capital; it was also a Japanese base during WWII. It's now a renowned playground for divers, with a series of fabulous wrecks lying just offshore. **Raiders Hotel** (☑ 7938017, 7494185, 32070; www.raidershotel.com; Tulagi; s S$550-990, d S$825-1265; ❇ 🛜), right on the waterfront (no beach), features tip-top rooms and has a professional dive shop that caters mainly to certified divers (no courses are offered). A single dive costs S$550 and diving-gear hire is S$450 per day. Wreck buffs will need a few days to explore the huge WWII wrecks lying just offshore, including the monster-sized USS *Kanawha,* the USS *Aaron Ward* and the *Moa.* Raiders Hotel can organise private transfers, or you can take an outboard-powered dinghy from the little beach next to Point Cruz Yacht Club in Honiara (about S$200 one way, or S$1800 if it's chartered). The passenger boat MV 360 Flyer/Discovery (p327) also travels between Honiara and Tulagi (S$200 one way, two hours) twice a week. For more details on dive sites in the area, see p36.

Though lying just 14km north of Guadalcanal, Savo is another great escape. Imagine an active volcano with a pair of dormant craters, coconut groves, a narrow strip of grey-sand beach and a few hot springs that are accessible by foot. The island also features a megapode field where hundreds of female birds lay their eggs in holes scratched into the hot sand. If you're lucky, you'll also spot pods of dolphins just offshore. **Sunset Lodge** (☑ 7498347; Kuila; full board per person S$450) has basic rooms and can arrange various tours as well as transfers from Honiara (S$400 per person return).

Henderson Airport Memorial Gardens
HISTORIC SITE

(Map p320; Henderson Airport) A small memorial outside the airport entrance honours US forces and their Pacific Islander allies. In front is a Japanese anti-aircraft gun. About 100m to the west of the terminal is the scaffold-style US WWII control tower, disused since the early 1950s.

Bloody Ridge
HISTORIC SITE

(Map p320) From Henderson airport, a track leads south to this area that's also called Edson's Ridge, after Edson's Raiders. Commanded by Colonel Merritt Edson, they defended the ridge against the Japanese in 1942 in their determined but unsuccessful attempts to seize the airfield. There's a humble pyramid-shaped US war memorial on the ridge. About 1km beyond Bloody Ridge, you'll come across a **Japanese war memorial** that honours the 2000 or more Japanese killed during these actions. There are great views of Mt Austen, the surrounding valleys and villages dotted around the hills.

★ WWII Museum
HISTORIC SITE

(Map p320; Tetere; admission S$100) A few metres before reaching the shore of **Tetere Beach**, a dirt track to the west leads to 30 or more abandoned amtracks (amphibious troop carriers). Many of these rusty relics are shielded by prickly thorns, adding to the poignancy of the site.

USS John Penn
DIVING

(Map p320) This large US-troop ship was bombed and sunk about 4km offshore, east of Honiara. For experienced divers only.

West of Honiara

Life becomes very sedate as one heads west through some of the north coast's divine scenery. Urban existence is left behind once the road traverses White River and crawls its way along the scenic coastline.

The area boasts a high historical significance. The seas between Guadalcanal's northwestern coast and Savo Island were the site of constant naval battles between August 1942 and February 1943. By the time the Japanese finally withdrew, so many ships had been sunk it became known as Iron Bottom Sound.

◉ Sights

Lela Beach
BEACH

(Map p320; admission S$30) Popular with locals and expats at weekends, this beach has black sand and is OK for swimming and bathing.

Turtle Beach
BEACH

(Map p320; admission S$30) Turtle Beach is an appealing strip of white coral sand fringed with coconut trees.

★ **Bonegi**   BEACH

(Map p320; admission S$30) About 12km west from Honiara, Bonegi is music to the ears of divers, snorkellers and sunbathers. Two large Japanese freighters sank just offshore on the night of 13 November 1942, and make for a magnificent playground for scuba divers, who call them Bonegi I and Bonegi II. As the upper works of Bonegi II break the surface, it can also be snorkelled. There's also a black-sand beach that is suitable for a picnic.

Sherman Tank   HISTORIC SITE

(Map p320; admission S$25) Just across the road from Bonegi beach, there's a bush track that heads inland and runs about 400m to a rusty US Sherman tank called *Jezebel,* which was used for wartime target practice once the Guadalcanal campaign was over.

★ **Vilu War Museum**   MUSEUM

(Map p320; admission S$100) About 25km from Honiara, a turn to the south from the coastal road brings you to this great open-air museum. Here there are US, Japanese, Australian, Fijian and New Zealand memorials, four large Japanese field guns and the remains of several US and Japanese aircraft, including a Betty bomber, a Lightning fighter and a Wildcat fighter whose wings can still be folded as they were for naval carrier-borne operations.

WORTH A TRIP

TAVANIPUPU ISLAND

If you've ever dreamed of having your own island paradise, **Tavanipupu Private Island Resort** (Map p320; ☏ 7378317; www.tavanipupu.com; d A$190-300) , on a small island off Guadalcanal's eastern tip, has all the key ingredients – exclusivity, seclusion and atmosphere. Digs are in six spacious bungalows scattered in a well-tended coconut grove that overlooks the beach. The restaurant uses only the freshest seafood (meals A$121 per person per day).

Snorkelling is excellent (gear provided), as is fishing, and you can work your tan on sandy beaches. Solomon Airlines flies two to three times a week from Honiara to Marau (S$1700 return, 30 minutes), from where it's a 15-minute boat ride to the resort.

Visale   VILLAGE

About 40km from Honiara is this timeless hamlet blessed with a majestic setting – it's wedged between the sea and a soaring, velvet-green hill. Soak up the rural atmosphere and make the most of the beach lapped by clear waters.

WESTERN PROVINCE

POP 76,600

Marovo Lagoon, Munda and Ghizo Island are the three unmissable destinations in the Western Province. Thanks to reliable inter-island boat and plane services, they can easily be combined and toured at a comfortable, leisurely pace.

Marovo Lagoon

On New Georgia's eastern side, Marovo Lagoon is the world's finest double-barrier-enclosed lagoon, bordered by the large New Georgia and Vangunu Islands on one side and a double line of long barrier islands on the other. It contains hundreds of beautiful small islands, most of which are covered by coconut palms and rainforest and surrounded by coral.

Don't expect sweeping expanses of silky sands, though. Although Marovo Lagoon boasts aquamarine water, it's not a beach-holiday destination. You come here to dive in fish soup, visit laid-back villages, picnic on deserted islands, take a lagoon tour, meet master carvers, kayak across the lagoon or take a walk through the rainforest or up awesome summits.

🏃 **Activities**

Diving & Snorkelling

Marovo Lagoon offers plenty of exhilarating dives for both experts and novices. Here's the menu: channels, caves, drop-offs, coral gardens, clouds of technicolour fish and a few wrecks thrown in for good measure. A few iconic sites include Uepi Point, General Store and Lumalihe Passage.

With dozens of lovely sites scattered throughout the lagoon, snorkelling is equally impressive. Lodges can organise lagoon tours and snorkelling trips, which cost anything from S$100 to S$300 per person depending on distance and duration. Bring your own gear.

For more on diving in the area, see p36.

Western Province

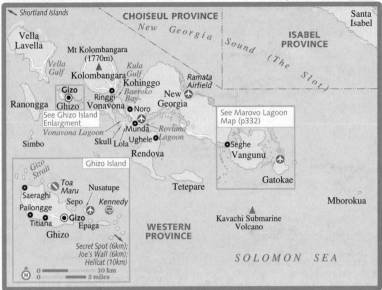

Solomon Dive Adventures
DIVING

(☑ 7469007; www.solomondiveadventures.com; Kahaini Island; 1-/2-tank dives S\$600/1200) This small outfit is based at Kahaini Guesthouse near Chea (North Marovo). The ebullient American owner, Lisa Roquette, runs dive trips to nearby islands, passages and reefs. Two-tank outings include a picnic lunch on a deserted island. Rental gear is available (S\$300 per day). Cash only.

Uepi Island Resort
DIVING, SNORKELLING

(www.uepi.com; Uepi island; single dive A\$75; ☺ by reservation) This outfit has a great reputation for service and professionalism and offers stunning dives for all levels of proficiency throughout Marovo Lagoon. It's also re-nowned for its certification courses and dedicated snorkelling trips. It caters mainly to the resort's guests; nonguests may be accepted, space permitting and by prior arrangement.

Dive Wilderness
DIVING

(☑ in Australia +61 2 9299 4633; www.diveadven tures.com.au; Peava, Gatokae Island; single dive A\$75) This modest operation caters to guests staying at the Wilderness Lodge and runs dive trips to Mbulo and Male Male Islands.

Kayaking

Diving is king in Marovo, but sea kayaking can be very rewarding, too.

Kayak Solomons
KAYAKING

(☑ in Australia +61 3 9787 7904; www.kayaksolo mons.com; per person per night A\$255) Based at Uepi Island Resort, this reputable outfit can arrange multiday kayaking trips, overnight-ing in villages along the way – an excellent way to discover the lagoon at a leisurely pace.

Walking

If you've got itchy feet, don't forget your walking shoes. Consider scaling Mt Mariu (887m) on Gatokae (two days), climbing the hill that lords over Chea village on Maro-vo Island (two hours) or tackling Mt Reku (520m) on Vangunu (half a day).

☞ Tours

All kinds of tours and activities, including village visits, guided walks, picnic trips and lagoon excursions, can be arranged through the region's lodges.

🛏 Sleeping

There's a small network of ecolodges on the lagoon. These rustic, family-run establish-ments are great places to meet locals and offer an authentic cultural experience. If you want to pamper yourself, opt for Uepi Island Resort.

Marovo Lagoon

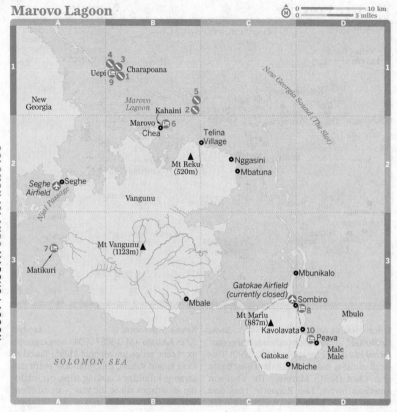

Matikuri Lodge   BUNGALOW **$**

(☑ 7467177; Matikuri Island; dm with full board S$400, bungalow per person S$490) Matikuri Lodge's drawcard is its soothing sense of isolation, sitting on the western arc of Marovo Lagoon. Digs are in three island-style, basic bungalows that face the sea; the four dorm-style rooms in the main house are rudimentary. Toilets and showers (cold water) are shared. No electricity, but kerosene lamps are provided.

The dining area has a large deck on stilts. There's good swimming just offshore and some great snorkelling spots nearby. A host of guided walks, village visits and lagoon tours can be organised, and there are kayaks for hire. One-way boat transfers to Seghe airstrip (20 minutes) are S$250 per person. Cash only.

Kahaini Guesthouse   GUESTHOUSE **$$**

(☑ 7469007; www.solomondiveadventures.com; Kahaini Island; per person with full board S$700–950) Run by American Lisa, this simple yet inviting guesthouse with a small on-site dive centre is on tiny Kahaini Island, just offshore from Chea village. Guests are accommodated in a large wooden house with three simply laid-out and clean rooms. There's a rudimentary outside shower and 24-hour electricity.

Aim for the slightly dearer East Room, which has its own toilet. Food is fresh and tasty, and there's excellent swimming and snorkelling around the islet. Although Kahaini Guesthouse mainly targets divers, it will also appeal to nature lovers – the atmosphere is delightfully chilled-out. Boat transfers to Seghe airstrip (30 minutes) are S$500 for two people one way. Cash only.

Ropiko Beach Resort   BUNGALOW **$$**

(☑ 23226, 7495805; www.ropikobeachresort.com.sb; Gatokae Island; d bungalow A$135; ☎) Entirely refurbished in 2015, this charming place grows on you quickly, with a clutch of well-proportioned bungalows nestled in a superb coconut grove. They're modern, well equipped

Marovo Lagoon

and comfy, but don't have terraces. Boat transfers to Mbunikalo wharf cost A$30 per boatload; to Seghe airstrip, it's A$300. Cash only.

Sunbathing is top-notch but swimming is not that enthralling, with very shallow waters; there's a tiny cove with deeper water nearby. Village visits, snorkelling trips, spearfishing and diving can be organised.

★**Uepi Island Resort**   RESORT **$$$**
(www.uepi.com; Uepi Island; s with full board A$245-330, d A$430-550; 🛜) This extremely well-run resort is very popular with Australian divers, who stay here to get thrilled by the sensational dive sites right on their doorstep. The best thing is that it also appeals to honeymooners, families and kayakers. The 10 spacious wooden bungalows are comfortable but not flash (no air-con and ordinary furnishings), and are scattered amid lovely bush gardens and coconut palms.

They're well spaced out and have large terraces. Snorkellers will get a buzz on the house reef that spreads from the end of the short jetty. And, joy of joys, there's a beach with safe swimming. The ethos here is laid-back and activity-oriented. Perks include a bar, a breezy dining room with excellent meals, a full dive shop and a good excursion program. Boat transfers to Seghe are A$153 per person return. Three nights minimum.

Wilderness Lodge   BUNGALOW **$$$**
(📇in Australia +61 2 9299 4633; www.diveadventures.com.au; Peava, Gatokae Island; s/d with full board A$165/250, bungalow A$356/400) Nestled in a coconut grove right by the lagoon, this

'lodge' features a large leafhouse with two bedrooms that share a bathroom as well as two seafront bungalows with private facilities (cold-water showers). Meals incorporate locally grown fruit and vegetables.

Various sea- and land-related excursions are available, including diving (there's a small on-site dive centre), hiking, crocodile-spotting and snorkelling along the house reef. Take note that the nearest airstrip is Seghe, a two-hour boat ride away (A$260 per boatload one way). Check if Gatokae airfield, which is a mere 10-minute boat ride away, has reopened when you book.

ⓘ Information

Marovo Lagoon is strongly Seventh Day Adventist, so you can't do much on Saturdays.

Marovo Lagoon has no ATMs and no banks, and credit cards are only accepted at Uepi Island Resort, so you'll need to bring a stash of cash to cover your entire bill (including accommodation, meals, activities and transport), plus some extra for surprise add-ons.

The mobile phone network doesn't cover Marovo Lagoon entirely; at the time of writing, South Marovo wasn't yet covered. Bookings for resorts and lodges can be made online or through SIVB in Honiara (p327).

ⓘ Getting There & Away

AIR

There are two main gateways to Marovo: Seghe (for North Marovo Lagoon) and Gatokae Island (for South Marovo Lagoon). Because of land disputes, the Gatokae airfield was closed at the time of writing.

Solomon Airlines (www.flysolomons.com) Connects Seghe with Honiara (S$1300, daily), and Munda (S$820) and Gizo (S$950) once a week.

BOAT

The cargo boat **MV Fair Glory** (p327) offers a weekly service between Honiara and Gizo via Marovo Lagoon (Mbunikalo, Mbatuna, Chea and Seghe). The Honiara–Mbunikalo trip costs S$380 in deck class and takes about 10 hours. It generally leaves Honiara on Sunday morning (return on Tuesday).

The cargo boat **MV Anjeanette** (p327) also offers a weekly service between Honiara and Gizo via Marovo Lagoon (Mbunikalo, Nggasini, Chea and Seghe). The Honiara–Mbunikalo trip costs S$380 and takes about 10 hours. It leaves Honiara on Saturday evening (return on Tuesday).

ⓘ Getting Around

If you've booked accommodation, your hosts will arrange airport transfers. Costs depend on distance travelled and number of passengers.

TETEPARE ISLAND

This large rainforest island is one of the Solomons' conservation jewels. The Tetepare Descendants' Association, which manages **Tetepare Island**, welcomes visitors in its rustic yet genuinely eco-friendly leafhouses (⌂ in Munda 62163; www.tetepare.org; full board per person S$500) – they have solar power, shared facilities and no air-con. What makes this place special is the host of environmentally friendly activities, including snorkelling with dugongs, spotting crocodiles, birdwatching and turtle-tagging.

Activities are free (except those that involve boat rides) and you'll be accompanied by trained guides. Food is fresh and organic. No alcohol is available, but it's BYO. Minuses: the cost and duration of transfers (S$2000 per boatload one way, at least 2½ hours from Munda).

Public transport does not exist. To get from South Marovo to North Marovo (or vice versa), you'll need to charter a boat; a ride between Wilderness Lodge and Uepi should set you back around S$2200.

West New Georgia

West New Georgia has its fair share of attractions as well as a few reliable accommodation options, a hatful of historic sites – from WWII relics to skull shrines – and thrilling dive sites.

It comprises the islands of Vonavona, Kohinggo, Rendova, Tetepare and New Georgia itself, together with many smaller neighbours. Given the lack of infrastructure, your best bet is to base yourself in Munda and take half- or full-day tours to nearby sights.

Munda & Around

The largest settlement, the little town of Munda on New Georgia, makes a convenient, if unglamorous, base for exploring the area's attractions. It's at its liveliest on Friday, which is market day.

⊙ Sights

Peter Joseph WWII Museum   MUSEUM
(⌂ 7432641, 7400387; Munda; admission S$50; ⊙ 6am-5pm) History buffs should consider this excellent private 'museum' of WWII relics. Run by knowledgeable Alphy Barney Paulson, it features lots of utensils, ammu-

nition, machine guns, shells, crockery, helmets, shavers and knives, all left behind by the Japanese and Americans. It's behind the soccer field, a 20- to 30-minute walk from the market, to the east.

★**Skull Island**   ISLAND
(admission S$50) A 30-minute boat ride from Munda, this tiny islet on Vonavona Lagoon is the final resting place for the skulls of countless vanquished warriors, as well as a shrine for the skulls of Rendovan chiefs. They date from the 1920s. The skull house is a small, triangular-shaped casket that also contains the chiefs' clamshell-ring valuables.

Baeroko Bay   HISTORIC SITE
(New Georgia Island) The Japanese garrison stationed in Baeroko Bay held the besieging US forces off for five weeks before finally being overwhelmed in August 1943. A silent reminder of this period is the *Casi Maru,* a sunken Japanese freighter near the shore. Its rusty masts protrude from the water. Enoghae, at the jutting northern lip of the bay, has several large Japanese WWII anti-aircraft guns still hidden in the scrub.

Kohinggo Island   ISLAND
On Kohinggo Island, a wrecked US Sherman tank lies at Tahitu on the northern shore. It was lost in action in September 1943 when US marines overran a Japanese strongpoint.

🕴 Activities

Munda is a destination of choice for demanding divers, with an exciting selection of wrecks, drop-offs, reefs and underwater caves. A few favourites include the atmospheric wrecks of the *Corsair* and a P-39 Airacobra. Top Shelf and Shark Point are awesome reef dives with plenty of fish life. For beginners, Susu Hite is a great spot, with a dense aggregation of reef species in less than 20m. For more on diving in the area, see p36.

Dive Munda   DIVING, SNORKELLING
(⌂ 7400328, 62156; www.mundadive.com; Agnes Lodge; 1-/2-tank dive S$650/1300; ⊙ by reservation) Based at Agnes Lodge, Dive Munda offers dive trips and certification courses. Snorkelling trips (S$500) and excursions to Skull Island (S$800) can also be arranged.

☞ Tours

The easiest way to get a broad look at the delights around West New Georgia is to take a half- or one-day tour.

Go West Tours TOUR
(☎62180; Agnes Lodge, Munda; ⊙by reservation) Based at Agnes Lodge, this small venture offers a range of excursions around West New Georgia. Prices start at S$850 for two people.

Sleeping & Eating

Qua Roviana GUESTHOUSE $
(☎7472472, 62123; quaroviana@gmail.com; Munda; s/d with shared bathroom S$250/500, r S$800; ❄📶) Just across the road from the market, this family-run abode is great value. The 15 rooms are simply furnished but serviceable, and the common lounge, bathrooms and kitchen are clean and well fitted out. The ground floor rooms are darker but come equipped with a kitchenette. Cash only.

Titiru Eco Lodge BUNGALOW $
(☎8593230; titiru.eco.resort@gmail.com; Rendova Island; full board per person S$500) After something well off the beaten track? This 'ecolodge' opened in 2014 on Rendova Island; it's a great place to sample authentic Melanesian life. Digs are in four rustic bungalows that share facilities, but that's part of the fun. It's close to Ughele village.

In a lovely setting, the property is filled with colourful flowers and it overlooks a scenic bay. Instead of sand at the front, it's mangrove, but your hosts will take you to a safe swimming area. Boat transfers to Munda airstrip (S$1600 per boatload return) take between 45 and 60 minutes and can be uncomfortable in bad weather.

Lolomo Eco Resort BUNGALOW $$
(☎7661222, 7495822; warren.paia@gmail.com; Kohinggo Island; d with shared bathroom S$450) Halfway between Munda and Gizo, this supremely relaxing place has three thatched-roof bungalows on stilts, but sadly it's not suitable for swimming; the shore is fringed with mangroves. The owners will happily take you to a nearby sandy island for a dip. The ablution block is squeaky clean and equipped with flush toilets and hot-water showers. The meals package costs S$310 per day.

Lolomo is very isolated but convenient nonetheless, as the shuttle operated by Rava stops here between Munda and Gizo. Private boat transfers to either Munda or Gizo cost S$1200 per boatload return. Cash only.

Agnes Lodge INN $$
(☎62133; www.agneslodge.com.sb; Munda; d S$770-1100, with shared bathroom S$440-550, ste S$1200-1400; ❄📶) This long-established venture right on the waterfront (no beach) has seen better days – some say it rests on its laurels – but it has a variety of rooms for all budgets, from fan-cooled, two-bed rooms to spacious self-contained units with air-con and a private terrace. Downside: rooms are tightly packed together. Amenities include a bar, a restaurant (mains S$80 to S$300) and a dive shop. It's a short walk from the airstrip. Credit cards are accepted.

Zipolo Habu Resort RESORT $$$
(☎7471105, 62178; www.zipolohabu.com.sb; Lola Island; bungalow with shared bathroom A$140-190, deluxe bungalow A$230-340; 📶) On Lola Island, about 20 minutes by boat from Munda, this small resort with a casual atmosphere satiates the white-sand beach, coconut-palm, azure-lagoon fantasy, with six spacious, fan-cooled bungalows scattered amid a nicely landscaped property. The cheaper ones are fairly basic leafhouses, while the two deluxe units boast private bathrooms and unobstructed views over the lagoon.

The restaurant (meals per day A$80) gets good reviews. This place offers village tours, lagoon excursions and sport-fishing charters, and there's a great beach with good swimming. Bonus: free kayaks. Return boat transfers to Munda cost A$120 per boatload. Divers can be picked up at the resort by the local dive centre. Credit cards are accepted.

Leaf Haus Cafe CAFETERIA $
(☎62136; Munda; mains S$30-60; ⊙7.30am-4.30pm) Located right on the main street, Leaf Haus Cafe is a handy spot for a cheap, uncomplicated, walk-in bite – think chilli chicken, fish and chips or toasted sandwiches. Keep your fluids up with a zesty milkshake (S$30) or a thick smoothie (S$30).

Information

Bank South Pacific (BSP; Munda; ⊙8.30am-3.30pm Mon-Fri) Changes currency and has an ATM (Visa only).

Our Telekom (Munda; per hr S$20; ⊙8am-noon & 1-4.30pm Mon-Fri) Internet access.

Getting There & Away

AIR

Solomon Airlines (☎62152; www.flysolomons.com; Munda) Connects Munda with Honiara (S$1500, daily), Gizo (S$800, daily) and Seghe (S$820, once a week).

BOAT

Rava (☎62180) Based at Agnes Lodge, this outfit offers a shuttle service to Gizo (S$250, two hours) stopping at various places en route, including Zipolo Habu Resort and Lolomo Eco Resort. It usually departs from Munda at 7.30am on Monday and Friday. It also operates on Wednesday if there's a minimum of six passengers.

The boat has a roof and rain jackets are provided, but expect to get wet if it's raining.

Ghizo

Little Ghizo Island is dwarfed by its neighbours, but it has the Solomons' second-biggest 'city', Gizo (pronounced the same, spelt differently), the most developed area outside the capital.

Gizo

POP 2900

Gizo is the hub around which the Western Province revolves. Sprawled along the waterfront with its steep hills behind, the town is not devoid of appeal, although the architecture is charmless. Apart from the bustling market on the waterfront, there are no specific sights, but there are some appealing lodgings a short boat ride away. Gizo is also a good base for divers, surfers and hikers.

🕺 Activities

Diving & Snorkelling

Most dive sites are less than a 20-minute boat ride from Gizo and include wrecks and reef dives that are suitable for all levels. A mere 15 minutes away north of Gizo, the *Toa Maru* is the best wreck dive around. There's fabulous snorkelling off Kennedy Island, just off Fatboys. Arrange a boat transfer to Fatboys (p339), hire snorkelling gear at the resort and snorkel to your heart's content. To the southeast of Kennedy Island, there's also a small Hellcat lying on a sandy floor in 9m. It's a fun dive that's usually combined with Secret Spot or Joe's Wall, two first-class dive sites famous for their schooling fish and atmospheric seascapes. For more on diving in the area, see p36.

Dive Gizo DIVING, SNORKELLING

(📞 60253; www.divegizo.com; Middenway Rd; introductory/2-tank dive A\$150/160; ⊙ 8am-5pm) This solid professional outfit at the western end of town leads a range of dives and can arrange dive certification courses and snorkelling trips. Their two-tank dive, which includes a picnic on a secluded island, is great. Gear rental is A\$40 per day.

World Fish Centre SNORKELLING

(📞 60022; Nusatupe Island; ⊙ by reservation) On Nusatupe Island (Gizo's airstrip), this clam farm and research centre is a good spot if you want to snorkel over giant clams of up to 1m long in the lagoon (bring your own gear). Boat transfers from Gizo cost about S\$200, or you can take the Solomon Airlines shuttle (S\$60 one way).

🛏 Sleeping

Cegily's Guesthouse GUESTHOUSE \$

(📞 60035, 7467982; r with shared bathroom S\$290-420) This small guesthouse with five fan-cooled rooms is very simple but clean, calm and secure. There's a well-kept communal kitchen, a tidy lounge area and a terrace with good ocean views. Angle for room 3, which gets more natural light and has the best views. It's just past the hospital, on a hillside.

Nagua Resthouse GUESTHOUSE \$

(📞 60012; s with shared bathroom S\$300, d with shared bathroom S\$400-450, d S\$500-600; ❄) A short (uphill) walk from town, this family-run guesthouse features plain, functional well-scrubbed rooms with air-con, and there's a nice communal kitchen. Upstairs bathrooms have hot showers. The place is well maintained, linen is fresh and the staff friendly, but quarters are a bit cramped. Rooms 8 to 11 afford dashing ocean views.

Rekona Moamoa Lodge GUESTHOUSE \$\$

(📞 60368; rekona.lodge@gmail.com; dm S\$160, d with shared bathroom S\$320, d S\$430-720; ❄�🛜) This great option has something for all purse strings. The cheaper rooms are fairly spartan, but at these rates you know you're not getting the Ritz. The dearer ones – especially rooms 16 to 20, upstairs – occupy a separate building and are way more inviting. They come with private bathrooms (hot showers), balconies with unobstructed views and air-con. There's a kitchen area for common use. Credit cards are accepted with no surcharge.

Gizo Hotel HOTEL \$\$

(📞 60199; www.gizohotel.com; Middenway Rd; d S\$650-720; ❄❄🛜) Gizo's only hotel has suffered in recent years from a lack of maintenance and TLC, and we've heard reports of poor service. That said, it's an acceptable fallback, with ordinary, motel-like rooms, a restaurant and a bar. Some rooms have sea views, while others open onto the garden. The pool at the back is a bit of a joke.

Gizo

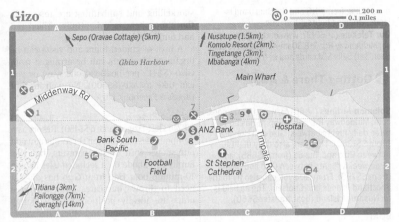

✗ Eating

Gizo has several well-stocked supermarkets, open Monday to Saturday.

Market   MARKET $
(Middenway Rd; ⊙6am-5pm Mon-Sat) Villagers from neighbouring islands arrive each morning by boat to occupy their little stands under the shade of tall trees. Stock up on fruit and vegetables, as well as fresh fish and delicious buns and scones. It's at its liveliest Monday and Friday mornings.

PT 109   SEAFOOD $$
(☑60257; Middenway Rd; mains S$50-80; ⊙11.30am-1.30pm & 5-8pm Mon-Fri; ☎) Named after John F Kennedy's WWII patrol boat that sank off Gizo, and situated in a great waterfront location, this place has a relaxed vibe. A blackboard displays a few simple dishes, such as fish and chips or burgers, as well as lobster.

Gizo Waterfront   SEAFOOD $$
(Middenway Rd; mains S$50-80; ⊙11.30am-1.30pm & 6-9pm) There aren't too many options at this Gilbertese-run eatery, but the daily specials are well prepared and won't blow your budget. Best of all, the open-air dining room overlooks the water.

☻ Drinking & Nightlife

The only drinking den in town is Gizo Waterfront, but it can get raucous in the evening – steer clear of inebriated patrons. During the day, nothing can beat a frothy tropical cocktail or a cold beer at SB Bar (p339) or Fatboys (p339) on Mbabanga Island.

⬛ Shopping

Dive Gizo has a wide selection of stonework and woodcarvings from Marovo.

ⓘ Information

ANZ Bank (Middenway Rd; ⊙9am-4pm Mon-Fri) Currency exchange. Has an ATM (Visa and MasterCard).

Bank South Pacific (BSP; Middenway Rd; ⊙9am-4pm Mon-Fri) Currency exchange. Has an ATM (Visa only).

Bmobile/Vodaphone (www.bmobile.com.sb; Middenway Rd; ⊙8am-4.30pm Mon-Fri, to noon Sat) Sells SIM cards and prepaid wi-fi cards.

Hospital (☑60224; Middenway Rd; ⊙8am-4pm) Has reliable medical services.

Immigration Office (off Middenway Rd; ⊙8-11.30am & 1-4.30pm Mon-Fri) Behind ANZ Bank. Can issue a visitor's permit for yachties proceeding from PNG and the Shortland Islands. Opening hours are erratic.

Our Telekom (☑ 60127; www.ourtelekom.com. sb; Middenway Rd; ⊗ 8.30am-4pm Mon-Fri, 9am-noon Sat) Sells SIM cards and wi-fi prepaid cards.

❶ Getting There & Away

AIR

Solomon Airlines (☑ 60173; www.flysolomons. com; Middenway Rd; ⊗ 8am-5pm) Has up to three daily flights between Gizo and Honiara (from S$1380). There are also daily flights between Gizo and Munda (from S$685), and three weekly flights between Gizo and Seghe (from S$790). From Gizo you can also fly to the Shortland Islands and Choiseul. The airfield is on Nusatupe Island (boat transfer S$60).

BOAT

MV Fair Glory (p327) Cargo boat offering a weekly service between Honiara and Gizo via Marovo Lagoon. The Gizo–Honiara trip costs S$480 in deck class (S$1490 per cabin) and takes about 27 hours. For Seghe, it's S$270. It generally leaves Gizo on Tuesday morning; check while you're here.

MV Anjeanette (p327) Cargo boat offering a weekly service between Gizo and Honiara via Marovo Lagoon. The Gizo–Honiara trip costs S$460 (S$500 in 'first class'). It leaves Gizo on Monday afternoon.

Rava (p335) This shuttle boat connects Gizo to Munda (S$250, two hours), stopping at various places en route. It usually leaves Gizo at 1pm on Monday and Friday. It also operates on Wednesday if there's a minimum of six passengers.

Around Gizo

The main road out of Gizo skirts the shore to **Saeraghi** at the island's northwestern end, which has lovely beaches. There's excellent point surfing off **Pailongge**, on Ghizo's southern coast. The October-to-April swell rises to 2m or more. There's a great left-hander near **Titiana** village, with a long paddle out to the reef's edge, and a right at Pailongge. To get to these spots, take a taxi from Gizo (S$200 to S$300 depending on distance). Bring your own board.

🛏 Sleeping & Eating

Urilolo Lodge BUNGALOW $$
(☑ 8624768; Saeraghi; bungalow s/d S$270/360) Saeraghi, at the northern tip of Ghizo, is a terrific place to kick off your shoes for a few days. This lovely haven consists of two charmingly simple bungalows that are right on a divine stretch of white sand, with Ranongga Island as a backdrop. Swimming,

snorkelling and sunbathing are top-notch, the atmosphere is delightfully chilled out and family-style meals are tasty.

A host of guided tours and visits can be organised. Transfers can be arranged from Gizo (S$415 per boatload one way) or you can take a taxi (S$300). No website, but there's a Facebook page.

Komolo Resort BUNGALOW $$
(☑ 7463365; Epaga Island; d S$450) 'Resort' is a pompous description for three plank-wood bungalows with bucket showers, but this family-run abode on a secluded islet lying a 10-minute boat ride from Gizo has all you need to throw your cares away. All three units are ideally positioned on a skinny stretch of white sand and offer killer views over the turquoise water.

Your host, Grace, can cook hearty meals (from S$60). There's not a great deal to do on the island apart from spending time in the water, but it's a great place to get away from it all while still being close to town. Boat transfers from/to cost S$100 per person.

Imagination Island BUNGALOW $$
(www.imaginationisland.com; Tingetange Island; r with shared bathroom A$60, bungalow d A$160-185, bungalow q A$190-225) This low-key resort, which opened in 2016, enjoys a great location on an islet lying a five-minute boat ride from Gizo. It comprises four sea-facing bungalows, a couple of miniscule budget rooms, a three-room house, a bar and an overwater restaurant. There's superb snorkelling offshore.

Oravae Cottage BUNGALOW $$$
(☑ 7400774, 7690026; www.oravaecottage.com; Sepo Island; d cottage with full board A$300) Just 20 minutes from Gizo on an isolated island, this lovely retreat has three handsomely designed plank-wood bungalows, two of which have private facilities. This is not a place for those looking to be pampered – air-con and hot showers are unknown – but for those who appreciate tropical charm and a laid-back atmosphere, look no further. Swimming and snorkelling are excellent.

It can accommodate two to 10 people at a time; families or groups of friends are preferred. Add A$140 per person extra.

Mbabanga Island

A mere 10-minute boat ride south of Gizo, this island has a brochure-esque appeal, with an expansive lagoon and a string of white-sand beaches.

🛏 Sleeping

Sanbis Resort RESORT $$$

(☑ 7443109; www.sanbisresort.com; Mbabanga Island; d A$270; 🖥) A place of easy bliss. Relax in your creatively designed bungalow, snorkel over healthy reefs just offshore, snooze in a hammock, treat yourself to a tasty meal at the laid-back over-the-water restaurant or kayak over translucent waters. There are only six units, which ensures intimacy. No air-con, but the location benefits from cooling breezes. The beach is thin but attractive.

It's a good base for honeymooners, divers (there's a small on-site dive shop) and fisherfolk (professional equipment is available for rent). No kids under 12.

Fatboys RESORT $$$

(☑ 7443107, 60095; www.solomonislandsfatboys. com.au; Mbabanga Island; d A$255-275; 🖥) This small complex consists of five sea-facing bungalows that blend tropical hardwoods and traditional leaf. It's quite spread out so you can get a decent dose of privacy. The defining factor, however, is the lovely bar and restaurant directly over the exquisite waters of the lagoon. The narrow beach is average, but the snorkelling is sensational.

Couples will opt for the snug Kusui bungalow, which is open-fronted and boasts an overwater terrace, while families will book the very spacious Haguma unit. Kayaks and snorkelling gear are free.

🍴 Eating

SB Bar INTERNATIONAL $$

(☑ 7443108; Sanbis Resort, Mbabanga Island; mains S$60-120; ⊗ 11am-4.30pm; 🖥) In a sublime location overlooking the turquoise lagoon, Sanbis Resort's overwater restaurant is an atmospheric place to sample a well-executed pizza, a burger or a plate of grilled fish at lunchtime. Call reception to arrange transfers from Gizo; there's generally a daily shuttle at 11.30am (with a return trip at 4.30pm).

Fatboys INTERNATIONAL $$$

(☑ 60095, 7443107; Mbabanga Island; mains S$120-200; ⊗ noon-2pm; 🖥) What a sensational setting! The dining room is on a pier that hovers over the turquoise waters of Vonavona Lagoon – it can't get more mellow than

SOLOMON ISLANDS GHIZO

BEST OF THE REST

If, after visiting Guadalcanal, Malaita, Central and Western Provinces, you still feel the urge for more off-the-beaten-track adventures, and if time is really no object, consider travelling to the other provinces.

Shortland Islands Like Choiseul, the Shortland Islands are culturally closer to Bougainville in PNG, which lies only 9km to the north.

Choiseul One of the least-visited provinces in the Solomons. Choiseul has two airfields, on Taro Island and in Kagau.

Isabel This province is a castaway's dream come true, especially if you can make it to the Arnarvon Islands, off the northwestern tip of Isabel. It's a conservation area and one of the world's largest nesting grounds for the hawksbill turtle. There's one basic guesthouse run by the rangers. Trips to Arnarvon Islands can be arranged through **Nature Conservancy** (Map p324; ☑ in Honiara 20940; www.nature.org; Mendana Ave; ⊗ 8am-4.30 Mon-Fri) in Honiara. On Isabel, **Papatura Island Retreat** (www.papatura.com) offers snorkelling, fishing and surfing outings. The gateways to Isabel are Buala and Suavanao.

Rennell & Bellona Both islands are Polynesia outliers, sharing similar languages and cultures. Geologically they're both rocky, uplifted-coral atolls. Rennell has **Lake Te'Nggano**, the South Pacific's largest expanse of fresh water.

Makira-Ulawa An untouched world only one hour from Honiara. Kirakira is the main gateway. Sensational surfing off **Star Harbour**.

Temotu Temotu Province lies at the Solomons' most easterly point. **Lata**, the provincial capital, on Santa Cruz Island, is the main launching pad for outlying islands, such as Reef Islands, Utupua and Vanikoro. One guesthouse on Pigeon Island (Reef Islands) is **Ngarando Faraway Resort** (☑ 7495914; tavakie@gmail.com; Pigeon Island, Temotu Province; bungalow s/d S$450/720), a two- to three-hour boat ride from Lata.

this. The choice is limited but the food is fresh and tasty. Good cocktails (from S\$60), too. Call the reception to arrange transfers from Gizo (S\$180/290 for one/two people).

After your meal, rent snorkelling gear (S\$30) or a kayak (S\$30) and explore the sandy shallows that extend to Kennedy Island.

Islands Around Ghizo

Natural attractions and a few war relics are the main drawcards of the islands surrounding Ghizo. Tourist infrastructure is minimal but all islands offer accommodation in the form of village stays.

The islands around Ghizo have no regular boat services. Your best bet is to find a shared ride at Gizo market. Dive Gizo (p336) can arrange excursions to Simbo and Kolombangara islands.

Simbo

Simbo is definitely worth a visit for its megapode hatcheries and its easily climbable volcano. There's also a sulphur-covered crater lake.

Kolombangara

A perfect cone-shaped volcano that rises to 1770m, Kolombangara looms majestically on the horizon, northeast of Ghizo Island. It rises from a 1km-wide coastal plain through flat-topped ridges and increasingly steep

---

DON'T MISS

HIKING IN KOLOMBANGARA

Growing weary of water activities? Consider climbing up to the crater's rim on Kolombangara (the big island facing Gizo). It's an exhilarating two-day/one-night hike. Take note that it's an arduous walk – it's wet and muddy all the way up, it's steep, and the path is irregular – so you'll need to be fit. But the atmosphere and views are surreal.

You'll need guides, porters and food. Dive Gizo (p336) and **Kolombangara Island Biodiversity Conservation Association** (KIBCA; ☑ 7401198, 60230; www.kolombangara.org) can arrange logistics. Plan on S\$2000 per person, excluding boat transfers from Gizo (S\$1700 per boatload return).

Kolombangara also has less challenging hikes, including crater walks and river walks.

---

escarpments to the rugged crater rim of Mt Veve. For history buffs, there are WWII Japanese relics scattered around the island.

MALAITA

POP 137,500

Easily reached from Guadalcanal, Malaita is a hauntingly beautiful island with narrow coastal plains, secluded bays and a rugged highland interior. As well as having a host of natural features to explore, Malaita has an equally fascinating ethnic heritage. It's a rare combination of being both an adventure island as well as a stronghold of ancient Melanesian traditions and cultures.

Unlike in Guadalcanal and the Western Province, the development of tourism is still in its infancy here. The main destinations (Auki and Langa Langa Lagoon) have enough infrastructure to travel safely on your own. Elsewhere it's virtually uncharted territory.

Auki & Around

POP 1600

Curled around a wonderfully shaped bay and surrounded by jungle-clad hills, Auki is the Solomons' third-largest town. It's a nondescript little port town, with a few low-slung buildings and a smattering of houses on stilts. Everything moves slowly except at the lively market and the bustling wharf, at the town's southern end.

◉ Sights & Activities

Lilisiana VILLAGE

With its traditional-style houses raised on stilts over the shore, the friendly fishing village of Lilisiana, about 1.5km from Auki, is photogenic to boot. Lilisiana's peaceful beach is a narrow, long, golden sand spit beside coral shallows.

Riba Cave CAVE

(admission S\$50) East of Auki is this haunting cave, with stalagmites, several large subterranean chambers and an underground river. Caveat: it's very slippery – wear sturdy walking shoes. From Auki, you can take a taxi (S\$100 return) then walk the final stretch (about five minutes) down to the entrance. It's best to go with a guide.

Kwaibala Waterfall WATERFALL

If you need to refresh yourself, make a beeline for Kwaibala Waterfall, about 3km from Auki. This little waterfall drops into a few pools that

Malaita Province

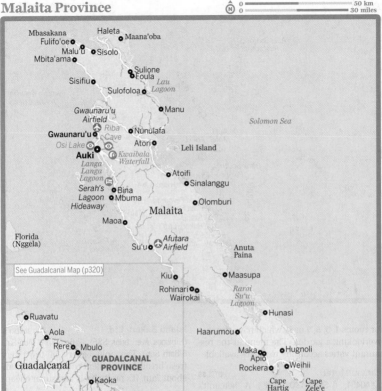

beg swimming. It's a 30-minute walk from town, or you can take a taxi (S$20) then walk the final stretch (about 20 minutes) along the Kwaibala River to the waterfall. It's not signposted; you'll need a guide to get there.

Osi Lake   LAKE
On the northern outskirts of Auki, this lake is a nature-lovers' paradise, home to colonies of seabirds. It can be explored in a dugout. You might be asked to pay a *kastom* (cultural) fee of S$50.

Tours

Discover Malaita Tours   TOUR
(☑7458201; silas.malai@yahoo.com) You'll need a guide to visit Riba Cave and Kwaibala Waterfall, which are difficult to find. Silas Diutee Malai is a freelance guide who charges S$200 for Riba Cave, S$200 for Kwaibala Waterfall and S$100 for Osi Lake. His prices are valid for a group of up to five people.

Kastom fees and taxi rides are not included in the prices he quotes. He can also arrange various village stays.

Sleeping

Auki Motel   HOTEL $
(☑7808884, 40014; aukimotel@solomon.com. sb; Loboi Ave; dm S$150, s with/without bathroom S$350/250, d S$450; ☀) This Auki stalwart caters to all budgets. On a shoestring? Opt for a bed in a neat three-bed dorm. In search of more privacy? Upgrade to a single. Want a few more creature comforts? The rooms with air-con and private facilities are your answer. It ain't fancy, but it's clean and there's an appealing terrace and communal kitchen.

Auki Lodge & Restaurant   LODGE $$
(☑40079; Batabu Rd; d S$620; ☀) Auki Lodge occupies a great location in the centre of town, near the post office. Rooms are plain and functional, with clean bathrooms; angle

Auki

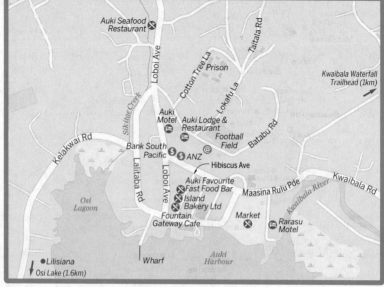

for rooms 1, 3, 5, 7 or 9, which have terraces overlooking a garden. The menu at the restaurant varies according to what's available.

Rarasu Motel HOTEL **$$**
(☑40454; d S$610-790; ❄️📶) A betelnut's throw from the market, this two-storey hotel is a good surprise. The rectangular building is nothing flash, but it's calm, tidy and well managed. Rooms are ordinary but spacious; those upstairs come with parquet flooring and a terrace.

🍴 Eating

Auki Favourite Fast Food Bar FAST FOOD **$**
(☑7369497; Hibiscus Ave; mains S$10-50; ⏰7.30am-5pm Mon-Fri) A very friendly bolt hole that's popular with locals any time of the day. Dig into budget savouries such as beef or chicken stews, omelettes or sweet-and-sour fish. In the morning, don't miss their freshly prepared roti (S$10).

Fountain Gateway Cafe INTERNATIONAL **$**
(☑7791763; Hibiscus Ave; mains S$40-50; ⏰8am-5pm Mon-Sat) This well-run venture with a kitschy dining room is a good-value stomach filler for those in need of some honestly prepared stews, soups, sandwiches and fish and chips at puny prices. Good roast chicken, too.

Island Bakery Ltd BAKERY **$**
(Hibiscus Ave; buns S$6; ⏰6am-8pm Mon-Sat, 6-8am Sun) The only bakery in town has fresh bread and excellent coconut buns from about 7am. It's pretty basic and super cheap.

Market MARKET **$**
The place to stock up on fruit and vegetables. You can also buy cakes.

Auki Seafood Restaurant SEAFOOD **$$**
(☑7540118; Loboi Ave; mains S$65-70; ⏰11am-2pm & 6.30-9.30pm Mon-Sat, 6.30-9.30pm Sun) The decor is bland but the food is tasty at this modest joint near the police station. The owner has worked as a cook for the Australian High Commission and serves up a mean garlic lobster accompanied with sweet potato chips. Enjoy.

ℹ️ Information

ANZ (Maasina Rulu Pde; ⏰9am-4pm Mon-Fri) Has one ATM (Visa and MasterCard) and changes major currencies.

Bank South Pacific (BSP; ☑40484; cnr Loboi Ave & Maasina Rulu Pde; ⏰8.30am-3pm Mon-Fri) Has one ATM (Visa only) and changes major currencies.

Our Telekom (Balabu Rd; per hr S$20; ⏰8.30am-4.30pm Mon-Fri, to 12.30pm Sat; 📶) Has a few computers as well as wi-fi access.

❶ Getting There & Away

Because of land disputes, flights were indefinitely suspended between Honiara and Auki at the time of writing.

Passenger boats **MV Express Pelican II** and **MV 360 Flyer/Discovery** (p327) run regular services between Honiara and Auki (from S$250 one way, three to four hours). The MV *360 Flyer/Discovery* stops at Tulagi twice weekly.

Langa Langa Lagoon

Langa Langa Lagoon is indisputably one of Malaita's highlights. Extending from 7km to 32km south of Auki, the lagoon is famous for its artificial islands built of stones and dead corals. It's also a strong centre for traditional activities, especially shell-money making and shipbuilding.

One proviso: 'lagoon' is a bit misleading. If it has recently rained, waters may be more chocolate than bright turquoise, and you won't find stunning beaches to sun yourself on. People rather come here for the laid-back tempo and the magical setting.

🛏 Sleeping & Eating

Serah's Lagoon Hideaway BUNGALOW **$$**
(📞7472344; serah_kei@yahoo.com.au; full board r per person S$550, bungalow S$650-800) This relaxing retreat run with flair by Serah Kei consists of one tiny bungalow on stilts and a much larger unit with a superb terrace overlooking the lagoon. Both are simply built and as clean as a whistle. There's also a much simpler four-room house. The ablution block is tip-top, with a proper shower and flush toilets, and the meals are memorable.

WORTH A TRIP

GWAUNARU'U

If you want to get a taste of rural life and enjoy superb scenery without travelling too far from Auki, make a beeline for Gwaunaru'u on Malaita. This sweet little village near the airfield, about 10km north of Auki, abuts a huge bay fringed by a 2km-long expanse of volcanic sand. It's at the mouth of a river that offers great swimming opportunities. Be warned: there are plenty of sand flies. Get here by taxi or contact Discover Malaita Tours (p341).

Beyond the river, amid a coconut grove, you'll find the graveyards of two missionaries – very Indiana Jones.

There's no electricity but solar lighting is available. Your host can arrange lagoon tours as well as cultural shows, such as a demonstration of shell-money making (S$300). No beach but there's good swimming and snorkelling. Offers transfers from Auki (about S$500 per boatload one way, 45 minutes).

UNDERSTAND THE SOLOMON ISLANDS

Solomon Islands Today

The RAMSI (Regional Assistance Mission to Solomon Islands) drawdown is well under way. The army has left and all the civilian positions have been transitioned into bilateral aid project positions. The police are the only RAMSI left and it's hoped that all RAMSI police will have withdrawn by 2017 or 2018. It depends on the ability of the Royal Solomon Islands Police Force (RSIPF) to take over the full security role. A staged rearmament of the local police is also under way.

With restored security, increased stability and better air connections from Australia, tourism is slightly on the rise. That said, the country remains one of the poorest in the Pacific. The improvement of transport infrastructure is widely acknowledged as vital for boosting the fragile economy.

History

Papuan-speaking hunter-gatherers from New Guinea were the only inhabitants of the Solomons for thousands of years, until Austronesian-speaking proto-Melanesians began moving in around 4000 BC. The Lapita people appeared between 2000 and 1600 BC. Polynesians from the east settled the outer islands such as Rennell, Bellona and Ontong Java between AD 1200 and 1600.

The first European visitor was Spaniard Don Alvaro de Mendaña y Neyra in 1568, who returned in 1595 to establish a settlement on Santa Cruz. There was almost no further contact with Europeans until 1767, when the British Captain Philip Carteret came upon Santa Cruz and Malaita. British, French and American explorers followed, and whalers began arriving in 1798. Sandalwood traders visited from the 1840s to late 1860s.

On 6 October 1893, Britain proclaimed a protectorate over the archipelago's southern islands, which was extended in 1897 and again in 1898. In 1899 Britain relinquished claims to Western Samoa, and in return Germany ceded the Shortlands, Choiseul, Ontong Java and Santa Isabel to Britain.

Between 1871 and 1903 blackbirders (slave traders) took 30,000 men from the Solomons to work in the cane fields of northern Australia and Fiji.

The year 1942 marked a turning point: in April the Japanese seized the Shortland Islands. Three weeks later Tulagi was taken and the Japanese began building an airstrip on Guadalcanal. United States troops landed on Guadalcanal in August 1942, but were severely defeated by a Japanese naval force that had left Rabaul in New Guinea to attack the US transports. However, the US forces gradually gained the upper hand. During the Guadalcanal campaign, six naval battles were fought and 67 warships and transports sunk – so many ships were sunk off the northern coast of Guadalcanal that this area is now called Iron Bottom Sound. Around 7000 American and 30,000 Japanese lives were lost on land and at sea. The Allies recovered all islands after the official Japanese surrender in 1945. The town of Tulagi was gutted during the war and the Quonset-hut township of Honiara replaced it as the capital.

A proto-nationalist postwar movement called Marching Rule sprang up in Malaita, opposed to cooperation with the British authorities, whose rule had been restored after WWII. Britain began to see the need for local government, and a governing council was elected in 1970. The British Solomon Islands Protectorate was renamed the Solomon Islands five years later and independence was granted on 7 July 1978.

Ethnic tensions started to fester; the Gwale people (people from Guadalcanal) resented the fact that their traditional land was being settled by migrants from Malaita. Early in 1999, the inevitable happened. Civil war broke out, and hundreds died in the fighting.

Following mediation by Australia and New Zealand, the Townsville Peace Agreement was signed between the two factions in October 2000. However, what began as ethnic tension descended into general lawlessness. Though the conflict was confined to Guadalcanal, 'events' started happening elsewhere, including in the Western Province. The whole country was crippled and traumatised, and the fragile economy collapsed.

On 24 July 2003, the RAMSI, an Australian-led coalition of police from Pacific Island states, was deployed throughout the whole country to restore law and order. However, this progress was seriously undermined in April 2006, when the election of controversial Snyder Rini as prime minister resulted in two days of rioting in the streets of Honiara, despite the presence of RAMSI. Australia flew in reinforcements for the RAMSI personnel, which brought calm to the Solomons' capital.

In early April 2007, a tsunami struck Western and Choiseul provinces. Aid workers arrived en masse to help rebuild the local economy.

The Culture

Solomon Islanders' obligations to their clan and village *bigman* (chief) are eternal and enduring, whether they live in the same village all their lives or move to another country. As in most Melanesian cultures, the *wantok* (clan or kinfolk) system is observed here. All islanders are born with a set of obligations to their *wantok*, but they're also endowed with privileges that only *wantok* receive. For most Melanesian villagers it's an egalitarian way of sharing community assets. There's no social security system and very few people are in paid employment, but the clan provides economic support and a strong sense of identity.

Melanesian culture is rooted in ancestor worship, magic and oral traditions. Villagers often refer to their traditional ways, beliefs and land ownership as *kastom;* it's bound up in the Melanesian systems of lore and culture.

The Solomons' 2014 population was estimated at 610,000. Melanesians represent 94% and Polynesians 4%. The large Micronesian communities who were resettled from Kiribati by the British in the 1960s are still called Gilbertese. The remainder of the population is made up of Asians and expats, mainly Aussies and Kiwis. Most of the population lives in rural villages.

JFK

In 1960 John F Kennedy invited two Solomon Islanders to his presidential inauguration in Washington DC. They were turned away because they spoke no English. In 1943 these two islanders had rescued 26-year-old skipper JFK and 10 survivors after their boat was sunk by Japanese during WWII.

About 96% of the population is Christian. Of these, 35% are members of the Anglican-affiliated Church of Melanesia and 20% are Roman Catholics.

Islanders still practise pre-Christian religions in a few remote areas, particularly on Malaita; in other places traditional beliefs are observed alongside Christianity.

Arts

Solomon Islanders are incredibly musical people – it's a must to go to a local church service to listen to the singing. The Malaitan pipe bands (or bamboo bands) are amazing. In ensembles of 12 or so members, the band plays bamboo pipes in all sizes bundled together with bushvine. They're played as panpipe and flutes, and as long tubes whose openings are struck with rubber thongs to make an unusual plinketty-plonk sound. One of the most famous panpipe groups is Narasirato (www.narasirato.com), from Malaita; this group has gained international recognition. They mix classic Malaitan pan-pipe music with contemporary beats.

There are also strong carving traditions in the Solomons. Carvings incorporate human, bird, fish and other animal motifs, often in combination, and they frequently represent deities and spirits. Woodcarvings are inlaid with nautilus or trochus shell. Decorated bowls and masks are widely available, as are stone replicas of traditional shell money.

Shell money is used in Malaita, while in the Temotu Islands red-feather coils are still used.

Environment

The islands of the Solomons form a scattered double chain that extends 1667km southeast from Bougainville in Papua New Guinea. The country's highest peak, Mt Makarakombu (2447m), is located on Guadalcanal. There are active volcanoes, and earthquakes are common.

The country is largely covered by tropical rainforest, but much of it has been degraded by logging operations. Excessive logging threatens the rich diversity of flora and fauna as well as the traditional lifestyle of villagers. Other possible negative effects include erosion, climate change, loss of water resources and disruption to coral reefs. In Marovo Lagoon, Isabel and other islands, the effects of logging are clearly being felt. That said, there are plans to reduce logging and thus the pressure on the environment.

The spectacular marine environment is home to a rich variety of fish, corals, anemones and many other creatures, including eight species of venomous sea snakes. Several islands are breeding grounds for green and hawksbill turtles.

The Solomons has 173 bird species, with 40 endemic. Native reptiles include the 1.5m-long monitor lizard, freshwater crocodiles and the very dangerous saltwater crocodile.

SURVIVAL GUIDE

❶ Directory A-Z

ACCOMMODATION

Tourist-class hotels are confined to Honiara, Tulago, Gizo and Munda. Although fairly basic by international standards, these hotels generally have rooms with or without private shower and air-con. Most have restaurants and bars, offer wi-fi service and take credit cards. There's also a handful of upmarket resorts in Honiara and the Western Province.

Elsewhere accommodation is offered in private houses, usually with only basic shared bathrooms, or in basic leafhouse-style lodges: traditional huts made from woven coconut thatch and other natural materials.

The visitor information centre in Honiara (p327) can make suggestions and help with bookings. You can also check out www.solomonislands-hotels.travel. This portal is a good source of information and offers online bookings, but its listings are not selective.

EMERGENCY
Police & Fire (📞999)

EMBASSIES & CONSULATES
Australian High Commission (Map p326; 📞21561; www.solomonislands.embassy.gov.au; Mud Alley, Honiara) In the centre of town.
French & German Consulates (📞7494820)
New Zealand High Commission (Map p326; 📞21502; www.nzembassy.com/solomon-islands; City Centre Bldg, Mendana Ave, Honiara; ⊗8am-noon & 1-4.30pm Mon-Fri) On the main drag.
Papua New Guinea High Commission (Map p326; 📞20561; www.pnghicom.com.sb; Tsilivi St; ⊗9am-noon & 1-4.30pm Mon-Thu) Off Mendana Ave.
UK High Commission (Map p326; 📞21705; www.gov.uk/government/world/solomon-islands; Heritage Park Hotel, Mendana Ave; ⊗8am-noon & 1-4pm Mon-Thu, to 3pm Fri) Inside the Heritage Park Hotel.

ⓘ SLEEPING PRICE RANGES

The following price ranges refer to a double room with bathroom:

$ less than S$500

$$ S$500–1000

$$$ more than S$1000

HOLIDAYS

New Year's Day 1 January

Easter March or April

Whit Monday May or June

Queen's Birthday First Monday in June

Independence Day 7 July

Christmas 25 December

National Thanksgiving Day 26 December

INTERNET ACCESS

➻ You'll find a few internet cafes in Honiara. Our Telekom (www.ourtelekom.com.sb) has public email facilities in Honiara, Gizo, Munda and Auki.

➻ Wi-fi is available at the better hotels and at a few cafes in Honiara, Auki, Munda and Gizo, but a fee usually applies. Our Telekom sells prepaid wi-fi access cards that can be used at hot spots around the country, including at some accommodation and a number of restaurants and cafes. These prepaid wi-fi cards are also available in some hotels.

➻ Most remote islands have no internet.

➻ Connections can be excruciatingly slow.

MONEY

ATMs There are ATMs at the ANZ bank and Bank South Pacific (BSP) in Honiara, and in Auki, Munda and Gizo. Note that ATMs at BSP only issue cash advances against Visa (not MasterCard). ANZ ATMs accept both Visa and MasterCard.

Credit cards The main tourist-oriented businesses, the Honiara branch of Solomon Airlines, a few dive shops and most upmarket hotels and resorts accept credit cards (usually with a 5% surcharge), but elsewhere it's strictly cash. The most commonly accepted cards are Visa and MasterCard.

Currency The local currency is the Solomon Islands' dollar (S$). A supply of coins and small-denomination notes will come in handy in rural areas, at markets, and for bus and boat rides.

Moneychangers The Bank South Pacific and ANZ will change money in most major currencies. There's also a bureau de change at the airport. Australian dollars are the best to carry, followed by US dollars. Euros are OK, but bank exchange rates are poor.

Taxes There's a 10% government tax on hotel and restaurant prices, but more basic places often don't charge it. All prices given include tax.

Tipping and bargaining Tipping and bargaining are not traditionally part of Melanesian culture.

OPENING HOURS

Banks 8.30am to 3pm Monday to Friday

Government offices 8am to noon and 1pm to 4pm Monday to Friday

Restaurants 11am to 9pm

Shops 8.30am to 5pm Monday to Saturday

TELEPHONE

Solomon Islands' country code is 677; there are no area codes. All landlines have five digits.

Mobile Phones

➻ Our Telekom (www.ourtelekom.com.sb) and Bmobile/Vodafone (www.bmobile.com.sb) offer GSM mobile phone service in most areas (but Marovo isn't entirely covered yet).

➻ Prepaid SIM cards are available for purchase. You can buy top-up cards in many outlets.

➻ Note that most foreign phones set up for global roaming won't work in the Solomons because the local providers don't have roaming agreements with foreign operators. That said, both operators have international roaming agreements with Telstra and Optus (Australia).

VISAS

Citizens from most Western countries don't need a visa to enter the Solomon Islands, just a valid passport, an onward ticket and sufficient funds for their stay. On arrival at the airport, you will be given an entry permit for up to six weeks.

WOMEN TRAVELLERS

➻ Exercise normal caution in Honiara – after dark, take a taxi and stay in busy areas.

➻ Melanesians are very sensitive about the display of female thighs, so shorts and skirts should be knee-length and swimwear should incorporate boardshorts rather than bikini bottoms.

ⓘ Getting There & Away

AIR

Most visitors arrive in the Solomons by air. All flights arrive at Henderson International Airport, 11km east of Honiara.

Access is easy from Australia, Fiji, Papua New Guinea and Vanuatu with direct flights. Coming

ⓘ EATING PRICE RANGES

Tipping is not expected in the Solomons and prices listed include tax. The following price ranges refer to standard mains:

$ less than S$60.

$$ S$60–120.

$$$ more than S$120.

from anywhere else, the easiest option is to travel to Brisbane, Sydney, Nadi, Vila or Port Moresby and connect with flights to Honiara.

Air Niugini (www.airniugini.com.pg) Flies from Port Moresby (Papua New Guinea) to Honiara three times a week. Also has a weekly flight from Honiara to Port Vila (Vanuatu) and a weekly flight from Honiara to Nadi (Fiji).

Fiji Airways (www.fijiairways.com) Has one weekly flight to Port Vila (Vanuatu) and two weekly flights to Nadi (Fiji) with onward connections to Auckland, Honolulu and Los Angeles.

Solomon Airlines (www.flysolomons.com) The national carrier has weekly flights between Honiara and Sydney and flies to Brisbane four times a week. Also has a weekly service between Honiara and Nadi (Fiji) via Port Vila (Vanuatu).

Virgin Australia (www.virginaustralia.com) Has three flights per week to/from Brisbane.

SEA

The Solomons is a favourite spot for yachties who take refuge in the lagoons during cyclone season. Along with Honiara, Korovou (Shortland Islands), Gizo, Ringgi and Tulagi are official ports of entry where you can clear customs and immigration.

ⓘ Getting Around

AIR

Solomon Airlines services the country's 20-odd airstrips. Honiara is the main hub. From the capital there are frequent flights to the main tourist gateways, including Gizo, Seghe (for Marovo Lagoon) and Munda, but be sure to confirm your flight at least 24 hours before your departure. Baggage allowance is 16kg per passenger.

BOAT
Dinghies

Outboard-powered dinghies are the most common form of transport in the Solomons. People pay a fare to travel a sector. Charters cost around S$1500 per day for boat and adriver; fuel is often not included (S$22 per litre in remote areas).

Inter-Island Ships

➡ There are a couple of reliable passenger boats from Honiara. The MV *360 Flyer/Discovery* (p327) has regular services between Honiara, Tulagi and Auki (Malaita), while the MV *Express Pelican II* (p327) has a twice-weekly service between Honiara and Auki. In Western Province, *Rava* (p335) operates a twice-weekly shuttle between Munda and Gizo.

➡ On top of passenger boats, there are also freighters that take passengers, including the MV *Anjeanette* (p327) and the MV *Fair Glory* (p327), which both operate between Honiara and the Western Province.

➡ Most shipping companies have offices near Honiara's main wharf.

PRACTICALITIES

➡ **Language** Solomon Islands Pijin, English and 67 indigenous languages

➡ **Newspapers & Magazines** The *Solomons Star* (www.solomonstarnews.com), the *Island Sun* and the web-only *Solomon Times* Online (www.solomontimes.com).

➡ **Electricity** The Solomons uses 240V, 50Hz AC and Australian-style three-pin plugs.

➡ **Weights and Measures** The metric system is used here.

➡ **Time** 11 hours ahead of GMT/UTC.

BUS

Public minibuses are found only in Honiara. Elsewhere, people pile into open-backed trucks or tractor-drawn trailers.

CAR & MOTORCYCLE

➡ The country has around 1300km of generally dreadful roads. International driving permits are accepted, as are most driving licences.

➡ Driving is on the left side of the road.

➡ Hire cars are available only in Honiara.

TAXI

Taxis are plentiful in Honiara and there are small fleets in Gizo and Auki. They are meterless, so agree on the price before you set off.

TOURS

Allways Dive Expeditions (www.allwaysdive.com.au) An Australian-based company that organises dive trips to the Solomons.

Battlefield Tours (www.battlefields.com.au) This Australian-based operator runs tours of important WWII battlefield sites and memorials around Honiara. All tours are led by historians.

Dive Adventures (www.diveadventures.com.au) Offers diving trips to the Solomons. Australian based.

Diversion Dive Travel (www.diversionoz.com) This Australian-based company specialises in diving trips.

MV Bilikiki (www.bilikiki.com) This highly reputable live-aboard dive boat offers regular cruises around the Russell Islands and Marovo Lagoon.

Sol Surfing (www.surfingsolomonislands.com) Specialises in community-based surf tours to Guadalcanal, Malaita, Isabel and Makira Islands.

Solomon Islands Dive Expeditions (www.solomonsdiving.com) Live-aboard dive trips around the Central Province and the Western Province. Trip lengths vary from three to 15 days.

Surf Solomons (www.surfsolomons.com) This specialist outfit organises community-based surfaris to Guadalcanal, Malaita, Isabel and Makira Islands.

Tahiti & French Polynesia

☏ 689 / POP 280,000

Best Places to Stay

➡ Ninamu (p407)

➡ Vanira Lodge (p363)

➡ Opoa Beach Hotel (p382)

➡ Intercontinental Bora Bora Resort & Thalasso Spa (p390)

Best Places to Eat

➡ Snack Mahana (p371)

➡ Chez Tara (p377)

➡ Maikai Bora Bora (p391)

➡ Restaurant Matira Beach (p392)

Why Go?

Just the name Tahiti conjures up centuries of legend and lifetimes of daydreams. Its 18th-century reputation as a wanton playground of flower-bedecked Polynesians in an Eden-like setting has morphed into a 21st-century image of a chic honeymoon haven. But there's more to the country than cocktails on the terrace of your overwater bungalow. Try hiking up a waterfall valley, paddling out on a turquoise lagoon or diving through sharky passes. This paradise is more affordable than you think. On top of ultraluxurious options, French Polynesia has plenty of family-run pensions that are easier on the wallet and offer local colour.

From the vast lagoons of the Tuamotu atolls to the culturally intense Marquesas Islands and the scenic mountainscapes of the Society Islands, French Polynesia's 118 islands provide enough diversity and surprises for several voyages.

When to Go
Pape'ete

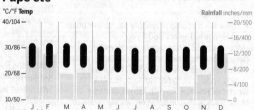

May–Jun & Sep–Nov Excellent times to visit. It's cool, dry and less windy than in July and August.

Jul–Aug Peak tourist season. Can be windy. The region comes to life for Heiva festival in July.

Dec–Apr The summer rainy season. Plenty of sun and cooling showers.

TAHITI

POP 186,909

What Tahiti lacks in wide, white-sand beaches, it makes up for in waterfall-laden, shadowy mountains, unpretentiously beautiful black-sand beaches, sheltered blue lagoons and a distinctly Polynesian, modern buzz. This is the heart of the islands, where the cultures from all the archipelagos are mixed in the cacaphonous, dusty, yet smiling and energetic capital of Pape'ete. Outside the city explore the majestic, mountainous interior on a 4WD tour, learn to dive in the translucent lagoon, wander amid mystical archaeological sites, and from July to October go whale watching. In July catch the country's most spectacular festival, the percussion- and dance-heavy Heiva. Head to Tahiti Iti to experience a more traditional pace of life.

ⓘ Getting There & Away

Pape'ete is the hub of all French Polynesian transport.

AIR

Faa'a (fa-ah-ah) airport is the aviation centre of French Polynesia. All international flights arrive here, and Air Tahiti flights to the other islands leave from here. Flights within each archipelago hop from one island to the next, but most connections between archipelagos are via Faa'a.

In Pape'ete, **Air Tahiti** (Map p358; ☑ 87 86 42 42, 40 47 44 00; www.airtahiti.pf; Rue du Maréchal Foch; ⊘ 8am-5pm Mon-Fri, to 11am Sat) is at the intersection with Rue Edouard Ahnne. It also has an office (⊘ 6am-4.30pm Mon-Fri, to 4pm Sat & Sun) at the airport.

BOAT

All passenger boats to other islands moor at the **Gare Maritime** (Map p357; Blvd Pomare). The numerous cargo ships to the different archipelagos work from the Motu Uta port zone, to the north of the city.

ⓘ Getting Around

Public transport in Tahiti is limited so you're best off renting a car.

CAR

Driving on Tahiti is quite straightforward and, although accident statistics are not encouraging, the traffic is fairly light once you get away from Pape'ete.

Rates start at about 4000 CFP per day with local companies but expect 8000 CFP or more per day from internationally run places. Prices drop after three days.

Most car-hire companies on Tahiti are based at Faa'a airport and stay open until the last departure. They can deliver vehicles to hotels and pensions on the west coast. Some companies also have desks at the bigger hotels.

Avis Pacificar (☑ 40 85 02 84; www.avis-tahiti.com; Faa'a International Airport) Also has a branch in Taravao.

Daniel Rent-a-Car (☑ 40 82 30 04, 40 81 96 32; www.daniel-location.com/en/; Faa'a International Airport) Old standby with a desk at the airport and good rates.

Ecocar Tahiti (Map p357; ☑ 89 50 44 77; www.ecocar-tahiti.com) Had the least expensive cars at the time of writing, starting from 4000 CFP. Reserve in advance for the best deals. Also rents scooters. Located across from Faa'a International Airport.

Europcar (☑ 40 86 61 96; www.europcarpolynesie.com; Faa'a International Airport)

Hertz (☑ 40 82 55 86; Faa'a International Airport)

Tahiti Auto Center (Map p354; ☑ 40 82 33 33; www.tahitiautocenter.pf; Pa'ea, PK20.2; ⊘ 7.30am-4.30pm Mon-Fri, 8-11.30am Sat) Cheaper vehicles need to be booked well in advance. No delivery to the airport.

Pape'ete

Metropolis this is not. Pape'ete is really just a medium-sized town (by Western standards) of moulding architecture with a lively port, lots of traffic, plenty of smiling faces and maybe a guy or two playing ukulele on the kerb. You'll either get its compact chaos and colourful clutter or you'll run quickly from its grimy edges and lack of gorgeous vistas. Sip an espresso at a Parisian-style pavement cafe, shop the vibrant market for everything and anything (from pearls to bright *pareu* – sarongs) or dine at a *roulotte* (mobile food van) in the balmy evening.

⊙ Sights

★**Marché de Pape'ete**　　　　MARKET
(Pape'ete Market; Map p358; cnr Rue Colette & Rue du 22 Septembre; ⊘ 7am-5pm Mon-Fri, 4-9am Sun) A Pape'ete institution. If you see one sight in town, make it this market, which fills an entire city block. Shop for colourful *pareu,* shell necklaces, woven hats and local produce in the main hall. Dotted among the meat and fish sellers are lunchtime hawkers selling takeaway *Ma'a Tahiti* (traditional Tahitian food), fresh fruit juices and local ice cream.

Tahiti & French Polynesia Highlights

1 Exploring the divinely lush and craggy interior of **Tahiti** (p349) by 4WD.

2 Diving with sharks and manta rays in Rangiroa's fantastic **Tiputa Pass** (p399).

3 Pampering yourself on ultragorgeous and over-the-top luxurious **Bora Bora** (p385).

4 Exploring the wild and rugged interior of **Nuku Hiva** (p408).

5 Pondering over French Polynesia's mysterious past at **Marae Taputapuatea** (p379) on Ra'iatea.

To the Marquesas
(100km, see Inset)

Same Scale as Main Map

The Marquesas

Hatutu
Motu One
Nuku Hiva ④
'Ua Huka
'Ua Pou
Hiva Oa
Tahuata
Fatu Hiva
THE MARQUESAS
140°W
10°S

Tepoto Nord
Napuka
Puka Puka
THE TUAMOTUS
Takume
Fangatau
Fakahina
tiu
Taenga
Raroia
Nihiru
Rekareka
Tauere
Makemo
Marutea Nord
Motutunga
Tekokota
Tatakoto
Haraiki
Hikueru
Reitoru
Amanu
Marokau
Ravahere
Hao
Pukarua
Nengonengo
Akiaki
Reao
Paraoa
Vahitahi
Manuhangi
Vairaatea
Nukutavake
Pinaki
Ahunui
Anuanuraro
Anuanurunga
Nukutepipi
Vanavana
Tureia
GLOUCESTER ISLANDS
Tenararo
Tenarunga
Marutea Sud
Vahanga
Matureivavao
Tematangi
Moruroa
Maria Island
Fangataufa
The Gambier Archipelago
Morane
Temoe

SOUTH PACIFIC OCEAN
140°W
136°W

⑥ Driving around **Mo'orea** (p364) and being awed by its mesmerising landscapes.

⑦ Leaving the world behind on little-known **Mataiva** (p406).

⑧ Finding your own slice of beach heaven on the unspoilt sands of **Sables Roses** (p403), Fakarava's most idyllic spot.

⑨ Taking life at a slower pace on **Maupiti** (p393), which is packed with quiet charm.

Society Islands

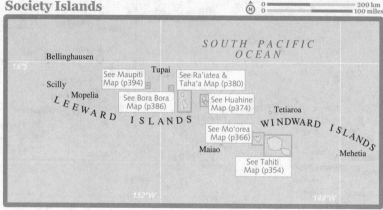

SOUTH PACIFIC OCEAN

Bellinghausen

Tupai
Scilly
Mopelia
See Maupiti Map (p394)
See Ra'iatea & Taha'a Map (p380)
See Bora Bora Map (p386)
See Huahine Map (p374)
Tetiaroa

LEEWARD ISLANDS
WINDWARD ISLANDS

See Mo'orea Map (p366)
Maiao
Mehetia

See Tahiti Map (p354)

Temple de Paofai
CHURCH

(Map p357; Blvd Pomare) Although the Catholic cathedral is placed squarely in the town centre, Tahiti remains predominantly Protestant, a lasting legacy of the London Missionary Society (LMS). The large pink Temple de Paofai makes an unforgettably colourful scene on Sunday morning, when it is bursting at the seams with a devout hat-wearing congregation dressed in white and belting out soul stirring *himene* (hymns).

Jardins de Paofai
GARDENS

(Map p357; Blvd Pomare) This is the main walking area along the waterfront, where you'll find paved walking paths that meander past blooming planter boxes and the occasional tree. While the traffic still buzzes by, it's an almost-relaxing place for a stroll. As you walk east there are racing *pirogues* (outrigger canoes) lined up on the pebbly shore.

Place Vaiete
SQUARE

(Map p358; Vaiete Sq) Place Vaiete is home to multiple *roulottes* and occasional live-music performances at night but is quite peaceful during the day. There are plenty of public benches where you can sit and watch the world go by.

Cathédrale Notre-Dame
CATHEDRAL

(Map p358; Ave du Général de Gaulle) Taking pride of place in the centre of town is the Cathédrale Notre-Dame.

Musée de la Perle
MUSEUM

(Pearl Museum; Map p358; ☑40 46 15 54; www.robertwan.com; Blvd Pomare; ⊙9am-5pm Mon-Sat) **FREE** This pearl museum was created by pearl magnate Robert Wan with aims of luring visitors into his glamorous shop. It's a worthwhile, small and modern museum that covers all facets of the pearl-cultivating business. Explanations of the displays are in English, and ogling Monsieur Wan's gorgeous, albeit uncommonly pricey, jewellery collection is almost as fun as the museum.

🛏 Sleeping

Central Pape'ete is not the place to stay if you're looking for tranquillity or anything resembling a tourist brochure; the options on the outskirts of town offer more palm-fringed, beachlike choices.

Fare Hau
PENSION $

(Map p357; ☑87 77 21 06, 49 90 05 89; www.farehau.pf; Faa'a; r with/without bathroom from 11,500/8500 CFP; ❄🅿) Close to the airport and to Pape'ete, this simple, welcoming place also has great views of Mo'orea from the terrace. The Moana room is the only room with its own bathroom and also has much more light, but the three other rooms are also good value. All prices include a delicious breakfast. Free airport transfers. Cash only.

Fare Suisse
GUESTHOUSE $

(Map p357; ☑40 42 00 30; www.fare-suisse.com; Rue des Poilus Tahitiens; d 9850 CFP; ❄🅿) This guesthouse is in a spotless and stylish cement home in a quiet area not far from the centre of town. The tiled rooms are simple but nicely decorated with bamboo furniture, and are bright and airy. But the best thing about this place is the owner Beni, who picks guests up free of charge at the airport, lets folks store their luggage and creates a super-pleasant atmosphere with his helpfulness.

Maison d'Hotes Tutehau   GUESTHOUSE $$

(Map p357; ☑87 31 19 84; www.faredhotestute-hau.com; Av du Chef Vairaatoa; s/d with shared bathroom from 8000/12,000 CFP, d/f with bathroom 15,000/18,000 CFP; ❄️📶) In Pape'ete, an 800m walk from the Gare Maritime this friendly, clean and colourful little nest is a secure spot in an otherwise unprepossessing part of town (although it's fine in daylight hours). Hosts are helpful finding you the best deals and there are plenty of hangout areas in the house proper and garden. Bikes and airport transfers are free.

Tiare Tahiti   HOTEL $$

(Map p358; ☑40 50 01 00; hoteltiaretahiti@mail.pf; Blvd Pomare; d 14,000-16,500 CFP; ❄️📶) This clean hotel has an excellent location overlooking the water in the hub of Pape'ete, but sadly is afflicted by traffic noise. A somewhat kitschy favourite with tour groups, it has 38 simply furnished, motel-like rooms that are expensive for what you get; the cheaper ones are at the back and lack views but are quieter. Breakfast costs 1000 CFP.

Intercontinental Resort Tahiti   RESORT $$$

(Map p357; ☑40 86 51 10; www.tahitiresorts.intercontinental.com; Faa'a, PK8; r & bungalow d from 30,500 CFP; ❄️📶🏊) Hands down, this is the best luxury resort on the island. The Intercontinental is as posh as Tahiti gets. Marble bathrooms, plush canopies and Mo'orea views from private balconies are standard both in the rooms and romantic overwater bungalows, which range from smallish to quite spacious.

🍴 Eating

⭐ Place Vaiete Roulottes   TAHITIAN $

(Map p358; Place Vaiete; mains from 900 CFP; ⏲6pm-late) The country's famous *roulottes* are a cultural and gastronomic delight. These little stalls sizzle, fry and grill up a storm every evening from around sunset and things don't quiet down until well into the night.

Place To'ata Snacks   TAHITIAN $$

(Map p357; Place To'ata; mains 1300-2700 CFP; ⏲11.30am-1.30pm & 6-10pm) This cluster of open-air *snacks* (snack bars) with outdoor seating – Vaimiti, Chez Jimmy, Mado, Moeata, Toa Sushi – near Place To'ata is a great place to chill with regulars and savour the most authentic and best-value food in town (but no alcohol is served). From *poisson cru* (raw fish) and burgers to crepes and sushi, each joint has its specialities.

TAHITI & FRENCH POLYNESIA IN...

One Week

Start on **Tahiti**. Spend two days driving around the island, and be sure to include **Tahiti Iti**, one of French Polynesia's hidden gems. Devote days three and four to **Mo'orea**, where you can splash around in the lagoon. Fly to **Bora Bora**, where cool hikes, boat tours on the vast turquoise lagoon and fancy restaurants await. Live it up for a couple of nights in an overwater bungalow before flying back to Pape'ete.

Two Weeks

Start with two days on **Tahiti** and the same on **Mo'orea** before flying to **Huahine** for a taste of Polynesian culture. Push on from here to **Bora Bora**, where you can spend a few days. Then it's time to change scene. Fly to **Rangiroa**, the largest coral atoll in the country. You'll need three days to do the atoll justice. Next, hop to **Fakarava** or **Tikehau**, where you can dive, snorkel and relax for a few days before returning to Tahiti.

Three Weeks

Split your time between three archipelagoes: the Society Islands, the Tuamotus and either the Marquesas or the Australs. In the Marquesas, it's easy to combine **Nuku Hiva** and **Hiva Oa**. In the Australs, try to visit **Rurutu** and **Raivavae**, because they perfectly complement each other.

Tahiti

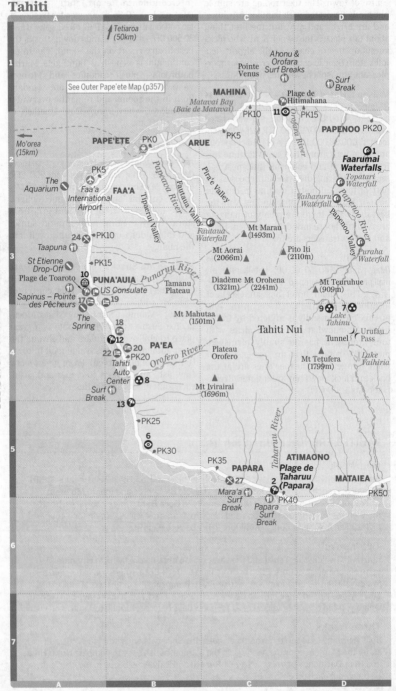

See Outer Pape'ete Map (p357)

TAHITI & FRENCH POLYNESIA PAPE'ETE

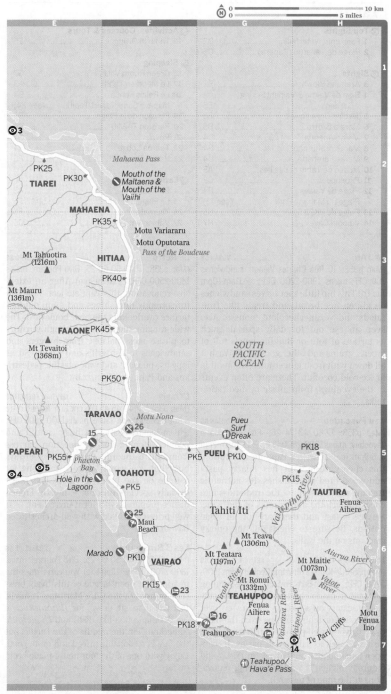

0 10 km
0 5 miles

PK25
PK30
TIAREI

Mahaena Pass
Mouth of the
Maltaena &
Mouth of the
Vaiihi

MAHAENA
PK35

Motu Variararu
Motu Oputotara
Pass of the Boudeuse

Mt Tahuotira
(1216m)
HITIAA

Mt Mauru
(1361m)
PK40

FAAONE PK45

SOUTH
PACIFIC
OCEAN

Mt Tevaitoi
(1368m)

PK50

TARAVAO *Motu Nono*
26
Pueu
Surf
Break

PAPEARI
15
AFAAHITI **PUEU**
PK55
PK5 PK10
PK18

Phaeton
Bay
TOAHOTU
PK15

Hole in the
Lagoon
PK5
TAUTIRA
Fenua
Aihere

Tahiti Iti
Vaitepiha River

25
Maui Beach

Mt Teava
(1306m)
Aiurua River

Marado
PK10
VAIRAO
Mt Teatara
(1197m)
Mt Maitie
(1073m)
*Vaiote
River*

PK15
23
Mt Ronui
(1332m)
Tirahi River
TEAHUPOO
Fenua
Aihere
Vaitarava River
Vaipoiri River

PK18
16
Teahupoo
21
14
Te Pari Cliffs
Motu
Fenua
Ino

Teahupoo/
Hava'e Pass

N

Tahiti

Le J'Am
VEGAN $$

(Map p358; 10 Rue Charles Viénot; sandwiches 700 CFP, mains 1900-2200 CFP; ⊗11am-10pm Tue-Fri) This hip little spot serves sandwiches on gluten-free bread, and treats like fruit salads and vegan chocolate mousse. Also keep an eye out for daily specials such as tartare of tofu or Buddha bowls full of greens, grains and other good stuff. Wash it all down with fresh ginger juice, a smoothie or ice-cold coconut. There are often events in the evenings, from music to meditation talks.

Lou Pescadou
ITALIAN $$

(Map p358; ☑40 43 74 26; Rue Anne-Marie Javouhey; mains 1200-2800 CFP; ⊗11.30am-2pm & 6-9pm Tue-Sat; ☑) A Pape'ete institution, this cheery restaurant has hearty pasta and wood-fired pizza dishes. It's authentic Italian, right down to the red-and-white check tablecloths and carafes of red wine. Service is fast and there are lots of vegie options. Be sure to check out the quirky cartoons on the walls.

Morrison's Café
FRENCH, TAHITIAN $$

(Map p358; ☑40 42 78 61; Vaima Centre; mains 1600-3200 CFP; ⊗6pm-5am Fri-Sun) Long-running yet still remarkably trendy, this casually elegant eatery on a rooftop with a view over the city is a delightful escape from the main drag. Savour well-prepared fish and meat dishes as well as salads and pastas. It stays open late and gets quite lively on Friday and Saturday nights. It was undergoing renovations at the time of research.

Le Rétro
BISTRO $$

(Map p358; ☑40 50 60 25; Blvd Pomare; mains 1800-2500 CFP; ⊗11am-9pm) After an extensive renovation, this Pape'ete icon now features trendy furnishings and a hip outdoor terrace overlooking the busy boulevard. The wide-ranging menu covers enough territory to please most palates, from burgers and sandwiches to fish grills and salads. Sit as long as you want and watch traffic, pedestrians and Pape'ete life buzz by.

L'Oasis
TAHITIAN, FRENCH $$

(Map p358; ☑40 45 45 01; cnr Rue Jeanne d'Arc & Rue du General de Gaulle; mains 1400-2600 CFP; ⊗6am-3pm Mon-Sat) In a busy, central and people-watching-worthy location across from the cathedral, this place is always busy, but you won't have to wait long for a table on the breezy terrace. The range of daily specials on offer – mostly French dishes prepared with local ingredients – is well priced and filled with well-orchestrated flavours.

Les 3 Brasseurs
BRASSERIE $$

(Map p358; ☑40 50 60 25; Blvd Pomare; mains 1800-2700 CFP; ⊗11am-late) You can't miss the inviting and open facade of this lively brasserie in front of the Gare Maritime. It might feel weird to sit down for *flammekueche* (an Alsatian pizza-like dish) and *choucroute* (sauerkraut) in the middle of the Pacific, but the fare is reasonably priced and quite good. Enjoy with one of the four house-made beers on tap.

Outer Pape'ete

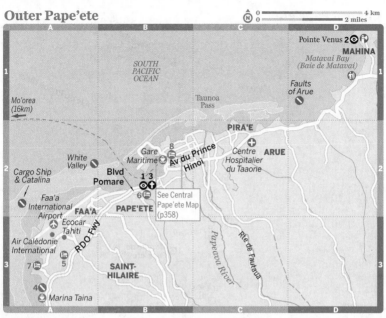

N
0 — 4 km
0 — 2 miles

Outer Pape'ete

Le Lotus　　　　　　　　FUSION **$$$**
(☑ 40 86 51 25; Intercontinental Resort Tahiti, Faa'a, PK8; mains 2000-4700 CFP; ⊗ noon-2.30pm & 6.30-9.30pm) Inside the Intercontinental Resort Tahiti, this uber-romantic restaurant on the edge of the lagoon is perfect for a special night out; a good excuse to put on your best, but still casual, outfit. Flickering candles, a breezy terrace and the gentle lap of waves will rekindle the faintest romantic flame. The food is suitably refined; flavourful French and Polynesian favourites are whipped into eye-pleasing concoctions.

🍷 Drinking & Entertainment

After a stay on other islands, where nightlife is just about nonexistent, Pape'ete could almost pass itself off as a city of wild abandon. Most restaurants at Marina Taina double as bars, so you can bar-hop on weekends for a low-key night out.

Top-end hotel bars are a focus of Pape'ete social life, especially on Friday and Saturday evenings. It's more fun than it might sound, pulling in a range of locals, residents and tourists. Consider the bars at the Pearl Beach Resort, the Intercontinental Resort Tahiti, the Manava Suite Resort and Le Méridien Tahiti.

🛍 Shopping

There's really not much to buy in Tahiti besides Tahitian pearls and a few handicrafts. Your best bet for

TAHITI & FRENCH POLYNESIA PAPE'ETE

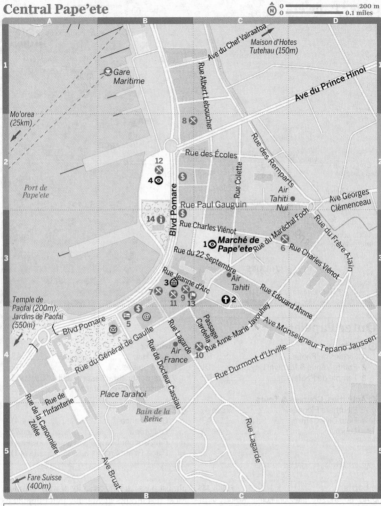

Central Pape'ete

everything from *pareu* to woven hats, pearls, vanilla and homemade *monoï* (fragranced coconut oil) is the Marché de Pape'ete. Watch out though – anything that seems to be mass produced probably is mass produced in China, Indonesia or the Philippines.

ℹ Information

There are banks (Banque Socredo, Banque de Tahiti and Banque de Polynésie) and ATMs scattered around Pape'ete and its suburbs. Banque Socredo has a branch at Faa'a airport, where there's also an ATM.

Ambulance (☑15)

Centre Hospitalier du Taaone (Map p357; ☑ 40 48 62 62, 24hr emergencies 40 42 01 01; Pira'e) The biggest hospital in French Polynesia, with good facilities and a range of medical specialities.

Cybernesia (Map p358; Vaima Centre; per hr 1000 CFP; ⊙8.30am-5pm Mon-Fri, 9am-1pm Sat)

Office du Tourisme de Tahiti et ses Îles (Tourist Office; Map p358; ☑40 50 40 30; www.tahiti-tourisme.com; Fare Manihini, Blvd Pomare; ⊙7.30am-5.30pm Mon-Fri, 8am-4pm Sat, 8am-noon Sun) Has lots of information on all of French Polynesia. Although Mo'orea and Bora Bora have tourist offices, the more remote islands don't, so if you have any queries, ask here. Very friendly and helpful.

Police (☑17)

Post office (OPT; Map p358; www.opt.pf; Blvd Pomare; ⊙7.30am-5pm Mon-Fri, to 11am Sat) Pape'ete's main post office is next to Parc Bougainville.

ℹ Getting Around

TO/FROM THE AIRPORT

The taxi drive to central Pape'ete will set you back 1800 CFP during the day and 2500 CFP at night (8pm to 6am).

TAXI

All the big hotels have taxi ranks, and there are plenty of taxis in central Pape'ete. Any trip of a reasonable length will approximate a day's car rental, so if you want wheels you may as well rent them.

Around Tahiti Nui

It's another world outside of Pape'ete; the sea is a deep blue, the jagged green mountains frame the sky and cars putter along at 50km/h.

THE HEIVA

If your visit is in July, stay on in Tahiti for the hugely popular Heiva, French Polynesia's premier festival, which is held at various venues in and near Pape'ete. It lasts about four weeks from late June to late July and is so impressive that it's almost worth timing your trip around. Expect a series of music, dance, cultural and sporting contests.

◉ Sights

The following is a 114km clockwise circuit around Tahiti Nui.

Pointe Vénus & Matavai Bay   HISTORIC SITE
(Map p357; PK10) Part of Captain Cook's mission on his three-month sojourn in 1769 was to record the transit of Venus across the face of the sun in an attempt to calculate the distance between the sun and the earth. Pointe Vénus, the promontory that marks the eastern end of Matavai Bay (Baie de Matavai), was the site of Cook's observatory.

Today Pointe Vénus is a popular beach stop. There are shady trees, a stretch of lawn, a nice black-sand beach, a couple of souvenir shops and an impressive lighthouse (1867).

Arahoho Blowhole   NATURAL SITE
(Map p354; PK22) When the swell is big enough, huge sprays of water shoot out from the *trou du souffleur* (blowhole) in a little park by the road just after the tunnel at PK22, coming from Pape'ete. The blowhole is at the end of the path and there's a small parking lot. Just past the blowhole is a fine sliver of black-sand beach, nice for a picnic.

★**Faarumai Waterfalls**   WATERFALL
(Map p354; PK22.1) Through the village of Tiarei where the road swoops around a black-sand beach, you'll see a sign on the mountain side of the road for the exceedingly high Faarumai Waterfalls. Unfortunately you can't swim here anymore since a tourist was hit on the head by a falling rock, so bring mosquito repellent and just enjoy the view.

Jardins Botaniques   GARDENS
(Map p354; PK51; 600 CFP; ⊙9am-5pm) The 137-hectare Jardins Botaniques has walking

paths that wind their way through the garden past ponds, palms, a massive banyan tree and a superb mape forest. The gardens were founded in 1919 by an American, Harrison Smith, who introduced many plants to Tahiti, including the large southeast Asian pomelo known on Tahiti as *pamplemousse,* the French word for grapefruit.

Bain de Vaima & Vaipahi Spring Gardens
GARDENS

(Map p354; PK49) Bain de Vaima (Vaima Pool) is where locals come from all over to bathe in the icy but exceptionally clear waters that are thought to have healing properties. Unfortunately there are so many visitors here on weekends and holidays that the 'clean' pools can get filled with rubbish.

The Vaipahi Spring Gardens further along is a beautifully landscaped garden with a magnificent natural waterfall.

★ Plage de Taharuu (Papara)
BEACH

(Map p354; PK39) Everybody loves Plage de Taharuu – locals taking the kids for a swim, tourists on day trips from Pape'ete and surfers catching some great waves. This gently curving black-sand beach is long, broad and fairly protected. It usually has some good swimming conditions. There's also a little *snack* right on the beach if you get peckish.

Mara'a Grotto
CAVE

(Map p354; PK28.5) Lush gardens, overhung caverns, crystal-clear pools and ferny grottoes are all standard features at gorgeous Mara'a Grotto. The fairy-tale park is found along the coastal road, and a manicured path runs throughout.

Plage du PK23.5
BEACH

(Map p354; PK23.5) This rather wide (by Tahiti standards) beach is popular with families and has public facilities. The sand is white-grey.

Marae Arahurahu
ARCHAEOLOGICAL SITE

(Map p354; PK22.5) Whether or not you believe in the powers of the *tiki* (sacred statue), it's hard to deny there is an amazing energy radiating from Marae Arahurahu in the Pa'ea district. Tranquil, huge and beautifully maintained, the *marae* (traditional temple) is undoubtedly the best-looking one on the island and even rivals those on other islands.

Plage du Mahana Park
BEACH

(Map p354; PK18.5) Plage du Mahana Park has calm waters and a snorkelling reef close to shore. On weekends there are kayaks for hire.

Plage de Vaiava
BEACH

(Plage du PK18; Map p354; PK18) Beloved by locals, Plage du PK18 is a stunning beach to sun yourself on, but not that great for swimming or snorkelling due to the shallow water. The sands can get jammed on weekends, but that's part of the scene.

Musée de Tahiti et des Îles
MUSEUM

(Museum of Tahiti & its Islands; Map p354; ☑40 54 84 36; PK15.1; 600 CFP; ☺9am-5pm Tue-Sun) Only 15km from Pape'ete along the west coast, this excellent museum, in Puna'auia, is divided into four sections: geography and natural history; pre-European culture; the European era; and outdoor exhibits. It's in a large garden and if you tire of the exhibits, you can wander out to the water's edge to watch the surfers at one of Tahiti's most popular breaks.

🏃 Activities

Diving & Whale Watching

There are some excellent diving opportunities to be had in Tahiti. Most dive shops lead whale-watching tours between July or August and October when humpbacks swim near the coasts. Half-day trips cost from 8000 CFP per person. Dolphin-watching tours run year-round and are slightly cheaper.

Eleuthera Plongée
DIVING, WHALE WATCHING

(Map p357; ☑40 42 49 29, 87 77 65 68; www.dive-tahiti.com; Marina Taina, PK9; single/two-tank dive 7900/13,230 CFP) A big dive outfit that also leads whale-watching excursions. It charges 7200 CFP for an introductory dive and 31,500/58,500 CFP for a five-/10-dive package. Nitrox dives are also offered. It's part of the Te Moana Diving Pass (p366).

Fluid Dive Centre
DIVING, WHALE WATCHING

(Map p357; ☑40 85 41 46, 87 70 83 75; www.fluidtahiti.com; Marina Taina, PK9; single/two-tank dives 7000/12,600 CFP) Fluid is known for friendly service and small groups. It also offers introductory dives (8000 CFP) as well as 10-dive packages (49,000 CFP).

Topdive
DIVING, WHALE WATCHING

(Map p357; ☑40 53 34 96; www.topdive.com; Intercontinental Tahiti Resort, PK8; single/two-tank dives 9800/19,000 CFP) This large and efficient operation offers a full range of dives, from

Nitrox to introductory dives (10,000 CFP). Six- and 10-dive packages (which can be used at their locations on other islands as well) are 50,000/80,000 CFP.

Hiking

Tahiti's interior is home to some of the most exquisite, and challenging, hikes in French Polynesia. Most trails require a guide as there's no waymark and it's easy to get lost. The following hikes are among the most popular.

Aito Rando HIKING
(☎ 87 76 20 25; www.facebook.com/aitorando987) Very dynamic guides who have made some new routes. Best contact is via Facebook.

Tahiti Reva Trek HIKING
(☎ 87 74 77 20; www.tahitirevatrek.com; hikes from 5900 CFP) Run by a female guide who has

lots of experience and offers a wide range of hikes for all levels.

Surfing

Polynesia is the birthplace of surfing, and Tahiti offers some fabulous beginner breaks, particularly at Papenoo and other beach breaks along the east coast. More advanced surfers can head to the Papara shore break and the reef breaks along the west coast and the big and small passes at Tahiti Iti. Tahiti's most famous, radical wave is at Hava'e Pass in Teahupoo on Tahiti Iti, where there's a big international surf contest held each August.

Several outfits offer tuition for beginners.

Aloha Surf School Tahiti SURFING
(☎ 89 33 82 09; www.alohasurfschooltahiti.com; group lessons 4500 CFP) Beginner classes on

---

INLAND THRILLS

Archaeological remains, mossy, velvet-green mountains and sensational vistas await you in Tahiti Nui's lush (and uninhabited) interior.

Papenoo to Relais de la Maroto

The 18km route from **Papenoo** (Map p354; PK17) on the north coast to the Relais de la Maroto follows the wide Papenoo Valley, the only valley to cut right through the volcanic interior of Tahiti. There are several waterfalls along the valley, as well as a well-preserved *marae* (sacred site). Then the track reaches the Relais de la Maroto.

Around the Relais de la Maroto

Originally built as accommodation quarters for workers on a hydroelectricity project, the Relais de la Maroto offers sensational mountain views. The restaurant is a great spot to break the journey.

The restored **Marae Farehape** (Map p354) site is almost directly below the ridge line on which the Relais de la Maroto perches; you can see an archery platform from where arrows were shot up the valley. Another archaeological site, **Marae Anapua** (Map p354), has also been beautifully restored and is worth a gander.

From Relais de la Maroto to Mataiea

From Relais de la Maroto, the track makes a very steep and winding climb to a pass and a 200m-long tunnel, at a height of around 800m, before plunging down to Lake Vaihiria (450m). Most tours stop here before returning via the same route; at the time of writing the road was closed further down the valley due to a barricade built by the area's residents. Legal proceedings were under way to ensure that the road would remain accessible both to visitors and Tahiti's hydroelectric-company workers. Check when you're on Tahiti.

Tours

The best way to explore the area is to join a 4WD tour. Specialised 4WD operators do the Papenoo-to-Vaihiria route regularly. Full-day trips cost 6500 CFP; children under 10 are half-price and hotel pick-up is included. You'll stop at Relais de la Maroto for lunch (not included). The following are a few favourite operators:

Tahiti Safari Expeditions (☎ 40 42 14 15, 87 77 80 76; www.tahiti-safari.com) This is the biggest operator, with reliable standards.

Ciao Tahiti (☎ 87 73 73 97; www.ciaotahiti.com) Comfy 4WDs and good credentials.

the beaches of Mahina and Papenoo, and more advanced sessions at Papara.

Tama He'e　　　　　　　　　　　　SURFING
(☑ 87 79 06 91; www.tahitisurfschool.com) Private and group surfing or bodyboarding classes with Michel Demont, world longboard champion in 1994. Prices vary.

🛏 Sleeping

There are a number of places to stay along the west coast, particularly around Puna'auia.

Pension Te Miti　　　　　　　　PENSION $
(Map p354; ☑ 40 58 48 61; www.pensiontemiti. com; PK18.6; dm with breakfast 2500 CFP, d with shared bathroom 6600-7600 CFP; @) Run by a young, friendly French couple, this fun place has a low-key backpacker vibe and is deservedly popular with budgeteers. It's on the mountain side of the main road in Pa'ea, about 200m from the beach. Digs are spread across two houses and include simple but clean four-bed dorms as well as fan-cooled rooms.

Taaroa Lodge　　　　　　　GUESTHOUSE $
(Map p354; ☑ 40 58 39 21; www.taaroalodge.com; PK18.2; dm/d/bungalows 2800/6400/10,600 CFP) Right on the waterfront, Taaroa Lodge has the most luxe location for the price tag on this coast. The dorm is basic and the one private en suite room downstairs is dark but comfortable. The two individual bungalows in the garden are definitely the highlight here and have lovely views of Mo'orea. There are kitchen facilities and a friendly atmosphere.

Pension de la Plage　　　　　　PENSION $
(Map p354; ☑ 40 45 56 12; www.pensiondela plage.com; PK15.4; s/d from 8500/9500 CFP; 🛜 🌊) Just across the road from Plage de Toaroto, this impeccably maintained place offers comfortable motel-style rooms in several garden-side buildings around a swimming pool. Each has tile floors and giant windows; some have kitchenettes. There's a bit of street noise but nothing to lose sleep over. Breakfast is available for 1000 CFP, dinner for 2600 CFP. Snorkel gear is complimentary.

Le Relais Fenua　　　　　　　　STUDIOS $
(Map p354; ☑ 40 45 01 98, 87 77 25 45; www. relaisfenua.fr; PK18.25; studios with/without kitchenette 10,900/8500 CFP; ❄ 🛜 🌊) A great, superfriendly option in Pa'ea, with seven immaculate, spacious and bright studios with TVs set around a little swimming pool.

Each little unit has its own back patio. Plage de Mahana Park is stumbling distance away, and there are a few affordable eating options just around the corner, all making this an even better deal for the price.

Le Méridien Tahiti　　　　　RESORT $$$
(Map p354; ☑ 40 47 07 07; www.lemeridien-tahiti. com; PK15; d from 25,000 CFP; ❄ @ 🛜 🌊) Le Méridien has truly lovely grounds dotted with lily ponds and fronted by a natural white-sand beach that has Mo'orea views; if you want a resort where you can swim in the lagoon this is your best bet. The overwater bungalows are stylishly built with hard woods and natural materials although parts of the resort are showing signs of wear.

Manava Suite Resort Tahiti　　RESORT $$$
(Map p354; ☑ 40 47 31 00; www.spmhotels.com/ resort/tahiti; PK10.8; studio/ste from 27,360/30,780 CFP; ❄ 🛜 🌊) This hotel is an odd mix of a resort and serviced apartments. Units are modern with clean lines and you won't have staff fawning over you during your stay, although the front desk is very helpful if you need them. The biggest draw is the fantastic infinity pool on a little white sand beach, all overlooking the silhouette of Mo'orea.

🍴 Eating

Most of Tahiti Nui's restaurants are along the west coast not far from Pape'ete. There are also plenty of tasty and inexpensive *roulottes* that open up along the roadside at night.

★ Blue Banana　　　FRENCH, POLYNESIAN $$
(Map p354; ☑ 40 41 22 24; http://bluebanana-tahiti.com; PK11.2; mains 1400-3500 CFP; ⏰ 11am-2pm Tue-Sun, 6.30-9.30pm Mon-Sat) Success has done nothing to dull the buzz at Blue Banana, a hip lagoonside restaurant in Puna'auia. The food is as good as the ambience – feast on innovative French and Polynesian dishes (small portions but artistically presented) and fine French vintages from the air-conditioned cellar. Pizzas also grace the menu.

Pink Coconut　　　　　　　　FRENCH $$
(Map p357; ☑ 40 41 22 23; www.tahitipinkcoco nut.com; Marina Taina, PK9; mains 1800-3600 CFP; ⏰ 11am-10pm Mon-Sat) We love this lively spot located right on Marina Taina with great views of stylish yachts at anchor. Dine on French-inspired fare with a contemporary twist. At night it's lit by candles and there's live music and dancing on the weekends.

Vahine Vata Beach
TAHITIAN, FRENCH **$$**

(Map p354; ☑40 45 50 10; PK36.8; pizzas 1300-2000 CFP, mains 1900-2800 CFP; ⊘11am-2pm & 6-9pm Tue-Sun) In a casual, yet beautiful and romantic setting on a verandah overlooking the black-sand beach of Papara, this place serves unique and tasty dishes. Expect fish with papaya sauce, cassoulet and especially good thin-crust pizzas, although the menu changes daily. There's occasional live music on weekends.

Casa Bianca
ITALIAN **$$**

(Map p357; ☑40 43 91 35; Marina Taina, PK9; mains 1300-2700 CFP; ⊘11am-10pm) If pasta offerings or pizzas make your stomach quiver with excitement, opt for this perky eatery with an outdoor dining area overlooking the marina. Come for the good fun, good mix of people, hearty dishes and wicked cocktails. Carnivores, don't miss out on *veau á la broche* (veal cooked on a spit) on Friday evenings.

Taumatai
FRENCH, TAHITIAN **$$**

(Map p354; ☑41 57 13 59; Taravao; mains 1700-3000 CFP; ⊘11.30am-2pm & 6.30-9pm Tue-Sat, 11.30am-2.30pm Sun) This delightful little place in Taravao serves fantastic French and Tahitian food in an elegant garden – it's by far the most peaceful and beautiful setting in Taravao and is a great spot for a romantic lunch or dinner. The shellfish in particular (try the *varo* – mantis shrimp – if available) is fresh and always prepared to perfection.

Tahiti Iti

Unpretentious and beautiful, the smaller loop of Tahiti's figure eight quietly attracts independent, outdoorsy folk looking for a more authentic glimpse of Polynesia. More commonly called the Presqu'île, Tahiti Iti has made a bit of a name for itself in recent years thanks to the promotion of its famous wave at Teahupoo. But despite its surfing fame, there's much more to do in Tahiti Iti than ride the waves. Exceptional walks, boat tours and horse riding are just a few of the options.

Taravao is this region's 'capital'. From this main hub, roads run along the north and south coasts of Tahiti Iti and to the interior, mountainous Tahiti Iti plateau.

◉ Sights & Activities

The south coast road runs past beaches and bays to **Teahupoo**. The size and hollowness of the waves at Teahupoo have earned it an international reputation. The road stops abruptly at the Tirahi River at PK18; from here it's a two-hour walk to **Vaipoiri Cave** (Map p354); another kilometre and a half along the coast from here the **Te Pari Cliffs** begin. You can hike the 8km of this coast dotted with archaeological treasures, waterfalls and caves, but only in good weather and if the swell isn't too big. A guide is essential.

Probably the most fun you can have in a day on Tahiti Iti is by taking a boat excursion, which invariably includes a picnic lunch, a visit to Vaipoiri Cave and, if the weather permits, Te Pari. All pensions in the area can arrange excursions.

Very few divers know that there's fantastic diving on Tahiti Iti. Most sites are scattered along the south coast, between Taravao and Teahupoo. You can expect pristine sites and fabulous drop-offs. **Tahiti Iti Diving** (Map p354; ☑40 42 25 33, 87 71 80 77; www.tahiti-iti-diving.com; PK58.1; single dive 5800 CFP; ⊘Tue-Sun) is based near Taravao on Tahiti Nui but runs dive trips to Tahiti Iti.

🛏 Sleeping & Eating

★Vanira Lodge
BUNGALOW **$$**

(Map p354; ☑40 57 70 18; www.vaniralodge.com; Teahupoo, PK15; bungalows 17,900-27,900 CFP; ❋⏾≋) Our favourite *pension* in Tahiti, this place is up a steep driveway on a miniplateau with vast views of the lagoon, surf, village and myriad island colours. The bungalows are fabulously eclectic and are all built from some combination of bamboo, thatch, rustic planks of wood, glass, adobe, coral and rock. One of the bungalows has an earth roof that's bursting with flowers.

Green Room Villa
RENTAL HOUSE **$$$**

(Map p354; www.vrbo.com/411295; Teahupoo, PK18; house from 21,000 CFP; ⏾) Rent this exquisite three-bedroom, two-bathroom house for a romantic getaway or bring up to seven other people (eight total) for a family or surfing get-together. The house is octagonal-shaped with a huge covered wooden deck, tons of windows, teak flooring, brightly painted walls and a fully equipped kitchen. The quiet, private property is a five-minute walk to Teahupoo's beach.

Reva
PENSION **$$**

(Map p354; ☑40 57 92 16, 87 77 14 28; www.reva-teahupoo.org; Fenua Aihere; bungalows per person with full board 13,000 CFP) 🌿 Reva is in a beautifully isolated place that's only accessible by boat from Teahupoo. It takes full advantage of the waterfront property, with a long pontoon jutting out over the lagoon – great for swimming. There are four well-designed bungalows scattered amid lush gardens. Plenty of activities are on offer to keep you busy if that's what you're after.

La Plage de Maui
TAHITIAN $$

(Map p354; ☑ 87 74 71 74; Vairao, PK7.6; mains 1600-3200 CFP; ☺ 10am-5pm) Dine with your toes in the sand and a view just out the window of fish darting around in the clear blue water – this is by far the best setting for a meal on Tahiti Iti. Best go with the Polynesian plates that usually include steamed fish and local produce like taro and breadfruit.

MO'OREA

POP 17,230

If you've been dreaming of holiday-brochure turquoise lagoons, white-sand beaches, vertical peaks and lush landscapes, you'd be hard pressed to find better than this gem of an island. Hovering less than 20km across the 'Sea of the Moon' from its big sister, Tahiti, Mo'orea absorbs its many visitors so gracefully that its feels surprisingly nontouristy.

Mo'orea has a healthy selection of top-end resorts, but it is also host to a good choice of smaller hotels. There are pretty white-sand beaches, but nothing big and sweeping. The drawcard is the limpid, warm water of the vibrant lagoon. If you need some action, take a hike, go on a whale- or dolphin-watching tour, hire a kayak, or go horse riding.

◉ Sights

The following circuit starts at the airport and moves in an anticlockwise direction, following the northern PK markers.

Temae Beach
BEACH

(Map p366; PK1) The best beach on the east coast, and the widest perhaps in all of French Polynesia, stretches from Teavaro round to the airport. The Sofitel Ia Ora Moorea Beach Resort occupies part of the beach, where there's superb snorkelling in the shallow water and out on the lagoon side of the fringing reef. The public section of Temae Beach, just north of the Sofitel, usually gets crowded on weekends. Do not leave valuables in your car.

★ Cook's Bay
BAY

(PK6 to PK11) The spectacular Cook's Bay is something of a misnomer because Cook actually anchored in Opunohu Bay. With Mt

Rotui as a backdrop, Cook's Bay is a lovely stretch of water. There's no real centre to Cook's Bay; shops, restaurants and hotels are simply dotted along the road.

Distillerie et Usine de Jus de Fruits de Moorea
DISTILLERY

(Map p366; ☑ 40 55 20 00; www.manuteatahiti. com; PK11; ☺ 8.30am-4.30pm Mon-Fri, to 12.30pm Sat) FREE About 300m inland from the coastal road, this juice-processing factory and distillery is well worth a stop. It produces various juices and alcoholic beverages, including yummy liqueurs and a devilish 'Tahitian punch'. The tasting of liqueurs and juices is free. Tours are available at 9am and 2pm from Monday to Thursday and last about 40 minutes. The gift shop sells drinks and souvenirs.

Ta'ahiamanu Beach
BEACH

(Mareto Beach; Map p366; PK14.5) At last, a public beach! Ta'ahiamanu (Mareto) Beach is one of the few public-access beaches on the island. This narrow stretch of white sand is a popular spot for both tourists and locals on weekends. Fear not, you'll find plenty of room to stretch out without bumping anyone else's beach towel. Despite the lack of facilities, it's ideal for splashing about, sunbathing or picnicking. Snorkellers will find plenty of coral and marine life right in front of the beach.

★ Opunohu Bay
BAY

(PK14 to PK18) Magnificent Opunohu Bay feels wonderfully fresh and isolated. The coastal road rounds Mt Rotui, and at about PK14 turns inland along the eastern side of Opunohu Bay. There is less development along here than around Cook's Bay, and it's one of the more tranquil and eye-catching spots on the island. At PK18, a road turns off inland along the Opunohu Valley to the valley *marae* and the *belvédère* (lookout).

Moorea Tropical Garden
FARM

(Map p366; ☑ 87 70 53 63; PK15.5; ☺ 8am-5pm Mon-Sat, to noon Sun) This delightfully peaceful property perched on a small plateau is heaven on earth for the sweet-toothed, who can sample (and buy) homemade organic jams, dried fruits, vanilla and delicious ice creams; there are lots of original flavours, such as *noni* and breadfruit (in season). Freshly squeezed juices are also on offer. If you happen to be there on Friday or Saturday, don't miss out on the Polynesian lunch menu (1500 CFP). Needless to say, the lagoon views are fantastic.

DON'T MISS

PAOPAO & OPUNOHU VALLEYS

From Mo'orea's two great bays, valleys sweep inland, meeting south of the coastal bulk of Mt Rotui. In the pre-European era the valleys were densely populated and the Opunohu Valley was dotted with *marae* (traditional temples), some of which have been restored.

A small *fare* (traditional-style houses) at the **Lycée Agricole** (Agricultural College; Map p366; ☑ 40 56 11 34; Opunohu Valley; ☺ 8.45am-4pm Mon-Sat) sells jams in local flavours and, on occasion, ice cream. If you've got itchy feet, there's a small network of **walking trails** that leads through the estate, in the basin of the caldera.

Past the agricultural college, the valley road comes to a parking area beside the huge **Marae Titiroa & Marae Ahu-o-Mahine** (Map p366; Opunohu Valley). A short way up the road is **Marae Fare Aito** (Map p366; Opunohu Valley) and an adjacent **archery platform**. Beyond Marae Fare Aito the road continues to climb steeply, winding up to the excellent **Belvédère** (Map p366; Opunohu Valley). This lookout is the island's highest point and offers superb views of Opunohu and Cook's Bays.

Magical Mountain VIEWPOINT

(Map p366; PK21; 300 CFP) At PK21, a cement road veers inland and makes a very steep climb to a lookout called 'Magical Mountain', at a height of 209m. It's an arduous, 45-minute walk, but the view over the northern part of the island and the lagoon is mesmerising. The access road is private, so permission must be obtained before entering the property; the owners live in the house across the road from the entrance of the property. Start early before it gets too hot.

Hauru Point BEACH

(PK25-PK30) The coastal road rounds Hauru Point, the northwestern corner of the island, between PK25 and PK30. Hauru Point has one of the best beaches on the island, a narrow but sandy stretch that extends for a couple of kilometres, with turquoise water and good snorkelling. That said, finding your way to the beach is not easy because there's no public access. Your best bet is to walk through the grounds of hotels and have a drink at their beachfront bar or restaurant.

Painapo Beach BEACH

(Map p366; PK33) You can't miss the huge (though falling apart) statue of a tattooed man holding a club at the entrance of this private property overlooking a lovely strip of white sand. In theory, there's an access fee to get to the beach – ask around.

Haapiti VILLAGE

(PK24) The largest village on the west coast, Haapiti is home to the splendid twin-towered Catholic **Église de la Sainte Famille**, which is made of coral and lime. The **Protestant Temple** is another notable building; it's at PK23.5, on the lagoon side of the road.

Vaiare VILLAGE

(PK4) The constant toing and froing of ferry boats and high-speed catamarans at the ferry quay, the busy market scene, and the cars, taxis and buses shuttling visitors around render the 100m or so near the dock area the busiest patch of real estate on Mo'orea.

Toatea Lookout VIEWPOINT

(Map p366; PK0.6) This spot really fits the picture-postcard ideal. Atop the hill north of the Sofitel la Ora Moorea Beach Resort, this lookout affords dazzling views of the hotel, the lagoon mottled with coral formations, the barrier reef and Tahiti in the background.

🏃 Activities

Diving & Snorkelling

Mo'orea is one of French Polynesia's main underwater playgrounds, which is no surprise considering its high visibility and clean waters. Although it can't rival the Tuamotus, it offers relaxed diving, and, for beginners, it's a great place to learn to dive and get certified.

For snorkelling, join an organised lagoon tour or DIY around Hauru Point and its *motu* (islet), around the interior of the reef beyond Temae Beach or off Ta'ahiamanu (Mareto) Beach.

Topdive DIVING

(Map p370; ☑ 40 56 31 44; www.topdive.com; PK25; introductory/single dive 10,000/9800 CFP; ☺ by reservation) This well-established dive shop at Intercontinental Moorea Resort & Spa offers the full range of scuba activities, with Nitrox dives at no extra cost. Six- and 10-dive packages go for 50,000/80,000 CFP and can be used at any of the Topdive centres in French Polynesia (Tahiti, Bora Bora,

Mo'orea

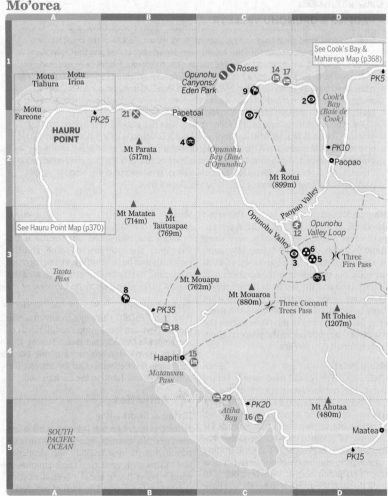

Map labels:
- Motu Tiahura
- Motu Irioa
- Motu Fareone
- PK25
- HAURU POINT
- Mt Parata (517m)
- Mt Matatea (714m)
- Mt Tautuapae (769m)
- Taota Pass
- Mt Mouapu (762m)
- PK35
- Haapiti
- Matauvau Pass
- SOUTH PACIFIC OCEAN
- Atiha Bay
- PK20
- Mt Mouaroa (880m)
- Mt Ahutaa (480m)
- Maatea
- PK15
- Papetoai
- Opunohu Canyons/Eden Park
- Roses
- Opunohu Bay (Baie d'Opunohu)
- Mt Rotui (899m)
- Opunohu Valley
- Paopao Valley
- Opunohu Valley Loop
- Three Firs Pass
- Three Coconut Trees Pass
- Mt Tohiea (1207m)
- See Cook's Bay & Maharepa Map (p368)
- PK5
- Cook's Bay (Baie de Cook)
- PK10
- Paopao
- See Hauru Point Map (p370)

Rangiroa and Fakarava). Snorkelling trips can be arranged. Free pick-up.

Moorea Blue Diving DIVING
(Map p368; ☑87 74 59 99, 40 55 17 04; www.mooreabluediving.com; PK5; introductory/single dive 8000/7500 CFP; ☺by reservation) At Moorea Pearl Resort & Spa, this small dive shop gets good reviews. If you've never been diving before, these are the people to see. Six-/10-dive packages are 42,000/64,000 CFP. Moorea Blue Diving is a member of **Te Moana Diving Pass** (www.temoanadiving.com; 10-dive pass 65,000 CFP), an interisland dive pass that's accepted in 16 dive shops in French Polynesia. Free pick-up.

Moorea Fun Dive DIVING
(Map p370; ☑40 56 40 38; www.moorea-fundive.com; PK26.7; introductory/single dive 7500/6600 CFP; ☺by reservation) This small operation at Hauru Point, on the beach, is the only dive shop on Mo'orea that's not part of a hotel. Run by a friendly French couple, it offers knowledgable and personal service. Two-tank dives (12,500 CFP) are excellent value. Add an extra 500 CFP per dive for Nitrox dives. Free pick-up.

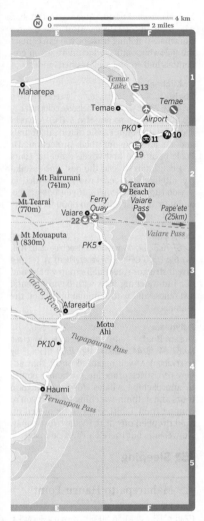

Mo'orea

Lagoon Excursions

The best way to discover Mo'orea's magnificent lagoon is by joining a lagoon excursion. Tours typically visit the Cook's and Opunohu Bays, stop to swim with the rays at a spot off the Intercontinental Moorea Resort & Spa, and picnic and snorkel on a *motu*.

Note that Mo'orea has a long history of shark and ray feeding, but mentalities are changing, and it's now illegal to feed the animals within the lagoon or near a pass. Be aware, though, that some tour guides still do 'bait', using tuna scraps they put in a box.

Hiking

Exhilarating hikes of varying difficulty tackle the lush inland area. Most trails are infrequently used and poorly marked, so it's necessary to use a guide. For a DIY hike, consider the trails at the Lycée Agricole.

Moorea Hiking   HIKING
(✆87 79 41 54; hirohiking@gmail.com; ⊙ by reservation) Hiro Damide is a reputable guide who's very knowledgable about local flora and geology. He charges 5300 CFP per person for the Three Coconut Trees Pass and 7400 CFP for the Opunohu Valley Loop. A minimum of two people is required.

Tahiti Evasion   HIKING
(✆87 70 56 18; www.tahitievasion.com; ⊙ by reservation) Run by a professional guide who offers a wide range of hikes for all levels. He charges

10,500 CFP for Mt Rotui, Mt Mouaputa or Opunohu Valley Loop. Half-day walks, including Three Coconut Trees Pass and Three Firs Pass, are 5200 CFP (minimum two people). This outfit can also organise canyoning outings. Prices include transfers.

Horse Riding

Ranch Opunohu Valley   HORSE RIDING
(Map p366; ☑ 87 78 42 47; Paopao Valley; 2hr rides 5500 CFP; ⊙ by reservation) Two-hour guided rides into the island's interior are available mornings and afternoons. The ranch is up in the Paopao Valley (it's signposted).

Whale & Dolphin Watching

This activity has exploded in recent years. You can count on finding dolphins year-round, but it's the whales, who migrate to Mo'orea from July (or August) to October, who draw in the crowds. Most dive centres run whale-watching trips, or you can contact the following outfits, which have green credentials and employ well-trained guides.

Dr Michael Poole   WILDLIFE WATCHING
(☑ 40 56 23 22; www.drmichaelpoole.com; half-day trip 8000 CFP; ⊙ morning Mon & Thu) A world specialist on South Pacific marine mammals and an advocate for their protection, Dr Poole began the first whale-watching tours and continues to lead the best ones available, although his boats can get crowded in season (up to 26 people). If you book a second tour, the price drops to 6000 CFP.

Moorea Deep Blue   WILDLIFE WATCHING
(☑ 87 76 37 27; www.moorea-deepblue.com; half-day trip 8000 CFP; ⊙ by reservation) A former dive instructor runs small-group whale- and dolphin-watching trips with environmental awareness and with minimal impact on the animals.

Polynesia Dream Boat   WHALE WATCHING, DOLPHIN WATCHING
(☑ 87 34 78 44; full-day trip 7500 CFP; ⊙ by reservation) A well-regarded outfit that adheres to strict procedures when it comes to approaching whales. Also runs lagoon tours and dolphin-watching tours. If you're coming from Tahiti, you can be picked up (and dropped off) at the Vaiare ferry quay. No website, but there's a Facebook page.

🛏 Sleeping

🛏 Maharepa to Hauru Point

Kaveka   RESORT $$
(Map p368; ☑ 40 56 50 50; www.hotel-kaveka-moorea.com; PK7.3; bungalows d 10,000-19,000 CFP; ❄🖭) Popular with English-speaking visitors (the owner is from New Zealand), this few-frills complex on the eastern shore of Cook's Bay has been around for years; although its 30 bungalows are showing their age a tad, they are serviceable and well organised. Note that the cheaper units are fan-cooled.

Motu Iti   BUNGALOW, DORM $$
(Map p366; ☑ 40 55 05 20, 87 74 43 38; www.pensionmotuiti.com; PK13.2; dm 1700 CFP, bungalows d 10,500-12,000 CFP; 🖭) This modest place is an acceptable standby for unfussy travellers. The

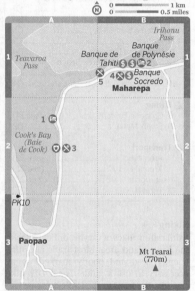

Cook's Bay & Maharepa

five bungalows are tightly packed together on a small property overlooking the lagoon. Be sure to book one of the three sea-facing bungalows (the garden units have blocked views). The 10-bed dorm is a blessing for those watching their francs, but the crude bathrooms downstairs lack maintenance.

Hilton Moorea
Lagoon Resort & Spa
RESORT $$$

(Map p366; ☑40 55 11 11; www.moorea.hilton.com; PK14; bungalows d from 58,000 CFP; ❄🏠🌊) Magnificently laid out with real style and class, the Hilton is one of Mo'orea's best resorts. Of the 103 guest units, 54 are built over the water and come with the requisite glass floor panels for fish-viewing and decks with steps down into the clear, waist-deep water. The garden bungalows have their own (small) plunge pool but are quite squeezed together.

Moorea Pearl Resort & Spa
RESORT $$$

(Map p368; ☑40 55 17 50; www.spmhotels.com; PK5; bungalows d 35,000-75,000 CFP; ❄🏠🌊) The infinity pool here is the island's best. There's a wide range of accommodation options, including duplex units for families as well as less expensive rooms in a two-storey building at the rear of the property. Pick of the bunch are the deluxe garden bungalows, which come with a private pool. Facilities include a restaurant, a spa and a dive centre.

🛏 Hauru Point

Unlike Cook's Bay, Hauru Point has a beach. Though narrow, it's pretty spectacular with turquoise water, a few *motu* out front to swim to and good snorkelling.

Fare Tokoau
BUNGALOW $

(Map p370; ☑87 35 21 98, 87 35 21 97; www. facebook.com/tokoau; PK28.3; bungalows d 9500 CFP; 🏠) Run by a friendly young couple, this great-value abode features a clutch of self-contained bungalows that are scattered on a neat property. The beach here is disappointingly thin, but you can paddle free kayaks out to the white-sand *motu* across the lagoon. It's within walking distance of shops and restaurants, and bikes are available for hire. Cash only.

Camping Nelson
CAMPGROUND, BUNGALOW $

(Map p370; ☑87 78 71 53, 40 56 15 18; www. camping-nelson.pf; PK27; campsites per person 1700-1800 CFP, dm 2400 CFP, d with shared bathroom 5200-5600 CFP, bungalows d from 6800-10,000 CFP; 🏠) A long-time budget favourite

(an easy distinction given the lack of competitors), Camping Nelson boasts a spiffing lagoon frontage (but no shade to speak of). Pitch your tent on the grassy plot within earshot of the gentle surf, or choose one of the claustrophobic cabins in a barrackslike building. For more privacy, consider one of the pricier, more comfortable bungalows.

Les Tipaniers
RESORT $$

(Map p370; ☑40 56 12 67; www.lestipaniers. com; PK25; d 9200 CFP, bungalows d 17,000-19,500 CFP; 🏠) It's a bustling hub of activity on this lovely knuckle of beach jutting out towards a coral-laden stretch of lagoon. Scattered amid a flowery garden, the 22 bungalows aren't going to win any architectural awards but are big, practical (most have kitchens and one to two bedrooms) and clean. Budget tip: it also harbours four cheaper, smaller rooms (book well ahead).

Fare Miti
BUNGALOW $$

(Map p370; ☑40 56 57 42, 87 21 65 59; www. mooreafaremiti.com; PK27.5; bungalows q 13,000-15,000 CFP; 🏠) Deservedly popular and occupying a thin but picturesque stretch of sand (with a small *motu* as a backdrop), Fare Miti has only eight few-frills-but-functional bungalows and a friendly, relaxed atmosphere. They were modernised in 2015 and can sleep up to four (at a pinch). Kayaks and snorkel gear are complimentary. It's all within walking distance of shops and restaurants.

Domloc
VILLA $$

(Map p370; ☑87 72 75 80; www.domlocpolynesie. com; PK25; bungalows from 18,000 CFP; ❄🏠) Domloc is actually a time-share vacation club, but it's run like a hotel – a cool hotel indeed, with eight well-appointed, fully equipped villas. They're closely packed but are buffered by lush gardens, and the beach is just a few steps away from the property. Prices fluctuate wildly according to seasons and school holidays. Free kayaks. Cash only.

Intercontinental
Moorea Resort & Spa
RESORT $$$

(Map p370; ☑40 55 19 19; www.moorea. intercontinental.com; PK25; r & bungalows d from 42,000 CFP; ❄🏠🌊) Spread over more than 10 hectares along the seashore, Mo'orea's biggest resort boasts 147 units and features a host of facilities and amenities, including two pools, two restaurants, two bars, a well-respected spa, a gift shop, a water-sports centre, a full dive shop and a marine-turtle rehabilitation centre.

TAHITI & FRENCH POLYNESIA MO'OREA

Hauru Point

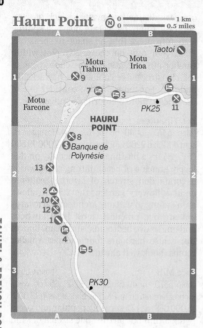

N 0 — 1 km
0 — 0.5 miles

Motu Tiahura
Motu Irioa
Taotoi
Motu Fareone
PK25
HAURU POINT
Banque de Polynésie
PK30

Hauru Point

Haapiti to Temae

Mark's Place Moorea BUNGALOW $
(Map p366; ☑ 40 56 43 02, 87 78 93 65; www.
marksplacemoorea.com; PK23.5; bungalows d/q from
8000/12,000 CFP; 🐾) The vast, lush garden and
creative, smartly finished bungalows – it helps

that the American owner is a carpenter –
make this a good option on Mo'orea, but
we've heard the odd grumble about variable
service. No two units are alike, but they are all
equipped to a high standard and competitively
priced. The amply sized Manu and Opuhi
units are ideal for families.

Moorea Surf B&B GUESTHOUSE $
(Map p366; ☑ 87 70 80 29; mooreasurfbnb.wix.
com/moorea-surf-bnb; PK20.3; d/q without bathroom incl breakfast 10,500/13,000 CFP; 🐾) More
a guesthouse than a B&B, this venture is
popular with unfussy travellers and surfers
lured by the proximity of the Haapiti surf
break. Owner Tama speaks English and can
guide you to the spot for 4000 CFP (two
hours). Accommodation-wise, it consists
of four pokey, wood-panelled rooms in a
chaletlike building. There's a communal
kitchen, or you can order a meal (2500 CFP).

★Résidence Linareva BUNGALOW $$
(Map p366; ☑ 40 55 05 65; www.linareva.com;
PK34.5; studios & bungalows d 16,700-23,100 CFP;
❄🐾) Résidence Linareva has a great reputa-
tion and features a cluster of well-furnished,
self-contained bungalows in a lush garden by
the lagoon. What's missing is a swimmable
beach, but there's great snorkelling off the
long pontoon jutting out over the lagoon.
If you don't mind the isolated location (a
vehicle is essential), it's a great place to stay.

Green Lodge BUNGALOW $$
(Map p366; ☑ 87 77 62 26, 40 56 31 00; www.
greenlodge.pf; Temae; d 16,000-20,000 CFP, bungalows d 20,000-33,000 CFP, all incl breakfast;
❄🐾🏊) This relaxing cocoon with a boutique feel offers all the luxuries of the fancy
resorts, but with enough intimacy and local
flavour to remind you that you're still in Polynesia. The sensitively furnished bungalows
come with all mod cons and orbit around
an alluring pool and a nicely laid-out tropical garden. Evening meals are available on
request (4500 CFP).

Tehuarupe BUNGALOW $$
(Map p366; ☑ 40 56 57 33; www.moorea-paradise.
com; PK22.2; bungalows d 12,000 CFP; 🐾🏊) On
the mountain side of the road, these four sea-
view units are a home away from home, with
lovingly finished interiors, wooden decks, vast
beds and tastefully chosen furniture (but no
air-con). They're spacious and self-contained.
Expect a bit of road noise during the day. The
catch? They're not on the lagoon (though
within hopping distance of the sea). Cash only.

Sofitel la Ora
Moorea Beach Resort RESORT $$$
(Map p366; ☑ 40 55 12 12; www.sofitel-moorea-iaora.com; Temae; bungalows d from 40,000 CFP; ✳ ❄ ☂) No, you're not hallucinating, the lagoon here is *that* turquoise. This excellent, modern Polynesian resort sports 114 units, including 39 opulent overwater bungalows and luxuriously appointed beach and garden units. It's on the best beach on the island. The list of facilities is prolific, with two restaurants, a wonderful spa, a small pool and a diving centre.

✗ Eating

There's a good range of independent restaurants on Mo'orea, and Maharepa, Cook's Bay and Hauru Point are the island's dining epicentres. Many hotels and resorts have in-house restaurants also open to nonguests.

There are quite a few supermarkets and smaller shops around the island where you can buy fresh baguettes and basic supplies.

✗ Maharepa & Cook's Bay

Caraméline CAFETERIA $
(Map p368; ☑ 40 56 15 88; Maharepa; mains 900-2300 CFP; ⊘ 7am-4pm Mon-Sat, to 2pm Sun; ☎) Get all-day American, French or Tahitian breakfasts (from 600 CFP), burgers, pizzas, salads, ice-cream treats and daily specials at this affordable and popular cafeteria right in the centre of Maharepa. Local gourmands rave about the French-style pastries and crepes.

Allo Pizza PIZZA $$
(Map p368; ☑ 40 56 18 22; PK7.8, Cook's Bay; mains 1400-1800 CFP; ⊘ 11am-2pm & 5-8.30pm; ☎) Despite its unpromising location across the road from the *gendarmerie* (police station), this is a great place to taste wood-fired pizzas. There's a huge variety of toppings, including fresh tuna. There's also a small selection of salads and steaks as well as a limited dessert menu – titillate your tastebuds with the unusual 'banana pizza' or a homemade chocolate mousse. Takeaway is available.

Moorea Beach Café TAHITIAN, FRENCH $$$
(Map p368; ☑ 40 56 29 29; www.mooreabeach-cafe.com; PK6.7, Maharepa; mains 1600-3200 CFP; ⊘ 11am-9pm; ☎) This hip lagoon-front restobar is as adept at serving up light bites as it is heartier meals. The menu is eclectic and inventive, and the breezy, sunset-friendly deck overlooking the water is

superatmospheric. In-house cocktails are very nice too. Free pick-up.

✗ Hauru Point

A L'Heure du Sud SANDWICHES $
(Map p370; ☑ 87 70 03 12; PK25; sandwiches 450-1000 CFP; ⊘ 10.30am-3pm Thu-Tue) Bargain! A great variety of well-stuffed sandwiches (think steak or fish and barbecue sauce stuffed in a baguette) are served at this blue *roulotte* in front of Le Petit Village shopping centre. It also dishes up generous burgers and voluminous salads that are best enjoyed at the tables behind the van. Cash only.

★ Snack Mahana TAHITIAN $$
(Map p366; ☑ 40 56 41 70; PK23.2; mains 1600-2300 CFP; ⊘ 11.30am-2.30pm Tue-Sat) In a sublime location overlooking the turquoise lagoon, breezy Mahana is a heart-stealing open-air *snack*. Linger over burgers, a plate of grilled *mahimahi* (dorado) or tuna sashimi while savouring the lagoon views. Light years away from the glitz usually associated with French Polynesia, it can't get more mellow than this. So Mo'orea. Cash only.

Crêperie Toatea CREPERIE $$
(Map p366; ☑ 40 55 11 11; Hilton Moorea Lagoon Resort & Spa, PK14; mains 1300-3100 CFP; ⊘ 6.30-10pm) Not your average creperie, this venture is renowned for its gourmet crepes prepared to order by an Alsatian chef. Where else could you savour a crepe stuffed with fresh fish in white-wine sauce? Another draw is the setting: it's inside the Hilton Moorea, on the pontoon that leads to the overwater bungalows (nonguests are welcome).

Le Lézard Jaune Café FUSION $$
(Map p370; ☑ 40 56 35 00; PK27.3; mains 2200-3100 CFP; ⊘ 6.30-9.30pm Wed-Sun; ☎) A surprisingly hip restaurant inside a house complete with dark-wood interior, this cool culinary outpost opened in 2015 specialises in creative fish and meat dishes *a la plancha* (grilled). For dessert, don't miss the impressive caramelised (or flambéed) banana or pineapple. Free pick-up.

Les Tipaniers FRENCH, ITALIAN $$
(Map p370; ☑ 40 56 12 67; PK25; mains 1500-2900 CFP; ⊘ 6.30-9.30pm) Part of the eponymous hotel, this elegant roadside restaurant serves up wholesome Italian and French-inspired dishes, including pizzas, pastas, salads, fish and meat dishes. Dim lighting contributes to romantic dining under a natural thatched roof.

Beach Café
INTERNATIONAL $$

(Map p370; ☑40 56 12 67; Les Tipaniers, PK25; mains 1400-2500 CFP; ☺11.30am-2.15pm) As the name suggests, this eatery has a fabulous beach frontage. After a morning spent paddling across the lagoon, reenergise with a copious salad, a juicy burger or a plate of spag. Good sandwiches (500 CFP) too. It's part of Les Tipaniers hotel, but nonguests are welcome.

Coco d'Isle
INTERNATIONAL $$

(Map p370; ☑40 56 59 07; PK27.3; mains 1400-3000 CFP; ☺6.30-9.30pm Mon-Sat) Don't be discouraged by the modest exterior and the unspectacular location on the main road. The cool sand floor – delicious between your toes – is a nice touch, although the plastic chairs mar the experience a bit. The food is a crowd-pleasing mix of steaks, fish dishes, seafood, salads and pizzas. Free pick-up.

★ Le Coco's Moorea
FUSION $$$

(Map p370; ☑40 55 15 14; PK24.8; lunch mains 2200 CFP, menus 6000-14,000 CFP; ☺6-9.30pm Mon-Thu, 11.30am-9.30pm Fri-Sun; ☏) This posh restaurant was designed with couples in mind – the widely spaced tables, attentive service, dim lighting and strong design-led interior create a suitably romantic atmosphere. The menu drips with panache, with an inventive mix of local ingredients and European flair. Lunch specials are a bargain. Needless to say, the wine list is top-notch. Alas, there are no direct lagoon views.

Le Mayflower
FRENCH $$$

(Map p370; ☑40 56 53 59; PK27; mains 2300-3600 CFP; ☺11.30am-1.45pm Wed-Fri, 6.30-9.30pm Tue-Sun) The G-spot for local gourmands. A neoclassical French menu puts the emphasis on fish and meat dishes with the addition of locally grown (or caught) ingredients. The signature dish? Lobster ravioli. Thanks to subdued lighting and elegant furnishings, it manages to be atmospheric and snug despite its location on the main road. Free pick-up.

✗ Motu Tiahura

Coco Beach
INTERNATIONAL $$

(Map p370; ☑87 72 57 26; Motu Tiahura; mains 1300-2700 CFP; ☺11.30am-2.30pm Wed-Sun, Tue-Sun during school holidays) This friendly eatery with a casual atmosphere has an idyllic setting on Motu Tiahura that is guaranteed to help you switch to 'relax' mode. The choice is limited and prices are a bit inflated, but the food is fresh and tasty – the octopus salad

will certainly win your heart. Bookings are essential on weekends. Cash only.

You can get a boat over to the *motu* (700 CFP per person return) from the mainland; call ahead.

🍷 Drinking & Entertainment

The big hotels have bars where all are welcome to enjoy a predinner drink, and many restaurants are good spots for a sunset tipple. A couple of times a week, the bigger hotels organise excellent Polynesian music and dance performances by local groups.

ℹ Information

Many hotels and pensions have wi-fi access. There's a medical centre in Afareaitu as well as several private doctors and three pharmacies. The Banque Socredo across from the quay at Vaiare has an ATM. There are banks and ATMs clustered around the small shopping centre in Maharepa near PK6. In Le Petit Village (the Hauru Point shopping centre) there is an ATM of the Banque de Polynésie.

ℹ Getting There & Away

There's less than 20km of blue Pacific between Tahiti and Mo'orea, and getting from one island to the other is simplicity itself.

AIR

Air Tahiti (☑40 86 42 42; www.airtahiti.pf) flies between Mo'orea and Pape'ete (4900 CFP one way, one to three daily), Huahine (14,000 CFP one way, three weekly), Ra'iatea (16,000 CFP one way, five weekly) and Bora Bora (22,000 CFP one way, daily).

BOAT

It's a breezy ride between Tahiti and Mo'orea. First departures in the morning are usually around 6am; the last trips are around 4.30pm or 5.30pm. If you are bringing a car, it's best to book in advance.

Aremiti 5 (Map p366; ☑40 56 31 10, 40 50 57 57; www.aremiti.pf; adult/child 1500/950 CFP) This catamaran jets to and from Mo'orea in about 35 minutes, three times daily from Monday to Friday. For a bike/car, it costs 250/5000 CFP.

Aremiti Ferry 2 (Map p366; ☑40 56 31 10, 40 56 57 57; www.aremiti.pf; adult/child 1500/950 CFP) Runs three to five times daily between Pape'ete and Mo'orea and takes about 45 minutes to cross. For a bike/car, it costs 250/5000 CFP.

Terevau (Map p366; ☑40 50 03 59; www.terevau.pf; adult/child 1200/600 CFP) Runs four to six times daily between Pape'ete and Mo'orea and takes about 35 minutes. It costs 240/4200 CFP for a bike/car.

❶ Getting Around

The coastal road is about 60km. Getting around Mo'orea without a car or scooter is not that easy. Distances aren't great but are often a bit too far to walk. Bear in mind that many of the restaurants will pick you up for free if you call them.

TO/FROM THE AIRPORT & QUAY

All ferries dock at the quay in Vaiare. In principle, buses (300 CFP) meet all *Aremiti 5* arrivals and departures but not the *Aremiti* ferry. Mo'orea's taxis are notoriously expensive: from the airport to the Intercontinental Moorea Resort & Spa will cost about 4500 CFP.

The airport is in the island's northeastern corner. Most hotels offer airport transfers.

CAR

On Mo'orea having your own wheels is very useful but expensive.

Albert Location (☑ 40 56 19 28, 40 56 33 75; www.albert-transport.net; ☺ daily by reservation) Has three outlets around the island and can deliver to your hotel. Scooters are 6000 CFP for 24 hours. Also rents bikes (2000 CFP a day).

Avis (☑ 40 56 32 61, 40 56 32 68; www. avis-tahiti.com) At the ferry quay at Vaiare, Intercontinental Moorea Resort & Spa and Club Bali Hai. It can deliver to your hotel. Negotiate, but figure on 8800 CFP per day for a small car.

Europcar (Map p366; ☑ 87 73 32 40, 40 56 28 64; www.europcar-tahiti.com; Vaiare) At ferry quay at Vaiare. Can deliver to your hotel. Prices start at 7700 CFP.

SCOOTER & BICYCLE

Bikes can be rented or are sometimes offered for free by many hotels and pensions.

Moorea Fun Bike (☑ 87 70 96 95; ☺ daily by reservation) Offers scooters/bikes for 5500/1900 CFP for 24 hours. It can deliver to your hotel.

Rent a Bike – Rent a Scooter (☑ 87 71 11 09; www.rent-a-bike-moorea.e-monsite.com; ☺ daily by reservation) Scooters cost 5500 CFP per 24 hours. It can deliver to your hotel.

HUAHINE

POP 6430

Huahine is immaculately tropical and effortlessly Polynesian. Lush and scarcely developed, this is an island to visit for extreme calm, communing with nature and a genuine taste of culture. There are plenty of opportunities for diving, surfing, snorkelling, exploring top-notch archaeological sites and horse riding, but the beauty of this place is just how easy it is to relax and do very little at all.

Huahine feels like one island but in fact it's two, connected by a short bridge: Huahine Nui (Big Huahine), to the north, is home to the bustling little village of Fare and most of the main tourist and administrative facilities. Rugged and isolated Huahine Iti (Little Huahine), to the south, offers the islands' best beaches, azure lagoons and a serene, get-away-from-it-all atmosphere.

◉ Sights

◉ Huahine Nui

This 60km clockwise circuit of the larger island starts at Fare.

Fare TOWN, BEACH

A visit to tiny Fare almost feels like stepping back in time, so perfectly does it capture the image of a sleepy South Seas port. There's not a lot to do, but that's part of Fare's appeal. Check out the colourful waterside market and a few creative boutiques, or hire a bicycle and just pedal around a bit.

Maeva VILLAGE

Prior to European influence, Maeva village, about 7km east of Fare, was the seat of royal power on the island. It's mostly famous for its concentration of pre-European **archaeological sites**, including a host of **marae** scattered along the shoreline and also up the slopes of Matairea Hill.

Le Jardin de Corail BEACH

If solitude is what you're seeking, head for this secluded beach at the southern tip of Motu Ovarei, just off the now-defunct Sofitel. It features shade trees, white sand, calm waters, and healthy coral gardens a few finkicks away.

Huahine Nui Pearls & Pottery FARM

(Map p374; ☑ 87 78 30 20; www.huahine-pearl farm.com; ☺ 10am-4pm Mon-Sat, to noon Sun) **FREE** This little pearl shop is located on a pearl farm in the middle of the lagoon and also features the work of the founder, renowned potter Peter Owen. From Faie a ferry departs for the studio every 15 minutes from 10am to 4pm. You'll be given a demonstration of pearl farming and have an opportunity to browse the pearl jewellery collection.

Huahine

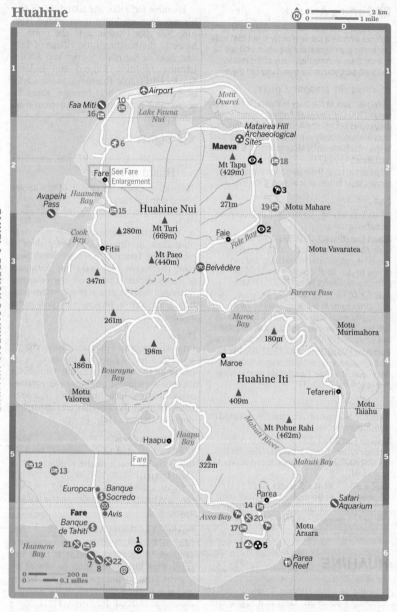

Faie VILLAGE

The coast road turns inland beside narrow Faie Bay to the village of Faie. Huahine's famous **blue-eyed eels** can be seen in the river just over the bridge – buy a can of sardines from the stand here and handfeed them if you're brave enough. Inland from Faie it's a steep climb to the **belvédère** on the slopes of Mt Turi. From this high point, the road drops even more steeply to the shores of Maroe Bay.

Huahine

◉ Huahine Iti

Start at the village of Maroe, on the south side of Maroe Bay, and head clockwise to **Marae Anini** (Map p374), the community *marae* on the island's southern tip. Made of massive coral blocks, this large coastal *marae* was dedicated to 'Oro (the god of war) and Hiro (the god of thieves and sailors). Beside Marae Anini, **Anini Beach** is a lovely spot for a picnic.

Some of the best **beaches** around Huahine Iti are found on the southern peninsula and along its western shore around Avea Bay.

⚡ Activities

Diving & Snorkelling

Huahine has two scuba centres offering magnificent dives for all experience levels.

Mahana Dive   DIVING
(☑87 73 07 17; www.mahanadive.com; single dive 6200 CFP) This outfit in Fare is run by English-speaking Annie and offers hands-on beginner dives as well as a slew of personalised trips for experienced divers. It also charges 7000 CFP for an introductory dive and 23,200 CFP for a four-dive package. It's part of the Te Moana Diving Pass.

Pacific Blue Adventure   DIVING
(☑40 68 87 21; www.divehuahine.com; single dive 6200 CFP; ☺Mon-Sat) A friendly centre on the quay at Fare. It's part of the Te Moana Diving Pass.

Lagoon Excursions

Various lagoon tours are offered on Huahine, with stops for snorkelling, swimming, a pearl-farm visit and a *motu* picnic. A minimum number of participants is required, so book ahead through your pension.

Horse Riding

La Petite Ferme   HORSE RIDING
(☑40 68 82 98; lapetiteferme@mail.pf; 2hr trips from 7500 CFP) To see the island from the back of a horse, head to this equestrian centre between Fare and the airport. The two-hour ride through coconut plantations and around the shore of Lake Fauna Nui is truly enchanting. Longer excursions include an all-day ride (18,000 CFP), which includes a visit to a vanilla plantation, and a stop for a picnic and snorkelling.

Hiking

There are no clearly marked trails on Huahine and the occasional paths in the interior grow over quickly if they're not maintained (which is usually the case) so DIY hikes are limited. The *marae* walk at Maeva is the most interesting option (although we suggest hiring a guide who can explain the cultural significance of the archaeological sites). Other walks require a guide.

Surfing

Huahine has some of the best and most consistent surf in French Polynesia, best tackled by experienced surfers. Local surfers can be very possessive, however, so be respectful.

Kayaking

Huahine provides opportunities to dip a paddle around the quiet lagoon. You can steer to Hana Iti Beach, Motu Araara or any other *motu*, but bear in mind that many of the *motu* belong to local families: don't treat the land as yours to explore without

WORTH A TRIP

HANA ITI BEACH

Here's a secret spot (shhh): the beach of the former Hana Iti Hotel. This dreamlike cove lapped by lapis-lazuli waters offers a nice patch of sand backed by lush hills, with a row of palm trees leaning over the shore. There's no access road; get there by kayak or hire a dinghy.

permission. Most places to stay either hire out or offer free sea kayaks for guests' use.

🛏 Sleeping

🛏 Huahine Nui

Most places are either right in town or a few kilometres to the north or south.

★ Tifaifai Motu Mahare   BUNGALOW $
(☎87 77 07 74; www.tifaifai-et-cafe.com; bungalows d/tr 8000/9900 CFP) This retreat on a dreamy, coconut-clad, surf-lapped *motu* has two authentic Polynesian (think: rustic), sand-floored, thatched bungalows with bathrooms (cold-water showers). Solar panels provide electricity. There are lovely swimming and snorkelling spots just offshore and the *motu* is edged with lovely white-sand beaches. Dinner is often available if you order in advance (2000 CFP) and there's an impeccable communal kitchen.

Tifaifai & Café   B&B $
(☎87 77 07 74; www.tifaifai-et-cafe.com; s/d incl breakfast 5900/7900 CFP; 🐾) Isolated out on Motu Ovarei, this is a place for a back-to-nature escape. Run by the affable Flora, it exudes low-key vibes and features two comfy rooms in the owner's house. The house overlooks a stretch of coral-and-sand beach that isn't swimmable, but La Jardin de Corail is a short walk away. You can order dinner (2000 CFP). Cash only.

Pension Fare Ara   PENSION $
(☎87 74 96 09; www.fare-ara.blog.fr; s/d 6000/7000 CFP, 2-bedroom apartment 8500-12,500 CFP; 🐾) One kilometre south of Fare, this hidden block of large, clean apartments and studios, all with kitchens, offers a great deal for self-caterers who want to be close to town. The units and flowery garden are impeccably kept by host Tinau, who takes many extra steps to ensure his guests are happy and comfortable.

Chez Guynette   GUESTHOUSE $
(☎40 68 83 75; www.pension-guynette-huahine. com; dm 2000 CFP, r from 4900 CFP; 🐾) This excellent-value place right in the centre of Fare – it's in front of the quay – offers seven simple but comfortable rooms with fans and bathrooms (with hot water). The eight-bed dorm is spacious and clean (though not at all private), there's a big communal kitchen and the reasonably priced terrace restaurant has the best people-watching this side of Pape'ete.

Meherio   PENSION $
(☎40 68 80 52; meherio.huahine@mail.pf; s/d incl breakfast 8400/10,500 CFP; 🐾) Situated about 150m from a stunning beach with great snorkelling, and only a short stroll from Fare, the rooms here surround a convivial little dining area and flowery garden. Room exteriors are woven bamboo, interiors have lots of colourful local fabrics, and two units are wheelchair accessible. Local-style three-course meals (dinner is 2650 CFP) are available on request.

Rande's Shack   BUNGALOW $$
(☎40 68 86 27; randesshack@mail.pf; bungalows 12,500-16,500 CFP; 🐾) Great for families and a long-time surfer favourite. American Rande and his lovely Tahitian wife give a character-filled welcome and offer two great-value self-catering houses, one of which sleeps up to six people. While the houses aren't fancy, they're spotless, have mosquito screens, are well-maintained and are located on a small beach perfect for swimming and snorkelling, a short walk from Fare.

Fare Maeva   BUNGALOW $
(☎40 68 75 53; www.fare-maeva.com; d/bungalows d 7500/13,000 CFP; ❄🐾🏊) On a coral-rock beach (not good for swimming), this place has elementary bungalows sleeping two to four people, all with kitchens. Five room units are smaller versions of the bungalows. The on-site restaurant won't win any dining awards but expect a great time when a band shows up (along with many local revellers) for dinner- and dancing-nights.

★ Maitai Lapita Village   RESORT $$$
(☎40 68 80 80; www.hotelmaitai.com; bungalows d from 29,000 CFP; ❄🐾🏊) 🏊 The Maitai isn't just another luxury resort. No overwater units here, but an array of creatively designed bungalows around a small lake complete with water-lilies. All units mimic *fare va'a* (outrigger-canoe huts). They're not just posh

and huge, they also blend into the environment. The beachfront restaurant serves fine food at reasonable prices and there's fantastic swimming mere steps away.

Huahine Iti

The (marginally) smaller island has several ideally situated places, as well as the most beautiful beaches and widest lagoon.

Hiva Plage   CAMPGROUND, GUESTHOUSE $
(⌨40 68 89 50, 87 78 19 10; teriitetumu@mail.pf; campsites for 1/2 people 1300/1800 CFP, s/d without bathroom 2800/5000 CFP; 🖥) Run by friendly Terii Tetumu (a licensed hiking guide) and his French wife, the green location here bordering a white coral seashore is the kind of place where you lose track of the days. Pitch your tent on the grass or choose one of the small, very basic rooms; wherever you chose you'll be lulled by trade winds and lapping waves.

Moana Lodge   PENSION $$
(⌨87 35 60 98; www.moanalodge.jimdo.com; bungalows incl breakfast 12,500-14,500 CFP; 🖥) This new place has three dark wooden bungalows that are spacious and sparsely elegant and only steps from an arc of white sand and blue lagoon. The whole place sits on a large lawn of soft Japanese grass – perfect for kids. Tailor-made boat tours are available (from 5000/9500 CFP for a half-/full day), as are fresh and healthy lunches and dinners (2500 CFP) on request.

Transfers, bikes, kayaks and snorkelling equipment are all free.

Relais Mahana   RESORT $$$
(⌨40 68 81 54; www.relaismahana.com; bungalows d 22,200-34,900 CFP; 🖥🖥🖥) This hotel is on what's arguably the best beach on Huahine, and there's a sensational coral garden just offshore. Bungalow interiors are tastefully decorated with local art in soothing muted colours, and most bathrooms have indoor-outdoor showers in private minigardens. Not all units have sea views, but there's a sense of luxury, especially with the pricier choices.

Eating

Chez Guynette   TAHITIAN $
(⌨40 68 83 75; mains 800-1900 CFP; ⊙7.30am-2.30pm Mon-Sat, to 1.30pm Sun) Fare's best coffee plus fresh fruit juices, breakfast dishes and light meals are served on a lively open-air terrace. The tuna steak and the

skewered *mahimahi* certainly won our heart. Brilliant value.

Roulottes   TAHITIAN, INTERNATIONAL $
(mains 1000-1500 CFP; ⊙11am-2pm & 6-9pm) The quayside *roulottes* are Huahine's best bargain for cheap eats. Huge portions of fish, chicken, burgers, steaks and chips are the order of the day, but there are also pizzas, crepes and ice cream. During the day walk a little further south and look for the vendor selling delicious *uru* (breadfruit) chips.

Huahine Yacht Club   TAHITIAN $$
(⌨40 68 70 81; mains 1600-2400 CFP; ⊙11am-2pm & 6-9pm) In a great location right on the lagoon, this lively restaurant is a favourite local watering hole and the best place to eat around Fare. With polished oyster shells nailed to the walls and lights strewn from the thatched ceiling, it has a beach-bar vibe and cooks a delicious shrimp curry.

★Chez Tara   TAHITIAN $$$
(⌨40 68 78 45; mains 1300-3500 CFP; ⊙11.30am-9pm) One of Huahine's unexpected gems, Chez Tara is easily the best place on the island to sample Tahitian specialities. Head here on Sundays for its legendary *ma'a Tahiti* (served buffet-style at noon; 3500 CFP), which should satisfy all but the hungriest of visitors. It's in a great location, right on the lagoon. Bookings essential.

ℹ Information

Ao Api New World (⌨40 68 70 99; per hour 1000 CFP; ⊙8.30am-7pm Mon-Fri) Internet access with a view of Fare's port. It's upstairs.

Banque de Tahiti (⊙8.15am-noon & 1-3.30pm Mon-Fri) Currency exchange and ATM.

Banque Socredo (⊙7.30-11am & 1.30-4pm Mon-Fri) Currency exchange and ATM.

Post Office (OPT; ⊙7.15am-3.15pm Mon-Thu, to 2.15pm Fri; 🖥) Internet and wi-fi access (with the Manaspot network).

ℹ Getting There & Away

Huahine, the first of the Leeward Islands, is 170km west of Tahiti and 35km east of Ra'iatea and Taha'a.

AIR

Air Tahiti (⌨40 86 42 42; www.airtahiti.pf) has an office on the main street in Fare. Destinations include Pape'ete (14,000 CFP, 35 minutes, daily), Ra'iatea (8200 CFP, 15 minutes, daily),

Bora Bora (10,500 CFP, 20 minutes, daily) and Mo'orea (16,300 CFP, 30 minutes, daily).

BOAT

Two cargo ships, the *Hawaiki Nui* and the *Taporo VII*, make two trips a week between Pape'ete and Bora Bora (via Huahine, Ra'iatea and Taha'a).

ℹ Getting Around

TO/FROM THE AIRPORT

Huahine's airport is 2.5km north of Fare. Pensions and hotels will arrange taxi transfers (sometimes included in the tariff).

CAR

A sealed road follows the coast all the way around both islands. Huahine's car-hire operators will deliver directly to the airport or to your hotel. Public rates are exorbitant – from 9200 CFP per day – but discounts are available if you book through your hotel or pension. There are two petrol stations in Fare.

Avis (☑ 40 68 73 34) Next to the Mobil petrol station in Fare, it also has a counter at the airport.

Europcar (☑ 40 68 82 59) The main agent is north of the centre of Fare near the post office; there are also counters at the airport and Relais Mahana (p377).

SCOOTER & BICYCLE

You can hire bicycles from Europcar for about 2000 CFP a day. For scooters, count on 6200 CFP for 24 hours.

RA'IATEA & TAHA'A

Ra'iatea and Taha'a are encircled by a common lagoon, but the two islands couldn't be more different. Ra'iatea is high, imposing and fiercely independent, has the second-biggest town in French Polynesia after Pape'ete and is considered by many to be the spiritual seat of the Polynesian Triangle (a region of the Pacific with three island groups at its corners: Hawai'i, Easter Island and New Zealand). Taha'a, on the other hand, has graceful low hills, is famous for its sweet-scented vanilla and is arguably the quietest of the Society Islands. Both islands are ideal places to explore a mysterious and wild-feeling Polynesia.

The islands have few beaches but the reef is dotted with secluded white-sand, palm-fringed, blue-lagoon *motu*.

Ra'iatea

POP 12,832

Ra'iatea is the second largest of the Society Islands after Tahiti and also the second most important economic centre, but its lack of beaches has left it relatively off the tourist radar. What dominates here are the high, steep mountains and the vast, reef-fringed lagoon. The capital, Uturoa, is the only real town; explore the rest of the island and you'll find an intensely calm, back-to-nature reality.

Ra'iatea is home to Marae Taputapuatea, once the most important traditional temple in Polynesia, which many believe still exudes power today. What is undeniable is that the island emanates a hard-to-pinpoint, mysterious energy that you won't feel anywhere else in French Polynesia.

◉ Sights

Bustling **Uturoa** blends seamlessly into **Avera**. From here the road follows the contours of the narrow and magnificent **Faaroa Bay**. After going round the base of the bay and crossing Faaroa River, you reach the inland turn-off to the south coast. From the turn-off, the road runs to a **belvédère**, with great views of Faaroa Bay, the coast and the surrounding mountains, before dropping down to the south-coast road. If you don't take the turn-off to the south coast, the road winds around the lush south coast of Faaroa Bay and through the village of **Opoa** to Marae Taputapuatea, which had immense importance to the ancient Polynesians.

The stretch of road from Marae Taputapuatea to **Tevaitoa** is the most remote part of Ra'iatea. The road wriggles along the coast past agriculture and mucky beaches backed by blue lagoon. The road then passes the megabucks **Apooiti Marina**. With a few shops, yacht-charter companies, a restaurant, a bar and a diving centre, it's a pleasant place to stop for a sunset cocktail. From the marina the road passes by the airport before circling back to Uturoa.

🏃 Activities

Diving & Snorkelling

There are about 15 dive sites along the east and west coasts and around Taha'a. Highlights include the superb **Teavapiti Pass** (Ra'iatea) and the **Nordby** (Ra'iatea), the only real wreck dive in French Polynesia.

MARAE TAPUTAPUATEA

The most important *marae* (traditional temple) in French Polynesia, sprawling Marae Taputapuatea dates from the 17th century. This was the centre of spiritual power in Polynesia when the first Europeans arrived, and its influence was international: *ari'i* (chiefs) from all over the Maohi (Polynesian) world, including the Australs, the Cook Islands and New Zealand, came here for important ceremonies.

The main part of the site is a large paved platform with a long *ahu* (altar) stretching down one side. At the very end of the cape is the smaller **Marae Tauraa**, a *tapu* (taboo) enclosure with a tall 'stone of investiture', where young *ari'i* were enthroned. The lagoonside **Marae Hauviri** also has an upright stone, and the whole site is made of pieces of coral.

Some of the reef *motu* are splendid and perfect for swimming or snorkelling. Ask at your hotel about renting a boat or joining a lagoon tour.

Hemisphere Sub   DIVING
(☑ 40 66 12 49, 87 72 19 52; www.hemispheresub. com; single/2-tank dive 6500/12,300 CFP) This operation based at the Apooiti Marina has excellent gear and well-trained staff. It offers dives on the east and west coasts as well as around Taha'a. It also charges 7500 CFP for an introductory dive and 36,000 CFP for a six-dive package and is included on the Te Moana Diving Pass (p366).

Te Mara Nui   DIVING
(☑ 40 66 11 88, 78 72 60 19; www.temaranui. pf; Uturoa Marina; single dive 6200 CFP) This small outfit offers personalised service. It charges 6800 CFP for an introductory dive and 37,500 CFP for a certification course.

Hiking

Good walking opportunities include the walk up to the **Temehani Plateau**; the short climb up **Mt Tapioi**, near Uturoa; and the **Three Waterfalls walk**, on the east coast.

With the exception of the walk to Mt Tapioi, a guide is required. Try **Thierry Laroche** (☑ 40 66 20 32, 87 77 91 23; raiatearando@mail. pf), who charges 4000 CFP per person (8000 CFP for Temehani Plateau).

Yachting

Ra'iatea's central position in the Society Islands, and its fine lagoon, have helped make it the yacht-charter centre of French Polynesia. Most operations will offer whatever a customer demands and prepare fully stocked and equipped boats. The following Ra'iatea-based companies are recommended.

Dream Yacht Charter   SAILING
(☑ 40 66 18 80; www.dreamyachtcharter.com) Offers catamaran and monohull cruises in all of French Polynesia's archipelagos.

Moorings   SAILING
(☑ 40 66 35 93; www.moorings.com; Apooiti Marina) This international outfitter has about 16 monohulls and 12 catamarans on offer for custom-crewed or bare-boat cruises in the Leeward Islands.

Sunsail   SAILING
(☑ 40 60 04 85; www.sunsailtahiti.com; Apooiti Marina) Operates a variety of bare-boat charters and crewed cruises in the Leeward Islands and the Tuamotu Islands. Offers monohulls and catamarans.

Tahiti Yacht Charter   SAILING
(☑ 40 66 28 80; www.tahitiyachtcharter.com; Apooiti Marina) Has catamarans and monohulls.

Lagoon Excursions

Boat tours are one of the most fun things you can do with your time. Full-day lagoon tours usually spend all of their their time on the island of Taha'a, but most companies are based on Ra'iatea and pick up from the pier in Uturoa.

Temehani   BOAT TOUR
(☑ 40 66 12 88, 87 77 54 87; www.vacances-tahiti. com) This half-day (7500 CFP) or full-day cruise (9500 CFP) on a monohull takes you to various scenic spots on the lagoon for swimming and snorkelling. The itinerary is flexible. Takes small groups only. Based in Ra'iatea.

Arii Moana Tours   BOAT TOUR
(☑ 87 79 69 72) The only operator that offers full-day tours of Ra'iatea that include snorkelling and swimming stops and a visit to Marae Taputapuatea (9000 CFP, including lunch).

Ra'iatea & Taha'a

N
0 — 5 km
0 — 2.5 miles

SOUTH
PACIFIC
OCEAN

Navette Route

2 ⊙ Patio 🛏11

14
22

🚶 Hipu

Lagon
Tau Tau

7

Motu
Tau Tau

Tapuamu

Taha'a

Tahaa
Location
Voitures

Col
Vaitoetoe

Mt Ohiri
(598m)

Haamene

Faaha

28

27

Motu
Mahae

25 Tiva

Monique
Locations

Haamene
Bay

13

🚶 Tau Tau

Hurepiti
Bay

Pati

3

17

Faaha Bay

Céran Pass (Toahotu Pass)
Motu Atger
(Motu Toahotu)

Joe
Dassin
Beach

21

Vaitoare

Tiva
Pass

Poutoru

Apu
Bay

Apu

Navette Route

Octopus
Hole

Uturoa

8

30
@

Ra'iatea

24

32

31

0 — 100 m

Airport

5
26

Uturoa

See Uturoa
Enlargement

33

PK0

Roses

20

Mt Tapioi
(294m)

6

9

Miri
Miri
Pass

19

PK10

Temehani
Plateau
(800m)

23

10

18

Tevaitoa

Mt Temehani
(821m)

Avera

15

Maire Pass (Iriru)

Motu Iriru

PK10

Faaroa
Bay

Ra'iatea

Te
Avamo'a
Pass

Mt Tefatua
(Toomaru)
(1017m)

PK25

Opoa

4

Tehurui

29

12 PK25

Faaroa River

16

Hotopu
Bay

Motu
Oatara
(500m)

Vaiaau

1

Mt Oropiro
(824m)

PK45

Mt Aahinui
(577m)

Puohine

Faatemu
Bay

PK40 Fetuna

Motu
Nao Nao

Ra'iatea & Taha'a

🛏 Sleeping

🛏 Uturoa & Around

Villa Tonoi   PENSION **$$**
(☑ 87 29 21 79; www.villatonoi.com; PK 1.5; bunga-
lows for up to 4 people 12,000 CFP; 🛜 🏊) It's well
worth the short but steep drive up to these
spotless, modern and comfortable kitch-
en-equipped bungalows with magnificent
views over the Teavapiti Pass to Huahine
(look for whales from your terrace from Oc-
tober to November). But what really stands
out here are friendly hosts Laura and Kevin,
who go above and beyond to ensure their
guests have a great time.

🛏 Around the Island

Pension Manava   PENSION **$**
(☑ 40 66 28 26; www.manavapension.com; PK6;
bungalows d 9500 CFP; 🛜) This is a friendly,
well-managed place with four spacious bun-
galows, all with kitchens and private bath-
rooms (hot water), dotting a tropical garden.
There's a bit of road noise, but nothing to lose
sleep over. For swimming and snorkelling ask
to be dropped off on nearby Motu Iriru (1500
CFP, minimum four people).

**★ Sunset
Beach Motel**   BUNGALOWS, CAMPGROUND **$$**
(☑ 40 66 33 47; www.sunset-raiatea.pf; PK5; camp-
sites per person 1500 CFP, bungalows d 12,000 CFP,
additional people 1500 CFP; 🛜) The location (on
an expansive coconut plantation fronting
the lagoon) alone would make this one of
Ra'iatea's best options, but the 22 bungalows – which are perhaps better described
as small homes – make this one of the best
deals in the islands. It's a particularly great
find for families as the kitchen-equipped
bungalows comfortably sleep four and
they're well spaced out.

Fare Vai Nui   BOUTIQUE HOTEL **$$**
(☑ 40 66 30 96; www.farevainui.com; PK 22.5,
Vaiaau; d 15,000C CFP; 🛜 🏊) A row of small yet
very comfortable and polished wooden bun-
galows line a gorgeous stretch of blue water
with Bora Bora in the distance. Even though
the road sits close by, this part of the island
is so peaceful that few cars drive by. Locals
drive all the way here in decent numbers to
dine at the respected restaurant.

The beach isn't great for swimming, but
you can jump off the pontoon, grab a free
kayak to explore the nearby *motu* or take a
dip in the tiny pool. Run by a French family,

the welcome isn't going to knock your socks off, but it's completely reasonable.

Raiatea Lodge
HOTEL $$

(☑ 40 66 20 00; www.raiateahotel.com; PK8.8; s/d from 19,500/23,500 CFP; ❄ 🛜 🛖) Raiatea Lodge pays elegant homage to colonial architecture, with a two-storey plantation-style building sitting quietly at the back of a coconut plantation. It's a good choice for those looking for comfortable rooms and amenities, including a restaurant and a pool, but with a boutique, intimate vibe. All rooms feature tropically inspired contemporary furnishings and are bright and inviting.

Opeha
PENSION $

(☑ 40 66 19 48; www.pensionopeha.pf; PK10.5; bungalows d incl breakfast 10,000 CFP; ❄ 🛜) A crisp and compact waterfront abode, Opeha has a handful of very white, very clean, kitchen-equipped bungalows, lined up in a row on a tiny, immaculate property. They're charmless but perfectly serviceable, and prices include a copious breakfast, kayaks and bikes. There's a pontoon, but the area is not good for swimming; for a dip, paddle to Motu Iriru.

★ Opoa Beach Hotel
RESORT $$$

(☑ 40 60 05 10; www.hotel-raiatea.com; PK37; bungalows 26,600-30,750 CFP; 🛜 🛖) This small resort with a boutique feel is one of Ra'iatea's top hotels, and it's easy to understand why. An effortless tropical charm pervades the collection of cottages set amid beautifully landscaped gardens. From the outside, the white facades and blue tin roofs lack the wow factor, but each one is artistically decorated with local materials and teak furnishings.

🍴 Eating & Drinking

You'll find small *snack*-style places and a few *roulottes* dotted around the island.

🍴 Uturoa & Around

Uturoa has several well-stocked supermarkets, open Monday to Saturday and some on Sunday morning.

Le Napoli
ITALIAN $$

(☑ 40 66 10 77; www.pizzerialenapoli.com; Uturoa; mains 1400-2400 CFP; ☺ noon-2pm Tue-Fri, 6.30-9pm Tue-Sun) In a reed hut decorated with loads of flowers, this congenial pizzeria near the Avis agency offers a long list of Italian dishes, including pasta, wood-fired pizzas and meat and fish specials.

Brasserie Maraamu
BISTRO $$

(☑ 40 66 46 54; mains 1200-2200 CFP; ☺ 6am-9pm Mon-Fri, noon-3pm Sat & Sun; 🖉) This popular joint serves huge plates of reasonably priced but not otherwise tantalising food, including a handful of tofu-based vegetarian options as well as steaks, poultry and fish. Hinano beer is on tap and breakfasts range from American eggs to Tahitian *poisson cru* (a raw fish dish) and *firifiri* (doughnuts).

La Cubana
BAR

(Uturoa; mains 1200-2200 CFP; ☺ noon-late) More of a watering hole than anything else, this big, open place has the best location in downtown Uturoa, overlooking the water from the port. There's live music, DJs and karaoke some nights but the food is mediocre, mostly pizza and simple fare. Still, it's the only logical place to eat or for a drink in town.

🍴 Around the Island

Bring a picnic if you're travelling around the island as there aren't many opportunities to find a meal during the day.

Vai Nui Restaurant
TAHITIAN $$

(☑ 40 66 30 96; Vaiaau; mains 1600-2900 CFP; ☺ 11.30am-1.30pm & 6.30-9pm Wed-Sun) This lovely little restaurant with views over the water (there's not much of a beach) is worth the drive. Choose from a more upscale, tasty menu of classic French Polynesian dishes like grilled meat or fish in Roquefort or vanilla sauce (among many other choices) or more simple dishes like chow mein and *poisson cru* (raw fish dish). Portions are huge.

Opoa Beach Hotel
SEAFOOD $$$

(☑ 40 60 05 10; PK37; set menu 5000 CFP; ☺ dinner by reservation) At the Opoa Beach Hotel, this is Ra'iatea's most glamorous dining spot. The chef earns raves for her high-flying creative dishes combining fresh produce (fish and shellfish in particular) and spices. The menu changes daily. The decor is elegant and the tables are candlelit, which is perfect for a tête-à-tête. Hotel guests have priority, so reserve early.

Raiatea Lodge
HOTEL RESTAURANT $$$

(☑ 40 66 20 00; PK8.8; mains 2200-3200 CFP; ☺ 11.30am-2pm & 6.30-9pm) For refined dining, opt for the Raiatea Lodge's on-site restaurant. The semioutdoor Zen-style setting is superb and is a great place for a drink as well as a meal. There's sure to be a dish on the extensive menu that suits your palate, but be sure to leave room for dessert.

ℹ Information

Banque de Polynésie (Uturoa; ⊘8.15am–noon & 1-3.30pm Mon-Fri) Currency exchange and ATM.

ITS (Uturoa; per 30min 500 CFP; ⊘8am–noon & 1-5pm Mon-Fri, 8-11.30am Sat) Internet access. Inside the *gare maritime* (boat terminal).

Socredo (Uturoa; ⊘8.15am–noon & 1-3.30pm Mon-Fri) Currency exchange and ATM.

ℹ Getting There & Away

Ra'iatea is 220km northwest of Tahiti and 40km southeast of Bora Bora.

AIR

Air Tahiti (www.airtahiti.pf) has an airport office. The airline operates direct flights from Tahiti (17,200 CFP, 40 minutes, seven to eight daily) with connections onward to Mo'orea (18,360 CFP). There are also direct flights to Bora Bora (8700 CFP, 20 minutes, daily), Huahine (8400 CFP, 20 minutes, daily) and Maupiti (9400 CFP, 20 minutes, two weekly).

BOAT

Ra'iatea is separated from Taha'a by a 3km-wide channel.The *navette* (shuttle boat) services on the **Te Haere Maru** (☑40 65 61 33) run between Uturoa and various stops on Taha'a twice a day, at 5.30am and 11.30am. There is no service on Saturday afternoon or Sunday. The one-way fare is 780 CFP.

There is also a **taxi-boat service** (☑87 74 72 22) between the two islands, which operates daily. It costs 7000 CFP to go to southern Taha'a and 13,700 CFP to get to the north of the island (prices are for two people).

The **Maupiti Express 2** (☑40 67 66 69) travels between Bora Bora, Taha'a and Ra'iatea three days a week. Fares are 5400 CFP one way between Ra'iatea and Bora Bora and 800 CFP to go from Ra'iatea to Taha'a.

The cargo ships *Taporo* and *Hawaiki Nui* also make a stop at Ra'iatea.

ℹ Getting Around

Most island accommodation will pick you up if you have booked (although there may be a charge). A sealed road hugs the coast all the way around the island. The best option to get around is to hire a car. Contact **Hertz** (☑40 66 35 35; www.herz-raiatea.com) or **Moana Rent a Car** (☑87 75 08 30; www.moanarentacar.com). An economy car costs from 6600 CFP for 24 hours.

Taha'a

POP 5301

Larger than you'd think (it's bigger than Mo'orea) and roughly orchid-shaped, this island specialises in two of the most pleasant things French Polynesia has to offer: vanilla and pearls. This befits the subtle and sweet personality of Taha'a, where smiles are as common as hibiscus flowers and the scent of vanilla wafts through the air. There's not much going on, but that's what's so wonderful about this island. Forget the world while soaking in the incredible quiet and natural beauty.

◉ Sights

A 70km sealed road winds around the island and the population is concentrated in eight villages on the coast. Tapuamu has the main quay, Patio is the main town, and Haamene is where the roads around the southern and northern parts of the island meet, forming a figure eight. Apu Bay to the south, Haamene Bay to the east and Hurepiti Bay to the west offer sheltered anchorages.

Maison de la Vanille FARM
(☑65 67 27; ⊘by reservation) FREE On the right of the road into Haamene is this small family-run operation where you can see vanilla preparation and drying processes and also purchase vanilla pods. If you haven't reserved, stop by and see if it's open anyway.

Love Here PEARL FARM
(☑40 65 62 62; ⊘8am-2pm Mon-Fri) FREE An exceptionally friendly, family-run pearl farm right on the seashore, approximately halfway between Tapuamu and Patio. Visitors learn about the technique of grafting to create cultured pearls, as well as the varieties and their characteristics. It has a gift shop that sells mounted and unmounted pearls as well as jewellery. Prices are great.

🏃 Activities

Diving & Snorkelling

Taha'a has one dive centre, but dive centres on Ra'iatea regularly use the sites to the east of the island and will collect you from lodgings in the south of Taha'a. As on Ra'iatea, you have to go to the *motu* for swimming and snorkelling. Some guesthouses will drop you on a *motu* for the day or you can join an organised *pirogue* tour. The healthiest coral gardens are off **Motu Tau Tau**.

JOE DASSIN BEACH

On Taha'a, if you're willing to take a bit of a walk you can get to deserted Joe Dassin Beach, on the southwest side of the island, a 15-minute walk along the coast north of Pati. The beach was once owned and is now named after a famous, classic French singer – sort of the Bing Crosby of France. Ask a local in Pati to show you the trailhead. Bring a picnic and snorkel gear: there's fantastic snorkelling just offshore.

Tahaa Diving   DIVING, SNORKELLING

(☑ 87 24 80 69, 40 65 78 37; www.tahaa-diving. com; single/2-tank dive 8750/15,600 CFP) This low-key operation is located at Le Taha'a Private Island & Spa. Most dive sites involve a 20- to 45-minute boat trip across the lagoon. Snorkelling trips are also on offer. It's part of the Te Moana Diving Pass (p366).

☞ Tours

Tours allow you to get out to those sandy *motu* for swimming and snorkelling and/or to visit local pearl farms, vanilla plantations and the interior via 4X4. Many tour operators are based in Ra'iatea and offer pick-up services from Ra'iatea if you just want to visit Taha'a for the day. Full-day tours range from 8500 CFP to 10,500 CFP. Book ahead as a minimum number of people (usually four) is required.

🛏 Sleeping

🛏 The Island

Chez Louise   CAMPGROUND $

(Tiva; 1000 CFP) Mamie Louise offers campsites on the waterfront next to her restaurant. The views of Bora Bora are sublime. Showers are rudimentary, toilets are inside the restaurant and you can use the kitchen for an extra 500 CFP per day. Louise has no phone or internet access, but she says to just show up, there's always room for everyone.

Titaina   PENSION $$

(☑ 87 29 17 13, 40 65 69 58; www.pension-titaina. com; Poutoru; bungalows d 12,500 CFP; ☎) Near the end of the road north of Poutoru, this delightfully secluded retreat has three bungalows spread out on grassy grounds surrounded by blooming tropical gardens. The bungalows are far from fancy but are prettily decorated and kept scrupulously clean. Your courteous hosts speak English and go above and beyond to ensure you enjoy your stay.

Hibiscus   HOTEL $$

(☑ 40 65 61 06; www.hibiscustahaa.com; Haamene Bay; bungalows d from 10,600 CFP; ☎) The haphazardly run Hibiscus gets mixed reviews, but its promo deals (stay three nights, pay for two) make it a bargain. Seven simply built bungalows of varying sizes and shapes are clustered in an Eden-like garden on a hillside overlooking Haamene Bay. They all have bathroom, terrace and fan, and there are eight free boat moorings with dock access.

Fare Pea Iti   PENSION $$$

(☑ 87 76 98 55; www.farepeaiti.pf; Patio; bungalows d garden/beach 20,000/40,000 CFP; ✳☎▩) This option offers lots of comfort and a beautiful, quiet, white-sand-beach setting with tons of individual attention and a low-key atmosphere. Bungalows are large and dotted with plenty of wood and bamboo touches but won't win any decoration awards. Lap up on-demand tours (3000 CFP) to the pension's own private, idyllic *motu* and plenty of other activity bargains.

🛏 The Motu

Motu digs are set in private paradises that rival (and some would say exceed) the settings of Bora Bora's better resorts.

Pension Atger   PENSION $

(☑ 87 28 26 81; atgertheodore@mail.pf; Motu Atger; bungalows full board per person s/d 10,000/9000 CFP; ☎) Hurrah for *motu* digs without the hefty price tag. This warm, family-run Polynesian retreat on Motu Toahotu has five clean, comfortable and large tiled en suite (cold water) bungalows that open onto the swishing blue Toahotu Pass with views that continue to the lagoon. The atmosphere is delightfully chilled out, swimming and snorkelling are excellent and kayaks are complimentary.

Vahine Island Private Island Resort   RESORT $$$

(☑ 40 65 67 38; www.vahine-island.com; Motu Tuuvahine; bungalows d 51,000-74,000 CFP; ✳☎) The setting here, on a white-beach-clad *motu* with a stretch of manicured coconut palms and views of blue in all directions, can't be matched. This boutique resort hosts an odd mix of a near-elegant style of shells and adornments that feels very Polynesian, with the detached, professional management approach of a chain resort – which many guests love.

La Pirogue Api   RESORT $$$

(☑ 87 27 56 00; www.hotellapirogueapi.com; bungalows d from 55,000 CFP; ☎) Recently relocated to a small and very private *motu*, the handful of massive bungalows here built from polished wood and thatch all have steps that lead directly into a swimming-pool-blue lagoon; views from the tiny islet take in the four high islands along with massive stretches of shimmering blue water. It's intimate, friendly and quite luxurious.

✕ Eating & Drinking

There are shops in each village and a few *roulottes* open around the island at night, but the dining options are very limited. The *motu* resorts all have their own bars, but otherwise your drinking options are limited.

Snack Bellevue   TAHITIAN $

(Faaha; mains 1200 CFP; ⊙ 7am-5pm Tue-Sun) High up on the Faaha crossing road, this rustic but agreeable little eatery has a fantastic view over Faaha Bay. Grab a crepe, sandwich or homemade cake to go, or stay awhile with a heaping portion of the fish of the day.

Tahaa Maitai   TAHITIAN $$

(☑ 40 65 70 85; Haamene; mains 1750-3500 CFP; ⊙ noon-10pm Tue-Sat, to 3pm Sun) Everyone recommends this restaurant right on Haamene Bay not only for its fabulous views but also for its delicious cuisine. The menu features lots of fresh seafood, local fruits and vegetables and delicious French desserts. There's also a long cocktail list, making this a popular local watering hole.

Chez Louise   TAHITIAN $$

(Tiva; mains 1400-1900 CFP; set menu 5500 CFP; ⊙ 8am-10pm) Right beside the lagoon, this very local-style (perhaps a little too local for some people) open-air terrace offers mesmerising views of Bora Bora to the west – a photographer's dream at sunset. Louise cooks simple but good Polynesian specialities, or you can splurge on the amazing 'marina menu', which includes an array of fresh, locally caught shellfish and fish. Cash only.

ⓘ Information

The post offices in Patio and Haamene have an ATM. The Banque Socredo in Patio and the Bank of Tahiti in Haamene also have ATMs. There's internet and wi-fi access at the post offices in Patio and Haamene (with the Manaspot network).

ⓘ Getting There & Away

There is no airport on Taha'a. From the southern tip of Taha'a, the airport on Ra'iatea is only 15 minutes across the lagoon and some hotels will pick up guests from the airport or from the ferry quay at Uturoa on Ra'iatea.

There is a *navette* service between Ra'iatea and Taha'a.

The **Maupiti Express 2** (☑ 40 67 66 99) ferry operates on Wednesday, Friday and Sunday between Bora Bora, Taha'a (Poutoru) and Ra'iatea.

ⓘ Getting Around

There is no public transport on Taha'a. Hiring a car or bike is the only way to see the island independently. **Monique Locations** (☑ 40 65 62 48; Haamene) hires out cars for 10,300 to 14,000 CFP for 24 hours, while **Tahaa Location Voitures** (☑ 40 65 66 75, 87 72 07 71; www.hotel-tahaa. com) charges 8000/10,000 CFP for eight/24 hours. You can save money on Taha'a's ridiculously expensive car costs by hiring a scooter on Ra'iatea and bringing it across on the *navette*.

BORA BORA

POP 9600

Ah, Bora Bora. As you arrive by plane the view says it all. How could you not be mesmerised by this stunning palette of sapphire, indigo and turquoise hues that mix together in modern-art abstractions? And these sand-edged *motu* and soaring rainforest-covered basaltic peaks? With such a dreamlike setting, Bora Bora is, unsurprisingly, a honeymooners' choice. But there's much more to do than clinking glasses with the loved one in a luxurious hotel. The good thing is that you can mix slow-paced sun-and-sand holidays with action-packed experiences. Diving, snorkelling, lagoon tours, hiking and parasailing are readily available.

◉ Sights

Matira Beach   BEACH

(Matira) Bora Bora's only real beach, this stunning stretch of snow white sand and pinch-me-I'm-dreaming turquoise sea is perfect for sunbathing and swimming (but less so for snorkelling). Matira Beach graces both sides

Bora Bora

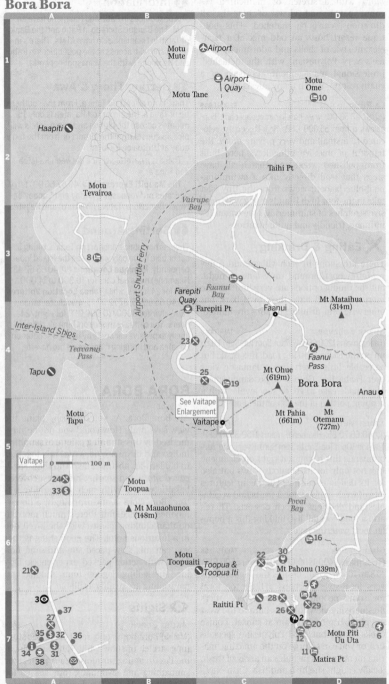

Motu Mute

Airport

Motu Tane

Airport Quay

Motu Ome
10

Haapiti

Motu Tevairoa

Taihi Pt

Vairupe Bay

8

Airport Shuttle Ferry

9

Farepiti Quay

Faanui Bay

Farepiti Pt

Faanui

Mt Mataihua (314m)

Inter-Island Ships

Teavanui Pass

Tapu

23

25

19

Mt Ohue (619m)

Faanui Pass

Bora Bora

Anau

See Vaitape Enlargement

Vaitape

Mt Pahia (661m)

Mt Otemanu (727m)

Motu Tapu

Vaitape

0   100 m

24
33

Motu Toopua

Mt Mauaohunoa (148m)

Povai Bay

21

16

3

37

Motu Toopuaiti

Toopua & Toopua Iti

22   30

Mt Pahonu (139m)

5

27

28   14

35   32

36

Raititi Pt

4   29

26

34   31

38

2

20

Motu Piti Uu Uta

17

6

12

11

Matira Pt

```
   0 _____ 2 km
N  0 _____ 1 mile
```

SOUTH
PACIFIC
OCEAN

☉1 Fitiiu Pt

Motu
Tofari

15🛏

13🛏

18🛏

Motu
Piti
Aau

Aponapu
Bay

Motu Ringo
(Motu Piti
Uu Tai)

7⛵
Motu
Fanfan

Tupitipiti
Pt

Bora Bora

◉ Sights

1	Coastal Defence Guns	E4
2	Matira Beach	D7
3	Vaitape	A7

✦ Activities, Courses & Tours

4	Eleuthera Bora Diving Centre	C7
	Topdive	(see 25)
5	La Plage	D6
	Manu Taxi Boat	(see 20)
6	Rohivai Tours	D7

🛏 Sleeping

7	Bora Bora Camping	E7
8	Bora Bora Pearl Beach Resort & Spa	A3
9	Bora Bungalove	C3
10	Chez Alice & Raphael	D1
11	Chez Robert & Tina	D7
12	Hotel Matira	D7
	Intercontinental Bora Bora Le Moana Resort	(see 12)
13	Intercontinental Bora Bora Resort & Thalasso Spa	F5
14	Le Maitai Bora Bora	D7
15	Le Méridien Bora Bora	F4
16	Rohotu Fare	D6
17	Sofitel Bora Bora Private Island	D7
18	St Régis Resort	F4
19	Sunset Hill Lodge	C4
20	Village Temanuata	D7

✖ Eating

21	Aloe Cafe	A6
22	Bloody Mary's	C6
23	Bora Bora Yacht Club	B4
	Fare Manuia	(see 20)
24	Le St James	A5
25	Maikai Bora Bora	C4
	Matira Beach Burger	(see 2)
26	Restaurant Matira Beach	C7
27	Roulottes	A7
28	Snack Matira	C7
29	Tama'a Maitai	D7
	Tiare Market	(see 5)

🍷 Drinking & Nightlife

| 30 | Tiki Bar | C6 |

ⓘ Information

31	Banque de Polynésie	A7
32	Banque de Tahiti	A7
33	Banque Socredo	A5
34	Bora Bora Tourist Office	A7

ⓘ Transport

35	Air Tahiti	A7
36	Bora Bora Rent a Car – Avis	A7
37	Europcar	A7
38	Maupiti Express 2	A7
	Totara Loca	(see 14)

TAHITI & FRENCH POLYNESIA BORA BORA

DON'T MISS

MAKING THE MOST OF THE MOTU

Aah, the tantalising *motu* (islets) on Bora Bora. All are private, so don't treat the land as yours to explore without permission. There are a few options, though.

La Plage (☑87 70 16 27, 87 28 48 66; www.laplage-borabora.com; Matira Beach; half-/full day 14,000/21,000 CFP; ☺8am-5pm) If you prefer setting your own pace and fancy tootling around the lagoon yourself, La Plage rents small four-seater motor boats that are easy to drive; no licence is required. A detailed map featuring the lagoon is provided, as well as life jackets, and petrol is included. It's based on the beach near hotel Maitai Polynesia Bora Bora. Call for transfers from your hotel.

Manu Taxi Boat (☑87 79 11 62; per person 3000 CFP; ☺9am-4.30pm) Can arrange transfers to **Motu Fanfan**, at the southernmost tip of Motu Piti Aau, for 3000 CFP. It's an idyllic spot, with sunloungers, hammocks, an ablution block and a sensational coral garden just offshore. Meals (3000 CFP, by reservation) and drinks are available. Bring your snorkel gear.

Rohivai Tours (☑87 32 60 46; ☺1-3.30pm) Can drop you off on private **Motu Ringo** (Motu Piti Uu Tai) for 3000 CFP. It usually departs at 1pm and returns at 3.30pm. The *motu* has sunloungers and an ablution block.

of **Matira Point**, a narrow peninsula that extends south into the lagoon.

Vaitape
VILLAGE

The island's main settlement, Vaitape is not the most evocative town, but it's a great place to do a bit of shopping, take care of banking needs and just get a feel for the way locals really live.

Coastal Defence Guns
HISTORIC SITE

(Fitiiu Point; 500 CFP) Up a small hill on the eastern coast, a track peels off to the east and leads to two massive WWII coastal guns and a concrete bunker that were left by the US troops. The walking trail along the ridge starts behind the first house (where you'll pay the entrance fee), at the sharp bend in the road. From the site there are fine views out over the lagoon to the *motu*.

🏃 Activities

Diving & Snorkelling

Diving in the bath-warm waters of Bora Bora is amazing. Sharks (including lemon sharks) rays and other marine life abound, and can be seen in quite shallow waters in the lagoon, or outside the reef. If you're a beginner, you've come to the right place – Bora Bora is a great place to learn to dive or to take a certification course.

No visit to Bora Bora would be complete without a bout of snorkelling. Alas, the best snorkelling spots can't be reached from the shore – you will have to rent a boat or opt for a lagoon tour.

Eleuthera Bora Diving Centre
DIVING

(☑87 77 67 46; www.boradivingcenter.com; Matira; introductory or single dive 9500 CFP; ☺by reservation) Right on Matira beach, this midsized operation (not too big, not too small) gets props for fostering a sociable vibe while maintaining a high standard of service. Two-tank dives (mornings only) cost 17,500 CFP. Various packages starting from 48,000 CFP for six dives (valid for two divers) are also offered. Free pick-up.

Topdive
DIVING

(☑40 60 50 50; www.topdive.com; Vaitape; introductory/single dive 10,000/9800 CFP; ☺by reservation) This well-oiled diving machine offers the full range of scuba activities and prides itself on offering Nitrox dives at no extra charge. Two-tanks dives are 19,000 CFP. It charges 50,000/80,000 CFP for a six-/10-dive package that can be used at any of the Topdive centres in French Polynesia (Tahiti, Mo'orea, Rangiroa and Fakarava). Free pick-up.

Lagoon Excursions

Taking a cruise around Bora Bora's idyllic lagoon will be one of the highlights of your trip to French Polynesia. You'll get the chance to swim and snorkel in otherwise inaccessible places. It will cost about 6000 CFP to 7000 CFP for half-day trips and 9500 CFP for whole-day trips. Full-day tours include a *motu* barbecue. There are plenty of operators available. You can book through your pension or hotel.

Undersea Walks

Aqua Safari WATER SPORTS

(☑87 28 87 77; www.aquasafaribora.com; trips 9500 CFP; ☺by reservation) This company provides the unique experience of walking underwater, wearing a diver's helmet and weight belt. Pumps on the boat above feed air to you during the 30-minute 'walk on the wet side', in less than 4m. Walks are available to everyone over the age of six. It's very reassuring that a dive instructor accompanies you on your walk.

Walking

You don't have to get all your thrills on or in the water. Draped in thick forest and dominated by bulky basaltic mountains, the island's interior has exceptional green treats. Arrange any hike with **Polynesia Island Tours** (☑87 29 66 60; polynesiaislandtours@mail.pf; half-/full-day hikes 6500/14,000 CFP; ☺by reservation) or **Bora Bora Mountain Trek** (☑87 72 98 45; borabora.mountaintrek@gmail.com; half-/full-day hikes 6500/13,500 CFP; ☺by reservation), which have professional walking guides who speak passable English. Count on 6500 CFP for a half-day walk and anything between 13,000 and 14,500 CFP for a longer walk.

☞ Tours

A couple of operators organise island tours aboard open 4WDs. These tours are good value if you don't want to rent a car.

Vavau Adventures CULTURAL TOUR

(☑87 72 01 21; www.vavau4x4adventures.com; 7500 CFP; ☺by reservation) Offers half-day trips that take in American WWII sites and various lookouts. Also includes fruit tasting.

Natura Discovery CULTURAL TOUR

(☑87 25 72 00; www.naturadiscovery.com; ☺by reservation) Natura Discovery runs a tour of the island's main attractions, including a couple of inland roads (for lookouts) and American WWII sites. The three-hour tour includes fruit tasting and transfers.

🛏 Sleeping

Glossy brochures and promotional literature focus on Bora Bora's ultraswish resorts, which are as luxurious and as expensive as the hype leads you to believe. That said, there's a smattering of affordable pensions that have sprung up over the last two decades (and are still largely ignored by most first-time visitors).

🛏 West Coast

★ Sunset Hill Lodge BUNGALOW $$

(☑87 79 26 48; www.sunsethilllodge.com; Vaitape; bungalows d 8000-15,500 CFP; ❄🛜) Although the location, on the northern outskirts of Vaitape, about 8km away from Matira Beach, doesn't exactly scream 'vacation', this is a real find if you're working to a tight budget. It's a convenient base – banks, supermarkets and restaurants are within walking distance – and accommodation options include four fully equipped apartments with air-con, and two cheaper, simpler fan-cooled units. They're all spotlessly clean.

Bora Bungalove BUNGALOW $$

(☑87 74 18 82, 40 67 73 58; www.boraboralove.com; Faanui; d/bungalows d 11,000/21,000 CFP; 🛜) You've got two options here: a comfy, spacious and kitchen-equipped bungalow with a terrace right on the water's edge and a rather cramped room with outside shower and toilets. OK, there's no air-con and you need wheels to stay here – Vaitape is 6km away and Matira Beach a further 8km away – but it's friendly, homey and well run. Bikes and kayaks are free.

Rohotu Fare BUNGALOW $$$

(☑87 70 77 99; www.rohotufarelodge.com; Povai Bay; bungalows d 26,000-30,000 CFP; ❄🛜) This upscale venture is a more intimate alternative to a resort, with three all-wood, fully equipped bungalows cocooned in exotic gardens on the mountainside overlooking Povai Bay. No beach nearby, but Matira Point is an easy bike ride away, or you can arrange transfer with Nir, your Israeli host, who speaks excellent English. Free transfers to Vaitape quay and free bikes.

🛏 Matira Point

Much of the island's accommodation is clustered around Matira Point, at the southern toe of Bora Bora. This area also features the island's best beach.

Chez Robert & Tina PENSION $

(☑87 73 53 89, 40 67 63 55; pensionrobertettina@mail.pf; Matira; d 10,100 CFP, without bathroom 8100-9100 CFP) This place is a heartbreaker. Right at the tip of Matira Point, it enjoys a sensational setting, with unobstructed views of the turquoise lagoon, and it's competitively priced (by Bora Bora standards) and within walking distance of various shops and restaurants. Sadly, we've heard reports of variable service, indifferent owners and lack of maintenance.

Le Maitai Bora Bora
RESORT $$$

(☑ 40 60 30 00; www.hotelmaitai.com; Matira; r/ bungalows d incl breakfast from 20,000/35,000 CFP; ✸ 🛜) This midrange resort prides itself on offering the cheapest overwater bungalows in French Polynesia. While much less exclusive and glamorous than the ones found at other hotels, they get the job done. Across the road from the beach, in the hills amid lush jungle foliage, the rooms are impersonal but well-tended and some upper-floor rooms have stunning lagoon views.

Hotel Matira
BUNGALOW $$$

(☑ 40 60 58 40, 40 67 70 51; www.hotel-matira. com; Matira; bungalows d 21,000-35,000 CFP; 🛜) Right on Matira Beach, this is surely one of the most divinely situated hotels in Bora Bora, especially if you score one of the dearer bungalows (Nos 1 and 11), which are just steps from the turquoise water. That said, the 14 units are in need of a lick of paint (and varnish) and don't have air-con. All told, it's about the location.

Village Temanuata
BUNGALOW $$$

(☑ 40 67 75 61; www.temanuata.com; Matira; bungalows d 20,000-24,000 CFP; 🛜) This long-standing institution is starting to show its age, especially the tired bathrooms. But overall it's not bad value given the irresistible location on Matira Beach and the promotional rates ('stay three nights, pay for two') when it's slack. The 14 bungalows are tightly packed together on a grassy property overlooking a narrow stretch of beach.

Intercontinental Bora Bora Le Moana Resort
RESORT $$$

(☑ 40 60 49 00; www.lemoana.intercontinental.com; Matira; bungalows d from 70,000 CFP; ✸ 🛜 🏊) If you're looking to do Bora Bora in style but don't want to feel cut off from the island, the Moana is your answer. It spreads along the eastern side of Matira Point (good for watching the sun rise), a thin stretch of beach is right out the front and there's sensational snorkelling offshore. It comprises beach bungalows and overwater bungalows that feature Polynesian designs.

🏕 The Motu

Staying on a *motu* ensures unrivalled tranquillity, a complete escape and great views of Bora Bora.

Bora Bora Camping
CAMPGROUND $

(☑ 87 70 22 08; Motu Piti Aau; campsites per person 2000 CFP) Camping in Bora Bora? Yes, it's possible, but don't hold your breath. This is a very modest place with limited amenities (cold showers, basic self-catering facilities), but its location on the southern tip of Motu Piti Aau is idyllic, with swaying palm trees, gin-clear waters and mesmerising views of the mountainous mainland. Transfers to Matira are 2000 CFP per person return.

★ Intercontinental Bora Bora Resort & Thalasso Spa
RESORT $$$

(☑ 40 60 76 00; www.tahiti.intercontinental.com; Motu Piti Aau; bungalows d from 90,000 CFP; ✸ 🛜 🏊) 🗷 The Intercontinental has one of the best resort reputations on the island, and the accolades are well deserved. Seen from above, the layout of the 80 overwater bungalows resembles two giant crab claws. The wow factor continues inside, with floor-to-ceiling windows and Starck-inspired decor. Two highlights: the lavish spa and the overwater wedding chapel, complete with a glass-floor aisle.

Sofitel Bora Bora Private Island
RESORT $$$

(☑ 40 60 56 00; www.sofitel.com; Motu Piti Uu Uta; bungalows d incl breakfast from 67,000 CFP; ✸ 🛜) One of Bora Bora's most popular honeymoon spots, this Sofitel strikes a perfect balance between luxury, seclusion, privacy (there are only 31 units) and convenience – on hilly Motu Piti Uu Uta, it's just five glorious minutes by shuttle boat from the main island.

St Régis Resort
RESORT $$$

(☑ 40 60 78 88; www.stregis.com/borabora; Motu Ome; bungalows d from 105,000 CFP; ✸ 🛜 🏊) This top-notch resort is a real treat for honeymooners or couples looking for a perfect high-style escape. Its superstylish public areas and gorgeous overwater bungalows and beach villas make it perfectly suited to romantic beach holidays. Though you would never guess it, the *motu* is landscaped for optimum beach space and features a series of turquoise channels and inner lagoons.

Chez Alice & Raphael
BUNGALOW $$$

(☑ 87 70 37 10; www.pensionaliceetraphaelborabora. com; Motu Ome; bungalow d incl breakfast 22,000 CFP) Simple hedonists will be hard-pressed to find a mellower spot to maroon themselves for a languid holiday. On Motu Ome, two well-proportioned bungalows are dotted around a vast coconut grove by the lagoon.

They were built using local materials in authentic Polynesian style, but the walls in the bathrooms don't make it to the ceilings and there's no air-con (only fans). Cash only.

Le Méridien Bora Bora
RESORT $$$

(☑40 60 51 51; www.lemeridien.com/borabora; Motu Piti Aau; bungalows d from 65,000 CFP; ❋ 🛜 ☒) While lavish, the Méridien offers affordable luxury in its 98 units, including 14 beach villas and 82 overwater bungalows. The *motu* is a stunner, with a vast infinity-edge pool, a lovely inner lagoon fringed with chalk white (artificial) beaches and an architecturally interesting space with timber and thatch for reception, restaurant and bar areas. Everything is luxurious, but nothing is over the top.

Bora Bora
Pearl Beach Resort & Spa
RESORT $$$

(☑40 60 52 00; www.spmhotels.com; Motu Tevairoa; bungalows d from 65,000 CFP; ❋🛜☒) Of all Bora Bora's top-end options, the Pearl has the strongest Polynesian feel. The 50 overwater bungalows are lovely, but the 20 garden suites, which come complete with their own swimming pool, and the 10 beach suites, equipped with an outdoor Jacuzzi, will really win your heart over. They all blend perfectly into the landscaped property.

🍴 Eating

There's a good choice of restaurants on Bora Bora, ranging from European gourmet dining to *roulottes* and *snacks*. Some top-end hotels have an in-house restaurant that is also open to nonguests.

All the luxury hotels have dance performances with buffet dinners several times a week, costing around 8000 CFP to 10,000 CFP.

🍴 West Coast

Roulottes
TAHITIAN $

(Vaitape; mains 1000-1600 CFP; ⊗6.30-9.30pm) If money matters, these cheap and cheerful food vans that take up position on the main square near the quay are the ideal pit stop. Fork out about 1200 CFP for a plate of grilled fish or a voluminous chow mein and you'll leave patting your tummy contentedly.

Aloe Cafe
CAFETERIA $$

(☑40 67 78 88; Vaitape; mains 1200-2300 CFP; ⊗7.30am-6pm Mon-Sat; 🛜) This busy place right in the centre of Vaitape has the most eclectic menu in town and is a good place for a light meal any time of the day (last order is at 4.30pm). Get things going with palate-pleasing salads, well-prepared fish and meat dishes, pasta or pizza. Good breakfasts (served until 10.30am) too and free wi-fi.

★ Maikai Bora Bora
FRENCH, TAHITIAN $$$

(☑40 60 38 00; www.maikaimarina.com; Vaitape; mains 1800-2900 CFP; ⊗noon-2pm & 6-9pm Mon-Sat; 🛜) This highly rated eatery offers excellent Polynesian cuisine with a refined twist, savoured in a vast and stylish dining room overlooking the lagoon (but only a few tables have lagoon views). Prices are surprisingly reasonable for the quality of the fare. On the northern outskirts of Vaitape. Free shuttle at dinner.

Bora Bora Yacht Club
FRENCH, TAHITIAN $$$

(☑40 67 60 47; www.boraborayachtclub.net; mains 1700-3500 CFP; ⊗noon-2pm & 6-9.30pm; 🛜) Yes, the food is pretty good, but the real draw here is the stunning wooden deck overlooking the lagoon – very romantic at sunset. The menu runs the gamut from grilled fish to meat dishes and salads to pasta. The tartares and the finely sliced carpaccios come recommended. For dessert, try the belt-bustingly good passionfruit cheesecake.

It's about 3km north of Vaitape. Free shuttle at dinner.

Le St James
FRENCH $$$

(☑40 67 64 62; www.boraborastjames.com; Vaitape; mains 2800-3000 CFP, lunch menu 2900 CFP, dinner menu 7000-9500 CFP; ⊗11.30am-2.30pm Tue-Wed & Fri-Sat, 6.30-9.30pm Mon-Sat; 🛜) Don't be deterred by the odd location – it's hidden in the back of a small shopping centre in Vaitape – for, once inside, you'll find a convivial space that combines style with informality and an enticing deck affording lovely bay views. Foodwise, the emphasis is on French specialities with a bow to local ingredients. Free shuttle at dinner.

Bloody Mary's
RESTAURANT $$$

(☑40 67 72 86; Povai Bay; lunch mains 1200-1800 CFP, dinner mains 3000-3700 CFP; ⊗11am-3pm & 6-9pm Mon-Sat; 🛜) Bloody Mary's isn't just a restaurant, it's an experience, especially at dinner (light meals only at lunchtime). You walk on sand floors, sit on coconut stools under a thatched roof and are surrounded by exotic plants. You choose your meal from an extensive display at the entrance, with a presentation in English.

🍴 Matira Point & Around

Snack Matira   TAHITIAN **$**
(☑40 67 77 32; Matira; mains 500-2200 CFP; ⊙10am-8pm Tue-Sat, to 4pm Sun) This unfussy little eatery could hardly be better situated: it's right on the beach at Matira (think terrific lagoon views). The menu concentrates on simply prepared fish and meat dishes as well as burgers, sandwiches and omelettes. Eat alfresco or grab your victuals and find your picnic spot on the beach.

Tiare Market   SUPERMARKET **$**
(Matira; ⊙6am-7pm Mon-Sat, 5.30am-1pm & 3-6pm Sun) Self-caterers can stock up the kitchenette at this local supermarket. It's well stocked with all the necessities, from wine and fresh bread to sunscreen and toothpaste.

Matira Beach Burger   BURGERS **$$**
(☑40 67 59 99; Matira Beach; mains 900-2000 CFP; ⊙11am-4pm Mon, to 7pm Tue-Sun) A seductive setting complete with an atmospheric terrace right on Matira Beach is the draw at this well-regarded joint. How about the food? It serves up a colourful assortment of palate pleasers, such as burgers, salads and a few grills.

Tama'a Maitai   INTERNATIONAL **$$**
(☑40 60 30 00; mains 1300-2800 CFP; ⊙11.30am-9pm; ☑) Part of Le Maitai Bora Bora hotel, Tama'a Maitai overlooks the lagoon and catches lots of breeze. All the usual suspects are featured on the menu, including salads, pizza, fish and meat dishes, as well as a few vegetarian options.

Fare Manuia   FRENCH, TAHITIAN **$$**
(☑40 67 68 08; Matira; mains 1200-3500 CFP; ⊙11.30am-3pm & 6-9.30pm) The hardest thing about eating at this local favourite is deciding between the excellent meat or fish dishes, crunchy salads and delicious pasta. Skip the pizzas, though. Big appetite? Opt for the huge wood-fired prime rib. Alas, no sea view – it's in an enclosed area beside the coastal road – but there's a small lounge section with a tiny pool at the back.

⭐**Restaurant**
Matira Beach   FRENCH, JAPANESE **$$$**
(☑40 67 79 09; www.restaurantmatirabeach.com; Matira; mains 1500-3900 CFP, dinner menu 5400-6000 CFP; ⊙11.30am-2pm & 6.30-9pm Wed-Sun)

This breezy, open-air restaurant provides an enchanting dining experience with delectable food. It's well known for its Japanese cuisine (sushi, nigiri, teppanyaki) as well as well-executed French and Polynesian dishes. Salads and burgers are also available at lunchtime. Another clincher is the gorgeous setting, with an agreeable deck overlooking the beach. Free shuttle at dinner.

🍷 Drinking & Nightlife

For an island that famous, the bar scene is very tame on Bora Bora. However, there are a few cool spots where you can cut loose over some sunset cocktails in pleasant surrounds. If it's just the setting you want to absorb, check out the bars in the big hotels. Many restaurants also have a bar section; check out Maikai Bora Bora (p391), which has great tapas and occasional live music, Bora Bora Yacht Club (p391) and Le St James (p391).

Tiki Bar   BAR
(☑40 67 57 36; Povai Bay; ⊙3pm-1am; 🛜) Opened in 2015, Tiki Bar is by far the most happening venue on Bora Bora. There's an interesting mix of people here, from hotel staff to tourists and locals, all drawn by the well-priced beer, cocktails, tapas and great atmosphere. It's usually packed on Friday and Saturday after 8pm. It hosts live bands certain evenings. Food is also served.

☆ Entertainment

If there's one thing you absolutely have to check out while you're on Bora Bora it's a traditional dance show held in one of the luxury hotels. You can usually get in for the price of a drink at the bar, or for between 8000 CFP and 10,000 CFP you can also feast on a buffet dinner. There are performances once or twice a week; ask at the reception desks about the schedule.

🔒 Shopping

Black-pearl jewellery is sold in many places around Bora Bora, at prices that are often higher than in Tahiti. Apart from pearls, shopping on Bora Bora tends to mean hopping between the few galleries and boutiques that are scattered around the island.

ⓘ Information

Most services are in Vaitape. There's a medical centre in Vaitape as well as numerous private doctors and a pharmacy.

Banque de Polynésie (Vaitape; ⊘7.45-11.45am & 12.45-4.15pm Mon-Thu, to 3.30pm Fri) Currency exchange and ATM (Visa only). Near the quay at Vaitape.

Banque de Tahiti Vaitape; ⊘8am-noon & 1-4pm Mon-Fri) Currency exchange and ATM. Near the quay at Vaitape.

Banque Socredo (Vaitape; ⊘7.30-11.30am & 1-3pm Mon-Fri) Currency exchange and ATM. At the northern end of Vaitape.

Bora Bora Tourist Office (☎40 67 76 36; www.borabora-tourisme.com; Vaitape; ⊘8.30am-noon & 1.30-4.30pm Mon-Fri, 8.30am-noon Sat) The office is on the quay at Vaitape and has pamphlets and other information.

Post Office (OPT; Vaitape; internet per hour 500 CFP; ⊘7.15am-3.15pm Mon-Thu, to 2.15pm Fri; 🛜) Internet and wi-fi access (with the Manaspot network). Has an ATM.

❶ Getting There & Away

Bora Bora is situated 270km northwest of Tahiti and can be reached by air or boat from there.

AIR

Air Tahiti (☎40 86 42 42; www.airtahiti.pf; Vaitape; ⊘7.30-11.30am & 1.30-4.30pm Mon-Fri, 8-11.30am Sat) flies between Bora Bora and Tahiti (24,000 CFP, 50 minutes, eight to 10 flights daily), Huahine (11,800 CFP, 20 minutes, one to two flights daily), Maupiti (8500 CFP, one to two flights weekly), Mo'orea (25,400 CFP, one hour, one to three flights daily) and Ra'iatea (9100 CFP, 15 minutes, one to three flights daily). Air Tahiti also has direct flights from Bora Bora to the Tuamotus, with a very handy flight to Rangiroa (31,500 CFP, 1¼ hours, three to four flights weekly) and onward connections to other atolls, including Tikehau and Fakarava.

BOAT

The **Maupiti Express 2** (☎40 67 66 69; Vaitape) serves Ra'iatea/Taha'a on Wednesday, Friday and Sunday (5400 CFP one way, two hours), departing for Ra'iatea and Taha'a at 7am on Wednesday and Friday and at 2pm on Sunday. Tickets can be bought on board or at the office on the Vaitape quay.

Two cargo ships, the *Hawaiki Nui* and the *Taporo VII*, make two trips a week between Pape'ete and Bora Bora (via Huahine, Ra'iatea and Taha'a).

❶ Getting Around

Bora Bora's 32km coast road hugs the shoreline almost all the way around the island.

TO/FROM THE AIRPORT

The airport is on Motu Mute, at the northern edge of the lagoon; transfers are offered to and from the Vaitape quay on two large catamaran ferries (included in the cost of your ticket). There's a shuttle bus from the quay to the hotels and pensions at Matira Point (500 CFP) but it has to be booked in advance by the place where you're staying.

When leaving by air, you need to be at the quay at least 1¼ hours before the flight. The top hotels transfer their visitors directly to and from the airport; all other passengers are picked up at the quay by the catamaran ferries (the cost of this is included in the ticket).

CAR & BICYCLE

Bora Bora Rent a Car – Avis (☎40 67 70 15; www.avis-borabora.com; Vaitape; ⊘7.30am-5.30pm Mon-Sat) Has its main office in the centre of Vaitape, as well as a desk near Matira Point. Cars cost from a whopping 11,900 CFP per 24 hours. It also has bikes (2100 CFP per 24 hours) and scooters (6800 CFP per 24 hours).

Europcar (Map p386; ☎87 71 73 31, 40 67 69 60; ⊘7.30am-5pm Mon-Fri, to 2pm Sat) Rents cars for 12,500 CFP per 24 hours. In the centre of Vaitape.

Totara Loca (☎87 72 74 33; Matira; ⊘8.30-11am) This small outfit in front of Le Maitai Bora Bora rents bikes from 1800 CFP per day. It also has scooters (6900 CFP per day). Prices drop to 4500 CFP per day for three days. It can also deliver the scooter to your hotel or pension. Outside hours, head to Le Maitai Bora Bora's reception.

MAUPITI

POP 1230

Bora Bora's discreet little sister, Maupiti is one of the most ravishing islands in French Polynesia. There's a shimmering lagoon with every hue from lapis lazuli to turquoise, a perfect ring of islets girdled with sand bars, palm trees leaning over the shore and large coral gardens. Although this little charmer is no longer a secret, it still remains a hideaway where visitors come to absorb the lazy lifestyle. There's only one road and virtually no cars, just bikes; there are no showy resorts, just a smattering of family-run pensions. And when you want to play, there's plenty of scope for activities on the water, such as kayaking, snorkelling and diving.

Maupiti

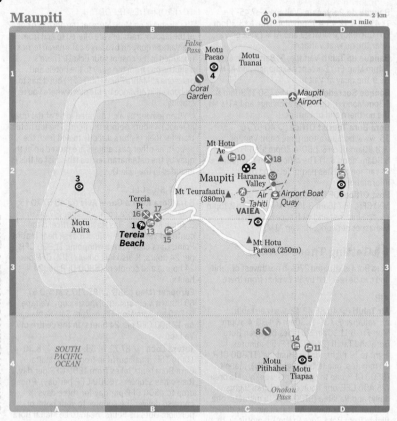

Maupiti

⊙ Top Sights
1 Tereia Beach..B3

⊙ Sights
2 Haranae Petroglyphs............................C2
3 Motu Auira..A2
4 Motu Paeao...C1
5 Motu Tiapaa...D4
6 Motu Tuanai...D2
7 Vaiea..C3

✪ Activities, Courses & Tours
8 Manta Point...C4
9 Mt Teurafaatiu..C2

🛏 Sleeping
10 Chez Ludo et Moyra..............................C2
11 Kuriri Village..D4
12 Maupiti Paradise....................................D2
13 Maupiti Résidence.................................B3
14 Papahani – Chez Vilna........................D4
15 Teheimana..B3

✗ Eating
16 Chez Mimi..B2
17 Espace Beach..B2
18 Tarona...C2

⊙ Sights

⊙ The Motu

Maupiti's star attractions are its five idyllic *motu*, spits of sand and crushed coral dotted with swaying palms, and floating in the jade lagoon that surrounds the main island. Besides acting as quiet retreats, the *motu* also offer good beaches.

Motu Auira
ISLAND

There's an important melon-production plantation on Motu Auira, as well as a lovely coral sand beach. At low tide you can reach it from the mainland by wading across the lagoon – the water is warm and only waist high, but keep an eye out for rays.

Motu Tuanai
ISLAND

The airport and a couple of pensions are found on Motu Tuanai, another picture-friendly islet. However, the lagoon is shallow along this *motu*, which doesn't make it good for swimming except for young children.

Motu Tiapaa
ISLAND

Motu Tiapaa has beautiful, sandy, white beaches and good snorkelling on its ocean and lagoon sides. It's also the most developed *motu*, with several pensions, so it can seem crowded by Maupiti standards.

Motu Paeao
ISLAND

Motu Paeao, at the northern end of the lagoon, is ideal for swimming and snorkelling, with fabulous coral gardens and jade waters.

⊙ The Main Island

★ Tereia Beach
BEACH

A more scenic spot you'd be hard-pressed to find. Here the lagoon is crystal clear and the bone-white beach is nearly all sand (no smashed coral or broken rock). This beach is a stunning place to sun yourself and the east side is deep enough for swimming. There are no facilities except two small beach restaurants. At sunset, the spot becomes downright romantic.

Haranae Petroglyphs
ARCHAEOLOGICAL SITE

Maupiti has some interesting petroglyphs etched into boulders in a rocky riverbed. The most impressive is a turtle image. To reach the petroglyphs, head north out of Vaiea and round the point before passing the basketball court near the church. You're now in the Haranae Valley; on the mountainside is a signposted track heading inland. Follow it for 200m to a small pumping station, and then follow the rocky riverbed. After only 100m, on the left, you'll find the petroglyphs.

Vaiea
VILLAGE

The village spreads along the east coast and is dominated by a sharp ridge running from north to south. Neat houses, brightened with hibiscus, are strung along the road and

they often have *uru* trees shading the family tombs fronting many of them.

🏃 Activities

Snorkelling & Lagoon Excursions

Maupiti's magnificent lagoon is crystal clear, bath warm and filled with all manner of tropical marine life, from schools of butterflyfish and parrotfish to manta rays and banks of flame-coloured coral. The best snorkelling sites are the reefs stretching north of Onoiau Pass (but beware of the currents) and Motu Paeao to the north.

The pensions run lagoon tours; figure between 5000 CFP and 6000 CFP for a full-day trip in a *pirogue,* gliding through the blue and stopping periodically to snorkel and free dive. In season, the pensions also offer snorkelling trips to the manta rays' cleaning station (about 2500 CFP).

Diving

Maupiti is an excellent underwater playground and a good place to learn to dive, with a couple of very safe dive sites in the lagoon, which are perfect for beginners. Maupiti's signature dive site is **Manta Point**, where you can observe manta rays in shallow waters.

Maupiti Diving
DIVING

(☑ 40 67 83 80; www.maupitidiving.com; introductory or single dive 7000 CFP; ⊙ by reservation) 🐟 This low-key diving venture specialises in small groups (maximum four divers) and offers an intimate feel on its aquatic adventures. A 10-dive package (valid for two divers) is 60,000 CFP. Book well ahead. Cash only. Free pick-up.

Kayaking

Sea kayaking is a popular activity of the DIY variety. Paddling around the quiet lagoon is very safe. Most accommodation places either rent or offer free sea kayaks for guests' use.

🛏 Sleeping & Eating

For the full Robinson Crusoe experience, places on the *motu* are hard to beat. If island life is your top priority, stay on the main island. Most people opt for half- or full board at their accommodation; if you're staying on the *motu* this will likely be your only option. Several small village shops sell basic supplies.

Chez Ludo et Moyra
PENSION $

(☑ 87 22 66 43, 40 67 84 07; www.pensionludo.com; s/d half board without bathroom 7500/15,000 CFP) An unpretentious pension with three modest guestrooms, which share bathrooms in the owners' house. Set in a verdant property 50m back from the coastal road, it offers few frills, just a genuine Polynesian welcome and hearty meals. It has no view to speak of, no direct lagoon access and no proper swimming area nearby, but Tereia Beach is a 10-minute bicycle ride away.

Teheimana   PENSION $
(☑ 40 67 81 45, 87 71 29 97; www.pensiontehei-mana.blogspot.com; s/d half board without bathroom 7500/15,000 CFP; 🛜) Tucked away in a beautifully landscaped garden, this pension with a definite family-run feel offers an affordable lagoonside tropical oasis. The house has three rooms that share bathrooms and a nice communal kitchen. It's very simple but clean, and the atmosphere is relaxed.

★Maupiti Résidence   BUNGALOW $$
(☑ 40 67 82 61; www.maupitiresidence.info; Tereia Beach; bungalows d 11,000-13,000 CFP, q 15,000-17,000 CFP; ❄🛜) The location, right on Tereia Beach, is to die for. While hardly glitzy, the two bungalows are spacious and serviceable, with a living room, two bedrooms, a terrace that delivers full-frontal lagoon views and a kitchen. Perks include free bicycles and kayaks, daily cleaning service, air-con (add 500 CFP) and washing machine, making this one of the best-value stays you'll have.

Maupiti Paradise   BUNGALOW $$
(☑ 87 71 09 70, 40 67 83 83; www.maupiti-paradise-lodge.com; Motu Tuanai; bungalows s/d half board 11,000/22,000 CFP) Here the setting is magical – the property opens onto the lagoon and the ocean, with both Bora Bora and the majestic silhouette of the main island in the background. The five bungalows are well proportioned, comfortable and inviting. Sunbathing is top notch, but swimming is not that enthralling, with very shallow waters; paddling to more idyllic swimming spots expands your possibilities.

Papahani – Chez Vilna   PENSION $$
(☑ 40 60 15 35; pensionpapahani@hotmail.fr; Motu Tiapaa; bungalows half board s 11,000-12,000 CFP, d 22,000-24,000; 🛜) An atmosphere of dreamlike tranquillity characterises this well-run pension with a fab lagoon frontage. Your biggest quandary here: go snorkelling (or kayaking) or snooze on the white-sand beach under the swaying palms? The four bungalows blend perfectly into the tropical gardens; the one that's right on the beach is well worth the few extra bucks.

Kuriri Village   BUNGALOW $$
(☑ 40 67 82 23, 87 74 54 54; www.maupiti-kuri-ri.com; Motu Tiapaa; bungalows half board s/d 15,300/26,300 CFP; 🛜) Watch dolphins frolicking in the waves from a little wooden deck (with Bora Bora as a backdrop), take a dip in the lagoon, relax in an attractive tropical garden – it can't get more laid-back than this. Digs are in four simply designed bungalows with a ramshackle charm. The property opens onto the lagoon and the ocean – two different settings, two different atmospheres.

Chez Mimi   TAHITIAN $
(Tereia Beach; mains 400-1000 CFP; ⊙9am-3pm) Feel the sand between your toes at this casual spot soothingly positioned right on Tereia Beach. Make sure you get there on the early side (ideally before 1pm) – only one round of food, usually grilled fish, raw fish and beef steak, is made for the day. Generous sandwiches are also available.

Espace Beach   TAHITIAN $
(☑ 40 67 81 54; Tereia Beach; mains 1200-1500 CFP; ⊙by reservation) Opening onto the lagoon, this is the best place on Maupiti for a lagoonside lunch or dinner (by reservation only). The emphasis is on simply prepared fish dishes, including tuna sashimi.

Tarona   TAHITIAN, CHINESE $
(☑ 40 67 82 46; mains 1300-1500 CFP; ⊙11.30am-1.30pm & 6-8pm Mon-Sat) Just north of Vaiea, this humble budget bite dishes up hearty portions of French Polynesian and Chinese staples at blessedly low prices. House specials include raw fish, grilled fish, tuna sashimi and chow mein. If you're really hungry after a day's Maupiti adventuring, the pork with taro will definitely fill you up.

❶ Getting There & Away

Maupiti is 320km west of Tahiti and 40km west of Bora Bora.

AIR

Air Tahiti (☑ 40 86 42 42, 40 67 81 24; www.air-tahiti.pf; ⊙8-11am Mon, Wed & Thu, 8.45am-1pm Tue & Fri) flies from Maupiti to Tahiti (18,500 CFP, 1½ hours, three to five flights weekly), Ra'iatea (9800 CFP, 25 minutes, two flights weekly) and Bora Bora (8500 CFP, 20 minutes, one or two flights weekly). Flights to/from Maupiti are in high demand so be sure to book well in advance.

BOAT

Because of strong currents and a tricky sandbar in the Onoiau Pass, the lagoon can only be navigated by smaller ships, which are occasionally forced to wait for appropriate tidal conditions. The **Maupiti Express 2** (☑ 40 67 66 69, 87 78 27 22) ferry used to run between Maupiti and Bora Bora twice weekly but this service was indefinitely suspended at the time of writing; check while you're there.

ⓘ Getting Around

If you've booked accommodation you'll be met at the airport, although some places charge for the trip (from 1000 CFP per person return).

It's simple to arrange a boat out to the *motu* from the village and vice versa. All the pensions on the mainland or *motu* can arrange these transfers.

TUAMOTU ISLANDS

The Tuamotus? It's the dream South Seas snapshot: the 77 atolls – narrow coral rings encircling turquoise lagoons – that make up this stunning archipelago are flung over an immense stretch of indigo blue ocean.

Life in the atolls is equal parts harsh and paradisiacal: hardly anything grows, so fruit and vegetables are in short supply, and the only drinking water is collected from the rain. Yet the silence, starry skies, coral beaches, blue lagoons, idyllic *motu* and languid pace of life captivate nearly everyone who makes it here. Most tourists visit Rangiroa, Tikehau and Fakarava, which have the bulk of tourist infrastructure, but it's also possible to explore lesser-known beauties such as Ahe, Mataiva and Makemo.

Anyone who loves the water will adore the Tuamotus. The vast, pristine marine area offers unparalleled opportunities to encounter the menagerie of marine life. For nondivers, fantastic lagoon excursions beckon.

Rangiroa

POP 2567

Rangiroa is one of the biggest atolls in the world, with a lagoon so vast that it could fit the entire island of Tahiti inside of it. While visitors coming directly from Bora Bora or Tahiti will probably find Rangi (as it's known to its friends) to be a low-key, middle-of-nowhere sort of a place, this is the big city for folks coming from anywhere else in the archipelago.

But it's only the beginning: Rangiroa's richest resource lies below the surface. It's a diving mecca, with world-renowned dive

sites blessed with prolific marine life just minutes from your bungalow.

For landlubbers the never-ending string of remote *motu* is the real draw and boat trips across the lagoon to scenic spots are not to be missed.

⊙ Sights

★**Île aux Récifs**   NATURAL SITE
(Island of Reef; Rangiroa) South of the atoll, an hour by boat from Avatoru, Île aux Récifs is an area dotted with raised *feo* (coral outcrops), weathered shapes chiselled by erosion into petrified silhouettes on the exterior reef. They stretch for several hundred metres, with basins and channels that make superb natural swimming pools. There's a good *hoa* (shallow channel) for swimming and a picturesque coconut grove by the beach. You'll need to take a lagoon excursion boat (p399) from Avatoru to get to Île aux Récifs.

★**Lagon Bleu**   NATURAL SITE
(Blue Lagoon; Rangiroa) This is what many people visualise when imagining a Polynesian paradise: a string of *motu* and coral reefs has formed a natural pool on the edge of the main reef, a lagoon within a lagoon. You can walk knee-deep across a (mostly dead) coral seabed to visit a bird island and laze on incredibly photogenic spits of white-and-pink coral sands. This intimate paradise is reached only on lagoon-excursion boats from Avatoru, about an hour away.

Avatoru   VILLAGE
Avatoru won't leap to the top of your list of preferred villages in French Polynesia, but its location, right by Avatoru Pass and the lagoon, is stunning. The two churches – one

Tuamotu Islands

400 km
250 miles

SOUTH PACIFIC OCEAN

Reao

Pukarua

Tatakoto

Vahitahi
Nukutavake

Tureia

Moruroa
Fangataufa

Maria Island

Gambier
Archipelago — Mangareva

Puka Puka

Napuka

Disappointment Islands

Fangatau
Fakahina

Takume
Raroia

Hao

Makemo

Katiu

Faaite
Tahanea
Anaa

Duke of Gloucester Islands

Manihi
Ahe
Takaroa
Takapoto
Arutua
Apataki
Aratika
Toau
Kauehi
Fakarava
Kaukura

Mataiva
Tikehau
Makatea

Tetiaroa
Mo'orea
Tahiti
Mehetia

The Society Islands

PAPE'ETE

See Rangiroa
Map (p400)

SOUTH PACIFIC OCEAN

Tropic of Capricorn

Catholic and one Mormon – are about the only buildings of interest.

Tiputa
VILLAGE

Very few visitors venture to this charmingly quiet village edging the eastern side of Tiputa Pass. Although it doesn't have tourist facilities (all accommodation options are on Avatoru), it's well worth the trip for its wonderfully relaxed atmosphere and to get a sense of atoll life; getting a boat across the Tiputa Pass adds to the whole experience. A track continues east from the the village through coconut plantations until it's halted by the next *hoa* (shallow channel).

Gauguin's Pearl
FARM

(☑ 40 93 11 30; www.gauguinspearl.com; ☺ guided tours 8.30am, 10.30am & 2pm Mon-Fri) **FREE**
There are free tours (in English) of the pearl farm next to the boutique. They include a pearl-grafting demonstration. Call for free pick-up.

🏃 Activities

Diving & Snorkelling

The number-one activity on Rangiroa is diving, and it's no wonder. The **Tiputa Pass** has achieved cult status in the diving community and offers some of the best drift dives in the world. Sharks, manta rays, eagle rays and dolphins are the big attractions, but you'll also encounter countless reef species as well as shoals of barracuda and trevallies.

Snorkelling is another great way to visit the lagoon. You can just grab a snorkel and splash around near your hotel or guesthouse, but to really experience life under the sea it's necessary to sign up with a dive centre or a boat tour operator and go out to further marine wonderlands.

Rangiroa Plongée
DIVING, SNORKELLING

(☑ 40 96 03 32, 87 77 65 86; www.rangiroaplongee. pf; introductory/single dive 7500/7000 CFP; ☺ by reservation) This small dive outfit provides personalised service at affordable prices and specialises in small groups. The dedicated two-hour snorkelling trip through the Tiputa Pass (5000 CFP) and at Motu Nuhi Nuhi comes highly recommended (no experience is required). Free pick-up.

Topdive
DIVING

(☑ 40 96 05 60; www.topdive.com; introductory/single dive 10,000/9800 CFP; ☺ by reservation) Topdive is a fully fledged, well-organised dive shop that offers the full range

---

---

of scuba activities. Prices are steep but Nitrox dives are offered at no extra charge. Six- and 10-dive packages go for 50,000/80,000 CFP and can be used at any of the Topdive centres in French Polynesia (Tahiti, Mo'orea, Bora Bora and Fakarava). Snorkelling trips can be arranged. Free pick-up.

Y'aka Plongée
DIVING

(☑ 87 20 68 98; www.yakaplongeerangiroa.com; introductory/single dive 8000/7600 CFP; ☺ by reservation) This welcoming outfit is run by Marco and Cathy, two of Rangiroa's long-standing dive instructors. They have plenty of experience, an excellent reputation for service and instruction, and offer great-value certification courses (from 42,000 CFP). Six- and 10-dive packages are 42,000/65,000 CFP. Add an extra 1000 CFP per dive for Nitrox dives. Also runs snorkelling trips through the Tiputa Pass. Free pick-up.

Lagoon Excursions

Organised tours are really the only way of exploring the most scenic spots on the lagoon and, if you happen upon a nice group, make for a wonderful day. The most popular excursions – the Lagon Bleu and Île aux Récifs – are to the opposite side of the lagoon from Avatoru, which takes at least an hour to cross and can be uncomfortable if the sea is rough. When the weather's bad or the winds are too high, excursions are cancelled. Usually a minimum of four to six people is required.

Full-day trips cost around 7500 CFP including lunch. All bookings can be made through your hotel or pension. Transfers are provided.

Rangiroa

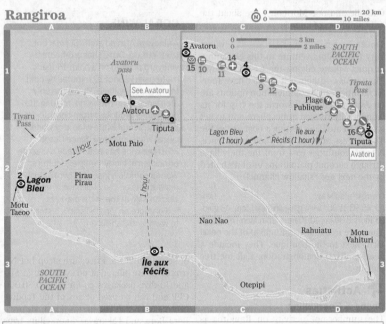

Rangiroa

🛏 Sleeping

Rangiroa has lots of simple, family-run pensions and a few more luxurious places.

★ Chez Cécile   PENSION $$

(☐ 87 77 55 72, 40 93 12 65; www.rangiroa-cecile.com; bungalows s half board 8000-11,000 CFP; d half board 16,000-22,000 CFP; 🛜) This solid-value option is run by a charming

Paumotu family who will go the extra mile to help travellers. It features nine spacious wood bungalows in a flowery garden. Most units line the 'beach', which is actually a breakwater filled in with coral gravel, but you can swim off a pier extending over the lagoon. The cheaper bungalows are set in the garden.

Turiroa Village – Chez Olga
BUNGALOW, DORM $

(☑40 96 04 27, 87 70 59 21; pension.turiroa@mail. pf; dm 3500 CFP, d without bathroom 7000 CFP, bungalows 10,500 CFP; ☏) Chez Olga may not have the Polynesian character of some of the other pensions, but it's a freakishly good deal for the Tuamotus, with three types of accommodation to suit all budgets. There's no beach, but a pontoon gives you access to a decent swimming area. No meals are provided except breakfast (500 CFP), but there's a well-equipped guest kitchen.

Rangiroa Plage
GUESTHOUSE, CAMPGROUND $

(☑87 75 43 40, 40 96 82 13; www.rangiroaplage. com; campsites per person 1400 CFP, dm 3000 CFP, d without bathroom 6500 CFP, d 8000-8500 CFP; ☏) The 'Plage' (beach) bit is a gross misnomer, but this no-frills backpackers housed in a ramshackle building in Avatoru village has a spiffing lagoonside location. Pitch your tent on a coral gravel plot just 10m from the lagoon, or choose one of the four shoebox-sized rooms with or without bathrooms. The two- and four-bed dorms are cramped but serviceable.

Raira Lagon
HOTEL $$

(☑40 93 12 30; www.raira-lagon.pf; bungalows s half board 16,000-17,500 CFP, bungalows d half board 29,000-32,000; ✴☏) A cross between a family-run place and a hotel, this is a re-assuring choice with no surprises (good or bad) up its sleeves. It features 10 bungalows that meet modern standards, including air-con. They're spread throughout a garden fringed by a satisfying swimming area (but no beach), and the more expensive ones come with a lagoon view. Bonuses: free kayaks, bikes and snorkelling gear.

Les Relais de Josephine
BUNGALOW $$

(☑40 96 02 00; www.relais-josephine-rangiroa.com; bungalows s/d half board 16,800/33,600 CFP; ☏) The setting of this very French interpretation of the Polynesian pension, right on the legendary Tiputa Pass, is arguably the prettiest on the atoll. The seven bungalows are decked out in minimalist colonial-style

elegance but are not luxurious. Lounging on the deck here is a truly decadent experience, as is dining on the elegant French-style food made from local ingredients.

Va'aitemoana
BUNGALOW, DORM $$

(☑87 32 36 16; www.vaaitemoana.com; dm 5000 CFP, d without bathroom 12,000 CFP, bungalows d 16,000-19,000 CFP, all include breakfast) Opened in late 2015, Va'aitemoana follows the stand-ard recipe for success: offer clean, light-filled, spacious accommodation with prim bath-rooms in a chilled-out setting. There are three bungalows in total (one of which comes equipped with a kitchenette), as well as a modern room and a four-bed dorm in the owners' house. The catch? There's no lagoon access. Free bikes. No wi-fi.

Dinners cost 3000 CFP.

Le Maitai Rangiroa
RESORT $$$

(☑40 93 13 50; www.hotelmaitai.com; bungalows d incl breakfast 29,000-42,000 CFP; ✴☏✸) Priva-cy is not Le Maitai's forte – the 34 few-frills-but-functional bungalows are tightly packed on a small property – but otherwise this low-key resort is well run and serviceable. The six units that are right on the shore and, at a pinch, the first row of Premium Garden bungalows, which offer good lagoon views, are well worth the extra bucks.

Kia Ora Resort & Spa
RESORT $$$

(☑40 93 11 11; www.eu.hotelkiaora.com; villas d from 60,000 CFP; ✴☏✸) Welcome to one of the swankiest options in French Polynesia, with 50 plush bungalows, including 10 enor-mous overwater units on a perfect turquoise lagoon. The ravishing garden villas come with their own pool and are dotted around a magnificent coconut plantation situated on a fine little stretch of white sand. It incor-porates restaurant, bar, spa and swimming pool.

Tevahine Dream
PENSION $$$

(☑40 93 12 75; www.tevahinedream-rangiroa. com; bungalows s half board 20,000-21,000 CFP, bungalows d half board 31,000-33,000 CFP; ☏) Tevahine Dream gets rave reviews from honeymooners who want something more personal and intimate than a hotel. Five rustic-chic bungalows, three of which face the lagoon, are designed in a Zen-meets-Polynesia style. That said, the odd layout of the bathrooms – no doors and no walls, only a curtain – may not be to everybody's taste. Prices include kayaks and snorkelling gear. Cash only.

✖ Eating

Many visitors opt for half board at their hotel or pension but there are also a few good independent eating options. Avatoru has a few supermarkets.

★ Mitivai   TAHITIAN, BURGERS $
(☑87 20 08 77; mains 1000-1950 CFP; ⊙11.30am-2.30pm) A favourite haunt of hungry divers (it's conveniently located between two busy dive shops) this trusty joint is one of Rangiroa's hottest spots for lunch and serves fine food to accompany the wonderful lagoon views. Gorge on yummy burgers, sandwiches, copious salads and tasty grilled fish. Leave room for the dangerously addictive desserts – *mmm*, the *profiteroles au chocolat*!

La Roulotte   FRENCH, SANDWICHES $
(☑40 96 82 13; mains 1000-1700 CFP; ⊙11am-1.30pm & 5.30-8.30pm Mon-Sat, 5.30-8.30pm Sun) Simple meals are the order of the day at this no-frills eatery at the eastern end of Avatoru village. The food's not fantastically exciting – fish, steaks and sandwiches (from 400 CFP) are the mainstays – but portions are large enough to satisfy the most voracious diver.

Puna   TAHITIAN $
(☑87 73 76 10; mains 1300-1500 CFP; ⊙11.30am-2pm Mon-Sat) Talk about location! The dining deck of this buzzing *snack* at the eastern tip of Avatoru is on the lagoon, literally. It features all the Polynesian classics as well as grills, sandwiches (550 CFP) and burgers. Mouthwatering crepes and waffles will finish you off sweetly. It's a good place to catch local vibes and enjoy plenty of local colour at lunchtime.

Chez Lili   INTERNATIONAL $$
(☑87 32 42 50; mains 1600-1700 CFP; ⊙11am-2pm Tue-Sun) For a menu that strays from the familiar 'raw fish in coconut milk' path, try this cute eatery at the eastern tip of Avatoru. Run by the energetic Lili (who is from Madagascar), it serves well-prepared daily specials, including chicken in Creole sauce and tuna tartare with mango.

Raira Lagon – Beach Raira FRENCH, TAHITIAN $$
(☑40 93 12 30; mains 1600-3500 CFP; ⊙11.30am-2pm & 6-9pm) Located inside Raira Lagon hotel (but open to nonguests), the well-respected Beach Raira is a terrific spot for a lagoonside meal, with alfresco tables overlooking the water. Prices are reasonable considering the location and the fresh ingredients – most dishes are under 2000 CFP.

Kia Ora Resort & Spa – Te Rairoa   INTERNATIONAL $$$
(☑40 93 11 11; mains 1600-3500 CFP; ⊙noon-2pm & 6.30-9pm) Rangiroa's standout resort restaurant is in Kia Ora Resort. Nab a seat on the lovely overwater dining deck and look forward to interesting combinations of Pacific, European and Asian flavours. Another reason to visit it is the twice-weekly island night and buffet (7500 CFP), where you can take your pick of lots of great dishes while enjoying a spectacular dance show.

🍷 Drinking & Nightlife

Te Mao   LOUNGE
(☑87 26 05 25; ⊙5-10pm Tue-Thu & Sun, to 11pm Fri & Sat; 🛜) A happening bar in Rangiroa? No, you're not dreaming. Run by a Parisian couple who fell in love with the atoll, this venture with a boho vibe and loungey feel will stun you with its relaxing atmosphere, wide choice of beers and cocktails (1200 CFP) and excellent tapas (from 800 CFP). It attracts tourists and locals alike.

❶ Information

Note that there are only two ATMs on Rangiroa: one in Avatoru and one in Tiputa.

Banque de Tahiti (Avatoru; ⊙7.30-11.30am & 1-4pm Mon-Fri) Currency exchange. In the village.

Banque Socredo (Avatoru; ⊙7.30-11.30am & 1.30-4pm Mon, Wed & Fri, 1.30-4pm Tue & Thu) Currency exchange. Has two 24-hour ATMs. Beside the airport terminal.

Centre Médical d'Avatoru (☑40 96 03 75; ⊙7.30am-3.30pm Mon-Fri) Medical centre. There are also two private doctors in Avatoru.

Gendarmerie (Police Station; ☑40 96 73 61)

Post Office (Avatoru; ⊙7am-3pm Mon-Thu, to 2pm Fri; 🛜) Internet and wi-fi access (with the Manaspot network).

❶ Getting There & Away

AIR

Within the archipelago, Rangiroa is the major flight hub. The airport is smack in between Avatoru (to the west) and Tiputa (to the east).

Air Tahiti (☑40 86 42 42; www.airtahiti.pf) offers two to three flights daily between Pape'ete and Rangiroa (one hour, 24,200 CFP). Rangiroa is also connected by air to Bora Bora and other atolls in the Tuamotus. One-way fares on offer include Bora Bora–Rangiroa 31,500 CFP,

Rangiroa–Tikehau 9500 CFP, Rangiroa–Fakarava 9500 CFP and Rangiroa–Mataiva 9500 CFP.

BOAT

A few cargo ships serve Rangiroa from Pape'ete.

✈ Getting Around

A sealed, entirely flat road runs the 10km from Avatoru village at the western end of the string of islets to the Tiputa Pass, at the eastern extremity.

If you have booked accommodation, your hosts will be at the airport to welcome you. If your pension is near the hotel, transfers will probably be free; places further away tend to charge (ask when you book).

CAR, BICYCLE & SCOOTER

The easiest way to get around is to hire a bicycle or a scooter (as it's hardly worth getting a car).
Arenahio Location (📱 87 73 92 84; ⊘ by reservation) Hires out cars/scooters/bicycles for 8500/5200/1300 CFP for a full day.
Rangi Rent a Car (📱 40 96 03 28; ⊘ by reservation) Car hire from 6500 CFP per day.

TAXI BOAT

Nova Transport (📱 87 26 78 06; ⊘ 7am-5pm) offers a shuttle service between Ohotu wharf and Tiputa village for 600 CFP return; taking a bicycle over costs 500 CFP extra. The crossing takes about five minutes.

Fakarava

One of the largest and most beautiful atolls in French Polynesia, Fakarava is the stuff of South Seas fantasy. Heavenly white and pink sand, ruffled coconut trees and an unbelievable palette of lagoon blues are the norm here. The atmosphere is supremely relaxed and the infrastructure is quite good, with an assortment of well-run pensions.

Fakarava is a great place to unwind, but for those looking for more than a suntan, it offers a number of high-energy distractions. The fantastic diving and snorkelling is legendary among divers, who come for a truly exhilarating experience in the two passes.

◉ Sights

★ Les Sables Roses   BEACH

(Pink Sands) A double crescent of dreamy beaches split by a narrow spit of white-and-pink coral sands, Les Sables Roses seems to come right out of central casting for tropical ideals. The turquoise water laps both sides of the sandy strip and there's

only one boat: yours. It's perfect for relaxing, swimming and evening up your sunburn. It's near the southernmost tip of the atoll, not far from Tetamanu, and is reached only on lagoon-excursion boats (p404).

Lagon Bleu (Motu Tehatea)   NATURAL SITE

(Blue Lagoon) Simply divine. Near the northwestern corner of Fakarava, Lagon Bleu features an indescribably lovely stretch of white-sand coral beach, turquoise water, palm trees leaning over the shore – and not a soul in sight. It's a fantastic place for a picnic or a bout of snorkelling and swimming. You'll need to take a boat tour to get to Lagon Bleu. One proviso: it's usually infested by *nono* (gnats).

Rotoava   VILLAGE

Most islanders live in Rotoava village at the northeastern end of the atoll, 4km east of the airport. Aside from Rangiroa's Avatoru, this is the most developed and busiest town in the Tuamotus, but it's still pretty quiet by most people's standards. With only a few streets, a couple of churches and stores, a town hall and a school, it's easy to explore.

Plage du PK9   BEACH

A bit of a local's secret, Plage du PK9 is – you guessed it – 9km west of Rotoava (go past the airport and follow the dirt track towards the northern pass; at the PK9 marker, take the path to the left). It's a thin, laid-back stretch of white coral sand backed by palms and lapped by sparkling turquoise waters. It's equally good for sunning and swimming and there's excellent snorkelling not far offshore. Bring plenty of water. Beware of falling coconuts.

PK10.5   NATURAL SITE

(PK10.5) The PK10.5 marks the end of the dirt road, just on the edge of the phenomenal Garuae Pass. By incoming or outgoing current, the pass gets really rough, with waves that can easily exceed 2m in the middle of the pass.

Tetamanu   VILLAGE

A handful of people also live in Tetamanu village, a tiny settlement on the edge of Tumakohua Pass, which is as backwater as backwater gets (despite the growing numbers of divers who stay in the nearby pensions). It has a cute coral chapel built in the 19th century and an old graveyard with coral tombstones.

Tetamanu is accessible by private boat only or during a lagoon excursion.

🏃 Activities

Diving & Snorkelling

Divers can't gush enough about the fabulous fish life, especially grey sharks, blacktip sharks, manta rays, tuna and barracuda, that can be found in the Garuae Pass (Northern Pass; Fakarava) (also known as 'Northern Pass') and Tumakohua Pass (Southern Pass; Fakarava) (also known as 'Southern Pass'). Another draw is the coral, which is much healthier than on Rangiroa. If you're based in or near Rotoava, day trips to the Southern Pass are regularly organised by local dive shops but they're weather-dependent and require a minimum number of divers.

Dive Spirit
DIVING

(☑87 32 79 87, 40 98 41 40; www.divespirit.com; PK4.2; introductory/single/2-tank dive 8500/8500/15,000 CFP; ☺ by reservation) Run by an efficient French-Spanish couple, this diving operation offers high standards and excellent service. It has daily outings to Garuae Pass as well as regular day trips to Tumakohua Pass (23,000 CFP, including two dives and lunch). Note that the boat doesn't have a roof, though. Six-/10-dive packages cost 42,000/68,000 CFP. Good English is spoken. Free pick-up.

Topdive
DIVING

(☑87 29 22 32, 40 98 43 76; www.topdive.com; PK1, Rotoava; introductory/single dive 10,000/9,800 CFP; ☺ by reservation) This reputable outfit in Rotoava also has an annex on a *motu* near Tetamanu (which caters for pensions in the south). Six- and 10-dive packages go for 50,000/80,000 CFP and can be used at any of the Topdive centres in French Polynesia (Tahiti, Bora Bora and Rangiroa). Day trips to Tumakohua Pass cost 31,000 CFP including lunch. Free pick-up.

Lagoon Excursions

As in other atolls, here organised tours are the only way of exploring the idyllic, remote spots on the lagoon, including Lagon Bleu, Tetamanu (if you're based in the north) and Les Sables Roses. Usually a minimum of four to six people is required.

Half-/full-day trips to Lagon Bleu cost around 7000/8500 CFP. A full-day excursion taking in Les Sables Roses, Tetamanu and a snorkelling stop in the southern pass usually costs 12,000 CFP, including a barbecued lunch at Tetamanu. All bookings can be made through your hotel or pension.

Note that it's at least a 90-minute boat ride to get to the southern sites from Rotoava. For Lagon Bleu, it takes about 30 minutes by boat from Rotoava.

🛏 Sleeping & Eating

Relais Marama
BUNGALOW, CAMPGROUND $

(☑87 76 12 29, 40 98 42 51; www.relais-marama.com; campsites per person 2800 CFP, bungalows s/d without bathroom 7000/14,000 CFP, all incl breakfast; 🖥) On the ocean side of Rotoava (no beach), this backpackerlike option is a great deal for solo travellers; eight no-frills, teeny but practical bungalows in a verdant compound, two well-scrubbed ablution blocks (with hot water) and a convenient location. Campers share the same facilities as the bungalows.

★ Havaiki Pearl Lodge
RESORT $$

(☑87 26 26 05, 40 93 40 15; www.havaiki.com; PK2, Rotoava; garden bungalows s/d half board 16,000/23,000 CFP, beach bungalows s/d half board 26,000/33,000 CFP; ❄🖥) At the southern end of Rotoava, this petite resort-style venue is the fanciest option in the north of the atoll, with 10 small but immaculate bungalows that offer a lovely lagoon frontage. They have been renovated in a modern, clean, white-and-brown colour scheme. There are also three garden units, which are built on stilts (nice views), but they don't have air-con.

Vaiama Village
PENSION $$

(☑87 70 81 99, 40 98 41 13; www.fakaravavaiama.com; PK6.8; bungalows s/d half board 12,700/19,700 CFP; 🖥) Each of the four bungalows here is crafted from a variety of local materials. Although they're packed rather closely together, they enjoy a splendid location, just steps from a fine ribbon of beach. All have attached bathrooms with coral-gravel floors and ferns for a tropical-oasis effect. There are also two garden bungalows with lagoon views.

Veke Veke Village
PENSION $$

(☑87 70 45 19, 40 98 42 89; www.pension-fakarava.com; PK4.1; bungalows s/d half board 12,800/19,000 CFP; 🖥) What an exquisite spot! Imagine a small, sandy bay fringed with coconut palms and lapped by turquoise waters. Choose between two family-sized semi-overwater bungalows or four smaller bungalows right on the beach. The dining area with coral-gravel floor is pleasingly simple, and there's also a picturesque, sunset-friendly pontoon. Kayaks and bikes are complimentary. Airport transfers are 1100 CFP return.

Raimiti
BUNGALOW $$$

(☑ 87 71 07 63; www.raimiti.com; bungalow full board for 2 nights s 54,000-61,000 CFP, d 99,000-112,000 CFP) Travellers in search of romance enthuse about this Crusoe-chic and very isolated spot with only nine units: five rustic but tastefully decorated lagoonside cabins constructed from local materials as well as four larger oceanside dark-wood bungalows. Food is a highlight, with refined meals. Prices include excursions and transfers (be warned that it's an open boat, which can be uncomfortable in bad weather).

Snack Kori Kori
TAHITIAN $

(☑ 87 79 57 46; PK4.2; mains 900-1500 CFP; ◷ 11.30am-2pm) A very pleasant spot for lunch, this family-run affair boasts an ace location right on the edge of the turquoise lagoon and whips up simple yet tasty meals as well as copious sandwiches and paninis (from 350 CFP).

Snack Elda
TAHITIAN $$

(☑ 87 23 66 42, 40 98 41 33; PK4.1; mains 1500-1900 CFP; ◷ 11.30am-1pm & 6.30-8pm) This unfussy little eatery could hardly be better situated: the dining deck is right on the lagoon. The menu concentrates on simply prepared seafood and meat dishes served in generous portions. Call ahead to make sure it's open. Free pick-up.

❶ Information

Post Office (OPT; Rotoava; ◷ 7-11.30am & 1-2.30pm Mon, Thu & Fri, to 2pm Wed; 🛜) Internet and wi-fi access (with the Manaspot network). Also has one 24-hour ATM, but we recommend bringing enough cash with you in case it's empty or not functioning.

❶ Getting There & Away

The atoll is 488km east-northeast of Tahiti.

AIR

Air Tahiti (☑ 40 86 42 42; www.airtahiti.pf) flies five times weekly from Pape'ete to Fakarava (24,200 CFP one way), three times weekly from Rangiroa to Fakarava (9500 CFP) and once or twice weekly from Fakarava to Rangiroa (9500 CFP).

BOAT

Some cargo ships stop at Fakarava and take passengers.

❶ Getting Around

The airport is 4km west of Rotoava. A scheduled visit by former French president Jacques Chirac

(he never actually showed up) brought funding to pave a 20km road from the airport to the southeast side of the atoll. From the airport, a dirt track goes as far as the edge of Garuae Pass, about 5.5km away to the west.

Fakarava Yacht Services (☑ 87 75 34 84; Rotoava; ◷ by reservation) hires out bikes (1500 CFP per day) and delivers to your pension.

Tikehau
POP 529

Tikehau is a joy. Its unparalleled beauty, endless coral beaches and low-key yet reasonably developed tourist infrastructure make it a real charmer. Time has eroded the ring of coral into sweeping, twisting *motu* of white and pink sands that engulf little bays, craggy nooks and the vivid turquoise lagoon. Idyllic picnic spots abound and the atoll's secluded shores are some of the best in the Tuamotus for lounging, loafing and lollygagging. And unlike on Rangiroa, you don't have to travel far to find that perfect strip of strand. Below the turquoise waters, a vast living world beckons divers of all levels.

⊙ Sights

Les Sables Roses
BEACH

(Pink Sands) The southeast shores of the atoll are fringed with truly amazing 'Pink Sands Beaches' that really do glow a light shade of pink, a result of finely pulverised coral.

Tuherahera
VILLAGE

Most islanders live in Tuherahera, in the southwest of the atoll. Find peace in this pretty village, bursting with *uru* (breadfruit), coconut trees, bougainvillea and hibiscus. Fancy a dip? Head to one of Tuherahera's coral beaches. The best one lies east of the village, near the airstrip. The sand is wide and the waters are calm and translucent. Another beauty lies at the western tip of the village; this strip is lapped by a glassy turquoise channel and has pinkish sands.

Motu Puarua
ISLAND

(Île aux Oiseaux, Bird Island) Lying almost in the middle of the lagoon, the rocky Motu Puarua hosts several species of ground-nesting birds, including brown noddies and *uaau* (red-footed boobies).

AHE & MATAIVA

Most tourists tend to visit only Rangiroa, Tikehau and Fakarava, which have the bulk of tourist infrastructure, but it's also possible to explore lesser-known beauties like Ahe and Mataiva.

Ahe

This 20km-long by 10km-wide ring of coral is a charmer. The many hues of its pure aqua-blue water, the foaming breakers around the reef and the thin strips of coral sand beach of its many deserted *motu* (islets) make for an enchanting scene.

The aim of the game on Ahe is to relax – but if you're keen to get the blood flowing a bit there are a few options available.

In a coconut plantation facing the lagoon, **Cocoperle Lodge** (☑ 40 96 44 08; www. cocoperlelodge.com; bungalows s half board 12,100-14,600 CFP, bungalows d half board 24,200-29,200 CFP) has a handful of shabby-chic bungalows. Activities include snorkelling, kayaking and excursions to the nearby bird *motu* or to a pearl farm. The place is run on solar power. **Chez Raita** (☑ 87 22 14 80; www.pension-raita.com; bungalows s/d half board 10,700/21,400 CFP) is a friendly and charming place on a white-sand *motu* on the east side of the atoll. Fancy diving? Contact **Dive N'Co** (☑ 87 22 14 80; www.divenco-ahe.com; introductory or single dive 7500 CFP; ☺ by reservation), which runs daily trips to Tiareroa Pass, a 30-minute boat ride away from the dive shop.

Air Tahiti (☑ 40 86 42 42; www.airtahiti.pf) flies from Pape'ete to Ahe three to four days weekly (24,200 CFP one way).

Mataiva

Like stepping into a time machine, this tiny, picturesque atoll is the sort of hideaway that you search your whole life to discover. Despite the limited tourist infrastructure, it provides a delightful escape holiday. There are superb coral beaches, a few good snorkelling and diving spots, lots of fish and one of the few noteworthy archaeological sites in the Tuamotus.

You can stay at **Ariiheevai** (☑ 87 76 73 23, 40 96 32 50; pensionariiheevai@gmail.com; dm incl breakfast 3500 CFP, bungalows s/d full board incl excursions 8500/17,000 CFP; ❄ 🛜). This place is one of the best deals in the Tuamotus, with 10 well-organised bungalows scattered on a well-tended property abutting the white-sand-fringed emerald lagoon. Rates include daily activities and excursions. Based at the pension, **Mataiva Plongée** (☑ 87 76 75 17, 40 96 32 84; www.mataivaplongee.com; introductory/single dive 8000/7500 CFP; ☺ by reservation) offers dive trips to the pass and beyond.

Air Tahiti (☑ 40 86 42 42; www.airtahiti.pf) has two Pape'ete–Mataiva flights (22,500 CFP one way) a week. One flight is via Rangiroa (9600 CFP one way). Maitaiva is not part of Air Tahiti island-hopping passes.

🏃 Activities

Diving & Snorkelling

The extraordinary **Tuheiava Pass**, to the west of the atoll, about 30 minutes by boat from Tuherahera village, is an unspoilt underwater idyll teeming with all sorts of fish and marine life. Inside the lagoon, the **Ferme aux Mantas** is another killer site. Every morning or so, several manta rays (up to four individuals) congregate around this site in order to be cleaned by wrasses that feed on parasites from the mantas' wings. Snorkellers and divers can easily approach these majestic creatures in less than 10m of waters.

Diving Safari Tikehau DIVING
(☑ 87 24 60 65; Tuherahera; introductory/single dive 8000/7000 CFP; ☺ by reservation) Run by a French couple, Diving Safari Tikehau offers small-group boat dives and certification courses. Two-tank dives in the morning cost 14,000 CFP. Snorkelling is also possible (4900 CFP). It's based at Tikehau Village. Free pick-ups.

Tikehau Plongée DIVING
(☑ 87 32 62 56, 40 96 22 44; introductory or single dive 8000 CFP; ☺ by reservation) This small yet well-organised dive outfit is based in the village and also runs an annex at Tikehau Pearl Beach Resort. It offers two-tank dives

(14,000 CFP) in the morning and has three/five two-tank-dive packages (39,500/61,200 CFP). At most dive sites, snorkelling is also possible (3500 CFP). Free pick-up.

Lagoon Excursions

The easiest way to get a broad look at the delights around the lagoon is to take a one-day tour. All pensions and hotels can organise excursions, sometimes through an outside operator, and trips cost from 8500 CFP per person. They usually take in La Ferme aux Mantas and Motu Puarua, and include a barbecue picnic on one of many paradisiacal *motu* dotted along the Sables Roses.

🛌 Sleeping

Most pensions on Tikehau are on white-sand beaches on the lagoon side of the atoll and a handful are on private *motu*.

Coconut Beach　　GUESTHOUSE, CAMPGROUND $
(☑40 96 23 86; pension.coconutbeachtikehau@gmail.com; Tuherahera; campsite for 2 persons half board 5500 CFP, s/d half board 7500/15,000 CFP, bungalow s/d half board 8500/17,000 CFP; 🖤) Jean-Louis, your friendly host, rents out two compact yet colourful and neat rooms in his modest house. For more privacy, opt for the snug bungalow (with private facilities) next door. The real appeal is the location – the property fronts a superb stretch of pinkish sand at the westen end of the village. Campers can pitch their tent right on the beach.

Tikehau Bed & Breakfast　　BUNGALOW, DORM $
(☑40 96 23 33; www.pensionhotu.com; Tuherahera; dm 3700 CFP, bungalows d 12,500 CFP, all incl breakfast; 🖤) This is the only pension in the village. You have two options here. The four bungalows won't knock your socks off but are in good nick. For solo travellers, the spacious six-bed dorm fits the bill, but expect plenty of mosquitoes – mercifully, mosquito nets are provided. The property opens onto the lagoon, but the shore here is fronted by some craggy coral formations.

Hotu　　BUNGALOW $$
(☑40 96 22 89; www.pensionhotu.com; Tuherahera; bungalows s/d half board 9700/19,400 CFP; 🖤) Occupying a divine stretch of sand, Hotu is a great place to enjoy the coral beach in low-key surroundings. It features five fan-cooled bungalows with private facilities, but the bathrooms don't have doors; they're teeny and feel a little past their prime on the inside, but get the job done. The daily rate includes the use of bikes and kayaks.

Chez Justine　　PENSION, CAMPGROUND $
(☑40 96 22 87, 87 72 02 44; campsite for 2 persons 3500 CFP, bungalows half board s 7500-8600 CFP, d 15,000-17,200 CFP; 🖤) This family-run pension offers a divine location, on a wide sandy beach lapped by topaz waters. Ask for one of the four individual beachfront bungalows here, which are slightly more expensive than the four basic, humbly furnished rooms tucked away behind (there are plans to refurbish them). Campers can pitch tents on a sandy, shady plot just 10m from the lagoon – bliss!

Tikehau Village　　PENSION $$
(☑40 96 22 86, 87 76 67 85; tikehauvillage@mail.pf; bungalows s/d half board 15,000/22,000 CFP; 🖤) You can't argue with the location. It's right on the beach, so your biggest worry is tracking sand into your bungalow. Beautiful views are augmented by simple yet well-appointed bungalows that are made from woven coconut thatch and other natural materials. The shady terraces look out over white-sand and turquoise-lagoon bliss. There are kayaks and bikes for guests' use. Some English is spoken.

★Ninamu　　BUNGALOW $$$
(☑87 28 56 88; www.motuninamu.com; bungalows s/d full board 38,000/76,000 CFP; 🖤) ⁄ Anchored on a private white- and pink-sand *motu* a 10-minute boat ride from the village, this Australian-run venture is the kind of haven stressed-out city slickers dream about. The massive bungalows are built from gnarled hunks of wood, coral stonework and coconut thatch, and the restaurant is another Crusoe-with-style masterpiece. There are only six units, which ensures intimacy.

Tikehau Pearl Beach Resort　　RESORT $$$
(☑40 96 23 00; www.spmhotels.com; bungalows d from 45,000 CFP; 🖳🖤🏊) A hot favourite with honeymooners, this intimate resort (there are only 38 units) boasts a stunning position between endless swaths of white- and pink-sand beaches and bright blue waters. The overwater suites offer the extra bonus of privacy and are so exquisitely designed that you might never want to leave your private dock. All options except the over-the-water standard bungalows have air-con.

🍴 Eating

Snack Ohina　　TAHITIAN $
(☑87 70 65 33; Tuherahera; mains 1000-1500 CFP; ⏰11am-2pm & 6-9pm Mon-Sat) There aren't too many options at this family-run eatery, but there are always invigorating Tahitian

favourites such as grilled *mahimahi*, tuna carpaccio and raw fish. Bonus: there's an enticing, shady terrace.

Snack Perarai – Chez Rowena TAHITIAN $
(☑ 87 74 94 08; Tuherahera; mains 700-1100 CFP; ⊙ 11am-2pm & 6-9pm Wed-Mon) This local-style eatery at the western end of the village serves voluminous portions of good chow mein and *steak frites* (steak and chips). Burgers are also available.

ℹ Information

There is no bank or ATM on Tikehau. There's wi-fi access (with the Manaspot network) near the post office.

ℹ Getting There & Away

Tikehau lies 300km northeast of Tahiti and 14km north of Rangiroa.

AIR
The airport is about 1km east of the village entrance. **Air Tahiti** (☑ 40 86 42 42; www.airtahiti.pf) has daily flights between Pape'ete and Tikehau (24,500 CFP). There are also several weekly flights between Rangiroa and Tikehau (9600 CFP).

BOAT
A few cargo ships offer transport to Tikehau from Pape'ete.

ℹ Getting Around

A 10km track goes around Tuherahera, and passes by the airport. If you've booked accommodation you'll be met at the airport.

MARQUESAS ISLANDS

Grand, brooding and powerful, nature's fingers have sculpted the Marquesas Islands into sharp sillhouettes that jut up dramatically

---

ℹ BITING FLIES

The Marquesas are *not* a beach destination, although there are a few enticing beaches.

As appealing as these beaches may look, the reality is they are invariably infested with *nono* – a small, aggressive biting fly. Fortunately they are found almost exclusively on beaches and in a few valleys and do not carry diseases. Cover yourself in lightweight trousers and long-sleeve shirts and whip out the jungle juice.

---

from the cobalt-blue ocean. Waterfalls taller than skyscrapers trickle down vertical canyons, the ocean thrashes towering cliffs, basalt pinnacles project from emerald forests, and scalloped bays are blanketed with desert arcs of white or black sand.

Some of the most inspirational hikes and horseback rides in French Polynesia are found here, allowing walkers and horse riders the opportunity to explore the islands' rugged interiors. Here the past is almost palpable, thanks to a wealth of archaeological remains dating from pre-European times.

Another highlight is the culture. In everything from cuisine and dances to language and crafts, the Marquesas do feel different from the rest of French Polynesia. But don't expect turquoise lagoons, swanky resorts and an electric nightlife – the Marquesas are an ecotourist's dream, not a beach-holiday destination.

Nuku Hiva
POP 3151

This huge, sparsely populated island (the second largest in French Polynesia after Tahiti) boasts a terrain of razor-edged basaltic cliffs pounded by crashing waves, deep bays blessed with Robinson Crusoe–like beaches, dramatically tall waterfalls and lush valleys that feel like the end of the world.

It's not all about inspiring landscapes, though. Nuku Hiva offers plenty of sites dating from pre-European times. And if you've got energy to burn, hiking and horseback riding will keep you busy.

Taiohae

Timeless little Taiohae, with its bay bobbing with sailboats and tattooed locals trotting through town on horseback, is the marvellous 'capital' of the Marquesas. Sitting peacefully at the base of soaring mountains, it spreads gracefully along a perfectly crescent-shaped bay. This is the obvious place to base yourself in Nuku Hiva.

◉ Sights

★ **Tohua Koueva** ARCHAEOLOGICAL SITE
(Map p410) It's believed that this extensive communal site, with its paved esplanade, belonged to the war chief Pakoko, who was killed by the French in 1845. Today it is a peaceful spot full of massive banyan trees and flowers. All the stone carvings are contemporary. This

massive *tohua* (open-air gathering site) is just over 1.3km up the Pakiu Valley on the Taipivai road, and 700m along a dirt track. Turn east from the main road at the 'Koueva' sign.

Pae Pae Piki Vehine
ARCHAEOLOGICAL SITE

(Map p412) Rebuilt for the 1989 Marquesas Festival, this *pae pae* (traditional meeting platform) contains modern sculptures and a dozen magnificent *tiki* made by the island's sculptors and artisans from Easter Island. Its central, breezy location makes it a popular hang-out for local kids.

Notre-Dame Cathedral
of the Marquesas Islands
MONUMENT

(Map p412) This striking building is built from wood and stones on a former sacred site venerated by the ancient Marquesans. The stones come from the archipelago's six inhabited islands. Pop in to see Marquesan carved religious figures or come for Sunday service at 8am for hauntingly beautiful harmonies.

🏃 Activities

Hiking

Nuku Hiva has a couple of exceptional walks that take in some awe-inspiring viewpoints, without another traveller in sight. A guide is essential because trails are not marked and it's easy to get lost. DIYers have two good options for solo walking: Colette Bay and from Hatiheu to Anaho. For a guide, contact Kimi Randonee (87 75 39 69; kimi.rando@ hotmail.fr; per full day 8000 CFP), who charges 8000 CFP per full day.

Horse Riding

Horse riding is a good way to soak up the drop-dead-gorgeous scenery.

Sabine Teikiteetini
HORSE RIDING

(40 92 01 56, 87 25 35 13; half-day rides incl transfers 10,000 CFP) Sabine is a qualified guide who can arrange lovely rides on Toovii Plateau. You don't need any riding experience, as Sabine caters to all levels of proficiency. Rides last about three hours.

🛏️ Sleeping & Eating

Moana Nui
HOTEL **$**

(Map p412; 40 92 03 30; pensionmoananui@ mail.pf; s/d incl breakfast 6360/9890 CFP, half board 10,110/17,390 CFP; ❄️ 🛜) All eight rooms are clean, well organised (air-con, a small balcony, private facilities, hot shower, daily cleaning) and utilitarian. Rooms 1 and 2 have good views of the bay and all are

Marquesas Islands

decorated in local fabrics and woven bamboo. The location doesn't get any more handy, right in the middle of the bay. The on-site restaurant is an added bonus.

Hee Tai Inn
HOTEL **$$**

(Map p412; 40 92 03 82; www.marquesas-hinn. com; r from 10,000 CFP; ❄️ 🛜) Hee Tai Inn has the eight tidiest rooms in town, all in a plain but comfortable motel-like building at the back of a garden teeming with endemic plants. The real draw here, however, is the owner, Rose Corser, an American woman who has spent decades learning and teaching others about all things Marquesan, from art history to botany.

Mave Mai
PENSION **$$**

(Map p412; 40 92 08 10; pension-mavemai@ mail.pf; s/d incl breakfast 9000/11,000 CFP, half board 11,000/15,000 CFP; ❄️ 🛜) Peacefully reposed over sloping grounds above the marina, this pension features eight rooms in a two-storey motel-style building. They're plain and not terribly Polynesian, but they're light and well appointed, with private facilities (hot water) and air-con, as well as a kitchenette in two of the rooms. The real draw is the small terrace (or balcony upstairs) overlooking the bay.

Nuku Hiva

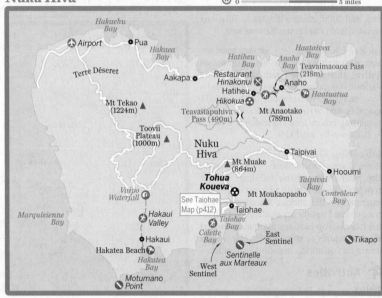

Keikahanui
Nuku Hiva Pearl Lodge
HOTEL **$$$**

(Map p412; ☑40 92 07 10; www.pearlodge.com; bungalows d 26,500-32,000 CFP; ✳@☎☎) Nuku Hiva's only upmarket option, the Keikahanui occupies a wonderfully peaceful domain at the tip of Colette Bay. Digs are in Polynesian-style bungalows hidden in a sea of greenery on a hillside. They are commodious and decked out with tapa and woodcarved panels. Each bungalow has a private balcony with an eye-popping view over the bay.

Café Vaeaki
TAHITIAN **$**

(Map p412; mains 800-1100 CFP; ☉5am-9pm; ☎) This friendly little godsend for yachties is right on the quay and offers simple but fresh dishes such as sashimi, grilled fish and chow mein alongside free wi-fi. There's also fresh juices and ice cream. Cash only.

Snack Tuhiva
TAHITIAN **$**

(Map p412; mains 1000-1200 CFP; ☉breakfast & lunch Mon-Sat) This low-key venue inside the market is a good spot to catch local vibes. Devour a comforting breakfast or munch on well-prepared fish dishes at lunchtime. It was being sold to a new owner when we passed by but it should continue to do more of the same. Cash only.

Hee Tai Restaurant
TAHITIAN, MARQUESAN **$$**

(Map p412; mains 1200-1600 CFP; ☉11.30am-2pm & 6-9pm Mon-Sat) In a lovely setting at the quiet western end of Taiohae Bay, this place takes pride in serving dishes from roast chicken to occasional roast pig feasts. There's also a full bar, perfect for cocktail hour.

ℹ Information

Banque Socredo (Map p412; ☉7.30-11.30am & 1.30-4pm Mon-Fri) Currency exchange, as well as two ATMs.

Hospital (Map p412; ☑40 91 20 00) Has a dentist, too.

Moetai Marine – Yacht Services (Map p412; ☑40 92 07 50; ☉8-11am & 12.30-3.30pm Mon-Fri; ☎) On the quay. Has laundry service (1000 CFP) and can help yachties with formalities. It's open extra hours 1 April to 30 July.

Post Office (Map p412; ☉7-11.30am & noon-3.30pm Mon-Thu, 7-11.30am & noon-2.30pm Fri; ☎) Internet access and wi-fi (with the Manaspot card).

Hatiheu

Hatiheu is a graceful little village dominated by a crescent of black sand, soaring peaks and immaculate, colourful gardens; it's no wonder that Robert Louis Stevenson was so charmed by this setting when he passed through in 1888. It's famous for its powerful archaeological sites, including the vast structures of **Kamuihei, Thakia & Teiipoka** as well as **Hikokua** (Map p410), all located on the outskirts of Hatiheu. They feature vast *tohua*, *tiki* and petroglyphs.

Eating

Restaurant Hinakonui　　MARQUESAN $$
(Chez Yvonne; Map p410; ☑ 40 92 02 97; mains 1800-2900 CFP; ⊙ 11am-1pm Mon-Sat, dinner by reservation) This authentic Marquesan restaurant is a relaxing spot, with an open-air thatched terrace opening onto the seafront. Signature dishes include lobster flambéed with whisky (from February to October) and a truly fantastic goat with coconut milk. Most meals come with a side of breadfruit and *cassava*. Bookings are recommended, otherwise you might find the kitchen closed if there aren't enough customers.

Hakaui Valley

Of all the marvels that Nuku Hiva offers, few equal the awe-inspiring majesty of the Hakaui Valley, which slices through the basaltic landmass, west of the island. On either side of the canyon, vertical walls rise to nearly 800m and **Vaipo Waterfall**, the highest in French Polynesia at 350m, plummets into a natural swimming pool at the end of the valley. In the drier months the volume of the falls lessens and can be reduced to a mere trickle.

Marquises Excursions (☑ 87 73 23 48, 40 92 08 75; www.marquises-excursions.net; halfday cruise for 2 people 17,000 CFP), **Nuku Hiva Tours** (☑ 87 22 68 72, 87 79 13 69) and **Thierry Tekuataaoa** (Map p412; ☑ 87 79 69 69; Yacht Service) can arrange guided trips to the waterfall. Expect to pay 14,000 CFP for two people for the full-day excursion without lunch. From Taiohae, it takes about 40 minutes by speedboat to reach Hakatea Bay, where the boat anchors. From the bay, allow about 2½ hours to reach the waterfall on foot. The path is flat and follows the river.

❶ Getting There & Away

AIR

Air Tahiti (Map p412; ☑ 91 02 25, 92 01 45, 86 42 42; www.airtahiti.pf; ⊙ 8am-noon & 1.30-4.30pm Mon-Thu, 8am-noon & 1.30-3.30pm Fri) has up to nine weekly flights between Pape'ete and Nuku Hiva (34,000 CFP one way, three hours). Within the Marquesas there are daily flights from Nuku Hiva to Hiva

---

ANAHO & HAATUATUA BAY

One of the best-kept secrets in the Marquesas is Anaho. This serene hamlet is only accessible by speedboat (15 minutes from Hatiheu, 7000 CFP) or a little less than 1½ hours by foot from Hatiheu. It's a popular anchorage for visiting yachts and, with the only coral reef on Nuku Hiva, the bay is lagoonlike and inviting.

If Anaho's not remote enough for you, head to Haatuatua Bay, a 30-minute stroll to the east, on an easy-to-follow trail. This crescent-shaped bay fringed with a yellow scimitar of sand, framed by lofty volcanic ridges, is the epitome of an island paradise...except for a few wicked *nono* to bring you back to reality.

Oa (15,500 CFP), and three to five flights per week from Nuku Hiva to 'Ua Huka and 'Ua Pou (both cost 15,000 CFP one way).

BOAT

The *Aranui* (p413) stops at Taiohae.

❶ Getting Around

TO/FROM THE AIRPORT

It takes a minimum of one hour to reach the airport from Taiohae along a winding road, longer if it has rained and the ground is muddy. Licensed 4WD taxis generally wait for each flight. It is nevertheless wise to book through your hotel or pension. Transfers to Taiohae cost 4000 CFP per person.

FOUR-WHEEL DRIVE

Four-wheel drives without driver can be hired from 11,300 to 13,600 CFP per day. Contact the hotel Moana Nui (p409) in Taiohae.

'Ua Huka

POP 630

This low-key, little-visited island feels entirely clean of the troubles of the world: the trees are heavy with fruit, wind whips over the mostly bare hills, surf swishes against the rocky cliffs – and good luck getting a signal on your cell phone outside of Vaipaee. Wood carving is the main activity here and this is the land of masters. There are only three villages, and after a day or two the small communities here seem to absorb you like a giant, friendly sponge. Watch the artisans at work, zigzag up the flanks of an extinct volcano to

Taiohae

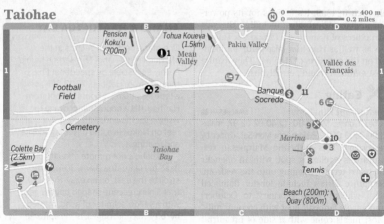

N 0 _____ 400 m
0 _____ 0.2 miles

Taiohae

reach mysterious archaeological sites in the jungle and delve right into Marquesan life.

◉ Sights

Vaipaee   VILLAGE
The island's main town is at the end of a very deep, narrow inlet, about 1km long and rightly named Invisible Bay. You'll find two stores, lots of fruit and flowers, and a few local carver's studios tucked back down the side roads.

Hane   VILLAGE
Experts believe that the first Polynesian settlement on the Marquesas was here, tucked away in a bay protected on the east by the impressive **Motu Hane**. The white house on the seafront contains the excellent village **craft centre** as well as a modest **marine museum** (free admission), which shows the evolution of traditional *pirogues* (outrigger canoes) as well as other artefacts.

Hokatu   VILLAGE
Tiny and scenic Hokatu, about 3km east of Hane, lies in a sheltered bay edged with a pebble beach pounded by azure seas with direct views of imposing, sugar-loafed Motu Hane. On the waterfront there's a small **museum** (free admission) that displays well-presented photographs of the petroglyphs around the island and just beyond is the **craft centre**, the island's biggest.

Meiaute   ARCHAEOLOGICAL SITE
High up in the valley of Hane, the site of Meiaute includes three 1m-high, red-tuff *tiki* that watch over a group of stone structures, *pae pae* and *me'ae*, which are partly overgrown. Two of these *tiki* have projecting ears, one has legs and a phallus, while the other two have only a head and trunk.

Vaikivi Petroglyphs   ARCHAEOLOGICAL SITE

This little-visited archaeological site on the Vaikivi Plateau is well worth the detour, if only for the walk or horse ride to get there. A guide is essential; ask at your pension. The petroglyphs represent an outrigger canoe, a human face, an octopus and various geometric designs.

🏃 Activities

Any chunk of the coastal route between Haavei Bay to the west and Hokatu to the east offers jaw-dropping views. For other walks, a guide is essential because the trails are unmarked. Ask at your pension for a guide; the usual cost is about 5000 CFP, picnic included.

Horse-riding trips can also be organised through your pension. A ride typically costs 6000 CFP for a half-day or 10,000 CFP for a full day, including a guide.

🛏 Sleeping & Eating

Chez Maurice et Delphine   PENSION $

(🗹 40 92 60 55; Hokatu; bungalows half board per person 6500 CFP) This pension has five very ramshackle but spacious bungalows on a little knoll in Hokatu, with sweeping views of Hokatu Bay and Motu Hane. Try to book the bungalow Mata Otemanu – lying on your bed you can see the bay and the *motu*. Meals are locally sourced and delicious; think: lobster, breadfruit and chicken soup and flambéed bananas for dessert.

Mana Tupuna Village   PENSION $

(🗹 40 92 60 08; manatupuna@mail.pf; Vaipaee; s/d with half board 7500/13,500 CFP; 🕾) These four clean and brightly coloured bungalows on stilts are perched on the side of a flowery hill. There are beautiful views over the valley from the bungalows but also from the restaurant/common area where they're framed by giant *tiki* carved by the owner, Raphael. The pension is run by Raphael's hip son Raiarii, who keeps it updated and fresh.

ℹ Information

Infrastructure is very limited on 'Ua Huka. Bring a wad of cash – there's no bank and no ATM, and credits cards are not accepted.

ℹ Getting There & Away

AIR

Air Tahiti (🗹 40 91 60 16, 40 92 60 44, 87 86 42 42; www.airtahiti.pf) has regular flights to Nuku Hiva (11,500 CFP), Hiva Oa (14,000 CFP) and 'Ua Pou (11,500 CFP). For Pape'ete, you'll have to change on Nuku Hiva.

BOAT

The *Aranui* (p413) stops at Vaipaee.

ℹ Getting Around

A surprisingly good 13km road links Vaipaee to Hokatu via Hane.

'Ua Huka's airport is on an arid plateau midway between Vaipaee and Hane. Pensions charge 2000 CFP return for airport transfers.

'Ua Pou

'Ua Pou's geology is fascinating. A collection of 12 pointy pinnacles seem to soar like missiles from the basaltic shield. Almost constantly shrouded in swirling mist and flecked by

---

DON'T MISS

THE ARANUI

If there's an iconic trip in French Polynesia, it's the **Aranui** (🗹 40 42 62 40; www.aranui. com). For over 25 years, this ship has been the umbilical cord between Tahiti and the Marquesas and a hot favourite with tourists. Its 14-day voyage, departing from Pape'ete, takes it to one atoll in the Tuamotus, the six inhabited islands of the Marquesas, as well as Bora Bora. There are 17 trips per year.

Its front half looks just like any other cargo ship of its size, with cranes and holds for all types of goods. The back, however, is like a cruise ship, with cabins, several decks and a swimming pool.

There are various classes of accommodation, from staterooms (from 540,000 CFP per person) and suites (from 720,000 CFP per person) to dorm-style beds with shared bathroom facilities (330,000 CFP per person). Prices include all meals, guided excursions and taxes. No nights are spent ashore; all shore visits last just a day or half-day and include multilingual guides. European and North American art history experts, archaeologists and ethnologists are invited on the cruise, providing cultural insights.

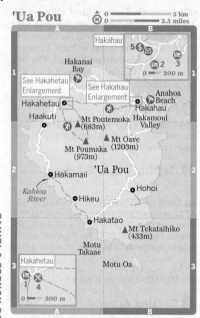

'Ua Pou

'Ua Pou	
Sleeping	
1 Pension Leydj	A3
2 Pension Vehine	B1
3 Pukuéé	B1
Eating	
Snack Vehine	(see 2)
4 Ti' Piero	A3
Information	
5 Banque Socredo	B1

bright sunlight, they form one of the Marquesas' most photographed scenes. 'Ua Pou's jewel-like natural setting will frame everything you do here, from hiking and horse riding across the island to visiting secluded hamlets. For culture buffs, the island musters up a handful of powerful archaeological sites.

Hakahau

'Ua Pou's largest settlement, Hakahau is blessed with a photogenic location. A huge bite chomped out of the fretted coastline of 'Ua Pou's northern coast, Hakahau Bay resembles a giant mouth about to swallow up its prey, with the iconic basalt peaks in the background. Hakahau is a relaxed coastal town blessed with a sweeping black-sand beach – fairly suitable for a dip. With a couple of pensions and useful services, it's a convenient base.

🏃 Activities

You can **walk** along the 4WD tracks that connect the villages. For deeper exploration, it's advisable to hire a guide since it's easy to get lost. Ask at your pension. Recommended hikes include the cross-island path from Hakahau to Hakahetau (about three hours) and the more challenging Poumaka loop (about four hours). A full-day guided walk is about 12,000 CFP for two.

🛏 Sleeping & Eating

Pukuéé　　　　　PENSION, RESTAURANT **$$**
(☎40 92 50 83, 87 72 90 08; pukuee.free.fr; s/d with half board 10,500/19,800 CFP; 🛜🍽) Reliable, friendly and fabulously situated on a hillside with swooning views of Hakahau Bay, Pukuéé offers two rooms in a wooden house surrounded by greenery. Owner Jérôme is great with arranging excursions, and his wife Elisa is a real cordon bleu cook.

Pension Vehine　　　　　PENSION **$$**
(☎40 92 53 21, 87 70 84 32; r incl breakfast/half board per person 6600/8800 CFP, 8800/17,600 CFP) In the centre of Hakahau, this *pension* offers two simple rooms with shared bathroom (hot-water showers) in a house and two beautifully finished bungalows in the garden (alas, no views). Meals are served at Snack Vehine, the family's restaurant. Cash only.

Snack Vehine　　　　　TAHITIAN **$**
(☎40 92 50 63; mains 1100-1900 CFP; ⊙11am-1.30pm & 6-8.30pm Mon-Sat) This casual eatery is your spot for chow mein, grilled or raw fish and steaks.

ℹ Information

Banque Socredo (⊙7.30am-noon & 1-3pm Mon-Fri) Currency exchange and an ATM.

Post Office (⊙7-11.30am & 12.15-3pm Mon-Thu, 7-11.30am & 12.15-2pm Fri) On the seafront. Internet and wi-fi access (with the Manaspot network). Has an ATM.

Hakanai Bay

Shortly beyond the airport at Aneou, this bay appears like a mirage from around a sharp bend: a long curve of wave-lashed beach, and the only footprints to be seen other than your own are those of crabs and insects (except at weekends, when locals enjoy picnics here). It has been named Plage aux Requins (Shark Beach) because of the sharks that are occasionally seen in the cove (it's safe for a dip nonetheless).

Hakahetau

This tranquil village springs up like an oasis after driving along the west coast on a dusty track. There aren't many things to see, but the addictive peaceful atmosphere could hold you captive longer than expected.

🛏 Sleeping & Eating

Pension Leydj PENSION $
(☑40 92 53 19; maka@mail.pf; r half board per person 6900 CFP) In a plum setting on a hill at the edge of Hakahetau, this mellow pension offers clean, well-swept yet impersonal rooms at a nice price. Bathrooms (hot water) are shared. Owner Tony is a renowned master carver and the living room is like a small art gallery – you won't find a better place to buy high-quality souvenirs.

Some seriously good Marquesan meals are served on the terrace with a view of the bay. Various excursions can be organised.

Ti' Piero MARQUESAN, FUSION $$
(☑40 92 55 82; mains 1800 CFP; ⊘by reservation Mon-Sat; 🛜) This family-run eatery does a wonderful job of preparing well-executed international specialities with a true Marquesan touch. Go the *chèvre de sept heures* (goat cooked for seven hours) and breadfruit rolls. A good place to recharge the batteries after the Hakahau–Hakahetau walk. Free wi-fi.

❶ Getting There & Away

AIR
Air Tahiti (p377) has regular flights to Nuku Hiva (15,000 CFP), Hiva Oa (15,500 CFP) and 'Ua Huka (13,500 CFP). For Pape'ete, you'll have to change on Nuku Hiva.

BOAT
The *Aranui* (p413) stops at Hakahau and Hakahetau.

❶ Getting Around

One dirt 4WD track runs most of the way around the island, with the only inaccessible bit being the section between Hakamaii and Hakatao.

The airport is at Aneou, about 10km west of Hakahau. Your hosts will come to collect you if you have booked accommodation; it usually costs 4000 CFP per person return.

Ask at your pension about hiring a 4WD with driver; expect to pay 15,000 CFP to 20,000 CFP per day.

Hiva Oa

POP 2447

Sweet Hiva Oa. Nowhere is the Marquesas' verdant, moody beauty better captured than here. This oh-so-mellow island is a picturesque mix of lush jungle, sea-smashed coastal cliffs and lofty volcanic peaks.

Atuona & Around

Winding around the mouth of a flower-laden bay, Atuona is the southern Marquesas group's tiny administrative capital. The village is framed at the back by forested mountains that give the whole place a close-in, cosy feel. It's the only town with any sort of bustle (by Marquesan standards) on Hiva Oa, and it has a small selection of restaurants and guesthouses.

Atuona is particularly famous for having once been home to Paul Gauguin and Belgian singer Jacques Brel (1929–78), whose memories are kept alive by a regular trickle of visitors.

◉ Sights

Calvaire Cemetery CEMETERY
(Map p416) A must-see for Gauguin and Brel devotees is the Calvaire Cemetery, perched on a hill overlooking Atuona. You will find this frangipani-filled graveyard an appropriately colourful place for Paul Gauguin's tomb. While most of the tombs are marked with white crosses, Gauguin's is a simple round stone with his name painted in white. Right behind, a replica of his statue *Oviri* (meaning 'wild') stands guard.

Smiling Tiki ARCHAEOLOGICAL SITE
(Map p416) Hiva Oa's most bizarre statue can be found near the road to the airport, about 10km from Atuona. About 1m in height, it stands alone in a clearing. To find it (no sign), ask your host to draw you a map.

Espace Culturel Paul Gauguin MUSEUM
(Map p416; adult/child 600/300 CFP; ⊘8-11am Mon-Fri, 2-5pm Mon-Thu, noon-4pm Fri) A homage to Gauguin that traces the artist's life through locally painted reproductions of his art. The main signs are translated into

Hiva Oa & Tahuata

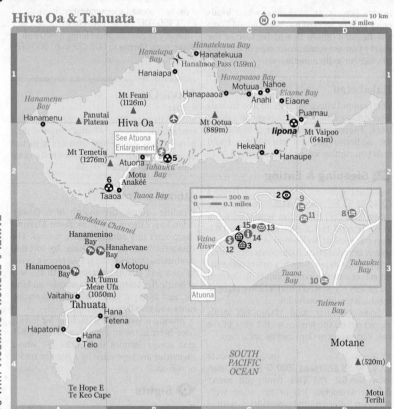

English but the detailed info with titbits about the individual works, alas, are only in French. The Maison du Jouir (House of Pleasure) is an abandoned-looking replica of Gauguin's house with a lifelike statue of the artist inside.

Centre Jacques Brel   MUSEUM
(adult/child 500/250 CFP; ⊘ 8-11am Mon-Fri, 2-5pm Mon-Thu, noon-4pm Fri) Behind the Espace Culturel Paul Gauguin you'll find a big aircraft hangar. In the centre is Jacques Brel's plane, *Jojo;* faded posters tracing the musician's life adorn the walls and his music plays dreamily over the sound system. There's not a word of English in any of the explanations.

Activities

Horse Riding

A network of trails leading to some of the most beautiful sites can be explored on horseback.

Hamau Ranch – Chez Paco   HORSE RIDING
(☑ 40 92 70 57, 87 28 68 21; hamauranch@mail.pf; rides 7000-14,000 CFP) Paco organises three-hour jaunts on the plateau near the airport. No previous experience is necessary. The ultimate is a full-day ride to Hanatekuua Bay, to the north of the island, along undulating ridges and the coastline. Riders must be at least six years old. Transfers can be arranged.

Boat Excursions

Taking a boat excursion to nearby Tahuata will be one of the main highlights of your visit to Hiva Oa and it's well worth the expense (especially given the lack of reliable boat services to Tahuata). Day-long trips usually include stops at Hapatoni and Vaitahu and a picnic lunch at Hanamenino Bay or Hanahevane Bay. Your pension will make arrangements with a local operator. Plan on 8500 CFP per person.

Hiva Oa & Tahuata

⌂ Sleeping

Accommodation options on Hiva Oa are fairly limited. All places are in (or near) Atuona, bar one in Puamau. Unless otherwise noted, credit cards are accepted.

★ Temetiu Village   PENSION $$
(☑ 40 91 70 60; www.temetiuvillage.com; Tahauku Bay; bungalows per person standard/large 9000/11,000 CFP; 🖥🖾) This well-run and friendly pension has four shiny-clean bungalows perched scenically on a lush hillside, each enjoying wraparound views of Tahauku Bay. There are also two older (and slightly cheaper) bungalows that are definitely less luxurious (linoleum floors instead of wood etc) but are more private and perfect for an unfussy couple or single traveler. The food is well respected.

Pension Kanahau – Chez Tania   PENSION $$
(☑ 40 91 71 31, 87 70 16 26; http://pensionkanahau.com; Tahauku Bay; s/d incl breakfast 10,600/13,500

CFP; 🖥) Tania, your chirpy host, does a superb job of keeping her place shipshape. Location-wise, this *pension* plays in the same league as nearby Temetiu Village, with a flower-filled garden and stupendous views of Tahauku Bay and the mountain amphitheatre. The four bungalows are well furnished, spacious and sparkling clean (hot water is available); two units are equipped with cooking facilities.

Relais Moehau   HOTEL $$
(☑ 40 92 72 69; www.relaismoehau.pf; Atuona; s/d incl breakfast from 8000/12,955 CFP; 🖥) Small and friendly like a pension, yet offering more independence, this classic South Pacific–feeling place is across the road from the waterfront and a short walk from town. The front rooms are light-filled and face a wide, bay-view terrace; those at the back face a dark hill. All rooms are pint-sized, but airy and have hot water, fan and plump bedding.

Hotel Hanakéé
Hiva Oa Pearl Lodge   HOTEL $$$
(☑ 40 92 75 87; www.pearlodge.com; bungalows d 24,000-33,000 CFP; ✳@🖥🖾) A secluded property on a mound overlooking Tahauku Bay, with Mt Temetiu as a backdrop, the 14 well-designed bungalows sit in a blooming tropical garden. There's a small pool and a good restaurant. Some units have views of the bay while others face the valley and the mountainous interior. One minus: it's quite isolated.

✕ Eating

Salon de The
Chez Eliane & Cyber Cafe   CREPERIE $
(crepes from 950 CFP; ⊙ 7.30am-5.30pm Mon-Fri, to 3.30pm Sat; 🖥) A cosy little lounge with wi-fi (500 CFP per hour) and a little snack bar serving crepes (sweet and savory), burgers, coffee and ice-cold coconuts. It's right next to the Espace Culturel Paul Gauguin.

Relais Moehau   TAHITIAN, PIZZA $$
(☑ 40 92 72 69; mains 1300-2000 CFP; ⊙11.30am-1.30pm & 6-9pm) Headliners here include *chaud froid de thon* (seared tuna), grilled wahoo, and marinated raw shrimp with coconut sauce, but the pizzas (available dinner only) are very good too. The tiled terrace overlooking Atuona bay is breezy and lovely. Credit cards are accepted (minimum 5000 CFP).

TAHITI & FRENCH POLYNESIA HIVA OA

DON'T MISS

MARQUESAS ARTS FESTIVAL

Powerful, grandiose, visceral – words do little justice to the Marquesas' premier festival, which lasts about one week and is held once every two years, usually in December, on one of the six inhabited islands. It revolves around a series of music, dance and cultural contests, with dance performances being the highlights. Most dancing contests take place on restored archaeological sites, which adds to the appeal.

The Marquesas Arts Festival is your top chance to immerse yourself in traditional Marquesan culture. All islanders take it very seriously. Book your Air Tahiti flight a few months in advance.

Bookmark December 2017 for the next festival, on Tahuata.

Hotel Hanakéé

Hiva Oa Pearl Lodge INTERNATIONAL $$
(Map p416; ☑40 92 75 87; mains 1500-4200 CFP; ☺lunch & dinner) Probably the number-one spot for fine dining in Hiva Oa, and certainly the most suitable place for a romantic soirée. The sweeping views from the terrace are impressive enough, but the excellent French-influenced cuisine is better still, and makes imaginative use of the island's rich produce. The Sunday brunch (3300 CFP) is a steal.

Temetiu Village MARQUESAN $$$
(Map p416; ☑40 91 70 60; set menu 3000 CFP; ☺lunch & dinner, by reservation) With panoramic views from the open-air dining room, a convivial atmosphere and delectable (and copious) Marquesan specialities such as seafood or goat, this place is worth the short drive. Credit cards are accepted.

ℹ️ Information

Banque Socredo (Map p416; ☑40 92 73 54; ☺7.30-11.30am & 1.30-4pm Mon-Fri) Currency exchange. Has a 24-hour ATM.

Cyberservices (☑40 92 79 85, 87 23 22 47; VHF 11) Laundry service, wi-fi and can help yachties with formalities (just call to be picked up).

Post Office (Map p416; ☺7am-noon & 12.30-3pm Mon-Thu, 7am-noon & 12.30-2pm Fri; 📶) Internet and wi-fi access (with the Manaspot card, available at the counter). Has an ATM, too.

Tourist Office (Map p416; ☑40 92 78 93; ☺8.30-11.30am & 2-4pm Mon-Fri) Right in the centre of town. Hands out useful brochures and sells sketch maps of most tourist sights. Opening hours are erratic.

Taaoa

This is a sweet, picturesque hamlet. About 7km southwest of Atuona, accessed by a scenic paved road, Taaoa really feels like the end of the line. It boasts a marvellous setting, with jagged green mountains as the backdrop, and an extensive archaeological site.

About 1.5km from Taaoa, high up in an uninhabited valley, **Tohua Upeke** (Map p416) doesn't have the impressive *tiki,* as at Iipona near Puamau, but its sheer size makes it just as interesting. On arrival at the site, you will find yourself facing a vast *tohua* built on several levels.

Puamau

Most tours visit this east-coast settlement to visit the **Iipona** (Map p416; admission 300 CFP) archaeological site lying on the outskirts of the village. Iipona is one of the best-preserved archaeological sites in French Polynesia. You'll be moved by its eeriness and impressed by the five monumental *tiki* – it pulsates with *mana* (spiritual force). Puamau itself is a delightful, timeless village that occupies a coastal plain bordered by an amphitheatre of mountains. On the way from Atuona you'll pass through the picturesque hamlets of **Motuua** and **Nahoe** and the incredibly scenic **Eiaone Bay**.

Hanaiapa

Picturesquely cradled by striking mountains carpeted with shrubs and coconut trees, Hanaiapa is a gem. Stretching for more than 1km along a single street, this neat and flower-filled village feels like the end of the line. The majestic Hanaiapa Bay is fringed with a pebble beach. An imposing rock sits in the middle of the bay.

Hanaiapa is a cul-de-sac, but you can walk to **Hanatekuua Bay**. One of Hiva Oa's best-kept secrets, this impossibly scenic bay is fringed with a pristine stretch of white-sand beach and backed by a lovely coconut grove. it is accessible by foot only (or by boat).

ℹ️ Getting There & Away

AIR

Air Tahiti (Map p416; ☑40 86 42 42, 40 92 70 90; www.airtahiti.pf) offers daily flights (not always direct) to Pape'ete (39,000 CFP), Nuku

Hiva (16,000 CFP, daily), 'Ua Pou (15,000 CFP, four weekly flights) and 'Ua Huka (15,000 CFP, three weekly flights).

BOAT

The *Aranui* (p413) stops at Atuona and Puamau. To get to Tahuata or Fatu Hiva, you can charter a private boat and share the costs with any other passengers.

ℹ️ Getting Around

The airport is 13km from Atuona. If you have booked your accommodation, your host will come and collect you for about 3600 CFP return.

Atuona Rent-a-Car (☑ 40 92 76 07, 78 72 17 17) and **Hiva Oa Location** (☑ 40 92 70 43, 78 24 65 05) rent 4WDs without driver for about 10,000CFP to 15,000 CFP per day.

Fatu Hiva

POP 630

As far away from the rest of the world as it's possible to get in these modern times (despite mobile phones and satellite TVs), Fatu Hiva is a marvellous 'stop the world and get off' place. When arriving by boat (there's no landing strip), expect a visual shock: wrinkled cliffs tumble into the ocean and splendid bays, including the iconic Bay of Virgins, indent the coastline.

It's a bit challenging to get to Fatu Hiva, but for travellers who relish the idea of being marooned for a few days, this hard-to-reach island way off most people's radar (bar yachties) is hard to beat.

⊙ Sights

Omoa   VILLAGE
Time moves at a crawl in Omoa. The most striking monument is the **Catholic church**, with its red roof, white facade and slender spire. It makes a colourful scene on Sunday morning, when it's bursting at the seams with a devout congregation neatly dressed and belting out rousing *himene*.

Hanavave   VILLAGE
Hanavave boasts a splendid setting, at the mouth of a steep-sided valley, best enjoyed from the sea (lucky yachties!). When the setting sun bounces purple halos off the towering basaltic cones of **Baie des Vierges**, with a cluster of yachts at anchor, it's a hallucinatory wonderland.

WORTH A TRIP

TAHUATA
....
Tahuata is accessible only by boat (there's no landing strip) from Hiva Oa. Given that there's no regular service, most travellers visit Tahuata on a day tour from Hiva Oa, which includes visits of Hapatoni, Vaitahu and a picnic on a beach at idyllic Hanamenino Bay, Hanamoenoa Bay or Hanahevane Bay.

🏃 Activities

Most activities on Fatu Hiva are of the DIY variety, including **walking** and **horse riding**. Follow the 17km-long track that links Omoa to Hanavave via the interior for a four-hour walk that's not too difficult and you can't get lost.

🛏️ Sleeping & Eating

Chez Lionel Cantois   PENSION **$**
(☑ 40 92 81 84, 78 70 03 71; chezlionel@mail.pf; Omoa; s/d incl breakfast 4500/6500 CFP, bungalows s/d incl breakfast 6500/9500 CFP; @) Basking in familial warmth, this pension at the far end of Omoa has an air of *Little House on the Prairie*. Lionel, who is from Normandy and who is a mine of local information (his English is passable), can take you virtually anywhere on the island, while his Marquesan wife Bernadette is a good cook (dinner from 1500 CFP).

ℹ️ Information

Bring a stash of cash – there's no bank on the island and credit cards are not accepted. There is a post office in Omoa.

ℹ️ Getting There & Away

Fatu Hiva is the most difficult island to get to in the Marquesas, but sorting out transport is manageable if you're flexible. In Hiva Oa, find out if boat charters to Fatu Hiva are being organised during your stay and you may be able to share the costs. There's no regular service. Another option is to hop on the *Aranui* (p413) when it stops at Atuona, Omoa or Hanavave. The crossing between Hiva Oa and Atuona takes anything from three to five hours, depending on the sea conditions. The journey can be very uncomfortable if the sea is choppy.

ℹ️ Getting Around

The only dirt road is 17km long and links Hanavave with Omoa, but it's quicker (and

TAHITI & FRENCH POLYNESIA FATU HIVA

cheaper) to hire a speedboat to travel between the two villages.

Inquire at your pension about renting a 4WD; expect to pay 15,000 CFP a day with driver.

THE AUSTRAL ISLANDS

Isolated and straddling the Tropic of Capricorn, the magnificent and pristine Austral Islands are arguably French Polynesia's most underrated destination. The climate is temperate, but everything else befitting of a tropical paradise is here: flower-filled jungles, sharp peaks, outrageously blue water and genuinely friendly people. The islands here have had less of a history with Europeans and less influx from the outside world, so have kept their culture alive.

Rurutu

POP 2400

The island's geology makes it unique; Rurutu is one of the South Pacific's largest raised atolls *(makatea)*. Vertical limestone cliffs pockmarked with caves line the coast, while the volcanic interior is a fertile, mind-bogglingly abundant jungle. While there's very little fringing reef, there are a few white-sand beaches where you can flake out. Feeling active? Various activities and lots of unique natural attractions will keep you busy.

◎ Sights

Ana Aeo
CAVE

This cave, with its massive, oozy-looking stalactites and stalagmites, is the most stunning on the island. It's 500m north of the Teautamatea pension; there's a signposted track going to the right that leads to the cave.

Ana Tane Uapoto
CAVE

On the eastern outskirts of the village of Moerai, near Arei Point, you'll find this large roadside cavern with stalactites and stalagmites. Traditionally this cave was used to salt (for preservation) and divide whale meat among the islanders.

🏃 Activities

Whale Watching

The whales come to Rurutu from around late July to mid-October to reproduce before heading back to the icy waters of the Antarctic. There are no promises that you will see

any (it's not uncommon to experience a few weeks in a row with no sightings), but the best chance of seeing the whales is in August and September; check with the local operators.

Tareparepa Baleines
WILDLIFE WATCHING

(☑ 87 79 48 86, 87 25 02 62; half-day tours 8500 CFP; ☺ by reservation) A well-trained operator who has plenty of experience. Small groups only.

Horse Riding

Viriamu
HORSE RIDING

(☑ 87 70 34 65, 40 93 02 93; 2/3hr rides 5000/7500 CFP; ☺ by reservation) Viriamu, from the Teautamatea pension, leads superb horse-riding excursions, suitable for all levels (children are welcome). The three-hour ride, during which you'll pass stunning viewpoints in the island's interior and clip-clop along the lagoon on the western coast, is truly enchanting.

🛏 Sleeping & Eating

Teautamatea
PENSION $$

(☑ 40 93 02 93, 87 70 34 65; www.teautamatea. blogspot.com; s/d half board 9000/13,800 CFP; 🛜) A more congenial place you'll be hard-pressed to find. Viriamu is from Rurutu, his wife Elin is Welsh, and you'll get the best of both worlds. There are three clean, well-swept and uncluttered rooms. They are in the owners' home but offer enough privacy.

Manotel
BUNGALOW $$

(☑ 40 93 02 25; www.lemanotel.com; bungalows s/d half board 11,500/16,400 CFP; 🛜) Run by a French-Rurutu couple, Manotel has seven pretty bungalows with fans, good bathrooms and particularly inviting terraces; it's across the road from a long stretch of white beach (not suitable for swimming due to the fringing reef) about 3km south of Moerai. The garden is blooming with colours, the owner runs reputable island tours and his wife is a real cordon bleu.

❶ Getting There & Away

Air Tahiti (☑ 40 86 42 42; www.airtahiti.pf) flies between Rurutu and Tahiti (23,600 CFP, three to five flights weekly), Tubuai (13,000 CFP, once or twice weekly), and Rimatara (10,800 CFP, once weekly). For Raivavae, you'll need to change on Tubuai.

If you've booked accommodation you'll be picked up at the airport. The best way to get around the island is to take a tour.

Austral Islands & Gambier Archipelago ⓝ

0 ⎯⎯⎯⎯⎯ 300 km
0 ⎯⎯⎯⎯⎯ 180 miles

Maria Island

Rurutu

Rimatara

The Australs

Tubuai

Tropic of Capricorn

Raivavae

The Gambier Archipelago

SOUTH PACIFIC OCEAN

To Gambier Archipelago (1000km; see inset)

Totegegie

Tarauru Roa

Mangareva

Mt Duff (441m) Rikitea

Taravai

Mt Mokoto (425m) Aukena

Akamaru

Agakauitai

Makaroa Manui
Kamaka

0 ⎯⎯⎯ 20 km
0 ⎯⎯⎯ 12 miles

Rapa Iti (Rapa)

Marotiri (Bass Rocks)

Tubuai

Although it lies in the shadow of Raivavae and Rurutu, this very scenic island is blessed with sandy beaches, a string of idyllic *motu*, a fantastic lagoon and a few archaeological sites. Two mountain ranges slope down to the flat plains by the sea and a low-lying central region bisects the two. You can stay at **Wipa Lodge** (☑ 87 73 10 02, 40 93 22 40; maletdoom@mail.pf; bungalows s/d half board 13,500/18,500 CFP; ☎).

Raivavae

POP 977

This is a paradise not only because of the sweeping blue lagoon, idyllic white-sand *motu* or the mountainous interior dominated by square-topped Mt Hiro (437m), but also because of the ultrawarm Polynesian welcome and extraordinary glimpse into a traditional way of life. Amazingly, though considered one of the great beauties of the South Pacific, the island receives only a trickle of tourists.

◉ Sights & Activities

All pensions offer lagoon tours and excursions to *motu* (5500 CFP to 7000 CFP) plus a tour of the island by car (about 1500 CFP).

Although the lagoon is the main highlight, Raivavae also has a few archaeological sites that are worth a peek.

Motu Piscine   BEACH
Raivavae's stunning lagoon, brimming with marine life and ringed by ironwood-covered *motu*, is one of the treasures of the South Pacific. Motu Piscine ('Motu Swimming Pool'; Motu Vaiamanu) is the best-known *motu*, fringed with white beaches and divided from its neighbour by a glassy turquoise channel that's teeming with tropical fish. Fabulous. All pensions can arrange a lagoon tour, including a picnic, on Motu Piscine.

🛏 Sleeping & Eating

Raivavae Tama   BUNGALOW $
(☑ 87 31 24 73, 40 95 42 52; www.raivavaetama. com; Anatonu; d half board without bathroom per person 6500 CFP, bungalows s/d half board 8500/15,000 CFP; ☎) Three rustic, coconut-thatched bungalows with bathrooms sit on a skinny stretch of white sand, with fabulous lagoon views; there are also two boxy rooms in the family's home (which is across the road) and two comfortable bungalows in the garden at the back. The local-style food and welcome here are extraordinary and excellent English is spoken.

TAHITI & FRENCH POLYNESIA FRENCH POLYNESIA TODAY

THE GAMBIER ARCHIPELAGO

If, after visiting the Society Islands, the Tuamotus, the Marquesas and the Australs, you still feel the urge for more off-the-beaten-track adventures, consider travelling to the Gambier, where visitors are an absolute rarity. All the makings of an island holiday paradise can be found in this jaw-droppingly beautiful archipelago, but it's so far away (about 1700km southeast from Tahiti) and expensive to get to that it remains one of the best-kept secrets in French Polynesia. The geology here is unique: one reef, complete with sandy *motu*, encircles a small archipelago of lush high islands dotting a blue lagoon that's as clear as air. Adding to the allure, the Gambier is the cradle of Polynesian Catholicism and houses some of the most eerie and interesting post-European structures in the country. It's also famous for its lustrous and colourful pearls.

Mangareva, the main island, has a couple of places to stay, including **Maro'i** (☑87 70 36 55, 40 97 84 44; www.pensionmaroi.com; bungalows 1-3 people 8000-9500 CFP; 🗑) and **Chez Bianca & Benoît** (☑40 97 83 76; www.chezbiancaetbenoit.pf; Rikitea; s/d half board 11,100/17,000 CFP, bungalows s/d half board 13,300/17,000 CFP; 🗑).

Tempted? Contact **Air Tahiti** (☑40 86 42 42; www.airtahiti.pf), which has regular flights to the Australs and the Gambier Islands.

Chez Linda
BUNGALOW **$**

(☑87 78 80 24, 40 95 44 25; www.pension lindaraivavae.pf; s/d half board 8500/12,500 CFP, bungalows s/d half board 10,600/14,000 CFP; 🗑) This is a reputable place with four Polynesian-style bungalows with private bathrooms and two adjoining tiny rooms at the back of the property. Food is a highlight, with delicious traditional dishes served at dinner. The lagoon is just across the road but swimming is not great, with shallow, murky waters. Bikes are available for hire and kayaks are free. Cash only.

Getting There & Away

Raivavae is 650km southeast of Tahiti and 200km southeast of Tubuai. **Air Tahiti** (☑40 86 42 42; www.airtahiti.pf) operates flights to/from Pape'ete three days a week (28,500 CFP), sometimes via Tubuai (13,000 CFP).

Pensions provide free airport transfers and bike hire. Cycling the flat 22km of coast road is easy.

UNDERSTAND TAHITI & FRENCH POLYNESIA

French Polynesia Today

While technically a part of France, French Polynesia is, for the most part, self-governing. Since 2004 the government has been in turmoil as the main political parties battle it out and try to woo members of the assembly to flip-flop the balance of power. While democratic elections decide how many assembly seats go to each party, once there the members can switch allegiances. When it's a fragile majority, which is usually the case, one or two changes can overturn the entire government. From 2004 to 2014 this happened 13 times, but Edouard Fritch is currently blowing the trend by remaining president since September 2014.

All these puzzle pieces make the big picture bad news for the French Polynesian people. They no longer have faith in their politicians or political systems, the economy is failing and France seems less and less inclined to offer large sums of money to keep everything afloat. There is hope that a new generation of politicians will come along who will bring the country forward, but so far these saviours are nowhere to be seen.

On the economic front, the situation is not rosy in French Polynesia. While elsewhere in the Pacific tourism is back on the rise, Tahiti's stats fell and now are rising only slightly; this makes the number of visitors per year not much greater than those of 1996 (around 150,000 – there were 180,000 visitors in 2014). This is a harsh blow to a country whose primary industry is tourism. Many blame the costly airfares but the country's reputation as a high-end-only destination may also be to blame. Another thing to think about: a large part of tourism is on cruise ships that don't impact local economies very much.

The pearl industry – which was once the second most important asset in French Polynesia's economy – is also in shambles. Today, with the price of Tahitian pearls at one quarter of what it was in 2000, only a few larger farms and a scattering of small family-run farms are still in business.

History

The isolated islands of Polynesia were among the last places on earth to be settled by humans and were also some of the last places to be colonised by Europeans. Without written language, little is known of the islands' history before Europeans arrived. Modern theories have Polynesian voyages originating from the Philippines or Taiwan, spurred on by territorial disputes or overpopulation.

European Arrival

European explorers first ventured into the region in 1595, although major expeditions didn't really get under way until the late 18th century. Don Alvaro de Mendaña y Neyra came upon the Marquesas Islands in 1595 on his second search for *terra australis incognita*, the nonexistent great southern continent. Mendaña named the islands after his patron, Marquesas de Mendoza, but his visit resulted in open warfare and 200 islanders were killed.

With his ship the *Dolphin*, Samuel Wallis anchored at Matavai Bay in Tahiti's lagoon in late June of 1767. He only stayed in Matavai Bay for a few weeks, just long enough to name the island King George's Land and to claim it for Britain.

With his ships *La Boudeuse* and *L'Étoile,* Louis-Antoine de Bougainville arrived on Tahiti in April 1768, less than a year after Wallis. At this time Wallis was still homeward bound, so Bougainville was unaware he was not the first European to set eyes on the island.

Unaware that the Union Jack had already flown over the island, Bougainville took time out to claim Tahiti for France but, like Wallis, he was soon overshadowed when the greatest Pacific explorer of them all, James Cook, arrived on the scene. In three great expeditions between 1769 and 1779, James Cook filled the map of the Pacific so comprehensively that future expeditions were reduced to joining the dots.

Already firmly established in South America, the Spanish looked upon the Pacific as their backyard and were less than happy to hear about other European navigators' visits. In 1772 Don Domingo de Boenechea sailed the *Aguilla* from Peru and anchored in the lagoon off Tautira on Tahiti Iti (Small Tahiti). For the third time, the island was claimed by a European nation.

Bounty Mutineers

In 1789 the infamous mutiny on the *Bounty* occurred after Bligh's crew had spent six long, comfortable months on Tahiti.

After the mutiny the mutineers returned to Tahiti and Tubuai in the Australs before sailing to a more remote hideaway on Pitcairn Island. Sixteen stayed behind on Tahiti, a move that changed the course of history.

Before the Europeans arrived, power had been a local affair. No ruler was strong enough to control more than a patch of land, and Tahiti was divided into a number of squabbling groups. However, once they realised the persuasive power of European weaponry, Tahitians pressed the *Bounty* mutineers to take sides in local conflicts. The mutineers became mercenaries to the highest bidder, the Pomare family.

That deal was the beginning of the Pomares' metamorphosis into a ruling dynasty. Pomare I, known as Tu, controlled most of Tahiti by the time he died in 1803; his son Pomare II took over, a trend that was to continue through the century.

Whalers, Missionaries & Depopulation

The London Missionary Society (LMS) landed at Tahiti's Point Vénus in March 1797 and did its best to rid the islanders of their wicked ways. Dancing, 'indecent' songs, tattoos, nudity, indiscriminate sex and even wearing flowers in the hair were banned once the missionaries got their patron, Pomare II, on their side.

Whalers and traders arrived in Polynesia in the 1790s, spreading diseases, encouraging prostitution and introducing alcohol and more weapons.

Plagued by diseases against which they had no natural immunity, the population plummeted. When Cook first visited, Tahiti's population was about 40,000. In 1800 it was less than 20,000 and by the 1820s it was down to around 6000. In the Marquesas, the population dropped from 80,000 to only 2000 in one century.

Pomares & the Missionaries

After 1815 the Pomares ruled Tahiti, with Protestant missionaries advising them on government and laws, and trying to keep whalers and Australian traders at arm's length. Pomare II died in 1821, leaving his son Pomare III to rule until his death six years later in 1827, at which point the young Queen Pomare IV assumed the throne for the next 50 years.

English Protestant missionaries were the major advisers to chiefs in the Society, Austral and Tuamotu Islands. But in the Gambier Archipelago and the Marquesas Islands, French Catholic missionaries were in control. In 1836 two French missionaries, Laval and Caret, visiting Pape'ete from the Gambier Archipelago, were caught up in this rivalry when the British promptly arrested and deported them.

French Takeover

The French saw the deportation of Laval and Caret as a national insult. Demands, claims, counterclaims, payments and apologies shuttled back and forth. In 1842 Admiral Dupetit-Thouars settled matters by turning up in *La Reine Blanche* and pointing the ship's guns at Pape'ete, forcing Queen Pomare to yield. French soldiers promptly landed, along with Catholic missionaries.

Queen Pomare, still hoping for British intervention, fled to Ra'iatea in 1844 and a guerrilla rebellion broke out on several islands. The rebels were subdued and by 1846 France controlled Tahiti and Mo'orea. The queen returned to Tahiti in 1847 as a mere figurehead.

Queen Pomare died in 1877; her son, Pomare V, had little interest in the position and abdicated in 1881. French power extended to include most of the other Society Islands in 1888. The Gambier Archipelago was annexed in 1881 and the Austral Islands in 1900–01.

Twentieth Century

Soon after the turn of the century an economic boom attracted colonists, mostly French. By 1911 there were about 3500 Europeans in the islands, adding to Chinese immigration, which had begun in 1864 with cotton production at Atimaono on Tahiti.

French Polynesia was directly involved in both world wars. In WWI almost 1000 Tahitian soldiers fought in Europe, and on 22 September 1914 two German cruisers patrolling the Pacific sank the French cruiser *Zélée* and shelled the Pape'ete market. In WWII 5000 US soldiers were based on Bora Bora, and a 2km runway was built in 1943.

Tahitian volunteers in the Pacific Battalion fought in North Africa and Europe.

In 1946 the islands became an overseas territory within the French Republic, sparking agitation for independence. On 22 July 1957 the territory officially became French Polynesia. The 1960s were a real turning point. In 1961 Faa'a airport was built, opening French Polynesia to the world. Shortly after, the filming of *Mutiny on the Bounty* on Tahiti poured millions of dollars into the economy. In 1963 the nuclear-testing Centre Expérimentation du Pacifique (CEP; Pacific Experimentation Centre) was established at Moruroa and Fangataufa.

From 1977 to 1996 French Polynesia took over internal management and autonomy from France. The nuclear testing of the era shook Polynesia physically, socially and economically: violent protests rocked Pape'ete in 1987 and 1995, and the CEP made French Polynesia economically dependent on France. The end to nuclear testing in 1996 also meant the end of the prosperity of the previous 30 years.

The Culture

The National Psyche

If French Polynesia had a national slogan it might be '*haere maru*' (take it slow). It's hard not to take it slow in the islands. With one road encircling most islands, you'll often get caught driving behind an old pick-up truck at 50km/h with no chance of passing; the internet takes an eternity if it works at all; and it seems holidays shut all the shops every week or so. Yet, somehow, everything works out.

Regardless of 'Tahiti time', Pape'ete manages to move at a pace fitting for a capital: there are traffic jams and everyone is on a mobile phone and uses social media. The modern world is quickly infiltrating the slow pace of life and this is most evident in the younger generations.

Lifestyle

The traditional Tahitian family is an open-armed force that is the country's backbone. Although modern girls are increasingly less likely to stay home and have baby after baby, an accidental pregnancy is considered more of a blessing than a hindrance, and babies are passed along to another eager, infant-loving family member. *Faamu* (adopted children) are not thought of as different to blood brothers and sisters, although the birth mother, and occasionally the father, sometimes remains a peripheral part of the child's life. Once a child is in a family, he or she is in no way obligated to stay; children move about to aunties, uncles and grandparents as they wish.

This family web is vitally important to an individual. When people first meet, the conversation usually starts with questions about family and most people are able to find a common relative between themselves within minutes. This accomplished, they are 'cousins' and fast friends.

But it's not all roses in what appears to be such a warm, fuzzy family framework. Domestic violence and incest are prevalent. This is closely connected with high rates of alcoholism. The government has launched numerous programs addressing these issues but little progress has been made.

Pakalolo (marijuana) and the Bob Marley lifestyle have been thoroughly embraced in French Polynesia, but harder drugs are rare. The exception is ice, a highly addictive methamphetamine that has rapidly gained popularity in the upper classes of Pape'ete.

Population

The majority of the population claims to be Polynesian (although most have some other ethnicity in the mix), 12% of the population is Chinese and the rest is European. Racial tension is rare but does exist. A few insults exist for each race, although they are usually only uttered on drunken binges or in schoolyards.

Paralleling worldwide patterns of urbanisation, French Polynesia's people have migrated towards the city and main island: 69% of the population currently make their home on Tahiti and 75% of those on Tahiti live in Pape'ete or its suburbs.

On all the islands the majority of the population lives in coastal zones. The rugged interior is virtually uninhabited.

Arts

The zealous work of the missionaries managed to rid the existing Polynesian art and culture of many of its symbols and practices. Among other things, temples and carvings were destroyed and tattooing and dancing were banned. Fortunately, some traditions survived this period, and in recent years there has been a revival of Polynesian culture.

Dance

The dances that visitors see are not created for tourists – they are authentic performances that take months of rehearsals and are based on rigorously standardised choreography depicting specific legends. In this land of oral traditions, dance is not merely an aesthetic medium but also a means of preserving the memory of the past.

Tahitian dance is taught in schools from a young age and those who become serious about it (and there are many) can continue on in a local troupe or at private dance schools. The best dance performances are held at the annual Heiva festival in July.

Many luxury hotels offer quality dance shows about twice a week. On Tahiti and Mo'orea they are performed by semiprofessional groups and range from small groups dancing to piped-in music (in the worst cases) to theatrical extravaganzas with live orchestras. These shows include a buffet and are open to all.

Music

Traditional Polynesian music, usually performed as an accompaniment to dance, is heard reverberating across the islands. Ukuleles and percussion instruments dominate, and the music is structured by a fast-paced and complex drumbeat. Sunday *himene* (hymns) at churches feature wonderful harmonies.

Modern Polynesian music by local artists is the blaring soundtrack to everyday life, whether it's in a bus, at a cafe or on the radio; some groups also perform in hotels and bars. This music ranges from rock to folksy ballads usually accompanied by a guitar or ukulele. A current popular local group (highly recommended) that you may see playing on Tahiti and Moorea is called Pepena.

Sculpture, Woodcarving & Tapa

Traditionally, the best sculptures and woodcarvings have come out of the Marquesas, where fine *tiki*, bowls, mortars and pestles, spears and clubs are carved from rosewood, *tou* wood or stone. You can find these pieces in the market of Pape'ete, as well as gift shops around the islands, but the best deals are had in the Marquesas themselves.

Traditionally made throughout the Pacific, tapa (paperlike cloth) is a nonwoven fabric made from the bark of *uru* (breadfruit), banyan or *aute* (paper mulberry) trees. It was the semidisposable clothing fabric of pre-European Polynesia. Finished pieces are dyed with the sap of various plants or decorated with traditional artwork. Today, designs are sometimes just drawn on with ink.

Tattoos

Since the early 1980s, tattooing has enjoyed a strong revival, becoming one of the most expressive and vibrant vehicles of Polynesian culture.

Young Tahitians have delved into their ancient traditions and have brought this ancestral form of bodily adornment, with its undisputed artistic qualities, completely up to date. Today many Polynesian men and women sport magnificent tattoos as symbols of their identity.

You'll find talented tattoo artists throughout the islands who will be happy to create an unforgettable souvenir on your skin.

Modern tattooing is completely for the sake of style or beautification; in ancient times it was a highly socially significant and sophisticated art.

Environment

The Land

French Polynesia's 118 islands are scattered over an expanse of the Pacific Ocean stretching more than 2000km – an area about the size of Western Europe. Five archipelagos, the Society, Tuamotu, Marquesas, Austral and Gambier, divide the country into distinct geological and cultural areas.

High islands – think Tahiti, Mo'orea and Bora Bora – are essentially mountains rising out of the ocean that are often encircled by a barrier reef. A protected, shallow lagoon, with that flashy blue colour of postcards and brochure fame, is formed by the reef.

The Tuamotus, east of the Society Islands, are classic low-lying coral atolls. An atoll is a ring of old barrier reef that surrounds a now-sunken high island. The remote Marquesas, north of the Tuamotus and not far from the equator, are rugged high islands but lack barrier reefs or lagoons. Finally, there are the even more remote and scattered Australs, also high islands, and the tiny Gambier Archipelago.

Wildlife

Basically, anything that couldn't swim, float or fly to French Polynesia has been introduced; therefore the flora and fauna is limited compared with that of the west Pacific. There are no snakes but plenty of insects and about 100 species of *manu* (birds). Seabirds include terns, petrels, noddies, frigate birds and boobies.

Any dismay about the lack of animal diversity on land is quickly made up for by the quantity of underwater species – it's all here. At the top of the food chain, sharks are found in healthy numbers throughout the islands. Blacktip and whitetip reef sharks are the most common and pose little danger. More aggressive and sometimes unnervingly curious, the grey reef shark is common in the Tuamotus. Other large creatures you are likely to encounter are graceful manta rays; smaller, spotted leopard rays; stingrays; and moray eels. Five of the seven species of sea turtle (all endangered) make their home in French Polynesia, but you're most likely to see the green and hawksbill turtles, which often come to feed in the lagoons.

Vegetation varies significantly from one archipelago to another. On the atolls, where the soil is poor and winds constant, bushy vegetation and coconut palms predominate. On the high islands, plant cover is more diverse and changes according to the altitude. The *tiare*, a small, white, fragrant gardenia, is the symbol of French Polynesia.

Marine reserves in French Polynesia in the past have been few: Scilly and Bellinghausen (remote islands in the Leeward group of Society Islands) and eight small areas within Mo'orea's lagoon are the only ones that have been protected long-term by the country itself. Fakarava and its surrounding atolls are a Unesco biosphere reserve. This is changing, however, with the likelihood of the creation of a 1-million-sq-km reserve around the Austral Islands; it's expected that this will become a reality by 2020. Another 700,000-sq-km area around the Marquesas Islands is hoped to be protected by 2017.

The only terrestrial reserves are the Marquesan Nature Reserves, which include the remote uninhabited islands of Motu One, Hatutu, Eiao and Motane. Several species are protected and there are limits placed on the fishing of some fish and crustaceans. Unfortunately, fish continue to be caught indiscriminately and shells are still collected. Although turtles are highly protected, they continue to be poached for their meat and their shells.

Environmental Issues

Atolls and high islands are ecologically fragile but French Polynesia has been slow to implement environmental protection. Despite a limited number of 'green' establishments that are springing up, and the rigorous requirements of public buildings and hotels to blend in with the landscape, pollution is steadily chipping away at the picture of paradise.

Although there are many low-lying atolls in French Polynesia, the effects of climate change, including rising sea level, have so far been minimal. Higher water temperatures are one of the biggest threats to the health of the country's coral reefs and, during El Niño years in particular, huge amounts of coral die, affecting the entire ecosystem.

The environmental repercussions of French nuclear testing are still hotly debated. It was confirmed in 1999 that Moruroa and Fangataufa were fissured by tests and that radioactivity has been allowed to escape from cracks in the atolls' coral cones. Evidence has been found of low-level activity in certain areas of the Gambiers but long-ranging conclusive evidence has yet to come forth.

SURVIVAL GUIDE

❶ Directory A–Z

ACCOMMODATION

Most people assume that a Tahitian holiday means staying at a resort but French Polynesia has a wide range of sleeping options, from camping upwards, depending on the island you choose. Double-occupancy bungalows, either at a resort, a small hotel or a family-run pension, are the most common option.

Camping & Hostels

Camping options come and go, but generally it's a matter of pensions having areas where you can pitch your tent and make use of their facilities; you'll pay anywhere from around 1200 CFP to 2500 CFP per person. You'll find camping on Tahiti, Mo'orea, Huahine, Ra'iatea, Bora Bora, Rangiroa, Fakarava and Tikehau. A scant number of guesthouses (on Tahiti, Mo'orea, Bora Bora, Rangiroa and Huahine) have dorm beds ranging from 2000 CFP to 3500 CFP per person per night.

Pensions & Small-Hotel Islands

Pensions are a godsend for travellers who baulk at the prices of the big hotels and enjoy more independence and contact with local culture. These little establishments, generally family-run affairs, are great places to meet locals and other travellers. Upmarket versions can be private, quite luxurious and have lots of amenities, but at the lower end of the scale you should brace yourself for cold showers, lumpy pillows and thin walls, but lap up the charm and culture.

Many pensions, particularly on islands where there are few to no other eating options available, offer half board (or *demi-pension*), which means breakfast and dinner. Young children usually stay for free, and children up to about 12 usually pay half-price.

Think ahead in terms of money, as many pensions do not take credit cards.

Small hotels are found mostly on the more touristed islands. The main difference between the two is the level of contact you're likely to have with the management: at pensions the owners usually take care of their guests almost like family, whereas small hotels will offer you services but leave you on your own and expect you to be more independent. Small hotels usually offer en-suite rooms in a building.

Resorts

If you are ever going to pamper yourself silly, French Polynesia is a great place to do it. The luxury hotels often manage to blend their opulent bungalows into the natural setting, be that perched over a blue lagoon or settled back into lush gardens. Many of the top hotels are on isolated *motu* (islets), and can only be reached by boat.

Holiday Rentals

Holiday rentals (private homes or rooms rented by an individual) are becoming more popular in French Polynesia, particularly on Mo'orea, although there are also some good options on Tahiti. These often self-catering options can be fun and economical for families or people travelling in larger groups who plan on staying in one place for more than a night or two.

> ### SLEEPING PRICE RANGES
>
> The following price ranges refer to a double room or bungalow with bathroom in high season. Unless otherwise stated, all taxes are included in the price.
>
> **$** less than 10,000 CFP
>
> **$$** 10,000–20,000 CFP
>
> **$$$** more than 20,000 CFP

CONSULATES

Given that French Polynesia is not an independent country, there are no foreign embassies, only consulates, and many countries are represented in Pape'ete by honorary consuls.

The consulates and diplomatic representatives are all located on Tahiti. Many are just single representatives and they do not have official offices, so you'll have to call or email them.

Australian & Canadian Consulate (⌨ 40 46 88 53; virginie.kiou.petropol@mail.pf)

New Zealand Consulate (Map p358; ⌨ 40 50 02 95; nzhonconsulate@mail.pf)

US Consulate (Map p354; ⌨ 40 42 65 35; www.usconsul.pf)

EMERGENCY

Ambulance ⌨ 15
Fire ⌨ 120
Police ⌨ 20

INTERNET ACCESS

➺ Thanks to the advent of smartphones, tablets and wi-fi, dedicated internet cafes have become a rarity in French Polynesia. Wi-fi access is increasingly the norm.

➺ Many post offices have internet posts but don't count too much on it – they are usually ancient models that are often not functioning.

➺ Free wi-fi is offered at many guesthouses and hotels (at least near the reception or the bar, if not always in each room, for which there's sometimes an additional charge for wi-fi access) and at a number of restaurants and cafes. Some places still charge a fee, though.

➺ Connections are fairly fast and reliable in the Society Islands, which have broadband internet; elsewhere, slow connections are the norm.

➺ If you're toting your own device through the Society, Marquesas or Austral Islands, consider buying a prepaid VinSpot card from the local post office or a code online (www.vinspot.pf) that allows you to access wi-fi zones provided by Mana in post offices and at some hotels, restaurants and public areas.

MONEY

The unit of currency in French Polynesia is the *Cour de Franc Pacifique* (CFP; Pacific franc),

referred to simply as 'the franc', and it's pegged to the euro.

ATMs

➺ Known as *distributeurs automatiques de billets* or DABs in French, ATMs will give you cash via Visa, MasterCard, Cirrus or Maestro networks.

➺ International cards generally work only at Banque Socredo ATMs; luckily most islands have at least one of these. You'll need a four-digit pin number.

➺ There's a Socredo ATM at Faa'a International Airport.

➺ Some post offices are also equipped with ATMs.

Credit Cards

All top-end and midrange hotels, restaurants, jewellery shops, dive centres and the bigger supermarkets accept credit cards, sometimes exclusively Visa or MasterCard, but they usually require a 2000 CFP minimum purchase. You can also pay for Air Tahiti flights with a card. Most budget guesthouses and many tour operators don't accept credit cards.

Money Changers

➺ There are three major banks operating in French Polynesia: Banque de Tahiti, Banque de Polynésie and Banque Socredo. They change major foreign currencies but a transaction fee applies, usually from 600 CFP to 950 CFP.

➺ The best currencies to bring are US dollars and euros.

➺ All the main islands in the Society group, apart from Maupiti, have at least one banking agency. In the Tuamotus, only Rangiroa has a permanent banking service. In the Marquesas there are Socredo agencies on 'Ua Pou, Nuku Hiva and Hiva Oa. In the Australs group, Rurutu and Tubuai have some banking services.

Tipping

Tipping is not a part of life in French Polynesia. The price quoted is the price you are expected to pay, which certainly simplifies things. In special circumstances, such as an excellent tour or great service by the hotel cleaning crew, a tip is appreciated.

OPENING HOURS

Typical business hours are as follows:

Banks 8am to noon and 1.30pm to 5pm Monday to Thursday, to 3pm Friday

Businesses 7.30am to 11.30am and 1.30pm to 5pm Monday to Saturday

Government offices 7.30am to noon and 1pm to 5pm Monday to Thursday, to 3pm Friday

Restaurants 11.30am to 2pm and 6.30pm to 9pm

EATING PRICE RANGES

The following price ranges refer to a standard main course.

$ less than 1400 CFP

$$ 1400–2400 CFP

$$$ more than 2400 CFP

Supermarkets 6.30am to 7pm Monday to Saturday, 6.30am to 11am Sunday

PUBLIC HOLIDAYS

Public holidays, when all businesses and government offices close, include the following.

New Year's Day 1 January

Arrival of the First Missionaries 5 March

Easter March/April

Labour Day 1 May

VE Day (Victory in Europe Day) 8 May

Ascension Late May

Pentecost & Pentecost Monday Early June

Internal Autonomy Day 29 June

Bastille Day 14 July

Assumption 15 August

All Saints' Day 1 November

Armistice Day 11 November

Christmas Day 25 December

TELEPHONE

➜ French Polynesia's country code is ☎ 689.

➜ There are no area codes in French Polynesia.

➜ To call overseas, dial ☎ 00 plus the country code followed by the phone number.

➜ From a landline, local phone calls cost 18 CFP per minute or 29 CFP per minute to a mobile phone.

➜ You can buy prepaid cards to call overseas at most post offices.

Mobile Phones

➜ There are two mobile phone operators in French Polynesia: Vini (www.vini.pf) and Vodaphone (www.vodafone.pf).

➜ Mobile phone services operate on 900 GSM and 98% of the inhabited islands have cellular coverage.

➜ Many foreign mobile services have coverage in Tahiti but roaming fees are usually quite high.

➜ You can buy a local SIM card for around 1000 CFP and use it in your own phone if it's unlocked (check with your provider before you leave).

➜ There are offices of both providers in Pape'ete. Top-ups can be purchased online or at various shops and most post offices.

➜ Local mobile-phone numbers begin with ☎ 87 or ☎ 89.

➜ 3G is available on Tahiti, Mo'orea, Huahine, Rai'atea and Bora Bora.

TIME

➜ TAHT (Tahiti Time) is 10 hours behind GMT/UTC. When it's noon in Pape'te, it's 10pm in London, 2pm or 3pm in Los Angeles and 9am (the next day) in Sydney; the region is just two hours east of the International Date Line.

PRACTICALITIES

Newspaper & Magazines If you read French, there is one Tahitian daily, *La Dépêche de Tahiti* (www.ladepeche.pf), while *Tahiti Infos* (www.tahitiinfos.com) is published five times a week.

Electricity French Polynesia uses 220V, 60Hz AC European-style two-pin plugs.

Languages Tahitian, French, Marquesan

Weights & Measures The international metric system is used here.

➜ The Marquesas are half an hour ahead of the rest of French Polynesia (noon on Tahiti is 12.30pm in the Marquesas).

➜ The Gambier Archipelago is one hour ahead of the rest of French Polynesia (noon on Tahiti is 1pm in the Gambier).

TOURIST INFORMATION

The main and only real tourist office is the Office du Tourisme de Tahiti et ses Îles (p359) in the centre of Pape'ete.

For information before you leave home, visit www.tahiti-tourisme.com, which has several international tourism office links.

VISAS

➜ Everyone needs a passport to visit French Polynesia. The regulations are much the same as for France: if you need a visa to visit France then you'll need one to visit French Polynesia.

➜ Anyone from an EU country can stay for up to three months without a visa, as can citizens of Argentina, Australia, Brazil, Canada, Chile, Japan, Mexico, New Zealand and Switzerland.

➜ Other nationalities need a visa, which can be applied for at French embassies.

➜ Apart from permanent residents and French citizens, all visitors to French Polynesia need to have an onward or return ticket.

WOMEN TRAVELLERS

➜ French Polynesia is a great place for solo women. Local women are very much a part of public life in the region, and it's not unusual to see Polynesian women out drinking beer together or walking alone, so you will probably feel pretty comfortable following suit.

➜ It is a sad reality that women are still required to exercise care, particularly at night, but this is the case worldwide. As with anywhere in the world, give drunks and their beer breath a wide berth.

➜ Perhaps it's the locals getting their own back after centuries of European men ogling Polynesian women, but there is reportedly a 'tradition' of Peeping Toms in French Polynesia, mainly in the outer islands. Take special care in places that seem to offer opportunities for spying on guests, particularly in the showers, and make sure your room is secure and locked at night.

ⓘ Getting There & Away

AIR

Most visitors to French Polynesia arrive at **Faa'a International Airport** (Map p354; www.tahiti-aeroport.pf), on Pape'ete's outskirts, 5km west of the capital. It is the only international airport in French Polynesia. The international check-in desks are at the terminal's eastern end.

Air Calédonie International (Aircalin; Map p357; www.aircalin.nc) Has flights between Noumea (New Caledonia) and Pape'ete.

Air France (Map p358; www.airfrance.com) Has flights between Paris and Pape'ete via Los Angeles.

Air New Zealand (Map p358; www.airnewzealand.com) Flies between Pape'ete and Auckland.

Air Tahiti Nui (Map p358; ☏ 40 45 55 55; www.airtahitinui.com) French Polynesia's national carrier has flights to France, the USA, Japan and New Zealand. There's an extra 23kg baggage allowance for divers, surfers and golfers.

Hawaiian Airlines (Map p358; www.hawaiianair.com) Flies between Honolulu (Hawaii) and Pape'ete.

LAN (Map p358; www.lan.com) Operates flights between Santiago (Chile) and Pape'ete via Easter Island.

SEA

Travelling to French Polynesia by yacht is entirely feasible: you can often pick up crewing positions from North America, Australia or NZ, or in the islands; ask at yacht clubs in San Diego, LA, San Francisco, Honolulu, Sydney, Cairns or Auckland.

It takes about a month to sail from the US west coast to Hawai'i and another month south from there to the Marquesas; with stops, another month takes you west to Tahiti and the Society Islands. Then it's another long leg southwest to Australia or New Zealand.

ⓘ Getting Around

Getting around French Polynesia is half the fun. Travelling between islands involves flights or boat travel and, thanks to French Government financial support, travel to the larger and more densely populated islands is relatively easy and reasonably priced.

AIR

➡ Air is the main way to cover long distances in French Polynesia. Domestic flights are run by the national carrier Air Tahiti (www.airtahiti.pf), which flies to 48 islands in all five of the major island groups.

➡ Note that Pape'ete is very much the hub for flights within French Polynesia and, with only a few exceptions, you'll generally have to pass through Pape'ete between island groups.

➡ Flight frequencies ebb and flow with the seasons, and extra flights are scheduled in the July–August peak season. Air Tahiti publishes a downloadable flight schedule, which is essential reading for anyone planning a complex trip around the islands.

➡ If you are making reservations from afar, you can reserve online and pay by credit card.

Air Passes

Because distances to the remote islands are so great, some of the full fares are quite high and the cheapest way to visit a number of islands by air is to buy one of Air Tahiti's air passes.

➡ Travel must commence in Pape'ete and you cannot connect back to Pape'ete until the end of the pass.

➡ Passes are valid for a maximum of 28 days and all flights must be booked when you buy your pass. Once you have taken the first flight on the pass the routing cannot be changed and the fare is nonrefundable.

➡ Check Air Tahiti's website for all details about air passes.

Discount Cards

Air Tahiti offers several cards that let you buy tickets at reduced prices, depending on whether the flight is classified as blue, white or red.

➡ If you're aged under 25, a *Carte Jeunes* (Youth Card), and if you're over 60 a *Carte Marama* (Third Age Card), gives you up to 50% reductions (depending on the colour of the flight) and costs 2500 CFP.

➡ A *Carte Famille* (Family Card) gives adults up to 50% and children up to 75% discount. It costs 3500 CFP. You need a passport and photos and the kids' birth certificates.

➡ These cards are issued on the spot, only in Pape'ete.

BICYCLE

Bicycles can often be rented for about 2000 CFP per day, and many guesthouses have bicycles for their guests, sometimes for free, though you might be riding an old rattler.

BOAT

Boat travel within the Society group isn't as easy as you'd hope unless you're only going to Mo'orea or taking a cruise or sailboat. A number of companies shuttle back and forth between Tahiti and Mo'orea each day; other routes between the islands are less frequent but served at least twice a week by cargo vessels.

In the other archipelagos travel by boat is more difficult. If you are short on time and keen to travel beyond the Society Islands you may need to consider flying at least some of the way.

Cargo ships, also known as *goélettes,* are principally involved in freight transport. Some take passengers, however, and for those who want to get off the beaten trail such a voyage can, depending on the circumstances, be anything from a memorable experience to an outright nightmare. The cargo boat companies' offices are in the Motu Uta port area in Pape'ete.

BUS

French Polynesia doesn't have much of a public transport system, and Tahiti is the only island where public transport is even an option. Buses stop at designated spots (marked with a blue clock) and supposedly run on a schedule – although times are hardly regular.

CAR & SCOOTER

➡ If you want to explore the larger islands of the Society group at your own pace, it is well worth renting a car.

➡ Car-hire agencies in French Polynesia only ask to see your national driving licence, so an international driving licence is unnecessary.

➡ There are many different car-hire agencies on the more touristy islands, but the prices really don't vary much. For a small car, expect to pay from 8000 CFP per day, which includes unlimited kilometres and insurance.

➡ At certain times of year (July, August and New Year's Eve) as well as on weekends, it's wise to book vehicles a few days in advance.

➡ In the Marquesas, rental vehicles are mainly 4WDs complete with a driver. Rental without a driver is possible only on Atuona (Hiva Oa) and Taiohae (Nuku Hiva).

➡ Driving is on the right-hand side in French Polynesia.

➡ Although the accident statistics are pretty grim, driving in French Polynesia is not difficult, and the traffic is light almost everywhere apart from the busy coastal strip around Pape'ete on Tahiti.

➡ Avis and Europcar both hire scooters on a number of islands. You'll pay around 6000 CFP a day.

TAHITI & FRENCH POLYNESIA GETTING AROUND

Tonga

☎ 676 / POP 106,000

Best Places to Stay

➜ Hideaway (p447)

➜ Port Wine Guest House (p458)

➜ Matafonua Lodge (p452)

➜ Sandy Beach Resort (p452)

➜ Nerima Lodge (p439)

Best Places to Eat

➜ Friends Cafe (p441)

➜ Tiger Inn (p441)

➜ Mariner's Cafe (p451)

➜ Aquarium Café (p460)

➜ Bellavista Cafe & Restaurant (p460)

Why Go?

Kiss the tourist hype goodbye – and say a warm *malo e lelei* (hello!) to the Kingdom of Tonga. Resolutely sidestepping flashy resorts and packaged cruise-ship schtick, Tonga is unpolished, gritty and unfailingly authentic. Life here ticks along at its own informal pace: church life is all pervasive, chickens and pigs have right of way, and there's nothing that can't wait until tomorrow. You don't have to seek out a cultural experience in Tonga – it's all around you!

Once you've shifted down into 'Tonga time', you'll find these islands awash with gorgeous beaches, low-key resorts, myriad snorkelling, diving, yachting and kayaking opportunities, hiking trails, rugged coastlines and affable locals (especially the kids!). Gear up for some active pursuits, then wind down with a cool sunset drink to the sound of waves folding over the reef. In Tonga, there really is nothing that can't wait until tomorrow.

When to Go
Nuku'alofa

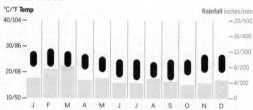

Jun–Oct
Peak season: stable weather, warm seas and buzzy waterside restaurants.

Apr–Aug
Cool, dry and less humid (winter) – when yachties turn up to play.

Nov–Mar
Warm and wet in the South Seas summer, but fine for water sports.

Map labels:

176°W   174°W

① Niuafo'ou

NIUA GROUP

Tafahi

Niuatoputapu

16°S

SOUTH PACIFIC OCEAN

N 0 _____ 100 km
   0 _____ 50 miles

Fonualei
Toku

18°S

VAVA'U GROUP

Late   **⑪ Vava'u**
        ① ⑦ Neiafu
        ⑥
Swallows' Cave

20°S

'Ofolanga
Kao
Tofua   Pangai Ha'ano
HA'APAI Ha'afeva Foa
GROUP   Kotu   **① Lifuka**
Tungua   'O'ua **④** Uiha
Tokulu
Nomuka
Fonuafo'ou Nomuk'iki   Telekivava'u
Hunga Tonga
Hunga
Ha'apai
        Ha'amonga a
        Maui Trilithon
Ha'atafu
Beach **⑨**
① ⑩ ③ 'Eue'iki   Tonga
Nuku'alofa **⑤** Tongatapu Trench
        ② 'Eua
TONGATAPU
GROUP

'Ata

Same Scale as Main Map
Minerva Reef   Inset

'inerva Reef
00km, See Inset)

Tonga Highlights

① Kayaking (p436) between the reefs and islands offshore from Nuku'alofa, Neiafu and Pangai.

② Hiking tropical rainforests and along sheer ocean clifftops on **'Eua** (p446).

③ Pondering Tongatapu's curious **Ha'amonga 'a Maui Trilithon** (p444), the 'Stonehenge of the South Pacific'.

④ Beach-bumming on the photogenic sands of **Uoleva** (p452), and (if you're lucky) watching whales breaching offshore.

⑤ Catching the cultural show at Tongatapu's **Oholei Beach & Hina Cave Feast & Show** (p444).

⑥ Swimming into **Swallows' Cave** (p462) on Kapa island in Vava'u.

⑦ Bouncing between bars and cafes in raffish **Neiafu** (p454).

⑧ Exploring far-off, doughnut-shaped **Niuafo'ou,** also known as Tin Can Island (p464) in the Niua Group.

⑨ Surfing the reef breaks at **Ha'atafu Beach** (p445) on Tongatapu.

⑩ Wandering aisles of produce and crafts at Nuku'alofa's **Talamahu Market** (p435).

⑪ Sailing (p455) through Vava'u's psychedelic web of waterways, islands and deserted beaches.

TONGATAPU

POP 75,500 / AREA 260 SQ KM

Low-lying Tongatapu (Sacred South) is Tonga's main island – and the landing and launching pad for most adventures in Tonga. Around two-thirds of Tonga's 106,000 residents live here, most of them in the capital Nuku'alofa (Abode of Love – how romantic), also home to the royal family. Outside Nuku'alofa, the island is a patchwork of dark-brown agricultural plots, small villages, a few chilled-out resorts, wild stretches of coastline and more churches than a year full of Sundays. And smiling kids are everywhere!

Tongatapu's key archaeological sights – such as Mu'a and the Ha'amonga 'a Maui Trilithon – are on the isle's eastern side, which also features caves, calm sandy coves and the airport. To the west are the Mapu'a Vaca Blowholes and the most of the resorts and surf breaks. North of Nuku'alofa are some lovely little day-trip islands. Give yourself a good few days to check it all out.

ⓘ Getting There & Away

AIR

Fua'amotu International Airport (Map p436; ☑ 35 415; www.tongaairports.com) is 21km southeast and a 30-minute drive from downtown Nuku'alofa. Air New Zealand, Fiji Airways and Virgin Australia all fly into Fua'amotu from overseas. In addition to local offices (p472), all are also bookable via Jones Travel (p443).

Real Tonga (Map p438; ☑ 23 777, 21 111; www.realtonga.to; Taufa'ahau Rd, Tungi Colonnade; ☺ 8.30am-12.30pm & 1-5pm Mon-Fri, 9am-1pm Sat) is Tonga's domestic airline, flying between Tongatapu, 'Eua, Ha'apai, Vava'u and (occasionally) the Niua Group.

BOAT

Regular ferries (p473) connect Tongatapu with Ha'apai, Vava'u and 'Eua.

ⓘ Getting Around

TO/FROM THE AIRPORT

Taxis meet all incoming flights, charging around T$40 between the airport and Nuku'alofa. Watch out for drivers taking you to a different guesthouse than the one you asked for! Many hotels and guesthouses arrange transfers if you pre-book (some for free).

The international and domestic airports are separate buildings; it's a short T$5 taxi fare between them.

BICYCLE

Some guesthouses have bicycles for guest use. Rent a bike from Kingdom Travel Centre (p435) in Nuku'alofa.

BOAT

Tongatapu's offshore island resorts all provide boat transport.

BUS

Buses around Tongatapu are run privately. There are no public buses and no fixed timetables. Nuku'alofa's two bus terminals are on the waterfront on Vuna Rd. Buses to outlying areas of Tongatapu depart from the western bus terminal, close to Vuna Wharf. Local Nuku'alofa buses leave from the eastern bus terminal, opposite the Visitor Information Centre. Most fares fall into the T$1 to T$2 category. Bus services run from about 8am to 5pm; there are no buses on Sundays.

CAR & SCOOTER

The following rental operators are all in Nuku'alofa.

Avis (Map p438; ☑ 21 179; www.avis.com; Asco Motors, Taufa'ahau Rd; ☺ 8.30am-5pm Mon-Fri, to 12.30pm Sat) Cars from T$100 per day.

Fab Rentals (Map p438; ☑ 23 077; www.tongaholiday.com/listing/fab-rentals; Salote Rd; ☺ 8am-5pm Mon-Fri, to noon Sat) Cars and vans from T$60 per day.

Friendly Islander Cruisers (☑ 849 2415; www.tongaholiday.com/listing/friendly-islander-cruisers; ☺ 9am-6pm Mon-Sat) Scooter hire per half-/full day from T$35/50. Organise your pick-up/drop-off location when you book.

Sunshine Rental (☑ 23 848; www.tongaholiday.com/listing/sunshine-rental; cnr Laifone & 'Unga Rds; ☺ 8am-5pm Mon-Fri, 8.30am-2pm Sat) Cars from T$80 per day.

TAXI

Taxis are unmetered: ask for the fare to your destination before you agree to pay or get in. From the airport into Nuku'alofa should be about T$40. Taxis have a 'T' on the licence plate. They're not permitted to operate on Sunday, but some guesthouses know secret Sunday taxi suppliers.

Holiday Taxi (☑ 25 169)

Wellington Taxi (☑ 24 744)

Nuku'alofa

POP 24,500

Raffish Nuku'alofa is the kingdom's seat of government and the home of the royal family. While it may not be a perfect Pacific paradise, Tonga's capital (aka 'Dirty Nuke') has hidden charm and promise if you blow the dust from the surface. The buzzy main street leads to the broad waterfront, from where there are

impressive views across the bay to coral islands, a short boat ride away. The market here
is a main line into Tongan life, there are a few
good places to eat and drink, and you'll still
see pigs and chickens careening around the
back streets.

◉ Sights

Royal Palace   PALACE
(Map p438; Vuna Rd) Encircled by expansive
lawns and casuarina trees, the white weather-
board Victorian-style Royal Palace, erected in
1867, is the pinnacle of Tongan grandeur. The
palace grounds are not open to visitors, but
you can get a good look through the gates
near the waterfront on the western side.

Centenary Chapel   CHURCH
(Map p438; ☑23 522; www.fwc.to; Wellington
Rd; free; ⊙daylight hours) Royal watchers and
rubberneckers (regardless of denomination)
head to this towering white church for a
glimpse of Tonga's royal family at Sunday
service, and to hear the congregation give
its vocal chords a workout (you can hear the
hymns a mile away). Dress sharp.

Royal Tombs   CEMETERY
(Map p438; Taufa'ahau Rd) Mala'ekula, the large
parklike area opposite the basilica, has been
the resting place of the royals since 1893. The
statue-studded white concrete tomb complex
is off limits to the public, but you can peer
across the lawns from the perimeter fence.

★ Talamahu Market   MARKET
(Map p438; ☑24 146; www.tongaholiday.com/list
ing/talamahu-marke; Salote Rd; ⊙8.30am-4.30pm
Mon-Sat) Want to see the real Nuku'alofa?
Wander through the aisles at Talamahu,
Tonga's main fresh-produce hub. You'll find
produce piled into handmade woven-frond
baskets, branches of bananas, colourful pyr-
amids of fruit and a few cooked-food stalls
– plus outstanding (and affordable) Tongan
arts and crafts. The whole place buzzes with
talk and commerce, particularly on Saturday
mornings.

🏃 Activities

Tongatapu is relatively flat: exploring by bicycle is an option if you're brimming with
energy.

You can also head out to the islands
(p446) you can see from Nuku'alofa – Pangaimotu, Fafá or 'Atata – for a day trip that
could include transfers, lunch, swimming
and snorkelling (don't miss the wreck off
Pangaimotu island). They're a good option on
a Sunday, when Tonga takes a 24-hour time
out, and good fun if you've got the kids in tow.

Kingdom Travel Centre   BICYCLE RENTAL
(Map p438; ☑28 000; www.kingdomtraveltonga.
to; cnr Vuna & Fatafehi Rds; ⊙8.30am-5pm Mon-
Fri, 9am-12.30pm Sat) Bikes with helmets and
locks for T$20 per day. On the Nuku'alofa
waterfront.

TONGA IN...

One Week
Acclimatise in the cafes in **Nuku'alofa**, then see the sights around Tonga's main island
of **Tongatapu**: take a day tour or hire a car. Jet north to **Vava'u** and explore this magical
maze of islands, beaches, reefs and sheltered waterways. Some time hanging out with the
yachties in the waterside bars and restaurants in **Neiafu** is a must. Fly back to Tongatapu
the day before your flight out.

Two Weeks
Throw in a visit to **Ha'apai** on your way back south from Vava'u. Lower than low-key, this
is the place to be if you're really on the run from the stresses of life elsewhere. Sleep, read,
eat, drink and strap on a snorkel at least once a day. Back on Tongatapu, fly out to nearby
'Eua, an emerging ecotourism destination which offers up hiking trails, rainforest and
raucous birdlife.

One Month
Consider using ferries to chug between the islands to really change down into 'Tonga
time'. A stay out by the **Ha'atafu Beach** surf is a great family option on Tongatapu.
Stretch out your stays in Vava'u, Ha'apai and on 'Eua (bring extra beach novels), or a trip
to the **Niua Group** could even be on the cards.

Tongatapu

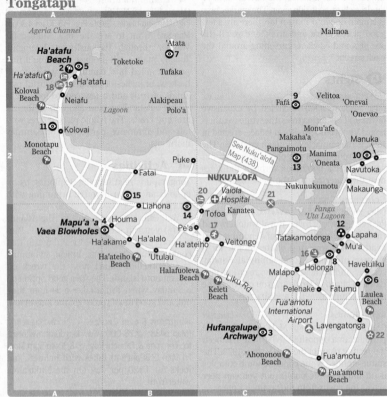

Ageria Channel

Malinoa

Ha'atafu Beach 2 5

'Atata 7

Toketoke

Tufaka

Ha'atafu 1

18 19 Ha'atafu

Kolovai Beach

Neiafu

Lagoon

Alakipeau
Polo'a

Fafá 9

Velitoa

'Onevai
'Onevao

11 Kolovai

Monotapu Beach

Manuka

Monu'afe

Makaha'a

Pangaimotu

Manima 10

13 'Oneata

Navutoka

Puke

See Nuku'alofa Map (438)

NUKU'ALOFA

Nukunukumotu

Makaunga

Fatai

Vaiola Hospital

21

Fanga 'Uta Lagoon

15

Liahona

14

Tofoa

Kanatea

12 Lapaha

**Mapu'a 'a 4
Vaea Blowholes**

Houma

Pe'a

17

Tatakamotonga

Mu'a

Ha'akame

Ha'alalo

Ha'ateiho

Veitongo

16

8

Haveluliku

Ha'ateiho Beach

'Utulau

Malapo

Holonga

Halafuoleva Beach

Liku Rd

Pelehake

Fatumu

6

Keleti Beach

Fua'amotu International Airport

Laulea Beach

Hufangalupe Archway 3

Lavengatonga

22

'Ahononou Beach

Fua'amotu

Fua'amotu Beach

Fatai Kayak Adventures   KAYAKING

(Map p436; ☑ 840 9175; www.tongaholiday.com/
listing/fatai-kayak-adventures; Holonga Village)
Based in Holonga Village in eastern Tongatapu, Fatai runs full-day kayak tours and offers
kayak rentals. Its 'Island Hop Adventure Tour'
takes paddlers out to Pangaimotu and Makaha'a islands (T$250). Single rental kayaks cost
T$40/60 per half-/full day, doubles T$60/90.

Ha'atafu Beach   SURFING, SNORKELLING

(Map p436; ☑ 41 088; www.surfingtonga.com;
🏄) Tongatapu's best breaks are peeling over
the reefs off Ha'atafu Beach in the island's
northwest. Check out Steve Burling's excellent website for tips on what to bring and
when to hit the waves. For the kids, an afternoon snorkelling in the shallows inside the
reef isn't hard to take.

Whale Swim, Fish & Dive   DIVING, SNORKELLING

(☑ 770 4984; www.whaleswimtours.com) Reliable small-group boat trips out into the

briny sea to go diving (from T$325 full day),
fishing (T$345 full day) or whale watching
(T$195 half-day, T$325 with swimming).
Boat tours with snorkelling also available
($T295 full day). Be aware that some ani-
mal welfare groups claim swimming with
whales is disruptive to their behaviour and
habitat: see (p461).

Royal Tongan Golf Club   GOLF

(Manamo'ui Golf Course; Map p436; ☑ 24 949;
Taufa'ahau Rd, Ha'ateiho; ⊙9am-4pm Mon-Sat)
Take a swing at Tonga's only golf course, a
relaxed nine-hole affair at Ha'ateiho on the
way to the airport. Green fees are T$30/40
for nine/18 holes with rental gear included.

Tonga Charters   FISHING, SNORKELLING

(☑ 771 5723; www.tonga-charters.com; half-day
fishing/snorkelling per group T$1000/500) Fish-
ing and snorkelling trips are on offer here.
Good for groups; pricey for soloists.

TONGA NUKU'ALOFA

👉 Tours

Tongatapu's main sights can be comfortably covered in a day tour – a good option for an otherwise somnolent Sunday. Most local accommodation operators will have a tour guide they recommend. See also Teta Tours (p443).

Ancient Tonga   CULTURAL TOUR
(☑786 3355, 25 510; www.ancienttonga.com; tours from T$140) Cultural full- and half-day tours around historic sites on Tongatapu, with activities that may include *umu* (earth oven), tapa- and mat-making demonstrations, *fale* (house) tours, dance performances and lunch. Call to discuss group numbers, options and prices.

Toni's Tours   TOUR
(☑21 049, 774 8720; www.tonisguesthouse.com; tours from T$60) Pile into Toni's van and do a lap of the island's main sights (minimum three people). Bring a sun hat, sunscreen, swimming gear and a preparedness to weather Toni's acerbic Lancashire wit. Pick up/drop off at your accommodation.

Supa Tours   TOUR
(☑771 6450; phlatohi@kalianet.to; tours from T$60) Big John's island tours operate daily, taking in all the main sights.

Pacific Ocean Tours   BOAT TOUR, SURFING
(☑24 933; www.pacificoceantours.com) Based in Nuku'alofa, these guys run boat trips out to surf breaks on the outer reefs (T$180, BYO boards), and offer fishing (T$150) and whale-watching (T$300) trips.

🛏 Sleeping

Ola's Guest House   GUESTHOUSE $
(Map p438; ☑25 154; olakoloi@hotmail.com; off Tupoulahi Rd, Ngele'ia; d T$150, s/d/f without bathroom T$70/90/180, all incl breakfast; ☎) Formerly Ali Baba's, this out-of-the-way

Nuku'alofa

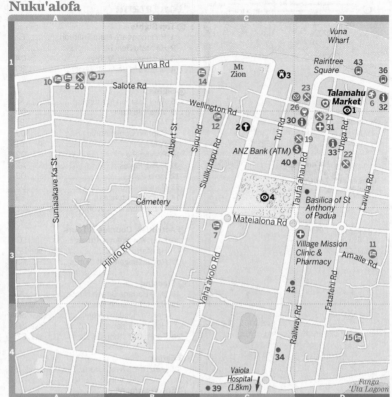

place is funky and friendly. Floors are chequered blue-and-gold, and the seven rooms (with two shared bathrooms) have TVs and their own colour schemes and themes. A welcoming host, Ola keeps things ultraclean and uptempo. It's about 1.5km from the post office.

Noa Guest House   GUESTHOUSE $

(Map p438; ☑21 810; www.noaenterprises. com; Wellington Rd; dm/s/d without bathroom T$35/70/90, d with bathroom T$150; ❋ ⓢ) Not far from church, town and sea, yellow-painted, two-tier Noa has a plumb location and plenty of rooms, from dorms to basic singles and doubles and en-suite doubles. The best are upstairs; the cheaper ones are out the back. Air-con in some rooms only, but all are clean and shipshape. Beaut communal kitchen.

Backpackers Townhouse   HOSTEL $

(Map p438; ☑771 6148; www.tongaholiday.com/ listing/backpackers-townhouse-nukualofa; cnr

Mateialona & Vaha'akolo Rds; dm/s/d T$25/60/80) This rickety hostel doesn't look like much from the dusty street out the front, but inside things quickly improve. There's a cheery communal kitchen-lounge, complete with beach books and a guitar to strum, free fruit from the owners' garden and reasonable rooms. The cheapest beds in downtown Nuku'alofa.

Toni's Guesthouses   GUESTHOUSE, HOSTEL $

(Map p436; ☑774 8720, 21 049; www.tonis guesthouse.com; Tofua; dm/s/d/house from T$25/50/50/180) Toni's is a brightly coloured budget complex in Tofoa, 3km south of Nuku'alofa. On the list are kava sessions, airport pick-ups (T$20), shuttles into town (T$2) and island tours (p437) in Toni's van. There are a lot of sleeping options from dorms to full houses, so check out the website. Toni knows Tongatapu backwards (a wry font of advice).

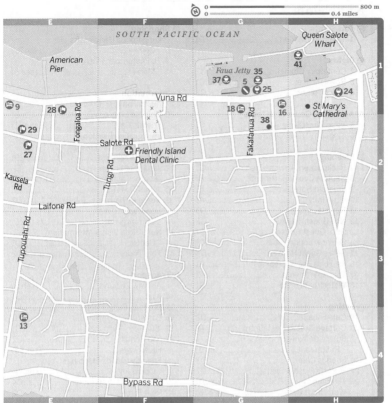

Sela's Guest House

GUESTHOUSE **$**

(Map p438; ☑ 25 040; www.tongaholiday.com/listing/selas-guesthouse; Longoteme Rd; dm/s/d T$25/80/100; ☎) Sela's is a long-running, warren-like and very basic guesthouse that wouldn't comply with many Western building codes. Still, it's a cheap and cheery outfit, with lavish cooked breakfasts with fruit (T$15). It's about a 1.5km hike from the post office.

★ Nerima Lodge

GUESTHOUSE **$$**

(Map p438; ☑ 25 533; www.nerimalodge.com; Amaile Rd; s/d T$80/115, s/d/tr without bathroom T$65/100/135, all incl breakfast; ☎) Simple, quiet, clean, friendly and a short walk to town – just how any good South Pacific guesthouse should be. Downstairs is a sunny communal lounge and breakfast room, where the morning menu changes daily (pancakes, bacon and eggs, toast with pawpaw-and-coconut jam). Upstairs are one en-suite room and six tidy private rooms with shared bathrooms. Great value.

'Utu'one Bed & Breakfast

B&B **$$**

(Map p438; ☑ 24 811; www.tongaholiday.com/listing/utuone-bed-and-breakfast; Vuna Rd; d incl breakfast T$150-250; ❄☎) Down near the ferry piers and the fish market, 'Utu'one is a bastion of cleanliness surrounded by things otherwise. It's a two-storey white hacienda, all rooms with en-suites or shared bathrooms across the hall. Free wi-fi and generous egg breakfasts, with a half-hour stroll into town to walk it off afterwards. Bit noisy on Saturday nights.

Captain Cook Apartments

APARTMENT **$$**

(Map p438; ☑ 25 600; www.captaincooktonga.com; Vuna Rd; d T$160, extra person T$25; ❄☎) Trim two-bedroom serviced apartments with full kitchen and living area, peeking at the sea through casuarina trees. The complex (six apartments) has been around a

Nuku'alofa

while and is showing its stylistic age, but it's still in good shape. Long-stay discounts.

Waterfront Lodge   HOTEL $$$
(Map p438; ☏25 260; www.tongawaterfront lodge.com; Vuna Rd; garden/sea-view d incl breakfast T$260/280, extra bed T$50; ❄☏) The rather boutiquey Waterfront is an elegant offering, with neat gardens and Victorian colonial aesthetics. The eight spacious rooms upstairs feature parquetry floors, teak and cane furnishings, tasteful prints and multi-head showers to banish the Nuku'alofa dust from your bones. The Waterfront Café (p442) downstairs is also a good'un.

Seaview Lodge   LODGE $$$
(Map p438; ☏23 709; www.seaview-lodge.com; Vuna Rd; d T$240-320, apt $320; ❄☏) This

endearing fave a short stroll from town has large rooms with island vibes. The priciest rooms have balconies from which to absorb the namesake views. Out the back there's a bungalow apartment with a kitchen; out the front is the house restaurant, which is about as classy as dinner in Nuku'alofa gets (mains T$39 to T$46). Hit-and-miss hot water.

Villa Apartments   APARTMENT $$$
(Map p438; ☏24 998; www.tongavilla.com/villa-apartments; Vuna Rd; 1-/2-bedroom apt from $265/395; ❄☏) Nuku'alofa's classiest beds? You could be right. These sassy New Zealand–owned apartments on Vuna Rd overlook the sea from a broad balcony, and tick all the up-market boxes. It's a two-storey beige edifice with an air of exclusivity about it, and a big

fence keeping anything that might interrupt your holiday at bay.

Emerald Hotel
HOTEL $$$

(Map p438; ☑22 888; www.emerald-tonga.com; Vuna Rd; d/tw/ste from T$250/250/349; ❄️🛜) One of Tonga's newer hotels has 20 bright, clean, spartan rooms over two levels. Air-con, friendly staff, in-room safe, wif-fi, minibar, the Emerald Chinese Restaurant (p442) downstairs, sea views from the best rooms... it's all here. A bit of soul is all that's lacking.

Little Italy
HOTEL $$$

(Map p438; ☑25 053; www.littleitalytonga. com; Vuna Rd; garden/ocean-view r incl breakfast T$290/330; ❄️🛜) There are two floors of Tuscan-toned rooms atop the buzzy Little Italy restaurant. Expect superprofessional staff and knock-out sea views from the best rooms (look at the ocean instead of the decor, which is a tad dated). The restaurant is open for breakfast and dinner (mains T$18 to T$44): pizza, pasta, scaloppine, paintings of pine trees and crooner tunes.

Eating

For self-caterers, Nuku'alofa's supermarkets stock a reasonable range of products (but not much fresh stuff: head to Talamahu Market, p435).

★Tiger Inn
CHINESE $

(Map p438; ☑777 8666; Tonga Post Food Court, Taufa'ahau Rd; mains $6-10; ⊗9am-6pm Mon-Fri, to 5pm Sat; 🛜) One of four quick-fire, perennially busy eateries on the ocean side of the Tonga Post building, Tiger Inn eschews the Western sausage-and-chips offerings of its neighbours and delivers authentic Chinese noodle soups. Order a spicy seafood version, laced with coriander, and slurp it down at one of the outside tables. Service can be surly.

★Friends Cafe
CAFE $$

(Map p438; ☑22 390; breakfast from T$7, mains T$10-26; ⊗7.30am-10pm Mon-Sat; 🛜) With a breezy charm, conversation, laughter and dependably good food, Friends is an irresistible social and culinary magnet for visitors and locals alike. Expect everything from panini to Thai beef curry to Moroccan spiced fish. Good coffee and free wi-fi to boot. There's also a tourist info (p443) wing off to one side.

Marco's Pizza & Pasta
ITALIAN $$

(Map p438; ☑22 144; www.tongaholiday.com/ listing/marcos-pizza-pasta; 'Unga Rd; mains $16-30; ⊗11am-2pm & 5-11pm Mon-Sat) Explore Nuku'alofa's back streets and you'll find plenty of places to eat: Korean, Singaporean, Indian, and Marco's – an unassuming little pizza and pasta joint. Chow down inside the modest shack, or sit out in the neat little garden area. Takeaways and occasional live music, too.

Cottage Breeze Restaurant
INTERNATIONAL $$

(Map p438; ☑28 940; Vuna Rd; mains T$20-30; ⊗4-10pm Mon-Sat) Earning a glowing reputation, this place on Vuna Rd west of the palace offers cheery service and consistently good food: everything from pork ribs to seafood grills. Kick back at your mosaic-topped table on the broad terrace and see the sea across the road.

SLEEPY SUNDAYS IN NUKU'ALOFA

Tonga comes to a screeching halt at midnight every Saturday night for 24 hours – Sunday is a day of rest and it's enshrined in Tongan law that it is illegal to work. There are no international or domestic flights, shops are closed, the streets are empty, sports are prohibited, and most Tongans are going to church, feasting and sleeping. Here are some suggestions to get you through till Monday morning:

➡ Go to church – magnificent singing and fiery sermons lift the soul (and almost the roof). At the Centenary Chapel (p435) you can tune your tonsils and worship alongside the king and the royal family.

➡ Take a round-the-island tour and explore Tongatapu's sights and attractions; try Toni's Tours (p437).

➡ Hire a bicycle and tootle around at your own pace.

➡ Visit one of the offshore island resorts for some sandy beaches and snorkelling.

➡ Truck out to Ha'atafu Beach and relax.

➡ Sleep and eat – that's what most of the locals will be doing!

Café Escape
CAFE **$$**

(Map p438; ☑21 212; www.tongaholiday.com/listing/cafe-escape; Fund Management House, Taufa'ahau Rd; breakfast from T$7, mains T$10-25; ⏱7.30am-late Mon-Fri, to 4pm Sat; 🛜) Slick Café Escape could be anywhere, but provides a refined air-conditioned retreat from the street and infuses the tropics into its mixed menu. Order the fab banana-and-pineapple porridge, or combat the starch in your diet with a big fruit salad. Free wi-fi, plus internet terminals and tourist brochures in the corner.

Emerald Chinese Restaurant
CHINESE **$$**

(Map p438; ☑24 619; www.emerald-tonga.com; Vuna Rd; mains T$6-25; ⏱10.30am-10.30pm Mon-Sat, 10.30am-2.30pm & 5.30-10.30pm Sun) Part of the Emerald Hotel, this place gets the nod for top Chinese restaurant in town. Good value, it's licensed, takeaway is available and (best of all) it's open on Sunday. Try the fried Szechuan chicken.

Waterfront Café
INTERNATIONAL, ITALIAN **$$$**

(Map p438; ☑25 260; www.tongawaterfrontlodge.com; Vuna Rd; mains T$22-43; ⏱6-10pm Mon-Sat) Downstairs at the Waterfront Lodge (p440), soak up the breezy South Seas vibes and chase a few sundowners with some Italian-style pasta, steak, lobster, lamb or seafood. It's a roomy room, spangled with colourful prints.

Lunarossa Restaurant
ITALIAN **$$$**

(Map p436; ☑26 324; www.tongaholiday.com/listing/lunarossa-restaurant; Umusi Rd, Ma'ufanga; mains T$20-40; ⏱7-10pm Mon-Fri) You'll need a car or taxi to get to the 'Red Moon', but it makes for a reasonably classy experience. The vibe is intimate with authentic Italian cuisine, the focus on ultrafresh seafood (the creed: 'a passion to redesign Tongan seafood with Italian cuisine').

🍸 Drinking & Nightlife

Tongans drink with gusto, but Nuku'alofa has a fairly limited bar scene. Ask a local about recommended kava circles (which you may be invited to join). Traditionally a male-only affair, both men and women are welcome around the kava bowl at Toni's Guesthouses (p438).

★ Billfish Bar & Restaurant
BAR

(Map p438; ☑24 084; www.billfish.co; Vuna Rd; ⏱11am-late Mon-Sat) This chilled-out open-air place down by the wharves is a long-time locals' haunt. There are hefty pub-style meals (mains T$14 to T$38; try the fish curry or the Hawaiian burger), chipper staff, Steinlager on tap, Dire Straits on the stereo and occasional live bands (also playing Dire Straits).

Reload
BAR

(Map p438; www.facebook.com/pages/reload-bar-tonga/156057704465308; Taufa'ahau Rd; ⏱noon-12.30am Mon-Fri, to 11.30pm Sat) 'Probably the best bar in Tonga' says the sign. We're not sure why it lacks confidence: the Ikale Lager is cold, the reggae is mellow and the upstairs balcony is surely the best spot for a beer in downtown Nuku'.

Ngutulei Bar & Restaurant
BAR

(Map p438; ☑22 666; tongawater@gmail.com; Vuna Wharf; ⏱8am-12.30am Mon-Fri, 8am-11.30pm Sat, 11am-9pm Sun) You can order a bang-up steak, chicken, lobster or swordfish meal at Ngutulei (mains T$18 to T$45), but most folks are here for a cold beer overlooking the fishing boats. With a stylish woody fit-out inside, it sits in a cordoned-off compound on the edge of a concrete sea (just look at the real sea, not the concrete).

Shopping

Langafonua Handicrafts Centre
ARTS

(Map p438; ☑21 014; www.madeintonga.com/langafonua; Taufa'ahau Rd; ⏱9am-5pm Mon-Fri, to 1pm Sat) A nonprofit artists co-op representing 300-plus local artists. Inside you'll find brilliant Tongan jewellery, carvings, baskets, weavings, canvasses...and trashy second-hand beach books!

Tu'imatamoana Fish Market
FOOD & DRINK

(Map p438; Vuna Wharf; ⏱5am-4.30pm Mon-Sat) Starts when the boats come in around 5am (get there early). There are trestle tables covered with bags of oysters, iridescent tropical fish, big crabs with taped-up claws, fish heads, slippery squid – a real briny bounty.

ℹ Information

EMERGENCY

Police Station (Map p438; ☑26 498, emergency 922; www.police.gov.to; Salote Rd) The local law-enforcement hub.

INTERNET ACCESS

Nuku'alofa has a clutch of internet cafes, the best of which are Café Escape (p442) and Friends Cafe (p441). Most local accommodation has wi-fi access for guests.

MEDICAL SERVICES

Friendly Island Dental Clinic (Map p438; ☑25 455; fidc@paluaviation.to; Fasi Village; ⏱5-7pm Mon-Sat)

Neeru's Pharmacy (Map p438; 📞 21 810; www.neeruspharmacy.com; Wellington Rd; ⊙9am-7pm Mon-Fri, to 3pm Sat) Downtown pharmacy.

Vaiola Hospital (Map p436; 📞 23 200; moh tonga@kalianet.to; Vaiola Rd, Tofoa; ⊙24hr) For emergencies and after-hours needs. There are also dentists here.

Village Mission Clinic & Pharmacy (Map p438; 📞 27 522; www.villagemissionclinic. org; Patco Business Centre, Taufa'ahau Rd; ⊙8.30am-5pm Mon-Fri, 10am-1.30pm Sat) This pharmacy has a doctor on duty every Friday between 9am and noon (or by appointment).

MONEY
There are plenty of ATMs around Nuku'alofa's main drag, most of them ANZ or Bank of South Pacific (BSP took over Tonga's Westpac branches in 2015 – the rebranding process is ongoing). There are also ANZ and BSP ATMs on Vuna Rd near the ferry terminal, and there's a BSP ATM and several money-change booths at Fua'amotu International Airport.

POST
Tonga Post (Map p438; 📞 21 700; www.tonga post.to; Taufa'ahau Rd; ⊙8.30am-4.30pm Mon-Fri, 9am-noon Sat) Down by the water in downtown Nuku'alofa.

TOURIST INFORMATION
Friends Cafe (Map p438; 📞 26 323; www. friendstonga.com; Taufa'ahau Rd; ⊙7.30am-10pm Mon-Sat; 🛜) This savvy little diner doubles up as a private tour-booking office, with plenty of details on what's happening around the kingdom. Also has internet access and books scooters for Friendly Islander Cruisers (p434).

Nuku'alofa Visitor Information Centre (Map p438; 📞 25 334; www.thekingdomoftonga. com; Vuna Rd; ⊙8.30am-4.30pm Mon-Sat) A government-run bureau with info on the whole of Tonga, maps and neat racks of brochures.

TRAVEL AGENCIES
Jetsave Taufonua (Map p438; 📞 23 052; in bound.taufonua@gmail.com; Fund Management Bldg, Taufa'ahau Rd; ⊙8.30am-4.30pm Mon-

Sat) Books day tours, rental cars and domestic package holidays to all island groups.

Jones Travel (Map p438; 📞 23 423; www. tonga-travel.travel; cnr Taufa'ahau & Wellington Rds; ⊙8.30am-4.30pm Mon-Sat) Flight bookings for Virgin Australia, Air New Zealand and Fiji Airways, plus local tours and scooter bookings for Friendly Islander Cruisers (p434).

Teta Tours (Map p438; 📞 23 363; www. tongaholiday.com/listing/teta-tours-and-travel-ltd; cnr Wellington & Railway Rds; ⊙8.30am-4.30pm Mon-Sat) Myriad tour and activity bookings across Tonga, including trips to Anahulu Cave (p444).

Around the Island

Buses are sporadic and taxis expensive, so the best way to see the sights is by island tour or rental car. The following points of interest run from Nuku'alofa in a clockwise direction around the island.

👁 Sights & Activities

👁 Eastern Tongatapu

Royal Residences   LANDMARK
(Map p436; Taufa'ahau Rd, Tofoa) South of Nuku'alofa, between Tofoa and Pe'a, you'll pass the private royal residences of the princess, adorned with white tigers and cannons, and the king, an austere European-style hilltop palace opposite (why are the princess's cannons pointing at the king?). After the 2015 coronation, it was unclear which royals would end up living in which houses (ask a passer-by!). No public access: views from the street only.

Captain Cook Landing Site   HISTORIC SITE
(Map p436; Taufa'ahau Rd, Holonga) A modest cairn above a mangrove inlet near Holonga village marks the spot where Captain Cook came ashore in 1777 (on his third trip to Tonga) and where Queen Elizabeth II popped by to commemorate it in 1970. Up-close access

---

JAPAN & CHINA: FUNDING FRENZY

Around Tongatapu you'll see neatly tarmacked roads emblazoned with 'China Aid' signs and hear people talking about the 'Japan road': they're referring to the sources of international funding used to construct these thoroughfares. China and Japan seem locked in a battle to see who can inject more money into Tonga's economy by financing civic projects: roads, hospitals, police stations, community health centres... Why? The international largesse is most welcome and Tonga is deeply indebted, but some cynical locals suggest that what China wants in return is to establish a naval base here, and that Japan is angling towards recommencing whaling in Tongan waters.

OHOLEI BEACH & HINA CAVE FEAST & SHOW

The pinnacle of Tongatapu entertainment is this fab feast and show at **Oholei Beach & Hina Cave Feast & Show** (Map p436; ☑ 11 783; www.oholeibeachresort.com; buffet & show adult/child T$40/20; ☺ 6pm Wed & Fri, buffet only 2pm Sun) in the island's southeast. The evening starts with a welcome on sandy Oholei Beach, followed by a hefty Tongan feast, including suckling pig roasted on a spit. The highlight is an enthusiastic traditional dance performance in the open-topped Hina Cave, culminating in an eye-popping fire dance.

There's a free shuttle to the show from Nuku'alofa. If you want to stay the night, bunk down in a *fale* at the resort (see the website).

was inhibited by a padlocked gate when we visited.

Mu'a　　　　　　　ARCHAEOLOGICAL SITE
(Map p436; off Taufa'ahau Rd, Mu'a; ☺ 24hr) The Mu'a area contains Tonga's richest concentration of archaeological remnants. In AD 1200 Tu'itatui, the 11th of the Tu'i Tonga kings, moved the royal capital from Heketa (near present-day Niutoua) to Mu'a. There are 28 royal stone tombs *(langi)* in the area, built with enormous limestone slabs. The most accessible of these are two monumental ancient burial sites off the dirt road towards the sea, just north of the Catholic church.

The structure closest to the main road is the Paepae 'o Tele'a (Platform of Tele'a), a pyramid-like stone memorial. Tele'a was a Tu'i Tonga who reigned during the 16th century. The other, the Langi Namoala, has a fine example of a *fonualoto* (vault for a corpse) on top.

Fishing Pigs　　　　　　LANDMARK
(Map p436; Taufa'ahau Rd, Manuka; ☺ daylight hours; 🚻) As you round the coast to the north of Mu'a, keep an eye out for Tonga's famed fishing pigs. When the tide is out, these unusual porkers trot out into the shallows and snuffle around in search of seafood. The word is they taste saltier than their land-based brethren. Not something you see every day! There are more fishing pigs along Vuna Rd west of Nuku'alofa.

★**Ha'amonga 'a Maui Trilithon**　　　ARCHAEOLOGICAL SITE
(Map p436; Taufa'ahau Rd, Niutoua; ☺ 24hr) FREE The South Pacific's equivalent of Stonehenge, the Ha'amonga 'a Maui (Maui's Burden) trilithon near Niutoua is one of ancient Polynesia's most intriguing monuments. Archaeologists and oral history credit its construction to Tu'itatui, the 11th Tu'i Tonga. Others say it was built by ancient Chinese explorers. Either way, the structure consists of three large coralline stones, each weighing about 40 tonnes, arranged into a trilithic gate. Mortised joints ensure the top stone won't fall off, as per Stonehenge!

A walking track winds northward past several *langi* (tombs; known as the Langi Heketa), including '**Esi Makafakinanga**, supposedly Tu'itatui's backrest. Such chiefly backrests were common in Polynesia: apparently Tu'itatui used this one as a shield against attack from behind while he oversaw the trilithon's construction.

'Anahulu Cave　　　　　　CAVE
(Map p436; ☑ 23 363; www.anahulucave.to; off Liku Rd, Haveluliku; T$10; ☺ 9am-4pm Mon-Sat) Tongatapu's most famous cave is an overloved, slightly eerie place full of stalactites and stalagmites, and blackened from the soot of flaming-frond torches and too much traffic. Inside is an underground freshwater pool where you can swim. The cave is managed by Teta Tours (p443): if there's no one from the company on site, the generator won't be working and you'll be venturing into the inky void (not advised).

⊙ Western Tongatapu

★**Hufangalupe Archway**　　　　LANDMARK
(Map p436; off Liku Rd; ☺ daylight hours) Near nowhere in particular is this impressive arch, aka 'the pigeon's doorway' – a natural land bridge over the pounding Pacific waves, formed when the roof of a sea cave collapsed. Walk across the top and peer into the pit, then gaze west along the craggy coast. No fences – watch your step.

★**Mapu'a 'a Vaea Blowholes**　　　LANDMARK
(Map p436; off Liku Rd, Houma; ☺ 24hr) On an especially good day at Mapu'a 'a Vaea (Chief's Whistles), hundreds of blowholes spurt skywards at once. Time your visit for a windy day with a strong swell, when the surf, forced up through eroded vents in the coralline limestone, jets 30m into the air. The blow-

hole-riddled rocks stretch for 5km along the south coast, near the village of Houma.

Triple-headed Coconut Tree   LANDMARK

(Map p436) If you think we must be scratching around for highlights to include a triple-headed coconut tree, then think again. Locals swear that this is the only coconut tree with three separate crowns in Tonga...some say in the whole South Pacific. Obligatory photo! The tree is on Loto Rd, just past Liahona.

Flying Foxes   LANDMARK

(Map p436) While you'll get the opportunity to see flying foxes (aka fruit bats, or *peka*) in many places in Tonga, one spot renowned for their presence is the village of Kolovai, up near the western tip of the island. They cling to the trees upside down in their hundreds – if you haven't seen bats before, it's a mind-blowing scene.

Abel Tasman Monument   HISTORIC SITE

(Map p436) At the northwestern tip of Tongatapu is a modest monument commemorating Dutchman Abel Tasman's 'discovery' of Tongatapu in 1643. He was on his way back to Batavia (present-day Jakarta) after firstly bumping into Tasmania, then New Zealand. With great European sensibility he named Tongatapu 'Amsterdam'.

★Ha'atafu Beach   BEACH

(Map p436; 🖈) On the sunset side of the island, Ha'atafu Beach is a sandy slice protected by a reef, where some of Tonga's best surf peels in (experienced surfers only need apply). There's sheltered swimming and snorkelling at high tide in the broad lagoon. If your timing is good (June to November), you can sometimes spy whales cavorting beyond the reef.

🛏 Sleeping & Eating

🛏 Western Tongatapu

There's a string of low-key (everything in Tonga is low-key) quasi-resorts facing onto Ha'atafu Beach in Tongatapu's northwest; the following are the pick of the bunch.

Heilala Holiday Lodge   BUNGALOW $$

(Map p436; 📞41 600; www.heilala-holiday-lodge.com; Palm Ave, Ha'atafu Beach; s/d lodges T$78/98, s/d/tr bungalows from T$138/168/198, all incl breakfast; 🛜) Photogenic thatched *fale* (sleeping three) are studded through tropical gardens at Heilala on fab Ha'atafu Beach. There's a restaurant for on-site dinners, or a communal kitchen if you'd rather DIY. Simple lodge rooms with shared bathrooms are a tad cheaper than the *fale*. Lots of free stuff (wi-fi, hammocks, snorkelling gear, bikes and books); airport pick-ups available. Nice one.

Ha'atafu Beach Resort   BUNGALOW $$

(Map p436; 📞41 088; www.surfingtonga.com; off Hihifo Rd, Ha'atafu Beach; bungalows per adult/child from T$150/75; 🛜) With a cosmic focus on surfing (owner Steve knows Tonga's waves backwards), this family-run set-up is laid-back and peaceful. Paths connect a range of thatched-roof *fale* to clean, shared facilities and the dining room (lots of organic stuff). Rates include breakfast and dinner. Free snorkelling gear,

---

THE REPUBLIC OF MINERVA

The Minerva Reefs, Tonga's southernmost extremity, 350km southwest of Tongatapu, has long served as a rest point for yachts travelling between Tonga and New Zealand. Awash most of the time, it contains a safe anchorage in an almost perfect circle of reef, and has a colourful history. Tonga first claimed the unpopulated reef in 1972 after the Phoenix Foundation, founded by Las Vegas property developer Michael Oliver, tried to create the tax-free Republic of Minerva there, barging in tonnes of sand from Australia. Currency was even pressed, before the Tongan king himself sailed south to tear down the republic's flag.

More recently, yachties have been warned to keep away from Minerva after a fracas between neighbours Fiji and Tonga. In 2005 Fiji stated that it did not recognise Tonga's maritime water claims to the reefs, and filed a complaint with the International Seabed Authority. Tonga counterfiled in opposition. Then in 2010 and again in 2011, the Fijian Navy took potshots at navigation lights on the reefs, before their boats were chased away by Tongan patrol boats. The UN was called in to calm everybody down.

In a bid to resolve the dispute, in 2014 Tonga reportedly offered the Minerva Reefs to Fiji in exchange for the Lau Islands, with which many Tongans have an affinity. But at the time of writing the future of Minerva was as cloudy as ever: watch this space!

WORTH A TRIP

DAY TRIPS TO TONGATAPU'S OFFSHORE ISLANDS

To the north of Tongatapu are a string of photoworthy islands that make for an interesting day trip (and a good way to fill a Sunday). All are only a short boat ride from Nuku'alofa. You can also visit some of these islands on a paddle tour with **Fatai Kayak Adventures** (p436).

Pangaimotu (Map p436; ☎ 771 5762; www.facebook.com/pangaimotu; day trip adult/child return incl lunch T$50/25; 🖼) The closest island resort to Nuku'alofa, Pangaimotu makes an easy day trip. Daily departures (including Sunday) chug out from the wharf beside the Fish Market at 11am, returning at 4pm (Sundays departing hourly 10am to 1pm, returning 4pm, 5pm and 6pm). The trip takes about 10 minutes. There's a decent beach, a good restaurant and shipwreck snorkelling – bring the kids!

If you want to stay the night, Pangaimotu Island Resort has simple *fale* (doubles from T$100).

Fafá (Map p436; ☎ 22 800; www.fafaislandresort.com; day trip adult/child incl lunch T$92/46) Honeymooners, start your engines! Fronting onto a magnificent beach, Fafá Island Resort is the most elegant on Tongatapu's offshore islands, but it makes a great day trip from Nuku'alofa too. Day-trip boats to Fafá depart Faua Jetty at 11am and return at 4.30pm daily.

The resort's traditional-style *fale* are perfect in their simplicity, with wood-shingle roofs and walls of woven palm leaves. Accommodation starts at T$400 per double (extra person T$90, half/full board T$110/135).

'Atata (Map p436; ☎ 21 254; www.royalsunset.biz; day trip adult/child T$70/35) 'Atata, 10km from Tongatapu, has beaut beaches and a little island village to wander through. Snorkelling, diving and fishing are near-essential. There is a resort here, but day trips are the best bet for visitors, including lunch and a snorkelling trip. Boats leave Nuku'alofa wharf at 10am, returning 4pm (20 minutes; Sunday too!).

kayaks and rides into town if Steve is heading that way.

Blue Banana Beach House CABIN $$
(Map p436; ☎ 41 575; www.bluebananastu dios.com; Ikalahi Rd, Ha'atafu Beach; d/q from T$170/350; 🖼) Looking for a simple, fetching, self-contained studio nested into the trees on the shore, all to yourself? The beautifully decorated Blue Banana *fale* provide the beauty of an offshore island with the convenience of the Tongatapu mainland. Great for snorkellers and self-caterers: catch the bus into Nuku'alofa and stock up.

Holty's Hideaway LODGE $$$
(Map p436; ☎ 41 720; www.holtyshideaway.com; off Hihifo Rd, Ha'atafu Beach; d/f from T$350/400, extra person T$80; 🖼🖼) Run by an expat Australian couple, Holty's is a simple, laid-back alternative to the resorts along Ha'atafu Beach. Book the large house (sleeping 10) or one of three *fale* (sleeping up to four). Great for groups of friends or families. There's also a cafe for weekend lunch, and surfboards and kayaks so you can paddle around at the beach.

'EUA

POP 5000 / AREA 87 SQ KM

Rugged 'Eua (pronounced 'a-wah'), 40km southeast of Tongatapu, is an unassuming slice of natural paradise. Known as 'the forgotten island', it's geologically the oldest island in Tonga (40 million years old!) and one of the oldest in the Pacific. There are steep hilly areas, cliff-top lookouts, hidden caves, sinkholes, a limestone arch and junglelike rainforest to explore. With its own species of plants, trees and the endemic *koki* (red shining parrot), 'Eua has a growing awareness of itself as a unique ecotourism destination.

'Eua's history is fascinating. In times past 'Euans had a reputation as the fiercest warriors in Tonga. Their sparsely populated island also became a haven for migrants moved from other islands. In 1860, when King Tupou I heard that European ships were capturing Tongans at the remote southern island of 'Ata for use as slaves, he resettled the island's entire population to 'Eua for their own protection. In 1946, after a nasty volcanic eruption at Niuafo'ou in the Niua Group, Queen Salote moved that island's population to 'Eua also.

◉ Sights & Activities

Activities on 'Eua are best booked via your guesthouse. Discuss what you want to do and everything will be arranged for you. 'Eua is the second-largest island in Tonga, and while fairly easy to navigate – just one long main road with a string of little villages along it – there's no public transport and distances are deceiving. Hideaway runs **4WD tours** to parts of 'Eua that are virtually inaccessible any other way. It's a great way to get the lay of the land: cliffs, forests, lookouts, beaches, rockpools...

For a cultural encounter, Hideaway also offers the chance for guests (and nonguests) to participate in community-orientated experiences such as **kava ceremonies** and **basket weaving** in the local village, as well as church visits and *umu* feasts on Sunday.

'Eua has some great **hiking** trails, particularly in **'Eua National Park** in the 'mountains' along the island's eastern coast. There are a number of options so discuss things with your hosts, get a map and organise a ride to the trailhead. Better yet, hire a guide for the day.

'Eua has some of the best **diving** in Tonga – its huge **Cathedral Cave** is becoming legendary. Book through your guesthouse. **Deep Blue Diving** (Map p438; ✆27 676; www.deepbluediving.to; Faua Jetty; snorkelling/diving from T$90/180), based in Nuku'alofa, also offers diving from its 'Eua base at Ovava Tree Lodge.

On the wildlife front, 'Eua is home to cacophonous **birds**, the star of which is the *koki* (red shining parrot). Others include *ngongo* (noddies), white-tailed *tavake* (tropic birds) and *pekapeka-tae* (swiftlets). The *peka* (fruit bat) also hangs around here (upside down in the trees). **Whales** come in very close to 'Eua. There are both whale-watching and whale-swim tours on offer between June and October, but it's very difficult to ensure that these are not intrusive or stressful experiences for the whales. Disruption to feeding, resting, nursing and other behaviour may have a long-term impact on populations.

🛏 Sleeping & Eating

Accommodation on 'Eua is budget all the way, baby. There aren't any restaurants, so the only place for visitors to eat is at their accommodation, where cooked meals are available daily (lunch and dinner mains are around T$15 to T$30).

★ Hideaway
GUESTHOUSE $

(✆50 255; www.hideawayeuatonga.com; West Coast Rd; s/d/tr incl breakfast T$65/95/120; 🛜) Hideaway is a chilled-out, sound-of-the-surf kinda joint with two rickety rows of rooms, a breezy bar-restaurant and a viewing platform out over the rocky shore (good sunsets and whale spotting). Rooms have bathrooms and slow-spinning fans (no air-con). Optional tours (4WD, hiking, horse riding, cultural encounters etc) can be booked on the spot. Rates include continental breakfast and transfers.

Ovava Tree Lodge
BUNGALOW $

(✆871 4536 22 840; www.deeplodge.to; Ohonua Village; bungalows s/d T$50/80, extra person T$15, all incl breakfast; 🛜) Across the road from the ferry wharf, sociable Ovava is 'Eua's new kid on the block, with six handsome wood-and-iron en-suite cabins set in lush gardens. There's a pizza oven in the restaurant-bar, and plenty of diving and snorkelling trips on offer. Airport transfers T$20.

Taina's Place
GUESTHOUSE $

(✆776 5002; www.tainasplace.com; Main Rd; camping per person T$20, cabins s/d/f T$45/60/110; 🛜) A little way inland near the forest, the cute red-and-white cabins at family-run Taina's revolve around trim gardens and a communal kitchen and bathrooms. There are tours aplenty, plus bike hire and a disco (!) on Friday and Saturday nights. Breakfast is T$15; wharf/airport transfers are T$12/8 return.

ℹ Information

MONEY
There is a Westpac bank near the ferry terminal on 'Eua, plus a Western Union and a couple of other money-transfer agencies, but opening hours are sporadic. Bring cash and a credit card.

TELEPHONE
There is mobile coverage in the villages but it's patchy on the hiking trails.

TOURIST INFORMATION
Bone-up on 'Eua info at Nuku'alofa Visitor Information Centre (p443) before you go, and have a look at www.eua-island-tonga.com.

ℹ Getting There & Around

AIR
Real Tonga makes the 10-minute hop from Tongatapu, reputedly the world's shortest scheduled commercial flight (don't fall asleep), at least once daily Monday to Saturday (one way T$96).

ⓘ TOP TONGAN TRAVEL TIPS

➡ Patience is a virtue: in Tonga, time is a flexible entity! Slow down and chill out.

➡ Respectful dress is important to Tongans: Tongan law prohibits being in a public place without a shirt (avoid singlets too), and wear long pants to church.

➡ Swimsuits should be worn only at resorts. Tongans swim fully dressed.

➡ 'Keeping face' is extremely important in Tonga. If things don't meet your expectations, don't escalate the situation by waving and shouting about it.

➡ Tonga closes down on Sundays: plan ahead accordingly.

➡ Double- and triple-check your ferry and Real Tonga flight schedules – things change!

BOAT

It's a 2½-hour ferry trip (p473) between Tongatapu and 'Eua.

CAR & BICYCLE

Accommodation hosts will pick you up at the wharf or airport; there's no car hire on the island. You can hire a bike at Hideaway (T$30 per day) if the local guy who owns them isn't in the midst of a maintenance program.

HA'APAI GROUP

POP 8200 / AREA 110 SQ KM

Isolated, thinly populated and untrammelled, the 62 Ha'apai islands – 45 of which are uninhabited – sprinkle themselves across the kingdom's central waters. Ha'apai appears on the horizon like a South Seas idyll: palm-fringed isles, vibrant reefs, breaching whales, deserted white beaches and even a couple of massive volcanoes.

That said, your initial arrival on Ha'apai may be a bit of a surprise, whether you arrive by plane or ferry. Simply put, there isn't much here, especially in the wake of category five Tropical Cyclone Ian, which lacerated the islands in 2014. If you were trying to get away from it all, pat yourself on the back – you've succeeded!

Online, have a look at www.haapai.to.

History

Archaeological excavations in southern Lifuka island reveal settlement dating back more than 3000 years.

The first European to turn up was Abel Tasman in 1643. He stopped for supplies at Nomuka and called the island 'Rotterdam' (feeling homesick that day?). Later, several notable events in Tongan history took place in Ha'apai. Captain Cook narrowly avoided the cooking pot in 1777; the mutiny on the *Bounty* occurred just offshore from Tofua in 1789; and the *Port-au-Prince*, with William Mariner (p453) aboard, was ransacked in 1806.

In 1831 Ha'apai was the first island group in Tonga to be converted to Christianity, following the baptism of its ruler Taufa'ahau. He took the name of Siaosi (George) after the king of England, and adopted the surname of Tupou. His wife was baptised Salote after Queen Charlotte. As King George Tupou I he united Tonga and established the royal line that continues through to the present day. Nuku'alofa's main street, Taufa'ahau Rd, is named after him.

ⓘ Getting There & Away

AIR

Ha'apai's Pilolevu Airport is 3km north of Pangai on Lifuka. The island's main north–south road passes right through the middle of the runway, meaning that the road is closed when aircraft are arriving or departing.

Real Tonga flies daily (except Sunday) between Ha'apai and Tongatapu, and three or four times a week between Ha'apai and Vava'u.

BOAT

MV *'Otuanga'ofa*, operated by Friendly Islands Shipping Company, stops weekly at Pangai on both its northbound and southbound runs between Tongatapu and Vava'u.

There are protected anchorages along the lee shores of Lifuka, Foa, Ha'ano and Uoleva.

ⓘ Getting Around

TO/FROM THE AIRPORT & WHARF

Organise tranport to your accommodation with your hosts, most of whom will pick you up at the airport or Pangai wharf. Taxis charge T$10 between the airport and Pangai.

BICYCLE

Lifuka and Foa are flat – a bicycle is the perfect way to explore. Mariner's Cafe (p451) rents out bikes for T$20 per day. Guests can use the bikes at Sandy Beach Resort (p452) and Matafonua Lodge (p452).

BOAT

The Pangai Visitor Information Centre (p451) may have some info on arranging boat transport

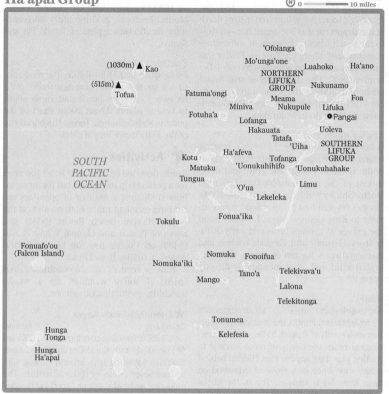

'Ofolanga
Mo'unga'one   Luahoko   Ha'ano
(1030m) ▲ Kao   NORTHERN   Nukunamo
(515m) ▲   LIFUKA
Tofua   Fatuma'ongi   GROUP   Foa
                            Meama
                   Miniva   Nukupule   Lifuka
Fotuha'a   Pangai
            Lofanga
            Hakauata   Uoleva
                   Tatafa
                          'Uiha   SOUTHERN
            Kotu   Ha'afeva   LIFUKA
SOUTH   Matuku   'Uonukuhihifo   Tofanga   GROUP
PACIFIC Tungua   'Uonukuhahake
OCEAN   'O'ua   Limu
                  Lekeleka

                Fonua'ika
      Tokulu

Fonuafo'ou
(Falcon Island)   Nomuka   Fonoifua
            Nomuka'iki
                   Tano'a   Telekivava'u
                Mango   Lalona
                        Telekitonga

                Tonumea
Hunga   Kelefesia
Tonga
Hunga
Ha'apai

around the Ha'apai group...or they might just send you to Mariner's Cafe!

TAXI

There are a couple of taxis based on Lifuka: book through Mariner's Cafe or your accommodation.

Lifuka Group

Most visitors to Ha'apai stay within the low-lying Lifuka Group of islands along the eastern barrier reef of Ha'apai. The airport, main ferry wharf and almost all of Ha'apai's accommodation and services are located here – with most of the action for visitors based on Lifuka, Foa and Uoleva islands.

It will take some serious planning, determination and rigour to get out to the remote Ha'apai islands, most of which are uninhabited: drop us a line and tell us about it if you do!

Lifuka

Pangai, Lifuka's main town, has basic services and a cool cafe, but struggles to be described as attractive, particularly with wreckage and rooflessness wrought by 2014's Tropical Cyclone Ian still littered around everywhere. The eastern side of the island is wild and windy; the western side is calm and protected. On hot afternoons the Pangai wharf is a mass of cooling-down kids, splashing around in the brine.

◉ Sights

The best way to get around the Lifuka island sights is by bicycle. The 14km (one way) ride to **Houmale'eia Beach** at the northern tip of Foa island is a good option.

Port-au-Prince
Massacre Monument   MONUMENT
(⊙ daylight hours) A few hundred metres north
of the airport runway is a signed turn-off west
to the beach where a monument commemorates the spot where the *Port-au-Prince* was
ransacked and its crew massacred on 1 December 1806. The ship's anchor was found
offshore in 2009; some of the ship's cannons
are lined up outside the former British embassy on Vuna Rd in Nuku'alofa.

Shirley Baker Monument
& European Cemetery   CEMETERY
(Holopeka Rd, Pangai; ⊙ daylight hours) About
800m north of Pangai, the grave and monument of the imperious-looking Reverend
Doctor Shirley Waldemar Baker (1836–1903),
Tonga's revered first prime minister and ad-
viser to King George Tupou I, stands amid
the graves of various 19th- and early-20th-
century German and English traders and
missionaries. A Tongan cemetery, with decorated sand and coral mounds, is directly
opposite.

Hihifo's
Archaeological Sites   ARCHAEOLOGICAL SITE
(⊙ daylight hours) Hihifo, the contiguous suburban area south of Pangai, hides some archaeological relics seemingly of more interest to
rooting pigs than anyone else. Hidden behind
a low stone fence in a grove of ironwood on
Loto Kolo Rd is **Olovehi Tomb**, the burial
ground for people holding the noble title of
Tuita.

Turn east at the Free Wesleyan Church
on Holopeka Rd to find the circular **Velata
Mound Fortress**, a 15th-century ditch-and-
ridge fortification, typical of Tonga, Fiji and
Samoa.

Southern Lifuka   AREA
(⊙ daylight hours) From Hihifo, the road continues south to **Hulu'ipaongo Point**, with
its sweep of white beach and views south
to Uoleva island. About 200m short of the
point is **Hulu'ipaongo Tomb**, the burial site
of the Mata'uvave line of chiefs.

🏃 Activities

Sandy, deserted beaches may be all you need
for a perfect trip to Ha'apai, but for more animated visitors, a number of operators are
running excellent tours, both on and off the
water. Ha'apai Beach Resort (p451) just
north of Pangai and Ha'apai Whale & Sail
(p452) on Uoleva also run boat trips and
watery activities from Lifuka.

Have a read of Whale-Watching Ethics
(p461) if you're weighing up a whale-
watching/-swimming experience.

⭐**Friendly Islands Kayak**
Company   KAYAKING
(☏ 874 8506; www.fikco.com; trips from T$1100; ⊛)
🖋 Friendly Islands Kayak Co runs all-inclusive,
multiday kayaking trips around Lifuka: sign
up for a seven-, nine- or 11-day adventure. The
moderate seven-day option (good for families
with older kids) includes accommodation and

FONUAFO'OU: NOW YOU SEE IT, NOW YOU DON'T

The Ha'apai group is home to Tonga's mysterious disappearing island, Fonuafo'ou. From
1781 to 1865 there were repeated reports of a shoal 72km northwest of Tongatapu and
60km west of Nomuka in the south of the Ha'apai group. An island was confirmed by the
HMS *Falcon* in 1865 and given the name Falcon Island. In 1885 the island was 50m high
and 2km long. Amid great excitement, Tonga planted its flag and claimed it as Fonuafo'ou,
meaning 'New Land'.

Then in 1894 Fonuafo'ou went missing! Two years later it reappeared at 320m high
before disappearing again. In 1927 it reemerged and in 1930 was measured at 130m high
and 2.5km long! By 1949 there was again no trace of Fonuafo'ou, which had once more
been eroded by the sea. Fonuafo'ou came back again, but at last report this geographical
freak had once more submerged.

The island is a submarine volcano that alternates between building itself up above sea
level and being eroded down below it. At present, its summit elevation is estimated at
17m below sea level. If the 'New Land' does come back, your best chance of spotting it is
if you are on a yacht.

In early 2015 volcanic hubbub 65km northwest of Nuku'alofa created another new
black-ash island, 2km long by 1km wide. Tongan officials have decided not to name it
(yet), with the expectation that, like Fonuafo'ou, the South Pacific surf will soon reclaim
it. What the sea wants, the sea shall have...

meals at Serenity Beaches Resort (p453) on Uoleva island; all the trips include snorkelling, a bit of hiking and plenty of beach time. Also runs trips in Vava'u (p456).

Whale Discoveries BOAT TOUR
(📋 873 7676; www.whalediscoveries.com; day trips from T$200) Excellent snorkelling day tours with lots of time in the water, some beach and bush walking, birdwatching, picnicking and Tongan cultural insights. Multiday live-aboard sailing trips and whale-watching/-swimming trips also available.

🛏 Sleeping

Fifita Guesthouse GUESTHOUSE $
(📋 731 8159, 60 213; www.tongaholiday.com/listing/fifita-guesthouse; Fau Rd, Pangai; s & d from T$70, s/d without bathroom from T$40/55, all incl breakfast) Morphing into the building upstairs/behind Mariner's Cafe and just a short walk from the wharf, red-and-white Fifita's remains a popular choice. It's rudimentary but friendly and clean enough, with back-and-forth travel banter flying around the communal kitchen. Rates include breakfast (or go downstairs to the cafe).

Lindsay Guesthouse GUESTHOUSE $
(📋 888 3531; www.tongaholiday.com/listing/lindsay-guesthouse; cnr Loto Kolo & Tuita Rds, Pangai; s/d/f T$60/60/75) A clean and friendly spot walking distance to downtown Pangai, with a broad verandah and communal sitting room and kitchen. Beds are distributed through sundry basic rooms: ask for a private one if you're not into dorm life. Breakfast is T$10. The scent of baking bread wafts across the lawn from the Matuku-ae-tau Bakery next door.

Ha'apai Beach Resort BUNGALOW $$
(📋 60 051; www.haapaibeachresort.com; Holopeka Rd, Lifuka; d T$190, s without bathroom T$85; 📶) Halfway between the airport and Pangai (about 1.5km from each), Ha'apai Beach Resort is chilled-out enclave of blue-and-white cabins on a grassy verge above the sand. Snorkelling, diving, kayaking, island trips, free wi-fi...it's all on offer. Head to the bar for a big TV and big breakfasts. Love the vintage *Mutiny on the Bounty* poster!

🍴 Eating

There's an informal market on the Pangai waterfront and a few shops with limited food supplies around town, but it would be a stretch to call them supermarkets. Plan ahead accordingly.

Matuku-ae-tau Bakery BAKERY $
(cnr Loto Kolo & Tuita Rds, Pangai; items from T$1; ⊙8am-5pm Mon-Sat, 5-8pm Sun) This basic bakery has two ovens to keep the island in bread, jam-filled rolls and *keki* (similar to doughnuts). There's a mad rush on Sunday afternoon.

★ Mariner's Cafe CAFE $$
(📋 60 374; www.tongaholiday.com/listing/mariners-cafe; Fau Rd, Pangai; mains $10-20; ⊙9am-late Mon-Sat, 6-9pm Sun; 📶) Pangai's prime dining option, cheery Mariner's is just off the main street. The menu, chalked up on little blackboards, features burgers, soups, stews and pastas, served to a soundtrack of Bryan Adams or Robbie Williams. Sit down with a beer or an iced coffee and soak up some local knowledge before heading on your adventures. Wi-fi is T$6 per hour.

ℹ Information

Tap water in Ha'apai is only fit for washing clothes and getting the sand off your bod. Drink bottled or rain water.

For money exchange and credit-card advances, there's a Western Union branch next to the visitor centre, and a Westpac bank branch on Holopeka Rd. There are no ATMs in Ha'apai (bring cash).

Niu'ui Hospital (📋 60 201; Holopeka Rd, Hihifo; ⊙24hr) Basic facilities and a pharmacy; for emergencies only.

Pangai Visitor Information Centre (📋 60 733; www.thekingdomoftonga.com; Holopeka Rd, Pangai; ⊙8.30am-4.30pm Mon-Fri, to 12.30pm Sat) Can assist with accommodation bookings, boat transport and directions (does it have a Pangai town map yet?). Next to the Western Union office.

Foa

To the north of Lifuka and connected by a wind-buffeted concrete causeway you can cycle over, Foa is a heavily wooded island. **Houmale'eia Beach**, on the western side of the northern tip, is the best beach on the Ha'apai 'mainland', with coral close to the shore, sublime views of Nukunamo and terrific snorkelling (or just a sunny patch of sand on which to sit and do nothing). On the eastern side of the northern tip, there are some ancient **petroglyphs** carved into a rocky ledge just offshore (only visible at low tide). Ask the bar staff at Matafonua Lodge to point you in the right direction.

🛏 Sleeping

★ Matafonua Lodge   BUNGALOW $$$
(☑ 69 766; www.matafonua.com; Faleloa, Foa; s & d bungalows T$210, extra adult/child T$60/30, all incl breakfast; 🛜) Right on the sandy northern tip of Foa, gazing across at Nukunamo island, family-friendly Matafonua was hammered by Tropical Cyclone Ian in 2014 but has been fully resurrected. Lovely water-view *fale* are totally comfortable, with freshwater showers in well-designed shared bathrooms. There's also an all-day cafe-bar, lagoon swimming and snorkelling, kayaks, bicycles and cultural tours to Ha'ano island.

★ Sandy Beach Resort   RESORT $$$
(☑ 69 600; www.sandybeach-tonga.com; Faleloa, Foa; s & d per person incl breakfast & dinner T$540; 🛜) Arguably Tonga's best resort, Sandy Beach really delivers (this is where the king stays when he's in Ha'apai). A row of elegant bungalows are oriented for sunset views over the sublime white-sand Houmale'eia Beach. The resort can organise activities daily, bookended by breakfast and dinner in its excellent restaurant. A library and open-air bar complete the experience. Paradise found.

ℹ Getting There & Around
If you're staying at either of the sleeping options, the operators will arrange to get you there. By bicycle from Pangai it takes around one hour; the taxi fare is about T$35.

Nukunamo
The small picture-postcard island you can see from the tip of Foa is Nukunamo, an uninhabited isle with a shining white beach littered with beautiful shells. You can kayak to Nukunamo across the channel from Foa, but don't try and swim over – the current ripping through here is truly powerful. If you're staying at Matafonua Lodge or Sandy Beach Resort, they have kayaks you can use.

Ha'ano
Travellers will get a dose of traditional Tongan life on the strikingly clean and friendly island of Ha'ano that lies to the north of Foa and Nukunamo.

Ask at Matafonua Lodge about occasional cultural day tours here, working in unison with the Ha'ano Women's Group. Trips include boat transfers, a school visit, a kava ceremony, handicraft demonstrations, a Tongan feast, some snorkelling and transport in a horse and cart around the island (there are only two cars on Ha'ano!).

Uoleva
Robbed a bank? On the run from tax-evasion allegations back home? The island of Uoleva, just south of Lifuka, is the perfect place to hide. Uninhabited apart from the accommodation providers (there are no villages here), it offers up an uncluttered, unharried South Pacific experience with little to do other than swim, snorkel, fish, read and relax (and figure out your escape route if the cops do come knocking). Whales swim close to the shore here during the migration season (June to October) – you can sometimes see them breaching just offshore.

🏃 Activities
Activity operators based on Lifuka will pick you up here if you're booked on one of their tours. See also Fanifo Lofa Kitesurf Tonga.

Ha'apai Whale & Sail   SAILING
(☑ 888 5800; www.uoleva.com; trips per half-/full day from T$70/155) Let the breeze sail you out into the day with Ha'apai Whale & Sail, based on Uoleva (it can also pick you up from Lifuka). Island-hopping and snorkelling are the names of the games. Whale-watching/-swimming trips are also available: have a read of Whale-Watching Ethics (p461) before you book.

🛏 Sleeping & Eating
There are no shops or restaurants on Uoleva – BYO food or eat at your accommodation.

Taiana's Resort   BUNGALOW $
(☑ 883 1722; www.tongaholiday.com/listing/tiannas-resort; Uoleva; bungalows s/d/f T$35/45/75, breakfast/dinner T$10/15) Ponder the stars and lapping west-coast waves at this budget beach-bum paradise. Simple tapa-lined *fale* have mats over sandy floors, comfy beds, mosquito nets, enclosed sitting areas, hammocks...and the sea is just 50m away! Homespun cooking completes the package (or you can BYO food if you like). Transfers from Pangai are T$30 one way.

Talitali'anga Eco Resort   SAFARI TENT $$
(☑ 868 5800; www.talitalianga.com; Uoleva; d T$185) 🗭 About halfway down Uoleva's becalmed west coast, this outfit comprises just two private, elevated safari tents, each with a bathroom (self-composting toilets), deck

WILLIAM MARINER

Thanks to a series of serendipitous events, the world has an extensive account of the customs, language, religion and politics of pre-Christian Tonga.

In 1805 15-year-old William Mariner went to sea on the privateer *Port-au-Prince*. The voyage took the ship across the Atlantic, around Cape Horn, up the west coast of South America, to the Sandwich (Hawaiian) Islands and finally into Tonga's Ha'apai Group. The crew anchored at the northern end of Lifuka and was immediately welcomed with yams and barbecued pork. The reception seemed friendly enough, but on 1 December 1806 an attack was launched, the crew murdered and the ship burned to the waterline.

Young Mariner, however, dressed in uniform, was captured and escorted ashore. Finau 'Ulukalala I, the reigning chief of Ha'apai, seeing the well-dressed young man, assumed that Mariner was the captain's son and ordered that his life be spared.

Mariner was taken under the wing of Finau and became privy to most of the goings-on in Tongan politics over the following four years. He learned the language well and travelled with the chief, observing and absorbing the finer points of Tongan ceremony and protocol.

After the death of Finau, the king's son permitted Mariner to leave Tonga on a passing English vessel. Back in England, an amateur anthropologist, Dr John Martin, was fascinated with Mariner's tale and suggested collaboration on a book. The result, *An Account of the Natives of the Tonga Islands,* is a masterpiece of Pacific literature.

The Port-au-Prince Massacre Monument (p450) is just north of the airport, near to where the wreck of the *Port-au-Prince* was found in 2012.

and sunset views as far as Foa. Drinks and meals at the sandy-floor bar (not included in accommodation prices); transfers from Pangai per person $T35 one way. And there's a resident turtle in the lagoon!

Serenity Beaches Resort BUNGALOW $$$
(☑873 4934; www.serenitybeaches.com; Uoleva; bungalow d with/without bathroom T$330/190, half/full board T$75/100; ☎) At the southern end of Uoleva, Serenity Beaches features beautifully constructed octagonal *fale* on both sides of the island. Food utilises fresh local ingredients (vegetarians rejoice!). There are free kayaks and snorkelling gear to entice you into the sea. Transfers from Pangai cost T$50 per person one way. If you've got the loot, stay here.

Fanifo Lofa Kitesurf Tonga BUNGALOW $$$
(☑845 8188; www.kitesurftonga.com; Uoleva; bungalows per person incl meals T$140; ☎) ✎ On the northern end of Uoleva, Fanifo Lofa is geared towards kitesurfers, but anyone can stay here regardless of whether they're prone to flying across the ocean waves or not. Elevated timber *fale* are solar-powered and supercomfortable. Rates include all meals and transfers, use of kayaks and stand-up paddle boards, and transport to kitesurfing hot spots (BYO equipment).

'Uiha

The conservative, traditional island of 'Uiha, to the south of Uoleva, is a friendly place with two little villages: 'Uiha, with a wharf, and Felemea, about 1.5km south.

In the centre of 'Uiha village is a large, elevated burial ground containing several royal tombs, once the official burial ground of the Tongan royal family until they moved to Nuku'alofa. At the village church are two cannons, souvenirs taken from a Peruvian blackbirding (slaving) ship that was attacked and destroyed by the locals in 1863.

A day trip to the island is good fun. Talk to the Pangai Visitor Information Centre (p451) about boat transport, or see if the folks at Ha'apai Beach Resort (p451) will ship you here.

VAVA'U GROUP

POP 18,000 / AREA 119 SQ KM

Shaped like a giant jellyfish with its tentacles dangling south, gorgeous Vava'u (va-vuh-ooh) is a photo opportunity at every turn. Those tentacles comprise myriad islands (61 of them!) intertwined with turquoise waterways and encircling reefs – one of the most famed sheltered yachting grounds on the planet.

To really experience it, get out onto the water. Vava'u has it all: charter sailing, sea kayaking, game fishing, surfing, diving and swimming with whales are the names of the games. Bunk down in town or head out to one of the islands for a remote tropical stay.

Vava'u plays host to around 500 visiting yachts each year, mainly during the May-to-October season as trans-Pacific yachts blow through heading west. Port of Refuge is one of the safest harbours in the South Pacific, attracting more than its share of yachts during cyclone season (November to April).

Online, have a look at www.vavau.to.

History

Vava'u is believed to have been settled for around 2000 years. The capital, Neiafu, looks out onto Port of Refuge, christened by Spaniard Don Francisco Antonio Mourelle, who sighted Vava'u on 4 March 1781 en route from Manila to Mexico. Mourelle claimed the new-found paradise, one of the last South Pacific island groups to be contacted by Europeans, for mother Spain. Captain Cook missed it a decade earlier when the Ha'apai islanders convinced him that there were no safe anchorages north of Ha'apai (ha-ha, Ha'apai).

William Mariner spent time here during Finau 'Ulukala I of Ha'apai's conquest of Vava'u in 1808. Later, on the death of 'Ulukala III, King George Tupou I added Vava'u to his realm when he formed a united Tonga in 1845.

ⓘ Getting There & Away

AIR
Lupepau'u Airport is a 15-minute drive north of Neiafu.

Real Tonga (Map p459; ☑71 115; www. realtonga.to; Tu'i Rd; ⊗8.30am-5pm Mon-Fri, 9am-1pm Sat) has a local office (domestic flights).

BOAT
The Friendly Islands Shipping Company runs long-haul ferries between Vava'u and Tongatapu, Ha'apai and occasionally the Niua Group.

ⓘ Getting Around

TO/FROM THE AIRPORT
Some accommodation, including island resorts, offers airport transfers for a price (from around T$15). Taxis charge T$30 for the airport–Neiafu trip.

BICYCLE
Vava'u is hilly but fairly manageable by bicycle. Café Tropicana (p458) in Neiafu rents out decent bikes with helmets from $15 per day.

BUS
Buses run from central stops on Tu'i Rd and Fatafehi Rd in Neiafu to most parts of Vava'u and its connected islands, leaving when full. They usually make the run into town in the morning and return in the afternoon, so they're not much good for day trips from town. Most fares are under T$2.

CAR
Rental cars are available in Neiafu. A Tongan visitor's driver's licence is probably prudent (T$40 from the police station) but operators may turn a blind eye if you don't have one. Don't park under coconut trees, and watch out for the usual maelstrom of kids, pigs, chickens and dogs throwing themselves into the road.

Coconut Car Rentals (☑755 6667; www. coconutcarrental.net) has a couple of small cars and a big Nissan pickup truck for rent, both from T$60 per day. Pick up and delivery anywhere in Neiafu.

TAXI
Taxis charge T$5 to T$10 around Neiafu, and T$30 to the airport, 'Ano and Hinakauea Beaches. You'll usually find one parked along Fatafehi Rd, across from the Westpac bank.

Neiafu

POP 6000

Strung around the fringes of Port of Refuge, surely one of the world's most photogenic harbours, Neiafu has a dishevelled charm. Home to a slew of decent restaurants and bars along the waterfront, the town itself is ramshackle and rakish (a great place to drink rum and write a novel). Over winter (June to October), with visiting yachties and a steady flow of visitors winging in, the ol' town buzzes with accents and activity.

⊙ Sights

★St Joseph's Cathedral   CATHEDRAL
(Map p459; Fatafehi Rd; free; ⊗daylight hours) A vision of colonial piety above Port of Refuge, St Joe's is Neiafu's defining piece of archiecture. Inside, the hypercoloured crucifixion scene behind the altar is something to behold. The stretch of Fatafehi Rd below the cathedral is called Hala Lupe (Way of Doves), named for the mournful singing of the female prisoners (convicted adulterers) who constructed it.

TOFUA & KAO

About 70km west of Lifuka are pyramidal Kao (1030m) and its smoking partner, Tofua (515m). On a good day this uninhabited pair is clearly visible from Lifuka.

Tofua is a flat-topped volcanic island that, like Niuafo'ou in the Niua Group, looks not unlike a huge floating life ring when viewed from above. It started life as a classic cone-shaped volcano but the top blew off in a violent eruption, creating a caldera, in the middle of which is a freshwater lake 38m above sea level. The crater rim is a tough one-hour climb from the Hokala landing site on the northern side of the island.

Adding to Tofua's intrigue, champion Swiss snowboarder Xavier Rosset decided to play modern-day Robinson Crusoe here in 2008 and spent 10 months on the island in survival mode. He took a satellite phone and blogged about his adventures – have a look online at www.xavierrosset.ch.

The four-hour hike up uninhabited Kao, a perfect volcanic cone 4km north of Tofua, is not recommended without a guide. The summit is the highest point in Tonga, but there is no marked track and the vegetation closes in around you in a green tropical embrace.

Unless you're on a yacht, reaching Tofua and Kao is not easy. Talk to the Pangai Visitor Information Centre (p451) or the boat-tour operators around Lifuka if you're keen. It should be considered a major expedition, not a day trip: taking along a local guide is a smart move.

Mt Talau National Park MOUNTAIN
(Map p456; off Tapueluefu Rd; ⊙daylight hours)
FREE A flat-topped mountain looming behind Port of Refuge, 131m Mt Talau (Mo'unga Talau) is protected as part of Mt Talau National Park. To check it out, from the centre of Neiafu truck west along Tapueluefu Rd for around 2km, where the road narrows into a bush track to the summit. Keep an eye out for flying foxes, the Tongan whistler and the *fokai* (banded lizard) en route.

Old Harbour HARBOUR
(Map p459; off Naufahu Rd; ⊙24hr) Head north on Tokongahahau Rd from the cathedral then turn east onto Naufahu Rd and you'll reach the low-key Old Harbour. It's much less developed than the main harbour over the hill: just a few houses, strings of *tapa* drying in the wind and the launch pad for boats to some of Vava'u's eastern islands.

🏃 Activities

Sailing

Vava'u is a world-famous yachtie hang-out. Charter a yacht, either bareboat or skippered, and cruise around the islands, stopping to snorkel and explore beaches as the mood strikes you (not a bad life).

Moorings BOATING
(Map p459; ☑70 016; www.tongasailing.com; waterfront, off Fatafehi Rd) Charters out catamarans and monohulls, sleeping up to 10 South Seas rapscallions. Prices vary with the seasons. Check the website for details, plus a handy Crusing Guide, maps and downloadable yachting info.

Melinda Sea Adventures BOATING
(Map p459; ☑889 7586; www.sailtonga.com; waterfront, off Fatafehi Rd) Fully crewed, full-day sailing trips on a luxury yacht, or three-night all-inclusive sailing experiences (beds, meals, skipper and cook). Rates depend on the season and number of passengers; check the website.

Vava'u Yacht Club BOATING
(Map p459; ☑70 650, 70 016; Mango Cafe, waterfront, off Fatafehi Rd; ⊙Fri Jun-Nov) On a balmy Friday afternoon, you can't beat knocking back some beers as the yachts race around Port of Refuge. If you want to crew, turn up at the Mango Cafe (p460), where the skippers meet around 4pm (5pm race start). Tons of fun at the bar, whether you're racing or not.

Diving

Vava'u's dive sites range from hard and soft coral gardens to barnacle-encrusted wrecks and vast sea caves – plenty of options for all levels and abilities. Most dive operators also offer whale-swim and snorkelling tours.

Beluga Diving DIVING
(Map p459; ☑70 327; www.belugadivingvavau.com; waterfront, off Fatafehi Rd; snorkelling/diving trips from T$200/350) With 25 years' experience, Beluga knows a thing or two about Tonga's undersea terrain. Diving, snorkelling, whale-watching and PADI dive courses available, plus occasional camping trips.

Vava'u Group

Dolphin Pacific Diving   DIVING
(Map p459; ☑70 292; www.dolphinpacificdiving.
com; waterfront, off Fatafehi Rd; full-day snorkelling/
diving trips from T$330/220) Dolphin Pacific
prides itself on being a relaxed, friendly operation. Down on the waterfront near the
white-elephant Puataukanave Hotel.

Fishing

If you're keen to bag a marlin, tuna or sailfish (then let it go), Vava'u is one of the best
game-fishing destinations in the Pacific
(more than 1km deep not far offshore).

Hakula Sport Fishing Charters   FISHING
(Map p456; ☑70 872; www.fishtonga.com; full-
day trips per 4 people from T$2000) Fishing trips
for experienced anglers on the MV *Hakula*.
Operates out of Hakula Lodge (p458).

Poppin' Tonga   FISHING
(☑873 3347, 71 075; www.talihaubeach.com; half-/
full day per 3 people incl equipment T$600/1000)
Operating out of Lucky's Beach Houses
(p462), and specialising in hooking giant
trevally (catch-and-release), either from land
or boat.

Water Sports

Island resorts and beachside accommodation
operators around Vava'u often provide kayaks
for guest use. There are some remote reef surf
breaks here, for expereinced wave hounds.

Friendly Islands Kayak Company   KAYAKING
(Map p456; ☑874 8506; www.fikco.com; 🖋)
🌿 These ecofriendly paddlers run magical three- to 10-day kayaking expeditions
around Vava'u (and Ha'apai, p450) with
knowledgeable local guides. Expect plenty of
snorkelling, beachcombing and village-visit
action, with myriad add-on options (whale
watching, mountain biking, diving...). Accommodation can be either camping out or
sleeping under more rigid roofs; check the
website for options.

Whale Watching

With a passing parade of humpback whales, Vava'u has become one of the world's top whale-watching destinations. The activity is not without controversy: see Whale-Watching Ethics (p461) for more.

There are 19 commercial whale-watching/-swimming licensees in Vava'u, all with similar prices (around T$350 to T$450 per person per day). The whales are generally here from June to late October.

☞ Tours

Land-based tours are the best way to see the main island of Vava'u, while several operators run day boat excursions that typically include Swallows' Cave, Mariner's Cave, lunch on an uninhabited island and snorkelling at an offshore reef.

Hakau Adventures   BOAT TOUR
(📞 755 8164; www.hakauadventures.com; tours per adult/child incl lunch T$140/70; 👶) Casual full-day boat trips that include a visit to Swallows' Cave on Kapa, reef snorkelling, swimming and picnic lunch on a remote beach (homemade chocolate brownies!). Trips to Vava'u's eastern islands also available.

Hakula Lodge Tours   TOUR
(Map p456; 📞 755 9279, 70 872; www.hakula lodge.com/tour; Fatafehi Rd; tours from T$70) Hakula Lodge (p458), just south of Neiafu, is a one-stop shop for tours and activities, both guided and unguided: fishing, snorkelling, sailing, bike-riding, diving, driving... Give them a call to discuss what you'd like to do: if they don't offer what you want, they'll suggest someone who does!

Vava'u Tours   TOUR
(📞 771 6148, 874 0000; www.vavau.to/portofrefuge villas) Salesi proudly shows visitors around his home island for T$75 (minimum two people). Island-hop boat tours also available (T$150).

> ### ℹ COCK-A-DOODLE-DOO
>
> Forget to set your alarm for your early flight? Don't worry: as per most South Pacific islands, Vava'u's roosters will ensure you're awake well before dawn even thinks about cracking. In a scrambled interpretation of International Date Line protocol, the birds here start crowing around 4am. Cock-a-doodle-don't... Bring your earplugs.

Vava'u Adventures   ADVENTURE TOUR
(Map p459; ☑ 751 2984, 874 6248; www.vavau guide.com/vavau-adventures-ltd-kart-safaris; s/d kart T$200/300) Upbeat, three-hour, 40km guided kart tours all over the main island. Take it all in (including wind-blown dust and dirt) while driving your own one- or two-seater petrol-powered kart.

🎊 Festivals & Events

Regatta Vava'u   SPORTS
(www.regattavavau.com) Held in early September each year, Regatta Vava'u is a blossoming party week with all sorts of action for yachties and landlubbers alike.

🛏 Sleeping

For rental houses, see www.vavauholiday homes.com.

★ Flying Annie Moa B&B   B&B $
(Map p456; ☑ 842 0325, 71 463; www.flyingann niemoavavau.com; Fatafehi Rd; r $T60-220; 🛜) Moas were flightless, weren't they? Regardless, this newish B&B soars above most Neiafu accommodation. It's immaculately clean for starters, without a cracked tile or broken fan in sight. Over two levels are a lovely lounge and broad balcony, bright singles and doubles (four en-suite), tidy bathrooms and a five-berth self-contained unit. Breakfast is eggs, cereal, toast and coffee. Nice one!

Backpackers Vava'u   HOSTEL $
(Map p459; ☑ 883 7080, 70 149; www.backpack ersvavau.com; Fatafehi Rd; dm/d T$35/200, s/d without bathroom T$75/100) This modern hostel in the middle of Neiafu makes a decent budget base from which to propel yourself into Vava'u's myriad activities and after-dark indulgences. Fan-cooled rooms are bright, clean and secure. The shared kitchen sees plenty of action, as does the sun-swathed terrace overlooking buzzy 'Utukalongalu Market.

★ Port Wine Guest House   GUESTHOUSE $$
(Map p459; ☑ 70 479; www.portwineguesthouse. com; Ha'amea Rd; s/d T$120/180, s/d without bathroom T$60/100, s/d bungalows T$180/250; 🛜) For a cheery Tongan family experience, head to smart-looking Port Wine, run by Lu'isa Tuiniua and her son Tai. Sleeping options include original guesthouse rooms (shared bathrooms), newer en-suite guesthouse rooms, and two private en-suite *fale* – all of which are superclean and proudly maintained. There's always a cold coconut in the fridge and fruit comes direct from the lush gardens.

Boathouse Apartments   APARTMENT $$
(Map p459; ☑ 70 016; www.boathousetonga.com; Fatafehi Rd; d/q from T$160/210; ❄) Propped up on the cliff above the harbour, this sky-blue apartment complex offers fabulous water views and four ship-shape apartments with kitchens – great for families and self-catering couples. Super location too, close to the cafes and the town hubbub.

Harbourview Resort   BUNGALOW $$
(Map p456; ☑ 70 687, 751 2149; www.harbour viewresort.com; off Fatafehi Rd, Toula; d/f from T$180/230; 🛜) The dodgy dirt road leading you here doesn't inspire, passing an old gas storage facility, but once you're ensconced in your motel-style cabin at Harbourview, you'll soon forgive. Set in immaculate tropical gardens (pink hibiscus blooms!) about 3km south of Neiafu, these nine units have kitchenettes and verandahs. Self-catering and family terrain. Taxis are T$10 from Neiafu.

Hakula Lodge   LODGE $$$
(Map p456; ☑ 70 872; www.hakulalodge.com; Fatafehi Rd; s/d/f T$195/275/350; ❄🛜) Top-end, terracotta-tiled units opening onto a full-length verandah overlooking Port of Refuge (good sunsets). Wander down through the tropical gardens to swim off the private jetty, from which the owners' various boat trips (p457) set sail. The lodge is about 2km south of Neiafu.

🍴 Eating

There are a few no-frills supermarkets and bakeries around town for self-caterers, plus the 'Utukalongalu Market (p460).

Café Tropicana   CAFE $
(Map p459; ☑ 71 322; www.vavau.to/tropicana; Fatafehi Rd; mains $5-16; ⏰8am-9pm Mon-Sat; 🛜🍴) Nab a seat in the shady interior or slouch into a deckchair on the terrace at this

Neiafu

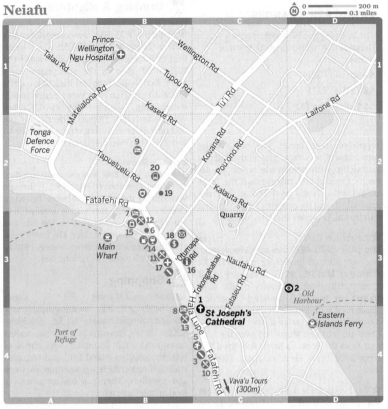

Neiafu

◎ Top Sights
1 St Joseph's Cathedral	C4

◎ Sights
2 Old Harbour	D3

✦ Activities, Courses & Tours
3 Beluga Diving	C4
4 Dolphin Pacific Diving	B3
Melinda Sea Adventures	(see 10)
5 Moorings	C4
6 Vava'u Adventures	B3
Vava'u Yacht Club	(see 13)

🛏 Sleeping
7 Backpackers Vava'u	B3
8 Boathouse Apartments	B4
9 Port Wine Guest House	B2

✕ Eating
10 Aquarium Café	C4
11 Bellavista Cafe & Restaurant	B3
12 Café Tropicana	B3
13 Mango Cafe	B4

🍷 Drinking & Nightlife
14 Bounty Bar	B3
Dancing Rooster	(see 11)

🛍 Shopping
15 'Utukalongalu Market	B3

ⓘ Information
ANZ Bank (ATM)	(see 6)
16 Neiafu Visitor Information Centre	B3
17 Universal Clinic & Pharmacy	B3
18 Westpac Bank (ATM)	B3

ⓘ Transport
Fatafehi Rd Bus Stop	(see 15)
19 Real Tonga	B2
20 Tu'i Rd Bus Stop	B2

> ### EATING PRICE RANGES
>
> The following prices ranges refer to the price of a main course, for lunch or dinner.
>
> **$** less than T$15
>
> **$$** T$15 to T$25
>
> **$$$** more than T$25

troppo-bohemian haunt. The menu wafts from burgers to wraps, pies and salads to sandwiches with homemade bread (wholemeal!). Cookies and cakes crowd the front cabinet, plus there's wi-fi and an internet terminal if you're suffering social media withdrawal. Espresso and bike hire too.

★**Aquarium Café** CAFE **$$**
(Map p459; ☏70 493; www.aquariumcafevavau. com; waterfront, off Fatafehi Rd; mains T$10-30; ☺9am-9pm Mon-Sat; 🛜) You can get it all at airy Aquarium: generous meals, fully stocked bar, free wi-fi, switched-on service, classic rock soundtrack, even the occasional live-music session around the kava bowl. There are winning views out over the harbour from the deck – a beaut spot for a few happy-hour beers (4pm to 7pm). Hard to beat!

★**Bellavista Cafe & Restaurant** ITALIAN **$$**
(Map p459; ☏71 035; www.tongaholiday.com/ listing/bellavista-cafe-restaurant; Gutenbeil Plaza, Fatafehi Rd; mains $19-26; ☺11am-2pm & 5-9pm Mon-Sat; 🛜🍽) Quiz a local about their favourite Neiafu eatery, and they'll most likely point you towards Bellavista – a romantic, top-floor Italian restaurant, complete with candlelight and red-and-white checked tablecloths. Terrific harbour views, attentive staff and disco hits (when was the last time you heard Andy Gibb?). Ask for some of the house-made chilli sauce on your pizza. Very kid-friendly, too.

Mango Cafe CAFE **$$**
(Map p459; ☏70 664; waterfront, off Fatafehi Rd; mains T$10-30; ☺9am-9pm Mon-Sat) This curvy-roofed, clubby cafe is right on the water (literally – you can see the sea through floorboards!) and is a fave with yachties who tie up their tenders out the front. Check the blackboard for daily offerings (the sesame-seed wasabi tuna is a knockout). Don't miss the yacht racing (p455) and a few ales here on Friday evenings (June to November).

🍷 Drinking & Nightlife

Bounty Bar BAR
(Map p459; ☏70 576; www.facebook.com/pag es/vavau-bounty-bar/728610520519671; water-front, off Fatafehi Rd; ☺10am-12.30am Mon-Fri, to 11.30pm Sat) Run by the unflappable Lawrence, Bounty Bar is as laid-back as it comes; ice-cold beers, harbour views and a highly entertaining *fakaleiti* show (p467) every Wednesday night (10pm). There's also the odd quiz night and a big screen on which to watch the big men collide in the rugby.

Dancing Rooster BAR
(Map p459; ☏70 886; www.vavauguide.com/danc ing-rooster; waterfront, off Fatafehi Rd; ☺9am-late Mon-Sat) On the waterfront below Bellavista Cafe & Restaurant, this joint is usually full of sea-salty expats, washed up on the tide and in need of a rum and a cigar. The food's passable (burgers, steaks, curries; mains T$10 to T$30) but it's mostly a drinking den.

🛍 Shopping

'Utukalongalu Market MARKET
(Map p459; ☏70 406; www.tongaholiday.com/ listing/utukalongalu-market; Tu'i Rd; ☺8.30am-4.30pm Mon-Fri, 7am-noon Sat) An open-walled harbourside hall crammed with racks of brightly coloured island fruit and veg, plus stalls selling locally hewn weavings, carvings and jewellery. There's a budget takeaway food arcade here too.

ℹ Information

There are Westpac and ANZ banks on Fatafehi Rd, both with ATMs.

The Aquarium Café has free wi-fi for customers; at Café Tropicana (p458) it's T$6 per hour (it also has an internet terminal).

Neiafu Visitor Information Centre (Map p459; ☏70 115; www.thekingdomoftonga. com; cnr Fatafehi & 'Otumapo Rds; ☺8.30am-4.30pm Mon-Sat) An open-walled, lime-green office stocked with neatly piled brochures. Helpful staff can assist with bookings, maps and accommodation reservations.

Police Station (Map p459; ☏26 498, emergency 922; www.police.gov.to; Tu'i Rd; ☺24hr) Ask about getting a Tongan visitor's drivers licence if you're renting a car.

Post Office (Map p459; www.tongapost.to; Pou'ono Rd; ☺8.30am-4.30pm Mon-Fri) Hard to find on the end of a little bank of shops, up a set of stairs.

Prince Wellington Ngu Hospital (Map p459; ☏70 201; Mateialona Rd; ☺24hr) On the hill behind town. For emergencies.

Universal Clinic & Pharmacy (Map p459; ☑70 213; Fatafehi Rd; ☺8.30am-5pm Mon-Fri, 11am-noon Sat) Pharmacy with a doctor on site between 9am and 4pm Monday, Thursday and Friday.

Around Vava'u

Neiafu is where everybody hangs out, but it's not at all typical of wider Vava'u, which is laced with farmland, little villages, some impressive lookouts and empty beaches. Take an island tour or hire a car for a day or two to get the true lay of the land.

South of the main island, **Pangaimotu** is a largish isle connected to the 'mainland' by A'hanga Causeway. Long, thin 'Utungake is in turn connected to Pangaimotu via another causeway.

◎ Sights

'Ene'io Botanical Garden   GARDENS
(Map p456; ☑71 048; www.eneio.com; 'Ene'io Beach, Tu'anekivale, Vava'u; ☺tours available 9am-5pm Mon-Sat) Developed by Tonga's former Minister of Agriculture, these gardens are brimming with botany (550 different plant varieties!). Access is via guided tour: book yourself onto a short garden walk (T$35), a three-hour birdwatching and hiking tour (T$85) or a full-day cultural tour (T$180). The cafe–gift shop sells everything from handicrafts to organic taro chips. 'Ene'io Beach is on the main island's eastern fringe – transport by arrangement. Bookings essential.

'Ano & Hinakauea Beaches   BEACH
(Map p456) Near the southern end of Pangaimotu are these two beaut beaches backed by vegetation, with sheltered waters, good snorkelling and a safe spot to anchor your yacht. A rewarding bike ride from Neiafu.

Ark Gallery Vava'u   GALLERY
(Map p456; ☑888 7998; www.tongavavauholiday.net/arkgalleryofvavau.htm; Anchorage 11, 'Ano Beach; ☺by appointment) Paintings, prints, local arts and crafts...on a boat! If you're keen to visit, phone first, then take a taxi to 'Ano Beach – you'll be picked up there. Or if you're on a yacht, sail up and use one of the Ark's moorings (one night for free with a

---

WHALE-WATCHING ETHICS

Tonga is an important breeding ground for humpback whales, which migrate to its warm waters between June and October. They can be seen raising young in the calm reef-protected waters and engaging in elaborate mating rituals. Humpbacks are dubbed 'singing whales' because the males sing during courtship routines. The low notes of their 'songs' can reach 185 decibels and carry 100km through the open ocean.

Humpback populations around the world have declined rapidly over the past 200 years, from 150,000 in the early 1800s to an estimated 12,000 today. The same predictable migration habits that once made the giants easy prey for whalers nowadays make them easy targets for whale watchers.

As Tonga's whale-watching industry has grown, so has concern over its impact. At the centre of the debate is the practice of swimming with whales. While it's undoubtedly one of the more unusual experiences you can have on the planet, some suggest that human interaction with whales – especially mothers and calves when they are at their most vulnerable – has a disruptive effect on behaviours and breeding patterns. Taking a longer view, others say that given humanity's historic propensity for slaughtering humpbacks by the tens of thousands, it's time we gave them a little peace and quiet.

In response to these concerns, in 2013 the Tongan government enacted a strict code of conduct for whale-watch operators and noncommercial yachts in the nation's waters, prohibiting unlicenced vessels within 300m of any whale, and banning swimming, diving, kayaking or jet-skiing near whales for anyone other than licenced operators.

If whale watching is a bucket-list essential for you, there are whale-watch and whale-swim operators in all of Tonga's island groups. Vava'u has most of the operators, but Ha'apai is probably a safer bet: there are only five operators here, which equates to less pressure on the whales. Make sure you go with a licensed operator – ask at the Nuku'alofa (p443) or Neiafu (p460) visitor information centres – and give yourself a few days to do it so that there is no pressure on the operator to 'chase' whales in order to keep you happy. If you feel your whale-swim operator has breached the boundaries and 'hassled' the whales in any way, make sure you report this to the info centres.

purchase from the gallery). The Ark was for sale at the time of writing – let us know if it has sailed away into the sunset!

🛏 Sleeping & Eating

Lucky's Beach Houses   BUNGALOW $
(Map p456; ☏ 71 075; www.luckysbeach.com; Talihau Village, 'Utungake; d bungalows/beach house from T$75/170; 📶) Lucky's overlooks the water at Talihau Beach at the tip of causeway-connected 'Utungake. Set up for self-caterers, there are two houses and two *fale* right by the water. Launch a kayak off the beach to explore 'Utungake, or paddle over to nearby Mala. Meals by request; two-night minimum stay. Lucky's also runs Poppin' Tonga (p456) fishing carters.

★ Vava'u Villa   GUESTHOUSE $$
(Map p456; ☏ 71 010; www.vavauvilla.com; A'hanga Causeway, Pangaimotu; d incl breakfast from T$190; 📶) Just across the causeway a short drive south of Neiafu, this bright white villa is run by an Australian couple (who also run the vanilla bean processing plant across the road – ask for a tour!). There are nine renovated en-suite rooms, upstairs and down, plus an airy terrace restaurant (mains T$8 to T$22 – terrific pancakes). 'Beer o'clock is any time'.

Mystic Sands   MOTEL $$$
(Map p456; ☏ 758 4148, 758 4027; www.mysticsands.net; 'Utungake Village, 'Utungake; d/f from T$345/365, 2-bedroom house T$555; 📶🏊) Upmarket (if not mystical) beachfront motel-style units on the northern end of 'Utungake, with one family-sized room and a two-bedroom house sleeping four (with kitchen). There isn't a restaurant on site; order room service, or taxi it back to Neiafu (10 minutes back over the causeway). Activity operators will pick you up from the jetty out the front.

Tongan Beach Resort   RESORT $$$
(Map p456; ☏ 70 380; www.thetongan.com; 'Utungake Village, 'Utungake; bungalows incl breakfast from T$590; 📶🏊) Right on Hikutamole Beach on 'Utungake, this relaxed resort gazes out onto the main channel into Port of Refuge (as many whales as yachts, at times). Up-tempo staff, decent rooms, a sandy-floor *fale* bar, beachfront restaurant and – that Tongan rarity – a swimming pool! Good for families.

Southern Vava'u Islands

Vava'u has an astounding number of islands and waterways weaving towards the south.

Visitors can head out to one of the growing number of island resorts, take it all in by boat, or sign up for a multiday kayak tour with Friendly Islands Kayak Company (p456). The resorts here can arrange all transfers.

Mala

Just south of 'Utungake, itself connected to 'mainland' Vava'u by causeways, the wee isle of Mala is just a few minutes' chug by boat from the road end (day-trip territory; talk to the Neiafu Visitor Information Centre, p460, about getting there). The island has a sandy swimming beach, a small resort and the **Japanese Gardens** – a brilliant snorkelling area between Mala and Kapa (though beware the strong current churning between these two islands and 'Utungake).

Kapa

Kapa island's big-ticket attraction is **Swallows' Cave** ('Anapekepeka; Map p456), cutting into a cliff on the west side of the island. It's actually inhabited by hundreds of swiftlets (not swallows) and you can swim right into it. The water is gin-clear, with the floor of the cave 18m below the surface. A regular inclusion in day tours, the only access is by boat.

🛏 Sleeping

Reef Resort   RESORT $$$
(Map p456; ☏ 755 9279; www.reefresortvavau.com; Otea; d T$480-550, extra person T$100-130, full board T$150; 📶) This German-run honeymooner is a top boutique outfit with perfect beach frontage and five roomy suites, decked out in classy castaway style. Euro-Polynesian meals are a real highlight, featuring fresh organic and local produce (seafood steals the show: expect lots of tuna, lobster, coral trout and snapper). Kayak to Swallows' Cave. Transfers T$60 per person.

Hunga & Foe'ata

In Vava'u's western fringes, the large, sheltered lagoon embraced by Hunga, Kalau and Fofoa islands offers safe anchorage and brilliant **snorkelling**. There's more good snorkelling off the island of Foe'ata, immediately south of Hunga, which has some glorious arcs of white sand.

🛏 Sleeping

Blue Lagoon Resort   BUNGALOW $$$
(Map p456; ☏ 867 1300; www.tongabluelagoon.com; Foe'ata; bungalows T$360-460, full board

T$140, transfers return T$175; ☎) One-of-a-kind Blue Lagoon has a show-stopping position on Foe'ata's northern tip. Each of the five en-suite bungalows here is uniquely constructed from local materials (lots of timber), with four of them on stilts over the water. Multiday package deals including accommodation, meals, transfers and whale watching from T$1750 per person. Wi-fi in the restaurant. No sign of Brooke Shields...

Nuapapu

Nuapapu is best known for **Mariner's Cave** (Map p456), a hidden underwater cave at the island's northern end. The main entrance is a couple of metres below the surface and the tunnel is about 4m long; use the swell to pull you towards it, then exit when the swell surges back out. Make sure you're with someone who knows what they are doing (this is dangerous stuff); snorkelling gear is essential.

'Eua'iki & 'Euakafa

In Vava'u's far southern reaches, the small atoll of 'Eua'iki has an amazing bright-white sandy beach, with a coral garden off the north shore (snorkelling supremacy).

A sandy beach also rings the north side of uninhabited 'Euakafa. From the island's eastern end a trail leads through the forest and mango trees to the summit (100m) and the overgrown tomb of Talafaiva, and ancient Tongan queen.

🛏 Sleeping

Treasure Island Eco-Resort BUNGALOW $$$
(☑ 847 6200; www.tongaislandresort.com; 'Eua'iki; bungalows d T$460, full board T$150; ☎) ✈ Want to see whales cavorting while you chew your breakfast? This solar-powered resort on 'Eua'iki features traditional thatched-roof *fale* spaced along the beachfront. There are deep sea channels on both sides of the island – whale commuter lanes. If your timing's good, they'll be trucking past while you sip your coffee. Snorkelling equipment and kayaks available.

Mounu & 'Ovalau

Almost as far south as Vava'u extends, little Mounu and 'Ovalau are perfectly far-flung sand-fringed islands. If you're looking for a romantic bolt-hole in which to express your amorous affections, look no further.

🛏 Sleeping

Mounu Island Resort RESORT $$$
(☑ 886 6403; www.mounuisland.com; Mounu; d T$430-670, full board T$150; ☎) On a tiny southern Vava'u atoll (just 6.5 acres), Mounu Island Resort comprises four wooden *fale* spaced around the island for perfect privacy (do your Tom-Hanks-in-*Castaway* impersonation at full volume). Meals and drinks at the bar; swimming, snorkelling and beach-bumming everywhere else. Good stuff.

Eastern Vava'u Islands

Mafana & 'Ofu

A short boat ride from Neiafu's Old Harbour, Vava'u's eastern islands are isolated without being too remote. 'Ofu's surrounding waters are the primary habitat of the prized but endangered *'ofu* shell (needless to say, we don't suggest you buy any).

🛏 Sleeping

Mafana Island Beach Backpackers HOSTEL $
(Map p456; ☑ 889 7679; www.mafanaislandbeach.com; Mafana; bungalows s/d from T$55/80) Budget accommodation on Vava'u's outer islands is as rare as turtle's teeth! Mafana offers treehouse-style bamboo and beachside *fale*, with a maximum of eight guests (book well ahead!). Guests self-cater, with a communal cooking area on the beach, and there are beach showers. Swim, snorkel, kayak, hike – great for families. Boat transfers T$15.

Mandala Resort BUNGALOW $$$
(Map p456; ☑ 849 1270; www.mandalaisland.com; Fetoko; s & d T$395-495, extra person T$65, half/full board T$70/100; ☎) Need an unpretentious, private Tongan island escape? Mandala fits the bill. Miniscule Fetoko Island is adrift midway between Mafana and 'Ofu, and plays host to Mandala's four brilliant en-suite bungalows. The tree house is built for couples; the two-bedroom villa is a winner for families. Meals are in the open-walled restaurant/bar. Transfers from T$17 one way.

NIUA GROUP

Tongan tradition is alive and kicking on these three small volcanic islands in Tonga's extreme northern reaches. The Niua group were the first Tongan islands to be eyeballed by Europeans (Dutchmen Schouten and Le

TAFAHI

Its fair to say that the Niua Group is 'OTBT' by definition, but that goes double for Tafahi. Nine kilometres north of Niuatoputapu, the perfect 560m cone of this extinct volcano (population 100) rises up from the sea. On the right tide you can cross by boat from Niuatoputapu to Tafahi in the morning and return in the afternoon. It's a good climb to the summit, from which on a good day you can see Samoa! Negotiate boat transfers with the local fishers if you're keen.

Maire in 1616); it may seem like little has changed since. The main islands of Niuatoputapu and Niuafo'ou are about 100km apart.

Unless you're on a yacht, any trip to the Niua Group should be approached with flexibility in mind as weather conditions often cause delays and cancellations of flights and ferry services.

ⓘ Getting There & Away

AIR
From Vava'u, Real Tonga flies to the grassy runways at Niuatoputapu (T$350 one way, weekly) and Niuafo'ou (T$420 one way, fortnightly).

BOAT
The ferry supposedly makes a trip from Vava'u to Niuatoputapu and Niuafo'ou, then back to Vava'u once a month. Sailings are reliant on unpredictable factors (ie there is no schedule): contact Friendly Islands Shipping Company (p473) for info.

Many visitors arrive on private yachts. Both islands are ports of entry to Tonga, but Niuafo'ou lacks a decent anchorage or landing site. Niuatoputapu has a pass in the reef on the northwest side of the island.

Niuatoputapu
POP 1300 / AREA 18 SQ KM

Niuatoputapu (Very Sacred Coconut) has a squashed sombrero shape, comprising a steep and narrow central ridge (a 157m-high eroded volcano) and surrounding coastal plains. The north coast is bounded by a series of reefs, and the island is surrounded by magnificent white beaches, easily circumnavigated on foot.

In 2009, following the Samoa earthquake, Niuatoputapu suffered extensive tsunami damage and nine people died.

Hihifo, the Niua Group's 'capital', has a police station, a post office and a small store. Cash and travellers cheques can be changed at the Treasury, though it sometimes runs out of cash: BYO *pa'anga* is a better idea. There is no ATM on the island.

Boat trips, including to nearby Tafahi, can be negotiated with local fishers. There's good **diving** outside the reef, but no diving equipment is available on the island.

Kaloloaine Guesthouse (☑ 758 5803; s/d from T$30/40) offers up warm hospitality in a village home with a spacious lounge and neat rooms. Guests can use the kitchen or book meals in advance. To find it, just ask a local to point the way.

Niuafo'ou
POP 735 / AREA 49 SQ KM

Remote Niuafo'ou, about 100km west of Niuatoputapu, looks like a huge doughnut floating in the ocean. But it's not fast food for giants – it's a collapsed volcanic cone (caldera), thought to have once topped 1300m in height. Today, the highest point on the caldera is 210m, and the lake it encloses is nearly 5km wide and 23m above sea level.

During the past 150 years, Niuafo'ou has experienced 10 major volcanic eruptions. After a particularly nasty one in 1946, the government evacuated the 1300 residents to 'Eua island, and Niuafo'ou was uninhabited until 200 homesick locals returned in 1957.

Niuafo'ou has no coral reef and no sandy beaches, just open ocean surrounds. A track leads right around the caldera and its impressive freshwater lake, **Vai Lahi** (Big Lake). Keep an eye out for Niuafo'ou's most unusual inhabitant, the turkeylike **Tongan megapode**, which uses the warm volcanic soil to incubate its eggs. Efforts to save this threatened bird have included transplanting chicks to the uninhabited volcanic islands of Late and Fonualei, two of Vava'u's outlying islands.

Real Tonga lands on Niuafo'ou Airport's grassy strip, winging in from Vava'u. There are a few campsites on the crater, although you should ask for permission from locals first. A handful of village houses offer guest rooms; contact the Nuku'alofa Visitor Information Centre (p443) in Tongatapu for details. There are several small shops scattered through the villages, but bring plenty of food and cash with you (no ATMs).

UNDERSTAND TONGA

Tonga Today

Politically, Tonga is in the midst of exciting times.

Before King George Tupou V was crowned in 2008, his lord chamberlain announced that the new king would relinquish much of his power to meet the democratic aspirations of his people. Changes were subsequently made to the electoral system, and in the November 2010 elections the people of Tonga gained the right to vote for 17 spots out of 26 in parliament. The other nine members are elected by the noble class from among themselves (there are 33 noble titles in Tonga).

Around 89% of eligible voters cast their ballots in this historic election. The Democratic Party of the Friendly Islands, led by long-term pro-democracy leader Akilisi Pohiva, won 12 of the 17 seats available to commoners. This wasn't quite enough, however: the other five seats were won by independents and they joined the nine nobles for a 14 to 12 majority in parliament and elected a noble, Lord Tu'ivakano, to be prime minister. This irked a number of political commentators, but democracy had taken root.

In 2014, after the unexpected death of King George Tupou V in 2012 and with his brother Tupou VI at the helm, all 26 seats were up for election, although the king retained the right to appoint nobles, nine of which again gained seats, with independents pinching three seats from the Democratic Party of the Friendly Islands to boost independent representation to eight seats. 'Akilisi Pohiva is now serving as prime minister.

Economically, Tonga is in the doldrums, reliant on limited tourism, agriculture and fishing. Remittances from Tongans living abroad are dropping as second-generation Tongans abroad need their hard-earned cash to raise their own families – rather than sending it back to Tonga. International aid is also apparently dropping, though aid work from China and Japan (p443) remains plainly visible.

Psychologically, however, Tongan national pride is soaring, with the lavish 2015 coronation of King Tupuo VI and Queen Nanasipau'u making global headlines and captivating the whole country (Tongans adore their royals). Still glowing from its historic defeat of France in the 2011 Rugby World Cup, the Tongan team went into the 2015 fixture in England with high hopes. A win over Namibia and a loss to eventual champions New Zealand was a reasonable return. All this excitement has done much to gloss over Tonga's various problems.

History

Tonga has a rich mythological tradition, and many ancient legends relate to the islands' creation. One tells that the Tongan islands were fished out of the sea by the mighty Polynesian god Tangaloa. Another story has Tonga plucked from the ocean by the demigod Maui, a temperamental hero well known throughout the Pacific.

The earliest date confirmed by radiocarbon testing for settlement of the Tongan group is 1100 BC. On Tongatapu, the Lapita people had their first capital at Toloa, near present-day Fua'amotu International Airport. Archaeological excavations in the village of Hihifo in Ha'apai unearthed Lapita pottery that has carbon dated settlement of this area to more than 3000 years ago. The Vava'u Group has been settled for around 2000 years.

The first king of Tonga, known as the Tu'i Tonga, was 'Aho'eitu. He came to power some time in the middle of the 10th century

TONGA TONGA TODAY

COOK'S 'FRIENDLY ISLANDS'

On Captain James Cook's third voyage – he later died in Hawai'i on this same trip – he spent from April to July 1777 in the Tongan islands. While visiting Lifuka in the Ha'apai Group, Cook and his men were treated to lavish feasting and entertainment by chief Finau, inspiring Cook to name his South Seas paradise the 'Friendly Islands'.

It was later learned, through William Mariner (p453), that the celebration had been part of a conspiracy to raid Cook's two ships Resolution and Discovery for their plainly visible wealth. The entertainment had been planned in order to gather the Englishmen in one spot so that they could be quickly dispatched and their ships looted. There was, however, a last-minute dispute between Finau and his nobles, and the operation was abandoned. Cook never learned how narrowly they had escaped! Not so friendly now, eh James?

AD and was the first in a line of almost 40 men to hold the title.

During the 400 years after the first Tu'i Tonga, the Tongans were aggressive colonisers, extending their empire over eastern Fiji, Niue and northward as far as the Samoas and Tokelau.

European Arrival

The first European arrivals in Tonga were Dutch explorers Willem Schouten and Jacob Le Maire, who bumped into the Niua Group in 1616.

Tongatapu's first European visitor was Dutchman Abel Tasman, who spent a few days trading with the locals in 1643. He named the island 'Amsterdam' (it didn't stick). In the same year, Tasman was also the first European to visit the Ha'apai Group.

The next European contact came in 1773 with James Cook, who buddied up with the 30th Tu'i Tonga, Fatafehi Paulaho.

Vava'u remained unseen by Europeans until Spaniard Don Francisco Antonio Mourelle showed up in 1781, making it one of the last South Pacific island groups to be contacted by Europeans.

House of Tupou

In 1831 missionaries baptised the ruling Tu'i Tonga, who took the Christian name George. As King George Tupou I, he united Tonga and, with the help of the first prime minister, Reverend Shirley Baker (yes, he was a man), came up with a flag, a state seal and a national anthem, then began drafting a constitution, which was passed in 1875. It included a bill of rights, a format for legislative and judicial procedures, laws for succession to the throne and a section on land tenure. It is also responsible for Tonga's heavily Christian laws today.

The second king, George Tupou II, who took over in 1893, lacked the charisma and fearlessness of his predecessor. He signed a Treaty of Friendship with Britain in 1900, placing Tonga under British protection and giving Britain control over Tonga's foreign affairs. When he died at the age of 45 in 1918, his 18-year-old daughter Salote became queen.

Queen Salote

A popular figure, Queen Salote's primary concerns for her country were medicine and education. With intelligence and compassion she made friends for Tonga throughout the world and was greatly loved by her subjects and foreigners alike. Her legendary attendance at Queen Elizabeth's coronation in 1953 won many hearts as she took part in the procession bareheaded in an open carriage through London, smiling resolutely at the crowds despite the pouring rain.

The World's Heaviest Monarch

King Taufa'ahau Tupou IV took over as ruler of Tonga on his mother's death in 1965. He reestablished full sovereignty for Tonga on 4 June 1970 and oversaw Tonga's admission to the Commonwealth of Nations and to the UN. In his later years, however, he made a number of unpopular decisions, including selling Tongan passports to anyone who wanted one and appointing an American to the dual role of financial advisor and official court jester, who oversaw the loss of T$50 million in funds.

An imposing figure who was renowned as the world's heaviest monarch, the 210kg king became a health role model for Tongans when he shed more than 75kg in weight. He was 88 when he died in September 2006.

In the last years of his life, the king resisted growing calls for democracy, which peaked in a 2005 strike by public servants that lasted for months and resulted in a huge growth of pro-democracy sentiment. Two months after his death, riots in Nuku'alofa killed eight, destroyed much of the business district, shocked the world and led to Australian and

TIN CAN ISLAND

Niuafo'ou is the 'Tin Can Island' legendary for its unique postal service. In days of old, since there was no anchorage or landing site, mail and supplies for residents were sealed up in a biscuit tin and tossed overboard from a passing supply ship. A strong swimmer from the island would then retrieve the parcel. Outbound mail was tied to the end of metre-long sticks, and the swimmer would carry them balanced overhead out to the waiting ship. This method persisted until 1931, when the mail swimmer became lunch for a passing shark.

In keeping with its postal tradition, special Niuafo'ou postage stamps, first issued by the Tongan government in 1983, are highly prized. To stamp collectors, Tin Can Island is legendary. The mail must go through...

FAKALEITI

One of the most distinctive features of Tongan culture are *fakaleiti,* a modern continuation of an ancient Polynesian tradition, known as *fa'afafine* in Samoa and *mahu* or *rae rae* in French Polynesia.

The term *fakaleiti* is made up of the prefix *faka-* (in the manner of) and *-leiti* from the English word 'lady'. Traditionally, if a Tongan woman had too many sons and not enough daughters she would need one of the sons to assist with 'women's work' such as cooking and housecleaning. This child would then be brought up as a daughter. These days, becoming a *fakaleiti* can also be a lifestyle choice. There is little stigma attached to *fakaleiti,* and they mix easily with the rest of society, often being admired for their style.

On Tongatapu, the Tonga Leitis' Association (TLA) is an active group – members prefer to call themselves simply *leiti* (ladies). The association sponsors several popular, well-attended events, including the international Miss Galaxy competition in July. On Vava'u, check out the *fakaleiti* show every Wednesday night at the Bounty Bar (p460).

New Zealand troops being sent to the supposedly peaceful Pacific paradise.

King George Tupou V

Following in the footsteps of his father, King George Tupou V was crowned in a lavish ceremony on 1 August 2008. The monocled bachelor, a graduate of Oxford and Sandhurst, came to power with the lord chamberlain making the following statement before his coronation: 'The sovereign of the only Polynesian kingdom...is voluntarily surrendering his powers to meet the democratic aspirations of many of his people...the people favour a more representative, elected parliament. The king agreed with them. He planned to guide his country through a period of political and economic reform for the 21st century.'

The King is Dead: Long Live the King!

In what was a shock to all Tongans, King George Tupou V died suddenly in Hong Kong in 2012. A hundred and fifty pallbearers carried him to his grave and the country mourned. His deeply religious and staunchly conservative younger brother is the new King Tupou VI, and was officially coronated in 2015, along with his wife Queen Nanasipau'u. The former crown prince, the new king previously voiced his opposition to democracy for Tonga and has a chequered history in charge, including a stint as prime minister that ended in his resignation. Tonga's economy plummeted during his leadership, leading to the calls for democracy his brother heeded. He was also involved in the demise of Royal Tongan Airlines, which lost the country millions. While many worry about the future under

the new king, others feel that as a family man with a wife and children (his brother was a bachelor) he will be a more caring king. And if his lengthy, hyperfestive coronation is any indication, he will be much adored!

The Culture

Tonga is a largely homogenous, church- and family-oriented society. Although most Tongans are open and extremely hospitable, due to cultural nuances foreigners can often feel a bit at arm's length.

Population

Tongans are proud Polynesians with a unique culture, different from other South Pacific nations. Tongans make up the vast majority of the people; there are a few *palangi* (Westerners) and a small but significant population of Chinese immigrants.

Tonga's total resident population is around 106,000. Tongatapu has more than 65% of the total population, with approximately 30% of the total living in and around Nuku'alofa (the island's and the nation's capital).

Estimates suggest there are as many Tongans living abroad as there are in the kingdom, mostly in New Zealand, Australia and the US. There are now many second- and third-generation Tongans living in these countries.

Religion

Tonga is, on the surface at least, a very religious country. Around 99% of the population identifies as being of Christian faith. The Free Wesleyan Church (the royal family's church of choice) claims the largest number

AMERICAN WWII SERVICEMEN: TONGA'S SAVIOURS?

Within 24 hours of the Japanese bombing of Pearl Harbour in 1941, Tonga declared war on Japan. Waves of fear swept the South Pacific: how far south would the Japanese war machine march? Between 1942 and 1945 it's estimated that 30,000 US servicemen passed through Tongatapu, either stationed here or en route to other regional bases. At the time, Tonga was a closeted nation of little more than 30,000 people itself, and was still reeling from the 1918 flu pandemic. Some suggest that the new bloodlines these thousands of GIs introduced into Tongan society were the saviour of Tonga, deepening the gene pool, bolstering immunity and building a platform for population growth.

of adherents, followed by the (Methodist) Free Church of Tonga, the Church of England, the Roman Catholics, Seventh Day Adventists and the wealthy and increasingly prominent Mormons (look for their tidy cream-and-blue complexes around the country).

Churches are central to everyday life and, as they are seen as social and community organisations, Tongans donate a lot of money to them. Because of this, Tongans are very conservative and bring religion into all kinds of aspects of their daily lives. For example, public displays of affection between the sexes are a no-no. Many Tongans, especially women, may go to church two, three or even four times every Sunday.

Many Tongans still believe in the spirits, taboos, superstitions, medical charms and gods of pre-Christian Polynesia. One such belief is that if a family member is suffering a serious illness, it is because the bones of their ancestors have been disturbed. Many will return to old family burial sites, dig up remains and rebury relatives to remedy their own ill health.

Lifestyle

Family is very important in Tongan life, with each member playing a role and elders commanding respect. A family unit often consists of extras including adopted children, cousins and other relatives living alongside the parents, children and grandparents. Everything is communal, from food to sleeping arrangements, and everyone is looked after. The patriarch is usually the head of the family and jobs are distributed according to gender.

You'll often see Tongans in conservative dress wearing distinctive pandanus mats called *ta'ovala* around their waists. In place of a *ta'ovala,* women often wear a *kiekie,* a decorative waistband of woven strips of pandanus. Men frequently wear a wraparound skirt known as a *tupenu* and women an ankle-length *vala* (skirt) and *kofu* (tunic).

Education

Tongans highly value education. The literacy rate is 99%, reflecting the large investment that Tonga – and some highly visible religious groups – have made in the people. English is taught in schools throughout the islands. At tertiary level, the University of the South Pacific (USP) has a large campus outside Nuku'alofa.

Check out the colourful school uniforms worn by Tongan kids, standard throughout the country. Children at government primary schools wear red and white, government secondary school students wear maroon, blue is the colour for Wesleyan schoolkids, orange is for Church of Tonga schools, and Mormon school students wear green.

Arts

Handicrafts

Tongan handicrafts are handmade from local materials and each piece is unique, not mass produced. A lot of time and effort has gone into making all those carved necklaces, wooden carvings, woven baskets, mother-of-pearl earrings and tapa mats that you're ogling in the markets and handicraft shops.

Women's groups often work together making handicrafts and especially tapa and woven mats, which are treasured possessions in every household and used for important occasions like weddings and funerals.

Tapa is made from beaten bark of the mulberry tree, and as women usually work together in a mat-making group to produce a large piece, it is often divided up later. Woven mats are made from pandanus leaves and used for floor coverings or as *ta'ovalas,* to be worn around the waist.

Visitors should avoid buying handicrafts made from turtleshell or whalebone while in Tonga – certainly nonsustainable materials.

TONGA ARTS

Music & Dance

Tongans love to sing, and conjure up some seriously sweet South Seas harmonies. They enthusiastically launch into song in church, at festivals, in cafes and bars, at dances, and with guitars and ukeleles around the kava bowl. They also love brass marching bands and every high school has one. Young Tongans, however, increasingly listen to imported Western music: hip hop is de rigeur and appropriately badass (but inexplicably, Elton John seems to emanate from every cafe, bar, car and construction site).

The most frequently performed traditional dance in Tonga is called the *lakalaka*. The *tau'olunga,* a female solo dance, is the most beautiful and graceful of all Tongan dances, while the most popular male dance is the intimidating *kailao* – the war dance (something akin to the famous Maori haka, but more kinetic).

At traditional feasts that visitors may attend, female dancers are often lathered in coconut oil and, as they dance, members of the audience approach and plaster paper money to their sticky bods. Far from an erotic prelude, this is good form and 'tips' given in this manner will be greatly appreciated.

Environment

The Kingdom of Tonga comprises 177 islands, scattered across 700,000 sq km of the South Pacific Ocean. Geographically Tonga is composed of four major island groups, which are, from south to north: Tongatapu and 'Eua, Ha'apai, Vava'u and the Niua Group.

Tonga sits on the eastern edge of the Indo-Australian plate, which has the Pacific tectonic plate sliding under it from the east, creating the Tonga Trench. This 2000km-long oceanic valley that stretches from Tonga to New Zealand is one of the deepest in the world – if Mt Everest was placed in the deepest part of the Tonga Trench, there would still be more than 2km of water on top of it. Tonga is moving southeast at 20mm a year (geologically speaking, that's really truckin'!), meaning that the region is a particularly volatile area for volcanic and earthquake activity.

Flora & Fauna

Tonga's national flower is the *heilala*, a small, pudgy pink-red bloom. The *heilala*, plus colourful and sweet-smelling hibiscus, frangipani and bird-of-paradise blooms,

create dazzling roadside colours. There are coconut groves and banana plantations amid fields of taro, *cassava* and yams. Papaya are everywhere. Huge rain trees (*kasia*), mango trees and banyans dot the landscape, while mangroves smother the mudflats.

Dolphins and migrating humpback whales swim in the waters around Tonga. The humpbacks come from June to October and can often be seen offshore from the major islands.

The only land mammal native to Tonga is the flying fox (fruit bat; *peka*). Interesting birdlife includes the *henga* (blue-crowned lorikeet); the *koki* (red shining parrot) of 'Eua; and the *malau* (megapode or incubator bird), originally found only on the island of Niuafo'ou, but introduced in recent years to uninhabited Late Island west of Vava'u in an effort to save it from extinction. Butterflies are a constant delight, right across the country.

Conservation Issues

A number of murky conservation issues cloud the waters of Tonga. These are mainly based around the environment being compromised for economic gain and include the following:

Swimming with dophins and whales There are arguments that swimming with whales alters their behaviour and habitat, and has a detrimental affect on both mothers and babies.

Green turtle conservation Tongans eat green turtles, often as part of religious ceremonies, and use turtle shell for jewellery, but turtle numbers are dwindling.

Sea cucumbers Asian culinary tastes mean that big dollars can be earned by exporting sea cucumbers to Asia. There is a fear that they are being overfished.

Aquarium fish It has been suggested that exporting brightly coloured aquarium fish to the USA is to the detriment of populations around Tongan reefs.

Litter Everywhere you go in Tonga you'll see piles of rubbish and non-biodegradable junk strewn along the roadsides. What a mess!

National Parks

Tonga has eight officially protected areas, including six national marine parks and reserves, Ha'atafu Beach Reserve on Tongatapu, and two national parks: the

449-hectare 'Eua National Park and Mt Talau National Park in Vava'u.

Food & Drink

Tonga is surrounded by the sea and Tongans will eat just about anything that comes out of it, from shellfish to shark to sea turtle. *'Ota'ika,* raw fish in coconut milk, is a favourite across the islands.

Pigs are prized family possessions and roam the streets, along with myriad chickens. For feasts, smaller pigs are roasted on spits over open fires while bigger ones are cooked in *umu* (underground ovens).

Starchy root crops such as taro, sweet potato and yams are easy to grow in Tonga, so take precedence over vegetables which are more high-maintenance.

Tropical fruits are everywhere, with coconuts, bananas and papaya available year-round. Summer is the season for mango, pineapple, passionfruit and guava.

Unfortunately, imported goods are having detrimental effects on Tongan diets and obesity is a problem. Canned meats from Australia and New Zealand, packets of chips (crisps), sugary drinks and high-carb instant noodles are some of the worst offenders.

There are bakeries throughout Tonga producing a wide variety of goodies. Tongans love *keki* (doughnuts).

Tongans have a growing taste for imported wine (mostly from Australia and New Zealand) and beer is available everywhere, also mostly imported (fine if you like Heineken). Look for the excellent Tongan-brewed Outrigger lager and Popao ale in bars and bottle shops.

As in other South Pacific countries, Tongan men drink kava, made from pepper roots. This is done as a social activity by groups of men in kava circles, usually in the evenings and late into the night.

SLEEPING PRICE RANGES

The following price ranges refer to a double room with bathroom: prices don't tend to vary much between seasons. Unless otherwise stated tax is included in the price.

$ less than T$100

$$ T$100 to T$200

$$$ more than T$200

Coffee grows well in Tonga's climate, but local cafes and restaurants haven't quite mastered the dark art of espresso. Weak and watery is the norm.

SURVIVAL GUIDE

ⓘ Directory A–Z

ACCOMMODATION

By lofty Western standards, accommodation in Tonga is basic, and maintenance is something to do tomorrow. The golden rule: even if prices seem expensive (and they often are), don't expect too much.

Tonga doesn't have much range in terms of international-style hotels, resorts or backpacker hostels. Instead, B&Bs and small boutique-style guesthouses have the market cornered, often with shared bathrooms and cooking facilities. Many of these are run by European expats.

Camping is generally discouraged and is illegal in Ha'apai and Vava'u unless part of a guided trip. Some guesthouses allow camping on their property.

CUSTOMS REGULATIONS

You may bring two cartons of cigarettes and 2.25L of spirits or 4.5L of wine or beer into Tonga duty free.

EMBASSIES & CONSULATES

The following foreign diplomatic representatives are all in Nuku'alofa. The nearest UK and US consulates are in Suva, Fiji.

Australian High Commission (Map p438; ☑ 23 244; www.tonga.embassy.gov.au; Salote Rd, Nuku'alofa; ⊘ 8.30am-4.30pm Mon-Fri) For visa applications head to the Australian Visa Application Centre in the Tonga Post (p443) building in Nuku'alofa.

Chinese Embassy (Map p438; ☑ 24 554; http://to.chineseembassy.org/eng; Vuna Rd, Nuku'alofa; ⊘ 9am-noon & 2.30-5pm Mon-Fri) On the waterfront.

Japanese Embassy (Map p438; ☑ 22 221; www.ton.emb-japan.go.jp; Salote Rd, National Reserve Bank Bldg, Nuku'alofa; ⊘ 8.30am-12.30pm & 1.30-4.30pm Mon-Fri)

New Zealand High Commission (Map p438; ☑ 23 122; www.nzembassy.com/tonga; Taufa'ahau Rd, Nuku'alofa; ⊘ 9am-3pm Mon-Fri)

EMERGENCY

☑ 911

FOOD

As per most South Pacific nations, food in Tonga is heavy on the protein and carbs: big serves, big people. See Food & Drink (p573) for more.

ℹ️ REAL TONGA SCHEDULING CHAOS

No doubt, Real Tonga plays a vital role in flying people between the isles of the Kingdom. But when it comes to concrete departure times, forget about it! Real Tonga's flight schedules are a movable feast, changing even within 24 hours of your next flight. They do try and email and phone your accommodation (if you've told them where you'll be!) to let you know, but otherwise beware. Reconfirm your booking as close as possible to your departure time, then arrive at the airport early – otherwise you may find yourself missing your flight, or with a long, desultory wait in a remote airport with nothing but bitterness to keep you company.

GAY & LESBIAN TRAVELLERS

Homosexuality is technically illegal but remains an accepted fact of life in Tonga: you'll see plenty of gay men around. The fine old Polynesian tradition of fakaleiti (p467) is alive and well, but the lesbian population is much more underground. Public displays of sexual affection are frowned upon, whether gay or straight.

INSURANCE

A comprehensive travel-insurance policy is a no-brainer for Tonga: check whether you're covered for 'dangerous' activities like surfing, snorkelling, diving etc.

Worldwide travel insurance is available at www.lonelyplanet.com/travel-insurance. You can buy, extend and claim online anytime – even if you're already on the road.

INTERNET ACCESS

Internet cafes crop up in Nuku'alofa and Nieafu. Charges are around T$6 per hour. Most guesthouses have wi-fi, often for free, but often with dazzlingly censorious browsing blockers in place (Tonga is a churchgoing nation – you're not supposed to be watching YouTube on a Sunday morning).

LEGAL MATTERS

Tonga is generally a very law-abiding country, and it's unlikely you'll need to have anything to do with the police. Watch out for speed cameras when driving on Tongatapu, especially between the airport and Nuku'alofa.

MONEY

Cash is king in Tonga (dig the new plastic notes to celebrate King Tupou VI's coronation): be sure to take plenty with you to Ha'apai and 'Eua, which are ATM-free. There are ATMs, however, in Tongatapu and Vava'u, and it's easy to change major currencies at local banks.

Credit cards are accepted at many tourist facilities but often attract a 4% to 5% transaction fee. Visa and MasterCard are the most common.

Tongans don't expect tips but you won't cause offence by rewarding good service with a few *pa'anga*.

OPENING HOURS

Following are some standard opening hours, but remember, time is a flexible entity in Tonga! Virtually everything is closed on Sundays.

Banks 9am to 4pm Monday to Friday

Bars 11am to 12.30am Monday to Friday, to 11.30pm Saturday

Cafes 7am to 10.30pm Monday to Saturday

Post Offices & Government Offices 8.30am to 4pm Monday to Friday

Shops 8am to 5pm Monday to Friday, to 1pm Saturday.

PUBLIC HOLIDAYS

In addition to New Year's Day, Easter, Christmas Day and Boxing Day, public holidays in Tonga include the following:

Anzac Day 25 April

Emancipation Day 4 June

King Tupou VI's Birthday 4 July

Crown Prince Tupouto'a-'Ulukalala's Birthday 17 September

Constitution Day 2 November

King George Tupou I Commemoration Day 4 December

SAFE TRAVEL

Tonga, in general, is a safe country to visit, though late nights and booze can be a bad mix: the big boys sometimes brawl in the bars.

Dogs can be aggressive: cross the street to avoid packs.

Watch out for coral cuts (p591), which tend to get infected.

TELEPHONE

The country code for Tonga is ☎ 676; there are no local area codes. Dial ☎ 913 for the international operator and ☎ 910 for directory enquiry.

There are public phones throughout Tonga (buy a phonecard to make calls), but a mobile (cell) phone is a more reliable bet. Most foreign phones set up for global roaming work here and coverage is reasonably good throughout the islands.

The two telecommunication companies are **Tonga Communications Corporation** (TCC; ☎ 27 006; www.tcc.to) and **Digicel** (☎ 876 1000;

PRACTICALITIES

➡ **Currency** The Tongan *pa'anga* (T$) comes in one, two, five, 10, 20 and 50 *pa'anga* notes, and coins in denominations of one, five, 10, 20 and 50 *seniti*.

➡ **Language** Tongan is the official language, but English is taught in schools and is widely spoken and understood.

➡ **Photography** Politeness goes a long way: always ask before taking pictures of people. Check out Lonely Planet's *Travel Photography* guide for inspiration.

➡ **Time** Tonga is 13 hours ahead of Greenwich Mean Time, making it the first country in the world to start each new day. Tonga does not observe daylight savings.

www.digiceltonga.com); a cheap local phone, including SIM, will cost you around T$60. Digicel also offers a T$20 Visitor SIM that expires after 30 days.

TOILETS

Tongan toilets are of the sit-down Western variety. Public toilets are few and far between, and are often closed for repairs.

TOURIST INFORMATION

Online, check out www.lonelyplanet.com/tonga for planning advice, recommendations and reviews.

The official Tongan tourism websites are www.thekingdomoftonga.com and www.tongaholiday.com.

'Eua Island (www.eua-island-tonga.com)
Ha'apai Islands (www.haapai.to)
Matangi Tonga (www.matangitonga.to)
Vavu'a Islands (www.vavau.to)

TRAVELLERS WITH DISABILITIES

Tonga isn't an easy place to visit for mobility- or vision-impared travellers: footpaths (sidewalks) are almost nonexistant, roadsides are potholed and dusty/muddy, and most accommodation, tours and transport aren't set up for wheelchairs.

VISAS

Most countries' citizens are granted a 31-day visitors' visa on arrival. You'll need a passport valid for at least six months and an onward ticket. One-month extensions are granted for

up to six months at T$69 per month: contact the **Immigration Division, Department of Foreign Affairs & Trade** (Map p438; ☑ 26 970; www.mic.gov.to; Salote Rd, Nuku'alofa).

Those intending to fly in and depart Tonga by yacht require a letter of authority from a Tongan diplomatic mission overseas or the Immigration Division.

VOLUNTEERING

Volunteering opportunities in Tonga are best organised through international agencies (p582). See also Lonely Planet's *Volunteer: A Traveller's Guide to Making a Difference Around the World* for useful information about volunteering.

WOMEN TRAVELLERS

Tonga is generally a safe and respectful place for women travelling solo, but exercise the usual precautions: don't walk around alone at night, avoid the bars at closing time, don't bother with hitchhiking etc.

WORK

There are penalties in place for working in Tonga whilst visiting on a tourist visa. Contact the Immigration Division, Department of Foreign Affairs & Trade for information before you arrive if you plan to conduct business or gain employment in Tonga.

🛈 Getting There & Away

AIR

Three international airlines fly into Tonga, with direct flights from New Zealand, Australia and Fiji.

Air New Zealand (Map p438; ☑ 23 192; www.airnewzealand.co.nz; Vuna Rd, Kingdom Travel Centre, Nuku'alofa; ⊙ 8.30am-5pm Mon-Fri, 9am-12.30pm Sat) Based at Kingdom Travel Centre on the Nuku'alofa waterfront. Jets into Tongatapu from Auckland.

Fiji Airways (Map p438; ☑ 24 021; www.fijiairways.com; Vuna Rd, 'Utu'one B&B, Nuku'alofa; ⊙ 8am-5pm Mon-Fri, 9am-noon Sat) Based at 'Utu'one B&B opposite the Nuku'alofa wharves. Flies Fiji to Nuku'aloka, and also operates some Real Tonga code-share flights between Nuku'alofa and Vava'u.

Virgin Australia (Map p438; ☑ 26 033; www.virginaustralia.com; Taufa'ahau Rd, Nuku'alofa; ⊙ 8.30am-5pm Mon-Fri, 9am-noon Sat) On Nuku'alofa's main street. Flies into Tongatapu from Australia via Auckland.

SEA

Trans-Pacific yachts ride the trade winds from Samoa, the Cook Islands and French Polynesia. Others come north from New Zealand. All vessels calling on Tonga must give customs 24-hour advance notice of arrival. To summon the harbour master and for emergencies in Tonga use VHF Channel 16.

Official entry ports include Nuku'alofa (Tongatapu), Neiafu (Vava'u), Pangai (Ha'apai), Falehau (Niuatoputapu) and Futu (Niuafo'ou). Contact **Ports Authority Tonga** (📞 21 168; www.ports authoritytonga.com) and see www.noonsite. com for more info.

ⓘ Getting Around

AIR

Flying is by far the easiest, fastest and most comfortable way to get around Tonga.

Real Tonga (p434) operates most of the domestic flights in Tonga. Fiji Airways (p472) also flies between Nuku'alofa and Vava'u, often as a code-share flight with Real Tonga. Flights are scheduled to work in with arriving and departing international flights (no flights on Sundays). Typical fares:

Route	Fare	Duration	Frequency
Ha'apai–Vava'u	T$204	30min	3-4 weekly
Tongatapu–'Eua	T$96	10min	1–2 daily
Tongatapu–Ha'apai	T$214	40min	2–3 daily
Tongatapu–Vava'u	T$310	1hr	2-3 daily
Vava'u–Niuafo'ou	T$420	1½hr	fortnightly
Vava'u–Niuatoputapu	T$350	70min	weekly

BOAT

The Nuku'alofa Visitor Information Centre (p443) lists ferry schedules, which must be re-checked prior to intended travel. See also www.tongaholiday.com/islands/transport.

Subsequent to the tragic sinking of the *Princess Ashika* in 2009 with the loss of 74 lives, all Tongan ferries and aircraft have come under intense scrutiny, and safety standards have risen dramatically.

Ferries to Ha'apai, Vava'u & the Niua Group

Friendly Islands Shipping Company (Map p438; 📞 22 582; www.fisa.to; Queen Salote Wharf, Nuku'alofa) operates the MV *'Otunga'ofa*, donated by the Japanese government in 2011. Once a week it plies the waters between Tongatapu, the Ha'apai Group and Vava'u (departing Tongatapu on Thursdays, getting back there on Saturdays), and occasionally heads to the Niua Group (unscheduled).

The following are adult fares; children aged 4–12 years pay half-price.

Route	Fare
Nuku'alofa–Neiafu (Vava'u)	T$99
Nuku'alofa–Pangai (Ha'apai)	T$79
Pangai (Ha'apai)–Neiafu (Vava'u)	T$71
Neiafu (Vava'u)–Niuafo'ou (Niuas)	T$121
Neiafu (Vava'u)–Niuatoputapu (Niuas)	T$121

Ferries to 'Eua

On a calm day the 2½-hour ferry trip between Tongatapu and 'Eua (T$23 one way) is a breeze. The **MV 'Onemato** (📞 24 755) leaves Nuku'alofa daily Monday to Saturday, returning from 'Eua the same day (sometimes it stays docked overnight in 'Eua; check when you buy your ticket). The **MV 'Alaimoana** (📞 21 326) sails for 'Eua on Tuesday and Thursday, returning from 'Eua the following morning.

The schedule does shift from time to time: check www.tongaholiday.com/islands/transport for the latest. Tickets are sold either at the ferry terminal or on board; get there an hour before sailing.

BUS

Tonga's privately owned buses have a handy interprative 'B' at the start of their licence plates. They run on Tongatapu, and in a more limited capacity on Vava'u and its causeway-linked islands. Fares range from T$0.70 to T$2 depending on distances travelled. Don't expect to get where you're going in a hurry...but riding a local bus is a cultural experience in itself!

CAR

The official line is that to drive in Tonga you need a visitor's driving licence (T$40) from the **Ministry of Infrastructure** (Map p438; 📞 Nuku'alofa 23 201, Vava'u 70 100; www.infrastructure. gov.to; Bypass Rd, Nuku'alofa; ⊗ 8.30am-4pm Mon-Fri), valid for three months (bring your passport, home drivers licence and international driving permit if you have one). But if it's only a one-day rental, some operators may turn a blind eye and require only your home licence.

People drive *veeery slooowly* on the left-hand side of the road. The speed limit is 50km/h in villages, 70km/h elsewhere. On the road, watch out for children, dogs, chickens and pigs, and don't park under coconut trees!

At the time of writing, petrol cost around T$2.50 per litre.

TAXI

Tonga's scrappy-looking taxis have a 'T' on their licence plates. There are plenty of taxis on Tongatapu and Vava'u, though it may not be an 'official' taxi that picks you up: if you ask someone to organise a taxi, it may be their husband, brother or nephew who comes to get you. Just pay the going rate; ask at your accommodation so you have a ballpark figure.

Vanuatu

🎵 678 / POP 281,500

Best Places to Stay

➡ Rocky Ridge Bungalows (p496)

➡ Havannah (p488)

➡ Traveller's Budget Motel (p482)

➡ Espiritu (p511)

➡ Lope Lope Adventure Lodge (p515)

Best Places to Eat

➡ Oyster Island (p515)

➡ Market Meal Booths (p512), Luganville

➡ Kesorn's Exotic Thai Kitchen (p485)

➡ L'Houstalet (p485)

Why Go?

Vanuatu is a Pacific island adventure far beyond any notions of cruise-ship ports and flashy resorts. Deserted beaches, ancient culture, remote and rugged islands and world-class diving are just a small part of the magnetism of this scattered 80-plus island archipelago.

Where else can you hike up a crater to stare down into a magma-filled active volcano then ashboard back down, snorkel in a blue hole and drink kava with the local village chief – all in the same day? The resorts and restaurants of Port Vila have little in common with traditional *kastom* (custom) village life in the outer islands, but it's contrasts like these that make Vanuatu a surprise and a challenge.

Vanuatu was slammed by Cyclone Pam in 2015, but its people, resilient and laid-back as ever, take life in smiling strides.

It takes a little time, effort and a healthy sense of adventure to truly explore Vanuatu's islands, but it's worth every bit of it.

When to Go
Port Vila

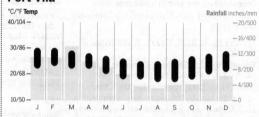

May–Jul Warm and dry; high season. Pentecost's land diving is in full swing.

Aug–Oct Avoid Australian school holidays and enjoy mostly dry sunny days.

Nov–Mar Wet (cyclone) season, so accommodation is plentiful but transport may be delayed.

EFATE

POP 66,000 / AREA 915 SQ KM

Efate is Vanuatu's main island, politically, economically, industrially and in terms of population and tourism. Even so, outside of the capital Port Vila it's pretty low-key, with some of the village life you'll find on other islands.

Efate has two of Vanuatu's best deep-water anchorages in Vila Bay and the expanding Havannah Harbour, as well as the principal airport. Drive around the island's sealed ring road (opened in 2011) to explore its bays and beaches, islands and inlets. It's also easy to access remote-feeling offshore islands such as Pele, Nguna, Moso and Lelepa.

Port Vila & Around

POP 44,000

Set around pretty Vila Bay and a series of lagoons, beaches and offshore islands, Port Vila is a surprisingly compact but energetic town. It's a little rough around the edges, with a few traffic-clogged main streets offering up a supply of souvenirs, markets, and waterfront restaurants and cafes with some lingering French influences. Beneath this veneer is an odd mix of holidaymakers, cruise-ship day trippers, expats and yachties, along with ni-Vanuata (local people) drawn from all over the archipelago.

This is the liveliest town in Vanuatu, with a mind-boggling array of tours and adventure activities, some excellent restaurants, bars, supermarkets, banks and markets. Vila is a place for comfort over culture, beach bars over basic bungalows – and that's reason enough to stay a while.

◎ Sights

★**National Museum of Vanuatu**   MUSEUM
(Map p481; ☑22129; Rue d'Artois; 1000VT, with guided tour 1500VT; ⊙9am-4.30pm Mon-Fri, to noon Sat; P) This excellent museum, in a soaring traditional building opposite the parliament, has a well-displayed collection of traditional artefacts such as *tamtam* (slit gongs or slit drums), outrigger canoes, ceremonial headdresses, shell jewellery and examples of Lapita and Wusi pottery. There's an interesting photographic display on the unearthing of Chief Roi Mata's burial site. One-hour guided tours include a traditional instrument demonstration and sand drawing.

Hideaway Island   ISLAND
(Map p478; ☑22963; http://hideaway.com.vu; opposite Mele Beach; marine park adult/child 1250/600VT; ⊙24hr; ⊕) Just 100m or so offshore from Mele Beach, Hideaway Island isn't all that hidden but it's one of Vila's favourite spots for snorkelling, diving or just enjoying lunch at the island's resort (nonguests can access the marine park until 4pm). The free ferry putts out from in front of the Beach Bar (p484) regularly, and once on the island you can snorkel in the marine sanctuary, join a dive tour and send a waterproof postcard from the world's only underwater post office.

Erakor   ISLAND
(Map p478; www.erakorislandresort.com; adult/child day pass 1000/500VT; ⊙24hr; ⊕) Erakor is one of Vila's excellent resort islands. Day trippers can swim and snorkel at the shallow white-sand beach, kayak around the island or dine in the Aqua Restaurant (the day pass is redeemable for food and drinks). The 24-hour ferry leaves from the end of the road past Nasama Resort.

★**Mele Cascades**   WATERFALL
(Map p478; adult/child 2000/1000VT; ⊙8.30am-5pm; P⊕) This popular and photogenic swimming spot is 10km from Port Vila. A series of clear aquamarine pools terrace up the hillside, culminating in an impressive 35m waterfall flowing into a natural plunge pool. A slippery path with guide ropes directs you to the top. There are toilets, change rooms and a cafe-bar with free wi-fi at the entrance. Go out by local minibus (250VT), or take a guided tour with Evergreen (Map p484; ☑23050; www.evergreenvanuatu.com; Lini Hwy; tours 3000VT).

Tanna Coffee Factory   FACTORY
(Map p478; ☑23661; Devil's Point Rd, Mele; ⊙8am-5pm Mon-Fri, to 1.30pm Sat; P) FREE Watch the roaster at work and learn the story of Tanna coffee over a strong brew (350VT) at this welcoming coffee-roasting factory and cafe.

Secret Garden   CULTURAL CENTRE
(Map p478; ☑26222; www.vanuatusecretgarden.com; adult/child 1000/500VT; ⊕) The beautiful botanic gardens here help bring some of Vanuatu's island flora and its cultural uses to life. There's a *kastom* magic show (adult/child 1500/750VT) on Friday morning and a popular 'Island Feast' (3500/1750VT) on Tuesday and Thursday evening.

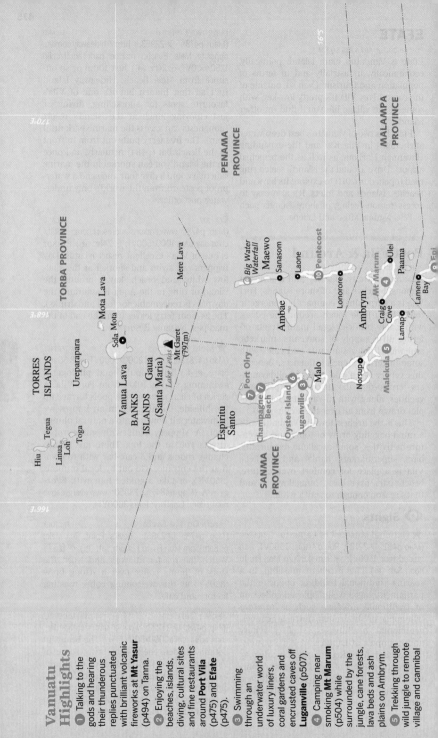

Vanuatu Highlights

1 Talking to the gods and hearing their thunderous replies punctuated with brilliant volcanic fireworks at **Mt Yasur** (p494) on Tanna.

2 Enjoying the beaches, islands, diving, cultural sites and fine restaurants around **Port Vila** (p475) and **Efate** (p475).

3 Swimming through an underwater world of luxury liners, coral gardens and encrusted caves off **Luganville** (p507).

4 Camping near smoking **Mt Marum** (p504) while surrounded by the jungle, cane forests, lava beds and ash plains on Ambrym.

5 Trekking through wild jungle to remote village and cannibal

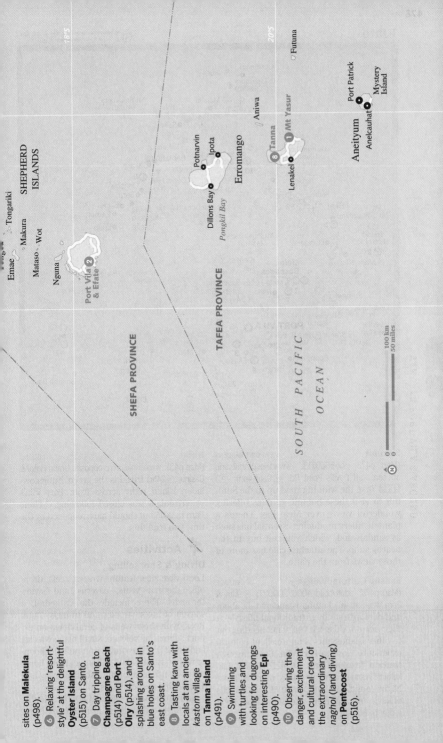

sites on **Malekula** (p498).

⑥ Relaxing 'resort-style' at the delightful **Oyster Island** (p515) on Santo.

⑦ Day tripping to **Champagne Beach** (p514) and **Port Olry** (p514), and splashing around in blue holes on Santo's east coast.

⑧ Tasting kava with locals at an ancient *kastom* village on **Tanna island** (p491).

⑨ Swimming with turtles and looking for dugongs on interesting **Epi** (p490).

⑩ Observing the danger, excitement and cultural cred of the extraordinary *naghol* (land diving) on **Pentecost** (p516).

SHEPHERD ISLANDS

Tongariki
Makura
Mataso
Wot
Emae
Nguna

Port Vila ②
& Efate

SHEFA PROVINCE

TAFEA PROVINCE

Potnarvin
Dillons Bay
Ipota
Pongkil Bay

Erromango

Aniwa

Tanna
⑧
Lenakel
① Mt Yasur

Futuna

Port Patrick
Mystery Island

Aneityum
Anelcauhat

SOUTH PACIFIC OCEAN

18°S

20°S

100 km
50 miles

Efate

Summit VIEWPOINT, GARDENS
(Map p478; ☏5660713; www.thesummitvanu
atu.com; off Devil's Point Rd; ☺9am-4pm; P)
FREE Take the winding road up to the Summit to visit these botanic gardens offering
wonderful views over Mele Bay. There's a
plant distillery producing essential oils such
as sandalwood, which you can buy in the
nearby shop. The attached cafe has more of
those views from the patio.

Ekasup Cultural Village VILLAGE
(Map p478; adult/child 4000/2000VT; ☺9am &
2pm Mon-Sat; ⚐) Futuna islanders talk about
and demonstrate their traditional lifestyle at
their *kastom* village. If you're not heading out
to other islands, this is an excellent cultural
experience close to Port Vila. Book through
Nafonu Tatoka Tours (☏24217, 7746734; tato
katours@vanuatu.com.vu). Friday night is 'Feast
Night' (adult/child 3100/1550VT), with shells
of kava, entertainment and buffet food. Book
a day in advance.

Iririki ISLAND
(Map p481; www.iririki.com; opposite Grand Hotel &
Casino; ☺24hr) Iririki is the green, bungalow-
laden island right across from Port Vila's
waterfront; it was closed following Cyclone
Pam in 2015 but should have reopened by the
time you read this..

🏃 Activities

Diving & Snorkelling
Local dive sites feature wrecks, reefs, drop-
offs, thermal vents, caverns and swim-
throughs. These include the Cathedral, a
warren of holes, stipples and tunnels; Paul's
Rock, with sheer walls of coral down an extinct submarine volcano; small plane wrecks;
and the *Star of Russia,* an iron-hulled schoon-
er with masts and hull still intact that's home
to thousands of colourful fish. Hideaway and
Tranquillity are popular island dive sites.

Introductory dives start at 8000VT, double
dives for certified divers from 11,000VT and

Efate

gear hire from 1500VT per dive. Transfers, boat trips and meals are extra. All operators offer Professional Association of Diving Instructors (PADI) courses from 32,000VT.

Big Blue Vanuatu   DIVING, SNORKELLING
(Map p484; ☑ 27518; www.bigbluevanuatu.com; single/double dive 6400/11,900VT, gear hire per dive 1500VT; ☺ 8am-4pm) PADI five-star operator with twice-daily dives in Port Vila Harbour and Mele Bay. Discover Scuba courses are 9500VT (free pool session first); Open Water course 42,500VT.

Nautilus Watersports   DIVING
(Map p481; ☑ 22398; nautilus@vanuatu.com.vu; Lini Hwy) Great resources: five-star PADI dive centre, dive boat and skills pool. Discover Scuba 8000VT; Open Water course 31,500VT.

Fishing

Vanuatu has some fabulous game-fishing opportunities and there are numerous experienced operators who will take you out for a half-day, full-day or liveaboard charter. Most big game fishing is on a tag-and-release basis.

Crusoe Fishing Adventures   FISHING
(Map p484; ☑ 7745490; www.crusoefishing.com. vu; half/full day 22,500/30,000VT) Fishing charters aboard the 34ft *Nevagivup* or *Reel Capture*, both fitted out for cruising and deep-sea fishing. Prices are for minimum four people.

Sportfish Vanuatu   FISHING
(Map p478; ☑ 7752433; www.sportfishvanuatu. com; half/full day maximum 3 people 40,000/ 70,000VT) Russ Housby holds many game-fishing records and will take you out on his 7m (23ft) customised fishing boat. He's based at the Wahoo Bar in Havannah Harbour.

Harbour Fishing Charters   FISHING
(Map p478; ☑ 7739539; www.melebeach.com. vu; 4/6/8 hours 48,000/65,000/85,000VT) Head out with Mitch and fish for marlin on the 6.7m Stabicraft *Dorado*. Trips over six hours' duration include lunch.

Lelepa Island Fishing Charters   BOAT TOUR
(☑ 22714; www.lelepaislandtours.com; half-/ full-day charter 45,000/55,000VT) Albert Solomon operates a 7m banana boat; the price includes snorkelling and island tour.

Light-tackle and reef fishing costs from around 7000VT per person.

Scenic Flights

Vanuatu Helicopters SCENIC FLIGHTS
(Map p484; ☑7744106, 25022; www.vanuatu helicopters.com; scenic flights 9000-38,000VT) Everything from a seven-minute whirl over Vila to a full circuit of Efate or a half-day flight over Ambrym's volcanoes.

Port Vila Parasailing ADVENTURE SPORTS
(Map p484; ☑5563288, 22398; www.portvila parasailing.com; single flight per person 9000VT) Parasail over the harbour. No experience necessary.

Swimming & Surfing

Surfers can get up-to-date info on www. surf-forecast.com. The best surf is down Pango way (between Breakers Beach Resort and Pango Point), along Devil's Point Rd or at Erakor. There's good swimming at Hideaway Island and Erakor.

Saltwater Players SURFING
(☑7775875; www.vanuatu-kitesurfing.com; 1hr/ half-day per person 3000/4500VT) Learn to surf, kitesurf or stand-up paddleboard with this outfit. Rates include equipment and transport, or you can just hire boards for 3000VT per day.

Water Sports

U-Power Zego Sea Adventures WATER SPORTS
(Map p484; ☑7760495; www.upowerzegovanu atu.com; Vila Outdoor Market; 30/60min tours per person from 4000/6500VT; ☺hourly 10am-4pm) Hit the bay in a high-speed Zego sports boat. Prices are for two people per boat but you can pay extra to ride solo.

Vila Flyboard WATER SPORTS
(Map p481; ☑7778007; Lini Hwy; adult/child 30min 14,000/12,500VT) Take water sports to another level with these space-age jet propulsion packs that can raise you up to 9m above the surface, or shoot you through the water like a human jet ski.

Tropic Thunder Jet BOATING
(Map p484; ☑5544107; http://tropicthunder jet.com; adult/child 6100/4700VT; ☺8am-5pm) Experience the high-speed 'Thrilla in Vila' 30-minute jet-boat ride around Vila Harbour, with 360s and other tricks. The one-hour tour (adult/child 6900/5500VT) goes further to Coco Beach Resort.

Land-Based Activities

Bellevue Ranch Equestrian Club HORSE RIDING
(Map p478; ☑7747318; www.bellevue-ranch. com; Montmartre; 2hr trail ride adult/child 5000/2500VT) Bellevue Ranch is run by experienced Tanna horseman Tom Nangam. Trail rides catering to all levels range from a two-hour rainforest ride to waterfall and sunset rides.

Club Hippique HORSE RIDING
(Map p478; ☑23347, 5566947; 1hr 4000VT; ☺9.30am & 2.30pm) Offers morning and afternoon horse rides by the lagoon and Erakor Beach.

Wet 'n' Wild Adventure Park ADVENTURE SPORTS
(Map p478; ☑5564353; www.wetnwildvanuatu. com; Devil's Point Rd; 2000-5000VT; ☺10am-4pm; ⛵) Downhill zorbing, a giant waterslide, go-karting and the 'human slingshot'. Great fun for kids.

Vanuatu Jungle Zipline ADVENTURE SPORTS
(Map p478; ☑5550423; http://vanuatujungle zipline.com; off Devil's Point Rd; adult/child 9000/4000VT; ☺10.45am & 2pm; ⛵) One of Vila's newest adventure thrills is the dramatic zip line from the Summit, about 13km from the town centre (book ahead for a pick-up). Once you're harnessed you can ride six lines through the jungle canopy.

Port Vila Golf & Country Club GOLF
(Map p478; ☑7710779; www.pvgcc.club; Rte de Mele; 18 holes 3500VT, club & buggy hire 2000VT, caddie 1000VT) A challenging course with palm-tree and ocean-front hazards, and an excellent 19th hole overlooking Mele Bay.

⏚ Tours

Native Round Island Tour BUS TOUR
(☑5450253; nativetours@hotmail.com; adult/child 7500/3500VT; ☺8.30am-5pm) This full-day tour includes swimming stops, nature walks, hot springs, Taka *kastom* village and lunch.

Vanuatu Ecotours ECOTOUR
(☑5403506; www.vanuatu-ecotour.com.vu; half-day tours 5900VT) Pascal Guillet leads you through lush gardens, down cascades, into rock pools and along riverbanks with three half-day tours: river kayaking, cycling or bushwalking. You can also hire bikes (per day 2500VT, free delivery). Book ahead.

Greater Port Vila

Greater Port Vila

Coongoola Day Cruise CRUISE

(Map p484; ☑25020; www.southpacdivecruise.
com.vu; adult/child 10,800/5400VT; ⚓) Sail to
Tranquillity Island on *Lady of the Sea,* a
romantic sailing ketch. Picnic on the beach,
visit the turtle sanctuary and snorkel or dive
in crystal-clear waters.

Buggy Fun Adventures TOUR

(Map p481; ☑22775, 7744092; www.buggyfun
rental.com.vu; safari rides 7000-8500VT) Guided
half-day all-terrain buggy adventures include the jungle safari and beach tours.

Vanuatu Adventures in Paradise TOUR

(Map p484; ☑25200; www.adventuresinparadise.
vu; Anchor Inn, Lini Hwy) Local tours as well
as Tanna overnight and full-day Pentecost
land-diving packages.

Reef Explorer BOAT TOUR, SNORKELLING

(Map p484; ☑23303; http://thereefexplorerva
nuatu.com; Lini Hwy; adult/child 3500/2500VT;

⊙10.30am & 2pm; ⚓) The semisubmersible
Reef Explorer is a good way to see marine
life without getting wet, but you can also
snorkel. Departs from Cafe du Village and
moors off Iririki island.

🛏 Sleeping

Port Vila has by far the greatest range of accommodation in Vanuatu, from backpacker boltholes to five-star resorts.

⭐ Traveller's Budget Motel   HOTEL $
(Map p481; ☑ 23940, 7756440; www.thetravel lersmotel.com; Ave du Stade; dm/d 3300/9500VT, d with air-con 9800VT; ❋ 🔊 🏊) Owners Jack and Janelle have created a hostel/ guesthouse you'll fall for, with spotless motel-style rooms orbiting a small pool and convivial bar area where you write down your drinks and food and pay later. It's a great place to meet other travellers and chat about onward plans. The dorm beds and vibe drag it back to the budget category.

Sportsmen's Hotel   HOTEL $
(Map p481; ☑ 25550; www.thesportsmenshotel vanuatu.com; Rue d'Artois; d per person with/without bathroom 3000/2000VT; ❋) Rooms at this budget hotel-bar-restaurant cater to visiting islanders as well as frugal travellers. The downstairs rooms share bathroom facilities, but the larger upstairs rooms with en suite are a steal. Great location (opposite the parliament building), well-kept and Emily's Cafe & Takeaway is on site. The owner is larger-than-life Aussie Bob.

Room with a View   B&B $
(Map p481; ☑ 7763860, 7793407; www.room withaview-vanuatu.com; Rue Renee Pujol; d/tw incl breakfast 5500/6700VT; 🔊) This lovely colonial building on a hilltop overlooking the harbour just north of town has three charming rooms and an expansive balcony. There's also a self-catering kitchen and guest piano.

⭐ Hideaway Island Resort   RESORT $$
(Map p478; ☑ 22963; www.hideaway.com.vu; dm 3750VT, d 8500-21,500VT, villas from 25,000VT; ❋ 🔊 🏊) Hideaway is a favourite with day trippers but also a great place to stay. Spacious, well-designed rooms and bungalows are all on the waterfront, while the luxurious one-bedroom villas come with private pool. The cheapest rooms have shared bathroom, and the dorm-style quad-share rooms are a good deal for backpackers.

Moorings Hotel   RESORT $$
(Map p481; ☑ 26800; www.mooringsvanuatu. com; Lini Hwy; d 15,000-17,000VT, f 18,000VT; ❋ 🔊 🏊) Moorings enjoys an excellent waterfront location with cute, chalet-style bungalows facing the harbour or orbiting a large pool. The restaurant is good and Wednesday is movie night.

Coconut Palms Resort   HOTEL $$
(Map p481; ☑ 23696; www.coconutpalms.vu; Rue Cornwall; d/apt 13,500/15,000VT, s/d without bathroom 6300/9500VT, all incl breakfast; ❋ 🔊 🏊) Coconut Palms has a wide range of rooms, from small but tidy singles and budget doubles with shared facilities to spacious self-contained family apartments. Facilities are good too, with engaging communal areas, restaurant, the Wild Pig bar, swimming pool, kitchen and barbecue area. Location is central but no water views.

Seachange Lodge   APARTMENT $$
(Map p481; ☑ 26551; www.seachangelodge.com; Captain Cook Ave, Seaside; studios/cottages/lodges 8000/15,000/23,000VT; ❋ 🔊 🏊) Orchids line the path as you meander down to the lovely cottages and studio apartments arranged around the garden or facing Erakor Lagoon.

VILA'S MARKETS

Vila Outdoor Market (Map p484; Lini Hwy; ⊙ open 24hr 6am Mon–noon Sat; 🚻) Vila's colourful waterfront covered market (also known as the Mama's Market) is open round the clock from Monday morning to noon on Saturday with women from all over the country wearing beautiful island dresses selling their fruit and vegetables. There's also a whiffy fish market here.

Hebrida Market Place (Map p484; Lini Hwy; ⊙ 8am-1pm & 2-5pm Mon-Fri, 7.30am-12.30pm Sat) Hebrida Market Place buzzes with the sound of sewing machines, as local women make island dresses to order. There's a range of hand-painted clothes, handmade souvenirs, woven bags, mats and trinkets for sale.

Vanuatu Handicraft Market (Map p481; ☑ 22277; www.vanuatuhandicraftmarket.com; Wharf Rd; ⊙ 8am-5pm Mon-Sat, plus Sun cruise-ship days; 🔊) With more than 140 stalls packed with traditional handicrafts, T-shirts, surf wear, jewellery and duty free, this giant shed is a one-stop souvenir shopping experience. Money exchange and ATM on-site, as well as cafes.

Cottages, sleeping up to five, are spacious and self-contained with kitchenette and TV.

Ripples on the Bay BUNGALOW $$
(Map p478; ☑7758080; www.ripplesresortva nuatu.com; Lot 19, Narpow Point; d incl breakfast 12,500VT; P🖨🛜🏊) In a secluded oceanfront location about 14km from Vila, Ripples is a boutique miniresort consisting of four private bungalows with sea views from their hammock-strewn verandahs. Apart from the serenity (strictly no kids) and opportunities for swimming and snorkelling, there's an excellent little restaurant serving local seafood and Asian dishes.

Vila Chaumières RESORT $$
(Map p478; ☑22866; www.vilachaumieres.com; Rte de la Teouma; r 10,500-14,000VT; 🖨🛜🏊) This romantic child-free resort has three private octagonal bungalows enshrouded in lush gardens and two upper-floor hotel-style rooms with spacious balcony overlooking Emten Lagoon. Absorb the ambience from the highly regarded lagoonside restaurant and take a kayak out for a paddle.

★Eratap Beach Resort RESORT $$$
(Map p478; ☑5545007; www.eratap.com; Eratap; d incl breakfast from 47,000VT, 2-/3-bedroom villas 50,000/60,000VT; P🖨🛜🏊) This is one of Vila's top resorts, set on a secluded peninsula 12km from town and boasting honeymoon rooms with private plunge pools and baths with views. The 16 waterfront villas have flat-screen TVs, fridge and open-air showers. Take a boat or kayak out on the lagoon or relax in the excellent restaurant.

Erakor Island Resort RESORT $$$
(Map p478; ☑26983; www.erakorislandresort. com; Erakor; d 17,500-28,500VT; spa bungalows 28,500-32,800VT, 4-bedroom houses 66,000VT; @🛜) Reached by a 24-hour ferry, Erakor is a stunning 6.5-hectare island with an air of exclusivity (although day visitors are welcome). There's a fine range of accommodation here, from motel-style rooms to beachfront spa villas and the deluxe four-bedroom Aqua Blue Beach House, plus catamarans, water sports, a day spa and the sublime Aqua restaurant.

Paradise Cove Resort & Restaurant RESORT $$$
(Map p478; ☑22701; www.paradisecoveresort. net; 1-/2-bedroom bungalows incl breakfast 26,500/32,800VT; 🛜🏊) This boutique resort has 10 self-contained, spacious and luxurious bungalows in a lovely waterfront garden out

Pango way. The popular poolside restaurant beneath a traditional *nakamal* (men's clubhouse) oozes romance and offers an international menu (mains 2500VT to 5000VT).

Poppy's on the Lagoon APARTMENT $$$
(Map p481; ☑23425; www.poppys.com.vu; d 18,000-29,500VT, 2-/3-bedroom apt 30,000/ 47,500VT; P🖨🛜) The absolute waterfront location on Erakor Lagoon is the big attraction at Poppy's, but there's also a lot to like about the various apartments and bungalows. All rooms have a kitchen and balcony; some have disabled access. The family cottages boast soaring ceilings and loads of space. Sea kayaks and kids' activities are free, and there's a day spa on-site.

Breaka's Beach Resort RESORT $$$
(Map p478; ☑23670; www.breakas.com; garden/ beachfront bungalows 22,400/29,600VT; P🛜🏊) On a sublime piece of Pango surf beach, Breaka's is an intimate child-free resort. Traditional individual bungalows in the garden or facing the beach have open-sky bathrooms and king-sized beds. There's a good poolside restaurant and bar and a regular program of cultural and feast nights.

Aquana Beach Resort RESORT $$$
(Map p478; www.aquana.com.au; Eratap; d incl breakfast 24,500-28,500VT, tr/q 27,500/31,000VT; P🖨🛜🏊) Aquana is a gorgeous little family-friendly resort with 16 one- and two-bedroom beachfront bungalows, all equipped with aircon, flat-screen TV and bar fridge. With easy access to ocean, reefs and islands but in a secluded location, Aquana is a cool little retreat. There's a great little restaurant, kids club and regular cultural entertainment.

🍴 Eating

★Jill's Cafe AMERICAN $
(Map p484; ☑25125; mains 350-900VT; ⏱7am-5pm Mon-Fri, to 1.30pm Sat; 🛜🚼) This bustling American-style diner is always buzzing with expats, tourists and locals, seeking out waffles, burgers, burritos and chilli cheese fries. Try Jill's homemade earthquake chilli and famous Port Vila thickshakes.

★Nambawan Cafe CAFE, PIZZA $
(Map p484; ☑7714826, 25246; mains 500-1600VT; ⏱6.30am-8pm; 🛜🚼) A great place to hang out by the harbour, this popular cafe has free wi-fi, snacks, tapas, pizzas, all-day breakfast and a full bar. The cafe is usually open from sunrise to sunset but Wednesday,

Central Port Vila

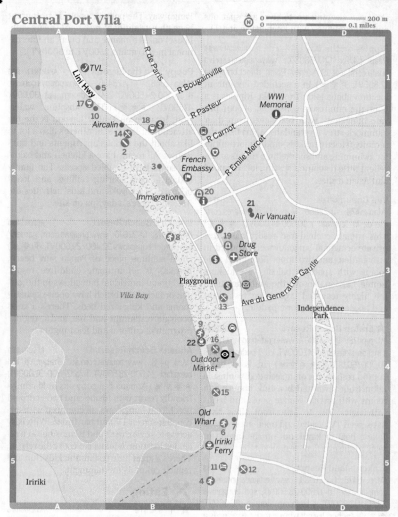

Saturday and Sunday are outdoor movie nights (from 6.45pm).

Vila Outdoor Market   HAWKER $

(Map p484; Lini Hwy; meals 400VT; ⊘ food stalls 11am-3pm Mon-Fri, to noon Sat) Join the locals on the communal benches to the side of the main market, where chicken, beef and fish meals piled with rice and vegetables are cooked to order.

Beach Bar   PIZZA $

(Map p478; ☑ 5601132; www.vanuatubeachbar. com; pizzas 1000-1450VT; mains 850-1850VT; ⊘ 8.30am-9pm; ☎⋒) Facing across to Hide-away Island, Beach Bar is a fun place with Tuesday movie nights (the screen is set up on the beach), a free (very popular) Friday night fire show, a Sunday circus and excellent wood-fired pizzas.

Emily's Cafe & Takeaway   CAFE $

(Map p481; Rue d'Artois; mains 600-1500VT; ⊘ 24hr; ☎) Emily's offers some of the best-value meals around. The 1000VT lunch specials – fish and chips, rump steak or chicken – are a steal and there are some good noodle dishes too.

Central Port Vila

★**Kesorn's Exotic Thai Kitchen**   THAI **$$**
(Map p481; ☑7731751, 29994; www.exotic-thai.
com; mains 1500-2200VT; ⊙10.30am-2.30pm &
5.30-10pm, dinner only Sun) Spicy aromas waft
from the kitchen onto the breezy elevated
deck at this authentic Thai place. Alongside
the fragrant curries (red curry duck, Penang
prawn curry) are pan-Asian dishes prepared
with fresh local ingredients. Book ahead for
the Thursday night buffet (2200VT).

★**L'Houstalet**   FRENCH **$$**
(Map p481; ☑22303; mains 890-2700VT; ⊙5-
10pm Mon-Sun, plus noon-2pm Wed) Still going
strong after more than 40 years, L'Houstalet is famous for its offbeat French creations
including stuffed flying fox, wild pigeon and
garlic snails. Simpler fare such as pizza and
pasta (from 900VT) is also available. It's well
worth a splurge for the rustic gastronomic
atmosphere.

**Brewery Bar
& Restaurant**   INTERNATIONAL, PIZZA **$$**
(Map p484; ☑28328; Lini Hwy; mains 800-
2000VT; ⊙10am-11pm; ☎) The street-front
deck at the Brewery usually attracts a crowd.
Try a pint of the local Nambawan draught
and peek into the open kitchen to see what's
cooking: there's a predictable menu but the
wood-fired pizzas are reliable (1000VT on
Monday and Tuesday).

Spice   INDIAN **$$**
(Map p481; ☑7766373; Lini Hwy; mains 1000-
2500VT; ⊙7.30am-3pm & 6-9pm Mon-Thu,
7.30am-3pm Fri, 6-10pm Sat, 6-9pm Sun) Spice
serves authentic and reasonably priced
Indian food in cosy surrounds. It's mostly
north Indian fare with chicken tikka masa-
la, rogan josh and aromatic Punjabi chicken
curry. There's a kids' menu (hold the spice!)
and a full bar with cocktails such as Bengali
booze.

Au Faré   FRENCH **$$**
(Map p481; ☑25580; Lini Hwy; mains 1300-
3200VT; ⊙9am-10pm Mon-Sat; ☎) A little bit
French, a little bit Pacific, Au Faré is a breezy
waterfront restaurant under an open-sided
thatched 'nakamal' with central bar. Sample
fresh local fish in ginger sauce, beef carpaccio
or Gallic steak dishes from the blackboard
menu. Saturday night sees fire dancing.

Chill   SEAFOOD **$$**
(Map p484; ☑22578; mains 1500-4000VT;
⊙11am-9pm; ❄☎❖) Chill enjoys a good
waterfront location, next to the market and
looking through large windows out to Iririki. It's a family friendly place specialising in
seafood: try the impressive seafood platter
or lobster pizza. The 1200VT lunch special is
a good deal until 5pm.

🍷 Drinking

Port Vila has a few atmospheric waterfront
bars and an abundance of kava bars with
bamboo walls and earthen floors; unlike on
some outer islands women are usually welcomed. The sunset kava cup (small/large
50/100VT), served in a coconut shell or plastic
bowl, is a ritual.

VANUATU PORT VILA & AROUND

Bamboo Nakamal
KAVA BAR

(Map p481; Rue Picarde; cup from 50VT; ⊙5-10pm) With its colourful murals, this is one of the numerous welcoming kava bars in Port Vila's Nambatu area, on the hill near the hospital.

War Horse Saloon
BAR

(Map p481; ✆26670; Wharf Rd; ⊙11am-late; 🗢) There's more than a hint of a Wild West theme at this popular expat bar and brewery. With a range of beers on tap (including Vanuatu Bitter), wagon wheels for chandeliers, bison heads on the wall and live music, it's a fun night out. Also a good place for burgers, ribs and Tex-Mex (mains 950VT to 6000VT).

Banyan Beach Bar
BAR

(Map p481; ✆7114689; Lini Hwy; ⊙noon-11pm) With fire pits and sunloungers on the beach, cocktails and shooters at 10 paces and a true beach bar close to the town centre, the Banyan makes for a fun night out.

Waterfront Bar & Grill
BAR

(Map p481; ⊙11am-late) A popular spot for yachties and expats (Yachting World is next door), the Waterfront is a fun place to kick back with a sunset cocktail and a seafood platter. Live music usually plays under the flag-strewn thatch roof.

Anchor Inn
BAR

(Map p484; ⊙10am-9pm Mon-Sat, 4-8pm Sun; 🗢) The timber deck of the Anchor Inn is a great place for a sundowner, and there's a welcoming local pub atmosphere, with draught beer, televised sports, live music on Friday nights, free wi-fi and good food.

Voodoo Bar
CLUB

(Map p484; Main St; ⊙9pm-late Wed-Sat) Port Vila's favourite nightclub and sports bar, Voodoo fills up with locals and expats after 11pm. Next door is Elektro, another late-night music venue.

☆ Entertainment

Most large resorts feature a Melanesian show at least once a week that includes buffet meal, kava tasting, string bands and *kastom* dancers. Prices range from 2400VT to 4500VT. The tourist office has a list.

There are casinos at the **Grand Hotel** (Map p484; ✆27344; www.grandvanuatu.com; Lini Hwy) and **Holiday Inn** (Map p481; ✆22040; www.ichotelsgroup.com/holidayinnresorts; Tassiriki Park; ❄🗢🏊).

Tana Cine
CINEMA

(Map p481; ✆7770444; Lini Hwy; tickets from 600VT, gold class from 1850VT; ⊙10am-10.30pm; 🖭) Vila's brand-new cinema complex shows mainstream movies in modern comfort; Gold Class features reclining seats and food and drink service.

Shopping

Apart from the markets, you'll find a number of shops selling duty-free products on Lini Hwy. They're reasonable for alcohol, perfume, fine china and jewellery. On cruise-ship days, prices at souvenir shops are known to unofficially increase.

Au Bon Marché
FOOD & DRINK

(Map p481; ⊙7.30am-10pm) There are several Au Bon Marché supermarkets around Vila, but the biggest and best is at the southern end of town. Good range of camping gear, books, groceries and alcohol.

Kava Emporium
DRINK

(Map p484; ✆26964; www.thekavaemporium.com; ⊙9am-5pm Mon-Fri, to noon Sat) Billed as the 'happiest shop in the world', this cool place deals in kava products from coconut drinks to kava chocolate and powdered kava. Even if you don't like the muddy stuff, this is worth a visit.

❶ Information

MEDICAL SERVICES

Drug Store (Map p484; ✆22789; ⊙7.30am-6pm Mon-Fri, to noon Sat, 8.30am-noon Sun) A well-stocked central pharmacy.

Port Vila Central Hospital (Map p481; ✆22100; ⊙emergency 24hr, outpatients 9am-6pm Mon-Fri) Has a dentist, private practitioners and dispensary; open for outpatients during business hours.

ProMedical (Map p481; ✆26996, 25566; www.promedical.com.vu; ⊙24hr) A 24-hour paramedic service with Vanuatu's only hyperbaric chamber.

MONEY

Upmarket resorts, restaurants and car hire companies accept credit cards (with a 4% to 5% surcharge), but cash (in vatu) is still king, especially outside Port Vila. Foreign exchange is provided by the following:

ANZ (Map p484; ✆22536; Lini Hwy; ⊙8am-3pm Mon-Fri) and **Westpac** (Map p484; ✆22084; Lini Hwy; ⊙9am-3.30pm Mon-Fri). Both have ATMs.

Goodies Money Exchange (Map p484; ✆23445; cnr Lini Hwy & Rue Pasteur; ⊙8am-

5.30pm Mon-Fri, 8am-1pm Sat, 8.30am-noon Sun) Generally gives the best rates. Has three offices on Lini Hwy in the centre of town.

POST

Post Office (Map p484; ☑ 22000; Lini Hwy; ⊙7.30am-5pm Mon-Fri, 8am-noon Sat) Poste restante; card-operated phones outside.

TOURIST INFORMATION

Vanuatu Tourism Office (VTO; Map p484; ☑ 22813; www.vanuatu.travel; Lini Hwy; ⊙ 8am-5pm Mon-Fri, to noon Sat, to 2pm weekends on cruise-ship days) Helpful staff; free maps and information about accommodation, activities, tours and the outer islands.

❶ Getting There & Away

AIR

Air Vanuatu (Map p484; ☑ 23848; www.air vanuatu.com; Rue de Paris; ⊙7.30am-4.30pm Mon-Fri, 8-11am Sat) Staff at this busy office book international and domestic flights.

BOAT

Big Sista (Map p484; ☑ 5683622) The Big Sista ferry departs from the harbour in front of the main market on its weekly run between Port Vila and Santo. The booking office is also here.

Vanuatu Ferry (Map p481; ☑ 26999; www.facebook.com/Vanuatu-Ferry-Limited-690422517676564/; Lini Hwy) Vanuatu Ferry operates between Port Vila and Santo weekly. Check the Facebook page for updated schedules.

❶ Getting Around

TO/FROM THE AIRPORT

Taxis charge around 1500VT from the airport. Several tour companies offer reliable pick-ups and drop-offs (1000VT per person), which are good for early or late flights. Try **Atmosphere** (☑ 7751520, 27870; www.atmosphere-vanuatu.com). If you don't have much luggage and arrive during the day, you can catch any minibus (300VT) from outside the neighbouring domestic terminal.

CAR & MOTORCYCLE

Major car-hire companies such as Budget, Hertz and Avis have offices in Port Vila.

Go2Rent (Map p481; ☑ 22775, 7744092; www.go2rent.com.vu; Nambatu; ⊙7.30am-5.30pm Mon-Sat, to 10am Sun) This is the place to go if you're after more than a car. Rents scooters (5000VT per day), motorbikes (7500VT), quad bikes (6500VT) and beach buggies (11,500VT), including mandatory insurance. All come with unlimited kilometres and discounts for two or more days. Credit cards accepted.

World Car Rentals (Map p481; ☑ 26515; www.vanuaturentalcars.com; Rue d'Artois, Nambatu; ⊙7.30am-5pm) Good-value car rental with compact cars and 4WDs from 6500VT per day and larger 4WDs from 9500VT.

MINIBUS & TAXI

The main roads are usually thick with minibuses between 6am and 7.30pm – this is the only place in Vanuatu where you can get stuck in traffic. In most cases, it's first in, first dropped off. Fares are a uniform 150VT around town. To travel further afield to, say, Hideaway Island or the Mele Cascades, costs 250VT.

Taxis, by contrast, cost around 500VT for a short trip across town and are only really worth using at night. Vila's main taxi stand is beside the outdoor market.

Efate Ring Road

Efate's sealed ring road (about 122km in total) makes a great day trip, with lots of interesting stopovers and jumping off points for offshore islands. Head anticlockwise east out of Port Vila. Past Teouma River (Efate's largest), take the dirt road detour down to the coastal road where the Pacific Ocean is fringed with screw-trunked pandanus palms and several waterfront restaurants.

⊙ Sights & Activities

Blue Lagoon   SWIMMING
(Map p478; Eton; admission 500VT; ⊙7.30am-5pm) Near Eton village, the Blue Lagoon is a popular swimming hole with ropes, swings and canoes. It's more green than blue but there's a pleasant garden with picnic tables, toilets and change rooms.

Eton Beach   BEACH
(Map p478; admission 500VT) About 2km on from the Blue Lagoon, Eton Beach is a dazzling white-sand, family-friendly beach with rock pools, safe swimming and a small river inlet.

Taka Kastom Village   VILLAGE
(Map p478) This cultural village near Takara welcomes visitors (it's on most round-island tours). A traditional buffet meal is 700VT per person and you can see music, dancing and weaving.

Matanawora WWII Relics   HISTORIC SITE, MUSEUM
(Map p478; ☑ 5427057; boat tour 2000VT) Two US WWII fighter planes lie in the shallows near Baofatu. They ran out of fuel coming in to land at Quoin Hill. If he's around, Erik will take you out in a boat to see them. The small museum of relics was closed at the time of writing.

Valeva Cave
CAVE

(Map p478; Siviri; 500VT) Turn off the Ring Rd to fragrant Siviri village (signposted), from where you can explore Valeva Cave in a kayak (1000VT). It has chambers, tunnels and an underground lake.

Havannah Harbour

Around 30km north of Port Vila via Klem's Hill, a soaring section of the Ring Rd, Havannah Harbour is a beautiful corner of Efate, with a handful of places to stay and eat and boats heading out to offshore islands.

🛏 Sleeping & Eating

Havannah Beach & Boat Club CAMPGROUND $
(Map p478; ☎5553578; www.havannahbeach andboatclub.com; Havannah Harbour; day use 1000VT, powered campsites per person 1000VT; 🅿) Campers can pitch a tent in this grassy picnic area and marina with free barbecues. Tent hire available.

Havannah Eco Lodge BUNGALOW $$
(Map p478; ☎5419949; www.havannahecolodge. com; d 9000-10,000VT; 🅿) There are four original bungalows here with kitchen facilities, bathroom and verandah, and two newer bungalows facing Havannah Harbour. All are on the waterfront and the excellent Gideon's Restaurant & Bar is on-site.

★Havannah RESORT $$$
(Map p478; ☎5518060; www.thehavannah.com; Efate Ring Rd; garden/pool villas 43,700/53,000VT, waterfront villas 64,000-95,000VT; 🅿✳🅰☀) The Havannah is a luxurious child-free resort with 20 villas. Choose from the cosy garden villas or go all out on the deluxe waterfront ones with elevated king-sized bed and private infinity plunge pool overlooking Havannah Bay. All have polished floors, ice-cold air-con and spacious bathrooms.

Resort facilities include a tennis court, free kayaks and stand-up paddleboards, a day spa, the top-class Point restaurant (dress code applies; guests can dine on the beach), and a free sunset catamaran cruise.

★Wahoo Bar INTERNATIONAL $$
(Map p478; Efate Ring Rd; mains 1500-3000VT; ☻10am-4pm Mon-Fri, to 8pm Sat & Sun) This laid-back bar and restaurant with a deck overlooking Havannah Harbour is a fine spot to stop for fresh fish or a cold beer. The fisherman's basket is a sight to behold and the steaks and burgers are good. Free snor-

kelling gear if you feel like a swim straight off the deck.

Francesca's ITALIAN $$$
(Map p478; ☎24733; www.francescas.com.vu; Havannah Harbour; mains 2200-3400VT; ☻11am-8pm Tue-Sun) Romantic waterfront dining at Havannah Harbour is the draw here and the food is upmarket Italian with a range of pizza, pasta and risotto dishes backed by local steak, seafood and fine wine.

West Coast Offshore Islands

Three very different islands opposite Havannah Harbour offer an interesting range of activities. Tranquillity Island (Moso) has a turtle sanctuary, dive base and rustic resort; Lelepa has spectacular Feles Cave, cave drawings and fishing adventures; and Hat Island (Eretoka) is the burial ground of Chief Roi Mata, a sacred place.

⊙ Sights & Activities

Chief Roi Mata Burial Site ARCHAEOLOGICAL SITE
(Map p478; 2hr/half-/full-day tour 2000/7500/9800VT) Chief Roi Mata's domain and burial site became Vanuatu's first World Heritage site in 2008. Roi Mata was a powerful 17th-century chief who, as legend has it, created peace among the islands of Efate. He died on Lelepa island and was buried, along with family and entourage (thought to be still alive at the time) at a mass funeral site on Hat Island. Local guides conduct tours; ask at tour operators in Port Vila.

Tranquillity Island Dive DIVING
(Map p478; ☎25020, 27211; www.tranquillitydive. com) Dive some 20 sites around Tranquillity Island (Moso); expect to see turtles and the occasional dugong. A two-dive day package, including transfers and lunch, is 11,500VT.

Lelepa Island Day Tours TOUR
(☎7763516, 7742714; www.lelepaislandtours.com; adult 9800VT; ☻8am Sun-Fri) An all-inclusive family-friendly adventure with fishing, snorkelling, BBQ lunch and village visit.

🛏 Sleeping

Tranquillity Island Resort RESORT $$
(Map p478; ☎27211, 25020; www.tranquil litydive.com; dm 3900VT, s bungalows/lodges 8500/11,900VT, d bungalow/lodge 11,250/12,750VT; 🛜) There are just eight traditional bungalows

here, fronting a private beach on rambling Tranquillity Island, all with comfy beds and thatched roofs; two (lodges) have en suites, while the others have private bathrooms outside. There's also a 10-bed dorm and a campsite (1600VT for two people). Accommodation packages usually include transfers and meals.

Nguna & Pele

NGUNA POP 1200; PELE POP 300

Only 45 minutes' drive from Port Vila at Emua village is the wharf leading to these two beautiful islands. Both have protected marine reserves (www.marineprotected area.com.vu), excellent snorkelling and a laid-back castaway vibe. Both islands were hard hit by Cyclone Pam but are steadfastly rebuilding. There's no mains electricity and not much running water.

◉ Sights & Activities

Nguna has a village feel, some nice stretches of beach, snorkel trails through exotic coral gardens and a couple of extinct volcanoes. Pele feels more remote with scattered villages, sublime beaches, a marine protected area and a **Giant Clam Garden**. The two islands are so close at one point that it's possible to swim between them.

Both islands are car-free and easily walkable. On Nguna, guides (1500VT) will take you up the island's extinct **volcano** (Mt Marou); the climb takes about three hours return and rewards with superb panoramas over the Shepherd Islands and much of Efate.

On Pele, head out in an outrigger canoe to see the villagers turtle tagging. Sponsor your own turtle, name it and see it back into the ocean.

👉 Tours

Evergreen TOUR
(☑ 25418, 23050; www.evergreenvanuatu.com; adult/child 9360/4680VT; ⊙ 8.30am) Evergreen offers a day tour to Pele island, which includes transfers from Port Vila, barbecue lunch, a village visit and time for snorkelling and swimming.

🛏 Sleeping & Eating

★ **Uduna Cove**
Beach Bungalows BUNGALOW $
(Map p478; ☑ 5497449; Taloa, Nguna; s/d without bathroom incl meals 3000/5000VT) Emma runs these five bright blue-and-yellow bunga-

lows in a landscaped garden facing a decent grey-sand beach. Clean bathrooms (bucket water), and there's a kitchen guests can use (otherwise meals are 500VT). Snorkel in the marine reserve right off the beach.

Paunvina Guesthouse GUESTHOUSE $
(Map p478; ☑ 7766263, 5348523; Unakapa, Nguna; per person incl meals 3000VT) This friendly guesthouse is in Unakapa village, facing across to Pele. There are three cramped rooms at the side but much better is the large double in the main house with verandah, well-stocked library and tile floor.

Napanga Bungalows BUNGALOW $
(Map p478; ☑ 5630315, 7787853; Pele; per person incl meals 3500VT) Kenneth has a very colourful bungalow set on a cute little bay on Pele's east side. Snorkel in crystal-clear waters off the rocky beach and look out for turtles and dugongs.

Sunset Frangipani Bungalow BUNGALOW $
(Map p478; ☑ 5348534; Pele; per person incl meals 3500VT) This single two-room bungalow (sleeps five) has a brilliant white-sand beachfront location on Pele's western tip across from Nguna.

Senna Papa Beach Bungalow BUNGALOW $
(Map p478; ☑ 5424728; Pele; per person incl meals 3500VT) Frank runs this colourful bungalow with floor matting, solar lighting and a shady verandah. It's in a garden setting just above the beach.

SPOTTING DUGONGS

Dugongs (also known as sea cows) inhabit warm tropical and subtropical coastal waters. But populations are declining worldwide due to hunting, drowning in fishing nets, pollution and loss of food resources, to the point of being considered vulnerable to extinction.

Dugongs can occasionally be seen around Lamen Bay and Lamen Island, as well as Malekula and the Maskelynes, and off Santo. Bondas, Lamen Bay's resident dugong, has been going to sea for months at a time so sightings are unpredictable, but if he's around you may find yourself snorkelling near him, watching his fat little snout swishing around on the ocean floor as he separates out his food.

Epi

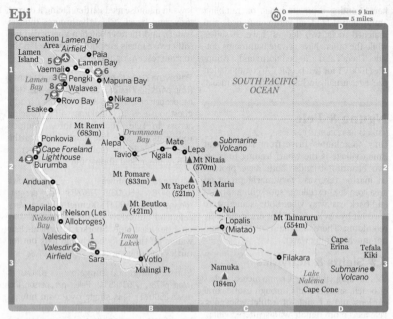

Epi

Sleeping
1 Epi Island Guesthouse A3
2 Nikaura Sunrise Bungalows B1
3 Paradise Sunset Bungalows................ A1

Transport
4 Cape Foreland Anchorage....................A2
5 Lamen Bay Anchorage..........................A1
6 Mapuna Anchorage A1
7 Rovo Bay Anchorage.............................A1
8 Walavea Anchorage...............................A1

Serety Sunset BUNGALOW $
(Map p478; ☑ 5630979, 7717113; Pele; per person incl meals 3500VT) On its own crescent of beach in front of the marine protected reserve, this place has a private and enviable location (it's a short walk to Piliura village). Solar lighting and flush toilet. Owner Charles is planning more bungalows.

Wora-Namoa Bungalow BUNGALOW $
(Map p478; ☑ 7790881; Laonama, Pele; per person incl meals 3500VT) This grand two-room beach bungalow is very much part of the community in Laonama village on Pele's eastern point. It was built by Australian secondary-schoolers as a school project and is made from local timbers and decorated with hand-dyed materials.

❶ Getting There & Around

Transport trucks to Emua Wharf depart from the bus stop near Port Vila's police station around 11am from Monday to Saturday (500VT); ask locals to point out the bus stop or ring ahead (☑ 7757410). The truck connects with an often-crowded boat to Nguna (500VT); the return trip departs at 5am.

If you're not arriving on the public truck, ask your accommodation host on Pele or Nguna about organising a private boat transfer, or just ask around Emua village; it's usually 2000VT to Pele, 3000VT to Nguna (one way) and 1000VT between the two islands.

EPI

POP 5200 / AREA 444 SQ KM

A 40-minute flight from Port Vila, Epi is an agreeably rugged and remote-feeling island where days can be spent snorkelling in search of dugongs or sampling ni-Van village life. Lamen Bay in the north is the main destination, from where you can head across by boat to Lamen Island (about 1km west) to spot turtles and lots of marine life in the fringing reef. An alternative entry point is Valesdir in the southwest.

📖 Sleeping & Eating

Paradise Sunset Bungalows BUNGALOW $
(Map p490; ☑5649107; Lamen Bay; per person incl breakfast & dinner 3500VT) This relaxed and friendly place is 15 minutes' walk from the Lamen Bay airfield. The rooms and shared facilities are basic, but the food and bay views are fine. Owner Tasso has snorkel gear and kayaks, and can arrange tours to Lamen Island. The restaurant is often busy with visiting yachties.

★Epi Island Guesthouse LODGE $$
(Map p490; ☑5528225; www.facebook.com/epiguesthouse; Valesdir Plantation; adult/child incl meals 15,000/7500VT; 🛜) Organic food and the relaxed lodge life of Epi Island Guesthouse draws people south to Valesdir. This arty ecolodge run by Alix and Rob Crapper features a large central room full of fascinating things (such as 1865–75 Enfield guns once owned by blackbirders) where you can chat with the family.

ℹ️ Getting There & Around

AIR

For a full Epi experience a good plan is to fly to Lamen Bay, make your way down the west coast by truck (8000VT) and then fly out of Valesdir (or vice versa). Epi's west coast road is rough, and there are only walking tracks in the east.

Air Vanuatu flies from Port Vila to Lamen Bay (8500VT) and Valesdir (7400VT) three or four times a week.

Air Taxi (☑5544206; http://airtaxivanuatu.com) runs full-day tours including a landing and lunch at Lamen Bay and a flight over Ambrym's volcanoes.

BOAT

Big Sista (☑23461, 5663851) stops at Epi (5500VT) on its weekly Port Vila–Santo run. Cargo ships also stop at Lamen Bay once or twice a week.

TANNA

POP 29,000 / AREA 565 SQ KM

If you visit only one island outside of Efate, this should be it. Tanna is an extraordinary place with the world's most accessible active volcano, sublime secluded beaches and some of Vanuatu's most intriguing traditional village life.

Apart from the fuming, furious Mt Yasur, the landscape features undisturbed rainforests, coffee plantations, mountains,

hot springs, blue holes and waterfalls, with some areas formed into marine and wildlife sanctuaries by local chiefs. *Kastom* is important in traditional villages, where all natural phenomena have a fourth dimension of spirituality and mystique, while strange cargo cults (John Frum and Prince Philip, in particular) still hold sway in some villages.

Lenakel is the main town with a market, port, several shops and a hospital, and it's near here that Tanna's more upmarket accommodation is located. The volcano and most of the island's basic bungalow accommodation is about 30km southeast on the rugged cross-island road via a central fertile, dense forest, aptly called Middlebush. The 'road' crosses Mt Yasur's remarkable ash plain on its way to Port Resolution.

🧭 Tours

You can get package deals in Vila that typically include airfares, transfers, accommodation, meals and visits to Mt Yasur and a *kastom* village (from 45,000VT), but if time isn't a factor it's cheaper to fly in and organise things yourself. Tours around the island can be arranged through your accommodation.

Air Safaris ADVENTURE TOUR
(☑7745206; www.airsafaris.vu; half-day tour 46,500VT) Air Safaris has a whirlwind half-day tour from Port Vila, flying past the crater and landing on the ash plain.

Air Taxi ADVENTURE TOUR
(☑5544206; http://airtaxivanuatu.com; day tour adult/child 39,000/26,000VT, overnight 46,000/31,000VT) Air Taxi flies to Tanna from Port Vila and offers a day tour with scenic flight over the volcano and 4WD trip across the island, and an overnight tour staying at Tanna Evergreen Bungalows.

ℹ️ Information

Take enough cash (vatu) for your whole time here. Credit cards are accepted at the large resorts with the usual 5% surcharge.

Tanna Evergreen Bungalows has free wi-fi if you're dining there.

Hospital (Map p492; ☑88659) At Lenakel.

NBV (Map p492; 🕗8.30am-3.30pm Mon-Thu, to 4pm Fri) The NBV bank in Lenakel will change cash only.

Tafea Tourism (http://tafeatourismcouncil.com) There's no tourist office but the website for Tafea Tourism (covering Tanna, Aniwa, Futuna, Erromango and Aneityum) is a useful resource.

Tanna

N 0 _____ 10 km
0 _____ 5 miles

Map labels (clockwise): Cape Enangiang, Lownapik Ruan, Lowital, Imafin, Analiwe Pt, Loanatit Pt, Ehniu, Mt Enuman (547m), Green Hill, SOUTH PACIFIC OCEAN, Black Sand Beach North, Enpek Lapen, Fetukai, Turtle Conservation Area, White Grass Plains, Mt Tangen (404m), Lenemtehin Pt, Whitegrass Airport, Middlebush, Louniel, White Sands, Imanaka, Lamnatu, Waesisi Bay, Ipai, Lownapkamei, Loanialu Lookout, Dip Point, Lownow, Yaneumakel, Sulphur Bay, Lowrapik, Mt Loanialu (552m), King's Cross, Isaka, Mt Yasur (361m), Ireupuow, Tanna Coffee Factory, Lenus, Tuan, Lenakel Wharf, Isangel, Yetpaleniel, Loanengo, Yakuveran, Lenakel, Imai, Yaohnanen, Imayo, Tapau, Manuapen, Ebul Bay, Bethel, Yakel, Turtle Bay, Cook's Hat, Black Sand Beach South, Imlao Point, Sharks Bay, Yatukwei, Ikeuti, Mt Melen (1047m), SOUTH PACIFIC OCEAN, Isakwai, Mt Tukosmera (1084m), Yenarpon, Green Pt, Yeruareng, Lapatua, Kwamera Bay, Kwamera, Yanuwao Pt

See Mt Yasur Area Map (p495)

Tanna

◉ Sights
1 Giant Banyan B3

◆ Activities, Courses & Tours
2 Blue Hole A2

⌂ Sleeping
3 Tanna Evergreen Bungalows A2
4 White Beach Bungalows A3
5 White Grass Ocean Resort A2

✸ Eating
6 White Grass Restaurant A2

ℹ Information
7 NBV B3
  TVL Internet .... (see 7)

TVL Internet (Map p492; Lenakel; per hour 500VT; ☺8-11.30am & 1.15-4pm Mon-Fri; 🖥) No computers, just a wi-fi hot spot.

ℹ Getting There & Around

Air Vanuatu (www.airvanuatu.com) flies between Vila and Tanna daily (13,000VT) except Friday and Saturday. If there are any spare seats, Air Taxi (p491) has standby fares for 10,000VT one way. Taxis (4WD trucks) and the odd minibus meet incoming flights. The fare to Lenakel from the airport is 2000/300VT by truck/bus (the truck price is for the whole truck).

For yachts, the official port of entry is at Lenakel (anchorage at Port Resolution is only possible after you've cleared immigration), and there are anchorages at Sulphur Bay and Waesisi Bay. Immigration and **Customs & Quarantine** (☺7.30am-noon & 1.30-4.30pm) are in Lenakel, opposite Lenakel Wharf.

The island's two main resorts are located just north of the airport; if you're staying in east Tanna, ask your bungalow to organise transport, or ask at the airport as soon as you arrive. Expect to pay 5000VT for the transfer for one or two people. The road is rough in places and the trip takes about an hour and a half.

East Tanna

East Tanna is the 'active' part of the island, in more ways than one. Mt Yasur dominates the landscape, its ash-laden smoke smothering the vegetation and creating a surreal monochrome scene on the western ash plain. There was once a large lake here, but following heavy rains in 2000 it burst its banks and drained out to sea through Sulphur Bay.

Along the coast to the north and east of Yasur are a string of black-sand and white-sand beaches, best explored from the headland of Port Resolution. Several *kastom* villages put on traditional dances for visitors and there are opportunities for jungle hikes and bathing in hot springs. If you're happy to stay in basic island bungalow accommodation, spending the night near Yasur (and climbing at sunrise) is an experience not to be missed.

◉ Sights & Activities

Bungalow owners and tour operators can arrange trips to: local villages to see *kastom* dancing; hot springs; surf beaches around Port Resolution; and Sharks Bay to see sharks feeding from the cliff-top.

Port Resolution   HARBOUR

(Map p495) Tanna's best anchorage is this beautiful bay with magnificent cliffs and easy access to east Tanna's best beaches. The Ireupuow village has a basic shop, a market and a couple of simple restaurants. To the left, a road leads up to the local cliff-top 'yacht club' and to a marine sanctuary at Yewao Point where you can snorkel in the calm water just before the coral reef finishes. Another path reaches a glorious white-sand beach and a top surf beach, with deep swells along 2.5km to Yankaren Para.

Port Resolution is 8km from the volcano entrance. A truck makes a return trip on Monday, Wednesday and Friday mornings from Port Resolution to Lenakel (2000VT), otherwise organise a charter.

John Frum Village   VILLAGE

(Map p495; Namakara; ⊘ Fri night) **FREE** At Namakara, this is one of the biggest John Frum villages on Tanna. Dances are held on Friday nights, when songs of praise are sung to the tunes of American battle hymns. It's free to attend but you'll need a local guide and transport from most bungalows is 2000VT.

Ashboarding   ADVENTURE SPORTS

(board hire 1000VT, guide 1000VT) Fancy boarding (like snowboarding or sandboarding) down the side of an active volcano? On Yasur's western side, where most of the ash clouds settle, it's possible to board from crater rim to ash plain in an exhilarating matter of minutes. It looks steep but the ash is far softer than snow! Ask at your bungalow about board hire.

🛏 Sleeping

Although most of the accommodation around Mt Yasur was flattened by Cyclone Pam, numerous operators have rebuilt and a few new ones have taken the opportunity to start up. Most offer meals and basic bungalow or tree-house accommodation, as well as camping. Generators usually provide electricity in the evenings (but don't expect it). If you can't get through by phone don't worry: just arrive and you'll find a bed.

★ Jungle Oasis   BUNGALOW $

(Map p495; ☑ 5448228, 7754933; camping per person 1000VT, s/d bungalows 2500/3500VT) Established 30 years ago, this was one of the original bungalow set-ups close to the volcano entrance and owner Kelson is still very active in the local tourism industry. Rebuilt from scratch after Cyclone Pam and set in black-sand gardens, the simple but quirky bungalows have shared bathroom and generator power (usually only in the evening).

A stilted restaurant-bar was under construction when we last visited.

Yasur View Lodge   BUNGALOW $

(Map p495; ☑ 7795634, 5686025; www.yasur viewlodge.com; camping per person 1000VT, s/d bungalows 1500/2500VT, s/d tree houses 2500/3500VT) Directly opposite the entrance to Mt Yasur (location, location!), the tree house here is good value. Owner Thomas has worked hard to restore his bungalows, garden and restaurant to a reasonably good standard.

Tanna Treetop Lodge   BUNGALOW $

(☑ 5417737; camping/tree houses per person 1000/2500VT) In a jungly garden setting just off the main road and about 500m from the Yasur entrance, this place does indeed have a head-spinning tree house atop a huge banyan tree (33 steps up!). Unfortunately the volcano views are

MT YASUR

Peering down into the rumbling, exploding lava storm of **Mt Yasur** (Map p495; 3350VT) is a sight you won't soon forget. The active volcano is so accessible that 4WD vehicles can get to within 150m of the crater rim. There are many tours up to see the old man, and although you can walk up without a guide (around 45 minutes from the entrance), or join a vehicle going up, it's still best to go with a guide.

Be sure to heed local warnings and take care around the crater rim – there are no safety rails or barriers. At the time of writing a new visitor centre was under construction at the entrance to the volcano road.

Although the ash plain to the west is desolate, the trip up to the crater from the entry gate on the southern slopes is through lush tree ferns and jungle. Along the path to the crater rim, there are whiffs of sulphur and whooshing, roaring sounds. Ahead are the silhouettes of people on the rim, bright orange fireworks periodically exploding behind them. Walk around to the west side of the central crater (furthest from the car park), which offers the best view into three smaller vents that take turns to spit rockets of red-molten rock and smoke. All is relatively calm until the ground trembles and the inevitable fountain of fiery magma shoots up with a deafening roar and spreads against the sky, sending huge boulders somersaulting back down into the broiling hole in the earth. Wait five minutes and it all happens again.

Some visitors find Yasur terrifying; others captivating. Photographers are beside themselves at the opportunity to capture nature at its most furious from such a vantage point. A sturdy tripod is essential for the best shots. The best times to visit Yasur are just before sunrise and for an hour or two after sunset. Absolute darkness is the ultimate thrill.

The level of activity within Yasur fluctuates between dangerous and relatively calm, but when it's hot, it's hot. It's often more active after the wet season; check www.geohazards. gov.vu and locals for the latest alert level. If the volcano is reaching activity levels three and four, entry to it won't be permitted. Take good walking shoes and a torch (flashlight), and bring a postcard to post at Volcano Post (www.vanuatupost.vu), the world's only postbox on top of a volcano. Vanuatu Post sells special 'singed' postcards for 200VT.

obscured by huge branches and the verandah is a bit pokey, but it's big enough for two double beds.

On the ground is a double-storey bungalow.

Port Resolution Yacht Club BUNGALOW **$**
(Map p495; ☎ 5376209, 5416989; wnarua@gmail. com; camping per person 1500VT, bungalows incl breakfast 3000-4000VT) Up on a bluff next to Ireupuow village, the grounds here overlook Port Resolution Bay, and one bungalow, with attached bathroom, tiled floor and balcony, has ocean views. The other two in the garden are cramped but sturdy, with shared bathroom.

It's not fancy as far as yacht clubs go, but the simple open-sided restaurant is strewn with international yachtie flags and pepped up by some threadbare but comfy old couches, and the bar serves the only cold beer for miles around. Owner Werry turns on the power in the evenings.

Island Dream BUNGALOW **$**
(Map p495; ☎ 5358595, 5621036; tannaisland dreambungalow@gmail.com; camping per person 1000VT, s/d 2000/4000VT, stilt huts d 5000VT, d with bathroom 8000VT,) Island Dream is in an interesting and slightly secluded location overlooking a small lake and Port Resolution on one side, mountains on the other. There are two basic bamboo-and-thatch bungalows, a nicer raised hut with mountain views, and a larger bungalow with tiled floor and attached bathroom.

There's a camping area if you have your own tent. The simple restaurant serves meals (from 800VT) and free breakfast.

Friendly Beach BUNGALOW **$$$**
(Map p495; ☎ 26856; www.friendlybeachvanu atu.com; d incl breakfast 18,800-28,000VT) The most upmarket accommodation in east Tanna, these three brand-new villas (well, fancy bungalows) face a lovely, secluded black-sand beach. They come with open-sky en-suite, queen-sized bed and airport transfers. Volcano tours and other activities are on offer. It's hard to justify the price tag, but if you can afford the extra style, this is your place.

✖ Eating

Ianiuia Surf Beach Restaurant   CAFE $
(Map p495; ☑547990; Port Resolution; meals 750VT; ⊙by arrangement) Chef Lea serves a range of chicken and vegetable dishes using a huge array of local produce, fresh herbs and flair. Book a day in advance (ask someone to help you find Lea).

Avoca Restaurant   CAFE $
(Map p495; ☑5633504; Port Resolution; lunch & dinner 700VT, coffee 300VT; ⊙by arrangement) This cute spot in Ireupuow village serves simple but delicious meals: chicken or fish with rice and vegetables or pancake fritters, and local Tanna coffee. Owner Serah lives next door so you can usually get a meal anytime.

West Tanna

All flights arrive at the coastal airstrip on west Tanna, 10km north of Lenakel, so this is likely to be your first view as you wing in. Tanna's upmarket resorts are a few minutes north of the airport.

Many travellers base themselves here and take a day trip to Mt Yasur (although we recommend at least one night in east Tanna). Lenakel has a lively produce market on Monday and Wednesday afternoons, and all day Friday, along with shops, mains electricity and a pretty little harbour. The kava bars offer some evening entertainment – but note that Tanna's mouth-numbing kava is regarded as the most potent in Vanuatu.

⊙ Sights & Activities

Any of the accommodation places can organise a variety of adventure or cultural tours. The most obvious is the day trip to Mt Yasur volcano (adult/child from 12,000/6000VT), leaving mid-afternoon and returning at about 8pm.

Also popular are visits to traditional **kastom villages** Lowinio (Yakel) or Ipai (from 8000VT), where you'll witness village life that hasn't changed in centuries. People gather nightly under a giant banyan at Yakel to drink kava, and dancing nights occur on a regular basis. The 'Black Magic' village tour (from 7000VT) is one of the best. Jungle trails take you past villages to a **giant banyan** as big as a soccer field near Lowrapik Tuan.

There's excellent snorkelling right along the west coast, with the reef face cascading down covered in coral, in and out of its

Mt Yasur Area   ⬆ N 0 ▬▬▬ 2 km / 0 ▬▬▬ 1 mile

Mt Yasur Area

⊙ Sights
1 John Frum Village	A1
Marine Sanctuary	(see 7)
2 Mt Yasur	A2
3 Port Resolution	B2

🛏 Sleeping
4 Friendly Beach	A1
5 Island Dream	B2
6 Jungle Oasis	A2
7 Port Resolution Yacht Club	B2
8 Yasur View Lodge	A2

✖ Eating
9 Avoca Restaurant	B2
10 Ianiuia Surf Beach Restaurant	B2

ℹ Information
11 Mt Yasur Crater Entry Gate	A2

ℹ Transport
Port Resolution	(see 3)

pocketed volcanic surface. A **blue hole** just north of White Grass Ocean Resort is like a fish nursery with coral wall decorations, and there's a second blue hole in front of Rocky Ridge Bungalows.

Walk about 2km north of Rocky Ridge to a **black-sand beach** that's good for swimming. Further north the **Blue Cave** makes for an interesting boat tour (7000VT).

Volcano Island Divers   DIVING
(☑30010; vanuatascuba@gmail.com; White Grass Ocean Resort; single shore/boat dive with full gear from 7000/10,500VT) This new PADI dive centre, based at White Grass Ocean Resort,

offers shore and boat dives along Tanna's west coast, as well as PADI Open Water courses.

🛏 Sleeping & Eating

⭐**Rocky Ridge Bungalows** BUNGALOW $
(📞5417220; http://rockyridgebungalows.word press.com; camping per person 1500VT, s/d/f incl breakfast 4000/8000/10,000VT) Tom and Margaret run this friendly place. Three simple but very comfortable bungalows have en suites with hot-water showers and small sea-facing balconies, while the larger family bungalow in front of the smaller ones has uninterrupted views. Free snorkelling gear and reef shoes are supplied for the blue hole directly out front.

Tours to Mt Yasur are 12,000VT per person, airport transfers 500VT (or it's a 3km walk).

White Beach Bungalows BUNGALOW $
(Map p492; 📞5949220; r 2000VT, s/d 3000/4000VT, beachfront d 5000VT) Down the road past the Tanna Coffee Factory you'll find a lovely, secluded white-sand beach, pounding surf, palm trees and these simple bungalows, some with attached bathroom. A restaurant was being built at the time of writing – breakfast is included and other meals are available.

⭐**Tanna**

Evergreen Bungalows BUNGALOW $$
(Map p492; 📞5588847; www.tannaevergreenre sorttours.com; s/d 14,000/16,000VT; 🛜) These ocean-front bungalows hide in lush gardens less than 1km north of the airport. All have soft beds, hot water and verandahs. New villas at the back were being planned at the time of writing. The resort is superfriendly and offers snorkel gear, babysitting, laundry, massage and the usual range of tours.

At **Tanna Evergreen Restaurant** (mains 1500-2500VT; ⊙6am-10pm; 🛜), the deck offers great views, free wi-fi and reliable meals from pasta to local lobster.

White Grass Ocean Resort BUNGALOW $$$
(Map p492; 📞30010; http://whitegrass tanna.com; d/tr/f incl breakfast 29,250/34,650/ 40,000VT; 🛜🏊) Tanna's top resort has 15 cosy bungalows with king-sized beds. Rambling grounds look out onto tiny rocky inlets, which are linked by timber bridges. There's a bar, hammocks, tennis, *pétanque* (boule) and a three-hole 'golf course'. Snorkelling gear and golf clubs are available and there's a dive outfit on site.

At **White Grass Restaurant** (Map p492; mains 2600-3800VT; ⊙7am-10pm; 🛜) the blackboard menu changes daily, with local seafood and beef steak the highlights. The timber deck overlooks the ocean with fabulous sunset views.

MALEKULA

POP 20,000 / AREA 2023 SQ KM

Second only to Santo in size, Malekula is a wild island famed for its tribal groups, cannibal sites, highland trekking and protected marine areas.

THE NEKOWIAR

About every three years (2015 being the most recent) come August, a great restlessness spreads across Tanna. The men scour the bush and villages for pigs and kava, counting, calculating. Finally one of the chiefs announces that his village will host the Nekowiar, a three-day extravaganza of song, dance and feasting during which the leaders of neighbouring villages organise marriages.

Preparations for the Nekowiar are exhaustive. Three complex dances are practised, and beauty magic takes over. Men, women, boys and girls use powders mixed with coconut oil to colour their faces a deep red, with black and yellow stripes.

The ceremony begins with the host village's young men dancing an invitation to the women. They respond with the Napen-Napen, a spectacular dance that represents their toil in the fields, and continues throughout the first night. The male guests watch and wait for dawn, when they dance the Toka, a pounding, colourful dance that shows scenes of daily life. If the Toka dancers make a circle around a woman, she's tossed up and down between them. During this stage a man may have sex with any woman who is willing.

On the third day the chief of the host village produces the *kweriya*, a 3m bamboo pole with white and black feathers wound around it and hawks' feathers on top. It announces that the Nao – the host village's dance – is to begin. This men's dance enacts events such as hunting and wrestling, followed by triumphant feasting.

Shaped like a sitting dog, Malekula has two highland areas connected by 'the dog's neck'. The uplands are extremely rugged and inhospitable, rising to over 800m and criss-crossed by narrow valleys.

Two of Malekula's major cultural groups are the Big Nambas and Small Nambas, named because of the size of the men's *namba* (penis sheath). Small Nambas men wear one leaf of dried fibre wound around the penis and tucked into a bark belt. Their semi-*kastom* communities are built around *tamtam*, ready to beat a rhythm, and a dance area.

Big Nambas men wind large purple pandanus fibres around their penis, securing the loose ends in a thick bark belt and leaving the testicles exposed. They had such an awesome warlike reputation that no foreigner dared venture into their territory. Even police expeditions, which came to punish them for killing traders, were ambushed and dispersed. They kept a stone fireplace where unwelcome outsiders were ritually cooked and eaten.

Big Nambas' *erpnavet* (grade-taking) ceremonies are preceded by lengthy rehearsals. The men cover themselves in charcoal and coconut oil, tie nut rattles around their ankles and wear feathers in their hair. At the highest level, a man has the powerful characteristics of a hawk, and a hawk dance is performed by a spirit man.

ⓘ Information

Hospital (Map p500; ☎ 48410; Norsup) The provincial hospital is in Norsup, about 5km north of Lakatoro.

Malampa Travel (Map p500; ☎ 7748030, 48888; www.malampa.travel) The Malampa Travel office, near the police station in the upper part of Lakatoro, can book accommodation or organise treks and tours on Malekula, as well as to Ambrym.

NBV (Map p500; Lakatoro; ☺ 8.30am-3.30pm Mon-Thu, to 4pm Fri) You can change major currencies (but not travellers cheques) at the bank in the LTC centre in Lakatoro, but don't count on it – bring plenty of vatu with you.

ⓘ Getting There & Around

AIR

There are daily flights with **Air Vanuatu** (Map p500; ☎ 23748, 23878) from Port Vila and Santo to Norsup, and three a week from Craig Cove, with usually one stopping at Lamap. The twice-weekly flight between Lamap and Norsup may be the only way to travel between these two places during the wet season, when rivers are flooded (and the flight can be cheaper than a boat or 4WD charter).

BOAT

The passenger ferry **Big Sista** (☎ 5625225; to Port Vila 7500VT, to Santo 3000VT) stops en route between Santo and Port Vila weekly, as does Vanuatu Ferry (p487). Both pick up and depart from the main wharf in Litslits, just south of Lakatoro.

VANUATU MALEKULA

THE JOHN FRUM MOVEMENT

Magic is a central force in ni-Vanuatu lives. So in 1936, when a mysterious man named John Frum came from the sea at Green Point and announced himself to some kava drinkers, they believed he was the brother of the god of Mt Tukosmera. He told the men that if the Europeans left Tanna, there would be an abundance of wealth. They spread the word. It was the beginning of a neopagan uprising, with followers doing things the missionaries had banned, such as traditional dancing – but not cannibalism, fortunately.

When US troops arrived a few years later, many Tannese went to Efate and Santo to work for them. There they met African American soldiers, who were colourful, with theatrical uniforms, decorations, badges, belts and hats. The African Americans had huge quantities of transport equipment, radios, Coca-Cola and cigarettes. But most of all, they were generous and friendly, treating the ni-Van as equals. Here was the wealth and way of life the ni-Van had been told about – John Frum was connected to America, they decided.

Some supporters made radio aerials out of tin cans and wire to contact John Frum. Others built an airfield in the bush and constructed wooden aircraft to entice his cargo planes to land. Still others erected wharves where his ships could berth. Small red crosses were placed all over Tanna and remain a feature in John Frum villages, where flags are raised daily to this god of their collective imagination.

An offshoot of John Frum, the Unity Movement, sees women in trances twirling themselves into the water at various places, such as Port Resolution, usually on a Wednesday.

A chartered speedboat ride from Wala in northern Malekula to Luganville on Santo costs around 25,000VT but will only go in calm weather. From Lamap to Craig Cove on Ambrym costs 12,000VT and takes about 90 minutes. Make sure the boat has life jackets.

All inhabited offshore islands (such as the Maskelynes) are linked to the mainland by speedboats or canoes; ask at your accommodation if you want to charter transport.

CAR, BUS & TRUCK

A dirt road runs from Lakatoro around the north coast and down the east coast to Lamap. The road south is rough and rutted and fords numerous rivers; in the wet season it's often impassable.

If you can hitch a ride on a truck it's 100VT from Norsup airport to Lakatoro, but 1000VT if you're stuck with a charter. On weekends there aren't many around; arrange a ride with your accommodation.

Jump in the tray of a truck to travel between Lakatoro and Lamap (1000VT, four hours) on weekdays. These leave Lamap between 3.30am and 5am and return from Lakatoro market at 1pm. On weekends or if you're in a hurry you'll need to charter (22,000VT). Trucks/charters run more frequently between Lakatoro and Veturah in the north (500/6500VT, one hour).

Most public transport leaves Lakatoro from the market. From Lakatoro to Lamap, you may be dropped at Black Sands, from where you can take a speedboat across to Port Sandwich or Levi's Beach Guesthouse (p502; 200VT per person). This avoids the long drive around the inlet.

Lakatoro & Around

Malekula's capital and main market town, Lakatoro is a relatively busy place with decent dirt roads, shops and power supply.

Set on two levels divided by a steep slope and a drawn-out lower main road, this is Malampa province's administrative capital. At the northern end of town is the LTC co-op, NBV bank, post office, bakery and Air Vanuatu office. The southern end has the MDC General Store and market.

About 4km north, at Norsup, is the main airstrip. A long stretch of beautiful coral reef stretches southwards from Aop Beach to Litslits, the main port for this area.

Tours to Small and Big Nambas cultural villages and to cannibal sites can be arranged through your accommodation (around 5000VT per person plus transfers), or Malampa Travel (p497).

◎ Sights

Lakatoro Cultural Centre   CULTURAL CENTRE
(Map p500; ☑5361223, 48651; adult/child 500/100VT; ☉7.30am-4.30pm Mon-Fri) On Lakatoro's upper ridge, this small cultural centre has some fascinating exhibits such as local carvings, photos and a library.

Malampa Handicrafts Centre   ARTS CENTRE
(Map p500; ☑5398633; ☉8.30am-4pm Mon-Fri) Behind the market in Lakatoro, this small handicrafts centre and store stocks locally made baskets, hats, mats, jewellery and coconut soaps and oils. Stop by for a chat and watch the workers weaving away.

🛏 Sleeping & Eating

★**Ameltoro
Resort & Restaurant**   BUNGALOW $
(Map p500; ☑7773387, 5368944; newmanrona@gmail.com; Norsup; bungalows incl breakfast 6500VT; ☎) These three spacious oval-shaped

---

MALEKULA TREKKING

Malekula has some of the wildest trekking country in Vanuatu, but it's also surprisingly well organised. Malampa Travel (p497) offers a number of itineraries that include guides, porters (one for two people) and village accommodation and meals. Jeep or boat transfers are often an extra charge so are best split with a group. Prices are for a minimum of two people.

Day hikes include the strenuous **Big Nambas Trek** (5500VT per person) from Lakatoro to Tenmaru and the half-day **Losinwei Cascades & Waterfall Walk** (3500VT per person). More challenging is the three-day coast-to-coast **Dog's Head Walk** (23,500VT per person), crossing from Small Nambas territory to Big Nambas territory and experiencing traditional village life along the way.

The ultimate adventure is the four-day **Manbush Trail** (29,700VT), which includes truck transfer from Norsup/Lakatoro to Unua, guide and porter, jungle and village stays, and accommodation at Lawa in a local guesthouse. It's no picnic, with up to six hours a day spent on bush trails, but it's an adventure. See Malampa Travel's website for trek details.

Malekula

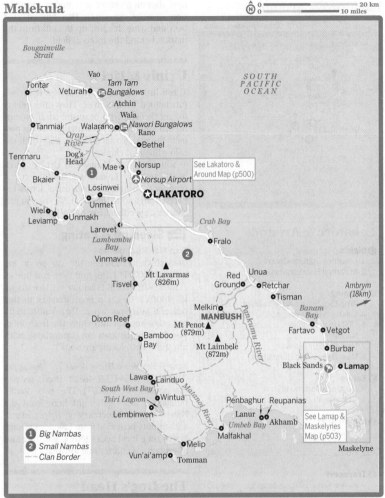

N
0 — 20 km
0 — 10 miles

Bougainville Strait

Tontar
Vao
Veturah○ Tam Tam Bungalows
Atchin
Wala
Walarano○ Nawori Bungalows
Rano
Bethel
○Tanmial
Orap River
Tenmaru
Dog's Head
Mae○
Norsup
○Norsup Airport
See Lakatoro & Around Map (p500)
✪LAKATORO
Bkaier
Losinwei
Unmet
Wiel○ ○Unmakh
Leviamp
Larevet
Lambumbu Bay
Vinmavis○
Mt Lavarmas (826m)
Tisvel○
Dixon Reef
Bamboo Bay
Mt Penot (879m)
Mt Laimbele (872m)
Lawa○ Lainduo
South West Bay
Tsiri Lagoon ○Wintua
Lembinwen
Melip
Vun'ai'amp○ Tomman

SOUTH PACIFIC OCEAN

Crab Bay
Fralo
Red Ground○
Unua
○Retchar
Tisman
MANBUSH
Melkin○
Punkumu River

Ambrym (18km)→

Banam Bay
Fartavo○ Vetgot
Burbar
Black Sands
Matanoui River
Penbaghur Reupanias
Lanur○○
Umbeb Bay Akhamb
Malfakhal

Lamap
See Lamap & Maskelynes Map (p503)
Maskelyne

1 Big Nambas
2 Small Nambas
-- Clan Border

VANUATU LAKATORO & AROUND

bungalows on the seafront across from Norsup island come with clean attached bathrooms, 24-hour mains power and solar hot water. Rona cooks up a French-influenced storm in the gorgeous brasserie-restaurant (meals 1300VT to 2000VT; by arrangement). It's about 1km north of the airport. Wi-fi costs 500VT.

Lakatoro Palm Lodge LODGE $

(Map p500; ☑ 5646285, 7721027; Lakatoro; r per person 2500VT, d bungalows 6000VT; ☎) A short walk from north Lakatoro on the road to Norsup, this welcoming, traditional-style place has three rooms in the main lodge with a shared lounge and kitchen and a separate private bungalow with balcony, all set in a sloping garden. Dinner is 800VT, or you can self-cater. Wi-fi is 300VT.

LTC Holiday Units MOTEL $

(Map p500; ☑ 549825; r 6500VT) These eight self-contained, one-bedroom units are tired looking and in an unappealing (but central) location behind the LTC co-op, but they're well-equipped with kitchenettes, white-tiled floors, attached bathroom and room enough to sleep six – good value for groups or families.

Lakatoro & Around

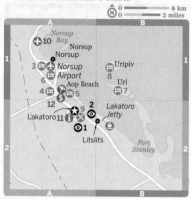

Nabelchel　　　　　　　　　　　BUNGALOW $
(Map p500; ☑5456402, 7740482; nabuchel
bungalows@gmail.com; Norsup; s/d incl breakfast
2500/5000VT; ☎) These simple bungalows
share a pleasant central sitting area and
are conveniently located a five-minute walk
north of the airport. Meals are 500VT and
beer is available. Wi-fi is 500VT per day.

Lakatoro
Community Cooperative　　　SUPERMARKET $
(LCC; Map p500; ⊙6.30am-7.30pm Mon-Fri,
6.30am-noon & 3-7.30pm Sat & Sun) Lakatoro's
best-stocked store by light years (though a

new shopping centre was under construction directly opposite). Has limited cold
beer and wine. It's just up the hill from the
market behind the football field.

Uripiv & Uri

These little islands have **marine reserves**
proclaimed by the chief. They offer plenty
for snorkellers, with beautiful coral, colourful fish and turtles. The sanctuary at Uri protects the mangroves and reef, and you'll see
colourful giant clams.

You can get to Uripiv and Uri by speedboat from the Lakatoro (Litslits) jetty. A
number of commuter boats travel across between 4pm and 4.30pm (200VT) or you can
charter a speedboat for 2000VT.

⊨ Sleeping & Eating

Nan Wat Bungalows　　　　　　BUNGALOW $
(Map p500; ☑5938523; Uri; per person incl
breakfast 2500VT) Lines and Jake run the secluded Nan Wat Bungalows on Uri island.
It's 1000VT to get a boat transfer to this
peaceful little spot where there's little to do
but relax, snorkel and enjoy the fresh food.
The three bungalows are comfortable, with
mosquito nets. Meals are 500VT.

Nawov Freswind Bungalows　　BUNGALOW $
(Map p500; ☑5497327, 48888; Uripiv; per person incl breakfast 2800VT) The two double
bungalows and restaurant here front the
Nawov Coastal Sanctuary on Uripiv island,
a 25-minute boat ride from Lakatoro Wharf.
Try to get a local boat (200VT, morning and
afternoon) or charter one for 1000VT.

The Dog's Head

The culture-filled, francophone zone of
Malekula's Dog's Head is home to several
cannibal sites as well as the Big and Small
Nambas tribal groups.

Kastom dancing tours go to Wala and
Vao to see Small Nambas dances; to Unmet
and Mae to see Big Nambas. Other tours go
to the spectacular **Yalo Cavern** near Tan-
mial and the islets of Wala (a cruise-ship
favourite) and Vao.

Accommodation places can usually arrange visits to tribal groups and the **Amel-
bati cannibal site** near Wala village, where
piles of bones and skulls tell a story of primi-
tive times less than a century ago. At the time

of writing the cannibal site on the island of Rano was off-limits due to a land dispute.

🛏 Sleeping & Eating

★ **Nawori Bungalows** GUESTHOUSE **$**
(Map p499; ☑5471005, 5685852; etieneet iasinmal@gmail.com; Wala; s/d incl breakfast 2500/5000VT; 🐚) Etienne and Lyn run this friendly place about an hour by truck north of Lakatoro. It's well placed for exploring the Dog's Head and the nearby island of Wala. There are three rooms in the main house with a communal dining room, and a separate lodge with four rooms and a sea-facing balcony.

THE SMALLER SOUTHERN ISLANDS

Aneityum & Mystery Island

Aneityum is the southernmost inhabited island in Vanuatu, but it's tiny Mystery Island just offshore – with its grass airstrip (built during WWII), glorious beaches, marine reserve and secluded bungalows – that will leave you slack-jawed. Garden paths criss-cross the island, and snorkelling is fantastic off the end of the airstrip (the island is a marine sanctuary). Aneityum people believe Mystery Island is the home of ghosts, so no one will live there. It's a favourite stopover with cruise ships, when it gets crowded and locals set up market stalls; at other times you'll probably have it to yourself.

Cross to Anelcauhat, Aneityum's main village, to see fascinating ruins of whaling-industry equipment, missionary Geddie's church and old irrigation channels. Take stunning walks from Anelcauhat to picturesque Port Patrick, impressive Inwan Leleghei Waterfall or to the top of Inrerow Atahein (853m), an extinct volcano.

Mystery Island Guesthouse (☑7799410; per bungalow 3000VT) has simple colourful bungalows and a basic central kitchen with a gas refrigerator (there's no electricity). You need to bring your own food and water, although someone will row across from Aneityum each day to see if you need anything. On Aneityum, Kenneth's Bungalows in the main village of Anelgauhat has two basic huts for 1500VT per person. Contact Tafea Tourism (http://tafeatourismcouncil.com) for more information.

Air Vanuatu has two scheduled flights a week from Tanna to the Mystery Island airstrip.

Erromango

The 'Land of Mangoes' is mountainous, with almost all the people living in two main villages on its rugged coast. Each village has a fertile garden, where taro, tomato, corn and sweet potato thrive among huge mango, coconut and pawpaw trees.

Dillon's Bay (Upongkor) is Erromango's largest settlement, with a huge crystal-clear swimming hole formed by the Williams River as it turns to the sea. Sandalwood trees still grow in the rainforest, and a rock displays the outline of John Williams, the first missionary here (locals laid his short, stout body on this rock and chipped around it prior to cooking and eating him in 1839).

Guided walks from Dillon's Bay include trips to a **kauri reserve** (2000VT) to see ancient 40m-high trees, and a three-day walk south and across to Ipota. At the mouth of Williams River, about 9km south of the Dillon's Bay airstrip, **Meteson's Guesthouse** (☑68677; Upongkor; s/d incl breakfast 2500/5000VT) sleeps eight in two rooms. Chief William arranges fishing trips and guides for treks.

Air Vanuatu flies weekly to Dillon's Bay from Port Vila and Tanna, as well as to Ipota on the remote southeastern side of the island.

Aniwa

This island is set around beautiful, clear-blue Itcharo Lagoon, with 1.5km of white-sand beach, coconut palms, a marine sanctuary and great snorkelling. The five colourful huts at **Aniwa Ocean View Bungalows** (☑5964778, 5616506; http://aniwaoceanviewbunga-lows.wordpress.com; s/d incl breakfast 2500/4000VT) are the only formal accommodation on Aniwa, and you'll get a friendly welcome (at the airstrip) from Jethro and Joshua. There's a restaurant (meals from 750VT) and island tours can be organised. Air Vanuatu flies to Aniwa from Tanna at least once a week.

Tam Tam Bungalows BUNGALOW $
(Map p499; ☑5548926; Veturah; dm 2000VT, bungalows per person 3500VT) These traditional bungalows with bathroom have been renovated and make a peaceful northern base for trekking and exploring the Small Nambas in Vao. There's snorkel gear and spear/canoe fishing, electricity from 6pm to 9pm and a restaurant. Transfers from Lakatoro are 6500VT.

Lamap

Lamap, with its nearby airstrip, is the entry point to Malekula in the south by air and boat (from Ambrym) and is the gateway to the Maskelyne islands. There's not much to the village itself: a church, school, a couple of guesthouses, dozens of kava bars and the reasonably well-stocked Levi's Store at the bottom of the hill heading into the village.

Organised activities in Lamap include *kastom village dances* (5000VT per person), a *dugong tour* to Gaspard Bay (2000VT) and the *Marieu Garden Tour* (2000VT per person). Ask at your accommodation or call Joseph (☑5435722) or Tito (☑5436814).

Your accommodation can organise transfers to/from the airport (1000VT) and Lakatoro (1500VT for a local truck, 25,000VT for a charter). The truck to Lakatoro departs between 3.30am and 5am on weekdays; check the night before. If you're coming to Lamap from Lakatoro, you may be dropped across the inlet at a place called Black Sands, from where a boat (200VT) will drop you at Port Sandwich or Levi's guesthouse.

🛏 Sleeping & Eating

**Lamap Ocean
View Guesthouse** GUESTHOUSE $
(Map p503; ☑7102018; s/d without bathroom 1800/3600VT) This neat and friendly guesthouse in the centre of Lamap village has four small rooms (three singles and a double), a sitting room with comfy couches and a kitchen. Clean shared bathrooms have flush toilet and shower. Meals are just 300VT.

Levi's Beach Guesthouse GUESTHOUSE $
(Map p503; ☑5934202, 5475656; r per person without bathroom incl breakfast 1500VT) This basic place on the waterfront next to Levi's Store has six rooms in two lodge-style buildings. The abominable shared toilet and shower were being replaced with more modern facilities at the time of writing. Limited power but comfy enough beds and Mary cooks up decent meals.

The Maskelynes

The lovely vehicle-free Maskelyne islands are only a short truck-and-boat trip from Lamap but seem a world away from mainland Malekula.

The main attractions, apart from the peaceful village life, are the coral reefs and marine conservation areas, swimming, snorkelling (BYO gear), canoeing or fishing, all of which can be experienced DIY or with organised tours.

The main island, Uliveo (Maskelyne), is a friendly place with the only accommodation – here you can watch the villagers make canoes, weave, string necklaces and hunt for edible sea creatures when the tide is out. You're welcome at the kava bars, and you can hire outrigger canoes (200/400VT half/full day or 1400VT with a guide). For tours and information, contact Sethrick at Batis Seaside Guesthouse or go online at www.maskelynetourism.blogspot.com.au.

The road from Lamap ends at a sandy beach, Point Doucere (transport from Lakatoro 1500VT), from where canoes and speedboats head out to the Maskelynes (2500VT). Point Doucere is a 20-minute walk south from the airport through coconut plantations.

⊙ Sights & Activities

**Ringi Te Suh
Marine Conservation Area** NATURE RESERVE
(Map p503; per person 1200VT) Take a guided tour by outrigger canoe to this marine sanctuary, a 100-hectare reef protected by the villagers of Pellonk (the name itself means 'leave it alone'). You can snorkel over the beautiful Giant Clam Garden and picnic on an artificial island.

🛏 Sleeping & Eating

There are just three bungalow operations on Uliveo island, including two side by side (owned by brothers) on the waterfront in Pellonk village. Malaflag Beach Bungalows, in Lutes village, was closed due to cyclone damage at the time of writing but may reopen in future.

Batis Seaside Guesthouse BUNGALOW $
(Map p503; ☑7751463, 5943885; batisseaside guesthouse.vanuatu@gmail.com; Pellonk; r per person without bathroom 2500VT, bungalows

5000VT) Two lemon-yellow waterfront bungalows with verandahs on stilts have their own toilet and shower at the back, while cheaper guesthouse rooms in the garden have comfy single beds and shared bathroom. Owner Sethrick can organise any activities on the islands or arrange boat charters. Lunch and dinner are 500VT and there's a small store and 24-hour solar power.

Senelich BUNGALOW $

(Map p503; ☑7117096, 7789547; senelich@gmail.com; Pellonk; r per person without bathroom 2500VT, bungalows 5000VT) Next to Batis Seaside Guesthouse and identical in most respects, the two sturdy waterfront bungalows have private bathrooms at the rear and verandahs over the water, and there are two more garden-facing rooms. There's also a lovely gazebo in the garden and a bar-cafe. Solar power.

Malog Bungalows BUNGALOW $

(Map p503; ☑7107905, 7783524; Peskarus; camping 500VT, dm 2000VT, s/d without bathroom incl breakfast 2800/5600VT; ☎) Owner Kalo has three traditional bungalows and a five-bed dorm on the muddy shore between the mangroves in Peskarus village, the largest on the island. The shared bathroom has flush toilets and showers and there's solar power. There are a couple of kayaks, or you can head out in an outrigger canoe. Lunch and dinner cost 700VT (1500VT if there's lobster).

AMBRYM

POP 7300 / AREA 680 SQ KM

Ambrym – called the Black Island because of its volcanic soils – has amazing twin volcanoes, Mt Marum and Mt Benbow, which keep volcanologists all over the world on the alert. Climbing one or both is the main attraction here – Ambrym isn't noted for its beaches and with few roads, getting around is mostly by boat or on foot.

Cultural attractions include Vanuatu's best tree-fern carvings and *tamtam*, and the Rom dances of northern and western Ambrym. Magic in Vanuatu is strongest on the islands with active volcanoes, and Ambrym is considered the country's sorcery centre. Sorcerers *(man blong majik* or *man blong posen)* are feared and despised. Many ni-Van have seen too many unexplained happenings, and would treat anyone who was found practising black magic severely. Tourists can visit

Lamap & Maskelynes

villages that feature traditional magic, but magic for tourists is not considered black.

Ambrym is known for sand drawings, with 180 sand designs, each referring to a specific object, legend, dance or creature.

✦ Festivals

There are three main festivals in north Ambrym (**Fanla Art Festival** and **North Ambrym Magic Festival** in July, and **Back to my Roots** in August), each an annual extravaganza of cultural demonstrations, ceremonies, fashion shows, Rom dances, magic and cooking lessons.

ⓘ Information

Malampa Travel (☑7748030, 48888; www.ambrym.travel) Malampa Travel, based in

VANUATU AMBRYM

Malekula, handles tourist information for Ambrym and is remarkably well organised. You can book guides and accommodation through here for an extra cost.

🛈 Getting There & Around

AIR

Air Vanuatu (📞 23748) flies between Craig Cove and Port Vila (10,000VT) and Santo (8000VT) three times a week. On Tuesday and Sunday the flight stops first at Ulei. Tour companies in Port Vila offer volcano adventure flights to Ambrym.

BOAT

The *Brisk* cargo ship makes its way from Vila to Santo on Saturdays, stopping at both Craig Cove and Ranon.

The best anchorages are at Craig Cove and Sanesup in the south (Port Vatu is OK in good weather), and Buwoma Bay, Ranvetlam, Ranon and Nobul in the north.

If you aren't concerned about deep ocean swells and fierce currents, you can travel from Ranon Beach Bungalows by speedboat from north Ambrym to Pangi in southwest Pentecost (13,000VT). You can also take a boat from Craig Cove to Lamap in Malekula (12,000VT) with Sam of Sam's Guest Bungalows. Both trips cross open oceans and are dependent on weather conditions. Speedboats also travel between Craig Cove and Ranvetlam or Ranon (12,000VT one way). Ask your bungalow host to arrange transport.

THE ROM DANCE

Ambrym's most striking traditional ceremony, the Rom dance combines *maghe* (grade-taking) elements with magic. When a man wishes to move up in the village structure, he must find someone who owns the design of a mask and ask to buy it, with pigs and cash. The owner makes his *nakamal* (men's clubhouse) *tabu* (taboo), and the buyer comes to discuss the purchase and learn the rules determining the colours and shapes of the mask. Once the design has been bought, the buyer invites men to pay to enter this *nakamal* where they practise the dance for days, cooking the food the buyer has provided. Finally there's a feast, and the next morning the dancers perform wearing the extraordinary costume: a tall, conical, brightly painted banana-fibre mask and a thick cloak of banana leaves.

TRUCK

If you're heading south from Craig Cove to Port Vatu, try to get a lift from the airport on one of the taxi trucks heading there (or hook up with other travellers), otherwise you'll need to charter (5000VT). If landing at Ulei, trucks run from Ulei to Endu (3000VT) on the east coast.

Central Ambrym

👁 Sights & Activities

The main reason to visit Ambrym is to hike up one or both of its volcanoes, preferably up one way and down another. On a clear and active night, the sky above them glows red.

Mt Benbow & Mt Marum   VOLCANO

(Map p505) The guided climb up these twin volcanoes is reasonably demanding and the view is often obscured by low cloud and volcanic smoke and ash. But on a clear day the reward for your climb will be peering into an active crater and seeing the red-hot magma boiling below like a satanic pot of tomato soup. Both volcanoes are closely monitored, climbing is occasionally suspended on high-activity days and evacuation plans are always ready.

To make the climb, you must be reasonably fit and comfortable walking on steep terrain, and you need a good guide (compulsory). Skin protection and plenty of drinking water are essential. There's a dry, slippery crust around both volcanoes so your boots need to be strong enough to kick toe holes. Ankle support is also necessary as there's some boulder hopping. Between the mountains, the walk over the razor-backed ridge gets very narrow and snakes nastily upwards, while vents all around spurt acrid smoke. Mother Nature does her best to be daunting.

The best idea is to trek up one way and down another (different guides will meet you on the caldera). There are three routes, two accessed from Craig Cove airport and one from Ulei airport:

North From Ranon or Ranvetlam, this is the only option for going up and back (Mt Marum only) in one day. From Ranon to North Camp it's two hours through jungle, then another three hours to the top. Return, or continue down (with camping) on the south or east routes.

Southwest From Port Vatu or Lalinda it's five to six hours slogging through jungle to the ash plain and the West Camp (overnight), then a steep 1½-hour trek to Mt Benbow or

Ambrym

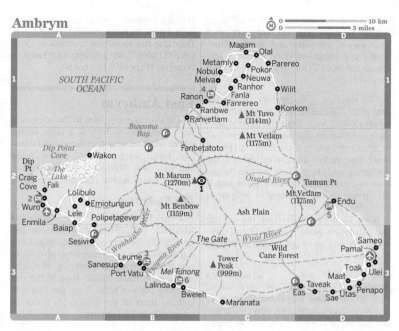

2½ hours to Mt Marum, from where you can continue down north or east.

East From Endu, 45 minutes north of Ulei airport, it's a testing 6½-hour trek to the ash plain, across Wisal River to East Camp. From there it's just 45 minutes to the top of Mt Marum. Return or continue north to Ranon or south to Port Vatu.

➡ Tours

Volcano tour guides usually have gear (tents, sleeping bags, hard hats, gloves, gas masks) should you want to hire anything. Ask if you need to bring extra food (meals are included).

Volcano climbs are well organised and costs for guides and transport are standardised. You can find a list of certified guides at www.ambrym.travel or posted at the airport at Craig Cove, but most travellers simply get hooked up through their accommodation.

➡ Costs

➡ **Full Day** (from Ranvetlam) – 7000VT per person (9000VT for solo travellers)

➡ **Two-day return** (from Port Vatu) – 11,900VT (15,850VT solo)

➡ **Three-day crossover** (from Ranvetlam, Port Vatu or Endu) – 21,150VT (23,100VT solo)

Ambrym

◎ Sights

1 Mt Benbow & Mt Marum....................C2

🛏 Sleeping

2 Jossie's Guesthouse............................A2
3 Karina Guesthouse...............................B3
4 Ranon Beach Bungalows..................... C1
Sam's Guest Bungalows............. (see 2)
5 Sea Roar Bungalows D2
Ter Ter Hot Spring
Bungalows .... (see 2)
6 Wola Volcano Guesthouse B3

West Ambrym

The village of **Craig Cove** is West Ambrym's tiny commercial centre, harbour and the island's main airport. It has several bungalows, a market and a few stores selling bread, canned food and hardware. From Craig Cove you can visit a number of **hot springs**; the best are at **Sesivi**, about 10km southeast.

🛏 Sleeping

Sam's Guest Bungalows   BUNGALOW **$**
(Map p505; ☑ 5944424, 7767129; Craig Cove; per person incl breakfast 3000VT) For a family welcome and volcano information, Sam's is

hard to beat in Craig Cove. There are three tidy rooms (with attached bathroom) in a quiet area of the village and another family or group bungalow. Good meals (lunch/dinner 500/800VT) and generator power in the evening.

Ter Ter Hot Spring Bungalows BUNGALOW $
(Map p505; ☏ 5493238, 7726534; Malvert; r per person 3500VT) Away from the main village, these seafront bungalows enjoy a fabulous location overlooking a small rock-and-coral beach cove. At low tide you can relax in the hot spring pools here. There are four bungalows in a palm-filled garden but the best is the private sea-facing bungalow with views out to Malekula.

It's a 15-minute walk from the airstrip through jungle paths; call ahead and owner Freddy will meet you at the airport or harbour.

Jossie's Guesthouse GUESTHOUSE $
(Map p505; ☏ 7741186; Craig Cove; r per person incl meals 2000VT) These simple but sturdy stone and palm-thatch bungalows in a village garden include two rooms in one building and a separate bungalow sleeping three. Long-drop toilet, bucket shower and a small shop on site.

North Ambrym

Most of Ambrym's northern coast has high volcanic cliffs rising straight out of the sea. The motorboat journey north from Craig Cove burbles past sheer angled cliffs, forests, rock caves, hot pools, coral reefs, turtles, dolphins and wild ducks.

The best **Rom dances** and **magic** (per person 5000VT) can be seen inland at **Fanla**, a 45-minute walk from Ranon. An island feast can be prepared for a group, and locals will bring out a terrific array of carvings for sale. It was once prohibited to access the volcano from here during yam season, but in line with the rest of the island this is no longer taboo.

Chief Joseph at Ranvetlam is the *kastom* owner of the northern approach to the volcanoes.

🛏 Sleeping

Ranon Beach Bungalows BUNGALOW $
(Map p505; ☏ 7758941, 5637502; Ranon; per person incl meals 3000VT) If you're climbing the volcano from the north, this is where you'll stay, in traditional bungalows on the beach or up the cliff. Owners Lann and Freddie

Douglas organise volcano tours as well as Rom dances in Fanla (5000VT per person). They also run speedboat transfers to Craig Cove (12,000VT, 45 minutes) and Pangi in Pentecost (13,000VT, two hours).

East Ambrym

Ulei is also an entry point to the volcanoes. **Toak**, near the airfield, is a large village where you'll see very traditional sand drawings, magic, *kastom* stories, dances, caves and waterfalls. Volcano tours depart from **Endu**, about 45 minutes north of the airport.

🛏 Sleeping

Sea Roar Bungalows BUNGALOW $
(Map p505; ☏ 7302577, 5357584; Endu; per person 2250VT) The two excellent double-storey traditional bungalows here sleep up to eight people and are set in a lovely garden with sea views in Endu village. Host Walter can organise volcano tours from the east and cultural tours of the village. It's about 45 minutes from Ulei airport.

South Ambrym

🛏 Sleeping

Karina Guesthouse GUESTHOUSE $
(Map p505; ☏ 7742661; www.vanuatuisland experience.com; Port Vatu; per person incl meals 2000VT) John Tasso runs this simple multibed guest bungalow in Port Vatu and guides volcano tours directly from here on the southwest route. A truck charter from Craig Cove airport is 5000VT.

Wola Volcano Guesthouse BUNGALOW $
(Map p505; ☏ 5487405; Lalinda; per person incl meals 2500VT) This thatched bungalow has two rooms sleeping five, with basic shared facilites. Owner Joses Wilfred is an experienced volcano guide, so this is a good alternative starting point to climb Mts Benbow and Marum, instead of nearby Port Vatu.

ESPIRITU SANTO

POP 40,000 / AREA 3677 SQ KM

Better known simply as Santo, this is Vanuatu's largest island and one of its most enjoyable. It doesn't have quite the activities and infrastructure of Port Vila, but it does have world-class diving, some excellent upmarket island resorts and some of the most jaw-droppingly beautiful beaches in the archipelago.

Espiritu Santo hides many of its secrets away from its small capital, Luganville, but there are plenty of tour operators to help get you to every corner of the island. Big attractions include the Millennium Cave, snorkelling or diving over dumped WWII memorabilia, the stunning east coast beaches and inviting blue holes. If you scuba dive, don't miss the SS *President Coolidge*, one of the world's most accessible wrecks.

Fanafo, north of Luganville, was where, in 1963, charismatic Jimmy Stevens formed the Nagriamel movement. Then, on 27 May 1980, eight weeks before national independence, he and his supporters staged a coup known as the Coconut Rebellion. Armed mainly with bows and arrows, they occupied Luganville and proclaimed Santo's independence, calling their new country Vemarana. However, the new nation collapsed with Stevens' arrest on 1 September.

Inland, villages are isolated and the locals totally self-sufficient. Southwest Santo has Vanuatu's highest mountains: Mt Tabwemasana (1879m), Mt Kotamtam (1747m), Mt Tawaloala (1742m) and Santo Peak (1704m), all of which can be climbed with local guides.

❶ Getting There & Away

AIR

Luganville's Pekoa International Airport receives a weekly international flight direct from Brisbane, Australia, and at least two flights daily to/from Port Vila. It's also the feeder airport for Vanuatu's northern islands, with direct flights from Santo to Malekula, Ambae, Pentecost and the Torres and Banks islands. Contact Air Vanuatu at its **Santo office** (Map p511; ☑ 37670; Main St; ⊙7.30am-4.30pm Mon-Fri, 8-11am Sat) or **airport office** (Map p514; ☑ 36506).

BOAT

Luganville has **Customs & Quarantine** (Map p511; ☑ 36225) and immigration facilities for yachts at or near the Main Wharf. Segond Channel, with its sandy bottom, is the town's main anchorage, but Aore island is the safest: 40m deep and away from the southeasterlies that hit the mainland.

Big Sista (Map p511; ☑ 23461) and Vanuatu Ferry (p487) both stop here on their weekly ferry trip between Port Vila and Santo.

❶ Getting Around

CAR & MOTORCYCLE

Santo's East Coast Rd is sealed from Luganville to Port Olry, so it's a good opportunity to self-drive; elsewhere travel by boat, 4WD truck or foot.

Deco Stop (Map p511; ☑ 36175; www.decostop.com.vu) The best place to rent a car (from 12,000VT per day) and the only place to rent a scooter (5000VT) or wicked dune buggy (10,000VT). Also rents out mountain bikes (2500VT).

Espiritu Car Hire (Map p511; ☑ 37539; Main St) Hire compact SUVs here from 9000VT per day.

MINIBUS & TAXI

Minibuses can be found around town but compact taxis far outnumber them in Luganville and are similarly priced at around 200VT for short trips. A minibus/taxi to the airport is 200/1000VT.

A minibus runs up the east coast from Luganville to Port Olry (600VT) from Monday to Saturday, leaving Unity Pacific Garage in Luganville between 2pm and 4pm. To return, stand by the roadside in Port Olry before 6.30am.

Luganville & Around

POP 13,200

Luganville is Vanuatu's 'second city', with a long, languid main road running parallel to the waterfront. Apart from the outlook across the channel to Aore island it's not a particularly attractive town, but with a good range of accommodation, some cool cafes and kava bars, plenty of dive and tour operators and a cheerful market, it's a fun place to hang out or base yourself for trips around Santo.

◉ Sights

★**Millennium Cave**   CAVE
(Map p508; ☑ 5470957; 7000VT; ⊙8am) Trek and trudge through the jungle, across creeks, along bamboo bridges and through cascades to this massive cave, 20m wide and 50m high, about 15km from Luganville. Climb down a bamboo ladder, and through a rocky pool dodging cascades and little bats, then out into the sunlight and into icy water to zap down the rapids past amazing towering rocks, gorgeous rainforest and waterfalls. An awesome, full-day, guided-tour experience; book through your accommodation or at the office near Sarakata Bridge.

Espiritu Santo

N

0 —————— 20 km
0 —————— 10 miles

A **B** **C** **D**

Cape
Cumberland

Hokua

Wunpuko

Cumberland
Peninsula

Petani

Cumberland Ranges

Pesena

Peamatsina

Nokuku

Lajmoli

Mt Lolohoe
(1547m)

Penaoru

Pialulup

Wunavae

Jeriviu

Big Bay

Matantas

Malao

SOUTH
PACIFIC
OCEAN

Cape
Quiros

Sakao
Peninsula

Sakao

Cape
Quiros

Port Olry 🔾 **2** Dolphin

Golden 🔾 **6**
Beach

Elephant
Island

8 **13**

Hog Harbour

Champagne
Beach

Lonnoc
Beach

Tasmate

Big Bay Hwy

Lowerie

Sara

Elia

Jordan River

Kole 1 **3**

14

Shark
Bay

Lataro

Lataroa

Mt Kotamtam
(1747m)

Bengie

Palon

5
Turtle **12**
Bay

Malwepe
(Oyster
Island)

Wusi

Mt Tabwemasana
(1879m)

Lape River

Mt Tananker
(784m)

Mavea

4

Linduri

Mt Tawaloala
(1742m)

Butmas

11

Barrier
Beach

Aese

Soari River

Santo Peak
(1704m)

**Millennium
Cave**

Fanafo

10
9

Tanmet

Nambel **1**

Saraoutou

Surunda

Toramaori

Marakae

Funaspef

Nampauk

Luganville

Tovu Tovu

Supenalao

Narango

La Roseraie

Kerevinumbu

Wailapa River

Adsone River

Vules Epe

Aore

See Around
Luganville &
Aore Island
Map (p511)

Tasiriki

Viase

Tangoa

Sasuli

Pelmol

Wailapa

Avunatari

Ambaghura

Ipayato

Tasmalum

Araki

Malo

Malo
Prospect

Cape
Lisburn

Pt Tsinoitariv

Nanuku

Asamaranda

Bougainville
Strait

Avorani

Ataripoi

A **B** **C** **D**

Espiritu Santo

Luganville Market MARKET
(Map p511; Main St; ⊙24hr) Villagers come from all over to sell their produce here. It's near the Sarakata Bridge.

Million Dollar Point DIVE SITE
(Map p514; 500VT) Million Dollar Point, where hundreds of tonnes of US military equipment was dumped, now shows its coral-encrusted machinery to snorkellers and divers. At low tide you'll find metal objects littering the beach for a kilometre in either direction. Don't leave your valuables around while you dive.

Aore Island ISLAND
(Map p514) Across the Segond Channel, Aore island is easily reached on the free resort ferry. There's not much regular transport on the island so you're limited to short walks and hanging out at the resort for a few hours (free if you buy lunch). The ferry departs Phillips Wharf at 8am, 11.30am and 2.30pm, returning at 11am, 1.30pm and 4pm.

Leweton Cultural Village VILLAGE
(Map p514; ☑5671114; 3000VT) Listen to women making water music and see other traditions from the Banks islands. Located near the airport; book in advance.

Ransuck Cultural Village VILLAGE
(Map p514; ☑5443973; 3000VT) Community members from Pentecost take you through a lush garden and show you how their beautiful mats are made. Near the airport.

🏃 Activities

Quadman Vanuatu ADVENTURE SPORTS
(Map p511; ☑5472051; http://quadmanvanuatu.com; half/full day 4000/7000VT) Hire a quad bike and head out for a day of adventure.

Santo Horse Adventures HORSE RIDING
(☑7774700; santohorseadventures@gmail.com; East Coast Rd; pony rides 4000VT, 2hr trail rides 7500VT) Experience a trail ride through jungle and along beaches. Megan's horse ranch is at Lope Lope Adventure Lodge around 11km north of Luganville.

Diving, Snorkelling & Fishing
Santo, particularly around Luganville and the offshore islands, is justifiably famous for its scuba diving, and snorkellers will find plenty to see just below the surface. Coral reefs are bright and healthy, the wrecks are world class and dive operators extremely professional, though you'll need to spend some time here to see the best of what's on offer. Look at operators' websites for some amazing images, such as MV *Henry Bonneaud,* one of the world's top night dives; SS *President Coolidge,* lying in 21m to 67m of water; and Tutuba Point, a spectacular drift dive with brilliant corals and marine life.

There are boat and offshore dives for beginners to experts. An intro dive costs about 10,000VT, single dives are 7000VT, diver certification courses cost from 48,000VT and equipment hire is 1500VT.

Allan Power Dive Tours DIVING
(Map p511; ☑36822; www.allan-power-santo.com; Main St; s/d dive 5000/10,000VT, gear hire per dive 2000VT) Allan Power is a legend in dive circles, having led more than 28,000 dives on the SS *President Coolidge* since 1969. Also dives at Million Dollar Point and other wrecks and offers PADI Open Water courses (49,000VT).

Aquamarine DIVING
(Map p511; ☑5551555; Main St) Experienced dive outfit based at the Espiritu hotel.

VANUATU LUGANVILLE & AROUND

Santo Island Dive & Fishing   DIVING, FISHING
(Map p511; 7758082; www.santodive.com; Main St; per dive 7000VT, full gear hire 2000VT) This operator offers wreck and reef diving and fishing charters in search of tuna, *mahimahi* and wahoo.

Island Fishing Santo   FISHING
(7740536; fabricemoderan@hotmail.com) Fabrice will take you out big-game fishing and snorkelling from his boat.

Hiking

Favourite Santo treks are through the Vatthe Conservation Area and the Loru Conservation Area. Wrecks to Rainforest can organise custom treks around the island.

Tours

Wrecks to Rainforest   TOUR
(Map p511; 37365, 5547001; www.wreckstorainforest.com; 7.30-11.30am & 1-5pm Mon-Fri, 7.30-11.30am Sat) With her office in front of the Espiritu hotel, owner Mayumi Green is a terrific source of knowledge and can organise custom two- to six-day treks (per day from 7000VT) through rainforest and mountains to *kastom* villages. Mayumi also runs tours with accommodation to the northern islands, Malekula and Ambrym.

Butterfly Adventure Tours   TOUR
(5660290; tours 5000-10,000VT) Glenn runs a wide range of tours, from bushwalking to birdwatching, beaches to historic sites.

Heritage Tours   TOUR
(36862, 7740968; www.heritagetours.com.vu) These island tours have been running for over 20 years; speak to Tim Rovu.

Paradise Tours   TOUR
(7747159; www.paradisetourssanto.net) Luke has been running tours for years. He picks you up from your accommodation and offers a mix of one- and half-day tours.

Island Time Kayaking   KAYAKING
(5695140; www.islandtimekayaking.net) Guided sea-kayaking tours at various locations along the east coast.

Sleeping

Luganville has a handful of good budget places and a few decent midrangers, but for the better resorts you'll need to head offshore or up the east coast.

★Hibiscus Le Motel   MOTEL $
(Map p511; 36727; lemotelhac@gmail.com; Rue Dumont D'Urville; r 3500VT;) Comfortable rooms, all with bathrooms and kitchenettes, sleep three and are set around a cramped but sociable central area. Central but quiet location, bargain priced and friendly French hosts.

Unity Park Motel   MOTEL $
(Map p511; 36052; www.unityparkmotel.com; Main St; s/d/tr/q 2200/3600/4500/6000, oceanview d 4000VT, with air-con 4500VT;) Facing the park of the same name, Unity is a friendly and reliable budget hotel. Upstairs are large airy rooms along a hallway (ask for a front one with shared balcony). Downstairs is more basic but clean and cheap. The shared kitchen and bathroom facilities are great.

Aqua Backpackers   HOSTEL $
(Map p511; 5554469; www.aquabackpackers.com; dm 2500-3000VT, d 5000VT;) This old-school backpackers has eight- and four-bed dorms and a small double in a loftlike space. Run by Mama Lou, it's built for

---

SANTO'S SUNKEN RICHES

Segond Channel was the Allies' base during WWII. For three years to September 1945, more than half a million military personnel, mainly Americans, were stationed here waiting to head into battle in the Pacific. There were sometimes 100 ships moored off Luganville. More than 10,000 ni-Van came to work for the troops. To them, the servicemen seemed fabulously wealthy and generous.

Unfortunately, **SS President Coolidge**, a luxury liner turned troopship, hit a friendly mine just offshore, where it sank with the loss of just one life. It's since become the world's largest accessible and diveable shipwreck. After the war, the USA offered the Condominium (p521) government the surplus equipment but the government didn't respond, so the lot was dumped. Everything from bulldozers, aeroplane engines and jeeps to crates of Coca-Cola went into the sea at what is now **Million Dollar Point**. The coral-encrusted equipment makes the point a popular diving and snorkelling spot.

Luganville

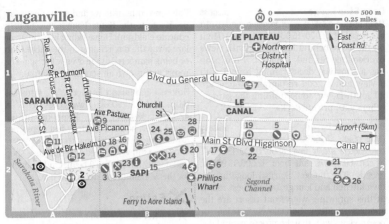

Luganville

⊙ Sights
1 Luganville Market	A2
Quonset Huts at Main Wharf	(see 27)
2 Steel Sea Walls	A2

⊙ Activities, Courses & Tours
3 Allan Power Dive Tours	B2
Aquamarine	(see 8)
4 Quadman Vanuatu	B2
5 Santo Island Dive & Fishing	C2
Wrecks to Rainforest	(see 8)

⊙ Sleeping
6 Aqua Backpackers	C2
7 Deco Stop Lodge	C1
8 Espiritu	B2
9 Hibiscus Le Motel	A2
10 Hotel Santo	B2
11 Tropicana Motel & Backpackers	A2
12 Unity Park Motel	A2

⊗ Eating
13 Attar Cafe	B2
Deco Stop Restaurant	(see 7)
14 Friends Cafe	B2
Market Meal Booths	(see 1)

⊙ Eating (cont.)
15 Natangora Café	B2
Tu Restaurant	(see 8)

⊙ Drinking & Nightlife
16 Club de Sanma	B2
17 Seaside Kava Bar	C2

⊙ Shopping
18 LCM	B2
19 Mama Handicrafts	C2

⊙ Information
20 ANZ Bank	B2
21 Customs & Quarantine	D2
22 Immigration Office	C2
23 Sanma Information & Call Centre	B2
24 Westpac Bank	B2

⊙ Transport
25 Air Vanuatu Town Office	B2
26 Big Sista	D2
Deco Stop	(see 7)
Espiritu Car Hire	(see 8)
27 Main Wharf	D2
28 Unity Pacific Garage	B2

travellers who like a good time, with a popular expat bar, pool table, live music on Fridays and a deck over the water.

Tropicana Motel & Backpackers   MOTEL **$**
(Map p511; ☑ 5372527, 36036; Cook St; dm/s/d 2000/3500/4500VT; ☎) Clean, modern rooms with en-suite bathrooms surround a courtyard garden (which acts like an echo chamber if it's busy). The industrial-sized communal kitchen is the best in Vanuatu and the dorms are only two-person bunk rooms.

★ Espiritu   HOTEL **$$**
(Map p511; ☑ 37539; www.the-espiritu.com; Main St; d 12,000-16,000VT; ☀☎☒) The Espiritu has transformed into an elegant boutique hotel and central Luganville's best midranger. First-floor rooms come with lounge, flat-screen TV and air-con, while the deluxe balcony rooms have king-sized beds and street views. There's a swanky pool and bar area at the back.

Deco Stop Lodge
LODGE $$

(Map p511; ☑36175; www.decostop.com.vu; d/f incl breakfast 12,000/16,000VT; ☀❄☲) High on the ridge behind Luganville, with views overlooking Segond Channel, Deco Stop has a convivial deck framing a pool with a view and a good restaurant. Rooms are all south-facing, some fronting the garden, others with private decks.

Beachfront Resort
LODGE $$

(Map p514; ☑36881; www.thebeachfrontresort. com; lodge s/d/tr from 8500/11,100/13,600VT; air-con bungalows s/d from 12,600/15,900VT; ☀❄☲) The 'budget' Starfish lodge has its own kitchen and lounge, but the best rooms at this sprawling waterfront resort are the spotless modern bungalows (garden or ocean view) with thatched roofs, verandahs, air-con and kitchenettes. There's a cool poolside area and restaurant. Cruising yachts often anchor out front.

Village de Santo
APARTMENT $$

(Map p514; ☑5623825, 36123; www.villagede santoresort.com; d incl breakfast 13,500VT; ❄☲) The 18 swish, traditionally designed, self-contained family units orbit a pool and lush gardens. It's close to the waterfront, the recommended Restaurant 1606 is on-site and it's walking distance (1.5km) to town. There's a Kids Club during school holidays.

Hotel Santo
HOTEL $$

(Map p511; ☑36250; s/d 8200/9300VT, upstairs s/d/tr 14,700/16,300/18,100VT; ☀❄☲) It's a bit of a time warp, but that's part of the appeal at this orange retro '70s hotel, with garden-facing units out the back and more elegant hotel-style rooms upstairs. Traditional touches include the fabulous *tamtam* in the foyer and the large *nakamal* in the back garden.

★ Aore Island Resort
RESORT $$$

(Map p514; ☑36705; http://aoreislandresorts. com; bungalow incl breakfast from 20,000VT; ❄☲) Spacious, well-designed bungalows (some in a child-free area, others for families), grassy slopes to the water, snorkel gear and kayaks: all are good, and the restaurant is a grand area (nonguests welcome). The ferry leaves from Phillips Wharf; ask for the schedule when you book. There's a dive shop and day spa.

★ Ratua Private Island Resort
RESORT $$$

(Map p514; ☑30020; www.ratua.com; Ratua; safari tents from 37,000VT, villas from 41,000VT; ☀@☲) This private island resort some 30 minutes' speedboat ride from Santo has

Bali-sourced bungalows and an eco bent (all profits go to the Ratua Foundation, to help educate children). Horse riding is popular, or laze away the day reading in the Yacht Club or being pampered at the over-water spa. The resort has its own air service (Air Ratua).

Bokissa Eco Island Resort
RESORT $$$

(Map p514; ☑30030; www.bokissa.com; d 42,000VT; ☀@☲) This luxurious private island resort boasts bungalows just steps from astounding reef snorkelling. It's a real getaway with everything you need: day spa, dive shop and quality dining. You'll be met in Luganville for the 25-minute speedboat ride here.

✕ Eating

★ Market Meal Booths
MARKET $

(Map p511; meals 400VT; ☉7.30am-10pm) The best budget dining in Santo. Choose one of the bright little tables next to the orange booths and a cheery woman will appear at the window with a glass of cordial, ready to take your order. Choose from chicken, fish or steak, piled with rice and vegetables, and watch it being cooked through the window.

★ Natangora Café
CAFE, JAPANESE $

(Map p511; ☑36811; Main St; meals 650-1500VT; ☉7.30am-4.30pm Mon-Fri, 8am-1.30pm Sat; ❄♿) This breezy open-air cafe (with a distant view of the water) specialises in breakfast, house-roasted coffee, hamburgers, juices and salads, but also does an interesting line in Japanese dishes: sushi, bento boxes, miso soup and Japanese curries.

Friends Cafe
CAFE $

(Map p511; Main St; meals 300-1300VT; ☉7.30am-4pm; ❄) A friendly little Euro-style cafe with excellent local Aore island coffee, homemade pies, burgers and sandwiches. Great spot for breakfast.

Attar Cafe
CAFE $

(Map p511; ☑37373; Main St; mains 500-1700VT; ☉7am-5pm; ❄) Excellent coffee, monster burgers, souvlaki and steaks – Attar does simple food with a smile.

Tu Restaurant
INTERNATIONAL $$

(Map p511; ☑37539; Main St; pizzas 1800VT, mains 2000-2500VT; ☉8am-8pm) At the Espiritu hotel, this elegant street-front restaurant serves a well-prepared local and global range of dishes from Santo scotch fillet to Thai green curry as well as all-day pizzas. Lunch features burgers and fish and chips. At the back is a stylish poolside lounge bar.

Restaurant 1606   INTERNATIONAL $$

(Map p514; Red Corner, Village de Santo; mains 1100-3400VT; ⊘7.30am-10pm) Regarded by some as Luganville's best restaurant, 1606 is worth a trip for its interesting selection of tapas (700VT to 1300VT), and mains such as seafood paella and crispy pork belly. Lunch offers the usual array of burgers and sandwiches.

Deco Stop Restaurant   INTERNATIONAL $$

(Map p511; ☑36175; Hospital Rd; mains 2200-2400VT; ⊘7am-3pm & 6-9pm) It's worth a trip up to the hilltop for the view alone, out to Segond Channel and Aore island. Dining is beside the pool with white wicker chairs on the terrace. The small but changing menu features fresh produce such as Santo scotch fillet, Thai curry, local lobster and pan-fried *poulet*. Full bar and friendly service.

Drinking & Nightlife

Luganville might be Vanuatu's second town, but it makes Vila look like Vegas. The Espiritu hotel has a very inviting poolside bar, as does Deco Stop Lodge, and there's weekly live music at Village de Santo. Kava bars are open from 5pm to 10pm – look out for a red or green light.

Seaside Kava Bar   KAVA BAR

(Map p511; Main St; cups from 50VT; ⊘from 5pm) This entertaining place has an unbeatable location with log benches right on the waterfront and other communal areas scattered around. Food is available and beer is only 300VT.

Club de Sanma   CLUB

(Map p511; ☑36039; Main St; ⊘10am-midnight Sun-Thu, to 3am Fri & Sat) Part nightclub, part sports bar and (upstairs) pokies joint, this is central Luganville's most happening nightspot. Occasional jazz and blues music on weekends.

Shopping

LCM   SHOPPING CENTRE

(Map p511; Main St; ⊘7.30am-5pm Mon-Sat) This modern shopping centre stocks a full supermarket range of groceries and liquor, as well as a surprisingly good line in fishing, camping and snorkelling gear. There's a useful noticeboard out front and credit cards are accepted.

Mama Handicrafts   SOUVENIRS

(Map p511; Main St; ⊘7.30am-5pm Mon-Sat) At the east end of town, this small shop is the best place to browse for locally made clothing, jewellery, carvings and woven bags.

ℹ Information

Luganville's main street has commercial banking facilities with ANZ and Westpac ATMs.

ANZ Bank (Map p511; ☑36711; ⊘8am-3pm Mon-Fri) Has an ATM.

Northern District Hospital (Map p511; ☑36345; ⊘24hr) Above the town in Le Plateau; usually hosts 'baby docs' (international doctors-in-training). Also has a good pharmacy.

Police (Map p511; ☑36222) Local police station.

Post Office (Map p511; Main St; ⊘8.30am-5pm Mon-Fri) Luganville's main post office.

Sanma Information & Call Centre (Map p511; ☑36616; www.santo.travel; Main St; ⊘7.30am-5pm Mon-Fri, plus weekends on cruise-ship days) Part tourist office, part private travel agency, Sanma (Santo and Malo) has helpful staff who can make local bookings.

Westpac Bank (Map p511; ☑36625; ⊘8am-4pm Mon-Fri) Has an ATM.

The East Coast Road

Santo's East Coast Rd between Luganville and Port Olry is only the second sealed road in Vanuatu (completed around the same time as the Efate Ring Rd in 2011), so it's an ideal region for a day trip. But with some excellent places to stay, play and dine, it's worth setting aside a few days.

◉ Sights & Activities

Loru Conservation Area   NATURE RESERVE

(Map p508; ☑5461731; guided tour per person 1000VT) Covering 220 hectares, Loru Conservation Area contains one of the last patches of lowland forest remaining on Santo's east coast. There are several excellent nature walks, many coconut crabs and a bat cave, which the villagers use as a cyclone shelter. Turn at the signpost off the East Coast Rd down a dirt road for 4km to Kole 1 Village. If you've come without a guide, ask for Kal. The guided walk takes about half an hour.

Lonnoc Beach   BEACH

In a beautiful coastal setting just off the East Coast Rd, this beach is all white sand and turquoise water, with views of Elephant Island. Drop into Lonnoc Beach Bungalows – day visitors can use the beach for free – and ask about kayak tours.

Around Luganville & Aore Island

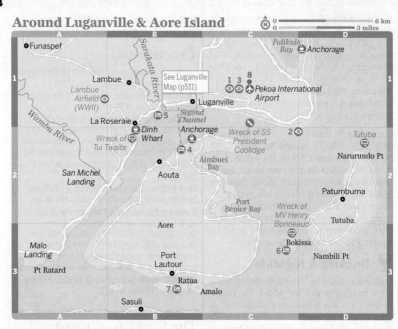

Around Luganville & Aore Island

Champagne Beach   BEACH

(per car 2000VT, or per person 500VT) Champagne Beach is a pretty horseshoe of soft white sand and turquoise water that gets rave (slightly overhyped) reviews and regular cruise-ship visitors. If you're driving, park the vehicle well back from the beach to avoid the extra charge. An impromptu souvenir market sets up when cruise ships are in.

★ **Port Olry**   VILLAGE

(Map p508) At the end of the sealed road you come to Port Olry, a small francophone fishing village with a stunning curve of white-sand beach and eye-watering shallow turquoise waters. Three offshore islands, which can be reached by kayak (500VT) or outrigger canoe (1000VT), have good reef snorkelling. There are a couple of good shack restaurants and bungalow operations here, making it a great place to chill out for a few days.

Secret Home Tour   ECOTOUR

(Map p508; ☑ 5685933, 5638219; East Coast Rd; per person 500VT) Drop in here, just before Port Olry, and local villagers will take you on this 30-minute garden and coastal walk, visiting caves, crab farms and a village garden, watching kava preparation and more.

Blue Holes

From south to north, stop at Riri Riri Blue Hole (Map p508; 500VT), where you can take an outrigger canoe up the river from the main road; pretty, jungle-clad Matevulu Blue Hole (Map p508; 500VT); or lovely Nanda Blue Hole (Map p508; 500VT).

OYSTER ISLAND

This small, forested island, less than 200m across from Santo's mainland, is home to a marine reserve and the excellent Oyster Island Restaurant & Resort. Take the signposted turn-off and summon the resort boat by banging on the gas cylinder – it operates on demand and nonguests are more than welcome.

The romantic **Oyster Island Restaurant & Resort** (Map p508; ☑ 36283; www.oyster-island.com; d units 12,500VT, d bungalows 21,000-23,000VT, family villas 30,000VT; ☎) consists of a scattering of individual traditional-style bungalows (the best are on the waterfront) and supremely comfortable units. With only 32 beds, there's a feel of exclusivity but also a welcoming, down-to-earth family vibe. A host of tours are offered, including the exclusive Mt Hope Waterfall tour (5000VT).

Much of the produce used in the **restaurant** (☑ 7782773; mains 1500-3000VT; ⊙ 7am-10pm) is sourced locally on the island – including the oysters. Call to order at least a few hours in advance for fresh oysters (1200VT for half a dozen). The Sunday lunch buffet (adult/child 2400/1200VT) is a legendary extravaganza.

🛏 Sleeping & Eating

★Port Olry Beach Bungalows & Restaurant　BUNGALOW $

(Map p508; ☑ 5990320; portolrybeachbun galow@gmail.com; s/d/f incl breakfast 4000/6000/7000VT) The three beautifully designed traditional bungalows here are a cut above most island huts, with solid timber decks and flooring, open-sky en suite and carved furniture. The beachfront restaurant and bar is also top-notch.

Reef Resort Backpackers　HOSTEL $

(Map p508; ☑ 7737627, 37627; www.reefresort santo.com.vu; East Coast Rd; dm/d/f 2500/7000/10,000VT) At pretty Turtle Bay, this waterfront garden backpackers is run by Honey. Rooms range from six-bed dorms or basic rooms in the main house to spacious family rooms with en suite, fridge, TV and private balcony. Kayaks, canoes, self-catering kitchen and a restaurant. Excellent value.

Lonnoc Beach Bungalows　BUNGALOW $

(Map p508; ☑ 5695140, 5906863; www.lon nocbeachbungalows.net; dm/s/d/f incl breakfast 2500/4500/6000/12,500VT) Fronting the captivating Lonnoc Beach, this well-organised budget resort has a dormitory lodge and a range of traditional stone and thatch bungalows with en suite. Free kayaks, generator power in the evenings and an excellent central restaurant make this a good deal.

Towoc Restaurant & Bungalows　BUNGALOW $

(Map p508; ☑ 5636173; towoc.bungalows@hot mail.com; s/d incl breakfast 2500/5000VT, beach-front 3500/7000VT) These simple bungalows are scattered around a garden setting on pretty Towoc Beach, a few minutes' walk to Champagne Beach (free access to guests). Solar lighting but evening generator in the friendly restaurant.

Bay of Illusions Guest House　BUNGALOW $

(Map p508; ☑ 5612525; d incl breakfast 2500VT) If you're heading inland to Big Bay or Vatthe Conservation Area, Bay of Illusions is the place to stay, with a two-room bungalow near a black-sand beach at Matantas. Meals available. Bookings and transport can also be arranged through Wrecks to Rainforest (p510) in Luganville.

Turtle Bay Lodge　LODGE $$

(Map p508; ☑ 37988; www.turtlebaylodge. vu; dm/d/f incl breakfast 3500/7600/12,600VT; ☑☎☒) With its private bit of beach, spacious units and welcoming restaurant-bar, Turtle Bay Lodge has an upmarket family feel with a reasonable price tag. Use the kayaks, rent the lodge car for a day or enjoy the serenity of Turtle Bay.

★Lope Lope Adventure Lodge　LODGE $$$

(Map p508; ☑ 36066; www.lopelopelodge.com; d fan/air-con 38,500/41,000VT; ☑☎) The four luxurious, romantic bungalows here are very private and have absolute water frontage with verandahs overlooking a perfect patch of sand. Boutique-styled accommodation with elevated king-sized beds facing the water, open-sky bathrooms, wi-fi, iPod, minibar and safe. The **Slipway Sports Bar & Grill** (mains 1450-3350VT; ☎) here is one of the best places to eat in Santo.

Sunrise Beach Cabanas Eco Resort   CABAÑAS $$$
(Map p508; ☑ 7799927, 36060; www.sunrise
beachcabanas.com; Barrier Beach; d 18,500-
29,300VT; P 🛜) The superb architect-
designed polygonal cabanas here provide a
romantic couples retreat on a private beach.
Thoughtful touches include boutique toilet-
ries, imported furniture, loaded iPod and
intercom for ordering meals. The welcoming
owners are building some cheaper guest-
house rooms, but it's strictly no kids.

Moyyan House by the Sea   GUESTHOUSE $$$
(Map p508; ☑ 30026; www.moyyan.com; d incl
breakfast 26,000-29,000VT; P 🛜) There's an
air of an old-fashioned planter's cottage
at exclusive little Moyyan, with a small
private beachfront on Barrier Beach, lush
gardens and an inviting communal deck.
Rooms are breezy but simple, focusing on
the guest experience, with privacy, free tablets, minibar and a reputable day spa.

Little Paradise Restaurant   SEAFOOD $$
(Map p508; ☑ 5483534; Port Olry; mains 1650-
2500VT) The original shack restaurant in Port
Olry (also called Harbour Beach Restaurant).
You might find local lobster and coconut
crab on the menu or ask about cheaper local
dishes. Service can be slow. There are a few
bungalows at the back (2500VT per person).

Velit Bay Plantation & 15° South   SEAFOOD $$
(Map p508; ☑ 5619687; www.velitbayplantation.
com; East Coast Rd; mains 1500-3000VT; ⊙ 7am-
4pm Mon-Fri, 9am-4pm Sat, 11.30am-4pm Sun; P)
The winding 2km drive down the rocky road
to spectacular Velit Bay is a visual sensation,
while the small, open-sided 15° South does
much to tempt the taste buds. Chill on the
private beach, where there are deckchairs
and a bunch of activities – kayaking, kitesurfing, snorkelling and beach volleyball –
or indulge in fresh seafood or pasta.

❶ Getting There & Away

There's a daily minibus service along the east
coast. Join the waiting crowd at Unity Pacific
Petrol Station in Luganville for the trip to Port
Olry (500VT) from around 2pm (check times in
advance). Taxis cost about 2000VT to Oyster
Island, 5000VT to Lonnoc Beach. To charter a
truck from Luganville to Matantas on Big Bay
costs around 8000VT one way. A cheaper option
is to take the local bus from Luganville, get off at
Sara village and organise a truck from there to
Matantas (around 2500VT; Monday to Friday).

PENTECOST, AMBAE & MAEWO

Pentecost

POP 16,800 / AREA 438 SQ KM

Pentecost is famously home to the *naghol*
(land diving), the most remarkable custom in
all of Melanesia, where men make spectacular leaps of courage from high towers as a gift
to the gods to ensure a bountiful yam harvest.

Pentecost is a long, thin island with a rugged interior, where truck travel can be pain-
fully slow. Most of the population lives along
the west coast, which has a high rainfall, attributed to local rainmakers. A rocky beach
extends 12km from just before Lonorore
airfield south to Ranputor. The south is the
home of the *naghol* (April to June). Pangi is
the largest village in the south but it's pretty
basic, with just a kava bar, clinic, a couple of
guesthouses and the NBV bank, which can
change foreign currency in an emergency.

◉ Sights & Activities

Apart from the land diving, you can take
jungle walks to waterfalls and banyans and
the stone ruins of a feasting hall, where 100
people were killed by the eel spirit. Other
tours include visits to villages to see *kastom*
dances. North of the airstrip is **Waterfall
Falls** (Map p518), tumbling down behind
Waterfall Village into pretty rockpools.

★ **Land Diving**   CULTURAL TOUR
(⊙ Apr-Jun) Land-dive towers are erected
at **Lonorore Airfield, Londot, Pangi** and
Rangusuksu (Map p518), though exact sites
change and are announced annually). **Luke
Fargo** (☑ 7734621; Mari Bungalows) arranges
official tours to the land diving (adult/child
12,000/6000VT). Most tourists come on
day packages (per person including flights
50,000VT) with Port Vila tour companies.

🛏 Sleeping & Eating

★ **Noda Guesthouse**   BUNGALOW $
(Map p518; ☑ 5473071, 7727394; www.pentecost
island.net/noda; Waterfall Village; per person incl
meals 3200VT) A great place to base yourself
in Waterfall Village (Vanu). The well-kept
house has six bedrooms and there are three
double-bed huts with shared bathroom. Silas is a great host who can organise tours to
kastom villages (7000VT), a nearby waterfall (800VT) and land diving (12,000VT),

and jungle treks (600VT). There's generator power in the evenings.

Mari Bungalows BUNGALOW $
(Map p518; ☑ 535514, 773462; Londot; s/d incl breakfast 3000/4000VT) These traditional thatched bungalows are set into the hills beside a land-dive site and opposite Londot beach. Luke Fargo operates land-diving tours from here. It's self-catering or 600VT per meal.

River Lodge GUESTHOUSE $
(Map p518; ☑ 5348846, 7723374; Baravet; d incl breakfast 3000VT) Set in a palm grove opposite a rocky beach a short drive north of the airstrip, this simple guesthouse has four rooms. Jonas arranges land diving, snorkelling, and waterfall and cave tours.

Nak Bungalow BUNGALOW $
(Map p518; ☑ 3573761; Pangi; per person without bathroom incl meals 3500VT) There are 12 beds in this basic guesthouse in the heart of Pangi village. The simple rooms are dressed with colourful sarongs and the shared bathrooms have bucket showers and flush toilets.

Panliki Bungalows BUNGALOW $
(Map p518; ☑ 5434412; Ranputur; per person incl meals 2500VT) In Ranputur village, Joseph runs the five simple beachfront rooms here. There's solar lighting and a friendly atmosphere.

❶ Getting There & Away

AIR
Lonorore airfield is the main point of entry for Pentecost. **Air Vanuatu** (☑ 23748) flies here from Port Vila and Santo at least twice a week. Transport from Lonorore airfield to Pangi by truck or boat is 4000VT. In the far north, Sara airfield is really only useful if you're taking the boat across to Maewo island.

BOAT
Pentecost has good protection from the south-eastern trade winds along the west coast, with many anchorages and landing places. Panas and Loltong are popular. In good conditions it's possible to arrive by speedboat from Ambae, Ambrym and Maewo.

Ambae

Ambae formed as part of a dramatic semi-active shield volcano, **Mt Lombenben** (1496m), which rumbles dynamically. A cone rose out of blue **Lake Manaro Lakua**, one of its famous crater lakes, in 2005, creating world news, then went back down. Hot and lime-green **Lake Vui** also sends volcanologists into a frenzy whenever it boils. Lake

---

THE LAND DIVERS OF PENTECOST

The men of Pentecost spend many weeks building towers up to 35m high by binding tree trunks, saplings and branches to a tall tree with vines. The tower sighs as it bends in the wind; you'll sigh, as you see the men make their spectacular leaps to ensure a successful harvest.

Each diver carefully selects his own liana vines, then an experienced elder checks to ensure that they're strong and elastic enough. The soil in front of the tower is cleared of rocks, then loosened. Fathers teach their young sons to dive from their shoulders. Boys practise diving from boulders into the sea. At age eight they are circumcised; then they can make their first jump.

Between 10 and 20 males per village will dive. Each man prepares in turn while his friends tie his vines. The women sing and dance below. As each man raises his hands he tells the crowd his most intimate thoughts; the people stop their singing and dancing, and stand quietly – these could be his last words.

Finally the diver claps his hands, crosses his arms and leans forward. In slow motion, falling, he arches his back. The platform breaks away. Snap. The vines abruptly stop him. Only his hair will touch the soil, to fertilise the yam crop. The crowd roars its appreciation, dancing, stomping and whistling in tribute.

The colour and sounds add to the atmosphere: men wearing small red-dyed *namba* (penis sheaths), clearly visible from so high above; women wearing white grass skirts made from wild hibiscus, spinning and twirling. It's a huge drawcard for tourists (even cruise ships pull in to Pangi), and has (controversially) morphed from an event that happened each Saturday for a month, to one that occurs more frequently from April to June. Commercial filming of the event is banned.

Pentecost

Manaro Ngoru, the third crater lake, is mostly dry with a central cold-water spring.

Guides and entry fees to the lakes cost 1000VT each, transfers 5000VT and meals 1000VT.

ⓘ Getting There & Away

Air Vanuatu flies to Longana from Santo three or four times a week and to Walaha at least once a week.

🛏 Sleeping & Eating

★**Tui Lodge**　　　　　　　GUESTHOUSE $
(Map p520; ☑ 5379267; bookattuilodge@gmail. com; Saratamata; per person incl meals 3000VT) This bright, modern six-room guesthouse is at Saratamata, not far from Longana airport. There's a guest kitchen, a restaurant and hot water, and the hosts can organise treks to Lake Vui and Lake Manaro Lakua. A truck from the airport costs 1000VT.

Duviara Last Stop Bungalows　BUNGALOW $
(Map p520; ☑ 5949740; Ambanga; per person 1500VT) Duviara Last Stop Bungalows is the closest place to the start of the treks to Lake Vui and Lake Manaro Lakua. Owner Paul can organise a guide (2000VT).

Toa Palms Bungalow　　　BUNGALOW $
(Map p520; ☑ 5637232, 7710800; Ndui Ndui; per person 1500VT) The best bet for exploring west Ambae is Toa Palms, with three comfortable en-suite bungalows. The owners can help organise a trek to the crater lakes.

Maewo

The 'Island of Water' has rivers, hot springs, deep cold pools and magnificent waterfalls. **Big Water waterfall**, in the north, is thought of locally as the Eighth Wonder of the World.

Down south, at Sanasom, is magnificent Hole of the Moon Cave (Maewo; 1500VT) and Malangauliuli, a cave with spectacular petroglyphs. Chief Jonah is *kastom* owner of the caves. Justin Ihu (☑7742605) can get you to them on his boat (7000VT).

Near Asanvari are the Lavoa Cascades, where you can swim or see a cultural show.

❶ Getting There & Away

Maewo's airstrip is located in the north, a few kilometres from Naone village. Air Vanuatu flies there once a week from Santo via Ambae. Another option is to fly into Ambae or Pentecost and take a speedboat (10,000VT) across to Asanvari in the south.

🛏 Sleeping & Eating

Mule Ocean View Guesthouse BUNGALOW $
(☑7742605; Asanvari; r per person incl breakfast 1700VT) Justin and Ericka run this simple but cosy guesthouse with two double bungalows near the fading Yacht Club in Asanvari. There's a restaurant as well as a kitchen for self-caterers, and fresh vegetables from the garden. Justin also has a boat.

**Sparkling Waters
Bar & Restaurant** SEAFOOD $$
(☑5442135; Asanvari; ⊗8am-8pm) Enjoy a cold beer on the verandah of this bar at Lavoa Cascades, or find out what's on the menu – seafood is the speciality.

BANKS & TORRES ISLANDS

These remote northerly groups of islands are popular with touring yachties and are accessible by Air Vanuatu, which flies from Santo to Gaua, Torres, Motalava and Vanua Lava in a loop two or three times a week.

Gaua (Santa Maria)

Gaua offers spectacular hikes, including a two-day test around the island's three major sights: pretty Lake Letas, one of the largest freshwater lakes in the Pacific; Mt Garet (797m), a semiactive volcano; and fabulous Siri Waterfall. Climb up to the lake (camp overnight) and canoe across to the volcano – a sulphurous mess that seeps orange into the lake. Then it's a vicious trek down to the falls, 120m of roaring power pummelling to the sea.

🛏 Sleeping

Wongrass Bungalow BUNGALOW $
(☑5690831, 7712879; per person incl meals 3500VT) The thatched two-bedroom Wongrass, near the airport, was the first in Gaua and is still going strong. Charles can arrange tours to the crater lake (3500VT).

Vanua Lava

The largest of the Banks islands, Vanua Lava offers waterfalls and excellent trekking. Sola, the island's capital, is the base for walks, such as the glorious day's hike (1000VT) via Mosina across the plateau overlooking Vureas Bay, through water-taro gardens, over streams and rapids to Waterfall Bay, where spectacular Sasara Falls tumbles over the cliff into the bay.

🛏 Sleeping

Leumerous Guesthouse GUESTHOUSE $
(☑7733426, 5391846; Sola; camping 500VT, bungalows per person incl meals 2500VT) In Sola, stay at beachfront Leumerous Guesthouse where six thatched bungalows sit along a garden path.

Motalava & Rah

Motalava is a small island in the Banks group, famous for its snake dance and treks to Sleeping Mountain (243m). A short canoe ride off the southwestern tip is stunning Rah island.

Air Vanuatu flies to Motalava from Santo once or twice a week. Wrecks to Rainforest (p510) in Santo can organise tours.

🛏 Sleeping

Rah Paradise Beach Bungalows BUNGALOW $
(☑7745650, 5945757; per person incl meals 4000VT) On a beautiful beach on a tiny island just off Motalava, this guesthouse is run by Father Luke and his wife Rona, who work closely with the village. Organised activities include a snake dance, treks to Sleeping Mountain, a legend tour of the Rock of Rah and reef-island trips.

Torres Islands

These are the most remote islands of Vanuatu, with some dazzling white-sand or coral beaches and good surfing. There's excellent snorkelling on most islands: Linua, with the Kamilisa guesthouse and the airstrip; Loh,

Ambae

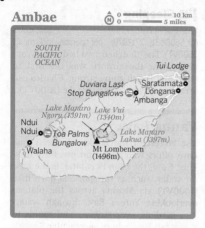

SOUTH PACIFIC OCEAN

Tui Lodge

Duviara Last Stop Bungalows — Saratamata — Longana — Ambanga

Lake Manaro Ngoru (1391m) Lake Vui (1340m)

Ndui Ndui — Toa Palms Bungalow

Lake Manaro Lakua (1397m)

Walaha — Mt Lombenben (1496m)

0 —— 10 km
0 —— 5 miles

across a tidal sandbank; Tegua and Hiu to the north (from where you can see the Solomon Islands on a clear day); and Toga, where most of the people live. Everyone gets around in outrigger canoes.

🛏 Sleeping

Kamilisa Memorial Resort GUESTHOUSE $
(☑ 7114506; Linua; per person incl meals 3000VT)
The delightful Kamilisa guesthouse has four bungalows in a delicate rainforest, right on the lagoon on Linua island. Phone coverage is patchy, but owner Whitely greets every flight.

UNDERSTAND VANUATU

Vanuatu Today

Vanuata is often called the 'Land of Smiles' – it was named the 'world's happiest place' in a 2006 Happy Planet Index – and when you see the beaming faces and hear the 'hallos' of the ni-Vanuatu (local people) it's hard not to agree. It has also been identified as one of the world's most dangerous places for natural disasters – cyclones, earthquakes, volcanic activity and drought.

Those smiles were tested when Cyclone Pam (p523) wrought havoc across the islands in March 2015, damaging or wiping out 90% of buildings (mostly village homes) along with vital crops and plantations.

Vanuatu's economy is largely agricultural – major exports include copra (dried coconut), beef, cocoa and kava – with some 80% of the population involved in farming and

fishing. Tourism is a vital source of income, though little filters through to the outer islands. Cruise ships provide two-thirds of annual visitors (most coming from Australia and New Zealand), who come ashore for a few hours to buy handicrafts or take adventure tours. Many young ni-Van leave their villages to work in the tourism and service industries in Efate and Espiritu Santo.

Corruption in Vanuatu politics is nothing new since independence, but a culture of backhanders and bribes was laid bare in October 2015 when 14 MPs, including Deputy Prime Minister Moana Carcasses, were found guilty of corruption and bribery and sent to prison for up to four years. Prime Minister Sato Kilman was not among those charged. Still, with half of his People's Progress Party in jail, governing became untenable and a snap election was called for 22 January 2016, resulting in a bloc of 36 newly elected MPs from 11 parties attempting to establish a new coalition government.

Foreign ownership remains a hot topic in Vanuatu. Foreigners are not permitted to buy land but they can lease it from traditional owners (up to 75 years for commercial property). Leasing land for fast cash has been tempting for many ni-Van owners, but with investors controlling some 90% of coastal land around Efate, tensions and disagreements often result.

History

In 2004 an archaeological dig at Teouma, near Port Vila, unearthed evidence of a Lapita culture dating back 3000 years. The site provided archaeologists with insights into the beliefs and rituals of these first people to settle, establish crops and keep domestic animals in Vanuatu. Lapita people are the ancestors of all Polynesian people, from Tahiti to Hawai'i to New Zealand. They had crossed the sea from the Solomon Islands.

Ancient Vanuatu

The people traditionally lived in clan-based villages, each with its own language because villages were separated by impassable mountains and rocky coastlines. Everyone lived in the shadow of their ancestors' spirits. Some spirits were benevolent, others hostile: famines, cyclones, enemy attack and other misfortunes could result if they became displeased. Magic was the main defence against angry spirits.

Interisland trade networks were established using large sailing canoes. Otherwise, villagers regarded their neighbours with deep suspicion. Skirmishes between villages were frequent, and usually the victor captured one or more male prisoners. It gave a chief great status to present a victim, ready for the pot, to chiefs of other villages. The victims' relatives would mount reprisals, so hostilities continued indefinitely.

Alongside this, the culture was steeped in agriculture. Yam cultivation decided the cycle of the year, with months named after yams.

European Explorers

The first recorded Europeans to visit Vanuatu, in May 1606, were on a Spanish expedition led by Pedro Fernández de Quirós, who was convinced that Santo was the fabled *terra australis incognita*. It was not until May 1768 that Louis-Antoine de Bougainville sailed between Malekula and Santo, proving that Vanuatu's largest island was not *terra australis*.

James Cook arrived on 16 July 1774, on his second Pacific expedition. He drew the first charts of the region, naming it New Hebrides, and naming other islands such as Tanna, Erromango, Ambrym and the Shepherd Islands.

In 1789, shortly after the famous mutiny on the *Bounty*, William Bligh sailed through the northern Banks group in his longboat. He sighted several previously unrecorded islands, and returned three years later to confirm his discoveries.

Missionaries & Traders

The first Christian missionary on the scene was the Reverend John Williams from the London Missionary Society (LMS). In 1839 he stepped ashore on Erromango, and was promptly eaten. After this inauspicious beginning, the church sent Polynesian teachers from Samoa, hoping they would be more acceptable. However, a number of them were also killed or died of malaria.

In 1848 the Reverend John Geddie arrived on Aneityum and made it the headquarters for the Vanuatu's Presbyterian mission, the major denomination on the southern islands. The Anglican Diocese of Melanesia followed in 1860 and became influential in the northern islands. Catholicism arrived in 1887.

Meanwhile, traders heard about the sandalwood trees on Erromango. There was great demand for the wood in China, where it was used for incense. Islanders traded tree trunks for guns, tobacco or men from enemy villages to be eaten at ceremonies. The best study of the turbulent times of the 19th-century sandalwood trade is Dorothy Shineberg's *They Came for Sandalwood* (1967).

Blackbirding developed as cheap labour was needed for the sugar-cane industries, coconut plantations and nickel mines of nearby countries. Blackbirders kidnapped shiploads of ni-Vanuatu but the missionaries stepped in, campaigning relentlessly until the practice was banned.

European Settlement

The first European settler was a cattle rancher who arrived in 1854, and other settlers arrived to set up cotton plantations. Intense rivalry existed between the French and English. Brawls were commonplace, as were clashes between settlers and ni-Vanuatu, who resented the loss of their land.

As elsewhere in the Pacific, the local inhabitants were decimated by European diseases. Some say Vanuatu's population was about one million in the early 19th century, but in 1935 only 41,000 ni-Vanuatu remained.

Condominium

With the Germans becoming influential in the region, the British and French governments established the Anglo–French Condominium of the New Hebrides, in an awkward moment of togetherness in 1906. Vanuatu would be ruled equally by the two colonial powers.

Cynics called the Condominium 'the Pandemonium', as the dual administration produced a bizarre duplication of authorities. Road rules epitomised the issue, as the English drove on the left, the French on the right. Anglo–French rivalry reached new levels of farce, as the height of each flag up each ministerial flagpole was measured every morning.

WWII

US forces arrived in Vanuatu in early 1942 and constructed bases, first at Havannah Harbour and Port Vila on Efate, then in southeastern Santo. With Japan's defeat in 1945, the US forces withdrew, leaving behind huge quantities of equipment. Some was sold, the remainder dumped into the sea near Luganville on Santo, creating Million Dollar Point.

Cargo cults appeared on several islands as ni-Van sought to secure the kind of wealth they'd seen in the camps – they believed that if they acted like Europeans, then 'cargo' would come their way.

VANUATU HISTORY

Independence

Land ownership had become Vanuatu's major political issue by the mid-1960s. It was the catalyst that spurred the country to seek independence.

At this time European settlers 'owned' about 30% of the country's land area. A movement based on *kastom* (custom; rules relating to traditional beliefs) called the Nagriamel sprang up under the leadership of the charismatic Jimmy Stevens. Operating from Santo, its aims were to protect ni-Vanuatu claims to their traditional land. By the late 1960s, Nagriamel had expanded to other islands in northern Vanuatu.

Another great leader, Father Walter Lini, formed the New Hebrides National Party in 1971. It was later called the Vanua'aku Party. His book *Beyond Pandemonium: from the New Hebrides to Vanuatu* (1980) tells of the lead-up to his country's independence.

The Condominium authorities agreed to hold the country's first general election in November 1979. The Vanua'aku Party was the clear winner. Independence was fixed for mid-1980.

Serious threats of secession were being made by the ni-Van on Santo and Tanna in early 1980; late in May matters came to a head. An insurrection on Tanna split that island between government supporters and rebels. On Santo, secessionists seized Luganville and hoisted the flag of the Independent Republic of Vemarana. Several other northern islands proclaimed their own secessions during June. They merged and announced the Provisional Government of the Northern Islands, under Jimmy Stevens.

Order was not restored until the new government brought in soldiers from Papua New Guinea following independence on 30 July, after which the secessionist ringleaders were arrested and the rebellion collapsed.

Post Independence

Since independence in 1980, the ni-Vanuatu government's desire has been for development that benefits everyone equally, while preserving customs and traditions. There were years with changing parties and leaders, much infighting and some high-profile scandals. As of 11 February 2016, Vanuatu's prime Minster is Charlot Salwai.

In 2005 Vanuatu qualified for the US Millennium Challenge (www.mcc.gov), a grant available to countries that show they will use it for sustainable economic growth. It was the only South Pacific country to be selected. The US$65 million was used to seal the Efate Ring Rd and the East Coast Rd on Santo.

Recent economic growth has been attributed to the services sector (including tourism) and the growth of aid programs. Other encouraging economic trends include: the 2 billion vatu earned annually by ni-Van workers under New Zealand's Recognised Seasonal Employer (RSE) scheme; the rising interest in copra; and the demand for Vanuatu beef, which consistently outstrips supply. Vanuatu joined the World Trade Organisation in October 2011. In 2015 work began on the US$93 million Luganville Wharf expansion project to be undertaken by China's Shanghai Construction Group.

Vanuatu's political problems resurfaced in late 2015 when 14 MPs, including the deputy prime minister, were found guilty of corruption and bribery and thrown into jail for between three and four years. A snap election, called by president Baldwin Lonsdale for January 2016, was contested by 265 candidates and resulted in an unwieldy coalition of 36 MPs from 11 different parties. This followed a period of national rebuilding and the involvement of international aid organisations in the wake of Cyclone Pam, which wiped out 90% of island homes.

The Culture

Vanuatu's culture and customs vary widely, yet there are common themes, particularly the obligation to pay for all services rendered and the finality of anything labelled *tabu,* which means 'sacred' as well as 'forbidden'. If a part of a traditional ceremony, a section of beach, a cave, anywhere at all, is *tabu,* it must be respected.

The National Psyche

Vanuatu's population is almost entirely ni-Vanuatu (Melanesian, although some islands have a strong Polynesian heritage), with most people living in rural areas, in villages of fewer than 50 people. There is a drift into towns, particularly Port Vila, by ni-Vanuatu in search of work.

Ownership of ancestral land, sea and reefs, and everything that comes from them, is fundamental to ni-Vanuatu life. It is held by ni-Van for the future, and the rhythm of the seasons dictates how those resources are used. They viewed with horror the European way of using the land; disputes over use and ownership are still serious issues. Always carry at least 1000VT with you as you never know when you'll have to pay a fee for swimming, fishing, or looking at or walking on a property. It is a matter of respect for the value of the resource and it is non-negotiable.

Everyone has a role to play in society. Each village is run by a chief (usually elected) who acts as a justice of the peace and village delegate. Their word is law. Even politicians must do what chiefs say when visiting their home villages.

In many areas, chiefs achieve their rank through *nimangki* (grade-taking) ceremonies, which include a lavish feast. Villagers who eat at the feast are then indebted to the chief, becoming a party of supporters who look to the chief for leadership and guidance. Each step up the village social ladder is accompanied by the ritual killing of pigs, so only men who have acquired enough pigs can hope to reach society's highest levels.

Lifestyle

The centre of village life is the *nakamal,* a men's clubhouse and clan meeting place, where men meet to discuss village and national issues. A traditional *nakamal* is always strictly *tabu* to women, and tourists may still be barred from entering in *kastom*-oriented areas. Women, too, have a meeting house, where they produce goods for sale.

Women spend many hours in the family garden and watching over the husband's pigs, while men tend their cash crops, fish, hunt, build boats, carve artefacts and discuss village matters. While the women prepare the evening meal, the men talk in the *nakamal* and drink kava.

There are strict rules in every village regarding dress. Islanders do not wear revealing clothing, and women's thighs are always covered. The village church is often the focal point on Sundays, when few people work.

Overall, the most pressing problem for ni-Van families is finding the money to pay their children's school fees each quarter.

Arts

Vanuatu's art and traditions vary from island to island, a diversity that contributes to the country's unique cultural identity.

The most common subject matters in ni-Vanuatu arts are the human form and traditional interpretations of what ancestral figures looked like. The most important artefacts are made for *nimangki*.

Carvings

While wood is the main carved material, objects are also made from tree fern, stone and coral. Serious carving is almost entirely created for ceremonies, while items for sale to tourists are usually small copies of the real thing.

Dances & Ceremonies

Traditional dances in Vanuatu require constant rehearsals. The timing is exquisite and the movements regimented; everyone turns, leaps and stomps together. Thus harmony and cooperation develop between people and villages. There are two major styles of dance: impersonation and participation.

CYCLONE PAM

Tropical Cyclone Pam hit Vanuatu in the early hours of 13 March 2015. Though many cyclones have threatened Vanuatu in the past, this Category 5 monster was always going to prove destructive. By the time it had petered out into the Pacific, Pam had become one of the worst natural disasters in Vanuatu's history.

Hardest hit were the southern provinces of Shefa (including the main island, Efate) and Tafea (including Tanna and Erromango). An estimated 90% of village homes were flattened, telecommunications knocked out, and important food crops and plantations decimated by sustained winds of up to 250km/h. Considering the destruction, loss of life was relatively low at an estimated 11 to 15 people.

In the following months, government and international aid organisations quickly set up temporary shelters, including tents for school classrooms, and delivered much-needed food, water and building materials.

Although islanders have largely rebuilt their homes and *nakamal* (men's clubhouses), the economic impact of the cyclone may not yet be known. Replacing valuable crops, water sources and agricultural land is the biggest challenge for many; encouraging tourists back to Vanuatu is another challenge.

Impersonation dances require more rehearsal, as each dancer pretends to be an ancestor or legendary figure and wears an elaborate mask or headdress, such as in the Rom dances of Ambrym.

Music

String bands developed during WWII, when ni-Van heard the US soldiers playing bluegrass. The singing is done with a pinched throat, forming a high-pitched lyrical note. Most local music tends to be a blend of reggae, country and rock, with an off beat that is a typical Toka dance rhythm. If you're in town in November, don't miss the contemporary music festival Fest' Napuan (www.festnapuan.info).

Vanuatu's *tamtam* (slit drums) are logs with hollowed-out slits and carved human faces (up to five, one above the other) set above the drum part. *Tamtam* are the largest free-standing musical instruments in the world.

Painting & Sand Drawing

Petroglyphs and rock paintings are the country's most ancient forms of pictorial art. The former are common and widespread, although their meanings have been lost and their main significance these days is to archaeologists. Several islands have caves where the walls are decorated with hand stencils and simple paintings of animals.

Styles of painting include bark art and body painting, a part of traditional ceremonies. Ni-Van create beautiful sand drawings on beaches and sandy spots, making many delicate loops and circles without raising their fingers, to leave messages or illustrate local legends, songs or ceremonies. The most elaborate and picturesque versions are made in Ambrym.

Traditional Dress

It's less common now, but in *kastom*-oriented parts of Tanna and Pentecost, men wore *namba* (penis sheaths) every day, while women dressed in grass skirts. On Santo, the men wore *mal mal* (loincloths), while some women wore an apron of leaves. In southern Malekula, women of the Small Nambas people traditionally wore raffia skirts, woven from banana-tree fibres.

In other parts of Vanuatu, grass skirts are fashioned from the bark of the *burao* (wild hibiscus). Most ni-Van wear traditional dress only to attend ceremonies, when

elaborate headgear is also worn. Masks are usually made from tree-fern material and represent the faces of demons and ancestral spirits. Others are constructed out of clay reinforced with coconut fibres and layered onto a wickerwork frame. Painted tree-fern face masks in southern Malekula are decorated with feathers and carved pigs' tusks.

Weaving

Baskets and mats are made throughout the country, as are traps for fish, shellfish and birds. Weaving is done mostly by women, using pandanus leaves and *burao* stalks. Wicker, coconut leaves and rattan are used when a more robust item is required.

Environment

Vanuatu lies squarely on the Pacific Ring of Fire, so it experiences frequent earth tremors, and rises or subsides by up to 2cm per year in some areas. There are nine active volcanoes (seven on land), and fumaroles (volcanic steam vents) and thermal springs are found throughout the archipelago.

Animals

Cats, dogs, cattle, horses, pigs and goats are all introduced to Vanuatu and have since run wild. Rats are the bane of village life and do much damage to the copra industry.

Native land mammals are limited to four flying-fox species and eight other bat species. Marine life includes more than 300 species of coral and 450 species of reef fish. The largest mammal is the dugong, the world's only herbivorous marine mammal.

Of Vanuatu's 121 bird species, 55 can be found on Santo, including all seven of the country's endemic species. One interesting species is the mound-building, fowl-like megapode (*namalao* in Bislama), which uses the warm volcanic soils to incubate its eggs.

BONNE ANNÉE

All through January, to welcome the new year, villagers prepare flower-embedded posts and set out together to walk as far as they can, dancing along and stopping at each village they pass to sing songs and chant, 'Happy, Happy, Bonne Année'. Then they dust their listeners with talcum powder and set off to the next village.

There are 19 native lizards, all small skinks and geckos, and one land snake, the harmless Pacific boa, which grows to 2.5m. While the yellow-bellied and banded sea snakes are extremely venomous, their small mouths and teeth aren't suitable for savaging humans.

Plants

About 75% of Vanuatu is natural vegetation, including rainforest and rain-shadow grasslands. Cyclones tear at the jungle regularly, renewing it but also making a mess of crops and plantations. Logging and subsistence farming hacks into a bit of land, but much of the country is a botanical wonderland.

The lord of most forests is the banyan tree, whose crown can be 70m or more across. Forests of mighty kauri trees are found on Erromango, while cloud forests dripping with moss and moisture are a magnificent feature of highland areas.

Vanuatu has around 20 species of palm, of which 14 are endemic. Orchids festoon the trees in many areas; there are 158 orchid species. Less enchanting are the introduced weeds, such as lantana and the widespread 'mile-a-minute' vine.

Conservation Areas

There are four official conservation areas in Vanuatu: Vatthe and Loru on Santo, the kauri reserve on Erromango, and the cloudforest area around Lake Manaro on Ambae. Marine Protected Areas (MPAs) include Nguna-Pele off Efate, USS *Coolidge* and Million Dollar Point off Santo and Uri-Narong Marine Park off Malekula.

SURVIVAL GUIDE

🛈 Directory A–Z

ACCOMMODATION

In Efate and Santo, you'll find all sorts of accommodation, from boutique resorts to backpacker beds. On the outer islands, accommodation is almost exclusively in simple island bungalows, usually thatched rooms with pandanus-leaf walls. Budget for a minimum of 2500VT per person per night, which often includes meals. Showers and toilets are usually separate from the bungalows and vary in cleanliness and usefulness, while electricity is supplied by solar power backed by diesel generators. Travel with some food supplies, toilet paper and a torch. In remote islands you might find communication difficult (no

phone), or bungalows deserted or nonexistent. 'Just go' is the best motto in Vanuatu; you'll find somewhere to stay. Most places will let you camp (for a fee). Ask the local chief for permission if you want to pitch your tent somewhere other than at a bungalow property.

Comfortable resorts and hotels can be found on Efate and Santo, and there are also a few on Tanna. In Port Vila there are some very decent hotel rooms for less than 5000VT, while luxury resorts start at around 20,000VT per double.

EMBASSIES & CONSULATES

Australian High Commission (Map p481; ☑ 22777; www.vanuatu.embassy.gov.au; Winston Churchill Ave, Port Vila; ☺ 8am-4.30pm Mon-Fri) One of the more impressive new buildings in Port Vila.

French Embassy (Map p484; ☑ 28700; www. ambafrance-vu.org; Lini Hwy) Also has the Alliance Française.

New Zealand High Commission (Map p481; ☑ 22933; www.nzembassy.com/vanuatu; Teoma St) Consular facilities.

EMERGENCIES

Ambulance ☑ 112
Fire ☑ 113
Police ☑ 111

HEALTH

Malaria is prevalent on some outer islands so take precautions. Tap water is OK to drink in Port Vila and tank water is usually safe on outer islands, but water can be in short supply, so consider carrying bottled water.

INTERNET ACCESS

Internet cafes have largely been replaced by (mostly) free wi-fi, which you'll find in many hotels and cafes in main towns. A local phone SIM with a good data plan will give you a 3G connection on most islands.

MONEY

The currency is the vatu (VT), which comes in notes of 100VT, 500VT, 1000VT, 2000VT and 5000VT, and coins of 5VT, 10VT, 20VT, 50VT and 100VT. A new series of coins (in the same denominations) was minted in 2015.

VANUATU DIRECTORY A–Z

You'll find ANZ, Westpac and Bred (Banque Populaire) ATMs in Port Vila and Luganville only.

Take plenty of vatu everywhere outside Port Vila and Luganville. You can change Australian and US dollars, and usually euros, at NBV banks in Lakatoro (Malekula), Lenakel (Tanna), Pangi (Pentecost), Craig Cove (Ambrym) and other main villages, but hours are limited, cash stocks may be low and they're always busy. Resorts, hotels, car rental companies and airlines routinely charge a 5% surcharge on credit cards.

OPENING HOURS

Government offices 7.30am to 11.30am and 1.30pm to 4.30pm Monday to Friday; sometimes Saturday morning.

Shops 7.30am to 6pm Monday to Friday (some close for lunch); to 11.30am Saturday. Chinese-run general stores open all weekend.

PUBLIC HOLIDAYS

New Year's Day 1 January
Lini Day 21 February
Custom Chiefs' Day 5 March
Good Friday, Easter Monday March/April
Labour Day 1 May
Ascension Day 17 May
Children's Day 24 July
Independence Day 30 July
Assumption Day 15 August
Constitution Day 5 October
Unity Day 29 November
Christmas Day 25 December
Family Day 26 December

TELEPHONE

Most of Vanuatu is covered by two mobile phone networks: the red Digicel (www.digicelvanuatu.com) or orange TVL (www.tvl.vu) signs are the most ubiquitous form of advertising you'll see around the islands. A Smile SIM-card package is 3000VT including 2500VT of calls, or you can get a Digicel SIM card for 2000VT. Coverage, service and pricing are similar but most islanders don't take any chances and have both SIM cards. If you plan on using 3G data, make sure you get a mobile internet plan.

TIME

Vanuatu time is GMT/UMT plus 11 hours. Noon in Port Vila is 1am in London, 6pm in Los Angeles and 1pm in Auckland. There's no daylight savings.

TOURIST INFORMATION

Vanuatu Tourism Office (p487) in Port Vila has free maps and information about accommodation, activities, tours and the outer islands.

VISAS

Entry visas are not required for nationals of the British Commonwealth and EU; see www.

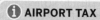

ⓘ AIRPORT TAX

There's an airport departure tax of 200VT on all domestic flights in Vanuatu. It's payable in cash after check-in (your boarding card will be stamped).

governmentofvanuatu.gov.vu. Most visitors get a free 30-day visa on arrival, which can be extended for up to four months (6000VT) at the Department of Immigration in Port Vila.

Nonexempt visitors should contact the **Principal Immigration Officer** (☏ 22354; immigration@vanuatu.gov.vu) to organise their visa application (3600VT). This must be finalised *before* you arrive.

ⓘ Getting There & Away

AIR

The following airlines have regular scheduled flights to Vanuatu.

Air New Zealand (☏ 22666; www.airnewzealand.co.nz) Direct flights from Auckland (from NZ$250 each way) to Port Vila.

Air Vanuatu (Map p484; ☏ 23848; www.airvanuatu.com; Rue de Paris, Port Vila) Air Vanuatu/Qantas (code-share) operates direct flights from Brisbane and Sydney to Port Vila. Return fares start at A$750. There is also a weekly direct flight to Espiritu Santo from Brisbane. From New Zealand, Air Vanuatu/Qantas flies direct from Auckland to Port Vila, and also has flights from Auckland via Nadi and Suva (Fiji), Honiara (Solomon Islands) and Noumea (New Caledonia).

Aircalin (Map p484; ☏ 22739; http://au.aircalin.com; Lini Hwy, Port Vila) New Caledonia's airline has flights to Port Vila from Nadi and Noumea.

Fiji Airways (Map p481; ☏ 22836; www.fijiairways.com; Lini Hwy) Flies to Port Vila from Nadi and Noumea.

Virgin Australia (☏ 22836; www.virginaustralia.com) Direct flights from Brisbane to Port Vila three times a week. Return fares start at A$500.

SEA
Yacht

The best source of general information on yachting matters is **Yachting World Vanuatu** (Map p481; www.yachtingworld-vanuatu.com; Lini Hwy; ☏ VHF16) in Port Vila. It has a sea-wall tie up and diesel dock and can arrange customs and quarantine inspections to your buoy.

The authorised ports of entry for touring yachts are Port Vila (Efate), Luganville (Santo), Lenakel (Tanna) and Sola (Vanua Lava). There are hefty fines if you make landfall in or depart from Vanuatu before customs and immigration have been cleared; 24 hours' notice is required for customs clearance. Port dues are 7875VT for the first 30 days and 100VT per day thereafter. Quarantine clearance is 3000VT and immigration clearance 4800VT.

Port Vila Boatyard (Map p478; www.portvilaboatyard.com) has many amenities and facilities in sheltered Pontoon Bay.

Getting Around

AIR

Air Vanuatu flies throughout the islands. Download its domestic flight schedule from www.airvanuatu.com, though it's not always up to date. You can book most flights via the Air Vanuatu website (fares listed in Australian dollars). If booking in person, show your international flight ticket with Air Vanuatu to receive a 20% discount. Children aged under 12 and students (student card required) receive a 50% and 25% discount respectively. It pays to book in advance if time is short but if you're flexible, seats are available on many flights at surprisingly short notice.

Air Safaris (☏ 7745207; www.airsafaris.vu) and **Air Taxi** (p491) run tours and are available for charter.

Belair Airways (☏ 29222, 5551290; www.belair.vu; Bauerfield International Airport) Vanuatu's newest scheduled airline with a single nineseater plane.

Unity Airlines (Map p481; ☏ 7744475, 24475; www.unity-airlines.com; Bauerfield International Airport) Flies tour groups to outer islands and is available for charter.

Airports

Port Vila's Bauerfield International Airport has an ANZ ATM, an NBV branch for currency exchange, a cafe and duty-free shopping. Port Vila's domestic airport has a Westpac ATM, a cafe, mobile phone outlets, and souvenir and book stall.

Near Luganville, Santo's Pekoa International Airport has an ANZ ATM, cafe, mobile phone outlets, duty-free shop and free wi-fi.

Tanna, Malekula (Norsup) and Pentecost have sealed airstrips; most other islands have grass airstrips with limited (or no) facilities.

BOAT
Canoe & Speedboat

When ni-Vanuatu talk of speedboats, they mean outboard-powered open dinghies. Canoes are dugout craft with outriggers, powered by paddle or sail. Speedboat prices are high, so it's best to wait for a scheduled service or a group rather than charter.

Passenger Boat

Big Sista (p487) This 33m passenger ferry runs a weekly service between Santo and Port Vila (9100VT), leaving Port Vila on Monday, returning Wednesday. It stops at Epi (5500VT)

KEEPING COSTS DOWN

Flexibility is the key to travelling Vanuatu's islands on a budget.

➡ Avoid travel on weekends: few places are open and you'll have to charter.

➡ Catch passenger ferries and the odd cargo ship and always go with the regular (shared) transport (both speedboat and truck) instead of expensive charters.

➡ Shop for fresh food at local markets and self-cater in Port Vila and Luganville.

➡ Remember that you'll have to pay landowners to visit many island beaches, caves, hot springs and blue holes.

---

and Malekula (7500VT). Travel business class for only 500VT more.

Vanuatu Ferry (p487) A weekly ferry between Port Vila and Santo (8000VT), via Malekula, departing Vila on Wednesday.

BUS & TAXI

Minibuses with a red 'B' on their number plates operate in Port Vila and Luganville. They don't run fixed routes but zoom to your destination. Flag them down by the roadside (150VT for short trips).

Taxis in Port Vila and Luganville are mostly sedans, but elsewhere they're 4WD open-tray trucks. Charges depend on distance, but also on the state of the 'road'. Ask your driver for a price: it will usually be honest and reasonable, unless you're chartering the vehicle. A short trip in Port Vila might cost 500VT, but a day charter will cost between 8000VT and 12,000VT. Local trucks meet flights at island airstrips, but may not be around on Sunday, public holidays or when there's no fuel on the island. Call your accommodation in advance.

CAR & MOTORCYCLE

You can hire cars, 4WDs and scooters in Port Vila and Luganville. The minimum age for renting a car is 23; for a scooter it's 17, provided you've held a valid driving licence for over a year. You don't need an International Driving Permit.

There's a speed limit of 50km/h in Port Vila and Luganville. Vehicles drive on the right.

EATING PRICE RANGES

The following price ranges refer to a standard main course:

$ less than 1500VT

$$ 1500VT–3000VT

$$$ more than 3000VT

Other Pacific Islands

Best On the Land

➡ Togo Chasm, Niue (p530)

➡ Christian's Cave, Pitcairn Island (p531)

➡ Funafuti Conservation Area islets, Tuvalu (p535)

➡ Île Fenua Fo'ou, Wallis (p536)

➡ Alofi island, Futuna (p537)

Best On the Water

➡ Diving in Niue (p529)

➡ St Paul's Pool, Pitcairn Island (p531)

➡ Fishing in Tokelau (p533)

➡ Funafuti Lagoon, Tuvalu (p535)

➡ Talava Arches, Niue (p530)

Why Go?

These South Pacific islands are as remote as they are unique. In some cases, a *looong* boat trip is the only means of access. And where intrepid airlines do ply the skies, flights are infrequent and usually involve a trip to another South Pacific access hub first.

But if you're brimming with adventurous spirit (and plenty of time), these islands offer unforgettable natural beauty: the coral atolls of Tokelau, the palmed-topped outer islets of Tuvalu, the craggy coastlines of Niue... Even more rewarding, the isolation of these isles has preserved some unique remnants of South Pacific culture, both ancient and more recent (there's nowhere on Earth quite like Pitcairn Island).

Disturbingly, global warming threatens the very existence of some of these islands: if sea levels continue to rise, low-lying territories such as Tuvalu and Tokelau may be underwater by the 22nd century. The time to visit is now!

When to Go

➡ **Jun–Oct** The southern hemisphere winter and spring deliver reliable weather in Niue.

➡ **Dec–Jan** Holiday time in Tuvalu, with lots of to-and-fro between Tuvalu and nearby Samoa.

➡ **Apr–Jun & Oct–Sep** Shoulder season in the Pitcairn Islands – not too chilly.

Niue

🎵 683 / POP 1200 / AREA 260 SQ KM

Niue (*new*-ay – which means 'behold the coconut') may be the world's smallest independent nation, but the Pacific island known as the 'Rock of Polynesia' (or just 'the Rock') packs in plenty of surprises for the bold traveller. The island sits in the middle of the triangle formed by Samoa, Tonga and the Cook Islands. This is rugged terrain: ditch the deckchair and unpack your hiking boots and sense of adventure.

You will need to walk, climb and sometimes swim to see the attractions hugging Niue's outrageously scenic perimeter. Get yourself a rental car or motorcycle and explore the numerous caves, snorkelling spots and cliff-encircled chasm pools en route.

As per many other South Pacific island groups (the Vava'u Group in Tonga springs to mind), from June to September humpback whales nurse their calves in Niue's safe warm waters. But give the whales a bit of space: instead, descend further to the indigo depths for some of the best diving in the South Pacific. Kayaking, fishing, caving and guided hiking trips are also on offer: check out www.niueisland.com/content/adventures for the low-down.

Niue's capital Alofi (population 1600) stretches out for several kilometres along the west coast, and has a reasonable range of budget and midrange guesthouses, plus cottages, motels, restaurants and a resort.

Curiously, in 2003 Niue became the world's first 'wi-fi nation', with free wireless internet available to everyone who lives here!

History

Polynesian explorers from Samoa first sailed south and settled Niue some time around AD 900. Marauding Tongans (not to be messed with) arrived from the west in the 16th century. A system of monarchy was established around 1700.

That Pacific paramour Captain James Cook caught sight of Niue in 1774, but the locals didn't exactly roll out the red carpet. In fact, Cook was unable to land. As he wrote in his his journal, 'The conduct and aspect of these islanders occasioned my giving it the name of Savage Island'.

Christian missionaries converted the Niue 'savages' in the 1840s, but it wasn't until 1900 that the island became a British protectorate. The Brits didn't protest too ardently when New Zealand annexed Niue in 1901. Niue finally gained autonomy from New Zealand in 1974, but Niueans continue to hold NZ passports and NZ still coordinates the nation's foreign affairs and military operations.

Culture

Niue is a pious place. Visitors are advised not to wear swimming gear in villages or towns, and not to go fishing or boating on a Sunday (but you can play golf, go for a swim or do some sightseeing – or better yet, go to church and belt out a few hymns with the locals).

Polynesian heritage in Niue is championed by a government strategy called 'Taoga Niue', an integrated community initiative aimed at preserving Niuean language, culture and traditions, all of which are on display at 'Village Show Days'. There are 14 of these events every year, with dancing, *umu* (earth oven) feasts, and local arts and crafts on display and for sale (check out the amazing weavings): try to time your visit so you can join in the fun.

Environment

Don't expect palm-fringed beaches or languid lagoons in Niue; instead, get set for a jagged landscape of limestone caverns, hidden sea caves and a rocky, untamed coast.

As with all South Pacific islands, tropical cyclones regularly threaten lives and wreak havoc here. Alofi's southern area was badly damaged by Tropical Cyclone Heta in 2004 and abandoned structures still punctuate the cliff tops. Reconstruction is ongoing across the whole country, but many locals chose not to rebuild and emigrated to New Zealand instead.

ℹ️ Information

CURRENCY
New Zealand dollar (NZ$)

LANGUAGES
English and Niuean

INTERNET
Free wi-fi (patchy but islandwide)

RESOURCES
www.niueisland.com

DON'T MISS

NIUE HIGHLIGHTS

➡ Diving with tangles of sea snakes at **Snake Gully** or negotiating twin underwater chimneys at **Ana Mahaga**.

➡ Hanging out in **Alofi** for a couple of very laid-back days.

➡ Soaking up some Pacific Ocean power at **Togo Chasm** and **Talava Arches**.

➡ Exploring the fish-filled reef pools near **Matapa Chasm**.

❶ Getting There & Away

AIR

Air New Zealand (www.airnewzealand.com) has a twice-weekly service to/from Auckland.

YACHT

Niue Yacht Club (www.nyc.nu) has a clutch of well-maintained moorings available.

Pitcairn Islands

📔 64 / POP 60 / AREA 47 SQ KM

The Pitcairn Islands – the last British Overseas Territory in the Pacific – comprises four remote islands: the namesake Pitcairn Island itself, plus the uninhabited Oeno, Henderson and Ducie. What's rarely mentioned about Pitcairn, between the infamous *Bounty* story and the 2004 sex-trials scandal, is that it's a place of incredible natural beauty. The island's 5-sq-km surface is almost entirely sloped and has a varied landscape, from desolate rock cliffs that look over an infinite expanse of sea to lush hillsides bursting with tropical plenty.

The nearest inhabited island to Pitcairn is Mangareva in French Polynesia, 480km or a 36-hour boat ride away. Besides a few hundred cruise ship passengers per year (who often only spend an hour or two on Pitcairn when the ship passes), the only visitors are a few yachts, occasional groups of boat-chartering birders and a handful of intrepid tourists.

History

In January 1790 the *Bounty* mutineers arrived on Pitcairn after a long search for a remote hideaway, far from the long arm of British naval justice. Led by Fletcher Christian, the party was made up of eight other mutineers, six Tahitian men, 12 Tahitian women and a child. Once they were settled on the island, the *Bounty* was burnt both to prevent escape and to avoid detection. Chaos and bloodshed ruled the first years, largely due to the English mutineers' slave-like treatment of the Polynesian men. By 1800, John Adams (who had recently discovered religion), was the sole surviving man along with 10 women and 23 children.

Adamstown was a neat little settlement of God-fearing Christians when American Captain Mayhew Folger rediscovered Pitcairn Island in 1809, solving the 19-year mystery of what had happened to Christian and the *Bounty* after the mutiny. By this time British attention was focused on Napoleon and there was no interest in the surviving mutineer who was guilty of a decades-old crime.

Pitcairn didn't hit world headlines again till 2004, when six men, including most heads of the community, were found guilty of a string of sex offences, including rape and indecent assault, on young girls. Life on Pitcairn changed irrevocably. Deep within the closest-knit society imaginable, sisters, daughters and wives were pitted against uncles, fathers and brothers and, just as often, each other. In response, Britain has paid more attention to this speck of a colony than it has since the days of Bligh. From a new jetty on the opposite side of the island to Bounty Bay, to a state-of-the-art telephone system, the island has gotten back on its feet and everyone hopes the years of sex abuse have ended.

Although Pitcairn's population grew to 223 before WWII, depopulation rather than overpopulation has become the major concern. With British funds being poured into the island for development since 2004, a few ex-islanders are being lured home. The presence of British officials and government workers has raised the population to around 60.

These days, the islanders do a busy trade turning out curios for visiting ships, including woven round pandanus baskets, models of the *Bounty* and a variety of *miro* wood carvings. Pots of local honey and Pitcairn Island stamps are other island must-haves.

Culture

Archaeological digs suggest that the Pitcairns were inhabited by Polynesians as recently as the 15th century, but periods of civil war and limited natural resources on the islands eventually lead to population exodus and/or extinction. So when Fletcher Christian arrived, the islands were uninhabited. It follows that today, Pitcairns' indigenous culture is inexorably bound to the *Bounty* and Britain, rather than to the centuries prior.

Life in the Pitcairns has had a reputation for restrictive formality over the years: smoking, dancing, kissing in public and drinking booze were all once banned here, but are (mercifully) now permitted.

As the island population is so small, any excuse for a celebration is valid: a birthday, the arrival of a cruise ship or even a yacht is reason enough for a communal feast.

Environment

The ocean surrounding the Pitcairns is arguably more interesting than the craggy landscapes of the islands themselves. In 2015 the UK government announced plans to create the world's largest Marine Protected Area (MPA) around the islands – an 834,000-sq-km zone in which commercial fishing will be banned, protecting upwards of 80 species of fish, coral and marine algae.

Above sea level, Henderson Island is populated by four species of endemic birds: the flightless Henderson rail, the colourful Stephen's lorikeet, the territorial Henderson fruit dove and the Henderson warbler. Because of its pristine condition and rare birdlife, Henderson Island was declared a Unesco World Heritage site in 1988.

Pitcairn Island

Exploring your way around craggy Pitcairn Island, you'll find a little **museum** with some *Bounty* artefacts as well as several other historical sights dotted around the place. **Down Rope** is the island's only beach. **St Paul's Pool** is a cathedral-like rock formation encircling a pool with the ocean waves surging in through gaps in the rocks. For walkers, there are several well-signposted trails snaking over the island, including an ecotrail leading up to **Christian's Cave**, which overlooks Adamstown. The only **mutineer's grave** you can visit is that of John Adams, in Adamstown (where else).

Henderson Island

Uninhabited bird-filled Henderson Island is 168km northeast of Pitcairn and is the largest island of the Pitcairn group. The usual landing spot is North Beach and, during certain tides, there is sometimes a freshwater spring in a cave at the north of the island. Visitors require a licence to visit, which is dependent on approval by the Pitcairn Island Council.

Interestingly, the wrecking of the whaling ship *Essex* on the island in 1820, after a charge by a sperm whale near the Marquesas, is believed to have provided the inspiration for Herman Melville's *Moby Dick*.

❶ Information

CURRENCY

New Zealand dollar (NZ$; official); US dollar (US$; for tourist goods and services)

LANGUAGES

English and Pitkern

RESOURCES

www.government.pn, www.visitpitcairn.pn

❶ Getting There & Away

BOAT

Check out the Pitcairn Island tourism website (www.visitpitcairn.pn) for information about passenger- and cargo-vessel transportation from New Zealand, visas and lodging with locals (various multiday packages are available).

CRUISE SHIP

About 10 cruise ships call at Pitcairn every year. Like cargo vessels, they anchor well offshore and, seas permitting, passengers are ferried to Bounty Bay.

YACHT

There is no sheltered anchorage at Pitcairn and boats must be moved when the winds change. Pitcairners are happy to sell fresh fruit and

---

DON'T MISS

PITCAIRN ISLANDS HIGHLIGHTS

➡ Taking a cool dip in the electric blue, glass-clear waters of **St Paul's Pool**.

➡ Climbing the precipice to **Christian's Cave** and imagining what must have gone through the mutineer's head as he sat there hundreds of years ago.

➡ Hanging out with locals on a Friday night at **Christian's Café** in Adamstown.

➡ Watching a flightless Henderson rail (that's a bird) trundle by as you relax on the mosquito-free shores of **Henderson Island**.

supply fresh water to yachties, but other supplies generally have to be imported from New Zealand and may be in short supply.

Tokelau

♪ 690 / POP 1400 / AREA 10 SQ KM

In a world where travel has become easy and accessible to the masses, travelling to Tokelau – a territory of New Zealand – still requires a dedication that dissuades all but the most committed visitors. It takes upwards of 24 hours to reach Tokelau by boat from its nearest neighbour, Samoa, and you can forget about flying – there's no airstrip. Once you're there, the ship that brought you is your only means of getting between the nation's three atolls – Fakaofo, Atafu and Nukunonu. It takes nine hours to travel between the two most distant ones (Fakaofo and Atafu). Your ship will also be your ticket home, so you'll have to be prepared to stay for at least five days until it's ready to leave, or wait for the next one in a week's time.

History

A thousand years ago Tokelau's three islands existed as independent societies with their own chiefs, occasionally feuding and often intermarrying.

From 1765 into the 1800s, several seafaring expeditions visited the islands, including ships from Britain and the USA, but it wasn't until French and British missionaries started arriving in 1845 that there was any in-house European influence here. Tragically, Peruvian slave traders raided the islands in 1863 and shanghaied most of the male population, many of whom subsequently died of smallpox and dysentery. Tokelau's population took many decades to recover.

Tokelau officially fell under the protective auspices of Britain in 1877, until the territory became part of New Zealand in 1949. In the 2000s, two referendums on a shift to self-governance narrowly failed to get across the line – for now, Tokelau remains part of NZ.

MUTINY ON THE BOUNTY

On 28 April 1789 Captain William Bligh and 18 crewmen of the HMS *Bounty* were involuntarily relieved of their duties and set adrift in an open boat off the island of Tofua in Tonga, with minimal supplies. It became the most famous naval mutiny in history.

The *Bounty*'s mission was to fetch breadfruit from Tahiti to feed England's African slave population in the Caribbean. Under the command of Bligh, an expert navigator who had trained under Captain James Cook, the expedition arrived in Tahiti in September 1788 after a particularly arduous 10-month journey. The breadfruit season was over and they had to wait six months in Tahiti before returning. Three weeks into the return journey, the crew, led by the master's mate Fletcher Christian, mutinied.

Whatever problems Bligh had with people skills, he was a brilliant navigator. Against the odds, he managed to get the longboat and most of his loyal crew 7000km from Tonga to Timor in the Dutch East Indies (modern-day Indonesia).

Under Christian's command the mutineers returned to Tahiti, then eventually split into two groups: Fletcher took a group of sailors and Tahitians off in search of Pitcairn Island, while a second group of 16 sailors stayed behind on Tahiti.

After Bligh returned to England, Captain Edward Edwards (a tyrant who made Bligh look like a saint) was sent in the *Pandora* to search for the mutineers. Edwards sailed past Ducie Atoll in the Pitcairn group, but he didn't see the larger island 470km to the west. However, Edwards did find and capture 14 of the 16 mutineers who had remained on Tahiti. Unfortunately, Edwards' sailing skills were not up to Bligh's standards and he ended up sinking the *Pandora* on the Great Barrier Reef. Of the surviving prisoners, three were ultimately hanged for the mutiny.

An American duo, Nordhoff and Hall, wrote three books on the *Bounty* mutiny and its aftermath in 1934. Several other books and films have ensued: check out young Marlon Brando as Fletcher Christian in the excellent *Mutiny on the Bounty* (1962), and the equally clean-cut Mel Gibson in *The Bounty* (1984).

Culture

Polynesian Tokelau aligns itself with the culture, art and language of both Samoa and Tuvalu, the latter having similar atoll-based geography. The Tokelauan lifestyle – 'Faka-Tokelau' – is focused squarely on community and family. Sharing of resources is a key societal trait. Within villages and towns, formal affairs are managed by councils of elders, local families nominating their representatives.

As in most South Pacific nations, religion plays a critical role in daily life here. Roman Catholicism is the denomination of choice, except on Atafu where most folks attend the Ekalehia Fakalapotopotoga Kelihiano Tokelau (EFKT) church. Respecting one's elders is a must in Tokelau, while violence and aggressive behaviour are absolute no-nos.

Environment

Land shortages have long forced emigration from Tokelau, and most of the country's people live overseas, predominantly in Samoa, New Zealand and Australia. Consisting only of low-lying coral atolls rising to a maximum of 5m, Tokelau faces great risk from global warming. It is predicted that all three atolls will be uninhabitable by the end of the 21st century, though some estimates give only another 30 years. While some Tokelauans regard these predictions as overly dramatic, others foresee the end to their 1000-year-old history.

On a more positive note, Tokelau is now completely self-sufficient in its energy needs through sustainable sources. A pilot program in solar energy on Fakaofo was such a success that the people of Tokelau extended it to the other atolls. Since 2012 the islanders have been generating 150% of their energy needs from the sun, saving the NZ$829,000 the country was spending annually on imported fuels.

Jaws fans rejoice: in 2011 Tokelau declared its surrounding Exclusive Economic Zone (319,031 sq km of ocean) a sanctuary for sharks.

ⓘ Information

Note that accommodation on Tokelau must be arranged before arrival through the **Tokelau Apia Liaison Office** (☑ 685-20822; www. tokelau.org.nz; PO Box 865, Apia; ⊘ 8am-5pm Mon-Fri) in Samoa. It's also the place to organise visitor permits and boat transport.

TOKELAU HIGHLIGHTS

➡ Dipping into gin-clear lagoons for memorable **snorkelling** or **diving**.

➡ **Pitching your tent** on an uninhabited island speck – a genuine castaway experience.

➡ Cutting the rug with the locals at a community **disco**.

➡ Heading out **fishing** with the experts.

CURRENCY
New Zealand dollar (NZ$)

LANGUAGES
Tokelauan, English, Samoan

RESOURCES
www.tokelau.org.nz

ⓘ Getting There & Away

BOAT
Several cargo and passenger ships service Tokelau from Apia in Samoa, with a departure roughly once a week. See the schedule on www.tokelau. org.nz for sailing times; book through the Tokelau Apia Liaison Office in Samoa.

YACHT
There are no official harbours in Tokelau and anchoring offshore is not easy, especially in an offshore wind. The sea floor drops off sharply beyond the coral reef, and the water is too deep for most anchor chains. The channels blasted through the coral are shallow and intended for dinghies only.

Tuvalu

☑ 688 / POP 9880 / AREA 26 SQ KM

Approaching these islands by plane – after endless miles of rolling ocean – a dazzling smear of turquoise and green appears, ringed with coral and studded with tiny, palm-topped islets, sitting vulnerably in the surrounding waters.

The landmass of Fongafale Islet (2.8 sq km), Tuvalu's main island, is so startlingly narrow that as the plane nears the airstrip it seems as if it's about to tip into the ocean. In fact, the airstrip is something of a social hub: kids play ball games on the runway in the late afternoons, young men race up and down it on their motorcycles and, on steamy summer nights, whole families may drag their sleeping mats and pillows out to spend the night on the tarmac (in the stifling heat it's the best place to catch breezes).

There's a small selection of accommodation on Fongafale that includes a hotel, a lodge, a motel and some family-run guesthouses. There's also a basic guesthouse on Funafala Islet.

Most restaurants on Tuvalu sell cheap, filling plates of Chinese-style food. Restaurants sometimes suffer from shortages when shipments don't arrive. Thursday to Saturday is party night on Fongafale, when the old-timers go to 'twists' (discos) and the youngsters go 'clubbing'.

History

In a familiar sequence of events right across the South Pacific, Polynesian explorers first settled Tuvalu more than 1000 years ago. Village life here progressed unchanged and unmolested until European traders started showing up in the 1820s, followed by British Christian missionaries in the 1860s, hellbent on converting the heathen realm.

The Brits put down less-theological roots in 1877, when Tuvalu (then known as the Ellice Islands) came under British protection as part of the Gilbert & Ellice Islands Protectorate. This status remained in place until a 1974 referendum returned a vote overwhelmingly in favour of independence. As part of this process, Tuvalu cut ties with the Gilbert Islands (now Kiribati) and became an independent member of the British Commonwealth in 1978, then a member of the United Nations in 2000.

During WWII the Ellice Islands were a staging point for Allied attacks on Nauru and the Gilbert Islands, then occupied by the Japanese. Airfields, naval bases, hospitals, seaplane ramps and port facilities were built around the Ellice Islands by US Marines, with a bit of muscle from the locals. All sorts of sorties were launched from here, with Funafuti being on the receiving end of Japanese air attacks in 1943. After the war finished in 1945, Funafuti airfield became Funafuti International Airport.

Culture

As in most Polynesian societies, family structures define the order of proceedings in Tuvalu, from meals and child care to farming and fishing. Within the community, each family has a *salanga* (task) to perform: fishing, construction, maintenance, crop planting, harvesting, repairing nets... Skills are passed down from generation to generation. Important community matters are thrashed out in *falekaupule* (meeting halls), which are also used for celebrations and dance performances (Tuvaluans love to dance).

On the food front, Tuvalans make do with what's around them: coconuts, fish, coconut milk, pork, coconut crabs, taro... and coconuts.

Environment

Unfortunately, environmental concerns have focused international attention on Tuvalu. As an atoll nation, the major long-term ecological threat to Tuvalu comes from global warming and rising sea levels. As well as shoreline erosion, water bubbles up through the porous coral on which the islands are based, and causes widespread salt contamination of areas used to grow staple crops. If sea levels continue to rise

TE ANO

While in Tuvalu, try to watch, or better still join in, a game of Tuvalu's unique sport, *te ano*. Almost completely incomprehensible to a first-timer, it's great fun and one of the few games that men and women play together.

To play *te ano* you need two round balls, about 12cm in diameter and woven from dried pandanus leaves. Two opposing teams face each other about 7m apart in five or six parallel rows of about six people, and nominate their *alovaka* (captain) and *tino pukepuke* (catcher), who stand in front of each team.

Team members hit the ball to each other with the aim of eventually reaching the catcher. Only the catcher can throw the ball back to the captain to hit back to the other team. To keep the game lively, two balls are used simultaneously. When either ball falls to the ground the other team scores a point, and the first to 10 points wins the game. Crazy stuff!

If you're more of a cricket fan, keep a look out for *kilikiti*, which puts a South Seas spin on the old game. To say that the rules are 'flexible' is probably fair comment.

as predicted – around 40cm in the next 100 years – much of Tuvalu will be underwater, with the remnants above sea level rendered uninhabitable.

What will happen to the population if Tuvalu does start to go under? The government has been in talks with Australia, which has twice rejected Tuvalu's pleas to open a migration channel. New Zealand has said it will absorb Tuvalu's population if it comes to that.

Population pressures and changing lifestyles also present a problem. Tiny Fongafale Islet, only about a third of which is habitable, is crammed with some 4500 people. Pits end up filled with waste, due to a lack of adequate garbage disposal and the reliance on imported packaged food – a common problem for Pacific islands of all sizes.

Funafuti Atoll & Fongafale Islet

Tuvalu's capital is technically Funafuti Atoll (population 6200), a hoop of 33 islets encircling a lagoon. The biggest islet in the atoll is Fongafale Islet (also spelled Fogafale or Fagafale), which is home to the main township and the seat of government. Tuvalu's answer to a metropolis, Fongafale is the only place in the country where tourists can change money, make international phone calls or use the internet.

The best thing about a visit to Fongafale is simply winding down to match the slow-paced island way of life. Take a stroll around town or hop on a bike or motorcycle to explore the islet from top to toe. There are also a handful of WWII relics here.

Funafuti Conservation Area, a half-hour motorboat ride west across the lagoon, is an amazing underwater world. Book a boat trip through the town council, which might include some time on one or two of the islets and perhaps some snorkelling.

To the south, Funafala Islet is a gorgeous little isle lined with talcum-powder beaches with basic accommodation right by the water.

Outer Islands

A trip to be made only if you've got plenty of time to spare and are a 'hard-core' traveller, Tuvalu's beautiful and remote outer islands have very little infrastructure for visitors. The cargo ships do a round trip lasting several days to each of the three island groups: the northern group comprises Nanumea

TUVALU HIGHLIGHTS

➡ Living out your desert-island fantasies on the palm-covered islets of the amazing **Funafuti Conservation Area**.

➡ Experiencing traditional island life with the few remaining families of **Funafala Islet**.

➡ Joining the locals for a sunset or early-morning dip in the luminous, cerulean **Funafuti Lagoon**.

➡ Catching a unique performance of Tuvalu's national dance, **fatele**.

Atoll, Niutao Atoll, Nanumaga Atoll and Nui Atoll; the central group is Vaitupu, Nukufetau Atoll and Fongafale Islet; and the southern group comprises Nukulaelae Atoll and Niulakita. The ships call in at each island for the best part of a day to unload and load supplies and passengers. So if you're prepared to spend your nights on board ship, you can explore the islands during the daytime. If you choose to get off the boat and plan to stay, be warned: it might be some weeks before the next transport arrives! Give advance warning of your arrival and come prepared to be pretty much self-sufficient.

ℹ Information

CURRENCY
Australian dollar (AUD$), Tuvaluan dollar (TUV$)

LANGUAGES
Tuvaluan, Gilbertese, English

RESOURCES
www.timelesstuvalu.com

ℹ Getting There & Away

AIR
Fiji Airways (www.fijiairways.com) plies the Suva–Funafuti route a couple of times a week; book well in advance to secure a seat.

Wallis & Futuna

📞 681 / POP 12,200 / AREA WALLIS 77.9 SQ KM, FUTUNA 64 SP KM

These two little-known French-funded volcanic specks lie smack in the centre of the Polynesia/Melanesia region. Wallis and Futuna, which lie 230km away from each other, are linked through French governance but

WALLIS & FUTUNA HIGHLIGHTS

➧ Visiting paradisaical Wallis lagoon islets such as **Île Fenua Fo'ou**.

➧ Gazing down the steep walls of **Lake Lalolalo** on Wallis.

➧ Finding shards of Lapita pottery in the king's path at **To'oga Toto**.

➧ Ogling the imposing tower and graceful tapa decorations at **Pierre Chanel Church** on Futuna.

that's where the connection ceases: Wallis has ancestral connections with Tonga, while Futuna traces its roots to Samoa. This is evident in the languages, which are quite different although mutually comprehensible, as well as the Samoan-like tapa designs of the Futunans and the Tongan-influenced designs found around Wallis. The two islands remain competitive with each other, but Wallis, being more populous (around 10,750 residents) and the centre of government, retains the upper hand.

History

Tongans on the move arrived in these parts 1000 years ago, before the Dutch bumped into Futuna in 1616. The British collided with Wallis in 1767, naming the islands after British explorer Samuel Wallis. But in 1837 it was French missionaries who settled here more permanently, France then declaring these islands a protectorate in 1842. A more official French takeover of the islands' three separate aristocratic monarchies – which are still in place – followed in 1888, when the islands were placed under the ministrations of New Caledonia. In 1961 Wallis and Futuna became a French Overseas Territory, ending the islands' deference to New Caledonia. The nomenclature shifted again in 2003 when Wallis and Futuna became a French Overseas Collectivity.

Culture

Wallis and Futuna islanders drive flashy 4WDs to and from their taro fields and enjoy satellite TV at night after a beer or maybe some kava. Free education and health and dental care here are propped up by French euros, but traditional island language, culture and intricate *coutume* (customs) have remained remarkably intact here.

Beneath the French umbrella, traditional royal hierarchies still hold sway. The islands maintain three kingdoms (*royaumes coutumiers*): Sigave, on the western side of Futuna; Alo, on Alofi and on the eastern side of Futuna; and Uvea, on Wallis. Today, all three kingdoms live in peaceful, if quite competitive, harmony with each other.

Interestingly, there are an estimated 17,000 Wallis and Futuna islanders living in New Caledonia – more than remain in Wallis and Futuna itself – plus a few thousand more living in France.

Environment

Wallis and Futuna are rather different environments. For starters, Wallis is flat-ish, rising gradually to 145m above sea level, while Futuna is peaky, jutting up to 524m. Wallis has a lagoon and barrier reef, but Futuna has craggy shores and is *sans* lagoon (to dip into local parlance). But both islands are green, green, green, with more than 3m of annual rainfall dumping on locals' rooftops. Aside from fairly regular tropical cyclone events in summer, Futuna sits near a collision point between underlying tectonic plates and is prone to earthquakes.

Wallis

What Wallis lacks in lofty emerald peaks and pearly white beaches it makes up for with its outrageously clear blue lagoon, weird circular crater lakes and extensive archaeological sites tucked back in the bush. It's a big, flat jungle of a place where traditional life is played out behind plain, modern concrete walls.

Mata'Utu is the country's sprawling administrative and business centre. The 35km island-circuit road is unsealed and at times fairly rough: it never actually runs along the coast, although in a few places there are detours that run along the water's edge. Unmarked side roads lead inland to archaeological sites such as **To'oga Toto**, and alluring-looking lakes, including the rather amazing circular **Lake Lalolalo**, with its sheer walls.

The calm, turquoise waters and impressive variety of islets of Wallis' **lagoon** are as much a reason to visit this island as the sights of the interior. Look forward to diving trips and watery explorations to islets such as **Île Fenua Fo'ou**.

In addition to a few restaurants, simple snack bars dot the island. There's a supermarket in the Fenuarama shopping centre.

Futuna & Alofi

Loaded up with flowers, sparkling beaches, traditional houses and vistas over Pacific blue, Futuna is storybook Polynesian-pretty. Yet since the islanders here have firmly decided not to develop tourism in order to preserve their lifestyle, it's a particularly difficult place to get around.

Uninhabited Alofi (area 51 sq km), with its tropical forest and beach, is just as photogenic and more wild. A strait less than 2km wide separates the two islands. Boats chug across to Alofi from Vele beach beside the airport.

Practical goings-on happen in Leava, Futuna's major centre, on the island's south coast. There are a couple of supermarkets here (stocked with an amazing but expensive variety of imported goods), the island's administrative headquarters (there's even a library) and a wharf. The few hotels on Futuna all have bar-restaurants.

It's a 33km circuit around Futuna but, with speed bumps on the good roads and potholes on the bad ones, it'll take at least 1½ hours to complete a lap. Along the route you'll come across a handful of some of the most beautiful churches in the Pacific, including the towering Pierre Chanel Church (called Petelo Sanele in Futunan), painstakingly decorated throughout with white-and-brown tapa. The chapel includes various relics of St Pierre (1803–1841; canonised in 1954), the first martyr of Oceania, including some of his clothes and the war club that is said to have dispatched him.

❶ Information

CURRENCY
Cour de Franc Pacifique (CFP), which is tied to the euro

LANGUAGES
Wallisian, Futunan, French

RESOURCES
www.outre-mer.gouv.fr (In French and English; select Wallis & Futuna on the map.)

❶ Getting There & Away

AIR
Aircalin (www.aircalin.com) flies from Noumea in New Caledonia to Wallis three times a week, continuing on to Nadi in Fiji. There are also daily commuter flights between Wallis and Futuna.

BOAT
Do let us know if the long-awaited Wallis-to-Futuna boat service has materialised!

YACHT
Yachts sometimes breeze into Wallis, with its welcoming lagoon, en route between Samoa and Fiji. Because there's not much room around the Mata'Utu wharf, yachts are encouraged to moor near the petroleum wharf at Halalo in the south of Wallis. Futuna does not have a protected lagoon, but there is an anchorage at Sigave Bay on the west coast.

OTHER PACIFIC ISLANDS WALLIS & FUTUNA

Understand South Pacific

South Pacific Today

The island nations of the South Pacific are a varied bunch: strewn across this vast ocean, it's not all kava, cocktails and good times. This region has a mindset all of its own, equal parts sleepy, stubborn and progressive. Political upheaval is par for the course here, but climate change presents a more profound threat than a coup or two – a threat to existence itself.

Best in Print

Blue Latitudes (Tony Horwitz; 2002) Retraces Captain Cook's voyages, comparing past and present.

The Sex Lives of Cannibals (J Maarten Troost; 2004) Laugh-a-minute escapades on a Kiribati atoll.

Mutiny on the Bounty (Nordhoff & Hall; 1932) Page-turning critique of Captain Bligh's management style.

The Happy Isles of Oceania (Paul Theroux; 1992) Theroux kayaks through the South Pacific.

Best on Film

Cast Away (director Robert Zemeckis; 2000) Tom Hanks befriends a volleyball and removes a tooth. Filmed in Fiji.

The Blue Lagoon (director Randal Kleiser; 1980) Brook Shields and Christopher Atkins hit puberty. Filmed in Fiji.

Mutiny on the Bounty (directors Frank Lloyd, Lewis Milestone & Roger Donaldson; 1935, 1962 & 1984 respectively) Captain Bligh and Fletcher Christian disagree. Filmed in Tahiti, Bora Bora and Mo'orea.

Tanna (directors Bentley Dean & Martin Butler; 2015) Romantic drama filmed entirely in Vanuatu.

A Changing Climate

If there's one issue on which all South Pacific nations are aligned, it's climate change. Low-lying island nations such as Tuvalu and Tokelau are most at risk from rising sea levels, but flow-on environmental effects come into play across all island groups. With rising seas comes rising soil salination, and any reduction in land area in the Pacific means less space for agriculture. The precious corals of Fiji and French Polynesia are also under threat, bleaching as sea temperatures rise. Warmer seas also mean more intense storms. Cyclone Pam, which leveled much of Vanuatu in 2015, is a prime example – the second-most savage storm ever recorded in the South Pacific. An ongoing drought is making it hard for crops to recover.

When member nations of the Pacific Islands Forum (PIF) convene, climate change is a hot topic (pardon the pun), along with reducing the region's reliance on fossil fuels. Member nations have pledged aid for research into climate change, improving food and water security and ensuring ecosystem protection. Ironically (if you don't factor in Australia's high per-capita emissions), the South Pacific region is one of Earth's lowest emitters of greenhouse gases, yet is among the hardest hit by the effects.

Colonial Powers & New Democracy

Right across the South Pacific, political freedom continues to tread a rocky road. A referendum for New Caledonia's independence from France is scheduled for some time before 2018, but the 2014 elections here handed power to anti-independence parties. Across in French Polynesia, former French Polynesian president Oscar Temaru pushed for independence for his country, but his pro-France successors Gaston Flosse and Édouard Fritch have set the independence cause back somewhat.

In 2010 Tongans voted for the first time in democratic elections, and did so again in 2014. Monarchy-linked nobles (who have reigned for centuries) won both elections, but democracy now has a foothold here. Fiji also held elections in 2014, with 2006 military coup leader Frank Bainimarama elected prime minister. However, critics suggest that democracy founded in the moods of one man is no democracy at all. Over in the Solomon Islands, peace-keeping forces from Australia, New Zealand, Tonga and Papua New Guinea deployed in 2003 to quell political unrest and violence were finally withdrawn in 2013 – the security situation in the country deemed to have stabilised. In Vanuatu in 2015, 14 MPs including the deputy prime minister (more than half of the serving government) were found guilt of corruption and bribery. Not completely unusual in Vanuatu but not ideal for regional democracy.

Beyond island shores, Australia and New Zealand continue to exert considerable influence in the South Pacific through their membership of the PIF. Lobbying from Australia resulted in the suspension of Fiji from the PIF in 2010 for its failure to host democratic elections. Fiji was reinstated in 2014 after elections that year. Australia continues to lobby for greater regionalism, pushing for Pacific nations to act collectively on trade, fishing, waste management and air transport. Under the Forum's *Pacific Plan* (2005; reviewed 2013), nations have removed regional trade barriers and have the facility to trade externally as a collective.

Meanwhile, France and the USA continue to bankroll their island territories in the Pacific. In 2015 France finally assented to paying compensation to South Pacific islanders affected by the French nuclear testing regime in the region, which ran until 1996.

Influences from the North

As old colonial power structures shift on the tide, new allegiances are emerging. In 2006 China signed the catchily titled *Action Plan of Economic Development and Cooperation,* offering trade with and aid to several Pacific nations. Today, China is one of the largest trading partners in the South Pacific, along with Australia and New Zealand. Cynics suggest that increased Chinese trade and (it has to be said) very welcome investment in island infrastructure (roads, hospitals, schools, community centres, police stations...even a massive new hotel in Tahiti) will grant China unprecedented access to regional minerals, timber and fisheries. Others suggest that China's motives are more poli-military, looking to undermine regional ties between the South Pacific nations and Australia, Japan and the USA, with an eye to tactical naval expansion in the South Seas. Regardless, the South Pacific – particularly Fiji, Vanuatu, the Solomon Islands and Tonga – is benefiting hugely from Chinese building programs and access to Chinese markets. Japan, too, has invested millions in South Pacific services and infrastructure. Again, the cynics cry 'foul', suggesting that Japanese whaling interests are behind such investment.

NUMBER OF SOUTH PACIFIC ISLANDS: **25,000**

POPULATION OF SOUTH PACIFIC ISLANDS: **2,504,445**

LANDMASS: **87,337 SQ KM**

PERCENTAGE OF THE EARTH'S SURFACE: **28%**

HIGHEST POINT: **MT POPMANASEU, SOLOMON ISLANDS (2335M)**

if the South Pacific were 100 people

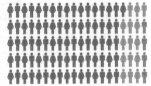

81 would be Pacific Islanders
15 would be of Asian origin
4 would be of European origin

belief systems
(% of population)

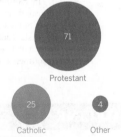

71 Protestant
25 Catholic
4 Other

population per sq km

SOUTH PACIFIC   SOLOMON ISLANDS   AMERICAN SAMOA

≈ 20 people

History

The Great Polynesian Migration is one of the world's most outlandish yet mysterious historical events. Imagine families and clans tossing chickens, dogs, pigs, vegies and the kids into canoes and sailing into an unknown, empty blue. Then they found islands, lots of them, using celestial navigation as well as now-forgotten methods of reading cloud reflections, wave formations and bird flight patterns. More than 3000 years after these people populated the Pacific, European explorers finally achieved the marine technology to 'discover' these tropical paradises.

Getting There is Half the Fun

The development of the outrigger canoe with its additional buoyant support, called *ama* in many Polynesian languages, allowed Austronesian people to journey vast distances across the Pacific.

About 50,000 years ago the first people reached the Pacific islands, arriving in New Guinea from Southeast Asia via Indonesia. These people, now known as Papuans, share ancestry with Australia's Aborigines. Moving slowly east, the Papuans' progress halted in the northern Solomon Islands about 25,000 years ago, due to the lack of marine technology needed to cross the increasingly wide stretches of ocean. Subsequent people, collectively known as Austronesians, moved into the area from the west, mingling with the Papuans and eventually becoming the highly diverse group of people known as 'Melanesians'. New Guinea and the Solomons were the only inhabited islands in the Pacific for many thousands of years.

The wide seas from the Solomons to Vanuatu were finally crossed in about 1500 BC by the Lapita people, who later gave rise to Polynesian culture.

The Melanesians of New Guinea and the Solomons mingled a little with the Lapita and followed them across the Pacific. Melanesians came to dominate New Guinea, the Solomons, Vanuatu, New Caledonia and Fiji.

The Lapitas' Polynesian descendants waited on Samoa and Tonga for a thousand years or so, until developing more advanced ocean vessels and skills. Some time around 200 BC, they crossed the long ocean stretches to the east, reaching the Society and Marquesas island groups (in modern French Polynesia). From there, voyaging canoes travelled southwest to Rarotonga and the southern Cook Islands, southeast to Rapa Nui (Easter

TIMELINE	50,000 years ago	1500 BC	200 BC
	The Papuans, related to Australia's Aborigines, settle the Pacific in Papua New Guinea and the Solomon Islands but are unable to travel further due to lack of technology.	Long-distance seafaring begins in earnest by the Lapita people in Vanuatu, New Caledonia, Fiji and central Polynesia, where they develop the culture now known as Polynesian.	Polynesians spread east to the Society and Marquesas Islands (modern-day French Polynesia). Melanesians following from New Guinea and the Solomon Islands come to dominate Vanuatu, New Caledonia and Fiji.

THE ANCIENT LAPITA CULTURE

The ancient race of people known as the Lapita is thought to be responsible for the wide distribution of Polynesian culture and Austronesian languages in the Pacific. It was in Tonga and Samoa that the Lapita developed into the people we now call Polynesians.

From 1500 BC to 500 BC, the Lapita held sway over a vast area of the Pacific, where their influence can be traced through the far-flung dispersal of their unique pottery. Lapita pottery has been found in Papua New Guinea, New Caledonia, in parts of Micronesia and in Fiji, Tonga, Samoa and Wallis and Futuna.

The Lapita were skilled sailors and navigators, able to cross hundreds of kilometres of open sea, and trade and settlement were important to them. They were also agriculturists and practised husbandry of dogs, pigs and fowl. Regarded as the first cultural complex in the Pacific, they traded obsidian (volcanic glass used in tool production) from New Britain (an island off PNG) with people up to 2500km away in Tonga and Samoa.

You can see Lapita artefacts in the national museums of Vanuatu and in Suva and Sigatoka in Fiji.

Island) in AD 300, north to Hawai'i around 400 and southwest past Rarotonga to Aotearoa (New Zealand) in 900.

Although the predominant direction of human movement was from west to east, population pressure and the occasional religious disagreement prompted constant movement of people across the oceans. So Polynesians can be found today in Melanesia's eastern islands, while the largely Melanesian Fiji is also home to many Polynesians and Micronesians.

Compared to the coast-hugging settlement patterns of contemporary Europeans, the settlement of the Pacific Ocean was the most remarkable feat of ocean sailing up to that time. All but the farthest-flung islands of the massive Pacific were colonised by 200 BC. By contrast it was more than 1000 years later that the Vikings crossed the (relatively small) Atlantic to make Europe's first cross-ocean settlement.

Melanesians embarked on regular trade and some war missions, but Polynesians travelled the broader stretches of open ocean. Almost no Pacific islands were cut off entirely from other cultures, and the presence of the *kumara* (sweet potato) in the Pacific islands confirms that at least some journeys were made as far east as South America, probably from the Marquesas or Austral Islands. Traditional stories also indicate exploratory journeys into Antarctic waters 'not seen by the sun'.

For a terrific summation of South Pacific history, with a particular bent towards Fiji, pick up a copy of *Worlds Apart: A History of the Pacific Islands* by IC Campbell (2003).

Voyaging & Navigation

Ancient Pacific islanders' voyages were motivated by war, trade, colonisation and the search for resources, or sometimes merely by curiosity and

AD 300–900	1568	1722	1768–79
The final major wave of Polynesian exploration leaves the Societies and Marquesas: north to Hawai'i, southwest to the Cook Islands, southeast to Easter Island and, lastly, to New Zealand.	Don Alvaro de Mendaña y Neyra lands on Santa Isabel Island finding traces of gold and, believing he has discovered King Solomon's Mines, names the islands the Solomons.	The Dutch arrive on Easter Island, rows of amazing stone *moai* and a few thousand Rapa Nui locals the only remnants of a population estimated to have been 15,000 a hundred years prior.	Captain James Cook 'boldly goes' on three voyages through the Pacific to explore more of the earth than anyone in history, before being killed in Hawai'i.

pride. The Tongans, known as the 'Vikings of the Pacific', ruled Samoa, Niue and eastern Fiji with an iron fist, and launched raids from Tuvalu to the Solomon Islands, 2700km to the west.

At the time of European contact, prodigious feats of navigation and voyaging still occurred, although not on as grand a scale as previously. The navigator-priest Tupaia, who boarded Cook's *Endeavour* in Tahiti, could name around 100 islands between the Marquesas and Fiji, and he directed Cook's search for islands west of Tahiti. For the entire circuitous journey to Java in Indonesia, Tupaia could always point in the direction of his homeland.

Top Archaeo-logical Sites

Easter Island

Taputapuatea, French Polynesia

Ha'amonga 'a Maui Trilithon, Tonga

Mangaia's burial caves, Cook Islands

Pulamelei Mound, Samoa

Canoes

The term 'canoe' (*vaka* or *va'a*) is misleading. In the South Pacific, the same word describes small dugouts used for river navigation, giant war vessels accommodating hundreds of men and 25m-long ocean-voyaging craft. Ocean-voyaging craft – either double canoes or single canoes with outriggers – carried one or more masts and sails of woven pandanus. Captain James Cook and contemporary observers estimated that Pacific canoes were capable of speeds greater than their own ships; probably 150km to 250km per day, so that trips of 5000km could be comfortably achieved with available provisions.

Navigation Techniques

Initial exploratory journeys often followed the migratory flights of birds. Once a new land had been discovered, the method of rediscovery was remembered and communicated mostly by which stars to follow. Fine-tuning of these directions was possible by observing the direction from which certain winds blew, the currents, wave fronts reflecting from islands and the flight of land birds.

European Arrival

Like Pacific islanders, European explorers came in search of resources (gold and spices initially), or were driven by curiosity and national pride. Europeans were also inspired by one overpowering myth: the existence and search for a great southern continent, Terra Australis.

Since the time of Ptolemy, scientists predicted the presence of a huge landmass in the southern hemisphere to counter the Earth's northern continents (otherwise, it was believed, the globe would be top heavy and fall over). In the absence of hard facts, Terra Australis was believed to be peopled with strange heathens and magical creatures, and rumoured to be rich in gold. The biblical tale of King Solomon had included vast gold mines in some unknown location. What could be a better spot than Terra Australis?

1785	1789	1812	1838
French explorer La Pérouse sets off to explore the Pacific. He visits Tonga, Samoa and Australia before mysteriously disappearing. His wrecked ship is discovered in the Solomon Islands in 2005.	Fletcher Christian famously relieves Captain Bligh of his duties. Christian, eight mutineers and a handful of Tahitian men and women leg it to Pitcairn Island; 16 mutineers remain on Tahiti.	King Pomare II of Tahiti seeks conversion to Protestantism, which leads to European support of his rule and allows him to centralise power; the missionaries essentially become the government.	After French Catholic missionaries are kicked off Tahiti, France sends in a gunboat, leading to bloody battles and the island being declared a French protectorate in 1842.

The Spanish

In 1521 the Portuguese Ferdinand Magellan led a Spanish expedition that discovered, at the southern tip of the Americas, an entrance to the ocean he named Mar Pacifico – the Pacific Ocean – for its calmness. Magellan spotted only two small, uninhabited islands until he had sailed northwest across almost the entire ocean to Guam in Micronesia.

MODERN VOYAGING

The voyaging skills of today's Pacific islanders may not match those of their ancestors, but the traditional knowledge of navigation is still put to everyday use. Both small inter-island trips and long-distance voyages have been used to test many theories about ocean voyaging.

Kon Tiki

Probably the most famous such voyage was that of Thor Heyerdahl's *Kon Tiki* from South America to the Tuamotus in 1947. The journey attempted to prove that Polynesia could have been populated from South America. While that theory has since been disproved by genetic evidence, the 8000km trip caused many historians to rethink their ideas about ancient Polynesian technology and ability to sail between islands.

Traditions Continue

Modern voyages along traditional routes have refined theories about canoe construction and navigational methods. Among such journeys, the 25m-long outrigger canoe *Tarratai* was sailed from Kiribati 2500km south to Fiji in 1976. That same year the voyage of the 20m *Hokule'a*, which used traditional navigation methods for the 4250km trip from Hawai'i to Tahiti, sparked a resurgence of interest in traditional navigation.

Other voyaging canoes include the 21m *Hawaiki Nui*, which sailed 4000km from Tahiti to Aotearoa in 1985. In 1995 *Te Au o Tonga*, captained by former prime minister of the Cook Islands Sir Thomas Davis (Papa Tom), sailed from Rarotonga to Tahiti, on to Hawai'i and back to Rarotonga. Part of the cargo on the last leg was less than traditional: Papa Tom's new 1200cc Harley-Davidson. The *Hokule'a* and *Te Au o Tonga*, among other great *vaka* (outrigger canoes), continue to make long voyages.

Te Mana O Te Moana

In April 2011 a group of seven traditional voyaging canoes, each skippered by a different Polynesian nation and calling themselves Te Mana O Te Moana (The Spirit of the Sea), set sail from New Zealand. Voyaging through Polynesia, the canoes arrived in Hawai'i for the Kava Bowl Summit that addressed the effects of climate change in the Pacific, then travelled onward to the West Coast of the USA, and eventually headed back through Polynesia to the Pacific Arts Festival in the Solomon Islands in 2012. Their overall goal: to raise environmental awareness of the great ocean.

Have a look at www.pacificvoyagers.org for more, including info on their voyages.

1841	1845	1864	1879
Pierre Louis Marie Chanel becomes patron saint of the Pacific islands after being killed for eroding the traditional power structure and gaining too many converts in Futuna.	Tonga's King George Tupou I takes the throne over a newly united nation and creates a governing system with a little help from his prime minister, Reverend Shirley Baker.	The first 'blackbirded' labourers from Vanuatu and the Solomon Islands arrive in Fiji. Meanwhile, the first 329 Chinese workers are brought to Tahiti to work at American-run cotton fields.	Following the outlawing of 'blackbirding', Britain introduces the first Indian indentured labourers to Fiji to work in the sugar-cane fields of the main island.

The Cook Islands were originally called the Hervey Islands by the modest Captain Cook. It was only after his death in the 1820s that the new name appeared in his honour on a Russian naval chart.

On Guam the first contact between Pacific islanders and Europeans followed a pattern that would become all too familiar. The islander belief that all property was shared meant that Guam's islanders helped themselves to one of the expedition's small boats and Magellan retaliated – seven islanders were killed. Magellan himself was killed two months later while in the Philippines, but not before he became the first person to circumnavigate the globe (having previously visited the Philippines from the other direction).

Spaniard Don Alvaro de Mendaña y Neyra sailed west across the Pacific in search of Terra Australis in 1567. In the Solomon Islands, conflict with the locals arose when islanders were unable to supply the resources Mendaña needed to resupply.

It took Mendaña nearly 30 years to gain approval for his disastrous second voyage during 1595. An estimated 200 islanders were killed in the Marquesas when conflict broke out. There was even more conflict with locals when the ship reached the Solomon Islands, and fighting also spread to the crew. Mendaña himself died of malaria, and the expedition limped to Peru under the command of the more humane Pedro Fernández de Quirós. Quirós led another expedition to the Pacific in 1605, 'discovering' the Tuamotu Islands and Vanuatu.

The Dutch

Jacob Le Maire and Willem Schouten's 1616 search for Terra Australis introduced Europe to the Tongan islands and Futuna. Jacob Roggeveen spotted Bora Bora in the Society Islands in 1722, and Tutuila and Upolu in Samoa. Abel Tasman became the most famous Dutch explorer of all, after charting Tasmania and the east coast of New Zealand in 1642 then landing on the islands of Tonga and Fiji.

Passing European seafarers reported many of Easter Island's famous *moai* had toppled over between 1722 and 1868, with oral stories pointing to a civil war that saw the statues pushed over to indicate defeat.

The French

The most famous French explorer, Louis-Antoine de Bougainville, came upon Tahiti and claimed it for France in 1768 (he didn't realise that Wallis had claimed it for England less than a year before). He went on to the Samoan islands, then continued to Vanuatu and Australia's Great Barrier Reef. Bougainville's impact was greater than dots on a map, however; his accounts of the South Pacific sparked massive interest back in Europe and created the myth of a southern paradise.

In 1827 Dumont d'Urville sailed the Pacific searching for his lost countryman, the comte de la Pérouse, whose boat had sunk near the Solomon Islands in 1788. D'Urville's writings of this and another journey (10 years later) were to establish the concept of the three great subdivisions of the Pacific: Melanesia, Micronesia and Polynesia.

1889–94	1890–1903	1899	1914
'Here he lies where he longed to be' – Robert Louis Stevenson abandons the chilly moors of Scotland for the warm delights of Samoa via French Polynesia.	French post-Impressionist Paul Gauguin retreats to Tahiti and the Marquesas to devote his life to art. His paintings strengthen the idyllic image of the South Pacific in the Western world.	Tripartite Treaty splits the Samoas between Germany and America; Britain steps out of the Samoas in exchange for the renunciation of German claims on Tonga, the Solomon Islands and Niue.	Concerned about the proximity of an enemy territory during WWI, New Zealand sends troops to occupy German territories in Samoa and meets no opposition.

The English
In 1767 Samuel Wallis – *still* searching for Terra Australis – landed on Tahiti, but the greatest of the English explorers was James Cook.

Cook's three journeys into the region – the first (1768–71) most famously 'discovered' Australia and New Zealand – saw detailed mapping and exploration that would later allow others to follow. His third and final journey was the first European visit to Hawai'i, where Cook was killed. His legacy can be seen throughout the Pacific with his detailed maps used until the 1990s and several places bearing his name, most notably the Cook Islands.

Following the most famous of maritime mutinies, Fletcher Christian captained the *Bounty* to discover Rarotonga in the southern Cook Islands in 1789.

For a cracking rendition of the story of the HMS *Bounty,* catch the debonair Marlon Brando as Fletcher Christian and Trevor Howard as William Bligh in *Mutiny On The Bounty* (1962).

Evangelisation of the Pacific
After a few largely unsuccessful Spanish Catholic forays into Micronesia during the 17th century, the first major attempt to bring Christianity to the Pacific was by English Protestants. The newly formed London Missionary Society (LMS) outfitted missionary outposts on Tahiti and Tonga, and in the Marquesas in 1797. These first missions failed – within two years the Tongan and Marquesan missions were abandoned. The Tahitian mission survived but its success was limited. For a decade there were only a handful of islanders who were tempted to join the new religion.

HISTORY EVANGELISATION OF THE PACIFIC

ST PIERRE CHANEL OF OCEANIA

Pierre Louis Marie Chanel was born into a French peasant family in 1802, and trained as a priest. He embarked for the Pacific islands with the newly formed Catholic Society of Mary (Marist) in 1836 and, the following year, was the first missionary to set foot on Futuna. The ruling king, Niuluki, welcomed him.

As missionaries gained converts and thus eroded the traditional power structure of the island, Niuluki became less keen on the newcomers. When Niuluki's son asked to be baptised, the king issued an edict that the missionaries cease their activities. On 28 April 1841 a band of warriors, probably condoned by Niuluki, attacked Pierre Chanel and killed him.

Despite this (or perhaps because of it) the island soon became fully Catholic as other Marist priests took up the challenge.

Pierre Chanel was declared venerable in 1857, beatified in 1889 and finally canonised as the patron saint of Oceania in 1954. He is also recognised as the first martyr to lay his life down for Oceania (Rev John Williams had been dead for two years at this stage, but he was a Protestant – and that doesn't count).

By Errol Hunt

1918–19	1942–43	1946	1947
Spanish influenza, an H1N1 virus that caused one of the biggest worldwide pandemics in history, ravages Tonga, Tahiti, Fiji and Samoa, wiping out approximately 20% of their populations.	Japanese and American forces battle post–Pearl Harbor on Guadalcanal in the Solomon Islands. The American win marks a turning point of WWII and halts Japanese expansion in the Pacific.	The first atomic testing in the Pacific begins: two bombs the size of those dropped on Nagasaki are detonated by the US on Bikini Atoll in the Marshall Islands.	Thor Heyerdahl sails the balsa raft *Kon Tiki* from Peru to the Tuamotus to prove that the Pacific was populated from the Americas. His theory is later disproved by genetics.

CAPTAIN JAMES COOK

If aliens ever visit Earth, they may wonder what to make of the countless obelisks, faded plaques and graffiti-covered statues of a stiff, wigged figure gazing out to sea from Alaska to Australia, from NZ to North Yorkshire, from Siberia to the South Pacific. James Cook (1728–79) explored more of the earth's surface than anyone in history, and it's impossible to travel the Pacific without encountering the captain's image and his controversial legacy in the lands he opened to the West.

For a man who travelled so widely, and rose to such fame, Cook came from an extremely pinched and provincial background. The son of a day labourer in rural Yorkshire, he was born in a mud cottage, had little schooling and seemed destined for farm work. Instead, Cook went to sea as a teenager, worked his way up from coal-ship servant to naval officer, and attracted notice for his exceptional charts of Canada. But Cook remained a little-known second lieutenant until, in 1768, the Royal Navy chose him to command a daring voyage to the South Seas.

In a converted coal ship called *Endeavour,* Cook sailed to Tahiti, and then became the first European to land at New Zealand and the east coast of Australia. Though the ship almost sank after striking the Great Barrier Reef, and 40% of the crew died from disease and accidents, the *Endeavour* limped home in 1771.

On a return voyage (1772–75), Cook became the first navigator to pierce the Antarctic Circle and circled the globe near its southernmost latitude, demolishing the ancient myth that a vast, populous and fertile continent surrounded the South Pole. Cook also criss-crossed the Pacific from Easter Island to Melanesia. Though Maori killed and cooked 10 sailors, the captain remained sympathetic to islanders. 'Notwithstanding they are cannibals,' he wrote, 'they are naturally of a good disposition.'

On Cook's final voyage (1776–79), in search of a northwest passage between the Atlantic and Pacific, he became the first European to visit Hawai'i, and coasted America from Oregon to Alaska. Forced back by Arctic pack ice, Cook returned to Hawai'i, where he was killed during a skirmish with islanders who had initially greeted him as a Polynesian god. In a single decade of discovery, Cook had filled in the map of the Pacific and, as one French navigator put it, 'left his successors with little to do but admire his exploits'.

But Cook's travels also spurred colonisation of the Pacific, and within decades of his death, missionaries, whalers, traders and settlers began transforming – and often devastating – island cultures. As a result, many indigenous people now revile Cook as an imperialist villain who introduced disease, dispossession and other ills to the Pacific (hence the frequent vandalising of Cook monuments). However, as islanders revive traditional crafts and practices, from tattooing to tapa, they have turned to the art and writing of Cook and his men as a resource for cultural renewal. For good and ill, a Yorkshire farm boy remains the single most significant figure in the shaping of the modern Pacific.

Tony Horwitz is a Pulitzer-winning reporter and nonfiction author. His latest book is BOOM: Oil, Money, Cowboys, Strippers, and the Energy Rush That Could Change America Forever. *He retraced Cook's voyages in his 2002 book* Blue Latitudes: Boldly Going Where Captain Cook Has Gone Before.

1958	1962	1963	1970
The camp musical *South Pacific,* based on James Michener's short story of the same title, is unleashed upon the world.	Western Samoa becomes the first Pacific nation to be given independence after being a UN Trust Territory administered by New Zealand since the end of WWII.	The first South Pacific Games (now called Pacific Games), a multi-sport mini Olympics, are held in Suva, Fiji. The games at first transpire at three-year intervals, later extended to four years.	After 96 years of colonial rule Fiji becomes independent, adopting a British model of parliament with two houses including a 'House of Lords' made up of Fijian chiefs.

Other Protestants soon joined the battle. New players in the South Pacific were the Wesleyan Missionary Society (WMS), fresh from moderate success in New Zealand, and the American Board of Commissioners for Foreign Missions (ABCFM), following their Christianising of Hawai'i. The WMS and ABCFM both floundered in the Marquesas, but fared better in Tonga.

In the 1830s French Catholic missions were established in the Marquesas and Tahiti. Catholic missionaries were often as pleased to convert a Protestant as a heathen, with the fierce rivalry between the different denominations extended to their island converts. Religious conflicts fitted easily into the already complex political melee of Pacific society, and local chiefs manipulated the two Christian camps for their own purposes.

Despite the slow start, missionary success grew. By the 1820s missionary influence on Tahiti was enormous. The Bible was translated into Tahitian, a Protestant work ethic was instilled, tattooing discouraged, promiscuity guarded against by nightly 'moral police' and the most 'heathen' practices such as human sacrifice were forbidden. From Tahiti, Tonga and Hawai'i, Christianity spread throughout the Pacific.

The missionaries' success was due to three major factors. Clever politics played a part, particularly the conversion of influential Tongan chief Taufa'ahau and the Tahitian Pomare family. The perceived link between European wealth and Christianity also played a part: missionaries 'civilised' as well as Christianised, and islanders obtained European tools and skills, such as literacy. Finally, the message of afterlife salvation fell on attentive ears as European arrival coincided with the massive depopulation through the spread of disease.

Missionaries shielded islanders from the excesses of some traders, and it was missionary pressure that finally put an end to the blackbirding (p551) trade. Putting Pacific languages into written form, initially in translations of the Bible, was another major contribution. While many missionaries deliberately destroyed 'heathen' Pacific artefacts and beliefs, others diligently recorded myths and oral traditions that would otherwise have been lost. A substantial portion of our knowledge of Pacific history and traditional culture comes from the work of missionary historians.

The church remains an important political player in many islands on the basis of its strong history. Ruling dynasties in Tonga, Tahiti and Fiji all owed their success to missionary backing, just as missionary success owed a lot to those dynasties.

Gold of the South Seas

Whaling

European whalers enthusiastically hunted in the Pacific from the late 18th century. Trade peaked in the mid-19th century, then declined as whale products were superseded by other materials. The effect on the

1971	1978	1978	1980
Establishment of the South Pacific Forum (now Pacific Islands Forum). Its aims include government cooperation to work towards economic and social well-being of the peoples of the South Pacific.	More than 20 years after crushing the nationalist movement, Britain grants independence for the Solomon Islands, with Chief Minister Sir Peter Kenilorea automatically assuming the role of prime minister.	After separating from the Ellis and Gilbert Islands under the Commonwealth and changing its name from Ellis Island to Tuvalu in 1974, Tuvalu becomes entirely independent. The Gilbert Islands are now Kiribati.	The islands known as the New Hebrides (which were co-governed by France and Great Britain) become independent with the new name of Vanuatu.

Pacific's whale population was catastrophic, but the effect on Pacific islanders was complex. There were opportunities for lucrative trade as ships resupplied, and many Pacific islanders, as always fond of travel, took the opportunity to embark on whaling ships. Some islanders, however, were effectively kidnapped and forced to travel without consent; whalers of the Pacific were not the most gentle of men.

Bêches-de-Mer

Also known as *trepang*, sea cucumbers or sea slugs, the *bêche-de-mer* is a marine organism related to starfish and urchins. An Asian delicacy, Pacific *bêches-de-mer* were sought by early-19th-century Europeans to trade for Chinese tea. *Bêches-de-mer* were relatively abundant, and important trading relations were forged with islanders. For the most part trade was mutually beneficial, with islanders trading eagerly for metal, cloth, tobacco and muskets. The trade in *bêches-de-mer* was largely nonviolent, in contrast with the sandalwood trade.

Sandalwood

When French Catholic missionaries were kicked out of Tahiti in 1836, France sent in a gunboat in 1838, which led to the island being declared a French protectorate in 1842.

Nineteenth-century Europeans trading with China found another valued Pacific resource in fragrant sandalwood, used in China for ornamental carving and cabinetmaking, as well as incense. By the 1820s these traders had stripped the sandalwood forests of Hawai'i, and looked to islands to the south. Extensive sandalwood forests on Fiji, Vanuatu, the Solomons and New Caledonia became the focus for traders keen to satisfy the demands of the Chinese market.

On each new island, payment for sandalwood was initially low. A small piece of metal, a goat or a dog was sometimes sufficient to buy a boatload of the aromatic wood. But as the supply of slow-growing sandalwood dwindled, the price rose – islanders demanded guns, ammunition, tobacco or assistance in war as payment.

While the sandalwood trade in Fiji was fairly orderly under the supervision of local chiefs, spheres of chiefly influence in the Solomons, Vanuatu and New Caledonia were much smaller and traders had difficulty establishing lasting relationships with islanders. Sandalwood was the most violent of any trades in the Pacific, and Melanesia's savage reputation in Europe was not improved. There were many attacks on ships' crews, sometimes motivated by a greed for plunder, but often a response to previous atrocities by Europeans. Melanesians assumed that all Europeans belonged to the one kin group, and thus were accountable for another's crimes.

The sandalwood trade was entirely unsustainable. Island after island was stripped of its forests, and the trade petered out in the 1860s with the removal of the last accessible stands.

Blackbirding

In the late 19th century, cheap labour was sought for various Pacific industries, such as mines and plantations. Pacific islanders were also 'recruited' to labour in Australia, Fiji, New Caledonia, Samoa and Peru. Satisfying the demand for labour was a major commercial activity from the 1860s.

In some cases islanders were keen to sign up, seeking to share the benefits of European wealth. Often, though, islanders were tricked into boarding ships, either being deceived about the length of time for which they were contracted, or sometimes enticed aboard by sailors dressed as priests. In many cases no pretence was even attempted: islanders were simply herded onto slaving ships at gunpoint.

The populations of many small, barely viable islands were devastated by blackbirders (a term used for the co-opting and sometimes kidnapping of islanders) – Tokelau lost almost half its population to Peruvian slave ships in 1863, while the Tongan island of 'Ata lost 40% of its population, and as a result is today uninhabited. People were also taken as slaves from Tuvalu, New Caledonia, Easter Island, Vanuatu and the Solomon Islands.

Blackbirding was outlawed by Britain's Pacific Islanders' Protection Act in 1872, largely due to persistent lobbying by missionaries. Their campaigns resulted in the banning of overseas-labour recruitment to Australia (in 1904), Samoa (in 1913) and Fiji (in 1916). The British government followed up the law with regular patrols of the region to prevent unscrupulous blackbirders, marking the beginning of a colonialist mentality of protection.

While some islanders returned to their homelands, others remained, such as the large Melanesian population in Queensland, Australia. In Fiji the large plantation economy looked elsewhere for cheap labour, transporting indentured labourers from India, who remain prominent in Fijian culture and society today.

'Once the people were on board they locked them up and sailed away. Two men escaped and swam back to shore, but the rest were never seen again.' Kelese Simona, in *Time and Tide: The Islands of Tuvalu,* recalls his father's account of blackbirders kidnapping much of the island's population.

HISTORY BLACKBIRDING

Flag Follows Trade

Once European traders were established in the Pacific, many began agitating for their home countries to intervene and protect their interests. Missionaries also lobbied for colonial takeover, hoping that European law would protect islanders from the lawless traders. European powers began following a policy of 'flag following trade' by declaring protectorates and then by annexing Pacific states.

Between 1878 and 1899 Germany annexed the Marshall Islands, northern Solomon Islands and Samoa. The latter treaty ceded American Samoa to the US, joining the Phoenix Islands (now in Kiribati), which the US and Britain had claimed in 1836. After annexing French Polynesia (1840s) and New Caledonia (1853), the French lost interest before claiming Wallis and Futuna (1880s) and going into partnership with Britain in Vanuatu in 1906.

2000	2001	2002	2002
George Speight heads a Fijian coup with hostages held in parliament for eight weeks; Speight is eventually charged with treason and given a life prison sentence.	Australia begins its Pacific Solution (2001–07), moving asylum seekers arriving in Australian waters by boat, to detention camps in PNG and Nauru rather than letting them land in Australia.	Tropical Cyclone Zoe, the most intense storm in recorded southern hemisphere history, blasts through parts of the Solomon Islands and Vanuatu. Amazingly, no-one is killed.	US reality series *Survivor* comes to French Polynesia with *Survivor Marquesas* – later seasons bring world attention to Fiji, Vanuatu and the Cook Islands.

Contrary to popular opinion, Britain was a reluctant Pacific-empire builder. However, it ended up with the largest of all Pacific empires, after being forced by various lobby groups to assume responsibilities for the Phoenix Islands in 1836, then Fiji, Tokelau, the Cooks, the Gilbert and Ellice Islands (modern Kiribati and Tuvalu), the southern Solomons and Niue between 1874 and 1900, and finally Vanuatu in 1906. Between 1900 and 1925, Britain happily offloaded the Cooks, Niue and Tokelau into the protection of New Zealand. Interestingly, the Kingdom of Tonga has never lost (or offered) its sovereignty to a colonial power, despite the British and the Tongan royals agreeing to a protective Treaty of Friendship in 1900.

Colonialism brought peace between warring European powers but an increase in tensions with islanders. The arrival of settlers brought diseases that had been unknown in the Pacific or had been experienced only in limited contact with explorers or traders, and these took a horrific toll. Cholera, measles, smallpox, influenza, pneumonia, scarlet fever, chickenpox, whooping cough, dysentery, venereal diseases and even the common cold had devastating effects. Most Polynesian populations were halved, while Micronesia and Melanesia's populations suffered even more. Some islands of Vanuatu were among the worst hit, dropping to just 5% of their original populations.

War in the Pacific

WWI had little impact on the Pacific, though German colonial rulers in Micronesia, Samoa and Nauru were exchanged for Japanese, New Zealand, Australian and British rule. Germany, slightly preoccupied with events in Europe at the time, didn't resist these Pacific takeovers.

In contrast, the Pacific was a major arena of conflict during WWII. The war with Japan was fought through the Micronesian territories Japan had won from Germany in WWI, in Papua New Guinea and in the Solomon Islands.

Initially Japan expanded south from its Micronesian territories almost unhindered and captured the Solomon Islands in 1942. They began building an airfield on Guadalcanal (which today is Henderson Airport) that would supply further advances south. Allied forces staged a huge offensive that saw more than 60 ships sunk in the surrounding waters that became known as Iron Bottom Sound. From 1944, US and Australian forces pushed the defending Japanese back, island by island. US bombers based in the Marianas punished Japanese cities for 10 months until 6 August 1945, when *Enola Gay* took off from Tinian (Northern Marianas) to drop an atomic bomb on Hiroshima. Days later another was dropped on Nagasaki and the Pacific war was over.

The suffering of islanders during the Pacific war was immense: Japanese forces in Micronesia forced the transport of large numbers

2006	2006	2007	2007
On 16 November riots erupt in the Tongan capital of Nuku'alofa as pro-democracy supporters express their anger at government inaction despite promises of reform.	After making demands about upcoming bills, Commodore Frank Bainimarama begins military manoeuvres that eventually depose the Fiji government, and declares himself acting president in a coup.	Samoa's King Malietoa Tanumafili II dies and the nation becomes a republic, electing Tuiatua Tupua Tamasese Efi as head of state for a five-year term.	The Solomon Islands are struck by an earthquake and tsunami killing 54 and making many thousands homeless; another devastating quake and tsunami hits in 2010, destroying some 200 homes.

of islanders between various islands, seemingly without motive. People were concentrated in areas without adequate food, thousands died from hunger and thousands more were executed by the Japanese as an Allied victory became apparent.

Soldiers from Fiji, the Solomon Islands, Samoa, Tonga, French Polynesia and New Caledonia served in the armed forces, seeing action in the Pacific, Africa and Europe. Their valour cemented relations with other allies.

WWII had a lasting effect on the region. Most obviously, Japan's Micronesian colonies were taken over by the US, becoming the Trust Territory of the Pacific islands. However, the war also left a legacy of more widespread and subtle effects. There was a huge improvement in roads and other infrastructure on many islands. There was also an input of money, food and other supplies that contributed towards the development of so-called cargo cults, whose devotees believed the goods were gifts from ancestral spirits. More biologically, in Tonga, the many thousands of American GIs stationed here in WWII are credited by some with the deepening of the local gene pool, bolstering immunity and providing a platform for sustained population growth.

WWII also hastened the end of traditional colonialism in the Pacific, the relative equality between white and black US soldiers prompting islanders to question why they were still subservient to the British and the French. Many independence leaders were influenced by wartime experiences.

Nuclear Fallout

In 1946, a US military officer met the people of the tiny Bikini Atoll in the Marshall Islands and asked if they'd be prepared to leave their island for 'the good of mankind and to end all world wars'. Over 160 Bikinians left their home to make way for 42,000 US personnel who would begin nuclear testing on this remote island.

Along with Enewetok and Kwajalein atolls, the area became known as the Pacific Proving Grounds where 105 atmospheric tests were conducted until 1962. The most disastrous test occurred in 1954, when a hydrogen bomb code-named Bravo was detonated in an intense 32km-high fireball that stripped branches from trees on surrounding islands. It was the largest US test, with fallout washing over other Marshall Islands along with a Japanese fishing boat, *Daigo Fukuryu Maru* (Lucky Dragon No 5). It was a beacon that blazed around the world, and eventually, in 1963, the Partial Test Ban Treaty was signed.

Some nations, however, didn't sign up. France began nuclear testing in 1966 on Moruroa Atoll, an isolated part of French Polynesia. More than 40 tests were conducted until 1974, when international pressure pushed testing literally underground. The French abandoned testing on Moruroa and drilled into the island itself, detonating a further 147 nuclear devices here

WWII Relics

Diveable shipwrecks in Vanuatu

Military wreckage across the Solomon Islands' Western Province

Guadalcanal, Solomon Islands

2008	2009	2010	2011
On 1 August George Tupou V is officially crowned king of Tonga. Three days before, he indicates his intention of relinquishing much of his power to the prime minister.	A 4.5m tsunami generated from an earthquake near Apia affects Tonga but devastates Samoa and American Samoa, killing more than 170 people and wiping out entire villages.	Tonga holds its first democratic elections. Nobles from the monarchy that has ruled for generations win when fringe parties join their ranks; 2014 delivers much the same result.	Samoa and Tokelau jump forward one day on the Date Line to make it easier for the countries' business relations with Australia and Asia.

and later at Fangataufa. The tests began to crack the atolls themselves and there were concerns that nuclear material would leak into the open seas. Protests (including those by Greenpeace ship *Rainbow Warrior*, which was bombed and sunk in Auckland harbour by French intelligence agents in 1985) eventually brought international condemnation and the last test was conducted in 1996 when France signed the Comprehensive Nuclear Test Ban Treaty.

While some French military who worked at the test sites have been compensated for health problems, Roland Oldham, President of Moruroa E Tatau, which represents former test-site workers in French Polynesia, claims that red tape and complicated court cases have prevented islanders from getting help from France. As for environmental clean-up, the French government has been strict about who it allows to the atolls and what information is given to the public, so it's difficult to gauge the impact of the tests or how any possible damage has been dealt with.

The impact of the testing in the area was huge. In 1968 the US declared Bikini Atoll habitable again and returned Bikinians to their homeland. They remained there for 10 years until a team of French scientists investigated reports of birth defects and cancer among Bikinians. A second evacuation followed and the US made a payment of US$150 million, which was spent removing and destroying the top half-metre of soil. Compensation claims are still being made today as Bikinians attempt to discover the half-life of US responsibility.

To (virtually) hop aboard the ill-fated *Rainbow Warrior* as it journeyed through the Pacific protesting against nuclear testing, read NZ journalist David Robie's *Eyes of Fire: The Last Voyage of the Rainbow Warrior* (1986).

Postcolonial Pacific

From Samoa in 1962 through to Vanuatu in 1980, most Pacific-island states gained independence (or partial independence) from their former colonial rulers. This was a relatively bloodless transition, with colonial masters as keen to ditch their expensive responsibilities as islanders were to gain independence. It took longer for the US to dismantle its Trust Territory of Micronesia, slowed by its desire to maintain a military presence in the region.

Only a handful of South Pacific territories remain in the hands of the US (American Samoa), France (New Caledonia, French Polynesia), Chile (Easter Island) and New Zealand (Rarotonga and the Cook Islands), with some gradually returning power to islanders. Self-government has not always been easy for Pacific nations, with Fiji and the Solomon Islands offering bellicose examples. Tonga, which was never officially colonised, remains the last monarchy in the Pacific, though the royal family has partly relinquished power in favour of democracy.

Today the Pacific's governments face new challenges, including global environmental problems such as climate change and rising sea levels, particularly for smaller islands such as Tuvalu and Kiribati, which are at great risk from these effects.

2012	2012	2014	2015
Commodore Frank Bainimarama lifts martial law in Fiji and announces he will open a national consultation process for developing a new constitution.	King George Tupou V of Tonga dies while visiting Hong Kong. His brother George Tupou VI steps into the fold, but isn't crowned until 2015.	With a new constitution (brought into effect in 2013), Fiji holds general elections. Frank Bainimarama of the FijiFirst Party is elected prime minister.	Tropical Cyclone Pam, the second-most intense storm in South Pacific history, devastates Vanuatu, with the loss of 16 lives.

Environmental Issues

The South Pacific islands are a long way from most of the world's population (and thus most of the world's problems) – but the islands' scale and ecological sensitivity means their environments are among the world's most fragile. Climate change tops the list of big issues across all island groups, while local environmental battles are being waged over whaling, overfishing, deforestation, soil salination, litter management and compensation and recovery from nuclear testing.

Geology

Down at a rock-and-dirt level, the South Pacific has three types of islands: continental, high and low. The 'high' ones are mostly the peaks of volcanoes, extinct or active; while the 'low' islands, or atolls, are formed by fringing reefs that encircle lagoons where volcanic peaks have eroded and sunk. Melanesia has the only large 'continental' islands in the region: large and stable islands sitting amid large and stable tectonic plates.

Climate Change

The most severe ecological danger to the nations of the South Pacific can be attributed to the developed world – climate change. As the polar ice caps melt, sea levels rise – a critical issue for the South Pacific islands, with low-lying coral atolls especially vulnerable. King tides are already threatening Tuvalu's nine low-lying atolls, and islanders from Papua New Guinea's Carteret group have had to relocate to Bougainville – we may soon see whole South Pacific populations on the move as climate-change refugees. And it's not just people under threat – mangroves are an important linchpin in Pacific ecosystems and are also vulnerable to rising sea levels.

El Niño

Further complicating climate-change scenarios, El Niño is a regularly (though unpredictably) occurring climatic event that causes drought in some South Pacific areas, wreaking havoc on crop production, and deluge in others. In normal circumstances, easterly trade winds tend to send warmer surface water towards the western Pacific, resulting in more rainfall in that region (Melanesia, Australia and New Zealand) than in the east.

An El Niño (more correctly El Niño Southern Oscillation) event occurs when the Christmas-period reversal in wind direction combines with high air pressure in the western Pacific and low air pressure in the east. The warm surface water is then blown back towards the eastern Pacific, carrying rain with it: western Pacific countries experience droughts at this time, while eastern islands suffer unusually heavy rains or cyclones. El Niños usually last for about a year and recur irregularly every four or five years.

Overfishing

To many visitors – treated to snorkelling trips above thriving sections of coral reef teeming with multicoloured fish – it may seem hard to believe that fish stocks across the South Pacific are under threat. Commercial fishing fleets working the Pacific catch around half of the world's fish – an annual harvest that approaches 100 million tonnes. While many seem to believe

When an El Niño ('the Boy') system develops in the Pacific, it is often followed by a La Niña ('the Girl') system, which reverses the El Niño – bringing storms to the western Pacific and droughts to the east.

that the Pacific Ocean is an infinite resource because of its vast size, others claim this catch is unsustainable. The UN has found that most commercially exploited fisheries worldwide are being fished beyond their capacity to recover, and has stated that the industry is 'globally nonsustainable' and that 'major ecological and economic damage is already visible'.

It is not only fish caught for consumption that are endangered – fishing fleets worldwide claim a 'bycatch' of almost 30 million tonnes per year. These are unwanted species such as dolphins, sharks and turtles that are pulled up along with the target species and then dumped. The infamous

GLOBAL WARMING & THE SOUTH PACIFIC

Tuvalu began to voice its concern about climate change internationally in the late 1980s. Our key concern then, and now, is sea-level rise, which has the potential to submerge the islands we call home. Successive governments in Tuvalu have amplified warnings of this threat.

Over 35 years ago, scientists hinted that human-made emissions of carbon dioxide and other greenhouse gases may be raising the earth's atmospheric temperature, causing glaciers and polar ice to melt and sea levels to rise.

Now, is the sea rising? We think it is, and this view is supported by a broad scientific consensus. Estimates of sea-level rise in the southwest Pacific range between 1mm and 2mm per year. This is what science tells us, and anecdotal evidence here in Tuvalu – just south of the equator, and west of the international dateline – suggests the same.

What we see in Tuvalu is marginally higher (peak) sea levels when tides are highest. This means annual high tides are creeping further ashore. There is crop damage from previously unseen levels of saltwater intrusion, and a higher incidence of wave washover during storms or periods of strong tidal activity.

Some commentators, journalists and scientists have attributed these phenomena to construction too close to fragile lagoon foreshores or ocean fronts, or to the loss of natural coastal protection from cutting down shoreline trees and shoreline mining. Whether or not this is true is debatable. If the sea is rising, no amount of natural or artificial coastal protection that is not prohibitively expensive will fend it off. So-called 'adaptation' measures, however beneficial, merely delay the inevitable. Unless, of course, the worldwide volume of greenhouse-gas production is cut drastically, and cut fast.

Tuvalu's nine small atolls and reef islands are geographically flat, rising no more than 4m above sea level. We cannot move away from our coastlines as all the land we inhabit is coastline. We have no continental interior to which we can relocate; no high interior, as is found on a volcanic island.

Confronting the Issues

Successive governments in Tuvalu have adopted the concept of sustainable development. But however much we try to put this concept into action locally, we also know it will not solve the problem of rising sea levels. So what else can we do?

As much as we try to meet the expectations of the international community, which demands that we include sustainable development in our national policy, our efforts on the ground have been mostly unsuccessful. (Other developing countries around the world share the same experience.)

In the context of climate change, it has become obvious to us that sustainable development is clearly not a defence against sea-level rise, no matter how hard the international debate tries to connect the two. As the former chairman of the Association of Small Island States, Tuiloma Neroni Slade, said: 'It may be that we manage to get our sustainable development polices right. Yet we will still face the risk that all will be undermined by climate change.' This reality is the situation we face in the Pacific. Human-made climate change is not a Pacific invention, nor are rising sea levels our problem to fix. There is only this: Tuvalu and other Pacific-island countries will be among the first to suffer the catastrophic consequences of sea-level rise.

Saufatu Sopoanga, an enduring political presence in Tuvalu, was prime minister of the country between 2002 and 2004.

drift nets, which are legally limited to 2.5km in length but are often much longer, claim a huge bycatch.

Remnants of drift nets are often found wrapped around dead whales that wash ashore. Nets and lines that have broken loose continue to drift through the oceans, catching and killing as they go. Longlines drifting loose on the surface of the South Pacific have decimated albatross populations, bringing some species near to extinction. Closer to the coast, blast fishing and cyanide fishing – both illegal – kill everything nearby including coral and shellfish rather than just their target species.

To resource-poor Pacific-island nations, selling licences to fish their relatively large Exclusive Economic Zones (EEZ) is one of few options available to bring in dollars. To fish, or not to fish, that is the question.

Taking a positive lead to combat overfishing, the Fijian government has declared its intent to protect 30% of its waters as marine parks by 2020 – potentially the largest marine-park network in the world.

Whaling

Australia and New Zealand have for years been trying to raise enough support among member countries in the International Whaling Commission (IWC; www.iwc.int) to declare a South Pacific whale sanctuary, but have consistently failed to gain the required three-quarters majority. The IWC pronounced a moratorium on commercial whaling in 1986, although Japan was allowed to continue to hunt whales under an agreed scientific-research clause (heavily criticised by opponents of whaling as being commercial whaling in disguise). Japan has tried to have the ban overturned, and won a vote on the 'eventual return of commercial whaling' by one vote in 2006. However, the ban was not lifted, and Japan continues it lobby for it to be so.

All three major players in the debate (Japan, Australia and New Zealand) are significant suppliers of foreign aid to Pacific nations, building roads, hospitals, police stations, schools...raising accusations of 'vote buying' at the IWC on both sides of the dispute.

Twelve Pacific countries and territories protect whales within economic exclusion zones. This area of 12 million sq km between French Polynesia and Australia acts as de facto whale sanctuary. Given the opposition it faces in the South Pacific, recently Japan has turned its attentions to whaling in the Southern Ocean around Antarctica, taking thousands of whales until another ban was enacted by the International Court of Justice (ICJ) in 2014, stating that Japan's whaling program was not for scientific purposes.

Deforestation & Salination

Easter Island led the world in its deforestation efforts a thousand years before Magellan sailed into the South Pacific. The resources put into constructing the island's famous *moai* statues turned the island into a desolate wasteland, and led to decline of the local population.

In modern times many South Pacific governments, with few other options, have embraced logging as a necessary evil. Logging is usually conducted by offshore companies: it's widely reported that graft and corruption is often involved in the granting of logging concessions by island governments. Foreign logging companies often have no long-term interests in Pacific countries beyond harvesting timber resources, sometimes operating at the very edge of legality. Locals rarely see net benefits from their traditional lands laid to waste in such fashion. Only larger Pacific islands like those in the Solomons, Vanuatu, New Caledonia, Fiji and Samoa have sufficient timber reserves to interest such companies. The Solomons' timber stocks continue to be perilously overharvested, with the annual deforestation rate running at about 0.2%. Much of this logging is illegal, run by well-organised international syndicates, and this fuels corruption, exploitation and violence. In 2007 the Anglican Church of Melanesia reported on widespread child sexual exploitation associated with an Asian logging company around Arosi in Makira Province in the Solomons. In 2015 the Solomon Islands' government announced renewed efforts to curtail illegal forestry activity.

As well as loss of habitat for native birds and animals, deforestation leads to massive soil loss, which is particularly serious on small coral islands such as Niue, whose soil quality has never been good. Increased run-off from deforested land also leads to pollution of waterways and muddying of coastal waters, which can severely retard the growth of coral. These impacts, in conjunction with the effects of rising saltwater tables, have lead to the salination of previously arable soils, rendering them unfit for the production of even the most hardy of South Pacific crops such as taro and coconut.

Nuclear Fallout

The Pacific Ocean has seen more than its fair share of nuclear explosions. In fact, in one respect it all started here: the world's only hostile uses of nuclear weapons, on Hiroshima and Nagasaki in 1945, were launched from the Northern Marianas in the northwestern Pacific. Subsequently, the US, the UK and France have all conducted nuclear testing here.

In 1971 the nuclear-testing issue loomed large at the first meeting of the South Pacific Forum (SPF; now Pacific Island Forum). In 1986 the SPF's *Treaty of Rarotonga* established the South Pacific Nuclear-Free Zone, banning nuclear weapons and the dumping of nuclear waste. This was ratified 10 years later by France, the US and the UK.

France's Pacific nuclear-testing program commenced with atmospheric tests in 1966 at Moruroa and Fangataufa in French Polynesia. Their early atmospheric tests caused measurable increases in radiation in several Pacific countries, as far away as Fiji, 4500km to the west. Atmospheric testing was abandoned in 1974 under severe international pressure, but underground tests (totalling 127 on Moruroa and 10 on Fangataufa) continued until 1996.

The effects of US atmospheric nuclear testing, which ceased in 1970, have rendered Rongelap and Bikini atolls in the Marshall Islands uninhabitable (although short-term visits are fine). Their people live in unhappy exile on neighbouring islands.

Fragile coral atolls were always a questionable place to detonate nuclear weapons, and the French Atomic Energy Commission confirmed the appearance of cracks in the coral structure of Moruroa and Fangataufa Atolls, and leakage of plutonium into the sea from Moruroa. The effect of large amounts of radioactive material leaking into the Pacific Ocean would be catastrophic and far reaching. Claims of high rates of birth defects and cancer on neighbouring islands of French Polynesia are denied by the French, but are impossible to confirm because of the secrecy attached to government health records.

In 2014 the French Polynesia Assembly initiated legal proceedings, planning to sue the French government for US$930 million in compensation. The French government bowed to pressure in 2015, offering an initial €10 million in compensation to affected South Pacific nations (and Algeria).

Nonbiodegradable Waste

Drive through any given South Pacific village and, chances are, along the roadside you'll see a whole lot of plastic rubbish: bottles, bags, lids, wrappers and – perhaps most distressingly – disposable kids' nappies (diapers). In Tonga you'll see little timber platforms built out the front of family homes, upon which mum and dad place used nappies bound-up in plastic bags. This is an attempt to keep dogs from ripping the bags open and nosing through the contents before the rubbish-removal operators can do their rounds. But it's a typically futile effort – nappies inevitably end up by the roadside. More positively, in French Polynesia there's much less rubbish around than there used to be – recycling efforts seem to be working.

Other plastic rubbish washes in from elsewhere on the ocean tides, sullying the region's otherwise-idyllic tropical beaches. This is a global issue, with plastic washing up on beaches everywhere from Tasmania to Alaska.

The Cook Islands are relatively litter-free compared to many South Pacific islands. There's also growing investment in solar power here, often partly funded by New Zealand. Vanuatu, too, is making moves towards alternative energy: wind in Port Vila, hydro on Espiritu Santo and coconut oil on Tanna.

Culture, Lifestyle & Religion

Spread across thousands of kilometres of open ocean, from the Solomon Islands in the west to Easter Island in the east, South Pacific culture is as diverse as these lonesome island groups themselves. Each nation is far enough from its neighbours to have developed a distinctive culture. Every generalisation here is paired with an exception: the more you try to define the South Pacific, the more it invites you back to the kava bowl and tells you to relax and reconsider.

The Lay of the Land

Geographically and culturally, the region breaks down into Polynesia (from Greek, meaning 'many islands') to the east, the un-PC-named Melanesia ('black islands') to the west, and the oft-forgotten Micronesia ('small islands') to the northwest. Many people here people share a common Lapita ancestry (from ancient Taiwan and Southeast Asia), though from this shared history each nation has developed a unique way of being.

The Pacific Psyche

At first glance the South Pacific beaches and reefs seem divine, but scratch the surface and it soon becomes clear that cultural and social realities here aren't always 100% heavenly.

Heaven on Earth

For people supposedly already living in heaven on Earth (as the first European visitors to these islands surmised), the rate of conversion to Christianity here was rapid and high. Tourist brochures still echo that the South Pacific is a paradise, but its denizens are far more diverse and complex than this.

Life here was, and remains, far from simple and free from rules: most Pacific islands share the common notion of *tapu* (or taboo, as it became pronounced in English), which holds certain objects or practices as sacred. And you only need to see how stringently many islanders now observe the Sabbath to lose any preconceptions of a carefree psyche.

Hierarchy & Reciprocation

Historically, Melanesian communities were generally small – less than a few hundred people – with a 'bigman' as ruler. Hereditary factors were important in selecting a Melanesian bigman, but the individual's ambition and nous in politics and war were equally important.

Power was hereditary on the male side only in some Polynesian societies, with the most senior male serving as *ariki, ari'i* or *ali'i* (chief) and with subchiefs and commoners beneath them, and it was strictly hierarchical in the islands of Tonga and Tahiti.

After the arrival of Europeans, these societies became single-ruler 'countries', resembling traditional monarchies. In egalitarian Samoa, *matai* (chiefs) were selected on the grounds of political acumen and ability rather than lines of descent. Today, the power of chiefs and monarchies has waned, with Tonga the only remaining kingdom.

The most widely read anthropology book of all time is Margaret Mead's *Coming of Age in Samoa* (1928), a brilliant but rose-tinted study that describes utopian society on the Samoan island of Ta'u in the 1920s.

The central role of reciprocity in Melanesian culture has created a reputation for generosity and friendliness. In the past, aid in the form of food or labour would be given out of a sense of duty, with the expectation of the favour being returned in the future. In Polynesia, the lack of a sense of ownership has diminished but you still might be offered an object if you comment that you like it, or be expected to give something of yours away when an islander praises it.

Family Ties

Family is key to islanders' perceptions of themselves, even when migrating to other countries. Ancestor worship took this reverence of kin to a spiritual level and many South Pacific islanders still believe strongly in the family unit, often sending money or gifts home to family when they emigrate. In relatively undeveloped countries like Tonga, many locals subsist on these monetary transactions.

In Polynesia in particular, tribal groups were based on extended family and the introduction of Christianity strengthened these ties. Today many small businesses are run by families, with extended families serving as additional employees or affiliates (don't be surprised if a guesthouse owner's cousin runs the local island tour or offers to taxi you to the airport).

Traditional Cultural Hot Spots

Easter Island

The Marquesas Islands, French Polynesia

Pentecost, Vanuatu

Navala, Fiji

The Niuas, Tonga

Ta'u, American Samoa

Rarotonga, Cook Islands

Fongafala Islet, Tuvalu

Lifestyle

Family is a vital element of islander society, reflecting the traditional clan basis of many South Pacific communities. You can expect to be asked about your own family on numerous occasions, and visiting couples may find themselves bombarded with questions like, 'When are you going to have children?' Raising children is a shared activity in many Pacific-island countries, with children often invited to join in communal activities. Disciplining by other parents is not uncommon.

Many islanders are seeing their traditions challenged by globalisation as they become more urbanised. The struggle between *kastom* (custom) and capitalism continues, played out in the abandonment of traditional music in favour of hip hop and reggae, and the eschewing of traditional diet in favour of processed Western food, which has led to high rates of obesity and type 2 diabetes among many islanders.

Women in the South Pacific

The role of women in the South Pacific is complex. Many cultures are matrilineal and women can wield considerable power in village affairs, even if they're not highly visible. For female visitors to the region, everyday sexism, such as being leered at while swimming or having the answers to their questions directed to male companions, can still be disturbing.

The women that live here are less bound to servitude than in the past, but they remain less likely to be employed and are usually more poorly paid. In fact, some studies estimate that less than a third of the female populations of Fiji and Tuvalu work outside of the home. A darker side of gender relations here is that domestic violence remains a well-documented problem. In some countries such as French Polynesia, however, women hold positions of political power and are gaining more equality.

Homosexuality

Attitudes to homosexuality in the Pacific vary considerably, and in some parts of the region it is technically illegal. In more conservative areas, religious leaders work themselves into a lather about it, as witnessed in Fiji in 2005 when 3000 Methodists took to the streets protesting 'ungodly acts'.

Elsewhere, attitudes are more tolerant. Tahitian *mahu* (men who act like women), for example, are respected within their culture. Similarly,

MEET & GREET

Want to get chatting with the locals? A good conversation starter is often sports such as rugby or netball: 'Can Fiji/Samoa/Tonga knock over the Kiwis at the next Commonwealth Games?' Given that many islanders travel around the world, they may want to talk about where you're from and they're almost guaranteed to have a relative who moved to Auckland, Sydney or Utah. Here are a few simple rules to follow which will help ingratiate you to your hosts in traditional villages:

➡ Remove your shoes when entering a home.

➡ Sit cross-legged on the floor, rather than with your feet pointing out.

➡ Avoid entering a house during prayers.

➡ Avoid walking between two people in conversation.

➡ Avoid extended direct eye contact at first meetings, which can be seen as an attempt to intimidate.

➡ Try to remain on a lower level than a chief to show respect.

in Tonga the cross-dressing skills of *fakaleiti* are celebrated in the annual Miss Galaxy Pageant, and at *fakaleiti* show nights in bars across the country. Their equivalent in Samoa are called *fa'afafine*. Attitudes towards lesbianism across the region, however, remain far less accepting.

Sport

From the cities to the smallest communities, recreational sport is an integral part of South Pacific life. Around sundown, everyone seems to come out and play, heading for the basketball court next to the church or the volleyball net down on the sand.

Rugby & Football

Football in several forms is played throughout the islands during winter, but rugby union reigns supreme, with many players from the South Pacific making a name for themselves on the world stage. The all-conquering New Zealand All Blacks wouldn't be the powerhouse team they are today without the input of islanders over the years like Tana Umaga, the first Samoan to captain New Zealand, and more recent hard-hitters like Ma'a Nonu (Samoa), Jerome Kaino (American Samoa) and Joe Rokocoko (Fiji).

Back home, rugby teams from Tonga, Fiji and Samoa compete in the fiercely competitive annual Pacific Nations Cup (www.worldrugby.org/pnc), which also includes teams from Canada, Japan and the USA. At the time of writing, Fiji had just clinched their third straight cup win. Fiji also won the 2014–15 World Rugby Sevens Series and were one of the first teams to qualify for the 2016 Rio de Janeiro Olympics. The Pacific's other rugby-obsessed countries include Vanuatu, Niue, the Cook Islands, the Solomon Islands and, to a lesser extent, French Polynesia. American NFL football holds sway in American Samoa.

Netball

In villages across the South Pacific, Saturday is the day for inter-village (and sometimes inter-island) netball, with games mostly in the winter season, though they can be played year-round. There's strong grassroots support in Samoa, Vanuatu, Tonga, Niue and the Solomon and Cook Islands – these countries often duke it out for top netball honours in the Pacific and Commonwealth Games. While netball provides an important way for women to keep up contact with other villages, it is also becoming popular among men, even in macho Samoa.

Cricket

Cricket – that most British of games – maintains a colonial foothold in Fiji and the Cook Islands, though you'll also hear the cracking of leather on willow in Tonga, Vanuatu and beyond in Papua New Guinea. In Samoa you'll find a cricket pitch in almost every village, but they are usually used for the local game, *kirikiti*. This sport has a lot in common with cricket, but throws an extra bowler into the mix and commonly features singing and dancing from the batting team. Tokelau's brand of cricket, *kilikiti*, uses a three-sided bat and has teams that include most of the local village. In Tonga, *lanita* puts yet another South Pacific spin on traditional cricket.

Canoeing

Not surprisingly, canoeing is another sport common to most Pacific nations. The sport is a great source of national pride at events such as the annual Hawaiki Nui *va'a* (canoe) race in French Polynesia and at the Pacific Games, held every four years (scheduled for Tonga in 2019).

Religion

Traditional Beliefs

French Polynesia's Heiva festival in July (www.heiva.pf) features plenty of splashy outrigger canoe racing, and highlights other traditional sports including coconut husking, rock lifting, fruit carrying (!) and javelin throwing.

Before Europeans arrived with their bibles, their Sundays and their crosses, ancestor worship and magic were common beliefs in Melanesia, while in Polynesia a whole range of gods were worshipped.

Melanesia's ancestor worship and sorcery were essential to every aspect of daily life, with spells cast for success in war, fishing and health. In remote areas, headhunting and cannibalism were practised as sacred rituals as late as the 1950s. In the Solomon Islands and Vanuatu, *kastom* continues to preserve the sacredness of traditions that have remained the same for centuries and which it is forbidden to question.

Across Polynesia, traditional religious beliefs were remarkably similar because of the islanders' common ancestry. The Polynesian pantheon was ruled by Tangaroa (Tangaloa or Ta'aroa) and included several lesser gods who divvied up the portfolios for the sea, the forest, war, crops and other important aspects of life. While there were many commonalities across Polynesia, in each island group the myths took on different variations.

Existing as a separate class alongside Polynesian chiefs, and often sharing their power, priests known as *tohunga* (*tohu'a* or *kahuna*) were the keepers of Polynesian religion. As well as having divine knowledge such as creation myths or rituals, these priests were also interpreters of the gods' wills for the village. They could really put the stoppers on an ambitious chief's plans, or form an alliance of considerable political power by joining with a chief to rule in tandem.

Christianity

Christianity arrived in its various forms in the early 19th century, and the race to convert the South Pacific was on! Many countries adopted several different Christian denominations: Anglican, Catholic, Wesleyan, Mormon, Jehovah's Witness... Many villages in Tonga, for example, have one church for each denomination, the relative local standing (and affluence) of each church obvious in the precision of lawnmowing and upkeep of paint.

Traditional islander beliefs were often incorporated into new Christian doctrines to help ease the passage of the new ways. But 100 years later, pure and pious Christianity has come to dominate spiritual life in the South Pacific. The popularity of church singing in both Micronesia and Polynesia is testament to the missionaries' early efforts: a visit to church to tune-in (and even sing along) is an essential Sunday experience, no matter what your beliefs. Only Fiji, with its large Hindu and Muslim Indo-Fijian population, has significant numbers of non-Christian believers, and at times there is tension between the different groups.

ANDERS RYMAN/GETTY IMAGES ©

Island Life

Pacific Island life trundles along at a slow, easy-going pace. Once you've slowed down too, you'll notice the small beauties of the day: a waft of frangipani, the last second of orange sunset. The cultures that have evolved in this balmy, bountiful region are diverse, but the ocean remains an ever-present bond.

Contents

Above Cook Islander boy blowing conch horn

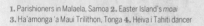

1. Parishioners in Malaela, Samoa 2. Easter Island's *moai*
3. Ha'amonga 'a Maui Trilithon, Tonga 4. Heiva i Tahiti dancer

People, History & Culture

More than 1700 years before the Vikings launched their longboats, before Chinese merchants and European explorers weighed anchor, Polynesian and Melanesian ancestors sailed their canoes from today's Taiwan and Southeast Asia and crossed 10,000km of ocean. Over the following centuries they populated the South Pacific islands: the South Pacific cultures were born.

Take Me to Church

Christianity has mostly replaced traditional religious beliefs here, but it's practised with all the heartfelt devotion of past religions. On Sundays many shops and businesses close, locals dress conservatively, and in some countries it's even illegal to go fishing! A trip to church here is unforgettable: dress in your best clothes, arrive in good time and let the locals welcome you. The hymnal harmonies will stay with you forever.

Ancient History

Isolated and utterly engaged with sea and sky, the South Pacific islanders turned to religion for reassurance and guidance. Ancient remnants stand as testament to their beliefs: the famous *moai* (statues) on Easter Island, dating back to 1250 AD; and lesser-known gems like the 13th-century Ha'amonga 'a Maui Trilithon in Tonga (the 'Stonehenge of the South Pacific'). In Samoa you'll find prehistoric 'star mounds' and the Pulemeilu Mound pyramid, possibly as old as 1100 AD.

Party Time

For a direct line into island life, time your visit with a major cultural festival. French Polynesia's Heiva i Tahiti (p24) is an incredibly colourful music, dance and sporting event held every June/July. Te Mire Kapa (p22), the Cook Islands' 'Dancer of the Year' competition, happens every April. Tapati Rapa Nui (p22) is Easter Island's annual big-ticket event in February, with much music, dance and audacious bareback horse racing.

1. Traditional Samoan tattoos 2. Cultural performance in Samoa
3. Fijian tapa cloth 4. Totemic woodcarving from Vanuatu

ANDERS RYMAN/GETTY IMAGES ©

KENT KOBERSTEEN/GETTY IMAGES ©

The Arts

Pacific islanders sure know how to have fun! Despite the cultural restrictions early missionaries placed on 'lewd' dancing, tattooing and even singing, none of these activities were ever entirely squelched. Today, these art forms are have made a real comeback.

Tattoos

Polynesians in particular are reviving their intricate tattoo designs. You'll see men with full-sleeve spectaculars everywhere in Tonga, Samoa and Tahiti in particular.

Music & Dance

Nights of sweet harmonies and breezy guitar and ukulele tunes are the South Seas soundtrack, from local bars to resort dining rooms. Dance-and-feast shows – from the soft Fijian sway to French Polynesia's high-speed hip blur and Tonga's mesmerising hand gestures – are as much a part of cultural heritage as they are a way to keep tourists entertained. 'Island Nights' in the Cook Islands are a great way to engage with local culture (beware: audience participation required).

Tapa

The performing arts may be evolving and flourishing, but other crafts such as making tapa (cloth made from mulberry bark) are becoming less common due to their labour-intensive nature and the availability of imported fabrics. Keep an eye out for Fijian tapa, in particular, which remains present in all stations and stages of local life.

Carvings

Art forms such as Marquesan and Vanuatuan woodcarvings are still in high demand. The finest examples of these take uncountable hours to create – often exclusively for ceremonial rather than commercial purposes – and thus come with a hefty price tag.

Kava preparation in Navua, F

Food & Drink

Pacific islanders love nothing more than to fill you up with hearty, bone-building traditional cuisine: fish, pork, taro, *cassava, kumara* and lashings of tropical fruit, topped off with a dousing of coconut cream!

Global Flavours

Alongside traditional island faves you'll find fiery Indian curries in Fiji, croissants in New Caledonia and French Polynesia, and modern New Zealand panache in Cook Islands' kitchens. You can get a quick-fire Chinese meal nearly everywhere, from noodle soups to lemon chicken.

Thirst Quenchers

Cold beer and the Tropic of Capricorn: they go together like snow and Sweden. Sip regional beers like Samoa's Vailima, Tonga's Popao, Tahiti's Hinano or a Fiji Bitter; or order a local rum cocktail (*oooh*, mai tais!). Fresh juices can be surprisingly hard to find; pineapple and green-skinned orange juice are the most common offerings. Decent espresso is rare – head for the expat cafes. Of course, the definitive South Pacific quencher is electrolyte-filled coconut water, sucked straight from the nut.

Kava

Kava is a muddy, slightly bitter, narcotic drink made from ground kava roots, that will mellow you down to the island pace of life. Sitting with locals and passing the kava cup, with the adjunct protocols of clapping, singing or spilling a bit for the spirits, is an unforgettable South Seas experience. Kava plays an important ceremonial role, and it's an honour to be invited to partake (take a sip even if you don't like it!).

Art & Influence

Welcome to a land (or rather, ocean) of rich artistic heritage and endeavour, where exquisite traditional arts and crafts are still produced to the highest standards, and customary dance and music are still performed with gusto. But watch how new media, from cinema to TV and hip hop to modern tattooing, is carrying the South Pacific's artistic soul into this new century.

The Arts

Dance

Dance was extremely important to Polynesian and Melanesian culture in ancient times. After being condemned by Christian leaders for over a century, it's now making a concerted comeback, sometimes with a modern twist.

Siva, the traditional Samoan dance, has a Hawaiian feel with slow hand movements that often relate a narrative. Trad Tongan dance is also big on hand motion – a captivating web of gestures, often set to modern beats. Fijian *meke* are melodic oral histories of battles, appointments of chiefs or gossip that use spears and fans as props. In the Cook Islands the rhythmic *hura* dance resembles the Hawaiian hula. The fast hip movements of *oro tahiti* (Tahitian dance) make it the most seductive dance of the Pacific and shows involve lavish costumes, live percussion orchestras and troupes of up to hundreds of dancers.

Music

Diversity is the byword for Pacific music, with enough variety to dispel any stereotyped grass-skirt preconceptions you might have had. Group singing is a part of many rituals across the islands, and with the arrival of Christianity, singing in church really took off. Take yourself to church on Sunday morning if you can (particularly in Tonga or Samoa) – the tight, high harmonies and all-round vocal enthusiasm lifts the rafters.

Contemporary South Pacific music often draws on traditional sounds and vocal styles – something you'll hear in the tunes of acoustic guitar groups at bars or around the kava bowl, and from artists that fuse trad and pop sounds. But increasingly islanders are nodding their heads to reggae or tuning in to hip-hop. In New Zealand, the music scene has benefited from Pacific migration to such a degree that New Zealand–based band Nesian Mystik coined the term *Polysaturated* for an album title that could readily describe the NZ recording industry. Small production studios are appearing in the Pacific, enabling recording by local groups and bolstering the hip-hop scene in Suva. In New Caledonia reggae is king, alongside popular local music known as Kaneka, a mixture of reggae and traditional Kanak rhythms. In French Polynesia, Tikahiri (www.tikahiri.com) is a badass Tahitian rock outfit with lots of fans.

Tapa

No art form is as characteristic of the Pacific as the beating of mulberry bark to create tapa cloth. Whether it's called *siapo* in Samoa, *ngatu* in Tonga, *hiapo* in Niue, *ahu* in the Pitcairn Islands, *mahute* on Easter Island

---

South Pacific Playlist

'Swing' by Savage (Samoa/New Zealand)

'Not Many' by Scribe (Samoa/New Zealand)

'Jonah Lomu' by Tyson (Cook Islands)

'Tama'i' by Matato'a (Easter Island)

'Paradisia' by Fenua (Tahiti)

'Mane Paina' by Narasirato (Solomon Islands)

'Nesian Style' by Nesian Mystik (Pacific Islands/New Zealand)

or *masi* in Fiji, this is much more than an everyday fabric. Fijian *masi* is essential to almost every stage of life: newborn babies are swaddled in it, coffins are covered with it and brides' mothers covet top pieces for their girls' wedding garb. In Tahiti it was made in huge sheets 3m wide and hundreds of metres in length, and signified the power of a chief.

Bark was stripped from mulberry (or sometimes breadfruit) trees then beaten into sheets on a specialised anvil. The thin sheets were then glued together using a substance such as manioc root paste.

Traditionally, the real value of tapa was based on the ritual surrounding its creation and the community that produced it. It was made exclusively by women in a communal ritual that revealed the strength of a tribe. When given to another tribal group it placed the group in debt to the giver, and the receiver would have to honour this debt.

With the arrival of calico and accompanying European values, the making of tapa declined. Tapa's legacy endures on several islands, though it is not made in the quantities it once was.

Tattoos

Pacific islanders of both sexes were tattooed to mark the onset of puberty and arrival into adulthood, and later to signify status within their tribal groups.

The most outrageous were seen on Marquesan warriors who 'wore' a full-body armour of tattoos, including on their eyelids and tongues. In Tahiti, Samoa and Tonga, tattoos were elaborate designs worn on the buttocks and hips, using natural pigments pounded into the skin with shell or bone tools. In Melanesia, scarring of the body was a popular alternative to tattooing, although tattoos also bestowed status.

While tattoos became popular with passing European seamen in the 19th century, Christian missionaries discouraged or forbade tattooing; Fijian tattooing (with its strong links to sexuality) became virtually extinct.

Samoan *tofuga* (tattooists) remain strongly traditional. The tattoo revival has seen full arm and leg designs becoming popular and even the full-body patterns are the order of the day, particularly among Tahiti's traditional dancers. Tongan *tatatau* (tattoos) were thought to be almost extinct, until a revival in the early 2000s.

Sculpture & Carving

Whether in wood, stone, coral or bone, distinctive sculpture is found right across the Pacific. Canoes were a common canvas; a prow's stylised bow could reveal an arriving crew's spiritual beliefs before they reached land. On war canoes the depiction of gods of battle and death would have explicitly declared the visitor's intentions. Other objects, such as bailers and paddles, were inlaid with symbolic motifs to bring protection or prosperity in fishing or conflict.

Objects of war were also crafted with considerable aesthetic skill. Marquesan *u'u* (war clubs) are prized by collectors for the fine-relief images of war gods carved into the hardwood. In Polynesia, woven or wooden shields often depicted protection deities.

Masks and headgear from around the region were not meant to be worn but to be destroyed in funeral pyres or preserved for hundreds of years and used in ongoing rituals. Other effigies and masks were built for long-dead ancestors to inhabit and watch over the clan.

Vanuatu was famous for its over-modelling of skulls, with clay, fibres or other materials being added to the bones to create elaborate effigies with eyes, teeth and hair, sometimes including earrings or other ornamentation.

The most recognisable icons of Pacific art are the enormous *moai* of Easter Island. *Moai* are similar to other eastern Polynesian statues, particularly the large stone *tiki* of the Marquesas and Tuamotu Islands. The

Traditional Samoan tattooing has gained recent exposure via some high-profile sportsmen with Samoan heritage. Check out the amazing tatts on Australian footballer Tim Cahill, New Zealand rugby renegade Sonny Bill Williams, and wrestler-turned-actor Dwayne 'The Rock' Johnson.

story of the *moai* and the dramatic shrinking of the indigenous culture that created them is intriguing: current consensus is that the stones were rolled into position using felled tree logs, the removal of trees causing soil erosion, which in turn caused the atrophy of Rapa Nui society (no dirt = nowhere to grow crops). Slave trading and European diseases didn't boost population growth either, but the amazing *moai* have endured.

Most wooden sculptures of the Pacific were either burnt by missionaries as idols or looted by souvenir-hunting Europeans. Many of the Pacific's most impressive artworks are in North American or European museums, such as the Marquesas collection at New York's Museum of Metropolitan Art or the pan-Pacific holdings of the British Museum.

Architecture

Traditional buildings throughout the Pacific were constructed knowing full well they would probably have to be rebuilt at some stage in the wake of storms or war. Modern building materials and techniques are used in housing today, but the historic design dictum remains in play (tropical cyclones here pack an increasingly weighty punch). Samoan and Tongan *fale* (houses) are designed without walls, but with woven blinds that can be lowered for harsher weather; while Fijian *bure* have walls and roofs of reeds or woven palms.

In Polynesia the *marae* (or *malae*) was the village meeting point. In western Polynesia, *marae* were village greens, sometimes walled off with matting, while in the east they became elaborate structures. In Easter Island, the Societies, Australs and Marquesas, *marae* were impressive open-air, paved temples with altars, carved-stone seating, platforms and walls, though only ruins and petroglyphs remain today.

Traditional men's houses (no women allowed!) are still widespread throughout Melanesia and are often a village's dominant building. With intricate carvings, towering facades and detailed interiors, they're made with complex joinery not using a single nail or screw. Throughout Melanesia secret councils of men still convene in these houses.

In terms of modern architecture a highlight is undeniably New Caledonia's Tjibaou Culture Centre (p153) in Noumea, which draws on traditional village architecture and mythology. Elsewhere in the Pacific you can see the vestiges of colonial architecture, including at Levuka on Ovalau in Fiji or Nuku'alofa's gracious timber Royal Palace (p435) in Tonga.

Cinema & TV

Film-makers have long been drawn to the locations of the Pacific, though many films only superficially explore its culture. Hollywood's take on James Michener's novels *Return to Paradise* (1953) and *South Pacific* (1958) have plenty of postcard images, even if the latter was filmed in Hawai'i, Malaysia and, ahem, Spain. The original *Blue Lagoon* (1949) and the Brooke Shields remake (1980) both feature Fiji's Yasawa Group, while Tom Hanks' *Cast Away* (2000) was also shot on location in Fiji. *Dead Calm* (1989) is a gripping South Pacific yacht thriller starring Nicole Kidman acting scared and Billy Zane acting scary. More recently, the goofy Vince Vaughn comedy *Couples Retreat* (2009) was filmed in Bora Bora in Tahiti. And of course, all three Hollywood takes on the story of the mutiny on the HMS *Bounty* (1935, 1962 and 1984) feature plenty of South Pacific scenes. You may want to have a look at the Kevin Costner–produced *Rapa-Nui* (1994), set on Easter Island (...then again, you may not).

Increasingly documentaries are exploring beneath the postcard veneer and showing the world the real Pacific. Highlighting this welcome genre is the annual Pacific International Documentary Film Festival (FIFO; www.fifo-tahiti.com) held in Pape'ete, which features films made by Pacific islanders. On the sporting front, surfing fans should check out *The Ultimate Wave*

Adorning the World: Art of the Marquesas Islands, published by the Metropolitan Museum of Art (2005), is a gorgeous coffee-table book exploring Marquesan art from collections around the world.

Tahiti 3D (2010), featuring evergreen surf champ Kelly Slater and Tahitian surfer Raimana Van Bastolaer carving up some serious South Seas waves.

One of the most successful Pacific islander ventures is the animated TV series *bro'Town,* made by a troupe calling themselves the Naked Samoans. The series was a politically incorrect look at the life of Samoan boys growing up in South Auckland, which ran through five series. Several of the Naked Samoans appear in the feature films *Sione's Wedding* (2006), *Sione's 2: Unfinished Business* (2012) and *Children of the Migration* (2004), which have different takes on Pacific islanders in NZ. In the US, Fijian Vilsoni Hereniko shows the real Pacific to Hollywood with his feature *Pear Ta Ma 'on Maf* (The Land Has Eyes; 2005).

But for many visitors the Pacific remains the land of the American *Survivor* TV series, with several series made in the region. In the same reality-TV vein, Britain's *Meet the Natives* (2007) followed villagers from Tanna in Vanuatu as they journeyed to the UK to meet their idol, Prince Philip. There was also a 2009 US version of the program, following similar lines (substitute Prince Philip for then-Secretary of State Colin Powell). And if you really must, the two-part season-six finale of US reality show *The Bachelorette* (2010) was filmed in Taha'a and Bora Bora in Tahiti (...she chose Roberto).

On the TV documentary front, *South Pacific* (2009) is an excellent six-part BBC nature documentary narrated by Benedict Cumberbatch. And if you can sidestep the fact that it was mostly filmed in Malta, the Norwegian-made and Oscar-nominated film *Kon-Tiki* (2012) is a dramatic re-enactment of Thor Heyerdahl's epic South Seas expedition of 1947.

Fiction & Nonfiction

The Pacific has a small but lively writing culture. Writers such as the influential Samoan Albert Wendt have found success in NZ and based themselves there. Other Pacific writers were born in NZ but have drawn on their Pacific heritage in their work. Tusiata Avia's first book of poetry, *Wild Dogs Under My Skirt,* takes a humorous look at her Samoan roots, while the Samoan novelist Sia Figiel received great praise for her debut title *Where We Once Belonged.* Maori-language publisher Huia (www.huia.co.nz) also publishes islander books, including *Island of Shattered Dreams* by Tahitian Chantal Spitz and the excellent anthology *Niu Voices.* Other estimable South Pacific writers to scan the shelves for include Tongan Epeli Hau'ofa, Fiji's Raymond Pillai, the Solomon Islands' John Saunana and Samoa's Fata Sano Malifa.

Hawai'i is another powerhouse of Pacific literature, with small presses like Tin Fish Press (www.tinfishpress.com) publishing and championing Pacific writers.

Of course, Westerners have been scribbling about the Pacific for centuries, from Jack London to Paul Theroux and Lloyd Jones (set in Bougainville in Papua New Guinea, the latter's Man Booker Prize–shortlisted 2006 novel *Mr Pip* (2006) is an essential South Pacific read). Robert Louis Stevenson relocated to Samoa, while Herman Melville based his *Typee* on four months' desertion from a whaling boat on the Marquesas Islands.

On the nonfiction front, *A Lesser Tale of the South Pacific: Reminiscences of World War II* by Edmund L DuBois (2011) tells DuBous' tale of sailing on a 1942 troopship convoy from Brooklyn to New Caledonia and beyond. Alan Rems' *South Pacific Cauldron: World War II's Great Forgotten Battlegrounds* (2015) sheds further light on WWII in the South Pacific. If you're into tattoos, *South Pacific Skin* by Amanda D Fornal (2012) is the definitive read. For foodies, *Me'a Kai: The Food And Flavours Of The South Pacific* by Robert Oliver (2010) will whet your appetite before your South Seas adventure.

Food & Drink

The food of the South Pacific is sturdy and fulfilling: don't expect to scale back the calories here! And don't worry about the indignity of piling your plate too high or going back for seconds – the more you eat, the more the islanders will love you for it. Expect lots of fish, chicken and pork, plus tropical fruits and some excellent South Seas beers to sluice it all down.

Staples & Specialities

South Pacific dietary staples were once dictated by what the ancient navigating peoples brought with them in their canoes: starchy root veggies, meat and fish have long comprised the bulk of the South Pacific diet, with green vegetables never playing much of a role. But these days each island nation has a distinctive culinary style, influenced by French, English or US colonisation and the presence of Chinese and Indian labourers. Root tubers, fish and pork now share a plate with pasta, rice and canned foods, from corned beef to foie gras.

> The tasty water inside a coconut is sterile and can be used in medical procedures, including for intravenous drips.

Breadfruit

The versatile breadfruit – trees of which Captain William Bligh, Fletcher Christian and the HMS *Bounty* were sent to the South Pacific to procure – is typically eaten unripe and roasted till charred on an open fire. Its flavour is somewhere between a potato and a chestnut. It can also be fried into chips, boiled or baked in the oven. The addition of coconut cream, kneaded into the cooked flesh, makes a sweet, doughy paste that can be eaten as is, or wrapped in leaves and baked to create a starchy pudding.

Many traditional cultures fermented breadfruit (and a few still do), both as a preservation technique and to add flavour to an otherwise bland diet (the fermented fruit develops a strong, sour taste).

Taro, Cassava & Kumara

Along with *cassava* and *kumara*, you'll encounter several varieties of taro across the South Pacific, all producing an oblong root tuber that is boiled in water or steamed in a traditional earthen pit oven. It's a firm, starchy, potato-like food that has a slightly gooey exterior when cooked just right. Covered with coconut milk, it exudes a hearty, gotta-be-good-for-you quality and makes a satisfying side dish.

The leaves of certain species of taro can also be eaten, usually mixed in savoury stews or eaten with coconut milk. They resemble spinach when cooked, and are the only traditional leafy green in Polynesia.

Coconut

Nothing invokes the flavours of the South Pacific more than that omni-present all-rounder, the humble coconut. It's an all-in-one food: meat, sugar, oil and water, all conveniently presented in its own sterile bowl. Each of the nut's four growth stages provides a different form of food or drink. The first stage is best for drinking because there's no flesh inside, except for a tasty jellylike substance. The best eating stage is the second, when the flesh is firm but thin and succulent. After this, the flesh becomes thick and hard – ideal for drying into copra. At its fourth stage, the milk inside goes spongy, making what is sometimes known as 'coconut ice cream'.

Fruit

While the Polynesian islands are generally dripping in fresh fruit (mangoes, papayas, pineapples, green-skin oranges, giant grapefruit, passionfruit, guava and the world's sweetest bananas), some parts of Melanesia are less well endowed – but you will still find tropical fruit here, as well as avocados and tomatoes. Most islanders source fruit from their own trees or from family and friends, so it can be surprisingly hard to buy fruit in urban shops throughout the Pacific. In most island groups, the best and cheapest places to stock up are local markets and informal roadside stalls – pull over and see what looks good. In many places, plantains and regular bananas are cooked and served as a side dishes, sometimes topped with coconut cream – delicious!

The milk you get across the South Pacific is almost always the long-life, heat-treated UHT variety: don't expect many creamy delights straight from the cow!

Fish & Meat

Fresh fish and shellfish are found on nearly every South Pacific restaurant menu and, as a general rule, are fabulous (the sea is a bountiful provider). Pigs were traditionally more highly valued than seafood; pork remains a regional staple. Dog was once eaten, but that's now a rare occurrence.

Regional meats include flying foxes (fruit bats) in eastern Polynesia and Melanesia, venison in New Caledonia and goat in the Marquesas Islands. High-quality lamb and beef imported from New Zealand are often available, as are low-quality frozen chicken cuts from the US.

Canned Influences

Ever-popular canned meat is cheap, easy and tasty – unfortunately, it's also full of fat, salt, nitrites and empty calories. The effect of this and other imports (especially soft drinks, instant noodles, potato chips and ice cream) on the weight and health of native Pacific peoples has been devastating. Obesity, heart problems, hypertension and diabetes are rife throughout the region.

Drinks

On a humid South Pacific afternoon, nothing sits in the belly better than some ice-cold coconut water (except for perhaps some ice-cold local lager). Coconut water is slightly sweet and is full of electrolytes – a healthy and reconstituting tonic. Sipping on a coconut straight from the tree, with a hole cut into it and a straw inserted, is a mandatory South Seas experience.

Conversely, freshly squeezed juices can be difficult to find, and you'll often have to buy a bottle or can that has been imported from somewhere far less appealing. Otherwise, go for filtered, boiled or bottled water – stay away from the tap water unless you've been assured by a reliable source that it's OK to drink.

Coffee

You can get a cup of coffee almost everywhere in the South Pacific, but aside from in New Caledonia and parts of Vanuatu, the quality of the brew can be questionable (regional interpretations of Italian-style espresso are sometimes rather abstract – weak and milky is the norm). For a stiff double-shot, head for the resort restaurants or expat-run cafes in urban areas. The further you get from the major towns, the more likely it is that it'll be instant coffee in your cup.

Kava

The drinking of kava remains a strong social tradition in many Pacific cultures, and is practised throughout almost all of Polynesia and much of Melanesia. As well as a form of welcome, it's used to seal alliances, kick off chiefly conferences and to commemorate births, deaths and marriages. To decline kava when it is offered is to decline friendship – so even though it may taste unusual (to put it mildly), try to gulp it down and appear impressed.

In many countries kava ceremonies have helped locals retain ancient customs. Many people also attribute a low crime rate to the calming, sedative effects of the drink, which, unlike alcohol, does not produce aggressive behaviour.

Kava Ceremonies

In more traditional areas, kava root is prepared by chewing it into a mush and spitting the hard bits onto leaves. Water is added to the mush, then it's all filtered through coconut fibres. This method produces a more potent brew, as saliva triggers the root's active ingredients. Modern techniques are slightly more hygienic, involving pounding the kava root in a bucket or preparing the brown brew from a commercially produced powder.

Kava is served in a coconut-shell cup – at formal ceremonies the chief and honoured guests usually drink first. Some cultures expect drinkers to down the kava in a single gulp, any remaining liquid being poured onto the ground. In Samoa a small amount is tipped out of the bowl before drinking. Sometimes kava is drunk in silence, but some cultures prefer a great deal of slurping to show appreciation. Your companions will sometimes clap while you drink, but other noises and conversation are generally kept to a minimum.

In some areas – particularly the more touristy ones where customs have become more lenient – the ultimate informal kava session may involve sitting around in a bar, passing the cup and strumming guitars. But this kind of scenario is generally for the entertainment and intrigue of tourists and expats, rather than for traditional ceremonial purposes.

Note that in most places, kava drinking remains an exclusively male activity – some say the original kava plant sprang from the loins of a woman, hence the *tapu* (taboo). Also note that kava makes the drinker's eyes sensitive to glare, so any strong lights, especially flash bulbs, are very intrusive.

Experiential Effects

Kava has a pungent, muddy taste and you'll begin to feel its effects within 10 to 25 minutes. If it's a strong brew, it'll make your lips go numb and cold like you've had a Novocaine injection, then your limbs will get heavy and your speech will slow. If it's really strong, you might get double vision and want to go to sleep. Even from the mildest form of the drink, you will feel slightly sedated and have a general sense of well-being. Some islanders claim to have repeated religious experiences after drinking kava.

Medicinal Uses

Broken down, kava is a cocktail of up to 14 analgesics and anaesthetics that work as natural pain and appetite suppressants. The root also has antibacterial, relaxant, diuretic and decongestant properties. Studies showing that kava may help to combat depression, reduce anxiety and even lower blood pressure led to a short-lived kava boom in Western countries during the 1990s. However, other studies have claimed the root could potentially cause liver damage, which has resulted in bans or warnings on kava beyond the South Pacific while research is continuing.

Alcoholic Drinks

The negative social effects of alcohol, such as domestic violence and drink-driving, have convinced some South Pacific communities to ban alcohol completely. But in most countries it's freely available at liquor stores and in restaurants and casual eateries. Most nations brew their own beers; Australian, NZ and US beers are also widely available. Wine – mostly

South Seas Beers

Hinano (Tahiti)

Vonu (Fiji)

Popoa (Tonga)

Vailima (Samoa)

Matutu (Cook Islands)

Solbrew (Solomon Islands)

Tusker (Vanuatu)

Mahina (Easter Island)

Manta (New Caledonia)

imported from NZ or Australia – is available in most large towns, but it usually comes with a high price tag. The French colonies offer a decent selection of French wines (Beaujolais on the beach, anyone?).

There aren't too many slick bars or nightclubs around the islands – laid-back waterside pubs and open-walled bars are the norm. But at swanky hotels and resorts you'll find all the tropical, coconut-and-pineapple cocktails you could dream of downing.

Party Time: Fire up the Umu

Traditionally, a big community celebration called for a feast prepared in a traditional earthen oven. For community chiefs, hosting a sizeable feast was a way to display power and wealth, as much as a meal to share with their people. Today, throughout the Pacific, a celebration still usually means an earthen *umu* (*ahima'a* in French Polynesia, *lovo* in Fiji), but nowadays anyone can throw a party. In general, Christian holidays, birthdays and weddings are the main excuses to chow down.

Every island group has its own method of preparing such feasts, but the common theme is that food, ranging from meat and fish to taro and cabbage, is neatly wrapped in banana leaves or wet cloth and cooked in a stone-lined, wood-fired pit covered with earth. The flavours and juices mingle for several hours and the resulting meal is steamy, tender and delectable.

In most island groups there are tourist-oriented local feasts of earthen cooked food (called 'Island Nights' in the Cook Islands, *fiafia* in Samoa, *meke* in Fiji, *laplap* in Vanuatu, *ma'a tahiti* in French Polynesia or *bougna* in New Caledonia). These usually also involve dance performances and make for a great night out.

Where to Eat & Drink

In many places, South Pacific islanders don't patronise restaurants, so eating establishments mostly serve the tourist or expat population and are concentrated in touristy areas. Bars aren't overly common, although some restaurants double as pubby, breezy watering holes.

The restaurants in the French territories can be superb, if your wallet can stand the heat. Most island groups have at least a handful of Western and Chinese places, and in Fiji you'll find sumptuous, reasonably priced Indian restaurants.

Markets are the best source of the freshest and cheapest foodstuffs, as more formal shops and supermarkets often rely on canned and pre-packaged goods.

Vegetarians & Vegans

Fish, pork or chicken form the basis of most South Pacific meals, so vegetarians will have to either pick through their food or get creative with self-catering. The exception to the rule is Fiji, which has a large Indian population and thus some terrific vegetarian options.

Habits & Customs

Eating habits and customs in the South Pacific vary according to the fare: Chinese and Japanese food is eaten with chopsticks; you should use your hands when eating traditional Pacific fare and some Indian specialities; and you can finally pick up a knife and fork for Western food. But for the most part, no one will complain if you fork through everything.

While many islanders eat copious breakfasts of fish or meat and rice, breadfruit or taro, visitors in hotels are more likely to encounter light breakfast fare: toast with a smear of butter and jam, coffee and sometimes fruit.

If you are invited to someone's home for dinner or a barbecue, it's not uncommon for the hosts to wait to eat until their guests have finished – so don't be shy, dig in (...but wait 'til everybody says grace, of course!).

Do

...try at least one meal cooked in a traditional earthen oven.

...wash your hands: you might be eating with your fingers.

...try a coconut, plucked straight from the palm.

...accept the kava cup if it comes your way.

Don't

...eat turtle. It's endangered and you'll be promoting an illegal trade.

...just dig in. Many locals say grace before a meal.

...count on a good coffee. Time to detox?

...count calories. Eating here is an indulgence!

Survival Guide

Directory A–Z

This Directory lists information applicable right across the South Pacific region; for country-specific info refer to destination chapters.

Electricity

The first plug shown is used in French Polynesia, New Caledonia and Easter Island, while the second one is used in all the other main countries in this book except American Samoa, which uses an American, two-square-pronged plug.

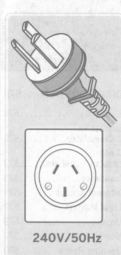

240V/50Hz

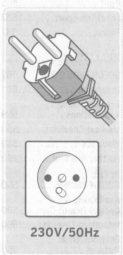

230V/50Hz

Embassies & Consulates

As a visitor to the South Pacific, you are bound by the laws of the country you're visiting – so if you commit a crime your embassy is powerless to intervene. Similarly, a crime committed against you would be a matter for local police (and possibly your travel insurer).

However, if you are in a dire emergency you might get some assistance, and if your passport has been lost or stolen, your embassy will help you get a new one. Embassies will normally only evacuate citizens in the event of a major natural disaster, war or sudden civil upheaval, such as a violent coup where all citizens of its country are affected.

Gay & Lesbian Travellers

Attitudes towards LGBTQI relations in the South Pacific are multilayered and complex. Due to the conservative Christian influences, being gay or lesbian is on one level regarded as unnatural and sinful. Yet in Polynesia – especially Tonga and Samoa – there are long traditions of male cross-dressing and transgenderism that are usually, though not always, associated with being gay. Melanesian countries tend to be less tolerant of gay men and lesbians, but this stance has noticeably softened over recent decades.

Being gay is technically illegal (although this is rarely enforced) in many South Pacific countries, including the Cook Islands, Niue, the Solomon Islands, Tokelau and Tonga. Lesbianism only gets an official mention in Samoa, where it is also illegal. But in Fiji and the more liberal French colonies of New Caledonia and French Polynesia, being gay or lesbian is legal.

Excessive public displays of affection – of any sexuality – are frowned upon in most South Pacific societies.

Insurance

Travel insurance that covers theft, loss and medical problems (p589) is essential. Note that some policies exclude 'dangerous activities', which can include scuba diving, surfing, motorcycling and even hiking. A locally acquired motorcycle licence is also not valid under some policies.

Worldwide travel insurance is available at www.lonelyplanet.com/travel-insurance. You can buy, extend and claim online anytime – even if you're already on the road.

Internet Access

Wi-fi in South Pacific accommodation is commonplace these days, especially if you're paying for more than budget digs: you'll generally be given a password with which to log on (unlimited use), or need to purchase a set amount of online time. Some resorts make the deliberate decision not to have blanket wi-fi access across their facilities, to help stressed-out guests really unwind. You'll also find wi-fi hot spots in major tourist and urban centres, and busy internet cafes.

Some of the more remote islands may not have any internet at all; others may surprise you with fast connections. In the Solomon Islands and Easter Island, however, connections are still slow.

Legal Matters

The nearest most travellers will get to local law enforcement protocols might be the odd speed camera on the roads. There's a degree of hypocrisy at play with regard to litter and drug laws in the region: you'll see plenty of rubbish along the roadsides and catch the scent of marijuana in many places in the South Pacific, but that doesn't mean that littering and smoking pot are legal here (they're not). Play it safe and don't do either.

Maps

Locally produced street and island maps from visitor information centres aren't particularly reliable in scale or content. If you're serious about old-school navigation with a tangible (rather than digital) map in your hands, do some research at home and make a purchase before you leave.

Money

The South Pacific has some rather exotic-sounding currencies: Vanuatu's vatu, Samoa's tala and the Tongan pa'anga. However, some South Pacific countries use US, Australian or New Zealand dollars, while the Pacific franc (the Cour de Franc Pacifique, or CFP) is legal tender in the French territories (New Caledonia, French Polynesia). See regional chapters for details, and p19 for exchange rates.

As with travel to any destination, it's best not to put all your monetary eggs into one basket. A credit/debit card, dedicated travel-cash card and a stash of notes will give you some options if an ATM swallows your plastic or the bank is closed.

ATMs & Credit Cards

Withdrawing cash via local ATMs – either from your home bank account or a dedicated travel-cash account – is the easiest way of accessing your money in the South Pacific. There are ATMs in most urban centres, at airports and many ferry docks, but not on remote islands, where cash is still king.

Credit cards are accepted at most tourist facilities but often attract a 4% to 5% transaction fee. Visa and MasterCard are the most common. Make a note of the applicable 'lost card' phone numbers before you depart.

You'll still encounter old-fashioned paper credit-card transaction slips here and there in the South Pacific. Be warned: dodgy shopkeepers have been known to quickly make several imprints of your card when you're not looking, and then copy your signature from the one that you authorise. Pay attention!

Bargaining

Bargaining and haggling isn't part of commercial culture in any South Pacific country – trying to do so is considered extremely rude. You might be able to shave a few dollars off a price in tourist shops and big-city markets, but in small villages locals will take their goods home rather than accept a lower price than what's asked. The one exception is in Fiji, where Indo-Fijians expect to bargain and will often initiate the process.

Cash

Nothing beats cash for convenience, paying for things in remote places...and risk. Very few travel insurers will come to your rescue if you lose your wad, and those that will compensate you limit the amount to somewhere around US$300. Withdraw moderate amounts from ATMs to minimise risk.

Changing Money

Fees, commissions, buy/sell exchange rates...changing currencies is always a losing game. If you're travelling to three South Pacific countries, try to get a handful of all three currencies before you leave home, rather than changing one for another on the road. But don't expect your local bank to stock obscure South Pacific currencies – banks and money changers in major gateway cities (eg Auckland, Brisbane, LA, Honolulu) are more likely to have a pile of Pacific tender in the vault

If you are exchanging currencies as you go, to redeem anything like face value it's best to get rid of cash in the country of origin before you leave.

Most airports and big hotels have exchange facilities or booths that are open outside of normal office hours. However, hotels are almost always the worst places for exchanging money. The best exchange rates are offered at banks – exchange bureaux generally offer worse rates or charge higher commissions.

Tipping

Attitudes to tipping vary across the South Pacific, but in general tipping is not expected. In Polynesian countries leaving a tip is fine if you feel inclined; in Melanesian countries, however, the issue is more complicated. In traditional Melanesian societies, a gift places obligation on the receiver to reciprocate somehow, and this can cause confusion and embarrassment when you're just trying to say thanks to the lady who cleans your hotel room –

particularly if you're about to leave. Always ask if unsure.

Travellers Cheques

These days, the only reason you'd carry travellers cheques rather than withdraw cash from a local ATM is the security cheques offer from loss and theft. American Express and Travelex/Thomas Cook travellers cheques are still accepted at banks across the region. Keep a record of cheque numbers, and ask about fees and commissions before you cash them in.

Value-Added Tax (VAT)

Value-added tax (VAT), known as TVA (*taxe sur la valeur ajoutée*) in French-speaking countries, is levied in some South Pacific nations such as French Polynesia, New Caledonia, the Cook Islands, Tonga and Fiji. It's added to the price of goods and services, including hotel and restaurant bills, and is usually included in the prices quoted.

Opening Hours

Opening hours vary across the region (and from season to season), but following are some typical business hours as a rough guide. Note that many local businesses close for a lunch hour (or two, in French-connected countries); and in some countries (eg Tonga) nothing at all is open on a Sunday.

Banks 9.30am to 4pm Monday to Friday

Bars 11am to late Monday to Saturday

Cafes 7am to 8pm

Post & government offices 9am to 4pm Monday to Friday, from 7.30am in countries with French ties

Shops 8am to 5pm Monday to Friday, to 1pm Saturday

Photography

As in all countries, a little politeness goes a long way: always ask before taking pictures of people, especially in ceremonial or religious circumstances.

Check out Lonely Planet's *Travel Photography* guide for inspiration.

Post

Postage costs vary from country to country, as does efficiency: the 'slowest post' award must go to Pitcairn Island – expect three months for letters either way (but the stamps are wonderful!).

It's more than a little outmoded these days, but major post offices do still provide poste-restante services. Ask people writing to you to print your name, underline your surname and mark the envelope 'Poste Restante (General Delivery)' with the name of the city and country. Bring your passport when you're collecting mail, and be prepared to pay a fee. If you can't locate your mail, check under your first name as well as your surname (or the name of your yacht!).

Public Holidays

Most major Western holidays – New Year's Day, Easter, Christmas Day and Boxing Day – are observed in South Pacific countries. See regional chapters for local public holiday listings.

Safe Travel

The South Pacific islands are safer travel destinations than most places in the world, and the locals are some of the friendliest you'll ever meet. But, as when travelling anywhere on the planet, it pays to use a little common sense.

Even in the larger cities, assaults and violent crime

are uncommon, but they do occur. Play it safe when walking around at night: stick to well-lit areas where there other people are hanging around, and avoid situations where you might be vulnerable.

You won't see many local ladies travelling solo, but the South Pacific is generally a safe and respectful region for visiting women to navigate alone.

More medically, grazes, coral cuts and even insect bites can quickly become infected in tropical climes: slather any lesions with antiseptic. Pay the tropical sun maximum respect and keep yourself hydrated. See the Health chapter for more.

In the Water

Many Pacific islands have sheltered lagoons inside protective reefs that offer safe swimming and snorkelling. But currents can be strong around passages and channels that drain the lagoon into the open sea on a falling tide. If there are no other swimmers around, ask a local before plunging in. Avoid swimming alone.

Watch out for venomous sea life – the lionfish is perhaps the most significant of these because it's mobile (though not aggressive) and has long venomous spines that cause extremely painful wounds. Most other beasties – eg sea urchins, stonefish, cone shells – sit placidly on the sea floor. The simple rule is look but don't touch; reef shoes (or old runners) can be useful. Stings and bites are extremely rare.

Shark attacks are also rare, but do occasionally happen. Swimming inside a reef offers some protection. Blacktip reef sharks look menacing, can grow to 2m long and sometimes swim in groups in shallow waters, but are harmless unless you pick a fight.

Mosquitoes

Malaria exists in western regions of the South Pacific – particularly the Solomon Islands and Vanuatu – but even where mosquitoes don't carry malaria, their bites can cause discomfort and, in some cases, dengue fever. Mosquitoes are less of a problem around the coast where sea breezes keep them away, but inland they can be a pest.

Theft

Petty thefts from hire cars, beach bags and hotel rooms do occur. Look after your valuables and keep them out of sight (passports, papers, tickets, cash). Money belts are a hassle in the heat – an ordinary wallet is better for cash. Valuables are normally safe in a locked hotel room if you're heading out for the day, but tuck them out of sight or stick them in a safe. Many South Pacific cultures have relaxed attitudes to property – it's best not to leave expensive gear lying around.

Telephone

Mobile Phones

Most mobile (cell) telephone carriers have global-roaming agreements with local providers in the South Pacific – but the costs of calling home, tweeting, posting on Facebook etc from your phone can be staggering. To give you some peace of mind, see if your carrier has a travel data package or similar, with capped call fees and data usage you can monitor.

If you're travelling within a specific country for a while, in most of the larger cities you can buy local SIM cards with data and calls allowances, which you can top up while on the road.

Mobile coverage in some South Pacific countries is still limited in remote areas, although it's rapidly expanding.

Phonecards

These days you'll be better off with your own mobile (cell) phone with global-roaming functionality or a local SIM. But phonecards are used in various Pacific countries – even Pitcairn Island has its own phonecards. That said, public telephones can be hard to find (and if you do find one, it often won't be working). At a pinch, you can usually find a shop owner who will let you use their phone for a local call. Some top-end hotels, however, charge steeply for the privilege of using their phones.

Phone Codes

To call abroad from the South Pacific, dial the international access code (IAC) for the country you're calling from (usually ⛉00 in the South Pacific, but ⛉05 in Fiji and ⛉19 in Wallis & Futuna), then

---

GOVERNMENT TRAVEL ADVICE

The following government websites offer travel advisories and information on current hot spots.

Australian Department of Foreign Affairs & Trade (www.smarttraveller.gov.au)

British Foreign & Commonwealth Office (www.gov.uk/fco)

Government of Canada (www.travel.gc.ca)

New Zealand Ministry of Foreign Affairs & Trade (www.safetravel.govt.nz)

US State Department (www.travel.state.gov)

the international telephone code (ITC) for the country you are calling, the local area code (if there is one, usually sans the leading zero) and finally the number.

For example, you are in the Cook Islands (IAC ⏚00) and you want to make a call to the USA (ITC ⏚1), San Francisco (area code ⏚212), number ⏚123 4567, then you dial ⏚00-1-212-123 4567. To call from Fiji (IAC ⏚05) to Australia (ITC ⏚61), Sydney (area code ⏚02), number ⏚1234 5678, then dial ⏚05-61-2-1234 5678 (dropping the zero from Sydney's area code).

There are no local area codes in countries of the South Pacific.

Time

Most South Pacific islands don't utilise daylight savings time, except for Fiji and Samoa. Double-check your airline tickets if you're winging in or out at the start or finish of daylight savings.

The International Date Line splits the South Pacific in half – running along the 180-degree longitude but detouring to the east to catch Tonga, Kiribati, Samoa and Tokelau in the same day – which makes time zones here complicated. Flying east across the International Date Line, you'll arrive at your destination before you left! Crossing from east to west, you'll lose a day.

Toilets

In South Pacific urban areas, most toilets are sit-down Western style. In some remote areas and outer islands (Vanuatu, the Solomon Islands), don't expect flushing toilets – handbuilt long-drop

toilets prevail, with BYO toilet paper. Public toilets can be few and far between, and are often closed for maintenance.

Tourist Information

Online, the quality of tourist information varies from one South Pacific country to the next, but even the most remote island groups have websites these days (though these may not be up to date).

The umbrella intergovernmental organisation is the South Pacific Tourism Organisation (www.spto.org), fostering regional cooperation in developing and promoting tourism. The SPTO serves as a tourist office for a few countries, though it doesn't offer whole a lot of advice for independent travellers.

On the ground, official visitor information centres swing from fairly professional outfits to erratically staffed shacks with dodgy maps and mildewy brochures – you'll soon know which you're dealing with once you walk in the door.

Travellers with Disabilities

South Pacific countries generally have poor facilities for disabled travellers. Wheelchair users will find getting around a problem: footpaths (sidewalks) can be patchy or nonexistent, domestic planes have steps and narrow doors, ferries may not have ramp access... Some larger international resorts offer rooms with disabled access, but it's not common.

That said, South Pacific cultures look after their elderly, disabled and infirm as integrated members of the community – there are no

special schools or aged-care facilities. Islanders won't simply look away if you need some help to get into a taxi or up some stairs – they'll rally up some helpers and pitch in.

Get in touch with your national support organisation before you travel to enquire about the countries you plan to visit.

Visas

As a sweeping generalisation, with a valid passport from most Western countries you can visit most South Pacific countries for up to three months, provided you have an onward or return ticket and sufficient means of support. You'll usually receive a visa or tourist permit at the airport or seaport on arrival – but not always. It's worth checking with the embassies or consulates of the countries you plan to visit before travelling, as visa requirements can change.

Volunteering

Volunteering is a great way to get to know the South Pacific and have an adventure while doing something worthwhile. There are all sorts of volunteering organisations in operation here, some requiring long-term commitments and experience or tertiary qualifications in specific fields, others based around the notion of short-term working holidays and community projects.

For more information, contact the following:

Australian Volunteers International (www.australianvolunteers.com)

Global Volunteers (www.globalvolunteers.org)

Madventurer (www.madventurer.com)

Projects Abroad (www.projects-abroad.org)

South Pacific Projects (www.southpacificprojects.org)

UN Volunteers (www.unv.org)

Vinaka Fiji (www.vinakafiji.com.fj)

Voluntary Service Overseas (www.vso.org.uk)

Volunteer Service Abroad (www.vsa.org.nz)

World Wildlife Fund (www.panda.org)

See also Lonely Planet's *Volunteer: A Traveller's Guide to Making a Difference Around the World* – an excellent resource for those interested in making a contribution to the South Pacific or elsewhere.

Work

Generally speaking, it's hard to get a work visa for South Pacific countries. For the low-down on working in a particular country, contact the relevant embassy, consulate or immigration office, or scan the websites.

Transport

GETTING THERE & AWAY

Flights, cars and tours can be booked online at lonelyplanet.com/bookings.

Entering the Region

Unless you're hoisting the spinnaker on a yacht or kicking back on a cruise ship, getting to the South Pacific will mean a long-haul flight, usually via a gateway city such as Auckland, Brisbane, Sydney, LA, Honolulu or Tokyo.

Passport

There are no passport restrictions when visiting South Pacific countries – everyone is welcome!

Air

Due to vast expanses of open ocean and the relatively small number of travellers visiting the region, just getting to the South Pacific can be expensive.

Airlines flying between the US, Australia, New Zealand and Japan stop off at a number of South Pacific destinations. There are also several smaller local airlines that only operate within the South Pacific region, but not all of these fly directly to all countries – you may find yourself having to detour through Auckland airport to get from one country to the next (not really a hassle – just a bit time-consuming).

Airlines

Air New Zealand, Qantas and Fiji Airways are the main carriers into the region. See individual destination chapters for other options.

Sea

Climbing aboard a cruise liner or an ocean-going yacht is a terrific way to see the sea.

Cruise Ship

Interestingly, the popularity of cruise ship travel is on the rise, which means more visitors will be slow-boating into the South Pacific in coming years. Cruise ships can be an expensive way to travel, and they usually only call into major tourist islands and rarely stay longer than a few hours. But if you've got the time, the cash and the inclination, go for it!

Yacht

Harnessing the South Pacific trade winds and sailing from one island idyll to the next – what a dream! If you've got the time, the cash and the inclination (and importantly, a friend with a yacht), go for it! Most island groups here have reef-protected lagoons or lee-side moorings (p586), and there's usually some nocturnal high-jinx to be had ashore wherever yachties pull in for the night (Neiafu in Tonga springs to mind).

GETTING AROUND

Air

Clambering into a light aircraft is the primary way of getting from A to B in the South Pacific. Don't expect cabin crew, complimentary meals or even a strip of tarmac in some cases (these small aircraft often land on grass airstrips on remote islands, where the terminal is a tin shed and a guy with a mobile phone). Some inter-island flights might operate just once or twice a week and can be heavily booked, so secure your seats well in advance.

Airlines in the South Pacific

The following carriers fly between and within South Pacific countries.

Air Niugini (www.airniugini.com.pg) Has flights between Port Moresby, Nadi in Fiji and Honiara in the Solomon Islands.

Air Tahiti (www.airtahiti.aero) Servicing French Polynesian destinations, extending to the Cook Islands.

Air Vanuatu (www.airvanuatu.com) Flies within Vanuatu, extending to Fiji, New Caledonia and the Solomon Islands.

Aircalin (www.aircalin.nc) Flies within New Caledonia, extending to Fiji, French Polynesia, Vanuatu and Wallis & Futuna.

Fiji Airways (www.fijiairways. com) Fiji's national carrier flies within Fiji, and from Fiji to the Solomon Islands, Samoa, Tonga, Tuvalu and Vanuatu.

Inter Island Airways (www.interislandair.com) Flies within and between Samoa and American Samoa.

Manu'a Airways (www. manuaair.com) New in American Samoa in 2016, with flights between Pago Pago and Ofu and Ta'u Islands, and between Ofu and Ta'u Islands.

Northern Air (www.northernair.com.fj) Domestic carrier within Fiji.

Polynesian Airlines (www. polynesianairlines.com) Flies between Samoa and American Samoa.

Real Tonga (www.realtonga. to) Tonga's domestic carrier, servicing the country's main island groups.

Solomon Airlines (www. solomonairlines.com.au) Flies to multiple destinations within the Solomon Islands, extending to Vanuatu and Fiji.

Boat

There are a few possibilities for those romantics taken with the idea of exploring the Pacific by sea. It's certainly much slower than flying and not necessarily any cheaper – but adventure is more important than any of that!

Cargo Ship

If you've got lots of time and don't mind roughing it, check the local supply-ship schedules. Cargo vessels, some of which carry passengers, travel between far-flung island groups, many of which are not serviced by air.

Other ships carry cargo and passengers across international borders. Cargo and dual-purpose cargo/passenger ships ply between Tuvalu and Fiji, Vanuatu and New Caledonia, Samoa and Tokelau, and Samoa and the Cook Islands. There's also a car ferry operating between Samoa and American Samoa.

Cruise Ship

Yes, yes, we know, cruise ships are the domain of the idle rich and the bourgeois, with spoon-fed culture and captive-audience entertainment filling the hours between cocktails. But if you can manage to fight your way free of the prepackaging and get a little solo shore time, in the South Pacific they can also be a handy way to get around without any hassle.

Fares vary enormously, but generally prices run upwards from US$250 per day. Major ports of call are Noumea (New Caledonia), Port Vila (Vanuatu), Rarotonga (Cook Islands) and Pape'ete, Mo'orea and Bora Bora (all in French Polynesia). Melanesian cruises usually depart from Australia's east coast, mostly from Sydney and Brisbane. Other cruises depart from US west-coast ports like Seattle, San Francisco, LA or Honolulu.

A few companies:

Adventure Life (www.adventure-life.com) Specialises in smaller, off-the-beaten-track cruises to South Pacific locales including Easter Island, the Pitcairn Islands and the Marquesas.

Carnival (www.carnival.com. au) Short-hop Pacific islands cruises from Sydney (usually six to 10 days).

Crystal Cruises (www.crystalcruises.com) LA to Sydney via American Samoa, Samoa, Fiji, Vanuatu and New Caledonia.

Holland America (www. hollandamerica.com) Cruises from the US to Australia and New Zealand via New Caledonia.

P&O Cruises (www.pocruises.com.au) Major global player with South Seas cruises from Australia and New Zealand.

Paul Gauguin Cruises (www.pgcruises.com) Sometimes combines French Polynesia with Fiji.

Princess Cruises (www.princess.com) South Pacific cruises departing Australia (Sydney, Brisbane and Melbourne).

Ferry

Within most South Pacific countries, passenger ferries ply the waters between various island groups and are a scenic and affordable (if not speedy or particularly comfortable) way to get from one island to the next. Tonga is a good example, with regular scheduled ferries (doubling as supply boats)

CLIMATE CHANGE & TRAVEL

Every form of transport that relies on carbon-based fuel generates CO_2, the main cause of human-induced climate change. Modern travel is dependent on aeroplanes, which might use less fuel per kilometre per person than most cars but travel much greater distances. The altitude at which aircraft emit gases (including CO_2) and particles also contributes to their climate change impact. Many websites offer 'carbon calculators' that allow people to estimate the carbon emissions generated by their journey and, for those who wish to do so, to offset the impact of the greenhouse gases emitted with contributions to portfolios of climate-friendly initiatives throughout the world. Lonely Planet offsets the carbon footprint of all staff and author travel.

chugging between the capital Nuku'alofa and the 'Eua, Ha'apai and Vava'u island groups.

Yacht

The South Pacific is a perennial playground for yachties. Between May and October, the harbours of the South Pacific swarm with cruising yachts from around the world. Almost invariably, yachts follow the favourable westerly winds from the Americas towards Asia, Australia or New Zealand.

Popular routes from the US west coast take in Hawai'i and Palmyra Atoll before following the traditional path through Samoa and American Samoa, Tonga, Fiji and New Zealand. From the Atlantic and Caribbean, yachties access the South Pacific via Panama, the Galápagos Islands, the Marquesas, the Society Islands and the Tuamotus. Possible stops include Suwarrow (northern Cook Islands), Rarotonga and Niue.

The tropical cyclone season begins in November and runs until April. Most yachties try to be well on their way to New Zealand by the early part of November.

The yachting community is an affable one and yachties are a good source of information about weather patterns, navigation and maritime geography. They're also often open to chatting about day charters, diving and sailing lessons.

RED TAPE

You must enter a country at an official 'port of entry' (usually the capital). If this means sailing past a dozen beautiful outlying islands on the way to an appointment with an official in a dull capital city, bad luck.

When you arrive, hoist your yellow quarantine flag (Q flag) and wait for the appropriate local official to contact you. Often, you are expected to alert them by VHF radio (usually on channel 16). Some countries charge visiting yachties entrance fees. Ask customs officials at the port of entry about requirements for visiting other islands in the country. Bear in mind that you are legally responsible

CREWING ON A YACHT

Yachties are often looking for crew – a super opportunity for those who like a bit of sea salt in their hair. It's not all hard work, either: most of the time, crew members will only be asked to take a turn on watch – to scan the horizon for cargo ships, stray containers and the odd reef – and possibly to cook or clean up the boat. In port, crew may be required to dive and scrape the bottom of the hull, paint or make repairs. In most cases, sailing experience is not necessary and crew members can learn as they go. Most yachties charge crew around US$20 per day for food and supplies.

If you'd like a crewing berth, try to find a yacht that has wind-vane steering, since the tedious job of standing at the wheel, staring at a compass all day and all night, is likely to be assigned to crew members of the lowest status (that's you). Comfort is also greatly increased on yachts that have a furling jib, a dodger to keep out the weather, a toilet and shower. Yachts rigged for ocean racing are usually more manageable than simple liveaboards. As a general rule, about 3m of length for each person aboard affords relatively uncrowded conditions.

If you're trying to find a berth on someone else's yacht (or trying to find crew for your own boat), ask at local yacht clubs and check noticeboards at marinas and yacht clubs. In the US, Honolulu and the west coast – San Francisco, Newport Beach and San Diego – are the places to start looking. Australia's northeastern seaboard (Brisbane to Cairns) is good and so are Auckland, Whangarei and the Bay of Islands in New Zealand. In the South Pacific, ask around in Pape'ete, Pago Pago, Apia, Nuku'alofa, Neiafu, Noumea or Port Vila.

Online resources:

⇒ **Noonsite** (www.noonsite.com) A terrific yachting catch-all, as broad as the sea is deep.

⇒ **Latitude 38** (www.latitude38.com) A handy resource for finding boats that need crew.

⇒ **Ocean Voyages** (www.oceanvoyages.com) Organises yacht charters in the South Pacific. Charter a whole boat or book a berth on a yacht sailing a particular route (a charter is about the only way to get to some remote islands and atolls if you don't have your own yacht).

⇒ **Boat Bureau** (www.boatbureau.com) Charters across the Pacific, with or without skipper.

for your crew's actions as well as your own.

Local Transport

Bicycle

On flat South Pacific islands, renting a bicycle can be an excellent way to get around. Most rental bikes won't come with a helmet or lock unless you ask for them – and be aware that maintenance often isn't a high priority. Watch for poor road surfaces, and check your travel insurance for disclaimers about hazardous activities. If you're bringing your own bike, ask the airline about costs and rules regarding dismantling and packing the bike.

Boat

Within a country, ferries and cargo boats are often the only way to get to some outer islands. Sometimes it'll come down to negotiating with the local fishers to get you there.

Bus

Large and populous islands usually have some kind of bus service. However, public transport here couldn't be described as ruthlessly efficient. Buses are often privately (or sometimes family) owned, and it's not unusual for owner-drivers to set their own schedules. Formal bus stops may or may not exist – just wave your arms around if not. If there aren't many people travelling on a particular day, the buses may stop altogether. Build flexibility into your plans.

Car & Motorcycle

Larger South Pacific islands and tourist destinations will usually have some car- or motorcycle-hire companies, either big international branches (Avis, Hertz etc) or locally run outfits. Prior to travel, check whether you need an International Driving Permit for the countries you're visiting – it's usually

a good idea to carry one regardless.

ROAD RULES & CONDITIONS

Driving in some countries here is on the right-hand side of the road (those affiliated with France or the US), and on the left-hand side in others (countries with English colonial lineage). Roads in rural areas may be no more than dirt tracks used mostly for foot traffic – conditions can be dreadful if there's recent cyclone or flood damage. Be super-watchful for kids and animals on the road, especially near villages. When you rent a car, ask about petrol availability if you're heading off the main routes. And don't park under coconut trees!

INSURANCE

Make sure you get the insurance rules and conditions explained before you drive away. Check your own travel insurance policy (p579) too: some do not cover damage on unsealed roads, windscreens, tyres or riding a motorcycle.

Hitching

In some South Pacific countries hitching is an accepted way of getting where you're going, and is practised by locals and tourists alike. In others, it's not the local custom and only tourists are seen trying it.

The main difficulty with hitching on the South Pacific islands is that rides tend not to be very long, perhaps only from one village to the next – it could take you a while to travel longer distances. But hitching can be a great way to meet locals and is an option for getting around when the buses aren't running. You might be expected to pay a small fee for a ride, so offer what you think the ride is worth – although offers of payment will often be refused.

Keep in mind that hitching is never entirely safe. If you do choose to hitch, don't go it alone. Women travelling on their own should definitely seek alternative conveyances.

Taxi

Taxis (and taxi drivers) in the South Pacific are a motley crew, ranging from company-owned and well-maintained minivans to rickety rust-buckets someone's uncle runs as a cab when he's not fishing. Either way, you can expect plenty of conversation with the driver, often extending to an invitation to call them directly tomorrow/next week/next month when you need a taxi again. Fare meters aren't always present (and it's a good idea to discuss price before you start driving, even if they are). Have the specific address of your destination ready to go, too, so you don't end up at the driver's sister's guesthouse instead of the one you've booked.

Tours

If you want to take the hassle out of planning, sign up for a South Pacific package tour or a dedicated activity-based tour.

Package Tours

The South Pacific endears itself to the package-tour market. Given the high price of flights to and within the region, and the often inflated price of accommodation once you arrive, a package tour can be a financial godsend. On the downside, package tours don't give you much leeway to explore independently. Also, you usually have to prebook a hotel or guesthouse for each destination before departure, meaning you can't swap resorts halfway through if you're not happy.

Diving package tours are another option, typically including flights, accommodation and multiple days down in the deep blue.

BOOKING

The websites of the airlines that service the region are good places to get a feel for pricing. But if you want more than a straightforward combo package, a good travel agent is essential – they can negotiate better prices at the larger hotels and handle internal flight bookings.

Most packages quote double-occupancy pricing; solo travellers have to pay a single-person supplement (it's not just half the double rate). Extra people can usually share a room, but there's a charge for the extra bed, which varies enormously from resort to resort.

Surfing Tours

Several operators specialise in surfing holidays in the South Pacific, including the following:

Perfect Wave (www.the perfectwave.com.au) Packaged-up surf holidays in Fiji, Samoa and Tahiti.

World Surfaris (www. worldsurfaris.com) Samoa, New Caledonia, Fiji and Tonga – the best breaks on surf trips customised by those in the know (Australians).

Wyndham Vacation Resorts (www.surfthesouth pacific.com) Resort-based family surf holidays in Fiji.

Health

Most travellers who come to the South Pacific won't experience anything worse than an upset stomach or a hangover. But if you have an immediate and serious health problem, phone or visit the nearest public hospital, or call into the nearest pharmacy for advice. The Solomon Islands and Vanuatu share the one serious health hazard: malaria. Elsewhere the main danger is from mosquito-borne dengue fever.

BEFORE YOU GO

A little planning before departure, particularly for preexisting illnesses, will avoid trouble down the line. A signed and dated letter from your physician describing your medical conditions and medications that you may have in your baggage, including generic names, is a good idea.

Insurance

A comprehensive travel and health insurance policy is essential for the South Pacific. Check whether you're covered for 'dangerous' activities (surfing, snorkelling, diving etc) and make sure your policy has provision for evacuation. Under these circumstances, hospitals will accept direct payment from major international insurers, but for all other health-related

costs cash upfront is usually required.

Worldwide travel insurance is available at lonelyplanet.com/travel-insurance. You can buy, extend and claim online anytime – even if you're already on the road.

American travellers Check whether your health plan covers expenses in American Samoa.

EU travellers You have the same rights in French Polynesia, New Caledonia, and Wallis & Futuna as you do in France, but remember to obtain the European Health Insurance Card (EHIC) before leaving home.

New Zealand travellers You may have free access to public but not private facilities in the Cook Islands.

Recommended Vaccinations

For all countries in the region, vaccinations are recommended for hepatitis A, hepatitis B and typhoid fever. A current influenza shot is also recommended. And check how long it's been since you had a tetanus booster (once every 10 years is the going rate).

Medical Checklist

Some of the following list will fall into the 'overkill' category for most travellers, but if you're serious about being ready for anything or if you're

heading into remote areas for any length of time, consider packing a nifty little bag with:

➡ acetaminophen (paracetamol) or aspirin

➡ antibiotics

➡ antidiarrhoeal drugs (eg loperamide)

➡ antihistamines (for hayfever and allergic reactions)

➡ anti-inflammatory drugs (eg ibuprofen)

➡ antibacterial ointment in case of cuts or abrasions

➡ steroid cream or cortisone (for allergic rashes)

➡ bandages, gauze, gauze rolls

➡ adhesive or paper tape

➡ scissors, safety pins, tweezers

➡ thermometer

➡ pocket knife

➡ DEET-containing insect repellent for the skin

➡ permethrin-containing insect spray for clothing, tents and bed nets

➡ sunscreen

➡ oral rehydration salts

➡ iodine tablets or water filter (for water purification)

Websites

For up-to-date information on health issues across the South Pacific, the World Health Organisation (www.who.int/en) is a font of knowledge. Government travel advice websites also list current health warnings:

Australian Department of Foreign Affairs & Trade (www.smarttraveller.gov.au)

British Foreign & Commonwealth Office (www.gov.uk/fco)

Government of Canada (www.travel.gc.ca)

New Zealand Ministry of Foreign Affairs & Trade (www.safetravel.govt.nz)

US State Department (www.travel.state.gov)

Further Reading

For a sobering reminder of the power of disease, have a read of *The Great Influenza: The Epic Story of the Deadliest Plague in History* by John M Barry (2004), concerning the 1918 influenza (or 'Spanish Flu') pandemic, which killed many thousands of islanders in the South Pacific.

IN THE SOUTH PACIFIC

Availability & Cost of Health Care

In Fiji, French Polynesia and American Samoa, there are doctors in private practice, and standard hospital and laboratory facilities with consultants and specialists. In the Cook Islands, New Caledonia, Samoa, Solomon Islands, Tonga and Vanuatu, specialised services may be limited but private general practitioners, dentists and pharmacies are present. On smaller islands there may be no services at all, or perhaps just a nurse. Medical costs vary between countries, but are generally comparable to Western prices.

Infectious Diseases

Dengue Fever

Risk All countries, especially in the hotter, wetter months

Symptoms & Treatment Mosquito-borne dengue fever causes a high fever, headache and severe muscle pains. A fine rash may also be present. Self-treatment includes par-acetamol (do *not* take aspirin), fluids and rest. Danger signs are prolonged vomiting, blood in the vomit, a blotchy dark red rash and/or bruising.

Eosinophilic Meningitis

Risk Cook Islands, French Polynesia, Fiji, Tonga

Symptoms & Treatment An illness manifested by scattered abnormal skin sensations, fever and sometimes meningitis symptoms (headache, vomiting, confusion, stiffness of the neck and spine). Eosinophilic meningitis is caused by a microscopic parasite – the rat lungworm – that contaminates raw food. There is no proven treatment, but symptoms may require hospitalisation. For prevention, pay strict attention to advice on food and drink.

Leptospirosis

Risk American Samoa, Fiji, French Polynesia, possibly elsewhere

Symptoms & Treatment Also known as Weil's disease, leptospirosis produces fever, headache, jaundice and, later, kidney failure. It's caused by the spirochaete organism found in water contaminated by rat and pig urine. Often confused with dengue fever, this disease is the more serious of the two. The organism penetrates skin, so swimming in flooded areas is a risk. If diagnosed early, it's cured with penicillin.

Malaria

Risk Solomon Islands (except outlying atolls), Vanuatu

Symptoms & Treatment Both malignant (falciparum) and less threatening but relapsing forms are present. Avoid getting bitten by mosquitoes and take antimalarial drugs before, during and after risk exposure. No antimalarial is 100% effective and there's no vaccine. The essence of the disease is fever. In a malarial zone it is best to assume that fever is due to malaria unless blood tests rule it out. This applies to up to a few months after leaving the area as well. Malaria is curable if diagnosed early.

Yaws

Risk Solomon Islands

Symptoms & Treatment A bacterial infection that causes multiple skin ulcers. Once thought to have been eliminated, there has been a recent resurgence. Infection is by direct contact. Treatment with penicillin produces a dramatic cure.

Environmental Hazards

Beyond the odd mosquito bite, threats to health from animals and insects are rare in the South Pacific. But there are a few things for travellers to be aware of.

TAP WATER

To steer yourself clear of diarrhoea, avoid tap water unless it has been boiled, filtered or chemically disinfected (with iodine tablets), and also avoid ice unless you've made it yourself from bottled water. This is a sensible overall precaution, but the municipal water supply in capital cities in the region can be trusted.

Bites & Stings

Jellyfish Watch out for the whip-like stings of the blue-coloured Indo-Pacific man-of-war. If you see these floating in the water or stranded on the beach, play it safe and stay on dry land. The sting is very painful and is best treated with vinegar or ice packs. Do not use alcohol.

Cone Shells Poisonous cone shells abound along shallow South Pacific coral reefs. Avoid handling them. Stings mainly only cause local reactions, but nausea, faintness, palpitations or difficulty in breathing are signs that medical attention is needed.

Sea Snakes As in all tropical waters, sea snakes may be seen around coral reefs. Unprovoked, sea snakes are extremely unlikely to attack – and their fangs will not penetrate a wetsuit (...in Tonga, locals joke that death by sea-snake bite is a voluntary undertaking – you'd have to force one to bite you!).

Sharks Sharks do swim around these warm tropical waters, but rarely pose a threat to humans. White-tip and black-tip reef sharks are too small to do any damage, but grey reef, tiger and bull sharks occasionally get nippy. If you're in the sea, remember that so are they.

Coral Ear

This is a fungal infection caused by seawater entering the ear canal. Seemingly trivial when it happens, it can be very, very painful and can spoil a holiday. Apart from diarrhoea it is the most common reason for tourists to consult a doctor. Self-treatment with an antibiotic-plus-steroid ear-drop preparation is very effective: see a doctor for a prescription, and stay out of the water until the pain and itch have subsided.

Staph Infection

Infection of cuts and scrapes is very common, with cuts from live coral particularly prone to infection. If you get a scrape, as soon as you can, cleanse the wound thoroughly (getting out all the little bits of coral or dirt), apply an antiseptic and cover with a dressing. You can get back in the water with these kinds of cuts, but healing time will be prolonged if you do. Change the dressing regularly, never let it sit wet and check often for signs of infection.

Diving Hazards

Because the South Pacific has wonderful opportunities for scuba diving, it is easy to get overexcited and neglect strict depth and time precautions. If you're inexperienced, make sure you're diving with a licensed operator who knows what they're doing, and has a realistic understanding of your limits. If you're not diving with a group, make sure you tell someone where you're going and when you'll be back.

Fish Poisoning

Ciguatera poisoning – a food-borne illness caused by eating toxic reef fish – is characterised by stomach upsets, itching, faintness, slow pulse and bizarre inverted sensations (cold feeling hot and vice versa). Ciguatera has been reported in many carnivorous reef fish, including red snapper, barracuda and even smaller reef fish. There is no safe test to determine whether a fish is poisonous or not and, although local knowledge is not entirely reliable, it is reasonable to eat what the locals are eating. Deep-sea tuna is perfectly safe.

Treatment consists of rehydration and if the pulse is very slow, medication may be needed. Healthy adults will make a complete recovery, although disturbed sensation may persist for some weeks – sometimes much longer.

Heat Sicknesses

Sunburn Apply sunscreen liberally and often, especially after swimming. And look after your eyes with a decent pair of sunglasses.

Heat Exhaustion Symptoms include dizziness, fainting, fatigue, nausea or vomiting, and pale, cool and clammy skin. Treatment consists of rest in a cool, shady place and fluid replacement with water or diluted sports drinks. Rule #1: stay hydrated.

Heat Stroke More dangerous than heat exhaustion, heat stroke happens when the cooling effect of sweating fails. This condition is characterised by muscle weakness and mental confusion. Skin will be hot and dry. If this occurs, 'put the heat out' by cooling the body with water on the outside and cold drinks for the inside. Seek urgent medical help.

Dogs

Dogs have free rein across most of the South Pacific island groups, but their bark is generally worse than their bite. Play it safe on the streets: cross the road to avoid packs and don't try to pat or befriend wandering mutts. And if you are barked at, don't hang around and continue the conversation.

Language

WANT MORE?

For in-depth language information and handy phrases, check out Lonely Planet's *South Pacific Phrasebook* and *Pidgin Phrasebook*. You'll find them at **shop.lonelyplanet.com**, or you can buy Lonely Planet's iPhone phrasebooks at the Apple App Store.

Which Language Where?

Here's an overview of the main languages of the South Pacific and where they are spoken, followed by some handy basics for the ones you're most likely to come across.

American Samoa	Samoan, English
Cook Islands	Rarotongan/Cook Islands Maori, English
Easter Island	Rapa Nui, Spanish
Fiji	Fijian, Fijian Hindi, English
New Caledonia	Kanak languages/Melanesian-Polynesian dialects, French
Rarotonga	Rarotongan, English
Samoa	Samoan, English
Solomon Islands	Solomon Islands Pijin, indigenous languages, English
Tahiti & French Polynesia	Tahitian (and others such as Austral, Marquesan & Tuamotuan), French
Tonga	Tongan, English
Vanuatu	Bislama, indigenous languages, English, French

Other Pacific Islands:

Niue	Niuean, English
Pitcairn Islands	Pitkern, English
Tokelau	Tokelauan, English
Tuvalu	Tuvaluan, Gilbertese, English
Wallis & Futuna	Wallisian, Futunan, French

BISLAMA

Bislama, a form of pidgin English, is Vanuatu's national language. English and French are also widely spoken, and schools teach in French or English. Vanuatu also has the greatest number of local languages per capita in the world, with about 120 still spoken.

Hello.	Alo.
Hello.	Alo olgeta.
Goodbye.	Bae.
See you.	Mi lukem yu.
How are you?	Olsem wanem?
I'm well, thanks.	I gud nomo, tankyu tumas.
Please.	Plis.
Thank you.	Tankyu tumas.
Sorry.	Sore.
Yes./No.	Olraet./No.
Do you speak English?	Yu tok tok Engglis?
I don't understand.	Mi no save.

COOK ISLANDS MAORI

See Rarotongan.

FIJIAN & FIJIAN HINDI

The majority of the local people in Fiji you're likely to come in contact with speak English, and all signs and official forms are also in English. However, indigenous Fijians speak Fijian at home. There are two major groups of Fijian dialects – western and eastern. The form understood throughout the islands is popularly known as *vosa vakabau* (Bauan).

Hello.	Bula.
Goodbye.	Moce.
Please.	Mada.
Thank you.	Vinaka.
Sorry.	Ni vosota sara.
Yes.	Io.
No.	Sega.
Do you speak English?	Oni kilaa na vosa vakavaalagi?
I don't understand.	E sega ni macala.

Indo-Fijians speak Fijian Hindi (also known as Fiji-Hindi or Fiji Hindustani). Note that in Fijian Hindi there are no equivalents for 'please' and 'thank you'. To be polite in making requests, people use the word *thoraa* (a little) and a special form of the verb ending in *-naa*, eg *thoraa nimak denaa* (please pass the salt). For 'thanks', people often just say *achhaa* (good).

Hello. (for Hindus)	Namaste.
Hello. (for Muslims)	Salaam alaykum.
Goodbye.	Fir milegaa.
How are you?	Kaise?
I'm well.	Tik.
Sorry.	Maaf karnaa.
Yes.	Ha.
No.	Nahi.
Do you speak English?	Aap/Tum English boltaa? (pol/inf)
I don't understand.	Ham nahi samajhtaa.

FRENCH

French is the official language in New Caledonia/French Polynesia, where indigenous Kanak (Melanesian-Polynesian) dialects are also spoken. French will also come in handy in Vanuatu and Tahiti, as well as Wallis and Futuna.

Hello.	Bonjour.
Goodbye.	Au revoir.
How are you?	Comment allez-vous?
I'm well, thanks.	Je vais bien, merci.
Please.	S'il vous plaît.
Thank you.	Merci.
Sorry.	Pardon.
Yes.	Oui.
No.	Non.
Do you speak English?	Parlez-vous anglais?
I don't understand.	Je ne comprends pas.

NEW CALEDONIAN

More than 30 indigenous Kanak (Melanesian-Polynesian) dialects are spoken in New Caledonia alongside French. There are 28 distinct Kanak languages (not counting dialects) and all belong to the Melanesian branch of the Austronesian language family, except for Faga Uvea (spoken on Uvea), which is a Polynesian language. The following are the basics for Drehu, the most widely spoken Kanak language (spoken in the Loyalty Islands).

Hello.	Bozu./Talofa.
Goodbye.	Tata./Iahni.
How are you? (only asked by an adult)	Hapeu laï?
I'm well.	Kaloi./Egöcatr.
Do you speak English?	Hapeu nyipë a qene papaale?

RAPA NUI

Spanish is the official language on Easter Island and it will get you by. The indigenous language is Rapa Nui, an eastern Polynesian dialect closely related to the languages of French Polynesia and Hawai'i. These days the language increasingly bears the influence of English and Spanish. Any attempt at a few basic phrases in Rapa Nui will be greatly appreciated by the locals.

The apostrophe (') in written Rapa Nui indicates a glottal stop (like the pause in the middle of 'uh-oh').

Hello.	'Iorana.
Goodbye.	'Iorana.
How are you?	Pehē koe/kōrua? (sg/pl)
I'm well.	Rivariva.
Thank you.	Maururu.

RAROTONGAN

Rarotongan (or Cook Islands Maori, as it's also known) is a Polynesian language similar to New Zealand Maori and Marquesan (from French Polynesia). There are minor dialectal differences between many of the islands, and some northern islands have their own languages. English is spoken as a second (or third) language by virtually everyone.

In Rarotongan, the glottal stop replaces the 'h' of similar Polynesian languages; for example, the Tahitian word for 'one', *tahi* (pronounced 'ta-hee'), is *ta'i* (pronounced 'ta-ee') in Rarotongan.

Hello.	Kia orana.
Goodbye. (if staying)	'Aere ra.
Goodbye. (if leaving)	'E no'o ra.

How are you?	Pe'ea koe?
Please.	Ine.
Thank you.	Meitaki.
Yes.	Ae.
No.	Kare.

SAMOAN

Samoan is the main language spoken in Samoa and American Samoa, although most people also speak English.

In Samoan, the 's' replaces the 'h' of many other Polynesian languages, 'l' replaces 'r', and a glottal stop replaces 'k'. Therefore, the Tahitian word for 'one', *tahi*, is *tasi* in Samoan, *rua* (two) is *lua*, and *ika* (Rarotongan for 'fish') is *i'a*. The soft 'ng' sound in Samoan is written as a 'g' (*palagi*, for example, is pronounced 'pah-lah-ngee').

Hello.	Tālofa.
Goodbye.	Tōfā soifua.
How are you?	'O ā mai 'oe?
I'm well, thanks.	Manuia lava, fa'afetai.
Please.	Fa'amolemole.
Thank you.	Fa'afetai.
Yes.	Ioe.
No.	Leai.

SOLOMON ISLANDS PIJIN

Officially, there are 67 indigenous languages and about 30 dialects in the Solomon Islands, so people from different villages often speak mutually incomprehensible languages. As a result, the national language is Solomon Islands Pijin, or Pijin for short. Educated people generally also speak English, which is the official language of the administration.

Hello.	Halo.
Goodbye.	Bae-bae.
How are you?	Oraet nomoa?
I'm well.	Oraet nomoa.
Please.	Plis.
Thank you.	Tanggio tumas.
Yes.	Ia.
No.	Nomoa.

SPANISH

Spanish is the official language on Easter Island. The indigenous population also speaks Rapa Nui.

Hello.	Hola.
Goodbye.	Adiós.

How are you?	¿Cómo está? (pol)
	¿Cómo estás? (inf)
I'm well, thanks.	Bien, gracias.
Please.	Por favor.
Thank you.	Gracias.
Sorry.	Perdón.
Yes./No.	Sí./No.
Do you speak	¿Habla inglés? (pol)
English?	¿Hablas inglés? (inf)
I don't understand.	No entiendo.

TAHITIAN (REO MAOHI)

The official languages of French Polynesia are French and Tahitian. Other languages on the islands include Austral, Marquesan and Tuamotuan, and much of the tourist industry uses English. If you venture to the more remote and less touristy islands, it's useful to know some French. On all islands, at least trying a few words in French – and even more so, Tahitian – will be appreciated.

Tahitian, also known as Reo Maohi, is a Polynesian language very similar to Hawaiian and Cook Islands Maori.

In Tahitian, a glottal stop replaces the consonants 'k' and 'ng' – for example, the Polynesian word *vaka* (canoe) is *va'a* in Tahitian.

Hello.	La ora na, nana.
Goodbye.	Pārahi, nana.
How are you?	E aha te huru?
Thank you.	Māuruuru roa.
Sorry.	E'e, aue ho'i e.
Yes.	E, 'oia.
No.	Aita.
I don't understand.	Aita i ta'a ia'u.

TONGAN

Tongan is a Polynesian language. It is the official language of Tonga, along with English, and the language most often used in everyday communication.

Note that the glottal stop is represented by an apostrophe (').

Hello.	Malo e lelei.
Goodbye. (if staying)	'Alu a.
Goodbye. (if leaving)	Nofo ā.
How are you?	Fefe hake?
I'm well, thanks.	Sai pe, malo.
Please.	Faka molemole.
Thank you.	Malo.
Yes.	'Io.
No.	Ikai.

GLOSSARY

ahu – raised altar on ancient *marae* (Polynesia)

'aiga – extended family (Samoa)

aitu – spirit (Polynesia)

ali'i – see *ariki*

ari'i – see *ariki*

ariki – paramount chief; members of a noble family

atoll – low-lying island built up from deposits of coral

Austronesians – people or languages from Indonesia, Malaysia and the Pacific

'ava – see *kava* (Samoa)

barrier reef – a long, narrow coral reef that is separated from the land by a deep lagoon and shelters the land from the sea

bêche-de-mer – lethargic, bottom-dwelling sea creature; sea cucumber

bigman – chief (Solomons, Vanuatu)

bilibili – bamboo raft (Fiji)

blackbirding – a 19th-century recruitment scheme little removed from slavery

bula – Fijian greeting

burao – wild hibiscus tree

bure – thatch dwelling (Fiji)

cagou – New Caledonia's national bird

Caldoche – white people born in New Caledonia with ancestral ties to the convicts or early French settlers

cargo cults – religious movements whose followers hope for the delivery of vast quantities of modern wealth (cargo) from supernatural forces or faraway countries

case – traditional *Kanak* house (New Caledonia); see also *grande case*

CFP – Cour de franc Pacifique (Pacific franc)

dalo – see *taro* (Fiji)

'ei – necklace (Cook Islands)

fa'a – see *faka*

fa'afafine – see *fakaleiti* (Samoa)

fafine – see *vahine*

faka – according to (a culture's) customs and tradition, eg *fa'a Samoa* or *faka Pasifika*

fakaleiti – man who dresses and lives as a woman (Tonga)

fale – house with thatched roof and open sides; often used to mean any building

fare – see *fale*

fenua – land

fiafia – dance performance (Samoa)

fono – governing council (Polynesian)

gîte – group of bungalows used for tourist accommodation (French territories)

grade-taking – process by which Melanesian men progress through castes, proving worth through feasts and gifts; see *nimangki*

grande case – big house where chiefs meet; see *case*

heilala – Tonga's national flower

honu – turtle (French Polynesia)

hôtel de ville – see *mairie*

i'a – see *ika*

kai – food

Kanak – indigenous New Caledonians

kastom – custom; rules relating to traditional beliefs (Solomons, Vanuatu)

kastom ownership – traditional ownership of land, objects or reef

kava – mud-coloured, mildly intoxicating drink made from the roots of the *Piper methysticum* plant

kikau – thatch-roofed

kilikiti – see *kirikiti*

kirikiti – cricket with many players on each side (French Polynesia, Samoa)

koutu – ancient open-air royal courtyard (Cook Islands)

kumara – sweet potato

la coutume – custom (New Caledonia); see *kastom*

Lapita – ancestors of the Polynesians

laplap – Vanuatu national dish

lava-lava – sarong-type garment; wide piece of cloth worn as a skirt

lei – see *'ei*

LMS – London Missionary Society

lovo – traditional feast (Fiji)

mahu – see *fakaleiti* (French Polynesia)

mairie – town hall (French Polynesia, New Caledonia)

makatea – a raised coral island; coral coastal plain around an island

malae – see *marae*

malo – Polynesian greeting

mana – spiritual power

manu – birds

Maohi – see *Maori*

Maori – indigenous people (Cook Islands, Society Islands)

marae – community village green (western Polynesia); pre-Christian sacred site (eastern Polynesia); ceremonial meeting ground (Cook Islands)

masi – bark cloth with designs in black and rust (Fiji)

matai – senior male, political representative of a family (Samoa, Tokelau and Tuvalu)

mataiapo – see *matai* (Cook Islands)

me'ae – see *marae*

meke – dance performance enacting stories (Fiji)

Melanesia – the western Pacific: Papua New Guinea, Solomons, Vanuatu, New

Caledonia and Fiji; the name is Greek for 'black islands'

Métro – someone from France (New Caledonia)

Micronesia – the northwestern Pacific: Palau, Northern Mariana Islands, Guam, FSM, Marshall Islands, Nauru and Kiribati; the name is Greek for 'small islands'

moai – large stone statues (Easter Island)

motu – island, islet

naghol – land-diving ritual (Vanuatu)

nakamal – men's clubhouse (New Caledonia, Vanuatu)

namba – traditional sheath (Vanuatu)

nimangki – status and power earned by *grade-taking* (Vanuatu)

niu – coconut

ni-Vanuatu – people from Vanuatu

nono – small gnats, sandflies (French Polynesia)

nuku – village (Polynesian)

nu'u – see *nuku*

ono – barracuda

pa'anga – Tongan currency

PADI – Professional Association of Dive Instructors

pae pae – paved *marae* floor

pakalolo – marijuana (French Polynesia)

palagi – see *palangi*

palangi – white person, westerner (Polynesia)

Papuans – ancient people who are among the ancestors of modern Melanesians

pareu – *lava-lava* (Cook Islands, French Polynesia, New Caledonia and Vanuatu)

pe'a – see *peka* (Samoa)

peka – bat, small bird

pelagic – creatures in the upper waters of the ocean

pilou – *Kanak* dance, performed for important ceremonies or events

Polynesia – a huge area bound by Hawai'i, New Zealand and Easter Island; includes the Cook Islands, French Polynesia, Niue, Pitcairn Island, the Samoas, Tokelau, Tonga, Tuvalu, and Wallis and Futuna; the name is Greek for 'many islands'

Polynesian Outliers – the islands of eastern Melanesia and southern Micronesia populated by Polynesians

pukao – topknot

pulenu'u – head man, village mayor (Polynesia)

quonset hut – WWII military storage shed

sevusevu – presentation of a gift to a village chief and, by extension, to the ancestral gods and spirits (Fiji)

siapo – *tapa* (Samoa)

snack – cheap cafe (French Territories)

SPF – South Pacific Forum

SPTO – South Pacific Tourism Organisation

swim-through – tunnel big enough to swim through

tabu – see *tapu*

tamtam – slit-gong, slit-drum; made from carved

logs with a hollowed-out section (Vanuatu)

ta'ovala – distinctive woven pandanus mats worn around the waist (Tonga)

tapa – see *masi*

tapu – sacred, prohibited

taro – plant with heart-shaped leaves, cultivated for its leaf and edible rootstock

tatau – tattoo

tiki – carved human figure (Polynesia)

tivaevae – colourful intricately sewn appliqué works (Cook Islands)

to'ona'i – Sunday lunch (Samoa)

tu' – see *tui* (Tonga)

tufuga – priest, expert (Samoa)

tui – paramount king (central Pacific)

tumunu – hollowed-out coconut-tree stump used to brew bush beer; also bush-beer drinking sessions

umu – earth oven

umukai – feast cooked in an *umu*

va'a – see *vaka*

vahine – woman (Polynesia)

vaka – canoe

vale – see *fale* (Fiji)

wantok – one talk; the western Melanesian concept that all who speak your language are allies (Solomon Islands)

yaqona – see *kava* (Fiji)

Behind the Scenes

SEND US YOUR FEEDBACK

We love to hear from travellers – your comments keep us on our toes and help make our books better. Our well-travelled team reads every word on what you loved or loathed about this book. Although we cannot reply individually to your submissions, we always guarantee that your feedback goes straight to the appropriate authors, in time for the next edition. Each person who sends us information is thanked in the next edition – the most useful submissions are rewarded with a selection of digital PDF chapters.

Visit **lonelyplanet.com/contact** to submit your updates and suggestions or to ask for help. Our award-winning website also features inspirational travel stories, news and discussions.

Note: We may edit, reproduce and incorporate your comments in Lonely Planet products such as guidebooks, websites and digital products, so let us know if you don't want your comments reproduced or your name acknowledged. For a copy of our privacy policy visit lonelyplanet.com/privacy.

OUR READERS

Many thanks to the travellers who used the last edition and wrote to us with helpful hints, useful advice and interesting anecdotes:

Alan Sedgwick, Allesia Frankie, Ann C Howell, Carina Karlsson, Catherine Waters, David Close, Jamie Sullivan, Jessica Lovatt, Joaquin Sitte, Ken Scott, Luigi Zeccardo, Mats Nilsson, Mike Griffin, Milton Lever, Murray Grindlay, Paolo Votino, Paul Chan, Simon Jackson

AUTHOR THANKS
Charles Rawlings-Way

Huge thanks to Tasmin for the gig: it had been far too long since I'd experienced the South Pacific any closer than 39,000 feet above the waves. Thanks also to the all-star in-house LP production staff in London and Melbourne, and kudos to my island-addled crew of co-authors (dirty job, someone's gotta do it, etc). Special praise and adoration as always to Meg and our daughters Ione and Remy, who held the fort at home while I reported in from sundry remote islands with stories of coral reefs, sunsets and cold beers.

Brett Atkinson

Meitaki ma'ata to all the friendly Cook Islanders I met on my travels, especially Christian Mani, Nane Teokotai Vainepoto Papa and Daniel Fisher at Cook Islands Tourism in Avarua. On 'Atiu thanks to Mata Arai, Roger Malcolm, and Mareta Atetu, and to Tangata and Teata Ateriano on Ma'uke. Final thanks to Carol for sharing this latest South Pacific adventure with me – especially the mammoth tuna sandwiches, bush-bashing excitement and lazy sunset cocktails.

Jean-Bernard Carillet

Heaps of thanks to the editorial and cartography teams at Lonely Planet for their great job. Coordinating author Charles Rawlings-Way deserves a *grand merci* for his support, as does DE Tasmin for her support and guidance. In Tahiti, a special mention goes to my second family, the Peirsegaeles in Mahina. In the Solomons, special thanks to Kerrie, Pam, Chris and Donaldson. And finally, once again a *gros bisou* to Christine and Eva.

BEHIND THE SCENES

Paul Harding

Many people helped with advice, information or just a good chat. Thanks in particular to Jack and Janelle, Kelson, Silas, Tom and Margaret, Sam and Helena, Sethrick and staff at Vanuatu Tourism Office in Port Vila. Thanks to Tasmin at Lonely Planet. Most of all, and as always, thanks to Hannah and Layla for your love and patience.

Craig McLachlan

A hearty thanks to everyone who helped me out on the road, but most of all to my exceptionally beautiful wife Yuriko.

Tamara Sheward

Fa'afetai tele and vinaka vaka levu to the wonderful folks of Samoa (Maria, Sophie, Jay, Killi and so many more), American Samoa (Fanua, Cita, Tom, Howard, et al) and Fiji (including superstars Miri, Lailanie, Alex and Viola). Frangipanis and South Sea smooches to my two crazy coconuts, Dušan and Masha.

ACKNOWLEDGEMENTS

Cover photograph: Lyretail anthias in Namena Marine Reserve, Fiji; Reinhard Dirscherl/Getty Images.
Climate map data adapted from Peel MC, Finlayson BL & McMahon TA (2007) 'Updated World Map of the Köppen-Geiger Climate Classification', Hydrology and Earth System Sciences, 11, 163344.

THIS BOOK

This sixth edition of Lonely Planet's South Pacific guidebook was researched and written by Charles Rawlings-Way, Brett Atkinson, Jean-Bernard Carillet, Paul Harding, Craig McLachlan and Tamara Sheward. The previous edition was also written by Brett, Jean-Bernard and Craig,

alongside Celeste Brash, Jayne D'Arcy and Virginia Jealous. This guidebook was produced by the following:

Destination Editor Tasmin Waby

Product Editor Joel Cotterell

Regional Senior Cartographer Diana Von Holdt

Book Designer Mazzy Princep

Coordinating Editor Andrea Dobbin

Assisting Editors Katie Connolly, Charlotte Orr

Assisting Cartographers Anita Banh, Julie Dodkins, Gabe Lindquist

Cover Researcher Naomi Parker

Thanks to Andi Jones, Anne Mason, Catherine Naghten, Karyn Noble, Susan Paterson, Alison Ridgway, Luna Soo, Ross Taylor and Angela Tinson

Index

Map Legend

Sights
- Beach
- Bird Sanctuary
- Buddhist
- Castle/Palace
- Christian
- Confucian
- Hindu
- Islamic
- Jain
- Jewish
- Monument
- Museum/Gallery/Historic Building
- Ruin
- Shinto
- Sikh
- Taoist
- Winery/Vineyard
- Zoo/Wildlife Sanctuary
- Other Sight

Activities, Courses & Tours
- Bodysurfing
- Diving
- Canoeing/Kayaking
- Course/Tour
- Sento Hot Baths/Onsen
- Skiing
- Snorkelling
- Surfing
- Swimming/Pool
- Walking
- Windsurfing
- Other Activity

Sleeping
- Sleeping
- Camping

Eating
- Eating

Drinking & Nightlife
- Drinking & Nightlife
- Cafe

Entertainment
- Entertainment

Shopping
- Shopping

Information
- Bank
- Embassy/Consulate
- Hospital/Medical
- Internet
- Police
- Post Office
- Telephone
- Toilet
- Tourist Information
- Other Information

Geographic
- Beach
- Gate
- Hut/Shelter
- Lighthouse
- Lookout
- Mountain/Volcano
- Oasis
- Park
- Pass
- Picnic Area
- Waterfall

Population
- Capital (National)
- Capital (State/Province)
- City/Large Town
- Town/Village

Transport
- Airport
- Border crossing
- Bus
- Cable car/Funicular
- Cycling
- Ferry
- Metro station
- Monorail
- Parking
- Petrol station
- Subway station
- Taxi
- Train station/Railway
- Tram
- Underground station
- Other Transport

Note: Not all symbols displayed above appear on the maps in this book

Routes
- Tollway
- Freeway
- Primary
- Secondary
- Tertiary
- Lane
- Unsealed road
- Road under construction
- Plaza/Mall
- Steps
- Tunnel
- Pedestrian overpass
- Walking Tour
- Walking Tour detour
- Path/Walking Trail

Boundaries
- International
- State/Province
- Disputed
- Regional/Suburb
- Marine Park
- Cliff
- Wall

Hydrography
- River, Creek
- Intermittent River
- Canal
- Water
- Dry/Salt/Intermittent Lake
- Reef

Areas
- Airport/Runway
- Beach/Desert
- Cemetery (Christian)
- Cemetery (Other)
- Glacier
- Mudflat
- Park/Forest
- Sight (Building)
- Sportsground
- Swamp/Mangrove

Craig McLachlan

New Caledonia An island enthusiast from way back, Craig has covered such varying spots as the Greek Islands, Okinawa, Tonga, New Caledonia and Oahu for Lonely Planet. A Kiwi with a passion for exploring, he loves New Caledonia, in particular the Loyalty Islands and Île des Pins. A 'freelance anything', Craig has an MBA from the University of Hawai'i and is also a pilot, karate instructor, tour leader, hiking guide, Japanese interpreter and budding novelist. See www.craigmclachlan.com.

Tamara Sheward

Fiji, Samoa, American Samoa Despite a hearty dislike of heat and humidity – not to mention that pesky mango allergy – Tamara not only lives in the tropics, but enjoys travelling them extensively. While researching the South Pacific, she rode in 50-plus boats, 14 aeroplanes, umpteen rattly open-air buses and one submarine; alas, no similar tally was kept on kava and coconut consumption. In addition to the islands in this book, Tamara has covered a incongruous miscellany of countries for Lonely Planet, including Serbia, northern Australia, Bulgaria and Russia.

OUR STORY

A beat-up old car, a few dollars in the pocket and a sense of adventure. In 1972 that's all Tony and Maureen Wheeler needed for the trip of a lifetime – across Europe and Asia overland to Australia. It took several months, and at the end – broke but inspired – they sat at their kitchen table writing and stapling together their first travel guide, *Across Asia on the Cheap*. Within a week they'd sold 1500 copies. Lonely Planet was born.

Today, Lonely Planet has offices in Franklin, London, Melbourne, Oakland, Beijing and Delhi, with more than 600 staff and writers. We share Tony's belief that 'a great guidebook should do three things: inform, educate and amuse'.

OUR WRITERS

Charles Rawlings-Way

Coordinating Writer, Tonga, Other Islands As a likely lad, Charles suffered in school shorts through Tasmanian winters. Ice on the puddles, snow on Mt Wellington...he dreamed of one day exploring tropical isles in a more humane climate. After dropping a windsurfer mast on a Texan tourist's head in Fiji in 1985 and chasing rats around an Aitutatki guesthouse in 2005, a trip to see what Tonga had to offer was well overdue. Charles has penned 30-something Lonely Planet guidebooks, and remains pathologically fixated on the virtues and vices of travel.

Brett Atkinson

Rarotonga & the Cook Islands From his home in Auckland, Brett Atkinson has travelled to many of the islands in his South Pacific backyard. For this extended research trip to the Cook Islands, he snorkelled and scootered around Aitutaki, drank bush beer and organic coffee on 'Atiu, and explored Rarotonga on two and four wheels with his wife Carol. Brett has covered more than 50 countries as a guidebook author and travel and food writer. See www.brett-atkinson.net for his most recent work and upcoming travels.

Jean-Bernard Carillet

Easter Island, Solomon Islands, Tahiti & French Polynesia Paris-based journalist and photographer Jean-Bernard is a die-hard island lover and diving instructor. He has clocked up numerous trips to the South Pacific, including five assignments to the Solomon Islands. On this research gig, his favourite experiences included diving the WWII wrecks off Tulagi, spending a day in Saeraghi, exploring Marovo Lagoon on a dinghy, visiting Gwaunau'ru with a local chief. Jean-Bernard has contributed to many Lonely Planet titles, in French and in English. He also writes for travel and dive magazines.

Paul Harding

Vanuatu As a writer and photographer Paul has been travelling around Asia, Australia and parts of the Pacific for nearly two decades, examining beaches and islands along the way. Vanuatu stands out though for its remote islands, pristine waters, friendly faces and ancient traditional culture. On this trip Paul climbed a volcano, drank too much kava and braved rough seas in very small boats. He has contributed to some 50 Lonely Planet guides.

OVER PAGE MORE WRITERS

Published by Lonely Planet Global Limited
CRN 554153
6th edition – December 2016
ISBN 978 1 78657 218 9
© Lonely Planet 2016   Photographs © as indicated 2016
10 9 8 7 6 5 4 3 2 1
Printed in China